About Pearson

Pearson is the world's learning company, with presence across 70 countries worldwide. Our unique insights and world-class expertise comes from a long history of working closely with renowned teachers, authors and thought leaders, as a result of which, we have emerged as the preferred choice for millions of teachers and learners across the world.

We believe learning opens up opportunities, creates fulfilling careers and hence better lives. We hence collaborate with the best of minds to deliver you class-leading products, spread across the Higher Education and Test Preparation spectrum.

Superior learning experience and improved outcomes are at the heart of everything we do. This product is the result of one such effort.

Your feedback plays a critical role in the evolution of our products and you can contact us – reachus@pearson.com. We look forward to it.

Electromagnetic Fields and Waves

Third Edition

S. Salivahanan
Vice Chancellor
Vel Tech Rangarajan Dr. Sagunthala
R&D Institute of Science and Technology
Avadi, Chennai

S. Karthie
Associate Professor
Department of ECE, SSN College of Engineering
Chennai

Senior Editor—Product: R. Dheepika
Senior Editor—Production: C. Purushothaman

ISBN 978-81-198-9667-7

First Impression

Published by Pearson India Education Services Pvt. Ltd, CIN: U72200TN2005PTC057128.

Head Office: 1st Floor, Berger Tower, Plot No. C-001A/2, Sector 16B, Noida - 201 301,
Uttar Pradesh, India.
Registered Office: Featherlite, 'The Address' 5th Floor, Survey No 203/10B,
200 Ft MMRD Road, Zamin Pallavaram, Chennai – 600 044.
Website: in.pearson.com, Email: companysecretary.india@pearson.com

Printed in India by Pushp Print Services

Dedicated
To
Our Beloved Parents

FOREWORD

It gives me an immense pleasure in introducing the third edition of the book, *Electromagnetic Fields and Waves,* published by Pearson Education and authored by Dr. S. Salivahanan, Vice Chancellor, Vel Tech Rangarajan Dr. Sagunthala R&D Institute of Science and Technology, Chennai, and Dr. S. Karthie, Associate Professor, Department of ECE, SSN College of Engineering, Chennai. This book is an outcome of several years of teaching and research experience of the authors. This book provides ample space for theory and practice in the field of electromagnetics. I have known Prof. S. Salivahanan very well as my student in PSG College of Technology, Coimbatore, a dedicated academician who is serving the cause of teaching and research, and an author of textbooks which are all-time bestsellers published by leading international publishers.

Electromagnetic Fields and Waves is one of the important core subjects in the field of Electrical Engineering, Electronics and Communication Engineering, Electronics and Instrumentation Engineering, and Applied Physics. There has been an increase in demand for a suitable textbook on this subject. The contents of the book are presented in a simple, precise and systematic manner which enable the students understand and apply the concepts in both efficient and effective ways. Numerous solved examples, self-explanatory sketches and a large number of exercise problems with answers have been presented in each chapter to aid conceptual understanding of the subject. Furthermore, the mode of presentation is set to enhance the interest of the readers towards self-directed learning.

Having been a teacher and resource person in the fields of Electrical and Computer Engineering for over a period of five decades, I am confident that this book shall fill the void felt by the academia for a good textbook on the subject of Electromagnetic Fields and Waves. I am sure that this book will enrich students' knowledge in the subject and would be welcomed by teachers and students. Making the copies of this book available in the libraries of all the universities, colleges and polytechnics will certainly help in enriching them. I strongly recommend this book to every electrical, electronics and communication engineering student. I wish the authors a grand success.

Dr. E. Balagurusamy
Former Vice Chancellor
Anna University, Chennai
Chairman, EBG Foundation, Coimbatore

PREFACE

Electromagnetism is the most pervasive force that exists in nature. Electromagnetic Fields is the study of characteristics of electric, magnetic and combined fields. The knowledge on electromagnetic fields and waves is essential for engineering graduates of Electrical and Electronics Engineering, Electronics and Communication Engineering and Electronics and Instrumentation Engineering. This book caters to the needs of B.E./B.Tech., M.Sc. (Electronics), B.Sc. (Physics), AMIE and Grade IETE degree programs.

We have designed the material to address the need for a comprehensive book covering the revised syllabi of various universities. Also, the book serves as a test-prep resource for competitive examinations. We are optimistic in our belief that this book shall enhance better and easy understanding of fundamental concepts of electromagnetics. Ensuring the availability of this book in the libraries of all universities, colleges and polytechnics will certainly help in enriching the knowledge of the readers. Various concepts of the subject have been arranged aesthetically in a sequential manner and presented in a simple reader-friendly language. For better understanding, a large number of numerical problems with step-by-step procedure for solutions have been provided. Further, the book includes comprehensively solved questions of university-level examinations. A set of review questions included at the end of each chapter focuses on helping the readers to test their understanding of the subject.

This book comprises of ten chapters. *Chapter 1* provides an in-depth discussion on vector analysis and different coordinate systems to provide strong mathematical foundation for the subject. *Chapter 2* deals with the concept of static electric fields and its understanding using Coulomb's law and Gauss's law. *Chapter 3* explains the electrical properties of conductors and dielectrics in electrostatics. Also, this chapter discusses electrostatic boundary conditions and solving boundary value problems using Laplace's and Poisson's equations. *Chapter 4* describes the concept of static magnetic field and its understanding using Biot-Savart's law and Ampere's law. *Chapter 5* explains the concept of magnetic forces and torque on current carrying conductors. The various types of magnetic materials, magnetostatic boundary conditions, concept of magnetic moment and magnetic dipole are explained as well. *Chapter 6* focuses on the concept of electromagnetic fields with special emphasis on time-varying fields. The formation of Maxwell's equations in differential and integral forms has been briefly discussed. *Chapter 7* elaborates the propagation of electromagnetic waves through different mediums with their characteristics of reflection, refraction and polarization. *Chapters 8 and 9* deal with the analysis of lossy and lossless transmission line equations and characteristic quantities, impedance matching, and the use of Smith chart for solving high-frequency transmission line problems. *Chapter 10* discusses the transmission of fields and waves in a confined medium like waveguides that support many possible field configurations.

We would like to sincerely thank the management of SSN College of Engineering, Chennai, for their constant encouragement and providing necessary facilities for completing this project. Also, we are thankful to our colleagues, G. R. Venkatakrishnan and V. Thiyagarajan, Associate Professors, Department of EEE, for their review and feedback to improve this book. We are indebted to R. Gopalakrishnan, A. Chakkarabani and K. Rajan of SSN College of Engineering, Chennai, for word-processing the manuscript of the entire text. We specially thank Pearson India Education Services Pvt. Ltd., for stimulating interest in this project and bringing out this book successfully in a short span of time.

Finally, we extend heartfelt gratitude to our family members, Kalavathy Salivahanan, S. Santhosh Kanna and S. Subadesh Kanna, and Devi Muthu Parvathy Karthie and Master K. Sundar, for their patience and cheerfulness throughout the project. We will appreciate any suggestions and constructive feedback from the readers for further improvement of this book at *salivahanans@hotmail.com*.

S. Salivahanan
S. Karthie

ABOUT THE AUTHORS

Dr. S. Salivahanan is the Vice Chancellor of Vel Tech Rangarajan Dr. Sagunthala R&D Institute of Science and Technology, Avadi, Chennai. Previously, he held the position of Principal at SSN College of Engineering, Chennai, for a span of 17 years. He earned his B.E. in Electronics and Communication Engineering from PSG College of Technology, Coimbatore, M.E. in Communication Systems from NIT Trichy, and Ph.D. in Microwave Integrated Circuits from Madurai Kamaraj University. With over four and a half decades of experience in teaching, research, administration, and industry, he has worked in various educational institutions in India and abroad.

Professor Salivahanan has taught at NIT Trichy, A.C. Government College of Engineering and Technology, Karaikudi, R.V. College of Engineering, Bangalore, and Mepco Schlenk Engineering College, Sivakasi. His industrial experience includes roles as a Scientist/Engineer at Space Applications Centre, ISRO, Ahmedabad, Telecommunication Engineer at State Organization of Electricity, Iraq, and Electronics Engineer at Electric Dar Establishment, Kingdom of Saudi Arabia.

Having authored a total of 68 well-received books, the author has left an indelible mark in the field of Electronics and Communication Engineering literature. Notable publications under Pearson Education, such as 'Control Systems Engineering' and Circuit Theory: Network Analysis and Synthesis', attest to his expertise. Additionally, he has produced bestsellers like 'Basic Electrical and Electronics Engineering', 'Electronic Devices and Circuits', and 'Linear Integrated Circuits', all published by McGraw-Hill Education. Noteworthy among his achievements is the translation of 'Digital Signal Processing' into Mandarin Chinese for McGraw-Hill International. His proficiency is further exemplified in the realm of 'Digital Circuits and Design', a publication under Oxford University Press.

Professor Salivahanan has received numerous accolades, including the Bharatiya Vidya Bhavan National Award for Best Engineering College Principal (2011), Lifetime Achievement Award from ISTE (2018), and the IEEE Outstanding Branch Counsellor and Advisor Award in the Asia-Pacific region (1996–97). He served as the Chairman of IEEE Madras Section for two years (2008–2009) and held leadership roles in IEEE Microwave Theory and Techniques Society chapter and IEEE Signal Processing Society chapter of IEEE Madras Section, and a Senate Member of the University of Madras.

As a Life Member of IEEE, Fellow of IETE, Fellow of Institution of Engineers (India), and life member of ISTE and the Society for EMC Engineers, Professor Salivahanan continues to contribute to various IEEE societies in Microwave Theory and Techniques, Communications, Signal Processing and Aerospace and Electronics. Additionally, he was a member of the DST expert group on Patent Facilitation Programme and the DST expert group on state Science and Technology councils.

Dr. S. Karthie is currently working as an Associate Professor in the Department of ECE, SSN College of Engineering, Chennai, and has over 21 years of teaching experience. He received his B.E. (ECE), first class with distinction, from National Engineering College, Kovilpatti, in 2001, M.E. (Applied Electronics) and Ph.D. degree from Anna University, Chennai in 2006 and 2020, respectively. He has published several research papers in International Journals and Conferences. He has also authored books on "Electromagnetic Field Theory" and "Physics for Electronics Engineering and Information Science," published by McGraw-Hill Education, New Delhi. His research interests include electromagnetics, electronic devices and circuits, RF/microwave filter design and microwave integrated circuits. He is an active member of IEEE – Microwave Theory and Techniques Society. He is also a Life member of IETE and ISTE.

CONTENTS

Foreword   *vii*
Preface   *ix*
About the Authors   *xi*

Chapter 1: Vector Analysis   **1**

1.1   Introduction   *1*
1.2   Basic Laws of Vector Algebra   *1*
    1.2.1   Vector Equality   *3*
    1.2.2   Vector Addition and Subtraction   *3*
    1.2.3   Position and Distance Vectors   *5*
    1.2.4   Vector Multiplication   *6*
1.3   Orthogonal Coordinate Systems   *14*
    1.3.1   Rectangular (Cartesian) Coordinates (x, y, z) *14*
    1.3.2   Cylindrical Coordinates (ρ, ϕ, z) *15*
    1.3.3   Spherical Coordinates (r, θ, ϕ) *17*
    1.3.4   Transformation between Cylindrical and Spherical Coordinates   *19*
1.4   Differential Elements of Length, Surface, and Volume   *27*
    1.4.1   Rectangular Coordinate System   *27*
    1.4.2   Cylindrical Coordinate System   *28*
    1.4.3   Spherical Coordinate System   *29*
    1.4.4   Comparison of Differential Elements for Coordinate Systems   *31*
1.5   Line, Surface, and Volume Integrals   *31*
    1.5.1   Line Integral   *31*
    1.5.2   Surface Integral   *34*
    1.5.3   Volume Integral   *36*
1.6   Vector Differential Operator   *38*
    1.6.1   Vector Differential Operator ∇ in Cylindrical Coordinates   *38*
    1.6.2   Vector Differential Operator ∇ in Spherical Coordinates   *39*
1.7   Gradient of a Scalar Field   *42*
1.8   Divergence of a Vector Field   *45*
1.9   Divergence Theorem   *50*
1.10   Curl of a Vector Field   *54*
1.11   Stokes's Theorem   *63*

1.12 Laplacian Operator *67*

1.13 Null Identities *70*

    1.13.1 Identity-I *70*

    1.13.2 Identity-II *71*

1.14 Helmholtz's Theorem *71*

Review Questions *73*

Chapter 2: Static Electric Fields   **77**

2.1 Introduction *77*

2.2 Coulomb's Law *77*

2.3 Electric Field Intensity *85*

2.4 Electric Field Due to Continuous Charge Distribution *89*

    2.4.1 Field due to a Line Charge *91*

    2.4.2 Field due to a Surface Charge *100*

    2.4.3 Field due to a Volume Charge *106*

2.5 Electric Flux Lines and Flux Density *107*

    2.5.1 Properties of Electric Field Lines *108*

2.6 Gauss's Law *109*

2.7 Gauss's Divergence Theorem *111*

2.8 Applications of Gauss's Law *118*

    2.8.1 Determination of Field due to a Point Charge *118*

    2.8.2 Determination of Field due to an Infinite Line of Charge *119*

    2.8.3 Determination of Field due to an Infinite Sheet of Charge *120*

    2.8.4 Determination of Field due to a Uniformly Charged Sphere *122*

    2.8.5 Determination of Field due to a Spherical Shell of Charge *124*

2.9 Equipotential Surfaces *126*

    2.9.1 Properties of Equipotential Surfaces *127*

2.10 Uniform and Non-uniform Field *127*

2.11 Electric Potential *134*

    2.11.1 Electric Potential due to Point Charge *144*

    2.11.2 Electric Potential due to Continuous Charge Distributions *149*

    2.11.3 Electric Potential and Field due to an Electric Dipole *154*

    2.11.4 Torque on an Electric Dipole in Electric Field *155*

    2.11.5 Torque on a Dipole due to Field of another Dipole *156*

2.12 Electrostatic Potential Energy *158*

2.13 Electrostatic Energy Density *163*

Review Questions *167*

Chapter 3: Conductors and Dielectrics   **175**

3.1 Introduction *175*

3.2 Material Properties *175*

3.3 Nature of Current and Current Density *176*

    3.3.1 Convection Current and Convection Current Density *177*

    3.3.2 Conduction Current and Conduction Current Density *178*

3.4 Conductors in Static Electric Field *179*

3.5 Dielectrics in Static Electric Field *182*
   3.5.1 Dielectric Polarization *182*
   3.5.2 Dielectric Constant and Dielectric Strength *183*
3.6 Continuity Equation and Relaxation Time *187*
3.7 Electric Boundary Conditions *191*
   3.7.1 Dielectric–Dielectric Boundary Conditions *191*
   3.7.2 Dielectric–Conductor Boundary Conditions *194*
   3.7.3 Free Space–Conductor Boundary Conditions *195*
   3.7.4 Conductor–Conductor Boundary Conditions *195*
   3.7.5 Analogy between Flux Density $\vec{D}$ and Current Density $\vec{J}$ *196*
3.8 Resistance *200*
   3.8.1 Joule's Law *203*
3.9 Determination of Capacitance *204*
   3.9.1 Capacitance of a Parallel Plate Capacitor *206*
   3.9.2 Capacitance of a Parallel Wire Transmission Line *213*
   3.9.3 Capacitance of a Coaxial Cable or Cylindrical Capacitor *216*
   3.9.4 Capacitance of an Isolated Charged Sphere *219*
   3.9.5 Capacitance of Spherical Capacitor *219*
   3.9.6 Composite Parallel Plate Capacitor *222*
3.10 Poisson's and Laplace's Equations *237*
   3.10.1 Laplacian Equation in Different Coordinate Systems *238*
   3.10.2 Uniqueness Theorem *239*
   3.10.3 General Procedure for Solving Poisson's or Laplace's Equation *240*
   3.10.4 Applications of Poisson's and Laplace's Equations *241*
3.11 Method of Images *255*
3.12 Applications of Static Electric Fields *262*
   3.12.1 Motion of Electron in Electric Field *262*
   3.12.2 Electrostatic Deflection in Cathode Ray Tube *264*
   3.12.3 Ink-jet printer *266*
   3.12.4 Electrostatic Voltmeter *267*
Review Questions *268*

Chapter 4: Static Magnetic Fields   **273**

4.1 Introduction *273*
4.2 Biot–Savart's Law *273*
   4.2.1 Magnetic Field due to a Straight Conductor *278*
   4.2.2 Magnetic Field due to a Circular Conductor *286*
4.3 Stokes's Theorem *292*
4.4 Ampere's Circuital Law *296*
   4.4.1 Point Form of Ampere's Circuital Law *296*
   4.4.2 Physical Interpretation of the Curl *299*
4.5 Applications of Ampere's Law *309*
   4.5.1 Magnetic Field due to an Infinite Line Current *309*
   4.5.2 Magnetic Field due to an Infinite Current Sheet *314*
   4.5.3 Magnetic Field due to an Infinitely Long Coaxial Cable *317*
   4.5.4 Magnetic Field inside a Toroidal Coil *321*

4.6   Magnetic Flux and Magnetic Flux Density *322*
4.7   Scalar And Vector Magnetic Potentials *328*
4.8   Derivation of Steady Magnetic Field Laws *344*
Review Questions *347*

Chapter 5: Magnetic Forces and Materials **351**

5.1   Introduction *351*
5.2   Force on a Moving Charge *351*
5.3   Force on a Differential Current Element *355*
5.4   Force Between Current Elements *360*
5.5   Force and Torque on a Closed Circuit *367*
5.6   Magnetic Dipole *379*
5.7   Nature and Classification of Magnetic Materials *382*
    5.7.1   Hysteresis Loop *384*
5.8   Magnetization and Permeability *387*
5.9   Boundary Conditions for Magnetic Fields *395*
    5.9.1   Boundary Conditions on Tangential Components *395*
    5.9.2   Boundary Conditions on Normal Components *396*
5.10   Magnetic Circuit *403*
    5.10.1   Fundamentals of Magnetic Circuits *403*
    5.10.2   Analysis of Simple Magnetic Circuit *403*
    5.10.3   Analysis of Series Magnetic Circuits *404*
    5.10.4   Analysis of Parallel Magnetic Circuits *405*
5.11   Inductance *414*
    5.11.1   Self Inductance *415*
    5.11.2   Mutual Inductance *415*
    5.11.3   Coefficient of Coupling *416*
5.12   Determination of Inductance *421*
    5.12.1   Inductance of a Solenoid *422*
    5.12.2   Inductance of a Toroid *426*
    5.12.3   Inductance of a Coaxial Cable *432*
    5.12.4   Inductance of a Parallel-Wire Transmission Line *434*
5.13   Energy Stored in Magnetic Fields *436*
5.14   Potential Energy and Forces on Magnetic Materials *437*
5.15   Applications of Static Magnetic Fields *440*
    5.15.1   Motion of Electron in Magnetic Field *440*
    5.15.2   Magnetic Deflection in Cathode Ray Tube *442*
    5.15.3   Hall Effect *443*
    5.15.4   Mass Spectrometer *445*
Review Questions *445*

Chapter 6: Time-Varying Fields and Maxwell's Equations **451**

6.1   Introduction *451*
6.2   Fundamental Relations for Electrostatic and Magnetostatic Fields *451*
6.3   Faraday's Law for Electromagnetic Induction *453*
6.4   Transformer and Motional EMFs *454*
    6.4.1   Stationary Conductor in Time-Varying Magnetic Field (Transformer emf) *455*

6.4.2   Moving Conductor in Static Magnetic Field (Motional emf) *458*
6.4.3   Moving Conductor in Time-Varying Magnetic Field *464*
6.5   Displacement Current *465*
6.6   Maxwell's Equations *477*
6.6.1   Maxwell's Equation from Gauss's law for Electrostatic fields *477*
6.6.2   Maxwell's Equation from Gauss's Law for Magnetostatic Fields *478*
6.6.3   Maxwell's Equation from Faraday's Law *478*
6.6.4   Maxwell's Equation from Ampere's Circuital Law *479*
6.7   Relation Between Field Theory and Circuit Theory *501*
6.8   Electromagnetic Boundary Conditions *504*
6.9   Potential Functions *507*
6.10   Wave Equations and their Solutions *510*
6.10.1   Solution of Wave Equations for Potentials *510*
6.10.2   Source-Free Wave Equations *513*
6.11   Time-Harmonic Fields *514*
6.11.1   Ratio between Conduction Current Density and Displacement Current Density *523*
6.11.2   Comparison of Different Types of Currents and Their Current Densities *523*
6.12   Electromagnetic Spectrum *529*
6.13   Applications of EM (Dynamic) Fields *531*
6.13.1   Transformer *531*
6.13.2   Betatron *534*
Review Questions *536*

Chapter 7: Electromagnetic Waves

541

7.1   Introduction *541*
7.2   Electromagnetic Wave Equations *541*
7.3   Wave Parameters *544*
7.4   Plane Wave Propagation *547*
7.4.1   Wave Propagation in Lossless Dielectrics *548*
7.4.2   Wave Propagation in Lossy Dielectrics *552*
7.4.3   Wave Propagation in Free Space *556*
7.4.4   Wave Propagation in Good Conductors *557*
7.5   Poynting Vector And Poynting's Theorem *579*
7.5.1   Instantaneous and Average Power Densities *581*
7.6   Wave Polarization *594*
7.6.1   Linear Polarization *594*
7.6.2   Circular Polarization *594*
7.6.3   Elliptical Polarization *595*
7.7   Reflection and Refraction of Plane Waves *595*
7.7.1   Normal Incidence at Perfect Conducting Boundary *595*
7.7.2   Oblique Incidence at Perfect Conducting Boundary *598*
7.7.3   Normal Incidence at Perfect Dielectric Boundary *602*
7.7.4   Oblique Incidence at Perfect Dielectric Boundary *605*
7.8   Surface Current, Surface Impedance and Power Loss in a Conductor *626*
7.8.1   Surface Current *626*
7.8.2   Surface Impedance *628*
7.8.3   Power Loss in a Conductor *628*
Review Questions *630*

Chapter 8: Transmission Lines-I (Transmission Line Theory)   **637**

8.1   Introduction   *637*
8.2   Transmission Line Parameters   *637*
8.3   Transmission Line Theory   *639*
8.4   Transmission Line Equations   *642*
8.5   Concepts of Infinite Line   *645*
8.6   Phase and Group Velocities   *647*
8.7   Types of Distortion   *649*
8.8   Conditions for Distortionless Line   *650*
8.9   Constants for the Line of Zero Dissipation and Minimum Attenuation   *651*
8.10 Types of Loading   *652*
Review Questions   *669*

Chapter 9: Transmission Lines–II (Impedance Matching in High Frequency Lines)   **671**

9.1   Introduction   *671*
9.2   Input Impedance Relations   *671*
9.3   Short Circuit and Open Circuit Lines   *672*
9.4   Reflection on a Line not Terminated With Z_0 *677*
9.5   Reflection Coefficient   *678*
9.6   Voltage Standing Wave Ratio (VsWr)   *680*
9.7   Impedance Matching and Impedance Transformation   *686*
9.8   Smith Chart-Configuration and Applications   *689*
9.9   Single Stub Matching   *691*
Review Questions   *717*

Chapter 10: Waveguides   **720**

10.1   Introduction   *720*
10.2   Electromagnetic Spectrum and Bands   *720*
10.3   Rectangular Waveguides   *722*
10.4   TM Mode Analysis and Field Expressions   *725*
10.5   TE Mode Analysis and Field Expressions   *728*
10.6   Characteristic Equation and Cut-Off Frequencies   *730*
10.7   Dominant and Degenerate Modes   *732*
10.8   Sketches of TM and TE Mode Fields in the Cross-Section   *732*
10.9   Phase and Group Velocities   *733*
10.10 Wavelengths and Impedance Relations   *734*
10.11 Impossibility of TEM Mode   *735*
10.12 Equation of Power Transmission   *735*
10.13 Microstrip Line   *743*
Review Questions   *748*
Objective Type Questions   *751*

Appendix A: Values of General Physical Constants   **755**

Appendix B: Electric and Magnetic Field Quantities and their Units   **756**

Appendix C: Conversion Factors and Prefixes   **757**

Appendix D   **758**

Rectangular (Cartesian) Coordinates (x, y, z) *758*
    Dot Product of unit vectors   *758*
    Cross Product of unit vectors   *758*
    Cross Product of two vectors $\vec{A}$ and $\vec{B}$ *758*
Cylindrical Coordinates (ρ, ϕ, z) *758*
    Dot Product of unit vectors   *758*
    Cross Product of unit vectors   *759*
    Cross Product of two vectors $\vec{A}$ and $\vec{B}$ *759*
Spherical Coordinates (r, θ, ϕ) *759*
    Dot Product of unit vectors   *759*
    Cross Product of unit vectors   *759*
    Cross Product of two vectors $\vec{A}$ and $\vec{B}$ *759*

Appendix E: Vector Identities   **760**

Appendix F: Gradient, Divergence, Curl and Laplacian Operators   **761**

Rectangular (Cartesian) Coordinates (x, y, z) *761*
Cylindrical Coordinates (ρ, ϕ, z) *761*
Spherical Coordinates (r, θ, ϕ) *762*

Appendix G   **763**

Governing Laws In Static Electric Fields   *763*
Governing Laws In Static Magnetic Fields   *763*

Appendix H: Governing Laws in Time-Varying (Dynamic) Fields   **764**

Maxwell's Equations in General Form   *764*
Maxwell's Equations For Free Space   *764*

Appendix I: Important Formulae   **765**

Trigonometric Identities   *765*
Indefinite integrals   *766*
Definite integrals   *768*
Binomial Series   *769*
Exponential Series   *769*

Index   **771**

VECTOR ANALYSIS

1.1 INTRODUCTION

Electromagnetics, in general, is a branch of physics that deals with the study of electric and magnetic phenomena. In the modern era of electronics, electromagnetics plays an important role in the design and operation of electronic devices such as diode, transistor, integrated circuit, laser, display screen, barcode reader, mobile phone, and microwave oven. Electromagnetic principles find extensive applications in the fields of microwave filters, antennas, electric machines, satellite communications, nuclear research, plasma, fiber optics, electromagnetic interference and compatibility (EMIC), micro electro mechanical systems(MEMS), remote sensing, etc. The design and application of these devices require a thorough understanding and insight of the laws and principles of electromagnetics.

Electromagnetics can be classified into three branches, namely, electrostatics, magnetostatics, and dynamics. Electric field is induced in electrostatics mainly due to static charges and magnetic field in magnetostatics due to steady currents. Both electrostatics and magnetostatics represent special cases of electromagnetics in which the induced electric and magnetic fields are not coupled with each other. Dynamics represents time-varying fields induced by time-varying sources in which both the induced electric and magnetic fields are coupled to each other, i.e., one field can be generated from another.

The concepts of electromagnetics can be best expressed using vector algebra. Vector analysis is a mathematical tool used to express and manipulate vector quantities in an efficient and convenient manner. Electric and magnetic fields, the two most significant quantities used in the study of electromagnetics, are vectors. The most commonly used coordinate systems in the study of vector quantities are rectangular (Cartesian), cylindrical, and spherical systems. The choice of a coordinate system to be used in a specific problem is mainly based on the geometry of the problem under consideration.

Vector algebra governs the laws of addition, subtraction, and multiplication of vectors in any coordinate system. This chapter covers the basic laws of vector algebra; vector representation in each coordinate system along with its transformation; vector operators (gradient, divergence, curl, and Laplacian); vector calculus (differentiation and integration of vectors); and the application of some useful theorems, namely, divergence, Stokes's theorem, and Helmholtz's theorems.

1.2 BASIC LAWS OF VECTOR ALGEBRA

A vector quantity is specified by both the magnitude and direction of that quantity. It is represented by a letter with an arrow on top, such as $\vec{A}$ and $\vec{B}$. Some vector quantities are velocity, force, displacement, torque, acceleration, electric field, and magnetic field. A scalar quantity is specified only by its magnitude, and it is represented simply by a letter, such as A and B. Examples of scalar quantities include mass, volume, time, temperature, work, and electric charge.

A field is a function that describes a physical quantity at all points in space and at any moment of time. A physical quantity may either be a scalar or vector. Therefore, the field can also be a scalar field or vector field. A scalar field is simply a scalar quantity that is a function of space and time. It is specified by its magnitude at all points in space and at any time. Some common examples of scalar fields include temperature, gas pressure, and altitude above sea level. An example of a scalar field in electromagnetism is electric potential.

A vector field is simply a vector quantity that varies as a function of space and time. It is specified by both magnitude and direction at all points in space and at any time. The gravitational force, velocity, and acceleration of a fluid are a few examples of vector fields. An example of a vector field in electromagnetism is electric field intensity.

A vector $\vec{A}$ has a magnitude $\left|\vec{A}\right|$ and a direction specified by unit vector $\vec{a}$, can be written as

$$\vec{A} = \left|\vec{A}\right|\vec{a} = A\vec{a} \tag{1.1}$$

where the unit vector $\vec{a}$ has a magnitude of unity, i.e., $\left|\vec{a}\right| = 1$. Its direction is given by

$$\vec{a} = \frac{\vec{A}}{\left|\vec{A}\right|} = \frac{\vec{A}}{A} \tag{1.2}$$

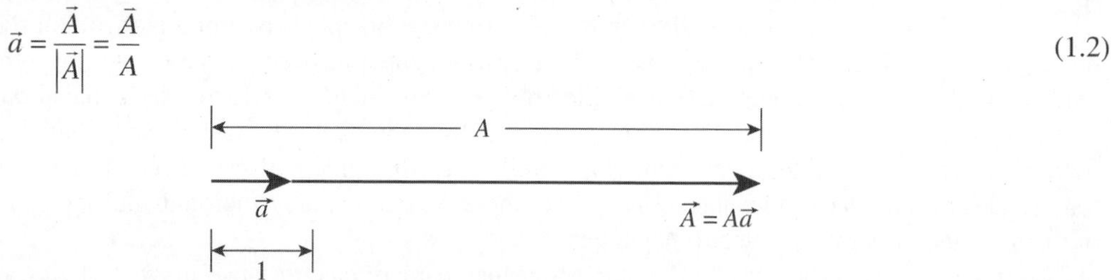

Figure 1.1 *Graphical representation of vector $\vec{A}$*

Figure 1.1 shows a graphical representation of the vector $\vec{A}$ as a straight line of magnitude A with its base pointing in the direction of $\vec{a}$. A vector $\vec{A}$ in rectangular (Cartesian) coordinate system, as shown in Figure 1.2, may be represented as

$$\vec{A} = A_x\vec{a}_x + A_y\vec{a}_y + A_z\vec{a}_z \tag{1.3}$$

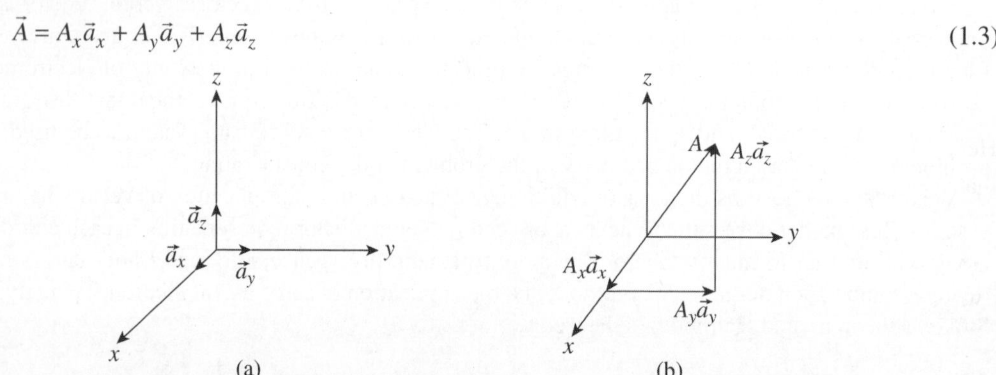

Figure 1.2 *Rectangular (Cartesian) coordinate system: (a) unit vectors and (b) components of $\vec{A}$*

The direction of x, y, and z coordinates is denoted by the three mutually perpendicular unit vectors $\vec{a}_x$, $\vec{a}_y$, and $\vec{a}_z$, which are called the base vectors. These unit vectors are shown in Figure 1.2(a) and the components of $\vec{A}$ along the coordinate axes are shown in Figure 1.2(b). The magnitude of vector represented by $\left|\vec{A}\right|$ is

$$\left|\vec{A}\right| = \sqrt{A_x^2 + A_y^2 + A_z^2} \tag{1.4}$$

Substituting Eqs (1.3) and (1.4) in Eq. (1.2), the unit vector $\vec{a}$ is given by

$$\vec{a} = \frac{\vec{A}}{\left|\vec{A}\right|} = \frac{A_x\vec{a}_x + A_y\vec{a}_y + A_z\vec{a}_z}{\sqrt{A_x^2 + A_y^2 + A_z^2}}$$

where A_x, A_y, and A_z denotes the components of $\vec{A}$ in a Cartesian coordinate system.

EXAMPLE 1.1

Given a vector $\vec{A} = 2\vec{a}_x + 2\vec{a}_y + \vec{a}_z$, determine the magnitude of vector $\vec{A}$, its unit vector, and the component of $\vec{A}$ along $\vec{a}_y$.

SOLUTION

The magnitude of vector $\vec{A}$ is

$$\left|\vec{A}\right| = \sqrt{A_x^2 + A_y^2 + A_z^2} = \sqrt{2^2 + 2^2 + 1^2} = 3$$

Its unit vector is

$$\vec{a}_A = \frac{\vec{A}}{\left|\vec{A}\right|} = \frac{2\vec{a}_x + 2\vec{a}_y + \vec{a}_z}{3}$$

The component of $\vec{A}$ along $\vec{a}_y$ is $A_y = 2$. ☐

1.2.1 Vector Equality

Two vectors $\vec{A}$ and $\vec{B}$ are said to be equal if they have equal magnitudes and identical unit vectors. For example, $\vec{A}$ and $\vec{B}$ are given by

$$\vec{A} = A\vec{a} = A_x\vec{a}_x + A_y\vec{a}_y + A_z\vec{a}_z \tag{1.5a}$$

$$\vec{B} = B\vec{b} = B_x\vec{b}_x + B_y\vec{b}_y + B_z\vec{b}_z \tag{1.5b}$$

Here, $\vec{A} = \vec{B}$ if and only if $\left|\vec{A}\right| = \left|\vec{B}\right|$ and $\vec{a} = \vec{b}$, which requires that $A_x = B_x$, $A_y = B_y$ and $A_z = B_z$. It is noted that vector manipulation is possible only if they have same unit vectors.

1.2.2 Vector Addition and Subtraction

Two vectors $\vec{A}$ and $\vec{B}$ can be added together to give the resultant vector $\vec{C}$ as given by

$$\vec{C} = \vec{A} + \vec{B} \tag{1.6}$$

Here, the vector addition is independent of the order in which the vectors are added, and the vectors obey both the *commutative law* and the *associative law* of addition. It is expressed as

$$\vec{A} + \vec{B} = \vec{B} + \vec{A} \qquad \text{(commutative property)}$$

$$\vec{A} + \left(\vec{B} + \vec{C}\right) = \left(\vec{A} + \vec{B}\right) + \vec{C} \qquad \text{(associative property)}$$

The vector addition can be carried out either by parallelogram method or head-to-tail method as shown in Figure 1.3. Here, Figure 1.3(a) shows the parallelogram rule, in which the resultant vector $\vec{C}$ is the diagonal of the parallelogram found by $\vec{A}$ and $\vec{B}$. The head-to-tail rule is possible when $\vec{A}$ is added to $\vec{B}$ or when $\vec{B}$ is added to $\vec{A}$. For example, when $\vec{B}$ is added to $\vec{A}$, it is positioned such that the tail of $\vec{B}$ starts at the tip of $\vec{A}$, by keeping its magnitude and direction unchanged. The sum vector $\vec{C}$ starts at the tail of $\vec{A}$ and ends at the tip of $\vec{B}$ as shown in Figure 1.3(b).

(a)   (b)

Figure 1.3   *Vector addition: (a) parallelogram rule and (b) head-to-tail rule*

The vector addition is carried out component by component. If (A_x, A_y, A_z) and (B_x, B_y, B_z) are the components of the vectors $\vec{A}$ and $\vec{B}$ in a rectangular coordinate system, then the vector addition can be written as follows:

$$\vec{C} = \vec{A} + \vec{B} = \left(A_x + B_x\right)\vec{a}_x + \left(A_y + B_y\right)\vec{a}_y + (A_z + B_z)\vec{a}_z$$

Similarly, vector subtraction can be written as

$$\vec{D} = \vec{A} - \vec{B} = \vec{A} + \left(-\vec{B}\right)$$

$$= \left(A_x - B_x\right)\vec{a}_x + \left(A_y - B_y\right)\vec{a}_y + \left(A_z - B_z\right)\vec{a}_z$$

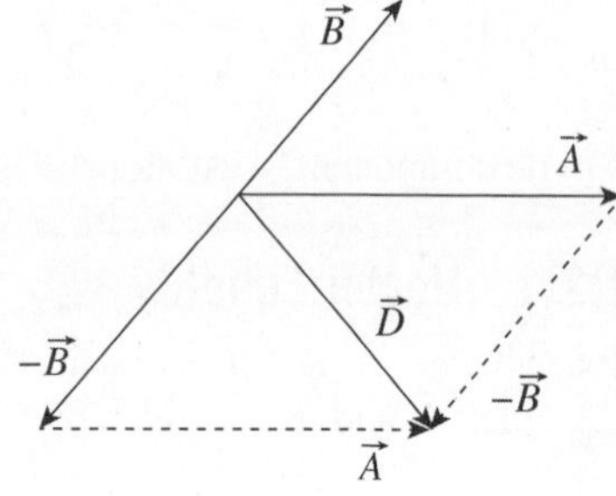

In graphical representation, the rules that are used for vector addition can also be applied to vector subtraction, as shown in Figure 1.4. The vector $(-\vec{B})$ can be drawn in the opposite direction of vector $\vec{B}$ with the same length.

Figure 1.4   *Vector subtraction*

If $\vec{A} = \vec{a}_x + 3\vec{a}_z$ and $\vec{B} = 5\vec{a}_x + 2\vec{a}_y - 6\vec{a}_z$, find (i) $\left|\vec{A} + \vec{B}\right|$, (ii) $5\vec{A} - \vec{B}$, (iii) the component of $\vec{A}$ along $\vec{a}_y$, and (iv) a unit vector parallel to $3\vec{A} + \vec{B}$.

SOLUTION

(*i*) $\vec{A} + \vec{B} = \left(\vec{a}_x + 3\vec{a}_z\right) + \left(5\vec{a}_x + 2\vec{a}_y - 6\vec{a}_z\right) = 6\vec{a}_x + 2\vec{a}_y - 3\vec{a}_z$

     $\left|\vec{A} + \vec{B}\right| = \sqrt{(6)^2 + (2)^2 + (-3)^2} = \sqrt{36 + 4 + 9} = 7$

(*ii*) $5\vec{A} - \vec{B} = 5\left(\vec{a}_x + 3\vec{a}_z\right) - \left(5\vec{a}_x + 2\vec{a}_y - 6\vec{a}_z\right) = -2\vec{a}_y + 21\vec{a}_z$

(*iii*)   The component of $\vec{A}$ along $\vec{a}_y$ is $A_y = 0$

(iv) $\quad 3\vec{A}+\vec{B} = 3\left(\vec{a}_x + 3\vec{a}_z\right) + \left(5\vec{a}_x + 2\vec{a}_y - 6\vec{a}_z\right) = 8\vec{a}_x + 2\vec{a}_y + 3\vec{a}_z$

Unit vector parallel to $3\vec{A}+\vec{B}$ is

$$\vec{a} = \frac{8\vec{a}_x + 2\vec{a}_y + 3\vec{a}_z}{\sqrt{(8)^2 + (2)^2 + (3)^2}} = \frac{8\vec{a}_x + 2\vec{a}_y + 3\vec{a}_z}{\sqrt{77}}$$

$$= 0.9117\vec{a}_x + 0.2279\vec{a}_y + 0.3419\vec{a}_z$$

1.2.3 Position and Distance Vectors

The position vector $(\vec{R})$ of a point P in space is defined as the vector from the origin O to point P. Here, points $P_1(x_1, y_1, z_1)$ and $P_2(x_2, y_2, z_2)$ in rectangular coordinate system are shown in Figure 1.5 and their position vectors are given by

$$\vec{R}_1 = \overrightarrow{OP_1} = x_1\vec{a}_x + y_1\vec{a}_y + z_1\vec{a}_z$$

$$\vec{R}_2 = \overrightarrow{OP_2} = x_2\vec{a}_x + y_2\vec{a}_y + z_2\vec{a}_z$$

The distance vector or separation vector $(\vec{R}_{12})$ is defined as the displacement from one point (P_1) to another point (P_2) as given by

$$\vec{R}_{12} = \overrightarrow{P_1P_2} = \vec{R}_2 - \vec{R}_1$$

$$= \left(x_2 - x_1\right)\vec{a}_x + \left(y_2 - y_1\right)\vec{a}_y + \left(z_2 - z_1\right)\vec{a}_z$$

The distance d between points P_1 and P_2 is equal to the magnitude of $\vec{R}_{12}$. Therefore,

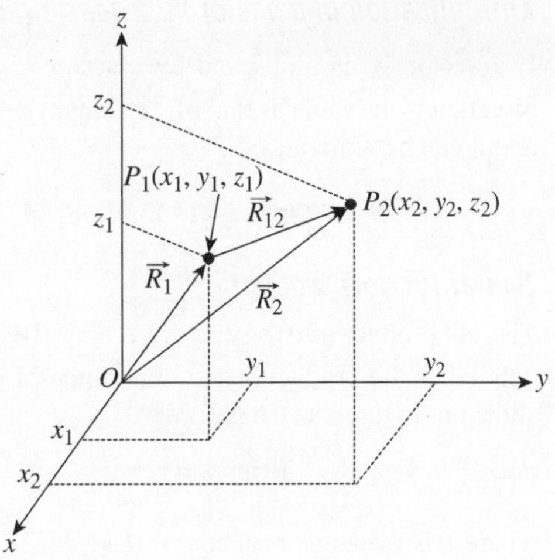
Figure 1.5 *Position and distance vectors*

$$d = \left|\vec{R}_{12}\right| = \sqrt{\left(x_2 - x_1\right)^2 + \left(y_2 - y_1\right)^2 + \left(z_2 - z_1\right)^2} \tag{1.7}$$

The first subscript of $\vec{R}_{12}$ in Eq. (1.7) denotes the location of the tail of vector $\vec{R}_{12}$ and the second subscript denotes the location of its head, as shown in Figure 1.5. It is noted that $\vec{R}_{12} \neq \vec{R}_{21}$ but $\left|\vec{R}_{12}\right| = \left|\vec{R}_{21}\right|$.

EXAMPLE 1.3

Determine the distance vector between the points $P_1(1,2,3)$ and $P_2(-1,-2,-3)$ in Cartesian coordinates and its magnitude.

SOLUTION

The distance vector is

$$\overrightarrow{P_1P_2} = \left(x_2 - x_1\right)\vec{a}_x + \left(y_2 - y_1\right)\vec{a}_y + \left(z_2 - z_1\right)\vec{a}_z$$

$$= \left(-1-1\right)\vec{a}_x + \left(-2-2\right)\vec{a}_y + \left(-3-3\right)\vec{a}_z$$

$$= -2\vec{a}_x - 4\vec{a}_y - 6\vec{a}_z$$

The magnitude of vector $\overrightarrow{P_1P_2}$ is

$$\left|\overrightarrow{P_1P_2}\right| = \sqrt{(-2)^2 + (-4)^2 + (-6)^2} = \sqrt{56}$$

1.2.4 Vector Multiplication

Vector products are of three types in vector algebra and they are simple product, scalar (or dot) product, and vector (or cross) product. When a vector is multiplied by a scalar, it is called simple product. When two vectors are multiplied, it results either in scalar product or vector product. Similarly, when three vectors are multiplied, only two products are possible – scalar triple product and vector triple product.

Multiplication of a vector by a scalar (simple product)

If a vector $\vec{A}$ is multiplied by a scalar k, the product is another vector $\vec{B}$ whose magnitude is kA and direction is the same as that of $\vec{A}$. This type of multiplication of a vector by a scalar is called simple product and it can be written as

$$\vec{B} = k\vec{A} = kA\vec{a} = \left(kA_x\right)\vec{a}_x + \left(kA_y\right)\vec{a}_y + \left(kA_z\right)\vec{a}_z \tag{1.8}$$

Scalar (or dot) product

The dot product of two vectors $\vec{A}$ and $\vec{B}$ is generally written as $\vec{A}\cdot\vec{B}$ and can be read as "$\vec{A}$ dot $\vec{B}$". It is defined as the product of the magnitude of two vectors and the cosine of the angle between $\vec{A}$ and $\vec{B}$, as shown in Figure 1.6. Therefore,

$$\vec{A}\cdot\vec{B} = \left|\vec{A}\right|\left|\vec{B}\right|\cos\theta_{AB} \tag{1.9}$$

where θ is the angle between $\vec{A}$ and $\vec{B}$. As the product of two vectors results in a scalar quantity, this dot product is also called a scalar product. When the two vectors are parallel ($\theta = 0°$), their dot product is maximum. When the two vectors are perpendicular or orthogonal ($\theta = 90°$) to each other, their dot product is zero.

The quantity $\left|\vec{B}\right|\cos\theta$ in the above dot product equation is the component of $\vec{B}$ along $\vec{A}$ and is equal to the projection of vector $\vec{B}$ on $\vec{A}$. Hence, the scalar projection of $\vec{B}$ on $\vec{A}$ is given by

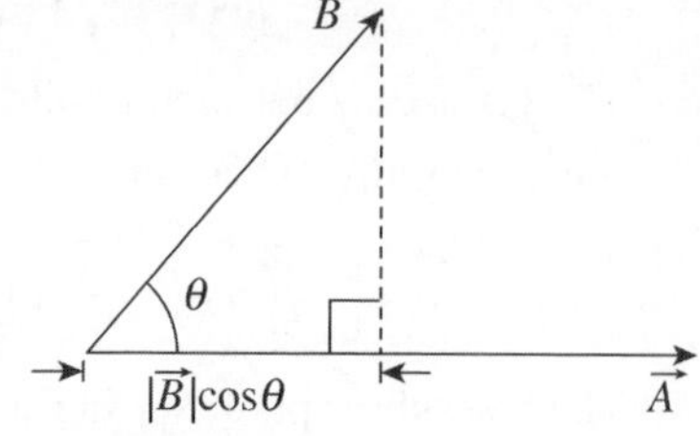

Figure 1.6 *Dot product*

$$\left|\vec{B}\right|\cos\theta = \frac{\vec{A}\cdot\vec{B}}{\left|\vec{A}\right|} = \vec{B}\cdot\vec{a}_A \qquad \left(\text{since } \vec{a}_A = \frac{\vec{A}}{\left|\vec{A}\right|}\right)$$

The vector projection of $\vec{B}$ on $\vec{A}$ can be defined by including the unit vector along $\vec{A}$ as given by

$$B\cos\theta\,\vec{a}_A = \left(\vec{B}\cdot\vec{a}_A\right)\vec{a}_A$$

The dot product equation can also be used to determine the angle between the two vectors $\vec{A}$ and $\vec{B}$ as given by

$$\cos\theta = \frac{\vec{A}\cdot\vec{B}}{\left|\vec{A}\right|\left|\vec{B}\right|} = \frac{\vec{A}\cdot\vec{B}}{AB}$$

If two unit vectors are parallel to each other, then their dot product is given by

$$\vec{a}_x \cdot \vec{a}_x = \vec{a}_y \cdot \vec{a}_y = \vec{a}_z \cdot \vec{a}_z = 1$$

and if two unit vectors are orthogonal to each other, then their dot product is given by

$$\vec{a}_x \cdot \vec{a}_y = \vec{a}_y \cdot \vec{a}_z = \vec{a}_z \cdot \vec{a}_x = 0$$

If $\left(A_x, A_y, A_z\right)$ and $\left(B_x, B_y, B_z\right)$ are the coordinates of the vectors $\vec{A}$ and $\vec{B}$ in a rectangular coordinate system, then their dot product is represented by

$$\vec{A} \cdot \vec{B} = \left(A_x \vec{a}_x + A_y \vec{a}_y + A_z \vec{a}_z\right) \cdot \left(B_x \vec{b}_x + B_y \vec{b}_y + B_z \vec{b}_z\right)$$

Using the dot product property of unit vectors, the above expression can be simplified as

$$\vec{A} \cdot \vec{B} = A_x B_x + A_y B_y + A_z B_z \tag{1.10}$$

The dot product of a vector $\vec{A}$ with itself results in

$$\vec{A} \cdot \vec{A} = |\vec{A}||\vec{A}| = |\vec{A}|^2 = A^2$$

Therefore, if the vector $\vec{A}$ is defined in a given coordinate system, then its magnitude can be determined as

$$A = |\vec{A}| = \sqrt{\vec{A} \cdot \vec{A}}$$

and if the vectors $\vec{A}$ and $\vec{B}$ are specified in a given coordinate system, then the smaller angle θ between them can be determined from

$$\theta = \cos^{-1}\left[\frac{\vec{A} \cdot \vec{B}}{|\vec{A}||\vec{B}|}\right] = \cos^{-1}\left[\frac{\vec{A} \cdot \vec{B}}{\sqrt{\vec{A} \cdot \vec{A}}\,\sqrt{\vec{B} \cdot \vec{B}}}\right] \tag{1.11}$$

The basic properties of dot product are:

Commutative: $\vec{A} \cdot \vec{B} = \vec{B} \cdot \vec{A}$

Distributive: $\vec{A} \cdot \left(\vec{B} + \vec{C}\right) = \vec{A} \cdot \vec{B} + \vec{A} \cdot \vec{C}$

Scaling: $k\left(\vec{A} \cdot \vec{B}\right) = \left(k\vec{A}\right) \cdot \vec{B} = \vec{A} \cdot \left(k\vec{B}\right)$

EXAMPLE 1.4

Given the two vectors $\vec{A} = 2\vec{a}_x - 5\vec{a}_y - 4\vec{a}_z$ and $\vec{B} = 3\vec{a}_x + 5\vec{a}_y + 2\vec{a}_z$, determine the dot product and the angle between the two vectors.

SOLUTION

Using Eq. (1.10), the dot product is

$$\vec{A} \cdot \vec{B} = A_x B_x + A_y B_y + A_z B_z = (2)(3) + (-5)(5) + (-4)(2) = -27$$

Since $\vec{A} \cdot \vec{B}$ is negative, the angle between the two vectors will be greater than 90°.

$$|\vec{A}| = \sqrt{(2)^2 + (-5)^2 + (-4)^2} = \sqrt{45}$$

$$\left|\vec{B}\right| = \sqrt{(3)^2 + (5)^2 + (2)^2} = \sqrt{38}$$

Therefore, $\theta_{AB} = \cos^{-1}\left[\dfrac{\vec{A}\cdot\vec{B}}{\left|\vec{A}\right|\left|\vec{B}\right|}\right] = \cos^{-1}\left(\dfrac{-27}{\sqrt{45}\sqrt{38}}\right) = 130.76°$

EXAMPLE 1.5

Show that the vectors $\vec{A} = 6\vec{a}_x + 4\vec{a}_y - 5\vec{a}_z$ and $\vec{B} = 5\vec{a}_x - 5\vec{a}_y + 2\vec{a}_z$ are perpendicular to each other.

SOLUTION

Two vectors $\vec{A}$ and $\vec{B}$ will be perpendicular to each other if $\vec{A}\cdot\vec{B} = 0$.

$$\begin{aligned}
\vec{A}\cdot\vec{B} &= A_x B_x + A_y B_y + A_z B_z \\
&= 6(5) - (4)(5) - (5)(2) = 0
\end{aligned}$$

Hence, the given vectors $\vec{A}$ and $\vec{B}$ are perpendicular to each other.

EXAMPLE 1.6

Given $\vec{A} = (y-1)\vec{a}_x + 2x\vec{a}_y$, determine the vector $\vec{A}$ at a point $(2, 2, 1)$ and the scalar projection of $\vec{A}$ on $\vec{B}$ where $\vec{B} = 5\vec{a}_x - \vec{a}_y + 2\vec{a}_z$.

SOLUTION

(a) Vector $\vec{A}$ at a point $(2, 2, 1) = (2-1)\vec{a}_x + (2)(2)\vec{a}_y = \vec{a}_x + 4\vec{a}_y$.

(b) Scalar projection of $\vec{A}$ on $\vec{B}$ is obtained by expressing the unit vector in the direction of the second vector $(\vec{a}_B)$, as shown in Figure E1.6, and then taking the dot product with $\vec{A}$ as given below:

Scalar projection of $\vec{A}$ on $\vec{B}$

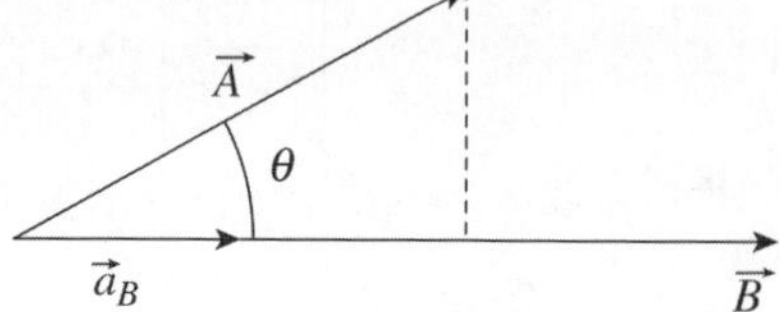

Figure E1.6

$$= \vec{A}\cdot\vec{a}_B = \frac{\vec{A}\cdot\vec{B}}{\left|\vec{B}\right|} = \frac{(1)(5)+(4)(-1)}{\sqrt{(5)^2+(-1)^2+(2)^2}} = \frac{1}{\sqrt{30}}$$

EXAMPLE 1.7

Given $\vec{A} = 5\vec{a}_x$ and $\vec{B} = 4\vec{a}_x + B_y\vec{a}_y$, determine B_y such that angle between $\vec{A}$ and $\vec{B}$ is $45°$. If $\vec{B}$ also has a term $B_z\vec{a}_z$, what relationship must exist between B_y and B_z?

SOLUTION

Given $\vec{A} = 5\vec{a}_x$, $\vec{B} = 4\vec{a}_x + B_y\vec{a}_y$, and $\theta = 45°$

$$\vec{A}\cdot\vec{B} = A_x B_x + A_y B_y + A_z B_z = (5\times4)+(0)+(0) = 20$$

But $\vec{A}\cdot\vec{B} = \left|\vec{A}\right|\left|\vec{B}\right|\cos\theta$

$$20 = \sqrt{(5)^2} \sqrt{(4)^2 + (B_y)^2} \cos 45°$$

$$\sqrt{16 + B_y^2} = 4\sqrt{2}$$

$$B_y^2 = 16$$

Hence, $B_y = \pm 4$

If $\vec{B}$ also has a term $B_z \vec{a}_z$, then

$$20 = \sqrt{(5)^2} \sqrt{(4)^2 + (B_y)^2 + (B_z)^2} \cos 45°$$

$$\sqrt{16 + B_y^2 + B_z^2} = 4\sqrt{2}$$

Therefore, $B_y^2 + B_z^2 = 16$

which gives the relation between B_y and B_z.

Vector (or cross) product

The cross product of two vectors $\vec{A}$ and $\vec{B}$ is generally written as $\vec{A} \times \vec{B}$ and can be read as "$\vec{A}$ cross $\vec{B}$". The cross product of two vectors results in a vector that is directed normal to the plane containing $\vec{A}$ and $\vec{B}$, as shown in Figure 1.7. The magnitude of the cross product is equal to the product of the magnitude of the vectors and the sine of the angle between them. The resultant product $\vec{C}$ is represented by

$$\vec{C} = \vec{A} \times \vec{B} = \vec{a}_n |\vec{A}||\vec{B}| \sin\theta \tag{1.12}$$

where θ is the angle between $\vec{A}$ and $\vec{B}$ and $\vec{a}_n$ is a unit vector normal to the plane of $\vec{A}$ and $\vec{B}$. The unit vector $\vec{a}_n$ points in the direction of motion of a right-handed screw rotating from $\vec{A}$ to $\vec{B}$, as shown in Figure 1.7(a).

The direction of unit vector $\vec{a}_n$ can also be determined by extending the fingers of the right hand, as shown in Figure 1.7(b). When the fore finger points in the direction of $\vec{A}$ and the middle finger in the direction of $\vec{B}$, the thumb points in the direction of the resultant product vector $\vec{C}$, i.e., the direction of the unit vector $\vec{a}_n$. As the product of two vectors results in a vector quantity, this cross product is also called vector product.

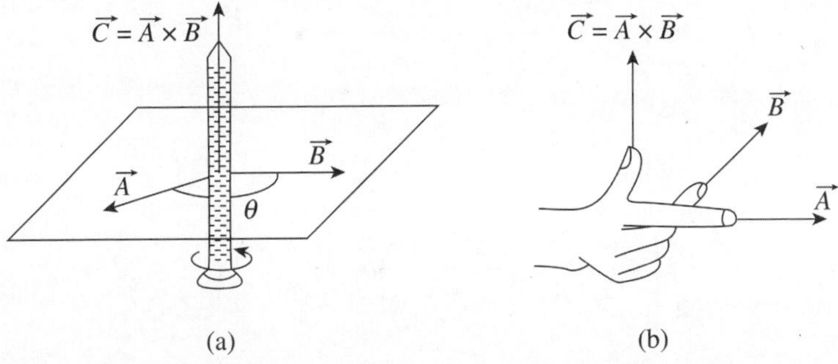

Figure 1.7   *Cross product: (a) right-hand screw rule and (b) right-hand rule*

If two unit vectors are parallel to each other, then their cross products are represented by

$$\vec{a}_x \times \vec{a}_x = \vec{a}_y \times \vec{a}_y = \vec{a}_z \times \vec{a}_z = 0$$

and if two unit vectors are orthogonal to each other, then their cross products are represented by

$$\vec{a}_x \times \vec{a}_y = \vec{a}_z \qquad \vec{a}_y \times \vec{a}_z = \vec{a}_x \qquad \vec{a}_z \times \vec{a}_x = \vec{a}_y$$

If $\left(A_x, A_y, A_z\right)$ and $\left(B_x, B_y, B_z\right)$ are the coordinates of the vectors $\vec{A}$ and $\vec{B}$ in a rectangular coordinate system, then their cross product is represented by

$$\vec{A} \times \vec{B} = \left(A_x \vec{a}_x + A_y \vec{a}_y + A_z \vec{a}_z\right) \times \left(B_x \vec{a}_x + B_y \vec{a}_y + B_z \vec{a}_z\right)$$

The above cross product equation can also be expressed in a simple determinant form as

$$\vec{A} \times \vec{B} = \begin{vmatrix} \vec{a}_x & \vec{a}_y & \vec{a}_z \\ A_x & A_y & A_z \\ B_x & B_y & B_z \end{vmatrix} \tag{1.13}$$

$$= \left(A_y B_z - A_z B_y\right)\vec{a}_x - \left(A_x B_z - A_z B_x\right)\vec{a}_y + \left(A_x B_y - A_y B_x\right)\vec{a}_z$$

The basic properties of cross product are:

Non-commutative: $\vec{A} \times B = -\vec{B} \times \vec{A}$

Distributive: $\vec{A} \times \left(\vec{B} + \vec{C}\right) = \vec{A} \times \vec{B} + \vec{A} \times \vec{C}$

Scaling : $k\left(\vec{A} \times \vec{B}\right) = \left(k\vec{A}\right) \times \vec{B} = \vec{A} \times \left(k\vec{B}\right)$

EXAMPLE 1.8

Given the two vectors $\vec{A} = 3\vec{a}_x + 4\vec{a}_y - 5\vec{a}_z$ and $\vec{B} = -6\vec{a}_x + 2\vec{a}_y + 4\vec{a}_z$, determine the unit vector normal to the plane containing the vectors $\vec{A}$ and $\vec{B}$.

SOLUTION

Given $\vec{A} = 3\vec{a}_x + 4\vec{a}_y - 5\vec{a}_z$ and $\vec{B} = -6\vec{a}_x + 2\vec{a}_y + 4\vec{a}_z$.

The unit vector normal to the plane containing the vectors $\vec{A}$ and $\vec{B}$ is the unit vector in the direction of cross product of $\vec{A}$ and $\vec{B}$.

From Eq. (1.13),

$$\vec{A} \times \vec{B} = \begin{vmatrix} \vec{a}_x & \vec{a}_y & \vec{a}_z \\ A_x & A_y & A_z \\ B_x & B_y & B_z \end{vmatrix}$$

$$= \begin{vmatrix} \vec{a}_x & \vec{a}_y & \vec{a}_z \\ 3 & 4 & -5 \\ -6 & 2 & 4 \end{vmatrix} = \begin{vmatrix} 4 & -5 \\ 2 & 4 \end{vmatrix}\vec{a}_x - \begin{vmatrix} 3 & -5 \\ -6 & 4 \end{vmatrix}\vec{a}_y + \begin{vmatrix} 3 & 4 \\ -6 & 2 \end{vmatrix}\vec{a}_z$$

$$= 26\vec{a}_x + 18\vec{a}_y + 30\vec{a}_z$$

The unit normal vector is

$$\vec{a}_n = \frac{\vec{A} \times \vec{B}}{\left|\vec{A} \times \vec{B}\right|} = \frac{26\vec{a}_x + 18\vec{a}_y + 30\vec{a}_z}{\sqrt{(26)^2 + (18)^2 + (19)^2}} = 0.596\vec{a}_x + 0.413\vec{a}_y + 0.688\vec{a}_z \qquad \square$$

EXAMPLE 1.9

Determine the angle θ between vectors $\vec{A} = 2\vec{a}_x + 3\vec{a}_y + 3\vec{a}_z$ and $\vec{B} = -\vec{a}_x - 5\vec{a}_y - \vec{a}_z$ using the cross product between them.

SOLUTION

We know that $\vec{A} \times \vec{B} = \vec{a}_n \left|\vec{A}\right| \left|\vec{B}\right| \sin\theta$

Therefore, $\sin\theta = \dfrac{\left|\vec{A} \times \vec{B}\right|}{\left|\vec{A}\right| \left|\vec{B}\right|}$

$$= \frac{\left|\left(2\vec{a}_x + 3\vec{a}_y + 3\vec{a}_z\right) \times \left(-\vec{a}_x - 5\vec{a}_y - \vec{a}_z\right)\right|}{\sqrt{22}\sqrt{27}}$$

$$= \frac{\left|12\vec{a}_x - \vec{a}_y - 7\vec{a}_z\right|}{\sqrt{22}\sqrt{27}} = \frac{\sqrt{144 + 1 + 49}}{\sqrt{22}\sqrt{27}} = 0.57$$

Hence, $\theta = \sin^{-1}(0.57) = 34.9°$ or $145.1°$ $\qquad \square$

EXAMPLE 1.10

If two vectors are expressed in rectangular coordinates as $\vec{A} = 2\vec{a}_x + \pi\vec{a}_y + \vec{a}_z$ and $\vec{B} = -\vec{a}_x + \dfrac{3\pi}{2}\vec{a}_y - 2\vec{a}_z$, then determine a unit vector perpendicular to the plane containing $\vec{A}$ and $\vec{B}$ as given by their cross product.

SOLUTION

We know that, $\vec{A} \times \vec{B} = \begin{vmatrix} \vec{a}_x & \vec{a}_y & \vec{a}_z \\ A_x & A_y & A_z \\ B_x & B_y & B_z \end{vmatrix} = \begin{vmatrix} \vec{a}_x & \vec{a}_y & \vec{a}_z \\ 2 & \pi & 1 \\ -1 & \dfrac{3\pi}{2} & -2 \end{vmatrix}$

$$= \left(-2\pi - \frac{3\pi}{2}\right)\vec{a}_x + (4-1)\vec{a}_y + 3(3\pi + \pi)\vec{a}_z$$

$$= -\frac{7\pi}{2}\vec{a}_x + 3\vec{a}_y + 4\pi\vec{a}_z$$

Therefore, the unit vector perpendicular to the plane containing $\vec{A}$ and $\vec{B}$ is

$$\vec{a}_n = \frac{\vec{A} \times \vec{B}}{\left|\vec{A} \times \vec{B}\right|}$$

$$= \frac{-\dfrac{7\pi}{2}\vec{a}_x + 3\vec{a}_y + 4\pi\vec{a}_z}{\sqrt{\left(\dfrac{7\pi}{2}\right)^2 + (3)^2 + \left(4\pi^2\right)}} = \frac{-3.5\pi\vec{a}_x + 3\vec{a}_y + 4\pi\vec{a}_z}{16.9651}$$

Hence, $\vec{a}_n = -0.648\vec{a}_x + 0.1768\vec{a}_y + 0.74\vec{a}_z$

EXAMPLE 1.11

Show that the vectors $\vec{A} = 6\vec{a}_x - 3\vec{a}_y + 3\vec{a}_z$ and $\vec{B} = -4\vec{a}_x + 2\vec{a}_y - 2\vec{a}_z$ are parallel to each other.

SOLUTION

Given $\vec{A} = 6\vec{a}_x - 3\vec{a}_y + 3\vec{a}_z$ and $\vec{B} = -4\vec{a}_x + 2\vec{a}_y - 2\vec{a}_z$.

Two vectors $\vec{A}$ and $\vec{B}$ are said to be parallel to each other if $\vec{A} \times \vec{B} = 0$.
That is,

$$\vec{A} \times \vec{B} = \begin{vmatrix} \vec{a}_x & \vec{a}_y & \vec{a}_z \\ 6 & -3 & 3 \\ -4 & 2 & -2 \end{vmatrix}$$

$$= [6-6]\vec{a}_x - [-12+12]\vec{a}_y + [12-12]\vec{a}_z = 0$$

Hence, the given vectors $\vec{A}$ and $\vec{B}$ are parallel to each other.

Scalar triple product

The dot product of a vector $\vec{A}$ with the cross product of other two vectors $\vec{B}$ and $\vec{C}$, results in a scalar, and hence, is called a scalar triple product. A scalar triple product obeys the following cyclic order $(ABCABC...)$ as given by

$$\vec{A} \cdot (\vec{B} \times \vec{C}) = \vec{B} \cdot (\vec{C} \times \vec{A}) = \vec{C} \cdot (\vec{A} \times \vec{B})$$

If $\left(A_x, A_y, A_z\right), \left(B_x, B_y, B_z\right)$, and $\left(C_x, C_y, C_z\right)$ are the coordinates of the vectors $\vec{A}$, $\vec{B}$, and $\vec{C}$, in a rectangular coordinate system, then the scalar triple product can be written in the form of a 3×3 determinant form as

$$\vec{A} \cdot (\vec{B} \times \vec{C}) = \begin{vmatrix} A_x & A_y & A_z \\ B_x & B_y & B_z \\ C_x & C_y & C_z \end{vmatrix} \tag{1.14}$$

However, the cross product of a vector $\vec{A}$ with the dot product of other two vectors $\vec{B}$ and $\vec{C}$, i.e., $\vec{A} \times (\vec{B} \cdot \vec{C})$ carries no meaning because $(\vec{B} \cdot \vec{C})$ results in a scalar, and the cross product of the vector $\vec{A}$ with a scalar is not defined under the rules of vector algebra.

Therefore, the only two useful products of three vectors are the scalar triple product and the vector triple product. If the vectors $\vec{A}$, $\vec{B}$, and $\vec{C}$ represent the sides of a parallelepiped, then its volume is determined by the scalar triple product. If the scalar triple product is zero, then the vectors will be coplanar.

Vector triple product

The cross product of a vector $\vec{A}$ with the cross product of other two vectors $\vec{B}$ and $\vec{C}$ results in a vector and hence, it is called a vector triple product, i.e., $\vec{A} \times \left(\vec{B} \times \vec{C} \right)$. Since each cross product yields a vector, the result of a vector triple product is also a vector. The vector triple product does not obey the associative law, i.e., $\vec{A} \times \left(\vec{B} \times \vec{C} \right) \neq \left(\vec{A} \times \vec{B} \right) \times \vec{C}$.

This shows that it is important to specify which cross multiplication is to be performed first. The vector triple product expression can be written by expanding the vectors $\vec{A}$, $\vec{B}$, and $\vec{C}$ in component form as

$$\vec{A} \times \left(\vec{B} \times \vec{C} \right) = \vec{B} \left(\vec{A} \cdot \vec{C} \right) - \vec{C} \left(\vec{A} \cdot \vec{B} \right) \tag{1.15}$$

which follows the "bac-cab" rule.

EXAMPLE 1.12

The three vector fields are given by $\vec{A} = 2\vec{a}_x - \vec{a}_z$, $\vec{B} = 2\vec{a}_x - \vec{a}_y + 2\vec{a}_z$ and $\vec{C} = 2\vec{a}_x - 3\vec{a}_y + \vec{a}_z$. Determine the scalar triple product and vector triple product.

SOLUTION

Given $\vec{A} = 2\vec{a}_x - \vec{a}_z$, $\vec{B} = 2\vec{a}_x - \vec{a}_y + 2\vec{a}_z$, and $\vec{C} = 2\vec{a}_x - 3\vec{a}_y + \vec{a}_z$.

The scalar triple product is given by

$$\vec{A} \cdot (\vec{B} \times \vec{C}) = \begin{vmatrix} 2 & 0 & -1 \\ 2 & -1 & 2 \\ 2 & -3 & 1 \end{vmatrix} = 14$$

The vector triple product is given by

$$\vec{A} \times (\vec{B} \times \vec{C}) = \vec{B}(\vec{A} \cdot \vec{C}) - \vec{C}(\vec{A} \cdot \vec{B})$$

where $\vec{A} \cdot \vec{C} = (2)(2) + (0)(-3) + (-1)(1) = 3$

and $\vec{A} \cdot \vec{B} = (2)(2) + (0)(-1) + (-1)(2) = 2$

Therefore, $\vec{A} \times (\vec{B} \times \vec{C}) = 3\vec{B} - 2\vec{C} = 3(2\vec{a}_x - \vec{a}_y + 2\vec{a}_z) - 2(2\vec{a}_x - 3\vec{a}_y + \vec{a}_z)$

$$= 2\vec{a}_x + 3\vec{a}_y + 4\vec{a}_z$$

EXAMPLE 1.13

Given the three vectors $\vec{A} = \vec{a}_x + 2\vec{a}_z$, $\vec{B} = \vec{a}_y + \vec{a}_z$, and $\vec{C} = -2\vec{a}_x + 3\vec{a}_z$, determine $\left(\vec{A} \times \vec{B} \right) \times \vec{C}$ and compare it with $\vec{A} \times \left(\vec{B} \times \vec{C} \right)$.

SOLUTION

The vector triple product can also be solved using determinant form as given by

$$\vec{A}\times\vec{B}=\begin{vmatrix} \vec{a}_x & \vec{a}_y & \vec{a}_z \\ 1 & 0 & 2 \\ 0 & 1 & 1 \end{vmatrix}$$
$$=-2\vec{a}_x-\vec{a}_y+\vec{a}_z$$

$$\vec{B}\times\vec{C}=\begin{vmatrix} \vec{a}_x & \vec{a}_y & \vec{a}_z \\ 0 & 1 & 1 \\ -2 & 0 & 3 \end{vmatrix}$$
$$=3\vec{a}_x-2\vec{a}_y+2\vec{a}_z$$

$$\left(\vec{A}\times\vec{B}\right)\times\vec{C}=\begin{vmatrix} \vec{a}_x & \vec{a}_y & \vec{a}_z \\ -2 & -1 & 1 \\ -2 & 0 & 3 \end{vmatrix}$$
$$=-3\vec{a}_x+4\vec{a}_y-2\vec{a}_z$$

$$\vec{A}\times\left(\vec{B}\times\vec{C}\right)=\begin{vmatrix} \vec{a}_x & \vec{a}_y & \vec{a}_z \\ 1 & 0 & 2 \\ 3 & -2 & 2 \end{vmatrix}$$
$$=4\vec{a}_x+4\vec{a}_y-2\vec{a}_z$$

Since $\vec{A}\times\left(\vec{B}\times\vec{C}\right)\neq\left(\vec{A}\times\vec{B}\right)\times\vec{C}$, the vector triple product does not obey the associative law. ◻

1.3   ORTHOGONAL COORDINATE SYSTEMS

The physical quantities used in electromagnetics are functions of both time and space. So, a three-dimensional coordinate system is more convenient to specify the location of a point in space or the direction of a vector quantity. An orthogonal coordinate system is one whose coordinates are mutually perpendicular to each other, whereas in a non-orthogonal coordinate system, all three coordinates are not mutually perpendicular.

The most commonly used orthogonal coordinate systems in the study of vector quantities are *rectangular* (Cartesian), *cylindrical*, and *spherical* systems. Any point P can be represented in the three coordinates as shown in Figure 1.8. The choice of coordinate system for a specific problem depends on the geometry of the problem under consideration. The properties of each orthogonal systems and transformation of coordinate variables and vector components from one coordinate system to another are discussed in this section.

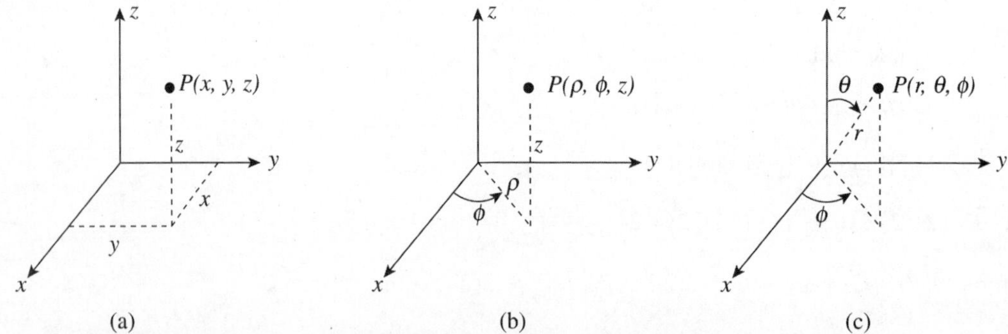

Figure 1.8   *Orthogonal coordinate systems: (a) Cartesian, (b) cylindrical, and (c) spherical*

1.3.1   Rectangular (Cartesian) Coordinates (x, y, z)

A rectangular coordinate system is a system formed by three mutually orthogonal straight lines and these lines are called the x, y, and z axes. The point of intersection of these axes is the origin. Any point P can be represented as (x, y, z) in rectangular coordinate system as shown in Figure 1.9(a). The ranges of the coordinate variables x, y, and z are $-\infty < x, y, z < \infty$. Therefore, a vector $\vec{A}$ in rectangular coordinates can be written as

$$\vec{A} = A_x \vec{a}_x + A_y \vec{a}_y + A_z \vec{a}_z \tag{1.16}$$

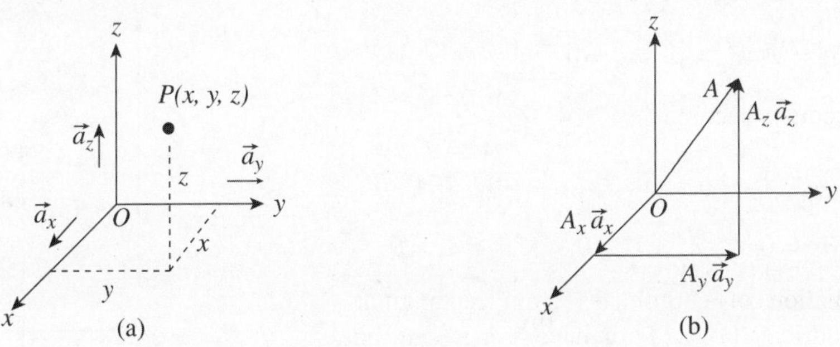

Figure 1.9 *Rectangular coordinate system: (a) representation of a point P and unit vectors and (b) components of A along $\vec{a}_x, \vec{a}_y$, and $\vec{a}_z$*

where $\vec{a}_x, \vec{a}_y$, and $\vec{a}_z$ denote the unit vectors that indicate the directions of the components of a vector along the x, y, and z axes, respectively. Here, A_x, A_y, and A_z denotes the magnitude components of $\vec{A}$ in a rectangular coordinate system, as shown in Figure 1.9(b). Since the three unit vectors are mutually orthogonal, their dot product becomes

$$\vec{a}_x \cdot \vec{a}_x = \vec{a}_y \cdot \vec{a}_y = \vec{a}_z \cdot \vec{a}_z = 1$$
$$\vec{a}_x \cdot \vec{a}_y = \vec{a}_y \cdot \vec{a}_z = \vec{a}_z \cdot \vec{a}_x = 0$$

and their cross product becomes

$$\vec{a}_x \times \vec{a}_y = \vec{a}_z, \qquad \vec{a}_y \times \vec{a}_z = \vec{a}_x, \qquad \vec{a}_z \times \vec{a}_x = \vec{a}_y$$
$$\vec{a}_x \times \vec{a}_x = 0, \qquad \vec{a}_y \times \vec{a}_y = 0, \qquad \vec{a}_z \times \vec{a}_z = 0$$

1.3.2 Cylindrical Coordinates (ρ, ϕ, z)

The cylindrical coordinate system is mainly considered when dealing with problems of circular or cylindrical symmetry. Any point P can be represented as (ρ, ϕ, z) in cylindrical coordinate system as shown in Figure 1.10. The coordinate ρ is the radius of the cylinder passing through P or the radial distance in the xy-plane, ϕ is the azimuth angle measured from the x-axis in the xy-plane and z is the same as in the Cartesian system. The ranges of the variables are $0 \le \rho < \infty$, $0 \le \phi < 2\pi$, and $-\infty < z < \infty$.

A vector $\vec{A}$ in cylindrical coordinates can be written as

$$\vec{A} = A_\rho \vec{a}_\rho + A_\phi \vec{a}_\phi + A_z \vec{a}_z \tag{1.17}$$

where $\vec{a}_\rho, \vec{a}_\phi$, and $\vec{a}_z$ are unit vectors in the ρ, ϕ, and z direction as shown in Figure 1.10. Therefore, the magnitude of A is

$$|\vec{A}| = \sqrt{\left(A_\rho^2 + A_\phi^2 + A_z^2\right)}$$

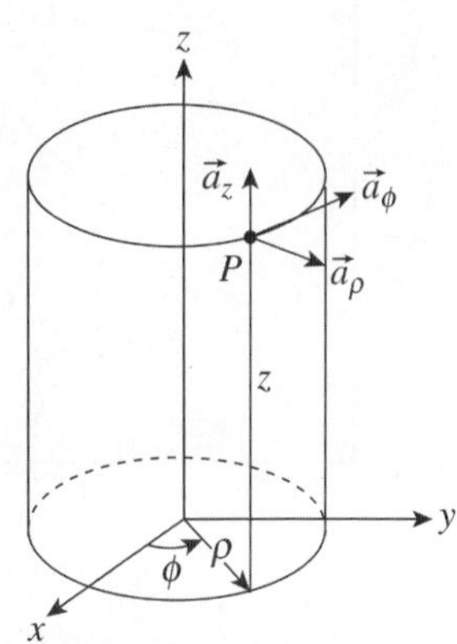

Figure 1.10 *Representation of a point P and unit vectors in the cylindrical coordinate system*

Since the coordinate system is orthogonal, unit vectors $\vec{a}_\rho, \vec{a}_\phi$, and $\vec{a}_z$ are mutually perpendicular. Here, $\vec{a}_\rho$ is in the direction of increasing ρ, $\vec{a}_\phi$ is in the direction of increasing ϕ, and $\vec{a}_z$ is in the positive z-direction. Since the three unit vectors are mutually orthogonal, their dot products become

$$\vec{a}_\rho \cdot \vec{a}_\rho = \vec{a}_\phi \cdot \vec{a}_\phi = \vec{a}_z \cdot \vec{a}_z = 1$$

$$\vec{a}_\rho \cdot \vec{a}_\phi = \vec{a}_\phi \cdot \vec{a}_z = \vec{a}_z \cdot \vec{a}_\rho = 0$$

and their cross products become

$$\vec{a}_\rho \times \vec{a}_\phi = \vec{a}_z, \quad \vec{a}_\phi \times \vec{a}_z = \vec{a}_\rho, \quad \vec{a}_z \times \vec{a}_\rho = \vec{a}_\phi$$

$$\vec{a}_\rho \times \vec{a}_\rho = 0, \quad \vec{a}_\phi \times \vec{a}_\phi = 0, \quad \vec{a}_z \times \vec{a}_z = 0$$

The transformation of coordinates from rectangular (x,y,z) to cylindrical (ρ,ϕ,z) or vice versa can be obtained using the relationship shown in Figure 1.11 and they can be written as

$$\rho = \sqrt{x^2 + y^2}, \quad \phi = \tan^{-1}\frac{y}{x}, \quad z = z$$

or

$$x = \rho\cos\phi, \quad y = \rho\sin\phi, \quad z = z$$

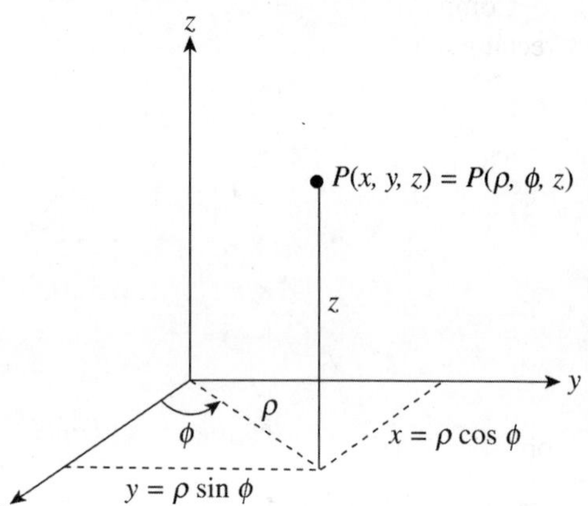

Figure 1.11 *Relationship between (x, y, z) and (ρ, φ, z)*

Similarly, the transformation of unit vectors from rectangular $\left(\vec{a}_x, \vec{a}_y, \vec{a}_z\right)$ to cylindrical $\left(\vec{a}_\rho, \vec{a}_\phi, \vec{a}_z\right)$ or vice versa can be obtained geometrically from Figure 1.12 as given by

$$\vec{a}_x = \cos\phi\,\vec{a}_\rho - \sin\phi\,\vec{a}_\phi \qquad \vec{a}_y = \sin\phi\,\vec{a}_\rho + \cos\phi\,\vec{a}_\phi \qquad \vec{a}_z = \vec{a}_z \qquad (1.18)$$

or

$$\vec{a}_\rho = \cos\phi\,\vec{a}_x + \sin\phi\,\vec{a}_y \qquad \vec{a}_\phi = -\sin\phi\,\vec{a}_x + \cos\phi\,\vec{a}_y \qquad \vec{a}_z = \vec{a}_z \qquad (1.19)$$

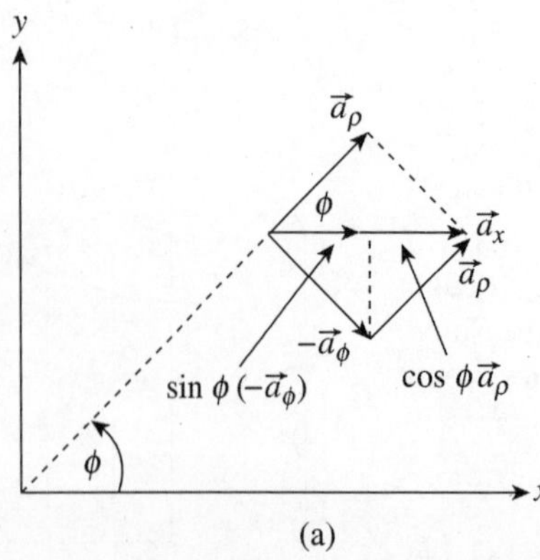

(a)

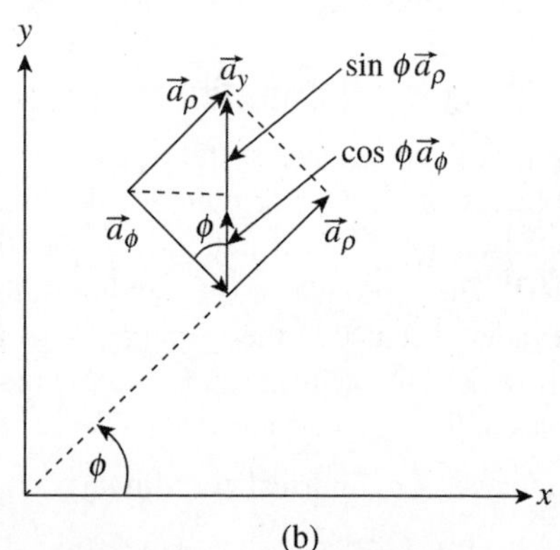

(b)

Figure 1.12 *Transformation of unit vectors: (a) cylindrical components of $\vec{a}_x$ (b) cylindrical component of $\vec{a}_y$*

Finally, the relationship between the vector components $\left(A_x, A_y, A_z\right)$ and $\left(A_\rho, A_\phi, A_z\right)$ is obtained by substituting Eq. (1.18) into Eq. (1.16) and rearranging the terms, we have

$$\vec{A} = A_x \left(\cos\phi\, \vec{a}_\rho - \sin\phi\, \vec{a}_\phi \right) + A_y \left(\sin\phi\, \vec{a}_\rho + \cos\phi\, \vec{a}_\phi \right) + A_z \vec{a}_z$$

$$= \left(A_x \cos\phi + A_y \sin\phi \right) \vec{a}_\rho + \left(-A_x \sin\phi + A_y \cos\phi \right) \vec{a}_\phi + A_z \vec{a}_z \tag{1.20}$$

Comparing Eq. (1.20) with Eq. (1.17), the cylindrical vector components can be written in terms of rectangular vector components as

$$A_\rho = A_x \cos\phi + A_y \sin\phi, \qquad A_\phi = -A_x \sin\phi + A_y \cos\phi, \qquad A_z = A_z$$

The above equations can be written in matrix form as

$$\begin{bmatrix} A_\rho \\ A_\phi \\ A_z \end{bmatrix} = \begin{bmatrix} \cos\phi & \sin\phi & 0 \\ -\sin\phi & \cos\phi & 0 \\ 0 & 0 & 1 \end{bmatrix} \begin{bmatrix} A_x \\ A_y \\ A_z \end{bmatrix}$$

Similarly, the transformation from cylindrical vector components to rectangular vector components is obtained by substituting Eq. (1.19) into Eq. (1.17) and rearranging the terms, we have

$$\vec{A} = A_\rho \left(\cos\phi\, \vec{a}_x + \sin\phi\, \vec{a}_y \right) + A_\phi \left(-\sin\phi\, \vec{a}_x + \cos\phi\, \vec{a}_y \right) + A_z \vec{a}_z$$

$$= \left(A_\rho \cos\phi - A_\phi \sin\phi \right) \vec{a}_x + \left(A_\rho \sin\phi + A_\phi \cos\phi \right) \vec{a}_y + A_z \vec{a}_z \tag{1.21}$$

Comparing Eq. (1.21) with Eq. (1.16), the rectangular vector components can be written in terms of cylindrical vector components as

$$A_x = A_\rho \cos\phi - A_\phi \sin\phi, \qquad A_y = A_\rho \sin\phi + A_\phi \cos\phi, \qquad A_z = A_z$$

The above equations can be written in matrix form as

$$\begin{bmatrix} A_x \\ A_y \\ A_z \end{bmatrix} = \begin{bmatrix} \cos\phi & -\sin\phi & 0 \\ \sin\phi & \cos\phi & 0 \\ 0 & 0 & 1 \end{bmatrix} \begin{bmatrix} A_\rho \\ A_\phi \\ A_z \end{bmatrix}$$

1.3.3 Spherical Coordinates (r, θ, φ)

The spherical coordinate system is mainly considered for problems of spherical symmetry. Any point P can be represented as (r, θ, ϕ) in spherical coordinate system as shown in Figure 1.13. The coordinate r is the distance from the origin to point P or the radius of a sphere centered at the origin and passing through P, θ is the zenith angle measured from the positive z-axis, and it describes conical surface with its apex at the origin and ϕ is the azimuth angle measured from the x-axis which is the same as in the cylindrical coordinate system. The ranges of these variables are $0 \le r < \infty$, $0 \le \theta \le \pi$, and $0 \le \phi < 2\pi$.

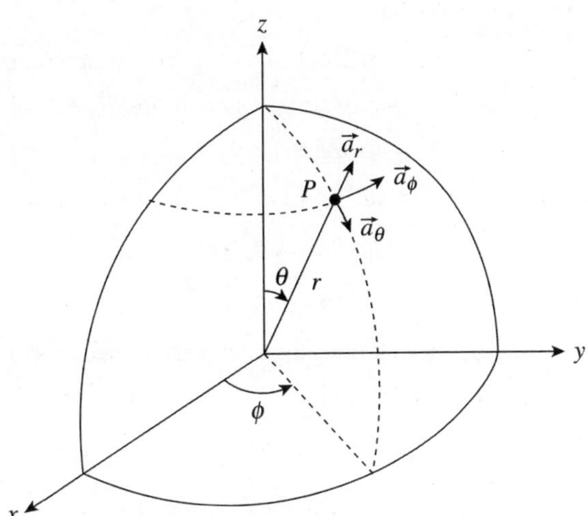

Figure 1.13 *Representation of a point P and unit vectors in spherical coordinate system*

A vector $\vec{A}$ in spherical coordinates can be written as

$$\vec{A} = A_r \vec{a}_r + A_\theta \vec{a}_\theta + A_\phi \vec{a}_\phi \tag{1.22}$$

where $\vec{a}_r, \vec{a}_\theta$, and $\vec{a}_\phi$ are unit vectors in the r, θ, and ϕ direction as shown in Figure 1.13. Therefore, magnitude of $\vec{A}$ is given by

$$\left| \vec{A} \right| = \sqrt{A_r^2 + A_\theta^2 + A_\phi^2}$$

Since the coordinate system is orthogonal, the unit vectors $\vec{a}_r, \vec{a}_\theta$, and $\vec{a}_\phi$ are mutually perpendicular. Here, $\vec{a}_r$ is in the direction of increasing $r, \vec{a}_\theta$ in the direction of increasing θ and $\vec{a}_\phi$ is in the direction of increasing ϕ. Since the three unit vectors are mutually orthogonal, their dot products become

$$\vec{a}_r \cdot \vec{a}_r = \vec{a}_\theta \cdot \vec{a}_\theta = \vec{a}_\phi \cdot \vec{a}_\phi = 1$$
$$\vec{a}_r \cdot \vec{a}_\theta = \vec{a}_\theta \cdot \vec{a}_\phi = \vec{a}_\phi \cdot \vec{a}_r = 0$$

and the cross products of unit vectors become

$$\vec{a}_r \times \vec{a}_\theta = \vec{a}_\phi, \qquad \vec{a}_\theta \times \vec{a}_\phi = \vec{a}_r, \qquad \vec{a}_\phi \times \vec{a}_r = \vec{a}_\theta$$
$$\vec{a}_r \times \vec{a}_r = 0, \qquad \vec{a}_\theta \times \vec{a}_\theta = 0, \qquad \vec{a}_\phi \times \vec{a}_\phi = 0$$

The transformation of coordinates from rectangular (x, y, z) to spherical (r, θ, ϕ) or vice versa can be obtained using the relationship shown in Figure 1.14(a) and they can be written as

$$r = \sqrt{x^2 + y^2 + z^2}, \quad \theta = \tan^{-1} \frac{\sqrt{x^2 + y^2}}{z}, \quad \text{and} \quad \phi = \tan^{-1} \frac{y}{x}.$$

Rectangular coordinates in terms of spherical coordinates can be written as

$$x = r\sin\theta\cos\phi, \quad y = r\sin\theta\sin\phi, \quad \text{and} \quad z = r\cos\theta$$

Similarly, the transformation of unit vectors from rectangular $\left(\vec{a}_x, \vec{a}_y, \vec{a}_z\right)$ to spherical $\left(\vec{a}_r, \vec{a}_\theta, \vec{a}_\phi\right)$ or vice versa are given by

$$\vec{a}_x = \sin\theta\cos\phi\,\vec{a}_r + \cos\theta\cos\phi\,\vec{a}_\theta - \sin\phi\,\vec{a}_\phi$$
$$\vec{a}_y = \sin\theta\sin\phi\,\vec{a}_r + \cos\theta\sin\phi\,\vec{a}_\theta + \cos\phi\,\vec{a}_\phi \tag{1.23}$$
$$\vec{a}_z = \cos\theta\,\vec{a}_r - \sin\theta\,\vec{a}_\theta$$

or

$$\vec{a}_r = \sin\theta\cos\phi\,\vec{a}_x + \sin\theta\sin\phi\,\vec{a}_y + \cos\theta\,\vec{a}_z$$
$$\vec{a}_\theta = \cos\theta\cos\phi\,\vec{a}_x + \cos\theta\sin\phi\,\vec{a}_y - \sin\theta\,\vec{a}_z \tag{1.24}$$
$$\vec{a}_\phi = -\sin\phi\,\vec{a}_x + \cos\phi\,\vec{a}_y$$

Finally, the relationship between the vector components $\left(A_x, A_y, A_z\right)$ and $\left(A_r, A_\theta, A_\phi\right)$ is obtained by substituting Eq. (1.23) in Eq. (1.16) and rearranging the terms. Therefore,

$$\vec{A} = \left(A_x \sin\theta\cos\phi + A_y \sin\theta\sin\phi + A_z \cos\theta\right)\vec{a}_r + \left(A_x \cos\theta\cos\phi + A_y \cos\theta\sin\phi - A_z \sin\theta\right)\vec{a}_\theta$$
$$+ \left(-A_x \sin\phi + A_y \cos\phi\right)\vec{a}_\phi \tag{1.25}$$

Comparing the above equation with Eq. (1.22), the spherical vector components can be written in terms of rectangular vector components as

$$A_r = A_x \sin\theta\cos\phi + A_y \sin\theta\sin\phi + A_z \cos\theta$$

$$A_\theta = A_x \cos\theta\cos\phi + A_y \cos\theta\sin\phi - A_z \sin\theta$$

$$A_\varphi = -A_x \sin\phi + A_y \cos\phi$$

The above equations can be written in matrix form as

$$\begin{bmatrix} A_r \\ A_\theta \\ A_\phi \end{bmatrix} = \begin{bmatrix} \sin\theta\cos\phi & \sin\theta\sin\phi & \cos\theta \\ \cos\theta\cos\phi & \cos\theta\sin\phi & -\sin\theta \\ -\sin\phi & \cos\phi & 0 \end{bmatrix} \begin{bmatrix} A_x \\ A_y \\ A_z \end{bmatrix}$$

Similarly, the transformation from spherical vector components to rectangular vector components is obtained by substituting Eq. (1.24) into Eq. (1.22), and rearranging the terms. Therefore,

$$\vec{A} = \left(A_r \sin\theta\cos\phi + A_\theta \cos\theta\cos\phi - A_\phi \sin\phi \right)\vec{a}_x + \left(A_r \sin\theta\sin\phi + A_\theta \cos\theta\sin\phi + A_\phi \cos\phi \right)\vec{a}_y$$

$$+ \left(A_r \cos\theta - A_\theta \sin\theta \right)\vec{a}_z \tag{1.26}$$

Comparing the above equation with Eq. (1.16), the rectangular vector components can be written in terms of spherical vector components as

$$A_x = A_r \sin\theta\cos\phi + A_\theta \cos\theta\cos\phi - A_\phi \sin\phi$$

$$A_y = A_r \sin\theta\sin\phi + A_\theta \cos\theta\sin\phi + A_\phi \cos\phi$$

$$A_z = A_r \cos\theta - A_\theta \sin\theta$$

The above equations can be written in matrix form as

$$\begin{bmatrix} A_x \\ A_y \\ A_z \end{bmatrix} = \begin{bmatrix} \sin\theta\cos\phi & \cos\theta\cos\phi & -\sin\phi \\ \sin\theta\sin\phi & \cos\theta\sin\phi & \cos\phi \\ \cos\theta & -\sin\theta & 0 \end{bmatrix} \begin{bmatrix} A_r \\ A_\theta \\ A_\phi \end{bmatrix}$$

1.3.4 Transformation between Cylindrical and Spherical Coordinates

Figure 1.14 shows the transformation relationship of coordinates, unit vectors, and vector components between cylindrical system and spherical system. The general relationship between rectangular, cylindrical, and spherical coordinates is shown in Figure 1.14(a).

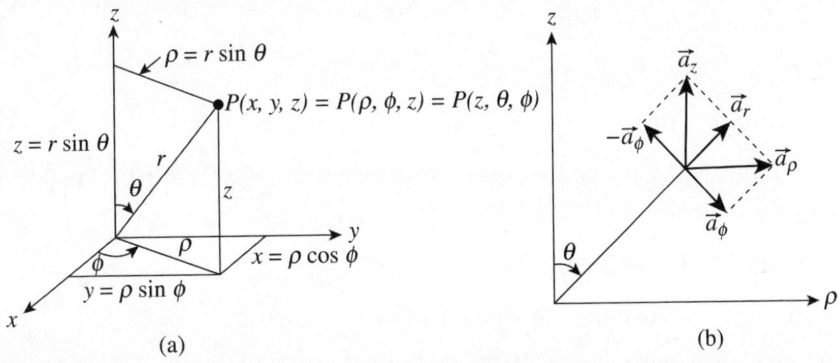

Figure 1.14 *Transformation between cylindrical and spherical coordinates: (a) relationship between coordinates and (b) unit vector transformation*

The transformation of coordinates from cylindrical (ρ,ϕ,z) to spherical (r,θ,ϕ) is obtained by expressing the spherical coordinates in terms of rectangular coordinates. Replacing the rectangular coordinates to cylindrical coordinates, we have

$$r = \sqrt{x^2 + y^2 + z^2} = \sqrt{\rho^2 + z^2} \qquad \text{(since } \rho = \sqrt{x^2 + y^2}\text{)}$$

$$\theta = \tan^{-1}\frac{\sqrt{x^2 + y^2}}{z} = \tan^{-1}\frac{\rho}{z}$$

$$\phi = \tan^{-1}\frac{y}{x} = \tan^{-1}\frac{\rho\sin\phi}{\rho\cos\phi} = \phi$$

Similarly, the transformation of coordinates from spherical (r,θ,ϕ) to cylindrical (ρ,ϕ,z) is obtained by expressing the cylindrical coordinates in terms of rectangular coordinates. Replacing the rectangular coordinates to spherical coordinates, we have

$$\rho = \sqrt{x^2 + y^2}$$

where $x = r\sin\theta\cos\phi$ and $y = r\sin\theta\sin\phi$.
That is,

$$\rho = \sqrt{(r\sin\theta\,\cos\phi)^2 + (r\sin\theta\,\sin\phi)^2} = \sqrt{r^2\sin^2\theta(\cos^2\phi + \sin^2\phi)} = r\sin\theta$$

$$\phi = \tan^{-1}\frac{y}{x} = \tan^{-1}\frac{r\sin\theta\sin\phi}{r\sin\theta\cos\phi} = \phi$$

$$z = r\cos\theta$$

The unit vector transformation for cylindrical and spherical coordinates is shown in Figure 1.14(b). Here, the transformation of unit vectors from cylindrical $(\vec{a}_\rho,\vec{a}_\phi,\vec{a}_z)$ to spherical $(\vec{a}_r,\vec{a}_\theta,\vec{a}_\phi)$ is given by

$$\vec{a}_r = \sin\theta\,\vec{a}_\rho + \cos\theta\,\vec{a}_z$$

$$\vec{a}_\theta = \cos\theta\,\vec{a}_\rho - \sin\theta\,\vec{a}_z \qquad (1.27)$$

$$\vec{a}_\phi = \vec{a}_\phi$$

Similarly, the transformation of unit vectors from spherical $(\vec{a}_r,\vec{a}_\theta,\vec{a}_\phi)$ to cylindrical $(\vec{a}_\rho,\vec{a}_\phi,\vec{a}_z)$ is given by

$$\vec{a}_\rho = \sin\theta\,\vec{a}_r + \cos\theta\,\vec{a}_\theta$$

$$\vec{a}_\phi = \vec{a}_\phi \qquad (1.28)$$

$$\vec{a}_z = \cos\theta\,\vec{a}_r - \sin\theta\,\vec{a}_\theta$$

Finally, the transformation of vector components from spherical (A_r,A_θ,A_ϕ) to cylindrical (A_ρ,A_ϕ,A_z) can be obtained by substituting Eq. (1.27) in Eq. (1.22). and rearranging the terms. Therefore,

$$\vec{A} = A_r(\sin\theta\,\vec{a}_\rho + \cos\theta\,\vec{a}_z) + A_\theta(\cos\theta\,\vec{a}_\rho - \sin\theta\,\vec{a}_z) + A_\phi\vec{a}_\phi$$

$$= (A_r\sin\theta + A_\theta\cos\theta)\vec{a}_\rho + A_\phi\vec{a}_\phi + (A_r\cos\theta - A_\theta\sin\theta)\vec{a}_z \qquad (1.29)$$

Comparing the above equation with Eq. (1.17), the cylindrical vector components can be written in terms of spherical vector components as

$$A_\rho = A_r \sin\theta + A_\theta \cos\theta$$

$$A_\phi = A_\phi$$

$$A_z = A_r \cos\theta - A_\theta \sin\theta$$

The above equations can be written in matrix form as

$$\begin{bmatrix} A_\rho \\ A_\phi \\ A_z \end{bmatrix} = \begin{bmatrix} \sin\theta & \cos\theta & 0 \\ 0 & 0 & 1 \\ \cos\theta & -\sin\theta & 0 \end{bmatrix} \begin{bmatrix} A_r \\ A_\theta \\ A_\phi \end{bmatrix}$$

Similarly, the transformation from cylindrical vector components to spherical vector components can be obtained by substituting Eq. (1.28) in Eq. (1.17) and rearranging the terms. Therefore,

$$\vec{A} = A_\rho(\sin\theta\,\vec{a}_r + \cos\theta\,\vec{a}_\theta) + A_\phi\vec{a}_\phi + A_z(\cos\theta\,\vec{a}_r - \sin\theta\,\vec{a}_\theta)$$

$$= (A_\rho \sin\theta + A_z \cos\theta)\vec{a}_r + (A_\rho \cos\theta - A_z \sin\theta)\vec{a}_\theta + A_\phi\vec{a}_\phi \qquad (1.30)$$

Comparing the above equation with Eq. (1.22), the spherical vector components can be written in terms of cylindrical vector components as

$$A_r = A_\rho \sin\theta + A_z \cos\theta$$

$$A_\theta = A_\rho \cos\theta - A_z \sin\theta$$

$$A_\phi = A_\phi$$

The above equations can be written in matrix form as

$$\begin{bmatrix} A_r \\ A_\theta \\ A_\phi \end{bmatrix} = \begin{bmatrix} \sin\theta & 0 & \cos\theta \\ \cos\theta & 0 & -\sin\theta \\ 0 & 1 & 0 \end{bmatrix} \begin{bmatrix} A_\rho \\ A_\phi \\ A_z \end{bmatrix}$$

Table 1.1 shows the summary of vector relations in three coordinate systems. The coordinate variables and its range, representation of a vector and its magnitude, position vector, dot product, cross product, and coordinate surfaces for all three coordinate systems are summarized in Table 1.1. The transformation relationship among the three coordinate systems is summarized in Table 1.2.

Table 1.1 *Summary of vector relations among coordinate systems*

	Coordinate systems		
	Rectangular	**Cylindrical**	**Spherical**
Coordinates	(x, y, z)	(ρ, ϕ, z)	(r, θ, ϕ)
Coordinate range	$-\infty < x < \infty$	$0 \le \rho < \infty$	$0 \le r < \infty$
	$-\infty < y < \infty$	$0 \le \phi < 2\pi$	$0 \le \theta \le \pi$
	$-\infty < z < \infty$	$-\infty < z < \infty$	$0 \le \phi < 2\pi$
Unit vector	$\vec{a}_x, \vec{a}_y, \vec{a}_z$	$\vec{a}_\rho, \vec{a}_\phi, \vec{a}_z$	$\vec{a}_r, \vec{a}_\theta, \vec{a}_\phi$

	Coordinate systems		
	Rectangular	**Cylindrical**	**Spherical**
Representation of vector, $\vec{A}$	$A_x \vec{a}_x + A_y \vec{a}_y + A_z \vec{a}_z$	$A_\rho \vec{a}_\rho + A_\phi \vec{a}_\phi + A_z \vec{a}_z$	$A_r \vec{a}_r + A_\theta \vec{a}_\theta + A_\phi \vec{a}_\phi$
Magnitude of vector, $\left\vert \vec{A} \right\vert$	$\sqrt{A_x^2 + A_y^2 + A_z^2}$	$\sqrt{A_\rho^2 + A_\phi^2 + A_z^2}$	$\sqrt{A_r^2 + A_\theta^2 + A_\phi^2}$
Position vector, $\overrightarrow{OP_1}$	$x_1 \vec{a}_x + y_1 \vec{a}_y + z_1 \vec{a}_z$ for $P\left(x_1, y_1, z_1\right)$	$\rho_1 \vec{a}_\rho + z_1 \vec{a}_z$ for $P\left(\rho_1, \phi_1, z_1\right)$	$r_1 \vec{a}_r$ for $P\left(r_1, \theta_1, \phi_1\right)$
Dot product, $\vec{A} \cdot \vec{B}$	$A_x B_x + A_y B_y + A_z B_z$	$A_\rho B_\rho + A_\phi B_\phi + A_z B_z$	$A_r B_r + A_\theta B_\theta + A_\phi B_\phi$
Cross product, $\vec{A} \times \vec{B}$	$\begin{vmatrix} \vec{a}_x & \vec{a}_y & \vec{a}_z \\ A_x & A_y & A_z \\ B_x & B_y & B_z \end{vmatrix}$	$\begin{vmatrix} \vec{a}_\rho & \vec{a}_\phi & \vec{a}_z \\ A_\rho & A_\phi & A_z \\ B_\rho & B_\phi & B_z \end{vmatrix}$	$\begin{vmatrix} \vec{a}_r & \vec{a}_\theta & \vec{a}_\phi \\ A_r & A_\theta & A_\phi \\ B_r & B_\theta & B_\phi \end{vmatrix}$
Coordinate surfaces	Plane $x = $ constant Plane $y = $ constant Plane $z = $ constant	Cylinder $\rho = $ constant Plane $\phi = $ constant Plane $z = $ constant	Sphere $r = $ constant Cone $\theta = $ constant Plane $\phi = $ constant

Table 1.2 *Transformation relationships among coordinates*

Transformation	Coordinate variables	Unit vectors	Vector components
Rectangular to cylindrical	$\rho = \sqrt{x^2 + y^2}$ $\phi = \tan^{-1} \dfrac{y}{x}$ $z = z$	$\vec{a}_\rho = \cos\phi\, \vec{a}_x + \sin\phi\, \vec{a}_y$ $\vec{a}_\phi = -\sin\phi\, \vec{a}_x + \cos\phi\, \vec{a}_y$ $\vec{a}_z = \vec{a}_z$	$A_\rho = A_x \cos\phi + A_y \sin\phi$ $A_\phi = -A_x \sin\phi + A_y \cos\phi$ $A_z = A_z$
Cylindrical to rectangular	$x = \rho\cos\phi$ $y = \rho\sin\phi$ $z = z$	$\vec{a}_x = \cos\phi\, \vec{a}_\rho - \sin\phi\, \vec{a}_\phi$ $\vec{a}_y = \sin\phi\, \vec{a}_\rho + \cos\phi\, \vec{a}_\phi$ $\vec{a}_z = \vec{a}_z$	$A_x = A_\rho \cos\phi - A_\phi \sin\phi$ $A_y = A_\rho \sin\phi + A_\phi \cos\phi$ $A_z = A_z$
Rectangular to spherical	$r = \sqrt{x^2 + y^2 + z^2}$ $\theta = \tan^{-1} \dfrac{\sqrt{x^2 + y^2}}{z}$ $\phi = \tan^{-1} \dfrac{y}{x}$	$\vec{a}_r = \sin\theta\cos\phi\, \vec{a}_x$ $\quad + \sin\theta\sin\phi\, \vec{a}_y$ $\quad + \cos\theta\, \vec{a}_z$ $\vec{a}_\theta = \cos\theta\cos\phi\, \vec{a}_x$ $\quad + \cos\theta\sin\phi\, \vec{a}_y$ $\quad - \sin\theta\, \vec{a}_z$ $\vec{a}_\phi = -\sin\phi\, \vec{a}_x + \cos\phi\, \vec{a}_y$	$A_r = A_x \sin\theta\cos\phi$ $\quad + A_y \sin\theta\sin\phi$ $\quad + A_z \cos\theta$ $A_\theta = A_x \cos\theta\cos\phi$ $\quad + A_y \cos\theta\sin\phi$ $\quad - A_z \sin\theta$ $A_\phi = -A_x \sin\phi + A_y \cos\phi$

Transformation	Coordinate variables	Unit vectors	Vector components
Spherical to rectangular	$x = r\sin\theta\cos\phi$ $y = r\sin\theta\sin\phi$ $z = r\cos\theta$	$\vec{a}_x = \sin\theta\cos\phi\,\vec{a}_r$ $\quad + \cos\theta\cos\phi\,\vec{a}_\theta$ $\quad - \sin\phi\,\vec{a}_\phi$ $\vec{a}_y = \sin\theta\sin\phi\,\vec{a}_r$ $\quad + \cos\theta\sin\phi\,\vec{a}_\theta$ $\quad + \cos\phi\,\vec{a}_\phi$ $\vec{a}_z = \cos\theta\,\vec{a}_r - \sin\theta\,\vec{a}_\theta$	$A_x = A_r\sin\theta\cos\phi$ $\quad + A_\theta\cos\theta\cos\phi$ $\quad - A_\phi\sin\phi$ $A_y = A_r\sin\theta\sin\phi$ $\quad + A_\theta\cos\theta\sin\phi$ $\quad + A_\phi\cos\phi$ $A_z = A_r\cos\theta - A_\theta\sin\theta$
Cylindrical to spherical	$r = \sqrt{\rho^2 + z^2}$ $\theta = \tan^{-1}\rho/z$ $\phi = \phi$	$\vec{a}_r = \sin\theta\,\vec{a}_\rho + \cos\theta\,\vec{a}_z$ $\vec{a}_\theta = \cos\theta\,\vec{a}_\rho - \sin\theta\,\vec{a}_z$ $\vec{a}_\phi = \vec{a}_\phi$	$A_r = A_\rho\sin\theta + A_z\cos\theta$ $A_\theta = A_\rho\cos\theta - A_z\sin\theta$ $A_\phi = A_\phi$
Spherical to cylindrical	$\rho = r\sin\theta$ $\phi = \phi$ $z = r\cos\theta$	$\vec{a}_\rho = \sin\theta\,\vec{a}_r + \cos\theta\,\vec{a}_\theta$ $\vec{a}_\phi = \vec{a}_\phi$ $\vec{a}_z = \cos\theta\,\vec{a}_r - \sin\theta\,\vec{a}_\theta$	$A_\rho = A_r\sin\theta + A_\theta\cos\theta$ $A_\phi = A_\phi$ $A_z = A_r\cos\theta - A_\theta\sin\theta$

The distance d between two points $P_1(\rho_1,\phi_1,z_1)$ and $P_2(\rho_2,\phi_2,z_2)$ in cylindrical coordinates is expressed as

$$d^2 = \rho_2^2 + \rho_1^2 - 2\rho_1\rho_2\cos(\phi_2 - \phi_1) + (z_2 - z_1)^2$$

The distance d between two points $P_1(r_1,\theta_1,\phi_1)$ and $P_2(r_2,\theta_2,\phi_2)$ in spherical coordinates is

$$d^2 = r_2^2 + r_1^2 - 2r_1r_2\cos\theta_2\cos\theta_1 - 2r_1r_2\sin\theta_2\sin\theta_1\cos(\phi_2 - \phi_1)$$

EXAMPLE 1.14

Given a point $P = (3,4,3)$ in Cartesian coordinates, express P in cylindrical coordinates.

SOLUTION

The transformation of coordinate from Cartesian to cylindrical is obtained by

$$\rho = \sqrt{x^2 + y^2} = \sqrt{(3)^2 + (4)^2} = 5$$

$$\phi = \tan^{-1}\frac{y}{x} = \tan^{-1}\frac{4}{3} = 53.1°$$

$z = 3$ (since z variable is same in both Cartesian and cylindrical coordinates)

Hence, $P(5, 53.1°, 3)$ is in cylindrical coordinates.

EXAMPLE 1.15

Given points $A\left(x = 2,\ y = 3,\ z = -1\right)$ and $B\left(\rho = 4,\ \phi = -50°,\ z = 2\right)$, determine the distance from A to B.

SOLUTION

Given point A in rectangular coordinates as $A\left(x = 2,\ y = 3,\ z = -1\right)$ and point B in cylindrical coordinates as $\rho = 4, \phi = -50°, z = 2$.

Converting point B into Cartesian coordinates, we get

$$x = \rho \cos\phi = 2.57, \qquad y = \rho \sin\phi = -3.06, \qquad z = 2$$

Therefore, the distance from A to B is given by

$$|AB| = \sqrt{\left(2.57 - 2\right)^2 + \left(-3.06 - 3\right)^2 + \left(2 + 1\right)^2} = 6.79$$

EXAMPLE 1.16

Convert the given coordinate point $P_1 = \left(1, 2, 0\right)$ from Cartesian to spherical coordinates.

SOLUTION

The transformation of coordinates from Cartesian to spherical is obtained by

$$r = \sqrt{x^2 + y^2 + z^2} = \sqrt{1^2 + 2^2} = 2.24$$

$$\theta = \tan^{-1}\frac{\sqrt{x^2 + y^2}}{z} = \tan^{-1}\frac{\sqrt{1^2 + 2^2}}{0} = 90°$$

$$\phi = \tan^{-1}\frac{y}{x} = \tan^{-1}\frac{2}{1} = 63.4°$$

Hence, the point P_1 in spherical coordinates are $\left(2.24, 90°, 63.4°\right)$.

EXAMPLE 1.17

Given the two points $A\left(x = 2, y = 3, z = -1\right)$ and $B\left(r = 4, \theta = 25°, \phi = 120°\right)$, find the (i) spherical coordinates of A and (ii) Cartesian coordinates of B.

SOLUTION

(i) Given $A\left(x = 2,\ y = 3,\ z = -1\right)$. Converting to spherical coordinates, we have

$$r = \sqrt{x^2 + y^2 + z^2} = \sqrt{\left(2\right)^2 + \left(3\right)^2 + \left(-1\right)^2} = \sqrt{14} = 3.7416$$

$$\theta = \tan^{-1}\frac{\sqrt{x^2 + y^2}}{z} = \tan^{-1}\left[\frac{\sqrt{13}}{-1}\right] = 105.5°$$

$$\phi = \tan^{-1}\frac{y}{x} = \tan^{-1}\frac{3}{2} = 56.31°$$

Hence, in spherical system, $A\left(3.7416, 105.5°,\ 56.31°\right)$.

(*ii*) Given $B\left(r = 4, \theta = 25^{\circ}, \phi = 120^{\circ}\right)$. Converting to Cartesian coordinates, we get

$$x = r\sin\theta\cos\phi = 4\sin 25^{\circ}\cos 120^{\circ} = -0.845$$

$$y = r\sin\theta\sin\phi = 4\sin 25^{\circ}\sin 120^{\circ} = 1.464$$

$$z = r\cos\theta = 4\cos 25^{\circ} = 3.625$$

Hence, in Cartesian system, $B\left(-0.845, 1.464, 3.625\right)$.

EXAMPLE 1.18

A point $P = \left(2\sqrt{3}, \dfrac{\pi}{3}, -2\right)$ is given in cylindrical coordinates. Express P in spherical coordinates.

SOLUTION

The transformation of coordinates from cylindrical to spherical is obtained by

$$r = \sqrt{\rho^2 + z^2} = \sqrt{\left(2\sqrt{3}\right)^2 + \left(-2\right)^2} = 4$$

$$\theta = \tan^{-1}\left(\frac{\rho}{z}\right) = \tan^{-1}\left(\frac{2\sqrt{3}}{-2}\right) = -60^{\circ} = -\frac{\pi}{3} \text{ or } \frac{2\pi}{3} \text{ rad}$$

$$\phi = \frac{\pi}{3} \text{ rad (since } \phi \text{ variable is same in both cylindrical and spherical coordinates)}$$

Hence, $P = \left(4, \dfrac{2\pi}{3}, \dfrac{\pi}{3}\right)$ in spherical coordinates.

EXAMPLE 1.19

Transform the vector $\vec{A} = \left(x + y\right)\vec{a}_x + \left(y - x\right)\vec{a}_y + z\vec{a}_z$ from Cartesian to cylindrical coordinates.

SOLUTION

Transforming the unit vectors and coordinate variables from Cartesian to cylindrical, we get

$$\vec{A} = \left(x + y\right)\vec{a}_x + \left(y - x\right)\vec{a}_y + z\vec{a}_z$$

$$= \left(\rho\cos\phi + \rho\sin\phi\right)\left(\cos\phi\,\vec{a}_\rho - \sin\phi\,\vec{a}_\phi\right) + \left(\rho\sin\phi - \rho\cos\phi\right)\left(\sin\phi\,\vec{a}_\rho + \cos\phi\,\vec{a}_\phi\right) + z\vec{a}_z$$

$$= \left(\cos^2\phi + \cos\phi\sin\phi + \sin^2\phi - \cos\phi\sin\phi\right)\rho\,\vec{a}_\rho + \left(-\sin\phi\cos\phi - \sin^2\phi + \sin\phi\cos\phi - \cos^2\phi\right)\rho\,\vec{a}_\phi + z\vec{a}_z$$

$$= \rho\,\vec{a}_\rho - \rho\,\vec{a}_\phi + z\vec{a}_z$$

EXAMPLE 1.20

A vector field is given by the expression $\vec{F} = \dfrac{1}{r}\vec{a}_r$ in the spherical coordinates. Determine $\vec{F}$ in Cartesian form at a point $x = 1$, $y = 1$, and $z = 1$.

SOLUTION

Given $\vec{F} = \dfrac{1}{r}\vec{a}_r$ in spherical coordinates.

The rectangular vector components can be written in terms of spherical vector components in matrix form as follows:

$$\begin{bmatrix} F_x \\ F_y \\ F_z \end{bmatrix} = \begin{bmatrix} \sin\theta\cos\phi & \cos\theta\cos\phi & -\sin\phi \\ \sin\theta\sin\phi & \cos\theta\sin\phi & \cos\phi \\ \cos\theta & -\sin\theta & 0 \end{bmatrix} \begin{bmatrix} F_r \\ F_\theta \\ F_\phi \end{bmatrix}$$

But $F_\theta = F_\phi = 0$ and $F_r = \dfrac{1}{r}$

Therefore, $F_x = F_r \sin\theta\cos\phi = \dfrac{1}{r}\sin\theta\cos\phi$

$$F_y = F_r \sin\theta\sin\phi = \frac{1}{r}\sin\theta\sin\phi$$

and $\qquad F_z = F_r \cos\theta = \dfrac{1}{r}\cos\theta$

At point, $x = 1$, $y = 1$, and $z = 1$, the spherical coordinates are given by

$$r = \sqrt{x^2 + y^2 + z^2} = \sqrt{3}, \quad \theta = \tan^{-1}\frac{\sqrt{x^2+y^2}}{z} = 54.735^\circ, \quad \phi = \tan^{-1}\frac{y}{x} = 45^\circ$$

Therefore, $F_x = \dfrac{1}{\sqrt{3}}\sin\left(54.735^\circ\right)\cos\left(45^\circ\right) = 0.333$

$$F_y = \frac{1}{\sqrt{3}}\sin\left(54.735^\circ\right)\sin\left(45^\circ\right) = 0.333$$

$$F_z = \frac{1}{\sqrt{3}}\cos\left(45^\circ\right) = 0.4082$$

Hence, in Cartesian form, $\vec{F} = 0.333\vec{a}_x + 0.333\vec{a}_y + 0.4082\vec{a}_z$. $\qquad\qquad\square$

EXAMPLE 1.21

Transform the vector $\vec{C} = \cos\phi\,\vec{a}_\rho - \sin\phi\,\vec{a}_\phi + \cos\phi\,\vec{a}_z$ from cylindrical to spherical coordinates and then evaluate it at $P = \left(2, \dfrac{\pi}{4}, 2\right)$.

SOLUTION

Transforming the unit vectors and coordinate variables from cylindrical to spherical, we get

$$C = \cos\phi\left(\sin\theta\,\vec{a}_r + \cos\theta\,\vec{a}_\theta\right) - \sin\phi\,\vec{a}_\phi + \cos\phi\left(\cos\theta\,\vec{a}_r - \sin\theta\,\vec{a}_\theta\right)$$

$$= \cos\phi\left(\sin\theta + \cos\theta\right)\vec{a}_r + \cos\phi\left(\cos\theta - \sin\theta\right)\vec{a}_\theta - \sin\phi\,\vec{a}_\phi$$

The transformation of point P from cylindrical to spherical coordinates is

$$P = \left(\sqrt{\rho^2 + z^2}, \tan^{-1}\left(\frac{\rho}{z}\right), \phi\right) = \left(\sqrt{2^2 + 2^2}, \tan^{-1}\left(\frac{2}{2}\right), \frac{\pi}{4}\right) = \left(2\sqrt{2}, 45^\circ, 45^\circ\right)$$

Therefore, at point $P = \left(2\sqrt{2}, 45^\circ, 45^\circ\right)$, the given vector is transformed from cylindrical to spherical coordinates as $\vec{C} = \vec{a}_r - 0.707\vec{a}_\phi$. $\qquad\qquad\square$

EXAMPLE 1.22

Transform the given vector $\vec{A} = \sin^2\theta\cos\phi\,\vec{a}_r + \cos^2\phi\,\vec{a}_\theta - \sin\phi\,\vec{a}_\phi$ from spherical to cylindrical coordinates and then evaluate it at $P = \left(2, \dfrac{\pi}{2}, \dfrac{\pi}{2}\right)$.

SOLUTION

Given $\vec{A} = \sin^2\theta\cos\phi\,\vec{a}_r + \cos^2\phi\,\vec{a}_\theta - \sin\phi\,\vec{a}_\phi$. Transforming the unit vectors and coordinate variables from spherical to cylindrical, we get

$$A = \sin^2\theta\cos\phi\,\vec{a}_r + \cos^2\phi\,\vec{a}_\theta - \sin\phi\,\vec{a}_\phi$$

$$= \sin^2\theta\cos\phi\left(\sin\theta\,\vec{a}_\rho + \cos\theta\,\vec{a}_z\right) + \cos^2\phi\left(\cos\theta\,\vec{a}_\rho - \sin\theta\,\vec{a}_z\right) - \sin\phi\,\vec{a}_\phi$$

$$= \left(\sin^3\theta\cos\phi + \cos\theta\cos^2\phi\right)\vec{a}_\rho - \sin\theta\,\vec{a}_\phi + \left(\cos\theta\sin^2\theta\cos\phi - \sin\theta\cos^2\phi\right)\vec{a}_z$$

Therefore, at point, $P = \left(2, \dfrac{\pi}{2}, \dfrac{\pi}{2}\right)$, $A = -\vec{a}_\phi$. ◻

1.4 DIFFERENTIAL ELEMENTS OF LENGTH, SURFACE, AND VOLUME

Differential quantities such as length, surface, and volume are mostly involved in the operation of differential calculus and are often required in the study of electromagnetism. The evaluation of differential quantities in a coordinate system requires the knowledge of differential elements of length, surface, and volume. This section deals with the construction of these differential elements in each coordinate system.

1.4.1 Rectangular Coordinate System

Consider the different elements in a rectangular coordinate system as shown in Figure 1.15 and its differential volume element is obtained by making differential changes dx, dy, and dz along the unit vectors $\vec{a}_x$, $\vec{a}_y$, and $\vec{a}_z$, respectively, as shown in Figure 1.15(a). The differential length element from P to Q in rectangular coordinates is a vector as represented by

$$d\vec{l} = dl_x\vec{a}_x + dl_y\vec{a}_y + dl_z\vec{a}_z = dx\vec{a}_x + dy\vec{a}_y + dz\vec{a}_z$$

where $dl_x = dx, dl_y = dy$, and $dl_z = dz$.

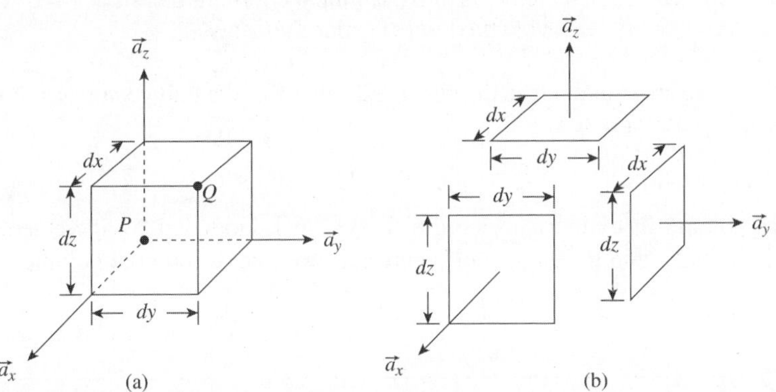

Figure 1.15 *Differential elements in a rectangular coordinate system: (a) differential volume and (b) expanded view*

The volume is enclosed by six differential surfaces and each surface is defined by a unit vector normal to that surface, as shown in the expanded view of Figure 1.15(b). The differential surface is defined as the product of two differential lengths with its direction pointed by a unit vector along the third direction. The differential surface area elements along the direction of unit vectors are given by

$$d\vec{s}_x = dy\,dz\,\vec{a}_x, \qquad d\vec{s}_y = dx\,dz\,\vec{a}_y, \qquad d\vec{s}_z = dx\,dy\,\vec{a}_z$$

The differential volume element in rectangular coordinate system is given by

$$dv = dx\,dy\,dz$$

The differential volume is generally defined as the product of all three differential lengths.

1.4.2 Cylindrical Coordinate System

Consider the differential elements in a cylindrical coordinate system as shown in Figure 1.16. The differential length element from P to Q in cylindrical coordinates is a vector as given by

$$\begin{aligned}
d\vec{l} &= dl_\rho \vec{a}_\rho + dl_\phi \vec{a}_\phi + dl_z \vec{a}_z \\
&= d\rho\,\vec{a}_\rho + \rho\,d\phi\,\vec{a}_\phi + dz\,\vec{a}_z
\end{aligned}$$

where $dl_\rho = d\rho, dl_\phi = \rho\,d\phi$, and $dl_z = dz$.

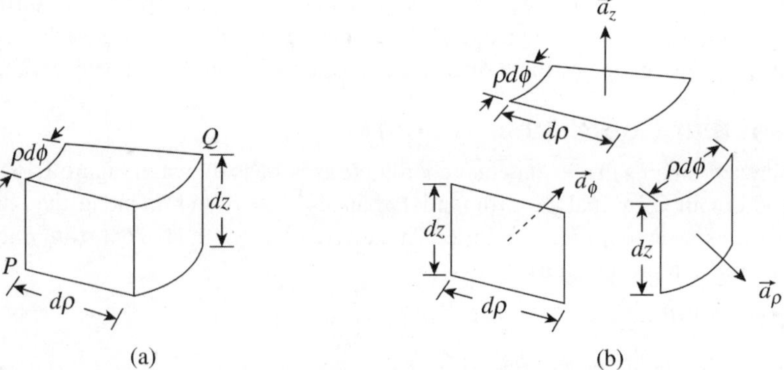

Figure 1.16 *Differential elements in a cylindrical coordinate system: (a) differential volume and (b) expanded view*

The differential surface area elements in the positive direction of the unit vectors, as shown in the expanded view of Figure 1.16(b), are given by

$$d\vec{s}_\rho = \rho\,d\phi\,dz\,\vec{a}_\rho, \qquad d\vec{s}_\phi = d\rho\,dz\,\vec{a}_\phi, \qquad d\vec{s}_z = \rho\,d\rho\,d\phi\,\vec{a}_z$$

The differential volume in cylindrical coordinate system is bounded by incrementing ρ, ϕ and z by $d\rho, d\phi$, and dz, respectively, and it is shown in Figure 1.16(a). The differential volume element is given by

$$dv = \rho\,d\rho\,d\phi\,dz$$

EXAMPLE 1.23

Using the cylindrical coordinate system, find the area of a curved surface on the right circular cylinder having radius 3 m and height 6 m and $30° \le \phi \le 120°$.

SOLUTION

The differential surface area element in cylindrical coordinates is $d\vec{s} = \rho\, d\phi\, dz\, \vec{a}_\rho$.

Integrating both the sides over s, the area of a curved surface on the right circular cylinder is obtained as

$$s = \int_{z=0}^{6} \int_{\phi=\pi/6}^{2\pi/3} \rho\, d\phi\, dz \Big|_{\rho=3} = 3\times 6 \times \left(\frac{2\pi}{3} - \frac{\pi}{6}\right) = 9\pi\,\text{m}^2 \qquad \square$$

Find the volume of a circular cylinder of radius $\rho = 3$cm, which is concentric with the z-axis and extends between $z = -2$cm and $z = 2$cm.

SOLUTION

The differential volume element in cylindrical coordinates is

$$dv = \rho\, d\rho\, d\phi\, dz$$

Integrating both the sides over v, the volume of the cylinder is obtained as

$$v = \int_{z=-2}^{2} \int_{\phi=0}^{2\pi} \int_{\rho=0}^{3} \rho\, d\rho\, d\phi\, dz$$

$$= \left[\frac{\rho^2}{2}\right]_0^3 \times [\phi]_0^{2\pi} \times [z]_{-2}^{2} = \frac{9}{2} \times 2\pi \times 4 = 113.04\ \text{cm}^3. \qquad \square$$

1.4.3 Spherical Coordinate System

Consider the differential element in a spherical coordinate system, as shown in Figure 1.17. The differential volume element from P to Q in spherical coordinates is a vector as given by

$$d\vec{l} = dl_r \vec{a}_r + dl_\theta \vec{a}_\theta + dl_\phi \vec{a}_\phi = dr\, \vec{a}_r + r d\theta\, \vec{a}_\theta + r\sin\theta\, d\phi\, \vec{a}_\phi$$

where $dl_r = dr, dl_\theta = r\, d\theta, dl_\phi = r\sin\theta\, d\phi$.

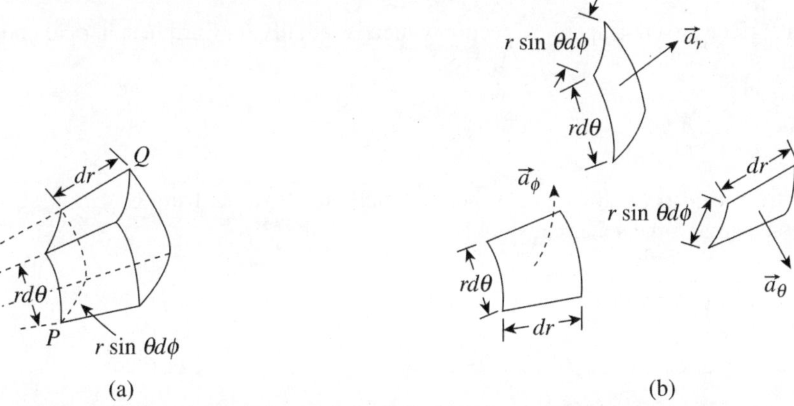

Figure 1.17 *Differential elements in a spherical coordinate system:*
(a) differential volume and (b) expanded view

The differential surface area elements along the direction of the unit vectors, as shown in the expanded view of Figure 1.17(b), are represented by

$$d\vec{s}_r = r^2 \sin\theta \, d\theta \, d\phi \, \vec{a}_r, \qquad d\vec{s}_\theta = r dr \sin\theta \, d\phi \, \vec{a}_\theta, \qquad d\vec{s}_\phi = r \, dr \, d\theta \, \vec{a}_\phi$$

The differential volume in spherical coordinate system, as shown in Figure 1.17(a), is obtained by incrementing r, θ, and ϕ by $dr, d\theta$, and $d\phi$, respectively. The differential volume element is given by

$$dv = r^2 \sin\theta \, dr \, d\theta \, d\phi$$

EXAMPLE 1.25

Using the concept of surface integral, find the surface area of a sphere of radius a.

SOLUTION

In spherical coordinates, the differential surface area in the perpendicular direction is

$$d\vec{s} = r^2 \sin\theta \, d\theta \, d\phi \, \vec{a}_r$$

Integrating both the sides over s, the surface area of the sphere is obtained as

$$s = \int_{\phi=0}^{2\pi} \int_{\theta=0}^{\pi} r^2 \sin\theta \, d\theta \, d\phi \Big|_{r=a}$$

$$= a^2 \times 2\pi \times \left(-\cos\theta\right)_0^\pi = 4\pi \, a^2 \, \text{m}^2$$

EXAMPLE 1.26

Using spherical coordinates, find the area of the region $0 \leq \phi \leq \alpha$ on the spherical shell of radius a. What is the area if $\alpha = 2\pi$?

SOLUTION

The differential surface area normal to r direction which is radially outward in spherical coordinate system is

$$d\vec{s} = r^2 \sin\theta \, d\theta \, d\phi \, \vec{a}_r$$

where radius $r = a$.

As ϕ varies from 0 to α for the given spherical shell and θ varies from 0 to π in spherical coordinate system, the surface area of the spherical shell is

$$s_r = r^2 \int_0^\alpha \int_0^\pi \sin\theta \, d\theta \, d\phi = r^2 \left(-\cos\theta\right)_0^\pi \left(\phi\right)_0^\alpha$$

$$= r^2 \left[-\cos\pi - \left(-\cos 0\right)\right]\alpha = 2r^2\alpha$$

Hence, the area of the given region of the spherical shell of radius a is $2a^2\alpha$. If $\alpha = 2\pi$, then the area of the region becomes $4\pi a^2$ which is same as the area of a sphere of radius a.

Obtain the expression for the volume of a sphere of radius a from the differential volume.

SOLUTION

The differential volume element in spherical coordinates is

$$dv = r^2 \sin\theta \, dr \, d\theta \, d\phi$$

Integrating both the sides over v, the volume of a sphere is obtained as

$$v = \int_{\phi=0}^{2\pi} \int_{\theta=0}^{\pi} \int_{r=0}^{a} r^2 \sin\theta \, dr \, d\theta \, d\phi = \left[\frac{r^3}{3}\right]_0^a \times \left[-\cos\theta\right]_0^{\pi} \times \left[\phi\right]_0^{2\pi} = \frac{4}{3}\pi a^3 \, \text{m}^3 \qquad \square$$

1.4.4 Comparison of Differential Elements for Coordinate Systems

The differential elements of length, surface, and volume for the rectangular, cylindrical, and spherical coordinate systems are summarized in Table 1.3.

Table 1.3 *Differential length, surface, and volume elements for the three coordinate systems*

Differential elements	Coordinate systems		
	Rectangular (Cartesian)	**Cylindrical**	**Spherical**
Length $d\vec{l}$	$dx\vec{a}_x + dy\vec{a}_y + dz\vec{a}_z$	$d\rho\,\vec{a}_\rho + \rho\,d\phi\,\vec{a}_\phi + dz\vec{a}_z$	$dr\vec{a}_r + rd\theta\vec{a}_\theta + r\sin\theta d\phi\vec{a}_\phi$
Surface $d\vec{s}$	$dy\,dz\vec{a}_x + dx\,dz\vec{a}_y + dx\,dy\,\vec{a}_z$	$\rho\,d\phi\,dz\vec{a}_\rho + d\rho\,dz\,\vec{a}_\phi$ $+\rho\,d\rho\,d\phi\,\vec{a}_z$	$r^2\sin\theta\,d\theta\,d\phi\,\vec{a}_r + r\,dr\sin\theta\,d\phi\,\vec{a}_\theta$ $+rdr\,d\theta\,\vec{a}_\phi$
Volume dv	$dx\,dy\,dz$	$\rho\,d\rho\,d\phi\,dz$	$r^2\sin\theta\,dr\,d\theta\,d\phi$

1.5 LINE, SURFACE, AND VOLUME INTEGRALS

The basic laws of electromagnetic fields are often expressed in terms of integrals of field quantities over volumes, across surfaces, and along lines in the desired region. For example, the potential function is defined in terms of the line integral of electric field intensity and the current through a conductor can be expressed as the surface integral of conduction current density. A better understanding of such spatial integrals is very much essential for the study of electromagnetic field theory.

1.5.1 Line Integral

Consider $f(x)$ be a continuous, single-valued function of x between the limits $x = a$ and $x = b$, as shown in Figure 1.18. The line integral of $f(x)$ is defined by dividing the interval from a to b into n small segments, which will approach zero in the limit. Hence, the line integral is then defined in terms of the limit of the sum as

$$\int_a^b f(x)\,dx = \underset{\substack{n\to\infty \\ \Delta x_i \to 0}}{Lt} \sum_{i=1}^{n} f_i \Delta x_i$$

Here, f_i is the value of $f(x)$ for the segment Δx_i which tends to zero. This general definition of the line integral can now be extended for a curve c in three-dimensional space, as shown in Figure 1.19.

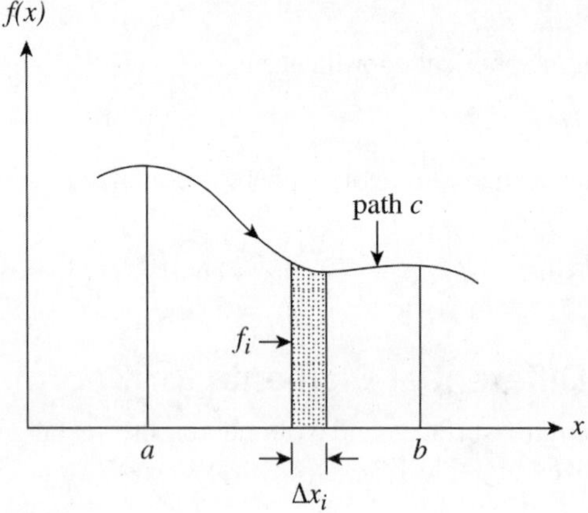

Figure 1.18   *Continuous, single-valued function*

First, a scalar field f is considered and its line integral is defined from a to b along c. Again, the interval between a and b is divided into n small sections, all of which reduces to zero in the limit. The small segments are length vectors. The position vectors for the ith element and their lengths are shown in Figure 1.19.

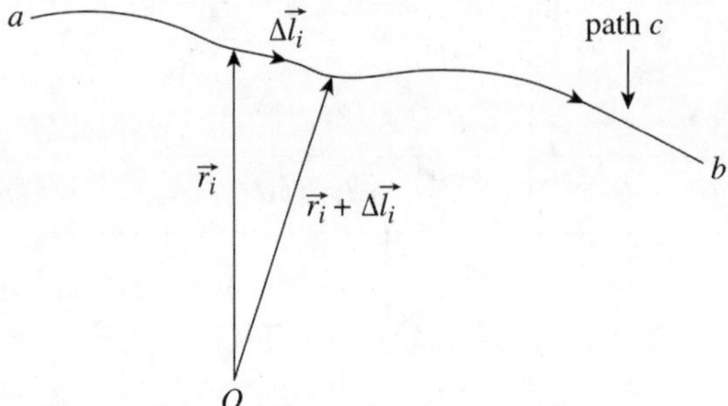

Figure 1.19   *Differential length element*

Hence, the line integral of f along c is then defined in the limit of the sum as

$$\int_c f\,d\vec{l} = \underset{\substack{n\to\infty \\ \Delta\vec{l}_i\to 0}}{Lt} \sum_{i=1}^{n} f_i \Delta\vec{l}_i$$

where f_i is the scalar function f within the length segment $\Delta\vec{l}_i$. Here, the line integral of f is a vector. Using the above expression, the scalar line integral for a vector field $\vec{F}$ along path c can be obtained by taking the dot product. Therefore,

$$\int_c \vec{F}\cdot d\vec{l} = \underset{\substack{n\to\infty \\ \Delta\vec{l}_i\to 0}}{Lt} \sum_{i=1}^{n} \vec{F}_i \cdot \Delta\vec{l}_i$$

Taking the cross product, the vector line integral of a vector field $\vec{F}$ along path c can be defined as

$$\int_c \vec{F} \times d\vec{l} = \underset{\substack{n \to \infty \\ \Delta \vec{l}_i \to 0}}{Lt} \sum_{i=1}^{n} \vec{F}_i \times \Delta \vec{l}_i$$

If the path of integration for the above integrals is a closed curve or contour, in which case the points a and b coincide, then such a closed path is usually denoted by the integral sign '$\oint$'.

For example, the line integral $\int_l \vec{F}$ for the path shown in Figure 1.20 is given by the integral of the tangential component of $\vec{F}$ along path l. It is defined by

$$\int_l \vec{F} \cdot d\vec{l} = \int_a^b |\vec{F}| \cos\theta \, d\vec{l}$$

If the path of integration is a closed curve such as *abca* in Figure 1.20, then the above equation becomes a closed contour integral as given by

$$\oint_l \vec{F} \cdot d\vec{l} \text{ or } \oint_c \vec{F} \cdot d\vec{l}$$

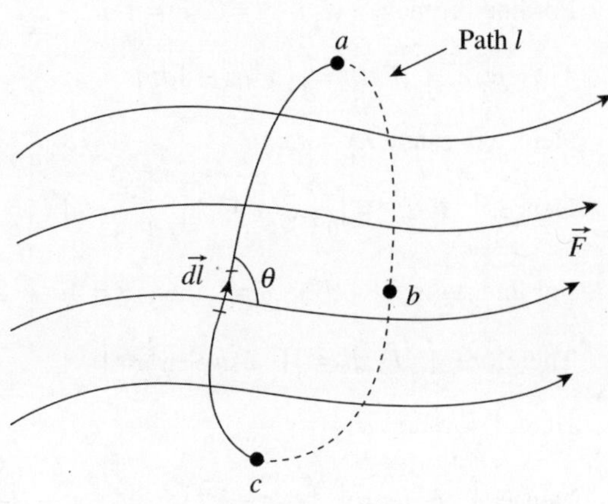

Figure 1.20 *Path of integration of $\vec{F}$*

EXAMPLE 1.28

Given the vector field, $\vec{F} = x^2 \vec{a}_x - xz \, \vec{a}_y - y^2 \vec{a}_z$, determine the circulation of $\vec{F}$ around the closed path shown in Figure E.1.28.

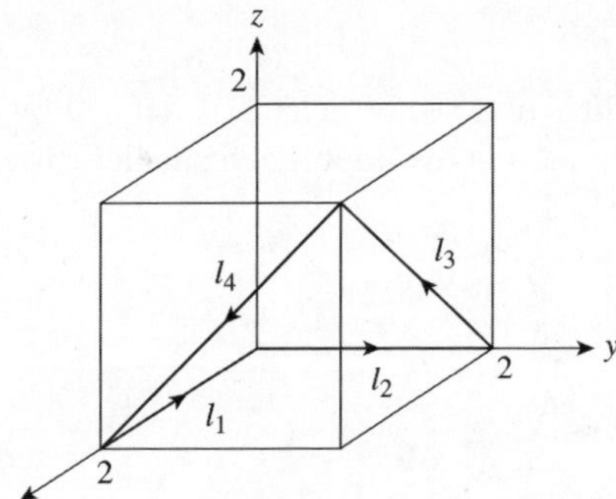

Figure E1.28

SOLUTION

The circulation of $\vec{F}$ around path l is

$$\oint_l \vec{F} \cdot d\vec{l} = \left(\int_1 + \int_2 + \int_3 + \int_4 \right) \vec{F} \cdot d\vec{l}$$

Here, the closed path is broken into four-line segments i.e., l_1, l_2, l_3 and l_4, as shown in Figure E.1.28. The circulation of $\vec{F}$ can be obtained by taking line integration over paths 1–4.

For line segment 1 (l_1), $y = z = 0$ then $\vec{F} = x^2 \vec{a}_x$ and $d\vec{l} = dx \, \vec{a}_x$.

Here, $d\vec{l}$ is taken along $+\vec{a}_x$ direction.

Hence, $\displaystyle \int_{l_1} \vec{F} \cdot d\vec{l} = \int_2^0 x^2 dx = \frac{x^3}{3} \bigg|_2^0 = -\frac{8}{3}$

For line segment 2 (l_2), $x = z = 0$, then $\vec{F} = -y^2\vec{a}_z$, and $d\vec{l} = dy\vec{a}_y$.

Hence, $\int_{l_2} \vec{F}\cdot d\vec{l} = 0$ (since $\vec{a}_z\cdot\vec{a}_y = 0$)

For line segment 3 (l_3), $y = 2$, $\vec{F} = x^2\vec{a}_x - xz\vec{a}_y - 4\vec{a}_z$, and $d\vec{l} = dx\vec{a}_x + dz\vec{a}_z$.

Therefore, $\int_{l_3} \vec{F}\cdot d\vec{l} = \int\left(x^2 dx - 4dz\right)$

Here, $x = z$, and $dx = dz$.

Hence, $\int_{l_3} \vec{F}\cdot d\vec{l} = \int_0^2\left(x^2 - 4\right)dx = \left[\dfrac{x^3}{3} - 4x\right] = -\dfrac{16}{3}$

For line segment 4 (l_4), $x = 2$, then $\vec{F} = 4\vec{a}_x - 2z\vec{a}_y - y^2\vec{a}_z$, and $d\vec{l} = dy\vec{a}_y + dz\vec{a}_z$.

Therefore, $\int_{l_4} \vec{F}\cdot d\vec{l} = \int\left(-2zdy - y^2 dz\right)$

Here, $z = y$, and $dz = dy$.

Hence, $\int_{l_4} \vec{F}\cdot d\vec{l} = \int_2^0\left(-2y - y^2\right)dy = \left[-y^2 - \dfrac{y^3}{3}\right]_2^0 = \dfrac{20}{3}$

Therefore, adding all the integrals over the closed path from 1 to 4, we get

$$\oint_l \vec{F}\cdot d\vec{l} = -\dfrac{8}{3} + 0 - \dfrac{16}{3} + \dfrac{20}{3} = -\dfrac{4}{3}$$

1.5.2 Surface Integral

The surface integral of a scalar field f or a vector field $\vec{F}$ is defined by dividing the given surface s into n small surfaces, which approaches to zero in the limit. Each smaller surface Δs_i has a corresponding vector surface $\Delta\vec{s}_i$ and is shown in Figure 1.21.

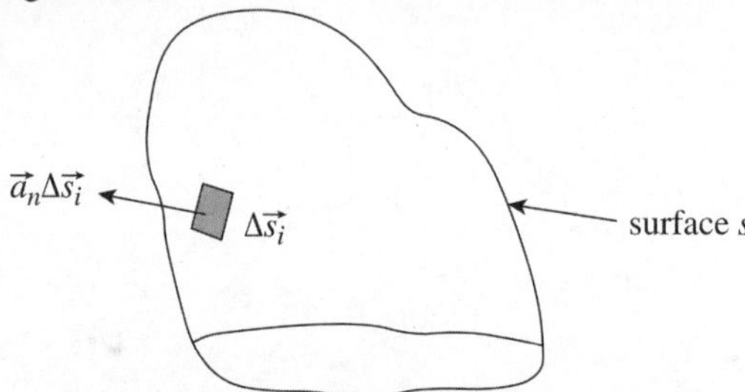

Figure 1.21 *Differential surface element*

The surface integral of f is obtained by multiplying f by each surface element and then adding their products for all n elements of s in the limit $\Delta\vec{s}_i \to 0$ as $n \to \infty$. This limit is called the surface integral of f over s as given by

$$\int_s f d\vec{s} = \underset{\substack{n\to\infty \\ \Delta\vec{s}_i\to 0}}{Lt} \sum_{i=1}^{n} f_i\Delta\vec{s}_i$$

where f_i is the value of the scalar function f over the elemental surface $\Delta\vec{s}_i$. The above equation shows that the surface integral of f is a vector.

Using this expression, the scalar surface integral for a vector field $\vec{F}$ can be obtained by taking the dot product. Therefore,

$$\int_s \vec{F} \cdot d\vec{s} = \underset{\substack{n \to \infty \\ \Delta \vec{s}_i \to 0}}{Lt} \sum_{i=1}^{n} \vec{F}_i \cdot \Delta \vec{s}_i$$

The vector surface integral of a vector field $\vec{F}$ can be obtained by taking the cross product as given by

$$\int_s \vec{F} \times d\vec{s} = \underset{\substack{n \to \infty \\ \Delta \vec{s}_i \to 0}}{Lt} \sum_{i=1}^{n} \vec{F} \times \Delta \vec{s}_i$$

For example, the surface integral $\int_s \vec{D}$ for the smooth surface shown in Figure 1.22 is given by the surface integral of the normal component of $\vec{D}$ across the surface s. It is defined by

$$\psi = \int_s \vec{D} \cdot \vec{a}_n \, ds$$

or simply, it can be written as

$$\psi = \int_s \vec{D} \cdot d\vec{s}$$

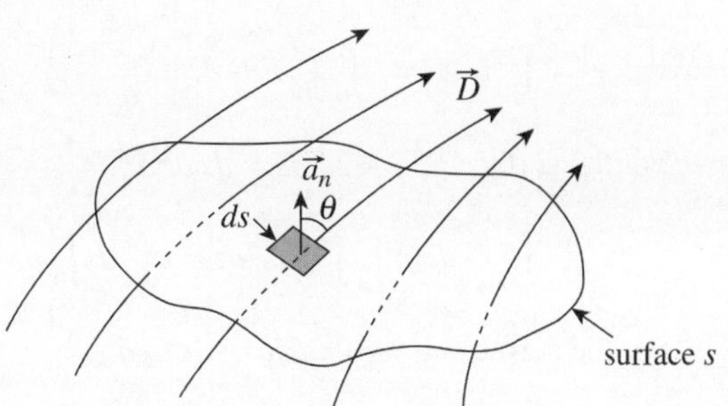

Figure 1.22 *Flux of a vector field $\vec{D}$ over surface s*

EXAMPLE 1.29

If $\vec{D} = \dfrac{1}{r}\vec{a}_r$, calculate $\displaystyle\int_s \vec{D} \cdot d\vec{s}$ over a hemispherical surface bounded by $r = 2$ and $0 \leq \theta \leq \dfrac{\pi}{2}$.

SOLUTION

In spherical coordinates, the surface area is given by $d\vec{s} = r^2 \sin\theta \, d\theta \, d\phi \, \vec{a}_r$.

Therefore, $\displaystyle\int_s \vec{D} \cdot d\vec{s} = \int_0^{2\pi} \int_0^{\pi/2} \left(\frac{1}{r}\right) \cdot \left(r^2 \sin\theta \, d\theta \, d\phi\right)\Big|_{r=2}$

$$= 4\pi \int_0^{\pi/2} \sin\theta \, d\theta = 4\pi$$

EXAMPLE 1.30

Evaluate $\displaystyle\oint \vec{r} \cdot d\vec{s}$ over the closed surface of the cube bounded by $0 \leq x \leq 2$, $0 \leq y \leq 2$, and $0 \leq z \leq 2$, where $\vec{r}$ is the position vector of any point on the surface of the cube.

SOLUTION

The six surfaces bounding the unit cube on which the surface integral is to be evaluated are shown in Figure E1.30.

The position vector of any point P on the surface is

$$\vec{r} = x\vec{a}_x + y\vec{a}_y + z\vec{a}_z$$

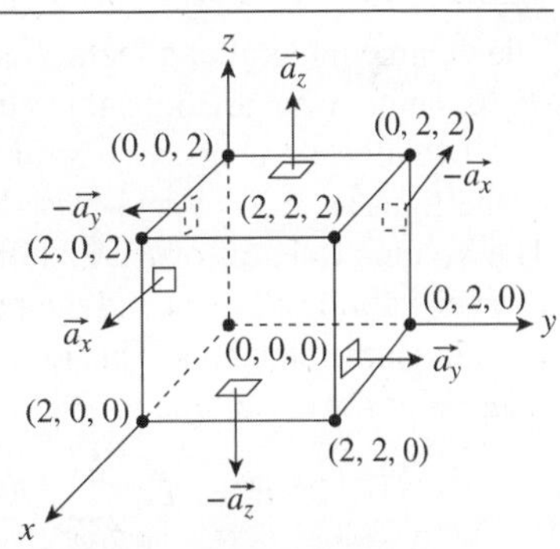

Figure E1.30

The surface integral is evaluated on each surface separately and then the results are added. Hence,

$$\oint_s \vec{r} \cdot d\vec{s} = \left(\int_{s1} + \int_{s2} + \int_{s3} + \int_{s4} + \int_{s5} + \int_{s6} \right) \vec{r} \cdot d\vec{s}$$

For the surface at $x = 2$: $d\vec{s} = dy\,dz\,\vec{a}_x$

$$\int_{s1} \vec{r} \cdot d\vec{s} = \int_0^2 \int_0^2 x\,dy\,dz = 2\int_0^2 dy \int_0^2 dz = 8$$

For the surface at $x = 0$: $d\vec{s} = -dy\,dz\,\vec{a}_x$

$$\int_{s2} \vec{r} \cdot d\vec{s} = -\int_0^2 \int_0^2 x\,dy\,dz = 0$$

For the surface at $y = 2$: $d\vec{s} = dx\,dz\,\vec{a}_y$

$$\int_{s3} \vec{r} \cdot d\vec{s} = \int_0^2 \int_0^2 y\,dx\,dz = 2\int_0^2 dx \int_0^2 dz = 8$$

For the surface at $y = 0$: $d\vec{s} = -dx\,dz\,\vec{a}_y$

$$\int_{s4} \vec{r} \cdot d\vec{s} = -\int_0^2 \int_0^2 y\,dx\,dz = 0$$

For the surface at $z = 2$: $d\vec{s} = dx\,dy\,\vec{a}_z$

$$\int_{s5} \vec{r} \cdot d\vec{s} = \int_0^2 \int_0^2 z\,dx\,dy = 2\int_0^2 dx \int_0^2 dy = 8$$

For the surface at $z = 0$: $d\vec{s} = -dx\,dy\,\vec{a}_z$

$$\int_{s6} \vec{r} \cdot d\vec{s} = -\int_0^2 \int_0^2 z\,dx\,dy = 0$$

Therefore, the sum of integrals taken on all surfaces is given by

$$\oint_s \vec{r} \cdot d\vec{s} = 8 + 0 + 8 + 0 + 8 + 0 = 24$$

1.5.3   Volume Integral

The volume integral of a scalar field f or a vector field $\vec{F}$ is defined by dividing the given volume v into n small volume elements, all of which approaches to zero in the limit as $n \rightarrow \infty$ and it is shown in Figure 1.23. The volume integral of f is obtained by multiplying f by each volume element and then adding their products for all volume elements. This limit is called the volume integral of f over volume v. Therefore,

$$\int_v f\,dv = \underset{\substack{n \to \infty \\ \Delta v_i \to 0}}{Lt} \sum_{i=1}^{n} f_i \Delta v_i$$

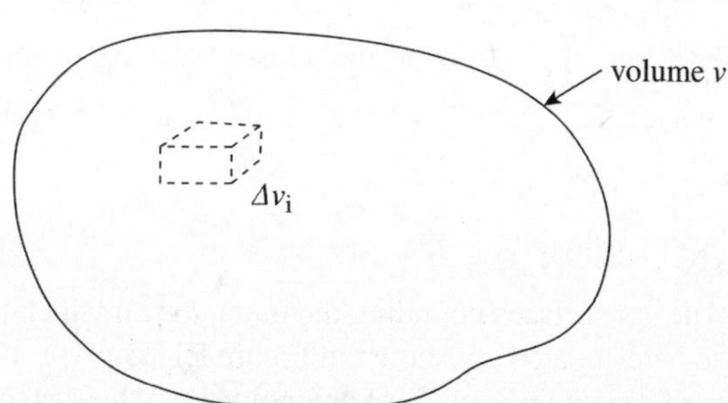

Figure 1.23   *Differential volume element*

Similarly, the volume integral of a vector field $\vec{F}$ is defined as

$$\int_v \vec{F}\, dv = \underset{\substack{n \to \infty \\ \Delta v_i \to 0}}{Lt} \sum_{i=1}^{n} \vec{F}_i \Delta v_i$$

and for a volume charge density ρ_v, the volume integral is given by $\int_v \rho_v dv$.

EXAMPLE 1.31

Obtain the expression for the volume of a sphere of radius a using the concept of volume integral.

SOLUTION

The differential volume in spherical coordinates is

$$dv = r^2 \sin\theta\, dr\, d\theta\, d\phi$$

where $0 \le r \le a$, $0 \le \theta \le \pi$, and $0 \le \phi \le 2\pi$.

Taking volume integral on both the sides of the above equation, the volume of the sphere is obtained as

$$v = \int_v r^2 \sin\theta\, dr\, d\theta\, d\phi$$

$$= \int_{\phi=0}^{2\pi} \int_{\theta=0}^{\pi} \int_{r=0}^{a} r^2 \sin\theta\, dr\, d\theta\, d\phi$$

$$= \frac{a^3}{3} \times 2\pi \times \left(-\cos\theta\right)_0^{\pi} = \frac{4}{3}\pi a^3 \ \text{m}^3$$

EXAMPLE 1.32

A sphere of radius 2 cm contains a volume charge density of $4\cos^2\theta$ C/m^3. Find the total charge Q contained in the sphere.

SOLUTION

The total charge contained in the sphere is

$$Q = \int_v \rho_v\, dv$$

$$= \int_{\phi=0}^{2\pi} \int_{\theta=0}^{\pi} \int_{r=0}^{0.02} \left(4\cos^2\theta\right) r^2 \sin\theta\, dr\, d\theta\, d\phi$$

$$= 4 \times \left(\frac{r^3}{3}\right)_0^{0.02} \times \int_0^{2\pi} \int_0^{\pi} \sin\theta \cos^2\theta\, d\theta\, d\phi$$

$$= \frac{32}{3} \times 10^{-6} \times \int_0^{2\pi} d\phi \times \left(-\frac{\cos^3\theta}{3}\right)_0^{\pi} = \frac{32}{9} \times 10^{-6} \times 2\pi \times 2$$

where $\int \sin\theta \cos^2\theta\, d\theta = -\frac{\cos^3\theta}{3}$.

Therefore, $Q = \frac{128\pi}{9} \times 10^{-6} = 44.68\ \mu\text{C}$.

1.6 VECTOR DIFFERENTIAL OPERATOR

The del operator, ∇, is generally called the vector differential operator, and it is used frequently in the study of electromagnetics. The del operator in rectangular or Cartesian coordinates (x, y, z) is written as

$$\nabla = \vec{a}_x \frac{\partial}{\partial x} + \vec{a}_y \frac{\partial}{\partial y} + \vec{a}_z \frac{\partial}{\partial z} \qquad \text{(rectangular)} \qquad (1.31)$$

This vector differential operator is also called the gradient operator, and it is not a vector in itself. But when it operates on a scalar function, it results in a vector. This operator is used in the definition of the following differential operations:

   (i) Gradient of a scalar V, represented by ∇V

   (ii) Divergence of a vector $\vec{E}$, represented by $\nabla \cdot \vec{E}$

  (iii) Curl of a vector $\vec{H}$, represented by $\nabla \times \vec{H}$

  (iv) Laplacian of a scalar V, represented by $\nabla^2 V$

The del operator can also be written in cylindrical and spherical coordinates by using the transformation formulae discussed in Sec. 1.3.

1.6.1 Vector Differential Operator ∇ in Cylindrical Coordinates

The transformation relationship from Cartesian (x, y, z) to cylindrical coordinates (ρ, ϕ, z) is given by

$$\rho = \sqrt{x^2 + y^2}, \qquad \phi = \tan^{-1}\frac{y}{x}, \qquad z = z$$

Taking partial derivative of ρ with respect to x, y, and z, we get

$$\frac{\partial \rho}{\partial x} = \frac{x}{\sqrt{x^2 + y^2}} = \frac{\rho \cos\phi}{\rho} = \cos\phi, \text{ where } x = \rho \cos\phi \qquad (1.32)$$

$$\frac{\partial \rho}{\partial y} = \frac{y}{\sqrt{x^2 + y^2}} = \frac{\rho \sin\phi}{\rho} = \sin\phi, \text{ where } y = \rho \sin\phi \qquad (1.33)$$

$$\frac{\partial \rho}{\partial z} = 0 \text{ where } z = z \qquad (1.34)$$

Taking partial derivative of ϕ with respect to x, y, and z, we get

$$\frac{\partial \phi}{\partial x} = \frac{(-y/x^2)}{1 + (y/x)^2} = \frac{-y}{x^2 + y^2} = \frac{-\rho \sin\phi}{\rho^2} = \frac{-\sin\phi}{\rho} \qquad (1.35)$$

$$\frac{\partial \phi}{\partial y} = \frac{(1/x)}{1 + (y/x)^2} = \frac{x}{x^2 + y^2} = \frac{\rho \cos\phi}{\rho^2} = \frac{\cos\phi}{\rho} \qquad (1.36)$$

$$\frac{\partial \phi}{\partial z} = 0 \qquad (1.37)$$

Taking partial derivative of z with respect to x, y, and z, we get

$$\frac{\partial z}{\partial x} = \frac{\partial z}{\partial y} = 0 \text{ and } \frac{\partial z}{\partial z} = 1 \qquad (1.38)$$

Hence $\dfrac{\partial}{\partial x}, \dfrac{\partial}{\partial y}$ and $\dfrac{\partial}{\partial z}$ of Eq. (1.31) can be written in cylindrical coordinates as

$$\frac{\partial}{\partial x} = \frac{\partial}{\partial \rho}\frac{\partial \rho}{\partial x} + \frac{\partial}{\partial \phi}\frac{\partial \phi}{\partial x} + \frac{\partial}{\partial z}\frac{\partial z}{\partial x} \tag{1.39a}$$

$$\frac{\partial}{\partial y} = \frac{\partial}{\partial \rho}\frac{\partial \rho}{\partial y} + \frac{\partial}{\partial \phi}\frac{\partial \phi}{\partial y} + \frac{\partial}{\partial z}\frac{\partial z}{\partial y} \tag{1.39b}$$

$$\frac{\partial}{\partial z} = \frac{\partial}{\partial \rho}\frac{\partial \rho}{\partial z} + \frac{\partial}{\partial \phi}\frac{\partial \phi}{\partial z} + \frac{\partial}{\partial z}\frac{\partial z}{\partial z} \tag{1.39c}$$

Substituting Eqs (1.32), (1.35), and (1.38) in Eq. (1.39a), we have

$$\frac{\partial}{\partial x} = \cos\phi\,\frac{\partial}{\partial \rho} - \frac{\sin\phi}{\rho}\frac{\partial}{\partial \phi} \tag{1.40}$$

Substituting Eqs (1.33), (1.36), and (1.38) in Eq. (1.39b), we have

$$\frac{\partial}{\partial y} = \sin\phi\,\frac{\partial}{\partial \rho} + \frac{\cos\phi}{\rho}\frac{\partial}{\partial \phi} \tag{1.41}$$

Substituting Eqs (1.34), (1.37), and (1.38) in Eq. (1.39c), we have

$$\frac{\partial}{\partial z} = 0\,\frac{\partial}{\partial \rho} + 0\,\frac{\partial}{\partial \phi} + 1\,\frac{\partial}{\partial z} = \frac{\partial}{\partial z} \tag{1.42}$$

From Sec. 1.3, the unit vector transformation from cylindrical $\left(\vec{a}_\rho, \vec{a}_\phi, \vec{a}_z\right)$ to rectangular $\left(\vec{a}_x, \vec{a}_y, \vec{a}_z\right)$ is represented by

$$\vec{a}_x = \cos\phi\,\vec{a}_\rho - \sin\phi\,\vec{a}_\phi, \qquad \vec{a}_y = \sin\phi\,\vec{a}_\rho + \cos\phi\,\vec{a}_\phi, \qquad \vec{a}_z = \vec{a}_z \tag{1.43}$$

Substituting Eqs. (1.40), (1.41), and (1.42) in Eq. (1.31) and making use of Eq. (1.43), the operator ∇, can be written in cylindrical coordinates (ρ, ϕ, z) as

$$\nabla = (\cos\phi\,\vec{a}_\rho - \sin\phi\,\vec{a}_\phi)(\cos\phi\,\frac{\partial}{\partial \rho} - \frac{\sin\phi}{\rho}\frac{\partial}{\partial \phi}) + (\sin\phi\,\vec{a}_\rho + \cos\phi\,\vec{a}_\phi)(\sin\phi\,\frac{\partial}{\partial \rho} + \frac{\cos\phi}{\rho}\frac{\partial}{\partial \phi}) + \vec{a}_z\,\frac{\partial}{\partial z}$$

Simplifying the above equation, we get

$$\nabla = \vec{a}_\rho\,\frac{\partial}{\partial \rho}(\cos^2\phi + \sin^2\phi) + \vec{a}_\phi\,\frac{\partial}{\partial \phi}\left(\frac{\sin^2\phi}{\rho} + \frac{\cos^2\phi}{\rho}\right) + \vec{a}_z\,\frac{\partial}{\partial z}$$

$$\nabla = \vec{a}_\rho\,\frac{\partial}{\partial \rho} + \vec{a}_\phi\,\frac{1}{\rho}\frac{\partial}{\partial \phi} + \vec{a}_z\,\frac{\partial}{\partial z} \qquad \text{(cylindrical)} \tag{1.44}$$

1.6.2 Vector Differential Operator ∇ in Spherical Coordinates

The transformation relationship from Cartesian (x, y, z) to spherical coordinates (r, θ, ϕ) is given by

$$r = \sqrt{x^2 + y^2 + z^2} \qquad \tan\theta = \frac{\sqrt{x^2 + y^2}}{z} \qquad \tan\phi = \frac{y}{x} \tag{1.45}$$

Taking partial derivative of r with respect to $x, y,$ and z, we get

$$\frac{\partial r}{\partial x} = \frac{x}{\sqrt{x^2 + y^2 + z^2}} = \frac{r\sin\theta\cos\phi}{r}, \text{ where } x = r\sin\theta\cos\phi$$

$$= \sin\theta\cos\phi \tag{1.46}$$

$$\frac{\partial r}{\partial y} = \frac{y}{\sqrt{x^2 + y^2 + z^2}} = \frac{r\sin\theta\sin\phi}{r}, \text{ where } y = r\sin\theta\sin\phi$$

$$= \sin\theta\sin\phi \tag{1.47}$$

$$\frac{\partial r}{\partial z} = \frac{z}{\sqrt{x^2 + y^2 + z^2}} = \frac{r\cos\theta}{r} = \cos\theta, \text{ where } z = r\cos\theta \tag{1.48}$$

Taking partial derivative of θ with respect to x, y, and z, we get

$$\frac{\partial\theta}{\partial x} = \frac{1}{1 + \left(\dfrac{\sqrt{x^2 + y^2}}{z}\right)^2} \times \frac{x}{z\sqrt{x^2 + y^2}} = \frac{xz}{(x^2 + y^2 + z^2)(\sqrt{x^2 + y^2})}$$

$$= \frac{(r\sin\theta\cos\phi)(r\cos\theta)}{r^2(r\sin\theta)}, \text{ where } x^2 + y^2 = (r\sin\theta)^2$$

$$= \frac{\cos\phi\cos\theta}{r} \tag{1.49}$$

$$\frac{\partial\theta}{\partial y} = \frac{yz}{(x^2 + y^2 + z^2)(\sqrt{x^2 + y^2})}$$

$$= \frac{(r\sin\theta\sin\phi)(r\cos\theta)}{r^2(r\sin\theta)} = \frac{\sin\phi\cos\theta}{r} \tag{1.50}$$

$$\frac{\partial\theta}{\partial z} = \frac{1}{1 + \left(\dfrac{\sqrt{x^2 + y^2}}{z}\right)^2} \times \frac{-\sqrt{x^2 + y^2}}{z^2} = \frac{z^2}{(x^2 + y^2 + z^2)} \times \frac{-\sqrt{x^2 + y^2}}{z^2}$$

$$= \frac{-r\sin\theta}{r^2} = \frac{-\sin\theta}{r} \tag{1.51}$$

Taking partial derivative of ϕ with respect to x, y, and z, we get

$$\frac{\partial\phi}{\partial x} = \frac{(-y/x^2)}{1 + (y/x)^2} = \frac{-y}{x^2 + y^2} = \frac{-r\sin\theta\sin\phi}{(r\sin\theta)^2} = \frac{-\sin\phi}{r\sin\theta} \tag{1.52}$$

$$\frac{\partial\phi}{\partial y} = \frac{(1/x)}{1 + (y/x)^2} = \frac{x}{x^2 + y^2} = \frac{r\sin\theta\cos\phi}{(r\sin\theta)^2} = \frac{\cos\phi}{r\sin\theta} \tag{1.53}$$

$$\frac{\partial\phi}{\partial z} = 0 \tag{1.54}$$

Hence $\dfrac{\partial}{\partial x}, \dfrac{\partial}{\partial y}$ and $\dfrac{\partial}{\partial z}$ of Eq. (1.31) can be written in spherical coordinates as

$$\frac{\partial}{\partial x} = \frac{\partial}{\partial r}\frac{\partial r}{\partial x} + \frac{\partial}{\partial \theta}\frac{\partial \theta}{\partial x} + \frac{\partial}{\partial \phi}\frac{\partial \phi}{\partial x} \tag{1.55a}$$

$$\frac{\partial}{\partial y} = \frac{\partial}{\partial r}\frac{\partial r}{\partial y} + \frac{\partial}{\partial \theta}\frac{\partial \theta}{\partial y} + \frac{\partial}{\partial \phi}\frac{\partial \phi}{\partial y} \tag{1.55b}$$

$$\frac{\partial}{\partial z} = \frac{\partial}{\partial r}\frac{\partial r}{\partial z} + \frac{\partial}{\partial \theta}\frac{\partial \theta}{\partial z} + \frac{\partial}{\partial \phi}\frac{\partial \phi}{\partial z} \tag{1.55c}$$

Substituting Eqs. (1.46), (1.49), and (1.52) in Eq. (1.55a), we have

$$\frac{\partial}{\partial x} = (\sin\theta\cos\phi)\frac{\partial}{\partial r} + \left(\frac{\cos\phi\cos\theta}{r}\right)\frac{\partial}{\partial \theta} - \left(\frac{\sin\phi}{r\sin\theta}\right)\frac{\partial}{\partial \phi} \tag{1.56}$$

Substituting Eqs. (1.47), (1.50), and (1.53) in Eq. (1.55b), we have

$$\frac{\partial}{\partial y} = (\sin\theta\sin\phi)\frac{\partial}{\partial r} + \left(\frac{\sin\phi\cos\theta}{r}\right)\frac{\partial}{\partial \theta} + \left(\frac{\cos\phi}{r\sin\theta}\right)\frac{\partial}{\partial \phi} \tag{1.57}$$

Substituting Eqs. (1.48), (1.51), and (1.54) in Eq. (1.55c), we have

$$\frac{\partial}{\partial z} = \cos\theta\frac{\partial}{\partial r} - \left(\frac{\sin\theta}{r}\right)\frac{\partial}{\partial \theta} \tag{1.58}$$

From Sec 1.3, the unit vector transformation from spherical $(\vec{a}_r\ \vec{a}_\theta\ \vec{a}_\phi)$ to rectangular $(\vec{a}_x, \vec{a}_y, \vec{a}_z)$ is given by

$$\vec{a}_x = \sin\theta\cos\phi\,\vec{a}_r + \cos\theta\cos\phi\,\vec{a}_\theta - \sin\phi\,\vec{a}_\phi \tag{1.59a}$$

$$\vec{a}_y = \sin\theta\sin\phi\,\vec{a}_r + \cos\theta\sin\phi\,\vec{a}_\theta + \cos\phi\,\vec{a}_\phi \tag{1.59b}$$

$$\vec{a}_z = \cos\theta\,\vec{a}_r - \sin\theta\,\vec{a}_\theta \tag{1.59c}$$

Substituting Eqs. (1.56), (1.57), and (1.58) in Eq. (1.31) and making use of Eqs. (1.59a) to (1.59c), the del operator ∇, can be written in spherical coordinates (r, θ, ϕ) as

$$\nabla = (\sin\theta\cos\phi\,\vec{a}_r + \cos\theta\cos\phi\,\vec{a}_\theta - \sin\phi\,\vec{a}_\phi)\left[(\sin\theta\cos\phi)\frac{\partial}{\partial r} + \left(\frac{\cos\phi\cos\theta}{r}\right)\frac{\partial}{\partial \theta} - \left(\frac{\sin\phi}{r\sin\theta}\right)\frac{\partial}{\partial \phi}\right]$$

$$+ (\sin\theta\sin\phi\,\vec{a}_r + \cos\theta\sin\phi\,\vec{a}_\theta + \cos\phi\,\vec{a}_\phi)\left[(\sin\theta\sin\phi)\frac{\partial}{\partial r} + \left(\frac{\sin\phi\cos\theta}{r}\right)\frac{\partial}{\partial \theta} + \left(\frac{\cos\phi}{r\sin\theta}\right)\frac{\partial}{\partial \phi}\right]$$

$$+ (\cos\theta\,\vec{a}_r - \sin\theta\,\vec{a}_\theta)\left[\cos\theta\frac{\partial}{\partial r} - \left(\frac{\sin\theta}{r}\right)\frac{\partial}{\partial \theta}\right]$$

Simplifying this equation, we get

$$\nabla = \vec{a}_r \frac{\partial}{\partial r}(\sin^2\theta\cos^2\phi + \sin^2\theta\sin^2\phi + \cos^2\theta) + \vec{a}_\theta \frac{\partial}{\partial\theta}\left(\frac{\cos^2\theta\cos^2\phi}{r} + \frac{\cos^2\theta\sin^2\phi}{r} + \frac{\sin^2\theta}{r}\right)$$

$$+\vec{a}_\phi \frac{\partial}{\partial\phi}\left(\frac{\sin^2\theta}{r\sin\theta} + \frac{\cos^2\theta}{r\sin\theta}\right)$$

$$\nabla = \vec{a}_r \frac{\partial}{\partial r} + \vec{a}_\theta \frac{1}{r}\frac{\partial}{\partial\theta} + \vec{a}_\phi \frac{1}{r\sin\theta}\frac{\partial}{\partial\phi} \qquad \text{(spherical)}$$

1.7   GRADIENT OF A SCALAR FIELD

The gradient of a scalar field V is defined as a vector that represents both the magnitude and the direction of the maximum rate of increase of V. The gradient can be expressed mathematically by calculating the difference in the field dV between points P_1 and P_2. Suppose that $V_1(x,y,z)$ is the voltage at point $P_1(x,y,z)$ and $V_2(x,y,z)$ is the voltage at a nearby point $P_2(x+dx,\ y+dy,\ z+dz)$ as shown in Figure 1.24. Here, the differential distances dx, dy and dz are the components of the differential distance vector $\vec{dl}$. Using differential calculus, the differential voltage $dV = V_2 - V_1$ is given by

$$dV = \frac{\partial V}{\partial x}dx + \frac{\partial V}{\partial y}dy + \frac{\partial V}{\partial z}dz \tag{1.60}$$

$$= \left(\frac{\partial V}{\partial x}\vec{a}_x + \frac{\partial V}{\partial y}\vec{a}_y + \frac{\partial V}{\partial z}\vec{a}_z\right)\cdot\left(dx\vec{a}_x + dy\vec{a}_y + dz\vec{a}_z\right)$$

where $\vec{A} = \dfrac{\partial V}{\partial x}\vec{a}_x + \dfrac{\partial V}{\partial y}\vec{a}_y + \dfrac{\partial V}{\partial z}\vec{a}_z$ and $\vec{dl} = dx\vec{a}_x + dy\vec{a}_y + dz\vec{a}_z$.

Hence, $dV = \vec{A}\cdot\vec{dl} = Adl\cos\theta$

That is,

$$\frac{dV}{dl} = A\cos\theta \tag{1.61}$$

where $\vec{dl}$ is the differential distance vector from P_1 to P_2 and θ is the angle between $\vec{A}$ and $\vec{dl}$. Here, the ratio $\dfrac{dV}{dl}$ is maximum when $\theta = 0°$ and $\vec{dl}$ is in the direction of $\vec{A}$. Therefore,

$$\left.\frac{dV}{dl}\right|_{\max} = \frac{dV}{dn} = A \tag{1.62}$$

where $\dfrac{dV}{dn}$ is the normal derivative. Hence, $\vec{A}$ has its magnitude and direction as those of the maximum rate of change of V. By definition, $\vec{A}$ is the gradient of V.

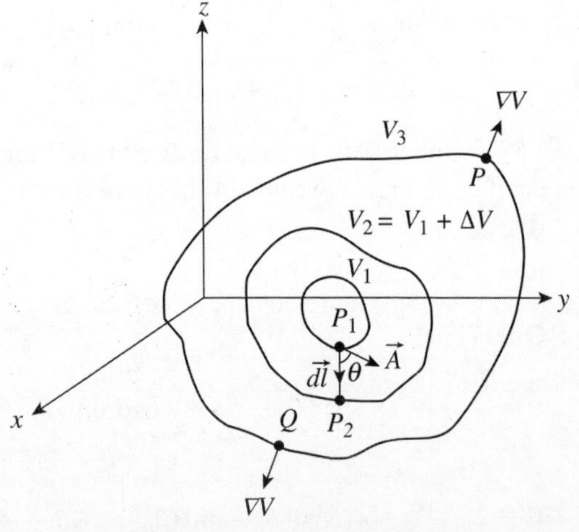

Figure 1.24   *Gradient of a scalar*

Therefore, for rectangular coordinates,

$$\text{Grad } V = \nabla V = \frac{\partial V}{\partial x}\vec{a}_x + \frac{\partial V}{\partial y}\vec{a}_y + \frac{\partial V}{\partial z}\vec{a}_z$$

The gradient operator is meaningful only when it operates on a scalar quantity. The result of this operation is a vector whose magnitude is equal to the maximum rate of change of the physical quantity per unit distance and whose direction is along the direction of maximum increase as given by Eq. (1.62).

The projection (or component) of V in the direction of a unit vector $\vec{a}_l$ is called the *directional derivative* of V along $\vec{a}_l$ and it is given by

$$\frac{dV}{dl} = \vec{A}\cdot\vec{a}_l = \nabla V \cdot \vec{a}_l$$

Using the del operator for cylindrical coordinates, the gradient of V is represented by

$$\nabla V = \frac{\partial V}{\partial \rho}\vec{a}_\rho + \frac{1}{\rho}\frac{\partial V}{\partial \phi}\vec{a}_\phi + \frac{\partial V}{\partial z}\vec{a}_z$$

For spherical coordinates, the gradient of V is represented by

$$\nabla V = \frac{\partial V}{\partial r}\vec{a}_r + \frac{1}{r}\frac{\partial V}{\partial \theta}\vec{a}_\theta + \frac{1}{r\sin\theta}\frac{\partial V}{\partial \phi}\vec{a}_\phi$$

EXAMPLE 1.33

Find the gradient of scalar system $t = x^2 y + e^z$ at point $P(1,5,-2)$.

SOLUTION

Given a scalar system, $t = x^2 y + e^z$.

$$\text{The gradient of } t = \nabla t = \frac{\partial t}{\partial x}\vec{a}_x + \frac{\partial t}{\partial y}\vec{a}_y + \frac{\partial t}{\partial z}\vec{a}_z$$

$$= 2xy\vec{a}_x + x^2\vec{a}_y + e^z\vec{a}_z$$

Therefore, at point, $P(1,5,-2)$, $\nabla t = 10\vec{a}_x + \vec{a}_y + e^{-2}\vec{a}_z$

EXAMPLE 1.34

Given a scalar field, $V = x^2 y + xy^2 + xz^2$, determine the gradient of V at $(1,-1,2)$.

SOLUTION

The gradient of V in rectangular coordinates is

$$\text{Grad } V = \nabla V = \frac{\partial V}{\partial x}\vec{a}_x + \frac{\partial V}{\partial y}\vec{a}_y + \frac{\partial V}{\partial z}\vec{a}_z$$

$$= \left(2xy + y^2 + z^2\right)\vec{a}_x + \left(x^2 + 2xy\right)\vec{a}_y + 2xz\vec{a}_z$$

Hence, $\nabla V\big|_{(1,-1,2)} = (-2+1+4)\vec{a}_x + (1-2)\vec{a}_y + 4\vec{a}_z$

$$= 3\vec{a}_x - \vec{a}_y + 4\vec{a}_z$$

EXAMPLE 1.35

For a scalar field, $V = x^2 y^2 + xyz$, determine ∇V and the direction derivative of V in the direction $3\vec{a}_x + 4\vec{a}_y + 12\vec{a}_z$ at $(2,1,0)$.

SOLUTION

The gradient of V in rectangular coordinates is

$$\nabla V = \frac{\partial V}{\partial x}\vec{a}_x + \frac{\partial V}{\partial y}\vec{a}_y + \frac{\partial V}{\partial z}\vec{a}_z$$

$$= \left(2xy^2 + yz\right)\vec{a}_x + \left(2x^2 y + xz\right)\vec{a}_y + \left(xy\right)\vec{a}_z$$

Therefore, at $(2,1,0)$, $\nabla V = 4\vec{a}_x + 8\vec{a}_y + 2\vec{a}_z$

The directional derivative of V is

$$\frac{dV}{dl} = \nabla V \cdot \vec{a}_l = \frac{\nabla V \cdot \vec{l}}{|\vec{l}|}$$

$$= \frac{\left(4\vec{a}_x + 8\vec{a}_y + 2\vec{a}_z\right) \cdot \left(3\vec{a}_x + 4\vec{a}_y + 12\vec{a}_z\right)}{\sqrt{(3)^2 + (4)^2 + (12)^2}} = \frac{68}{13}$$

EXAMPLE 1.36

Determine the directional derivative of $V = \rho z^2 \cos 2\phi$ along the direction of $2\vec{a}_\rho - \vec{a}_z$ and evaluate it at $\left(1, \dfrac{\pi}{2}, 3\right)$.

SOLUTION

The gradient of V in cylindrical coordinates is

$$\nabla V = \frac{\partial V}{\partial \rho}\vec{a}_\rho + \frac{1}{\rho}\frac{\partial V}{\partial \phi}\vec{a}_\phi + \frac{\partial V}{\partial z}\vec{a}_z$$

$$= \left(z^2 \cos 2\phi\right)\vec{a}_\rho - \left(2z^2 \sin 2\phi\right)\vec{a}_\phi + \left(2\rho z \cos 2\phi\right)\vec{a}_z$$

The directional derivative of V is

$$\frac{dV}{dl} = \nabla V \cdot \vec{a}_l = \frac{\left\{\left(z^2 \cos 2\phi\right)\vec{a}_\rho - \left(2z^2 \sin 2\phi\right)\vec{a}_\phi + \left(2\rho z \cos 2\phi\right)\vec{a}_z\right\} \cdot \left\{2\vec{a}_\rho - \vec{a}_z\right\}}{\sqrt{5}}$$

$$= \frac{2z^2 \cos 2\phi - 2\rho z \cos 2\phi}{\sqrt{5}}$$

Therefore,

$$\frac{dV}{dl}\bigg|_{\left(1,\frac{\pi}{2},3\right)} = \frac{2\times 9\cos\pi - 2\times 3\cos\pi}{\sqrt{5}} = -\frac{12}{\sqrt{5}}$$

□

EXAMPLE 1.37

Determine the gradient of the given scalar field, $V = 5r\sin^2\theta\cos\phi$ in spherical coordinates.

SOLUTION

Gradient of V in spherical coordinates is

$$\nabla V = \frac{\partial V}{\partial r}\vec{a}_r + \frac{1}{r}\frac{\partial V}{\partial\theta}\vec{a}_\theta + \frac{1}{r\sin\theta}\frac{\partial V}{\partial\phi}\vec{a}_\phi$$

$$= 5\sin^2\theta\cos\phi\,\vec{a}_r + 5\sin 2\theta\cos\phi\,\vec{a}_\theta - 5\sin\theta\sin\phi\,\vec{a}_\phi$$

□

EXAMPLE 1.38

Find the gradient of the given scalar field, $V = V_0\left(\dfrac{a}{r}\right)\cos 2\theta$ in spherical coordinates and then evaluate it at the given point $P(4a,0,\pi)$.

SOLUTION

The gradient of V in spherical coordinates is

$$\nabla V = \left(\vec{a}_r\frac{\partial}{\partial r} + \vec{a}_\theta\frac{1}{r}\frac{\partial}{\partial\theta} + \vec{a}_\phi\frac{1}{r\sin\theta}\frac{\partial}{\partial\phi}\right)V_0\left(\frac{a}{r}\right)\cos 2\theta$$

$$= -\frac{V_0 a}{r^2}\cos 2\theta\,\vec{a}_r - \frac{2V_0 a}{r^2}\sin 2\theta\,\vec{a}_\theta$$

$$= -\frac{V_0 a}{r^2}\left(\cos 2\theta\,\vec{a}_r + 2\sin 2\theta\,\vec{a}_\theta\right)$$

Therefore, the gradient at point $P(4a,0,\pi)$ is

$$\nabla V = -\frac{V_0}{16a}\vec{a}_r$$

□

1.8 DIVERGENCE OF A VECTOR FIELD

An isolated, positive point charge Q induces an electric field $\vec{E}$ in the space around it. The direction of $\vec{E}$ is in the outward direction away from the charge and its magnitude is proportional to Q. Such a vector field $\vec{E}$ is usually represented by field lines as shown in Figure 1.25. The arrowhead denotes the direction of the field at the point and the length of the line indicates the magnitude of field. The flux density of the electric field $\vec{E}$ at the surface boundary is defined as the amount of outward flux crossing the unit surface $d\vec{s}$. Therefore,

$$\text{Flux density of }\vec{E} = \frac{\vec{E}\cdot d\vec{s}}{|d\vec{s}|} = \frac{\vec{E}\cdot\vec{a}_n ds}{ds}$$

where $\vec{a}_n$ is normal to the surface of $d\vec{s}$. The total flux crossing a closed surface s as shown in Figure 1.25, is obtained from the integral $\oint_s \vec{E}\cdot d\vec{s}$.

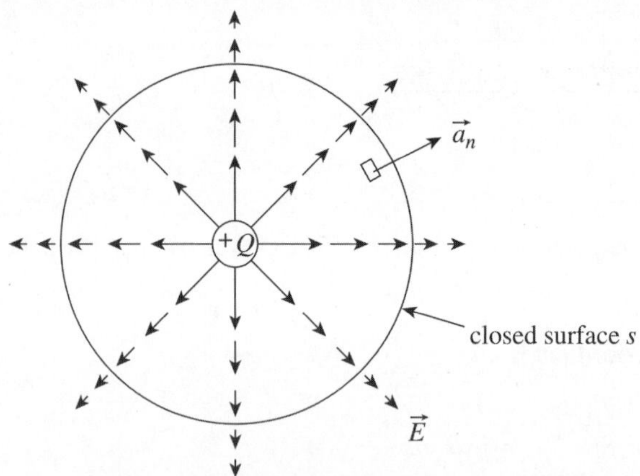

Figure 1.25   *Flux lines of the electric field $\vec{E}$ due to a positive charge Q*

The *divergence* of a vector field $\vec{E}$ at any point is defined as the net outward flow of flux per unit volume over a closed surface s as the volume shrinks about that point.

$$\text{Div } \vec{E} = \nabla \cdot \vec{E} = \lim_{\Delta v \to 0} \frac{\oint_s \vec{E} \cdot d\vec{s}}{\Delta v}$$

where Δv is the volume enclosed by the closed surface s.

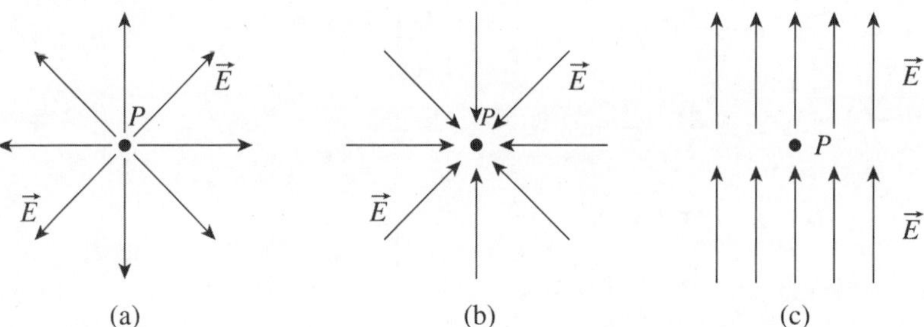

(a)   (b)   (c)

Figure 1.26   *Representation of the divergence of a vector field $\vec{E}$ at P:*
(a) positive divergence, (b) negative divergence, and (c) zero divergence

Figure 1.26 shows the divergence of a vector field $\vec{E}$ at a given point and it is a measure of how much the field diverges or emanates from that point. When the vector field diverges or spreads out, the divergence at P is positive as shown in Figure 1.26(a). When it converges, the divergence at P is negative as shown in Figure 1.26(b). The vector field having zero divergence at P is said to be divergenceless and it is shown in Figure 1.26(c).

Figure 1.27 shows a differential rectangular parallelepiped, such as a cube, whose edges are oriented with the axes of the Cartesian coordinate system. Here, the lengths of the edges are Δx along x, Δy along y, and Δz along z, respectively. A vector field $\vec{E}$ exists in the region of space containing the parallelepiped, and the flux of $\vec{E}$ can be determined over the closed surface s by adding the fluxes over all six sides. The flux through any side is defined as the outward flux from the volume Δv through that side. A vector field $\vec{E}$ in Cartesian coordinate system is given by

$$\vec{E} = E_x \vec{a}_x + E_y \vec{a}_y + E_z \vec{a}_z \tag{1.63}$$

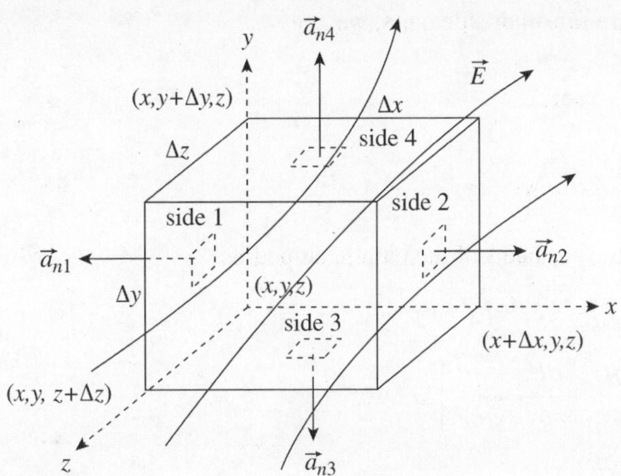

Figure 1.27 *Flux lines of a vector field $\vec{E}$ through a differential rectangular parallelepiped*

The area of the side 1 in Figure 1.27 is defined as $\Delta y\,\Delta z$, and its unit vector is along negative x-direction, i.e., $\vec{a}_{n1} = -\vec{a}_x$. Hence, the outward flux F_1 through side 1 is

$$F_1 = \int_{side1} \vec{E}\cdot\vec{a}_{n1}\,ds$$

$$= \int_{side1}\left(E_x\vec{a}_x + E_y\vec{a}_y + E_z\vec{a}_z\right)\cdot\left(-\vec{a}_x\right)dydz$$

$$= -E_x(1)\Delta y\Delta z \tag{1.64}$$

where $E_x(1)$ is the value of E_x at the center of side 1.

Similarly, the flux flowing out of side 2 with its unit vector along positive x-direction $\left(\vec{a}_{n2} = \vec{a}_x\right)$, is

$$F_2 = E_x(2)\Delta y\Delta z \tag{1.65}$$

where $E_x(2)$ is the value of E_x at the center of side 2. As the differential volume under consideration is very small, $E_x(2)$ is related to $E_x(1)$ using a differential separation Δx method. It is given by

$$E_x(2) = E_x(1) + \frac{\partial E_x}{\partial x}\Delta x \tag{1.66}$$

Here, higher-order terms involving $(\Delta x)^2$ and higher powers are ignored as their contributions are negligibly small when Δx is very small. Substituting Eq. (1.66) in Eq. (1.65), we get

$$F_2 = \left[E_x(1) + \frac{\partial E_x}{\partial x}\Delta x\right]\Delta y\Delta z \tag{1.67}$$

Adding Eqs (1.64) and (1.67), the sum of the fluxes out of side 1 and side 2 is obtained by

$$F_1 + F_2 = \frac{\partial E_x}{\partial x}\Delta x\Delta y\Delta z$$

Repeating this procedure for other side pairs, we get

$$F_3 + F_4 = \frac{\partial E_y}{\partial y} \Delta x \Delta y \Delta z$$

$$F_5 + F_6 = \frac{\partial E_z}{\partial z} \Delta x \Delta y \Delta z$$

The total flux through the surface s of the parallelepiped is

$$\oint_s \vec{E} \cdot d\vec{s} = F_1 + F_2 + F_3 + F_4 + F_5 + F_6$$

$$= \left(\frac{\partial E_x}{\partial x} + \frac{\partial E_y}{\partial y} + \frac{\partial E}{\partial z} \right) \Delta x \Delta y \Delta z$$

$$= \left(\text{div} \vec{E} \right) \Delta v \tag{1.68}$$

where $\Delta v = \Delta x \Delta y \Delta z$ and div $\vec{E}$ is a differential function called the *divergence* of $\vec{E}$ or $\nabla \cdot \vec{E}$ and it can be defined in Cartesian coordinates as

$$\text{div } \vec{E} = \nabla \cdot \vec{E} = \frac{\partial E_x}{\partial x} + \frac{\partial E_y}{\partial y} + \frac{\partial E_z}{\partial z} \tag{1.69}$$

Shrinking the volume Δv to zero, the divergence of $\vec{E}$ at a point can be defined as the net outward flux per unit volume over a closed surface. Therefore, from Eq. (1.68), we get

$$\text{div } \vec{E} = \underset{\Delta v \to 0}{Lt} \frac{\oint_s \vec{E} \cdot d\vec{s}}{\Delta v} \tag{1.70}$$

where s encloses the elemental volume Δv. The divergence is a differential operator, which operates only on vectors and the result is a scalar. This is in contrast with the gradient operator, which can operate only on scalars and the result is a vector.

Using the del operator for cylindrical coordinates, the divergence of $\vec{E}$ is represented by

$$\nabla \cdot \vec{E} = \frac{1}{\rho} \frac{\partial}{\partial \rho} \left(\rho E_\rho \right) + \frac{1}{\rho} \frac{\partial E_\phi}{\partial \phi} + \frac{\partial E_z}{\partial z}$$

Similarly, for spherical coordinates, the divergence of $\vec{E}$ is represented by

$$\nabla \cdot \vec{E} = \frac{1}{r^2} \frac{\partial}{\partial r} \left(r^2 E_r \right) + \frac{1}{r \sin \theta} \frac{\partial}{\partial \theta} \left(E_\theta \sin \theta \right) + \frac{1}{r \sin \theta} \frac{\partial E_\phi}{\partial \phi}$$

The properties involving divergence are:

(*i*)   The divergence of a vector field is always a scalar.

(*ii*)   The divergence of a scalar field V, i.e., $\nabla \cdot V$ carries no meaning in vector algebra.

(*iii*) $\nabla \cdot \left(\vec{A} + \vec{B} \right) = \nabla \cdot \vec{A} + \nabla \cdot \vec{B}$ (Distributive property)

(*iv*) $\nabla \cdot \left(V \vec{A} \right) = V(\nabla \cdot \vec{A}) + \vec{A} \cdot \nabla V$ (Scaling property)

(*v*)   If $\nabla \cdot \vec{A} = 0$, then the vector field $\vec{A}$ is said to be solenoidal or continuous.

EXAMPLE 1.39

Find the divergence of $\vec{A} = x^2 \vec{a}_x + (xy)^2 \vec{a}_y + 24(xyz)^2 \vec{a}_z$.

SOLUTION

The divergence of $\vec{A}$ in rectangular coordinates is

$$\nabla \cdot \vec{A} = \frac{\partial A_x}{\partial x} + \frac{\partial A_y}{\partial y} + \frac{\partial A_z}{\partial z}$$

$$= \frac{\partial}{\partial x}\left(x^2\right) + \frac{\partial}{\partial y}\left(x^2 y^2\right) + 24\frac{\partial}{\partial z}\left(x^2 y^2 z^2\right)$$

$$= 2x + 2x^2 y + 48 x^2 y^2 z$$

EXAMPLE 1.40

Given a vector $\vec{A} = \rho \cos\phi\, \vec{a}_\rho + \rho \sin\phi\, \vec{a}_\phi + 3z \vec{a}_z$, find the divergence of $\vec{A}$ at point $(2,0,3)$.

SOLUTION

The divergence of $\vec{A}$ in cylindrical coordinates is

$$\nabla \cdot \vec{A} = \frac{1}{\rho}\frac{\partial}{\partial \rho}\left(\rho A_\rho\right) + \frac{1}{\rho}\frac{\partial A_\phi}{\partial \phi} + \frac{\partial A_z}{\partial z}$$

$$= \frac{1}{\rho}\frac{\partial}{\partial \rho}\left(\rho^2 \cos\phi\right) + \frac{1}{\rho}\frac{\partial}{\partial \phi}\left(\rho \sin\phi\right) + \frac{\partial}{\partial z}\left(3z\right)$$

$$= 2\cos\phi + \cos\phi + 3$$

Therefore,

$$\left.\left(\nabla \cdot \vec{A}\right)\right|_{(2,0,3)} = 2 + 1 + 3 = 6$$

EXAMPLE 1.41

For the vector field, $\vec{E} = \frac{1}{r^2}\cos\theta\, \vec{a}_r + r\sin\theta\cos\phi\, \vec{a}_\theta + \cos\theta\, \vec{a}_\phi$, determine the divergence.

SOLUTION

The divergence of $\vec{E}$ in spherical coordinates is

$$\nabla \cdot \vec{E} = \frac{1}{r^2}\frac{\partial}{\partial r}\left(r^2 E_r\right) + \frac{1}{r\sin\theta}\frac{\partial}{\partial \theta}\left(E_\theta \sin\theta\right) + \frac{1}{r\sin\theta}\frac{\partial E_\phi}{\partial \phi}$$

$$= \frac{1}{r^2}\frac{\partial}{\partial r}\left(\cos\theta\right) + \frac{1}{r\sin\theta}\frac{\partial}{\partial \theta}\left(r\sin^2\theta\cos\phi\right) + \frac{1}{r\sin\theta}\frac{\partial}{\partial \phi}\left(\cos\theta\right)$$

$$= 0 + \frac{1}{r\sin\theta}2r\sin\theta\cos\theta\cos\phi + 0$$

$$= 2\cos\theta\cos\phi$$

EXAMPLE 1.42

Show that the vector $\vec{A} = 5y^4 z^2 \vec{a}_x + 4x^3 z^2 \vec{a}_y + 3x^2 y^2 \vec{a}_z$ is solenoidal.

SOLUTION

A vector $\vec{A}$ is said to be solenoidal if $\nabla \cdot \vec{A} = 0$.

$$\nabla \cdot \vec{A} = \frac{\partial A_x}{\partial x} + \frac{\partial A_y}{\partial y} + \frac{\partial A_z}{\partial z}$$

$$= \frac{\partial}{\partial x}\left(5y^4 z^2\right) + \frac{\partial}{\partial y}\left(4x^3 z^2\right) + \frac{\partial}{\partial z}\left(3x^2 y^2\right)$$

$$= 0$$

Since $\nabla \cdot \vec{A} = 0$, the given vector $\vec{A}$ is solenoidal.

1.9 DIVERGENCE THEOREM

Divergence theorem states that the total outward flux of a vector field $\vec{D}$ through the closed surface s is equal to the volume integral of the divergence of $\vec{D}$. The result given by Eq. (1.68) for a differential volume Δv can be extended to relate the volume integral of $\nabla \cdot \vec{D}$ over any volume v to the flux of $\vec{D}$ through the closed surface s that encloses volume v. Mathematically, *divergence theorem* is expressed as

$$\oint_s \vec{D} \cdot d\vec{s} = \int_v \left(\nabla \cdot \vec{D}\right) dv$$

and this relationship is used extensively in electromagnetics.

Proof   Consider the volume v as shown in Figure 1.28, and it is subdivided into n number of small cells. If the nth cell has volume Δv_n and is bounded by surface s_n, then the surface integral of a vector field $\vec{D}$ over the closed surface s is represented by

$$\oint_s \vec{D} \cdot d\vec{s} = \sum_n \oint_{s_n} \vec{D} \cdot d\vec{s} = \sum_n \frac{\oint_{s_n} \vec{D} \cdot d\vec{s}}{\Delta v_n} \Delta v_n \qquad (1.71)$$

Here, the outward flux to one cell is inward to neighboring cells. This results in cancellation of every interior surface, and the sum of all the surface integrals over s_n is the same as the surface integral over the surface s.

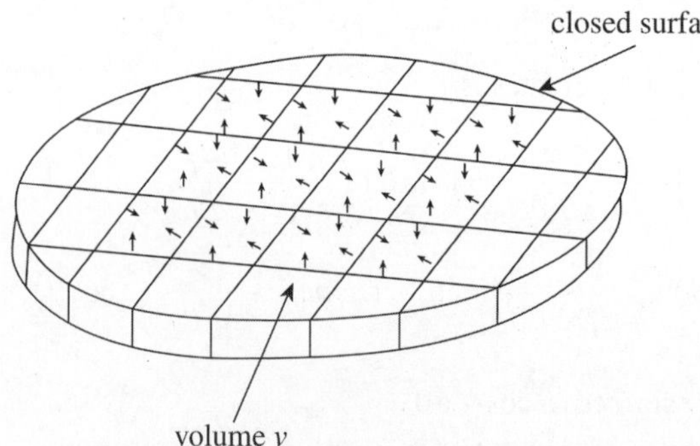

Figure 1.28   *Illustration of divergence theorem*

Taking the limit on the right-hand side (RHS) of Eq. (1.71) as $\Delta v_n \to 0$ and comparing with Eq. (1.70), we get

$$\underset{\Delta v \to 0}{Lt} \sum_n \frac{\oint_{s_n} \vec{D} \cdot d\vec{s}}{\Delta v_n} \Delta v_n = \int_v \left(\nabla \cdot \vec{D} \right) dv \tag{1.72}$$

Comparing the above equation with Eq. (1.71), we get

$$\oint_s \vec{D} \cdot d\vec{s} = \int_v \left(\nabla \cdot \vec{D} \right) dv \tag{1.73}$$

This equation represents divergence theorem. If the vector field $\vec{D}$ is continuous or solenoidal, then $\nabla \cdot \vec{D} = 0$. For a continuous vector field such as the flow of an incompressible fluid through a pipe or the magnetic lines of field surrounding a magnet, there is no net outward flow of flux. Therefore, its net outward of flux over the closed surface s is zero, i.e., $\oint_s \vec{D} \cdot d\vec{s} = 0$.

EXAMPLE 1.43

Given that $\vec{A} = \left(\dfrac{5r^2}{4} \right) \vec{a}_r$ is in spherical coordinates, evaluate both sides of the divergence theorem for the volume enclosed by $r = 4\text{m}$ and $\theta = \dfrac{\pi}{4}$ shown in Figure E1.43.

SOLUTION

By divergence theorem,

$$\oint_s \vec{A} \cdot d\vec{s} = \int_v \left(\nabla \cdot \vec{A} \right) dv$$

where $\vec{A}$ has only a radial component and $\vec{A} \cdot d\vec{s}$ has a non-zero value on the surface $r = 4\text{m}$.

Evaluating the left-hand side (LHS) of divergence theorem, we get

$$\oint_s \vec{A} \cdot d\vec{s} = \int_0^{2\pi} \int_0^{\frac{\pi}{4}} \left\{ \frac{5(4)^2}{4} \vec{a}_r \right\} \cdot \left\{ (4)^2 \sin\theta \, d\theta \, d\phi \, \vec{a}_r \right\}$$

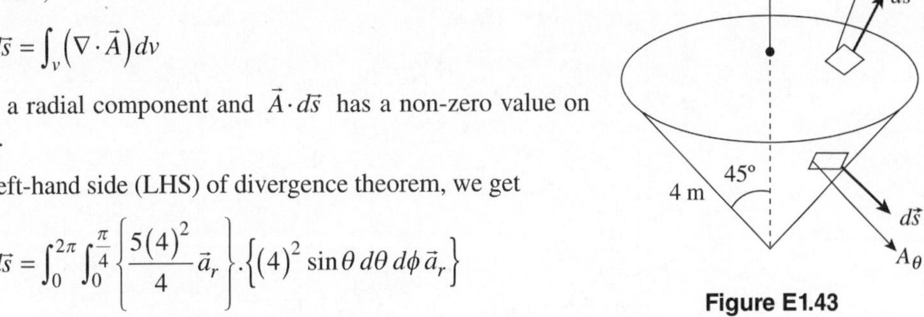

Figure E1.43

$$= 5(4)^3 \int_0^{2\pi} \int_0^{\frac{\pi}{4}} \sin\theta \, d\theta \, d\phi = 589.1$$

where $d\vec{s} = r^2 \sin\theta \, d\theta \, d\phi \, \vec{a}_r$ in spherical coordinates.

Divergence of $\vec{A}$ in spherical coordinates is given by

$$\nabla \cdot \vec{A} = \frac{1}{r^2} \frac{\partial}{\partial r} \left(r^2 A_r \right) + \frac{1}{r \sin\theta} \frac{\partial}{\partial \theta} \left(A_\theta \sin\theta \right) + \frac{1}{r \sin\theta} \frac{\partial A_\phi}{\partial \phi}$$

$$= \frac{1}{r^2} \frac{\partial}{\partial r} \left(r^2 \frac{5r^2}{4} \right) = 5r$$

Evaluating the RHS of divergence theorem, we get

$$\int_{v}\left(\nabla\cdot\vec{A}\right)dv = \int_{0}^{2\pi}\int_{0}^{\frac{\pi}{4}}\int_{0}^{4}\left(5r\right)r^{2}\sin\theta\,dr\,d\theta\,d\phi$$

$$= 5\left(4\right)^{3}\int_{0}^{2\pi}\int_{0}^{\frac{\pi}{4}}\sin\theta\,d\theta\,d\phi = 589.1$$

where $dv = r^{2}\sin\theta\,dr\,d\theta\,d\phi$ in spherical coordinates.

EXAMPLE 1.44

Using divergence theorem, evaluate $\oint_{s}\vec{A}\cdot d\vec{s}$, where $\vec{A} = 2xy\vec{a}_{x} + y^{2}\vec{a}_{y} + 4yz\vec{a}_{z}$ and s is the surface of the cube bounded by the planes $x = 0, x = 1; y = 0, y = 1$; and $z = 0, z = 1$.

SOLUTION

By divergence theorem,

$$\oint_{s}\vec{A}\cdot d\vec{s} = \int_{v}\left(\nabla\cdot\vec{A}\right)dv$$

$$\nabla\cdot\vec{A} = \left(\vec{a}_{x}\frac{\partial}{\partial x} + \vec{a}_{y}\frac{\partial}{\partial y} + \vec{a}_{z}\frac{\partial}{\partial z}\right)\cdot\left(2xy\vec{a}_{x} + y^{2}\vec{a}_{y} + 4yz\vec{a}_{z}\right)$$

$$= \frac{\partial}{\partial x}\left(2xy\right) + \frac{\partial}{\partial y}\left(y^{2}\right) + \frac{\partial}{\partial z}\left(4yz\right)$$

$$= 2y + 2y + 4y = 8y$$

$$\int_{v}\left(\nabla\cdot\vec{A}\right)dv = \int_{0}^{1}\int_{0}^{1}\int_{0}^{1} 8y\,dx\,dy\,dz = \int_{0}^{1}\int_{0}^{1}\left[8yz\right]_{0}^{1}dxdy = \int_{0}^{1}\int_{0}^{1}8y\,dx\,dy$$

$$= \int_{0}^{1}\left[8\frac{y^{2}}{2}\right]_{0}^{1}dx = 4\int_{0}^{1}dx$$

$$= 4\left[x\right]_{0}^{1} = 4$$

Therefore, using divergence theorem, we get $\oint_{s}\vec{A}\cdot d\vec{s} = \int_{v}\left(\nabla\cdot\vec{A}\right)dv = 4$

EXAMPLE 1.45

Verify the divergence theorem for the given field $\vec{A} = 2xy\vec{a}_{x} + x^{2}\vec{a}_{y}$ and the rectangular parallelepiped formed by the planes $x = 0, x = 1; y = 0, y = 2$; and $z = 0, z = 3$.

SOLUTION

By divergence theorem,

$$\oint_{s}\vec{A}\cdot d\vec{s} = \int_{v}\left(\nabla\cdot\vec{A}\right)dv$$

Evaluating the RHS of divergence theorem, we get

$$\nabla\cdot\vec{A} = \left(\vec{a}_{x}\frac{\partial}{\partial x} + \vec{a}_{y}\frac{\partial}{\partial y} + \vec{a}_{z}\frac{\partial}{\partial z}\right)\cdot\left(2xy\vec{a}_{x} + x^{2}\vec{a}_{y}\right)$$

$$= \frac{\partial}{\partial x}(2xy) + \frac{\partial}{\partial y}(x^2) + 0$$

$$= 2y + 0 = 2y$$

$$\int_v (\nabla \cdot \vec{A})\, dv = \int_{x=0}^{1} \int_{y=0}^{2} \int_{z=0}^{3} 2y\, dx\, dy\, dz = \int_0^1 \int_0^2 [2yz]_0^3 \, dx\, dy$$

$$= \int_0^1 \int_0^2 6y\, dx\, dy = \int_0^1 \left[6\frac{y^2}{2} \right]_0^2 dx = \int_0^1 12\, dx = [12x]_0^1 = 12$$

Evaluating the LHS of divergence theorem, we get

$$\oint_s \vec{A} \cdot d\vec{s} = \int_0^3 \int_0^2 (A)_{x=0} \cdot (-dydz\,\vec{a}_x) + \int_0^3 \int_0^2 (A)_{x=1} \cdot (dydz\,\vec{a}_x) + \int_0^3 \int_0^1 (A)_{y=0} \cdot (-dxdz\,\vec{a}_y)$$

$$+ \int_0^3 \int_0^1 (A)_{y=2} \cdot (dxdz\,\vec{a}_y)$$

$$= -\int_0^3 \int_0^2 (A_x)_{x=0}\, dydz + \int_0^3 \int_0^2 (A_x)_{x=1}\, dydz - \int_0^3 \int_0^1 (A_y)_{y=0}\, dxdz + \int_0^3 \int_0^1 (A_y)_{y=2}\, dxdz$$

Here, $(A_x)_{x=0} = 0, (A_x)_{x=1} = 2y$ and $(A_y)_{y=0} = (A_y)_{y=2} = x^2$.
Therefore,

$$\int_s \vec{A} \cdot d\vec{s} = \int_0^3 \int_0^2 (2y)\, dydz - \int_0^3 \int_0^1 (x^2)\, dxdz + \int_0^3 \int_0^1 (x^2)\, dxdz$$

$$= 4\int_0^3 dz - \frac{1}{3}\int_0^3 dz + \frac{1}{3}\int_0^3 dz = 12 - 1 + 1 = 12$$

Since $\oint_s \vec{A} \cdot d\vec{s} = \int_v (\nabla \cdot \vec{A})\, dv = 12$, the divergence theorem is verified. ☐

EXAMPLE 1.46

Verify the divergence theorem for the vector field, $\vec{E} = 2r\vec{a}_r$ in spherical coordinates.

SOLUTION

Divergence theorem is $\oint_s \vec{E} \cdot d\vec{s} = \int_v (\nabla \cdot \vec{E})\, dv$

Evaluating LHS, $\oint_s \vec{E} \cdot d\vec{s} = \int_{\phi=0}^{2\pi} \int_{\theta=0}^{\pi} (2r\vec{a}_r) \cdot (r^2 \sin\theta\, d\theta\, d\phi\, \vec{a}_r)$

$$= (2r^3)(-\cos\theta)_0^\pi (\phi)_0^{2\pi} = 8\pi r^3$$

Evaluating RHS, $\nabla \cdot \vec{E} = \frac{1}{r^2}\frac{\partial}{\partial r}(r^2 E_r) = \frac{1}{r^2}\frac{\partial}{\partial r}(2r^3) = 6$

$$\int_v \left(\nabla \cdot \vec{E}\right) dv = \int_0^{2\pi} \int_0^{\pi} \int_0^{r} 6r^2 \sin\theta \, dr \, d\theta \, d\phi$$

$$= 6\left(\frac{r^3}{3}\right)_0^r (-\cos\theta)_0^{\pi} (\phi)_0^{2\pi} = 8\pi r^3$$

Hence, the divergence theorem is verified. $\square$

1.10 CURL OF A VECTOR FIELD

The curl operator is another fundamental operator used in vector analysis, other than the gradient and the divergence operators. The curl of any vector field $\vec{B}$ denotes the rotational property or the circulation of $\vec{B}$. For a closed contour c or closed path l, the circulation of $\vec{B}$ is defined as the line integral of $\vec{B}$ around c. It is given by

$$\text{Circulation of } \vec{B} = \oint_c \vec{B} \cdot d\vec{l} \ \text{ or } \ \oint_l \vec{B} \cdot d\vec{l}$$

The physical meaning of curl operation can be best understood by means of the following two examples. First, consider a uniform field along positive x-direction given by $\vec{B} = B_0 \vec{a}_x$, whose field lines are shown in Figure 1.29(a). For the rectangular contour $abcda$, the circulation of $\vec{B}$ is given by

$$\text{Circulation of } \vec{B} = \int_a^b B_0 \vec{a}_x \cdot dx\, \vec{a}_x + \int_b^c B_0 \vec{a}_x \cdot dy\, \vec{a}_y + \int_c^d B_0 \vec{a}_x \cdot (-dx\, \vec{a}_x) + \int_d^a B_0 \vec{a}_x \cdot (-dy\, \vec{a}_y)$$

$$= B_0 \Delta x - B_0 \Delta x = 0.$$

where $\Delta x = b - a = c - d$. Since $\vec{a}_x \cdot \vec{a}_y = 0$, the second and fourth integration terms are zero. The above equation shows that the circulation of $\vec{B}$ in a uniform field is zero.

Next, consider the case of magnetic field of flux density $\vec{B}$ induced by an infinite wire carrying current I. If the wire is in free space and having orientation along the z-direction, then the magnetic field is represented by

$$\vec{B} = \frac{\mu_0 I}{2\pi\rho} \vec{a}_\phi$$

where μ_0 is the permeability of free space and ρ is the radial distance from the wire carrying current in the xy-plane. The direction of $\vec{B}$ is along the azimuth direction $\vec{a}_\phi$ and the field lines of $\vec{B}$ are concentric circles around the current source, as shown in Figure 1.29(b).

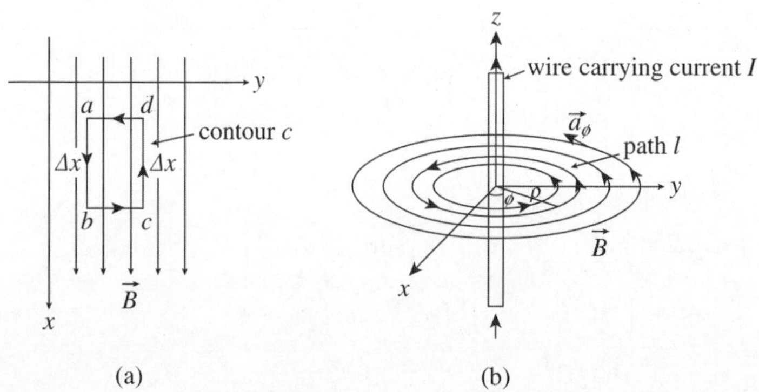

Figure 1.29 *Circulation of $\vec{B}$: (a) uniform field and (b) azimuthal field*

For a circular path of radius ρ, the differential length vector $d\vec{l} = \rho\,d\phi\,\vec{a}_\phi$ and the circulation of $\vec{B}$ around l is given by

$$\text{Circulation of } \vec{B} = \oint_l \vec{B} \cdot d\vec{l}$$

$$= \int_0^{2\pi} \left(\frac{\mu_0 I}{2\pi\rho}\, \vec{a}_\phi \right) \cdot \left(\rho\,d\phi\,\vec{a}_\phi \right), \qquad \text{where } \vec{a}_\phi \cdot \vec{a}_\phi = 1$$

$$= \frac{\mu_0 I}{2\pi} \int_0^{2\pi} d\phi = \mu_0 I$$

The above equation shows that the circulation of magnetic field around the closed path l or closed contour c is not zero. Suppose if the path l or contour c is perpendicular to the xy-plane, then $d\vec{l}$ will not have a $\vec{a}_\phi$ component and the line integral results in a net circulation of zero. In other words, the circulation of $\vec{B}$ depends on the choice of path l or contour c. The curl of a vector field $\vec{B}$ is denoted as curl $\vec{B}$ or $\nabla \times \vec{B}$. It is given by

$$\nabla \times \vec{B} = \underset{\Delta s \to 0}{Lt} \frac{1}{\Delta s} \left[\oint_c \vec{B} \cdot d\vec{l} \right]_{\max} \vec{a}_n \tag{1.74}$$

The physical significance of curl of a vector field $\vec{B}$ is that it represents the circulation of $\vec{B}$ per unit area, with the area Δs of the closed path l being oriented such that the circulation is maximum. According to the right-hand rule, the direction of curl $\vec{B}$ is along $\vec{a}_n$ (unit normal of Δs) with the four fingers of the right hand following the direction of closed path $d\vec{l}$ in anticlockwise direction and the thumb points along $\vec{a}_n$ as shown in Figure 1.30.

The curl of any vector field at a point P is generally considered as a measure of the circulation or curling of the field around P as shown in Figure 1.31. The curl of the vector field $\vec{B}$ shown in Figure 1.31(a) is zero and the curl of a vector field $\vec{B}$ around P shown in Figure 1.31(b) is directed out of the page.

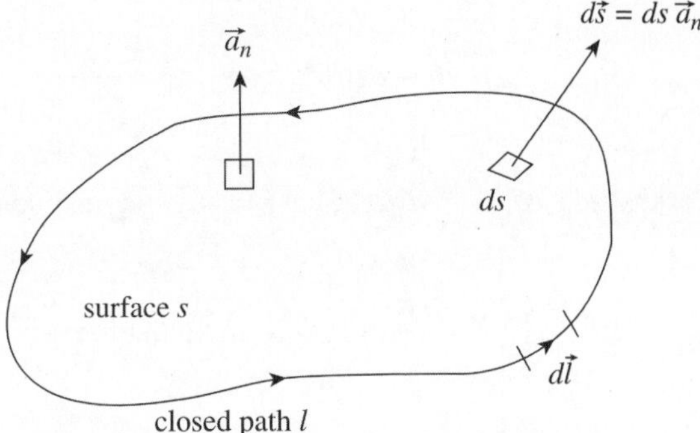

Figure 1.30 *Right-hand rule to define unit normal vector $\vec{a}_n$ of curl*

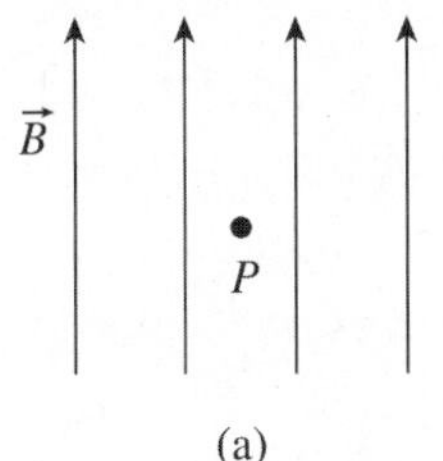

(a)

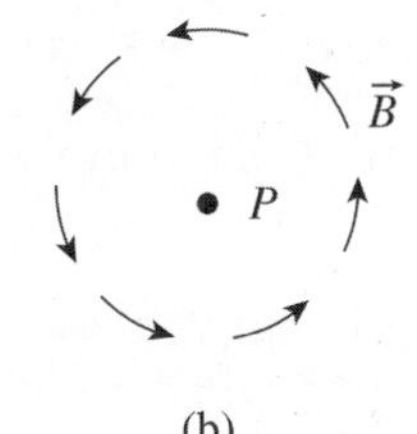

(b)

Figure 1.31 *Representation of curl operation: (a) zero curl at P and (b) non-zero curl at P (directed out of page)*

The expression for $\nabla \times \vec{B}$ can be obtained by considering the differential area in the yz-plane as shown in Figure 1.32. The line integral along the closed path l can be written as

$$\oint_l \vec{B} \cdot d\vec{l} = \left(\int_{ab} + \int_{bc} + \int_{cd} + \int_{da} \right) \vec{B} \cdot d\vec{l} \tag{1.75}$$

A three-dimensional Taylor series expansion of B_x about P is

$$B_x(x,y,z) = B_x(x_0,y_0,z_0) + (x-x_0)\frac{\partial B_x}{\partial x}\bigg|_P + (y-y_0)\frac{\partial B_x}{\partial y}\bigg|_P + (z-z_0)\frac{\partial B_x}{\partial z}\bigg|_P + \text{higher-order terms}$$

The field components of Eq. (1.75) can be expanded about the center point $P(x_0,y_0,z_0)$ by using Taylor series expansion and the corresponding line integral can be determined on all sides.

On side ab, $d\vec{l} = dy\vec{a}_y$, and $z = z_o - \dfrac{dz}{2}$ its line integral is given by

$$\int_{ab} \vec{B} \cdot d\vec{l} = dy\left[B_y(x_0,y_0,z_0) - \frac{dz}{2}\frac{\partial B_y}{\partial z}\bigg|_P \right] \tag{1.76}$$

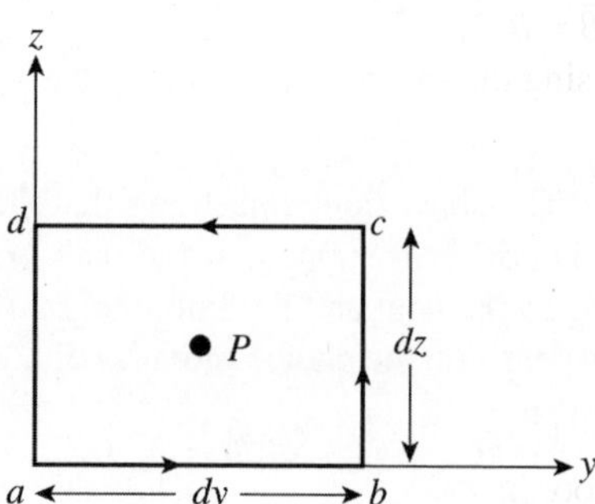

Figure 1.32 *Contour used in the evaluation of* $\nabla \times \vec{B}$ *at* $P(x_o,y_o,z_o)$

On side bc, $d\vec{l} = dz\vec{a}_z$, and $y = y_0 + \dfrac{dy}{2}$, its line integral is given by

$$\int_{bc} \vec{B} \cdot d\vec{l} = dz\left[B_z(x_0,y_0,z_0) + \frac{dy}{2}\frac{\partial B_z}{\partial y}\bigg|_P \right] \tag{1.77}$$

On side cd, $d\vec{l} = dy\vec{a}_y$, and $z = z_0 + \dfrac{dz}{2}$, its line integral is given by

$$\int_{cd} \vec{B} \cdot d\vec{l} = -dy\left[B_y(x_0,y_0,z_0) + \frac{dz}{2}\frac{\partial B_y}{\partial z}\bigg|_P \right] \tag{1.78}$$

On side da, $d\vec{l} = dz\vec{a}_z$, and $y = y_0 - \dfrac{dy}{2}$, its line integral is given by

$$\int_{da} \vec{B} \cdot d\vec{l} = -dz\left[B_z(x_0,y_0,z_0) - \frac{dy}{2}\frac{\partial B_z}{\partial y}\bigg|_P \right] \tag{1.79}$$

Substituting Eq. (1.76) to (1.79) in Eq. (1.75), we get

$$\oint_l \vec{B} \cdot d\vec{l} = -\frac{dydz}{2}\frac{\partial B_y}{\partial z} + \frac{dzdy}{2}\frac{\partial B_z}{\partial y} - \frac{dydz}{2}\frac{\partial B_y}{\partial z} + \frac{dzdy}{2}\frac{\partial B_z}{\partial y}$$

Therefore, $\oint_l \dfrac{\vec{B} \cdot d\vec{l}}{dydz} = \dfrac{\partial B_z}{\partial y} - \dfrac{\partial B_y}{\partial z}$

Since, $\Delta s = dydz$, the x, y and z-components of curl of $\vec{B}$ are given by

$$(\nabla \times \vec{B})_x = \lim_{\Delta s \to 0}\frac{1}{\Delta s}\oint_l \vec{B} \cdot d\vec{l} = \frac{\partial B_z}{\partial y} - \frac{\partial B_y}{\partial z}$$

$$\left(\nabla \times \vec{B}\right)_y = \frac{\partial B_x}{\partial z} - \frac{\partial B_z}{\partial x}$$

$$\left(\nabla \times \vec{B}\right)_z = \frac{\partial B_y}{\partial x} - \frac{\partial B_x}{\partial y}$$

The definition of $\nabla \times \vec{B}$ in Eq. (1.74) is independent of the coordinate system. For a vector $\vec{B} = B_x \vec{a}_x + B_y \vec{a}_y + B_z \vec{a}_z$ specified in rectangular or Cartesian coordinates, the curl of $\vec{B}$ is easily found using the determinant form. Therefore,

$$\nabla \times \vec{B} = \begin{vmatrix} \vec{a}_x & \vec{a}_y & \vec{a}_z \\ \dfrac{\partial}{\partial x} & \dfrac{\partial}{\partial y} & \dfrac{\partial}{\partial z} \\ B_x & B_y & B_z \end{vmatrix} = \left[\frac{\partial B_z}{\partial y} - \frac{\partial B_y}{\partial z}\right]\vec{a}_x + \left[\frac{\partial B_x}{\partial z} - \frac{\partial B_z}{\partial x}\right]\vec{a}_y + \left[\frac{\partial B_y}{\partial x} - \frac{\partial B_x}{\partial y}\right]\vec{a}_z$$

Using coordinate and vector transformation methods used in section 1.3, the curl of $\vec{B}$ in cylindrical coordinates is represented by

$$\nabla \times \vec{B} = \frac{1}{\rho} \begin{vmatrix} \vec{a}_\rho & \rho\vec{a}_\phi & \vec{a}_z \\ \dfrac{\partial}{\partial \rho} & \dfrac{\partial}{\partial \phi} & \dfrac{\partial}{\partial z} \\ B_\rho & \rho B_\phi & B_z \end{vmatrix}$$

In spherical coordinates, it is represented by

$$\nabla \times \vec{B} = \frac{1}{r^2 \sin\theta} \begin{vmatrix} \vec{a}_r & r\vec{a}_\theta & r\sin\theta\,\vec{a}_\phi \\ \dfrac{\partial}{\partial r} & \dfrac{\partial}{\partial \theta} & \dfrac{\partial}{\partial \phi} \\ B_r & rB_\theta & r\sin\theta B_\phi \end{vmatrix}$$

The properties involving curl are:

(*i*)   The curl of a vector field is always a vector.

(*ii*)   The curl of a scalar field V, i.e., $\nabla \times V$ carries no meaning in vector algebra.

(*iii*)   The divergence of the curl of a vector field is zero, i.e., $\nabla \cdot \left(\nabla \times \vec{A}\right) = 0$.

(*iv*) $\nabla \times \left(\vec{A} + \vec{B}\right) = \nabla \times \vec{A} + \nabla \times \vec{B}$ (Distributive property)

(*v*)   The curl of the gradient of a scalar field is zero, i.e., $\nabla \times \left(\nabla V\right) = 0$.

(*vi*)   If $\nabla \times \vec{A} = 0$, then the field $\vec{A}$ is irrotational or conservative.

EXAMPLE 1 47

Determine curl $\vec{H}$ if $\vec{H} = \left(2\rho\cos\phi\,\vec{a}_\rho - 4\rho\sin\phi\,\vec{a}_\phi + 3\vec{a}_z\right)$.

SOLUTION

Given $\vec{H} = \left(2\rho\cos\phi\,\vec{a}_\rho - 4\rho\sin\phi\,\vec{a}_\phi + 3\vec{a}_z\right)$ and it is represented in cylindrical coordinate system. The curl $\vec{H}$ in cylindrical coordinate system is

$$\nabla \times \vec{H} = \frac{1}{\rho} \begin{vmatrix} \vec{a}_\rho & \rho\,\vec{a}_\phi & \vec{a}_z \\ \dfrac{\partial}{\partial \rho} & \dfrac{\partial}{\partial \phi} & \dfrac{\partial}{\partial z} \\ 2\rho\cos\phi & \rho(-4\rho\sin\phi) & 3 \end{vmatrix}$$

$$= \frac{1}{\rho}\vec{a}_\rho\left[\frac{\partial(3)}{\partial\phi} - \frac{\partial}{\partial z}\rho(-4\rho\sin\phi)\right] - \frac{1}{\rho}\left(\rho\vec{a}_\phi\right)\left[\frac{\partial(3)}{\partial\rho} - \frac{\partial}{\partial z}(2\rho\cos\phi)\right]$$

$$+ \frac{1}{\rho}\vec{a}_z\left[\frac{\partial}{\partial\rho}\rho(-4\rho\sin\phi) - \frac{\partial}{\partial\phi}(2\rho\cos\phi)\right]$$

$$= \frac{1}{\rho}\vec{a}_\rho\left[0-0\right] - \vec{a}_\phi\left[0-0\right] + \frac{1}{\rho}\vec{a}_z\left[-8\rho\sin\phi - 2\rho(-\sin\phi)\right]$$

$$= -6\sin\phi\,\vec{a}_z$$

EXAMPLE 1.48

Given $\vec{A} = (y\cos ax)\vec{a}_x + (y + e^x)\vec{a}_z$, determine $\nabla \times \vec{A}$ at the origin.

SOLUTION

Given $\quad \vec{A} = (y\cos ax)\vec{a}_x + (y + e^x)\vec{a}_z$.

Therefore, $A_x = y\cos ax,\ A_y = 0,\ A_z = y + e^x$

$$\nabla \times \vec{A} = \begin{vmatrix} \vec{a}_x & \vec{a}_y & \vec{a}_z \\ \dfrac{\partial}{\partial x} & \dfrac{\partial}{\partial y} & \dfrac{\partial}{\partial z} \\ y\cos ax & 0 & y + e^x \end{vmatrix}$$

$$= \vec{a}_x\frac{\partial}{\partial y}\left(y + e^x\right) + \vec{a}_y\left(\frac{\partial}{\partial z}[y\cos ax] - \frac{\partial}{\partial x}\left[y + e^x\right]\right) - \vec{a}_z\frac{\partial}{\partial y}(y\cos ax)$$

$$= \vec{a}_x - e^x\vec{a}_y - \cos ax\,\vec{a}_z$$

Hence, $\nabla \times \vec{A} = \vec{a}_x - e^x\vec{a}_y - \cos ax\,\vec{a}_z$

Therefore, at the origin, $x = 0, y = 0, z = 0$

$$\nabla \times \vec{A} = \vec{a}_x - \vec{a}_y - \vec{a}_z$$

EXAMPLE 1.49

Determine $\nabla \times \vec{A}$ at $(2, 0, 3)$ in cylindrical coordinates for the vector field given by

$$\vec{A} = 10e^{-2\rho}\cos\phi\,\vec{a}_\rho + 10\sin\phi\,\vec{a}_z.$$

SOLUTION

The curl of $\vec{A}$ in cylindrical coordinates is

$$\nabla \times \vec{A} = \frac{1}{\rho} \begin{vmatrix} \vec{a}_\rho & \rho\vec{a}_\phi & \vec{a}_z \\ \dfrac{\partial}{\partial \rho} & \dfrac{\partial}{\partial \phi} & \dfrac{\partial}{\partial z} \\ A_\rho & \rho A_\phi & A_z \end{vmatrix}$$

$$= \left(\frac{1}{\rho} \frac{\partial A_z}{\partial \phi} - \frac{\partial A_\phi}{\partial z} \right) \vec{a}_\rho + \left(\frac{\partial A_\rho}{\partial z} - \frac{\partial A_z}{\partial \rho} \right) \vec{a}_\phi + \frac{1}{\rho} \left(\frac{\partial}{\partial \rho} \rho A_\phi - \frac{\partial A_\rho}{\partial \phi} \right) \vec{a}_z$$

$$= \left(\frac{1}{\rho} \frac{\partial}{\partial \phi} (10 \sin \phi) \right) \vec{a}_\rho + \left(\frac{\partial}{\partial z} \left(10 e^{-2\rho} \cos \phi \right) - \frac{\partial}{\partial \rho} (10 \sin \phi) \right) \vec{a}_\phi - \frac{1}{\rho} \left(10 e^{-2\rho} \cos \phi \right) \vec{a}_z$$

$$= \frac{10 \cos \phi}{\rho} \vec{a}_\rho + \frac{10 e^{-2\rho}}{\rho} \sin \phi \, \vec{a}_z$$

Therefore, $\nabla \times \vec{A} \big|_{(2,0,3)} = 5 \vec{a}_\rho$

EXAMPLE 1.50

Find $\nabla \times \vec{A}$ at $\left(3, \dfrac{\pi}{6}, 0 \right)$ in spherical coordinates for the vector field given by $\vec{A} = 12 \sin \theta \, \vec{a}_\theta$.

SOLUTION

Given $\vec{A} = 12 \sin \theta \, \vec{a}_\theta$. Here $A_r = 0, A_\theta = 12 \sin \theta$ and $A_\phi = 0$.

The curl of $\vec{A}$ in spherical coordinates is

$$\nabla \times \vec{A} = \frac{1}{r^2 \sin \theta} \begin{vmatrix} \vec{a}_r & r\vec{a}_\theta & r\sin\theta \, \vec{a}_\phi \\ \dfrac{\partial}{\partial r} & \dfrac{\partial}{\partial \theta} & \dfrac{\partial}{\partial \phi} \\ A_r & rA_\theta & r\sin\theta A_\phi \end{vmatrix} = \frac{1}{r^2 \sin \theta} \begin{vmatrix} \vec{a}_r & r\vec{a}_\theta & r\sin\theta \, \vec{a}_\phi \\ \dfrac{\partial}{\partial r} & \dfrac{\partial}{\partial \theta} & \dfrac{\partial}{\partial \phi} \\ 0 & r(12\sin\theta) & 0 \end{vmatrix}$$

$$= \frac{1}{r^2 \sin \theta} \times r \sin \theta \left[\frac{\partial}{\partial r} (12r \, \sin\theta) \right] \vec{a}_\phi$$

$$= \frac{12 \sin \theta}{r} \vec{a}_\phi$$

Therefore, $\nabla \times \vec{A} \big|_{\left(3, \frac{\pi}{6}, 0 \right)} = 4 \sin 30° \vec{a}_\phi = 2 \vec{a}_\phi$

EXAMPLE 1.51

Show that $\vec{A} = x^2 \vec{a}_x + y^2 \vec{a}_y + z^2 \vec{a}_z$ is an irrotational vector field.

SOLUTION

The given vector $\vec{A}$ is conservative or irrotational if $\nabla \times \vec{A} = 0$.

The curl of $\vec{A}$ is

$$\nabla \times \vec{A} = \begin{vmatrix} \vec{a}_x & \vec{a}_y & \vec{a}_z \\ \dfrac{\partial}{\partial x} & \dfrac{\partial}{\partial y} & \dfrac{\partial}{\partial z} \\ x^2 & y^2 & z^2 \end{vmatrix}$$

$$= \vec{a}_x\left[\frac{\partial}{\partial y}\left(z^2\right) - \frac{\partial}{\partial z}\left(y^2\right)\right] - \vec{a}_y\left[\frac{\partial}{\partial x}\left(z^2\right) - \frac{\partial}{\partial z}\left(x^2\right)\right] + \vec{a}_z\left[\frac{\partial}{\partial x}\left(y^2\right) - \frac{\partial}{\partial y}\left(x^2\right)\right]$$

$$= \vec{a}_x(0) + \vec{a}_y(0) + \vec{a}_z(0) = 0$$

This shows that $\vec{A}$ is an irrotational or a conservative vector field.

EXAMPLE 1.52

If vector $\vec{P} = \left(2x + y + lz\right)\vec{a}_x + \left(mx + 4y - 3z\right)\vec{a}_y + \left(2x + ny + 3z\right)\vec{a}_z$ is irrotational, then determine the constants l, m and n.

SOLUTION

For a vector $\vec{P}$ to be "irrotational", $\nabla \times \vec{P} = 0$. Taking curl $\vec{P}$, we get

$$\nabla \times \vec{P} = \begin{vmatrix} \vec{a}_x & \vec{a}_y & \vec{a}_z \\ \dfrac{\partial}{\partial x} & \dfrac{\partial}{\partial y} & \dfrac{\partial}{\partial z} \\ \left(2x+y+lz\right) & \left(mx+4y-3z\right) & \left(2x+ny+3z\right) \end{vmatrix}$$

$$= \left[\frac{\partial}{\partial y}\left(2x+ny+3z\right) - \frac{\partial}{\partial z}\left(mx+4y-3z\right)\right]\vec{a}_x - \left[\frac{\partial}{\partial x}\left(2x+ny+3z\right) - \frac{\partial}{\partial z}\left(2x+y+lz\right)\right]\vec{a}_y$$

$$+ \left[\frac{\partial}{\partial x}\left(mx+4y-3z\right) - \frac{\partial}{\partial y}\left(2x+y+lz\right)\right]\vec{a}_z$$

$$= \left(n+3\right)\vec{a}_x - \left(2-l\right)\vec{a}_y + \left(m-1\right)\vec{a}_z$$

As $\nabla \times \vec{P} = 0$, we get $l = 2, m = 1$ and $n = -3$

EXAMPLE 1.53

For a vector field $\left(\vec{A}\right)$, show that the divergence of curl of the vector field is zero i.e., $\nabla \cdot \left(\nabla \times \vec{A}\right) = 0$.

SOLUTION

Assume vector $\vec{A} = A_x\vec{a}_x + A_y\vec{a}_y + A_z\vec{a}_z$.

$$\nabla \times \vec{A} = \begin{vmatrix} \vec{a}_x & \vec{a}_y & \vec{a}_z \\ \dfrac{\partial}{\partial x} & \dfrac{\partial}{\partial y} & \dfrac{\partial}{\partial z} \\ A_x & A_y & A_z \end{vmatrix}$$

$$= \vec{a}_x \left(\frac{\partial A_z}{\partial y} - \frac{\partial A_y}{\partial z} \right) - \vec{a}_y \left(\frac{\partial A_z}{\partial x} - \frac{\partial A_x}{\partial z} \right) + \vec{a}_z \left(\frac{\partial A_y}{\partial x} - \frac{\partial A_x}{\partial y} \right)$$

Taking divergence, we get

$$\nabla \cdot \left(\nabla \times \vec{A} \right) = \frac{\partial}{\partial x} \left[\frac{\partial A_z}{\partial y} - \frac{\partial A_y}{\partial z} \right] - \frac{\partial}{\partial y} \left[\frac{\partial A_z}{\partial x} - \frac{\partial A_x}{\partial z} \right] + \frac{\partial}{\partial z} \left[\frac{\partial A_y}{\partial x} - \frac{\partial A_x}{\partial y} \right]$$

$$= \frac{\partial^2 A_z}{\partial x \partial y} - \frac{\partial^2 A_y}{\partial x \partial z} - \frac{\partial^2 A_z}{\partial y \partial x} + \frac{\partial^2 A_x}{\partial y \partial z} + \frac{\partial^2 A_y}{\partial z \partial x} - \frac{\partial^2 A_x}{\partial z \partial y}$$

$$= 0$$

Hence $\nabla \cdot \left(\nabla \times \vec{A} \right) = 0$ ☐

EXAMPLE 1.54

For a scalar field V, show that the curl of the gradient of the scalar field vanishes, i.e., $\nabla \times \nabla V = 0$.

SOLUTION

We know that, $\nabla V = \dfrac{\partial V}{\partial x} \vec{a}_x + \dfrac{\partial V}{\partial y} \vec{a}_y + \dfrac{\partial V}{\partial z} \vec{a}_z$

Taking curl of ∇V, we get

$$\nabla \times \nabla V = \begin{vmatrix} \vec{a}_x & \vec{a}_y & \vec{a}_z \\ \dfrac{\partial}{\partial x} & \dfrac{\partial}{\partial y} & \dfrac{\partial}{\partial z} \\ \dfrac{\partial V}{\partial x} & \dfrac{\partial V}{\partial y} & \dfrac{\partial V}{\partial z} \end{vmatrix}$$

$$= \vec{a}_x \left[\frac{\partial^2 V}{\partial y \partial z} - \frac{\partial^2 V}{\partial y \partial z} \right] - \vec{a}_y \left[\frac{\partial^2 V}{\partial x \partial z} - \frac{\partial^2 V}{\partial x \partial z} \right] + \vec{a}_z \left[\frac{\partial^2 V}{\partial x \partial y} - \frac{\partial^2 V}{\partial x \partial y} \right] = 0$$

Hence, $\qquad \nabla \times \nabla V = 0$ ☐

EXAMPLE 1.55

Determine the divergence and curl of the given field $\vec{F} = 30\vec{a}_x + 2xy\vec{a}_y + 5xz^2\vec{a}_z$ at $(1,1,-0.2)$ and hence, state the nature of the field.

SOLUTION

Given $\vec{F} = 30\vec{a}_x + 2xy\vec{a}_y + 5xz^2\vec{a}_z$.

$$\nabla \cdot \vec{F} = \frac{\partial F_x}{\partial x} + \frac{\partial F_y}{\partial y} + \frac{\partial F_z}{\partial z} = 0 + 2x + 10xz$$

At point $P(1,1,-0.2)$, $\nabla \cdot \vec{F} = 2 - 2 = 0$

As divergence is zero, $\overline{F}$ is solenoidal field.

$$\nabla \times \vec{F} = \begin{vmatrix} \vec{a}_x & \vec{a}_y & \vec{a}_z \\ \dfrac{\partial}{\partial x} & \dfrac{\partial}{\partial y} & \dfrac{\partial}{\partial z} \\ F_x & F_y & F_z \end{vmatrix} = \begin{vmatrix} \vec{a}_x & \vec{a}_y & \vec{a}_z \\ \dfrac{\partial}{\partial x} & \dfrac{\partial}{\partial y} & \dfrac{\partial}{\partial z} \\ 30 & 2xy & 5xz^2 \end{vmatrix}$$

$$= \vec{a}_x \left(0-0\right) - \vec{a}_y \left(5z^2 - 0\right) + \vec{a}_z \left(2y - 0\right)$$

$$= -5z^2 \vec{a}_y + 2y\vec{a}_z$$

At point $P(1,1,-0.2)$, $\nabla \times \vec{F} = -5(-0.2)^2\, \vec{a}_y + 2(1)\vec{a}_z$

Hence, $\nabla \times \vec{F} = -0.2\vec{a}_y + 2\vec{a}_z \neq 0$

As curl is not zero, $\vec{F}$ is rotational field. Hence, the given field is solenoidal and rotational in nature. ☐

EXAMPLE 1.56

Verify whether the vector field $\vec{E} = yz\vec{a}_x + xz\vec{a}_y + xy\vec{a}_z$ is both solenoidal and irrotational.

SOLUTION

$$\nabla \cdot \vec{E} = \frac{\partial E_x}{\partial x} + \frac{\partial E_y}{\partial y} + \frac{\partial E_z}{\partial z}$$

$$= \frac{\partial}{\partial x}\left(yz\right) + \frac{\partial}{\partial y}\left(xz\right) + \frac{\partial}{\partial z}\left(xy\right) = 0$$

Therefore, the vector field $\vec{E}$ is solenoidal.

$$\nabla \times \vec{E} = \begin{vmatrix} \vec{a}_x & \vec{a}_y & \vec{a}_z \\ \dfrac{\partial}{\partial x} & \dfrac{\partial}{\partial y} & \dfrac{\partial}{\partial z} \\ yz & xz & xy \end{vmatrix} = \vec{a}_x\left(x-x\right) - \vec{a}_y\left(y-y\right) + \vec{a}_z\left(z-z\right) = 0$$

Therefore, the vector field $\vec{E}$ is irrotational. Hence, the given field is both solenoidal and irrotational. ☐

EXAMPLE 1.57

Given $\vec{A} = \rho\cos\phi\, \vec{a}_\rho + \rho^2\vec{a}_z$, determine $\nabla \times \vec{A}$ and $\int_s \left(\nabla \times \vec{A}\right) \cdot d\vec{s}$ over the area s as shown in the Figure E1.57.

SOLUTION

Given $\vec{A} = \rho\cos\phi\, \vec{a}_\rho + \rho^2\vec{a}_z$.

In cylindrical coordinates, the curl of a vector $\vec{A}$ is

$$\nabla \times \vec{A} = \frac{1}{\rho} \begin{vmatrix} \vec{a}_\rho & \rho\vec{a}_\phi & \vec{a}_z \\ \dfrac{\partial}{\partial \rho} & \dfrac{\partial}{\partial \phi} & \dfrac{\partial}{\partial z} \\ \rho\cos\phi & 0 & \rho^2 \end{vmatrix}$$

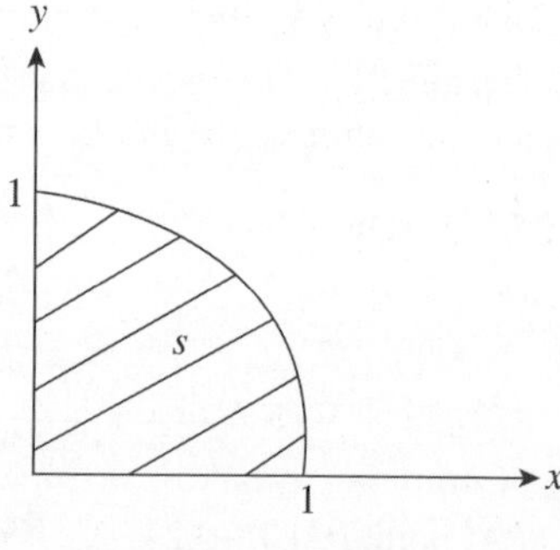

Figure E1.57

$$= \frac{1}{\rho}\left[-\rho\vec{a}_\phi\left(2\rho\right)+\vec{a}_z\,\rho\sin\phi\right]$$

$$= -2\rho\,\vec{a}_\phi + \sin\phi\,\vec{a}_z$$

The differential surface area along z in cylindrical coordinates is $d\vec{s} = \rho\,d\rho\,d\phi\,\vec{a}_z$.

Therefore, $\displaystyle\int_s\left(\nabla\times\vec{A}\right)\cdot d\vec{s} = \int_s\left(-2\rho\,\vec{a}_\phi + \sin\phi\,\vec{a}_z\right)\cdot\left(\rho\,d\rho\,d\phi\,\vec{a}_z\right)$

$$= \int_0^{\pi/2}\int_0^1 \rho\sin\phi\,d\rho\,d\phi = \int_0^1 \rho\,d\rho\int_0^{\pi/2}\sin\phi\,d\phi$$

$$= \left[\frac{\rho^2}{2}\right]_0^1\left[-\cos\phi\right]_0^{\pi/2} = \frac{1}{2}\qquad\square$$

1.11 STOKES'S THEOREM

Stokes's theorem states that the line integral (circulation) of a vector field $\vec{H}$ around a closed path l is equal to the surface integral of the curl of $\vec{H}$ over any open surface s surrounded by l. Mathematically, *Stokes's theorem* is expressed as

$$\oint_l \vec{H}\cdot d\vec{l} = \int_s\left(\nabla\times\vec{H}\right)\cdot d\vec{s} \tag{1.80}$$

and this relationship is extensively used in electromagnetics.

Proof The proof of Stokes's theorem is similar to that of the divergence theorem. Consider the surface s as shown in Figure 1.33 and it is subdivided into n number of small cells. If the nth cell has surface area Δs_n and is bounded by path l_n, then the line integral of a vector field $\vec{H}$ around a closed path l is represented by

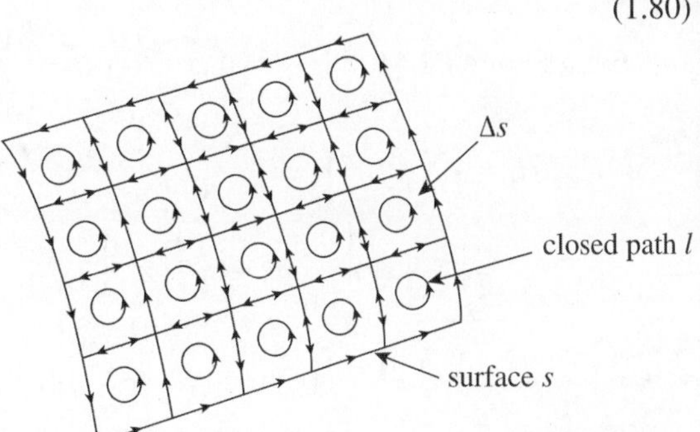

Figure 1.33 *Illustration of Stokes's theorem*

$$\oint_l \vec{H}\cdot d\vec{l} = \sum_n \oint_{l_n}\vec{H}\cdot d\vec{l} = \sum_n \frac{\oint_{l_n}\vec{H}\cdot d\vec{l}}{\Delta s_n}\Delta s_n \tag{1.81}$$

Here, it is seen that the path along the internal cells gets cancelled and the sum of the line integrals around l_n is equal to the line integral around the outer closed path l. Taking the limit on the RHS of Eq. (1.81) as $\Delta s_n \to 0$ and comparing with Eq. (1.74), we get

$$\underset{\Delta s\to 0}{Lt}\sum_n \frac{\oint_{l_n}\vec{H}\cdot d\vec{l}}{\Delta s_n}\Delta s_n = \int_s\left(\nabla\times\vec{H}\right)\cdot d\vec{s} \tag{1.82}$$

Comparing Eq. (1.81) with Eq. (1.82), we get

$$\oint_l \vec{H}\cdot d\vec{l} = \int_s\left(\nabla\times\vec{H}\right)\cdot d\vec{s}$$

This equation represents Stokes's theorem. It is noted that the divergence theorem relates a surface integral to a volume integral whereas the Stokes's theorem relates a line integral to a surface integral. The conversion of one integral form to another integral form is extensively used in solving electromagnetic problems. If the vector field $\vec{H}$ is conservative or irrotational, then $\nabla \times \vec{H} = 0$. Hence, the circulation $\overrightarrow{H}$ over the closed path l represented by the LHS of the above equation is zero i.e., $\oint_l \vec{H} \cdot d\vec{l} = 0$.

EXAMPLE 1.58

For the vector field, $\vec{A} = xy\vec{a}_x - \left(x^2 + 2y^2\right)\vec{a}_y$, verify Stokes's theorem by evaluating (a) $\oint_l \vec{A} \cdot d\vec{l}$ around the triangular path shown in Figure E1.58 and (b) $\int_s \left(\nabla \times \vec{A}\right) \cdot d\vec{s}$ over the area of the triangle.

SOLUTION

By Stokes's theorem,

$$\oint_l \vec{A} \cdot d\vec{l} = \int_s \left(\nabla \times \vec{A}\right) \cdot d\vec{s}$$

The three lines of the triangle are represented by the equations $y = 0$, $x = 1$ and $y = x$ in addition to the independent condition $z = 0$.

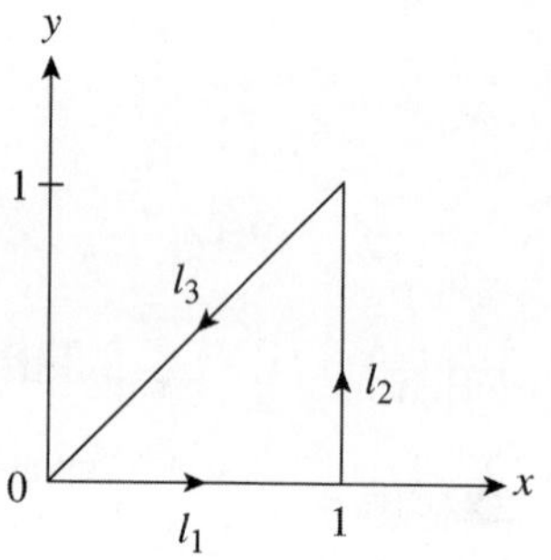

Figure E1.58

(*a*) From Figure E1.61, it is seen that $\oint_l \vec{A} \cdot d\vec{l} = \left(\int_1 + \int_2 + \int_3\right) \vec{A} \cdot d\vec{l} = l_1 + l_2 + l_3$

$$l_1 = \oint \vec{A} \cdot d\vec{l} = \int \left(xy\vec{a}_x - \left(x^2 + 2y^2\right)\vec{a}_y\right) \cdot \left(dx\vec{a}_x + dy\vec{a}_y + dz\vec{a}_z\right)$$

$$= \int_{x=0}^{1}(xy)\Big|_{\substack{y=0,\\z=0}} dx - \int_{y=0}^{0}\left(x^2 + 2y^2\right)\Big|_{z=0} dy + \int_{z=0}^{0}(0)\Big|_{y=0} dz = 0$$

$$l_2 = \oint \vec{A} \cdot d\vec{l} = \int \left(xy\vec{a}_x - \left(x^2 + 2y^2\right)\vec{a}_y\right) \cdot \left(dx\vec{a}_x + dy\vec{a}_y + dz\vec{a}_z\right)$$

$$= \int_{x=1}^{1}(xy)\Big|_{z=0} dx - \int_{y=0}^{1}\left(x^2 + 2y^2\right)\Big|_{\substack{x=1,\\z=0}} dy + \int_{z=0}^{0}(0)\Big|_{x=1} dz$$

$$= 0 - \left(y + \frac{2y^3}{3}\right)\Bigg|_{0}^{1} + 0 = \frac{-5}{3}$$

$$l_3 = \oint \vec{A} \cdot d\vec{l} = \int \left(xy\vec{a}_x - \left(x^2 + 2y^2\right)\vec{a}_y\right) \cdot \left(dx\vec{a}_x + dy\vec{a}_y + dz\vec{a}_z\right)$$

$$= \int_{x=1}^{0}(xy)\Big|_{\substack{y=x,\\z=0}} dx - \int_{y=1}^{0}\left(x^2 + 2y^2\right)\Big|_{\substack{x=y,\\z=0}} dy + \int_{z=0}^{0}(0)\Big|_{y=x} dz$$

$$= \left(\frac{x^3}{3}\right)\Bigg|_{1}^{0} - \left(y^3\right)\Big|_{1}^{0} + 0 = \frac{2}{3}$$

Therefore, $\oint_l \vec{A} \cdot d\vec{l} = 0 - \frac{5}{3} + \frac{2}{3} = -1$

(b) $\quad \nabla \times \vec{A} = \begin{vmatrix} \vec{a}_x & \vec{a}_y & \vec{a}_z \\ \dfrac{\partial}{\partial x} & \dfrac{\partial}{\partial y} & \dfrac{\partial}{\partial z} \\ xy & -\left(x^2 + 2y^2\right) & 0 \end{vmatrix} = \vec{a}_x\left(0\right) - \vec{a}_y\left(0\right) + \vec{a}_z\left(-2x - x\right) = -3x\vec{a}_z$

$$\int_s \left(\nabla \times \vec{A}\right) \cdot d\vec{s} = \int_{x=0}^{1} \int_{y=0}^{x} \left(-3x\vec{a}_z\right) \cdot \left(dy\,dx\,\vec{a}_z\right)\Big|_{z=0}$$

$$= -\int_{x=0}^{1} \int_{y=0}^{x} 3x\,dy\,dx = -\int_{x=0}^{1} 3x\left(x - 0\right)dx$$

$$= -\left(x^3\right)\Big|_0^1 = -1$$

Hence, Stokes's theorem is verified. $\qquad\qquad\qquad\qquad\qquad\qquad\qquad\qquad$ ❏

EXAMPLE 1.59

Verify Stokes's theorem for the vector $\vec{B} = \rho\cos\phi\,\vec{a}_\rho + z\sin\phi\,\vec{a}_z$ by evaluating:

(a) $\oint_l \vec{B} \cdot d\vec{l}$ over the path l of the wedge defined by $0 \le \rho \le 2$, $0 \le \phi \le 60°$, $z = 0$ as shown in Figure E1.59.

(b) $\int_s \left(\nabla \times \vec{B}\right) \cdot d\vec{s}$ over the surface of the wedge shown in Figure E1.59.

SOLUTION

(a) $\quad \oint_l \vec{B} \cdot d\vec{l} = \left(\int_1 + \int_2 + \int_3\right) \vec{B} \cdot d\vec{l} = l_1 + l_2 + l_3$

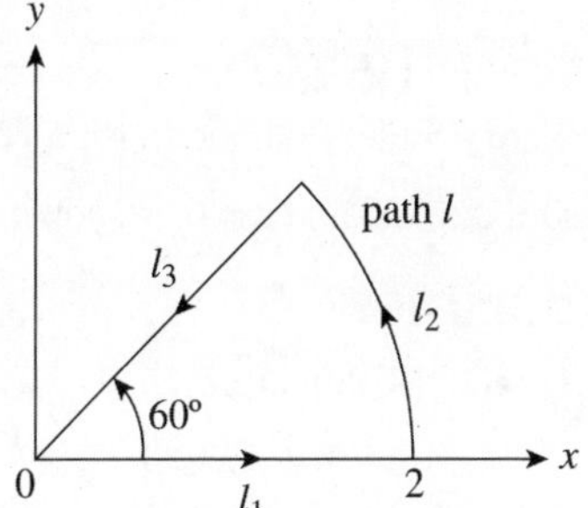

Figure E1.59

Along path 1, $l_1 = \int \vec{B} \cdot d\vec{l} = \int_0^2 \left(\rho\cos\phi\,\vec{a}_\rho + z\sin\phi\,\vec{a}_z\right) \cdot \left(d\rho\,\vec{a}_\rho\right)$

$$= \int_0^2 \rho\cos\phi\,d\rho\Big|_{\phi=0} = \left[\frac{\rho^2}{2}\right]_0^2 = 2$$

Along path 2, $l_2 = \int \vec{B} \cdot d\vec{l} = \int_{\phi=0}^{60°} \left(\rho\cos\phi\,\vec{a}_\rho + z\sin\phi\,\vec{a}_z\right) \cdot \left(\rho\,d\phi\,\vec{a}_\phi\right) = 0$

Along path 3, $l_3 = \int \vec{B} \cdot d\vec{l} = \int_2^0 \left(\rho\cos\phi\,\vec{a}_\rho + z\sin\phi\,\vec{a}_z\right) \cdot \left(d\rho\,\vec{a}_\rho\right)$

$$= \int_2^0 \rho\cos\phi\,d\rho\Big|_{\phi=60°} = \left[-\frac{\rho^2}{2}\right]_2^0 \left[\frac{1}{2}\right] = -1$$

Therefore, $\oint_l \vec{B} \cdot d\vec{l} = l_1 + l_2 + l_3 = 2 + 0 - 1 = 1$

(b) $\nabla \times \vec{B} = \dfrac{1}{\rho} \begin{vmatrix} \vec{a}_\rho & \rho\vec{a}_\phi & \vec{a}_z \\ \dfrac{\partial}{\partial \rho} & \dfrac{\partial}{\partial \phi} & \dfrac{\partial}{\partial z} \\ B_\rho & \rho B_\phi & B_z \end{vmatrix} = \dfrac{1}{\rho} \begin{vmatrix} \vec{a}_\rho & \rho\vec{a}_\phi & \vec{a}_z \\ \dfrac{\partial}{\partial \rho} & \dfrac{\partial}{\partial \phi} & \dfrac{\partial}{\partial z} \\ \rho\cos\phi & 0 & z\sin\phi \end{vmatrix}$

$$= \frac{z\cos\phi}{\rho}\,\vec{a}_\rho + \sin\phi\,\vec{a}_z$$

$$d\vec{s} = \rho\,d\rho\,d\phi\,\vec{a}_z$$

$$\int_s \left(\nabla \times \vec{B}\right)\cdot d\vec{s} = \int_0^{60°}\int_0^2 \left(\frac{z\cos\phi}{\rho}\,\vec{a}_\rho + \sin\phi\,\vec{a}_z\right)\cdot\left(\rho\,d\rho\,d\phi\,\vec{a}_z\right)$$

$$= \int_0^{60°}\int_0^2 \rho\sin\phi\,d\rho\,d\phi$$

$$= \left[\frac{\rho^2}{2}\right]_0^2 \left[\cos\phi\right]_0^{60°} = 2\left(-\frac{1}{2}+1\right) = 1$$

Hence, Stokes's theorem is verified.   ◻

EXAMPLE 1.60

Verify Stokes's theorem for a vector field $\vec{F} = \rho^2\cos\phi\,\vec{a}_\rho + z\sin\phi\,\vec{a}_z$ around the path l defined by $0 \le \rho \le 3$, $0 \le \phi \le 45°$ and $z = 0$ as shown in the Figure E1.60.

SOLUTION

By Stokes's theorem,

$$\oint_l \vec{F}\cdot d\vec{l} = \int_s \left(\nabla \times \vec{F}\right)\cdot d\vec{s}$$

To evaluate LHS, first divide the given path l into three sections and then add the line integral of all the three sections.

$$\oint_l \vec{F}\cdot d\vec{l} = \left(\int_1 + \int_2 + \int_3\right)\vec{F}\cdot d\vec{l} = l_1 + l_2 + l_3$$

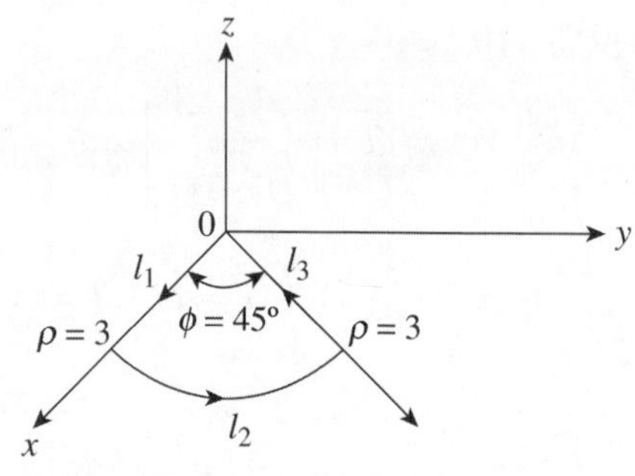

Figure E1.60

Along path 1, $l_1 = \int \vec{F}\cdot d\vec{l} = \int_0^3 \left(\rho^2\cos\phi\,\vec{a}_\rho + z\sin\phi\,\vec{a}_z\right)\cdot\left(d\rho\,\vec{a}_\rho\right)$

$$= \int_0^3 \rho^2\cos\phi\,d\rho\,\Big|_{\phi=0} = \left[\frac{\rho^3}{3}\right]_0^3 = \frac{27}{3} = 9$$

Along path 2, $l_2 = \int \vec{F}\cdot d\vec{l} = \int_{\phi=0}^{45°} \left(\rho^2\cos\phi\,\vec{a}_\rho + z\sin\phi\,\vec{a}_z\right)\cdot\left(\rho\,d\phi\,\vec{a}_\phi\right) = 0$

Along path 3, $l_3 = \int \vec{F}\cdot d\vec{l} = \int_3^0 \left(\rho^2\cos\phi\,\vec{a}_\rho + z\sin\phi\,\vec{a}_z\right)\cdot\left(d\rho\,\vec{a}_\rho\right)$

$$= \int_3^0 \rho^2 \cos\phi \, d\rho \Big|_{\phi=45°} = \cos 45° \left[\frac{\rho^3}{3}\right]_3^0$$

$$= 0.7071\left[-\frac{27}{3}\right] = -6.3639$$

Therefore, $\oint_l \vec{F} \cdot d\vec{l} = l_1 + l_2 + l_3 = 9 + 0 - 6.3639 = 2.6361$

To evaluate RHS, first find $\nabla \times \vec{F}$ in cylindrical coordinates as given by

$$\nabla \times \vec{F} = \frac{1}{\rho}\begin{vmatrix} \vec{a}_\rho & \rho\,\vec{a}_\phi & \vec{a}_z \\ \frac{\partial}{\partial\rho} & \frac{\partial}{\partial\phi} & \frac{\partial}{\partial z} \\ F_\rho & \rho F_\phi & F_z \end{vmatrix} = \left[\frac{1}{\rho}\frac{\partial F_z}{\partial\phi} - \frac{\partial F_\phi}{\partial z}\right]\vec{a}_\rho + \left[\frac{\partial F_\rho}{\partial z} - \frac{\partial F_z}{\partial\rho}\right]\vec{a}_\phi + \left[\frac{1}{\rho}\frac{\partial(\rho F_\phi)}{\partial\rho} - \frac{1}{\rho}\frac{\partial F_\rho}{\partial\phi}\right]\vec{a}_z$$

where $F_\rho = \rho^2\cos\phi$, $F_\phi = 0$, $F_z = z\sin\phi$.

Therefore, $\nabla \times \vec{F} = \left[\frac{1}{\rho}\times 2\cos\phi - 0\right]\vec{a}_\rho + [0-0]\vec{a}_\phi + \left[\frac{1}{\rho}(0) - \frac{1}{\rho}(\rho^2)(-\sin\phi)\right]\vec{a}_z$

$$= \frac{2\cos\phi}{\rho}\vec{a}_\rho + \rho\sin\phi\,\vec{a}_z$$

As the given surface is in $\rho\phi$-plane for which the normal direction is $\vec{a}_z$, its differential surface area is given by $d\vec{s}_z = \rho\, d\rho\, d\phi\,\vec{a}_z$.

Therefore, $\int_s \left(\nabla \times \vec{F}\right)\cdot d\vec{s} = \int_s \left(\rho\sin\phi\,\vec{a}_z\right)\cdot\left(\rho\, d\rho\, d\phi\,\vec{a}_z\right)$

$$= \int_{\phi=0}^{45°}\int_{\rho=0}^{3} \rho^2 \sin\phi\, d\rho\, d\phi = \left[\frac{\rho^3}{3}\right]_0^3 \left[-\cos\phi\right]_0^{45°}$$

$$= (9)\left[-0.707 - (-1)\right] = 9\times 0.293 = 2.637$$

LHS = RHS
Hence, Stokes's theorem is verified. ❐

1.12 LAPLACIAN OPERATOR

Differential operations that were discussed in the previous sections deal mostly with first-order differential operators. The second-order differential operator that occurs frequently in the study of electromagnetics is called the *Laplacian operator*, and it is symbolically written as ∇^2. The symbol ∇^2 is pronounced as "del square."

Laplacian of the scalar field V is defined as the divergence of the gradient of V. For a scalar function V, defined in rectangular coordinates, its gradient is given by

$$\nabla V = \frac{\partial V}{\partial x}\vec{a}_x + \frac{\partial V}{\partial y}\vec{a}_y + \frac{\partial V}{\partial z}\vec{a}_z$$

Therefore, Laplacian of the scalar field V is represented by

$$\nabla^2 V = \nabla \cdot (\nabla V) = \left(\vec{a}_x \frac{\partial}{\partial x} + \vec{a}_y \frac{\partial}{\partial y} + \vec{a}_z \frac{\partial}{\partial z} \right) \cdot \left(\frac{\partial V}{\partial x} \vec{a}_x + \frac{\partial V}{\partial y} \vec{a}_y + \frac{\partial V}{\partial z} \vec{a}_z \right)$$

$$\text{Hence, } \nabla^2 V = \frac{\partial^2 V}{\partial x^2} + \frac{\partial^2 V}{\partial y^2} + \frac{\partial^2 V}{\partial z^2} \tag{1.83}$$

The above equation shows that Laplacian of the scalar field V results in a scalar. Similarly, Laplacian of the scalar field V in cylindrical is represented by

$$\nabla^2 V = \frac{1}{\rho} \frac{\partial}{\partial \rho} \left(\rho \frac{\partial V}{\partial \rho} \right) + \frac{1}{\rho^2} \frac{\partial^2 V}{\partial \phi^2} + \frac{\partial^2 V}{\partial z^2} \tag{1.84}$$

and in spherical coordinates, it is represented by

$$\nabla^2 V = \frac{1}{r^2} \frac{\partial}{\partial r} \left(r^2 \frac{\partial V}{\partial r} \right) + \frac{1}{r^2 \sin \theta} \frac{\partial}{\partial \theta} \left(\sin \theta \frac{\partial V}{\partial \theta} \right) + \frac{1}{r^2 \sin^2 \theta} \frac{\partial^2 V}{\partial \phi^2} \tag{1.85}$$

A scalar field V is harmonic in a given region if its Laplacian vanishes in that region. In other words, if $\nabla^2 V = 0$ is satisfied in the region, the solution for V is harmonic and this equation is called *Laplace's equation*.

Since the Laplacian operator ∇^2 is a scalar operator, it is also possible to define the Laplacian of a vector $\vec{A}$. A vector field $\vec{A}$ defined in Cartesian coordinates is represented by

$$\vec{A} = A_x \vec{a}_x + A_y \vec{a}_y + A_z \vec{a}_z$$

The Laplacian of a vector $\vec{A}$ is written as

$$\nabla^2 \vec{A} = \left(\frac{\partial^2}{\partial x^2} + \frac{\partial^2}{\partial y^2} + \frac{\partial^2}{\partial z^2} \right) \vec{A}$$

$$= \nabla^2 A_x \vec{a}_x + \nabla^2 A_y \vec{a}_y + \nabla^2 A_z \vec{a}_z \tag{1.86}$$

The above equation shows that the Laplacian of a vector field $\vec{A}$ results in a vector, whose components are equal to the Laplacian of the vector components. The Laplacian of a vector $\vec{A}$ should not be considered as the divergence of the gradient of $\vec{A}$, which carries no meaning. However, $\nabla^2 \vec{A}$ is defined as the gradient of the divergence of $\vec{A}$ minus the curl of the curl of $\vec{A}$. It can be written as $\nabla^2 \vec{A} = \nabla(\nabla \cdot \vec{A}) - \nabla \times (\nabla \times \vec{A})$.

EXAMPLE 1.61

Find the Laplacian of the following scalar fields:

(*i*) $V = 4xy^2 z^3$,

(*ii*) $V = xy + yz + zx$,

(*iii*) $V = \rho^2 z \cos 2\phi$, and

(*iv*) $V = e^{-r} \sin \theta \cos \phi$

SOLUTION

(*i*) The Laplacian of the scalar field V in Cartesian coordinates is

$$\nabla^2 V = \frac{\partial^2 V}{\partial x^2} + \frac{\partial^2 V}{\partial y^2} + \frac{\partial^2 V}{\partial z^2}$$

$$= \frac{\partial^2}{\partial x^2}\left(4xy^2 z^3\right) + \frac{\partial^2}{\partial y^2}\left(4xy^2 z^3\right) + \frac{\partial^2}{\partial z^2}\left(4xy^2 z^3\right)$$

$$= 8xz^3 + 24xy^2 z$$

(*ii*) $\nabla^2 V = \dfrac{\partial^2}{\partial x^2}(xy + yz + zx) + \dfrac{\partial^2}{\partial y^2}(xy + yz + zx) + \dfrac{\partial^2}{\partial z^2}(xy + yz + zx) = 0$

(*iii*) The Laplacian of the scalar field V in cylindrical coordinates is

$$\nabla^2 V = \frac{1}{\rho}\frac{\partial}{\partial \rho}\left(\rho\frac{\partial V}{\partial \rho}\right) + \frac{1}{\rho^2}\frac{\partial^2 V}{\partial \phi^2} + \frac{\partial^2 V}{\partial z^2}$$

$$= \frac{1}{\rho}\frac{\partial}{\partial \rho}\left(2\rho^2 z\cos 2\phi\right) - \frac{1}{\rho^2}4\rho^2 z\cos 2\phi + 0$$

$$= 4z\cos 2\phi - 4z\cos 2\phi = 0$$

(*iv*) The Laplacian of the scalar field V in spherical coordinates is

$$\nabla^2 V = \frac{1}{r^2}\frac{\partial}{\partial r}\left(r^2\frac{\partial V}{\partial r}\right) + \frac{1}{r^2\sin\theta}\frac{\partial}{\partial \theta}\left(\sin\theta\frac{\partial V}{\partial \theta}\right) + \frac{1}{r^2\sin^2\theta}\frac{\partial^2 V}{\partial \phi^2}$$

$$= \frac{1}{r^2}\frac{\partial}{\partial r}\left[r^2(-1)e^{-r}\sin\theta\cos\phi\right] + \frac{1}{r^2\sin\theta}\frac{\partial}{\partial \theta}\left[\sin\theta\, e^{-r}\cos\theta\cos\phi\right]$$

$$+ \frac{1}{r^2\sin^2\theta}\frac{\partial}{\partial \phi}\left[-e^{-r}\sin\theta\sin\phi\right]$$

$$= -\frac{\sin\theta\cos\phi}{r^2}\frac{\partial}{\partial r}\left(e^{-r}r^2\right) + \frac{e^{-r}\cos 2\theta\cos\phi}{r^2\sin\theta} - \frac{e^{-r}\sin\theta\cos\phi}{r^2\sin^2\theta}$$

$$= -\frac{\sin\theta\cos\phi}{r^2}\left(2re^{-r} - e^{-r}r^2\right) + \frac{e^{-r}\cos\phi}{r^2\sin\theta}\left(\cos 2\theta - 1\right)$$

$$= \sin\theta\cos\phi\left(e^{-r} - \frac{2}{r}e^{-r}\right) - \frac{e^{-r}}{r^2}\frac{\cos\phi}{\sin\theta}\left(1 - \cos 2\theta\right)$$

$$= \sin\theta\cos\phi\left(e^{-r} - \frac{2}{r}e^{-r}\right) - \frac{e^{-r}}{r^2}\frac{\cos\phi}{\sin\theta}\,2\sin^2\theta$$

$$= \sin\theta\cos\phi\left(e^{-r} - \frac{2}{r}e^{-r}\right) - \frac{e^{-r}}{r^2}\,2\sin\theta\cos\phi$$

$$= e^{-r}\sin\theta\cos\phi\left(1 - \frac{2}{r} - \frac{2}{r^2}\right)$$

EXAMPLE 1.62

Given the vector field, $\vec{E} = \left(x^2 + y^2\right)\vec{a}_x + \left(x + y\right)\vec{a}_y$, find $\nabla^2\vec{E}$.

SOLUTION

We know that, $\nabla^2\vec{E} = \left(\nabla^2 E_x\right)\vec{a}_x + \left(\nabla^2 E_y\right)\vec{a}_y + \left(\nabla^2 E_z\right)\vec{a}_z$

where $\nabla^2 = \left(\dfrac{\partial^2}{\partial x^2} + \dfrac{\partial^2}{\partial y^2} + \dfrac{\partial^2}{\partial z^2}\right)$.

Since E_y component is linear, $\nabla^2 E_y$ will be zero and $\nabla^2 E_z$ also vanishes to zero, as there is no E_z component in the given vector field.

Therefore, $\nabla^2\vec{E} = \nabla^2 E_x\vec{a}_x = \left(\dfrac{\partial^2}{\partial x^2} + \dfrac{\partial^2}{\partial y^2} + \dfrac{\partial^2}{\partial z^2}\right)\left(x^2 + y^2\right)\vec{a}_x$

$$= \left(2 + 2\right)\vec{a}_x = 4\vec{a}_x$$

1.13 NULL IDENTITIES

The two null identities with del (∇) functions involving divergence and curl operations in vector analysis form a significant part in the study of electromagnetism. These identities are used particularly in defining the potential function, which will be discussed in the later chapter. The two identities are discussed separately as given below.

1.13.1 Identity-I

From the properties involving curl, it is known that the curl of the gradient of any scalar field is zero.

That is, $\nabla \times \left(\nabla V\right) = 0$ (1.87)

By Stokes's theorem, the surface integral of $\nabla \times \left(\nabla V\right)$ over any surface is equal to the line integral of ∇V around the closed path bounding the surface.

That is, $\int_s \left[\nabla \times \left(\nabla V\right)\right] \cdot d\vec{s} = \oint_l \left(\nabla V\right) \cdot d\vec{l}$ (1.88)

Since $dV = \left(\nabla V\right) \cdot d\vec{l}$, the above equation becomes

$$\oint_l \left(\nabla V\right) \cdot d\vec{l} = \oint_l dV = 0$$ (1.89)

Substituting Eq. (1.89) in Eq. (1.88), we get

$$\int_s \left[\nabla \times \left(\nabla V\right)\right] \cdot d\vec{s} = 0$$ (1.90)

The above equation states that the surface integral of $\nabla \times \left(\nabla V\right)$ over any surface is zero, leading to the first null identity denoted in Eq. (1.87). This identity is a general one and is invariant with the selection of any coordinate systems.

Conversely, the null identity-I can also be stated that if the curl of any vector field is zero, then it can be defined as the gradient of a scalar field. For a vector field $\vec{E}$, if $\nabla \times \vec{E} = 0$, then the scalar field V can be expressed such that $\vec{E} = -\nabla V$. Also, it is known that if the curl of a vector is zero, then the vector field is said to be conservative or irrotational. Using the converse statement of null identity-I, a conservative vector field can also be defined as the gradient of a scalar field.

1.13.2 Identity-II

From the properties involving divergence and curl, it is also known that the divergence of the curl of any vector field is zero.

That is, $\nabla \cdot \left(\nabla \times \vec{A} \right) = 0$ 　　　　　(1.91)

By divergence theorem, the volume integral of $\nabla \cdot \left(\nabla \times \vec{A} \right)$ over any volume is equal to the surface integral of $\nabla \times \vec{A}$ through the closed surface.

That is, $\int_{v} \nabla \cdot \left(\nabla \times \vec{A} \right) dv = \oint_{s} \left(\nabla \times \vec{A} \right) \cdot d\vec{s}$ 　　　(1.92)

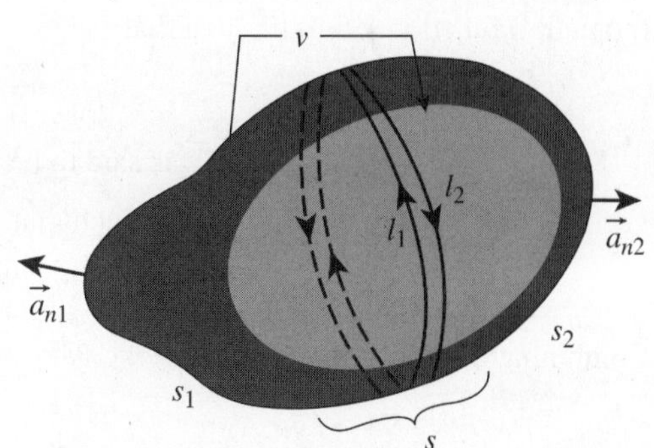

Figure 1.34　*Arbitrary volume v enclosed by surface s*

Consider the arbitrary volume v enclosed by a surface s as shown in Figure 1.34. Assume that the closed surface s is split into two open surfaces, s_1 and s_2, with a common boundary that is twice as l_1 and l_2. Applying Stokes's theorem to surface s_1 bounded by l_1, and surface s_2 bounded by l_2, the RHS of the above equation is written as

$$\oint_{s} \left(\nabla \times \vec{A} \right) \cdot d\vec{s} = \int_{s_1} \left(\nabla \times \vec{A} \right) \cdot \vec{a}_{n1} d\vec{s} + \int_{s_2} \left(\nabla \times \vec{A} \right) \cdot \vec{a}_{n2} d\vec{s}$$

$$= \oint_{l_1} \vec{A} \cdot d\vec{l} + \oint_{l_2} \vec{A} \cdot d\vec{l} \qquad (1.93)$$

Here, $\vec{a}_{n1}$ and $\vec{a}_{n2}$ are the unit normal vectors directed outwards to surfaces s_1 and s_2 following the right-hand rule with the path directions of l_1 and l_2. As the paths l_1 and l_2 share same common boundary between s_1 and s_2, the two-line integrals on the right side of the above equation follow the same path but in opposite directions.

That is, $\oint_{s} \left(\nabla \times \vec{A} \right) \cdot d\vec{s} = \oint_{l_1} A \cdot d\vec{l} - \oint_{l_2} A \cdot d\vec{l} = 0$ 　　　(1.94)

Substituting Eq. (1.94) in Eq. (1.92), we get

$$\int_{v} \nabla \cdot \left(\nabla \times \vec{A} \right) dv = 0 \qquad (1.95)$$

The above equation states that the volume integral of $\nabla \cdot \left(\nabla \times \vec{A} \right)$ over any volume is zero, leading to the second null identity denoted in Eq. (1.91).

Conversely, the null identity-II can also be stated that if the divergence of a vector field is zero, then it can be defined as the curl of another vector field. For a vector field $\vec{B}$, if $\nabla \cdot \vec{B} = 0$, then the vector field $\vec{A}$ can be expressed such that $\vec{B} = \nabla \times \vec{A}$. Also, it is known that if the divergence of a vector is zero, then the vector field is said to be solenoidal. Using the converse statement of null identity-II, a solenoidal vector field can also be defined as the curl of a vector field.

1.14　HELMHOLTZ'S THEOREM

Helmholtz's theorem states that a vector field is uniquely described within a region by its divergence and curl. Both the divergence and the curl of the vector field in an unbounded region vanish at infinity. If the vector field is confined within a region bounded by a surface, then the divergence and curl can be determined throughout the region.

In general, any vector field or vector point function $\vec{F}$ can be determined by decomposing it into an irrotational part $\vec{F_i}$ and a solenoid part $\vec{F_s}$.

That is, $\vec{F} = \vec{F_i} + \vec{F_s}$ (1.96)

If the vector field $\vec{F_i}$ is said to be irrotational, i.e., $\nabla \times \vec{F_i} = 0$, then by using null identity-I, the scalar (potential) function V will be such that

$$\vec{F_i} = -\nabla V \qquad (1.97)$$

Similarly, if the vector field $\vec{F_s}$ is said to be solenoidal, i.e., $\nabla \cdot \vec{F_s} = 0$, then by using null identity-II, the vector (potential) function $\vec{A}$ will be such that

$$\vec{F_s} = \nabla \times \vec{A} \qquad (1.98)$$

Combining the above two equations, we get

$$\vec{F} = -\nabla V + (\nabla \times \vec{A})$$

The above equation shows that any general vector field $\vec{F}$ can be written as the sum of the gradient of a scalar field V and the curl of a vector field $\vec{A}$. Helmholtz's theorem is considered as a basic constituent in the study of electromagnetic field theory.

EXAMPLE 1.63

Given a vector function $\vec{F} = (6y - b_1 z)\vec{a}_x + (b_2 x - 4z)\vec{a}_y - (b_3 y + z)\vec{a}_z$. (i) Find the constants b_1, b_2, and b_3 if $\vec{F}$ is irrotational and, (ii) find the scalar potential function V whose negative gradient equals $\vec{F}$.

SOLUTION

(*i*) We know that for an irrotational vector $\vec{F}$, its $\nabla \times \vec{F} = 0$.

$$\text{That is, } \nabla \times \vec{F} = \begin{vmatrix} \vec{a}_x & \vec{a}_y & \vec{a}_z \\ \dfrac{\partial}{\partial x} & \dfrac{\partial}{\partial y} & \dfrac{\partial}{\partial z} \\ 6y - b_1 z & b_2 x - 4z & -(b_3 y + z) \end{vmatrix} = (-b_3 + 4)\vec{a}_x - b_1 \vec{a}_y + (b_2 - 6)\vec{a}_z = 0$$

Since each component of $\nabla \times \vec{F}$ vanish to zero, we obtain the constants as $b_1 = 0, b_2 = 6$ and $b_3 = 4$.

(*ii*) From the null identity-I, an irrotational vector $\vec{F}$ can be expressed as the negative gradient of a scalar function V.

$$\text{That is, } \vec{F} = -\nabla V = -\frac{\partial V}{dx}\vec{a}_x - \frac{\partial V}{dy}\vec{a}_y - \frac{\partial V}{dz}\vec{a}_z$$

$$6y\vec{a}_x + (6x - 4z)\vec{a}_y - (4y + z)\vec{a}_z = -\frac{\partial V}{dx}\vec{a}_x - \frac{\partial V}{dy}\vec{a}_y - \frac{\partial V}{dz}\vec{a}_z$$

Equating the components on both the sides of the above equation, we have

$$\frac{\partial V}{\partial x} = -6y \tag{1}$$

$$\frac{\partial V}{\partial y} = -6x + 4z \tag{2}$$

$$\frac{\partial V}{\partial z} = 4y + z \tag{3}$$

Integrating Eq. (1) with respect to x, we get

$$V = -6xy + f_1(y,z) \tag{4}$$

where $f_1(y,z)$ is a function of y and z, which is to be determined. Similarly, integrating Eq. (2) with respect to y and integrating Eq. (3) with respect to z results in

$$V = -6xy + 4yz + f_2(x,z) \tag{5}$$

and

$$V = 4yz + \frac{z^2}{2} + f_3(x,y) \tag{6}$$

By looking into Eqs. (4), (5), and (6), the scalar potential function can be written as

$$V = -6xy + 4yz + \frac{z^2}{2} \tag{7}$$

Adding any constant to the above equation will result in a possible answer for scalar potential function V. This constant can be determined either by a boundary condition or the condition at infinity.

REVIEW QUESTIONS

1. What is a scalar quantity? Give some examples of scalars.
2. What is a vector quantity? Give some examples of vectors.
3. Define scalar field and vector field. Give examples for each.
4. What are the sources of electromagnetic fields?
5. What is a unit vector? Give its significance.
6. How will you determine the position vector and distance vector in rectangular coordinate system?
7. Determine the distance vector between $P(0,-2,1)$ and $Q(-2,0,3)$ in rectangular coordinates.
8. If $\vec{A} = \vec{a}_x + \vec{a}_y + \vec{a}_z$ and $\vec{B} = 4\vec{a}_x + 4\vec{a}_y + \vec{a}_z$ are the two position vectors, what is the distance vector from $\vec{A}$ to $\vec{B}$? What is its magnitude?
9. Determine the unit vector normal to both vectors $\vec{A} = 4\vec{a}_x - 3\vec{a}_y + \vec{a}_z$ and $\vec{B} = 2\vec{a}_x + \vec{a}_y - \vec{a}_z$.
10. Verify the commutative law for addition of vectors.
11. Show that the necessary and sufficient condition for two non-zero vectors $\vec{A}$ and $\vec{B}$ to be perpendicular is that $\vec{A} \cdot \vec{B} = 0$.
12. Show that $\vec{A} = 6\vec{a}_x + 5\vec{a}_y - 10\vec{a}_z$ and $\vec{B} = 5\vec{a}_x + 2\vec{a}_y + 4\vec{a}_z$ are orthogonal vectors.

13. Prove that the vectors obey the distributive law for the scalar product and cross product.

14. Prove that two non-zero vectors are parallel if and only if their cross product is zero.

15. List the three types of vector product.

16. Define dot product.

17. Explain the significance of dot product and its applications.

18. What is the right-hand rule?

19. Define cross product.

20. Explain the significance of cross product and its applications.

21. What is the direction of $\vec{A} \times \vec{B}$?

22. Give some physical examples of dot product and cross product.

23. Write the properties of dot product and cross product.

24. Define scalar triple product and vector triple product.

25. By expansion in rectangular component form, prove that $\vec{A} \times (\vec{B} \times \vec{C}) = \vec{B}(\vec{A} \cdot \vec{C}) - \vec{C}(\vec{A} \cdot \vec{B})$.

26. Determine the volume of the parallelepiped formed by the lengths of the vectors $\vec{A} = -2\vec{a}_x - 3\vec{a}_y + \vec{a}_z$, $\vec{B} = 2\vec{a}_x - 5\vec{a}_y + 3\vec{a}_z$ and $\vec{C} = 4\vec{a}_x + 2\vec{a}_y + 6\vec{a}_z$.

27. Find the value of B_z such that the angle between the vectors $\vec{A} = 2\vec{a}_x + \vec{a}_y + 4\vec{a}_z$ and $\vec{B} = -2\vec{a}_x - \vec{a}_y + B_z\vec{a}_z$ is 45°.

28. For the vectors $\vec{A} = 2\vec{a}_x - 2\vec{a}_y + \vec{a}_z$ and $\vec{B} = 3\vec{a}_x + 5\vec{a}_y - 2\vec{a}_z$ find $\vec{A} \cdot \vec{B}$, $\vec{A} \times \vec{B}$, and show that $\vec{A} \times \vec{B} = -(\vec{B} \times \vec{A})$.

29. Show that $\vec{A} = 4\vec{a}_x - 2\vec{a}_y - \vec{a}_z$ and $\vec{B} = \vec{a}_x + 4\vec{a}_y - 4\vec{a}_z$ are mutually perpendicular vectors.

30. Determine the angle between $\vec{A}$ and $\vec{B}$ for the vectors given by $\vec{A} = 3\vec{a}_x + 4\vec{a}_y + \vec{a}_z$ and $\vec{B} = 2\vec{a}_y - 5\vec{a}_z$.

31. Find the angle between the vectors $\vec{A} = 2\vec{a}_x + 4\vec{a}_y - \vec{a}_z$ and $\vec{B} = 3\vec{a}_x + 6\vec{a}_y - 4\vec{a}_z$ using dot product and cross product.

32. Consider two vectors $\vec{P} = 4\vec{a}_y + 10\vec{a}_z$ and $\vec{Q} = 2\vec{a}_x + 3\vec{a}_y$. Find the projection of $\vec{P}$ and $\vec{Q}$.

33. Mention the criteria for choosing an appropriate coordinate system for solving a field problem easily. Explain with an example.

34. Explain rectangular and cylindrical system and the procedure for conversion from one to another.

35. Derive the relationship between Cartesian and spherical system.

36. How are the unit vectors defined in cylindrical and spherical coordinate systems?

37. What are the three steps required in vector transformation?

38. Convert the given rectangular coordinate $A(x = 2, y = 3, z = 1)$ into the corresponding cylindrical coordinate.

39. Transform the vector $5\vec{a}_x$ at $Q(x = 3, y = 4, z = -2)$ to the cylindrical coordinates.

40. Given the two points $A(x = 2, y = 3, z = -1)$ and $B(r = 4, \theta = -25°, \phi = 120°)$, find the spherical coordinates of A, Cartesian coordinates of B and distance AB.

41. Given the two points $A(x=2, y=3, z=-1)$ and $B(\rho=4, \phi=-50°, z=2)$, find the distance from A to B.

42. Give the expression for distance between the points (ρ_1, ϕ_1, z_1) and (ρ_2, ϕ_2, z_2) in cylindrical coordinates.

43. Calculate the distance between two points given in cylindrical coordinates as $P(5, \pi/6, 5)$ and $Q(2, \pi/3, 4)$.

44. Determine the distance between two points given in spherical coordinates as $P(10, \pi/4, \pi/3)$ and $Q(2, \pi/2, \pi)$. What is the distance vector from P to Q?

45. Transform a vector $\vec{A} = y\vec{a}_x - x\vec{a}_y + z\vec{a}_z$ into cylindrical coordinates.

46. A vector $\vec{F} = 3x\vec{a}_x + 0.5y^2\vec{a}_y + 0.25x^2y^2\vec{a}_z$ is given at point $P(3,4,12)$ in the rectangular coordinate system. Express this vector in the spherical coordinate system.

47. Given point $P(-2,6,3)$ and vector $\vec{A} = y\vec{a}_x + (x+z)\vec{a}_y$, express P and A in cylindrical and spherical coordinates. Evaluate A at P in the Cartesian, cylindrical and spherical coordinate systems.

48. State the elementary vector lengths in Cartesian, cylindrical, and spherical coordinate system.

49. State the various differential surface elements in three coordinate systems.

50. State the expressions for differential volume element in three coordinate systems.

51. Define line integral, surface integral, and volume integral.

52. Evaluate $\oint_l \vec{\rho} \cdot d\vec{l}$ along the closed circular path of radius b in the xy-plane.

53. Determine $\oint_s \vec{r} \cdot d\vec{s}$ over the closed surface of a sphere of radius b.

54. For a given vector, $\vec{F} = xy^2\vec{a}_x + (x^2y + y)\vec{a}_y$, evaluate (*a*) $\oint_l \vec{F} \cdot d\vec{l}$ along the circumference of a circle of radius 3 and (*b*) $\oint_s \vec{F} \cdot d\vec{s}$ over the surface of the same circle.

55. Determine the volume of a region bounded by the xy-plane $(z=0)$ and $z = 4 - x^2 - y^2$.

56. What do you mean by gradient? State the gradient in three coordinate systems.

57. Mention the properties of gradient of a scalar.

58. Define divergence of a vector field and express the divergence of a vector field in three coordinate systems.

59. If $\vec{B} = -xy\vec{a}_x + 3x^2yz\vec{a}_y + z^3x\vec{a}_z$, find $\nabla \cdot \vec{B}$ at $P(1,-1,2)$.

60. Prove that $\nabla \cdot \vec{r} = 3$, where $\vec{r}$ is the position vector of any point P in space.

61. State the curl of a vector in three coordinate systems.

62. Find the curl of the vector $\vec{A} = xyz\vec{a}_x + 3x^2y\vec{a}_y + (xz^2 - y^2z)\vec{a}_z$.

63. Give the physical interpretation of divergence and curl of vector field.

64. Using the Cartesian coordinate system, verify the following statements:

(*i*)   Divergence of the curl of a vector function is zero

(*ii*) Curl of the gradient of a scalar function is zero

65. Give practical examples for diverging and curling fields.

66. Given the field $\vec{E} = E_0 \cos\theta\, \vec{a}_r - E_0 \sin\theta\, \vec{a}_\theta$, find $\nabla \cdot \vec{E}$ and $\nabla \times \vec{E}$.

67. Using the rectangular coordinate system, verify that (a) $\nabla \cdot (\nabla \times \vec{A}) = 0$ and (b) $\nabla \times (\nabla f) = 0$.

68. Explain the terms irrotational and solenoidal as applied to vector $\vec{A}$.

69. Show that the vector field $\vec{E} = yz\vec{a}_x + xz\vec{a}_y + xy\vec{a}_z$ is both continuous (solenoidal) and conservative (irrotational).

70. State and prove divergence theorem.

71. For the vector field $\vec{D} = 3r^2\vec{a}_r$, evaluate both sides of the divergence theorem for the region enclosed between the spherical shells defined by $r = 1$ and $r = 2$.

72. Given $\vec{F} = x\vec{a}_x$, evaluate $\oint_s \vec{F} \cdot d\vec{s}$ where s is taken over the surface y of a cube of side $2a$, centered about the origin. Then, evaluate the volume integral $\nabla \cdot \vec{F}$ for the cube and show that the two results are equivalent.

73. Given $\vec{F} = x^3\vec{a}_x + x^2y\vec{a}_y + x^2z\vec{a}_z$, verify the divergence theorem when the region is bounded by a cylinder $x^2 + y^2 = 25$ and planes at $z = 0$ and $z = 4$.

74. State and prove Stokes's theorem.

75. If $\vec{C} = 3y^2\vec{a}_x + 4z\vec{a}_y + 6y\vec{a}_z$, verify Stokes's theorem for the open surface $z^2 + y^2 = 4$ in the $x = 0$ plane.

76. Verify Stokes's theorem over a hemispherical surface at $r = 2$ and $0 \leq \theta \leq \dfrac{\pi}{2}$ for the field $\vec{E} = 100\cos\theta\,\vec{a}_r$.

77. Describe the importance of divergence theorem and Stokes's theorem.

78. Give the expressions for Laplacian of a scalar field V in three coordinate systems.

79. If $f = x^3y^2z$, determine (i) ∇f and (ii) $\nabla^2 f$ at $P(2,3,5)$.

80. Determine the Laplacian of the following scalar functions:

(*i*) $V = 10r\sin^2\theta\cos\phi,$ (*ii*) $V = 5e^{-r}\cos\phi$, and (*iii*) $V = xy^2z^3$.

81. State and prove the null identities involving divergence and curl operations.

82. State Helmholtz's theorem.

83. Show how a vector function $\vec{F}$ can be expressed in terms of scalar potential function (V) and vector potential function $(\vec{A})$.

84. Give the difference between a solenoidal field and an irrotational field.

STATIC ELECTRIC FIELDS

2.1 INTRODUCTION

The electrostatic field theory is the study of time-invariant fields established by charges at rest. Electrostatics corresponds to stationary charges i.e., charges are at rest, which means an electrostatic field is produced by a static charge distribution. The source of electric field is electric charge or charge density. A charge can be either concentrated at a point or distributed in any manner. In any case, the charge is assumed to be constant in time and hence, the field produced by the charge will be time-invariant. Therefore, this electrostatic field is also called a time-invariant field.

Electrostatics has diverse areas of applications, and many electronic devices and systems are based on the principles of electrostatics. They include X-ray machines, oscilloscopes, inkjet electrostatic printers, copying machines, touch pads, capacitance keyboards, liquid crystal displays (LCD) and many solid state control devices. The electrostatics field concept is used in the design of medical diagnostic sensors, such as the electrocardiogram (ECG) and the electroencephalogram (EGG) as well as in numerous industrial applications.

The study of electrostatics begins with the discussion of Coulomb's law and Gauss's law which govern the static electric fields. Both these laws are based on experimental studies and they are interdependent. Coulomb's law is used to determine the force between two charged particles. The concept of electric field intensity is introduced and applied to discrete point charges and continuous charge distributions (line, surface and volume charges) based on Coulomb's law. The idea of electric lines of force or electric flux lines is also discussed, which is an important concept used in the representation, visualization and description of the electric field.

Although Coulomb's law is applicable to determine the electric field intensity due to any charge distribution, it is easier to use Gauss's law when the charge distribution is symmetrical. The problems related to electrostatic field can easily be solved by using Gauss's law when compared to Coulomb's law.

In this chapter, the fundamental concepts that are applicable to static electric fields (electrostatics) in vacuum or free space are discussed. The electric potential, known as a scalar field, is defined in terms of electric field intensity and an expression for the energy required in moving a charge from one location to another in an electrostatic field is derived. As electric potential is a scalar quantity, it is always easier to work with such a scalar quantity when compared to electric field, which is a vector quantity. The electrostatic energy and energy density are also derived in terms of electric field intensity.

2.2 COULOMB'S LAW

Electrostatics is based on the experimental analysis of Coulomb's law which determines the electric force that a charged particle exerts on another point charge. A point charge is a charge that is located on a body whose dimensions are much smaller than other dimensions and its unit is coulomb (C).

Coulomb's law states that the force F between two point charges Q_1 and Q_2 in free space is

(*i*) directly proportional to the product of their charges

(*ii*) inversely proportional to the square of the distance (R) between them

(*iii*) directed along the line joining them and

(*iv*) attractive (repulsive) for unlike (like) charges.

Therefore, Coulomb's law can be mathematically expressed as

$$F \alpha \frac{Q_1 Q_2}{R^2}$$

(2.1)

i.e.,

$$F = \frac{k Q_1 Q_2}{R^2} = \frac{Q_1 Q_2}{4 \pi \varepsilon_0 R^2}$$

where the proportionality constant k is denoted by

$$k = \frac{1}{4 \pi \varepsilon_0} = 9 \times 10^9 \text{ m/F}$$

and the constant ε_0 is called electrical *permittivity of free space* which is measured in farad per metre. Its value is given by

$$\varepsilon_0 = \frac{1}{36 \pi} \times 10^{-9} = 8.854 \times 10^{-12} \text{ F/m}$$

For any material with permittivity ε, the force F between two point charges Q_1 and Q_2 is given by

$$F = \frac{Q_1 Q_2}{4 \pi \varepsilon R^2}$$

(2.2)

where $\varepsilon = \varepsilon_0 \varepsilon_r$ in which ε_r is called *relative permittivity or dielectric constant* of the material. The unit of force F is newton (N).

Figure 2.1 shows two point charges Q_1 and Q_2 situated at points with position vectors $\vec{r}_1$ and $\vec{r}_2$ respectively, in free space. Therefore, the electric force $\vec{F}_{12}$ on Q_2 due to Q_1 is represented by

$$\vec{F}_{12} = \frac{Q_1 Q_2}{4 \pi \varepsilon_0 R_{12}^2} \vec{a}_{12}$$

(2.3)

where R_{12} is the distance between two point charges Q_1 and Q_2, and $\vec{a}_{12}$ is a unit vector in the direction of distance vector $\vec{R}_{12}$

Therefore, $\vec{a}_{12} = \dfrac{\vec{R}_{12}}{\left|\vec{R}_{12}\right|} = \dfrac{\vec{R}_{12}}{R_{12}} = \dfrac{\vec{r}_2 - \vec{r}_1}{\left|\vec{r}_2 - \vec{r}_1\right|}$

Substituting the above unit vector $\vec{a}_{12}$ in Eq. (2.3), we get

$$\vec{F}_{12} = \frac{Q_1 Q_2 \left(\vec{r}_2 - \vec{r}_1\right)}{4 \pi \varepsilon_0 \left|\vec{r}_2 - \vec{r}_1\right|^3}$$

(2.4)

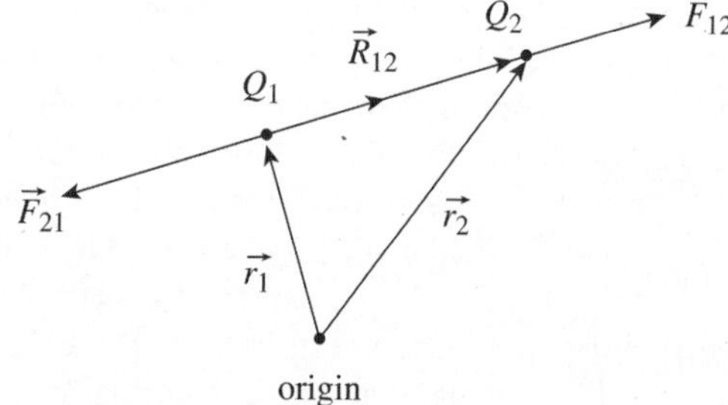

Figure 2.1   *Electric force between two point charges in vector form*

which is known as the *vector form of Coulomb's law*. It is valid not only for charged particles such as electrons and protons but also for point charges. Charged bodies can be considered as point charges as long as their sizes are much less than the distance between them. If two point charges, each having a charge of 1 coulomb, are separated by a distance of 1m, then the magnitude of the force experienced by each charge in free space is 9×10^9 newton.

Here, the force exerted on Q_1 by Q_2 is equal in magnitude but opposite in direction to the force exerted on Q_2 by Q_1. Therefore,

$$\vec{F}_{21} = \left|\vec{F}_{12}\right|\vec{a}_{21} = \left|\vec{F}_{12}\right|\left(-\vec{a}_{12}\right) \tag{2.5}$$

Since $\vec{a}_{21} = -\vec{a}_{12}$, we can write, $\vec{F}_{21} = -\vec{F}_{12}$.

Coulomb's force also obeys the *principle of superposition.* If there are more than two point charges i.e., multiple point charges, then the superposition principle can be used to determine the force on a particular charge due to other charges. Superposition principle states that, if there are n point charges $Q_1, Q_2,..., Q_n$ situated at points with position vectors $\vec{r}_1, \vec{r}_2,..., \vec{r}_n$, then the total force $\vec{F}_t$ acting on a point charge Q with position vector $\vec{r}$ is the vector sum of the forces exerted individually by each charge on Q. Figure 2.2 shows the force experienced by a charge Q in a system of n point charges with distance vectors $\vec{R}_1, \vec{R}_2, \vec{R}_3,..., \vec{R}_n$, between the charges.

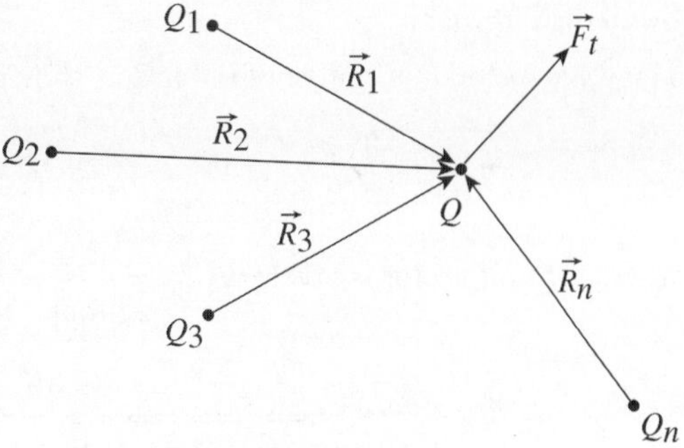

Figure 2.2 *Coulomb's Force for multiple point charges*

Using superposition principle, the total force $\vec{F}_t$ can be written as

$$\vec{F}_t = \frac{QQ_1\left(\vec{r}-\vec{r}_1\right)}{4\pi\varepsilon_0 \left|\vec{r}-\vec{r}_1\right|^3} + \frac{QQ_2\left(\vec{r}-\vec{r}_2\right)}{4\pi\varepsilon_0 \left|\vec{r}-\vec{r}_2\right|^3} + \cdots + \frac{QQ_n\left(\vec{r}-\vec{r}_n\right)}{4\pi\varepsilon_0 \left|\vec{r}-\vec{r}_n\right|^3}$$

The above expression can be simplified as

$$\vec{F}_t = \frac{Q}{4\pi\varepsilon_0} \sum_{i=1}^{n} \frac{Q_i\left(\vec{r}-\vec{r}_i\right)}{\left|\vec{r}-\vec{r}_i\right|^3}$$

EXAMPLE 2.1

In xy-plane, $Q_1 = 100$ μC at $(2, 3, 0)$ m experiences a repulsive force of 7.5 N because of Q_2 at $(10, 6, 0)$ m. Find Q_2.

SOLUTION

The distance R_{12} between two point charges Q_1 and Q_2 is

$$\vec{R}_{12} = \vec{r}_2 - \vec{r}_1 = (10-2)\vec{a}_x + (6-3)\vec{a}_y + (0-0)\vec{a}_z = 8\vec{a}_x + 3\vec{a}_y$$

$$R_{12} = \left|\vec{R}_{12}\right| = \left|\vec{r}_2 - \vec{r}_1\right| = \sqrt{(8)^2 + (3)^2} = \sqrt{73}$$

From Coulomb's law, the magnitude of force exerted on charge Q_1 by charge Q_2 in free space is

$$\left|\vec{F}_{21}\right| = \left|\vec{F}_{12}\right| = \frac{Q_1 Q_2}{4\pi\varepsilon_0 R_{12}^2}$$

$$7.5 = \frac{100 \times 10^{-6} \times Q_2}{4\pi \times \dfrac{10^{-9}}{36\pi} \times 73} = 12.328 \times 10^3 \times Q_2$$

Therefore, $Q_2 = \dfrac{7.5}{12.328 \times 10^3} = 0.608 \times 10^{-3} = 608\ \mu C$ ∎

EXAMPLE 2.2

Find the force on charge of 0.3 mC at (1, 2, 3) m due to a charge of -0.1 mC at (2, 0, 5) m in the free space.

SOLUTION

The force exerted on charge of 0.3 mC as shown in Figure E2.2 is

$$\vec{F}_{12} = \frac{Q_1 Q_2}{4\pi\varepsilon_0 R_{12}^2}\,\vec{a}_{12}$$

where the unit vector is given by $\vec{a}_{12} = \dfrac{\vec{R}_{12}}{\left|\vec{R}_{12}\right|} = \dfrac{\vec{r}_2 - \vec{r}_1}{\left|\vec{r}_2 - \vec{r}_1\right|}$

$$\vec{a}_{12} = \frac{(1-2)\vec{a}_x + (2-0)\vec{a}_y + (3-5)\vec{a}_z}{\sqrt{(-1)^2 + (2)^2 + (-2)^2}} = \frac{-\vec{a}_x + 2\vec{a}_y - 2\vec{a}_z}{3}$$

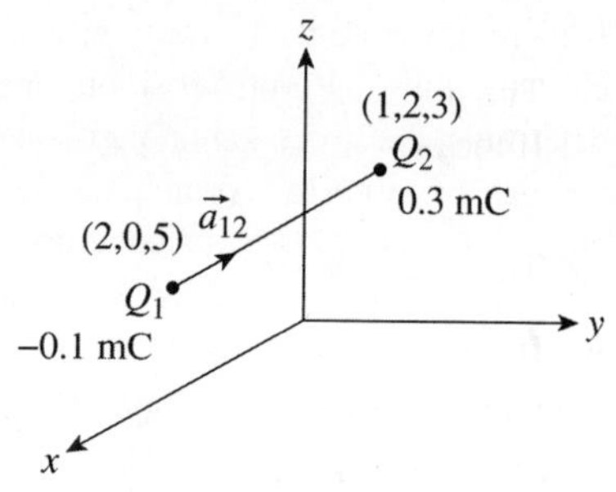

Figure E2.2

Therefore, $\vec{F}_{12} = \dfrac{Q_1 Q_2}{4\pi\varepsilon_0 R_{12}^2}\,\vec{a}_{12} = \dfrac{0.3 \times 10^{-3} \times -0.1 \times 10^{-3}}{4\pi \times 8.854 \times 10^{-12} \times (3)^2} \times (\vec{a}_{12}),$ where $R_{12} = 3$

$$= -29.97 \times \left(\frac{-\vec{a}_x + 2\vec{a}_y - 2\vec{a}_z}{3}\right)$$

$$= 9.99\vec{a}_x - 19.98\vec{a}_y + 19.98\vec{a}_z\ N$$

Hence, the magnitude of the force is

$$\left|\vec{F}_{12}\right| = \sqrt{(9.99)^2 + (-19.98)^2 + (19.98)^2} = 29.97\ N$$ ∎

EXAMPLE 2.3

Find the force of interaction between two charges spaced 10 cm apart in vaccum. The charges are 4×10^{-8} C and 6×10^{-5} C. If the same charges are separated by the same distance in kerosene with $\varepsilon_r = 2$, what is the force of interaction?

SOLUTION

From Coulomb's law, the magnitude of the force is

$$F = \frac{Q_1 Q_2}{4\pi\varepsilon R^2} = \frac{Q_1 Q_2}{4\pi\varepsilon_0 \varepsilon_r R^2}$$

where $R = 10$ cm $= 0.1$ m and $\varepsilon_r = 2$ for kerosene.

Therefore, $F = \dfrac{4 \times 10^{-8} \times 6 \times 10^{-5}}{4\pi \times 8.854 \times 10^{-12} \times 2 \times (0.1)^2} = 1.0785\ N$ ∎

EXAMPLE 2.4

Given that two small identical conducting spheres have charges of 2×10^{-9} C and -1×10^{-9} C respectively. When they are placed 4 cm apart, what is the force between them? If they are brought into contact and then separated by 4 cm, what is the force between them?

SOLUTION

From Coulomb's law, the force between the conducting spheres is

$$F = \frac{Q_1 Q_2}{4\pi\varepsilon_0 R^2} = \frac{2\times10^{-9}\times\left(-1\times10^{-9}\right)}{4\pi\times8.854\times10^{-12}\times\left(4\times10^{-2}\right)^2} = -11.234\,\mu\text{N}$$

The negative sign indicates that the force is attractive.
If the two charges are brought into contact, the charge on both spheres becomes their average value.

Therefore, $Q_1 = Q_2 = \dfrac{\left(2\times10^{-9}\right)+\left(-1\times10^{-9}\right)}{2} = 0.5\times10^{-9}\,\text{C}$

In this case, the force between the conducting spheres is

$$F = \frac{Q_1 Q_2}{4\pi\varepsilon_0 R^2} = \frac{0.5\times10^{-9}\times0.5\times10^{-9}}{4\pi\times8.854\times10^{-12}\times\left(4\times10^{-2}\right)^2} = -1.404\,\mu\text{N}$$

The positive sign indicates that the force is repulsive. $\qquad\qquad\square$

EXAMPLE 2.5

A point charge $Q_1 = 300\,\mu\text{C}$ located at $(1,-1,-3)$ m experiences a force $\vec{F} = 8\vec{a}_x - 8\vec{a}_y + 4\vec{a}_z\,\text{N}$ due to point charge Q_2 at $(3,-3,-2)$ m. Find the charge Q_2.

SOLUTION

From Coulomb's law,

$$\vec{F} = \frac{Q_1 Q_2}{4\pi\varepsilon_0 R^2}\,\vec{a}_R$$

where distance vector is $\vec{R} = (1-3)\vec{a}_x + \left[-1-(-3)\right]\vec{a}_y + \left[-3-(2)\right]\vec{a}_z$

$$= -2\vec{a}_x + 2\vec{a}_y - \vec{a}_z$$

and its magnitude is $R = \left|\vec{R}\right| = \sqrt{4+4+1} = 3$

Therefore, the unit vector is

$$\vec{a}_R = \frac{\vec{R}}{\left|\vec{R}\right|} = \frac{-2\vec{a}_x + 2\vec{a}_y - \vec{a}_z}{3}$$

Therefore, $\vec{F} = \dfrac{300\times10^{-6}\times Q_2}{4\pi\times\left(\dfrac{10^{-9}}{36\pi}\right)\times(3)^2}\left[\dfrac{-2\vec{a}_x + 2\vec{a}_y - \vec{a}_z}{3}\right]$

i.e., $8\vec{a}_x - 8\vec{a}_y + 4\vec{a}_z = 10^5 Q_2 \left(-2\vec{a}_x + 2\vec{a}_y - \vec{a}_z \right)$

Equating coefficients of $\vec{a}_x$, we get

$$-2 \times 10^5 Q_2 = 8$$

Hence, $Q_2 = -\dfrac{8}{2 \times 10^5} = -40\,\mu\text{C}$

EXAMPLE 2.6

Given that four point charges of 10 µC each are located in free space at $(-3,0,0)$, $(3,0,0)$, $(0,-3,0)$ and $(0,3,0)$ in Cartesian coordinate system. Determine the force on a 20 µC charge located at $(0,0,4)$. All distances are in metres.

SOLUTION

The position vectors of four point charges, Q_1 to Q_4, each of 10 µC, located in free space at $(-3,0,0)$, $(3,0,0)$, $(0,-3,0)$ and $(0,3,0)$, respectively, in Cartesian coordinate system, as shown in Figure E2.6, are given by

$$\vec{r}_1 = -3\vec{a}_x, \quad \vec{r}_2 = 3\vec{a}_x, \quad \vec{r}_3 = -3\vec{a}_y, \quad \vec{r}_4 = 3\vec{a}_y$$

Here, the position vector of point charge Q of 20 µC is $\vec{r} = 4\vec{a}_z$.
The force acting on a charge Q of 20 µC by each point charge can be obtained as

$$\vec{F}_1 = \frac{QQ_1 (\vec{r} - \vec{r}_1)}{4\pi\varepsilon_0 |\vec{r} - \vec{r}_1|^3} = \frac{QQ_1}{4\pi\varepsilon_0} \times \frac{\left(4\vec{a}_z + 3\vec{a}_x \right)}{125} = \frac{QQ_1}{500\pi\varepsilon_0} \left(4\vec{a}_z + 3\vec{a}_x \right)$$

$$\vec{F}_2 = \frac{QQ_2 (\vec{r} - \vec{r}_2)}{4\pi\varepsilon_0 |\vec{r} - \vec{r}_2|^3} = \frac{QQ_2}{4\pi\varepsilon_0} \times \frac{\left(4\vec{a}_z - 3\vec{a}_x \right)}{125} = \frac{QQ_2}{500\pi\varepsilon_0} \left(4\vec{a}_z - 3\vec{a}_x \right)$$

$$\vec{F}_3 = \frac{QQ_3 (\vec{r} - \vec{r}_3)}{4\pi\varepsilon_0 |\vec{r} - \vec{r}_3|^3} = \frac{QQ_3}{4\pi\varepsilon_0} \times \frac{\left(4\vec{a}_z + 3\vec{a}_y \right)}{125} = \frac{QQ_3}{500\pi\varepsilon_0} \left(4\vec{a}_z + 3\vec{a}_y \right)$$

$$\vec{F}_4 = \frac{QQ_4 (\vec{r} - \vec{r}_4)}{4\pi\varepsilon_0 |\vec{r} - \vec{r}_4|^3} = \frac{QQ_4}{4\pi\varepsilon_0} \times \frac{\left(4\vec{a}_z - 3\vec{a}_y \right)}{125} = \frac{QQ_4}{500\pi\varepsilon_0} \left(4\vec{a}_z - 3\vec{a}_y \right)$$

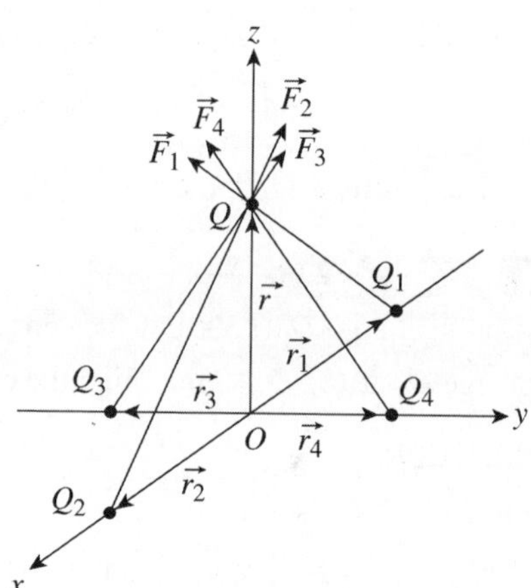

Figure E2.6

Using superposition principle, the total force $\vec{F}_t$ on a 20 µC charge is

$$\vec{F}_t = \vec{F}_1 + \vec{F}_2 + \vec{F}_3 + \vec{F}_4$$

$$= \frac{20 \times 10^{-6} \times 10 \times 10^{-6}}{500\pi\varepsilon_0} \times \left(16\vec{a}_z \right)$$

$$= \frac{32 \times 10^{-12}}{5\pi \times 8.854 \times 10^{-12}} \vec{a}_z = 0.23\vec{a}_z \qquad \left(\text{since } \varepsilon_0 = 8.854 \times 10^{-12} \right)$$

Therefore, the force on a 20 µC charge is $0.23\vec{a}_z$ N.

EXAMPLE 2.7

Given that four point charges are located in free space as shown in Figure E2.7. Find the force experienced by the 1 µC charge.

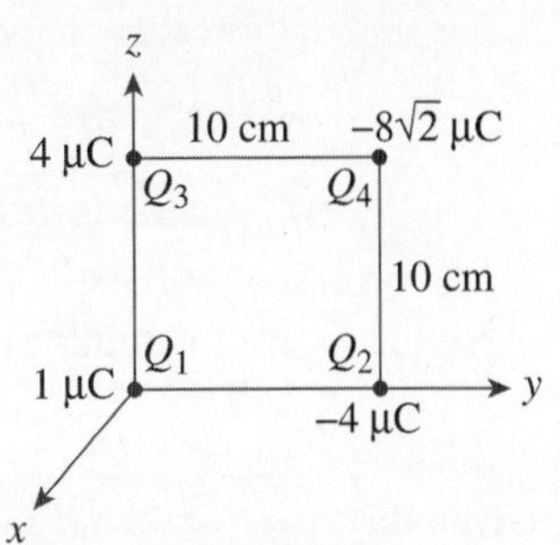

Figure E2.7

SOLUTION

Given $Q_1 = 1\,\mu C$ at $(0,0,0)$, $Q_2 = -4\,\mu C$ at $(0,0.1,0)$, $Q_3 = 4\,\mu C$ at $(0,0,0.1)$ and $Q_4 = -8\sqrt{2}\,\mu C$ at $(0,0.1,0.1)$ Therefore, the force experienced by $Q_1 = 1\,\mu C$ is obtained from the superposition principle as

$$\vec{F} = \vec{F}_1 + \vec{F}_2 + \vec{F}_3$$

$$= \frac{1}{4\pi\varepsilon_0}\left[\frac{Q_1 Q_2}{R_{21}^2}\vec{a}_{R21} + \frac{Q_1 Q_3}{R_{31}^2}\vec{a}_{R31} + \frac{Q_1 Q_4}{R_{41}^2}\vec{a}_{R41}\right]$$

$$= Q_1 \times 9\times 10^9 \times \left[\frac{Q_2}{R_{21}^2}\vec{a}_{R21} + \frac{Q_3}{R_{31}^2}\vec{a}_{R31} + \frac{Q_4}{R_{41}^2}\vec{a}_{R41}\right]$$

where $\dfrac{1}{4\pi\varepsilon_0} = 9\times 10^9$.

Here, the unit vectors are

$$\vec{a}_{R21} = \frac{\vec{R}_{21}}{R_{21}} = \frac{(0,0,0)-(0,0.1,0)}{\sqrt{(-0.1)^2}} = \frac{-0.1\vec{a}_y}{0.1} = -\vec{a}_y$$

$$\vec{a}_{R31} = \frac{\vec{R}_{31}}{R_{31}} = \frac{(0,0,0)-(0,0,0.1)}{\sqrt{(-0.1)^2}} = \frac{-0.1\vec{a}_z}{0.1} = -\vec{a}_z$$

and $\vec{a}_{R41} = \dfrac{\vec{R}_{41}}{R_{41}} = \dfrac{(0,0,0)-(0,0.1,0.1)}{\sqrt{(-0.1)^2+(-0.1)^2}} = \dfrac{-0.1\vec{a}_y - 0.1\vec{a}_z}{0.1\sqrt{2}} = \dfrac{-\vec{a}_y - \vec{a}_z}{\sqrt{2}}$

Therefore, $\vec{F} = 10^{-6}\times 9\times 10^9 \left[\dfrac{-4\times 10^{-6}}{0.1^2}(-\vec{a}_y) + \dfrac{4\times 10^{-6}}{0.1^2}(-\vec{a}_z) - \dfrac{8\sqrt{2}\times 10^{-6}}{\left(0.1\sqrt{2}\right)^2}\left(\dfrac{-\vec{a}_y - \vec{a}_z}{\sqrt{2}}\right)\right]$

$$= 9\times 10^3 \times 10^{-6}\left[400\vec{a}_y - 400\vec{a}_z + 400\vec{a}_y + 400\vec{a}_z\right] = 7.2\,\vec{a}_y$$

$$\vec{F} = 7.2\,\vec{a}_y\,\text{N}$$

EXAMPLE 2.8

Given that three point charges of Q coulombs are placed in air at the vertices of an equilateral triangle of side d. Determine the magnitude and direction of the force on one charge due to other charges.

SOLUTION

Let us find the force on charge at *A* due to the other two charges situated at points *B* and *C*. Using Coulomb's law, the magnitude of force on charge at *A* due to charge at *B* is

$$\left|\vec{F}_{BA}\right| = \frac{Q_1 Q_2}{4\pi\varepsilon_0 R^2} = \frac{Q^2}{4\pi\varepsilon_0 d^2}$$

Similarly, the magnitude of force on charge at *A* due to charge at *C* is

$$\left|\vec{F}_{CA}\right| = \frac{Q^2}{4\pi\varepsilon_0 d^2}$$

From Figure E2.8, it is seen that the horizontal components of the total force cancel out. Hence, the total force acts along the upward direction and its magnitude is given as

$$\left|\vec{F}\right| = \left|\vec{F}_{BA}\right|\cos 30° + \left|\vec{F}_{CA}\right|\cos 30°$$

Therefore, $\left|\vec{F}\right| = \dfrac{2Q^2}{4\pi\varepsilon_0 d^2} \times \cos 30° = \dfrac{Q^2}{2\pi\varepsilon_0 d^2} \times \dfrac{\sqrt{3}}{2} = \dfrac{\sqrt{3}Q^2}{4\pi\varepsilon_0 d^2}$

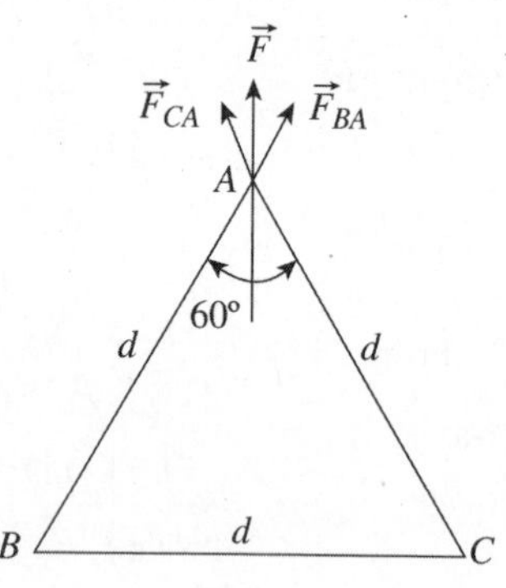

Figure E2.8

EXAMPLE 2.9

Given that concentrated charges of 0.25 µC are located at the vertices of an equilateral triangle of 10 m side as shown in Figure E2.9. Determine the magnitude and direction of force on one charge due to other two charges.

SOLUTION

Given that charges of 0.25 µC are located at the vertices of an equilateral triangle of 10 m side as shown in Figure E2.9. Assume the charges are located at $(0,0,0), (10,0,0)$ and $\left(5,\sqrt{75},0\right)$.

The force on one charge due to other two charges is obtained by using superposition principle. Therefore, the total charge at the origin due to other charges is

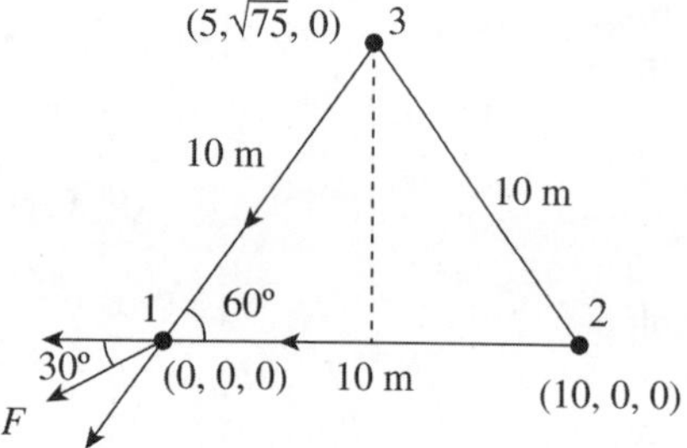

Figure E2.9

$$\vec{F} = \vec{F}_{21} + \vec{F}_{31} = \frac{Q^2}{4\pi\varepsilon_0 R_{21}^2}\vec{a}_{R21} + \frac{Q^2}{4\pi\varepsilon_0 R_{31}^2}\vec{a}_{R31}$$

Here, the unit vectors are

$$\vec{a}_{R21} = \frac{\vec{R}_{21}}{R_{21}} = \frac{(0,0,0)-(10,0,0)}{\sqrt{(-10)^2}} = \frac{-10\,\vec{a}_x}{10} = -\vec{a}_x$$

and $\vec{a}_{R31} = \dfrac{\vec{R}_{31}}{R_{31}} = \dfrac{(0,0,0)-\left(5,\sqrt{75},0\right)}{\sqrt{5^2+75}} = \dfrac{-5\,\vec{a}_x - \sqrt{75}\,\vec{a}_y}{10} = -0.5\,\vec{a}_x - 0.866\,\vec{a}_y$

Therefore, $\vec{F} = \dfrac{Q^2}{4\pi\varepsilon_0}\left[\dfrac{\vec{a}_{R21}}{R_{21}^2} + \dfrac{\vec{a}_{R31}}{R_{31}^2}\right]$

$$= \left(0.25\right)^2 \times 10^{-12} \times 9 \times 10^9 \left[\frac{-\vec{a}_x}{100} + \frac{-0.5\,\vec{a}_x - 0.866\,\vec{a}_y}{100}\right]$$

$$= \frac{0.56 \times 10^{-3}}{100}\left[-\vec{a}_x - 0.5\vec{a}_x - 0.866\vec{a}_y\right]$$

$$= \left(-8.4\vec{a}_x - 4.85\vec{a}_y\right) \mu\text{N}$$

Therefore, the magnitude of force, $\left|\vec{F}\right| = \sqrt{(-8.4)^2 + (-4.85)^2} = 9.7\,\mu\text{N}$

From Figure E2.9, it is seen that the direction of force is, $\theta = \tan^{-1}\left(\frac{-4.85}{-8.4}\right) = 30°$ to the negative of x-axis. The magnitude of force can also be obtained by using the expression derived in Example 2.8 as

$$\left|\vec{F}\right| = \frac{\sqrt{3}Q^2}{4\pi\varepsilon_0 d^2} = \frac{\sqrt{3} \times \left(0.25 \times 10^{-6}\right)^2}{4\pi \times 8.864 \times 10^{-12} \times 10^2} = 9.7 \ \mu\text{N} \qquad \qquad \square$$

2.3 ELECTRIC FIELD INTENSITY

The force exerted on a unit charge in an electric field is called *electric field intensity* ($\vec{E}$) or *electric field strength*. The field intensity exists everywhere in space surrounding the charge. When another charge is brought into this electric field, it experiences force acting on it. The electric field intensity is defined as the force per unit charge as given by

$$\vec{E} = \frac{\vec{F}}{Q} \tag{2.6}$$

The unit of electric field intensity $\vec{E}$ is newton per coulomb (N/C), which is dimensionally equivalent to volt per metre (V/m). Though the electric field intensity is defined as the force per unit charge, it is common to express in terms of volt per metre. The direction of electric field intensity $\vec{E}$ is always in the direction of force $\vec{F}$.

If $\vec{E}$ is the electric field intensity at a point P in space, then the force $\vec{F}$ acting on a charge Q at that point is represented by

$$\vec{F} = Q\vec{E} \tag{2.7}$$

This equation can be used to compute the electrostatic force experienced by a charge placed in an electric field.

Using Coulomb's law in vector form due to a point charge Q, the electric field intensity $\vec{E}$ at any point P due to a point charge Q can be written as

$$\vec{E} = \frac{Q}{4\pi\varepsilon_0 R^2}\vec{a}_R = \frac{Q\left(\vec{r}_2 - \vec{r}_1\right)}{4\pi\varepsilon_0 \left|\vec{r}_2 - \vec{r}_1\right|^3} \tag{2.8}$$

where $\vec{a}_R$ is a unit vector in the direction of $\vec{R}$.

Using Coulomb's law for multiple point charges, the electric field intensity at any point P with position vector $\vec{r}$ due to n point charges is represented by

$$\vec{E} = \frac{Q_1\left(\vec{r} - \vec{r}_1\right)}{4\pi\varepsilon_0 \left|\vec{r} - \vec{r}_1\right|^3} + \frac{Q_2\left(\vec{r} - \vec{r}_2\right)}{4\pi\varepsilon_0 \left|\vec{r} - \vec{r}_2\right|^3} + \cdots + \frac{Q_n\left(\vec{r} - \vec{r}_n\right)}{4\pi\varepsilon_0 \left|\vec{r} - \vec{r}_n\right|^3}$$

The above equation can be simplified as

$$\vec{E} = \frac{1}{4\pi\varepsilon_0} \sum_{i=1}^{n} \frac{Q_i\left(\vec{r} - \vec{r}_i\right)}{\left|\vec{r} - \vec{r}_i\right|^3} \tag{2.9}$$

where $\vec{r}_i$ is the position vector from the origin O to charge Q_i and $\vec{r} - \vec{r}_1$ is the distance vector directed from the location of the charge Q_i towards the point of measurement of $\vec{E}$.

Here, the electric field intensity obeys the principle of linear superposition and the electric field $\vec{E}$ at any point in space is equal to the vector sum of the electric fields intensities induced by all the individual charges. For example, the electric field intensity at point P in space due to two point charges Q_1 and Q_2 having position vectors $\vec{r}_1$ and $\vec{r}_2$ from origin is shown in Figure 2.3.

Therefore, the electric field intensity at point P with position vector $\vec{r}$ from origin is represented by

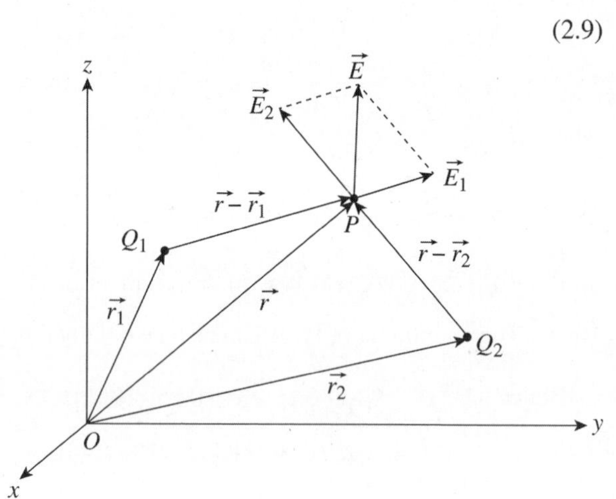

Figure 2.3   *Electric field at P due to two point charges*

$$\vec{E} = \vec{E}_1 + \vec{E}_2 = \frac{1}{4\pi\varepsilon_0}\left[\frac{Q_1\left(\vec{r} - \vec{r}_1\right)}{\left|\vec{r} - \vec{r}_1\right|^3} + \frac{Q_2\left(\vec{r} - \vec{r}_2\right)}{\left|\vec{r} - \vec{r}_2\right|^3}\right] \tag{2.10}$$

EXAMPLE 2.10

Find the electric field intensity $\vec{E}$ at $(0,3,4)$ m in Cartesian coordinates due to a point charge $Q = 1\,\mu\text{C}$ at the origin.

SOLUTION

The electric field intensity $\vec{E}$ at $(0,3,4)$ m in Cartesian coordinates due to a point charge $Q = 1\,\mu\text{C}$ at the origin is

$$\vec{E} = \frac{Q}{4\pi\varepsilon_0 R^2}\,\vec{a}_R$$

where unit vector, $\vec{a}_R = \dfrac{(0-0)\vec{a}_x + (3-0)\vec{a}_y + (4-0)\vec{a}_z}{\sqrt{(0)^2 + (3)^2 + (4)^2}} = \dfrac{3\vec{a}_y + 4\vec{a}_z}{5} = 0.6\vec{a}_y + 0.8\vec{a}_z$

and the magnitude of the distance vector, $R = \sqrt{(3)^2 + (4)^2} = 5$

Therefore, $\vec{E} = \dfrac{1\times10^{-6}}{4\pi \times 8.854\times10^{-12} \times (5)^2} \times \left(\vec{a}_R\right) = 360 \times \left(0.6\vec{a}_y + 0.8\vec{a}_z\right)$

$$= 216\,\vec{a}_y + 288\,\vec{a}_z \text{ V/m}$$

EXAMPLE 2.11

Determine the electric field intensity at point $P\left(-0.2, 0, -2.3\right)$ due to a point charge Q of $+5$ nC at point $\left(0.2, 0.1, -2.5\right)$ in air.

SOLUTION

The electric field intensity $\vec{E}$ at point $P(-0.2, 0, -2.3)$ due to a point charge of $+5$ nC at point $(0.2, 0.1, -2.5)$ is

$$\vec{E} = \frac{Q}{4\pi\varepsilon_0 R^2}\,\vec{a}_R$$

where $\vec{a}_R$ is the unit vector in the direction of $\vec{R}$.

i.e., $\displaystyle \vec{a}_R = \frac{\vec{R}}{|\vec{R}|} = \frac{(-0.2-0.2)\vec{a}_x + (0-0.1)\vec{a}_y + [-2.3-(-2.5)]\vec{a}_z}{\sqrt{(-0.4)^2 + (-0.1)^2 + (0.2)^2}}$

$$= \frac{-0.4\vec{a}_x - 0.1\vec{a}_y + 0.2\vec{a}_z}{0.45825}$$

Hence, $\displaystyle \vec{E} = \frac{5\times10^{-9}}{4\pi\times8.854\times10^{-12}\times(0.45825)^2} \times \frac{-0.4\vec{a}_x - 0.1\vec{a}_y + 0.2\vec{a}_z}{0.45825}$

$$= 44.96\times\frac{-0.4\vec{a}_x - 0.1\vec{a}_y + 0.2\vec{a}_z}{(0.45825)^3} = 467.22 \times \left(-0.4\,\vec{a}_x - 0.1\,\vec{a}_y + 0.2\,\vec{a}_z\right)$$

$$= -186.89\vec{a}_x - 46.72\vec{a}_y + 93.44\vec{a}_z$$

Therefore, $\vec{E} = -186.89\vec{a}_x - 46.72\vec{a}_y + 93.44\vec{a}_z$ V/m ☐

EXAMPLE 2.12

Find the total electric field intensity at the origin due to charge of 10^{-8} C located $P(0, 4, 4)$ m and charge of -0.5×10^{-8} C at Q (4,0,2) m.

SOLUTION

The total electric field intensity at the origin is equal to the vector sum of the electric field intensities induced by the individual charges as given by

$$\vec{E} \text{ at origin} = \vec{E} \text{ due to } Q_P + \vec{E} \text{ due to } Q_Q$$

$$= \frac{Q_P}{4\pi\varepsilon_0 R_1^2}\,\vec{a}_{R1} + \frac{Q_Q}{4\pi\varepsilon_0 R_2^2}\,\vec{a}_{R2}$$

From Figure E2.12, the unit vectors are in the direction of $\vec{R}_1$ and $\vec{R}_2$. Therefore,

$$\vec{a}_{R1} = \frac{\vec{R}_1}{|\vec{R}_1|} \text{ and } \vec{a}_{R2} = \frac{\vec{R}_2}{|\vec{R}_2|}$$

where $\quad \vec{R}_1 = (0-0)\vec{a}_x + (0-4)\vec{a}_y + (0-4)\vec{a}_z = -4\vec{a}_y - 4\vec{a}_z,$

$$|\vec{R}_1| = \sqrt{(-4)^2 + (-4)^2} = \sqrt{32},$$

$$\vec{R}_2 = (0-4)\vec{a}_x + (0-0)\vec{a}_y + (0-2)\vec{a}_z = -4\vec{a}_x - 2\vec{a}_z$$

and $\quad |\vec{R}_2| = \sqrt{(-4)^2 + (-2)^2} = \sqrt{20}.$

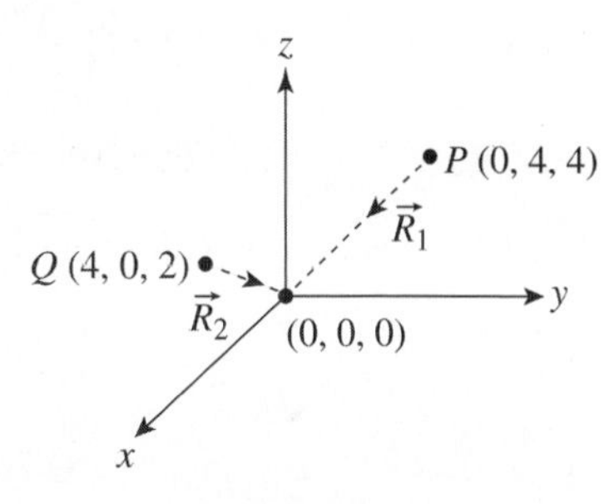

Figure E2.12

Therefore, $\vec{E} = \dfrac{1}{4\pi \times 8.854 \times 10^{-12}} \left[\dfrac{\left(10^{-8}\right)}{\left(\sqrt{32}\right)^2} \dfrac{\left(-4\vec{a}_y - 4\vec{a}_z\right)}{\sqrt{32}} + \dfrac{\left(-0.5 \times 10^{-8}\right)}{\left(\sqrt{20}\right)^2} \dfrac{\left(-4\vec{a}_x - 2\vec{a}_z\right)}{\sqrt{20}} \right]$

$$= -1.986\vec{a}_y - 1.986\vec{a}_z + 2\vec{a}_x + \vec{a}_z$$

$$= 2\vec{a}_x - 1.986\vec{a}_y - 0.986\vec{a}_z \text{ V/m}$$

EXAMPLE 2.13

Given that two point charges 2 mC and -4 mC are located at $(3,2,-1)$ and $(-1,-1,4)$, respectively. Calculate the electric force on a 20 nC charge located at $(0, 3, 1)$ and the electric field intensity at that point.

SOLUTION

Given $Q = 20$ nC at $(0, 3, 1)$, $Q_1 = 2$ mC at $(3, 2, -1)$ and $Q_2 = -4$ mC at $(-1,-1,4)$.

Using superposition principle, the force is

$$\vec{F} = \vec{F}_1 + \vec{F}_2$$

The electric force due to Q_1 on a 20 nC charge located at $(0, 3, 1)$ is

$$\vec{F}_1 = \dfrac{QQ_1\left(\vec{r} - \vec{r}_1\right)}{4\pi\varepsilon_0 \left|\vec{r} - \vec{r}_1\right|^3} = \dfrac{20 \times 10^{-9} \times 2 \times 10^{-3}}{4\pi\varepsilon_0} \left\{ \dfrac{(0-3)\vec{a}_x + (3-2)\vec{a}_y + (1+1)\vec{a}_z}{\left(3^2 + 1^2 + 2^2\right)^{3/2}} \right\}$$

$$= 360 \times 10^{-3} \left(\dfrac{-3\vec{a}_x + \vec{a}_y + 2\vec{a}_z}{52.38} \right) \qquad \left(\text{since } \dfrac{1}{4\pi\varepsilon_0} = 9 \times 10^9 \right)$$

The electric force due to Q_2 on a 10 nC charge located at $(0, 3, 1)$ is

$$\vec{F}_2 = \dfrac{QQ_2\left(\vec{r} - \vec{r}_2\right)}{4\pi\varepsilon_0 \left|\vec{r} - \vec{r}_2\right|^3} = \dfrac{20 \times 10^{-9} \times \left(-4 \times 10^{-3}\right)}{4\pi\varepsilon_0} \left\{ \dfrac{(0+1)\vec{a}_x + (3+1)\vec{a}_y + (1-4)\vec{a}_z}{\left(1^2 + 4^2 + 3^2\right)^{3/2}} \right\}$$

$$= -720 \times 10^{-3} \left(\dfrac{\vec{a}_x + 4\vec{a}_y - 3\vec{a}_z}{132.57} \right)$$

Therefore, $\vec{F} = 360 \times 10^{-3} \left(\dfrac{-3\vec{a}_x + \vec{a}_y + 2\vec{a}_z}{52.38} \right) - 720 \times 10^{-3} \left(\dfrac{\vec{a}_x + 4\vec{a}_y - 3\vec{a}_z}{132.57} \right)$

$$= -26.05\vec{a}_x - 14.85\vec{a}_y + 30.039\vec{a}_z \text{ mN}$$

Hence, the electric field intensity at $(0, 3, 1)$ is

$$\vec{E} = \dfrac{\vec{F}}{Q} = \left(-26.05\vec{a}_x - 14.85\vec{a}_y + 30.039\vec{a}_z\right) \times \dfrac{10^{-3}}{20 \times 10^{-9}}$$

$$= -1302.5\vec{a}_x - 742.55\vec{a}_y + 1501.95\vec{a}_z \text{ kV/m}$$

EXAMPLE 2.14

Consider that two point charges, $-Q$ and $+Q/2$, are located at the origin and at a point $(a, 0, 0)$ respectively. At what point does the electric field intensity vanish?

SOLUTION

Given the point charge $-Q$ located at $(0, 0, 0)$ and $+Q/2$ located at $(a, 0, 0)$. The electric field due to two point charges is

$$\vec{E} = \frac{-Q\vec{a}_{R1}}{4\pi\varepsilon R_1^2} + \frac{(Q/2)\vec{a}_{R2}}{4\pi\varepsilon R_2^2}$$

At point P, $\vec{E} = 0$.

Therefore, $\left|\dfrac{-Q\vec{a}_{R1}}{4\pi\varepsilon R_1^2}\right| = \left|\dfrac{(Q/2)\vec{a}_{R2}}{4\pi\varepsilon R_2^2}\right|$

$$\left|\frac{1}{R_1^2}\right| = \left|\frac{1}{2R_2^2}\right|$$

$$R_1^2 = 2R_2^2$$

The distance vectors are

$$\vec{R}_1 = (x,0,0) - (0,0,0) = x\vec{a}_x \text{ and } \vec{R}_2 = (x,0,0) - (a,0,0) = (x-a)\vec{a}_x$$

Since $\qquad R_1^2 = 2R_2^2$

$$x^2 = 2(x-a)^2$$

i.e., $\quad \sqrt{2}(x-a) = \pm x$

$$\sqrt{2}x \pm x = \sqrt{2}a$$

Hence, $\qquad x = \dfrac{\sqrt{2}}{(\sqrt{2}\pm 1)}a$

i.e., $\qquad x = 0.585a \text{ or } 3.414a$

Since the force is attractive, the point P lies away from the charges. Hence, at point $P(3.141a, 0, 0)$, the field vanishes. $\qquad\square$

2.4 ELECTRIC FIELD DUE TO CONTINUOUS CHARGE DISTRIBUTION

The concept of electric field due to discrete point charges can now be extended to continuous charge distributions along a line, across a surface, or over a volume. These different charge distributions are shown in Figure 2.4.

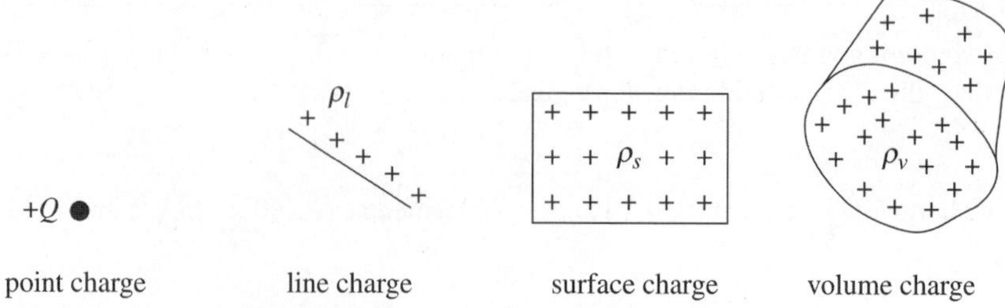

Figure 2.4   *Different charge distributions*

When the charge is distributed along a line or a linear element, the *line charge density* ρ_l is defined as the charge per unit length as given by

$$\rho_l = \underset{\Delta l \to \infty}{Lt} \frac{\Delta Q}{\Delta l} \ \text{C/m}$$

When the charge is distributed across a surface, the *surface charge density* ρ_s is defined as the charge per unit area as given by

$$\rho_s = \underset{\Delta s \to \infty}{Lt} \frac{\Delta Q}{\Delta s} \ \text{C/m}^2$$

If the charge is confined within a volume, the *volume charge density* ρ_v is defined as the charge per unit volume as given by

$$\rho_v = \underset{\Delta v \to \infty}{Lt} \frac{\Delta Q}{\Delta v} \ \text{C/m}^3$$

Figure 2.5 shows the electric charge distribution by volume charge density ρ_v over a volume v. Using Coulomb's law, the differential electric field intensity at any point P in free space due to a differential amount of charge $dQ = \rho_v dv$ contained in a differential volume dv is represented by

$$d\vec{E} = \frac{dQ}{4\pi\varepsilon_0 R^2}\vec{a}_R = \frac{\rho_v dv}{4\pi\varepsilon_0 R^2}\vec{a}_R$$

where R is the distance between the point P and the differential amount of charge $dQ = \rho_v dv$ and $\vec{a}_R$ is the unit vector in the direction of $\vec{R}$.

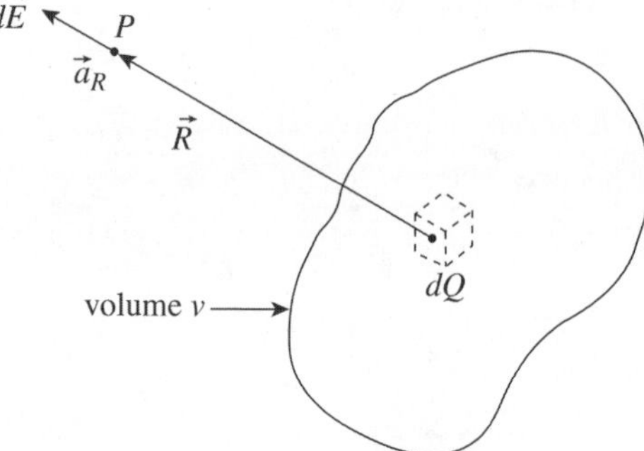

Figure 2.5   *Electric field intensity due to volume charge distribution*

Applying the principle of linear superposition, the total electric field intensity $\vec{E}$ can be obtained by integrating the fields contributed by all the charges forming the charge distribution. Therefore, the electric field intensity for volume charge distribution is given by

$$\vec{E} = \int_v d\vec{E} = \frac{1}{4\pi\varepsilon_0}\int_v \frac{\rho_v dv}{R^2}\vec{a}_R$$

Here, both R and $\vec{a}_R$ vary as a function of position over the volume integral. Suppose if the charge is distributed across a surface s with surface charge density ρ_s, then $dQ = \rho_s ds$ and the electric field intensity for surface charge distribution is given by

$$\vec{E} = \int_s d\vec{E} = \frac{1}{4\pi\varepsilon_0}\int_s \frac{\rho_s ds}{R^2}\vec{a}_R$$

Similarly, if the charge is distributed along a line l with line charge density ρ_l, then $dQ = \rho_l dl$ and the electric field intensity for line charge distribution is given by

$$\vec{E} = \int_l d\vec{E} = \frac{1}{4\pi\varepsilon_0} \int_l \frac{\rho_l\, dl}{R^2}\, \vec{a}_R$$

EXAMPLE 2.15

A square plate in the xy-plane is situated in the space defined by $-3\,\text{m} \le x \le 3\,\text{m}$ and $-3\,\text{m} \le y \le 3\,\text{m}$. Find the total charge on the plate if the surface charge density is given by $\rho_s = 4y^2\ \mu\text{C/m}^2$.

SOLUTION

The total charge on the plate is

$$Q = \int_s \rho_s\, ds, \qquad \text{where } \rho_s = 4y^2 \times 10^{-6}$$

$$= \int_{-3}^{3}\int_{-3}^{3} 4y^2 \times 10^{-6}\, dx\, dy = \left[\frac{4y^3}{3}\right]_{-3}^{3} \times [x]_{-3}^{3} \times 10^{-6}$$

$$= 432\ \mu\text{C}$$

EXAMPLE 2.16

A spherical shell centered at origin extends between $r = 0.02$ m and $r = 0.03$ m. If the volume charge density is given by $\rho_v = 3r \times 10^{-4}\ \text{C/m}^3$, find the total charge contained in the shell.

SOLUTION

The total charge contained in the shell is

$$Q = \int_v \rho_v\, dv, \qquad \text{where } \rho_v = 3r \times 10^{-4}\ \text{C/m}^3 \ \text{ and } \ dv = r^2 \sin\theta\, dr\, d\theta\, d\phi$$

$$= \int_{\phi=0}^{2\pi} \int_{\theta=0}^{\pi} \int_{r=0.02}^{0.03} \left(3r \times 10^{-4}\right)\left(r^2 \sin\theta\, dr\, d\theta\, d\phi\right)$$

$$= 3\times 10^{-4} \left[\frac{r^4}{4}\right]_{0.02}^{0.03} \times [-\cos\theta]_0^{\pi} \times [\phi]_0^{2\pi}$$

$$= \frac{3\times 10^{-4}}{4}\left[(0.03)^4 - (0.02)^4\right] \times 2 \times 2\pi = 0.61 \times 10^{-9}$$

$$= 0.61\ \text{nC}$$

2.4.1 Field due to a Line Charge

A finite line charge with uniform charge density ρ_l from C to D along the z-axis is shown in Figure 2.6. The differential charge element dQ associated with differential element dl of the line is

$$dQ = \rho_l dl = \rho_l dz'$$

where the differential line element is at a distance of z' from the origin.

In Figure 2.6, the field point is specified by (x, y, z) and the source point is denoted by $(0, 0, z')$. The electric field intensity $\vec{E}$ at a point $P(x, y, z)$ due to linear charge distribution ρ_l can be obtained as

$$\vec{E} = \int_l d\vec{E} = \frac{1}{4\pi\varepsilon_0} \int_l \frac{\rho_l dl}{R^2} \vec{a}_R \tag{2.11}$$

The differential line element is given by

$$dl = dz' \tag{2.12}$$

The distance vector $\vec{R}$ between the differential line element $(0, 0, z')$ and the arbitrary point $P(x, y, z)$ can be written as

$$\vec{R} = \left(x\vec{a}_x + y\vec{a}_y + z\vec{a}_z\right) - z'\vec{a}_z = x\vec{a}_x + y\vec{a}_y + \left(z - z'\right)\vec{a}_z$$

In cylindrical coordinates, the distance vector $\vec{R}$ is denoted by

$$\vec{R} = \rho\,\vec{a}_\rho + \left(z - z'\right)\vec{a}_z$$

Therefore, $R^2 = \left|\vec{R}\right|^2 = x^2 + y^2 + \left(z - z'\right)^2 = \rho^2 + \left(z - z'\right)^2$

and $\dfrac{\vec{a}_R}{R^2} = \dfrac{\vec{R}}{\left|\vec{R}\right|} \times \dfrac{1}{R^2} = \dfrac{\rho\,\vec{a}_\rho + \left(z - z'\right)\vec{a}_z}{\sqrt{\rho^2 + \left(z - z'\right)^2}} \times \dfrac{1}{\rho^2 + \left(z - z'\right)^2}$

$$= \frac{\rho\,\vec{a}_\rho + \left(z - z'\right)\vec{a}_z}{\left[\rho^2 + \left(z - z'\right)^2\right]^{\frac{3}{2}}} \tag{2.13}$$

Substituting Eq. (2.12) and Eq. (2.13) into Eq. (2.11), we get

$$\vec{E} = \frac{\rho_l}{4\pi\varepsilon_0} \int \frac{\rho\,\vec{a}_\rho + \left(z - z'\right)\vec{a}_z}{\left[\rho^2 + \left(z - z'\right)^2\right]^{\frac{3}{2}}} dz' \tag{2.14}$$

From Figure 2.6, it is seen that to determine $\vec{E}$, it is necessary to define R and z'. Hence, using trigonometry, we get

$$R = \left[\rho^2 + \left(z - z'\right)^2\right]^{1/2} = \rho\sec\alpha$$

$$z' = z - \rho\tan\alpha \tag{2.15a}$$

$$dz' = -\rho\sec^2\alpha\,d\alpha \tag{2.15b}$$

Substituting Eq. (2.15a) and Eq. (2.15b) into Eq. (2.14), we get

$$\vec{E} = \frac{-\rho_l}{4\pi\varepsilon_0} \int_{\alpha_1}^{\alpha_2} \frac{\rho\,\vec{a}_\rho + \rho\tan\alpha\,\vec{a}_z}{\rho^3 \sec^3\alpha} \rho\sec^2\alpha\,d\alpha$$

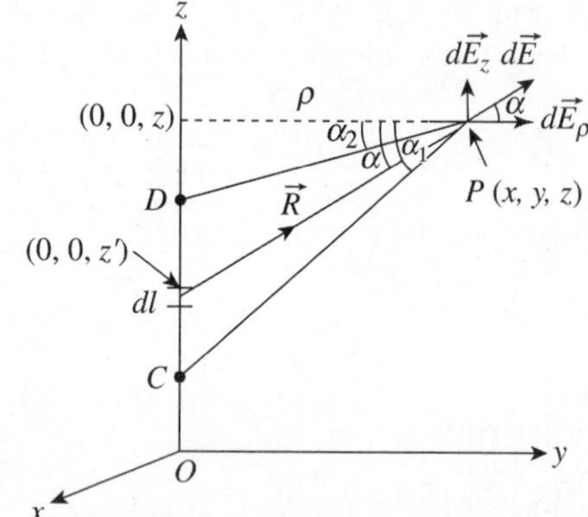

Figure 2.6 *Determination of electric field $\vec{E}$ due to a line charge distribution*

$$= \frac{-\rho_l}{4\pi\varepsilon_0} \int_{\alpha_1}^{\alpha_2} \frac{\left[\vec{a}_\rho + \dfrac{\sin\alpha}{\cos\alpha}\vec{a}_z\right]}{\rho\sec\alpha}\, d\alpha$$

$$= -\frac{\rho_l}{4\pi\varepsilon_0\rho} \int_{\alpha_1}^{\alpha_2} \left[\cos\alpha\,\vec{a}_\rho + \sin\alpha\,\vec{a}_z\right] d\alpha$$

Therefore, for a *finite line charge*, the electric field intensity is represented by

$$\vec{E} = \frac{\rho_l}{4\pi\varepsilon_0\rho}\left[-\left(\sin\alpha_2 - \sin\alpha_1\right)\vec{a}_\rho + \left(\cos\alpha_2 - \cos\alpha_1\right)\vec{a}_z\right] \tag{2.16}$$

An *infinite line charge* is a special case of Figure 2.6 in which the line charge is of infinite extent along the z-axis from $C\,(0,0,-\infty)$ to $D\,(0,0,\infty)$ such that $\alpha_1 = 90°$ and $\alpha_2 = -90°$. Thus, the z-components vanish and the electric field intensity can be written as

$$\vec{E} = \frac{\rho_l}{2\pi\varepsilon_0\rho}\vec{a}_\rho \tag{2.17}$$

The above equation shows that the electric field intensity has only $\vec{E}_\rho$ component and there is lack of variation of field with ϕ and z. If the line is not along the z-axis, ρ is the perpendicular distance from the line to the point of observation P and $\vec{a}_\rho$ is a unit vector along that distance directed from the source point to the field point.

EXAMPLE 2.17

A uniform line charge, infinite in extent with $\rho_l = 40\,\text{nC/m}$ lies along the z-axis. Determine the electric field $\vec{E}$ at (6, 8, 3) m.

SOLUTION

A uniform line charge, infinite in extent with $\rho_l = 40\,\text{nC/m}$ lying along the z-axis is shown in Figure E2.17. Any point on the line charge along the z-axis is (0, 0, z). As the uniform line charge is along z-axis, the electric field $\vec{E}$ cannot have any component along z-direction. Hence, z co-ordinate is not considered while calculating $\vec{R}$.

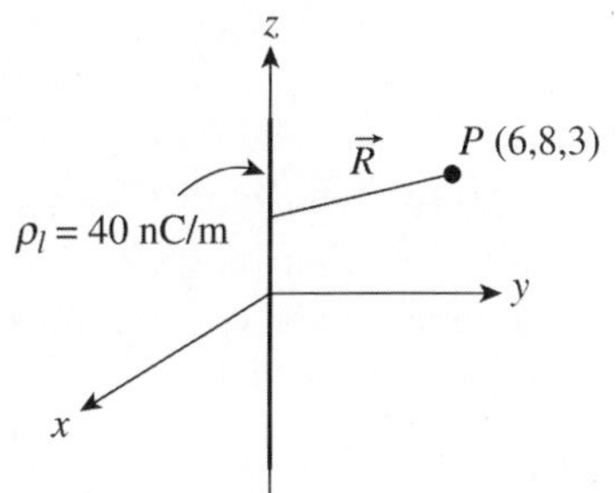

Figure E2.17

Therefore, $\vec{R} = (6-0)\vec{a}_x + (8-0)\vec{a}_y$

and its magnitude is written as

$$R = \left|\vec{R}\right| = \sqrt{6^2 + 8^2} = 10$$

The unit vector along $\vec{R}$ direction is

$$\vec{a}_\rho = \frac{\vec{R}}{\left|\vec{R}\right|} = \frac{6\vec{a}_x + 8\vec{a}_y}{\sqrt{6^2 + 8^2}} = \frac{6\vec{a}_x + 8\vec{a}_y}{10} = 0.6\vec{a}_x + 0.8\vec{a}_y$$

The electric field intensity due to an infinite line of charge is

$$\vec{E} = \frac{\rho_l}{2\pi\varepsilon_0\rho}\vec{a}_\rho$$

where $\rho = R = 10$.

Therefore, $\vec{E} = \dfrac{40 \times 10^{-9}}{2\pi \times 8.854 \times 10^{-12} \times 10}\left[0.6\vec{a}_x + 0.8\vec{a}_y\right]$

$$= 43.16\vec{a}_x + 57.56\vec{a}_y \text{ V/m}$$

EXAMPLE 2.18

A line charge density of 24 nC/m is located in free space on the line $y = 1, z = 2$. Determine the electric field intensity at $P(6, -1, 3)$.

SOLUTION

The line charge density of 24 nC/m is located at $y = 1, z = 2$. As the line charge is on the yz-plane i.e., x-axis, the electric field intensity cannot have any component along x-direction. The radial distance between the line charge and point $P(6, -1, 3)$ is

$$R = \sqrt{(-1-1)^2 + (3-2)^2} = \sqrt{5}$$

The electric field intensity is

$$\vec{E} = \frac{\rho_l}{2\pi\varepsilon_0\rho}\vec{a}_\rho$$

where the unit vector, $\vec{a}_\rho = \dfrac{\vec{R}}{|\vec{R}|} = \dfrac{(-1-1)\vec{a}_y + (3-2)\vec{a}_z}{\sqrt{5}} = \dfrac{-2\vec{a}_y + \vec{a}_z}{\sqrt{5}}$

Therefore, $\vec{E} = \dfrac{24 \times 10^{-9}}{2\pi \times 8.854 \times 10^{-12} \times \sqrt{5}} \times \dfrac{-2\vec{a}_y + \vec{a}_z}{\sqrt{5}}$ where $\rho = R = \sqrt{5}$

$$= -172.76\vec{a}_y + 86.37\vec{a}_z \text{ V/m}$$

EXAMPLE 2.19

A uniform line charge $\rho_l = 25$ nC/m lies on the line $x = -3$ m and $y = 4$ m in free space. Determine the electric field intensity at a point $(2, 3, 15)$ m.

SOLUTION

A uniform line charge is shown in Figure E2.19 and it lies on the line with $x = -3$ m and $y = 4$ m. It is a line parallel to z-axis and hence, z can take any value. The electric field intensity due to an infinite line of charge can be written as

$$\vec{E} = \frac{\rho_l}{2\pi\varepsilon_0\rho}\vec{a}_\rho$$

As the line charge is parallel to z-axis, $\vec{E}$ cannot have any component in $\vec{a}_z$ direction. Hence, z co-ordinate is not considered

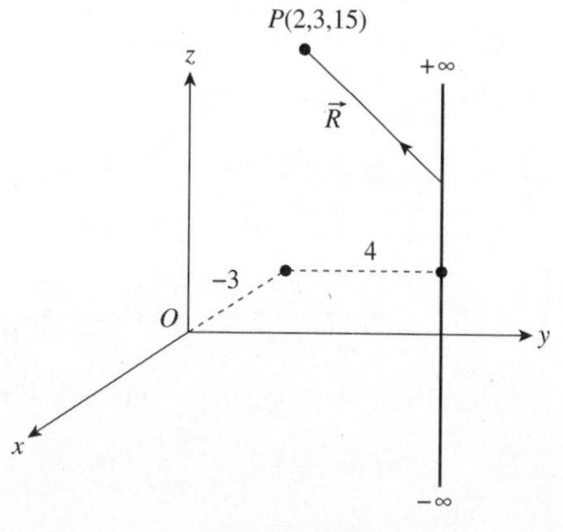

Figure E2.19

while calculating $\vec{R}$. The distance vector $\vec{R}$ between the point of observation $P(2,3,15)$ and other point $(-3,4,z)$ on the line charge is

$$\vec{R} = \left[2-(-3)\right]\vec{a}_x + \left[3-4\right]\vec{a}_y = 5\vec{a}_x - \vec{a}_y$$

and its magnitude is

$$R = \left|\vec{R}\right| = \sqrt{(5)^2 + (-1)^2} = \sqrt{26} = \rho$$

The unit vector along $\vec{R}$ direction is

$$\vec{a}_\rho = \frac{\vec{R}}{\left|\vec{R}\right|} = \frac{5\vec{a}_x - \vec{a}_y}{\sqrt{26}}$$

Therefore, the electric field intensity is

$$\vec{E} = \frac{\rho_l}{2\pi\varepsilon_0\rho}\vec{a}_\rho = \frac{\rho_l}{2\pi\varepsilon_0} \times \frac{1}{\sqrt{26}}\left(\frac{5\vec{a}_x - \vec{a}_y}{\sqrt{26}}\right)$$

$$= \frac{25\times10^{-9}\times\left(5\vec{a}_x - \vec{a}_y\right)}{2\pi\times8.8854\times10^{-12}\times26} = 17.3\times\left(5\vec{a}_x - \vec{a}_y\right)$$

$$= 86.5\vec{a}_x - 17.3\vec{a}_y \ \text{V/m}$$

EXAMPLE 2.20

An infinitely long uniform line charge is located at $y = 5, z = 3$ with $\rho_l = 30\,\text{nC/m}$. Determine the field intensity $\vec{E}$ at (i) Origin (ii) $P(0,6,1)$ and (iii) $P(5,6,1)$.

SOLUTION

An infinitely long uniform line charge is shown in Figure E2.20 and it is parallel to x-axis. As line charge is parallel to x-axis, $\vec{E}$ cannot have any component in $\vec{a}_x$ direction. Hence, x-coordinate is not considered while calculating $\vec{R}$.

(i) To find the field intensity $\vec{E}$ at origin $(0,0,0)$, first determine the distance vector $\vec{R}$ between point $P(0,0,0)$ and other point $\left(x,3,5\right)$ on the line charge. Therefore,

$$\vec{R} = \left(0-5\right)\vec{a}_y + \left(0-3\right)\vec{a}_z = -5\vec{a}_y - 3\vec{a}_z$$

and its magnitude is

$$R = \left|\vec{R}\right| = \sqrt{(-5)^2 + (-3)^2} = \sqrt{34} = \rho$$

Therefore, the electric field intensity is

$$\vec{E} = \frac{\rho_l}{2\pi\varepsilon_0\rho}\vec{a}_\rho = \frac{\rho_l}{2\pi\varepsilon_0\rho}\left(\frac{\vec{R}}{\left|\vec{R}\right|}\right)$$

$$= \frac{30\times10^{-9}}{2\pi\times8.854\times10^{-12}\times\sqrt{34}}\left[\frac{-5\vec{a}_y - 3\vec{a}_z}{\sqrt{34}}\right]$$

$$= -80\vec{a}_y - 48\vec{a}_z \ \text{V/m}$$

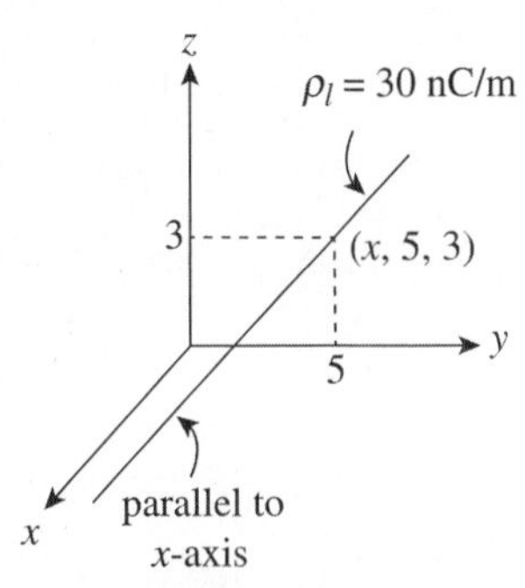

Figure E2.20

(ii) To find the field intensity $\vec{E}$ at $P(0,6,1)$, the distance vector $\vec{R}$ between point $P(0,6,1)$ and other point $(x,5,3)$ on the line charge is determined first. Therefore,

$$\vec{R} = (6-5)\vec{a}_y + (1-3)\vec{a}_z = \vec{a}_y - 2\vec{a}_z$$

and its magnitude is

$$R = |\vec{R}| = \sqrt{(1)^2 + (-2)^2} = \sqrt{5} = \rho$$

Therefore, the electric field intensity is

$$\vec{E} = \frac{\rho_l}{2\pi\varepsilon_0\rho}\vec{a}_\rho = \frac{30\times10^{-9}}{2\pi\times8.854\times10^{12}\times\sqrt{5}}\left[\frac{\vec{a}_y - 2\vec{a}_z}{\sqrt{5}}\right]$$

$$= 108\vec{a}_y - 216\vec{a}_z \text{ V/m}$$

(iii) As the electric field $\vec{E}$ does not have any component in x-direction and y, z-coordinates are same as in (ii), the electric field intensity $\vec{E}$ also remains same as obtained in (ii). Therefore, the electric field intensity at $P(5,6,1)$ is

$$\vec{E} = 108\vec{a}_y - 216\vec{a}_z \text{ V/m} \qquad \square$$

EXAMPLE 2.21

A semi-infinite line extending from $-\infty$ to 0 along the z-axis carries a uniform charge distribution of 200 nC/m. Determine the electric field intensity at point $P(0,0,2)$. If a charge of 1 μC is placed at P, calculate the force acting on it.

SOLUTION

Assume a differential charge element $dQ = \rho_l dz'$ at $z = z'$ from the origin, as shown in Figure E2.21. The distance vector from z' to P is

$$\vec{r} - \vec{r}' = (z - z')\vec{a}_z$$

and its magnitude is

$$|\vec{r} - \vec{r}'| = z - z'$$

Using Coulomb's law in vector form, the electric field intensity $\vec{E}$ at any point P due to a point charge Q can be written as

$$\vec{E} = \frac{Q}{4\pi\varepsilon_0 R^2}\vec{a}_R = \frac{Q(\vec{r}_2 - \vec{r}_1)}{4\pi\varepsilon_0|\vec{r}_2 - \vec{r}_1|^3}$$

where $\vec{a}_R$ is a unit vector in the direction of $\vec{R}$. Substituting the distance vector and its magnitude in the above field expression, the differential electric field intensity due to dz' at point P is

$$d\vec{E} = \frac{dQ}{4\pi\varepsilon_0(z - z')^2}\vec{a}_z$$

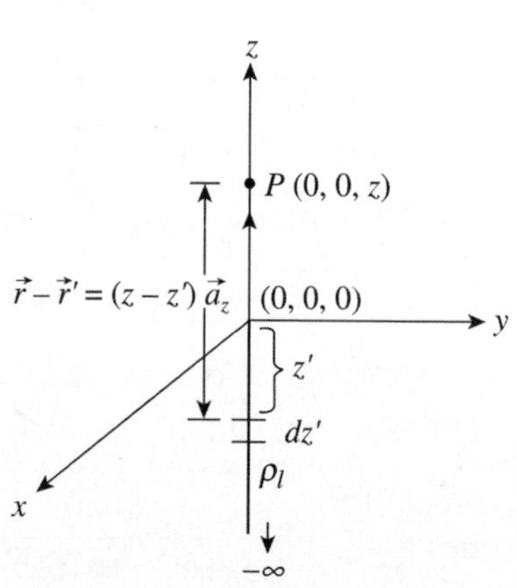

Figure E2.21

The total electric field intensity due to a semi-infinite line along the z-axis is obtained by integrating the above equation from $-\infty$ to 0 as

$$\vec{E} = \int_{-\infty}^{0} d\vec{E} = \frac{\rho_l}{4\pi\varepsilon_0} \int_{-\infty}^{0} \frac{dz'}{(z-z')^2} \vec{a}_z$$

$$= \frac{\rho_l}{4\pi\varepsilon_0 z} \vec{a}_z$$

Substituting $\rho_l = 200$ nC/m and $z = 2$, we get

$$\vec{E} = \frac{9\times10^9 \times 200\times10^{-9}}{2} \vec{a}_z = 900\vec{a}_z \text{ V/m}$$

where $\dfrac{1}{4\pi\varepsilon_0} = 9\times10^9$.

Therefore, the force acting on a charge of 1 μC at $z = 2$ is

$$\vec{F} = Q\vec{E} = 1\times10^{-6} \times 900\vec{a}_z = 900\vec{a}_z \text{ μN}$$

EXAMPLE 2.22

A circular ring of radius b carries a uniform line charge density of ρ_l and is placed on the xy-plane. Find the electric field intensity $\vec{E}$ at a point $P(0,0,h)$ along the axis of the ring at a distance h from its center.

SOLUTION

Consider a circular ring of radius b with uniform line charge density of ρ_l as shown in Figure E2.22(a). Here, the electric field generated by a differential segment of the ring (segment 1) situated at point $(b,\phi,0)$ in xy-plane. The differential segment length is denoted by $dl = bd\phi$ and the differential charge associated with this segment length is

$$dQ = \rho_l dl = \rho_l b d\phi$$

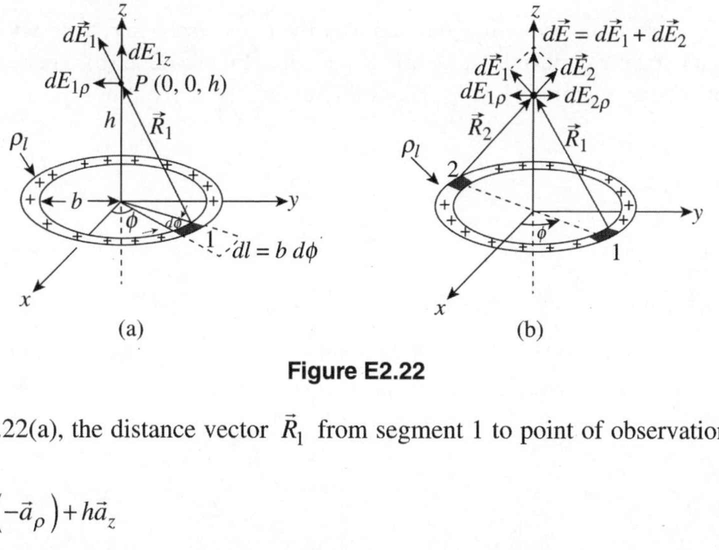

Figure E2.22

From Figure E2.22(a), the distance vector $\vec{R}_1$ from segment 1 to point of observation $P(0,0,h)$ can be written as

$$\vec{R}_1 = b\left(-\vec{a}_\rho\right) + h\vec{a}_z$$

and its magnitude is

$$R_1 = \left|\vec{R}_1\right| = \sqrt{b^2 + h^2}$$

Therefore, the unit vector is

$$\vec{a}_{R1} = \frac{\vec{R}_1}{\left|\vec{R}_1\right|} = \frac{-b\vec{a}_\rho + h\vec{a}_z}{\sqrt{b^2 + h^2}}$$

The electric field intensity at $P(0,0,h)$ due to the charge of segment 1 is

$$d\vec{E}_1 = \frac{dQ}{4\pi\varepsilon_0 R_1^2}\,\vec{a}_{R1} = \frac{\rho_l dl}{4\pi\varepsilon_0 R_1^2}\,\frac{\vec{R}_1}{\left|\vec{R}_1\right|}$$

$$= \frac{\rho_l b}{4\pi\varepsilon_0}\,\frac{\left(-b\vec{a}_\rho + h\vec{a}_z\right)}{\left(b^2 + h^2\right)^{3/2}}\,d\phi$$

The field intensity $d\vec{E}_1$ has component $dE_{1\rho}$ along $-\vec{a}_\rho$ direction and component dE_{1z} along $\vec{a}_z$ direction. Due to the symmetry of the charge distribution shown in Figure E2.22(b), the field is generated by differential line segment 2 located diametrically opposite to the location of differential line segment 1. It is identical with $d\vec{E}_1$ except that the $\vec{a}_\rho$ component of $d\vec{E}_2$ is opposite to that of $d\vec{E}_1$. Hence, the $\vec{a}_\rho$ components of $d\vec{E}_1$ and $d\vec{E}_2$ get cancelled and $d\vec{E}$ has only z-component.

Therefore, the electric field intensity due to both segment 1 and 2 is represented by

$$d\vec{E} = d\vec{E}_1 + d\vec{E}_2 = \frac{\rho_l b}{4\pi\varepsilon_0}\,\frac{\left(-b\vec{a}_\rho + h\vec{a}_z\right)}{\left(b^2 + h^2\right)^{3/2}}\,d\phi + \frac{\rho_l b}{4\pi\varepsilon_0}\,\frac{\left(b\vec{a}_\rho + h\vec{a}_z\right)}{\left(b^2 + h^2\right)^{3/2}}\,d\phi$$

$$= \frac{\rho_l bh}{2\pi\varepsilon_0}\,\frac{d\phi}{\left(b^2 + h^2\right)^{3/2}}\,\vec{a}_z \tag{1}$$

For every ring segment in the semicircle defined over the range $0 \le \phi \le \pi$, there will be a corresponding segment situated diametrically opposite at $(\phi + \pi)$, as shown in Figure E2.22(b). Therefore, the total electric field intensity is obtained by integrating Eq. (1) over the semicircle as given by

$$\vec{E} = \frac{\rho_l bh}{2\pi\varepsilon_0\left(b^2 + h^2\right)^{3/2}}\,\vec{a}_z \int_0^\pi d\phi$$

$$= \frac{\rho_l bh}{2\varepsilon_0\left(b^2 + h^2\right)^{3/2}}\,\vec{a}_z \tag{2}$$

The above equation shows that the electric field intensity $\vec{E}$ has only z-component and it is determined at a point P along the axis of the circular ring of radius b at a distance h from its center. Since the charge is uniformly distributed, the line charge density is expressed by

$$\rho_l = \frac{Q}{2\pi b} \tag{3}$$

Substituting Eq. (3) in Eq. (2), we get

$$\vec{E} = \frac{Qh}{4\pi\varepsilon_0 \left(b^2 + h^2\right)^{3/2}}\,\vec{a}_z$$

As the radius of the circular ring tends to zero, i.e., $b \to 0$, then the electric field is same as that of the field due to a point charge.

$$\vec{E} = \frac{Q}{4\pi\varepsilon_0 h^2}\,\vec{a}_z$$

In general, $\vec{E} = \dfrac{Q}{4\pi\varepsilon_0 R^2}\,\vec{a}_R$ (4)

This is the general expression for electric field intensity $\vec{E}$ at a point P due to a point charge Q located at the origin. ◻

EXAMPLE 2.23

A circular ring of charge of radius 2 m lies in the $z = 0$ plane, with the center at the origin. If it has uniform charge density $\rho_l = 10\,\text{nC/m}$, find the point charge Q at the origin which would produce the same electric field intensity $\vec{E}$ at $(0,0,5)\,\text{m}$.

SOLUTION

Figure E2.23 shows a circular ring of radius $b = 2\,\text{m}$ placed on the $z = 0$ plane with charge density $\rho_l = 10\,\text{nC/m}$.

From Example 2.22, the electric field intensity due to the circular ring at $(0,0,5)$ is

$$\vec{E} = \frac{\rho_l bh}{2\varepsilon_0 \left(b^2 + h^2\right)^{3/2}}\,\vec{a}_z$$

$$= \frac{10\times 10^{-9} \times 2 \times 5}{2 \times 8.854 \times 10^{-12} \times \left(2^2 + 5^2\right)^{3/2}}\,\vec{a}_z = 36.16\,\vec{a}_z\ \text{V/m}$$

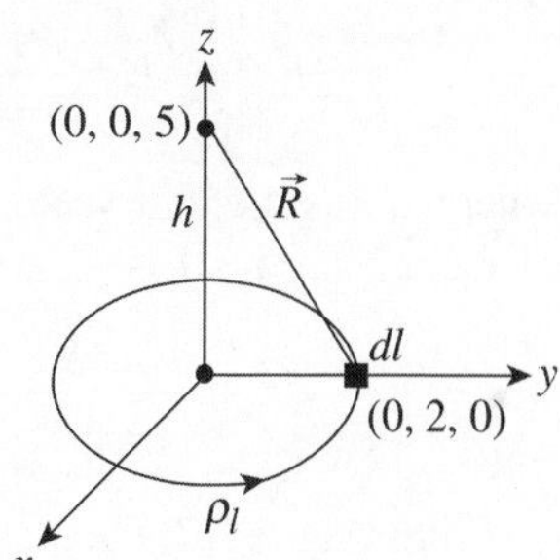

Figure E2.23

Similarly, the electric field intensity due to a point charge Q at the origin is

$$\vec{E} = \frac{Q}{4\pi\varepsilon_0 h^2}\,\vec{a}_z$$

If the electric field intensity is same at both the points, then

$$36.16\,\vec{a}_z = \frac{Q}{4\pi\varepsilon_0 \times 5^2}\,\vec{a}_z$$

$$Q = 100.4\,\text{nC}$$

◻

2.4.2 Field due to a Surface Charge

An infinite sheet of charge in the *xy*-plane with uniform surface charge density ρ_s is shown in Figure 2.7. The differential charge associated with differential elemental area *ds* is

$$dQ = \rho_s ds$$

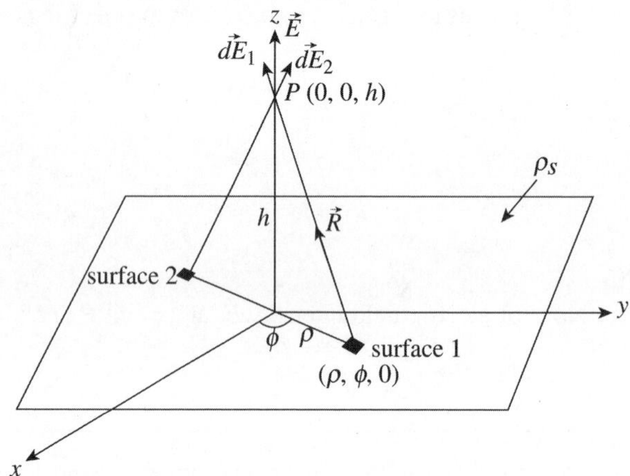

Figure 2.7 *Determination of electric field $\vec{E}$ due to surface charge distribution*

The electric field intensity $\vec{E}$ at a point $P(0,0,h)$ due to both elemental surfaces 1 and 2 is represented by

$$\vec{E} = \int_s d\vec{E} = \frac{1}{4\pi\varepsilon_0}\int_s \frac{\rho_s ds}{R^2}\vec{a}_R$$

where $\vec{a}_R$ is the unit vector along the direction of $\vec{R}$ and the differential electric field intensity due to the elemental surface 1 is

$$d\vec{E}_1 = \frac{dQ}{4\pi\varepsilon_0 R^2}\vec{a}_R = \frac{\rho_s ds}{4\pi\varepsilon_0 R^2}\frac{\vec{R}}{\left|\vec{R}\right|} \tag{2.18}$$

From Figure 2.7, the distance vector $\vec{R}$ between the elemental surface 1 $(\rho,\phi,0)$ and the arbitrary point $P(0,0,h)$ can be written as

$$\vec{R} = (0-\rho)\vec{a}_\rho + (h-0)\vec{a}_z = -\rho\vec{a}_\rho + h\vec{a}_z \tag{2.19}$$

and its magnitude is

$$R = \left|\vec{R}\right| = \sqrt{\rho^2 + h^2} \tag{2.20}$$

The differential charge in cylindrical coordinates is represented by

$$dQ = \rho_s ds = \rho_s \rho\, d\phi\, d\rho \tag{2.21}$$

Substituting Eqs. (2.19) to (2.21) in Eq. (2.18), we get

$$d\vec{E}_1 = \frac{\rho_s \rho\, d\phi\, d\rho\left(-\rho\vec{a}_\rho + h\vec{a}_z\right)}{4\pi\varepsilon_0\left(\rho^2 + h^2\right)^{3/2}} \tag{2.22}$$

Here, the field $d\vec{E}_1$ has component $dE_{1\rho}$ along $-\vec{a}_\rho$ direction and component dE_{1z} along $\vec{a}_z$ direction. From symmetry considerations, it is seen that the field is generated by the elemental surface 2 which is located diametrically opposite to the location of elemental surface 1. It is identical with $d\vec{E}_1$ except that the $\vec{a}_\rho$ component of $d\vec{E}_2$ is opposite to that of $d\vec{E}_1$. Hence, the contributions to $\vec{E}_\rho$ adds to zero and $\vec{E}$ has only z-component.

Therefore, the electric field intensity due to surface charge is represented by

$$\vec{E} = \int d\vec{E}_z = \frac{\rho_s}{4\pi\varepsilon_0} \int_{\phi=0}^{2\pi} \int_{\rho=0}^{\infty} \frac{h\rho\, d\rho\, d\phi}{\left[\rho^2 + h^2\right]^{3/2}} \vec{a}_z$$

For an infinite sheet charge, the limits for ρ are from 0 to ∞ and the limits for ϕ are from 0 to 2π.

$$\vec{E} == \frac{\rho_s h}{4\pi\varepsilon_0} \int_{\phi=0}^{2\pi} d\phi \int_0^{\infty} \frac{\rho\, d\rho}{\left[\rho^2 + h^2\right]^{3/2}} \vec{a}_z = \frac{2\pi\rho_s h}{4\pi\varepsilon_0} \int_0^{\infty} \frac{\rho\, d\rho}{\left[\rho^2 + h^2\right]^{3/2}} \vec{a}_z$$

To evaluate the integral, let $\rho^2 + h^2 = t^2$. Then $2\rho\, d\rho = 2t\, dt$. The limits are from h to ∞.

Therefore, $\vec{E} = \dfrac{\rho_s h}{4\pi\varepsilon_0} \displaystyle\int_h^{\infty} \frac{t\, dt}{t^3} \vec{a}_z = \dfrac{\rho_s h}{2\varepsilon_0} \displaystyle\int_h^{\infty} \frac{dt}{t^2} \vec{a}_z = \dfrac{\rho_s h}{2\varepsilon_0}\left(\dfrac{1}{h}\right) \vec{a}_z$

$$= \frac{\rho_s}{2\varepsilon_0} \vec{a}_z \tag{2.23}$$

Here, the electric field intensity $\vec{E}$ has only z-component and it is also independent of the distance between the sheet and the point of observation P. In general, for an *infinite sheet of charge*, the electric field intensity can be written as

$$\vec{E} = \frac{\rho_s}{2\varepsilon_0} \vec{a}_n \tag{2.24}$$

where $\vec{a}_n$ is a unit vector normal to the sheet. The above expression can be used to find the electric field intensity between the two plates in a parallel-plate capacitor with equal and opposite charges.

Therefore, $\vec{E} = \dfrac{\rho_s}{2\varepsilon_0} \vec{a}_n + \dfrac{-\rho_s}{2\varepsilon_0}\left(-\vec{a}_n\right) = \dfrac{\rho_s}{\varepsilon_0} \vec{a}_n$

EXAMPLE 2.24

Determine the electric field intensity at a point $P(0,0,h)$ in free space at a height h on the z-axis due to a circular disc of charge in the xy-plane with uniform surface charge density of ρ_s. Also, evaluate the field intensity $\vec{E}$ for the infinite sheet case.

SOLUTION

To determine the electric field intensity at a point $P(0,0,h)$ due to a circular disc of charge, the expression for the electric field intensity due to a circular ring of charge, derived in Example 2.22 can be used. The circular disc is shown in Figure E2.24 and it can be treated as a set of concentric rings in order to determine its field.

Assuming $\rho = r$ in cylindrical coordinates, the surface area of a circular ring of radius r along z is

$$ds = r\, dr\, d\phi = 2\pi r\, dr$$

and the differential charge associated with differential elemental area *ds* is

$$dQ = \rho_s\,ds = 2\pi\rho_s r\,dr$$

From Example 2.22, the electric field intensity due to a circular ring of charge is

$$\vec{E} = \frac{\rho_l bh}{2\varepsilon_0\left(b^2 + h^2\right)^{3/2}}\,\vec{a}_z = \frac{hQ}{4\pi\varepsilon_0\left(b^2 + h^2\right)^{3/2}}\,\vec{a}_z \quad (1)$$

where $Q = 2\pi b\rho_l$ is the total charge contained in the ring.

Replacing *b* with *r* in Eq. (1), the expression for the differential electric field intensity due to a circular ring can be written as

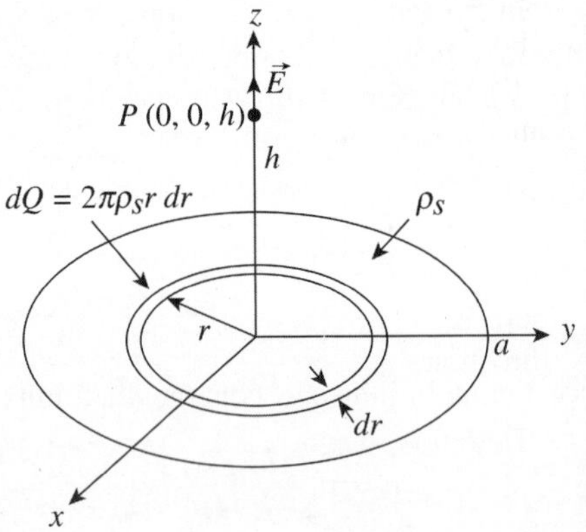

$$d\vec{E} = \frac{h\,dQ}{4\pi\varepsilon_0\left(b^2 + h^2\right)^{3/2}}\,\vec{a}_z = \frac{h\left(2\pi\rho_s\,r\,dr\right)}{4\pi\varepsilon_0\left(r^2 + h^2\right)^{3/2}}\,\vec{a}_z$$

$$= \frac{\rho_s h r\,dr}{2\varepsilon_0\left(r^2 + h^2\right)^{3/2}}\,\vec{a}_z \tag{2}$$

Therefore, the total electric field intensity at *P* is obtained by integrating the above equation over the region from $r = 0$ to $r = a$ as given by

$$\vec{E} = \int_{r=0}^{r=a} d\vec{E} = \frac{\rho_s h}{2\varepsilon_0}\int_0^a \frac{r\,dr}{\left(r^2 + h^2\right)^{3/2}}\,\vec{a}_z$$

$$= \pm\frac{\rho_s}{2\varepsilon_0}\left[1 - \frac{|h|}{\sqrt{a^2 + h^2}}\right]\vec{a}_z \tag{3}$$

The electric field intensity $\vec{E}$ due to circular disc of charge is determined by using the above equation. Here, the plus sign corresponds to $h > 0$ (above the disc) and the minus sign corresponds to $h < 0$ (below the disc).

When *a* tends to ∞, the circular disc of charge becomes an *infinite sheet of charge* and its electric field is

$$\vec{E} = \frac{\rho_s}{2\varepsilon_0}\,\vec{a}_z \tag{4}$$

For an infinite sheet of charge, the above equation shows that the electric field is in *+ve* *z*-direction i.e., above the *xy*-plane. For points located below the *xy*-plane, the unit vector $\vec{a}_z$ is replaced with $-\vec{a}_z$ and the electric field will be in *–ve z* direction.   ❑

Figure E2.24

EXAMPLE 2.25

A uniform surface charge of $\rho_s = 2\,\mu\text{C/m}^2$ is situated at $z = 2$ plane. Determine the electric field intensity at $P(1,1,1)$.

SOLUTION

The $z = 2$ plane is shown in Figure E2.25 and point $P(1,1,1)$ is located below the plane.

For an infinite sheet of charge with surface charge density of ρ_s, the electric field intensity for points located below the $z = 2$ plane is

$$\vec{E} = \frac{\rho_s}{2\varepsilon_0}\vec{a}_n = \frac{\rho_s}{2\varepsilon_0}\left(-\vec{a}_z\right)$$

where $\vec{a}_n$ is a unit vector normal to the sheet and it is in the $-ve$ z-direction.

Therefore, $\vec{E} = \dfrac{2\times10^{-6}}{2\times8.854\times10^{-12}}\left(-\vec{a}_z\right) = -112.94\vec{a}_z$ kV/m □

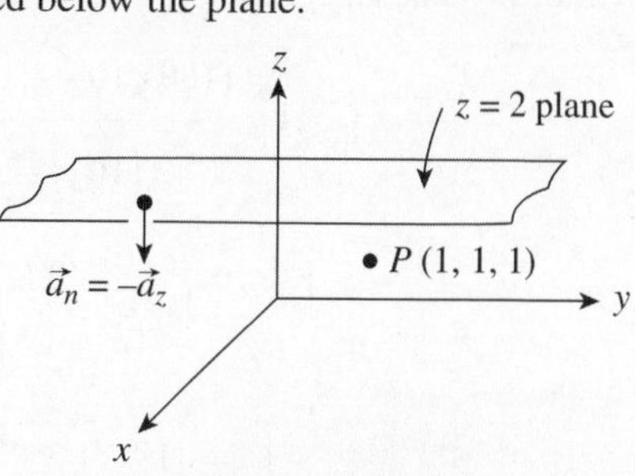

Figure E2.25

EXAMPLE 2.26

Find the force on a point charge of 100 μC at $(0,0,5)$ m due to a charge of 500π μC that is uniformly distributed over the circular disc with $r \le 5$ m, $z = 0$ m as shown in Figure E2.26.

SOLUTION

The surface charge density is

$$\rho_s = \frac{Q}{A} = \frac{500\pi\times10^{-6}}{\pi(5)^2} = 0.2\times10^{-4}\ \text{C/m}^2$$

Assume the radius $\rho = r$ in cylindrical coordinates.
From Fig. E2.26, the distance vector in cylindrical coordinates is

$$\vec{R} = -r\vec{a}_r + 5\vec{a}_z$$

and it magnitude is

$$R = \left|\vec{R}\right| = \sqrt{r^2 + 25}$$

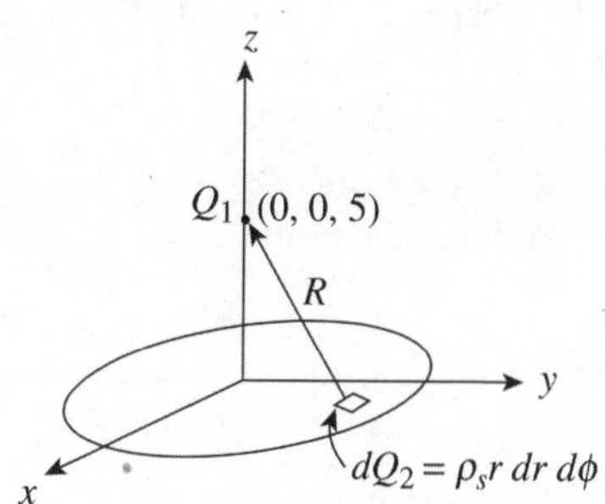

Figure E2.26

From Coulomb's law, the force between the charges is

$$\vec{F} = \frac{Q_1 Q_2}{4\pi\varepsilon_0 R^2}\vec{a}_R$$

Then, each differential charge results in a differential force which can be written as

$$d\vec{F} = \frac{dQ_1 dQ_2}{4\pi\varepsilon_0 R^2}\vec{a}_R = \frac{dQ_1 \rho_s ds}{4\pi\varepsilon_0 R^2}\frac{\vec{R}}{\left|\vec{R}\right|}$$

where the surface area along the radial direction in cylindrical coordinates is

$$ds = r\, dr\, d\phi$$

Therefore, $d\vec{F} = \dfrac{\left(100\times10^{-6}\right)\left(\rho_s r\, dr\, d\phi\right)}{4\pi\left(10^{-9}/36\pi\right)\left(r^2 + 25\right)}\left(\dfrac{-r\vec{a}_r + 5\vec{a}_z}{\sqrt{r^2 + 25}}\right)$

Due to symmetrical charge distribution in a circular disc, the radial components get cancelled and only $\vec{a}_z$ will be present. Integrating the above equation over ϕ and r, we get

$$\vec{F} = \int_0^{2\pi} \int_0^5 \frac{\left(100 \times 10^{-6}\right)\left(0.2 \times 10^{-4}\right) 5r\, dr\, d\phi}{4\pi \left(10^{-9}/36\pi\right)\left(r^2 + 25\right)^{3/2}} \vec{a}_z$$

$$= 90 \int_0^{2\pi} d\phi \int_0^5 \frac{r\, dr}{\left(r^2 + 25\right)^{3/2}} \vec{a}_z$$

$$= 180\pi \left[\frac{-1}{\sqrt{r^2 + 25}}\right]_0^5 \vec{a}_z = 33.12\, \vec{a}_z \ \text{N} \qquad \square$$

<hr>

EXAMPLE 2.27

The charge lies on the circular disc $r \le 4$ m, $z = 0$ with density $\rho_s = \left(10^{-7}/r\right)$ C/m^2. Determine the electric field intensity $\vec{E}$ at $r = 0$, $z = 3$ m.

SOLUTION

The electric field intensity for surface charge distribution is

$$\vec{E} = \int_s d\vec{E} = \frac{1}{4\pi\varepsilon_0} \int_s \frac{\rho_s ds}{R^2} \vec{a}_R$$

Assume the radius $\rho = r$ in cylindrical coordinates. The differential electric field intensity is

$$d\vec{E} = \frac{\left(10^{-7}/r\right) r\, dr\, d\phi}{4\pi\varepsilon_0 \left(r^2 + 9\right)} \left(\frac{-r\vec{a}_r + 3\vec{a}_z}{\sqrt{r^2 + 9}}\right) \qquad (\text{since } ds = r\, dr\, d\phi)$$

For a circular disc, the radial component vanishes by symmetry and only $\vec{a}_z$ exists. Integrating the above equation, we have

$$\vec{E} = \left(2.7 \times 10^3\right) \int_0^{2\pi} d\phi \int_0^4 \frac{dr}{(r^3 + 9)^{3/2}} \vec{a}_z$$

$$= 2.7 \times 10^3 \times 2\pi \left[\frac{r}{9\sqrt{r^2 + 9}}\right]_0^4 = 1.51 \vec{a}_z \ \text{kV/m} \qquad \square$$

<hr>

EXAMPLE 2.28

The charge lies in the $z = -3$ m plane in the form of a square sheet defined by $-2 \le x \le 2$ m, $-2 \le y \le 2$ m with charge density $\rho_s = \left(x^2 + y^2 + 9\right)^{3/2}$ nC/m^2. Find $\vec{E}$ at the origin.

SOLUTION

From Figure E2.28, the distance vector between the origin (0,0,0) and the charge dQ at $(x, y, -3)$ is

$$\vec{R} = -x\vec{a}_x - y\vec{a}_y + 3\vec{a}_z$$

and its magnitude is

$$R = \left|\vec{R}\right| = \sqrt{x^2 + y^2 + 9}$$

The charge with surface charge density is

$$dQ = \rho_s ds = \rho_s dxdy = \left(x^2 + y^2 + 9\right)^{3/2} \times 10^{-9}\, dx\, dy$$

Therefore, the electric field intensity for surface charge distribution is

$$\vec{E} = \int_s d\vec{E} = \frac{1}{4\pi\varepsilon_0} \int_s \frac{\rho_s ds}{R^2}\, \vec{a}_R$$

where the unit vector is $\vec{a}_R = \dfrac{\vec{R}}{\left|\vec{R}\right|}$.

Hence, the differential electric field intensity is

$$d\vec{E} = \frac{\left(x^2 + y^2 + 9\right)^{3/2} \times 10^{-9}\, dx\, dy}{4\pi\varepsilon_0 \left(x^2 + y^2 + 9\right)} \left[\frac{-x\vec{a}_x - y\vec{a}_y + 3\vec{a}_z}{\sqrt{x^2 + y^2 + 9}}\right]$$

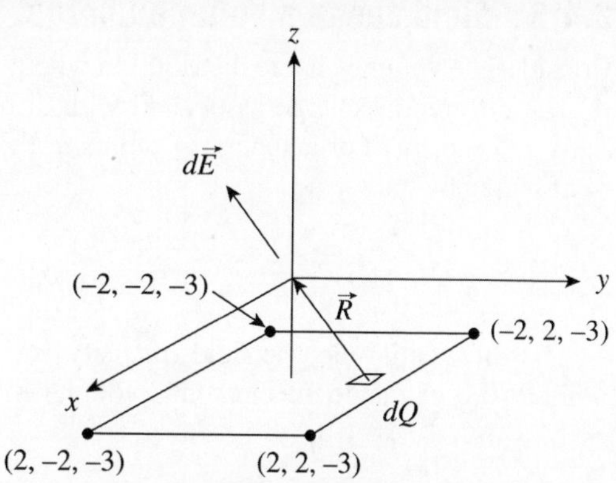

Figure E2.28

Due to symmetry, only the z component of $\vec{E}$ exists. Integrating the above equation, we get

$$\vec{E} = \int_{-2}^{2}\int_{-2}^{2} \frac{3\times 10^{-9}\, dx\, dy}{4\pi\varepsilon_0}\, \vec{a}_z = \frac{3\times 10^{-9}}{4\pi \times \dfrac{10^{-9}}{36\pi}} \int_{-2}^{2} dx \int_{-2}^{2} dy\, \vec{a}_z$$

$$= 27 \times \left[x\right]_{-2}^{2} \times \left[y\right]_{-2}^{2}\, \vec{a}_z = 432\, \vec{a}_z\ \text{V/m}$$

EXAMPLE 2.29

A circular disc of 10 cm radius is charged uniformly with a total charge of 100 μC. Determine the electric field intensity at a point 20 cm on its axis.

SOLUTION

Consider a circular disc of radius $a = 10$ cm placed in the xy-plane. The electric field intensity due to a circular disc of charge 100 μC at a height $h = 20$ cm on its axis is

$$\vec{E} = \frac{\rho_s}{2\varepsilon_0}\left[1 - \frac{h}{\sqrt{a^2 + h^2}}\right]\vec{a}_z$$

where surface charge density, $\rho_s = \dfrac{Q}{A} = \dfrac{100\times 10^{-6}}{\pi a^2} = 3.184 \times 10^{-3}\, \text{C/m}^2$

Therefore, $\vec{E} = \dfrac{3.184\times 10^{-3}}{2\times 8.854\times 10^{-12}}\left[1 - \dfrac{0.2}{\sqrt{0.1^2 + 0.2^2}}\right]\vec{a}_z = 18.97\times 10^{6}\, \vec{a}_z\, \text{V/m}$

2.4.3 Field due to a Volume Charge

Consider the volume charge distribution with a uniform charge density ρ_v as shown in Figure 2.8.

The differential charge associated with differential volume dv is $dQ = \rho_v dv$. For a sphere of radius a, the total charge is represented by

$$Q = \int_v \rho_v dv = \rho_v \int_v dv = \frac{4\pi a^3}{3}\,\rho_v$$

The differential electric field intensity $d\vec{E}$ at an arbitrary point $P(0,0,z)$ due to the elemental volume is

$$d\vec{E} = \frac{\rho_v dv}{4\pi\varepsilon_0 R^2}\,\vec{a}_R$$

where $\vec{a}_R = \cos\alpha\,\vec{a}_z + \sin\alpha\,\vec{a}_\rho$. From symmetry considerations, the x or y-component of the electric field intensity sum up to zero and only z-component exists. Hence, the electric field intensity along z is given by

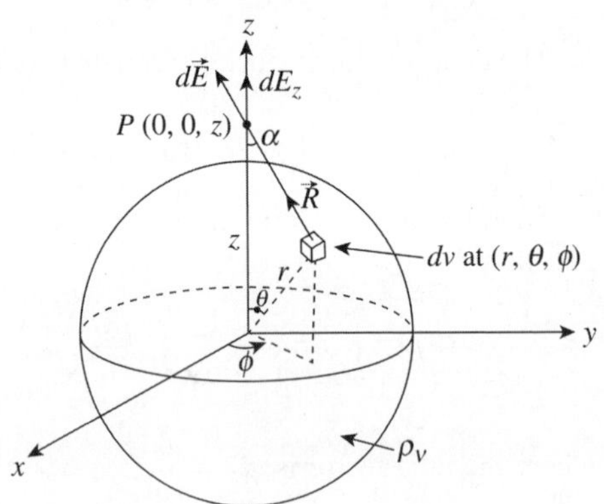

Figure 2.8 *Determination of electric field $\vec{E}$ due to volume charge distribution*

$$E_z = \vec{E}\cdot\vec{a}_z = \int_v dE\cos\alpha = \frac{\rho_v}{4\pi\varepsilon_0}\int_v \frac{\cos\alpha}{R^2}dv \tag{2.25}$$

The differential volume in spherical coordinates is written as

$$dv = r^2 \sin\theta\, dr\, d\theta\, d\phi$$

Applying the cosine rule to Figure 2.8, the distance R between the elemental volume at (r,θ,ϕ) and the arbitrary point P at $(0,0,z)$ can be written as

$$R^2 = z^2 + r^2 - 2zr\cos\theta$$

and the distance from origin to elemental volume is written as

$$r^2 = z^2 + R^2 - 2zR\cos\alpha$$

The integration over the electric field is performed in terms of R and r. Using trignometry, $\cos\theta, \cos\alpha$ and $\sin\theta\,d\theta$ can be expressed in terms of R and r as

$$\cos\alpha = \frac{z^2 + R^2 - r^2}{2zR} \text{ and } \cos\theta = \frac{z^2 + r^2 - R^2}{2zr} \tag{2.26}$$

Differentiating the above equation with respect to θ with z and r as constants, we get

$$\sin\theta\,d\theta = \frac{R\,dR}{zr}$$

Substituting the above terms in Eq. (2.25), we get

$$E_z = \frac{\rho_v}{4\pi\varepsilon_0}\int_v r^2 \sin\theta\, dr\, d\theta\, d\phi\,\frac{\cos\alpha}{R^2}$$

$$= \frac{\rho_v}{4\pi\varepsilon_0}\int_{\phi=0}^{2\pi} d\phi \int_{r=0}^{a}\int_{R=z-r}^{z+r} r^2\,\frac{R\,dR}{zr}\,\frac{z^2+R^2-r^2}{2zR}\,\frac{1}{R^2}$$

$$= \frac{2\pi\rho_v}{8\pi\varepsilon_0 z^2} \int_{r=0}^{a} \int_{R=z-r}^{z+r} r\left[1 + \frac{z^2 - r^2}{R^2}\right] dR\, dr$$

$$= \frac{\pi\rho_v}{4\pi\varepsilon_0 z^2} \int_0^a r \left[R - \frac{\left(z^2 - r^2\right)}{R} \right]_{z-r}^{z+r} dr$$

$$= \frac{\pi\rho_v}{4\pi\varepsilon_0 z^2} \int_0^a 4r^2\, dr = \frac{\pi\rho_v}{4\pi\varepsilon_0 z^2}\left[4\frac{r^3}{3}\right]_0^a$$

$$= \frac{1}{4\pi\varepsilon_0 z^2}\left(\frac{4}{3}\pi a^3\, \rho_v\right) = \frac{Q}{4\pi\varepsilon_0 z^2}$$

where Q = charge density $\times$ volume.

The electric field intensity $\vec{E}$ along z-direction at $P(0,0,z)$ can also be written as

$$\vec{E} = \frac{Q}{4\pi\varepsilon_0 z^2}\vec{a}_z$$

Due to the symmetry of the charge distribution, the electric field along r-direction at $P(r,\theta,\phi)$ is given by

$$\vec{E} = \frac{Q}{4\pi\varepsilon_0 r^2}\vec{a}_r \tag{2.27}$$

The above equation is identical to the electric field expression at the same point P due to a point charge Q located at the origin or at the center of the spherical charge distribution.

2.5 ELECTRIC FLUX LINES AND FLUX DENSITY

Electric flux lines are the lines of electric fields and its direction at any point is in the direction of the electric field intensity at that point. Assume a test charge is placed at one point in an electric field and it is allowed to move. The force acting on the test charge will move it along a certain path. This path is called electric lines of force or electric field pattern or simply flux lines.

By placing the test charge at a new location, another line of force can be created. Therefore, many lines of force can be created by repeating the process. The number of lines of force due to a charge is equal to the magnitude of the charge in coulomb. Hence, the unit of electric flux is coulomb. The field lines are used to represent the electric flux. The idea of electric lines of force or electric flux lines is an important concept used in the representation, visualization and description of the electric field.

For an isolated positive point charge, the electric flux points radially outward as shown in Figure 2.9(a). The electric field pattern or flux lines for a pair of equal and opposite point charges i.e., electric dipole is indicated in Figure 2.9(b). The flux lines between two positively charged bodies are represented in Figure 2.9(c).

From Figure 2.9, it is observed that the electric field intensity at any point is tangential to the electric flux lines. The magnitude of electric flux depends solely upon the charge from which it originates and it is independent of the medium. The electric field intensity also satisfies these constraints but its magnitude depends on the permittivity of the medium. Hence, the electric flux density $\vec{D}$ can be defined in terms of electric field intensity $\vec{E}$ as

$$\vec{D} = \varepsilon_0 \vec{E}$$

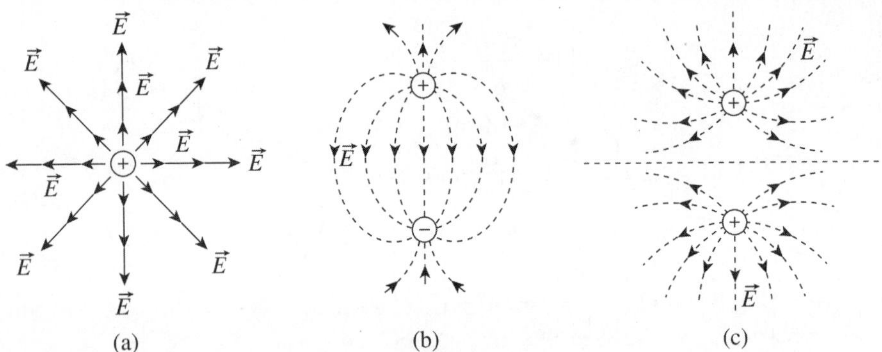

Figure 2.9 *Electric flux lines: (a) for a point charge (b) for electric dipole and (c) between two +ve charges*

where ε_0 is the permittivity of free space. As the electric field intensity $\vec{E}$ at any point is tangential to the electric flux lines, the electric flux density $\vec{D}$ is also tangential to the flux lines.

Substituting for $\vec{E}$ due to a point charge Q in the above equation, we get

$$\vec{D} = \varepsilon_0 \frac{Q}{4\pi\varepsilon_0 r^2}\,\vec{a}_r$$

$$= \frac{Q}{4\pi r^2}\,\vec{a}_r$$

Here, the electric flux density $\vec{D}$ has the units of coulomb per square metre (C/m^2). The *electric flux density* $\vec{D}$ can also be defined as the ratio of flux (Ψ) or charge (Q) per unit area. Therefore,

$$\vec{D} = \frac{\Psi}{A} = \frac{Q}{A}$$

The unit of flux is coulomb. Therefore, the electric flux Ψ can be defined in terms of flux density $\vec{D}$ as

$$\psi = Q = \int_s \vec{D}\cdot d\vec{s}$$

where $d\vec{s}$ is the differential surface element on surface s, as shown in Figure 2.10. The flux passing through s is maximum if $\vec{D}$ and $d\vec{s}$ are in the same direction.

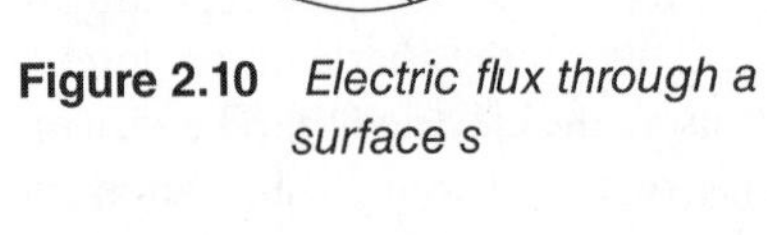

Figure 2.10 *Electric flux through a surface s*

2.5.1 Properties of Electric Field Lines

The properties of electric field lines or flux lines are:

(*i*) The direction of the electric field intensity $\vec{E}$ at a point is tangential to the field lines.

(*ii*) Electric field lines or flux lines never cross each other.

(*iii*) The field lines must begin on a positive charge and terminate on a negative charge.

(*iv*) Electric flux lines are most dense around objects with the greatest amount of charge.

(*v*) The number of field lines that originate from a positive charge or terminate on a negative charge must be proportional to the magnitude of the charge.

2.6 GAUSS'S LAW

Gauss's law states that the net outward flux passing through a closed surface s is equal to the charge Q enclosed by that surface as given by

$$\oint_s \vec{D} \cdot d\vec{s} = \psi = Q \tag{2.28}$$

To prove Gauss's law, assume a point charge Q is enclosed at point O by an arbitrary surface s, as shown in Figure 2.11. Since $\vec{D} = \varepsilon_0 \vec{E}$, the electric flux density for a point charge Q at point P on the closed surface s is represented by

$$\vec{D} = \frac{Q}{4\pi R^2} \vec{a}_R \tag{2.29}$$

where the distance vector from O to P is denoted by $\vec{R} = \vec{r} - \vec{r}' = R\vec{a}_R$.

Figure 2.11 shows the electric flux flowing outwards through a closed surface s from a point charge Q enclosed by s. The electric flux Ψ passing through the closed surface s is given by

$$\psi = \oint_s \vec{D} \cdot d\vec{s} = \frac{Q}{4\pi} \oint_s \frac{\vec{a}_R \cdot \vec{a}_n\, ds}{R^2} \tag{2.30}$$

The integrand on the right hand side of the above equation is the solid angle $d\Omega$, subtended by the surface ds at O as shown in Figure 2.11. Therefore, the above equation can be written as

$$\psi = \frac{Q}{4\pi} \oint_s d\Omega$$

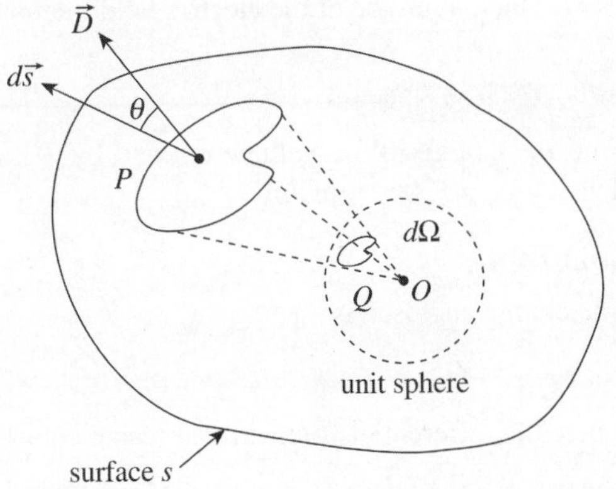

The solid angle $d\Omega$ subtended by any closed surface is denoted by 4π steradian or square radian, which is the unit of solid angle. Hence, the total flux passing through the closed surface is

Figure 2.11 *Electric Flux from a point charge Q enclosed by a closed surface s*

$$\psi = \oint_s \vec{D} \cdot d\vec{s} = \frac{Q}{4\pi} 4\pi = Q$$

Therefore, $\oint_s \vec{D} \cdot d\vec{s} = Q$ $\tag{2.31}$

The above equation is a mathematical statement of Gauss's law and the surface over which the integral is taken is called *Gaussian surface*. It is clear that the charge outside the closed surface does not contribute to the total charge enclosed. As $\vec{D} = \varepsilon_0 \vec{E}$, Gauss's law can also be expressed in terms of electric field intensity $\vec{E}$ in free space as

$$\oint_s \vec{E} \cdot d\vec{s} = \frac{Q}{\varepsilon_0}$$

Suppose if the charge distribution is characterized by volume charge density ρ_v, then Gauss's law is written as

$$\oint_s \vec{D} \cdot d\vec{s} = Q = \int_v \rho_v\, dv \tag{2.32}$$

Similarly, Eq. (2.32) can be written in terms of line charge density and surface charge density if the charges are distributed over a surface or a linear element. This equation is called the *integral form of Gauss's law* which states that the outward flow of flux $\vec{D}$ through a surface is proportional to the enclosed charge Q.

Gauss's law constitutes one of the fundamental laws of electromagnetism. It can be used to determine the total charge enclosed if the electric field intensity or flux density is known at all points on the surface. Gauss's law is applicable if the charge distribution is symmetric and the flux density is constant over the chosen surface. As a result, it greatly reduces the complexity of field problems.

The following steps may be useful when applying Gauss's law for solving field problems:

(*i*) First, the symmetry associated with the charge distribution is identified.

(*ii*) Then a Gaussian surface is identified and the direction of electric field is determined.

(*iii*) The field space associated with the charge distribution is divided into different regions. For each region, the net charge enclosed by the Gaussian surface, Q_{enc} is calculated.

(*iv*) Then the electric flux Ψ through the Gaussian surface for each region is found.

(*v*) The magnitude of the electric field intensity is deduced by equating Ψ with $\dfrac{Q_{enc}}{\varepsilon}$.

EXAMPLE 2.30

Find the charge in the volume defined by $0 \le x \le 1$ m, $0 \le y \le 1$ m and $0 \le z \le 1$ m, if the volume charge density $\rho_v = 120\,x^2 y$ μC/m^3.

SOLUTION

The charge enclosed is

$$Q = \int_v \rho_v \, dv$$

where the differential volume in cartesian coordinates is

$$dv = dx\,dy\,dz$$

Therefore, $Q = \int_0^1 \int_0^1 \int_0^1 \left(120 x^2 y \times 10^{-6}\right) dx\,dy\,dz$

$$= 120 \times 10^{-6} \left[\frac{x^3}{3}\right]_0^1 \left[\frac{y^2}{2}\right]_0^1 [z]_0^1 = 120 \times 10^{-6} \times \frac{1}{3} \times \frac{1}{2}$$

$$= 20\,\mu C$$

EXAMPLE 2.31

If $\rho_v = \dfrac{5\cos^2\phi}{r^4}$ C/m^3, determine the charge in the volume defined by $1 \le r \le 2$ m in spherical coordinates.

SOLUTION

The total charge contained in the volume is

$$Q = \int_v \rho_v \, dv$$

where the differential volume in spherical coordinates is

$$dv = r^2 \sin\theta \, dr \, d\theta \, d\phi$$

Therefore, $Q = \int_0^{2\pi} \int_0^{\pi} \int_1^2 \left(\dfrac{5\cos^2\phi}{r^4} \right) r^2 \sin\theta \, dr \, d\theta \, d\phi$

$$= 5 \times \int_0^{2\pi} \cos^2\phi \, d\phi \times \int_0^{\pi} \sin\theta \, d\theta \times \int_1^2 \left(\dfrac{1}{r^2} \right) dr$$

$$= 5 \times \dfrac{1}{2} \times \left[\phi + \dfrac{\sin 2\phi}{2} \right]_0^{2\pi} \times \left[-\cos\theta \right]_0^{\pi} \times \left[\dfrac{-1}{r} \right]_1^2 \qquad \left(\text{since } \cos^2\phi = \dfrac{1 + \cos 2\phi}{2} \right)$$

$$= 5 \times \dfrac{1}{2} \times 2\pi \times 2 \times \dfrac{1}{2} = 5\pi \, \text{C} \qquad \square$$

2.7 GAUSS'S DIVERGENCE THEOREM

The divergence theorem states that the volume integral of the divergence of any vector over a volume v is equal to the total outward flux of that vector through the surface s enclosing volume v. Therefore, for an electric flux density vector $\vec{D}$, the *Gauss's divergence theorem* is expressed as

$$\int_v \left(\nabla \cdot \vec{D} \right) dv = \oint_s \vec{D} \cdot d\vec{s}$$

The divergence theorem applies to both time-varying fields and static fields in any coordinate system. This theorem is mostly used in derivations where it becomes necessary to change a closed surface integration to volume integration. But it may also be used to convert the volume integral of the divergence of a vector field into a closed surface integral. The proof for this theorem is explained in section 1.9 of Chapter 1.

Since $\oint_s \vec{D} \cdot d\vec{s} = Q = \int_v \rho_v \, dv$, Gauss's divergence theorem becomes

$$\int_v \left(\nabla \cdot \vec{D} \right) dv = \int_v \rho_v \, dv$$

Comparing the integrands on both sides of the above equation, we get

$$\nabla \cdot \vec{D} = \rho_v \tag{2.33}$$

This equation is called the *point or differential form of Gauss's law*. For a positive charge density, the electric flux lines flow outwards from any point in space whereas for a negative charge density, the flux lines converge towards the point. The above equation shows that the electric flux density is always a measure of free charges present in a region.

EXAMPLE 2.32

The electric flux density in a charge free region is given by $\vec{D} = 10x\,\vec{a}_x + 5y\,\vec{a}_y + kz\,\vec{a}_z \, \mu\text{C/m}^2$. Find the constant k.

SOLUTION

For a charge free region, $\rho_v = 0$ and $\nabla \cdot \vec{D} = \rho_v = 0$

$$\nabla \cdot \vec{D} = \dfrac{\partial D_x}{\partial x} + \dfrac{\partial D_y}{\partial y} + \dfrac{\partial D_z}{\partial z} = 0$$

$$10 + 5 + k = 0$$

Therefore, $k = -15$ $\qquad \square$

EXAMPLE 2.33

Given the electric flux density, $\vec{D} = \left(y + e^x\right)\vec{a}_x - ye^{-y}\vec{a}_y + z\vec{a}_z$ C/m^2, determine the volume charge density in the electric field.

SOLUTION

From point form of Gauss's law,

$$\nabla \cdot \vec{D} = \rho_v$$

In Cartesian system, the volume charge density ρ_v is

$$\rho_v = \nabla \cdot \vec{D} = \frac{\partial D_x}{\partial x} + \frac{\partial D_y}{\partial y} + \frac{\partial D_z}{\partial z}$$

$$= \frac{\partial\left(y + e^x\right)}{\partial x} + \frac{\partial\left(-ye^{-y}\right)}{\partial y} + \frac{\partial(z)}{\partial z}$$

$$= e^x - \left[ye^{-y}(-1) + e^{-y}(1)\right] + 1$$

$$= e^x + ye^{-y} - e^{-y} + 1 = e^x + e^{-y}(y - 1) + 1$$

EXAMPLE 2.34

Prove that the divergence of the electric field intensity and that of electric flux density in charge free region is zero.

SOLUTION

From point form of Gauss's Law,

$$\nabla \cdot \vec{D} = \rho_v$$

$$\nabla \cdot \left(\varepsilon_0 \vec{E}\right) = \rho_v$$

Therefore, $\nabla \cdot \vec{E} = \dfrac{\rho_v}{\varepsilon_0}$

As $Q = 0$ in charge free region, no charge density ρ_v exists in such a region. Substituting $\rho_v = 0$ in the above equation, we get

$$\nabla \cdot \vec{D} = \nabla \cdot \vec{E} = 0$$

Hence, the divergence of flux density $\vec{D}$ and field intensity $\vec{E}$ are zero in a charge free region.

EXAMPLE 2.35

Given $\vec{D} = z\rho \cos^2 \phi \, \vec{a}_z$ C/m^2, calculate the charge density at $\left(1, \dfrac{\pi}{4}, 3\right)$ and the total charge enclosed by the cylinder of radius $\rho = 1$ m with $-2 \leq z \leq 2$ m.

SOLUTION

From point from of Gauss's law, the volume charge density is

$$\rho_v = \nabla \cdot \vec{D} = \frac{\partial D_z}{\partial z} = \rho \cos^2 \phi$$

The point is given in cylindrical coordinates as $\left(1,\dfrac{\pi}{4},3\right)$ and ρ_v at this point can be written as

$$\rho_v = \cos^2\left(\pi/4\right) = 0.5\,\text{C/m}^3$$

Therefore, the charge enclosed by the cylinder is

$$Q = \int_v \rho_v\,dv = \int_v \rho\cos^2\phi\,\rho\,d\rho\,d\phi\,dz$$

where $dv = \rho\,d\rho\,d\phi\,dz$ in cylindrical coordinates.

Therefore, $Q = \displaystyle\int_{\rho=0}^{1}\rho^2\,d\rho\int_{\phi=0}^{2\pi}\cos^2\phi\,d\phi\int_{z=-2}^{2}dz$

$$= \frac{4\pi}{3}C$$

EXAMPLE 2.36

Show that the divergence of flux density due to point charge and uniform line charge is zero.

SOLUTION

The flux density $\vec{D}$ due to a point charge in spherical coordinates is

$$\vec{D} = \frac{Q}{4\pi r^2}\,\vec{a}_r$$

Hence, for $r > 0$, $D_r = \dfrac{Q}{4\pi r^2}, D_\theta = D_\pi = 0$

The divergence of flux density in spherical coordinates is

$$\nabla\cdot\vec{D} = \frac{1}{r^2}\frac{\partial}{\partial r}\left(r^2 D_r\right) + \frac{1}{r\sin\theta}\frac{\partial}{\partial\theta}\left(D_\theta\sin\theta\right) + \frac{1}{r\sin\theta}\frac{\partial D_\phi}{\partial\phi}$$

$$= \frac{1}{r^3}\frac{\partial}{\partial r}\left(r^2\frac{Q}{4\pi r^2}\right) + 0 + 0 = \frac{1}{r^2}\frac{\partial}{\partial r}\left(\frac{Q}{4\pi}\right)$$

$$= 0 \qquad \left(\text{since }\frac{Q}{2\pi}\text{ is constant}\right)$$

Hence, the divergence of flux density due to point charge is zero.

The flux density $\vec{D}$ due to a uniform line charge in cylindrical coordinates, is

$$\vec{D} = \frac{\rho_l}{2\pi\rho}\,\vec{a}_\rho$$

Hence, for $\rho > 0$, $D_\rho = \dfrac{\rho_l}{2\pi\rho}$ and $D_\phi = D_\pi = 0$

The divergence of flux density in cylindrical coordinates is

$$\nabla\cdot D = \frac{1}{\rho}\frac{\partial}{\partial\rho}\left(\rho D_\rho\right) + \frac{1}{\rho}\frac{\partial D_\phi}{d\phi} + \frac{\partial D_z}{dz}$$

$$= \frac{1}{\rho}\frac{\partial}{\partial \rho}\left[\rho\,\frac{\rho_l}{2\pi\rho}\right] + 0 + 0 = \frac{1}{\rho}\frac{\partial}{\partial \rho}\left(\frac{\rho_l}{2\pi}\right)$$

$$= 0 \qquad \left(\text{since } \frac{\rho_l}{2\pi}\text{ is constant}\right)$$

Therefore, the divergence of the flux density due to uniform line charge is zero everywhere except at $\rho = 0$. As $\vec{D} = \varepsilon_0 \vec{E}$ and ε_0 is a constant, the divergence of electric field $\vec{E}$ due to point charge and uniform line charge is also zero everywhere except at $r = 0$ and $\rho = 0$ where it is indeterminate. ☐

EXAMPLE 2.37

Show that $\vec{D} = \varepsilon_0 \vec{E}$ using Gauss's law.

SOLUTION

Consider a point charge Q at the origin as shown in Figure E2.37. Let P be the point at which flux density $\vec{D}$ has to be obtained. Assume the Gaussian surface as shown in Figure E2.37 in which $\vec{D}$ is directed outward in $\vec{a}_r$ direction.

Therefore, the differential surface $d\vec{s}$ and flux density $\vec{D}$ at point P in spherical coordinates is

$$d\vec{s} = ds\,\vec{a}_n = r^2 \sin\theta\, d\theta\, d\phi\, \vec{a}_r$$

$$\vec{D} = D_r \vec{a}_r$$

By Gauss's law,

$$Q = \oint_s \vec{D}\cdot d\vec{s} = \int_{\phi=0}^{2\pi}\int_{\theta=0}^{\pi}\left(D_r\vec{a}_r\right)\cdot\left(r^2 \sin\theta\, d\theta\, d\phi\, \vec{a}_r\right)$$

where $\vec{a}_r \cdot \vec{a}_r = 1$.

Therefore, $Q = 4\pi r^2 D_r$

Hence, the radial component of $\vec{D}$ is

$$D_r = \frac{Q}{4\pi r^2}$$

Therefore, the flux density $\vec{D}$ is

$$\vec{D} = \frac{Q}{4\pi r^2}\,\vec{a}_r$$

By Coulomb's law, the electric field intensity $\vec{E}$ due to a point charge is

$$\vec{E} = \frac{Q}{4\pi\varepsilon_0 r^2}\,\vec{a}_r = \frac{\vec{D}}{\varepsilon_0}$$

Therefore, $\vec{D} = \varepsilon_0 \vec{E}$ is proved using Gauss's law. ☐

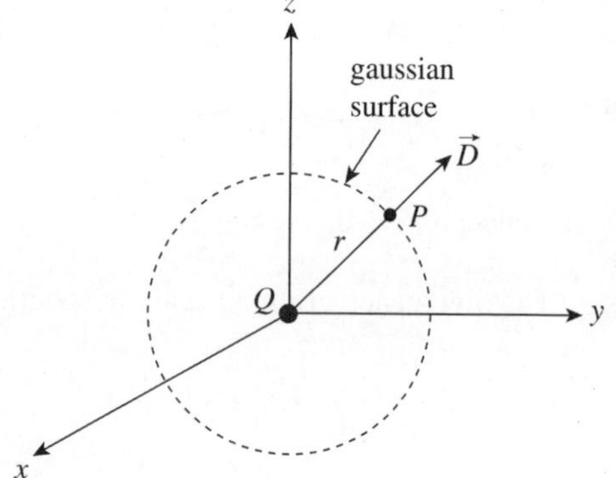

Figure E2.37

EXAMPLE 2.38

The region $r \leq a$ in spherical coordinates has electric flux density $\vec{D} = \frac{\rho r}{3}\,\vec{a}_r\ \mathrm{C/m^2}$. Evaluated both sides of the divergence theorem for this vector field. For s, choose the spherical surface $r = b \leq a$.

SOLUTION

By Gauss's divergence theorem,

$$\int_v \left(\nabla \cdot \vec{D}\right) dv = \oint_s \vec{D} \cdot d\vec{s}$$

where $\vec{D}$ has only a radial component and $\vec{D} \cdot d\vec{s}$ has a non-zero value on the surface $r = b \le a$. First evaluating the right hand side of divergence theorem, we get

$$\oint_s \vec{D} \cdot d\vec{s} = \int_0^{2\pi} \int_0^{\pi} \left(\frac{\rho b}{3}\vec{a}_r\right) \cdot \left(b^2 \sin\theta \, d\theta \, d\phi \, \vec{a}_r\right)$$

$$= \frac{\rho b^3}{3}\int_0^{\pi} \sin\theta \, d\theta \int_0^{2\pi} d\phi$$

$$= \frac{4\pi\rho b^3}{3}$$

where $d\vec{s} = r^2 \sin\theta \, d\theta \, d\phi \, \vec{a}_r$ in spherical coordinates.

Divergence of $\vec{D}$ in spherical coordinates is

$$\nabla \cdot \vec{D} = \frac{1}{r^2}\frac{\partial}{\partial r}\left(r^2 D_r\right) + \frac{1}{r\sin\theta}\frac{\partial}{\partial\theta}\left(D_\theta \sin\theta\right) + \frac{1}{r\sin\theta}\frac{\partial D_\phi}{\partial\phi}$$

$$= \frac{1}{r^2}\frac{\partial}{\partial r}\left(r^2\frac{\rho r}{3}\right) = \frac{\rho}{3r^2}\times 3r^2 = \rho$$

Next evaluating the left hand side of divergence theorem, we get

$$\int_v \left(\nabla \cdot \vec{D}\right) dv = \int_0^{2\pi}\int_0^{\pi}\int_0^b \rho r^2 \sin\theta \, dr \, d\theta \, d\phi$$

$$= \rho \int_0^b r^2 \, dr \int_0^{\pi} \sin\theta \, d\theta \int_0^{2\pi} d\phi$$

$$= \frac{4\pi\rho b^3}{3}$$

where $dv = r^2 \sin\theta \, dr \, d\theta \, d\phi$ in spherical coordinates. Hence, the divergence theorem is examined on both sides. ☐

EXAMPLE 2.39

Given $\vec{D} = \left(\dfrac{5x^3}{3}\right)\vec{a}_x$ C/m^2, evaluate both sides of the divergence theorem for the volume of a cube, 2 m on an edge, centered at the origin and with edges parallel to the axes.

SOLUTION

By Gauss's divergence theorem,

$$\int_v \left(\nabla \cdot \vec{D}\right) dv = \oint_s \vec{D} \cdot d\vec{s}$$

From Figure E2.39, it is seen that $\vec{D}$ has only an x-component. Therefore, $\vec{D} \cdot d\vec{s}$ is zero on all faces except the faces at $x = 1$ m and $x = -1$ m.

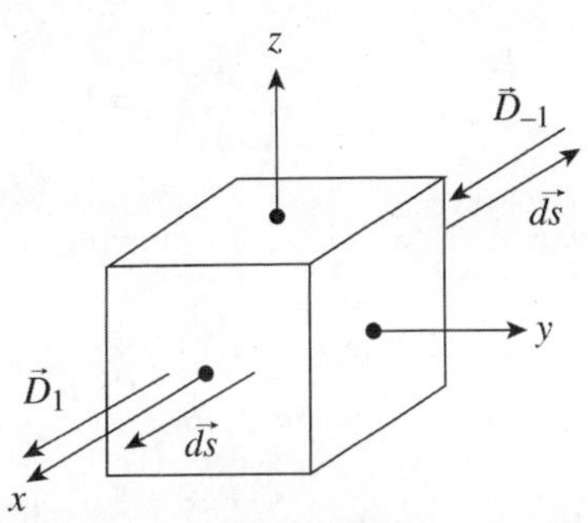

Figure E2.39

Evaluating RHS, we get

$$\oint_s \vec{D} \cdot d\vec{s} = \int_{-1}^{1}\int_{-1}^{1}\left(\frac{5(1)}{3}\vec{a}_x\right)\cdot(dy\,dz\,\vec{a}_x) + \int_{-1}^{1}\int_{-1}^{1}\frac{5(-1)}{3}\vec{a}_x\cdot dy\,dz(-\vec{a}_x)$$

$$= \frac{20}{3} + \frac{20}{3} = \frac{40}{3}\,C$$

Since $\nabla\cdot\vec{D} = 5x^2$, evaluating LHS, we get

$$\int_v(\nabla\cdot\vec{D})dv = \int_{-1}^{1}\int_{-1}^{1}\int_{-1}^{1}(5x^2)dx\,dy\,dz$$

$$= 5\int_{-1}^{1}\int_{-1}^{1}\left[\frac{x^3}{3}\right]_{-1}^{1} dy\,dz = \frac{40}{3}\,C$$

Hence, the divergence theorem is verified.

EXAMPLE 2.40

Given $\vec{D} = \dfrac{5\rho^3}{4}\vec{a}_\rho\ C/m^2$ in cylindrical coordinates, evaluates both sides of the divergence theorem for the volume enclosed by $\rho = 1$ m, $\rho = 2$ m, $z = 0$ and $z = 10$ m as shown in Figure E2.40.

SOLUTION

From Figure E.2.40, it is seen that $\vec{D}$ has no z-component. Therefore, $\vec{D}\cdot d\vec{s}$ is zero on the top and bottom surfaces. On the inner cylindrical surface, $d\vec{s}$ is in the direction of $-\vec{a}_\rho$.

By Gauss's divergence theorem,

$$\int_v(\nabla\cdot\vec{D})dv = \oint_s \vec{D}\cdot d\vec{s}$$

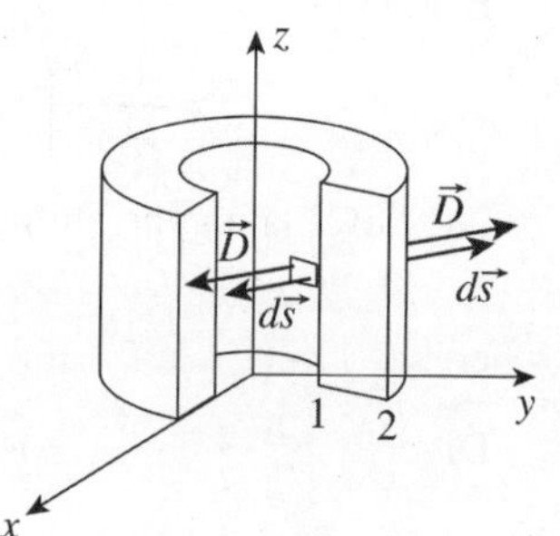

Figure E2.40

Evaluating RHS, we get

$$\oint_s \vec{D}\cdot d\vec{s} = \int_0^{10}\int_0^{2\pi}\left(\frac{5\rho^3}{4}\vec{a}_\rho\right)\cdot\left(\rho\,d\phi\,dz(-\vec{a}_\rho)\right)\Big|_{\rho=1} + \int_0^{10}\int_0^{2\pi}\left(\frac{5\rho^3}{4}\vec{a}_\rho\right)\cdot\left(\rho\,d\phi\,dz\,\vec{a}_\rho\right)\Big|_{\rho=2}$$

$$= \frac{-100\pi}{4} + 16\left(\frac{100\pi}{4}\right) = 375\pi\,C$$

where $d\vec{s} = \rho\,d\phi\,dz\,\vec{a}_\rho$ in cylindrical coordinates. Divergence of $\vec{D}$ in cylindrical coordinates is

$$\nabla\cdot\vec{D} = \frac{1}{\rho}\frac{\partial}{\partial\rho}(\rho D_\rho) + \frac{1}{\rho}\frac{\partial D_\phi}{\partial\phi} + \frac{\partial D_z}{\partial z}$$

$$= \frac{1}{\rho}\frac{\partial}{\partial\rho}\left(\frac{5\rho^4}{4}\right) = 5\rho^2$$

From LHS of the divergence theorem,

$$\int_v \left(\nabla \cdot \vec{D}\right) dv = \int_0^{10} \int_0^{2\pi} \int_1^2 \left(5\rho^2\right) \rho \, d\rho \, d\phi \, dz = 375\pi \, \text{C}$$

Hence, the divergence theorem is verified. ❐

Given $\vec{A} = 30e^{-\rho}\vec{a}_\rho - 3z\vec{a}_z$ in cylindrical coordinates, determine both sides of the divergence theorem for the volume enclosed by $\rho = 2$, $z = 0$ and $z = 5$ as shown in Figure E2.41.

SOLUTION

By divergence theorem,

$$\int_v \left(\nabla \cdot \vec{A}\right) dv = \oint_s \vec{A} \cdot d\vec{s}$$

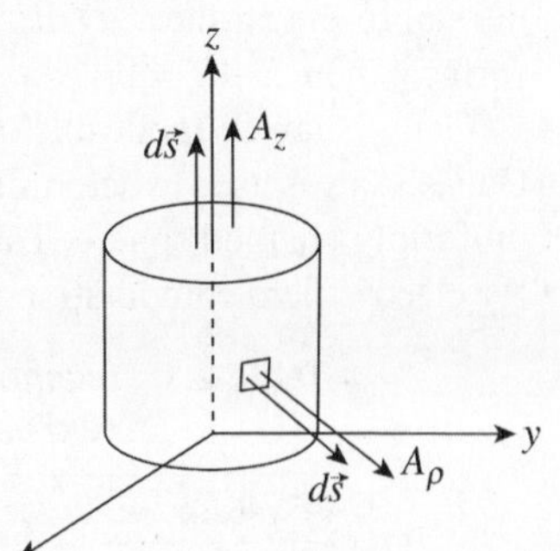

Figure E2.41

From the given vector $\vec{A}$, it is noted that $A_z = 0$ for $z = 0$ and hence, $\vec{A} \cdot d\vec{s}$ is zero over that part of the surface.

Evaluating RHS, we get

$$\oint_s \vec{A} \cdot d\vec{s} = \int_0^5 \int_0^{2\pi} \left(30e^{-2}\vec{a}_\rho\right) \cdot \left(2\,d\phi\,dz\,\vec{a}_\rho\right) + \int_0^{2\pi} \int_0^2 \left(-3(5)\vec{a}_z\right) \cdot \left(\rho\,d\rho\,d\phi\,\vec{a}_z\right)$$

$$= 60e^{-2}(2\pi)(5) - 15(2\pi)(2) = 2\pi(40.6 - 30) = 66.56$$

where $d\vec{s}_\rho = \rho\,d\phi\,dz\,\vec{a}_\rho$ and $d\vec{s}_z = \rho\,d\rho\,d\phi\,\vec{a}_z$ in cylindrical coordinates.

Divergence of $\vec{A}$ in cylindrical coordinates is

$$\left(\nabla \cdot \vec{A}\right) = \frac{1}{\rho}\frac{\partial}{\partial \rho}\left(\rho A_\rho\right) + \frac{1}{\rho}\frac{\partial A_\phi}{\partial \phi} + \frac{\partial A_z}{\partial z}$$

$$= \frac{1}{\rho}\frac{\partial}{\partial \rho}\left(30\rho\,e^{-\rho}\right) + \frac{\partial}{\partial z}(-3z)$$

$$= \frac{30e^{-\rho}}{\rho} - 30e^{-\rho} - 3$$

Now evaluating LHS, we get

$$\int_v \left(\nabla \cdot \vec{A}\right) dv = \int_0^5 \int_0^{2\pi} \int_0^2 \left(\frac{30e^{-\rho}}{\rho} - 30e^{-\rho} - 3\right) \rho\,d\rho\,d\phi\,dz$$

$$= \int_0^2 \left(\frac{30e^{-\rho}}{\rho} - 30e^{-\rho} - 3\right) \rho\,d\rho \times \int_0^{2\pi} d\phi \times \int_0^5 dz = 66.56$$

where $dv = \rho\,d\rho\,d\phi\,dz$ in cylindrical coordinates. Hence, the divergence theorem is evaluated on both sides. ❐

2.8 APPLICATIONS OF GAUSS'S LAW

When the charge distribution possesses symmetry properties, Gauss's law is used to determine the flux density $\vec{D}$ and field intensity $\vec{E}$. At every point on the surface, the direction of $\vec{ds}$ is along its outward normal and only the normal component of $\vec{D}$ at the Gaussian surface contributes to the integral form of Gauss's law.

Gauss's law can be applied successfully by choosing the surface s such that, $\vec{D}$ is constant in magnitude and its direction is either normal or purely tangential at every point of each subsurface of s. When $\vec{D}$ is normal to the surface, $\vec{D} \cdot \vec{ds} = D \cdot ds$ because $\vec{D}$ is constant on the surface. When $\vec{D}$ is tangential to the surface, then $\vec{D} \cdot \vec{ds} = 0$.

Gauss's law is applicable only to systems with planar, cylindrical and spherical symmetry. In this section, Gauss's law is used to determine the field due to a point charge, infinite line charge, infinite sheet of charge and uniformly charged sphere. Table 2.1 list some examples of systems in which Gauss's law can be applicable for electric field computation with the corresponding Gaussian surface.

Table 2.1 *Examples of systems having Gaussian surface for computing electric field using Gauss's law*

System	Symmetry	Gaussian Surface
Point charge	Spherical	Concentric sphere
Infinite rod	Cylindrical	Coaxial cylinder
Inifinite plane	Planar	Gaussian Pillbox
Sphere, Spherical shell	Spherical	Concentric sphere

2.8.1 Determination of Field due to a Point Charge

The integral form of Gauss's law can be used to determine the field intensity due to a single isolated charge Q by constructing a closed spherical surface of arbitrary radius r centered at Q as shown in Figure 2.12. Symmetry conditions will be satisfied by choosing a spherical surface.

When the charge Q is positive, the direction of $\vec{D}$ must be radially outward along the unit vector $\vec{a}_r$. The magnitude of $\vec{D}$ is constant at all points on the Gaussian surface as $\vec{D}$ is normal to the surface considered. Thus, at any point on the surface, defined by the position vector $\vec{r}$, $\vec{D} = D_r \vec{a}_r$ and $\vec{ds} = ds\,\vec{a}_r$.

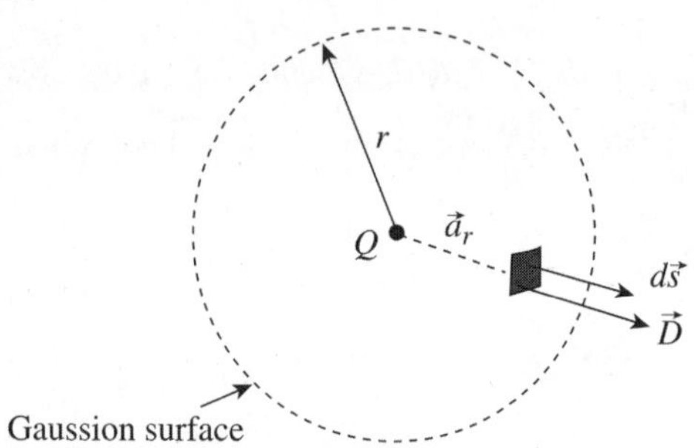

Figure 2.12 *Gaussian surface about an isolated point charge*

Applying Gauss's law, we get

$$Q = \oint_s \vec{D} \cdot \vec{ds} = \oint_s \left(D_r \vec{a}_r \right) \cdot \left(ds\,\vec{a}_r \right) = \oint_s D_r\,ds$$

$$= D_r \oint_s ds = D_r \int_{\phi=0}^{2\pi} \int_{\theta=0}^{\pi} r^2 \sin\theta\, d\theta\, d\phi$$

$$= D_r \left(4\pi r^2 \right) \tag{2.34}$$

where $\oint_s ds = 4\pi r^2$ is the surface area of the Gaussian surface which is spherical.

Therefore, the magnitude of electric flux density is represented by

$$D_r = \frac{Q}{4\pi r^2} \tag{2.35}$$

In vector form,

$$\vec{D} = \frac{Q}{4\pi r^2}\vec{a}_r \tag{2.36}$$

The electric field intensity $\vec{E}$ induced by an isolated point charge in a medium with permittivity ε_0 is represented by

$$\vec{E} = \frac{\vec{D}}{\varepsilon_0} = \frac{Q}{4\pi\varepsilon_0 r^2}\vec{a}_r \tag{2.37}$$

The electric field intensity due to an isolated point charge is identical to the one obtained using Coulomb's law. For an isolated point charge, either Coulomb's law or Gauss's law can be used to find electric field intensity $\vec{E}$. Though Coulomb's law can be used to find $\vec{E}$ for any specified charge distribution, Gauss's law is easier to apply than Coulomb's law but its applicability is limited to symmetrical charge distributions.

2.8.2 Determination of Field due to an Infinite Line of Charge

Consider a line of infinite extent with uniform charge density of ρ_l C/m lying along the z-axis. The electric flux density $\vec{D}$ can be determined by choosing a cylindrical surface which satisfies symmetry condition as shown in Figure 2.13. It is seen that $\vec{D}$ is constant and normal to the chosen cylindrical Gaussian surface. Symmetry considerations show that $\vec{D}$ must be in radial direction $\vec{a}_\rho$ and must not depend on ϕ or z. Therefore, $\vec{D} = D_\rho \vec{a}_\rho$. Here, a cylindrical Gaussian surface of radius ρ is constructed around the line of charge. The total charge contained within the cylinder is $Q = \rho_l h$ where h is the height of the cylinder.

Applying Gauss's law, we get

$$Q = \oint_s \vec{D} \cdot d\vec{s} = \oint_s \left(D_\rho \vec{a}_\rho\right) \cdot \left(ds\,\vec{a}_\rho\right) = \oint_s D_\rho\, ds$$

$$= D_\rho \oint_s ds = D_\rho \int_{z=0}^{h}\int_{\phi=0}^{2\pi} \rho\, d\phi\, dz$$

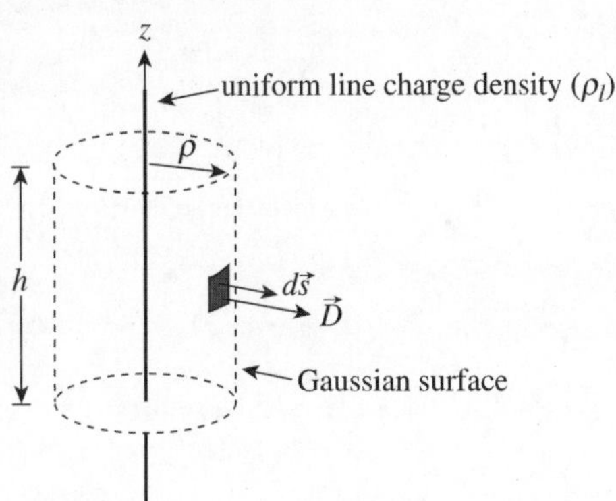

Figure 2.13 *Gaussian surface around an infinite line charge*

i.e.,

$$\rho_l h = D_\rho \left(2\pi\rho h\right) \tag{2.38}$$

where $\oint_s ds = 2\pi\rho h$ is the surface area of the Gaussian surface which is cylindrical. Since $\vec{D}$ is along the radial direction $\vec{a}_\rho$, the top and bottom surfaces of the cylinder do not contribute to the surface integral on the left hand side of Gauss's law and only the side surface contributes to the integral. This results in $\vec{D}$ with ρ-component only and not with ϕ or z-component.

From Eq. (2.38), the magnitude of electric flux density is represented by

$$D_\rho = \frac{\rho_l h}{2\pi\rho h} = \frac{\rho_l}{2\pi\rho}$$

In vector form, $\quad \vec{D} = \dfrac{\rho_l}{2\pi\rho}\vec{a}_\rho \tag{2.39}$

Therefore, the electric field intensity $\vec{E}$ due to an infinite line of charge in a medium with permittivity ε_0 is given by

$$\vec{E} = \frac{\vec{D}}{\varepsilon_0} = \frac{\rho_l}{2\pi\varepsilon_0\rho}\,\vec{a}_\rho \qquad (2.40)$$

This electric field intensity due to an infinite line of charge is identical to the one obtained using Coulomb's law.

2.8.3 Determination of Field due to an Infinite Sheet of Charge

Consider a sheet of infinite extent with uniform charge density ρ_s C/m^2 lying on the xy-plane. The flux density $\vec{D}$ can be determined by choosing a rectangular box which is symmetrical about the sheet of charge and has two of its faces parallel to the sheet as shown in Figure 2.14. It is seen that $\vec{D}$ is constant and normal to the chosen rectangular Gaussian surface. Symmetry considerations show that $\vec{D}$ must be in $\vec{a}_z$ direction and must not depend on x or y. As $\vec{D}$ is normal to the sheet, $\vec{D} = D_z\vec{a}_z$.

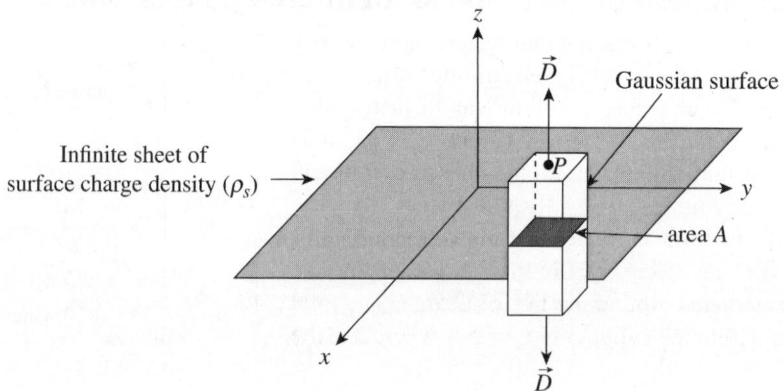

Figure 2.14 *Gaussian surface about an infinite sheet of charge*

Applying Gauss's law, we get

$$Q = \oint_s \vec{D}\cdot d\vec{s} = \oint_s \left(D_z\vec{a}_z\right)\cdot\left(ds\,\vec{a}_z\right) = \oint_s D_z\,ds$$

i.e., $\qquad \rho_s\int ds = D_z\oint_s ds = D_z\left[\int_{top} ds + \int_{bottom} ds\right] \qquad (2.41)$

Since $\vec{D}$ is along $\vec{a}_z$ direction, the sides of the rectangular box do not contribute to the surface integral on the left hand side of Gauss's law and only the top and bottom sides contribute to the integral. This shows that $\vec{D}$ has only z-component and no x or y-component. If the top and bottom areas of the box have area A, then the above equation becomes

$$\rho_s A = D_z\oint_s ds = D_z\left[A + A\right]$$

Therefore, the magnitude of electric flux density is $D_z = \dfrac{\rho_s}{2}$.

Representing in vector form, we get $\vec{D} = \dfrac{\rho_s}{2}\vec{a}_z \qquad (2.42)$

Hence, the electric field intensity $\vec{E}$ due to an infinite sheet of charge in a medium with permittivity of free space ε_0 is given by

$$\vec{E} = \frac{\vec{D}}{\varepsilon_0} = \frac{\rho_s}{2\varepsilon_0}\vec{a}_z \tag{2.43}$$

This electric field intensity due to an infinite sheet of charge is identical to the one obtained using Coulomb's law.

EXAMPLE 2.42

A uniform line charge of $\rho_l = 6\,\mu\text{C/m}$ lies along the z-axis and a concentric circular cylinder of radius 2 m has $\rho_s = \left(-1.5/4\pi\right)\mu\text{C/m}^2$. Both distributions are infinite in extent with z. Use Gauss's law, find $\vec{D}$ in all regions.

SOLUTION

Figure E2.42 shows the Gaussian surface A for a uniform line charge and Gaussian surface B for a concentric circular cylinder of radius $\rho = 2$ m with surface charge distribution.

From Gauss's law, the electric flux density $\vec{D}$ due to an infinite line of charge in the Gaussian surface A is

$$\vec{D} = \frac{\rho_l}{2\pi\rho}\vec{a}_\rho = \frac{6\times10^{-6}}{2\pi\rho}\vec{a}_\rho$$

$$= \frac{0.955}{\rho}\vec{a}_\rho \ \mu\text{C/m}^2 \text{ for } 0 < \rho < 2$$

Gaussian surface B encloses both the line charge and surface charge distributions. Therefore, the enclosed charge is the sum of both charge distributions as given by

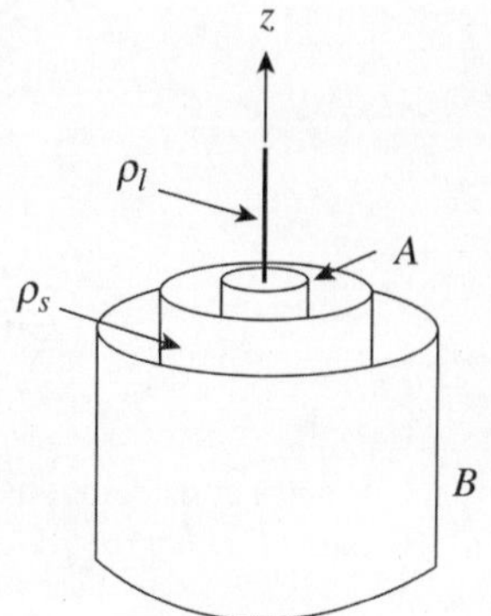

Figure E2.42

$$Q_{enc} = Q \text{ due to line charge } +Q \text{ due to surface charge}$$

$$= \rho_l l + \rho_s \left(2\pi\rho l\right)$$

where $\rho = 2$ is the radius of the cylinder and l is the length of both the surfaces A and B.

Using Gauss's law,

$$Q_{enc} = \oint \vec{D}\cdot d\vec{s}$$

$$\left(\rho_l + 4\pi\rho_s\right)l = D_\rho\left(2\pi\rho l\right)$$

Therefore, the electric flux density due to both charge distributions in the Gaussian surface B can be written as

$$D_\rho = \frac{\rho_l + 4\pi\rho_s}{2\pi\rho} = \frac{6\times10^{-6} + 4\pi\left(-1.5/4\pi\right)\times10^{-6}}{2\pi\rho}$$

$$= \frac{0.717\times10^{-6}}{\rho}$$

Therefore, in vector form, we have

$$\vec{D} = \frac{0.717}{\rho}\vec{a}_\rho \ \mu\text{C/m}^2 \text{ for } \rho > 2 \qquad \square$$

2.8.4   Determination of Field due to a Uniformly Charged Sphere

Consider a sphere of radius a with uniform volume charge density of ρ_v C/m^3. The electric flux density $\vec{D}$ can be determined by constructing Gaussian surfaces for cases $r \le a$ and $r \ge a$ separately as shown in Figure 2.15 (a) and (b). Since the charge has spherical symmetry, it is obvious that a spherical surface is an appropriate Gaussian surface.

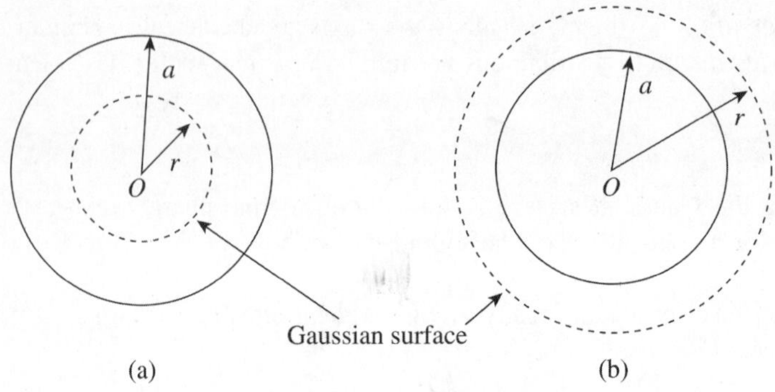

Figure 2.15   *Gaussian surface for a uniformly charged sphere when (a) $r \le a$ and (b) $r \ge a$*

Symmetry considerations show that $\vec{D}$ must be in $\vec{a}_r$ direction and must not depend on θ or ϕ. As $\vec{D}$ is normal to the sphere, $\vec{D} = D_r\vec{a}_r$. For $r \le a$, the total charge enclosed by the spherical surface of radius r is represented by

$$Q_{enc} = \int \rho_v dv = \rho_v \int_{\phi=0}^{2\pi}\int_{\theta=0}^{\pi}\int_{r=0}^{r} r^2 \sin\theta \, dr \, d\theta \, d\phi$$

$$= \rho_v\left(\frac{4}{3}\pi r^3\right)$$

Applying Gauss's law, we get

$$\psi = \oint_s \vec{D}\cdot d\vec{s} = \oint_s \left(D_r\vec{a}_r\right)\cdot\left(ds\vec{a}_r\right) = D_r\oint_s ds$$

$$= D_r\int_{\phi=0}^{2\pi}\int_{\theta=0}^{\pi} r^2 \sin\theta \, d\theta \, d\phi$$

$$= D_r\left(4\pi r^2\right)$$

The total flux Ψ is equal to the charge enclosed Q_{enc} i.e., $\psi = Q_{enc}$. Hence, by equating the corresponding expressions, we get

$$D_r\left(4\pi r^2\right) = \rho_v\left(\frac{4}{3}\pi r^3\right)$$

$$D_r = \frac{\rho_v\left(\dfrac{4}{3}\pi r^3\right)}{\left(4\pi r^2\right)} = \frac{r\rho_v}{3}$$

Hence, the electric flux density is given by

$$\vec{D} = \frac{r\rho_v}{3}\vec{a}_r, \qquad 0 < r \le a \tag{2.44}$$

For $r \ge a$, the total charge enclosed by the spherical surface is the entire charge as given by

$$Q_{enc} = \int \rho_v \, dv = \rho_v \int_{\phi=0}^{2\pi} \int_{\theta=0}^{\pi} \int_{r=0}^{a} r^2 \sin\theta \, dr \, d\theta \, d\phi$$

$$= \rho_v \left(\frac{4}{3}\pi a^3 \right)$$

By Gauss's law, the total flux through the Gaussian surface of radius r is

$$\psi = \oint_s \vec{D} \cdot d\vec{s} = \oint_s \left(D_r \vec{a}_r \right) \cdot \left(ds\, \vec{a}_r \right) = D_r \oint_s ds$$

$$= D_r \int_{\phi=0}^{2\pi} \int_{\theta=0}^{\pi} r^2 \sin\theta \, d\theta \, d\phi = D_r \left(4\pi r^2 \right)$$

The total flux Ψ is equal to the enclosed charge Q_{enc} i.e., $\psi = Q_{enc}$. Hence, by equating the corresponding expressions, we get

$$D_r \left(4\pi r^2 \right) = \rho_v \left(\frac{4}{3}\pi a^3 \right)$$

$$D_r = \frac{\rho_v \left(\dfrac{4}{3}\pi a^3 \right)}{\left(4\pi r^2 \right)} = \frac{a^3 \rho_v}{3r^2}$$

Hence, the electric flux density is represented by

$$\vec{D} = \frac{a^3 \rho_v}{3r^2}\vec{a}_r, \qquad r \ge a \tag{2.45}$$

Therefore, the electric field intensity $\vec{E}$ due to a uniformly charged sphere in free space is expressed by

$$\vec{E} = \frac{\vec{D}}{\varepsilon_0} = \begin{cases} \dfrac{r\rho_v}{3\varepsilon_0}\vec{a}_r, & 0 < r \le a \\[3mm] \dfrac{a^3 \rho_v}{3\varepsilon_0 r^2}\vec{a}_r, & r \ge a \end{cases} \tag{2.46}$$

The variation of magnitude of $\vec{E}$ over the radius r for a uniformly charged sphere is shown in Figure 2.16. It is seen that, for $r \le a$, the magnitude of electric field density $\vec{E}$ increases as it is directly proportional to r and for $r \ge a$, $\left|\vec{E}\right|$ decreases as it is inversely proportional to r^2. At $r = a$, $\left|\vec{E}\right| = \dfrac{a\rho_v}{3\varepsilon_0}$ depends on the radius of the charged sphere. For $r > a$, the graph of $\left|\vec{E}\right|$ versus r is parabolic as shown in Figure 2.16. The graph of $\left|\vec{D}\right|$ vs r is exactly similar in nature as $\left|\vec{E}\right|$ vs r.

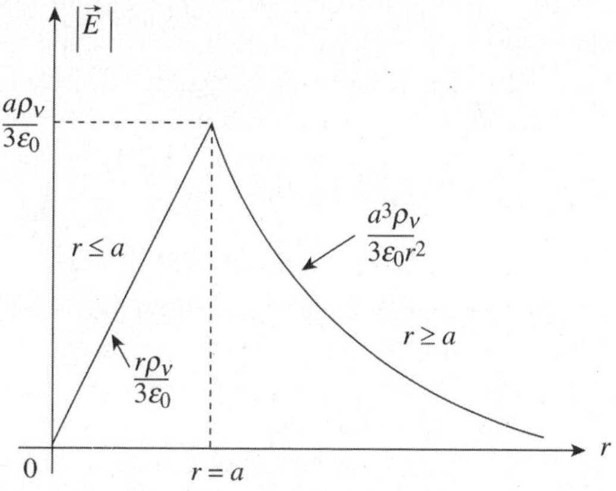

Figure 2.16 *Variation of $\left|\vec{E}\right|$ over the radius r for a uniformly charged sphere*

EXAMPLE 2.43

The volume in cylindrical coordinates between $\rho = 2\,\text{m}$ and $\rho = 4\,\text{m}$ contains a uniform charge density $2\rho_v\ \text{C/m}^3$. Using Gauss' law, determine the electric flux density $\vec{D}$ in all regions.

SOLUTION

From Figure E2.43, $\vec{D}$ can be obtained using Gauss's law in three regions, namely, $0 < \rho < 2\,\text{m}$, $2 \le \rho \le 4\,\text{m}$ and $\rho > 4\,\text{m}$.

For $0 < \rho < 2\,\text{m}$,, using Gauss's law, we get

$$Q_{enc} = \oint \vec{D}\cdot d\vec{s} = D(2\pi\rho l)$$

Since there is no charge enclosed in this region i.e., $Q_{enc} = 0$, the flux density will be zero. Therefore, $\vec{D} = 0$.

For $2 \le \rho \le 4\,\text{m}$, using Gauss's law, we get

$$(2\rho_v)(2\pi l)\left(\frac{\rho^2 - 4}{2}\right) = D(2\pi\,\rho l)$$

$$\pi(2\rho_v)l(\rho^2 - 4) = D(2\pi\,\rho l)$$

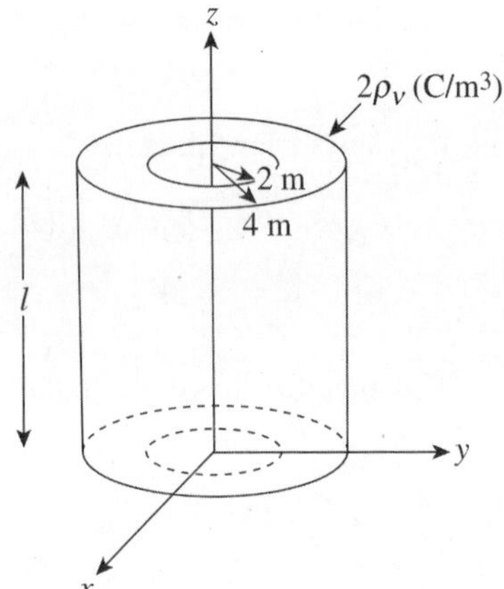

Figure E2.43

Here, $Q_{enc} = \int_v 2\rho_v\, dv = 2\rho_v \int_0^l \int_0^{2\pi} \int_0^4 \rho\, d\rho\, d\phi\, dz$ in cylindrical coordinates.

Therefore, $\vec{D} = \dfrac{\rho_v}{\rho}\left(\rho^2 - 4\right)\vec{a}_\rho\ \text{C/m}^2$

For $\rho > 4$ m, using Gauss's law, we get

$$12\pi(2\rho_v)l = D(2\pi\,\rho l)$$

Hence, $\vec{D} = \dfrac{12\rho_v}{\rho}\vec{a}_\rho\,\text{C/m}^2$ ☐

2.8.5 Determination of Field due to a Spherical Shell of Charge

Consider a spherical shell of radius a with uniform distribution of charge over its entire surface as shown in Figure 2.17 and it has a surface charge density of $\rho_s\ \text{C/m}^2$. The electric flux density $\vec{D}$ and electric field intensity $\vec{E}$ can be determined using Gauss's law by constructing Gaussian surfaces for cases $r > a$ and $r < a$ separately as shown in Figure 2.17 (a) and (b). Let r be the distance from the center of the spherical shell to the point P at which $\vec{D}$ and $\vec{E}$ have to be determined using Gauss's law.

Case (i): Point P outside the shell (r > a)

Consider a point P at a distance r from the origin such that $r > a$ as shown in Figure 2.17 (a). The Gaussian surface passing through point P is a concentric sphere of radius r. Due to spherical Gaussian surface, the flux lines are directed radially outwards and normal to the surface. Hence, the electric flux density $\vec{D}$ is also directed radially outwards at point P and has component only in $\vec{a}_r$ direction such that $\vec{D} = D_r\vec{a}_r$. Assume the differential surface area ds at P is normal to $\vec{a}_r$ direction and hence, in spherical coordinate system, $d\vec{s}$ can be written as

$$d\vec{s} = ds\,\vec{a}_r = r^2 \sin\theta\, d\theta\, d\phi\,\vec{a}_r$$

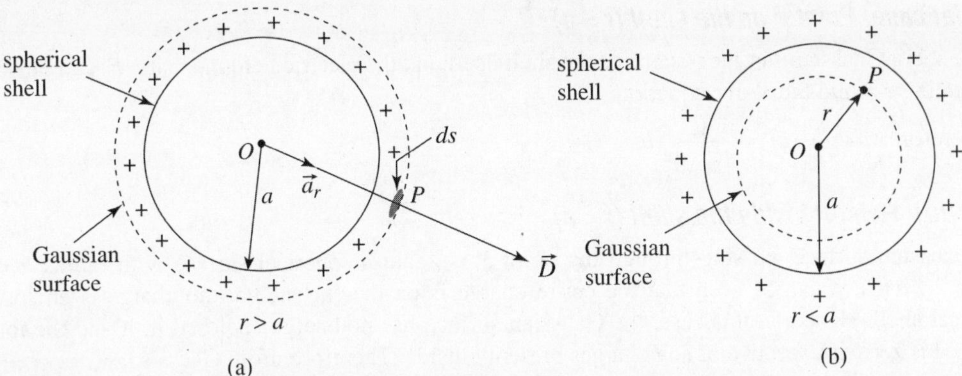

Figure 2.17 *Gaussian surface for a spherical shell of charge when (a) r > a and (b) r < a*

For $r > a$, the total charge enclosed by the spherical surface of radius a is represented by

$$Q = \int \rho_s \, ds = \rho_s \int_{\phi=0}^{2\pi} \int_{\theta=0}^{\pi} r^2 \sin\theta \, d\theta \, d\phi$$

$$= \rho_s a^2 \left[-\cos\theta\right]_0^{\pi} \left[\phi\right]_0^{2\pi}$$

$$= \rho_s \left(4\pi a^2\right)$$

Using Gauss's law, the total flux through the Gaussian surface of radius r is

$$\psi = \oint_s \vec{D} \cdot d\vec{s} = \oint_s \left(D_r \vec{a}_r\right) \cdot \left(ds \, \vec{a}_r\right) = D_r \oint_s ds$$

$$= D_r \int_{\phi=0}^{2\pi} \int_{\theta=0}^{\pi} r^2 \sin\theta \, d\theta \, d\phi$$

$$= D_r r^2 \left[-\cos\theta\right]_0^{\pi} \left[\phi\right]_0^{2\pi} = D_r \left(4\pi r^2\right)$$

The total flux Ψ is equal to the charge Q enclosed by spherical surface i.e., $\Psi = Q$. Hence, by equating the corresponding expressions, we get

$$D_r \left(4\pi r^2\right) = \rho_s \left(4\pi a^2\right)$$

$$D_r = \frac{\rho_s a^2}{r^2}$$

Hence, the electric flux density is given by

$$\vec{D} = D_r \vec{a}_r = \frac{\rho_s a^2}{r^2} \vec{a}_r \tag{2.47}$$

and the electric field intensity is given by

$$\vec{E} = \frac{\vec{D}}{\varepsilon_0} = \frac{\rho_s a^2}{\varepsilon_0 \, r^2} \vec{a}_r = \frac{Q}{4\pi\varepsilon_0 r^2} \vec{a}_r \tag{2.48}$$

Therefore, for $r > a$, electric field intensity $\vec{E}$ is inversely proportional to the square of the distance from the origin.

Special case: Point P on the shell (r = a)

On the shell, Gaussian surface is same as the shell itself and the electric field intensity $\vec{E}$ can be obtained by substituting $r = a$ in the above equation.

$$\text{Therefore,}\quad \vec{E} = \frac{\rho_s}{\varepsilon_0}\vec{a}_r = \frac{Q}{4\pi\varepsilon_0 a^2}\vec{a}_r \tag{2.49}$$

Case (iii): Point P inside the shell (r < a)

The Gaussian surface, passing through the point P is again a spherical surface with radius $r < a$. From Figure 2.17 (b), it can be seen that the entire charge is on the surface and no charge is enclosed by the spherical shell. Hence, in this case, the Gaussian surface has no charge enclosed in it and the total charge enclosed is zero, irrespective of any charges present outside. Therefore, from Gauss's law,

$$\psi = Q = \oint_s \vec{D}\cdot d\vec{s} = 0$$

As the total charge enclosed inside the spherical shell is zero, the electric flux density and field intensity should also be zero.

$$\text{Hence,}\quad \vec{D} = 0 \text{ and } \vec{E} = \frac{\vec{D}}{\varepsilon_0} = 0. \tag{2.50}$$

Therefore, the electric flux density and electric field intensity at any point inside a spherical shell is zero. The variation of magnitude of $\vec{E}$ vs the radial distance r measured from the origin is shown in Figure 2.18.

Hence, the electric field intensity $\vec{E}$ due to a spherical shell in free space is expressed by

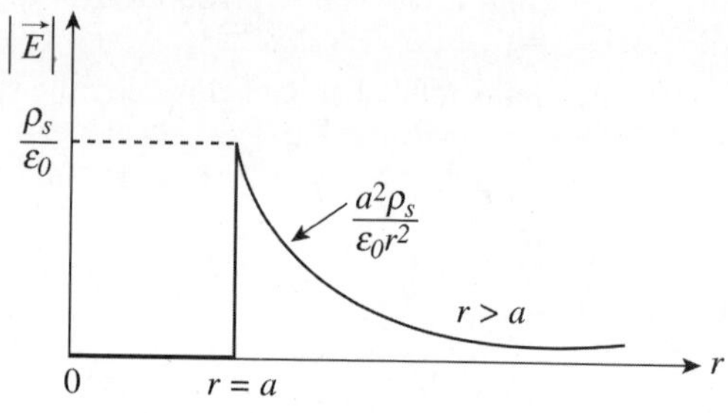

Figure 2.18 *Variation of $|\vec{E}|$ vs r for a spherical shell*

$$\vec{E} = \frac{\vec{D}}{\varepsilon_0} = \begin{cases} 0, & r < a \\[2mm] \dfrac{\rho_s}{\varepsilon_0}\vec{a}_r, & r = a \\[2mm] \dfrac{a^2\rho_s}{\varepsilon_0\, r^2}\vec{a}_r, & r > a \end{cases} \tag{2.51}$$

Here, at $r = a$ the electric field intensity $\vec{E}$ is independent of the radius of the spherical shell and for $r > a$, it is inversely proportional to the square of the distance r from the origin. The variation of magnitude of $\vec{D}$ vs r is also similar to variation of $\vec{E}$ vs r. For the medium other than the free space, ε_0 must be replaced by $\varepsilon = \varepsilon_0\varepsilon_r$.

2.9 EQUIPOTENTIAL SURFACES

Equipotential surface is the surface on which the electric potential is same at every point. The intersection of an equipotential surface and a plane results in a path or a line which is known as an equipotential line. The voltage difference between two points is equal to the line integral of electric field intensity $\vec{E}$ between the two points. Therefore,

$$V_{21} = V_2 - V_1 = \int_{P_1}^{P_2} \vec{E}\cdot d\vec{l} \tag{2.52}$$

When no work is done in moving a charge from one point to another along an equipotential line or surface i.e., $V_2 - V_1 = 0$, the line integral of electric field intensity $\vec{E}$ between the two points on the line or surface is equal to zero as given by

$$\int_{P_1}^{P_2} \vec{E} \cdot d\vec{l} = 0 \tag{2.53}$$

Here, it is observed that the electric lines of force or flux lines or the direction of $\vec{E}$ are always normal to equipotential surfaces. Figure 2.19 shows the equipotential surfaces and field lines for a point charge and a dipole.

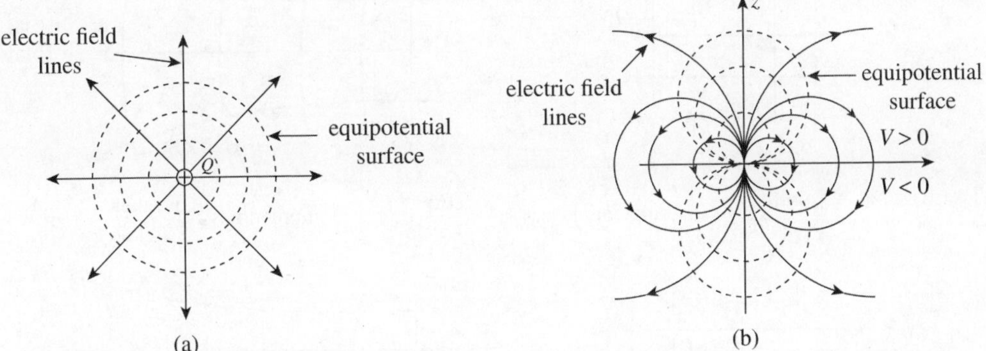

Figure 2.19 *Equipotential surfaces and field lines: (a) point charge and (b) electric dipole*

Also, it is seen that the direction of $\vec{E}$ is normal to the equipotential lines everywhere. Equipotential surfaces are important in the study of conductors. A perfect conductor is an equipotential medium in which the electric potential is same at every point in the conductor surface.

2.9.1 Properties of Equipotential Surfaces

The properties of equipotential surfaces are:

(*i*) The electric field lines are perpendicular to the equipotential surfaces and directed from higher to lower potentials.

(*ii*) The tangential component of the electric field along the equipotential surface is zero.

(*iii*) No work is required to move a particle along an equipotential surface.

(*iv*) The equipotential surfaces for a flat surface with uniform charge distribution are the planes that are parallel to the surface.

(*v*) The equipotential surfaces for a point charge or a sphere with uniform charge distribution are spheres concentric with the charge.

(*vi*) The equipotential surfaces for a line charge or a cylinder with uniform charge distribution are concentric cylinders centered on the axis of the charge distribution.

2.10 UNIFORM AND NON-UNIFORM FIELD

Uniform field is a field in which the electric field lines $\vec{E}$ are parallel and the equipotential lines form a parallel orthogonal set of lines as shown in Figure 2.20(a). These equipotentials are plane surfaces perpendicular to $\vec{E}$. For any fixed voltage increment ΔV, these equipotentials are spaced uniformly.

Figure 2.20(c) represents the three dimensional view of uniform fields with equipotential planes spaced uniformly.

Non-uniform field is a field in which the electric field lines $\vec{E}$ diverge from a stronger to a weaker field region and the equipotential surfaces become more widely spaced in the weaker field region as shown in Figure 2.20(b). These equipotential are curved surfaces perpendicular to $\vec{E}$ and for any fixed voltage increment ΔV, the equipotential spacing increases as the field becomes weaker.

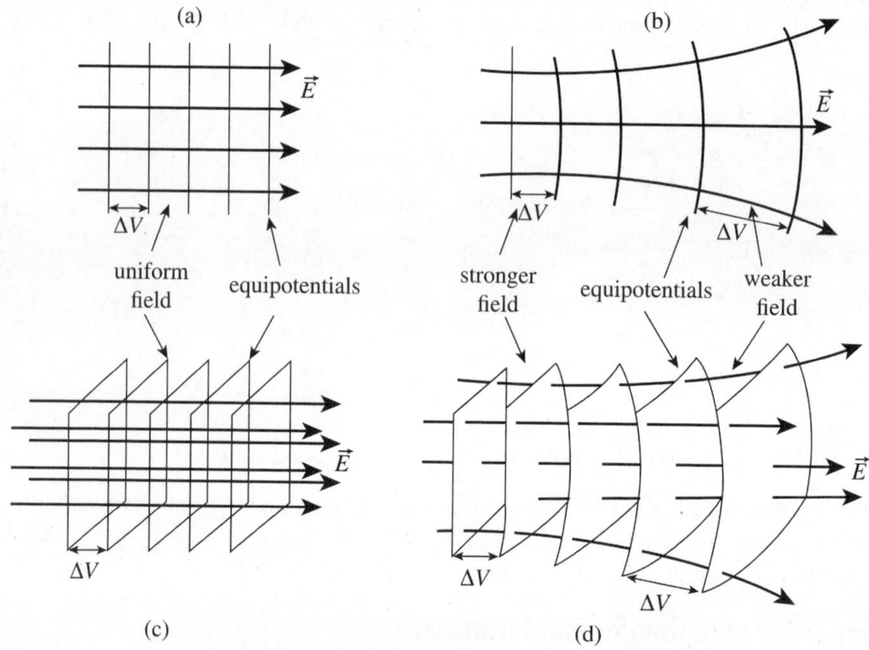

Figure 2.20 *Uniform and Non-uniform fields*

Figure 2.20(d) represents the three dimensional view of non-uniform fields with curved equipotential surfaces spaced non-uniformly. From Figure 2.20, it is seen that the electric field lines and equipotentials are everywhere orthogonal for both uniform and non-uniform fields.

EXAMPLE 2.44

A uniform surface charge of density $\rho_s = 2\ \mu\text{C/m}^2$ is situated at $z = 2$ m plane. What is the value of flux density at $P(1,1,1)$ m ?

SOLUTION

For an infinite sheet of charge, the electric field intensity is

$$\vec{E} = \frac{\rho_s}{2\varepsilon_0}\vec{a}_n$$

Therefore, the electric flux density $\vec{D}$ due to surface charge density is

$$\vec{D} = \varepsilon_0 \vec{E} = \frac{\rho_s}{2}\vec{a}_n = \frac{2\times10^{-6}}{2}\vec{a}_n$$

$$= 10^{-6}\,\vec{a}_n\ \text{C/m}^2$$

If $P(1,1,1)$ with $z = 1$ is below the plane $z = 2$ m, then $\vec{a}_n = -\vec{a}_z$.

Therefore, $\vec{D} = -10^{-6}\vec{a}_z = -\vec{a}_z$ μC/m^2 ☐

EXAMPLE 2.45

A point charge, $Q = 120\,\mu\text{C}$ is located at the origin in Cartesian coordinate system. Determine the electric flux density $\vec{D}$ at $(2,3,4)$.

SOLUTION

The electric flux density due to a point charge is

$$\vec{D} = \varepsilon_0\vec{E} = \varepsilon_0\frac{Q}{4\pi\varepsilon_0 R^2}\vec{a}_R = \frac{Q}{4\pi R^2}\vec{a}_R$$

$$= \frac{120\times10^{-6}}{4\pi\left(2^2+3^2+4^2\right)}\left(\frac{2\vec{a}_x+3\vec{a}_y+4\vec{a}_z}{\sqrt{2^2+3^2+4^2}}\right)$$

$$= 0.329\left(\frac{2\vec{a}_x+3\vec{a}_y+4\vec{a}_z}{\sqrt{29}}\right)\times10^{-6}$$

$$= 0.12\vec{a}_x+0.18\vec{a}_y+0.24\vec{a}_z \text{ μC/m}^2$$ ☐

EXAMPLE 2.46

Determine the electric flux density $\vec{D}$ in the region about a uniform line charge of 8 nC/m lying along the z-axis with $\rho = 3$ m in free space.

SOLUTION

The electric field intensity due to a line charge is

$$\vec{E} = \frac{\rho_l}{2\pi\varepsilon_0\rho}\vec{a}_\rho$$

$$= \frac{8\times10^{-9}}{2\pi\times8.854\times10^{-12}\times3}\vec{a}_\rho = 47.9\vec{a}_\rho \text{ V/m}$$

Therefore, the electric flux density $\vec{D}$ due to a line charge is

$$\vec{D} = \varepsilon_0\vec{E} = 8.854\times10^{-12}\times47.9\vec{a}_\rho$$

$$= 0.42\vec{a}_\rho \text{ nC/m}^2$$ ☐

EXAMPLE 2.47

The electric flux density is given as $\vec{D} = \frac{r}{4}\vec{a}_r$ nC/m^2 in free space. Calculate (*i*) the electric field intensity of a sphere at $r = 0.25$ m, (*ii*) the total charge within a sphere of $r = 0.25$ m and (*iii*) the total flux leaving the sphere of $r = 0.35$ m.

SOLUTION

(*i*) The electric field intensity $\vec{E}$ at $r = 0.25$ is

$$\vec{E} = \frac{\vec{D}}{\varepsilon_0} = \frac{r \times 10^{-9}}{4\varepsilon_0}\,\vec{a}_r = \frac{0.25 \times 10^{-9}}{4 \times 8.854 \times 10^{-12}}\,\vec{a}_r = 7.06\,\vec{a}_r\,\text{V/m}$$

(*ii*) By Gauss's law, the total charge enclosed or the total flux is equal to the net outward normal flux passing through the closed surface as given by

$$Q = \psi = \oint_s \vec{D} \cdot d\vec{s}$$

The differential area $d\vec{s}$ normal to $\vec{a}_r$ in spherical coordinates is $r^2 \sin\theta\, d\theta\, d\phi$.

Hence, $\displaystyle \oint_s \vec{D} \cdot d\vec{s} = \oint_s \left(\frac{r \times 10^{-9}}{4}\,\vec{a}_r\right) \cdot \left(r^2 \sin\theta\, d\theta\, d\phi\, \vec{a}_r\right)$

$$= \oint_s \frac{r^3 \times 10^{-9}}{4} \sin\theta\, d\theta\, d\phi \qquad\qquad \left(\text{since } \vec{a}_r \cdot \vec{a}_r = 1\right)$$

$$Q = \frac{r^3 \times 10^{-9}}{4} \int_{\phi=0}^{2\pi}\int_{\theta=0}^{\pi} \sin\theta\, d\theta\, d\phi = \frac{r^3 \times 10^{-9}}{4}\left[-\cos\theta\right]_0^\pi \left[\phi\right]_0^{2\pi}$$

$$= \pi r^3 \text{ nC}$$

Therefore, the total charge enclosed in a sphere of radius $r = 0.25$ m is

$$Q = \pi \times (0.25)^3 \times 10^{-9} = 0.04906\,\text{nC} = 49.06\,\text{pC}$$

(*iii*) According to Gauss's law, the total flux leaving the sphere is same as the charge enclosed.

Therefore, the total flux leaving the sphere of $r = 0.35$ m is

$$\psi = \pi \times (0.35)^3 \times 10^{-9} = 134.63\,\text{pC} \qquad\qquad\qquad \square$$

EXAMPLE 2.48

Consider that the point charges of 20 nC each are symmetrically located at $(4, 4, 0)$, $(4, -4, 0)$, $(-4, 4, 0)$ and $(-4, -4, 0)$ and a uniform line charge of 50 nC/m lies at $x = 0$, $y = 8$ and $z = 0$. Determine the electric flux density $\vec{D}$ at the origin.

SOLUTION

Figure E.2.48 shows the location of point charges and line charge. At the origin, the flux due to four point charges cancels each other. Hence, the electric flux density at the origin is only due to line charges as given by

$$\vec{D} = \varepsilon_0\vec{E} = \varepsilon_0 \frac{\rho_l}{2\pi\varepsilon_0 R}\,\vec{a}_R = \frac{\rho_l}{2\pi R}\,\vec{a}_R$$

where the unit vector is

$$\vec{a}_R = \frac{\vec{R}}{|\vec{R}|} = \frac{(0-0)\vec{a}_x + (0-8)\vec{a}_y + (0-0)\vec{a}_z}{8} = -\vec{a}_y$$

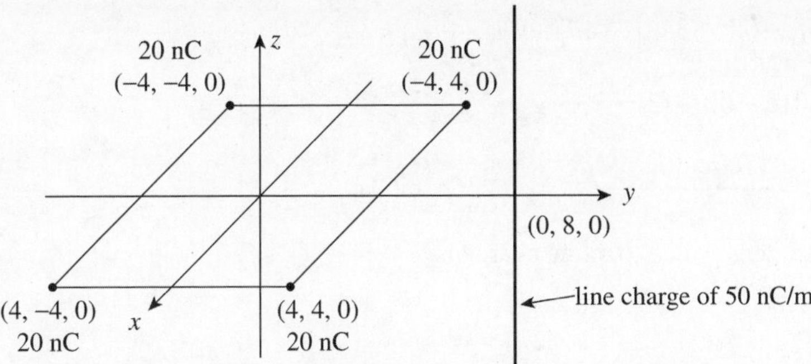

Figure E.2.48

The radial distance between the line charge (0,8,0) and the origin (0,0,0) is

$$R = \left|\vec{R}\right| = \sqrt{(0)^2 + (-8)^2 + (0)^2} = 8$$

Therefore, $\vec{D} = \dfrac{\rho_l}{2\pi R}\, \vec{a}_R = -\dfrac{50 \times 10^{-9}}{2\pi \times 8}\, \vec{a}_y = -0.995\, \vec{a}_y \text{ nC/m}^2$ ☐

EXAMPLE 2.49

Determine the electric flux density $\vec{D}$ at $(4,0,3)$ if there is a point charge -10π mC at $(4,0,0)$ and a line charge 6π mC/m along the y-axis.

SOLUTION

Figure E2.49 shows the electric flux density $\vec{D}$ due to a point charge and an infinite line charge.

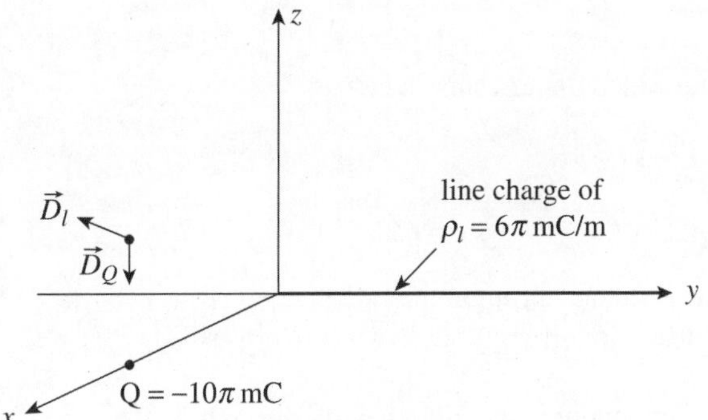

Figure E2.49

The electric flux density $\vec{D}$ at $(4,0,3)$ is determined by the sum of flux densities due to a point charge $\left(\vec{D}_Q\right)$ and a line charge $\left(\vec{D}_l\right)$. The electric flux density due to a point charge is

$$\vec{D}_Q = \frac{Q}{4\pi R^2}\, \vec{a}_R = \frac{Q\left(\vec{r} - \vec{r}_1\right)}{4\pi\left|\vec{r} - \vec{r}_1\right|^3}$$

where $\vec{r} - \vec{r}_1 = \left(4\vec{a}_x + 0\vec{a}_y + 3\vec{a}_z\right) - \left(4\vec{a}_x + 0\vec{a}_y + 0\vec{a}_z\right) = 3\vec{a}_z$

and $\left|\vec{r} - \vec{r}_1\right| = \sqrt{(0)^2 + (0)^2 + (3)^2} = 3$

Therefore, $\vec{D}_Q = \dfrac{-10\pi \times 10^{-3} \times 3\vec{a}_z}{4\pi \times 3^3} = -0.276\vec{a}_z \, \text{mC/m}^2$

The electric flux density due to a line charge is

$$\vec{D}_l = \frac{\rho_l}{2\pi\rho}\vec{a}_\rho$$

where $\quad \vec{a}_\rho = \dfrac{\vec{R}}{\left|\vec{R}\right|} = \dfrac{4\vec{a}_x + 3\vec{a}_z}{\sqrt{4^2 + 3^2}} = \dfrac{4\vec{a}_x + 3\vec{a}_z}{5}$

and $\quad \rho = \left|\vec{R}\right| = \sqrt{4^2 + 3^2} = 5$

Hence, $\quad \vec{D}_l = \dfrac{6\pi}{2\pi \times 5} \times \dfrac{\left(4\vec{a}_x + 3\vec{a}_z\right)}{5} = 0.48\vec{a}_x + 0.36\vec{a}_z \, \text{mC/m}^2$

Therefore, the total electric flux density is

$$\vec{D} = \vec{D}_Q + \vec{D}_l = \left(-0.276\vec{a}_z + 0.48\vec{a}_x + 0.36\vec{a}_z\right) \, \text{mC/m}^2$$

$$= 480\,\vec{a}_x + 84\,\vec{a}_z \, \mu\text{C/m}^2$$

EXAMPLE 2.50

Given $\vec{D} = z\rho\cos^2\phi\,\vec{a}_z \, \text{C/m}^2$, determine the total charge enclosed by the cylinder of radius $\rho = 1$ m with $-2 \le z \le 2\,\text{m}$.

SOLUTION

The total charge can be determined using Gauss's law as

$$Q = \psi = \oint_s \vec{D}\cdot d\vec{s}$$

$$= \left(\int_s + \int_t + \int_b\right)\vec{D}\cdot d\vec{s} = \psi_s + \psi_t + \psi_b$$

where ψ_s, ψ_t and ψ_b are the fluxes through the sides, the top surface, and the bottom surface of the cylinder respectively as shown in Figure E2.50.

Since $\vec{D}$ does not have component along $\vec{a}_\rho$, the flux through the side surfaces will be zero i.e., $\psi_s = 0$. For the flux through the top surface ψ_t, the surface area in cylindrical coordinates is $d\vec{s} = \rho\,d\rho\,d\phi\,\vec{a}_z$.

Therefore, $\psi_t = \int_{\rho=0}^{1}\int_{\phi=0}^{2\pi} z\rho\cos^2\phi\,\rho\,d\rho\,d\phi\bigg|_{z=2}$

$$= 2\int_0^1 \rho^2 d\rho\int_0^{2\pi}\cos^2\phi\,d\phi = 2\left(\frac{1}{3}\right)\pi = \frac{2\pi}{3}$$

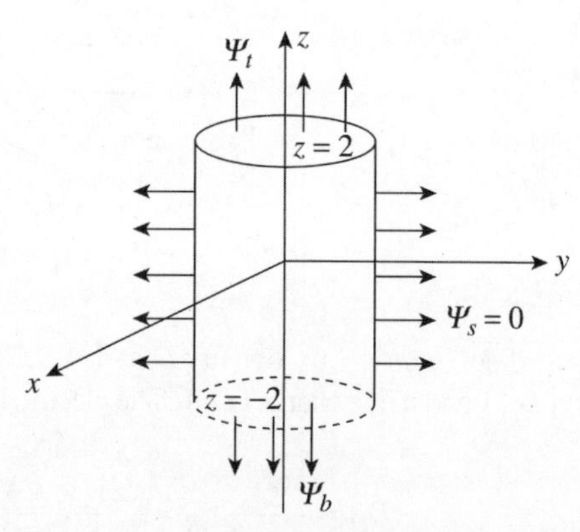

Figure E.2.50

and for the flux through the bottom surface ψ_b, the surface area in cylindrical coordinates is $d\vec{s} = -\rho\, d\rho\, d\phi\, \vec{a}_z$.

Therefore, $\psi_b = -\int_{\rho=0}^{1}\int_{\phi=0}^{2\pi} z\,\rho\cos^2\phi\,\rho\,d\rho\,d\phi\Big|_{z=-2}$

$$= 2\int_0^1 \rho^2 d\rho \int_0^{2\pi}\cos^2\phi\,d\phi = \frac{2\pi}{3}$$

Hence, the total charge enclosed by the cylinder is

$$Q = \psi = 0 + \frac{2\pi}{3} + \frac{2\pi}{3} = \frac{4\pi}{3}\,\text{C}$$

EXAMPLE 2.51

Consider that three charged cylindrical sheets are present in three spaces with $\rho_s = 5$ C/m^2 at $R = 2$ m, $\rho_s = -2$ C/m^2 at $R = 4$ m and $\rho_s = -3$ C/m^2 at $R = 5$ m. Determine the flux density at $R = 1, 3, 4.5$ and 6 m.

SOLUTION

Consider three cylindrical sheets as shown in Figure E2.51.

   The charge enclosed by the cylinder is,

Q = charge density × area = $\rho_s \times A$

Let the length of each cylindrical sheet be l and its area $= 2\pi R \times l$

   When $R = 2$ m, the charge in cylindrical sheet 1, $Q_1 = 5 \times 2\pi \times 2 \times l = 20\pi l$

   When $R = 4$ m, the charge in cylindrical sheet 2, $Q_2 = -2 \times 2\pi \times 4 \times l = -16\pi l$

   When $R = 5$ m, the charge in cylindrical sheet 3, $Q_3 = -3 \times 2\pi \times 5 \times l = -30\pi l$

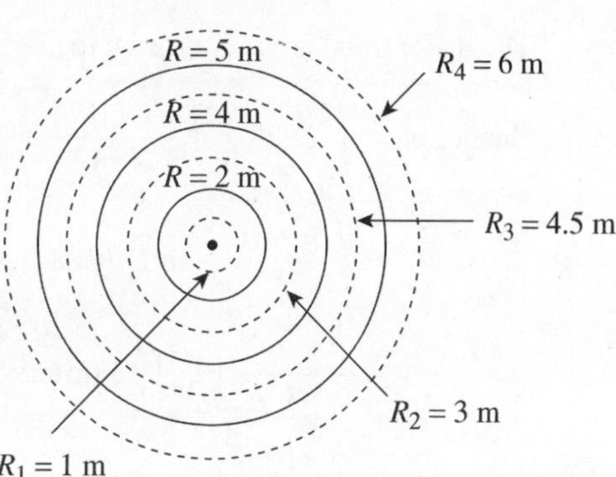

Figure E2.51

   The flux density is given by

$$\vec{D} = \frac{\text{charge enclosed}}{\text{area of cylinderical shell considered}}\,\vec{a}_r$$

For $R_1 = 1$ m, Q = Charge enclosed = 0

$$\vec{D} = \frac{Q}{2\pi R_1 l}\,\vec{a}_r = 0$$

For $R_2 = 3$ m, $Q = Q_1 = 20\pi l$

$$\vec{D} = \frac{Q}{2\pi R_2 l}\,\vec{a}_r = \frac{20\pi l}{2\pi \times 3 \times l}\,\vec{a}_r = 3.33\vec{a}_r\ \text{C/m}^2$$

For $R_3 = 4.5$ m, $Q = Q_1 + Q_2 = 20\pi l - 16\pi l = 4\pi l$

$$\vec{D} = \frac{Q}{2\pi R_3 l}\,\vec{a}_r = \frac{4\pi l}{2\pi \times 4.5 \times l}\,\vec{a}_r = 0.444\vec{a}_r\ \text{C/m}^2$$

For $R_4 = 6$ m, $Q = Q_1 + Q_2 + Q_3 = 20\pi l - 16\pi l - 30\pi l = -26\pi l$

$$\vec{D} = \frac{Q}{2\pi R_4 l}\,\vec{a}_r = \frac{-26\pi l}{2\pi \times 6 \times l}\,\vec{a}_r = -2.167\vec{a}_r\ \text{C/m}^2$$

EXAMPLE 2.52

The flux density given by $\vec{D} = \dfrac{r}{3}\vec{a}_r$ nC/m^2 is in the free space. Determine (*i*) the field intensity $\vec{E}$ of the sphere at $r = 0.2$ m (*ii*) the total electric flux leaving the sphere of $r = 0.2$ m and (*iii*) the total charge within the sphere of $r = 0.3$ m.

SOLUTION

(*i*) The electric field intensity $\vec{E}$ at $r = 0.2$ m is

$$\vec{E} = \frac{\vec{D}}{\varepsilon_0} = \frac{r \times 10^{-9}}{3\varepsilon_0}\vec{a}_r = \frac{0.2 \times 10^{-9}}{3 \times 8.854 \times 10^{-12}}\vec{a}_r = 7.53\,\vec{a}_r \text{ V/m}$$

(*ii*) By Gauss's law, the total charge enclosed or the total flux is equal to the net outward normal flux passing through the closed surface as given by

$$Q = \psi = \oint_s \vec{D} \cdot d\vec{s}$$

The differential area $d\vec{s}$ normal to $\vec{a}_r$ in spherical coordinates is $r^2 \sin\theta\, d\theta\, d\phi$.

Hence, $\psi = \oint_s \vec{D} \cdot d\vec{s} = \oint_s \left(\dfrac{r \times 10^{-9}}{3}\vec{a}_r \right) \cdot \left(r^2 \sin\theta\, d\theta\, d\phi\, \vec{a}_r \right)$

$$= \oint_s \frac{r^3 \times 10^{-9}}{3} \sin\theta\, d\theta\, d\phi \quad (\text{since } \vec{a}_r \cdot \vec{a}_r = 1)$$

$$= \frac{r^3 \times 10^{-9}}{3} \int_{\phi=0}^{2\pi} \int_{\theta=0}^{\pi} \sin\theta\, d\theta\, d\phi$$

$$= \frac{r^3 \times 10^{-9}}{3} \left[-\cos\theta \right]_0^\pi \left[\phi \right]_0^{2\pi}$$

$$= \frac{4}{3}\pi r^3 \text{ nC}$$

At $r = 0.2$ m, $\psi = \dfrac{4}{3}\pi \times (0.2)^3 \times 10^{-9}$

$$= 0.0335 \text{ nC} = 33.51 \text{ pC}$$

(*iii*) The total charge within the sphere of $r = 0.3$ m is

$$Q = \frac{4}{3}\pi \times (0.3)^3 \times 10^{-9}$$

$$= 0.113 \text{ nC} = 113.097 \text{ pC}$$

2.11 ELECTRIC POTENTIAL

Coulomb's law is generally used to determine the electric field intensity $\vec{E}$ due to any charge distribution. The electric field intensity $\vec{E}$ can also be obtained using Gauss's law when the charge distribution is symmetric. Another method of obtaining $\vec{E}$ is from the scalar electric potential V.

If a positive test charge Q is placed in an electric field intensity $\vec{E}$, it will experience a force which is represented by $\vec{F} = Q\vec{E}$. Under the influence of this force, the charge moves a differential distance $\vec{dl}$ as shown in Figure 2.21(a). If the charge moves, then work is being done by the electric field. The differential amount of work done in displacing the charge by $\vec{dl}$ is

$$dW_e = \vec{F} \cdot \vec{dl} = Q\vec{E} \cdot \vec{dl}$$

It is noted that a positive test charge always moves in the direction of the electric field intensity when the work is done by the electric field. If the test charge is moved against the direction of the field by an external force $\vec{F}_{ext}$, then the differential work done by the external force is given by

$$dW_e = -\vec{F}_{ext} \cdot \vec{dl} = -Q\vec{E} \cdot \vec{dl}$$

Here, the minus sign indicates that the charge is moved in a direction opposite to the electric field intensity. The external force is assumed to balance the electric force, as shown in Figure 2.21(b) in order to avoid consideration of any kinetic energy that may be acquired by a moving charge.

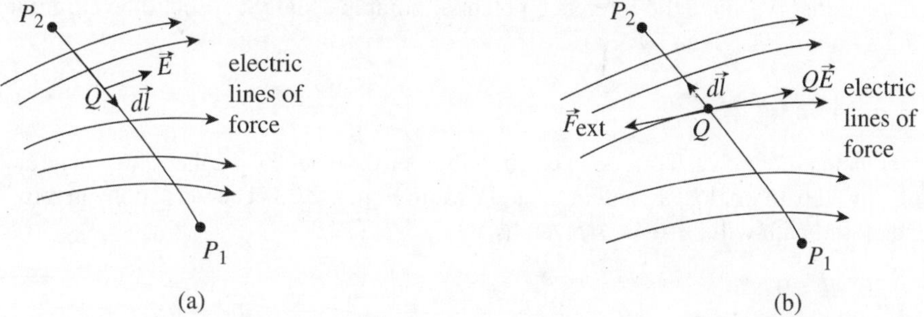

Figure 2.21 *Movement of test charge in an electric field caused by (a) the electric field and (b) the external force*

Therefore, the total work done or the potential energy required to move the test charge Q from point P_1 to P_2 is represented by

$$W = \int_{P_1}^{P_2} dW_e = -Q\int_{P_1}^{P_2} \vec{E} \cdot \vec{dl}$$

The *potential difference* between any two points P_1 and P_2 is defined as the electric energy per unit charge as given by

$$V_{21} = V_2 - V_1 = \frac{W}{Q} = -\int_{P_1}^{P_2} \vec{E} \cdot \vec{dl}$$

The unit of potential difference is joule per coulomb (J/C) or volt (V) whereas the electric field intensity is measured in volt per metre (V/m). The potential difference V is also called an *electrostatic potential* or *electric potential*.

In electrostatics, the potential difference between two points P_1 and P_2 is same irrespective of the path used for obtaining the line integral of the electric field intensity between them. Figure 2.22 shows the different paths (path 1 to path 3) for determining the potential difference between two points P_1 and P_2. The line integral taken on the right hand side of the above equation should be independent of the path taken between two points P_1 and P_2. Therefore, the potential remains same irrespective of the considered path.

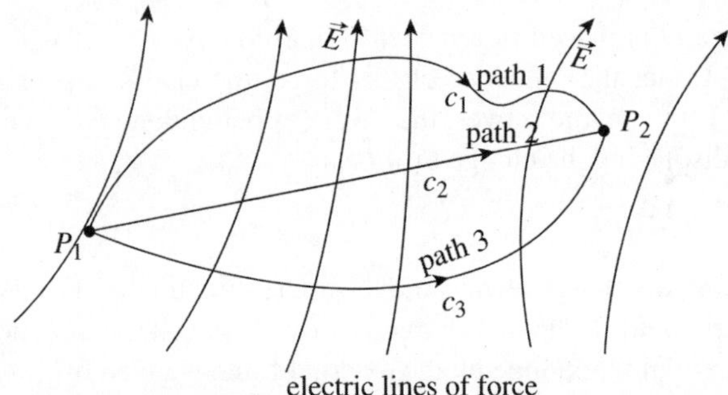

Figure 2.22 *Different paths to determine the potential difference between points P_1 and P_2*

The electric potential V at any point P in space is obtained with respect to some reference point and it is called the *absolute electric potential*. In electric circuit theory, absolute voltage at a point in a circuit has no meaning without considering the reference voltage point (ground). The same principle also applies to electric potential V in field theory. Since the reference potential point is usually chosen to be at infinity, the electric potential V at any point P is given by

$$V = -\int_{\infty}^{P} \vec{E} \cdot d\vec{l} \tag{2.54}$$

The above equation shows that, if one point is at infinity, then the potential is called an absolute electric potential.

Consider a closed path or closed contour c, as shown in Figure 2.23. The work done in moving the charge around such a closed path will be zero as given by

$$\oint_c \vec{E} \cdot d\vec{l} = 0$$

A vector field whose line integral around any closed path is zero is said to be an irrotational or a conservative field. Here, the electrostatic field $\vec{E}$ is called irrotational or conservative. However, a field is also said to be conservative if its curl is zero. It is mathematically expressed as

$$\nabla \times \vec{E} = 0 \tag{2.55}$$

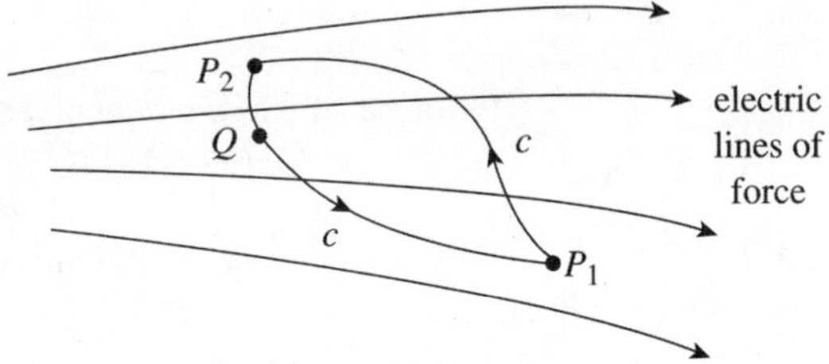

Figure 2.23 *Motion of charge Q around a closed path c in an electric field*

If the curl of a vector field is zero, then the vector field can be represented in terms of the gradient of a scalar field. Therefore, the electric field $\vec{E}$ is expressed in terms of a scalar field V as

$$\vec{E} = -\nabla V \tag{2.56}$$

Here, the minus sign indicates that the work done in moving a positive charge is against the electric field and ∇ is the gradient or the vector differential operator. Hence, the electric field can be called the negative gradient of V. The gradient is in the direction of the maximum rate of change of the potential V and in a direction opposite to that of the field.

As V is expressed in terms of a line integral over $\vec{E}$, the inverse relationship is also possible by expressing $\vec{E}$ in differential form of V. The differential electric potential can be written as

$$dV = -\vec{E} \cdot d\vec{l} \tag{2.57}$$

A scalar differential function V can be written as

$$dV = \nabla V \cdot d\vec{l} \tag{2.58}$$

where ∇ is the vector differential operator. Comparing Eqs. (2.57) and (2.58), we get

$$\vec{E} = -\nabla V \tag{2.59}$$

The above equation shows that $\vec{E}$ can be expressed in differential form of V and simply it is called the negative gradient of V. This relationship between V and $\vec{E}$ in differential form allows us to determine $\vec{E}$ for any charge distribution by first determining V and then obtaining the negative gradient of V.

The electric potential approach to determine the field intensity $\vec{E}$ is a two-step process which involves scalar sums and integrals. Hence, it is much easier to use this approach when compared to vector sums and integrals in determining $\vec{E}$ using Coulomb's law.

EXAMPLE 2.53

Given the potential $V = \dfrac{10}{r^2}\sin\theta\cos\phi,$ calculate the work done in moving a charge of 10 μC from point $A(1,30°,120°)$ to point $B(4,90°,60°).$

SOLUTION

The work done in moving a charge is

$$W_e = -Q\int_A^B \vec{E}\cdot d\vec{l}$$

$$= QV_{BA} = Q\left(V_B - V_A\right)$$

$$= 10\times10^{-6}\left[\frac{10}{4^2}\sin 90°\cos 60° - \frac{10}{1^2}\sin 30°\cos 120°\right]$$

$$= 10\times10^{-6}\left[\frac{10}{32} - \frac{(-10)}{4}\right] = 28.13\times10^{-6}$$

$$= 28.13\,\mu J$$

EXAMPLE 2.54

An electrostatic field intensity is given by $\vec{E} = \left(\dfrac{x}{2}+2y\right)\vec{a}_x + 2x\,\vec{a}_y$ V/m. Find the work done in moving a point charge $Q = -10\,\mu C$ (*i*) from the origin to $(4,0,0)$ m and (*ii*) from $(4,0,0)$ m to $(4,2,0)$ m.

SOLUTION

(*i*) The first path is along the x-axis, so that $d\vec{l} = dx\,\vec{a}_x.$

Therefore, the differential work done in moving the charge is

$$dW = -Q\vec{E}\cdot d\vec{l} = \left(10\times10^{-6}\right)\left(\frac{x}{2}+2y\right)\vec{a}_x\cdot dx\,\vec{a}_x$$

Integrating this equation, we get

$$W = \left(10 \times 10^{-6}\right) \int_0^4 \left(\frac{x}{2} + 2y\right) dx$$

$$= 10 \times 10^{-6} \times \left[\frac{x^2}{4}\right]_0^4 = 40\,\mu\text{J}$$

(*ii*) The second path is in the $\vec{a}_y$ direction, so that $d\vec{l} = dy\,\vec{a}_y$.

Therefore, the work done in moving the charge is

$$W = \left(10 \times 10^{-6}\right) \int_0^2 2x\,dy\Big|_{x=4} = 160\,\mu\text{J}\qquad\square$$

EXAMPLE 2.55

The potential distribution of $V = ax^2 + 6y^2 - 3\sqrt{z}$ V exists in an electric field intensity of $\vec{E} = -8x\vec{a}_x - 12y\vec{a}_y + \dfrac{1.5}{\sqrt{z}}\vec{a}_z$. Find the value of a.

SOLUTION

The electric field intensity in terms of potential is

$$\vec{E} = -\nabla V = -\left(\frac{\partial V}{\partial x}\vec{a}_x + \frac{\partial V}{\partial y}\vec{a}_y + \frac{\partial V}{\partial z}\vec{a}_z\right)$$

$$= -\left(2ax\vec{a}_x + 12y\vec{a}_y - \frac{3}{2\sqrt{z}}\vec{a}_z\right)$$

Comparing the above expression with the given expression of the electric field intensity $\vec{E}$, we get

$$2a = 8$$

Therefore, $a = 4$ $\qquad\square$

EXAMPLE 2.56

Given the field $\vec{E} = \left(\dfrac{-16}{r^2}\right)\vec{a}_r$ V/m in spherical coordinates, find the potential of point $\left(2, \pi, \dfrac{\pi}{2}\right)$ with respect to $(4, 0, \pi)$.

SOLUTION

The equipotential surfaces are concentric spherical shells. Consider A as $r = 2$ m and B as $r = 4$ m. The potential is

$$V_{AB} = -\int_B^A \vec{E} \cdot d\vec{l} = \int_4^2 \left(\frac{-16}{r^2}\right) dr = -4\text{V}\qquad\square$$

EXAMPLE 2.57

Given that the potential $V = 2x^2y - 5z$ V. At point $P(-4,6,3)$, determine (i) the potential V (ii) electric field intensity $\vec{E}$ (iii) the direction of $\vec{E}$ (iv) electric flux density $\vec{D}$ and (v) volume charge density ρ_v.

SOLUTION

(*i*) The potential V at point $P(-4,6,3)$ is

$$V_p = 2(-4)^2(6) - 5(3) = 192 - 15 = 177\text{ V}$$

(*ii*) The electric field intensity $\vec{E}$ is

$$\vec{E} = -\nabla V = -\left(\frac{\partial V}{\partial x}\vec{a}_x + \frac{\partial V}{\partial y}\vec{a}_y + \frac{\partial V}{\partial z}\vec{a}_z\right)$$

$$= -4xy\vec{a}_x - 2x^2\vec{a}_y + 5\vec{a}_z \text{ V/m}$$

Hence, the electric field intensity $\vec{E}$ at point $P(-4,6,3)$ is

$$\vec{E}_P = -4(-4)(6)\vec{a}_x - 2(-4)^2\vec{a}_y + 5\vec{a}_z$$

$$= 96\vec{a}_x - 32\vec{a}_y + 5\vec{a}_z \text{ V/m}$$

The magnitude of $\vec{E}_P$ is

$$\left|\vec{E}_p\right| = \sqrt{(96)^2 + (-32)^2 + (5)^2} = 101.32 \text{ V/m}$$

(*iii*) The direction of $\vec{E}$ at point $P(-4,6,3)$ is along the unit vector $\vec{a}_E$ as given by

$$\vec{a}_E = \frac{\vec{E}_P}{\left|\vec{E}_P\right|} = \frac{96\vec{a}_x - 32\vec{a}_y + 5\vec{a}_z}{101.32}$$

$$= 0.947\vec{a}_x - 0.316\vec{a}_y + 0.049\vec{a}_z$$

(*iv*) The electric flux density $\vec{D}$ at point $P(-4,6,3)$ is

$$\vec{D} = \varepsilon_0\vec{E} = 8.854\times10^{-12}\left[-4xy\vec{a}_x - 2x^2\vec{a}_y + 5\vec{a}_z\right]$$

$$= 35.4xy\vec{a}_x - 17.71x^2\vec{a}_y + 44.27\vec{a}_z \text{ pC/m}^2$$

At point $P(-4,6,3)$, $\vec{D}_p = 849.6\vec{a}_x - 283.36\vec{a}_y + 44.27\vec{a}_z \text{ pC/m}^2$

(*v*) The volume charge density ρ_v at point $P(-4,6,3)$ is

$$\rho_v = \nabla \cdot \vec{D} = \left(\frac{\partial V}{\partial x}\vec{a}_x + \frac{\partial V}{\partial y}\vec{a}_y + \frac{\partial V}{\partial z}\vec{a}_z\right)\cdot\left(-35.4xy\vec{a}_x - 17.71x^2\vec{a}_y + 44.27\vec{a}_z\right)$$

$$= -35.4\,y \text{ pC/m}^3$$

At point P, $\rho_v = -35.4\times6 = -212.4 \text{ pC/m}^3$

EXAMPLE 2.58

An electric potential is given by, $V = \dfrac{60\sin\theta}{r^2}V$. Find the potential and electric field at $P(3,60°,25°)$.

SOLUTION

The point $P(3,60°,25°)$ is given in spherical coordinates where $r = 3$, $\theta = 60°$ and $\phi = 25°$.

At point $P(3,60°,25°)$, the potential is

$$V = \frac{60\sin60°}{(3)^2} = 5.774 \text{ V}$$

The electric field intensity $\vec{E}$ in spherical coordinates is given by

$$\vec{E} = -\nabla V = -\left(\frac{\partial V}{\partial r}\vec{a}_r + \frac{1}{r}\frac{\partial V}{\partial \theta}\vec{a}_\theta + \frac{1}{r\sin\theta}\frac{\partial V}{\partial \phi}\vec{a}_\phi \right)$$

where $\dfrac{\partial V}{\partial r} = 60\sin\theta\,(-2)\,r^{-3} = -\dfrac{120\sin\theta}{r^3},$ θ constant

$$\frac{\partial V}{\partial \theta} = \frac{60}{r^2}\cos\theta, \qquad\qquad r \text{ constant}$$

$$\frac{\partial V}{\partial \phi} = 0, \qquad\qquad \phi \text{ constant}$$

Hence, $\vec{E} = -\left[-\dfrac{120\sin\theta}{r^3}\vec{a}_r + \dfrac{1}{r}\dfrac{60}{r^2}\cos\theta\,\vec{a}_\theta \right]$

At $P\left(3,60°,25°\right)$, $\vec{E} = \dfrac{120\sin 60°}{(3)^3}\vec{a}_r - \dfrac{60}{(3)^3}\cos 60°\,\vec{a}_\theta$

$$= 3.849\,\vec{a}_r - 1.111\vec{a}_\theta \text{ V/m}$$

EXAMPLE 2.59

If $V = 2x^2 y + 20z - \dfrac{4}{x^2 + y^2}$ V, determine $\vec{E}, \vec{D}$ and ρ_v at $P\left(6,-2.5,3\right)$.

SOLUTION

$$\vec{E} = -\nabla V = -\left[\frac{\partial V}{\partial x}\vec{a}_x + \frac{\partial V}{\partial y}\vec{a}_y + \frac{\partial V}{\partial z}\vec{a}_z \right]$$

where $\dfrac{\partial V}{\partial x} = 2y(2x) + 0 - 4\left[\dfrac{-(2x)}{\left(x^2 + y^2\right)^2} \right] = 4xy + \dfrac{8x}{\left(x^2 + y^2\right)^2}$

$$\frac{\partial V}{\partial y} = 2x^2 + 0 - 4\left[\frac{-2y}{\left(x^2 + y^2\right)^2} \right] = 2x^2 + \frac{8y}{\left(x^2 + y^2\right)^2}$$

$$\frac{\partial V}{\partial z} = 0 + 20 - 0 = 20$$

Hence, $\vec{E} = -\left\{ \left[4xy + \dfrac{8x}{\left(x^2 + y^2\right)^2} \right]\vec{a}_x + \left[2x^2 + \dfrac{8x}{\left(x^2 + y^2\right)^2} \right]\vec{a}_y + 20\vec{a}_z \right\}$

At point $P(6,-2.5,3)$,

$$\vec{E} = -\left\{ [-60 + 0.0268]\vec{a}_x + [72 - 0.0112]\vec{a}_y + 20\vec{a}_z \right\}$$

$$= 59.97\,\vec{a}_x - 71.99\,\vec{a}_y - 20\,\vec{a}_z \text{ V/m}$$

and $\qquad \vec{D} = \varepsilon_0 \vec{E} = 8.854 \times 10^{-12} \times \left(59.97 \vec{a}_x - 71.99 \vec{a}_y - 20 \vec{a}_z \right)$

$$= 0.531 \vec{a}_x - 0637 \vec{a}_y - 0.177 \vec{a}_z \ \ nC/m^2$$

From point form of Gauss's law, the volume charge density is

$$\rho_v = \nabla \cdot \vec{D}$$

$$= \nabla \cdot \left(\varepsilon_0 \vec{E} \right) = \left(\nabla \cdot \vec{E} \right) \varepsilon_0$$

Therefore, $\nabla \cdot \vec{E} = \dfrac{\partial E_x}{\partial x} + \dfrac{\partial E_y}{\partial y} + \dfrac{\partial E_z}{\partial z}$

$$= -\frac{\partial}{\partial x} \left[4xy + \frac{8x}{\left(x^2 + y^2 \right)^2} \right] - \frac{\partial}{\partial y} \left[2x^2 + \frac{8y}{\left(x^2 + y^2 \right)^2} \right] - \frac{\partial}{\partial z} (20)$$

$$= - \left[4y + \left\{ \frac{\left(x^2 + y^2 \right)^2 8 - 8x \times 2 \left(x^2 + y^2 \right)(2x)}{\left(x^2 + y^2 \right)^4} \right\} \right]$$

$$- \left[0 + \left\{ \frac{\left(x^2 + y^2 \right)^2 (8) - 8y \times 2 \left(x^2 + y^2 \right)(2y)}{\left(x^2 + y^2 \right)^4} \right\} \right] - 0$$

$$= -4y - \frac{8}{\left(x^2 + y^2 \right)^2} + \frac{32x^2}{\left(x^2 + y^2 \right)^3} - \frac{8}{\left(x^2 + y^2 \right)^2} + \frac{32y^2}{\left(x^2 + y^2 \right)^3}$$

At P, $x = 6, y = -2.5$ and $z = 3$.

Hence, $\nabla \cdot \vec{E} = 10 - 4.482 \times 10^{-3} + 15.27 \times 10^{-3} - 4.482 \times 10^{-3} + 2.65 \times 10^{-3}$

$$= 10 - 8.8956 \times 10^{-3} \approx 10$$

$$\rho_v = \left(\nabla \cdot \vec{E} \right) \varepsilon_0 = 10 \times 8.854 \times 10^{-12}$$

$$= 88.54 \ pC/m^3$$

EXAMPLE 2.60

Given the potential $V = \dfrac{10}{r^2} \sin \theta \cos \phi$ V, find the electric flux density at $\left(2, \dfrac{\pi}{2}, 0 \right)$.

SOLUTION

The electric field intensity is $\vec{E} = -\nabla V$.

where $\nabla V = \left(\dfrac{\partial V}{\partial r} \vec{a}_r + \dfrac{1}{r} \dfrac{\partial V}{\partial \theta} \vec{a}_\theta + \dfrac{1}{r \sin \theta} \dfrac{\partial V}{\partial \phi} \vec{a}_\phi \right)$ in spherical coordinates.

Therefore, $\vec{E} = -\left(\dfrac{\partial V}{\partial r} \vec{a}_r + \dfrac{1}{r} \dfrac{\partial V}{\partial \theta} \vec{a}_\theta + \dfrac{1}{r \sin \theta} \dfrac{\partial V}{\partial \phi} \vec{a}_\phi \right)$

$$= \frac{20}{r^3} \sin \theta \cos \phi \, \vec{a}_r - \frac{10}{r^3} \cos \theta \cos \phi \, \vec{a}_\theta + \frac{10}{r^3} \sin \phi \, \vec{a}_\phi$$

Given the point in spherical coordinates $\left(2, \dfrac{\pi}{2}, 0 \right)$ where $r = 2$, $\theta = \dfrac{\pi}{2}$ and $\phi = 0$.

The electric flux density at $\left(2, \dfrac{\pi}{2}, 0 \right)$ is

$$\vec{D} = \varepsilon_0 \vec{E} = \varepsilon_0 \left(\frac{20}{8} \right) \vec{a}_r$$

$$= 2.5 \varepsilon_0 \vec{a}_r = 2.5 \times 8.854 \times 10^{-12} \, \vec{a}_r$$

$$= 22.13 \, \vec{a}_r \,\, \text{pC/m}^2$$

EXAMPLE 2.61

If the potential field is given by $V = 100\left(x^2 - y^2 \right) V$, determine V and $\vec{E}$ at a point $(2, -1, 3)$ and the equation represents the locus of all points having a potential of 300 V.

SOLUTION

Given $V = 100\left(x^2 - y^2 \right) \text{V}$.

At $(2, -1, 3)$, the potential is

$$V = 100 \left[(2)^2 - (-1)^2 \right] = 300 \, \text{V}$$

The electric field intensity is

$$\vec{E} = -\nabla V = -\left(\frac{\partial V}{\partial x} \vec{a}_x + \frac{\partial V}{\partial y} \vec{a}_y + \frac{\partial V}{\partial z} \vec{a}_z \right)$$

$$= -\left(200x \vec{a}_x - 200y \vec{a}_y \right)$$

$$= -200x \vec{a}_x + 200y \vec{a}_y$$

Hence, at $(2, -1, 3)$, $\vec{E} = -400 \, \vec{a}_x - 200 \, \vec{a}_y$ V/m

For a potential of 300V, the equation representing the locus of all points is

$$300 = 100\left(x^2 - y^2 \right)$$

i.e., $x^2 - y^2 = 3$

EXAMPLE 2.62

Given field intensity $\vec{E} = 40xy \vec{a}_x + 20x^2 \vec{a}_y + 2 \vec{a}_z$ V/m, calculate the potential difference between two points $P(1, -1, 0)$ and $Q(2, 1, 3)$.

SOLUTION

Given $\vec{E} = 40xy\vec{a}_x + 20x^2\vec{a}_y + 2\vec{a}_z$ V/m.

The potential difference is

$$V_{PQ} = -\int_Q^P \vec{E} \cdot d\vec{l}, \quad \text{where} \quad d\vec{l} = dx\vec{a}_x + dy\vec{a}_y + dz\vec{a}_z$$

Now $\vec{a}_x \cdot \vec{a}_x = \vec{a}_y \cdot \vec{a}_y = \vec{a}_z \cdot \vec{a}_z = 1$ and all other dot products are zero.

$$\vec{E} \cdot d\vec{l} = 40xy\,dx + 20x^2\,dy + 2dz$$

Therefore, $V_{PQ} = -\int_Q^P \left(40xy\,dx + 20x^2\,dy + 2dz\right)$

As the line integral does not depend on the path from $Q(2,1,3)$ to $P(1,-1,0)$, we can divide the path into

Path 1, $\quad Q(2,1,3)$ to $(1,1,3)$ $\longrightarrow$ only x varies, $y = 1$, $z = 3$

Path 2, $\quad (1,1,3)$ to $(1,-1,3)$ $\longrightarrow$ only y varies, $x = 1$, $z = 3$

Path 3, $\quad (1,-1,3)$ to $P(1,-1,0)$ $\longrightarrow$ only z varies, $x = 1$, $y = -1$

Hence, the potential difference between two points $P(1,-1,0)$ and $Q(2,1,3)$ is

$$V_{PQ} = -\left[\int_{x=2}^{x=1} 40xy\Big|_{y=1}\,dx + \int_{y=1}^{y=-1} 20x^2\Big|_{x=1}\,dy + \int_{z=3}^{z=0} 2dz\right]$$

$$= -\left(40\left[\frac{x^2}{2}\right]_2^1 + 20[y]_1^{-1} + 2[z]_3^0\right)$$

$$= -\{20(1-4) + 20(-1-1) + 2(0-3)\}$$

$$= -(-60 - 40 - 6) = 106\ \text{V}$$

EXAMPLE 2.63

Given below the electric field intensity variation, find the odd one out:

(i) $\vec{E} = c\left[xy\vec{a}_x + 2yz\vec{a}_y + 3xz\vec{a}_z\right]$

(ii) $\vec{E} = c\left[y^2\vec{a}_x + \left(2xy + z^2\right)\vec{a}_y + 2yz\vec{a}_z\right]$

Determine the potential for the possible field using the origin as reference point. Verify the answer by computing ∇V.

SOLUTION

The odd field can be found by checking whether the curl of the given electric field vector function is zero or not, i.e, $\nabla \times \vec{E} = 0$.

(i) $\vec{E} = c\left[xy\vec{a}_x + 2yz\vec{a}_y + 3xz\vec{a}_z\right]$

$$\nabla \times \vec{E} = c\begin{vmatrix} \vec{a}_x & \vec{a}_y & \vec{a}_z \\ \dfrac{\partial}{\partial x} & \dfrac{\partial}{\partial y} & \dfrac{\partial}{\partial z} \\ xy & 2yz & 3xz \end{vmatrix} = c\left[(0-2y)\vec{a}_x - (3z)\vec{a}_y + (-x)\vec{a}_z\right]$$

$$= c\left(-2y\vec{a}_x - 3z\vec{a}_y - x\vec{a}_z\right)$$

$$\nabla \times \vec{E} \neq 0$$

Since the curl of the electric field intensity is not equal to zero, the given vector function cannot describe an electric field.

(ii) $\vec{E} = c\left[y^2\vec{a}_x + \left(2xy + z^2\right)\vec{a}_y + 2yz\vec{a}_z\right]$

$$\nabla \times \vec{E} = c\begin{vmatrix} \vec{a}_x & \vec{a}_y & \vec{a}_z \\ \dfrac{\partial}{\partial x} & \dfrac{\partial}{\partial y} & \dfrac{\partial}{\partial z} \\ y^2 & 2xy + z^2 & 2yz \end{vmatrix}$$

$$= c\left(\left(2z - 2z\right)\vec{a}_x - \left(0 - 0\right)\vec{a}_y + \left(2y - 2y\right)\vec{a}_z\right)$$

$$\nabla \times \vec{E} = 0$$

Since the curl of the electric field intensity is equal to zero, the given vector function can describe an electric field.

To calculate the electric potential V at an arbitrary point (x, y, z) using $(0, 0, 0)$ as a reference point, we have to evaluate the line integral of $\vec{E}$ between $(0, 0, 0)$ and (x, y, z). Since the line integral of $\vec{E}$ is independent of the path, we are free to choose the most convenient integration path.

Consider the following integration path:

$$(0,0,0) \longrightarrow (x,0,0) \longrightarrow (x,y,0) \longrightarrow (x,y,z)$$

The potential at (x_1, y_1, z_1) for this field is

$$V = -\int_0^l E \cdot dl = -\left[\int_0^x cy^2\Big|_{y=0} dx + \int_0^y c\left(2xy + z^2\right)\Big|_{z=0} dy + \int_0^z c\left(2yz\right)dz\right]$$

$$= -c\left(xy^2 + yz^2\right)\text{V}$$

The answer can be verified by determining the gradient of V as given by

$$\nabla V = \frac{\partial V}{\partial x}\vec{a}_x + \frac{\partial V}{\partial y}\vec{a}_y + \frac{\partial V}{\partial z}\vec{a}_z$$

$$= -c\left[y^2\vec{a}_x + \left(2xy + z^2\right)\vec{a}_y + 2yz\vec{a}_z\right] = -\vec{E}$$

2.11.1 Electric Potential due to Point Charge

For a point charge Q located at the origin of a spherical coordinate system, the electric field intensity $\vec{E}$ at a distance r is represented by

$$\vec{E} = \frac{Q}{4\pi\varepsilon_0 r^2}\vec{a}_r$$

The choice of integration path between the two end points in potential equation is arbitrary. Hence, it will be convenient to choose the path along the radial direction $\vec{a}_r$, in which case $d\vec{l} = dr\,\vec{a}_r$ and

$$V = -\int_{\infty}^{r} \vec{E} \cdot d\vec{l} = -\int_{\infty}^{r}\left(\frac{Q}{4\pi\varepsilon_0 r^2}\vec{a}_r\right)\cdot(dr\,\vec{a}_r)=\frac{Q}{4\pi\varepsilon_0 r} \tag{2.60}$$

Suppose if the charge Q is not located at the origin, but at a point whose position vector is $\vec{r}_i$, then the potential V at $\vec{r}$ becomes

$$V(\vec{r}) = \frac{Q}{4\pi\varepsilon_0 |\vec{r} - \vec{r}_i|} \tag{2.61}$$

where $|\vec{r} - \vec{r}_i|$ is the distance between the point of observation and the location of charge Q. The basic idea of finding the electric potential due to a point charge is applied to other types of charge distribution because any charge distribution can be regarded as consisting of point charges. The superposition principle applied to the electric field intensity $\vec{E}$ can also be applied to find the electric potential V. For n discrete point charges $Q_1, Q_2, \ldots, Q_n$ located at points with position vectors $\vec{r}_1, \vec{r}_2, \ldots, \vec{r}_n$, the electric potential at $\vec{r}$ is expressed by

$$V(\vec{r}) = \frac{1}{4\pi\varepsilon_0}\sum_{i=1}^{n}\frac{Q_i}{|\vec{r} - \vec{r}_i|} \tag{2.62}$$

EXAMPLE 2.64

Determine the potential difference between two points due to a point charge Q at the origin.

SOLUTION

The electric field intensity $\vec{E}$ at a radial distance r from a point charge Q is

$$\vec{E} = \frac{Q}{4\pi\varepsilon_0 r^2}\vec{a}_r$$

If the distances of two points A and B from the charge Q at the origin are r_1 and r_2 respectively, then the potential difference is

$$V_{AB} = -\int_{r_2}^{r_1}\vec{E}\cdot d\vec{l} = -\int_{r_2}^{r_1}\left(\frac{Q}{4\pi\varepsilon_0 r^2}\vec{a}_r\right)\cdot(dr\vec{a}_r)$$

$$= -\frac{Q}{4\pi\varepsilon_0}\int_{r_2}^{r_1}\frac{1}{r^2}\,dr = \frac{Q}{4\pi\varepsilon_0}\left[\frac{1}{r_1} - \frac{1}{r_2}\right]$$

$$V_{AB} = V_A - V_B$$

where V_A and V_B are the absolute potentials at A and B, respectively.

If $r_2 \to \infty$, then the potential of point A with respect to point B at infinity is known as the absolute potential. Hence, the absolute potential of point A at $r_1 = R$ is

$$V_A = \frac{Q}{4\pi\varepsilon_0 R}$$

EXAMPLE 2.65

A point charge of 2 nC is located at the origin. What is the value of potential at $P(1,0,0)$ m?

SOLUTION

Given that a point charge of $Q = 2\,\text{nC} = 2\times10^{-9}\,\text{C}$ is located at the origin. The potential due to a point charge at point $P(1,0,0)$ is

$$V = \frac{Q}{4\pi\varepsilon_0 r}$$

Here, $\quad r = \sqrt{(1-0)^2 + 0^2 + 0^2} = 1$

Therefore, $V = \dfrac{2\times10^{-9}}{4\pi \times 8.854\times10^{-12}\times1} = 17.98\,\text{V}$

EXAMPLE 2.66

Determine the potential at $r_B = 15\,\text{m}$ with respect to $r_A = 5\,\text{m}$ due to a point charge $Q = 100\,\text{pC}$ at the origin and zero reference at infinity.

SOLUTION

The potential due to a point charge is

$$V_{AB} = \frac{Q}{4\pi\varepsilon_0}\left(\frac{1}{r_A} - \frac{1}{r_B}\right)$$

In order to find the potential difference at the origin, the zero reference is not needed.

$$V_{AB} = \frac{100\times10^{-12}}{4\pi\times8.854\times10^{-12}}\left(\frac{1}{5} - \frac{1}{15}\right) = 0.12\,\text{V}$$

The zero reference at infinity may be used to find V_5 and V_{15}.

$$V_A = V_5 = \frac{Q}{4\pi\varepsilon_0}\left(\frac{1}{5}\right) = 0.18\,\text{V}$$

$$V_B = V_{15} = \frac{Q}{4\pi\varepsilon_0}\left(\frac{1}{15}\right) = 0.06\,\text{V}$$

Therefore, $V_{AB} = V_A - V_B = 0.12\,\text{V}$

EXAMPLE 2.67

Determine the potential difference between the points A and B which are at a distance of 0.5 m and 0.1 m respectively from a negative charge of $20\times10^{-10}\,\text{C}$ and $\varepsilon_0 = 8.854\,\text{pF/m}$.

SOLUTION

The potential due to a point charge is

$$V = \frac{Q}{4\pi\varepsilon_0 r}$$

The potential between two point charges at A and B is

$$V_{AB} = V_A - V_B = \frac{Q}{4\pi\varepsilon_0}\left[\frac{1}{r_A} - \frac{1}{r_B}\right]$$

$$= \frac{-20 \times 10^{-10}}{4\pi \times 8.854 \times 10^{-12}} \left[\frac{1}{0.5} - \frac{1}{0.1} \right] = 143.88 \, \text{V}$$

EXAMPLE 2.68

Given that two point charges $-4 \, \mu\text{C}$ and $5 \, \mu\text{C}$ are located at $(2,-1,3)$ and $(0,4,-2)$, respectively. Find the potential at $(2,0,2)$ assuming zero potential at infinity.

SOLUTION

Given $Q_1 = -4 \, \mu\text{C}$ and $Q_2 = 5 \, \mu\text{C}$. The potential V at $\vec{r}$ is

$$V(\vec{r}) = \frac{Q_1}{4\pi\varepsilon_0 |\vec{r} - \vec{r}_1|} + \frac{Q_2}{4\pi\varepsilon_0 |\vec{r} - \vec{r}_2|} + B_0$$

If $V(\infty) = 0$, then $B_0 = 0$. The distance vector between the point $(2,0,2)$ and the charge Q_1 located at $(2,-1,3)$ is

$$|\vec{r} - \vec{r}_1| = \sqrt{(2-2)^2 + (0+1)^2 + (2-3)^2} = \sqrt{2}$$

and the distance vector between the point $(2,0,2)$ and the charge Q_2 located at $(0,4,-2)$ is

$$|\vec{r} - \vec{r}_2| = \sqrt{(2-0)^2 + (0-4)^2 + (2+2)^2} = \sqrt{36} = 6$$

Therefore, the potential at $(2,0,2)$ is

$$V_{\text{at}(2,0,2)} = 9 \times 10^9 \times 10^{-6} \left[\frac{-4}{\sqrt{2}} + \frac{5}{6} \right] \qquad \left(\text{since} \frac{1}{4\pi\varepsilon_0} = 9 \times 10^9 \right)$$

$$= 9 \times 10^3 \left(-2.828 + 0.833 \right) = -17.96 \, \text{kV}$$

EXAMPLE 2.69

What is the potential at the center of a square with side $a = 2 \, \text{m}$ while charges $2 \, \mu\text{C}, -4\mu\text{C}, 6\mu\text{C}$ and $2 \, \mu\text{C}$ are located at its four corners?

SOLUTION

Figure E2.69 shows the arrangement of charges at four corners of the square. The potential at a point center point P due to a point charge is

$$V = \frac{Q}{4\pi\varepsilon_0 R}$$

where R is the distance between the charge and point P.

Therefore, the potential of P due to Q_A is $V_{P1} = \dfrac{Q_A}{4\pi\varepsilon_0 R_1}$

where $R_1 = \sqrt{2}$ is the distance from the charge at A to point P.

Similarly $V_{P2} = \dfrac{Q_B}{4\pi\varepsilon_0 R_2}$, where $R_2 = \sqrt{2}$

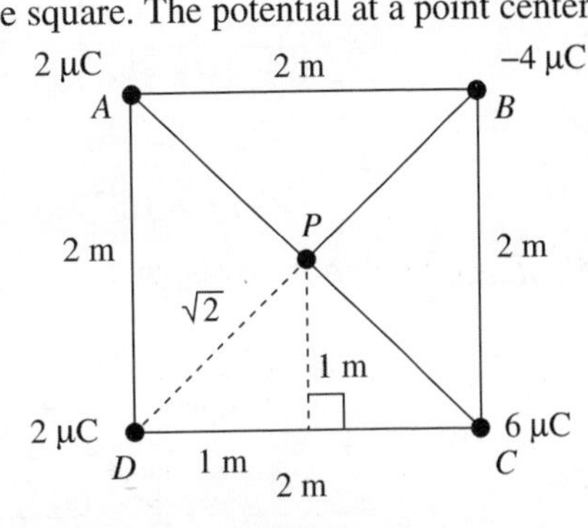

Figure E2.69

$$V_{P3} = \frac{Q_C}{4\pi\varepsilon_0 R_3}, \qquad \text{where } R_3 = \sqrt{2}$$

$$V_{P4} = \frac{Q_D}{4\pi\varepsilon_0 R_4}, \qquad \text{where } R_4 = \sqrt{2}$$

Therefore, by superposition principle, the total potential at the center of the square is

$$V_P = \sum_{i=1}^{4} V_{Pi} = \frac{1}{4\pi\varepsilon_0 R}\left[Q_A + Q_B + Q_C + Q_D\right]$$

where $R = R_1 = R_2 = R_3 = R_4 = \sqrt{2}$ m.

Hence, the potential is

$$V_P = \frac{1}{4\pi \times 8.854 \times 10^{-12} \times \sqrt{2}}\left[2 - 4 + 6 + 2\right] \times 10^{-6} = 38.16\,\text{kV} \qquad \square$$

EXAMPLE 2.70

A hollow sphere is charged to 5 μC. Determine the potential (i) at its surface (ii) inside the sphere and (iii) at a distance 0.5 m from the surface. The radius of the sphere is 0.2 m. Calculate the potential with respect to r, which is the distance of the point from the center of the sphere for $0 < r < \infty$.

SOLUTION

Given $\varepsilon = \varepsilon_0$ in free space, charge $Q = 5 \times 10^{-6}\,\text{C}$ and radius of the sphere, $a = 0.2$ m. The potential difference $V_a - V_\infty$ gives absolute potential at a distance r_1 from center as given by

$$V_a - V_\infty = -\int_{r_1}^{a} \frac{Q\,dr}{4\pi\varepsilon_0 r^2} - \int_{\infty}^{r_1} \frac{Q\,dr}{4\pi\varepsilon_0 r^2}$$

Case (i): At the surface: $r_1 = a$

$$V = -\int_{a}^{a} \frac{Q\,dr}{4\pi\varepsilon_0 r^2} - \int_{\infty}^{a} \frac{Q\,dr}{4\pi\varepsilon_0 r^2}$$

$$= -\int_{\infty}^{a} \frac{Q\,dr}{4\pi\varepsilon_0 r^2} = -\frac{Q}{4\pi\varepsilon_0}\left[-\frac{1}{r}\right]_{\infty}^{a}$$

$$= -\frac{Q}{4\pi\varepsilon_0}\left[-\frac{1}{a} + \frac{1}{\infty}\right] = \frac{Q}{4\pi\varepsilon_0 a}$$

$$= \frac{5 \times 10^{-6}}{4\pi \times 8.854 \times 10^{-12} \times 0.2} = 224.69\,\text{kV}$$

Case (ii): Inside the sphere

$$V = -\int_{r_1}^{a} \frac{Q\,dr}{4\pi\varepsilon_0 r^2}$$

$$= -\frac{Q}{4\pi\varepsilon_0}\left[-\frac{1}{r}\right]_{r_1}^{a} = -\frac{Q}{4\pi\varepsilon_0}\left[-\frac{1}{a} + \frac{1}{r_1}\right]$$

$$= \frac{Q}{4\pi\varepsilon_0}\left[\frac{1}{0.2} - \frac{1}{r_1}\right] = \frac{5\times10^{-6}}{4\pi\times8.854\times10^{-12}}\left[5 - \frac{1}{r_1}\right]$$

$$= 44.94\times10^3\left(5 - \frac{1}{r_1}\right) = 44.94\left(5 - \frac{1}{r_1}\right)\text{ kV}$$

where r_1 is the distance from the center to the point at which the potential is measured.

Case (iii): At a point 0.5 m from the surface

The radius of the sphere is 0.2 m. Hence, the point is at 0.7 m from the center.

$$V = -\int_\infty^{0.7}\frac{Q\,dr}{4\pi\varepsilon_0 r^2} = -\frac{Q}{4\pi\varepsilon_0}\left[-\frac{1}{r}\right]_\infty^{0.7}$$

$$= -\frac{Q}{4\pi\varepsilon_0}\left[-\frac{1}{0.7} + \frac{1}{\infty}\right]$$

$$= \frac{5\times10^{-6}}{4\pi\times8.854\times10^{-12}\times0.7} = 64.196\text{ kV} \qquad\qquad \square$$

2.11.2 Electric Potential due to Continuous Charge Distributions

For a continuous charge distribution specified over a given volume v, or across a surface s, or along a line l, the charge Q_i in Eq. (2.62) is replaced with $\rho_l dl, \rho_s ds$ or $\rho_v dv$ and the summation is converted into an integration, the potential V at $\vec{r}$ becomes

$$V = \frac{1}{4\pi\varepsilon_0}\int_l \frac{\rho_l dl}{|\vec{r} - \vec{r_i}|} \qquad\qquad \text{(line charge distribution)}$$

$$V = \frac{1}{4\pi\varepsilon_0}\int_s \frac{\rho_s ds}{|\vec{r} - \vec{r_i}|} \qquad\qquad \text{(surface charge distribution)}$$

$$V = \frac{1}{4\pi\varepsilon_0}\int_v \frac{\rho_v dv}{|\vec{r} - \vec{r_i}|} \qquad\qquad \text{(volume charge distribution)}$$

where $\vec{r_i}$ refers to the position vector of source point and $\vec{r}$ denotes the position vector of field point at which V is to be determined.

EXAMPLE 2.71

A uniform line charge of 1nC/m is situated along x-axis between the points $(-500,0)$ mm and $(500,0)$ mm. Find the electric scalar potential at $(0,1000)$ mm.

SOLUTION

Figure E2.71 shows a uniform line charge of $\rho_l = 1$ nC/m along x-axis. Consider a differential charge dQ on a differential length dx at distance x from the origin as given by $dQ = \rho_l dx$. The distance of point A from charge dQ is $R = \sqrt{x^2 + 1}$.

The differential voltage due to differential charge is

$$dV_A = \frac{dQ}{4\pi\varepsilon_0 R} = \frac{\rho_l dx}{4\pi\varepsilon_0\sqrt{x^2 + 1}}$$

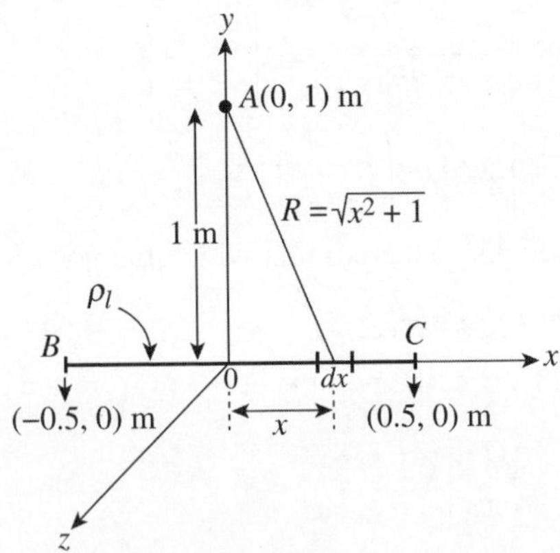

Figure E2.71

Integrating this equation, we get

$$V_A = \int_{-0.5}^{0.5} \frac{\rho_l dx}{4\pi\varepsilon_0 \sqrt{x^2+1}} = 2\int_0^{0.5} \frac{\rho_l dx}{4\pi\varepsilon_0 \sqrt{x^2+1}}$$

$$= \frac{2\rho_l}{4\pi\varepsilon_0} \int_0^{0.5} \frac{dx}{\sqrt{x^2+1}}$$

$$= \frac{2\rho_l}{4\pi\varepsilon_0} \left[\ln\left(x + \sqrt{x^2+1}\right) \right]_0^{0.5}$$

$$= \frac{2\times 1\times 10^{-9}}{4\pi\times 8.854\times 10^{-12}} \left[\ln\left(0.5 + \sqrt{0.5^2+1}\right) - \ln(1) \right] = 8.65\,\text{V}$$

Therefore, the electric scalar potential at $A(0,1)\,$m is $V_A = 8.65\,$V.

EXAMPLE 2.72

A charged ring of radius b carries a uniform linear charge distribution. Determine the potential and the electric field intensity at any point on the axis of the ring.

SOLUTION

Figure E2.72 shows an uniformly charged circular ring of radius b with linear charge density of ρ_l. The potential at point $P(0,0,z)$ due to linear charge density of ρ_l on the z-axis is

$$V = \frac{1}{4\pi\varepsilon_0} \int_l \frac{\rho_l dl}{|\vec{r} - \vec{r}_i|}$$

where $dl = bd\phi$ is the differential length along $\vec{a}_\phi$ direction in cylindrical coordinates and $|\vec{r} - \vec{r}_i| = \sqrt{b^2 + z^2}$.

Therefore, the potential on the axis of the charged circular ring is

$$V(z) = \frac{1}{4\pi\varepsilon_0} \int_0^{2\pi} \frac{\rho_l b\, d\phi}{\sqrt{b^2 + z^2}}$$

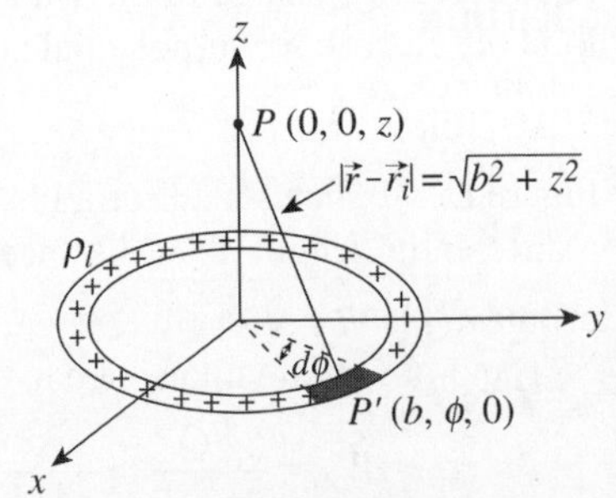

Figure E2.72

$$= \frac{1}{4\pi\varepsilon_0} \frac{\rho_l b}{\sqrt{b^2 + z^2}} \int_0^{2\pi} d\phi$$

$$V(z) = \frac{\rho_l b}{2\varepsilon_0 \sqrt{b^2 + z^2}}$$

At the center of the ring, $z = 0$. Then the above potential reduces to

$$V = \frac{\rho_l}{2\varepsilon_0}$$

The electric field intensity is defined as the negative gradient of potential as given by

$$\vec{E} = -\nabla V$$

$$= -\frac{\partial V(z)}{\partial z} \vec{a}_z$$

$$= -\frac{\rho_l b}{2\varepsilon_0} \frac{\partial}{\partial z} \left(\frac{1}{\sqrt{b^2 + z^2}} \right) \vec{a}_z$$

$$\vec{E} = \frac{\rho_l bz}{2\varepsilon_0 \left(b^2 + z^2 \right)^{3/2}} \vec{a}_z$$

If the point P is along the axis of the ring at a distance h from its center i.e., $z = h$, then the above equation can be written as

$$\vec{E} = \frac{\rho_l bh}{2\varepsilon_0 \left(b^2 + h^2 \right)^{3/2}} \vec{a}_z$$

Due to symmetrical charge distribution, the electric field intensity $\vec{E}$ at the center of the ring, $z = 0$, is zero. The above expression is identical to Eq. (2) derived in Example 2.22. ❏

EXAMPLE 2.73

The charge of 80 nC is uniformly distributed around a circular ring of radius 2 m. Determine the potential at a point on the axis 5 m from the plane of the ring. Also, find the potential if all charges are at the origin in the form of a point charge.

SOLUTION

The line charge density is defined as the ratio of charge per unit length as

$$\rho_l = \frac{Q}{l} = \frac{80 \times 10^{-9}}{2\pi(2)} = \frac{20 \times 10^{-9}}{\pi} \ \text{C/m}$$

From Example 2.72, the potential due to charged circular ring at a point on its axis is

$$V = \frac{\rho_l b}{2\varepsilon_0 \sqrt{b^2 + z^2}}$$

$$= \frac{\left(20 \times 10^{-9} / \pi\right) \times 2}{2\left(10^{-9} / 36\pi\right)\sqrt{2^2 + 5^2}} = 133.7\,\text{V}$$

If charge is concentrated at the origin, then the expression for the potential of a point charge is applied. Therefore,

$$V = \frac{Q}{4\pi\varepsilon_0 z} = \frac{80 \times 10^{-9}}{4\pi\varepsilon_0 (5)} = 144\ \text{V} \qquad\qquad \square$$

EXAMPLE 2.74

Determine the potential due to charged circular disc having uniform surface charge density of ρ_s C/m^2 at a height h on its axis. Also, find the electric field intensity.

SOLUTION

Figure E2.74 shows a circular disc of radius ρ placed in the xy-plane with z as its axis. The disc is charged with uniform surface charge density of ρ_s. The differential surface area ds contains a charge $dQ = \rho_s ds$.

As ds is in xy-plane, its normal direction is along $\vec{a}_z$ and the differential surface area along z-direction is written in cylindrical coordinates as $ds = \rho\,d\rho\,d\phi$. Hence, $dQ = \rho_s ds = \rho_s \rho\,d\rho\,d\phi$ where ρ is the radius of the circular disc. The potential due to charged disc at point P is

$$dV = \frac{dQ}{4\pi\varepsilon_0 R} = \frac{\rho_s \rho\,d\rho\,d\phi}{4\pi\varepsilon_0 \sqrt{\rho^2 + h^2}}, \quad \text{where} \quad R = \sqrt{\rho^2 + h^2}$$

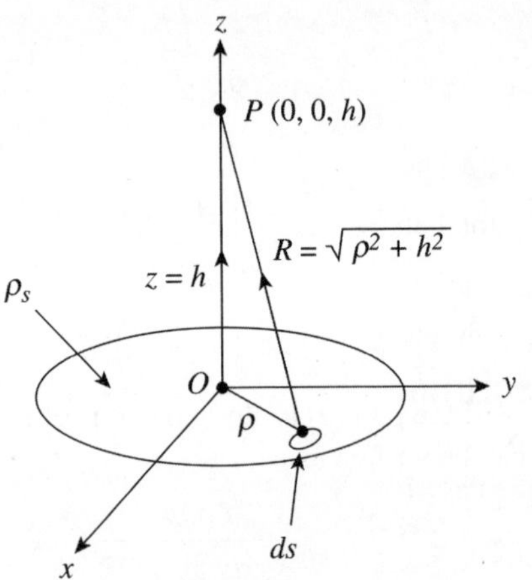

Figure E2.74

Integrating the above equation over ρ and ϕ, we get

$$V = \int_{\phi=0}^{2\pi}\int_{\rho=0}^{a} \frac{\rho_s \rho\,d\rho\,d\phi}{4\pi\varepsilon_0 \sqrt{\rho^2 + h^2}}$$

Substituting $\rho^2 + h^2 = u^2$ and differentiating, we get

$$2\rho\,d\rho = 2u\,du$$

For $\rho = 0, u_1 = h$ and $\rho = a, u_2 = \sqrt{a^2 + h^2}$

Therefore, $V = \displaystyle\int_{\phi=0}^{2\pi}\int_{u_1}^{u_2} \frac{\rho_s u\,du\,d\phi}{4\pi\varepsilon_0 u} = \frac{\rho_s}{4\pi\varepsilon_0}\left[u\right]_{u_1}^{u_2}\left[\phi\right]_0^{2\pi}$

$$= \frac{2\pi\rho_s}{4\pi\varepsilon_0}\left[u_2 - u_1\right]$$

$$= \frac{\rho_s}{2\varepsilon_0}\left[\sqrt{a^2 + h^2} - h\right]\text{V}$$

This is the required potential due to charged disc of radius $\rho = a$ at a height h along its axis.
Now, the electric field intensity $\vec{E}$ is

$$\vec{E} = -\nabla V = -\left[\frac{\partial V}{\partial \rho}\vec{a}_\rho + \frac{1}{\rho}\frac{\partial V}{\partial \phi}\vec{a}_\phi + \frac{\partial V}{\partial z}\vec{a}_z\right]$$

$$= -\frac{\partial}{\partial z}\left[\frac{\rho_s}{2\varepsilon_0}\left(\sqrt{a^2+z^2}-z\right)\right]\vec{a}_z, \text{where the component of } \vec{a}_\rho \text{ and } \vec{a}_\phi \text{ is } 0$$

$$= \frac{\rho_s}{2\varepsilon_0}\left[\left(1-\frac{z}{\sqrt{a^2+z^2}}\right)\right]\vec{a}_z$$

Therefore, electric field intensity $\vec{E}$ due to a charged circular disc of radius $\rho = a$ at a height $z = h$ along its axis is

$$\vec{E} = \frac{\rho_s}{2\varepsilon_0}\left[\left(1-\frac{h}{\sqrt{a^2+h^2}}\right)\right]\vec{a}_z$$

The above equation is identical to Eq. (3) derived in Example 2.24. When the radius a tends to ∞ in the above equation, the charged circular disc becomes an *infinite sheet of charge* and its electric field is

$$\vec{E} = \frac{\rho_s}{2\varepsilon_0}\vec{a}_z$$

$\square$

EXAMPLE 2.75

A total charge of $\dfrac{20}{3}$ nC is uniformly distributed in the form of a circular disc of radius 2 m. Determine the potential due to this charge at a point on the axis, 2 m from the disc. Also, find the potential if all the charges are at the center of the disc.

SOLUTION

The surface charge density is defined as the ratio of charge per unit area as given by

$$\rho_s = \frac{Q}{A} = \frac{\left(\dfrac{20}{3}\right)\times 10^{-9}}{\pi\rho^2} = \frac{5\times 10^{-9}}{3\pi}\,\text{C/m}^2$$

From Example 2.74, the potential due to charged circular disc at a point on its axis is

$$V = \frac{\rho_s}{2\varepsilon_0}\left[\sqrt{\rho^2+h^2}-h\right]$$

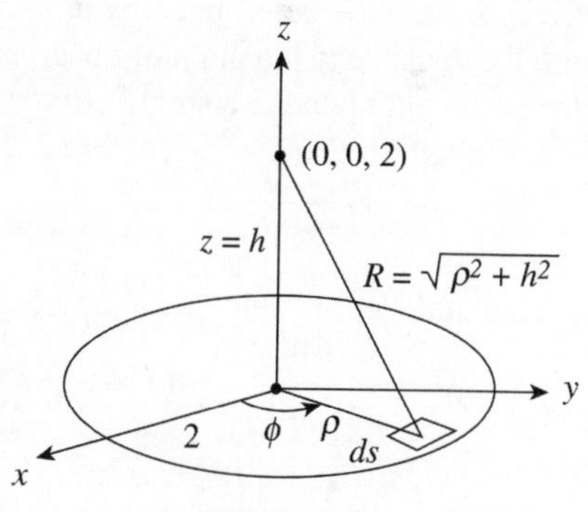

Figure E2.75

where $\rho = 2$ is the radius of the circular disc and $h = 2$ is the distance from the center of the disc to the point of observation on its axis, as shown in Figure E2.75.

$$\text{Therefore, } V = \frac{\left(5\times 10^{-9}/3\pi\right)}{2\times\left(10^{-9}/36\pi\right)}\left[\sqrt{2^2+2^2}-2\right] = 30\times 0.828 = 24.84\,\text{V}$$

If the charge is at the centre of the disc, the expression for potential due to a point charge is

$$V = \frac{Q}{4\pi\varepsilon_0 z} = \frac{\dfrac{20}{3}\times 10^{-9}}{4\pi\times\left(10^{-9}/36\pi\right)\times 2}, \text{ where } z = 2$$

$$= 30\,\text{V}$$

$\square$

2.11.3 Electric Potential and Field due to an Electric Dipole

An electric dipole is defined as a pair of point charges with equal magnitude and opposite polarity, separated by a small distance, as shown in Figure 2.24(a). Assume that the magnitude of each charge is Q and the separation between them is d.

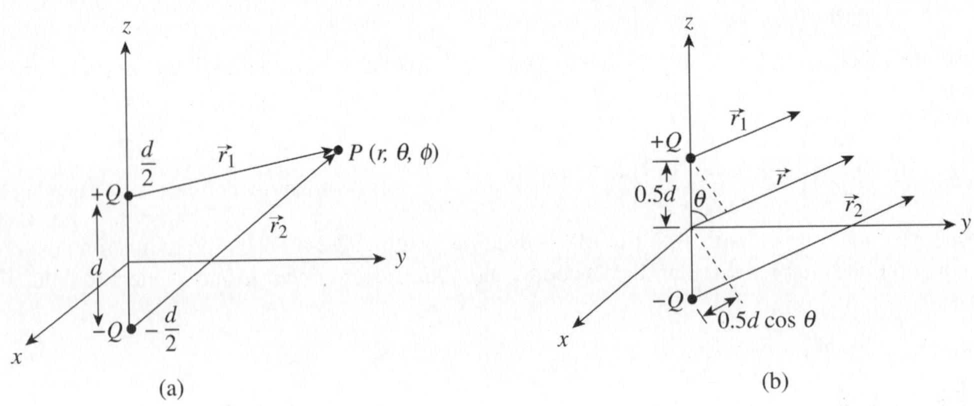

Figure 2.24 *Electric dipole: (a) when point P at (r, θ, φ) and (b) when P is far away from dipole with distance approximations*

The electric potential V and electric field intensity $\vec{E}$ established by the dipole at any point $P(r,\theta,\phi)$ in free space, can be determined by assuming that the separation between the charges is very small compared with the distance to the point of observation P i.e., $d \ll r$, where r is the distance from the charges to P. The electric potential due to a single point charge is given by

$$V = \frac{Q}{4\pi\varepsilon_0 r}$$

The total electric potential at any point P due to two point charges i.e., dipole is given by

$$V = V_1 + V_2 = \frac{Q}{4\pi\varepsilon_0}\left(\frac{1}{r_1} + \frac{-1}{r_2}\right) = \frac{Q}{4\pi\varepsilon_0}\left(\frac{r_2 - r_1}{r_1 r_2}\right) \tag{2.63}$$

If the charges are symmetrically placed along the z-axis and the point of observation is quite far away so that $r \gg d$, the lines are labeled as r_1 and r_2, as shown in Figure 2.24(b). These lines are approximately parallel to each other and the following approximations can be applied here.

$$r_1 \approx r - 0.5\,d\cos\theta, \qquad r_2 \approx r + 0.5\,d\cos\theta$$

and $\qquad r_1 r_2 = r^2 - (0.5\,d\cos\theta)^2 \approx r^2$

Substituting the above approximations in Eq. (2.63), we get

$$V = \frac{Qd\,\cos\theta}{4\pi\varepsilon_0 r^2} \tag{2.64}$$

Here, it is observed that the potential V at any point in the plane bisecting the dipole is zero when $\theta = 90°$. Hence, there is no expenditure of energy if a charge is moved from one point to another in this plane.

By defining $\vec{p}$ as a dipole moment vector with magnitude $p = Qd$ and direction along the line from the negative to the positive charge such that, $\vec{p} = Qd\,\vec{a}_z$, the potential at point P due to a dipole can now be written as

$$V = \frac{p\cos\theta}{4\pi\varepsilon_0 r^2} = \frac{\vec{p}\cdot\vec{a}_r}{4\pi\varepsilon_0 r^2} \qquad (\text{since } \vec{a}_z = \cos\theta\,\vec{a}_r - \sin\theta\,\vec{a}_\theta) \tag{2.65}$$

where $\vec{a}_r$ is the unit vector pointing from the center of the dipole towards the point of observation. The equation shows that the potential is inversely proportional to the square of the distance for a dipole, whereas the potential is inversely proportional to the distance for a point charge or a monopole. The unit of dipole moment is coulmb metre (C·m).

The electric field intensity due to the dipole with center at the origin in spherical coordinates is

$$\vec{E} = -\nabla V = -\left(\frac{\partial V}{\partial r}\vec{a}_r + \frac{1}{r}\frac{\partial V}{\partial \theta}\vec{a}_\theta + \frac{1}{r\sin\theta}\frac{\partial V}{\partial \phi}\vec{a}_\phi\right)$$

$$= -\frac{\partial}{\partial r}\left(\frac{Qd\cos\theta}{4\pi\varepsilon_0 r^2}\right)\vec{a}_r - \frac{1}{r}\frac{\partial}{\partial \theta}\left(\frac{Qd\cos\theta}{4\pi\varepsilon_0 r^2}\right)\vec{a}_\theta$$

$$= \frac{Qd\cos\theta}{2\pi\varepsilon_0 r^3}\vec{a}_r + \frac{Qd\sin\theta}{4\pi\varepsilon_0 r^3}\vec{a}_\theta$$

$$= \frac{Qd}{4\pi\varepsilon_0 r^3}\left(2\cos\theta\,\vec{a}_r + \sin\theta\,\vec{a}_\theta\right) \tag{2.66}$$

The expressions for electric potential V and electric field intensity $\vec{E}$ for a dipole are applicable only when $r \gg d$. Here, $\vec{E}$ is inversely proportional to r^3 for a dipole, whereas $\vec{E}$ is inversely proportional to r^2 for a point charge or a monopole. The concept of electric dipole is very useful in explaining the behavior of dielectric material when it is placed in an electric field.

2.11.4 Torque on an Electric Dipole in Electric Field

The torque on the dipole is equal to the cross product of the dipole moment $\vec{p}$ and the electric field intensity $\vec{E}$. It can be expressed as

$$\vec{T} = \vec{p} \times \vec{E}$$

The unit of torque on an electric dipole is newton metre (N·m). Consider an electric dipole in a uniform electric field intensity $\vec{E}$ as shown in Figure 2.25. Let the dipole axis makes an angle θ with the field and the distance between the charges be d.

The magnitude of force on the dipole is $\vec{F} = Q\vec{E}$. Then, the torque is defined as

$$T = (\text{Force})\,(\text{Distance}) = Fl = QEl$$

where l is the perpendicular distance between the field and charge.

From Figure 2.25, $\qquad \sin\theta = \dfrac{l}{d}$ or $l = d\sin\theta$

Therefore, $\qquad T = QEd\sin\theta = pE\sin\theta$

i.e., $\qquad \vec{T} = \vec{p} \times \vec{E}$

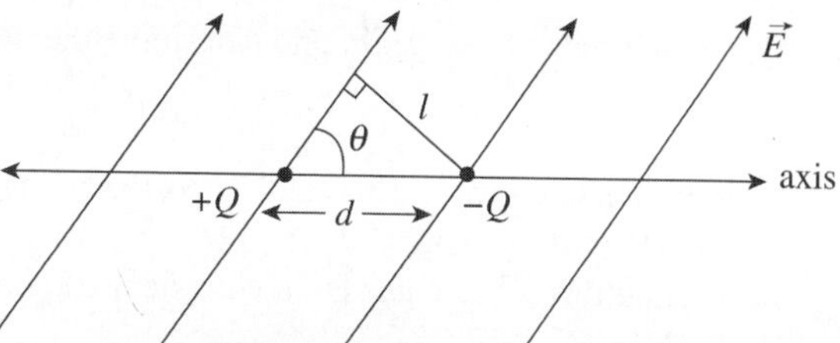

Figure 2.25 *Torque on an electric dipole*

where $p = Qd$ is the magnitude of dipole moment. Thus, the torque on the dipole is equal to the cross product of the dipole moment and the electric field intensity. The direction of the torque is perpendicular to the dipole plane.

2.11.5 Torque on a Dipole due to Field of another Dipole

Consider two pure dipoles with dipole moments $\vec{p}_1$ and $\vec{p}_2$ located in free space separated by a distance r. Assume that $\vec{p}_1$ is directed along the z-axis. From Eq. (2.66), the electric field at radial distance r due to dipole $\vec{p}_1$ in spherical coordinates is

$$\vec{E}_1 = \frac{p_1}{4\pi\varepsilon_0 r^3}\left(2\cos\theta\,\vec{a}_r + \sin\theta\,\vec{a}_\theta\right)$$

The torque on $\vec{p}_2$ due to the electric field $\vec{E}_1$ is

$$\vec{T} = \vec{p}_2 \times \vec{E}_1$$

Since $\vec{p}_2$ depends on r, we have $\vec{p}_2 = p_2\vec{a}_r$

Therefore, $\vec{T} = \left(p_2\vec{a}_r\right) \times \dfrac{p_1}{4\pi\varepsilon_0 r^3}\left(2\cos\theta\,\vec{a}_r + \sin\theta\,\vec{a}_\theta\right)$

$$= \frac{p_2 p_1}{4\pi\varepsilon_0 r^3}\sin\theta\left(\vec{a}_r \times \vec{a}_\theta\right) = \frac{p_2 p_1 \sin\theta}{4\pi\varepsilon_0 r^3}\vec{a}_\phi$$

The above equation shows that the dipole $\vec{p}_2$ rotates along the $\vec{a}_\phi$ direction.

EXAMPLE 2.76

An electric dipole of $100\,\vec{a}_z$ pC·m is located at the origin. Find the scalar potential V at the point $P(0,0,10)$.

SOLUTION

The potential at point P due to a dipole is

$$V = \frac{\vec{p}\cdot\vec{a}_r}{4\pi\varepsilon_0 r^2}$$

where $\vec{a}_r = (10-0)\vec{a}_z = 10\vec{a}_z$ and $r = 10$.

Therefore, $V = \dfrac{\left(100\times10^{-12}\vec{a}_z\right)\cdot\left(10\vec{a}_z\right)}{4\pi\times8.854\times10^{-12}\times10^2} = 0.0899 = 89.9\,\text{mV}$ $\square$

EXAMPLE 2.77

Given that two point charges 1.5 nC at $(0,0,0.1)$ and -1.5 nC at $(0,0,-0.1)$ are in free space. Treat the two charges as a dipole at the origin and determine the potential at $P(0.3,0,0.4)$.

SOLUTION

The dipole is shown in Figure E2.77 and the point $P(0.3,0,0.4)$ is given in cartesian coordinates where $x = 0.3, y = 0$ and $z = 0.4$.

Converting the coordinates from cartesian to spherical, we get

$$r = \sqrt{x^2 + y^2 + z^2} = 0.5$$

$$\theta = \cos^{-1}\left[\frac{z}{r}\right] = \cos^{-1}\left[\frac{0.4}{0.5}\right] = 36.87°$$

$$\phi = \tan^{-1}\left[\frac{y}{x}\right] = 0°$$

Therefore, the potential due to a dipole at the origin $(0,0,0)$ is

$$V = \frac{Qd\cos\theta}{4\pi\varepsilon_0 r^2} = \frac{1.5\times10^{-9}}{4\pi\times8.854\times10^{-12}}\left[\frac{0.2\times\cos(36.87°)}{(0.5)^2}\right]$$

$$= 8.63\,\text{V} \qquad \square$$

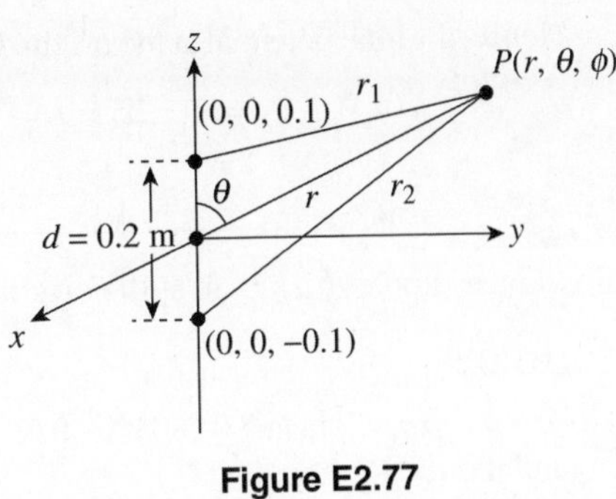

Figure E2.77

EXAMPLE 2.78

Given that two dipoles with dipole moments $-5\vec{a}_z$ nC·m and $9\vec{a}_z$ nC·m are located at points $(0,0,-2)$ and $(0,0,3)$ respectively. Determine the potential at the origin.

SOLUTION

The potential at the origin $(0,0,0)$ due to a dipole with dipole moment $\vec{p}$ of $-5\vec{a}_z$ nC·m located at a point $(0,0,-2)$ is

$$V_1 = \frac{\vec{p}\cdot\vec{a}_r}{4\pi\varepsilon_0 r_1^2}$$

where $\quad \vec{a}_r = \dfrac{\vec{r}-\vec{r}'}{|\vec{r}-\vec{r}'|} = \dfrac{\left(0\vec{a}_x - 0\vec{a}_y + 0\vec{a}_z\right) - \left(0\vec{a}_x + 0\vec{a}_y - 2\vec{a}_z\right)}{\sqrt{(2)^2}} = \dfrac{2\vec{a}_z}{2} = \vec{a}_z$

and $\quad r_1 = |\vec{r}-\vec{r}'| = \sqrt{(0)^2 + (0)^2 + (2)^2} = 2$

Therefore, $\quad V_1 = \dfrac{\vec{p}\cdot\vec{a}_r}{4\pi\varepsilon_0 r_1^2} = 9\times10^9\left(\dfrac{-5\times10^{-9}\,\vec{a}_z\cdot\vec{a}_z}{2^2}\right) \qquad \left(\text{since}\,\dfrac{1}{4\pi\varepsilon_0} = 9\times10^9\right)$

$$= -11.25\,\text{V}$$

The potential at the origin $(0,0,0)$ due to a dipole with dipole moment $\vec{p}$ of $9\vec{a}_z$ nC·m located at a point $(0,0,3)$ is

$$V_2 = \frac{\vec{p}\cdot\vec{a}_r}{4\pi\varepsilon_0 r_2^2}$$

where $\quad \vec{a}_r = \dfrac{\vec{r}-\vec{r}'}{|\vec{r}-\vec{r}'|} = \dfrac{\left(0\vec{a}_x + 0\vec{a}_y + 0\vec{a}_z\right) - \left(0\vec{a}_x + 0\vec{a}_y + 3\vec{a}_z\right)}{\sqrt{(-3)^2}} = \dfrac{-3\vec{a}_z}{3} = -\vec{a}_z$

and $\quad r_2 = |\vec{r}-\vec{r}'| = \sqrt{(0)^2 + (0)^2 + (-3)^2} = 3$

Therefore, $\quad V_2 = \dfrac{\vec{p}\cdot\vec{a}_r}{4\pi\varepsilon_0 r_2^2} = 9\times10^9\left(\dfrac{-9\times10^{-9}\,\vec{a}_z\cdot\vec{a}_z}{3^2}\right) = -9\,\text{V}$

Hence, the total potential at the origin due to two dipoles is the sum of potentials due to each dipole. Therefore,

$$V = V_1 + V_2 = -11.25 - 9 = -20.25 \text{ V}$$

EXAMPLE 2.79

For a pure dipole $p\,\vec{a}_z$ C·m at the origin in free space, find the potential at a point $A\left(r, \theta, \dfrac{\pi}{2}\right)$.

SOLUTION

Given $\vec{p} = p\,\vec{a}_z$ C·m at $(0,0,0)$ in free space. The potential at point $A\left(r, \theta, \dfrac{\pi}{2}\right)$ is to be determined. The potential due to a dipole is

$$V = \frac{\vec{p} \cdot \vec{a}_r}{4\pi\varepsilon_0 r^2} = \frac{p\,\vec{a}_z \cdot \vec{a}_r}{4\pi\varepsilon_0 r^2}$$

where $\vec{a}_z \cdot \vec{a}_r = \cos\theta$. Therefore, the potential becomes

$$V = \frac{p\cos\theta}{4\pi\varepsilon_0 r^2} \text{ V}$$

Note: If the dipole is along the z-axis, V does not vary with ϕ.

EXAMPLE 2.80

Compute the torque for a dipole comprising 1μC charge in an electric field $\vec{E} = 10^3 \left(z\vec{a}_x - \vec{a}_y - \vec{a}_z \right)$ V/m separated by 1 mm and located on the z-axis at the origin.

SOLUTION

Given $Q = 1\mu\text{C} = 1 \times 10^{-6}\text{C}$, $d = 1$ mm, $\vec{d} = 10^{-3}\vec{a}_z$ and $\vec{E} = 10^3 \left(z\vec{a}_x - \vec{a}_y - \vec{a}_z \right)$ V/m.

The torque on a dipole is

$$\vec{T} = \vec{p} \times \vec{E}$$

where $\vec{p} = Q\vec{d} = Qd\,\vec{a}_z = 10^{-6} \times 10^{-3}\vec{a}_z = 10^{-9}\vec{a}_z$.

Therefore,

$$\vec{T} = \left(10^{-9}\vec{a}_z\right) \times 10^3 \left(z\vec{a}_x - \vec{a}_y - \vec{a}_z \right) = 10^{-6} \begin{vmatrix} \vec{a}_x & \vec{a}_y & \vec{a}_z \\ 0 & 0 & 1 \\ z & -1 & -1 \end{vmatrix}$$

$$= 10^{-6}\left[\vec{a}_x + z\vec{a}_y \right] = \left[\vec{a}_x + z\vec{a}_y \right] \mu\text{N·m}$$

2.12 ELECTROSTATIC POTENTIAL ENERGY

The energy stored in an electric field is determined in terms of sources i.e., group of discrete point charges. The expression for the energy in an electrostatic system derived for discrete charges can also be extended to any continuous charge distribution.

Consider a region without any electric field, and the charges are located at infinity as shown in Figure 2.26. Assume that there are *n* point charges, each at an infinite distance away from the region under consideration. As the region is initially charge free and devoid of electric field, no work is needed to transfer the charge Q_1 from infinity to point *a* i.e., $W_1 = 0$, and the charge did not experience any force. The presence of point charge Q_1 creates a potential distribution in the region. If another charge Q_2 is moved from infinity to point *b*, then the work done is

$$W_2 = Q_2 V_{ba} = \frac{Q_1 Q_2}{4\pi\varepsilon R}$$

where V_{ba} is the potential at point *b* due to charge Q_1 at point *a* and R is the distance between the two charges. The reference point for the potential is chosen to be at infinity. The total energy required or the work done to bring the two charges from infinity to point *a* and *b* is given by

$$W_e = W_{e1} + W_{e2} = 0 + Q_2 V_{ba} = \frac{Q_1 Q_2}{4\pi\varepsilon R} \qquad (2.67)$$

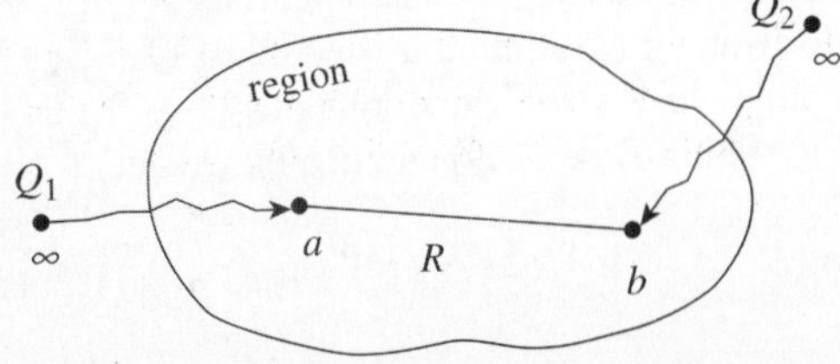

Figure 2.26 *Potential energy between two point charges*

The potential energy between two point charges separated by a distance R in any medium is represented by the above equation. Suppose if the process is reversed by first bringing Q_2 to point *b* in the region free of electric fields, no work is done to transfer the charge Q_2 from infinity to point *b* i.e., $W_2 = 0$. Now the potential at point *a* due to charge Q_2 at point *b* is expressed by

$$V_{ab} = \frac{Q_2}{4\pi\varepsilon R}$$

The energy required to bring another charge Q_1 from infinity to point *a* is written as

$$W_1 = Q_1 V_{ab} = \frac{Q_1 Q_2}{4\pi\varepsilon R}$$

The total energy required or the work done for this reversed process is represented by

$$W_e = W_{e1} + W_{e2} = 0 + Q_1 V_{ab} = \frac{Q_1 Q_2}{4\pi\varepsilon R} \qquad (2.68)$$

From Eqs (2.67) and (2.68), it is seen that the energy required for both the cases is same and it does not really matter which charge is transferred first.

Now, the above process can be extended to a system of three point charges Q_1, Q_2 and Q_3 which are to be moved from infinity to points *a*, *b* and *c* respectively, as shown in Figure 2.27. The energy expended to move the charge is expressed by

$$W_e = W_{e1} + W_{e2} + W_{e3} = 0 + Q_2 V_{ba} + Q_3 \left(V_{ca} + V_{cb} \right) \qquad (2.69)$$

$$= \frac{1}{4\pi\varepsilon} \left(\frac{Q_2 Q_1}{R_{21}} + \frac{Q_3 Q_1}{R_{31}} + \frac{Q_3 Q_2}{R_{32}} \right) \qquad (2.70)$$

where V_{ca} and V_{cb} are the potentials at point *c* due to charges Q_1 and Q_2 respectively and the work done in positioning Q_3 at point *c* is equal to $Q_3 \left(V_{ca} + V_{cb} \right)$.

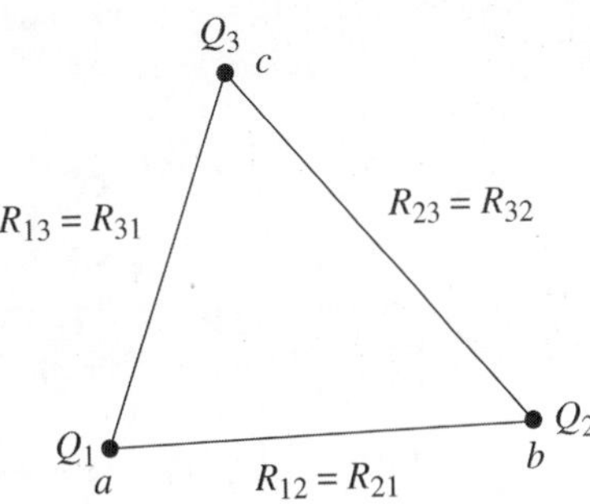

Figure 2.27 *Potential energy in a system of three point charges*

Suppose if three charges are moved to their respective positions in reverse order, the total energy required or the work done is

$$W_e = W_{e3} + W_{e2} + W_{e1} = 0 + Q_2 V_{bc} + Q_1 \left(V_{ac} + V_{ab} \right) \tag{2.71}$$

$$= \frac{1}{4\pi\varepsilon} \left(\frac{Q_2 Q_3}{R_{23}} + \frac{Q_1 Q_3}{R_{13}} + \frac{Q_1 Q_2}{R_{12}} \right) \tag{2.72}$$

where V_{ac} and V_{ab} are the potentials at point a due to charges Q_3 and Q_2 respectively and the work done in positioning Q_1 at point a is equal to $Q_1 \left(V_{ac} + V_{ab} \right)$. Equations (2.70) and (2.72) are identical and hence, in both the cases, the work done increases the amount of energy stored in the system of charges.

Adding Eqs. (2.69) and (2.71), we get

$$W_e = \frac{1}{2} \left[Q_1 \left(V_{ac} + V_{ab} \right) + Q_2 \left(V_{ba} + V_{bc} \right) + Q_3 \left(V_{ca} + V_{cb} \right) \right] \tag{2.73}$$

Therefore, the potential at point a due to charges at points c and b is

$$V_1 = V_{ac} + V_{ab} = \frac{1}{4\pi\varepsilon} \left(\frac{Q_3}{R_{13}} + \frac{Q_2}{R_{12}} \right)$$

The potential at point b due to charges at points a and c is

$$V_2 = V_{ba} + V_{bc}$$

The potential at point c due to charges at points a and b is

$$V_3 = V_{ca} + V_{cb}$$

From Eq. (2.73), the total energy is

$$W_e = \frac{1}{2} \left[Q_1 V_1 + Q_2 V_2 + Q_3 V_3 \right] = \frac{1}{2} \sum_{k=1}^{3} Q_k V_k$$

Hence, the generalized equation for a system of n point charges is

$$W_e = \frac{1}{2} \sum_{k=1}^{n} Q_k V_k \tag{2.74}$$

The above equation is used to determine the *electrostatic potential energy* for a group of n discrete point charges. For a *continuous charge distribution*, the electrostatic potential energy is given by

$$W_e = \frac{1}{2} \int_v \rho_v V \, dv \quad \text{(volume charge)} \tag{2.75}$$

where ρ_v is the volume charge density within volume v. The above equation is the general expression for the energy of a system of charges in terms of volume charge density and potential V. Similarly, for surface charge and line charge distribution, the electrostatic potential energy is

$$W_e = \frac{1}{2} \int_s \rho_s V \, ds \quad \text{(surface charge)} \tag{2.76}$$

$$W_e = \frac{1}{2} \int_l \rho_l V \, dl \quad \text{(line charge)} \tag{2.77}$$

EXAMPLE 2.81

Given that three point charges -1nC, 4nC and 3nC are located at $(0,0,0,)$, $(0,0,1)$ and $(1,0,0)$ respectively. Determine the energy stored in the system.

SOLUTION

From Eq. (2.74), the total energy stored in the system is

$$W_e = \frac{1}{2}\sum_{k=1}^{3} Q_k V_k = \frac{1}{2}\left(Q_1 V_1 + Q_2 V_2 + Q_3 V_3\right)$$

$$= \frac{Q_1}{2}\left[\frac{Q_2}{4\pi\varepsilon_0(1)} + \frac{Q_3}{4\pi\varepsilon_0(1)}\right] + \frac{Q_2}{2}\left[\frac{Q_1}{4\pi\varepsilon_0(1)} + \frac{Q_3}{4\pi\varepsilon_0(\sqrt{2})}\right] + \frac{Q_3}{2}\left[\frac{Q_1}{4\pi\varepsilon_0(1)} + \frac{Q_2}{4\pi\varepsilon_0(\sqrt{2})}\right]$$

$$= \frac{1}{4\pi\varepsilon_0}\left(Q_1 Q_2 + Q_1 Q_3 + \frac{Q_2 Q_3}{\sqrt{2}}\right)$$

$$= 9\times10^9\left(-4-3+\frac{12}{\sqrt{2}}\right)\times10^{-18} \qquad \left(\text{since}\,\frac{1}{4\pi\varepsilon_0} = 9\times10^9\right)$$

$$= 9\left(-7+\frac{12}{\sqrt{2}}\right)\times10^{-9} = 13.37\text{ nJ} \qquad \square$$

EXAMPLE 2.82

Given that three point charges 1, 2 and 3 coulombs are situated in free space at the corners of an equilateral triangle of side 1 m. Determine the energy stored in the system.

SOLUTION

Figure E2.82 shows three point charges situated at the corners of an equilateral triangle.

When Q_1 alone is placed at one corner and no other charges present, then the work done is zero.

i.e., $W_{e1} = 0$

When Q_2 is placed, Q_1 is present. Then, the work done is

$$W_{e2} = Q_2 V_{21} = Q_2\left[\frac{Q_1}{4\pi\varepsilon_0 R_{21}}\right]$$

$$= 2\left[\frac{1}{4\pi\varepsilon_0(1)}\right] = \frac{2}{4\pi\varepsilon_0}\text{ J}$$

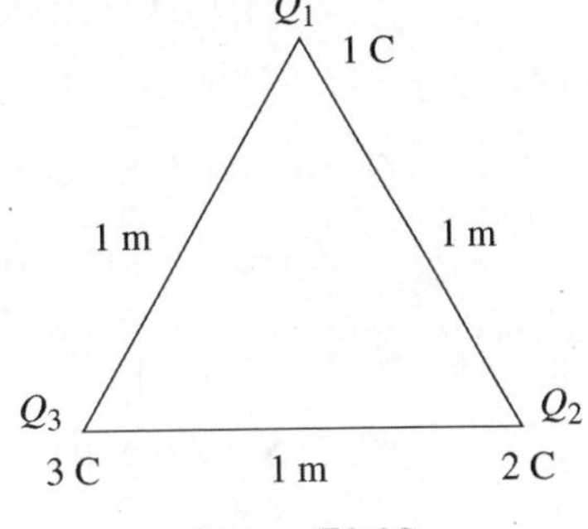

Figure E2.82

When Q_3 is placed, both Q_1 and Q_2 are present. Then, the work done is

$$W_{e3} = Q_3 V_{31} + Q_3 V_{32} = Q_3\left[\frac{Q_1}{4\pi\varepsilon_0 R_{31}}\right] + Q_3\left[\frac{Q_2}{4\pi\varepsilon_0 R_{32}}\right]$$

$$= 3\left[\frac{1}{4\pi\varepsilon_0(1)}\right] + 3\left[\frac{2}{4\pi\varepsilon_0(1)}\right] = \frac{9}{4\pi\varepsilon_0}\text{ J}$$

Hence, the total energy stored in the system is

$$W_e = W_{e1} + W_{e2} + W_{e3} = 0 + \frac{2}{4\pi\varepsilon_0} + \frac{9}{4\pi\varepsilon_0}$$

$$= \frac{11}{4\pi \times 8.854 \times 10^{-12}} = 9.89 \times 10^{10}\,\text{J}$$

Therefore, the total energy stored in the system is $W_e = 9.89 \times 10^{10}\,\text{J}$.

EXAMPLE 2.83

A metallic sphere of radius 10 cm has a surface charge density 10 nC/m^2. Calculate the electric energy stored in the system.

SOLUTION

The potential on the surface of the sphere is

$$V = \int_s \frac{\rho_s ds}{4\pi\varepsilon_0 r}$$

where the surface area of the sphere is $s = \int_s ds = r^2 \int_0^\pi \sin\theta\, d\theta \int_0^{2\pi} d\phi$.

Therefore, $V = \dfrac{10 \times 10^{-9}}{4\pi \times \dfrac{10^{-9}}{36\pi} \times 0.1} \times (0.1)^2 \times \int_0^\pi \sin\theta\, d\theta \int_0^{2\pi} d\phi$

$$= 9 \times \left[-\cos\theta\right]_0^\pi \times \left[\phi\right]_0^{2\pi} = 113.1\,\text{V}$$

The energy stored in the system is determined in terms of sources i.e., charges. Therefore,

$$W_e = \frac{1}{2}\int_s \rho_s V ds = \frac{1}{2} Q_t V$$

where Q_t is the total charge on the sphere. For uniform charge distribution, the total charge is

$$Q_t = \text{area} \times \text{charge density} = 4\pi r^2 \times \rho_s$$

$$= 4\pi (0.1)^2 \times 10 \times 10^{-9} = 1.257\,\text{nC}$$

Therefore,

$$W_e = \frac{1}{2} \times 1.257 \times 10^{-9} \times 113.1 = 71.08 \times 10^{-9} = 71.08\,\text{nJ}$$

EXAMPLE 2.84

Find the work done in moving a point charge $Q = 10\,\mu\text{C}$ from the origin to $\left(2, \dfrac{\pi}{4}, \dfrac{\pi}{2}\right)$ in spherical coordinates, in the field given by $\vec{E} = 5e^{-r/4}\vec{a}_r + \dfrac{10}{r\sin\theta}\vec{a}_\phi$ V/m.

SOLUTION

Choose the path as shown in Figure E2.84 and the differential length in spherical coordinates is

$$d\vec{l} = dr\,\vec{a}_r + rd\theta\,\vec{a}_\theta + r\sin\theta\, d\phi\,\vec{a}_\phi$$

Along segment 1, $d\theta = d\phi = 0$ and the differential work done in moving the charge along $\vec{a}_r$ direction is

$$dW_{e1} = -Q\,dV = -Q\vec{E}\cdot d\vec{l} = \left(-10\times10^{-6}\right)\left(5e^{-r/4}\,dr\right)$$

Along segment 2, $dr = d\theta = 0$ and the differential work done in moving the charge along $\vec{a}_\phi$ direction is

$$dW_{e2} = -Q\vec{E}\cdot d\vec{l} = \left(-10\times10^{-6}\right)\left(10\,d\phi\right)$$

Along segment 3, $dr = d\phi = 0$ and the differential work done in moving the charge along $\vec{a}_\theta$ direction is

$$dW_{e3} = -Q\vec{E}\cdot d\vec{l} = 0$$

Therefore, the total work done by the field on the charge is

$$W_e = \left(-50\times10^{-6}\right)\int_0^2 e^{-r/4}\,dr + \left(-100\times10^{-6}\right)\int_0^{\frac{\pi}{2}} d\phi + 0$$

$$= \left(-78.7\times10^{-6}\right) + \left(-157\times10^{-6}\right) = -235.7\,\mu\text{J} \qquad \square$$

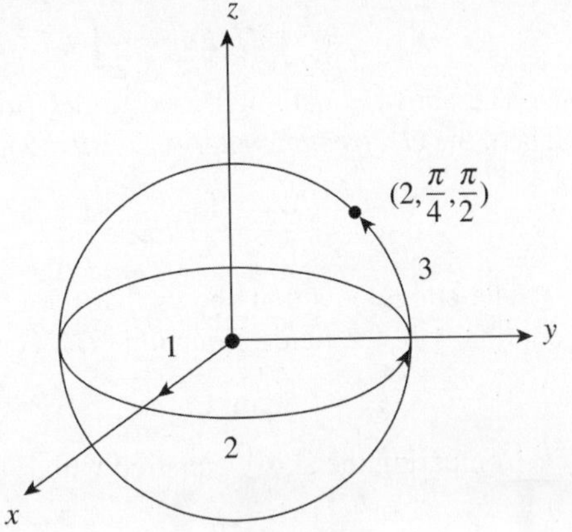

Figure E2.84

2.13 ELECTROSTATIC ENERGY DENSITY

The electrostatic energy density is defined as the electrostatic energy per unit volume and it is determined from the energy expression derived in terms of field quantities. As $\nabla\cdot\vec{D} = \rho_v$ by Gauss's law, Eq. (2.75) can be written as

$$W_e = \frac{1}{2}\int_v V(\nabla\cdot\vec{D})\,dv \qquad (2.78)$$

But for any vector $\vec{D}$ and scalar V, the vector identity is

$$V(\nabla\cdot\vec{D}) = \nabla\cdot(V\vec{D}) - \vec{D}\cdot(\nabla V)$$

Substituting the above vector identity in Eq. (2.78), the expression for energy is obtained as

$$W_e = \frac{1}{2}\int_v\left[\nabla\cdot(V\vec{D}) - \vec{D}\cdot(\nabla V)\right]dv$$

$$= \frac{1}{2}\left[\int_v \nabla\cdot(V\vec{D})\,dv - \int_v \vec{D}\cdot(\nabla V)\,dv\right] \qquad (2.79)$$

Applying divergence theorem to the first term on the right hand side of the above equation, we get

$$W_e = \frac{1}{2}\left[\oint_s (V\vec{D})\cdot d\vec{s} - \frac{1}{2}\int_v \vec{D}\cdot(\nabla V)\,dv\right] \qquad (2.80)$$

The choice of the volume v in the above integral is arbitrary but the only constraint is that the surface s bounds volume v. If the integration is done over such a large volume that potential V and electric flux density $\vec{D}$ are negligibly small on the bounding surface, then the surface integral tends to zero in the above equation. Hence, the electrostatic energy stored in the electrostatic system reduces to

$$W_e = -\frac{1}{2}\int_v \vec{D}\cdot(\nabla V)\,dv \qquad (2.81)$$

Since $\vec{E} = -\nabla V$ and $\vec{D} = \varepsilon \vec{E}$,

$$W_e = \frac{1}{2}\int_v \vec{D}\cdot\vec{E}\,dv = \frac{1}{2}\int_v \varepsilon E^2\,dv \tag{2.82}$$

The above equation is used to determine the electrostatic potential energy in terms of field quantities. Then, the *electrostatic energy density*, defined as the energy per unit volume, is given by

$$w_e = \frac{dW_e}{dv} = \frac{1}{2}\vec{D}\cdot\vec{E} = \frac{1}{2}\varepsilon E^2 = \frac{D^2}{2\varepsilon} \tag{2.83}$$

The above equation shows that the energy density may be non-zero all over the space because of the continuity of the fields. Equation (2.82) can be expressed in terms of energy density as

$$W_e = \int_v w_e\,dv \tag{2.84}$$

Comparing the above equation with Eq. (2.75), the expression for energy density can be obtained as

$$w_e = \frac{1}{2}\rho_v V \tag{2.85}$$

Equation (2.84) shows that the volume integral of energy density gives the total energy W_e.

EXAMPLE 2.85

The electric field between two concentric cylindrical conductors at $\rho = 0.01\,\text{m}$ and $\rho = 0.05\,\text{m}$ is given by $\vec{E} = \left(10^6 / \rho\right)\vec{a}_\rho$ V/m and fringing is neglected. Determine the energy stored in a 0.5 m length. Assume free space.

SOLUTION

The energy stored in the electric field is

$$W_e = \frac{1}{2}\int_v \varepsilon_0 E^2\,dv$$

$$= \frac{\varepsilon_0}{2}\int_h^{h+0.5}\int_0^{2\pi}\int_{0.01}^{0.05}\left(\frac{10^6}{\rho}\right)^2 \rho\,d\rho\,d\phi\,dz$$

$$= \frac{10^{-9}}{36\pi}\times\frac{1}{2}\times 0.5\times 2\pi\times\left(10^6\right)^2\times\ln[\rho]_{0.01}^{0.05}$$

$$= 22.35\,\text{J}$$

EXAMPLE 2.86

The potential field in free space is given by, $V = \dfrac{50}{r}$ V, $a \le r \le b$ in spherical coordinates.

(*i*) Show that $\rho_v = 0$ for $a < r < b$.

(*ii*) Determine the energy stored in the region $a < r < b$.

SOLUTION

(*i*) Given that, $V = \dfrac{50}{r}$ V, where $a \le r \le b$ in spherical coordinates.

Therefore, $\vec{E} = -\nabla V = -\left[\dfrac{\partial V}{\partial r}\vec{a}_r + \dfrac{1}{r}\dfrac{\partial V}{\partial \theta}\vec{a}_\theta + \dfrac{1}{r\sin\theta}\dfrac{\partial V}{\partial \phi}\vec{a}_\phi\right]$

where $\dfrac{\partial V}{\partial r} = -\dfrac{50}{r^2}$ and $\dfrac{\partial V}{\partial \theta} = \dfrac{\partial V}{\partial \phi} = 0.$

Hence, the electric field intensity is

$$\vec{E} = \frac{50}{r^2}\,\vec{a}_r\ \text{V/m}$$

and the electric flux density is

$$\vec{D} = \varepsilon_0 \vec{E} = \frac{50\varepsilon_0}{r^2}\,\vec{a}_r\ \text{C/m}^2$$

Therefore, ρ_v in spherical coordinates is

$$\rho_v = \nabla \cdot \vec{D} = \frac{1}{r^2}\frac{\partial}{\partial r}\left(r^2 D_r\right)$$

$$= \frac{1}{r^2}\frac{\partial}{\partial r}\left[r^2 \times \frac{50\varepsilon_0}{r^2}\right] = \frac{1}{r^2}\frac{\partial}{\partial r}\left[50\varepsilon_0\right] = 0$$

(ii) The energy stored is

$$W_e = \frac{1}{2}\int_v \varepsilon_0 E^2\ dv$$

where $E^2 = \dfrac{(50)^2}{r^4}$ and $dv = r^2 \sin\theta\,dr\,d\theta\,d\phi.$

Therefore,

$$W_e = \frac{\varepsilon_0}{2}\int_{\phi=0}^{2\pi}\int_{\theta=0}^{\pi}\int_{r=a}^{b} \frac{50^2}{r^4}\,r^2 \sin\theta\,dr\,d\theta\,d\phi$$

$$= \frac{2500\varepsilon_0}{2}\left[-\frac{1}{r}\right]_a^b \left[-\cos\theta\right]_0^\pi \left[\phi\right]_0^{2\pi} = 1250\varepsilon_0\left[-\frac{1}{b}-\left(-\frac{1}{a}\right)\right](2)(2\pi)$$

$$= 0.139\left[\frac{1}{a}-\frac{1}{b}\right]\mu\text{J}$$

EXAMPLE 2.87

A metallic sphere of radius 10 cm has a surface charge density of 10 nC/m^2. Calculate the electric energy stored in the system.

SOLUTION

The expression for electric energy is

$$W_e = \int_v w_e\,dv = \frac{1}{2}\int_v \vec{D}\cdot\vec{E}\,dv$$

where w_e is the electrostatic energy density.

Since the charge distribution is on the surface of the sphere, the energy density within the sphere is zero. Gauss's law is used to determine the electric flux density $\vec{D}$ at any point in space for a spherical Gaussian surface as given by

$$\oint_s \vec{D}\cdot d\vec{s} = Q$$

Therefore, $\vec{D} = \dfrac{Q}{4\pi r^2}\,\vec{a}_r = \dfrac{\rho_s\,ds}{4\pi r^2}\,\vec{a}_r$

$$= \dfrac{10\times10^{-9}\times 4\pi \times (0.1)^2}{4\pi r^2}\,\vec{a}_r = \dfrac{0.1\times10^{-9}}{r^2}\,\vec{a}_r$$

Thus, the total energy in the system is

$$W_e = \frac{1}{2}\int_v \vec{D}\cdot\vec{E}\,dv = \frac{1}{2}\int_v \frac{D^2}{\varepsilon_0}\,dv$$

$$= \frac{1}{2}\int_v \frac{(0.1)^2\times10^{-18}}{\varepsilon_0 r^4}\,r^2\sin\theta\,dr\,d\theta\,d\phi$$

$$= \frac{(0.1)^2\times10^{-18}}{2\times 8.854\times10^{-12}}\int_{r=0.1}^{\infty}\frac{1}{r^2}\,dr\int_{\theta=0}^{\pi}\sin\theta\,d\theta\int_{\phi=0}^{2\pi}d\phi$$

$$= 71.08\times10^{-9} = 71.08\,\text{nJ}$$

This solution is same as the one obtained in Example 2.83.

EXAMPLE 2.88

A parallel-plate capacitor, for which $C = \varepsilon_0 A / d$, has a constant voltage V applied across the plates. Determine the energy stored in the electric field.

SOLUTION

Figure E2.88 shows a parallel-plate capacitor with A as the surface area of the plates and d as the spacing between the plates. The electric field is $\vec{E} = \dfrac{V}{d}\,\vec{a}_n$ between the plates and $\vec{E} = 0$ elsewhere. Therefore, the energy stored in the electric field is

$$W_e = \frac{1}{2}\int_v \varepsilon_0 E^2\,dv$$

$$= \frac{\varepsilon_0}{2}\left(\frac{V}{d}\right)^2\int dv = \frac{\varepsilon_0}{2}\left(\frac{V}{d}\right)^2 (A\times d)$$

$$= \frac{\varepsilon_0 A V^2}{2d} = \frac{1}{2}CV^2$$

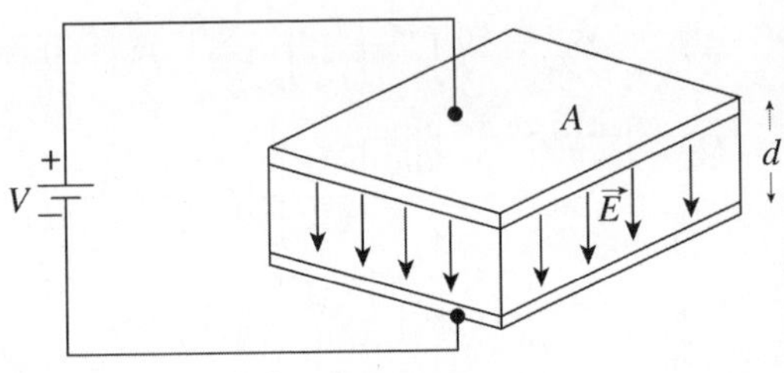

Figure E2.88

EXAMPLE 2.89

The radii of the inner and outer conductors of a coaxial cable are 2 cm and 5 cm, respectively and the insulating material between them has a relative permittivity of 4. The charge density on the outer conductor is $\rho_l = 10^{-4}$ C/m. Calculate the total energy stored in a 10 cm length of the cable.

SOLUTION

Given $\varepsilon_r = 4$, $l = 0.1$ m and $\rho_l = 10^{-4}$ C/m.

From Gauss' law, the magnitude of electric field due to coaxial cable with charge density ρ_l is

$$E = \frac{\rho_l}{2\pi\varepsilon\rho}$$

where ρ is the radius of the conductor cable. The total energy stored in the electric field is

$$W_e = \frac{1}{2}\int_v \varepsilon E^2\, dv = \frac{l\varepsilon}{2}\int_{\rho=2}^{\rho=5} E^2(2\pi\rho\, d\rho)$$

where $dv = 2\pi\rho\, l\, d\rho$.

Therefore, $W_e = \dfrac{l\varepsilon}{2}\displaystyle\int_2^5 \left(\frac{\rho_l}{2\pi\varepsilon\rho}\right)^2 (2\pi\rho\, d\rho)$

$$= \frac{\rho_l^2 l}{4\pi\varepsilon}\int_2^5\left(\frac{d\rho}{\rho}\right) = \frac{\rho_l^2 l}{4\pi\varepsilon}\ln[\rho]_2^5$$

$$= \frac{\rho_l^2 l}{4\pi\varepsilon_0\varepsilon_r}\ln\left[\frac{5}{2}\right]$$

$$= 9\times10^9 \times \frac{\left(10^{-4}\right)^2 \times 0.1}{4}\times 0.916 \qquad \left(\text{since}\,\frac{1}{4\pi\varepsilon_0} = 9\times10^9\right)$$

$$= 2.06\ \text{J}$$

REVIEW QUESTIONS

1. Define Coulomb's law in vector form.

2. State and explain Coulomb's law and the equation of force between two point charges indicating clearly the units of the quantities.

3. Obtain an expression for total force experienced by a point charge due to infinite number of point charges around it.

4. Determine the electric force acting on a point charge of 1 µC situated at the origin if a point charge of 200 nC is located at $(0.2, 0.3, 0)$ m and a charge of -1300 nC is located at $(0.5, 0.7, -1.3)$ m.

5. A point charge of 2 µC is situated at $P(0, 4, 0)$ and a second charge of 10 µC is located at $S(3, 0, 0)$. Calculate the force experienced by each charge.

6. Given that four point charges, each $20\,\mu\text{C}$ are on the x and y-axes at $\pm 4\,\text{m}$. Determine the force on a $200\,\mu\text{C}$ point charge at $(0, 0, 3)$ m.

7. A charge $Q_2 = 121\times10^{-9}\,\text{C}$ is located in vacuum at $P_2(-0.03,\ 0.01,\ 0.04)$ m. Find the force on Q_2 due to $Q_1 = 110\ \mu\text{C}$ at $P_1(0.03,\ 0.08, -0.02)$ m.

8. Calculate the force on a unit positive charge at P on x-axis whose coordinates are ($z = 3$ m, $y = 0$) due to the following two charges: A positive charge of 10^{-9}C is situated in air at ($z = 0$, $y = 0$) and a negative charge of $-2\times10^{-9}\text{C}$ and on the z-axis ($z = 2$ m, $y = 0$).

9. Given that the point charges of 4 nC are situated at three corners of a square, whose side is 0.3 m. Find the magnitude and direction of the electric field at the vacant corner point of the square.

10. Given that four identical point charges Q Coulombs each are placed at the four corners of a square of side b. Find the force on a 1 C charge located at the centre of any one side.

11. What is electric field intensity?

12. Prove that newton per coulomb is dimensionally same as volt per metre.

13. Define point charge.

14. Give the formula for electric field intensity at a point P due to n number of point charges.

15. If the electric field is 200 V/m at a distance of 2 m from the point charge Q, then find Q in free space.

16. Find $|\vec{E}|$ at a distance of 20 cm from a charge of 20pC in vacuum.

17. Write the formula for electric field intensity due to infinite line charge.

18. Define line charge, surface charge and volume charge.

19. Write the expression for electric field intensity due to line charge, surface charge and volume charge.

20. Write a short note on principle of superposition as applied to charge distribution.

21. Find the electric field due to n charges.

22. Determine the electric field intensity at $P(-0.2, 0, -2.3)$ due to a point charge of $+5\,\text{nC}$ at $Q(0.2, 0.1, -2.5)$ in air. All dimensions are in metres.

23. What are the types of charge distributions? Give one example of each.

24. Determine the electric field intensity due to infinite long straight line.

25. Give the electric field intensity due to charged circular ring placed in xy-plane, at a point on its axis at a distance z.

26. Give the electric field intensity due to infinite sheet of charge.

27. Give the electric field intensity due to charged circular disc with uniform charge density ρ_s at a distance h on its axis.

28. Mention any two sources of electromagnetic field.

29. Define electric field intensity. Obtain an expression for the electric field intensity at a point which is at a distance of R from a point charge Q.

30. State the units of electric field intensity $\vec{E}$ and explain the method of obtaining $\vec{E}$ at a point in Cartesian system, due to a point charge Q.

31. Obtain an expression for total electric field intensity at a point due to infinite number of point charges.

32. Given that two point charges with $Q_1 = 2 \times 10^{-5}\,\text{C}$ and $Q_2 = -4 \times 10^{-5}\,\text{C}$ are located in free space at $(1, 3, -1)\,\text{m}$ and $(-3, 1, -2)\,\text{m}$ respectively, in a Cartesian coordinate system. Find (a) the electric field $\vec{E}$ at $(3, 1, -2)\,\text{m}$ and (b) the force on a $8 \times 10^{-5}\,\text{C}$ charge located at that point.

33. Find the force on a point charge Q located at $(0, 0, h)$ due to surface charge density of $\rho_s\,\text{C/m}^2$ uniformly distributed over the circular disc $r \le a$, $z = 0$.

34. Explain the various types of charge distributions.

35. State the units of line charge density, surface charge density and volume charge density.

36. Obtain an expression for an electric field due to infinite line charge having density of $\rho_l\,\text{C/m}$ placed along z-axis, at a point P on y-axis at a distance of d from the z-axis.

37. Obtain an expression for an electric field intensity due to charged circular ring of radius h placed in xy-plane, at a point $P(0,0,z)$ having uniform line charge density of ρ_l C/m.

38. Derive the expression for the electric field intensity due to infinite sheet of charge placed in xy-plane, having surface charge density of ρ_s C/m^2.

39. A circular disc of radius a is charged uniformly with a charge density of σ C/m^2. Find the electric intensity at a point h from the disc along its central axis.

40. A uniform line charge with $\rho_l = 10$ µC/m line along x-axis. Find $\vec{E}$ at $(5,2,3)$.

41. A charge is distributed on y-axis of Cartesian system having a line charge density of $5y^{3.5}$ µC/m. Find the total charge over the length of 15 m.

42. Find the total charge inside a volume having volume charge density as $15z^3 e^{-0.3x} \sin \pi y$ mC/m^3. The volume is defined between $-1 \le x \le 1, 0 \le y \le 1$ and $2 \le z \le 5$.

43. Explain the procedure of obtaining $\vec{E}$ due to the line charge, surface charge and volume charge.

44. Find the total charge contained in the specified volume:

   (*i*) A cube with edges 1 m long and parallel to axes, lying in the first octant $(x,y,z \ge 0)$ with one corner at the origin: Charge density is $\rho = 2xy/(z+1)$.

  (*ii*) A sphere with radius of 1 m centred at the origin: Charge density is $\rho = R(1+\cos\theta)\sin\dfrac{\phi}{2}$.

45. A charge of +10 C is located at the point $x = 0$ and $y = 1$ and charge of –5C is at the point $x = 0$ and $y = -1$. Find the point on y-axis at which net $\vec{E} = 0$.

46. A point charge of 20 nC is located at the origin. Determine the magnitude and direction of $\vec{E}$ at point $P(1,3,-4)$ m.

47. A circular disc of 10 cm radius is charged uniformly all over the surface with total charge of 100 µC. Find $\vec{E}$ at a point 20 cm away from the disc along its axis.

48. Calculate the force on a point charge of $50\,\mu$C placed at a point $(0,0,5)$ m due to a charge of 500 µC that is uniformly distributed over a circular disc of radius 5 m and placed in the xy-plane.

49. Given that two parallel infinite lines with equal and opposite but uniform line charge distributions of 100 nC/m are separated by a distance of 1 mm. Determine the force per unit length. What is the nature of this force?

50. A ring of radius 6m is placed in yz-plane with line charge density of 18 nC/m and is centered at origin. Find the electric field intensity at point $(8,0,0)$ m.

51. A charge is distributed along the z-axis between ± 6 m with uniform charge density of 25 nC/m. Calculate $\vec{E}$ at a point $(2,0,0)$ m in free space.

52. The infinite line charge parallel to z-axis is at $x = 6$, $y = 10$. Find $\vec{E}$ at the general point $P(x,y,z)$ in Cartesian system.

53. Find $\vec{E}$ at $(10,0,0)$ due to a charge of 10 nC which is distributed uniformly along x-axis between $x = -5$ to +5 m in free space.

54. Find the electric field $\vec{E}$ at $P(0,0,2)$ m due to the infinite sheet of charge in xy-plane with density 10 nC/m^2.

55. Given that two infinite sheets of charge each with density ρ_s are located at $x = \pm 2$ m. Determine $\vec{E}$ in all directions.

56. A sheet of charge with $\rho_s = 2$ nC/m^2 is in the plane $x = 2$ in free space and a line charge $\rho_l = 20$ nC/m is located at $x = 1$ and $z = 4$. Find $\vec{E}$ at $P(0,0,0)$ and at $P(4,5,6)$. What is the force per unit length on the line charge?

57. Find the force on a point charge Q located at $(0,0,h)$ due to charge of surface charge density ρ_s C/m^2 uniformly distributed over the circular disc $r \le a$, $z = 0$m.

58. A uniform surface charge of $\rho_s = 2$ μC/m^2 is situated at $z = 2$ plane. What is the value of electric field intensity at $P(1,1,1,)$?

59. Find $\vec{E}$ at $(0,0,2)$m due to charged circular disc in x-plane with $\rho_s = 20$ nC/m^2 and radius 1m.

60. Find the electric field intensity at a point at a distance above the plane and along the axis of a square loop carrying uniformly distributed charge of λ C/m . The square loop has side a m.

61. A circular disc of 10 m radius is charged uniformly with a total charge of Q coulombs. Find the electric field intensity at a point 40 cm away from the disc along its axis.

62. What is a line of force?

63. Define electric flux and electric flux density.

64. Explain the concept of electric flux density.

65. Express the electric flux density at a point in field in a vector form.

66. Define electric flux density at a point due to a point charge Q.

67. Derive the expression for $\vec{D}$ due to a point charge and thus, deduce the relationship between $\vec{D}$ and $\vec{E}$.

68. State and prove Gauss's law.

69. State the conditions to be satisfied by the special Gaussian surfaces.

70. Derive the expression for $\vec{D}$ due to a point charge using Gauss's law.

71. Explain Gauss's law applied to the case of infinite line charge and derive the expression for $\vec{D}$ due to an infinite line charge.

72. A uniform line charge with $\rho_l = 5\mu$ C/m lies along the x-axis. Find $\vec{D}$ at $(3,2,1)$m .

73. A uniform surface charge of $\rho_s = 2$ μC/m^2 is situated at $z = 2$ plane. What is the value of flux density at $P(1,1,1)$?

74. Find $\vec{D}$ at $(4,0,3)$ due to a point charge of -15.734 mC at $(4,0,0)$ and a line charge of 9.427 mC/m along the y-axis.

75. Consider a coaxial cable with inner radius a and outer radius b. Derive the expression for $\vec{D}$ for the region $a < r < b$ using Gauss's law.

76. Derive the expression for $\vec{D}$ due to the infinite sheet of charge placed in $z = 0$ plane, using Gauss's law and hence, derive the expression for $\vec{D}$ in all regions. Sketch the variation of $|\vec{D}|$ vs radius r.

77. Using Gauss's law, derive $\vec{D}$ in all the regions for a uniformly charged sphere having volume charge density ρ_v C/m^3. Sketch the variation of $|\vec{D}|$ vs radius r.

78. Find $\vec{D}$ at $P(6,8,-10)$ caused due to (i) a point charge of 30 mC at the origin. (ii) a uniform line charge $\rho_l = 40$ μC/m on the z-axis and (iii) a uniform $\rho_s = 57.2$ μC/m^2 on the plane $x = 9$.

79. A uniform surface charge density $\rho_s = 5$ nC/m^2 is situated at $x = 2$ m plane. What is $\vec{D}$ at $(3,1,1)$m ?

80. A spherical shell of charge density $\rho_s = 2$ nC/m^2 has a radius $r = 3$ m . Find $\vec{D}$ at $r = 6$ m and $r = 1$ m .

81. A uniformly charged sphere of radius 2m has charge density of 20 nC/m^3. Find $\vec{D}$ at $r = 5$ m .

82. Prove that a symmetrical charge distribution in the form of a sphere is equivalent to a concentrated point charge at the centre of the sphere as far as the external fields are concerned. Assume that the charge density is function of radius only.

83. Starting from the Gauss's law as applied to the differential volume element, explain the concept of divergence.

84. State and prove Gauss's divergence theorem.

85. State the physical significance of divergence of a vector field.

86. State the various properties of divergence of a vector field.

87. Using the Cartesian coordinate system, verify the following statements:

  (*i*) Divergence of the curl of a vector function is zero.

  (*ii*) Curl of the gradient of a scalar function is zero.

88. Given the $\vec{D} = zr\cos^2\phi\,\vec{a}_z$ C/m^2, calculate the charge density at $(1, \pi/4, 3)$ and the total charge enclosed by the cylinder of radius 1m with $-2 \le z \le 2$m.

89. A spherical symmetrical charge distribution has

$$\rho_v = \begin{cases} \dfrac{\rho_0 r}{a}, & 0 \le r \le a \\ 0, & r > a \end{cases}$$ Determine $\vec{D}$ and $\vec{E}$ everywhere.

90. Using Gauss's law, compute the electric field intensity and electric flux density at any point due to a uniform charge distribution on an infinite plane sheet of charge.

91. If $\vec{D} = 20xy^2(z+1)\vec{a}_x + 20x^2y(z+1)\vec{a}_y + 10x^2y^2\vec{a}_z$ C/m^2, calculate the charge density at $P(0.3, 0.4, 0.5)$.

92. If $\vec{D} = 2xy\vec{a}_x + 3yz\vec{a}_y + 4zx\vec{a}_z$ C/m^2, find the charge enclosed by $-1 \le x \le 2$, $0 \le z \le 4$ and $y = 3$ plane.

93. If $\vec{D} = 10xy^2\vec{a}_x + 15x^2y\vec{a}_y + 20x^2y^2z\vec{a}_z$, find ρ_v at $(1,1,1)$.

94. If $\vec{D} = 5x^2y^2z^2\vec{a}_x + 2x^3y^2z\vec{a}_y + 6x^4y^3z^2\vec{a}_z$, find ρ_v at $(2,3,5)$.

95. Given the flux density in free space $\vec{D} = \dfrac{r}{4}\vec{a}_r$ C/m^2. Determine (i) total flux leaving a sphere of $r = 0.4$ m (ii) total charge enclosed in a sphere of $r = 0.4$ m and (iii) field intensity at $r = 0.3$ m.

96. Given that $\vec{D} = \dfrac{5x^3}{2}\vec{a}_x$ C/m^2, evaluate both sides of the divergence theorem for the volume of a cube 1 m on an edge, centered at the origin and with edges parallel to the axes.

97. Evaluate $\int \vec{D}\cdot d\vec{s}$ if $\vec{D} = yxz\vec{a}_x - y^2\vec{a}_y + yz\vec{a}_z$ and the unit cube is bounded by $x = 0$, $x = 1$, $y = 0$, $y = 1$, $z = 0$, $z = 1$. Also, verify the divergence theorem.

98. A vector field $\vec{D} = \left(\dfrac{5r^2}{4}\right)\vec{a}_r$ is given in spherical co-ordinates. Evaluate both sides of divergence theorem for the volume enclosed between $r = 1$ and $r = 2$.

99. Mention the applications of Gauss's law.

100. Consider that concentric cylindrical conductor with radii $r_a = 0.01$ m and $r_b = 0.08$ m have charge densities $\rho_{sa} = 40$ C/m^3 and ρ_{sb} such that $\vec{D}$ and $\vec{E}$ fields exist between the two cylinders, but are zero elsewhere. Find ρ_{sb}.

101. Obtain the expressions for $\vec{D}$ and $\vec{E}$ using Gauss's law for a uniformly charged sphere.

102. Describe any two applications of Gauss's law.

103. Prove $\nabla \cdot \vec{D} = \rho_v$ using Gauss's law.

104. State the relationship between electric field intensity and electric flux density.

105. State and sketch the variation of $\vec{E}$ vs the radial distance r measured from the origin for the spherical shell of radius a.

106. Sketch the variation of $\vec{E}$ vs the radial distance r for a uniformly charged sphere of radius a.

107. Why Gauss's law cannot be applied to determine the electric field due to finite line charge?

108. Deduce Coulomb's law from Gauss's law.

109. What is the physical significance of $\nabla \cdot \vec{D}$?

110. Show that $\vec{D} = \varepsilon_0 \vec{E}$ by using Gauss's law.

111. Determine the total charge enclosed by a cube of 2 m side, centered at the origin with the edges parallel to the axes when $\vec{D}$ over the cube is $5x^3 \vec{a}_x$ C/m^2.

112. What is an equipotential surface?

113. Show the equipotential surfaces for a point charge.

114. Define equipotential line and show that equipotential and field lines are orthogonal.

115. Give an account of the nature and characteristics of equipotential lines in an electrostatic field.

116. Given that two long thin parallel wires carrying charges $+\lambda$ and $-\lambda$ C/m are situated d metres apart. Determine an expression for the potential at a point between the wires. Sketch the pattern of equipotential lines around the wires.

117. Write notes on uniform and non-uniform electric fields.

118. State the nature of conservative field.

119. Define a work done and obtain the integral to calculate the work done in moving a point charge Q in an electric field $\vec{E}$.

120. Define electric potential.

121. Distinguish between potential and potential difference.

122. State the principle of superposition as applied to an electric potential of a point.

123. State the general expressions for the potential at a point due to line charge, surface charge and volume charge.

124. State the potential difference between the two points due to infinite line charge.

125. Give the relation between electric field and potential.

126. Give the properties of gradient of a scalar.

127. Explain the term 'potential gradient' and establish its relation with electric field intensity.

128. A point charge $+2\,\text{nC}$ is located at the origin. What is the value of potential at $P(1,0,0)\text{m}$?

129. The potential distribution of $V = ax^2 + 6y^2 - 3\sqrt{z}$ V exists in an electric field intensity of $\vec{E} = -16\vec{a}_x - 12y\,\vec{a}_y + \dfrac{1.5}{\sqrt{z}}\vec{a}_z$ V/m. Calculate the value of 'a'.

130. A scalar potential is given by $V = 7y^2 + 12x$ V. Determine $\vec{E}$ and its value at $(0,0,0), (4,0,0)$ and $(0,4,0)$.

131. A scalar potential is given by $V = 5x + 4y^2 + 2z^3$ V. Determine $\vec{E}$ at $(2,3,4)$.

132. The potential in a certain region is given as $V = x^2 + 3y^2 + 9z$ V. Determine the electric field intensity at $P(1,-2,3)$.

133. Given $V = \dfrac{120\sin\theta}{r^2}$ V in free space. Determine the electric potential and field intensity at the point P located at $r = 3\,\text{m}$, $\theta = 60°$ and $\phi = 25°$.

134. If $V = 3x^2 - y + 3z$, determine V, $\vec{E}$ and $\left|\vec{D}\right|$ at $(3,-2,4)$.

135. If $\vec{E} = -8xy\vec{a}_x - 4x^2\vec{a}_y + \vec{a}_z$ V/m, then find the work done in carrying a 6C charge from $(1,8,5)$ to $(2,18,6)$ along the path $y = 3x^2 + z, z = x + 4$.

136. Explain why $\oint_l \vec{E}\cdot d\vec{l} = 0$ in electrostatic fields.

137. Given a field $\vec{E} = \left(\dfrac{-6y}{x^2}\right)\vec{a}_x + \left(\dfrac{6}{x}\right)\vec{a}_y + 5\vec{a}_z$ V/m, determine the potential difference V_{AB} for $A(-5,1,2)$ and $B(4,0,3)$.

138. A point charge Q_1 is located at the origin in the free space. Determine the work done in carrying a charge Q_2 from $B(r_b,\theta_B,\phi_B)$ to $C(r_A,\theta_B,\phi_B)$ with θ and ϕ held constant.

139. If three point charge, $3\mu C, -4\mu C$ and $5\mu C$ are located at $(0,0,0),(2,-1,3)$ and $(0,4,-2)$ respectively, determine the potential at $(-1,5,2)$ assuming $V(\infty) = 0$.

140. A total charge of $\dfrac{40}{3}$ nC is uniformly distributed over a circular disc of radius 2m. Determine the potential on the axis of the disc 2 m from the plane of the disc.

141. A point charge of 15 nC is situated at the origin and another point charge of $-12\,\text{nC}$ is located at the point $(3,3,3)$ m. Determine the potential at the point $(0,-3,-3)$.

142. A uniform line charge of 0.8 nC/m lies along the z-axis in free space. Determine the potential at $P(3,4,5)$ if the potential at $Q(2,8,3)$ is zero.

143. A point charge of 16 nC is located at $Q(2,3,5)$ in free space and a uniform line charge of 5 nC/m is at the intersection of the planes $x = 2$ and $y = 4$. If the potential at the origin is 100V, find V at $(4,1,3)$.

144. A charged ring of radius a carries a uniform charge distribution. Determine the potential and the electric field intensity at any point on the axis of the ring.

145. A negative point charge of magnitude $2\,\mu C$ is located in air at the origin, and two positive point charge of $1\mu C$ each are at points $y = \pm 3\text{m}$, calculate the electric potential at a point 4m from the origin on the x-axis.

146. Calculate the potential V_{AB} for $r_A = 6\text{m}$ with respect to $r_B = 8\,\text{m}$ due to a point charge $Q = 500\text{pC}$ at the origin.

147. A positive point charge of magnitude $10\mu C$ is situated at point $x = 0$, $y = +2\text{m}$ and negative point charge of $-10\mu C$ is situated at point $x = 0$, $y = -2\text{m}$. Calculate V at $x = 0$, $y = -1\text{m}$.

148. Derive an expression for potential at a point inside a sphere of radius R with uniform volume charge density ρ. A spherical volume of radius $R = 1.5\text{m}$ has a uniform charge density of $\rho = 0.5\text{C/m}^3$. Calculate the electric field and potential V at (i) $r = 0.5\text{m}$ and (ii) $r = 3.0\,\text{m}$ (outside the sphere).

149. Derive the expression for potential due to charged disc. From potential, derive its electric field intensity.

150. A positive charge of 100 pC is uniformly distributed throughout a spherical volume 0.5m diameter. Calculate and plot the variation of electric field and potential as a function of radius r from the centre of the sphere to a distance of 1m.

151. Consider that three point charges are located in free space as follows: $+5\times10^{-9}$ C at $(0,0)$ m , $+4\times10^{-9}$ C at $(3,0)$ m and -6×10^{-9} C at $(0,4)$ m

    (*i*) Determine the potential, electric field intensity and flux density at $(3,4)$ m .

    (*ii*) What is the total electric flux over a sphere of 5m radius with centre at $(0,0)$ m .

152. Establish the relation between potential and electric field.

153. A charge of Q coulomb is distributed homogeneously throughout the volume of a sphere of radius R metre, and the sphere is in vacuum. Find the flux density, the field strength and the potential as a function of the distance from the centre of the sphere for $0 \leq R \leq \alpha$; assume $V(\alpha)=0$.

154. What is an electric dipole?

155. Define electric dipole moment. Give its units.

156. Give the potential at a point due to an electrical dipole.

157. Give an electric field $\vec{E}$ at a point due to an electric dipole.

158. Given that point charges $+3\,\mu C$ and $-3\,\mu C$ are located at $(0,0,1)$ and $(0,0-1)$ respectively, in free space. (i) Find the dipole moment $\vec{p}$ and (ii) find $\vec{E}$ at $P(r=2,\theta=40°,\phi=50°)$.

159. An electric dipole of $100\,\vec{a}_z$ pC·m is located at the origin. Find the scalar potential V at $(0,0,10)$.

160. Derive the expression for potential due to an electric dipole at any point P. Also, find electric field intensity at the same point.

161. Show that the electric field intensity due to an electric dipole represents a conservative field.

162. Point charges $+Q$ and $-Q$ are located at $(0,0,d/2)$ and $(0,0,-d/2)$. Show that the potential at a point $P(r,\theta,\phi)$ is inversely proportional to r^2 noting that $r \gg d$.

163. Given that two charges $\pm10^{-9}$ C are separated by a small distance of 10 mm. What is the dipole-moment of the combination? If this dipole is situated with its axis at an angle of 60° to the orientation of a uniform electric field of 10 V/m, determine the translational force on the dipole and also, the torque that tends to align the dipole-axis with the field.

164. Show that the torque on a physical dipole $\vec{p}$ in a uniform electric field $\vec{E}$ is given by $\vec{p}\times\vec{E}$. Extend this result to a pure dipole.

165. Derive an expression for potential energy stored in the system of n point charges.

166. Give the energy in terms of $\vec{E}$ and $\vec{D}$.

167. If $V = x-y+xy+2z$ V, find $\vec{E}$ at $(1,2,3)$ and the electrostatic energy stored in a cube of side 2 m centered at the origin.

168. Given that three charges of 100 nC, 200 nC and 300 nC are so arranged that the separation between any two charges is 5 cm. What is the total energy stored in the system?

169. Given that two parallel plates, each measuring 20 cm × 20 cm, are separated by a gap of 1 mm. The plates have equal but opposite uniform surface charge density of 250 nC/m^2. Compute the energy stored if the dielectric constant of the medium is 2.

170. Derive the expression for the energy density in electric field.

171. If $V = \rho^2 z \sin\phi$, calculate the energy within the region defined by $1<\rho<4$, $0<\phi<\pi/3$ and $-2<z<2$.

172. Prove that the energy stored in the electric field in the electrostatic case is $\int_v \frac{1}{2}\vec{D}\cdot\vec{E}\,dv$.

173. Show that the energy stored in a capacitor is proportional to its capacitance and square of the voltage.

CONDUCTORS AND DIELECTRICS

3.1 INTRODUCTION

Materials are generally classified as conductors and nonconductors based on their electrical properties. The electrical properties of these materials are discussed in this chapter to understand the concepts of current and current density. Nonconducting materials are known as insulators or dielectrics. The characteristics of dielectric materials such as permittivity, susceptibility, dielectric strength, and polarization are also explained. The concepts of boundary conditions for electrostatics at the interface of two different mediums are introduced.

In this chapter, the concept of determining the capacitance for parallel plate capacitor, parallel wire transmission line, coaxial cable, and spherical capacitor is explained. Boundary value problems that involve electrostatic conditions at some boundaries are solved using Laplace's equation and Poisson's equation. The capacitance for different geometries is also derived using Laplace's equation. The determination of electric potential, electric field intensity, and charge density using method of images and applications of static electric fields are also discussed.

3.2 MATERIAL PROPERTIES

Any material in a static electric field medium is characterized by its constitutive parameters like electrical permittivity ε and conductivity σ. Materials are broadly classified as conductors and dielectrics based on their conductivity values. The conductivity of a material depends on the movement of electrons through the material under the influence of an external electric field. A material with high conductivity ($\sigma > 1$) is called a conductor or a metal, and a material with low conductivity ($\sigma < 1$) is called a dielectric or an insulator.

The valence electrons in a conductor are loosely bound to the atoms and these electrons migrate from one atom to another under the application of external electric field. The movement of electrons is in a direction opposite to that of the applied electric field and their movement is characterized by an average velocity called the drift velocity $\bar{u}$. This results in high conductivity for good conductor or metal. The conductivity σ of metals is in the range of 10^6 to 10^7 S/m.

But in a dielectric material, the valence electrons are tightly bound to the nucleus of the atoms and hence, it is very difficult to remove these electrons under the influence of external electric field. The small movement of electrons inside the dielectric material results in poor conductivity. The conductivity of dielectric or insulator is in the range of 10^{-10} to 10^{-17} S/m. Any dielectric material can also be characterized by its permittivity. The permittivity of dielectric material is used to determine the dielectric strength of that material. A perfect conductor is a material with $\sigma = \infty$ and a perfect dielectric is a material with $\sigma = 0$.

Materials, such as silicon and germanium, having conductivity values between that of conductors and dielectrics are known as semiconductors. The conductivity of silicon is 4.4×10^{-4} S/m and that of germanium is 2.2 S/m. The conductivity of a material depends on temperature and on the amount of impurities. As the temperature decreases, the conductivity of metals increases. At very low temperatures ($T = 0$K), some conductors act as superconductors because their conductivities reach infinite values. The conductivity of lead at a temperature of 4K is in the order of 10^{20} S/m.

The values of conductivity of some common materials at 20° C are given in Table 3.1. Here, copper, silver, and aluminum are conductors, whereas silicon and germanium are semiconductors and water, paper, and glass are insulators as listed in Table 3.1.

Table 3.1 *Conductivity of some common materials at 20° C for conductors, semiconductors and insulators.*

Materials	Conductivity σ in (S/m)
Conductors	
Silver	6.1×10^7
Copper	5.8×10^7
Gold	4.1×10^7
Aluminum	3.5×10^7
Zinc	1.7×10^7
Iron	1×10^7
Mercury	1×10^6
Carbon	3×10^4
Semiconductors	
Pure germanium	2.2
Pure silicon	4.4×10^{-4}
Insulators	
Water (distilled)	10^{-4}
Bakelite	10^{-10}
Paper	10^{-11}
Glass	10^{-12}
Mica	10^{-15}
Wax	10^{-17}

3.3 NATURE OF CURRENT AND CURRENT DENSITY

The current is generally defined as the rate of flow of charge in a conducting medium as given by

$$I = \frac{dQ}{dt} \tag{3.1}$$

where dQ is the amount of charge that flows in time dt. The motion of charges inside a conductor constitutes a current. The current denoted by uppercase letter I indicate steady current which is constant in time and it is called a direct current (dc). When the current is represented by lowercase letter i, it indicates the current as a function of time and it is called an alternating current (ac). The unit of current is ampere (A). A current of one ampere corresponds to the movement of one coulomb of charge in one second.

The current density J is generally defined as the flow of current per unit area as given by

$$J = \frac{I}{A} \tag{3.2}$$

The unit of current density is ampere per square metre (A/m^2). In general, there are two types of currents namely, convection current and conduction current. The corresponding current densities are known as convection current density and conduction current density.

In general, electric charge in motion constitutes an electric current and any medium carrying current is called a conductor. In conductors or metals, the charge is carried by electrons whereas in plasma or gaseous conductors, the charge is carried by negative electrons and positive ions. For example, ionosphere of the earth is made of positive ions and of free electrons in plasma.

The charge is carried by both positive and negative ions in liquid conductors or electrolytes whereas in semiconductors, the charge is carried by both positively charged holes and negatively charged electrons.

3.3.1 Convection Current and Convection Current Density

The steady current flowing through an insulating medium such as liquid, gas, plasma, or free space (vacuum) due to movement of charged particles is called convection current. The motion of electrons in a cathode ray tube (CRT) or picture tube in television is a classic example of convection current. In this case, the electrons emitted from the cathode move very slowly and those electrons that are close to the anode attain very high velocities. This is mainly because the electrons will not collide with one another in their path of travel from cathode to anode. A charged thunder cloud in the atmosphere also gives rise to convection current.

Consider a region of charge with volume charge density ρ_v in free space as shown in Figure 3.1. The charges are moving with an average velocity $\vec{u}$ along the axis of the tube under the influence of an electric field. These charges will move a distance $d\vec{l}$ in time Δt such that $d\vec{l} = \vec{u}\Delta t$ in which the differential elemental length is in the same direction as the mean velocity.

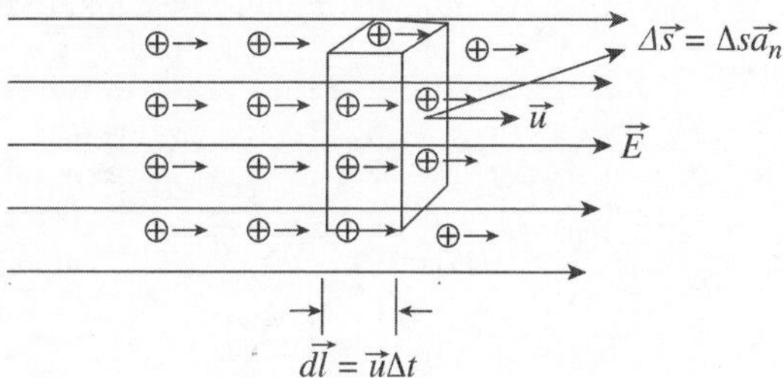

Figure 3.1 *Movement of charges in free space under the influence of electric field*

When an imaginary window with surface area $\Delta \vec{s}$ normal to the drift velocity is considered, the differential charge moving through this window is represented by

$$\Delta Q = \rho_v dv = \rho_v \Delta \vec{s} \cdot d\vec{l} = \rho_v \Delta \vec{s} \cdot \vec{u}\Delta t$$

and the corresponding differential current ΔI through the surface $\Delta \vec{s}$ is

$$\Delta I = \frac{\Delta Q}{\Delta t} = \rho_v \vec{u} \cdot \Delta \vec{s} = \vec{J} \cdot \Delta \vec{s}$$

where $\vec{J} = \rho_v \vec{u}$ is defined as the convection current density and its unit is measured in A/m^2. The convection current density is related linearly to charge density as well as to velocity. The total current flowing through any arbitrary surface s is represented by

$$I = \int_s \vec{J} \cdot d\vec{s} \tag{3.3}$$

This current is called the convection current. Here, the current I in a region can be described by the surface in which the charges are passing. Since the current density $\vec{J}$ is represented by a vector function, it is more useful in describing the fields instead of current I. This current density $\vec{J}$ is also referred to as volume current density.

3.3.2   Conduction Current and Conduction Current Density

The steady current flowing through a conductor due to movement of free electrons is called conduction current. The free charge carriers are mostly electrons in metals like copper, silver, and gold. These electrons form the valence electrons of an atom and contribute to the conduction process. The current through a conducting metal is an example of conduction current, which is simply due to the flow of electrons.

When a battery is connected across the two ends of a conductor, difference in potential exists between the two ends. This will result in an electric field inside the conductor and this electric field within the conductor exerts a force on the free electron of the conductor. The force on an electron with charge $-e$ or $-Q$ in the electric field $\vec{E}$ is represented by $\vec{F} = -e\vec{E}$.

As the electrons are not in free space, they will not be accelerated under the influence of electric field. But they will collide with each other in the atom and drift from one atom to another. The electric field makes the electrons to move with random velocity, known as drift velocity, which causes the electrons to drift gradually in a particular direction. The net drift of electrons in that direction results in conduction current through the conductor. The direction of conventional current is opposite to that of the movement of electrons.

If an electron with mass m is moving in an electric field with mean drift velocity $\vec{u}$, then the average rate at which an electron loses momentum in collisions is $\dfrac{m\vec{u}}{\tau}$, where τ is the mean time per collision. The average rate at which an electron gains momentum from the electric force is $-e\vec{E}$. According to Newton's law, under steady-state conditions, the rate of loss of momentum must be equal to the rate of gain of momentum. Therefore,

$$\frac{m\vec{u}}{\tau} = -e\vec{E} \tag{3.4}$$

Then, the drift velocity can be written as

$$\vec{u} = -\frac{e\tau \vec{E}}{m} = -\mu_e \vec{E} \tag{3.5}$$

where the constant of proportionality $\mu_e = \dfrac{e\tau}{m}$ is called the electron mobility. Here, the drift velocity of an electron in a conducting medium is proportional to the applied electric field intensity.

If there are N electrons per unit volume, then the electron charge density is given by $\rho_v = -Ne$, where e is the magnitude of the charge on the electron. Hence, the conduction current density in the conducting medium is

$$\vec{J} = \rho_v \vec{u} = Ne\mu_e \vec{E} = \sigma \vec{E} \tag{3.6}$$

or

$$\vec{J} = \sigma \vec{E} \tag{3.7}$$

where the constant of proportionality $\sigma = Ne\mu_e$ is the conductivity of the medium in siemens per metre (S/m) or ohm inverse per metre (Ω^{-1}/m).

Equation (3.7) is known as the *point form of Ohm's law*, which states that the conduction current density at any point in a conducting medium is proportional to the electric field intensity. The reciprocal of conductivity is called the resistivity, i.e., $\rho = \dfrac{1}{\sigma}$. The unit of resistivity is ohm metre ($\Omega\cdot$m).

In general, conduction current requires conductors, whereas convection current does not need any conductors. As both these types of current are generated by different physical mechanisms, conduction current obeys Ohm's law, whereas convection current does not obey Ohm's law.

3.4 CONDUCTORS IN STATIC ELECTRIC FIELD

Under the influence of externally applied electric field $\vec{E}$ to a conducting material, the valence electrons in the conductor move with electron drift velocity $\vec{u}_e = -\mu_e\vec{E}$ where μ_e is called the electron mobility. The electric charge in motion constitutes an electric current in a conductor, whereas in a semiconductor, the current is due to flow of both charge carriers, namely electrons and holes. As holes are positive charge carriers, they are associated with hole drift velocity $\vec{u}_h = \mu_h\vec{E}$ where μ_h is the hole mobility. The movement of holes is in the same direction of applied electric field $\vec{E}$ and the movement of electrons is in the direction opposite to that of the field.

For a medium of charges with volume density ρ_v of charges moving with a velocity $\vec{u}$, the current density is represented by $\vec{J} = \rho_v\vec{u}$. In semiconductors, the total current density is the sum of $\vec{J}_e$ due to electrons and $\vec{J}_h$ due to holes as given by

$$\vec{J} = \vec{J}_e + \vec{J}_h = \rho_{ve}\vec{u}_e + \rho_{vh}\vec{u}_h \tag{3.8}$$

Substituting the expression for drift velocity of electrons and holes in Eq. (3.8), we get

$$\vec{J} = (-\rho_{ve}\mu_e + \rho_{vh}\mu_h)\vec{E} = \sigma\vec{E}$$

where the conductivity σ of the semiconductor is given by

$$\begin{aligned}
\sigma &= -\rho_{ve}\mu_e + \rho_{vh}\mu_h \\
&= (N_e\mu_e + N_h\mu_h)e
\end{aligned} \tag{3.9}$$

in which $\rho_{ve} = -N_e e$ and $\rho_{vh} = N_h e$ with N_e and N_h represent the number of free electrons per unit volume and the number of free holes per unit volume respectively, and $e = 1.602 \times 10^{-19}$ C represents the absolute charge of a single hole or electron.

In a good conductor, the electrons are the only charge carriers. The free electrons in the outermost shell of an atom move in random directions with variable speeds in the absence of an external electric field. This random motion of electrons produces zero average current through the conductor. On application of external electrical field $\vec{E}$, the electrons migrate from one atom to another along a direction opposite to that of the applied field with a drift velocity $\vec{u}_e = -\mu_e\vec{E}$. For a good conductor, $N_h\mu_h \ll N_e\mu_e$. Then the conductivity expression given in Eq. (3.9) reduces to

$$\sigma = N_e\mu_e e = -\rho_{ve}\mu_e$$

Hence, the current density in a conductor is represented by

$$\vec{J} = \vec{J}_e = \rho_{ve}\vec{u}_e = -\rho_{ve}\mu_e\vec{E}$$
$$\vec{J} = \sigma\vec{E}$$

which is the *point form of Ohm's law*. A perfect conductor with $\sigma = \infty$ results in $\vec{E} = \dfrac{\vec{J}}{\sigma} = 0$. This means that the electric field inside the conductor vanishes to maintain a finite current density. According to Gauss's law, if $\vec{E} = 0$, then the charge density ρ_v must be zero, which shows that a perfect conductor cannot contain an electrostatic field within it.

A perfect conductor is an equipotential medium in which the electric potential is the same at every point in the conductor, which is based on the fact that $\vec{E} = -\nabla V$. Since $\vec{E} = 0$ everywhere in the perfect conductor, the potential difference between two points will also be zero. Hence, under static conditions, inside a perfect conductor, $\sigma = \infty$, $\vec{E} = 0$, $\rho_v = 0$, and potential between any two points is zero.

EXAMPLE 3.1

A conductor of uniform cross section and 150 m long has a voltage drop of 1.3 V and a current density of 4.65×10^5 A/m^2. What is the conductivity of the material in the conductor?

SOLUTION

Given $J = 4.65 \times 10^5$ A/m^2, $V = 1.3$ volts, and $l = 150$ m.

From Ohm's law, $J = \sigma E$.

Therefore, conductivity is

$$\sigma = \frac{J}{E} = \frac{Jl}{V} \qquad \left(\text{since } E = \frac{V}{l} \right)$$

$$= \frac{4.65 \times 10^5 \times 150}{1.3} = 5.37 \times 10^7 \text{ S/m}$$

EXAMPLE 3.2

The current flowing through a 100 m long conducting wire of uniform cross section has a density of 3×10^5 A/m^2. Find the voltage drop across the length of the wire if the wire material has a conductivity of 2×10^7 S/m.

SOLUTION

Given $J = 3 \times 10^5$ A/m^2, $\sigma = 2 \times 10^7$ S/m, and $l = 100$ m.

We know that $V = El$. From Ohm's law, the electric field intensity is $E = \dfrac{J}{\sigma}$ and the voltage drop across the length of the wire is

$$V = \frac{Jl}{\sigma} = \frac{3 \times 10^5 \times 100}{2 \times 10^7} = 1.5 \text{ V}$$

EXAMPLE 3.3

What is the density of free electrons in aluminum for a mobility of 0.0015 m^2/V·s and a conductivity of 3.5×10^7 S/m?

SOLUTION

Given $\sigma = 3.5 \times 10^7$ S/m and $\mu_e = 0.0015$ m^2/V·s.

We know that,

$$\sigma = N_e \mu_e e$$

Therefore, the density of free electrons is

$$N_e = \frac{\sigma}{\mu_e e} = \frac{3.5 \times 10^7}{0.0015 \times 1.602 \times 10^{-19}} = 1.46 \times 10^{29} \text{ electrons/m}^3 \qquad \square$$

EXAMPLE 3.4

An aluminum conductor is 600 m long with a circular cross section and a diameter of 20 mm. If a dc voltage of 1.2 V is applied between them, find (i) the current density, (ii) the current, and (iii) power dissipated using the knowledge of circuit theory. Assume $\sigma = 3.82 \times 10^7$ S/m for aluminum.

SOLUTION

Given $l = 600$ m, $d = 20 \times 10^{-3}$ m, $\sigma = 3.82 \times 10^7$ S/m, and $V = 1.2$ V.

We know that,

$$E = \frac{V}{l}$$

Therefore, $E = \dfrac{1.2}{600} = 2 \times 10^{-3}$ V/m

(*i*) From Ohm's law, the current density is

$$J = \sigma E = 3.82 \times 10^7 \times 2 \times 10^{-3} = 76.4 \times 10^3 \text{ A/m}^2$$

(*ii*) The current, $I = JA = J\left(\dfrac{\pi d^2}{4}\right) = 76.4 \times 10^3 \times \dfrac{\pi}{4} \times \left(20 \times 10^{-3}\right)^2 = 24$ A

(*iii*) The power dissipated is

$$P = VI = 1.2 \times 24 = 28.8 \text{ W} \qquad \square$$

EXAMPLE 3.5

A wire of diameter 2 mm with the conductivity 5×10^7 Ω/m has 10^{29} free electrons per m^3. It is subjected to an electric field of 10 mV/m. Find (i) the free electron charge density, (ii) the current density, (iii) the current in the wire, and (iv) the drift velocity of the electrons. Given that the charge of one electron, $e = -1.602 \times 10^{-19}$ C.

SOLUTION

Given $\sigma = 5 \times 10^7$ S/m, $E = 10$ mV/m, $N_e = 10^{29}$ electrons/m^3, and $e = -1.602 \times 10^{-19}$ C.

(*i*) The volume charge density of free electrons is

$$\rho_{ve} = -N_e e$$

$$= -10^{29} \times \left(1.602 \times 10^{-19}\right) = -1.602 \times 10^{10} \text{ C/m}^3$$

(*ii*) From Ohm's law, the current density is

$$J = \sigma E = 5 \times 10^7 \times 10 \times 10^{-3} = 500 \times 10^3 \text{ A/m}^2$$

(*iii*) The current flowing in the wire is

$$I = \text{Current density} \times \text{Area} = JA$$

$$= J\left(\frac{\pi d^2}{4}\right) = 500\times10^3 \times \frac{\pi}{4} \times \left(2\times10^{-3}\right)^2 = 1.57 \text{ A}$$

(iv) We know that $\vec{J} = \rho_{ve}\vec{u}_e$. Therefore, the electron drift velocity is

$$\vec{u}_e = \frac{\vec{J}}{\rho_{ve}} = \frac{500\times10^3}{-1.6\times10^{10}} = -312.5\times10^{-7} = -3.125\times10^{-5} \text{ m/s}$$

The negative sign indicates that $\vec{u}_e$ is in the direction opposite to that of the applied electric field. $\square$

3.5   DIELECTRICS IN STATIC ELECTRIC FIELD

In a conductor, the free electrons that are able to move freely, whereas in a dielectric the electrons in the outermost shell of an atom are tightly bound to the atom. Though the charges in a dielectric are not able to move freely, a small displacement can be observed when an external force is applied.

To understand the effect of an electric field on a dielectric, consider a dielectric atom consisting of a negative charge $-Q$ (electron cloud) and a positive charge $+Q$ (nucleus) as shown in Figure 3.2. The electrons form a symmetrical cloud around the nucleus in the absence of an external electric field. Here, the center of the cloud coincides with the center of the nucleus as shown in Figure 3.2(a).

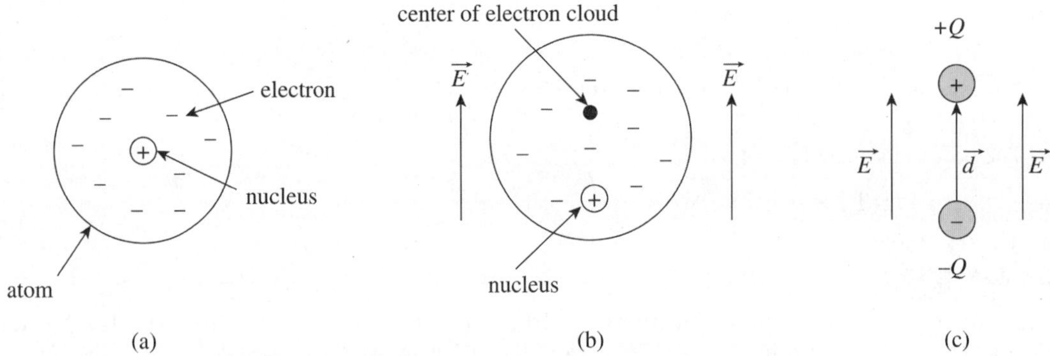

Figure 3.2   *Polarization of a non-polar atom: (a) non-polar atom with $\vec{E} = 0$ and (b) $\vec{E} \neq 0$, and (c) electric dipole*

When an external electric field $\vec{E}$ is applied to the dielectric, movement of charges is not possible as these charges are not able to move freely. But the electric field will polarize the atoms or molecules in the material by moving the center of the electron cloud away from the nucleus as shown in Figure 3.2(b). The polarized atom or molecule may be represented by an electric dipole consisting of charge $+Q$ at the center of the nucleus and charge $-Q$ at the center of the electron cloud as shown in Figure 3.2(c).

3.5.1   Dielectric Polarization

A smaller displacement that takes place between the positively charged nucleus and the negatively charged electron cloud in a dielectric atom or molecule due to the application of an externally applied electric field $\vec{E}$ results in polarization. The polarization process is illustrated in Figure 3.3, which transform a non-polar atom to polar.

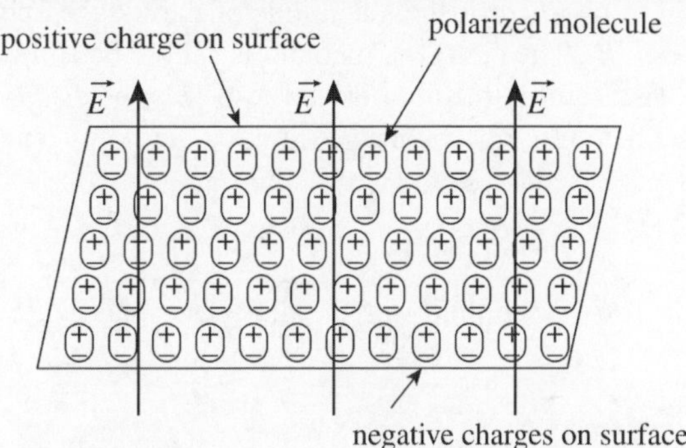

Figure 3.3 *Polarization of dielectric medium*

The dipole created by displacement due to the external field sets up a small internal electric field, pointing from the positively charged nucleus to the negatively charged electron cloud. This induced electric field is called polarization field, and it is generally weaker and opposite in direction to external field. Consequently, the net electric field present in the dielectric material is smaller than the external field $\vec{E}$.

At the microscopic level, each dipole exhibits a dipole moment characterized by $\vec{p} = Q\vec{d}$, where $\vec{d}$ is the distance vector from $-Q$ to $+Q$. These dipoles align themselves linearly inside the dielectric material by the external field as shown in Figure 3.3. This linear arrangement of dipole results in positive and negative surface charge densities along the upper and lower ends of the material. If there are n such dipoles in a small volume Δv of the dielectric, then the total dipole moment due to the electric field is represented by

$$Q_1\vec{d}_1 + Q_2\vec{d}_2 + \ldots\ldots + Q_n\vec{d}_n = \sum_{i=1}^{n} Q_i\vec{d}_i$$

The internal induced field due to dipoles is called an *electric polarization field* $\vec{P}$, and it can also be defined as the dipole moment per unit volume of the dielectric. The unit of polarization field is in coulomb/square metre and the field $\vec{P}$ is denoted by

$$\vec{P} = \underset{\Delta v \to 0}{Lt} \frac{\sum_{i=1}^{n} Q_i\vec{d}_i}{\Delta v} \tag{3.10}$$

The non-polar dielectric molecules do not possess dipoles or permanent dipole moments. Under the application of external electric field $\vec{E}$, these non-polar molecules get polarized. On removal of the external field, these molecules return to their original unpolarized state. Examples of such dielectrics are oxygen, nitrogen, hydrogen, and rare gases. But in some materials like water, SiO_2, and HCl, the molecules have built in permanent dipoles that are randomly oriented. Such materials with permanent dipoles are said to be polar. Under the influence of external electric field, these permanent dipoles align themselves along the direction of the electric field.

3.5.2 Dielectric Constant and Dielectric Strength

The electric field intensity $\vec{E}$ and flux density $\vec{D}$ are related by ε_0 in free space, i.e., $\vec{D} = \varepsilon_0\vec{E}$ whereas in dielectric, the presence of dipoles alters this relationship by the inclusion of induced polarization field $\vec{P}$ as given by

$$\vec{D} = \varepsilon_0\vec{E} + \vec{P} \tag{3.11}$$

A dielectric medium is said to be *linear* if the magnitude of the induced polarization field $\vec{P}$ is directly proportional to the magnitude of $\vec{E}$. The dielectric medium is said to be *isotropic* if the direction of $\vec{P}$ and $\vec{E}$ are in the same direction. A dielectric medium is said to be *homogeneous* if its parameters ε, μ, and σ are constant throughout the medium. For a linear, isotropic, and homogeneous dielectric medium, $\vec{P}$ is directly proportional to $\vec{E}$ as expressed by

$$\vec{P} = \chi_e \varepsilon_0 \vec{E} \tag{3.12}$$

where χ_e is known as the electric susceptibility of the dielectric material. Substituting Eq. (3.12) in Eq. (3.11), we get

$$\vec{D} = \varepsilon_0 \vec{E} + \chi_e \varepsilon_0 \vec{E} = \varepsilon_0 (1 + \chi_e) \vec{E}$$
$$= \varepsilon_0 \varepsilon_r \vec{E} = \varepsilon \vec{E} \tag{3.13}$$

where ε_0 is called the permittivity of free space, which is equal to $\dfrac{10^{-9}}{36\pi}$ or 8.854×10^{-12} F/m and ε_r is called the dielectric constant or relative permittivity. From Eq. (3.13), the relative permittivity ε_r of the dielectric material can be written as

$$\varepsilon_r = 1 + \chi_e \tag{3.14}$$

It should be noted that ε_r and χ_e are dimensionless whereas ε and ε_0 are in F/m. The relative permittivity ε_r is the ratio of the permittivity of dielectric to that of free space. For free space, $\varepsilon_r = 1$ and for most conductors such as metals, $\varepsilon_r \approx 1$. Table 3.2 gives the dielectric constants of some common materials. Here, it is evident that ε_r is always greater than or equal to unity.

The discussion on the dielectric theory considers only ideal dielectric materials. But, practically, no material is with ideal characteristics. In reality, if the applied electric field intensity $\vec{E}$ exceeds a certain critical value, it will pull the electrons completely out of molecules and the dielectric becomes conducting. As a result, sparking occurs and permanent damage can occur in the dielectric due to electron collision with the molecular structure. When the dielectric becomes conducting, dielectric breakdown is said to have occurred. This breakdown occurs in all kinds of dielectric materials such solid, liquid, or gas depending on the nature of the material, humidity, temperature, and the amount of time that the field is applied.

The maximum magnitude of electric field up to which the material can sustain or withstand without breakdown is called the *dielectric strength* of the dielectric material. The values of dielectric strength are also listed in Table 3.2 for some common dielectric materials. For example, lightning happens due to the dielectric breakdown of air. When the electric field of a charged thunder cloud exceeds the dielectric strength of air (3 MV/m), ionization occurs and the discharge of ions results in lightning.

Table 3.2 *Dielectric constant or relative permittivity (ε_r) and dielectric strength of common dielectric materials*

Dielectric Material	Dielectric constant, ε_r	Dielectric strength, E (MV/m)
Air	1	3
Petroleum oil	2.1	12
Paraffin	2.2	30
Quartz	5	30
Bakelite	5	20

Dielectric Material	Dielectric constant, ε_r	Dielectric strength, E (MV/m)
Glass	5–10	35
Mica	6	200
Paper	7	12

EXAMPLE 3.6

Determine the electric field intensity $\vec{E}$ in a material for which the electric susceptibility is 3.5 and $\vec{P} = 2.3 \times 10^{-7} \vec{a}_z$ C/m^2.

SOLUTION

Given $\chi_e = 3.5$ and $\vec{P} = 2.3 \times 10^{-7} \vec{a}_z$ C/m^2.

For a dielectric material, $\vec{P} = \chi_e \varepsilon_0 \vec{E}$

Assuming that $\vec{P}$ and $\vec{E}$ are in the same direction, the electric field intensity is

$$\vec{E} = \frac{\vec{P}}{\chi_e \varepsilon_0} = \frac{2.3 \times 10^{-7} \vec{a}_z}{3.5 \times 8.854 \times 10^{-12}} = 7.42 \times 10^3 \vec{a}_z \text{ V/m}$$

EXAMPLE 3.7

Find the magnitude of $\vec{D}$ and $\vec{P}$ for a dielectric material in which $\left|\vec{E}\right| = 0.15$mV/m and $\chi_e = 4.25$.

SOLUTION

Given $\chi_e = 4.25$ and $\left|\vec{E}\right| = 0.15$mV/m.

For a dielectric medium, $\varepsilon_r = 1 + \chi_e = 1 + 4.25 = 5.25$
Therefore,

$$\vec{D} = \varepsilon_0 \varepsilon_r \vec{E}$$

That is,

$$\left|\vec{D}\right| = 8.854 \times 10^{-12} \times 5.25 \times 0.15 \times 10^{-3} = 6.97 \times 10^{-15} \text{ C/m}^2$$

and

$$\vec{P} = \chi_e \varepsilon_0 \vec{E}$$

That is,

$$\left|\vec{P}\right| = 4.25 \times 8.854 \times 10^{-12} \times 0.15 \times 10^{-3} = 5.64 \times 10^{-15} \text{ C/m}^2$$

EXAMPLE 3.8

The polarization field of $\vec{P} = -0.2\vec{a}_x + 0.7\vec{a}_y + 0.3\vec{a}_z \mu$ C/m^2 exists in a region with $\varepsilon_r = 2.7$. Find (*i*) $\vec{E}$, (*ii*) $\vec{D}$, and (*iii*) the magnitude of electric field intensity.

SOLUTION

We know that, $\vec{P} = \chi_e \varepsilon_0 \vec{E}$.

   (*i*) The electric field intensity is

$$\vec{E} = \frac{\vec{P}}{\varepsilon_0(\varepsilon_r - 1)} = \frac{(-0.2\vec{a}_x + 0.7\vec{a}_y + 0.3\vec{a}_z) \times 10^{-6}}{8.854 \times 10^{-12} \times 1.7}$$

$$= -13.29\vec{a}_x + 46.5\vec{a}_y + 19.93\vec{a}_z \text{ kV/m}$$

  (*ii*) The electric flux density is

$$\vec{D} = \frac{\varepsilon_r}{(\varepsilon_r - 1)}\vec{P} = \frac{2.7}{1.7} \times (-0.2\vec{a}_x + 0.7\vec{a}_y + 0.3\vec{a}_z) \times 10^{-6}$$

$$= -0.318\vec{a}_x + 1.111\vec{a}_y + 0.476\vec{a}_z \ \mu \text{ C/m}^2$$

(*iii*) The magnitude of electric field intensity is

$$\left|\vec{E}\right| = \sqrt{(-13.29)^2 + (46.5)^2 + (19.93)^2} = 52.31 \text{ kV/m}$$

EXAMPLE 3.9

A spherical dielectric shell has its center at origin and its internal and external radii are 49 and 50 cm, respectively. The shell has a polarization of $3\vec{a}_r$ nC/m^2. Considering the bound surface density on the outer surface, find the potential of the dielectric shell if $\varepsilon_r = 4$.

SOLUTION

Given a spherical dielectric shell with center at the origin, inner radius $a = 49$ cm $= 0.49$ m and outer radius $b = 50$ cm $= 0.5$ m. The shell has a polarization $\vec{P} = 3\vec{a}_r$ nC/m^2.

   We know that,

$$\vec{P} = \chi_e \varepsilon_0 \vec{E}$$

where the electric susceptibility, $\chi_e = \varepsilon_r - 1 = 4 - 1 = 3$

   Therefore,

$$\vec{P} = 3\varepsilon_0 \vec{E}$$

$$\vec{E} = \frac{10^{-9}\,\vec{a}_r}{\varepsilon_0} \text{ F/m} = 113\vec{a}_r \text{ F/m}$$

Also, the potential of the dielectric shell is

$$V = -\int_a^b \vec{E} \cdot d\vec{l} = -\int_{0.49}^{0.5} \left(\frac{10^{-9}}{\varepsilon_0}\vec{a}_r\right) \cdot (dr\vec{a}_r)$$

$$= \frac{-10^{-9}}{\varepsilon_0}\int_{0.49}^{0.5} dr = \frac{-10^{-9}}{\varepsilon_0}[r]_{0.49}^{0.5}$$

$$= \frac{-10^{-9}}{8.854 \times 10^{-12}}[0.5 - 0.49] = -1.13 \text{ V}$$

3.6 CONTINUITY EQUATION AND RELAXATION TIME

Consider a conducting region with volume charge density ρ_v bounded by a closed surface s as shown in Figure 3.4. The total current crossing the closed surface in the outward direction can be described in terms of volume current density $\vec{J}$ as given by

$$I = \oint_s \vec{J} \cdot d\vec{s} \qquad (3.15)$$

As the current is simply a flow of charges per second, an outward flow of charges decreases the charge concentration by the same amount within the region bounded by s. Due to principle of conservation of charge, the time rate of decrease of charge in the bounded region must be equal to the net current flowing in the outward direction through the closed surface. Therefore, the total current flowing in the outward direction can also be expressed as

$$I = -\frac{dQ}{dt} \qquad (3.16)$$

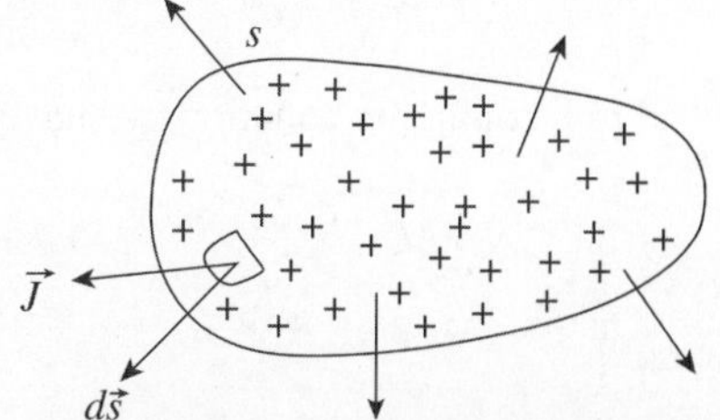

Figure 3.4 *Conducting region bounded by a closed surface with outward current flow*

where Q is the total charge enclosed by the surface and it can be written in terms of volume charge density ρ_v as

$$Q = \int_v \rho_v \, dv \qquad (3.17)$$

Combining Eqs. (3.15), (3.16), and (3.17), we get

$$\oint_s \vec{J} \cdot d\vec{s} = -\frac{d}{dt} \int_v \rho_v \, dv \qquad (3.18)$$

which is called the *integral form of continuity equation*. It is a mathematical expression for principle of conservation of charge which states that, charge can neither be created nor be destroyed but can only be transferred. To obtain the continuity equation in differential form, the closed surface integral on the left-hand side of the above equation can be transformed into a volume integral by applying the divergence theorem.

That is,

$$\int_v (\nabla \cdot \vec{J}) \, dv = -\frac{d}{dt} \int_v \rho_v \, dv = -\int_v \frac{\partial \rho_v}{\partial t} \, dv \qquad (3.19)$$

Comparing the integrands on both the sides of the above equation, we have

$$\nabla \cdot \vec{J} = -\frac{\partial \rho_v}{\partial t} \qquad (3.20)$$

which is called the *differential (point) form of continuity equation*. It states that the time-varying volume charge density ρ_v is the source of volume current density $\vec{J}$.

The charge density through the closed surface within a conductor decreases exponentially with time. The relaxation time T_r is defined as the time taken by the charge density to decay to 36.8% of its initial value at a given point. It is expressed as

$$T_r = \frac{\varepsilon}{\sigma}$$

where ε is the permittivity of the medium and σ is the conductivity of the medium. The relaxation time depends only on the properties of the medium.

Consider a linear and homogeneous medium with constants σ and ε through which current is flowing with current density $\vec{J}$. From Ohm's law, we have

$$\vec{J} = \sigma \vec{E} = \sigma \frac{\vec{D}}{\varepsilon}$$

From continuity equation, we have

$$\nabla \cdot \vec{J} = -\frac{\partial \rho_v}{\partial t}$$

That is,

$$\nabla \cdot \left(\frac{\sigma}{\varepsilon} \right) \vec{D} = -\frac{\partial \rho_v}{\partial t}$$

$$\frac{\sigma}{\varepsilon} \left(\nabla \cdot \vec{D} \right) = -\frac{\partial \rho_v}{\partial t}$$

$$\frac{\sigma}{\varepsilon} \rho_v = \frac{-\partial \rho_v}{\partial t} \qquad \text{(since } \nabla \cdot \vec{D} = \rho_v)$$

Therefore,

$$\frac{\partial \rho_v}{\partial t} + \frac{\sigma}{\varepsilon} \rho_v = 0$$

This is the first-order linear differential equation. By using separation of variables method, we get

$$\frac{\partial \rho_v}{\rho_v} = -\frac{\sigma}{\varepsilon} \partial t$$

Taking integration on both sides, we get

$$\ln \rho_v = -\frac{\sigma t}{\varepsilon} + \ln \rho_{v0}$$

where $\ln \rho_{v0}$ is the constant of integration.

Hence,

$$\rho_v = \rho_{v0} e^{-\sigma t / \varepsilon} = \rho_{v0} e^{-t/T_r}$$

where the time constant $T_r = \dfrac{\varepsilon}{\sigma}$ is the relaxation time in seconds and ρ_{v0} is the initial charge density, i.e., ρ_v at $t = 0$.

At $t = T_r$, $\rho_v = \dfrac{\rho_{v0}}{e} = 0.368 \rho_{v0}$

Therefore, the relaxation time $T_r = \dfrac{\varepsilon}{\sigma}$ is the time taken for the charge density to decay to 36.8% or $(1/e)$ times its initial value as shown in Figure 3.5.

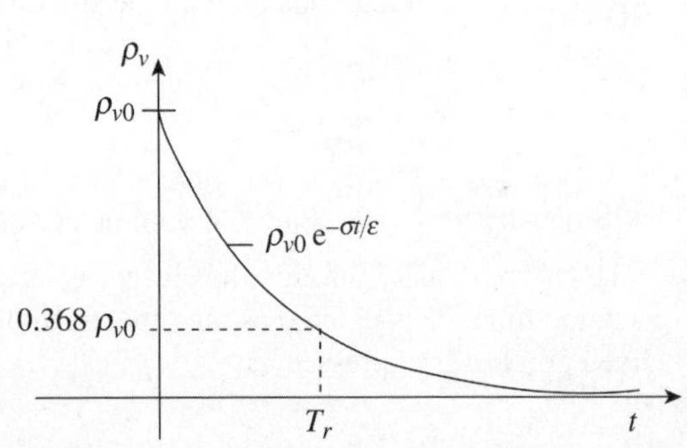

Figure 3.5 *Charge density and relaxation time*

EXAMPLE 3.10

In cylindrical coordinates, the current density is given by $\vec{J} = 10e^{-100\rho}\vec{a}_\phi$ A/m^2. Find the current crossing through the region $0.01 \leq \rho \leq 0.02$ m, $0 < z \leq 1$ m and intersection of this region with $\phi = $ constant plane.

SOLUTION

The current crossing through the given region can be obtained by the integral form of the continuity equation. Therefore,

$$I = \oint_s \vec{J} \cdot d\vec{s}$$

Since the given current density $\vec{J}$ is in $\vec{a}_\phi$ direction, the surface normal pointing to $\vec{a}_\phi$ direction, in cylindrical coordinates is $d\vec{s} = d\rho\, dz\, \vec{a}_\phi$.

Therefore, the current is

$$I = \oint_s \vec{J} \cdot d\vec{s} = \int\limits_{z=0}^{1} \int\limits_{\rho=0.01}^{0.02} \left(10e^{-100\rho}\vec{a}_\phi\right) \cdot \left(d\rho\, dz\vec{a}_\phi\right)$$

$$= \int\limits_{z=0}^{1} \int\limits_{\rho=0.01}^{0.02} 10e^{-100\rho} d\rho\, dz, \qquad \text{(since } \vec{a}_\phi \cdot \vec{a}_\phi = 1\text{)}$$

$$= 10\left[\frac{e^{-100\rho}}{-100}\right]_{0.01}^{0.02} \times [z]_0^1 = 10\left[\frac{e^{-2}}{-100} - \frac{e^{-1}}{-100}\right]$$

$$= 10\left(-1.353 \times 10^{-3} + 3.678 \times 10^{-3}\right) = 23.25 \times 10^{-3}$$

$$= 23.25 \text{ mA}$$

Hence, the current crossing the given region is 23.25 mA.

EXAMPLE 3.11

Find the total current in outward direction from a cube of 1 m, with one corner at the origin and edges parallel to the coordinate axes if $\vec{J} = 2x^2\,\vec{a}_x + 2xy^3\,\vec{a}_y + 2xy\vec{a}_z$ A/m^2.

SOLUTION

From continuity equation and divergence theorem, we know that

$$I = \oint_s \vec{J} \cdot d\vec{s} = \int_v (\nabla \cdot \vec{J}) dv$$

Since the cube is a volume, we use volume integral. The differential volume is $dv = dx\, dy\, dz$.
Therefore,

$$\nabla \cdot \vec{J} = \frac{\partial J_x}{\partial x} + \frac{\partial J_y}{\partial y} + \frac{\partial J_z}{\partial z} = \frac{\partial\left[2x^2\right]}{\partial x} + \frac{\partial\left[2xy^3\right]}{\partial y} + \frac{\partial[2xy]}{\partial z}$$

$$= 4x + 6xy^2$$

Hence, the current is

$$I = \int_v (\nabla \cdot \vec{J})\,dv = \int_v \left(4x + 6xy^2\right)dx\,dy\,dz$$

$$= \int_{z=0}^{1} \int_{y=0}^{1} \int_{x=0}^{1} (4x + 6xy^2)\,dx\,dy\,dz = \int_{z=0}^{1} \int_{y=0}^{1} \left[\frac{4x^2}{2} + \frac{6x^2y^2}{2}\right]_0^1 dy\,dz$$

$$= \int_{z=0}^{1} \int_{y=0}^{1} \left(2 + 3y^2\right)dy\,dz = \int_{z=0}^{1} \left[2y + \frac{3y^3}{3}\right]_0^1 dz$$

$$= \int_{z=0}^{1} 3\,dz = 3[z]_0^1 = 3\text{A}$$

Therefore, the total outward current from a cube of 1 m is 3A.

EXAMPLE 3.12

Find the current in the circular wire of radius 2 mm if the current density is given by $\vec{J} = 15\left(1 - e^{-1000\rho}\right)\vec{a}_z$ A/m^2.

SOLUTION

Figure E3.12 shows the current density $\vec{J}$ of the circular wire in $\vec{a}_z$ direction. Here, the surface normal points to $\vec{a}_z$ direction in cylindrical coordinates is $d\vec{s} = \rho\,d\rho\,d\phi\,\vec{a}_z$.

We know that, $I = \oint_s \vec{J} \cdot d\vec{s}$. Therefore, the current in the circular wire is

$$I = \int_{\phi=0}^{2\pi} \int_{\rho=0}^{0.002} \left[15\left(1 - e^{-1000\rho}\right)\vec{a}_z\right] \cdot \left(\rho\,d\rho\,d\phi\,\vec{a}_z\right)$$

$$= 15 \int_0^{2\pi} d\phi \int_0^{0.002} \left(1 - e^{-1000\rho}\right)\rho\,d\rho$$

$$= 15 \times 2\pi \left[\left(\frac{\rho^2}{2}\right) - \frac{e^{-1000\rho}}{(-1000)^2}(-1000\rho - 1)\right]_0^{0.002}$$

$$= 30\pi \times \left[2 \times 10^{-6} - 0.594 \times 10^{-6}\right] = 132.44\,\mu\text{A}$$

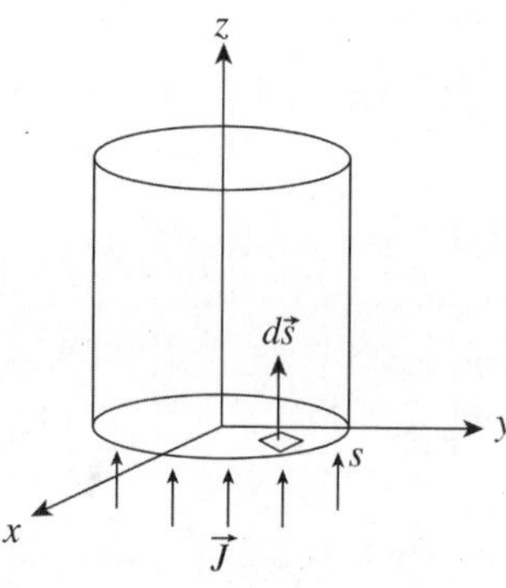

Figure E3.12

EXAMPLE 3.13

Find the total current in a circular conductor of radius 4 mm if the current density varies according to $J = \left(\dfrac{10^4}{\rho}\right)$ A/m^2.

SOLUTION

We know that, $I = \oint_s \vec{J} \cdot d\vec{s}$. Assuming given $\vec{J}$ in $\vec{a}_z$ direction, $d\vec{s}_z = \rho\,d\rho\,d\phi\,\vec{a}_z$.

Therefore, the total current in a circular conductor is

$$I = \oint_s \vec{J} \cdot d\vec{s} = \int_{\phi=0}^{2\pi} \int_{\rho=0}^{0.004} \left[\frac{10^4}{\rho} \vec{a}_z \right] \cdot \left(\rho\, d\rho\, d\phi\, \vec{a}_z \right)$$

$$= \int_0^{2\pi} \int_0^{4\times10^{-3}} 10^4 \, d\rho\, d\phi = 10^4 \left[\rho \right]_0^{4\times10^{-3}} \left[\phi \right]_0^{2\pi}$$

$$= 10^4 \times 4 \times 10^{-3} \times 2\pi = 80\pi \text{ A}$$

3.7 ELECTRIC BOUNDARY CONDITIONS

The conditions that govern the behavior of electric fields at the boundary (interface) between the two mediums are called boundary conditions. These boundary conditions can be obtained on either side of the interface and they are helpful in determining the field on one side of the interface, if the field on the other side is known. Boundary conditions specify how the tangential and normal components of the electric field in one medium are related to the components of the field across the boundary in another medium.

The boundary conditions are derived in this section for dielectric–dielectric interface, dielectric–conductor interface, free space–conductor interface, and conductor–conductor interface based on the material used in the medium. The boundary conditions derived for electrostatic fields are equally valid for time-varying electric fields.

3.7.1 Dielectric–Dielectric Boundary Conditions

Consider an interface between dielectric medium 1 with permittivity ε_1 and another dielectric medium 2 with permittivity ε_2 as shown in Figure 3.6. Here, the electric field intensities $\vec{E}_1$ and $\vec{E}_2$ in terms of tangential and normal directions for media 1 and 2 can be written as

$$\vec{E}_1 = \vec{E}_{t1} + \vec{E}_{n1}$$
$$\vec{E}_2 = \vec{E}_{t2} + \vec{E}_{n2}$$

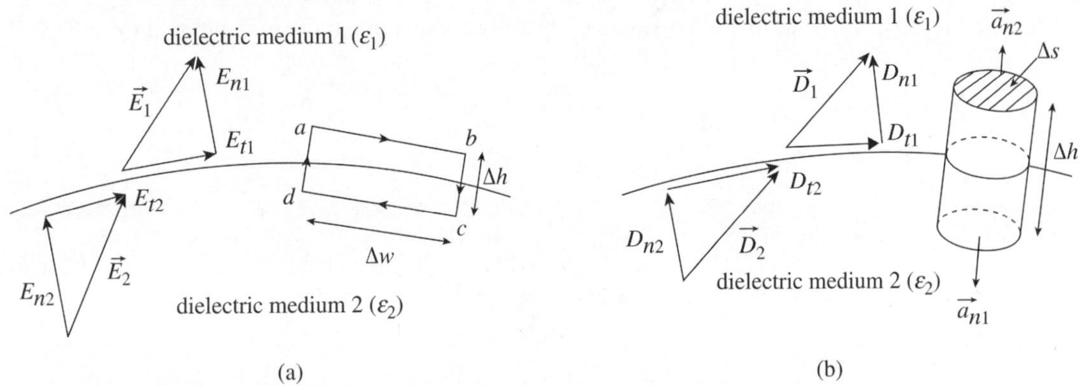

Figure 3.6 *Boundary between two dielectrics: (a) tangential component of $\vec{E}$ and (b) normal component of $\vec{D}$*

Assume a closed rectangular loop *abcda* as shown in Figure 3.6(a), to derive the boundary conditions for the tangential components of $\vec{E}$. Due to conservative property of the electric field, the line integral of the field around a closed path is always zero. By making $\Delta h \to 0$, the contributions to the line integral by segments *bc* and *da* vanish. Hence, the line integral of the electric field around a closed path is denoted by

$$\oint_l \vec{E} \cdot d\vec{l} = \int_a^b \vec{E}_1 \cdot d\vec{l} + \int_c^d \vec{E}_2 \cdot d\vec{l} = 0 \tag{3.21}$$

where $\vec{E}_1$ and $\vec{E}_2$ are the electric field intensities in medium 1 and 2, respectively.

From Figure 3.6(a), it is seen that, over the segment *ab*, $\vec{E}_{t1}$ and Δw have the same direction but over segment *cd*, $\vec{E}_{t2}$ and Δw are in opposite direction. Hence, the above equation can be written in magnitude form as

$$E_{t1}\Delta w - E_{t2}\Delta w = 0$$

Therefore,

$$E_{t1} = E_{t2} \tag{3.22}$$

The above equation shows that the tangential components of the electric field intensity are the same on the two sides of the boundary and is said to be continuous across the boundary between any two dielectric mediums. In other words, the tangential component of the electric field intensity E_t does not undergo any change on the boundary. Here, the conservative property of electric field intensity $\vec{E}$ led to the result that the tangential component of $\vec{E}$ is continuous across the boundary. Since $D_{t1} = \varepsilon_1 E_{t1}$ and $D_{t2} = \varepsilon_2 E_{t2}$, the boundary condition of the tangential components of the electric flux density is represented by

$$\frac{D_{t1}}{\varepsilon_1} = \frac{D_{t2}}{\varepsilon_2} \tag{3.23}$$

Here, the tangential component of the electric flux density D_t undergoes change on the boundary due to its permittivity. Hence, D_t is said to be discontinuous across the boundary.

Consider a small cylinder or pill box (Gaussian surface) as shown in Figure 3.6(b) to derive the boundary conditions for the normal components of $\vec{E}$ and $\vec{D}$. The normal components of the field can be obtained by using the Gauss's law. According to Gauss's law, the total outward flux of $\vec{D}$ through the top, bottom, and side surfaces of the pill box shown in Figure 3.6(b) must be equal to the total charge enclosed in the cylinder. By allowing the height of cylinder $\Delta h \to 0$, the contribution to the total flux through the side surface goes to zero.

If the mediums have free charge densities, then the only charge remaining in the closed cylinder is that distributed on the boundary as given by $Q = \rho_s \Delta s$. Applying Gauss's law to the pill box, we get

$$\oint_s \vec{D} \cdot d\vec{s} = Q$$

$$\int_{top} \vec{D}_1 \cdot \vec{a}_{n2} ds + \int_{bottom} \vec{D}_2 \cdot \vec{a}_{n1} ds = \rho_s \Delta s \tag{3.24}$$

where $\vec{a}_{n1}$ and $\vec{a}_{n2}$ are the outward normal unit vectors of the bottom and top surfaces, respectively. It is noted that the normal unit vector at the surface of any medium is always defined to be in the outward direction away from that medium. Since $\vec{a}_{n1} = -\vec{a}_{n2}$, the above equation is simplified to

$$\vec{a}_{n2} \cdot (\vec{D}_1 - \vec{D}_2) = \rho_s$$

Thus, the normal component of $\vec{D}$ in magnitude form is

$$D_{n1} - D_{n2} = \rho_s \tag{3.25}$$

where ρ_s is the surface charge density at the boundary. Thus, the normal component of $\vec{D}$ undergoes a change at the boundary between the two dielectric mediums and the amount of change is equal to the surface charge density ρ_s at the boundary. Here, the divergence property of $\vec{D}$ led to the result that the normal component of $\vec{D}$ changes by ρ_s across the boundary. The corresponding boundary condition for normal component of $\vec{E}$ is

$$\varepsilon_1 E_{n1} - \varepsilon_2 E_{n2} = \rho_s \tag{3.26}$$

If there are no free charges available at the interface, i.e., $\rho_s = 0$, then the normal component of $\vec{D}$ reduces to

$$D_{n1} = D_{n2}$$

Thus, the normal component of $\vec{D}$ is continuous across the boundary and it undergoes no change at the boundary. The corresponding boundary condition for $\vec{E}$ is

$$\varepsilon_1 E_{n1} = \varepsilon_2 E_{n2} \tag{3.27}$$

Here, the normal component of $\vec{E}$ is discontinuous at the boundary. Therefore, if the electric field intensity on one side of the boundary is known, then the boundary condition can be used to determine the electric field intensity on the other side of the boundary.

The boundary conditions derived above can also be used to determine the refraction of the electric field across the interface. Let θ_1 and θ_2 be the angles between the normal to the interface and the fields in either of the mediums as shown in Figure 3.7. The boundary equation for tangential component of $\vec{E}$ is represented by

$$E_{t1} = E_{t2}$$
$$E_1 \sin\theta_1 = E_2 \sin\theta_2$$

The boundary equation for normal component of $\vec{D}$ for a charge free boundary ($\rho_s = 0$) is given by

$$D_{n1} = D_{n2}$$
$$\varepsilon_1 E_1 \cos\theta_1 = \varepsilon_2 E_2 \cos\theta_2$$

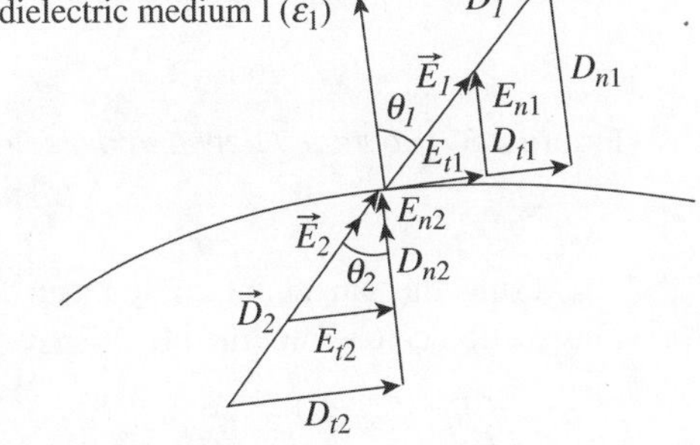

Figure 3.7 *Refraction of electric field at dielectric–dielectric boundary*

Dividing the tangential component by the normal component of $\vec{E}$, we get

$$\frac{E_1 \sin\theta_1}{\varepsilon_1 E_1 \cos\theta_1} = \frac{E_2 \sin\theta_2}{\varepsilon_2 E_2 \cos\theta_2}$$

Therefore,

$$\frac{\tan\theta_1}{\varepsilon_1} = \frac{\tan\theta_2}{\varepsilon_2} \tag{3.28}$$

Since $\varepsilon_1 = \varepsilon_{r1}\varepsilon_0$ and $\varepsilon_2 = \varepsilon_{r2}\varepsilon_0$, the above equation can be written as

$$\frac{\tan\theta_1}{\tan\theta_2} = \frac{\varepsilon_{r1}}{\varepsilon_{r2}} \tag{3.29}$$

This equation is called the *law of refraction* of the electric field at the charge-free boundary.

3.7.2 Dielectric–Conductor Boundary Conditions

Consider an interface in which medium1 is a dielectric material with permittivity $\varepsilon = \varepsilon_0 \varepsilon_r$ and medium 2 is a perfect conductor with $\sigma = \infty$ as shown in Figure 3.8. The procedure for determining the boundary conditions at the interface between the dielectric and conductor is similar to the one derived for dielectric–dielectric interface. The only difference is that, in a perfect conductor, $\vec{E} = \vec{D} = 0$ everywhere inside the conductor. Hence, $E_2 = D_2 = 0$ for a conductor medium 2. This means that the tangential and normal components of E_2 and D_2 are zero.

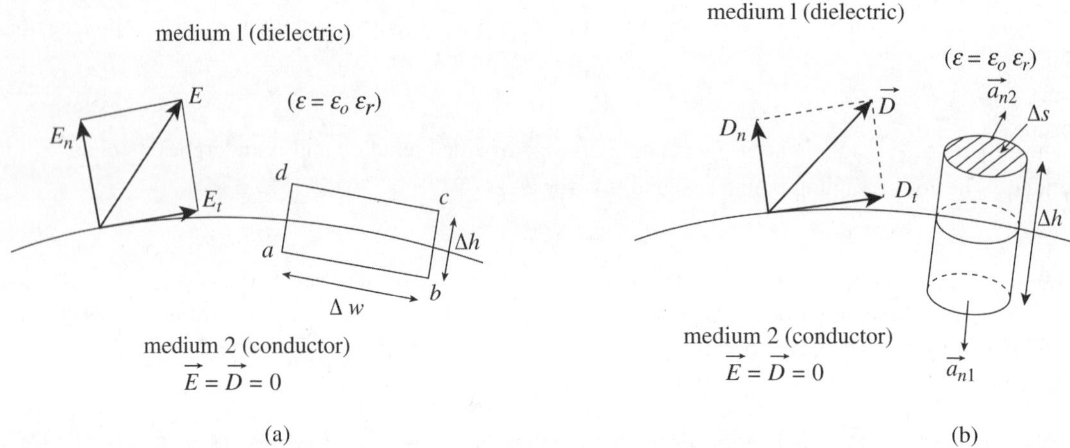

Figure 3.8 *Boundary between dielectric–conductor interface: (a) tangential component of $\vec{E}$ and (b) normal component of $\vec{D}$*

As a result, the tangential component of $\vec{E}$ and $\vec{D}$ derived for dielectric–dielectric interface in the previous section can be modified to

$$E_{t1} = E_{t2} = 0$$

and
$$D_{t1} = D_{t2} = 0$$

The normal components of $\vec{E}$ and $\vec{D}$ derived for dielectric–dielectric interface in the previous section can also be modified as

$$D_{n1} = \rho_s$$
$$\varepsilon_1 E_{n1} = \rho_s$$

Therefore, the normal component of $\vec{E}$ in the dielectric medium 1 with permittivity ε_1 is represented by

$$E_{n1} = \frac{\rho_s}{\varepsilon_1}$$

At the conductor surface, the boundary conditions of the dielectric–conductor interface can be combined into

$$D_1 = \varepsilon_1 E_1 = \vec{a}_n \rho_s \tag{3.30}$$

where $\vec{a}_n$ is a unit vector directed normally outward from the conductor surface. This means that the electric field lines point directly away from the conductor surface when ρ_s is positive and directly toward the conductor surface when ρ_s is negative. Table 3.3 summarizes the electric field boundary conditions for different types of medium.

Table 3.3 *Electric field—Boundary Conditions*

Field Component	Any two media	Medium 1 Dielectric ε_1	Medium 2 Dielectric ε_2	Medium 1 Dielectric ε_1	Medium 2 Conductor
Tangential $\vec{E}$	$E_{t1} = E_{t2}$	$E_{t1} = E_{t2}$		$E_{t1} = E_{t2} = 0$	
Tangential $\vec{D}$	$\dfrac{D_{t1}}{\varepsilon_1} = \dfrac{D_{t2}}{\varepsilon_2}$	$\dfrac{D_{t1}}{\varepsilon_1} = \dfrac{D_{t2}}{\varepsilon_2}$		$D_{t1} = D_{t2} = 0$	
Normal $\vec{E}$	$\vec{a}_n \cdot (\varepsilon_1 \vec{E}_1 - \varepsilon_2 \vec{E}_2) = \rho_s$	$\varepsilon_1 E_{n1} - \varepsilon_2 E_{n2} = \rho_s$		$E_{n1} = \dfrac{\rho_s}{\varepsilon_1}$	$E_{n2} = 0$
Normal $\vec{D}$	$\vec{a}_n \cdot (\vec{D}_1 - \vec{D}_2) = \rho_s$	$D_{n1} - D_{n2} = \rho_s$		$D_{n1} = \rho_s$	$D_{n2} = 0$

3.7.3 Free Space–Conductor Boundary Conditions

The free space is regarded as a special dielectric for which $\varepsilon_r = 1$. The boundary condition between free space and a conductor is a special case of dielectric–conductor boundary condition discussed in Sec. 3.7.2. Figure 3.9 shows medium 1 as a free space and medium 2 as a conductor.

The boundary conditions at the interface between free space and a conductor can be obtained by replacing $\varepsilon_r = 1$ in the boundary conditions of dielectric–conductor obtained in previous section. Therefore, the boundary conditions for free space–conductor interface can be written as

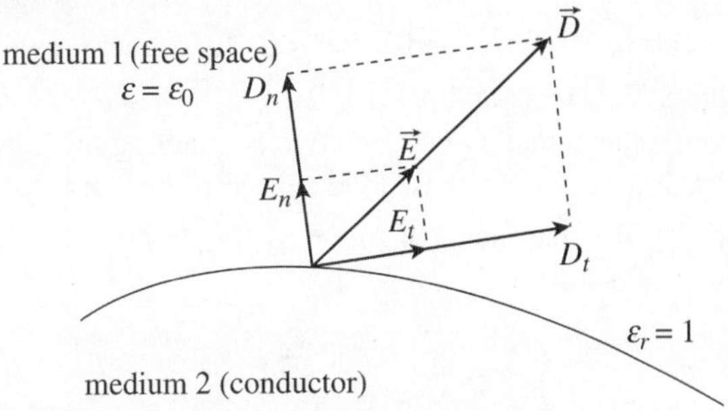

$$D_t = \varepsilon_0 E_t = 0 \quad \text{and} \quad D_n = \varepsilon_0 E_n = \rho_s \quad (3.31)$$

where ε_0 is the permittivity of free space. It is seen that the electric field is external to the conductor and normal to its surface.

Figure 3.9 *Boundary between free space–conductor*

3.7.4 Conductor–Conductor Boundary Conditions

Consider an interface in which both medium 1 and medium 2 are conductors with conductivities σ_1 and σ_2 as shown in Figure 3.10. Since both the mediums are conducting surfaces, the electric fields give rise to current densities $\vec{J}_1$ and $\vec{J}_2$. As $\vec{J} = \sigma \vec{E}$, $\vec{J}_1$ is proportional to $\vec{E}_1$ and $\vec{J}_2$ is proportional to $\vec{E}_2$.

For any two media, the tangential components of the electric field intensity are same across the boundary as represented by

$$E_{t1} = E_{t2}$$

From $\vec{J} = \sigma \vec{E}$, the tangential components of the current density are written as

$$\frac{J_{t1}}{\sigma_1} = \frac{J_{t2}}{\sigma_2} \quad (3.32)$$

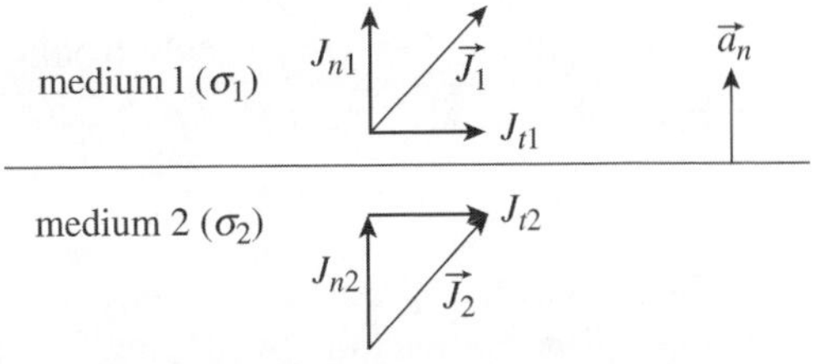

Figure 3.10 *Boundary between two conductors*

Here, the ratio of tangential components of the current densities at the interface is equal to the ratio of the conductivities. The tangential components J_{t1} and J_{t2} represent the current flowing in the two mediums in a direction parallel to the boundary and hence, no transfer of charge is involved between them.

If the normal components of current densities are not equal, i.e., $J_{n1} \neq J_{n2}$, there will be a difference in the amount of charge entering the boundary and leaving it. Therefore, the surface charge density ρ_s changes and it cannot remain constant with time. But it violates the condition of electrostatics, which requires all fields and charges to be constant. Therefore, the normal component of $\vec{J}$ has to be continuous $(J_{n1} = J_{n2})$ across the boundary between two conducting mediums to satisfy electrostatic conditions.

3.7.5   Analogy between Flux Density $\vec{D}$ and Current Density $\vec{J}$

Under static or time invariant conditions, it is seen that there exists an analogy between electric flux density $\vec{D}$ and current density $\vec{J}$. Therefore, both these fields can be described by equations of the same mathematical form. For example, in case of a steady current, $\nabla \cdot \vec{J} = 0$ and in case of a charge-free region, $\nabla \cdot \vec{D} = 0$. Since $\vec{J} = \sigma \vec{E}$, $\vec{D} = \varepsilon \vec{E}$, and $\nabla \times \vec{E} = 0$, for a linear medium with constant permittivity ε and conductivity σ, we have $\nabla \times \vec{D} = 0$ and $\nabla \times \vec{J} = 0$.

At the boundary between two conducting mediums, the normal components of $\vec{J}$ are continuous as given by $J_{n1} = J_{n2}$, whereas at the charge-free boundary between two dielectric mediums, the normal components of $\vec{D}$ are continuous as given by $D_{n1} = D_{n2}$. From the boundary conditions on the tangential components, we have

$$\frac{D_{t1}}{D_{t2}} = \frac{\varepsilon_1}{\varepsilon_2}$$

and

$$\frac{J_{t1}}{J_{t2}} = \frac{\sigma_1}{\sigma_2}$$

From the above expressions, it is seen that an equation in terms of $\vec{J}$ can be obtained from an equation in terms of $\vec{D}$ by relating $\vec{D}$ with $\vec{J}$, and ε with σ.

EXAMPLE 3.14

The xy-plane is a boundary separating two dielectric mediums with permittivities ε_1 and ε_2 as shown in Figure E3.14. If the electric field in medium 2 is $\vec{E}_2 = 2\vec{a}_x - 3\vec{a}_y + 3\vec{a}_z$ V/m, $\varepsilon_1 = 2\varepsilon_0$, and $\varepsilon_2 = 8\varepsilon_0$, determine $\vec{E}_1$ (i) in a charge-free boundary and (ii) in a boundary with surface charge density $\rho_s = 3.54 \times 10^{-11}$ C/m^2.

SOLUTION

From Figure E3.14, it is seen that the normal to the boundary is $\vec{a}_z$. At the boundary between the two dielectric mediums, the x- and y-components of the electric field are tangential to the boundary and the z-components are normal to the boundary.

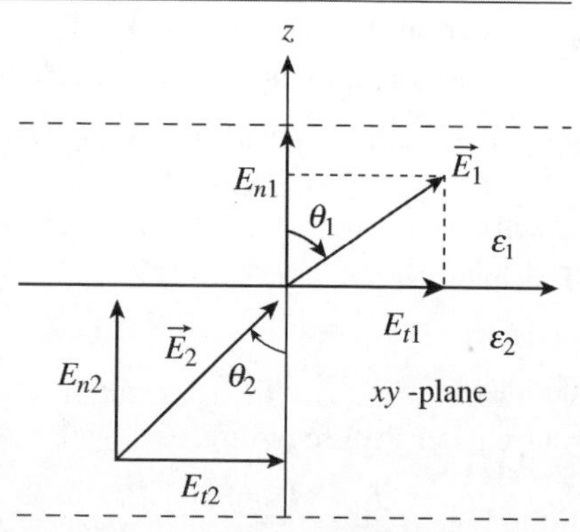

Figure E3.14

(*i*) At a charge-free interface $(\rho_s = 0)$, the tangential components of $\vec{E}$ and the normal components of $\vec{D}$ are continuous, i.e., $\vec{D}_{n1} = \vec{D}_{n2}$ and $\vec{E}_{t1} = \vec{E}_{t2}$. Therefore, the x- and y- components of the electric field in the two dielectric mediums are equal and they are given by

$$E_{1x} = E_{2x} = 2 \quad \text{and} \quad E_{1y} = E_{2y} = -3$$

The z-components of the flux density in the two dielectric mediums are equal. Therefore,

$$D_{1z} = D_{2z}$$
$$\varepsilon_1 E_{1z} = \varepsilon_2 E_{2z}$$

Here, the z-component of $\vec{E}_1$ is

$$E_{1z} = \frac{\varepsilon_2}{\varepsilon_1} E_{2z} = \frac{8\varepsilon_0}{2\varepsilon_0}(3\vec{a}_z) = 12\vec{a}_z$$

Hence, the electric field intensity in dielectric medium 1 for a charge-free boundary is

$$\vec{E}_1 = 2\vec{a}_x - 3\vec{a}_y + 12\vec{a}_z \, \text{V/m}$$

(*ii*) For a boundary with surface charges, the normal component of $\vec{D}$ undergoes a change at the boundary between the two dielectric mediums and the amount of change is equal to the surface charge density ρ_s on the boundary, i.e., $D_{n1} - D_{n2} = \rho_s$.

Since the normal component of $\vec{D}$ is along $\vec{a}_z$,

$$D_{1z} - D_{2z} = \rho_s$$
$$\varepsilon_1 E_{1z} - \varepsilon_2 E_{2z} = \rho_s$$

Therefore,

$$E_{1z} = \frac{\rho_s + \varepsilon_2 E_{2z}}{\varepsilon_1} = \frac{3.54 \times 10^{-11} + (8\varepsilon_0 \times 3)}{2\varepsilon_0}$$

$$= \frac{3.54 \times 10^{-11}}{2 \times 8.54 \times 10^{-12}} + 12 = 14$$

Hence, the electric field intensity in dielectric medium 1 for a charged boundary is

$$\vec{E}_1 = 2\vec{a}_x - 3\vec{a}_y + 14\vec{a}_z \, \text{V/m} \qquad \square$$

EXAMPLE 3.15

The interface between two dielectrics is defined by $x = 0$ plane. For dielectric 1, $x > 0$, $\varepsilon_{r1} = 3$ while for dielectric 2, $x < 0$, $\varepsilon_{r2} = 4$. If the electric flux density in region 1 is given by $\vec{D}_1 = 4\vec{a}_x + 6\vec{a}_y + 8\vec{a}_z \, \text{C/m}^2$, determine $\vec{D}_2$.

SOLUTION

From Figure E3.15, it is seen that at the dielectric—dielectric boundary, the normal direction to $x = 0$ plane is $\vec{a}_x$. Therefore, $\vec{a}_x$ is normal component of $\vec{D}_1$. Hence, the normal component of flux density in the dielectric medium 1 is given by $\vec{D}_{n1} = 4\vec{a}_x$ and the tangential component of flux density in the dielectric medium 1 is $\vec{D}_{t1} = 6\vec{a}_y + 8\vec{a}_z$.

The boundary equation for normal component of $\vec{D}$ for a charge-free boundary ($\rho_s = 0$) is $D_{n1} = D_{n2}$. Therefore, $\vec{D}_{n2} = 4\vec{a}_x$. At the dielectric–dielectric boundary,

$$\frac{D_{t1}}{D_{t2}} = \frac{\varepsilon_1}{\varepsilon_2} = \frac{\varepsilon_{r1}}{\varepsilon_{r2}}$$

$$\vec{D}_{t2} = \frac{\varepsilon_{r2}}{\varepsilon_{r1}}\vec{D}_{t1} = \frac{4}{3}\times\left[6\vec{a}_y + 8\vec{a}_z\right]$$

$$= 8\vec{a}_y + 10.67\vec{a}_z$$

Hence, the electric flux density in dielectric 2 is

$$\vec{D}_2 = \vec{D}_{n2} + \vec{D}_{t2}$$

$$= 4\vec{a}_x + 8\vec{a}_y + 10.67\vec{a}_z \ \text{C/m}^2$$

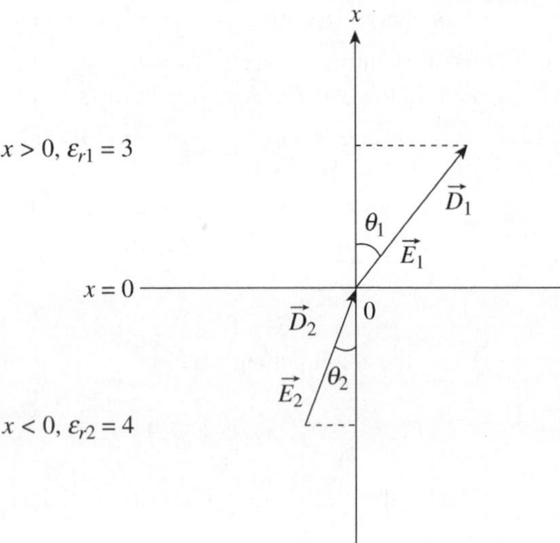

Figure E3.15

EXAMPLE 3.16

Consider that two dielectric media with permittivities ε_1 and ε_2 are separated by a charge-free boundary as shown in Figure E3.16. The electric flux density in medium 1 at the point P_1 has a magnitude D_1 and makes an angle θ_1 with normal. Determine the magnitude and direction of electric flux density and electric field intensity at point P_2 in medium 2.

SOLUTION

Let $\vec{D}_1$ (and $\vec{E}_1$) make an angle θ_1 with normal to the surface as shown in Figure E3.16. Since the normal components of $\vec{D}_1$ are continuous for a charge-free boundary,

$$D_{n1} = D_1 \cos\theta_1 = D_2 \cos\theta_2 = D_{n2}$$

The ratio of tangential components of $\vec{D}$ is

$$\frac{D_{t1}}{D_{t2}} = \frac{\varepsilon_2}{\varepsilon_1}$$

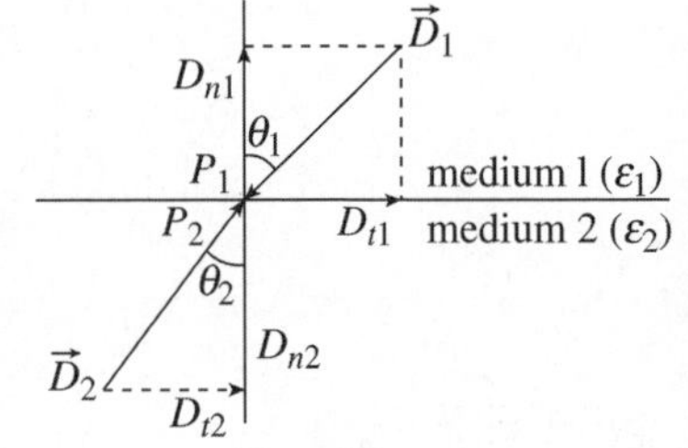

Figure E3. 16

Therefore,

$$\frac{D_{t1}}{D_{t2}} = \frac{D_1 \sin\theta_1}{D_2 \sin\theta_2} = \frac{\cos\theta_2 \sin\theta_1}{\cos\theta_1 \sin\theta_2} = \frac{\tan\theta_1}{\tan\theta_2} = \frac{\varepsilon_1}{\varepsilon_2}$$

Since $\vec{D} = \varepsilon\vec{E}$, the direction of field intensity $\vec{E}$ on each side of boundary is identical with the direction of flux density $\vec{D}$.

The magnitude of $\vec{D}$ in region 2 can be obtained from the above two equations. Therefore,

$$\frac{D_2}{D_1} = \frac{\cos\theta_1}{\cos\theta_2} \quad \text{and} \quad \frac{D_2}{D_1} = \frac{\varepsilon_2 \sin\theta_1}{\varepsilon_1 \sin\theta_2}$$

$$\cos\theta_2 = \frac{D_1}{D_2}\cos\theta_1 \quad \text{and} \quad \sin\theta_2 = \left(\frac{D_1}{D_2}\right)\left(\frac{\varepsilon_2}{\varepsilon_1}\right)\sin\theta_1$$

We know that, $\cos^2\theta_2 + \sin^2\theta_2 = 1 = \left(\frac{D_1}{D_2}\right)^2\left[\cos^2\theta_1 + \left(\frac{\varepsilon_2}{\varepsilon_1}\right)^2\sin^2\theta_1\right]$

Hence, $D_2 = D_1\sqrt{\cos^2\theta_1 + \left(\frac{\varepsilon_2}{\varepsilon_1}\right)^2\sin^2\theta_1}$

The magnitude of $\vec{E}_2$ is $E_2 = E_1\sqrt{\sin^2\theta_1 + \left(\frac{\varepsilon_1}{\varepsilon_2}\right)^2\cos^2\theta_1}$

It is evident from these equations that $\vec{D}$ is larger in the region of larger permittivity unless $\theta_1 = \theta_2 = 0°$ where the magnitude is unchanged. Also, $\vec{E}$ is larger in the region of smaller permittivity unless $\theta_1 = \theta_2 = 90°$ where its magnitude is unchanged. $\qquad\square$

EXAMPLE 3.17

An electric field in a medium whose relative permittivity is 7 enters another medium of relative permittivity 2. If $\vec{E}$ makes an angle of 60° with the boundary normal, what angle does the field makes with the normal in the second dielectric?

SOLUTION

Given, two dielectric materials with $\varepsilon_{r1} = 7$ and $\varepsilon_{r2} = 2$; $\theta_1 = 60°$.

We know that, at the boundary

$$\frac{\tan\theta_1}{\tan\theta_2} = \frac{\varepsilon_{r1}}{\varepsilon_{r2}}$$

$$\tan\theta_2 = \frac{\varepsilon_{r2}}{\varepsilon_{r1}} \times \tan\theta_1 = \frac{2}{7}\tan 60° = 0.4948$$

Therefore, $\theta_2 = \tan^{-1}(0.4948) = 26.33°$ $\qquad\square$

EXAMPLE 3.18

Given $z < 0$ is a region of a linear dielectric of relative permittivity 6.5 and $z > 0$ is free space. The electric field intensity in the free space region is $\left(-3\vec{a}_x + 4\vec{a}_y - 2\vec{a}_z\right)$ V/m. Find (i) $\vec{D}$ for $z > 0$ (ii) tangential components of $\vec{D}$ and $\vec{E}$ on the boundary of $z < 0$ region.

SOLUTION

Figure E3.18 shows dielectric region 1 for $z < 0$ and free space region 2 for $z > 0$.

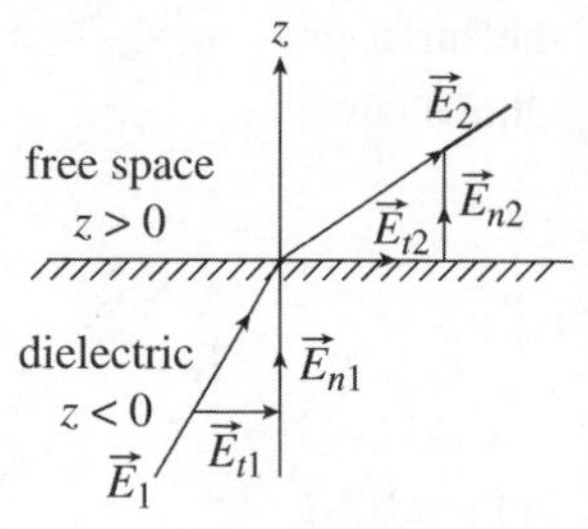

Figure E3.18

Given $\varepsilon_{r1} = 6.5$, $\varepsilon_{r2} = 1$ and $\vec{E}_2 = -3\vec{a}_x + 4\vec{a}_y - 2\vec{a}_z$.

(*i*) For $z > 0$,

$$\vec{D}_2 = \varepsilon_2 \vec{E}_2 = 8.854 \times 10^{-12} \times \left(-3\vec{a}_x + 4\vec{a}_y - 2\vec{a}_z \right)$$

$$= \left(-26.56\vec{a}_x + 35.41\vec{a}_y - 17.7\vec{a}_z \right) \times 10^{-12} \text{ C/m}^2$$

(*ii*) The tangential and normal components of $\vec{D}_1, \vec{E}_1, \vec{D}_2$ and $\vec{E}_2$ are shown in Figure E3.18.

Here,

$$\vec{E}_2 = \vec{E}_{t2} + \vec{E}_{n2}$$

Therefore,

$$\vec{E}_{n2} = -2\vec{a}_z$$

and

$$E_{t2} = \vec{E}_2 - \vec{E}_{n2} = -3\vec{a}_x + 4\vec{a}_y - 2\vec{a}_z + 2\vec{a}_z = -3\vec{a}_x + 4\vec{a}_y$$

At the boundary, the tangential components of electric field are continuous and they are given by

$$\vec{E}_{t1} = \vec{E}_{t2} = -3\vec{a}_x + 4\vec{a}_y$$

$$\left| \vec{E}_{t1} \right| = \left| \vec{E}_{t2} \right| = \sqrt{(-3)^2 + 4^2} = 5 \text{ V/m}$$

The tangential components of electric flux density are given by

$$\vec{D}_{t1} = \varepsilon \vec{E}_{t1} = \varepsilon_0 \varepsilon_r \left(-3\vec{a}_x + 4\vec{a}_y \right)$$

$$= 8.854 \times 10^{-12} \times 6.5 \times \left(-3\vec{a}_x + 4\vec{a}_y \right)$$

$$= \left(-0.173\vec{a}_x + 0.23\vec{a}_y \right) \times 10^{-9} \text{ C/m}^2$$

Therefore,

$$\left| \vec{D}_{t1} \right| = 0.287 \text{ nC/m}^2$$

and

$$\left| \vec{D}_{t2} \right| = \frac{\varepsilon_2}{\varepsilon_1} \left| \vec{D}_{t1} \right| = \frac{1}{6.5} (0.287 \times 10^{-9}) = 0.044 \text{ nC/m}^2 \qquad \square$$

3.8 RESISTANCE

The resistance of a conductor (R) is defined as the ratio of voltage across the conductor (V) to current through the surface of the conductor (I). The voltage across the conductor is equal to the negative line integral of $\vec{E}$ over a path l between two points and the current is equal to the surface integral of $\vec{J}$ through the surface s of the conductor. Therefore, the resistance of a conductor of length l can be obtained from Ohm's law in terms of the field quantities $\vec{E}$ and $\vec{J}$ as

$$R = \frac{V}{I} = \frac{-\int_l \vec{E} \cdot d\vec{l}}{\int_s \vec{J} \cdot d\vec{s}} \tag{3.33}$$

Consider a conductor of length l and uniform cross section A, as shown in Figure 3.11. The conductor axis is placed along the x-axis between two points x_1 and x_2. The length of the conductor along the x-axis is given by $x_2 - x_1$. When a voltage V is applied across the conductor terminals, it establishes an electric field along the x-axis as represented by $\vec{E} = E_x \vec{a}_x$.

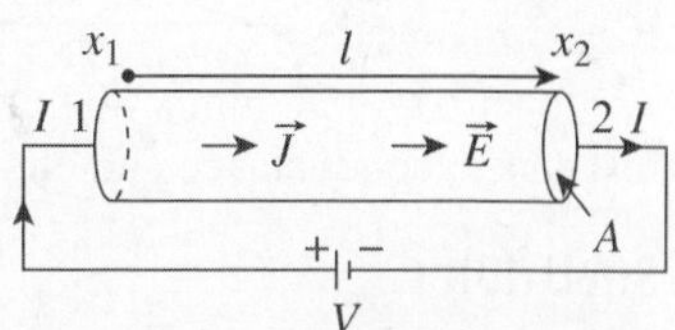

Figure 3.11 *Resistor of cross section A and length l*

Here, the direction of electric field intensity $\vec{E}$ is from the point with higher potential (point 1) to the point with lower potential (point 2). The potential difference between two points x_1 and x_2 obtained by integrating $\vec{E}$ along the path between them is represented by

$$V = V_1 - V_2 = -\int_{x_2}^{x_1} \vec{E} \cdot d\vec{l}$$

$$= -\int_{x_2}^{x_1} (E_x \vec{a}_x) \cdot (dl\vec{a}_x) = E_x l \tag{3.34}$$

The current flowing through the uniform cross section A is equal to the surface integral of $\vec{J}$ through the surface of the conductor. Therefore,

$$I = \int_A \vec{J} \cdot d\vec{s} = \int_A \sigma \vec{E} \cdot d\vec{s}$$

$$= \int_A \sigma (E_x \vec{a}_x) \cdot (ds\vec{a}_x) = \sigma E_x A \tag{3.35}$$

Substituting Eq. (3.34) and Eq. (3.35) in Eq. (3.33), we get

$$R = \frac{V}{I} = \frac{-\int_l \vec{E} \cdot d\vec{l}}{\int_s \vec{J} \cdot d\vec{s}} = \frac{E_x l}{\sigma E_x A}$$

$$= \frac{l}{\sigma A} \tag{3.36}$$

The unit of resistance is ohm (Ω). The reciprocal of resistance is conductance G as denoted by

$$G = \frac{1}{R} = \frac{\sigma A}{l} \tag{3.37}$$

The unit of conductance is ohm inverse (Ω^{-1}) or siemens (S).

Find the resistance of a copper wire of length 200 km and uniform cross-section area 40 mm^2. Given that the conductivity of copper is 5.8×10^7 S/m.

SOLUTION

The resistance of the copper wire is

$$R = \frac{l}{\sigma A} = \frac{200 \times 10^3}{5.8 \times 10^7 \times 40 \times 10^{-6}} = 86.2\,\Omega \qquad \square$$

EXAMPLE 3.20

A copper bar of 30 mm × 80 mm in cross section and 2 m in length has 50 mV applied between its ends. Find resistance, conductance and electric field.

SOLUTION

For copper, $\sigma = 5.8 \times 10^7$ S/m

The resistance is

$$R = \frac{l}{\sigma A} = \frac{2}{5.8 \times 10^7 \times 30 \times 80 \times 10^{-6}} = 14.368 \times 10^{-6}\,\Omega$$

The conductance is

$$G = \frac{1}{R} = \frac{10^6}{14.368} = 0.0696 \times 10^6\,\Omega^{-1}$$

The electric field intensity is

$$E = \frac{V}{d} = \frac{50 \times 10^{-3}}{2} = 25 \times 10^{-3}\,\text{V/m} = 25\ \text{mV/m} \qquad \square$$

EXAMPLE 3.21

The radii of the inner and outer conductors of a coaxial cable of length l are a and b, respectively. The insulation material between the two conductors has conductivity σ. Obtain an expression for conductance per unit length between the conductors.

SOLUTION

Figure E3.21 shows a coaxial cable of length l with inner conductor radius a and outer conductor radius b. When a voltage (V_{ab}) is applied between the inner and outer conductors, the current I flows from the inner conductor to outer conductor through the insulation material.

The area through which the current flows is

$$A = 2\pi rl$$

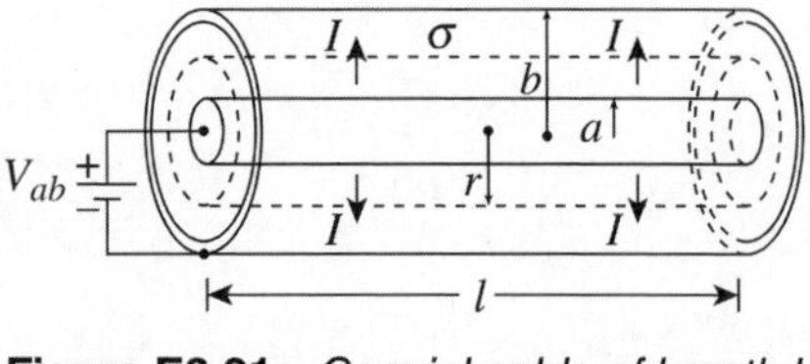

Figure E3.21 *Coaxial cable of length l*

where r is the radial distance from the axis of the center conductor. As the flow of current is along the radial distance, the current density is written as

$$\vec{J} = \frac{I}{A}\vec{a}_r = \frac{I}{2\pi rl}\vec{a}_r$$

From point form of Ohm's law, $\vec{J} = \sigma\vec{E}$, the electric field intensity $\vec{E}$ is

$$\vec{E} = \frac{\vec{J}}{\sigma} = \frac{I}{2\pi\sigma r l}\vec{a}_r$$

As current flows from a higher potential to a lower potential in a resistor, the inner conductor must be at a higher potential than the outer conductor. Hence, the voltage difference between the conductors is

$$V_{ab} = -\int_b^a \vec{E}\cdot d\vec{l}$$

$$= -\int_b^a \frac{I}{2\pi\sigma l}\vec{a}_r \cdot \frac{dr}{r}\vec{a}_r$$

$$= -\frac{I}{2\pi\sigma l}\ln\left[r\right]_b^a \qquad (\text{since } \vec{a}_r \cdot \vec{a}_r = 1)$$

Hence, $V_{ab} = \dfrac{I}{2\pi\sigma l}\ln\left[\dfrac{b}{a}\right]$

Therefore, $R = \dfrac{V_{ab}}{I} = \dfrac{\ln(b/a)}{2\pi\sigma l}\,\Omega$

and $G = \dfrac{1}{R} = \dfrac{I}{V_{ab}} = \dfrac{2\pi\sigma l}{\ln(b/a)}\,\Omega^{-1}$

Hence, the conductance per unit length is

$$G' = \frac{G}{l} = \frac{2\pi\sigma}{\ln(b/a)}\,\Omega^{-1}/\text{m} \qquad\qquad \square$$

3.8.1 Joule's Law

Consider a medium in which the charges are moving with a mean velocity $\vec{u}$ under the influence of an electric field intensity $\vec{E}$. If ρ_v is the volume charge density, the force experienced by the charge in a volume dv is

$$\vec{F} = q\vec{E} = \rho_v v\vec{E} \tag{3.38}$$

These charges move a distance $d\vec{l}$ in time dt such that $d\vec{l} = \vec{u}dt$. Then, the work done by the electric field is represented by

$$dW = d\vec{F}\cdot d\vec{l} = \rho_v dv\vec{E}\cdot\vec{u}dt$$

$$= \rho_v\vec{u}\cdot\vec{E}\,dv\,dt = \vec{J}\cdot\vec{E}\,dv\,dt$$

where $\vec{J} = \rho_v\vec{u}$. Since power is the rate at which work is done, the power supplied by the electric field intensity is given by

$$dp = \frac{dW}{dt} = \vec{J}\cdot\vec{E}dv \tag{3.39}$$

If the power density p is defined as the power per unit volume such that $dp = pdv$, then the above equation can be written as

$$p = \vec{J}\cdot\vec{E} \tag{3.40}$$

Equation (3.40) is called the *point form of Joule's law*, which states that the power delivered per unit volume by the electric field is a scalar product of electric field intensity $\vec{E}$ and volume current density $\vec{J}$. The power associated with the volume v is

$$P = \int_v p\, dv = \int_v (\vec{J} \cdot \vec{E})\, dv \tag{3.41}$$

The unit of power is measured in watt (W). This equation is called the *integral form of Joule's law*. For a conductor, $\vec{J} = \sigma\vec{E}$, the power density is represented by

$$p = \vec{J} \cdot \vec{E} = \sigma\vec{E} \cdot \vec{E} = \sigma E^2$$

The total power dissipation is

$$P = \int_v \sigma E^2\, dv \tag{3.42}$$

If V is the potential difference between the two ends of a conductor of length l and uniform cross section A, then the total power lost by the conductor as heat is represented by

$$P = \int_v \sigma \left(\frac{V}{l} \right)^2 dv = \frac{\sigma V^2 A l}{l^2}$$

$$= \frac{\sigma A V^2}{l} = \frac{V^2}{R} \tag{3.43}$$

where $R = \dfrac{l}{\sigma A}$ is the resistance of the conductor. This equation is an equivalent form of Joule's law, which is commonly used in electric circuit theory to determine the power dissipated as heat by a resistor.

EXAMPLE 3.22

A 50-m long copper wire has a circular cross section with radius $r = 4$ cm. Given that the conductivity of copper is 5.8×10^7 S/m, determine a) the resistance of the wire and b) the power dissipated in the wire if the voltage across its length is 1.5 mV.

SOLUTION

(a) The resistance of the wire is

$$R = \frac{l}{\sigma A} = \frac{50}{5.8 \times 10^7 \times \pi \times (0.04)^2} = 1.72 \times 10^{-4}\,\Omega$$

(b) From Joule's law, the power dissipated in the wire is

$$P = \frac{V^2}{R} = \frac{\left(1.5 \times 10^{-3}\right)^2}{1.72 \times 10^{-4}} = 1.3 \times 10^{-2} = 13 \text{ mW}$$

3.9   DETERMINATION OF CAPACITANCE

When two conductors carrying equal and opposite charges are separated by a dielectric medium, it forms a capacitor. The conductors may be of any arbitrary shape and size. When a dc voltage is applied across the conducting plates, charges of equal and opposite polarity are transferred to the surface of conducting plates as shown in Figure 3.12.

The positive charge will accumulate on the surface of the conductor *a* connected to the positive terminal of the dc voltage source and the negative charge will accumulate on the surface of the conductor *b* connected to the negative terminal of the source.

The separation of charges establishes an electric field $\vec{E}$ in the dielectric medium and thereby, a potential difference between the conductors. The electric field lines originate at the surface of one conductor with charge $+Q$ and terminate at the surface of another conductor with charge $-Q$. The potential difference between the two conductors is proportional to the charge transferred. Therefore,

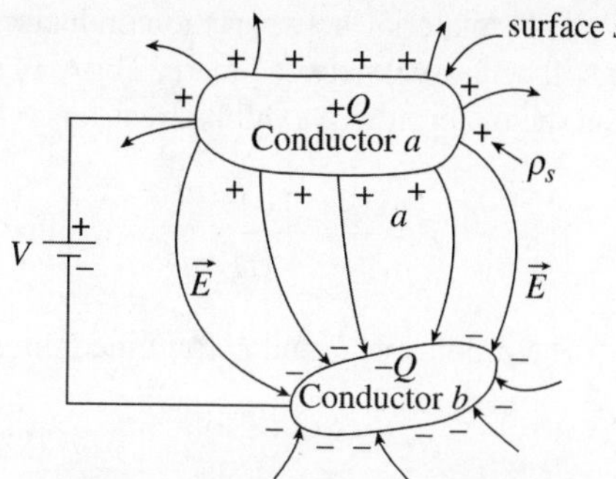

Figure 3.12 *A charged capacitor*

the capacitance of a two-conductor capacitor is defined as the ratio of charge (Q) on one of the conducting plates to the potential difference (V) between them as given by

$$C = \frac{Q}{V} \tag{3.44}$$

where C is the capacitance measured in farad (F).

From electrostatic boundary conditions, it is known that the tangential component of electric field $\vec{E}$ is always zero at the surface of the conductor and it is always perpendicular to the conductor surfaces. Hence, the normal component of electric field intensity $\vec{E}$ at any point on the surface of either conductor is written as

$$E_n = \vec{E} \cdot \vec{a}_n = \frac{\rho_s}{\varepsilon} \qquad (\text{since } D_n = \varepsilon E_n = \rho_s) \tag{3.45}$$

where $\vec{a}_n$ is the outward normal unit vector at that point, ε is the permittivity of the dielectric medium between the conductors and ρ_s is the surface charge density at the same point. The charge Q is equal to the surface integral of ρ_s over surface *s* as given by

$$Q = \int_s \rho_s \cdot d\vec{s}$$

Since $\rho_s = \varepsilon \vec{E} \cdot \vec{a}_n$, we get

$$Q = \int_s \varepsilon \vec{E} \cdot \vec{a}_n d\vec{s} = \int_s \varepsilon \vec{E} \cdot d\vec{s} \tag{3.46}$$

It is known that the voltage V is related to the electric field intensity $\vec{E}$ by

$$V = V_{ab} = -\int_{P_2}^{P_1} \vec{E} \cdot d\vec{l} \tag{3.47}$$

where P_1 and P_2 are any two points of the conducting surfaces *a* and *b*, respectively. Substituting Eqs. (3.46) and (3.47) in Eq. (3.44), we get

$$C = \frac{Q}{V} = \frac{\int_s \varepsilon \vec{E} \cdot d\vec{s}}{-\int_l \vec{E} \cdot d\vec{l}} \tag{3.48}$$

where *l* is the path of integration from conductor *b* to conductor *a*. As the above equation involves electric field intensity $\vec{E}$ in both numerator and denominator, the capacitance obtained for any specific configuration is always independent of the field intensity $\vec{E}$. But the capacitance depends on the permittivity of the dielectric medium between the conductors, the size, shape and relative position of the two conductors.

If the material between the conductors is not a perfect dielectric, then a small amount of conductivity σ will be present between them. This will result in a current flow through the material between the conductors and the material will exhibit a resistance R. The expression for resistance R of any resistor is represented by

$$R = \frac{V}{I} = \frac{-\int_l \vec{E} \cdot d\vec{l}}{\int_s \sigma \vec{E} \cdot d\vec{s}}$$

The product of R and C for a medium with uniform σ and ε results in

$$RC = \frac{\varepsilon}{\sigma} = T_r \tag{3.49}$$

This relationship is called the *time constant or relaxation time T_r* and it can be used to find R if C is known, or vice versa.

The determination of the capacitance for (i) parallel plate capacitor, (ii) parallel wire transmission line, (iii) coaxial cable or cylindrical capacitor, (iv) isolated charged sphere, and (v) spherical capacitor is discussed below.

3.9.1 Capacitance of a Parallel Plate Capacitor

Consider that two parallel conducting plates, each of area A and separated by a distance d, form a parallel plate capacitor. The capacitance is to be determined for a parallel plate capacitor filled with a dielectric medium having permittivity ε. By knowing the capacitance of this parallel plate capacitor, the resistance and the energy stored in the medium can also be obtained. Assume that the bottom plate of the capacitor is placed in xy-plane and the top plate of the capacitor is in $z = d$ plane as shown in Figure 3.13.

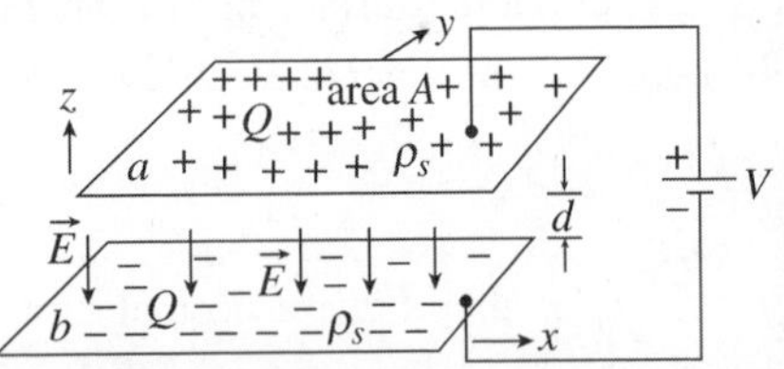

Figure 3.13 *Parallel plate capacitor*

Here, the charge on the top plate a is $+Q$ and on the bottom plate b, it is $-Q$. These charges will induce a uniform electric field from top plate to bottom plate in the negative z-direction. The charge density on the top plate is

$$\rho_s = \frac{Q}{A}$$

The electric field intensity between the conductors is $\vec{E} = -E\vec{a}_z$ and the magnitude of $\vec{E}$ at the conductor–dielectric boundary is $E = \dfrac{\rho_s}{\varepsilon} = \dfrac{Q}{\varepsilon A}$. Therefore, the potential difference between the plates is

$$V = -\int_0^d \vec{E} \cdot d\vec{l} = -\int_0^d (-E\vec{a}_z) \cdot (dz\vec{a}_z)$$

$$= \frac{Q}{\varepsilon A} \int_0^d dz = \frac{Qd}{\varepsilon A}$$

Hence, the capacitance of the parallel plate capacitor is

$$C = \frac{Q}{V} = \frac{\varepsilon A}{d}$$

For an imperfect dielectric, $RC = \dfrac{\varepsilon}{\sigma}$

where σ is the conductivity of the imperfect dielectric medium between the two parallel plate conductors. Therefore, the resistance between the two plates is

$$R = \frac{\varepsilon}{\sigma C} = \frac{\varepsilon}{\sigma} \times \frac{d}{\varepsilon A} = \frac{d}{\sigma A}$$

The energy stored in the dielectric medium of a parallel plate capacitor is

$$W_e = \frac{1}{2}\int_v \varepsilon E^2 dv = \frac{1}{2}\frac{Ad}{\varepsilon}\rho_s^2 \qquad \left(\text{since } E = \frac{\rho_s}{\varepsilon}\right)$$

$$= \frac{1}{2}\frac{d}{\varepsilon A}Q^2 = \frac{1}{2C}Q^2 = \frac{1}{2}CV^2$$

EXAMPLE 3.23

A parallel plate capacitor has an area of 0.8 m^2, separation of 0.1 mm with a dielectric for which $\varepsilon_r = 1000$ and a field of 10^6 V/m. Determine the capacitance and the voltage across the two plates.

SOLUTION

Given $A = 0.8$ m^2, $d = 0.1$ mm, $\varepsilon_r = 1000$ and $E = 10^6$ V/m.

The capacitance, $C = \dfrac{\varepsilon A}{d}$

$$= \frac{\varepsilon_0 \varepsilon_r A}{d} = \frac{8.854 \times 10^{-12} \times 1000 \times 0.8}{0.1 \times 10^{-3}} = 70.83\,\mu\text{F}$$

The voltage across the two plates,

$$V = Ed = 10^6 \times 0.1 \times 10^{-3} = 100\text{ V}$$

EXAMPLE 3.24

A capacitor consists of two similar square aluminum plates each of 10 cm $\times$ 10 cm mounted parallel and opposite to each other. What is the capacitance when the distance between them is 1 cm and dielectric is air?

SOLUTION

Given area of the plates, $A = 10 \times 10^{-2} \times 10 \times 10^{-2} = 10^{-2}$ m^2 and the distance between the plates, $d = 1$ cm $= 10^{-2}$ m.

For air dielectric, $\varepsilon_r = 1$, $\varepsilon_0 = \dfrac{10^{-9}}{36\pi} = 8.854 \times 10^{-12}$

Therefore, the capacitance, $C = \dfrac{\varepsilon A}{d} = \dfrac{\varepsilon_r \varepsilon_0 A}{d} = \dfrac{\varepsilon_0 A}{d}$

$$= \frac{8.854 \times 10^{-12} \times 10^{-2}}{10^{-2}} = 8.854\text{ pF}$$

EXAMPLE 3.25

A condenser is composed of two plates separated by a sheet of insulating material 3 mm thick and of relative permittivity $\varepsilon_{r1} = 4$. The distance between the plates is increased to allow the insulation of a second sheet of 5 mm thick and relative permittivity ε_{r2}. If the capacitance of the condenser so formed is 1/3 of the original capacitance, find ε_{r2}.

SOLUTION

The capacitance of a parallel plate capacitor is $C = \dfrac{\varepsilon_0 \varepsilon_r A}{d}$

$$\text{Therefore, } C_1 = \frac{\varepsilon_0 \varepsilon_{r1} A}{d_1} = \frac{\varepsilon_0 \times 4 \times A}{3 \times 10^{-3}} = \frac{4 \times 10^3}{3} \varepsilon_0 A$$

$$C_2 = \frac{\varepsilon_0 \varepsilon_{r2} A}{d_2} = \frac{\varepsilon_0 \varepsilon_{r2} A}{5 \times 10^{-3}} = \frac{10^3}{5} \varepsilon_0 \varepsilon_{r2} A$$

When $C_2 = \dfrac{1}{3} C_1$, the above equations can be equated as

$$\frac{10^3}{5} \varepsilon_0 \varepsilon_{r2} A = \frac{1}{3} \times \frac{4 \times 10^3}{3} \varepsilon_0 A$$

Hence,
$$\varepsilon_{r2} = \frac{20}{9} = 2.222$$

EXAMPLE 3.26

A parallel plate capacitor has three similar plates, the outside two being joined together. The inner plate is movable so that it can be used as a variable capacitor. If C_1 is the capacitance when the inner plate is exactly midway between the outer plates and C_2 is the capacitance when the inner plate is 3 times as near one plate as the other, find $\dfrac{C_1}{C_2}$.

SOLUTION

(a) To determine the capacitance C_1:

Consider Figure E3.26(a) representing a parallel plate capacitor in which the inner plate is exactly midway between the outer plates.

$$C_1 = \frac{\varepsilon A}{d/2} + \frac{\varepsilon A}{d/2}$$

$$= 4 \cdot \frac{\varepsilon A}{d}$$

(b) To determine the capacitance C_2

Consider Figure E3.26(b) representing a parallel plate capacitor in which the inner plate is 3 times as near one plate as the other.

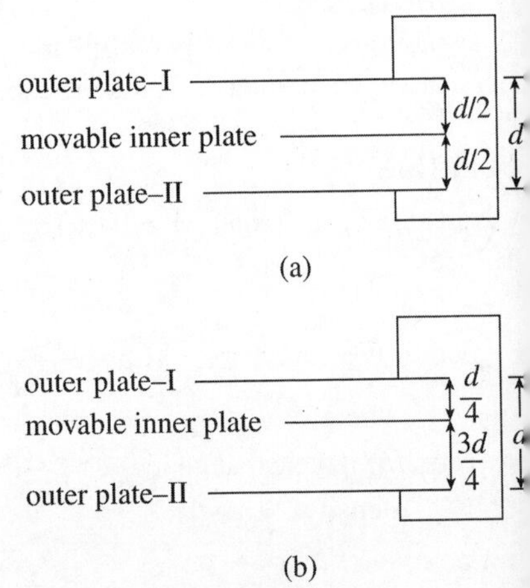

Figure E.3.26

$$C_2 = \frac{\varepsilon A}{d/4} + \frac{\varepsilon A}{3d/4}$$

$$= \frac{16}{3}\left(\frac{\varepsilon A}{d}\right)$$

$$= 4 \cdot \left(\frac{\varepsilon A}{d}\right) \cdot \frac{4}{3}$$

Therefore, $\dfrac{C_1}{C_2} = \dfrac{3}{4}$

EXAMPLE 3.27

The capacitance of the condenser formed by the two parallel metal sheets, each 100 cm^2 in area separated by a dielectric 2 mm thick is 2×10^{-4} μF. A potential of 20 kV is applied to it. Find (i) electric flux, (ii) potential gradient in kV/m, (iii) the relative permittivity of the material, and (iv) electric flux density.

SOLUTION

Given $A = 100 \text{ cm}^2$, $d = 2 \text{ mm}, C = 2 \times 10^{-4}$ μF and $V = 20 \text{ kV}$.

(*i*) The capacitance of the parallel plate condenser is

$$C = \frac{Q}{V}$$

$$2 \times 10^{-4} \times 10^{-6} = \frac{Q}{20 \times 10^3}$$

Hence, $Q = 4$ μC

The electric flux ψ is same as the charge.

Therefore, $\psi = Q = 4$ μC

(*ii*) The electric field intensity is

$$E = \frac{V}{d} = \frac{20 \times 10^3}{2 \times 10^{-3}} = 10 \times 10^6 \text{ V/m or } 100 \text{ kV/cm}$$

(*iii*) The capacitance between the parallel plates is

$$C = \frac{\varepsilon_0 \varepsilon_r A}{d}$$

$$2 \times 10^{-4} \times 10^{-6} = \frac{8.854 \times 10^{-12} \times \varepsilon_r \times 100 \times 10^{-4}}{2 \times 10^{-3}}$$

Therefore, $\varepsilon_r = 4.5177$

(*iv*) At the conductor–dielectric boundary, the normal component of $\vec{D}$ must be equal to the surface charge density ρ_s of the conductor and the flux density is

$$D_n = \rho_s = \frac{Q}{A} = \frac{4 \times 10^{-6}}{100 \times 10^{-4}} = 4 \times 10^{-4} \text{ C/m}^2$$

EXAMPLE 3.28

Find the capacitance of a capacitor consisting of two parallel plates of 30 cm × 30 cm surface area, separated by 5 mm in air. What is the total energy stored in the capacitor when charged to a potential difference of 500 V? What is the energy density?

SOLUTION

Given $A = 0.3 \times 0.3 = 0.09 \, \text{m}^2$, $d = 5 \times 10^{-3} \, \text{m}$, $\varepsilon_0 = 8.854 \times 10^{-12}$ and $\varepsilon_r = 1$ for air.

The capacitance of a parallel plate capacitor is

$$C = \frac{\varepsilon A}{d} = \frac{\varepsilon_0 \varepsilon_r A}{d}$$

$$= \frac{8.854 \times 10^{-12} \times 0.09}{5 \times 10^{-3}} = 159.2 \times 10^{-12} = 159.2 \, \text{pF}$$

The total energy stored in the capacitor is

$$W_e = \frac{1}{2} C V^2$$

$$= \frac{1}{2} \times 159.2 \times 10^{-12} \times (500)^2 = 19.9 \times 10^{-6} = 19.9 \, \mu\text{J}$$

The energy density, $w_e = \frac{1}{2} \varepsilon E^2 = \frac{1}{2} \varepsilon_0 E^2$

where

$$E = \frac{V}{d} = \frac{500}{5 \times 10^{-3}} = 10^5 \, \text{V/m}.$$

Therefore,

$$w_e = \frac{1}{2} \times 8.854 \times 10^{-12} \times 10^{10}$$

$$= 4.427 \times 10^{-2} \, \text{J/m}^3$$

EXAMPLE 3.29

An air capacitor with plate separation of 1 mm and plate area of $36\pi \, \text{cm}^2$ has charges of ± 50 nC on the plates without disturbing the charges. To what value should the separation of the plates be changed to double the (i) voltage, (ii) energy stored, (iii) capacitance, (iv) electric field intensity, and (v) surface charge density.

SOLUTION

Given $d = 1 \, \text{mm} = 10^{-3} \, \text{m}$, $A = 36\pi \times 10^{-4} \, \text{m}^2$, $Q = \pm 50 \text{nC}$.

We know that, $C = \dfrac{\varepsilon_0 A}{d} = \dfrac{8.854 \times 10^{-12} \times 36\pi \times 10^{-4}}{1 \times 10^{-3}} = 100 \, \text{pF}$

Since $C = \dfrac{Q}{V}$, the voltage is

$$V = \frac{Q}{C} = \frac{50 \times 10^{-9}}{100 \times 10^{-12}} = 500 \text{ V}$$

(*i*) To double the voltage, capacitance should be reduced to half value. Therefore, d should be doubled, i.e., separation of plates = 2 mm.

(*ii*) The energy stored, $W_e = \dfrac{1}{2} C V^2 = \dfrac{1}{2} \dfrac{Q^2}{C} = \dfrac{1}{2} \cdot \dfrac{d Q^2}{\varepsilon_0 A}$

To double the energy stored (W_e), the capacitance C should be reduced to half value. Therefore, d should be doubled, i.e., separation of plates = 2 mm.

(*iii*) To double the capacitance, distance d should be halved. Therefore, separation of plates, $d = 0.5$mm.

(*iv*) The electric field intensity, $E = \dfrac{V}{d}$

To double the electric field intensity, the separation of the plates should be halved, i.e., $d = 0.5$ mm.

(*v*) The surface charge density, $\rho_s = \dfrac{\varepsilon_0}{d}$

To double the surface charge density, the separation of the plates should be halved, i.e., separation of plates = 0.5 mm. ◻

EXAMPLE 3.30

The parallel conducting disks in Figure E3.30 are separated by 6 mm and contain a dielectric for which $\varepsilon_r = 4$. Determine the charge densities on the disks.

SOLUTION

The magnitude of electric field intensity is

$$E = \frac{\Delta V}{d} = \frac{270 - 90}{6 \times 10^{-3}} = 3 \times 10^4 \text{ V/m}$$

The direction of field intensity is along $\vec{a}_z$ direction.

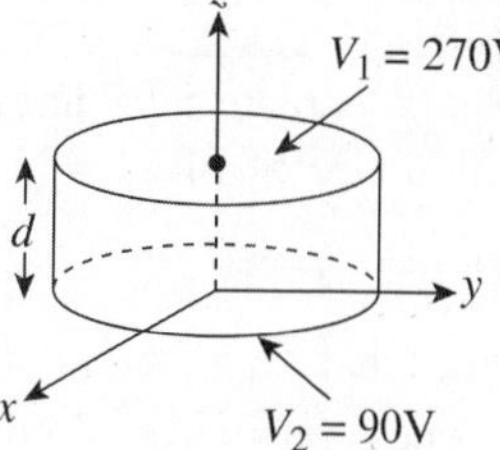

Figure E3.30

Therefore, $\qquad \vec{E} = -\nabla V = -3 \times 10^4 \, \vec{a}_z$ V/m

The flux density is $\vec{D} = \varepsilon_0 \varepsilon_r \vec{E} = 8.854 \times 10^{-12} \times 4 \times \left(-3 \times 10^4 \right) = -10.62 \times 10^{-7} \vec{a}_z$ C/m^2

Since $\vec{D}$ is constant between the disks, and $D_n = \rho_s$ at a conductor surface,

$$\rho_s = \pm 10.62 \times 10^{-7} = \pm 1.062 \, \mu\text{C/m}^2$$

The charge density is +ve on the upper plate and −ve on the lower plate. ◻

EXAMPLE 3.31

An air condenser consisting of a parallel square plate of 50 cm side is charged to a potential difference of 250 V when the plates are 1mm apart. Find the work done in separating the plates from 1 to 3 mm. Assume perfect insulation.

SOLUTION

Given the area of the plate, $A = 50 \times 10^{-2} \times 50 \times 10^{-2} = 25 \times 10^{-2}$ m.

When $d_1 = 1 \times 10^{-3}$ m, the capacitance, $C_1 = \dfrac{\varepsilon_0 A}{d_1} = \dfrac{8.854 \times 10^{-12} \times 25 \times 10^{-2}}{1 \times 10^{-3}}$

$$= 0.22135 \times 10^{-8} \text{ F}$$

When $d_2 = 3 \times 10^{-3}$ m, the capacitance, $C_2 = \dfrac{\varepsilon_0 A}{d_2} = \dfrac{8.854 \times 10^{-12} \times 25 \times 10^{-2}}{3 \times 10^{-3}}$

$$= 0.07333 \times 10^{-8} \text{ F}$$

The energy stored in capacitor C_1 is $W_{e1} = \dfrac{1}{2} C_1 V^2$

The energy stored in the capacitor C_2 is $W_{e2} = \dfrac{1}{2} C_2 V^2$

Therefore, work done in separating the plates from 1mm to 3mm is

$$W_e = W_{e1} - W_{e2} = \frac{1}{2} C_1 V^2 - \frac{1}{2} C_2 V^2 = \frac{1}{2} V^2 (C_1 - C_2)$$

$$= \frac{1}{2} (250)^2 (0.22135 - 0.07333) \times 10^{-8}$$

$$= 4.583 \times 10^{-5} \text{ J}$$

EXAMPLE 3.32

A parallel plate capacitor is of area 2 m^2 and has a separation of 2 mm. The space between the plates is filled with dielectric of $\varepsilon_r = 25$. If 1,000 V is applied, find the force squeezing the plates together.

SOLUTION

Given that, $A = 2\,\text{m}^2$, $d = 2\,\text{mm}$, $\varepsilon_r = 25$ and $V = 1000\,\text{V}$.

The capacitance of a parallel plate capacitor is

$$C = \frac{\varepsilon A}{d} = \frac{\varepsilon_0 \varepsilon_r A}{d}$$

$$= \frac{8.854 \times 10^{-12} \times 25 \times 2}{2 \times 10^{-3}} = 221.35 \text{ nF}$$

The charge induced on the plates is

$$Q = CV = 221.35 \times 10^{-9} \times 1000 = 221.35 \times 10^{-6} \text{ C}$$

If the plate separation is considered as x, then the capacitor of the parallel plate capacitor is $C = \dfrac{\varepsilon A}{x}$ and the energy stored in a capacitor $= \dfrac{1}{2} CV^2$. For the fixed voltage V across the plates,

$$V \frac{\partial Q}{\partial x} = V \frac{\partial (CV)}{\partial x} = V^2 \frac{\partial C}{\partial x}$$

Therefore, $\dfrac{\partial W_e}{\partial x} = \dfrac{\partial}{\partial x}\left(\dfrac{1}{2}CV^2\right) = \dfrac{1}{2}V^2\dfrac{\partial C}{\partial x}$

The force between the plates is

$$F = -\frac{\partial W_e}{\partial x} + V\frac{\partial Q}{\partial x} = -\frac{1}{2}V^2\frac{\partial C}{\partial x} + V^2\frac{\partial C}{\partial x}$$

$$= \frac{1}{2}V^2\frac{\partial C}{\partial x}, \text{ where } C = \frac{\varepsilon A}{x}$$

Hence, $\dfrac{\partial C}{\partial x} = \dfrac{-\varepsilon A}{x^2}$

Substituting $\dfrac{\partial C}{\partial x}$ in the above force equation, we get

$$F = -\frac{1}{2}V^2\frac{\varepsilon A}{x^2}, \text{ where } x = d = 2 \text{ mm}$$

Therefore, the force squeezing the plates together is

$$F = -\frac{(1000)^2 \times 8.854 \times 10^{-12} \times 25 \times 2}{2 \times \left(2 \times 10^{-3}\right)^2} = -55.34 \text{ N}$$

3.9.2   Capacitance of a Parallel Wire Transmission Line

Consider a parallel wire conductor of radius a separated by a distance d as shown in Figure 3.14. Both conductor A and conductor B has a line charge density of ρ_l C/m. The electric field intensity at any point P with a distance r from the conductor A is algebraic sum of electric field intensity at P due to conductor A and conductor B.

Therefore,

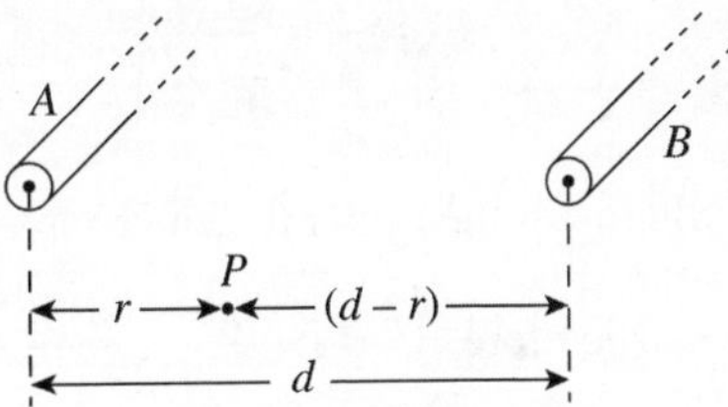

Figure 3.14   *Parallel wire conductor*

$$E = \frac{\rho_l}{2\pi\varepsilon r} + \frac{\rho_l}{2\pi\varepsilon(d-r)}$$

$$= \frac{\rho_l}{2\pi\varepsilon}\left(\frac{1}{r} + \frac{1}{d-r}\right)$$

The potential difference between the conductors is

$$V = -\int \vec{E}\cdot d\vec{l} = -\int (E\vec{a}_r)\cdot(dr\vec{a}_r) = -\int E\,dr$$

$$= -\frac{\rho_l}{2\pi\varepsilon}\int_{d-a}^{a}\left(\frac{1}{r} + \frac{1}{d-r}\right)dr = -\frac{\rho_l}{2\pi\varepsilon}\left(\ln\frac{a}{d-a} + \ln\frac{a}{d-a}\right)$$

$$= -\frac{\rho_l}{2\pi\varepsilon}\left(2\ln\frac{a}{d-a}\right)$$

$$V = \frac{\rho_l}{\pi\varepsilon}\ln\left(\frac{d-a}{a}\right)$$

The capacitance per unit length between two parallel conductors is

$$C' = \frac{C}{l} = \frac{Q}{Vl} = \frac{\rho_l}{V} = \frac{\pi\varepsilon}{\ln\left(\dfrac{d-a}{a}\right)} \qquad \left(\text{since } \rho_l = \frac{Q}{l}\right)$$

If $d \gg a$, then

$$C' = \frac{\pi\varepsilon}{\ln\left(\dfrac{d}{a}\right)} \ \text{F/m}$$

If the dielectric medium between two conductors is air (for transmission lines), then $\varepsilon_r = 1$ and the capacitance is

$$C' = \frac{\pi\varepsilon_0}{\ln\left(\dfrac{d}{a}\right)} \ \text{F/m}$$

EXAMPLE 3.33

Find the capacitance per unit length between two parallel cylindrical conductors in air of radius 1.5 cm and with a center to center separation of 85 cm.

SOLUTION

The capacitance per unit length between two parallel cylindrical conductors in air is

$$C' = \frac{C}{l} = \frac{\pi\varepsilon_0}{\ln\left(\dfrac{d}{a}\right)}$$

where d is the center to center separation and a is the radius of the conductor.

$$\text{Therefore, } C' = \frac{\pi\times8.854\times10^{-12}}{\ln\left(\dfrac{85}{1.5}\right)} = 6.89 \ \text{pF/m}$$

EXAMPLE 3.34

Calculate the capacitance per km length of two identical parallel wires of diameter 1 cm each and placed 1 m apart. Also, find the potential difference between them, which will make the maximum electric field intensity at the conductor surface just 4×10^6 V/m.

SOLUTION

Given that, the radius of the parallel wire, $a = 0.5\times10^{-2}$ m and the distance between the two identical parallel wires is $d = 1$m. The electric field intensity is given as $E = 4\times10^6$ V/m.

The capacitance per km length of parallel wire conductor is

$$C' = \frac{C}{l} = \frac{\pi\varepsilon_0}{\ln\left(\dfrac{d}{a}\right)} = \frac{\pi\times8.854\times10^{-12}}{\ln\left(\dfrac{1}{0.5\times10^{-2}}\right)} = 5.25 \ \text{pF}$$

We know that, $E = \dfrac{V}{d}$

Therefore, $\quad V = Ed = 4\times10^6 \times 1 = 4\times10^6$ V $\qquad\square$

EXAMPLE 3.35

The conductors of two-wire transmission line of length 4 km are spaced 45 cm between centers. If each conductor has a diameter of 1.5 cm, then calculate the capacitance of the line.

SOLUTION

The capacitance of the two-wire transmission line is

$$C = \dfrac{\pi \varepsilon_0 l}{\ln\left(\dfrac{d}{a}\right)}$$

where $l = 4\,\text{km} = 4\times10^3\,\text{m}$, $d = 45\,\text{cm} = 0.45\,\text{m}$ and $a = \dfrac{1.5}{2}\,\text{cm} = 0.75\times10^{-2}\,\text{m}$.

Hence,

$$C = \dfrac{\pi \times 8.854 \times 10^{-12} \times 4\times10^3}{\ln\left(\dfrac{0.45}{0.75\times10^{-2}}\right)} = 0.02717\times10^{-6} = 27.17\,\text{nF} \qquad\square$$

EXAMPLE 3.36

Consider that two copper wires of 1.29 mm diameter are parallel with separation d between the axes. Determine d so that the capacitance between the wires in air is $30\,\text{pF/m}$.

SOLUTION

The capacitance of a pair of parallel wires per km is

$$C' = \dfrac{C}{l} = \dfrac{\pi \varepsilon_0}{\ln\left(\dfrac{d}{a}\right)}$$

where a is the radius of the wire and d is the distance between two wires.

$$30\times10^{-12} = \dfrac{\pi \times 8.854 \times 10^{-12}}{\ln\left(\dfrac{d}{a}\right)}$$

$$\ln\left(\dfrac{d}{a}\right) = \dfrac{\pi \times 8.854}{30} = 0.927$$

$$\dfrac{d}{a} = e^{0.927} = 2.53$$

Therefore, $d = 2.53a = 2.53\times\dfrac{1.29\times10^{-3}}{2} = 1.63\,\text{mm}$ $\qquad\square$

3.9.3 Capacitance of a Coaxial Cable or Cylindrical Capacitor

Consider a coaxial line of length l with inner conductor having radius a and outer conductor having radius b, such that $b > a$, as shown in Figure 3.15. The two conductors are separated by a dielectric medium with permittivity ε. When a voltage V is applied across the capacitor, charges $+Q$ and $-Q$ will accumulate on the surfaces of the inner and outer conductors with uniform distribution.

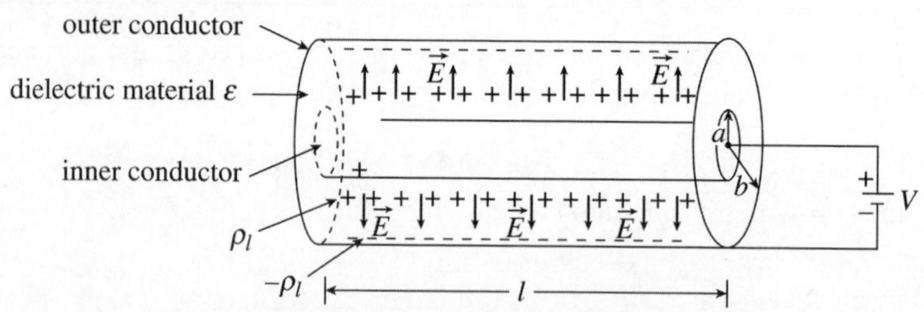

Figure 3.15 *Coaxial capacitor*

Applying Gauss's law to an arbitrary Gaussian cylindrical surface of radius ρ $(a < \rho < b)$, we get

$$Q = \oint_s \varepsilon \vec{E} \cdot d\vec{s} = \varepsilon \oint_s E_\rho \vec{a}_\rho \cdot ds\,\vec{a}_\rho = \varepsilon \oint_s E_\rho \cdot ds$$

$$= \varepsilon E_\rho 2\pi\rho l$$

Therefore, the electric field intensity is

$$E_\rho = \frac{Q}{2\pi\varepsilon\rho\, l}$$

In vector form, $\vec{E} = \dfrac{Q}{2\pi\varepsilon\rho\, l}\, \vec{a}_\rho$

The potential difference between the inner and outer cylindrical conductors is

$$V = -\int_b^a \vec{E} \cdot d\vec{l} = -\int_b^a \left(\frac{Q}{2\pi\varepsilon\rho l}\, \vec{a}_\rho \right) \cdot \left(d\rho\, \vec{a}_\rho \right)$$

$$= -\frac{Q}{2\pi\varepsilon\, l} \int_b^a \frac{1}{\rho}\, d\rho = \frac{Q}{2\pi\varepsilon\, l} \ln\left(\frac{b}{a} \right)$$

Hence, the capacitance of the coaxial cable is

$$C = \frac{Q}{V} = \frac{2\pi\varepsilon\, l}{\ln\left(\dfrac{b}{a} \right)}$$

The capacitance per unit length of the coaxial line is

$$C' = \frac{C}{l} = \frac{2\pi\varepsilon}{\ln\left(\dfrac{b}{a} \right)}\ \text{F/m}$$

The coaxial cable can also be considered as a coaxial cylindrical capacitor.
For an imperfect dielectric,

$$RC = \frac{\varepsilon}{\sigma}$$

where σ is the conductivity of the imperfect dielectric medium between the two cylindrical conductors. Therefore, the resistance between the two conductors is

$$R = \frac{\varepsilon}{\sigma C} = \frac{\varepsilon}{\sigma} \times \frac{\ln\left(\dfrac{b}{a}\right)}{2\pi\varepsilon l}$$

$$= \frac{\ln\left(\dfrac{b}{a}\right)}{2\pi\sigma l}$$

EXAMPLE 3.37

Calculate the capacitance of the coaxial cable with the radii of inner conductor $a = 10\text{mm}$ and outer conductor $b = 15\text{mm}$ and the dielectric medium has $\varepsilon_r = 3.5$. The inner conductor is at potential 1 kV and the outer shield is grounded. The cable is 8 km long.

SOLUTION

Given $a = 10\text{mm}$, $b = 15\text{mm}$, $\varepsilon_r = 3.5$ and $l = 8\,\text{km}$.

The capacitance of the coaxial cable is

$$C = \frac{2\pi\varepsilon l}{\ln\left(\dfrac{b}{a}\right)} = \frac{2\pi \times 3.5 \times 8.854 \times 10^{-12} \times 8 \times 10^3}{\ln\left(\dfrac{15}{10}\right)} = 3.84\,\mu\text{F}$$

EXAMPLE 3.38

Find the capacitance per unit length of a coaxial conductor with outer radius 4 mm and inner radius 0.5 mm if the dielectric has $\varepsilon_r = 5.2$.

SOLUTION

The capacitance per unit length of a coaxial conductor is

$$C' = \frac{C}{l} = \frac{2\pi\varepsilon_0\varepsilon_r}{\ln\left(\dfrac{b}{a}\right)} = \frac{2\pi \times 8.854 \times 10^{-12} \times 5.2}{\ln\left(\dfrac{4 \times 10^{-3}}{0.5 \times 10^{-3}}\right)} = 139.116\ \text{pF/km}$$

EXAMPLE 3.39

Calculate the capacitance per km of a coaxial cable with inner diameter of 2 mm, outer diameter of 5 mm and the region between them being filled with a dielectric of $\varepsilon_r = 4$.

SOLUTION

Given that, $\varepsilon_r = 4$, inner diameter $a = 2\ \text{mm} = 2 \times 10^{-3}\ \text{m}$ and outer diameter $b = 5\ \text{mm} = 5 \times 10^{-3}\ \text{m}$.

The capacitance of coaxial cable, $C = \dfrac{2\pi\varepsilon l}{\ln\left(\dfrac{b}{a}\right)}$

The capacitance per unit length (km), $C' = \dfrac{C}{l} = \dfrac{2\pi\varepsilon}{\ln\left(\dfrac{b}{a}\right)}$

Therefore,

$$C' = \frac{2\pi \times 8.854 \times 10^{-12} \times 4}{\ln\left(\dfrac{5 \times 10^{-3}}{2 \times 10^{-3}}\right)} = \frac{2.225 \times 10^{-10}}{0.9163} = 242.9 \times 10^{-12}\,\text{F} = 242.9\,\text{pF}$$

EXAMPLE 3.40

A single core coaxial cable is designed for 10 kV with rubber dielectric having allowable field strength 50×10^6 V/m. If the inner conductor is a solid wire with radius 50 mm, determine the minimum radial thickness of dielectric required.

SOLUTION

Given, $V = 10$ kV, $E = 5 \times 10^6$ V/m, inner radius $r_{in} = 50$ mm and outer radius $r_{out} = r_{in} + t$, where t is the thickness of dielectric.

Electric field strength, $E = \dfrac{V}{r_{in} \ln\left(\dfrac{r_{out}}{r_{in}}\right)}$

$$50 \times 10^6 = \frac{10 \times 10^3}{50 \times 10^{-3} \ln\left(\dfrac{r_{in} + t}{50 \times 10^{-3}}\right)}$$

$$\ln\left(\frac{r_{in} + t}{50 \times 10^{-3}}\right) = \frac{10 \times 10^3}{50 \times 10^6 \times 50 \times 10^{-3}}$$

$$\ln\left(\frac{r_{in} + t}{50 \times 10^{-3}}\right) = 0.004$$

$$\frac{r_{in} + t}{50 \times 10^{-3}} = e^{0.004} = 1.004$$

$$50 \times 10^{-3} + t = 1.004 \times 50 \times 10^{-3} = 0.0502$$

Therefore,

$$t = 0.0502 - 0.05 = 2 \times 10^{-4} = 0.2\,\text{mm}$$

EXAMPLE 3.41

A cylindrical capacitor has radius $a = 2$ cm and $b = 4$ cm. If the space between the plates is filled with a non-homogeneous dielectric with relative permittivity $\varepsilon_r = (20 + \rho)/\rho$, where ρ is in cm, determine the capacitance per metre of the capacitor.

SOLUTION

The potential difference between the inner and outer cylindrical conductors is

$$V = -\int_b^a \vec{E} \cdot d\vec{l} = -\int_b^a \left(\frac{Q}{2\pi\varepsilon_0 \varepsilon_r \rho l} \vec{a}_\rho \right) \cdot \left(d\rho\, \vec{a}_\rho \right)$$

$$= -\frac{Q}{2\pi\varepsilon_0 l} \int_b^a \frac{1}{\varepsilon_r \rho} d\rho = -\frac{Q}{2\pi\varepsilon_0 l} \int_b^a \frac{d\rho}{\left(\dfrac{20+\rho}{\rho} \right)\rho}$$

$$= -\frac{Q}{2\pi\varepsilon_0 l} \int_b^a \frac{d\rho}{20+\rho} = -\frac{Q}{2\pi\varepsilon_0 l} \ln\left(20+\rho\right)_b^a$$

$$= \frac{Q}{2\pi\varepsilon_0 l} \ln\left(\frac{20+b}{20+a} \right)$$

When $l = 1\,\mathrm{m}$, the capacitance per metre is

$$C = \frac{Q}{V} = \frac{2\pi\varepsilon_0}{\ln\left(\dfrac{20+b}{20+a} \right)} = 2\pi \times \frac{10^{-9}}{36\pi} \times \frac{1}{\ln\left(\dfrac{24}{22} \right)}$$

$$= 0.639 \times 10^{-9} = 639\ \mathrm{pF/m}$$

3.9.4 Capacitance of an Isolated Charged Sphere

Consider a sphere of radius r having charge Q coulombs as shown in Figure 3.16. The potential is the work done per unit charge in carrying a positive test charge from infinity to the sphere.

Therefore, the absolute potential is

$$V = -\int_\infty^r E \cdot dr = -\frac{Q}{4\pi\varepsilon} \int_\infty^r \frac{dr}{r^2}$$

$$= \frac{Q}{4\pi\varepsilon r}$$

The capacitance of an isolated sphere is

$$C = \frac{Q}{V} = 4\pi\varepsilon r$$

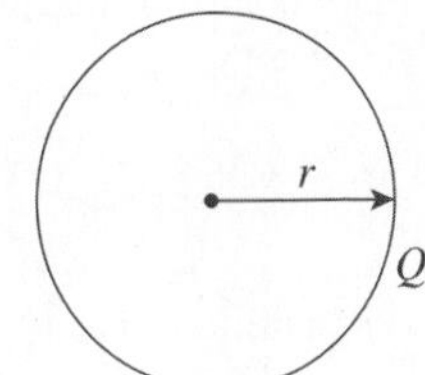

Figure 3.16 *Isolated charge sphere*

where $\varepsilon = \varepsilon_0 \varepsilon_r$.

If the medium is air, then the capacitance C becomes

$$C = 4\pi\varepsilon_0 r$$

3.9.5 Capacitance of Spherical Capacitor

Figure 3.17 shows two concentric spherical conductors with inner sphere having radius a and outer sphere having radius b, such that $b > a$. The two spherical conductors are separated by a dielectric medium with permittivity ε. When a voltage V is applied across the spherical capacitor, charges $+Q$ and $-Q$ will accumulate on the surfaces of the inner and outer conductors with uniform distribution.

Applying Gauss's law to an arbitrary Gaussian spherical surface of radius r $(a < r < b)$, we get

$$Q = \oint_s \varepsilon \vec{E} \cdot d\vec{s} = \varepsilon \oint_s E_r \vec{a}_r \cdot ds\vec{a}_r = \varepsilon \oint_s E_r \cdot ds$$

$$= \varepsilon E_r \left(4\pi r^2\right)$$

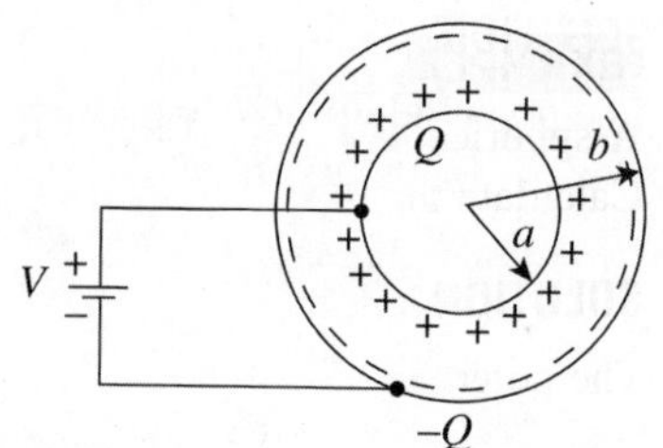

Figure 3.17   *Spherical capacitor*

Therefore, the electric field intensity is $E_r = \dfrac{Q}{4\pi\varepsilon r^2}$

In vector form,

$$\vec{E} = \frac{Q}{4\pi\varepsilon r^2}\vec{a}_r$$

The potential difference between the inner and outer spherical conductor is

$$V = -\int_b^a \vec{E} \cdot d\vec{l} = -\int_b^a \left(\frac{Q}{4\pi\varepsilon r^2}\vec{a}_r\right) \cdot \left(dr\vec{a}_r\right)$$

$$= -\frac{Q}{4\pi\varepsilon}\int_b^a \frac{1}{r^2}\,dr = \frac{Q}{4\pi\varepsilon}\left(\frac{1}{a} - \frac{1}{b}\right)$$

Hence, the capacitance of the spherical capacitor is

$$C = \frac{Q}{V} = \frac{4\pi\varepsilon}{\left(\dfrac{1}{a} - \dfrac{1}{b}\right)} = \frac{4\pi\varepsilon ab}{(b-a)}$$

A single isolated sphere is formed by the inner conducting plate with radius a having charge $+Q$. Since the outer plate is at infinite distance, i.e., $b = \infty$, the capacitance of the spherical capacitor becomes

$$C = \frac{4\pi\varepsilon}{\left(\dfrac{1}{a} - \dfrac{1}{\infty}\right)} = 4\pi\varepsilon\, a$$

The isolated sphere is the special case of a spherical capacitor at a large distance from other conductors and the above expression is identical with the one obtained in Sec. 3.9.4.

For an imperfect dielectric,

$$RC = \frac{\varepsilon}{\sigma}$$

where σ is the conductivity of the imperfect dielectric medium between the two spherical conductors. Therefore, the resistance between the two conductors is

$$R = \frac{\varepsilon}{\sigma C} = \frac{\varepsilon}{\sigma} \times \frac{(b-a)}{4\pi\varepsilon ab}$$

$$= \frac{(b-a)}{4\pi\sigma ab}$$

EXAMPLE 3.42

A spherical capacitor with radius $a = 2$ cm and $b = 4$ cm has a non-homogeneous dielectric of $\varepsilon = \dfrac{10\varepsilon_0}{r}$.
Calculate the capacitance of the capacitor.

SOLUTION

The potential difference between the inner and outer spherical conductor is

$$V = -\int_b^a \vec{E} \cdot d\vec{l} = -\int_b^a \left(\frac{Q}{4\pi\varepsilon\, r^2} \vec{a}_r \right) \cdot (dr\vec{a}_r)$$

$$= -\frac{Q}{4\pi} \int_b^a \frac{dr}{\varepsilon r^2} = -\frac{Q}{4\pi} \int_b^a \frac{dr}{\dfrac{10\varepsilon_0}{r} r^2}$$

$$= -\frac{Q}{40\pi\varepsilon_0} \int_b^a \frac{dr}{r} = \frac{Q}{40\pi\varepsilon_0} \ln\left(\frac{b}{a}\right)$$

Hence, the capacitance of the spherical capacitor is

$$C = \frac{Q}{V} = \frac{40\pi\varepsilon_0}{\ln(b/a)} = \frac{40\pi}{\ln(4/2)} \times \frac{10^{-9}}{36\pi} = 1.6 \text{ nF}$$

EXAMPLE 3.43

The radii of inner and outer spheres are 10 and 20 cm, respectively. The space between the two spheres is
filled with insulating material of $\varepsilon_r = 3$. Find the capacitance formed by the two concentric spheres.

SOLUTION

Given the radius of the inner sphere $a = 10$ cm $= 0.1$ m and the radius of the outer sphere $b = 20$cm $= 0.2$ m.
The capacitance formed by two concentric spheres is

$$C = \frac{4\pi\varepsilon}{\left(\dfrac{1}{a} - \dfrac{1}{b}\right)} = \frac{4\pi\varepsilon_0\varepsilon_r}{\left(\dfrac{1}{0.1} - \dfrac{1}{0.2}\right)}$$

$$= \frac{4\pi \times 8.854 \times 10^{-12} \times 3}{5} = 66.76 \times 10^{-12} \text{ F} = 66.76 \text{ pF}$$

EXAMPLE 3.44

The radii of two spheres differ by 4 cm with air as dielectric and the capacitance of the spherical capacitor is
$\dfrac{160}{3}$ pF. If the outer sphere is grounded, determine the radii.

SOLUTION

The capacitance of spherical capacitor is

$$C = 4\pi\varepsilon_0 \left(\frac{ab}{b-a} \right)$$

Here,

$$(b-a) = 4 \times 10^{-2} \tag{1}$$

$$C = 4\pi \times 8.854 \times 10^{-12} \frac{ab}{4 \times 10^{-2}} = \frac{160}{3} \times 10^{-12}$$

Hence,

$$ab = \frac{160 \times 10^{-12} \times 4 \times 10^{-2}}{3 \times 4\pi \times 8.854 \times 10^{-12}} = 0.019\,\text{m}^2 \tag{2}$$

Solving Eqs. (1) and (2), we get

$$a = 0.12\,\text{m} \quad \text{and} \quad b = 0.16\,\text{m} \qquad \qquad \square$$

EXAMPLE 3.45

The radii of two concentric spheres are 0.1 cm and 0.25 cm and the space between them is filled with a dielectric of $\varepsilon_r = 2.5$ with $Q = 1\text{C}$. Determine the capacitance of this spherical capacitor and also find the greatest electric field in the dielectric.

SOLUTION

Let the radii of inner and outer concentric spheres be a and b, respectively.

Given $a = 0.1\,\text{cm} = 0.1 \times 10^{-2}\,\text{m}$ and $b = 0.25\,\text{cm} = 0.25 \times 10^{-2}\,\text{m}$.

(*i*) The capacitance, $C = \dfrac{4\pi\varepsilon}{\left(\dfrac{1}{a} - \dfrac{1}{b}\right)} = \dfrac{4\pi \times 8.854 \times 10^{-12} \times 2.5}{\left(\dfrac{1}{0.1 \times 10^{-2}} - \dfrac{1}{0.25 \times 10^{-2}}\right)}$

$$= 4.635 \times 10^{-13}\,\text{F} = 0.464\,\text{pF}$$

(*ii*) The potential, $V = \dfrac{Q}{C} = \dfrac{1}{0.464 \times 10^{-12}} = 2.15 \times 10^{12}\,\text{V}$

The maximum electric field, $E_{\max} = \dfrac{V}{(b-a)\ln\left(\dfrac{b}{a}\right)} = \dfrac{2.15 \times 10^{12}}{1.5 \times 10^{-3} \times \ln\left(\dfrac{0.25}{0.1}\right)}$

$$= 1.56 \times 10^{15}\,\text{V/m} \qquad \qquad \square$$

3.9.6   Composite Parallel Plate Capacitor

Two parallel conducting plates separated by a dielectric is generally known as a capacitor. The composite parallel plate capacitor is one in which the space between the parallel plates is filled with more than one dielectric material. The dielectric materials can be placed parallel to the conducting plates or normal to the plates.

Case (i): Dielectric interface parallel to plates

Consider a composite capacitor with the space between the two plates filled with two different dielectric materials with permittivity ε_1 and ε_2 as shown in Figure 3.18(a). The two dielectrics are placed parallel to the conducting plates with the space d_1 being filled by dielectric 1 with permittivity ε_1 and the space d_2 being filled by dielectric 2 with permittivity ε_2. Assume the charge on each plate is Q, the electric field intensity in region d_1 is $\vec{E}_1$ and the electric field intensity in region d_2 is $\vec{E}_2$.

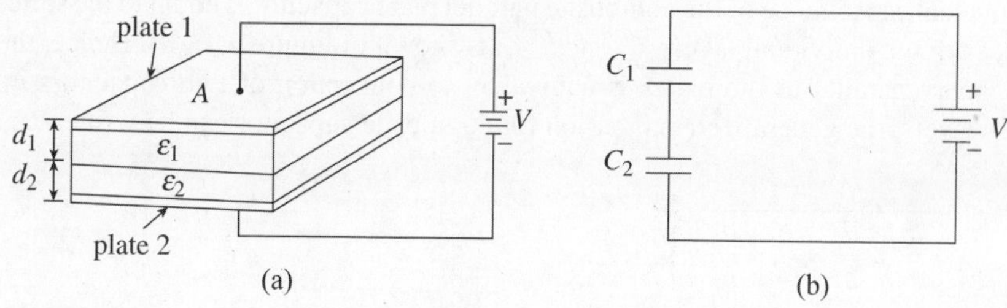

Figure 3.18 *Composite parallel plate capacitor: (a) with dielectric parallel to plates and its (b) its equivalent circuit*

Therefore, the potential across dielectric 1 is $V_1 = E_1 d_1$ and the potential across dielectric 2 is $V_2 = E_2 d_2$ where E_1 and E_2 are the magnitudes of the two intensities. Hence, the total potential across the two parallel conducting plates is given by

$$V = V_1 + V_2 = E_1 d_1 + E_2 d_2 \tag{3.50}$$

From boundary conditions, it is seen that the normal component of flux density is equal to surface charge density at each dielectric–conductor interface. Hence, at the two dielectric–conductor interfaces, $D_{n1} = D_{n2} = \rho_s$. The flux density in the two dielectric layers can be written in terms of electric field intensity as $D_1 = \varepsilon_1 E_1$ and $D_2 = \varepsilon_2 E_2$. Substituting $E = \dfrac{D}{\varepsilon}$ in Eq. (3.50), we get

$$V = \frac{D_1}{\varepsilon_1} d_1 + \frac{D_2}{\varepsilon_2} d_2$$

Since the magnitude of flux density is same on each plate, i.e., $D_1 = D_2 = \rho_s$, the potential can be written as

$$V = \rho_s \left(\frac{d_1}{\varepsilon_1} + \frac{d_2}{\varepsilon_2} \right)$$

Therefore, the capacitance is given by

$$C = \frac{Q}{V} = \frac{Q}{\rho_s \left(\dfrac{d_1}{\varepsilon_1} + \dfrac{d_2}{\varepsilon_2} \right)} \qquad \text{(since } Q = \rho_s A\text{)}$$

$$= \frac{\rho_s A}{\rho_s \left[\dfrac{d_1}{\varepsilon_1} + \dfrac{d_2}{\varepsilon_2} \right]} = \frac{A}{\dfrac{d_1}{\varepsilon_1} + \dfrac{d_2}{\varepsilon_2}}$$

Therefore, $C = \dfrac{1}{\dfrac{d_1}{\varepsilon_1 A} + \dfrac{d_2}{\varepsilon_2 A}} = \dfrac{1}{\dfrac{1}{C_1} + \dfrac{1}{C_2}} = \dfrac{C_1 C_2}{C_1 + C_2}$ $\hspace{2cm}$ (3.51)

where $C_1 = \dfrac{\varepsilon_1 A}{d_1}$ and $C_2 = \dfrac{\varepsilon_2 A}{d_2}$.

Here, the equivalent capacitance of the composite parallel plate capacitor is equal to the series combination of the capacitances of the individual layers C_1 and C_2, as shown in Figure 3.18(b). Hence, the arrangement of dielectric boundary parallel to the plates is equivalent to connection of two capacitors in series. For n parallel dielectric layers, the generalized expression for composite capacitor can be written as

$$C = \dfrac{A}{\dfrac{d_1}{\varepsilon_1} + \dfrac{d_2}{\varepsilon_2} + \dfrac{d_3}{\varepsilon_3} + \cdots + \dfrac{d_n}{\varepsilon_n}}$$

Case (ii): Dielectric interface normal to plates

Consider the composite capacitor in which dielectric boundary is normal to the conducting plates as shown in Figure 3.19(a). Here, it is seen that the dielectric 1 with permittivity ε_1 occupies an area A_1 of the plates and the dielectric 2 with permittivity ε_2 occupying area A_2.

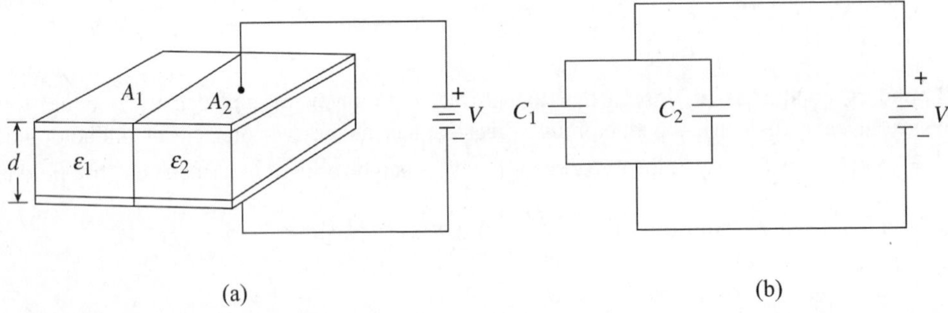

Figure 3.19 *Composite parallel plate capacitor: (a) with dielectric normal to plates and its (b) its equivalent circuit*

The total potential across the two plates is V and distance between the plates is d. Hence, the magnitude of electric field or potential gradient is given by

$$E = \dfrac{V}{d}$$

From boundary conditions, it is seen that the tangential components of field intensities are equal at a dielectric–dielectric interface. Hence, $E_{t1} = E_{t1} = E_1 = E_2 = \dfrac{V}{d}$. The flux density in the two dielectric layers can be written in terms of electric field intensity as $D_1 = \varepsilon_1 E_1$ and $D_2 = \varepsilon_2 E_2$.

Therefore, $D_1 = \dfrac{\varepsilon_1 V}{d}$ and $D_2 = \dfrac{\varepsilon_2 V}{d}$

The charge is divided into two parts on the plate. The charge density is $\rho_{s1} = D_1$ on area A_1 whereas on area A_2, the charge density is $\rho_{s2} = D_2$. Therefore, the total charge on plates is

$$Q = Q_1 + Q_2$$

$$= \rho_{s1} A_1 + \rho_{s2} A_2 = D_1 A_1 + D_2 A_2$$

$$= \frac{\varepsilon_1 V A_1}{d} + \frac{\varepsilon_2 V A_2}{d}$$

Therefore, the capacitance is given by

$$C = \frac{Q}{V} = \frac{\varepsilon_1 A_1}{d} + \frac{\varepsilon_2 A_2}{d}$$

Therefore,

$$C = C_1 + C_2 \tag{3.52}$$

Hence, the arrangement of dielectric boundary normal to the plates is equivalent to connection of two capacitors in parallel to the plates as shown in Figure 3.19(b).

EXAMPLE 3.46

A capacitor consists of two parallel metal plates each of area 2000 cm^2 and 5 mm apart. The space between the plates is filled with a layer of paper 2 mm thick and a sheet of glass 3 mm thick. The relative permittivities of paper and glass are 2 and 8, respectively. A potential difference of 5 kV is applied between the plates. Calculate the (*i*) capacitance of the capacitor, (*ii*) potential gradient in each dielectric, and (*iii*) total energy stored in capacitor.

SOLUTION

Given area, $A = 2000 \times 10^4$ m^2, $\varepsilon_{rp} = 2$, $\varepsilon_{rg} = 8$ and $V = 5000$ V.

The total distance between plates, $d = 5 \times 10^{-3}$ m, $d_p = 2 \times 10^{-3}$ m and $d_g = 3 \times 10^{-3}$ m.

(*i*) The capacitance of paper,

$$C_p = \frac{\varepsilon_0\, \varepsilon_{rp}\, A}{d_p} = \frac{8.854 \times 10^{-12} \times 2 \times 2000 \times 10^{-4}}{2 \times 10^{-3}} = 1.771 \text{ nF}$$

The capacitance of glass,

$$C_g = \frac{\varepsilon_0 \varepsilon_{rg} A}{d_g} = \frac{8.854 \times 10^{-12} \times 8 \times 2000 \times 10^{-4}}{3 \times 10^{-3}} = 4.722 \text{ nF}$$

Hence, the total capacitance,

$$C = C_p + C_g = (1.771 + 4.722)\, \text{nF} = 6.493\, \text{nF}$$

(*ii*) The voltage across each dielectric is

$$V_p = \frac{C_g}{C_p + C_g} \times V = \frac{4.722 \times 10^{-9}}{6.493 \times 10^{-9}} \times 5000 = 3636.22 \text{ volt}$$

$$V_g = \frac{C_p}{C_p + C_g} \times V = \frac{1.771 \times 10^{-9}}{6.493 \times 10^{-9}} \times 5000 = 1363.78 \ \text{volt}$$

The potential gradient in each dielectric is

$$E_{paper} = \frac{V_p}{d_p} = \frac{3636.22}{2 \times 10^{-3}} = 1818.11 \ \text{kV/m}$$

$$E_{glass} = \frac{V_g}{d_g} = \frac{1363.78}{3 \times 10^{-3}} = 454.6 \ \text{kV/m}$$

(*iii*) The total energy stored, $W_e = \frac{1}{2} CV^2$

$$= \frac{1}{2} \times 6.493 \times 10^{-9} \times (5 \times 10^3)^2 = 0.08116 \ \text{J}$$

EXAMPLE 3.47

Determine the voltage across each dielectric in the series-plate capacitor containing two dielectrics, $\varepsilon_{r1} = 3$ and $\varepsilon_{r2} = 1$ when the applied voltage is 200 V. Here $A = 1 \, \text{m}^2$, $d_1 = 1$ mm and $d_2 = 4$ mm.

SOLUTION

We know that,

$$C_1 = \frac{\varepsilon_0 \varepsilon_r A}{d_1} = \frac{\varepsilon_0 \times 3 \times 1}{10^{-3}} = 3000 \, \varepsilon_0$$

$$C_2 = \frac{\varepsilon_0 \times 1}{4 \times 10^{-3}} = 250 \, \varepsilon_0$$

The net capacitance is

$$C = \frac{C_1 C_2}{C_1 + C_2} = 230.77 \, \varepsilon_0 = 230.77 \times 8.854 \times 10^{-12} = 2.043 \ \text{nF}$$

Since the flux density is equal to charge density at the conductor surface,

$$D_n = \rho_s = \frac{Q}{A} = \frac{CV}{A} = \frac{2.043 \times 10^{-9} \times 200}{1} = 4.086 \times 10^{-7} \ \text{C/m}^2$$

Hence, the electric field intensities are

$$E_1 = \frac{D}{\varepsilon_0 \varepsilon_{r1}} = \frac{4.086 \times 10^{-7}}{8.854 \times 10^{-12} \times 3} = 15.4 \times 10^3 \ \text{V/m}$$

$$E_2 = \frac{D}{\varepsilon_0 \varepsilon_{r2}} = \frac{4.086 \times 10^{-7}}{8.854 \times 10^{-12} \times 1} = 46.15 \times 10^3 \ \text{V/m}$$

Therefore, the voltage across each dielectric is

$$V_1 = E_1 d_1 = 15.4 \times 10^3 \times 10^{-3} = 15.4 \ \text{V}$$

$$V_2 = E_2 d_2 = 46.15 \times 10^3 \times 4 \times 10^{-3} = 184.6 \ \text{V}$$

EXAMPLE 3.48

Given that two identical air capacitors are connected in series and the combination is maintained at the constant potential difference of 50V. If a dielectric sheet of $\varepsilon_r = 10$ and thickness equal to one-tenth of the air gap is inserted into one of the capacitors, calculate the voltage across this capacitor.

SOLUTION

Initially, the capacitances of two identical air capacitors are

$$C_1 = C_2 = \frac{\varepsilon_0 A}{d}$$

Then, if a dielectric sheet of $\varepsilon_r = 10$ and thickness of $0.1d$ is inserted into the second capacitor, the capacitance of the second capacitor becomes

$$C_{i2} = \frac{\dfrac{\varepsilon_0 A}{0.9d} \times \dfrac{\varepsilon_0 10A}{0.1d}}{\dfrac{\varepsilon_0 A}{0.9d} + \dfrac{\varepsilon_0 10A}{0.1d}} = \frac{1000}{910}\frac{\varepsilon_0 A}{d}$$

When C_1 and C_2 are connected in series, the voltage across capacitor C_{i2} is

$$V_{i2} = \frac{C_1}{C_1 + C_{i2}} \times V = \frac{\dfrac{\varepsilon_0 A}{d}}{\dfrac{\varepsilon_0 A}{d} + \dfrac{1000}{910}\dfrac{\varepsilon_0 A}{d}} \times 50$$

$$= \frac{910}{1910} \times 50 = 23.822 \text{ V}$$

EXAMPLE 3.49

A parallel plate capacitor consists of two plates each 30 cm $\times$ 30 cm spaced 2 mm apart and two dielectrics each 1 mm thick having relative permittivity of 3 and 5. If the potential difference between the plates is 5000V, calculate the voltage gradient in each dielectric.

SOLUTION

Given area, $A = 30$ cm $\times$ 30 cm $= 0.09$ m^2, thickness of dielectric $d_1 = d_2 = 1$ mm $= 10^{-3}$ m, relative permittivity of dielectrics $\varepsilon_{r1} = 3$, $\varepsilon_{r2} = 5$ and $V = 5000$ V.

Therefore, the capacitances are given by

$$C_1 = \frac{\varepsilon_0 \varepsilon_{r1} A}{d_1} = \frac{\varepsilon_0 (3)(0.09)}{1 \times 10^{-3}} = 270\varepsilon_0$$

$$C_2 = \frac{\varepsilon_0 \varepsilon_{r2} A}{d_2} = \frac{\varepsilon_0 (5)(0.09)}{1 \times 10^{-3}} = 450\varepsilon_0$$

Since $Q = C_1 V_1 = C_2 V_2$ and $V_1 + V_2 = V$, the potential across each dielectric is

$$V_1 = \frac{C_2}{C_1 + C_2} V = \frac{450\varepsilon_0}{720\varepsilon_0} \times 5000 = 3125 \text{ V}$$

$$V_2 = \frac{C_1}{C_1 + C_2} V = \frac{270\,\varepsilon_0}{720\,\varepsilon_0} \times 5000 = 1875 \text{ V}$$

The potential gradient of dielectric 1 is $E_1 = \dfrac{V_1}{d_1} = \dfrac{3125}{1 \times 10^{-3}} = 3125 \times 10^3 \text{ V/m}$

The potential gradient of dielectric 2 is $E_2 = \dfrac{V_2}{d_2} = \dfrac{1875}{1 \times 10^{-3}} = 1875 \times 10^3 \text{ V/m}$

EXAMPLE 3.50

Find the capacitance of cylindrical (coaxial) capacitor shown in Figure E3.50. Here, each dielectric occupies one-half the volume with $a = 3$ cm, $b = 12$ cm, $\varepsilon_{r1} = 2.5$ and $\varepsilon_{r2} = 4$. The voltage difference is 50 V.

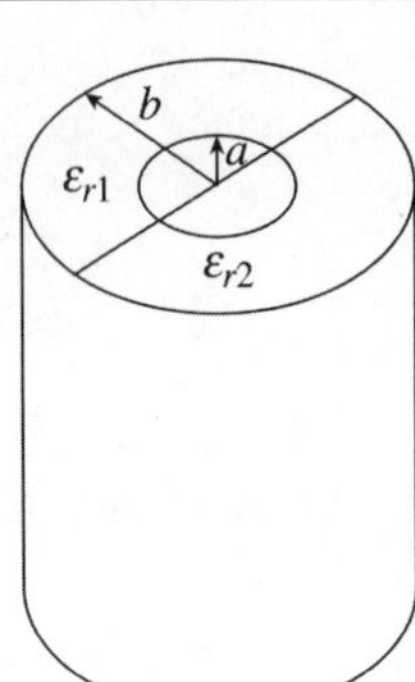

Figure E3.50

SOLUTION

As the dielectric interface is parallel to $\vec{D}$ and $\vec{E}$, the configuration is considered as two capacitors in parallel, as shown in Figure E3.50.

Since each capacitor carries half the charge as that of complete cylinder, the capacitances per unit length are

$$C_1 = \frac{\pi\,\varepsilon_0 \varepsilon_{r1}}{\ln\left(\dfrac{b}{a}\right)} \quad \text{and} \quad C_2 = \frac{\pi\,\varepsilon_0 \varepsilon_{r2}}{\ln\left(\dfrac{b}{a}\right)}$$

Therefore, the net capacitance is

$$C = C_1 + C_2 = \frac{\pi\,\varepsilon_0(\varepsilon_{r1} + \varepsilon_{r2})}{\ln\left(\dfrac{b}{a}\right)}$$

$$= \frac{\pi \times 8.854 \times 10^{-12}(2.5 + 4)}{\ln\left(\dfrac{12}{3}\right)} = 130.642 \text{ pF/m}$$

EXAMPLE 3.51

Referring to Figure E3.51, determine (i) the capacitance per unit length of the cable and (ii) the maximum electric field intensity in each dielectric from the following data: $V_0 = 1.2\text{kV}, \varepsilon_{r1} = 4.5, \varepsilon_{r2} = 3$ and $r_3 = 2r_2 = 4r_1 = 40$ mm.

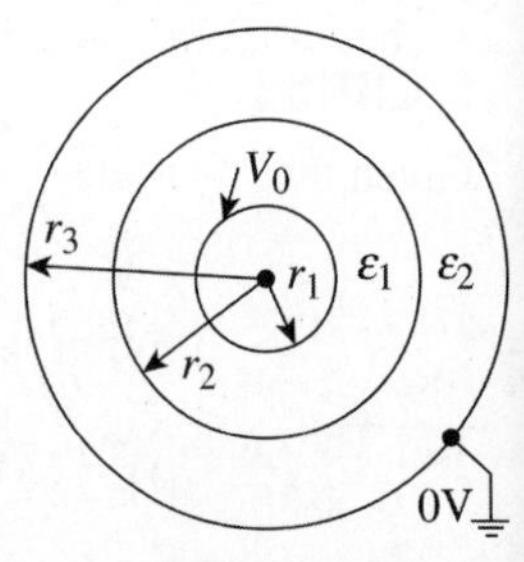

Figure E3.51

SOLUTION

(*i*) The capacitance of the coaxial cable is

$$C_1 = \frac{2\pi\,\varepsilon_1}{\ln\left(\dfrac{r_2}{r_1}\right)} \quad \text{and} \quad C_2 = \frac{2\pi\,\varepsilon_2}{\ln\left(\dfrac{r_3}{r_2}\right)}$$

Since the capacitances are in series, the capacitance per unit length of the cable is

$$C = \frac{C_1 C_2}{C_1 + C_2} = \frac{2\pi \, \varepsilon_1 \varepsilon_2}{\varepsilon_2 \ln\left(\dfrac{r_2}{r_1}\right) + \varepsilon_1 \ln\left(\dfrac{r_3}{r_2}\right)}$$

(*ii*) To find maximum electric field intensity in each dielectric:

$$C_1 = \frac{2\pi \times 8.854 \times 10^{-12} \times 4.5}{\ln 2} = 0.36 \text{ nF/m}$$

and

$$C_2 = \frac{2\pi \times 8.854 \times 10^{-12} \times 3}{\ln 2} = 0.24 \text{ nF/m}$$

Then, $\dfrac{V_2}{V_1} = \dfrac{C_1}{C_2} = \dfrac{0.36}{0.24} = 1.5$ and $V_1 + V_2 = 1200\,\text{V}$

Upon solving, we get $V_1 = 480\text{V}$ and $Q = C_1 V_1 = 0.36 \times 10^{-9} \times 480 = 172.8 \text{ nC/m}$.

Here, $E_{r\,max}$ occurs at the inner surface of each dielectric as given by

$$E_{r\,max} = \frac{\rho_s}{\varepsilon} = \frac{Q}{2\pi \, r\varepsilon}$$

Hence, at $r = r_1$,

$$E_{r\,max} = \frac{172.8 \times 10^{-9}}{2\pi \times 0.01 \times 8.854 \times 10^{-12} \times 4.5} = 69.1 \text{ kV/m}$$

At $r = r_2 = 2r_1$, $E_{r\,max} = \dfrac{172.8 \times 10^{-9}}{2\pi \times 0.02 \times 8.854 \times 10^{-12} \times 3} = 51.8 \text{ kV/m}$

$$V_2 = 720\,\text{V}, \; C_2 = 0.24 \text{ nF/m}, \; Q = C_2 V_2 = 172.8 \text{ nC/m}$$

EXAMPLE 3.52

If two parallel plates of area 4 m^2 are separated by 6 mm, find the capacitance between these two plates. If a rubber sheet of 4 mm thick with $\varepsilon_r = 2.4$ is introduced in between the plates leaving a gap of 1 mm on both sides, determine the capacitance.

SOLUTION

Given that, $A = 4\text{m}^2$ and $d = 6 \times 10^{-3}\,\text{m}$.

(*i*) The capacitance, $C = \dfrac{\varepsilon_0 A}{d} = \dfrac{8.854 \times 10^{-12} \times 4}{6 \times 10^{-3}} = 5.902 \times 10^{-9} \text{ F}$

(*ii*) The capacitance after introducing rubber

$$C = \frac{\varepsilon_0 A}{d_1} + \frac{\varepsilon_0 \varepsilon_r A}{d_2} + \frac{\varepsilon_0 A}{d_3} \;, \text{ where } d_1 = d_3 = 1\text{ mm and } d_2 = 4\text{ mm}$$

$$= \frac{8.854\times10^{-12}\times4}{10^{-3}} + \frac{8.854\times10^{-12}\times2.4\times4}{4\times10^{-3}} + \frac{8.854\times10^{-12}\times4}{10^{-3}}$$

$$= 35.416\times10^{-9} + 21.25\times10^{-9} + 35.416\times10^{-9}$$

$$= 92.082\times10^{-9} \text{ F} = 92.082 \text{ nF}$$

EXAMPLE 3.53

Find the capacitance of a parallel plate capacitor containing two dielectrics, $\varepsilon_{r1} = 1.5$ and $\varepsilon_{r2} = 3.5$, each comprising one half the volume as shown in Figure E3.53 in which $A = 4 \text{ m}^2$ and $d = 10^{-3}$ m.

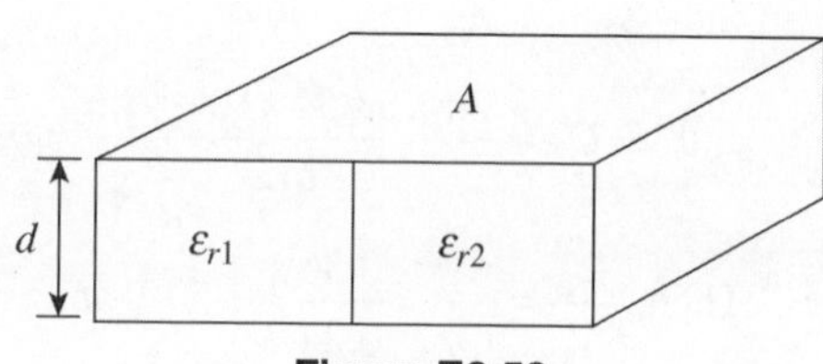

Figure E3.53

SOLUTION

Figure E3.53 shows a parallel plate capacitor with two dielectric materials. Since $\vec{E}$ and $\vec{D}$ are parallel to the dielectric interface, the capacitor can be treated as consisting of two capacitors C_1 and C_2 in parallel.

The capacitance values of these capacitors are given by

$$C_1 = \frac{\varepsilon_0 \varepsilon_{r1} A_1}{d}, \quad \text{where } A_1 = \frac{A}{2}$$

$$= \frac{8.854\times10^{-12}\times1.5\times2}{10^{-3}} = 26.6\times10^{-9} = 26.6 \text{ nF}$$

and

$$C_2 = \frac{\varepsilon_0 \varepsilon_{r2} A_2}{d}, \quad \text{where } A_2 = \frac{A}{2}$$

$$= \frac{8.854\times10^{-12}\times3.5\times2}{10^{-3}} = 61.9\times10^{-9} = 61.9 \text{ nF}$$

Since the two capacitors are in parallel, the equivalent capacitance is

$$C_{eq} = C_1 + C_2 = (26.6 + 61.9)\times10^{-9} = 88.5 \text{ nF}$$

EXAMPLE 3.54

Find the capacitance of a parallel plate capacitor containing two dielectrics, $\varepsilon_{r1} = 1.5$ and $\varepsilon_{r2} = 3.5$, each occupying one half of the space between the plates but the interface is parallel to the plates, as shown in Figure E3.54, in which $A = 4 \text{ m}^2$ and $d = 10^{-3}$ m.

SOLUTION

Figure E3.54 shows a parallel plate capacitor with two dielectric materials. Since $\vec{E}$ and $\vec{D}$ are normal to the dielectric interface, the capacitor can be treated as consisting of two capacitors C_1 and C_2 in series.

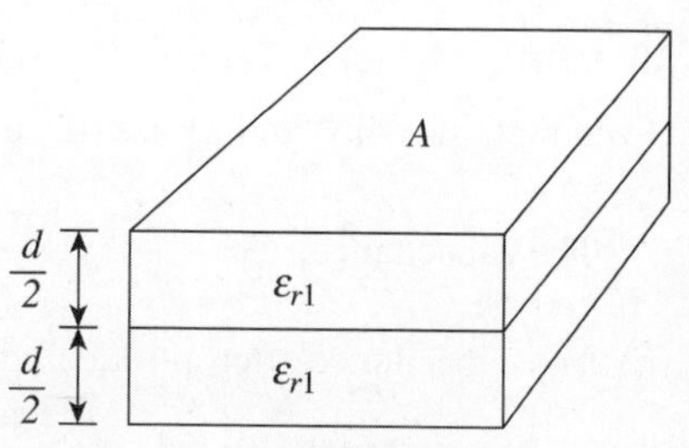

Figure E3.54

The capacitance values of these capacitors are given by

$$C_1 = \frac{\varepsilon_0 \varepsilon_{r1} A}{d_1} = \frac{\varepsilon_0 \varepsilon_{r1} A}{d/2}$$

$$= \frac{8.854 \times 10^{-12} \times 1.5 \times 4}{10^{-3}/2} = 106.2 \text{ nF}$$

and

$$C_2 = \frac{\varepsilon_0 \varepsilon_{r2} A}{d_2} = \frac{\varepsilon_0 \varepsilon_{r2} A}{d/2}$$

$$= \frac{8.854 \times 10^{-12} \times 3.5 \times 4}{10^{-3}/2} = 247.9 \text{ nF}$$

Since the two capacitors are in series, the equivalent capacitance is

$$C_{eq} = \frac{C_1 C_2}{C_1 + C_2} = \frac{\left(106.2 \times 10^{-9}\right) \times \left(247.9 \times 10^{-9}\right)}{106.2 \times 10^{-9} + 247.9 \times 10^{-9}} = 74.35 \text{ nF}$$

EXAMPLE 3.55

A capacitor with two dielectric materials is as follows: Plate area = 100 cm^2, Dielectric 1 thickness = 3 mm, $\varepsilon_{r1} = 3$, Dielectric 2 thickness = 2 mm, $\varepsilon_{r2} = 2$. If a potential of 100 V is applied across the plates, find the energy stored in each dielectric and potential gradient in each dielectric.

SOLUTION

Figure E3.55 shows a capacitor with two dielectric materials. Since $\vec{E}$ and $\vec{D}$ are normal to the dielectric interface, the capacitor can be treated as consisting of two capacitors C_1 and C_2 in series.

The capacitance values of these capacitors are

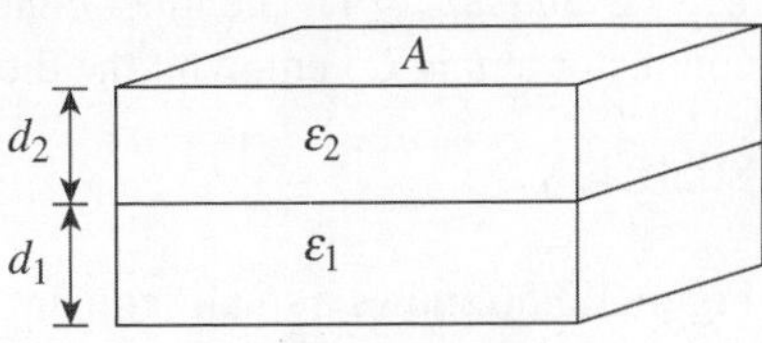

Figure E3.55

$$C_1 = \frac{\varepsilon_1 A}{d_1} = \frac{\varepsilon_0 \varepsilon_{r1} A}{d_1}$$

$$= \frac{8.854 \times 10^{-12} \times 3 \times 100 \times 10^{-4}}{3 \times 10^{-3}} = 88.54 \times 10^{-12} \text{ F}$$

$$C_2 = \frac{\varepsilon_2 A}{d_2} = \frac{\varepsilon_0 \varepsilon_{r2} A}{d_2}$$

$$= \frac{8.854 \times 10^{-12} \times 2 \times 100 \times 10^{-4}}{2 \times 10^{-3}} = 88.54 \times 10^{-12} \text{ F}$$

The total capacitance is

$$C = \frac{C_1 C_2}{C_1 + C_2} = 44.27 \times 10^{-12} \text{ F}$$

We know that, $C = \dfrac{Q}{V}$

Therefore, $Q = CV = 44.27 \times 10^{-12} \times 100 = 4.427 \times 10^{-9} = 4.427\,\text{nC}$

The charge Q remains same for both C_1 and C_2, Using C_1 and Q, the potential in dielectric 1 is

$$V_1 = \frac{Q}{C_1} = \frac{4.427 \times 10^{-9}}{88.54 \times 10^{-12}} = 50\,\text{V}$$

Similarly, the potential in dielectric 2 is

$$V_2 = \frac{Q}{C_2} = \frac{4.427 \times 10^{-9}}{88.54 \times 10^{-12}} = 50\,\text{V}$$

Hence, the energy stored in each dielectric is

$$W_{e1} = W_{e2} = \frac{1}{2}C_1 V_1^2 = \frac{1}{2}C_2 V_2^2 = 0.1106\,\mu\text{J}$$

Therefore, the potential gradients are given by

$$E_1 = \frac{V_1}{d_1} = \frac{50}{3 \times 10^{-3}} = 16.667\,\text{kV/m}$$

and

$$E_2 = \frac{V_2}{d_2} = \frac{50}{2 \times 10^{-3}} = 25\,\text{kV/m}$$

EXAMPLE 3.56

Calculate the voltage across each dielectric in Figure E3.56, where $\varepsilon_{r1} = 2$ and $\varepsilon_{r2} = 4$. The inner conductor is at $a = 2$ cm and the outer conductor at $b = 2.5$ cm, with the dielectric interface halfway between.

SOLUTION

Figure E3.56 shows a small segment with angle θ and its capacitance is $\dfrac{\theta}{2\pi}$ times that of complete coaxial capacitor.

Therefore, $C_1 = \left(\dfrac{\theta}{2\pi}\right)\dfrac{2\pi\,\varepsilon_0 \varepsilon_{r1} l}{\ln\left(\dfrac{2.25}{2}\right)}$

$$= \left(\frac{\theta}{2\pi}\right)\frac{2\pi \times 8.854 \times 10^{-12} \times 2 \times l}{\ln\left(\dfrac{2.25}{2}\right)}$$

$$= \theta\, l\,(1.5 \times 10^{-10})$$

$$C_2 = \left(\frac{\theta}{2\pi}\right)\frac{2\pi\,\varepsilon_0 \varepsilon_{r2} l}{\ln\left(\dfrac{2.5}{2.25}\right)} = \left(\frac{\theta}{2\pi}\right)\frac{2\pi \times 8.854 \times 10^{-12} \times 4 \times l}{\ln\left(\dfrac{2.5}{2.25}\right)}$$

$$= \theta\, l\,(3.36 \times 10^{-10})$$

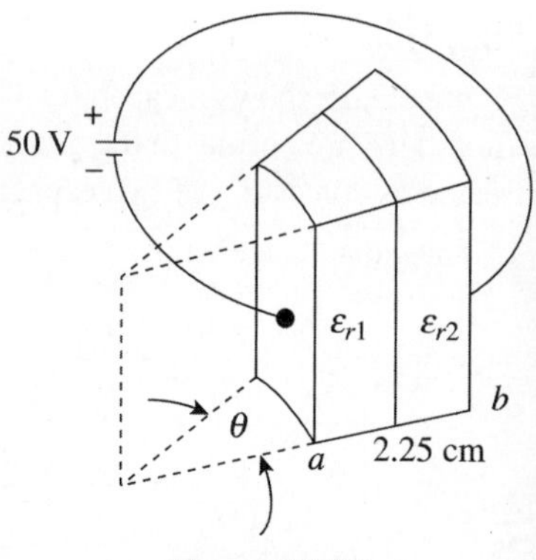

Figure E3.56

We know that,

$$Q = C_1 V_1 = C_2 V_2 \quad \text{and} \quad V_1 + V_2 = V = 50$$

The voltage across each dielectric is

$$V_1 = \frac{C_2}{C_1 + C_2} \times V = \frac{3.36}{1.5 + 3.36}(50) = 34.56 \text{ V}$$

$$V_2 = \frac{C_1}{C_1 + C_2} \times V = \frac{1.5}{1.5 + 3.36}(50) = 15.43 \text{ V}$$

EXAMPLE 3.57

Find the capacitance of a conductor sphere of 2 cm in diameter, covered with a layer of polyethylene with $\varepsilon_r = 2.26$ and 3 cm thick.

SOLUTION

Figure E3.57 shows a sphere of diameter 2 cm (radius $a = 1$ cm) covered with a layer of polyethylene having thickness $t = 3$ cm. The distance from the center to the outer surface is given by $r_1 = a + t = 1 + 3 = 4$. This forms two capacitors in series.

The capacitance due to spherical arrangement of concentric spheres is

$$C_1 = \frac{4\pi\varepsilon}{\left(\dfrac{1}{a} - \dfrac{1}{b}\right)} = \frac{4\pi\varepsilon\, ab}{b - a} \quad \text{where } a = 1 \text{ cm and } b = r_1 = 4 \text{ cm}$$

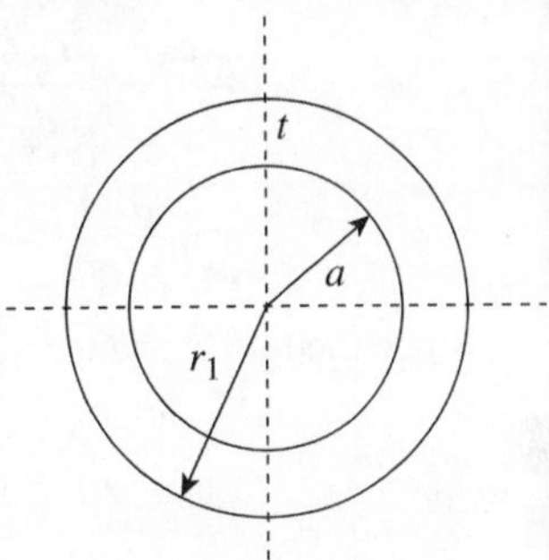

Figure E3.57

Therefore,

$$C_1 = \frac{4\pi\varepsilon_0\varepsilon_r\, ab}{b - a} = \frac{4\pi \times 8.854 \times 10^{-12} \times 2.26 \times 1 \times 4}{(4-1)\times 10^{-2}} = 3.35 \times 10^{-12} \text{ F}$$

The capacitance due to isolated sphere of $r_1 = 4$ cm is

$$C_2 = 4\pi\varepsilon\, r_1$$

The dielectric is free space having permittivity ε_0 between the sphere of radius r_1 and the sphere at infinity. Therefore,

$$C_2 = 4\pi\varepsilon_0 r_1 = 4\pi \times 8.854 \times 10^{-12} \times 4 \times 10^{-2} = 4.45 \times 10^{-12} \text{ F}$$

Since the two capacitors are in series, the equivalent capacitance is

$$C_{eq} = \frac{1}{\dfrac{1}{C_1} + \dfrac{1}{C_2}} = \frac{C_1 C_2}{C_1 + C_2}$$

$$= \frac{3.35 \times 10^{-12} \times 4.45 \times 10^{-12}}{10^{-12}(3.35 + 4.45)} = 1.91 \times 10^{-12} = 1.91 \text{ pF}$$

EXAMPLE 3.58

Determine the voltage across each dielectric in the capacitor shown in Figure E3.58 when the applied voltage is 200 V.

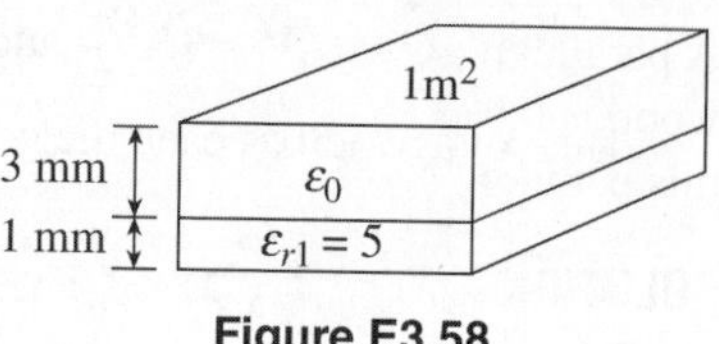

Figure E3.58

SOLUTION

As shown in Figure E3.58, the arrangement of dielectrics forms two capacitors connected in series. For first dielectric, $\varepsilon_{r1} = 5$, $d_1 = 1 \times 10^{-3}$ m and $A = 1$ m². Therefore, the capacitance due to first dielectric is

$$C_1 = \frac{\varepsilon_1 A}{d_1} = \frac{\varepsilon_0 \varepsilon_{r1} A}{d_1}$$

$$= \frac{\varepsilon_0 \times 5 \times 1}{10^{-3}} = 5000\,\varepsilon_0$$

Since the second dielectric is made of air, its permittivity is ε_0 and the capacitance due to second dielectric is

$$C_2 = \frac{\varepsilon_2 A}{d_2} = \frac{\varepsilon_0 A}{d_2} \quad \text{where } A = 1 \text{ m}^2 \text{ and } d_2 = 3 \times 10^{-3} \text{ m}$$

$$= \frac{\varepsilon_0 \times 1}{3 \times 10^{-3}} = \frac{1000\,\varepsilon_0}{3}$$

Since the two capacitors are in series, the equivalent capacitance is

$$C_{eq} = \frac{C_1 C_2}{C_1 + C_2} = \frac{(5000\,\varepsilon_0) \times \left(\dfrac{1000\,\varepsilon_0}{3}\right)}{5000\,\varepsilon_0 + \dfrac{1000\,\varepsilon_0}{3}}$$

$$= \frac{5 \times 10^6 \times 8.854 \times 10^{-12}}{16000} = 2.77 \times 10^{-9} = 2.77\,\text{nF}$$

At the dielectric conductor boundary, the normal component of flux density $\vec{D}$ must be equal to the surface charge density as given by

$$D_n = \rho_s = \frac{Q}{A} = \frac{CV}{A} = \frac{2.77 \times 10^{-9} \times 200}{1} = 5.54 \times 10^{-7} \text{ C/m}^2$$

The electric fields in the two capacitors are

$$E_1 = \frac{D}{\varepsilon_0 \varepsilon_{r1}} = \frac{5.54 \times 10^{-7}}{8.854 \times 10^{-12} \times 5} = 1.25 \times 10^4 \text{ V/m}$$

and

$$E_2 = \frac{D}{\varepsilon_0} = \frac{5.54 \times 10^{-7}}{8.854 \times 10^{-12}} = 6.25 \times 10^4 \text{ V/m}$$

The voltage across each dielectric in the capacitor is

$$V_1 = E_1 d_1 = 1.25 \times 10^4 \times 10^{-3} = 12.5 \text{ V}$$

and

$$V_2 = E_2 d_2 = 6.25 \times 10^4 \times 3 \times 10^{-3} = 187.5 \text{ V}$$

EXAMPLE 3.59

A parallel plate capacitor has an area $1\ m^2$ with the distance between the plate is 0.01 m and thickness of the wood is 0.002 m. The relative dielectric constant of wood is 6 times that of air. Calculate the capacitance of this parallel plate capacitor.

SOLUTION

Figure E3.59 shows dielectric 1 filled with air and dielectric 2 filled with wood.

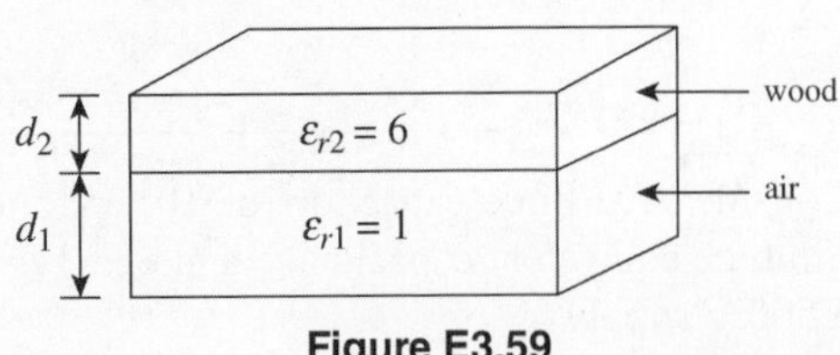

Figure E3.59

Given that, the area of parallel plate, $A = 1\,m^2$, distance between the plate $d = 0.01\,m$, thickness of the wood, $d_2 = 0.002\,m$ and $\varepsilon_{r2} = 6$.

Therefore, $d = d_1 + d_2 = 0.01$

$$d_1 = 0.01 - 0.002 = 0.008 \text{ m}$$

We know that,

$$C_1 = \frac{\varepsilon_1 A}{d_1} \text{ and } C_2 = \frac{\varepsilon_2 A}{d_2}$$

The arrangement of dielectrics parallel to plates as shown in Figure E3.59 is equivalent to two capacitors in series.

Therefore,
$$C_1 = \frac{\varepsilon_0 \varepsilon_{r1} A}{d_1} = \frac{8.854 \times 10^{-12} \times 1 \times 1}{0.008} = 1.11\,nF$$

and
$$C_2 = \frac{\varepsilon_0 \varepsilon_{r2} A}{d_2} = \frac{8.854 \times 10^{-12} \times 6 \times 1}{0.002} = 26.56\,nF$$

Therefore, for two capacitors in series, the equivalent capacitance is

$$C_{eq} = \frac{C_1 C_2}{C_1 + C_2} = \frac{1.11 \times 10^{-9} \times 26.56 \times 10^{-9}}{1.11 \times 10^{-9} + 26.56 \times 10^{-9}}$$

$$= 1.06 \times 10^{-9}\,F = 1.06\ nF$$

EXAMPLE 3.60

Consider that two capacitors of $10\,\mu F$ and $25\,\mu F$ are connected in (i) series and (ii) parallel. Find the equivalent value of capacitance in each case.

SOLUTION

Given $C_1 = 10\,\mu F$ and $C_2 = 25\,\mu F$.

(*i*) When two capacitors are connected in series, the equivalent capacitance C becomes

$$\frac{1}{C} = \frac{1}{C_1} + \frac{1}{C_2}$$

Therefore, $\quad C = \dfrac{C_1 C_2}{C_1 + C_2} = \dfrac{10 \times 25}{10 + 25} = \dfrac{250}{35}\mu F = 7.142\,\mu F$

(*ii*) When two capacitors are connected in parallel, the equivalent capacitance C becomes

$$C = C_1 + C_2$$
$$= 10\mu F + 25\mu F = 35\mu F$$

EXAMPLE 3.61

Consider that three capacitors of 10, 25, and 50 microfarads are connected in (*i*) series and (*ii*) parallel. Find the equivalent capacitance and energy stored in each case, when the combination is connected across a 500 V supply.

SOLUTION

Given $C_1 = 10\,\mu F$, $C_2 = 25\,\mu F$ and $C_3 = 50\,\mu F$ and applied potential, $V = 500$ V.

(*i*) When three capacitors are connected in series, the equivalent capacitance C_s becomes

$$\frac{1}{C_s} = \frac{1}{C_1} + \frac{1}{C_2} + \frac{1}{C_3}$$

$$= \left(\frac{1}{10} + \frac{1}{25} + \frac{1}{50} \right) \times \frac{1}{10^{-6}}$$

Therefore, $\qquad C_s = 6.25\mu F$

The energy stored, $\qquad W_e = \dfrac{1}{2} C_s V^2$

$$= \frac{1}{2} \times 6.25 \times 10^{-6} \times (500)^2 = 0.781\,\text{J}$$

(*ii*) When three capacitors are connected in parallel, the equivalent capacitance C_p becomes

$$C_p = C_1 + C_2 + C_3 = (10 + 25 + 50)\mu F = 85\mu F$$

Hence, the energy stored, $W_e = \dfrac{1}{2} C_p V^2 = \dfrac{1}{2} \times 85 \times 10^{-6} \times (500)^2 = 10.625$ J

EXAMPLE 3.62

A 4 mF capacitor is charged by connecting it across 100 V dc. The supply is disconnected and another uncharged 2 mF capacitor is connected across it. If leakage charge is negligible, determine the potential between the plates.

SOLUTION

The arrangement of two capacitors in parallel is shown in the Figure E3.62.

Initially when C_1 is charged to 100 V dc, the energy stored is

$$E = \frac{1}{2} C_1 V^2 = \frac{1}{2} \times 4 \times 10^{-3} \times 100^2 = 20\,\text{J}$$

If voltage across the two plates is same as V_{eq}, then the energy must remain same. So, the total energy in the new arrangement is

$$E = \frac{1}{2}C_1 V_{eq}^2 + \frac{1}{2}C_2 V_{eq}^2$$

$$20 = \frac{1}{2} \times 4 \times 10^{-3} \times V_{eq}^2 + \frac{1}{2} \times 2 \times 10^{-3} \times V_{eq}^2 = 3 \times 10^{-3} V_{eq}^2$$

That is $V_{eq}^2 = 6666.67$

Hence, $V_{eq} = 81.65\,\text{V}$

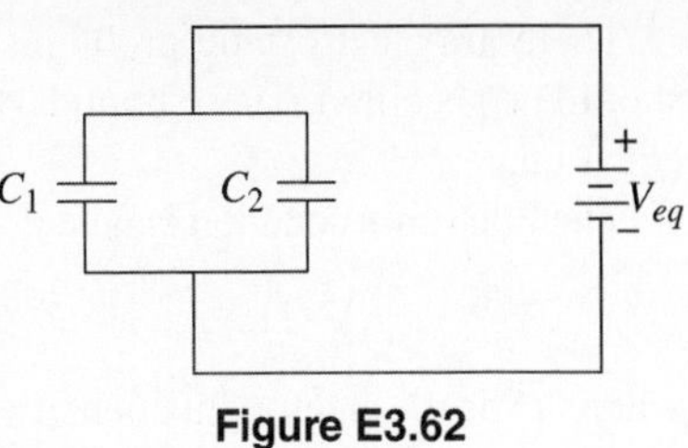

Figure E3.62

EXAMPLE 3.63

Determine the capacitance of a sphere having two dielectric layers, which has the dielectric material $\varepsilon = \varepsilon_1$ from $r = a$ to $r = r_1$ and $\varepsilon = \varepsilon_0$ from $r = r_1$ to $r = \infty$.

SOLUTION

The electric flux density is $D_r = \dfrac{Q}{4\pi r^2}$

The electric field density is $E_r = \dfrac{Q}{4\pi \varepsilon_1 r^2} \qquad (a < r < r_1)$

$$E_r = \frac{Q}{4\pi \varepsilon_0 r^2} \qquad (r_1 < r < \infty)$$

Hence, the potential difference of the sphere,

$$V_a - V_\infty = -\int_{r_1}^{a} \frac{Q\,dr}{4\pi\,\varepsilon_1\,r^2} - \int_{\infty}^{r_1} \frac{Q\,dr}{4\pi\,\varepsilon_0\,r^2}$$

$$= \frac{Q\,dr}{4\pi\,\varepsilon_0\,r^2}\left[\frac{1}{\varepsilon_1}\left(\frac{1}{a} - \frac{1}{r_1}\right) + \frac{1}{\varepsilon_0 r_1}\right]$$

Therefore, the capacitance, $\displaystyle C = \frac{Q}{V} = \frac{4\pi}{\left[\dfrac{1}{\varepsilon_1}\left(\dfrac{1}{a} - \dfrac{1}{r_1}\right) + \dfrac{1}{\varepsilon_0 r_1}\right]}$

3.10   POISSON'S AND LAPLACE'S EQUATIONS

When the charge distribution is known, the electric field intensity $\vec{E}$ and flux density $\vec{D}$ can be determined by using either Coulomb's law or Gauss's law. When the potential distribution is known, the field can be determined by using the relationship $\vec{E} = -\nabla V$. However, in practical cases, both charge distribution and potential distribution are unknown.

There are electrostatic problems that involve boundary surfaces on which either the charge or potential should be specified. These boundary value problems can be solved by using Poisson's equation or Laplace's equation.

The Poisson's equation can be derived from the differential or point form of Gauss's law, as represented by

$$\nabla \cdot \vec{D} = \rho_v$$

where $\vec{D}$ is the electric flux density and ρ_v is the volume charge density. It is known that for a homogeneous, isotropic and linear medium, electric flux density $\vec{D}$ and electric field intensity $\vec{E}$ are directly proportional. Therefore,

$$\vec{D} = \varepsilon \vec{E}$$

Hence, $\nabla \cdot (\varepsilon \vec{E}) = \rho_v$

$$\nabla \cdot \vec{E} = \frac{\rho_v}{\varepsilon} \tag{3.53}$$

Substituting $\vec{E} = -\nabla V$ in the above equation, we obtain

$$\nabla \cdot (-\nabla V) = \frac{\rho_v}{\varepsilon} \tag{3.54}$$

The above equation can be written in simplified form as

$$\nabla^2 V = -\frac{\rho_v}{\varepsilon} \tag{3.55}$$

The above equation is known as *Poisson's equation*, which states that the potential distribution in a region depends on the charge distribution in that region. It is applicable in homogeneous medium where ε is constant.

In conductors, the charge distribution exists only on the surface of the conductors. Hence, the free volume charge density is zero, i.e., $\rho_v = 0$ in the region of interest. Therefore, Eq. (3.55) becomes

$$\nabla^2 V = 0 \tag{3.56}$$

which is generally called *Laplace's equation*. The potential function in a charge-free region can be obtained using Laplace's equation subjected to the boundary conditions. The Laplacian operator is denoted by ∇^2.

The solution of Laplace's equation should satisfy the boundary conditions. The Poisson's equation and Laplace's equation are useful in determining the electrostatic potential and field in regions with the known boundary conditions.

3.10.1 Laplacian Equation in Different Coordinate Systems

The potential V can be expressed in any of the three coordinate systems as $V(x,y,z)$, $V(\rho,\phi,z)$ or $V(r,\theta,\phi)$. Depending upon coordinate system, the ∇^2 operator must be used for Laplace's equation.

In Cartesian coordinate system,

$$\nabla V = \frac{\partial V}{\partial x} \vec{a}_x + \frac{\partial V}{\partial y} \vec{a}_y + \frac{\partial V}{\partial z} \vec{a}_z$$

Therefore, $$\nabla \cdot \nabla V = \frac{\partial}{\partial x}\left(\frac{\partial V}{\partial x}\right) + \frac{\partial}{\partial y}\left(\frac{\partial V}{\partial y}\right) + \frac{\partial}{\partial z}\left(\frac{\partial V}{\partial z}\right)$$

where
$$\nabla = \vec{a}_x \frac{\partial}{\partial x} + \vec{a}_y \frac{\partial}{\partial y} + \vec{a}_z \frac{\partial}{\partial z}.$$

Hence,
$$\nabla^2 V = \frac{\partial^2 V}{\partial x^2} + \frac{\partial^2 V}{\partial y^2} + \frac{\partial^2 V}{\partial z^2} = 0 \tag{3.57}$$

The above equation is called Laplace's equation in the form of Cartesian coordinates.
In cylindrical coordinate system,

$$\nabla V = \frac{\partial V}{\partial \rho}\vec{a}_\rho + \frac{1}{\rho}\frac{\partial V}{\partial \phi}\vec{a}_\phi + \frac{\partial V}{\partial z}\vec{a}_z$$

Therefore, the Laplace's equation is

$$\nabla^2 V = \frac{1}{\rho}\frac{\partial}{\partial \rho}\left(\rho\frac{\partial V}{\partial \rho}\right) + \frac{1}{\rho^2}\left(\frac{\partial^2 V}{\partial \phi^2}\right) + \frac{\partial^2 V}{\partial z^2} = 0 \tag{3.58}$$

In spherical coordinate system,

$$\nabla V = \frac{\partial V}{\partial r}\vec{a}_r + \frac{1}{r}\frac{\partial V}{\partial \theta}\vec{a}_\theta + \frac{1}{r\sin\theta}\frac{\partial V}{\partial \phi}\vec{a}_\phi$$

Therefore, the Laplace's equation is

$$\nabla^2 V = \frac{1}{r^2}\frac{\partial}{\partial r}\left(r^2\frac{\partial V}{\partial r}\right) + \frac{1}{r^2\sin\theta}\frac{\partial}{\partial \theta}\left(\sin\theta\frac{\partial V}{\partial \theta}\right) + \frac{1}{r^2\sin^2\theta}\frac{\partial^2 V}{\partial \phi^2} = 0 \tag{3.59}$$

3.10.2 Uniqueness Theorem

The uniqueness theorem states that the Laplace's equation has only one solution, irrespective of the method adopted. Therefore, any solution of Laplace's equation, which satisfies the boundary conditions must be the only solution. The uniqueness theorem can be applied to any solution of Poisson's or Laplace's equation in a given region.

Proof

Assume that the Laplace's equation has two solutions, V_1 and V_2, at the boundary. Then, the Laplace equations are $\nabla^2 V_1 = 0$ and $\nabla^2 V_2 = 0$. At the boundary on the equipotential surface, the potentials at different points are equal, i.e., $V_1 = V_2$. If there exists a potential difference between V_1 and V_2, then $V_d = V_1 - V_2$.

Using Laplace's equation for potential difference V_d, we have

$$\nabla^2 V_d = \nabla^2\left(V_1 - V_2\right) = 0$$

where $V_d = 0$ on the boundary.

Consider the vector identity

$$\nabla\cdot\left(\alpha\vec{A}\right) = \alpha\left(\nabla\cdot\vec{A}\right) + \vec{A}\cdot\left(\nabla\alpha\right)$$

For any vector $\vec{A}$ and constant α, let $\alpha = V_1 - V_2$ and $\vec{A} = \nabla\left(V_1 - V_2\right)$.

Then,
$$\nabla\cdot\left[\left(V_1 - V_2\right)\nabla\left(V_1 - V_2\right)\right] = \left(V_1 - V_2\right)\left(\nabla\cdot\nabla\left(V_1 - V_2\right)\right) + \nabla\left(V_1 - V_2\right)\cdot\nabla\left(V_1 - V_2\right)$$

or
$$\nabla\cdot\left(V_d\nabla V_d\right) = V_d\nabla^2 V_d + \nabla V_d\cdot\nabla V_d$$

Taking volume integration on both sides, we get

$$\int_v \nabla \cdot \left(V_d \nabla V_d\right) dv = \int_v \left(V_d \nabla^2 V_d\right) dv + \int_v \left(\nabla V_d \cdot \nabla V_d\right) dv$$

Applying divergence theorem to any vector $\vec{B}$, we have

$$\int_v \left(\nabla \cdot \vec{B}\right) dv = \oint_s \vec{B} \cdot d\vec{s}$$

If $\vec{B} = V_d \nabla V_d$, then $\int_s \left(V_d \nabla V_d\right) \cdot d\vec{s} = \int_v \left(V_d \nabla^2 V_d\right) dv + \int_v \left(\nabla V_d \cdot \nabla V_d\right) dv$

But $\nabla^2 V_d = 0$ at the boundary. Hence,

$$\int_s \left(V_d \nabla V_d\right) \cdot d\vec{s} = \int_v \left(\nabla V_d \cdot \nabla V_d\right) dv$$

Since V_d is also zero at the boundary,

$$\int_v \left(\nabla V_d \cdot \nabla V_d\right) dv = 0$$

We know that, $\nabla V_d \cdot \nabla V_d = \left|\nabla V_d\right|^2$

Therefore, $\int_v \left|\nabla V_d\right|^2 dv = 0$
That is,

$$\int_v \left|\nabla\left(V_1 - V_2\right)\right|^2 dv = 0$$

The above integral equation is possible if the quantity in the integration is either zero or has equal and opposite regions. Since the integration is always positive, we have

$$\left|\nabla\left(V_1 - V_2\right)\right|^2 = 0$$

$$\nabla\left(V_1 - V_2\right) = 0$$

Therefore,

$$\nabla V_d = 0$$

or

$$V_d = V_1 - V_2 = 0$$

Hence, $V_d = 0$ or $V_1 = V_2$ everywhere, shows that V_1 and V_2 cannot have different solutions to the same problem. If a solution to Laplace's equation satisfies the boundary conditions, then the solution is unique.

3.10.3   General Procedure for Solving Poisson's or Laplace's Equation

The general procedure for solving any boundary value problem involving Poisson's or Laplace's equation is given below:

(*i*) Solve Poisson's equation (if $\rho_v \neq 0$) or Laplace's equation (if $\rho_v = 0$) to determine V using the direct method of integration or separation of variables method. The solution obtained is not unique due to presence of unknown constants of integration which are to be determined.

(*ii*) Determine the constants of integration by applying the given boundary conditions. The solution for V obtained in step (i) with constants determined using boundary conditions forms a unique solution.

(*iii*) The electric field intensity $\vec{E}$ can then be obtained from the potential V, using $\vec{E} = -\nabla V$.

(*iv*) For homogeneous medium, $\vec{D}$ can be obtained from $\vec{D} = \varepsilon \vec{E}$.

(*v*) At the conductor surface, the normal component of $\vec{D}$ is equal to the surface charge density ρ_s, i.e., $D_n = \rho_s$. Hence, the charge induced Q on the conductor surface can be found from $Q = \int_s \rho_s ds$.

(*vi*) By knowing the potential V and the charge Q, the capacitance C between two conductors can be obtained by $C = \dfrac{Q}{V}$.

3.10.4 Applications of Poisson's and Laplace's Equations

Both Poisson's and Laplace's equations are used to solve electrostatic problems by applying boundary conditions. Poisson's equation can be applied in a region where the charge density is specified.

If the medium is a charge free, i.e., $\rho_v = 0$, then Laplace's equation can be applied to solve the electrostatic boundary problems. Laplace's equation is mainly used to determine the electric potential and field in parallel plate capacitor, coaxial cable, and spherical conductor.

EXAMPLE 3.64

If $V = 2$ V at $x = 1$ mm and $V = 0$ at $x = 0$ and volume charge density ρ_v is $-10^6 \varepsilon_0$ C/m^3 constant throughout the region between $x = 0$ to $x = 1$ mm, calculate V at $x = 0.5$ mm and E_x at $x = 1$ mm in free space.

SOLUTION

As ρ_v is not zero, Poisson's equation can be used to solve this problem to find V.

For Poisson's equation, $\nabla^2 V = -\dfrac{\rho_v}{\varepsilon}$

$$\text{Therefore,} \qquad \nabla^2 V = \frac{-\left(-10^6 \varepsilon_0\right)}{\varepsilon_0} = 10^6 \qquad (1)$$

where $\varepsilon = \varepsilon_0$ in free space. The given potential V is the function of x only. Therefore, Eq. (1) in rectangular coordinates is

$$\nabla^2 V = \frac{\partial^2 V}{\partial x^2} = 10^6 \qquad (2)$$

Integrating the above equation, we get

$$\frac{\partial V}{\partial x} = \int 10^6 dx + c_1 = 10^6 x + c_1$$

Integrating once again, we obtain

$$V = \int \left(10^6 x + c_1\right) dx + c_2$$

$$= \frac{10^6 x^2}{2} + c_1 x + c_2 \qquad (3)$$

Using the given boundary conditions,

at $x = 0$, $V = 0$ i.e., $c_2 = 0$

at $x = 1\text{ mm} = 10^{-3}\text{ m}$, $V = 2\text{ V}$

$$2 = \frac{10^6}{2}\left(10^{-3}\right)^2 + c_1\left(10^{-3}\right)$$

Therefore, $c_1 = 1500$

Substituting the constant values c_1 and c_2 in Eq. (3), we get

$$V = 0.5\times10^6 x^2 + 1500x$$

At $x = 0.5\text{ mm} = 0.5\times10^{-3}\text{ m}$, the potential is

$$V = 0.5\times10^6\left(0.5\times10^{-3}\right)^2 + 1500\times\left(0.5\times10^{-3}\right) = 0.875 \text{ volt}$$

From V, the electric field intensity can be obtained using the relation $\vec{E} = -\nabla V$ and it is written in rectangular coordinates as

$$\vec{E} = -\nabla V = -\frac{\partial V}{\partial x}\vec{a}_x$$

$$= -\frac{\partial}{\partial x}\left(0.5\times10^6 x^2 + 1500\,x\right)\vec{a}_x = \left(-1\times10^6 x - 1500\right)\vec{a}_x$$

Hence, $\qquad E_x = -10^6 x - 1500 \text{ V/m}$

Therefore, at $x = 1\text{ mm} = 1\times10^{-3}\text{ m}$, the electric field intensity along x-direction is

$$E_x = -10^6\times1\times10^{-3} - 1500 = -2500 \text{ V/m} \qquad\qquad \square$$

EXAMPLE 3.65

Given the volume charge density $\rho_v = -2\times10^7\,\varepsilon_0\sqrt{x}\text{ C/m}^3$ in free space. Assume $V = 0$ at $x = 0$ and $V = 2\text{ volt}$ at $x = 2.5\text{ mm}$. Find V at $x = 1\text{ mm}$.

SOLUTION

As $\rho_v \neq 0$, we can use Poisson's equation as given by

$$\nabla^2 V = -\frac{\rho_v}{\varepsilon} = -\frac{\left(-2\times10^7\,\varepsilon_0\sqrt{x}\right)}{\varepsilon_0} = 2\times10^7\sqrt{x} \tag{1}$$

where $\varepsilon = \varepsilon_0$ in free space. The given potential V is the function of x only. Therefore, Eq. (1) in rectangular coordinates is

$$\nabla^2 V = \frac{\partial^2 V}{\partial x^2} = 2\times10^7 x^{1/2}$$

Integrating, we get

$$\frac{\partial V}{\partial x} = \frac{2\times10^7 x^{3/2}}{3/2} + c_1 = 13.33\times10^6 x^{3/2} + c_1$$

Integrating once again, we obtain

$$V = \int \left(13.33 \times 10^6 \, x^{3/2} + c_1 \right) dx + c_2$$

$$= \frac{\left(13.33 \times 10^6 \, x^{5/2} \right)}{5/2} + c_1 x + c_2$$

Therefore, $V = 5.33 \times 10^6 \, x^{5/2} + c_1 x + c_2$ (2)

Using the given boundary conditions,

at $x = 0, V = 0,$ i.e., $c_2 = 0$

at $x = 2.5 \, \text{mm}, V = 2$ volt

$$2 = 5.33 \times 10^6 \left(2.5 \times 10^{-3} \right)^{5/2} + c_1 \left(2.5 \times 10^{-3} \right)$$

Therefore, $c_1 = 133.75$

Substituting the values of c_1 and c_2 in Eq. (2), we get

$$V = 5.33 \times 10^6 \, x^{5/2} + 133.75 \, x$$

At $x = 1 \, \text{mm} = 10^{-3} \, \text{m},$ the potential is

$$V = 5.33 \times 10^6 \left(1 \times 10^{-3} \right)^{5/2} + 133.75 \left(1 \times 10^{-3} \right) = 0.302 \text{ V}$$

EXAMPLE 3.66

The region between two concentric right circular cylinders with radius r contains a uniform charge density ρ_v. Use Poisson's equation to find V.

SOLUTION

For Poisson's equation, $\nabla^2 V = \dfrac{-\rho_v}{\varepsilon}$.

Since r is the radius of the given cylinder, the coordinate ρ in cylindrical system can be replaced by r. Therefore, the Poisson's equation in cylindrical coordinates can be written as

$$\frac{1}{r} \frac{\partial}{\partial r} \left(r \frac{\partial V}{\partial r} \right) + \frac{1}{r^2} \left(\frac{\partial^2 V}{\partial \phi^2} \right) + \frac{\partial^2 V}{\partial z^2} = \frac{-\rho_v}{\varepsilon}$$

Since the region is a function of r alone, Poisson's equation reduces to

$$\frac{1}{r} \frac{\partial}{\partial r} \left(r \frac{\partial V}{\partial r} \right) = \frac{-\rho_v}{\varepsilon}$$

$$\frac{\partial}{\partial r} \left(r \frac{\partial V}{\partial r} \right) = \frac{-r \rho_v}{\varepsilon}$$

Integrating, we get

$$r \frac{\partial V}{\partial r} = \frac{-r^2 \rho_v}{2\varepsilon} + c_1$$

$$\frac{\partial V}{\partial r} = \frac{-r\rho_v}{2\varepsilon} + \frac{c_1}{r}$$

Integrating once again, we have the potential function as

$$V = \frac{-r^2\rho_v}{4\varepsilon} + c_1 \ln r + c_2$$

where c_1 and c_2 are constants of integration.

EXAMPLE 3.67

A charge density of $\rho_v = 10^{-8}\cos(z/z_0)\,\text{C/m}^3$ exists in the region $\dfrac{-\pi}{2} < \dfrac{z}{z_0} < \dfrac{\pi}{2}$ and is zero elsewhere as shown in Figure E3.67. Determine V and $\vec{E}$ using Poisson's equation and compare it with the results derived from Gauss's law.

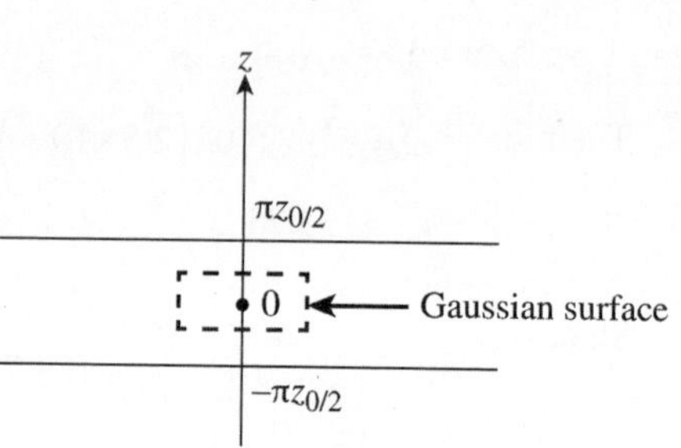

Figure E3.67

SOLUTION

Since V is not a function of x and y, Poisson's equation in rectangular coordinates reduces to

$$\frac{\partial^2 V}{\partial z^2} = \frac{-\rho_v}{\varepsilon} = \frac{-10^{-8}\cos(z/z_0)}{\varepsilon}$$

Integrating the above equation, we get

$$\frac{\partial V}{\partial z} = \frac{-10^{-8} z_0 \sin(z/z_0)}{\varepsilon} + c_1$$

Integrating once again, we have the potential function as

$$V = \frac{10^{-8} z_0^2 \cos(z/z_0)}{\varepsilon} + c_1 z + c_2$$

The electric field intensity can be determined using the relation, $\vec{E} = -\nabla V$. Since V is a function of z, $\vec{E}$ will also be a function of z.

Therefore,

$$\vec{E} = -\frac{\partial V}{\partial z}\vec{a}_z = -\frac{\partial}{\partial z}\left(\frac{10^{-8} z_0^2 \cos(z/z_0)}{\varepsilon} + c_1 z + c_2\right)\vec{a}_z$$

$$= \left(\frac{10^{-8} z_0 \sin(z/z_0)}{\varepsilon} - c_1\right)\vec{a}_z\,\text{V/m}$$

But, due to symmetry of the charge distribution, the field intensity must vanish on $z = 0$ plane. Therefore, $c_1 = 0$ and the field intensity $\vec{E}$ is

$$\vec{E} = \left(\frac{10^{-8} z_0 \sin(z/z_0)}{\varepsilon}\right)\vec{a}_z\,\text{V/m} \qquad (1)$$

This equation can also be obtained using Gauss's law by constructing a Gaussian surface centered about $z = 0$ as shown in Figure E3.67.

Here, it is evident that flux density $\vec{D}$ passes only through the top and bottom surfaces and each surface is having an area A. Since the charge distribution is symmetrical about $z = 0$, the flux density on the top surface is $\vec{D}_1 = D\vec{a}_z$ and on the bottom surface, it is $\vec{D}_2 = -D\vec{a}_z$. From Gauss's law, $\oint \vec{D} \cdot d\vec{s} = Q$ where $Q = \int_v \rho_v dv$.

$$D\oint_1 d\vec{s} + D\oint_2 d\vec{s} = \int_{-z}^{z} \iint 10^{-8} \cos(z/z_0)\, dxdydz$$

$$2DA = 2z_0 A \times 10^{-8} \sin(z/z_0)$$

$$D = z_0 \times 10^{-8} \sin(z/z_0) \qquad \text{for} \qquad 0 < z < \frac{\pi z_0}{2}$$

Therefore, the electric flux density is

$$\vec{D} = 10^{-8} z_0 \sin(z/z_0)\vec{a}_z \ \text{C/m}^2 \qquad \text{for} \qquad -\frac{\pi z_0}{2} < z < \frac{\pi z_0}{2}$$

Since $\vec{D} = \varepsilon \vec{E}$, the electric field intensity is

$$\vec{E} = \frac{\vec{D}}{\varepsilon} = \left(\frac{10^{-8} z_0 \sin(z/z_0)}{\varepsilon} \right)\vec{a}_z \ \text{V/m} \tag{2}$$

This equation obtained using Gauss's law is identical with Eq. (1) obtained using Poisson's equation. ❑

EXAMPLE 3.68

Solve one dimensional Laplace's equation to obtain the field inside a parallel plate capacitor and also, find the expression for the surface charge density at two plates.

SOLUTION

Figure E3.68 shows a parallel plate capacitor placed on the xy-plane with lower plate at ground potential and upper plate at V_0 potential.

The two plates are separated by a distance d. Hence, the potential V is a function of z alone. Laplace's equation is

$$\nabla^2 V = 0$$

For the charge-free region between the plates, Laplace's equation reduces to

$$\frac{\partial^2 V}{\partial z^2} = 0$$

Integrating the above equation, we get

$$\frac{\partial V}{\partial z} = c_1$$

Integrating once again, we get

$$V = \int c_1\, dz + c_2 = c_1 z + c_2$$

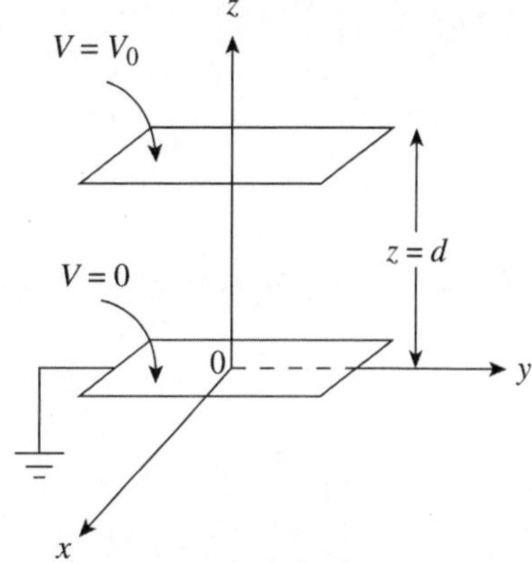

Figure E3.68

where c_1 and c_2 are constants to be obtained using the boundary conditions. Therefore, at $z = 0$, $V = 0$ and at $z = d$, $V = V_0$. Substituting the boundary conditions in the solution for potential V, we get

$$0 = c_1 \times 0 + c_2 \qquad \text{i.e., } c_2 = 0$$

and $\qquad V_0 = c_1 d + c_2 \qquad \text{i.e., } c_1 = \dfrac{V_0}{d}$

Hence, the potential is

$$V = \frac{V_0 z}{d} \tag{1}$$

Equation (1) shows that the potential varies linearly in a parallel plate capacitor. Now, the electric field intensity is

$$\vec{E} = -\nabla V = -\frac{\partial V}{\partial z} \vec{a}_z$$

$$= -\frac{\partial}{\partial z}\left[\frac{V_0 z}{d}\right]\vec{a}_z = -\frac{V_0}{d}\vec{a}_z \text{ V/m}$$

$$\vec{D} = \varepsilon\, \vec{E} = -\frac{\varepsilon V_0}{d}\vec{a}_z \text{ C/m}^2 \tag{2}$$

Since the normal component of $\vec{D}$ must be equal to the surface charge density ρ_s on a conductor, the surface charge density on the lower plate is

$$\rho_s\big|_{z=0} = -\frac{\varepsilon V_0}{d} \text{ C/m}^2 \tag{3}$$

and the surface charge density on the upper plate is

$$\rho_s\big|_{z=d} = \frac{\varepsilon V_0}{d} \text{ C/m}^2 \tag{4}$$

From Eq. (3) and Eq. (4), it is seen that the charge density is negative on the lower plate and positive on the upper plate. $\qquad\square$

EXAMPLE 3.69

Consider that two parallel conducting plates are separated by a distance d and filled with a dielectric medium having ε_r as relative permittivity. Using Laplace's equation, derive an expression for capacitance per unit length of a parallel plate capacitor, if it is connected to a dc source supplying 'V' volt.

SOLUTION

Referring to Example 3.68, the surface charge density is

$$\rho_s = \left|\vec{D}\right| = D_n = \frac{\varepsilon V_0}{d} = \frac{\varepsilon V}{d}$$

where $V_0 = V$. Assume that the surface area of the plate is A m^2. Therefore, the charge induced on the plate is

$$Q = \rho_s \times A = \frac{\varepsilon V}{d} \times A$$

Hence, the capacitance of a parallel plate capacitor is

$$C = \frac{Q}{V} = = \frac{\varepsilon A}{d}$$

❒

Using Laplace's equation, find the capacitance per unit length of a coaxial cable with inner radius 'a' m and outer radius 'b' m. Assume $V = V_0$ at $\rho = a$ and $V = 0$ at $\rho = b$.

SOLUTION

The coaxial cable is shown in the Figure E3.70.

Assume a cylindrical coordinate system for a coaxial cable in which the field intensity $\vec{E}$ is in radial direction from inner cylinder to outer cylinder. Hence, V is a function of radius ρ only and not the function of ϕ and z. The radius of the inner cylinder is $\rho = a$ and the radius of the outer cylinder is $\rho = b$.

For Laplace's equation,

$$\nabla^2 V = 0$$

Laplace's equation is written in cylindrical coordinates as

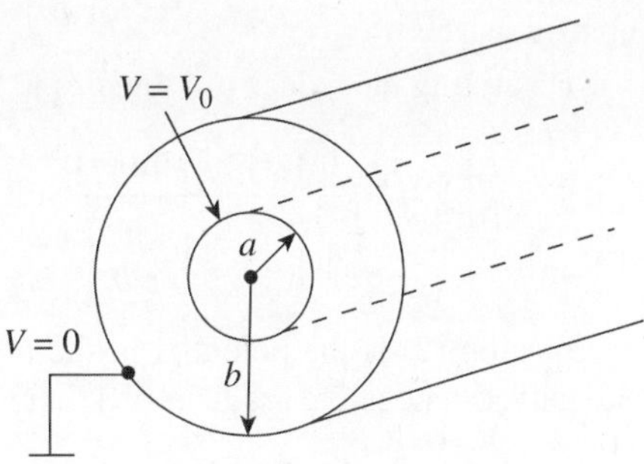

Figure E3.70

$$\nabla^2 V = \frac{1}{\rho}\frac{\partial}{\partial \rho}\left(\rho\frac{\partial V}{\partial \rho}\right) + \frac{1}{\rho^2}\left(\frac{\partial^2 V}{\partial \phi^2}\right) + \frac{\partial^2 V}{\partial z^2} = 0$$

Since V is a function of ρ only, we get

$$\frac{1}{\rho}\frac{\partial}{\partial \rho}\left(\rho\frac{\partial V}{\partial \rho}\right) = 0$$

i.e.,

$$\frac{\partial}{\partial \rho}\left(\rho\frac{\partial V}{\partial \rho}\right) = 0$$

Integrating the above equation, we get

$$\rho\frac{\partial V}{\partial \rho} = c_1$$

i.e.,

$$\frac{\partial V}{\partial \rho} = \frac{c_1}{\rho}$$

Integrating once again, the potential equation is

$$V = c_1 \ln(\rho) + c_2 \tag{1}$$

where c_1 and c_2 are the constants of integration. These constants can be determined by using the given boundary conditions.

At $\rho = b$, $V = 0$ i.e., $0 = c_1 \ln(b) + c_2$

and at $\rho = a$, $V = V_0$ i.e., $V_0 = c_1 \ln(a) + c_2$

Subtracting these two equations of boundary conditions, we get

$$V_0 = c_1\left[\ln(a) - \ln(b)\right] = c_1 \ln\left(\frac{a}{b}\right)$$

Therefore, $c_1 = \dfrac{V_0}{\ln\left(\dfrac{a}{b}\right)}$

and $\qquad c_2 = -c_1 \ln(b) = \dfrac{-V_0 \ln(b)}{\ln\left(\dfrac{a}{b}\right)}$

Substituting the values of c_1 and c_2 in Eq. (1), we get

$$V = \frac{V_0 \ln(\rho)}{\ln\left(\dfrac{a}{b}\right)} - \frac{V_0 \ln(b)}{\ln\left(\dfrac{a}{b}\right)} \text{ volt} \tag{2}$$

Equation (2) is the potential in the region between the inner and outer cylinder. Now, the electric field intensity as a negative gradient of V in cylindrical coordinates is

$$\vec{E} = -\nabla V = -\frac{\partial V}{\partial \rho}\,\vec{a}_\rho \qquad \text{(since V is a function of ρ only)}$$

$$= -\frac{\partial}{\partial \rho}\left[\frac{V_0 \ln(\rho)}{\ln\left(\dfrac{a}{b}\right)}\right]\vec{a}_\rho = -\frac{V_0}{\ln\left(\dfrac{a}{b}\right)}\left[\frac{\partial}{\partial \rho}\ln(\rho)\right]\vec{a}_\rho = -\frac{V_0}{\rho \ln\left(\dfrac{a}{b}\right)}\,\vec{a}_\rho \text{ V/m}$$

We know that, $\vec{D} = \varepsilon \vec{E}$

Hence, $\qquad \vec{D} = \dfrac{-\varepsilon V_0}{\rho \ln\left(\dfrac{a}{b}\right)}\,\vec{a}_\rho = \dfrac{\varepsilon V_0}{\rho \ln\left(\dfrac{b}{a}\right)}\,\vec{a}_\rho \text{ C/m}^2$

The flux density $\vec{D}$ is normal to the conductor surface as per the conductor–dielectric boundary conditions. Therefore, the normal component of $\vec{D}$ is

$$D_n = \left|\vec{D}\right| = \frac{\varepsilon V_0}{\rho \ln\left(\dfrac{b}{a}\right)}$$

Since the normal component of $\vec{D}$ must be equal to the surface charge density ρ_s on a conductor, the surface charge density ρ_s is

$$\rho_s = \frac{\varepsilon V_0}{\rho \ln\left(\dfrac{b}{a}\right)} \text{ C/m}^2$$

where ρ is the radius of the cylinder. The surface charge density exists on entire surface area of inner cylinder and the total charge on the surface area of the inner cylinder is

$$Q = \rho_s \times \text{surface area of inner cylinder}$$

$$= \frac{\varepsilon V_0}{\rho \ln\left(\dfrac{b}{a}\right)} \times 2\pi\rho \times l = \frac{2\pi\varepsilon l V_0}{\ln\left(\dfrac{b}{a}\right)} \tag{3}$$

The potential difference between the two cylinders is V_0. From Eq. (3), the capacitance is

$$C = \frac{Q}{V} = \frac{Q}{V_0} = \frac{2\pi\varepsilon l}{\ln\left(\dfrac{b}{a}\right)} \text{ F} \tag{4}$$

The capacitance per unit length is,

$$C' = \frac{C}{l} = \frac{2\pi\varepsilon}{\ln\left(\dfrac{b}{a}\right)} \text{ F/m} \tag{5}$$

The above equation derived using Laplace's equation is identical to the expression derived in section 3.9.3. ∎

EXAMPLE 3.71

Solve the Laplace's equation for the potential field in the homogeneous region between the two concentric conducting spheres with radii a and b, such that $b > a$ if potential $V = 0$ at $r = b$ and $V = V_0$ at $r = a$. Also, find the capacitance between the two concentric spheres.

SOLUTION

The concentric conducting spheres are shown in Figure E3.71.

Assume a spherical coordinate system for concentric spheres in which the field intensity $\vec{E}$ is in radial direction from inner to outer sphere. Hence, V is a function of radius r only and not the function of θ and ϕ. The radius of inner sphere is $r = a$ and the radius of outer sphere is $r = b$.

For Laplace's equation,

$$\nabla^2 V = 0$$

Laplace's equation is written in spherical coordinates, as

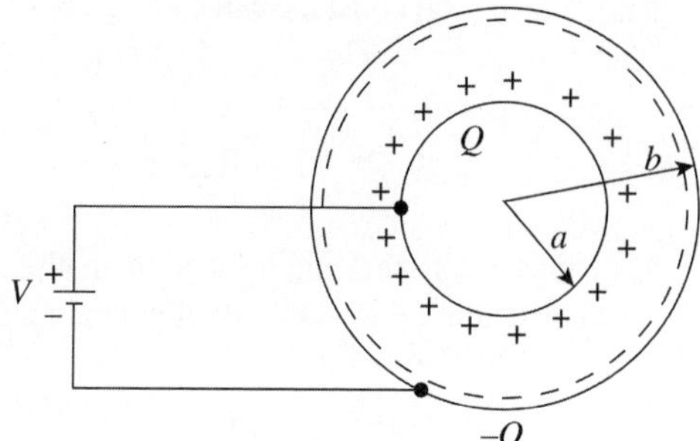

Figure E3.71

$$\nabla^2 V = \frac{1}{r^2}\frac{\partial}{\partial r}\left(r^2\frac{\partial V}{\partial r}\right) + \frac{1}{r^2\sin\theta}\frac{\partial}{\partial\theta}\left(\sin\theta\frac{\partial V}{\partial\theta}\right) + \frac{1}{r^2\sin^2\theta}\frac{\partial^2 V}{\partial\phi^2} = 0$$

Since V is a function of r only, we get

$$\frac{1}{r^2}\frac{\partial}{\partial r}\left(r^2\frac{\partial V}{\partial r}\right) = 0$$

$$\frac{\partial}{\partial r}\left(r^2\frac{\partial V}{\partial r}\right) = 0$$

Integrating the above equation, we get

$$r^2 \frac{\partial V}{\partial r} = c_1$$

$$\frac{\partial V}{\partial r} = \frac{c_1}{r^2} = c_1 r^{-2}$$

Integrating once again, the potential is

$$V = \int c_1 r^{-2} + c_2 = -\frac{c_1}{r} + c_2 \tag{1}$$

where c_1 and c_2 are the constants of integration. These constants can be determined by using the given boundary conditions.

At $r = b$, $V = 0$ i.e., $0 = -\frac{c_1}{b} + c_2$

and at $r = a$, $V = V_0$ i.e., $V_0 = -\frac{c_1}{a} + c_2$

Subtracting the above equations of two boundary condition, we have

$$V_0 = c_1 \left(\frac{1}{b} - \frac{1}{a} \right)$$

Therefore, $c_1 = \dfrac{V_0}{\left(\dfrac{1}{b} - \dfrac{1}{a} \right)}$ and $c_2 = \dfrac{c_1}{b} = \dfrac{V_0}{b \left(\dfrac{1}{b} - \dfrac{1}{a} \right)}$

Substituting the constant values c_1 and c_2 in Eq. (1), we get

$$V = \frac{-V_0}{r \left(\dfrac{1}{b} - \dfrac{1}{a} \right)} + \frac{V_0}{b \left(\dfrac{1}{b} - \dfrac{1}{a} \right)} \text{ volt} \tag{2}$$

Equation (2) is the potential field in the region between the two spheres. Now, the electric field as a negative gradient of V in spherical coordinates is

$$\vec{E} = -\nabla V = -\frac{\partial V}{\partial r} \vec{a}_r \qquad \text{(since } V \text{ is a function of } r \text{ only)}$$

$$= -\frac{\partial}{\partial r} \left[\frac{-V_0}{r \left(\dfrac{1}{b} - \dfrac{1}{a} \right)} \right] \vec{a}_r = \frac{V_0}{\left(\dfrac{1}{b} - \dfrac{1}{a} \right)} \left[\frac{\partial}{\partial r} \left(\frac{1}{r} \right) \right] \vec{a}_r$$

$$= \frac{-V_0}{\left(\dfrac{1}{b} - \dfrac{1}{a} \right) r^2} \vec{a}_r \text{ V/m}$$

We know that, $\vec{D} = \varepsilon \vec{E}$.

Hence,

$$\vec{D} = \frac{-\varepsilon V_0}{\left(\dfrac{1}{b} - \dfrac{1}{a}\right) r^2} \vec{a}_r = \frac{\varepsilon V_0}{\left(\dfrac{1}{a} - \dfrac{1}{b}\right) r^2} \vec{a}_r \; \text{C/m}^2$$

The flux density $\vec{D}$ is normal to the conductor surface as per the conductor–dielectric boundary conditions. Therefore, the normal component of $\vec{D}$ is

$$D_n = \left|\vec{D}\right| = \frac{\varepsilon V_0}{\left(\dfrac{1}{a} - \dfrac{1}{b}\right) r^2}$$

Since the normal component of $\vec{D}$ must be equal to the surface charge density ρ_s on a conductor, the surface charge density ρ_s is written as

$$\rho_s = \frac{\varepsilon V_0}{\left(\dfrac{1}{a} - \dfrac{1}{b}\right) r^2} \; \text{C/m}^2$$

The total charge on the surface of the sphere of radius r is

$$Q = \rho_s \times \text{surface area of sphere of radius } r$$

$$= \frac{\varepsilon V_0}{\left(\dfrac{1}{a} - \dfrac{1}{b}\right) r^2} \times 4\pi r^2 = \frac{4\pi \varepsilon V_0}{\left(\dfrac{1}{a} - \dfrac{1}{b}\right)} \tag{3}$$

The potential difference between the two spheres is V_0. From Eq. (3), the capacitance is

$$C = \frac{Q}{V} = \frac{Q}{V_0} = \frac{4\pi\varepsilon}{\left(\dfrac{1}{a} - \dfrac{1}{b}\right)}$$

$$= \frac{4\pi\varepsilon\, ab}{(b - a)} \; \text{F} \tag{4}$$

Equation (4) is derived using Laplace' equation is identical to the expression derived in section 3.9.5. ☐

EXAMPLE 3.72

Given the potential field, $V = \dfrac{50\sin\theta}{r^2}$ V in free space, determine whether V satisfies Laplace's equation.

SOLUTION

$\nabla^2 V = 0$ is the Laplace's equation. Given V in spherical coordinates, the Laplacian operator $\nabla^2 V$ is written in spherical coordinates as

$$\nabla^2 V = \frac{1}{r^2}\frac{\partial}{\partial r}\left[r^2 \frac{\partial V}{\partial r}\right] + \frac{1}{r^2 \sin\theta}\frac{\partial}{\partial\theta}\left[\sin\theta \frac{\partial V}{\partial\theta}\right] + \frac{1}{r^2 \sin^2\theta}\frac{\partial^2 V}{\partial\phi^2}$$

$$= \frac{1}{r^2}\frac{\partial}{\partial r}\left[r^2 \times 50\sin\theta \frac{(-2)}{r^3}\right] + \frac{1}{r^2 \sin\theta}\frac{\partial}{\partial\theta}\left[\sin\theta \times \frac{50}{r^2} \times \cos\theta\right] + 0$$

$$= \frac{1}{r^2} \frac{\partial}{\partial r}\left[\frac{-100\sin\theta}{r} \right] + \frac{1}{r^2 \sin\theta} \frac{\partial}{\partial\theta}\left[\frac{50\sin\theta\cos\theta}{r^2} \right]$$

$$= \frac{1}{r^2}(-100\sin\theta)\left[-\frac{1}{r^2} \right] + \frac{1}{r^2 \sin\theta} \times \frac{1}{r^2} \frac{\partial}{\partial\theta}\left[\frac{50}{2} \times \sin 2\theta \right]$$

$$= \frac{100\sin\theta}{r^4} + \frac{1}{r^4 \sin\theta} \times 25 \times 2\cos 2\theta$$

$$= \frac{100\sin\theta}{r^4} + \frac{50}{r^4 \sin\theta}\left[1 - 2\sin^2\theta \right]$$

$$= \frac{100\sin\theta}{r^4} + \frac{50}{r^4 \sin\theta} - \frac{100\sin\theta}{r^4}$$

$$= \frac{50}{r^4 \sin\theta}$$

Since $\nabla^2 V \neq 0$, the given potential field does not satisfy the Laplace's equation. ▫

EXAMPLE 3.73

Show that the expression for the potential due to an electric dipole satisfies the Laplace equation.

SOLUTION

From Section 2.11.3 of Chapter 2, the potential due to dipole is

$$V = \frac{Qd\cos\theta}{4\pi\varepsilon_0 r^2} = \frac{K\cos\theta}{r^2}, \quad \text{where } K = \frac{Qd}{4\pi\varepsilon_0} \text{ is a constant}$$

Since the dipole potential is expressed in spherical coordinates, the Laplacian operator in spherical coordinates is

$$\nabla^2 V = \frac{1}{r^2} \frac{\partial}{\partial r}\left[r^2 \frac{\partial V}{\partial r} \right] + \frac{1}{r^2 \sin\theta} \frac{\partial}{\partial\theta}\left[\sin\theta \frac{\partial V}{\partial\theta} \right] + \frac{1}{r^2 \sin^2\theta} \frac{\partial^2 V}{\partial\phi^2}$$

$$= \frac{1}{r^2} \frac{\partial}{\partial r}\left[r^2 K\cos\theta\left(-\frac{2}{r^3} \right) \right] + \frac{1}{r^2 \sin\theta} \frac{\partial}{\partial\theta}\left[\sin\theta \frac{K}{r^2}(-\sin\theta) \right] + 0$$

$$= \frac{-2K\cos\theta}{r^2} \frac{\partial}{\partial r}\left(\frac{1}{r} \right) - \frac{K}{r^4 \sin\theta} \frac{\partial}{\partial\theta}\left(\sin^2\theta \right)$$

$$= \left(\frac{-2K\cos\theta}{r^2} \right)\left(\frac{-1}{r^2} \right) - \left(\frac{K}{r^4 \sin\theta} \right)(2\sin\theta\cos\theta)$$

$$= \frac{2K\cos\theta}{r^4} - \frac{2K\cos\theta}{r^4} = 0$$

Since $\nabla^2 V = 0$, the potential due to an electric dipole satisfies Laplace's equation. ▫

EXAMPLE 3.74

In a charge-free region of free space, a potential field is given as, $V(x, y) = 5x^3 + f(x) - 2y^2$ V. Find $f(x)$ if E_x and V are both zero at origin.

SOLUTION

Given $V(x,y) = 5x^3 + f(x) - 2y^2$ V.

At origin, $V(0,0) = f(0) = 0$

We know that $\vec{E} = -\nabla V = -\left(\dfrac{\partial V}{\partial x}\vec{a}_x + \dfrac{\partial V}{\partial y}\vec{a}_y + \dfrac{\partial V}{\partial z}\vec{a}_z \right)$

$$= -\left[\left(15x^2 + \frac{\partial f(x)}{\partial x} \right)\vec{a}_x - 4y\vec{a}_y \right]$$

Therefore, $E_x = -\left[15x^2 + \dfrac{\partial f(x)}{\partial x} \right]$

Since $E_x = 0$ at origin, $\dfrac{\partial f(x)}{\partial x} = 0$ at origin.

For a charge-free region, $\nabla^2 V = 0$

$$\frac{\partial^2 V}{\partial x^2} + \frac{\partial^2 V}{\partial y^2} + \frac{\partial^2 V}{\partial z^2} = 0$$

$$\frac{\partial V}{\partial x} = 15x^2 + \frac{\partial f(x)}{\partial x}, \qquad \frac{\partial V}{\partial y} = -4y, \qquad \frac{\partial V}{\partial z} = 0$$

$$\frac{\partial^2 V}{\partial x^2} = 30x + \frac{\partial^2 f(x)}{\partial x^2}, \qquad \frac{\partial^2 V}{\partial y} = -4, \qquad \frac{\partial^2 V}{\partial z^2} = 0$$

Therefore, $30x + \dfrac{\partial^2 f(x)}{\partial x^2} - 4 = 0$

That is,

$$\frac{\partial^2 f(x)}{\partial x^2} = 4 - 30x$$

Integrating the above equation, we get

$$\frac{\partial f(x)}{\partial x} = \int (4 - 30x)\,dx + c_1$$

$$= 4x - \frac{30x^2}{2} + c_1 = 4x - 15x^2 + c_1$$

Since at origin, $\dfrac{\partial f(x)}{\partial x} = 0$. Hence, $c_1 = 0$

Integrating again, we get

$$f(x) = \int \left(4x - 15x^2 \right)dx + c_2 = \frac{4x^2}{2} - \frac{15x^3}{3} + c_2 = 2x^2 - 5x^3 + c_2$$

But $f(x) = 0$ at origin, So, $c_2 = 0$

Therefore, $f(x) = 2x^2 - 5x^3$

EXAMPLE 3.75

Determine whether or not the following potential fields satisfy the Laplace's equation: (i) $V = x^2 - y^2 + z^2$, (ii) $V = \rho \cos\phi + z$, and (iii) $V = r\cos\theta + \phi$

SOLUTION

(i) Given $V = x^2 - y^2 + z^2$ in rectangular coordinates.

We know that, $\nabla^2 V = \dfrac{\partial^2 V}{\partial x^2} + \dfrac{\partial^2 V}{\partial y^2} + \dfrac{\partial^2 V}{\partial z^2}$

$$= \dfrac{\partial^2}{\partial x^2}\left(x^2 - y^2 + z^2\right) + \dfrac{\partial^2}{\partial y^2}\left(x^2 - y^2 + z^2\right) + \dfrac{\partial^2}{\partial z^2}\left(x^2 - y^2 + z^2\right)$$

$$= \dfrac{\partial}{\partial x}(2x) + \dfrac{\partial}{\partial y}(-2y) + \dfrac{\partial}{\partial z}(2z)$$

$$= 2 - 2 + 2 = 2$$

Since $\nabla^2 V \neq 0$, the given potential field V does not satisfy the Laplace's equation.

(ii) Given $V = \rho\cos\phi + z$ in cylindrical coordinates.

We know that, $\nabla^2 V = \dfrac{1}{\rho}\dfrac{\partial}{\partial \rho}\left(\rho\dfrac{\partial V}{\partial \rho}\right) + \dfrac{1}{\rho^2}\left(\dfrac{\partial^2 V}{\partial \phi^2}\right) + \dfrac{\partial^2 V}{\partial z^2}$

$$\dfrac{\partial V}{\partial \rho} = \dfrac{\partial}{\partial \rho}(\rho\cos\phi + z) = \cos\phi$$

$$\dfrac{\partial V}{\partial \phi} = \dfrac{\partial}{\partial \phi}(\rho\cos\phi + z) = -\rho\sin\phi$$

and $\dfrac{\partial^2 V}{\partial \phi^2} = \dfrac{\partial}{\partial \phi}(-\rho\sin\phi) = -\rho\cos\phi$

$$\dfrac{\partial V}{\partial z} = \dfrac{\partial}{\partial z}(\rho\cos\phi + z) = 1 \text{ and hence, } \dfrac{\partial^2 V}{\partial z^2} = \dfrac{\partial}{\partial z}(1) = 0$$

Therefore,

$$\nabla^2 V = \dfrac{1}{\rho}\dfrac{\partial}{\partial \rho}(\rho\cos\phi) + \dfrac{1}{\rho^2}(-\rho\cos\phi)$$

$$= \dfrac{\cos\phi}{\rho} - \dfrac{\cos\phi}{\rho} = 0$$

Since $\nabla^2 V = 0$, the given potential field V satisfies the Laplace's equation.

(iii) Given $V = r\cos\theta + \phi$ in spherical coordinates.

We know that, $\nabla^2 V = \dfrac{1}{r^2}\dfrac{\partial}{\partial r}\left(r^2\dfrac{\partial V}{\partial r}\right) + \dfrac{1}{r^2\sin\theta}\dfrac{\partial}{\partial \theta}\left(\sin\theta\dfrac{\partial V}{\partial \theta}\right) + \dfrac{1}{r^2\sin^2\theta}\dfrac{\partial^2 V}{\partial \phi^2} = 0$

$$r^2\dfrac{\partial V}{\partial r} = r^2\dfrac{\partial}{\partial r}(r\cos\theta + \phi) = r^2\cos\theta$$

$$\sin\theta\,\frac{\partial V}{\partial\theta} = \sin\theta\,\frac{\partial}{\partial\theta}\big(r\cos\theta + \phi\big) = -r\sin^2\theta$$

$$\frac{1}{r^2\sin^2\theta}\frac{\partial^2 V}{\partial\phi^2} = \frac{1}{r^2\sin^2\theta}\frac{\partial^2}{\partial\phi^2}\big(r\cos\theta + \phi\big) = \frac{1}{r^2\sin^2\theta}\frac{\partial}{\partial\phi}(1) = 0$$

Therefore,

$$\nabla^2 V = \frac{1}{r^2}\frac{\partial}{\partial r}\Big(r^2\cos\theta\Big) + \frac{1}{r^2\sin\theta}\frac{\partial}{\partial\theta}\Big(-r\sin^2\theta\Big)$$

$$= \frac{1}{r^2}\times 2r\cos\theta + \frac{1}{r^2\sin\theta}\big(-r\times 2\sin\theta\cos\theta\big)$$

$$= \frac{2\cos\theta}{r} - \frac{2\cos\theta}{r} = 0$$

Since $\nabla^2 V = 0$, the given potential field V satisfies the Laplace's equation. ◻

3.11 METHOD OF IMAGES

The method of images is commonly used to determine V, $\vec{E}$, and $\vec{D}$ at any point in free space due to charges above the grounded conductor. It can also be used to determine surface charge distribution ρ_s on the conducting plate. This method cannot be used to solve all electrostatic field problems, but it reduces a complex problem into a simple one. For example, consider an electrostatic problem in which a point charge Q is placed at a distance d above a perfectly conducting plane as shown in Figure 3.20(a).

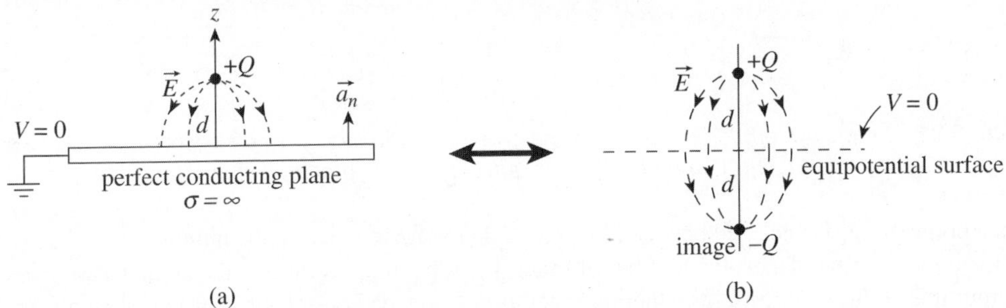

Figure 3.20 *Image system for a point charge Q: (a) charge above conducting plane and (b) its equivalent configuration with image*

To determine the electric field intensity $\vec{E}$ due to a point charge as shown in Figure 3.20(a), three methods can be employed. The first method is based on the Coulomb's law. This method needs information on the magnitudes and locations of all the charges contributing to $\vec{E}$ at a given point in space. But in Figure 3.20(a), the charge Q induces an unknown and non-uniform distribution of charge on the conductor surface. Hence, Coulomb's method cannot be used.

The second method, based on Gauss's law, is also difficult to use. Here, the construction of a Gaussian surface is complex in which $\vec{E}$ is always totally tangential or totally normal at every point on that surface. The third method is based on gradient approach in which the electric field intensity is obtained using $\vec{E} = -\nabla V$, after solving Poisson's or Laplace's equation for V to satisfy the boundary conditions. Here, the solution involves complicated mathematics and thus, gradient approach cannot be used.

Alternatively, this electrostatic field problem can be solved with great ease using image theory or method of images. The image theory states that any given charge configuration above an infinite, grounded perfect conducting plane is electrically equivalent to the combination of the charge configuration and its image by removing the conducting plane. In other words, using image theory, any charge configuration above an infinite, perfectly conducting plane may be replaced by the charge configuration itself, its image and an equipotential surface in place of the conducting plane.

Figure 3.20 shows an image system for point charge. The image equivalent to the charge Q above a conducting plane is shown in Figure 3.20(b). The charge $-Q$ is said to be the image of the real charge Q. The electric field intensity due to the two isolated charges can now be easily determined at any point (x, y, z) by applying Coulomb's law. By symmetry, the combination of the two charges will always produce a potential $V = 0$ at every point in the plane previously occupied by the conducting surface.

In the method of images, the imaginary charge obtained is a fictitious charge and it must be located in the region of the conducting plane. Such a conducting plane is an equipotential surface in which the potential is zero or constant. The method of images is not only applicable to point charges but also to any charge distributions such as the line and volume charge distributions as shown in Figure 3.21. The line and volume charge distributions above a conducting plane is shown in Figure 3.21(a) and their equivalent configuration with image is shown in Figure 3.21(b).

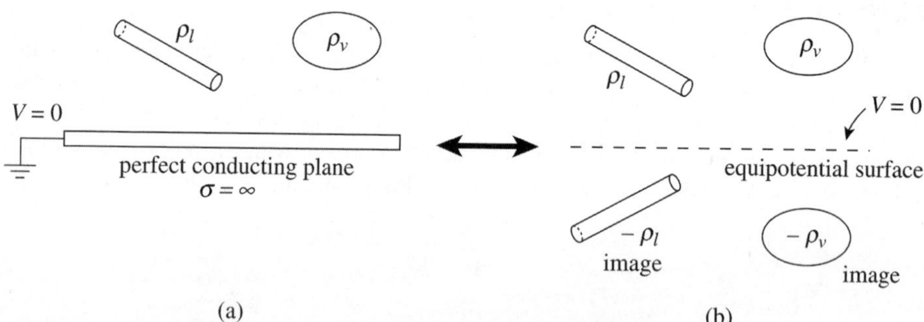

Figure 3.21 *Image system for line and volume charge distributions: (a) charge distributions above conducting plane and (b) its equivalent configuration with image*

When a point charge is enclosed between two parallel conducting planes, the number of images is infinite. But, for the two bisecting planes, the number of images will be finite as long as the angle between the planes is a sub-multiple of 360°. In general, when the method of images is used for a system with a point charge between two semi-infinite conducting planes inclined at an angle θ, the number of images is represented by

$$N = \left(\frac{360°}{\theta} - 1\right)$$

(3.60)

where the charge and its images lie on a circle. For example, in a point charge as shown in Figure 3.20, $\theta = 180°$ and it will have only one image, i.e., $N = 1$. For $\theta = 90°$, the number of images $N = 3$ and for $\theta = 60°$ the number of images $N = 5$.

EXAMPLE 3.76

A point charge $+Q$ is located above the surface of a conducting plane of infinite extent and depth. Using image theory, determine the potential V and electric field intensity $\vec{E}$ at any point P in free space. Show that the total charge induced on the surface of the plane is $-Q$.

SOLUTION

Figure E3.76(a) shows a point charge $+Q$ located at $(0,0,d)$ above the surface of a conducting plane. By image theory, any given charge configuration above an infinite, grounded perfect conducting plane is electrically equivalent to the combination of the given charge configuration and its image configuration, with the conducting plane removed.

Therefore, to determine the field intensities, an imaginary charge $-Q$ is placed at $(0,0,-d)$ by temporarily ignoring the existence of the plane as shown in Figure E3.76(b). The electric field intensity due to point charges at any point $P(x,y,z)$ and for $z \geq 0$ is represented by

$$\vec{E} = \vec{E}_{+Q} + \vec{E}_{-Q} = \frac{Q\vec{R}_1}{4\pi\varepsilon_0 R_1^3} + \frac{-Q\vec{R}_2}{4\pi\varepsilon_0 R_2^3} \tag{1}$$

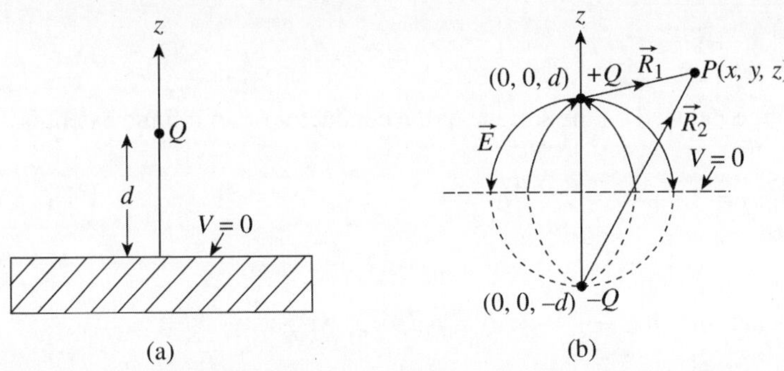

Figure E3.76 *Image system for point charge Q: (a) charge above conducting plane and (b) its equivalent configuration with image*

The distance vectors $\vec{R}_1$ and $\vec{R}_2$ are given by

$$\vec{R}_1 = x\vec{a}_x + y\vec{a}_y + (z-d)\vec{a}_z$$

$$\vec{R}_2 = x\vec{a}_x + y\vec{a}_y + (z+d)\vec{a}_z$$

Equation (1) can now be written as

$$\vec{E} = \frac{Q}{4\pi\varepsilon_0}\left[\frac{x\vec{a}_x + y\vec{a}_y + (z-d)\vec{a}_z}{\left[x^2 + y^2 + (z-d)^2\right]^{3/2}} - \frac{x\vec{a}_x + y\vec{a}_y + (z+d)\vec{a}_z}{\left[x^2 + y^2 + (z+d)^2\right]^{3/2}} \right] \tag{2}$$

Here, when $z = 0$, $\vec{E}$ will have only the z-component which confirms that $\vec{E}$ is normal to the conducting surface.

By superposition principle, the potential V due to two point charges at P for $z \geq 0$ is

$$V = V_{+Q} + V_{-Q} = \frac{Q}{4\pi\varepsilon_0 R_1} + \frac{-Q}{4\pi\varepsilon_0 R_2} = \frac{Q}{4\pi\varepsilon_0}\left(\frac{1}{\sqrt{x^2 + y^2 + (z-d)^2}} - \frac{1}{\sqrt{x^2 + y^2 + (z+d)^2}} \right) \tag{3}$$

Here, when $z = 0$, the potential $V = 0$ as $R_1 = R_2$.

On the surface of the conducting plane, i.e., $z = 0$, the electric field intensity equation reduces to

$$\vec{E} = \frac{-2Qd\,\vec{a}_z}{4\pi\varepsilon_0\left[x^2 + y^2 + d^2\right]^{3/2}}$$

At the conductor–dielectric boundary, the normal component of the flux density $\vec{D}$ must be equal to the surface charge density on the surface of the conductor at $z = 0$.

Therefore,

$$\rho_s = D_n = \varepsilon_0 E_n\big|_{z=0}$$

$$= \frac{-Qd}{2\pi\left[x^2 + y^2 + d^2\right]^{3/2}}$$

Thus, the total charge induced on the surface of the conductor of an infinite extent is

$$Q_i = \int \rho_s\, ds = \int_{-\infty}^{\infty} \frac{-Qd\, dx\, dy}{2\pi\left[x^2 + y^2 + d^2\right]^{3/2}}$$

By changing variables, $\rho^2 = x^2 + y^2,\;\; dx\, dy = \rho\, d\rho\, d\phi$, we get

$$Q_i = -\frac{Qd}{2\pi}\int_0^{\infty} \frac{\rho\, d\rho}{\left[\rho^2 + d^2\right]^{3/2}} \int_0^{2\pi} d\phi$$

$$= -\frac{Qd}{2\pi} \times 2\pi \times \left[-\frac{1}{\left(\rho^2 + d^2\right)^{1/2}}\right]_0^{\infty} \qquad \left(\text{since } \int \frac{\rho\, d\rho}{\left(\rho^2 + d^2\right)^{3/2}} = -\frac{1}{\left(\rho^2 + d^2\right)^{1/2}}\right)$$

$$= Qd\left[\frac{1}{\left(\rho^2 + d^2\right)^{1/2}}\right]_0^{\infty} = Qd\left[\frac{1}{\infty} - \frac{1}{d}\right] = -Q$$

Thus, the total charge induced on the surface of the conducting plane is $-Q$. $\qquad\qquad\square$

<hr>

EXAMPLE 3.77

An infinite charge with density ρ_l C/m is located at distance d from the grounded conducting plane $z = 0$. Using image theory, determine the potential V and electric field intensity $\vec{E}$ at any point P in free space. Show that the charge density induced on the surface of the plane is $-\rho_l$.

SOLUTION

Assume that an infinite charge with density ρ_l C/m is located at distance d from the grounded conducting plane $z = 0$. The image system shown in Figure E3.76(b) for a point charge can be extended to line charge also, by replacing Q with ρ_l.

Consider the infinite line charge ρ_l to be at $x = 0, z = d$ and its image charge $-\rho_l$ at $x = 0, z = -d$ so that the two are parallel to the y-axis. The electric field due to line charge density ρ_l at any point $P(x, y, z)$ and for $z \geq 0$ is represented by

$$\vec{E} = \vec{E}_{+\rho_l} + \vec{E}_{-\rho_l} = \frac{\rho_l}{2\pi\varepsilon_0\rho_1}\vec{a}_{\rho 1} + \frac{-\rho_l}{2\pi\varepsilon_0\rho_2}\vec{a}_{\rho 2} \tag{1}$$

where $\vec{a}_{\rho 1} = \dfrac{\rho_1}{|\rho_1|}$ and $\vec{a}_{\rho 2} = \dfrac{\rho_2}{|\rho_2|}$.

The distance vectors $\vec{\rho}_1$ and $\vec{\rho}_2$ are given by

$$\vec{\rho}_1 = x\vec{a}_x + (z - d)\vec{a}_z$$
$$\vec{\rho}_2 = x\vec{a}_x + (z + d)\vec{a}_z$$

Equation (1) can now be written as

$$\vec{E} = \frac{\rho_l}{2\pi\varepsilon_0}\left[\frac{x\vec{a}_x + (z - d)\vec{a}_z}{x^2 + (z - d)^2} - \frac{x\vec{a}_x + (z + d)\vec{a}_z}{x^2 + (z + d)^2}\right] \tag{2}$$

Here, when $z = 0$, $\vec{E}$ will have only the z-component which confirms that $\vec{E}$ is normal to the conducting surface.

The potential V for $z \geq 0$ is obtained by taking the line integral over the electric field $\vec{E}$ using $V = -\int \vec{E} \cdot d\vec{l}$. Therefore,

$$V = V_{+\rho_l} + V_{-\rho_l} = -\frac{\rho_l}{2\pi\varepsilon_0}\ln\rho_1 - \frac{-\rho_l}{2\pi\varepsilon_0}\ln\rho_2$$

$$= -\frac{\rho_l}{2\pi\varepsilon_0}\ln\left(\frac{\rho_1}{\rho_2}\right) \tag{3}$$

where $\rho_1 = |\vec{\rho}_1| = \left[x^2 + (z - d)^2\right]^{1/2}$ and $\rho_2 = |\vec{\rho}_2| = \left[x^2 + (z + d)^2\right]^{1/2}$

Substituting the magnitudes of ρ_1 and ρ_2 in Eq. (3), we get

$$V = -\frac{\rho_l}{2\pi\varepsilon_0}\ln\left[\frac{x^2 + (z - d)^2}{x^2 + (z + d)^2}\right]^{1/2} \tag{4}$$

Here, when $z = 0$, the potential $V = 0$ as $\rho_1 = \rho_2$.

At the conductor–dielectric boundary, the normal component of the flux density $\vec{D}$ must be equal to the surface charge density on the surface of the conductor at $z = 0$. Therefore,

$$\rho_s = D_n = \varepsilon_0 E_z\big|_{z=0} = \frac{-\rho_l d}{\pi\left(x^2 + d^2\right)}$$

The induced charge density on the conducting plane is

$$\rho_i = \int \rho_s \, dx = -\frac{\rho_l d}{\pi}\int\limits_{-\infty}^{\infty}\frac{dx}{x^2 + d^2}$$

$$= -\frac{\rho_l d}{\pi}\left[\frac{1}{d}\tan^{-1}\frac{x}{d}\right]_{-\infty}^{\infty} \qquad \left(\text{since}\int\frac{dx}{x^2+d^2}=\frac{1}{d}\tan^{-1}\frac{x}{d}\right)$$

$$= -\frac{\rho_l}{\pi}\times\left[\frac{\pi}{2}-\left(\frac{-\pi}{2}\right)\right]=-\frac{\rho_l}{\pi}\times\pi$$

$$= -\rho_l$$

Thus, the charge density induced on the surface of the plane is $-\rho_l$.

EXAMPLE 3.78

A charge of 50 nC is placed at $(2,3,0)$ between two infinite planes having $90°$ angle of intersection. Using method of images, find the electric potential and electric field intensity at point $P(2,4,0)$.

SOLUTION

Figure E3.78 shows that a point charge is placed between two infinite planes having $90°$ angle of intersection. For such an arrangement, the number of images using method of images is

$$N=\left(\frac{360°}{\theta}-1\right)=\left(\frac{360°}{90°}-1\right)=3$$

Hence, three imaginary charges are needed as shown in Figure E3.78. If (x,y,z) are the general coordinates of point P, then the distance between the real charge and point P is

$$R_1=\left[(x-2)^2+(y-3)^2+z^2\right]^{1/2}$$

The distance between the three imaginary charges and point P is

$$R_2=\left[(x+2)^2+(y-3)^2+z^2\right]^{1/2}$$

$$R_3=\left[(x+2)^2+(y+3)^2+z^2\right]^{1/2}$$

$$R_4=\left[(x-2)^2+(y+3)^2+z^2\right]^{1/2}$$

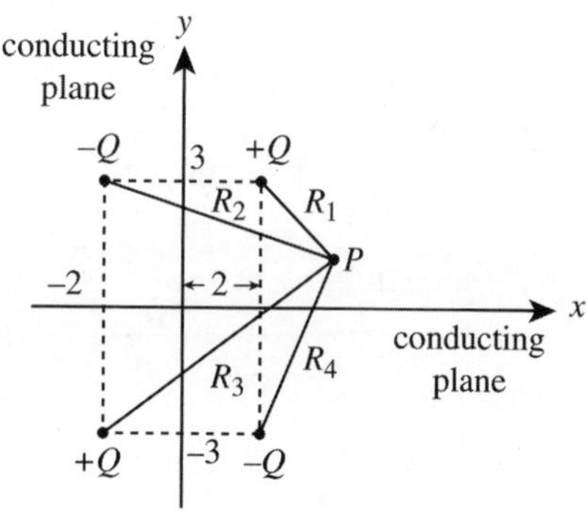

Figure E3.78

At point $P(2,4,0)$, $R_1=1$, $R_2=\sqrt{17}$, $R_3=\sqrt{65}$, $R_4=\sqrt{49}$

The potential at free space is

$$V=\frac{Q}{4\pi\varepsilon_0}\left[\frac{1}{R_1}-\frac{1}{R_2}+\frac{1}{R_3}-\frac{1}{R_4}\right]$$

where $\dfrac{1}{4\pi\varepsilon_0}=9\times10^9$.

Hence, the potential at $P(2,4,0)$ is

$$V = 9 \times 10^9 \times 50 \times 10^{-9} \times \left[1 - \frac{1}{\sqrt{17}} + \frac{1}{\sqrt{65}} - \frac{1}{\sqrt{49}} \right] = 333$$

Therefore, the electric field intensity is

$$\vec{E} = -\nabla V = -\frac{\partial V}{\partial x}\vec{a}_x - \frac{\partial V}{\partial y}\vec{a}_y - \frac{\partial V}{\partial z}\vec{a}_z$$

where

$$\frac{\partial V}{\partial x} = 450 \left[-\frac{x-2}{R_1^3} + \frac{x+2}{R_2^3} - \frac{x+2}{R_3^3} + \frac{x-2}{R_4^3} \right]$$

At $P(2,4,0)$,

$$\frac{\partial V}{\partial x} = 22$$

$$\frac{\partial V}{\partial y} = 450 \left[-\frac{y-3}{R_1^3} + \frac{y-3}{R_2^3} - \frac{y+3}{R_3^3} + \frac{y+3}{R_4^3} \right]$$

Similarly, at $P(2,4,0)$, $\dfrac{\partial V}{\partial y} = -440.51$

and

$$\frac{\partial V}{\partial z} = 0$$

Hence, the electric field intensity at $P(2,4,0)$ is

$$\vec{E} = -22\vec{a}_x + 440.51\vec{a}_y \, \text{V/m}$$

EXAMPLE 3.79

A wire of 6 mm in diameter and 5 km in length is suspended at a constant height of 10 m above seawater. Calculate the capacitance between conductor and earth using method of images.

SOLUTION

Figure E3.79 shows a wire of radius $a = 3$ mm and length $l = 5$ km is suspended at a height $h = 10$ m above sea water. By image theory, any charge configuration above a ground plane is electrically equivalent to the combination of the given charge and its image, with the conducting plane removed.

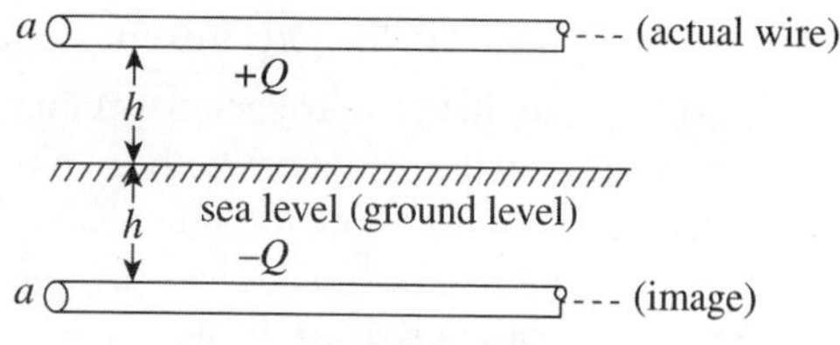

Figure E3.79

Referring to Sec. 3.9.2, the potential difference between parallel wires of charges Q is

$$V = \frac{Q}{\pi \varepsilon_0 l} \ln\left(\frac{d-a}{a} \right) \qquad \left(\text{since } \rho_l = \frac{Q}{l} \right)$$

Here, the distance d between the actual wire and its image is $2h$. The potential between the actual wire and the ground will be half of V.

Therefore,

$$V = \frac{1}{2}\frac{Q}{\pi\varepsilon_0 l}\ln\left(\frac{2h-a}{a}\right)$$

$$= \frac{1}{2}\frac{Q}{\pi\varepsilon_0 l}\ln\left(\frac{2h}{a}\right) \qquad \left(\text{since } h \gg a,\ 2h-a \approx 2h\right)$$

Hence, the capacitance per unit length of the long conductor with the earth as the other conductor is

$$C' = \frac{C}{l} = \frac{Q}{Vl} = \frac{2\pi\varepsilon_0}{\ln\left(\dfrac{2h}{a}\right)}$$

$$= \frac{2\pi \times 8.854 \times 10^{-12}}{\ln\left(\dfrac{2\times 10}{3\times 10^{-3}}\right)} = 6.315 \times 10^{-12}\ \text{F}$$

For a length of $l = 5\,\text{km}$, the total capacitance between conductor and earth is

$$C = C'l = 6.315 \times 10^{-12} \times 5 \times 10^3 = 31.58\,\text{nF}$$

3.12 APPLICATIONS OF STATIC ELECTRIC FIELDS

The applications of static electric fields are mainly based on the fundamental concepts studied in electrostatics. Here, the motion of an electron in the electric field is described first and it is followed by some applications of static electric fields.

3.12.1 Motion of Electron in Electric Field

The assumptions for the analysis of motion of electron in electric fields are made as follows:

(*i*) the charge density is low enough so that the mutual repulsive force may be neglected,

(*ii*) the movement of the charged particle is in high vacuum so that no collision with gas atoms or ions occur, and

(*iii*) the mass of the charged particle is extremely small so that the gravitational force may be neglected as compared to the forces exerted by the fields.

Consider a parallel plate capacitor with uniform electric field in between the plates. If an electron enters the region between the two plates with an initial velocity u_{0x} in the $+x$-direction, the electron is made to move in a parabolic path. Referring to Figure 3.22, the electric field intensity $\vec{E}$ is in the $-y$-direction, and no other fields are existing in other directions.

The initial conditions at $t = 0$ are

$$u_x = u_{0x}, \quad x = 0$$

$$u_y = 0, \quad y = 0$$

$$u_z = 0, \quad z = 0$$

Let us analyze the fields in the different axes.

z-axis: Since no field is present in this direction, force is zero (since $F = QE$). As the force is zero, the acceleration along the z-direction is also zero (since $F = ma$). The zero acceleration means no change in the velocity component in z-direction. Since the initial velocity $u_z = 0$, the final velocity must also be zero. Hence, there is no movement of electron in the z-direction.

x-axis: The electron moves with a constant velocity of u_{0x} in the x-direction, for the same reasons given above.

y-axis: The field is in the $-y$-direction, which is uniform. Hence, F is also uniform and constant, which makes the electrons with mass m to have a constant

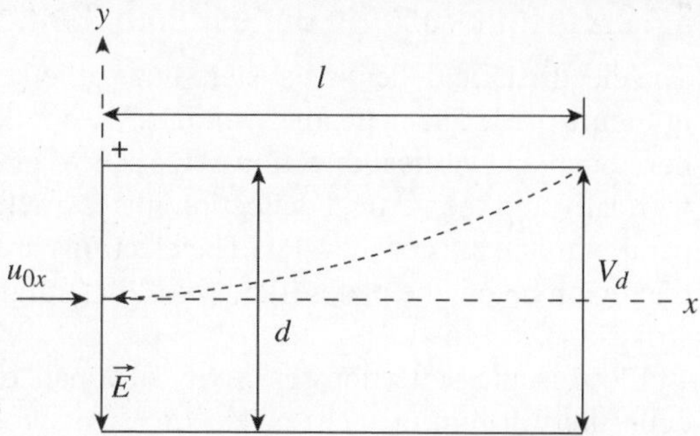

Figure 3.22 *Motion of an electron in an electric field*

acceleration along the y-direction. The motion in the y-direction is represented by

$$u_y = a_y t, \qquad y = \frac{1}{2} a_y t^2 \tag{3.61}$$

where a_y is the acceleration along the y-direction, and using Newton's second law, we have

$$a_y = Q \frac{E_y}{m} = Q \frac{V_d}{md} \tag{3.62}$$

Here, $E = \dfrac{V_d}{d}$

where V_d is the potential across the plates and d is the separation. The above equations indicate an upward motion of the electron in the region between the plates. The velocity component u_y changes from point to point, whereas the velocity component u_x remains unchanged. The distance covered by an electron along the x-direction is given by

$$x = u_{0x} t \tag{3.63}$$

Combining Eqs. (3.61) and (3.63), we get

$$y = \frac{1}{2} a_y t^2 = \frac{1}{2} a_y \left(\frac{x}{u_{0x}} \right)^2$$

$$= \frac{1}{2} \left(\frac{a_y}{u_{0x}^2} \right) x^2$$

Therefore,

$$y = kx^2, \text{ where } k = \frac{1}{2} \left(\frac{a_y}{u_{0x}^2} \right) \tag{3.64}$$

The above equation shows that the electron moves in a parabolic path in the region between the plates.

Some of the applications of the static electric fields such as electrostatic deflection in cathode ray tube, ink-jet printer, and electrostatic voltmeter are discussed in this section.

3.12.2 Electrostatic Deflection in Cathode Ray Tube

The electrostatic deflection system in a cathode ray tube (CRT) uses a pair of deflection plates as shown in Figure 3.23. The deflecting voltages are applied between the two plates. For deflecting the beam in the horizontal and vertical directions, two sets of plates are required. The horizontal deflection plates are kept vertically and the vertical deflection plates are kept horizontally. However, the plane of the plates is kept parallel to the axis of the CRT. The electrons are attracted toward the positive plates and when they leave the region below the plates, they travel in straight line, at an angle with the axis. Then, the electron beam strikes the screen at a point.

Electrostatic deflection sensitivity of a pair of deflection plates of a CRT is defined as the amount of deflection (in mm or inch) of electron spot produced when a voltage of 1 V dc is applied between the corresponding deflection plates. The deflection sensitivity of the plates may be different for X-X and Y-Y plates. The amount of deflection produced may be calculated by knowing (i) the dimensions of the tube components and (ii) deflecting voltage.

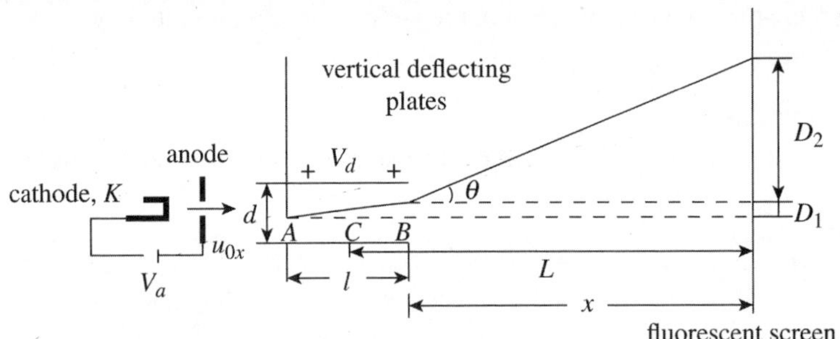

Figure 3.23 *Electrostatic deflection system in a CRT*

Figure 3.23 shows the configuration of the electrostatic deflection system in a CRT. Two plates of length l and spacing d are kept at a distance x from the screen. Let the voltage applied between the plates be V_d and u_{0x} be the velocity of an electron on entering the field of deflection plates.

Then,

$$u_{0x} = \sqrt{\frac{2Q}{m}V_a} = 5.94 \times 10^5 \sqrt{V_a} \text{ m/s}$$

where V_a is the final anode voltage (in volt), Q is the charge of an electron in coulomb, and m is the mass of an electron in kilogram.

As the beam passes through the field of the deflection plates, the electrons are attracted toward the positive plate by a force equal to

$$F = QE = Q\frac{V_d}{d} \tag{3.65}$$

The force produces an acceleration of a m/s^2, which is equal to the force divided by mass m of an electron. This mass may be supposed to be the mass at rest because the deflecting voltage is hardly even greater than 2000 V. Therefore, the acceleration is represented by

$$a = \frac{F}{m} = \frac{QE}{m} = \frac{QV_d}{dm} \tag{3.66}$$

The forward motion however continues at velocity u_{0x}. Then, the time taken by an electron to traverse the field of the plates is $\dfrac{l}{u_{0x}}$. Therefore, the upward velocity attained by an electron in this time interval is u_y which is given by

$$u_y = \frac{l}{u_{0x}} \cdot a = \frac{l}{u_{0x}} \cdot \frac{QV_d}{dm} \tag{3.67}$$

Then, the ratio of upward velocity to forward velocity at the instant the electron leaves the field is

$$\frac{u_y}{u_{0x}} = \frac{QlV_d}{dm\, u_{0x}^2}$$

The electron follows a curved path from A, the point of entrance, to point B, the point leaving the field. Let D_1 be the vertical displacement as represented by

$$D_1 = \frac{1}{2} a \left(\frac{l}{u_{0x}} \right)^2 = \frac{1}{2} \frac{QV_d\, l^2}{dm\, u_{0x}^2} \tag{3.68}$$

If θ is the angle with the axis that the electron beam makes after emerging out from the field of the deflection plates, then

$$\tan \theta = \frac{u_y}{u_{0x}} = \frac{D_2}{x}$$

or

$$D_2 = x \cdot \frac{u_y}{u_{0x}} = \frac{V_d}{d} \cdot \frac{Q}{m} \cdot \frac{l}{u_{0x}^2} \cdot x \tag{3.69}$$

Adding Eqs. (3.68) and (3.69), the total deflection is given by

$$D = D_1 + D_2 = \frac{V_d \cdot Ql \left[\dfrac{l}{2} + x \right]}{dm\, u_{0x}^2}$$

$$= \frac{V_d \cdot QlL}{dm\, u_{0x}^2} \qquad \left(\text{since } L = \frac{l}{2} + x \right) \tag{3.70}$$

The total deflection of the spot will be same as an electron travelling in a straight line path at angle θ from point C instead of B.

Here,

$$u_{0x}^2 = \frac{2QV_a}{m} \tag{3.71}$$

where V_a is the final anode voltage.

Substituting Eq. (3.71) in Eq. (3.70), we get

$$D = \frac{V_d \cdot}{V_a} \times \frac{lL}{2d} \tag{3.72}$$

For a given CRT, the quantities l, L, and d are fixed. Hence, the deflection D of the spot can be changed only by changing the ratio $\dfrac{V_d}{V_a}$. The electrostatic deflection sensitivity of a CRT is defined as the deflection in metre on the screen per volt of deflecting voltage.

The deflection sensitivity is represented by

$$S = \frac{D}{V_d} = \frac{lL}{2dV_a} \text{ cm/V} \tag{3.73}$$

where l is the length of the deflecting plates in m, L is the distance from the center of the plate to the screen in m, V_a is the accelerating potential in V, and d is the separation between the two plates in m.

From the above equation, it is seen that the deflection sensitivity is

(*i*)   directly proportional to the length of the deflection plates l,

(*ii*)   directly proportional to the distance L between the screen and the center of the deflection plates, and

(*iii*) inversely proportional to the spacing d between the deflection plates and inversely proportional to the final anode voltage V_a.

3.12.3   Ink-jet printer

One of the main applications of static electric field is the operation of ink-jet printer. The printing technique involved in an ink-jet printer is based on the principle of electrostatic deflection. This electrostatic deflection mechanism increases the speed of the printing process and also it enhances the quality of the print. Figure 3.24 shows the component of ink-jet printer. An ink-jet printer consists of a nozzle vibrating at ultrasonic frequency and it sprays ink in the form of tiny-sized droplets with small spacing. These droplets will attain charge, based on the type of character to be printed while moving through a set of charged plates. The vertical displacement of an ink droplet is proportional to its charge based on a fixed potential between the vertical deflection plates. Without imparting any charge to the ink droplets, a blank space between characters can be achieved.

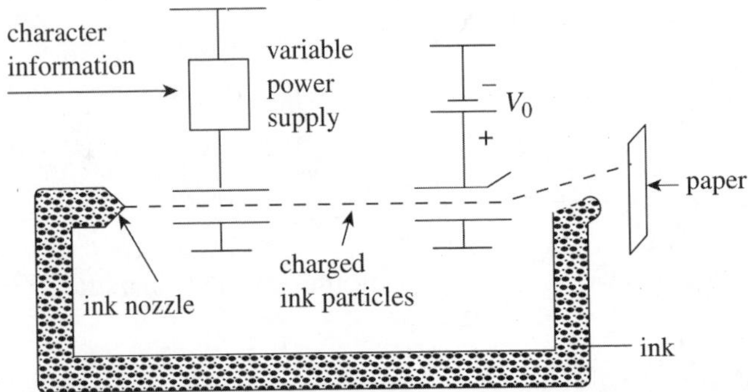

Figure 3.24   *Components of ink-jet printer*

The horizontal deflection of electrons is obtained by varying the potential difference between the horizontal deflection plates in a CRT, whereas in an ink-jet printer, the printer head is moved horizontally at a constant speed. The path or trajectory of an ink droplet is similar to the path of an electron in a CRT. Here, the characters can be printed at the rate of 100 characters per second. Since there are very few moving parts, ink-jet printers are highly reliable, versatile, and quiet in operation.

3.12.4 Electrostatic Voltmeter

Another application involving static electric field concept is the working principle of electrostatic voltmeter. The electrostatic voltmeter is mainly used to measure the rms voltage based on the potential difference concept studied in static electric fields. This type of voltmeter is also used to measure both dc and ac voltages.

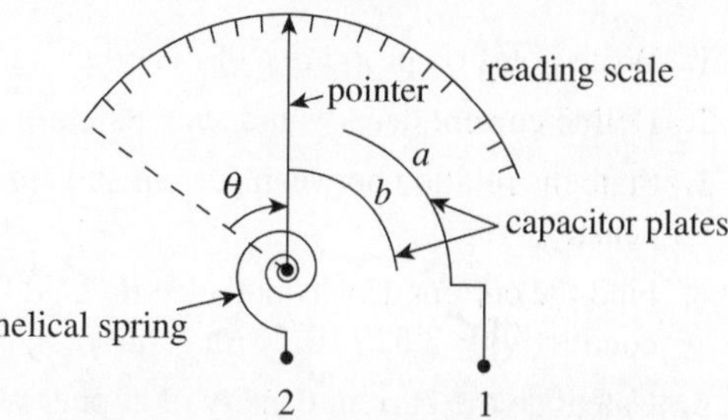

Figure 3.25 *Electrostatic voltmeter*

An electrostatic voltmeter with its components is shown in Figure 3.25. It consists two capacitor plates a and b, a helical spring, a pointer, and a reading scale. Here, the capacitor plate a is fixed to terminal 1 and plate b is movable along with pointer. When a voltage is applied between terminals 1 and 2, the capacitance value of the plates increases based on the movement of the pointer to the right. The helical spring is used to control the movement of the pointer. It is also used to establish an electrical contact between the movable plate b and terminal 2. When the pointer makes an angle θ with the applied constant voltage, there will be an increase in electrostatic energy and it is equal to the amount of work done.

The potential difference between the capacitor plates in an electrostatic voltmeter is given by

$$dV = d\left(\frac{Q}{C}\right) = \frac{1}{C}dQ - \frac{Q}{C^2}dC \tag{3.74}$$

When the applied voltage is constant, i.e., $dV = 0$, Eq. (3.74) becomes

$$\frac{1}{C}dQ = \frac{Q}{C^2}dC \tag{3.75}$$

The change in electrostatic energy is represented by

$$dW_e = d\left(\frac{Q^2}{2C}\right) = \frac{Q}{C}dQ - \frac{Q^2}{2C^2}dC = \frac{Q^2}{2C^2}dC \tag{3.76}$$

The amount of work done in the electric field can be written in terms of torque T and angular displacement $d\theta$ as

$$dW_e = Td\theta \tag{3.77}$$

Equating Eqs. (3.76) and (3.77), we get

$$T = \frac{Q^2}{2C^2}\frac{dC}{d\theta} = \frac{1}{2}V^2\frac{dC}{d\theta} \tag{3.78}$$

Here, $T = \tau\theta$ in the equilibrium position where τ is the torsional constant of the spring and θ is the deflection angle of the pointer.

Therefore, the deflection angle of the pointer is given by

$$\theta = \frac{1}{2\tau}V^2\frac{dC}{d\theta} \tag{3.79}$$

Here, the deflection angle is proportional to the square of the applied voltage V if $\dfrac{dC}{d\theta}$ is constant.

REVIEW QUESTIONS

1. Write notes on properties of materials and their classification based on conductivity.
2. Define current density and state its unit.
3. State the relation between current and current density. Also, state how current density is related to charge density.
4. Find the current density and electric field for an aluminum having drift velocity of electrons 5.3×10^{-4} m/s, conductivity 3.82×10^{-4} S/m , and $\mu_e = 0.0014$ m^2/V$\cdot$s.
5. Calculate the current density of copper wire having conductivity of 5.8×10^{7} S/m and $|\vec{E}| = 20$ V/m .
6. What is mobility? Obtain its unit.
7. Distinguish between conduction current and convection current.
8. Derive the relation between $\vec{J}$ and ρ_v.
9. State continuity equation in integral and differential forms.
10. State and derive the point form of Ohm's law.
11. State the effect of temperature on resistivity and conductivity.
12. State the properties of conductor.
13. Derive the expression for continuity equation of current in differential form.
14. What do you understand by current continuity equation of current?
15. Determine the time rate of change of the volume charge density if the volume current density in the medium is $\vec{J} = \sin(10x)\vec{a}_x + y\vec{a}_y + e^{-3z}\vec{a}_z$ A/m^2 .
16. Given $\vec{J} = 10^{4}\sin\theta\,\vec{a}_r$ A/m^2 in spherical system, find the current passing the spherical shell of $r = 0.2$ m .
17. What is the difference between homogeneous medium and non-homogeneous medium?
18. What is the difference between linear and non-linear mediums?
19. What is polarization?
20. State the mathematical equation for polarization and state its unit.
21. Define dielectric strength of material. Give its unit. State its value for the air.
22. Define the term relative permittivity.
23. Describe the polarization in dielectric materials.
24. Define electric susceptibility of dielectric material.
25. Explain the properties of dielectric materials.
26. Obtain a relationship between polarization and electric field intensity.
27. Write notes on dielectric breakdown voltage and dielectric strength of a dielectric material with example.
28. Derive an expression for the normal flux density $\vec{D}$ in a dielectric material in terms of the electric field intensity $\vec{E}$ and the dielectric constant ε_r.
29. Explain what is meant by "breakdown strength" of a dielectric.
30. Why is the electrostatic potential continuous at a boundary?
31. Define the boundary conditions for the conductor–free space boundary in electrostatic field.

32. Derive the boundary conditions of the tangential and normal components of electric field at the interface of two mediums with different dielectrics.

33. The electric field strength 1.2 V/m is entering a dielectric medium of $\varepsilon_r = 4$ from air. The orientation of $\vec{E}$ in air is 65° with respect to boundary. Determine the orientation of $\vec{E}$ in the dielectric and its strength in the dielectric.

34. The electric field intensity $\vec{E}$ in air above a block of paraffin $(\varepsilon_r = 2.1)$ is at an angle of 45° with respect to the plane surface of the block. Find the angle between $\vec{E}$ and the surface in the paraffin.

35. The electric field strength in a mass of porcelain (relative permittivity 6) in air is 2000 V/cm. At the inner surface of the porcelain, the field makes an angle 45° to the normal and emerges into the air. Find the angle of emergence of the external field and its magnitude.

36. Write down the boundary conditions at the interface between different dielectric mediums in both scalar and vector forms.

37. Explain the law of refraction at dielectric–dielectric interface.

38. Find the angle by which the direction of $\vec{E}$ changes, as it crosses the boundary between two dielectrics with dielectric constants 4 and 5. The incident angle is 50° with the normal.

39. A potential field is given by $V = 150\left(x^2 - y^2\right)$. The point $P(4, -2, 1)$ lies on the boundary of the conductor and free space. At point P, obtain the magnitudes of (i) V, (ii) $\vec{E}$, (iii) E_n, (iv) E_{tan}, (v) $\vec{D}$, and (vi) ρ_s.

40. Obtain the expression for resistance of a conductor.

41. Derive the expression for resistance and conductance of a coaxial cable.

42. A copper wire of area 1 cm^2 carries a uniformly distributed current of 200 A. If the electron density in copper is 8.5×10^{28} electrons per cubic metre, determine the average drift velocity of the electrons. What is the electric field intensity in the wire? If the wire is 100 km long, calculate the potential difference between its ends. What is the resistance of the wire?

43. State and explain Joule's law.

44. A wire of length 10 m and radius 0.5 mm carries a current of 2 A when a potential difference of 12 V is applied between its ends. What is the resistance of the wire? What is its conductivity?

45. A copper wire 10 km in length and 1.3 mm in diameter is connected to an EMF source of 24 V. Determine (i) the resistance of the wire, (ii) the current through the wire, (iii) the current density in the wire, (iv) the power dissipated as heat by the wire, and (v) the power supplied by the source.

46. Compare conductor, dielectric, and capacitor.

47. Derive the expression for capacitance of parallel plate capacitor.

48. Determine the capacitance of a parallel plate capacitor having tin foil sheets, 25 cm square plates separated through a glass dielectric 0.5 cm thick with relative permittivity 6.

49. A parallel plate capacitor has voltage of 25 V across the plates. If the distance between the plates is doubled, find the new voltage across the plates.

50. Determine the capacitance of a capacitor with two parallel plates 30 cm × 30 cm separated by 5 mm in air. What is the energy stored in the capacitor if it is charged to a potential drop of 500 V?

51. Obtain the expression for capacitance of co-axial cable.

52. Determine the capacitance of spherical capacitor.

53. Derive the expression for capacitance of isolated sphere.

54. Derive the expression for capacitance of composite parallel plate capacitor with two different dielectric materials parallel and normal to plates.

55. Find the capacitance of a parallel plate capacitor, if the plates are of area 1.5m^2, the distance between plates is 2 mm, potential gradient is 10^5V/m, and ρ_s is $2.5 \,\mu\text{C/m}^2$.

56. A capacitor is composed of two parallel plates each having a surface area 2m^2. Their distance of separation is 2.5 mm in free space. A 200 V battery is connected across them and then removed. Calculate the magnitude of electric flux density $\vec{D}$, charge density ρ_s, and energy density W_e. A sheet of dielectric 1 mm thick and surface area 2 m^2 is inserted between the plates. Calculate $\vec{D}$, ρ_s, and W_e for this new capacitor.

57. A condenser is composed of two plates separated by a sheet of insulating material 3 mm thick and $\varepsilon_r = 6$. The distance between the plates is increased to allow the insulation of a second sheet 5 mm thick of $\varepsilon_{r2} = x$. If the capacitance of the condenser so formed is 1/3 of the original capacitance, find x.

58. Consider that two parallel conducting plates are each 10 cm × 10 cm and separated by 2 mm. The region between plates is filled with a perfect dielectric for which $\varepsilon_r = (1 + 200x)^2$, where x is the distance from one plate. Assume uniform surface charge density of 10 nC/m^2 on the positive plate. Determine density D_x and capacitance C.

59. A capacitor is composed of two parallel plates and separated by an insulating medium of 3 mm thickness and of relative permittivity 4. The distance between the plates is increased to allow the insertion of a second sheet which is 5 mm thick and of relative permittivity ε_{r2}. If the capacitance of the capacitor so formed is 1/3 of the original capacitance, find the value of ε_{r2}.

60. A parallel plate capacitor with a separation $d = 1\text{cm}$ has 29 kV applied when free space is the only dielectric. Assume air has a dielectric strength of 30 kV/cm. Show why the air breaks down when a thin piece of glass $(\varepsilon_r = 6.5)$ with a dielectric strength of 290 kV/cm and thickness $d_2 = 0.2\,\text{cm}$ is inserted.

61. An electrolytic condenser consisting of an oxidized aluminum sheet with an effective surface area of 400 cm^2 has a capacitance of 8 F and the dielectric constant of Al_2O_3 is 8. A potential difference of 10 V is applied between the aluminum and the electrolyte. What are the field strength and total dipole moment induced in the oxide layer?

62. Find the capacitance of a parallel plate capacitor,

(*i*)   when the plates are of area 1m^2, distance between the plates 1 mm, voltage gradient is 10^5V/m, and the $\rho_s = 2\,\mu\text{C/m}^2$.

(*ii*)   when the stored energy is 5 mJ and the voltage across the plates is 5 V.

63. A cylindrical capacitor consists of an inner conductor of radius a and an outer conductor whose inner radius is b. The space between the conductors is filled with a dielectric of permittivity ε, and the length of the capacitor is l. Determine its capacitance.

64. A single core coaxial cable is designed for 10 kV with rubber dielectric having an allowable field strength of 3×10^6 V/m. If the inner conductor is a solid wire with radius 50 mm, then determine the minimum radial thickness of dielectric required to satisfy the above specifications.

65. A spherical capacitor consists of an inner conducting sphere of radius R_i and an outer conductor with a spherical inner wall of radius R_0. The space in between is filled with a dielectric of permittivity ε. Determine the capacitance.

66. Consider that two concentric spheres of radii 2 and 4 cm are separated by vacuum. Find the capacitance.

67. The radii of two concentric spheres forming a spherical capacitor are 0.20 and 0.06 m and the space between them is filled with a dielectric of relative permittivity 2.1. Find the greatest field in V/m in the dielectric when the potential difference between the spheres is 50 kV. Show that for a given radius of the surrounding sphere, the greatest electric field will be a minimum when the radii are in the ratio 2 to 1.

68. Determine the capacitance in picofarads of an air-insulated capacitor with 9 parallel plates each of $0.2 \, \text{m}^2$ with plane separation of 0.2 cm.

69. Consider the two conducting plates, each $3 \, \text{cm} \times 6 \, \text{cm}$ and three slabs of dielectric each $1 \, \text{cm} \times 3 \, \text{cm} \times 6 \, \text{cm}$ having relative dielectric constants of π, 2π, and 3π are assembled into a capacitor with a separation of 3 cm. Compute the two values of capacitance obtained by two possible methods of assembling the capacitor.

70. Derive, from fundamentals, an expression for the equivalent capacitance of two capacitors in series and in parallel.

71. Prove that $C_{eq} = \dfrac{C_1 C_2}{C_1 + C_2}$ if the capacitors C_1 and C_2 are connected in series.

72. If $C_1 = 100 \, \mu\text{F}$ and $C_2 = 50 \, \text{mF}$, then what is the combined capacitance C for series combination and for parallel combination?

73. Derive Poisson's and Laplace's equations.

74. State the applications of Poisson's and Laplace's equations.

75. Write down the expressions for Laplacian of a scalar potential V in (i) Cartesian form, (ii) cylindrical form, and (iii) spherical form.

76. Define Poisson's equation for a homogenous medium.

77. The conductivity of a homogenous conducting medium is bounded by $10 \, \text{cm} \leq r \leq 20 \, \text{cm}$, $30° \leq \theta \leq 45°$, and $\pi/6 \leq \phi \leq \pi/3$ is $0.4 \, \text{S/m}$. The surface at $\theta = 45°$ is at a ground potential and the surface at $\theta = 30°$ is at 100 V. Using Laplace's equation, determine the resistance of the medium.

78. Obtain the capacitance of parallel plate capacitor using Laplace's equation.

79. Write the capacitance of spherical plate capacitor using Laplace's equation.

80. Derive the capacitance of two spherical shells of radius a and b using Laplace's equation. The inner shell is at a potential of V_0 and the outer shell is grounded. What is the surface charge density on the inner shell?

81. Calculate the capacitance of two concentric spherical shells of radii 5 and 10 cm using Laplace's equation. The inner shell is at a potential of 500 V and the outer shell is grounded. What is the surface charge density on the inner shell? The dielectric constant of the medium is 9. Determine the potential difference and the electric field in the medium.

82. Obtain the capacitance of coaxial cable capacitor using Laplace's equation.

83. In cylindrical coordinates, $V = 75 \, \text{V}$ at $r = 5 \, \text{mm}$ and $V = 0$ at $r = 60 \, \text{mm}$. Find the voltage at $r = 130 \, \text{mm}$, if the potential depends only on r.

84. Consider that long concentric and right conducting cylinders in free space, at $r = 5 \, \text{mm}$ and $r = 25 \, \text{mm}$, in cylindrical coordinates, have voltages 0 and V_0, respectively. If $\vec{E} = -8.28 \times 10^3 \, \vec{a}_r \, \text{V/m}$ at $r = 5 \, \text{mm}$, find V_0 and ρ_s on the outer conductor by using Laplace's equation.

85. Find the potential V at the point P (2, 3, 4) for the field of two coaxial conducting cylinders, given $V = 6 \, \text{V}$ at $r = 3 \, \text{mm}$ and $V = 10 \, \text{V}$ at $r = 5 \, \text{m}$.

86. Find the potential at P (1, 2, 3,) for the field of two infinite radial conducting plates, given $V = 40\text{V}$ at $\phi = 15°$ and $V = 15\text{V}$ at $\phi = 40°$.

87. Find the potential between two coaxial cones using Laplace's equation with $V = V_1$ at $\theta = \theta_1$ and $V = V_0$ at $\theta = \theta_2$.

88. Find V at $\theta = 20°$ for the field between two conducting cones with $V = 0$ at $\theta = 30°$ and $V = 100\text{V}$ at $\theta = 10°$. Also, calculate θ for a voltage to be 50 V.

89. Find a solution to Laplace's equation subject to the boundary conditions $V = 100$ volt at $z = 0.01$ and $V = -33$ volt at $z = 0.02$.

90. Solve one-dimensional Laplace equation to obtain the field inside a parallel plate capacitor and also, find the expression for the surface charge density at two plates.

91. Show that the potential function (in cylindrical coordinates) $V = \dfrac{V_0 zr (\cos\phi + \sin\phi)}{a^2}$ satisfies Laplace's equation.

92. Show that the electrostatic potential V in regions where charges are present, satisfies Poisson's equation $\nabla^2 V = -\dfrac{\rho}{\varepsilon}$ where ρ is the charge density and ε is the permittivity of the medium.

93. Obtain Poisson's equation from Gauss's law.

94. State the difference between Poisson's and Laplace's equations.

95. When can we use Laplace's equation to determine the potential distribution in a conducting medium carrying steady current?

96. A uniform volume charge distribution of $-10^{-8}\,\text{C/m}^3$ occupies the region between two coaxial conducting cylinders of radii 20 and 50 mm. If the electric field and potential are both zero on the inner cylinder, find the potential on the outer cylinder using Poisson's equation.

97. Explain the importance of Poisson's equation and Laplace's equation regarding static electric fields.

98. A point charge Q is placed at a distance d from the center of a grounded conducting sphere of radius a. Calculate the surface charge density on the sphere.

99. Write notes on the applications of static electric fields.

100. Describe the motion of electrons in electric field.

101. Explain how electrostatic deflection takes place in a cathode ray tube.

102. Discuss the working principle of ink-jet printer.

103. Explain the construction and working principle of electrostatic voltmeter.

STATIC MAGNETIC FIELDS

4.1 INTRODUCTION

The static electric field is produced by stationary charges whereas static magnetic field is produced by steady currents. The movement of charges with constant velocity gives rise to constant current flow, i.e., direct current, which in turn results in static or steady magnetic field. Such a static magnetic field is also called magnetostatic field. The study of magnetic field begins with the discussion of two major laws, namely, Biot–Savart's law and Ampere's law, which govern magnetostatic fields. Biot–Savart's law is the general law of magnetostatics which is similar to Coulomb's law in electrostatics. Ampere's law is a special case of Biot–Savart's law and is similar to Gauss's law in electrostatics.

The determination of magnetic field strength or intensity due to linear and circular conductors carrying current is based on Biot–Savart's law. Similarly, Ampere's law is used to determine the magnetic field for different current distributions such as line current, surface current, and volume current. Ampere's law is applicable only for symmetric current distributions like Gauss's law to symmetric charge distributions in electrostatics.

The static electric fields are characterized by electric field intensity $\vec{E}$ and electric flux density $\vec{D}$. Similarly, the static magnetic fields are characterized by magnetic field intensity $\vec{H}$ and magnetic flux density $\vec{B}$. For a linear and isotropic medium, $\vec{D}$ and $\vec{E}$ are related as $\vec{D} = \varepsilon\vec{E}$ in electrostatics whereas $\vec{H}$ and $\vec{B}$ in magnetostatics are related as $\vec{B} = \mu\vec{H}$. The applications of Biot–Savart's law, Ampere's law, and magnetic potential are discussed in this chapter.

4.2 BIOT–SAVART'S LAW

Biot–Savart's law states that the differential magnetic field intensity $d\vec{H}$ produced at a point P due to a steady current I flowing through a differential elemental length $d\vec{l}$ of a wire is given by

$$d\vec{H} = k\frac{I d\vec{l} \times \vec{a}_R}{R^2} \tag{4.1}$$

where $k = \dfrac{1}{4\pi}$ is the constant of proportionality and $\vec{a}_R = \dfrac{\vec{R}}{R}$

i.e., $\vec{R} = R\vec{a}_R$ is the distance vector between $d\vec{l}$ and the point of observation P, as shown in Figure 4.1.

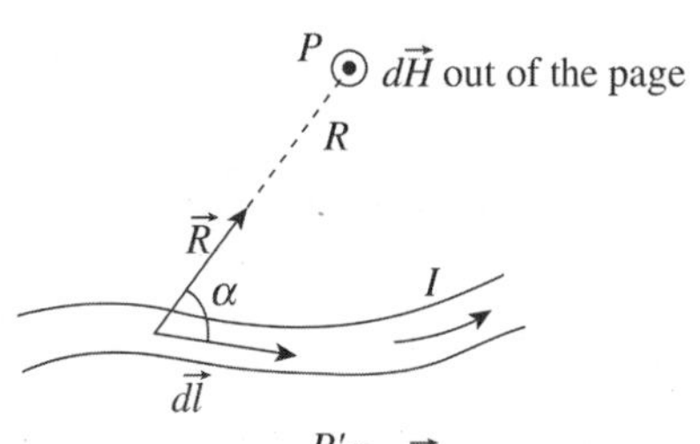

Figure 4.1 *Magnetic field $d\vec{H}$ produced at a point P due to a current element $I d\vec{l}$*

The unit of magnetic field intensity is ampere per metre (A/m). Substituting the values of proportionality constant and unit vector in Eq. (4.1), the differential magnetic field intensity can be written as

$$d\vec{H} = \frac{Id\vec{l} \times \vec{R}}{4\pi R^3} \tag{4.2}$$

Using the magnitude of cross product i.e., $\left|d\vec{l} \times \vec{R}\right| = dl\,R\sin\alpha$ in the above equation, the magnitude of differential magnetic field intensity becomes

$$dH = \frac{Idl\sin\alpha}{4\pi R^2} \tag{4.3}$$

From Biot–Savart's law, it is seen that the magnitude of differential magnetic field intensity dH is directly proportional to the product Idl and the sine of angle α between the current element and the line joining the observation point P to the element and inversely proportional to the square of the distance R between point P and current element.

The conventional representation of magnetic field intensity is shown in Figure 4.1 in which the direction of $d\vec{H}$ is out of the page (a small circle with a dot sign) at point P and the direction of $d\vec{H}$ is into the page (a small circle with a cross sign) at point P'.

The direction of magnetic field $d\vec{H}$ can be determined by the right-hand rule. Here, the thumb points in the direction of the current and the remaining four fingers surrounding the wire represent the direction of the magnetic field $d\vec{H}$, as shown in Figure 4.2(a). The direction of $d\vec{H}$ can also be determined using the right-hand screw rule. Here, the tip of the screw moving downwards points in the direction of current I and the direction of rotation of the screw gives the direction of $d\vec{H}$, as shown in Figure 4.2(b).

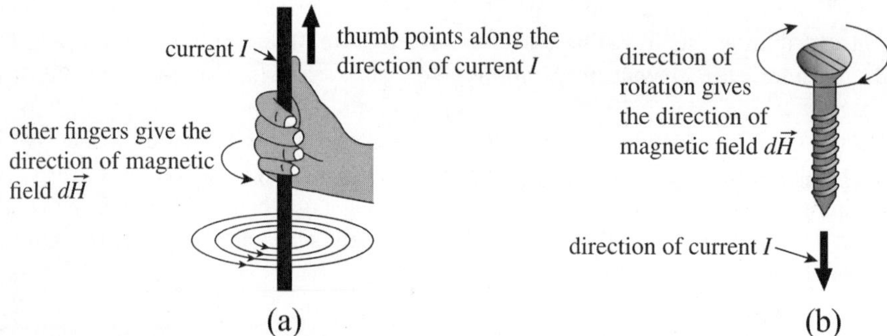

Figure 4.2 *Direction of magnetic field $d\vec{H}$: (a) right-hand rule and (b) right-hand screw rule*

Both magnetic field and electric field intensities are inversely proportional to R^2. The direction of electric field intensity $\vec{E}$ is along the distance vector $\vec{R}$ joining the charge to the point of observation whereas the direction of magnetic field intensity $\vec{H}$ is perpendicular to the plane containing the direction of the current element $Id\vec{l}$ and the distant vector $\vec{R}$.

The total magnetic field intensity at a point due to a conductor of finite size can be obtained by integrating the contributions due to all current elements of the conductor. Therefore, the Biot–Savart's law can be written as

$$\vec{H} = \frac{I}{4\pi}\int_{l}\frac{d\vec{l} \times \vec{a}_R}{R^2} \tag{4.4}$$

where the current flows along the line path l.

As the electric field exists for different charge distributions, the magnetic field also exists for different current distributions such as line current, surface current, and volume current, as shown in Figure 4.3. Hence, Biot–Savart's law can also be expressed in terms of distributed current sources such as the *volume current density* $\vec{J}$ (in A/m^2) or the *surface current density* $\vec{K}$ or $\vec{J}_s$ (in A/m). The surface current density is generally applicable to currents that flow on the surface of thin conducting sheets.

If the current sources are defined in terms of $\vec{J}$ over a volume v or in terms of $\vec{K}$ over a surface s, then the relation between the source elements is written as

$$I d\vec{l} = \vec{K} ds = \vec{J} dv$$

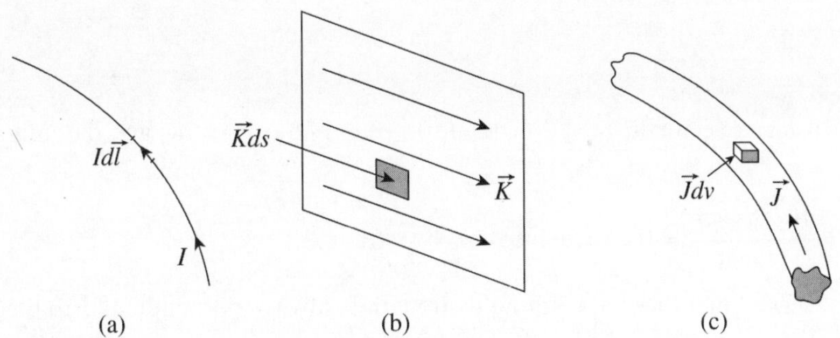

Figure 4.3 *Different current distributions: (a) line current (b) surface current and (c) volume current*

Thus, the Biot–Savart's law can be expressed in terms of distributed current sources as follows:

$$\vec{H} = \frac{1}{4\pi} \int_v \frac{\vec{J} dv \times \vec{a}_R}{R^2} \qquad \text{(volume current)} \tag{4.5a}$$

$$\vec{H} = \frac{1}{4\pi} \int_s \frac{\vec{K} ds \times \vec{a}_R}{R^2} \qquad \text{(surface current)} \tag{4.5b}$$

$$\vec{H} = \frac{1}{4\pi} \int_l \frac{I d\vec{l} \times \vec{a}_R}{R^2} \qquad \text{(line current)} \tag{4.5c}$$

EXAMPLE 4.1

A steady current element of $10^{-3}\,\vec{a}_z$ A·m is located at the origin in free space. (i) What is the magnetic field intensity due to this current element at $(1,0,0)$? (ii) What is the magnetic field at $(0,0,1)$?

SOLUTION

(*i*) Using Biot–Savart's law, the differential magnetic field intensity at $(1,0,0)$ due to the current element located at $(0,0,0)$ is

$$d\vec{H} = \frac{I d\vec{l} \times \vec{a}_R}{4\pi R^2}$$

where the distance vector is $\vec{R} = (1-0)\vec{a}_x + (0-0)\vec{a}_y + (0-0)\vec{a}_z = \vec{a}_x.$

Therefore, the unit vector is

$$\vec{a}_R = \frac{\vec{R}}{\left|\vec{R}\right|} = \frac{\vec{a}_x}{\sqrt{1^2}} = \vec{a}_x$$

Since the current element $Id\vec{l} = 10^{-3}\,\vec{a}_z\ \text{A}\cdot\text{m},$ the differential magnetic field intensity is

$$d\vec{H} = \frac{10^{-3}\,\vec{a}_z \times \vec{a}_x}{4\pi} = \frac{10^{-3}}{4\pi}\vec{a}_y\ \text{A/m}, \qquad \text{where } R = 1$$

(*ii*)   The differential magnetic field strength at $(0,0,1)$ due to the current element located at $(0,0,0)$ is

$$d\vec{H} = \frac{Id\vec{l} \times \vec{a}_R}{4\pi R^2}$$

where the distance vector is $\vec{R} = (0-0)\vec{a}_x + (0-0)\vec{a}_y + (1-0)\vec{a}_z = \vec{a}_z$ and the unit vector is $\vec{a}_R = \vec{a}_z$. Therefore,

$$d\vec{H} = \frac{10^{-3}\,\vec{a}_z \times \vec{a}_z}{4\pi \times 1} = 0 \qquad (\text{since } \vec{a}_z \times \vec{a}_z = 0)$$

Hence, it is observed that the magnetic field strength is always perpendicular to the current carrying element.   ∎

EXAMPLE 4.2

Find the magnetic field intensity at the origin due to a current element, $Id\vec{l} = 3\pi\left(\vec{a}_x + 2\vec{a}_y + 3\vec{a}_z\right)\mu\text{A}\cdot\text{m}$ at $(3,4,5)$ in free space.

SOLUTION

Using Biot–Savart's law, the differential magnetic field intensity due to the current element shown in Figure E4.2 is

$$d\vec{H} = \frac{Id\vec{l} \times \vec{a}_R}{4\pi R^2}$$

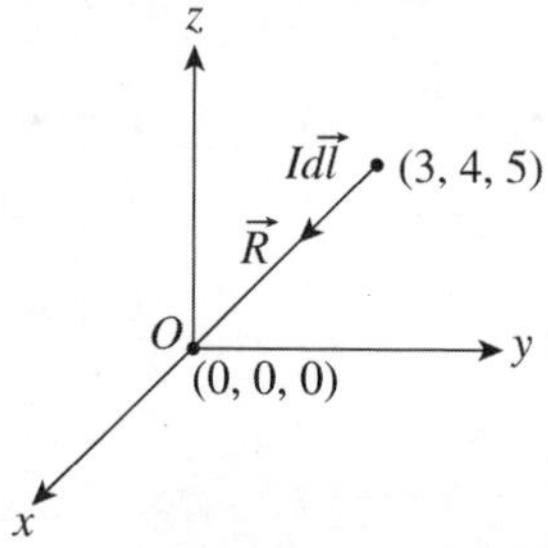

where the distance vector is $\vec{R} = -3\vec{a}_x - 4\vec{a}_y - 5\vec{a}_z$. Therefore, the unit vector is

$$\vec{a}_R = \frac{\vec{R}}{\left|\vec{R}\right|} = \frac{-3\vec{a}_x - 4\vec{a}_y - 5\vec{a}_z}{\sqrt{3^2 + 4^2 + 5^2}}$$

$$= -0.4242\vec{a}_x - 0.5656\vec{a}_y - 0.7071\vec{a}_z$$

Figure E4.2

Since $Id\vec{l} = 3\pi\left(\vec{a}_x + 2\vec{a}_y + 3\vec{a}_z\right)\mu\text{A}\cdot\text{m},$

$$Id\vec{l} \times \vec{a}_R = \begin{vmatrix} \vec{a}_x & \vec{a}_y & \vec{a}_z \\ 3\pi & 6\pi & 9\pi \\ -0.4242 & -0.5656 & -0.7071 \end{vmatrix} \times 10^{-6}$$

$$= (-13.322\vec{a}_x - 12\vec{a}_y - 5.33\vec{a}_z + 8\vec{a}_z + 6.661\vec{a}_y + 15.983\vec{a}_x) \times 10^{-6}$$

$$= (2.661\vec{a}_x - 5.339\vec{a}_y + 2.67\vec{a}_z) \times 10^{-6}$$

Hence, $d\vec{H} = \dfrac{(2.661\vec{a}_x - 5.339\vec{a}_y + 2.67\vec{a}_z)\times 10^{-6}}{4\pi \times \left(\sqrt{50}\right)^2}$ $\left(\text{since } R = \left|\vec{R}\right| = \sqrt{50}\right)$

$$= 4.24\vec{a}_x - 8.51\vec{a}_y + 4.25\vec{a}_z \text{ nA/m} \qquad \square$$

EXAMPLE 4.3

Find the incremental field strength at P_2 due to the current element $2\pi\vec{a}_z \, \mu\text{A}\cdot\text{m}$ at P_1. The co-ordinates of P_1 and P_2 are $(4,0,0)$ and $(0,3,0)$, respectively.

SOLUTION

Figure E4.3 shows the current element $I_1 d\vec{l}_1$ at P_1. Given the co-ordinates of P_1 and P_2 are $(4,0,0)$ and $(0,3,0)$, respectively.

According to Biot–Savart's law, the incremental field strength at P_2 due to the current element of $2\pi\vec{a}_z \, \mu\text{A}\cdot\text{m}$ at P_1 is

$$d\vec{H}_2 = \frac{I_1 d\vec{l}_1 \times \vec{a}_{R12}}{4\pi \, R_{12}^2}$$

where the distance vector between points P_1 and P_2 is

$$\vec{R}_{12} = (0-4)\vec{a}_x + (3-0)\vec{a}_y + 0\vec{a}_z = -4\vec{a}_x + 3\vec{a}_y$$

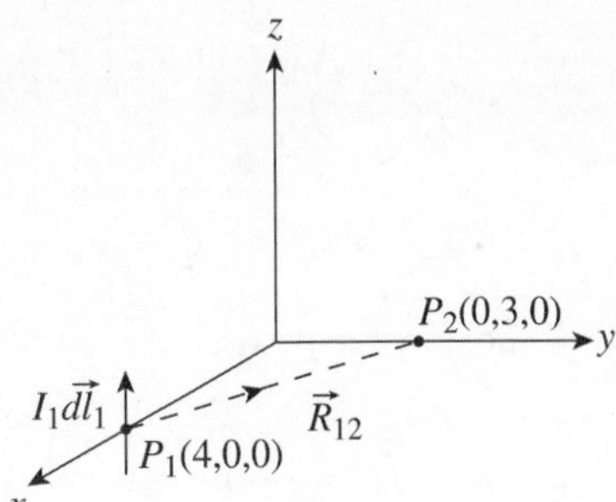

Figure E4.3

Therefore, the unit vector is

$$\vec{a}_{R12} = \frac{\vec{R}_{12}}{\left|\vec{R}_{12}\right|} = \frac{-4\vec{a}_x + 3\vec{a}_y}{\sqrt{16+9}} = \frac{-4\vec{a}_x + 3\vec{a}_y}{5}$$

Since $I_1 d\vec{l}_1 = 2\pi\vec{a}_z \, \mu\text{A}\cdot\text{m}$,

$$I_1 \, d\vec{l}_1 \times \vec{a}_{R12} = \begin{vmatrix} \vec{a}_x & \vec{a}_y & \vec{a}_z \\ 0 & 0 & 2\pi \\ -\dfrac{4}{5} & \dfrac{3}{5} & 0 \end{vmatrix} = \left(-\frac{3}{5}\times 2\pi\right)\vec{a}_x - \left(\frac{4}{5}\times 2\pi\right)\vec{a}_y = -\frac{2\pi}{5}\left[3\vec{a}_x + 4\vec{a}_y\right]$$

Hence, $d\vec{H}_2 = \dfrac{-\dfrac{2\pi}{5}\left[3\vec{a}_x + 4\vec{a}_y\right]}{4\pi\times(5)^2} = -4\times 10^{-3}\left[3\vec{a}_x + 4\vec{a}_y\right] \, \mu\text{A/m}$

$$= -12\vec{a}_x - 16\vec{a}_y \text{ nA/m} \qquad \square$$

EXAMPLE 4.4

A filamentary current of 10 A is directed inward from infinity to the origin on the positive x-axis and then outward to infinity along the positive y-axis. Using Biot–Savart's law, find the magnetic field strength at $P(0,0,1)$.

SOLUTION

From Biot–Savart's law, the differential magnetic field strength is

$$d\vec{H} = \frac{Id\vec{l} \times \vec{a}_R}{4\pi R^2} = \frac{Id\vec{l} \times \vec{R}}{4\pi R^3}$$

For x-axis, the distance vector $\vec{R} = -x\vec{a}_x + \vec{a}_z$ and the current element is $Id\vec{l} = 10dx\vec{a}_x$. Therefore,

$$\vec{H}_1 = \frac{10}{4\pi} \int_\infty^0 \frac{(dx\vec{a}_x) \times (-x\vec{a}_x + \vec{a}_z)}{\left[\sqrt{(1+x^2)}\right]^3} = -\frac{5}{2\pi} \int_\infty^0 \frac{dx\vec{a}_y}{(1+x^2)^{3/2}} \qquad \left(\text{since } \vec{a}_x \times \vec{a}_z = -\vec{a}_y\right)$$

$$= -\frac{5}{2\pi} \frac{x}{\sqrt{(1+x^2)}}\bigg|_\infty^0 \vec{a}_y = \frac{5}{2\pi}\vec{a}_y \text{ A/m}$$

Similarly, for y-axis,

$$\vec{H}_2 = \frac{5}{2\pi} \int_0^\infty \frac{(dy\vec{a}_y) \times (-y\vec{a}_y + \vec{a}_z)}{\left[\sqrt{1+y^2}\right]^3} = \frac{5}{2\pi} \int_0^\infty \frac{dy\vec{a}_x}{(1+y^2)^{3/2}} \qquad \left(\text{since } \vec{a}_y \times \vec{a}_z = \vec{a}_x\right)$$

$$= \frac{5}{2\pi} \frac{y}{\sqrt{(1+y^2)}}\bigg|_0^\infty \vec{a}_x = \frac{5}{2\pi}\vec{a}_x \text{ A/m}$$

The total magnetic field intensity is the combination of the two fields due to currents flowing in x-axis and y-axis. Hence,

$$\vec{H}_t = \vec{H}_1 + \vec{H}_2 = \frac{5}{2\pi}\vec{a}_y + \frac{5}{2\pi}\vec{a}_x = 0.796\left[\vec{a}_y + \vec{a}_x\right] \text{ A/m} \qquad \square$$

4.2.1 Magnetic Field due to a Straight Conductor

Consider a straight conductor of finite length l carrying current I is placed along the z-axis, as shown in Figure 4.4(a).

The magnetic field intensity at point P located at a distance ρ in the xy-plane in free space can be determined using Biot–Savart's law. The current carrying conductor is placed along the z-axis such that its upper end is at $z = l/2$ and the lower end is at $z = -l/2$. Both the ends are also inclined at angles α_1 and α_2 with the point of observation P, as shown in Figure 4.4(b). First, the contribution of differential magnetic field intensity $d\vec{H}$ due to an incremental current element $d\vec{l}$ is to be obtained using Biot–Savart's law. From Eq. (4.1), we get

$$d\vec{H} = \frac{I}{4\pi} \frac{d\vec{l} \times \vec{a}_r}{r^2} \tag{4.6}$$

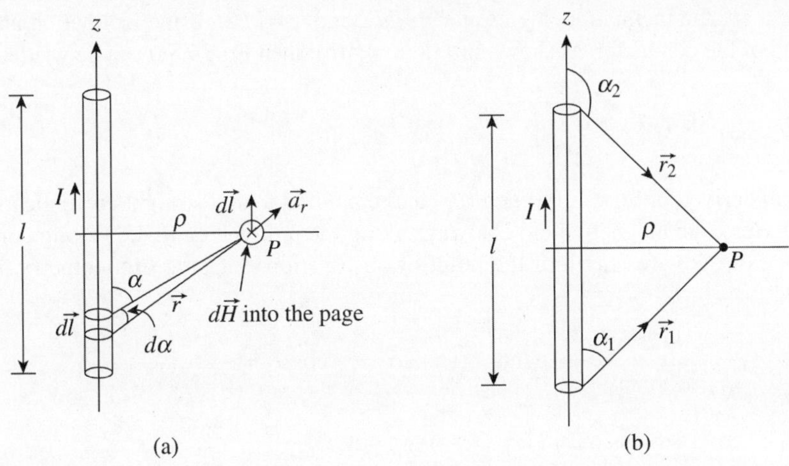

Figure 4.4   *Determination of magnetic field due to a straight conductor: (a) field at point P due to element $\vec{dl}$ and (b) conductor with limiting angles at its ends*

Here, the small current element $\vec{dl} = dz\vec{a}_z$ and $\vec{dl} \times \vec{a}_r = dz(\vec{a}_z \times \vec{a}_r) = \vec{a}_\phi \sin\alpha \, dz$ where $\vec{a}_\phi$ is the azimuth direction and α is the angle between $\vec{dl}$ and $\vec{a}_r$.

Then, the total magnetic field intensity due to a conductor of finite size can be obtained by integrating the contributions due to all current elements of the conductor. Integrating Eq. (4.6) over z, we get

$$\vec{H} = \frac{I}{4\pi} \int_{z=-l/2}^{z=l/2} \frac{\vec{dl} \times \vec{a}_r}{r^2}$$

$$= \frac{I}{4\pi} \int_{z=-l/2}^{z=l/2} \frac{\sin\alpha}{r^2} dz \, \vec{a}_\phi \tag{4.7}$$

Converting the integration variable from z to α, we get

$$r = \rho \, \mathrm{cosec}\, \alpha$$

$$z = -\rho \cot \alpha$$

$$dz = \rho \, \mathrm{cosec}^2 \alpha \, d\alpha$$

Substituting the above transformations in Eq. (4.7), we have

$$\vec{H} = \frac{I}{4\pi} \int_{\alpha_1}^{\alpha_2} \frac{(\sin\alpha)(\rho \, \mathrm{cosec}^2 \alpha \, d\alpha)}{(\rho \, \mathrm{cosec}\, \alpha)^2} \vec{a}_\phi$$

$$= \frac{I}{4\pi\rho} \int_{\alpha_1}^{\alpha_2} \sin\alpha \, d\alpha \, \vec{a}_\phi$$

$$= \frac{I}{4\pi\rho} \left(\cos\alpha_1 - \cos\alpha_2\right) \vec{a}_\phi \tag{4.8a}$$

where α_1 and α_2 are the inclination angles at $z = -l/2$ and $z = l/2$. If the inclination angle α_2 is taken inside the top end of the conductor, as shown in Figure 4.4(b), then Eq. (4.8a) can be written as

$$\vec{H} = \frac{I}{4\pi\rho}\left(\cos\alpha_1 + \cos\alpha_2\right)\vec{a}_\phi \tag{4.8b}$$

The expression derived in Eqs. 4.8(a) and (b) can be applied to any straight current carrying conductor of *finite* length l. Here, the magnetic field is always along the unit vector $\vec{a}_\phi$ i.e., along concentric circular paths, irrespective of the wire length or the point of observation P. Using trigonometry in Figure 4.4(b), we get

$$\cos\alpha_1 = \frac{l/2}{\sqrt{\rho^2 + (l/2)^2}} \qquad \text{and} \qquad \cos\alpha_2 = -\cos\alpha_1 = \frac{-l/2}{\sqrt{\rho^2 + (l/2)^2}}$$

Substituting the above expressions in Eq. (4.8a), we get

$$\vec{H} = \frac{Il}{2\pi\rho\sqrt{4\rho^2 + l^2}}\vec{a}_\phi \tag{4.9}$$

When $l \gg \rho$, the above equation reduces to

$$\vec{H} = \frac{I}{2\pi\rho}\vec{a}_\phi \tag{4.10}$$

The above equation corresponds to the magnetic field due to a current carrying conductor of *infinite* length. Also, it is noted that the magnetic field is proportional to the current I and inversely proportional to the perpendicular distance ρ with the direction of $\vec{H}$ along ϕ. Here, the magnetic field $\vec{H}$ is tangential to the concentric circles around the conductor and follows the right-hand rule.

EXAMPLE 4.5

A semi-infinite linear conductor extends between $z = 0$ and $z = \infty$ along the z-axis. If the current I in the conductor flows along the positive z-direction, find the magnetic field $\vec{H}$ at a point in xy-plane at a radial distance ρ from the conductor.

SOLUTION

From Eq. (4.8a), the magnetic field $\vec{H}$ due to a current carrying conductor of length l is

$$\vec{H} = \frac{I}{4\pi\rho}\left(\cos\alpha_1 - \cos\alpha_2\right)\vec{a}_\phi$$

Referring to Figure 4.4(b), for a semi-infinite linear conductor extending between $z = 0$ and $z = \infty$, $\alpha_1 = \frac{\pi}{2}$ and $\alpha_2 = \pi$, the magnetic field becomes

$$\vec{H} = \frac{I}{4\pi\rho}\left(\cos\frac{\pi}{2} - \cos\pi\right)\vec{a}_\phi$$

$$= \frac{I}{4\pi\rho}(0+1)\vec{a}_\phi = \frac{I}{4\pi\rho}\vec{a}_\phi \text{ A/m} \qquad \square$$

EXAMPLE 4.6

A filament of current of 10A is directed inward from infinity to the origin on the positive x-axis and then outward to infinity along y-axis. Find the magnetic field intensity at point $P(5,8,0)$.

SOLUTION

Given $I = 10$A. The current filament is shown in Figure E4.6. From Eq. (4.8b), the magnetic field intensity due to a finite length wire is

$$\vec{H}_1 = \frac{I}{4\pi\rho}\left(\cos\alpha_1 + \cos\alpha_2\right)\vec{a}_\phi$$

To determine the magnetic field intensity at $P(5,8,0)$:

Since one end of the line is at infinity on x-axis,

$$\alpha_1 = 0°,\ \cos\alpha_1 = 1 \text{ and } \cos\alpha_2 = \frac{5}{\sqrt{5^2+8^2}} = 0.53.$$

For the first filament, $\rho_1 = 8$ and its magnetic field intensity is

$$\vec{H}_1 = \frac{10}{4\pi(8)}\left(1+0.53\right)\vec{a}_\phi = 0.152\vec{a}_\phi \text{ A/m}$$

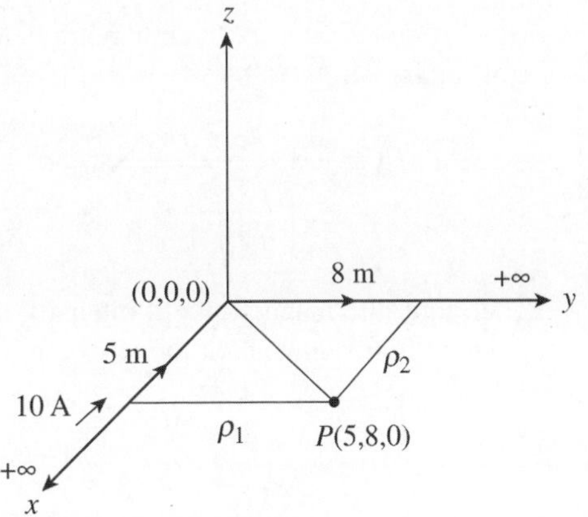

Figure E4.6

Consider another semi-infinite current filament on y-axis extending from zero to infinity.

Since one end of the line is at infinity, $\alpha_2 = 0°$, $\cos\alpha_2 = 1$ and $\cos\alpha_1 = \frac{8}{\sqrt{5^2+8^2}} = 0.848.$

For the second filament, $\rho_2 = 5$ and its magnetic field intensity is

$$\vec{H}_2 = \frac{10}{4\pi(5)}\left(0.848+1\right)\vec{a}_\phi = 0.294\ \vec{a}_\phi \text{ A/m}$$

The total magnetic field intensity at point P is

$$\vec{H} = \vec{H}_1 + \vec{H}_2$$
$$= 0.152\,\vec{a}_\phi + 0.294\,\vec{a}_\phi = 0.446\,\vec{a}_\phi \text{ A/m}$$

Since the current is flowing in a clockwise direction in the xy-plane, the direction of magnetic field will be in negative $\vec{a}_z$ direction according to right-hand rule i.e., $\vec{a}_\phi = -\vec{a}_z$. Hence, the magnetic field intensity is $\vec{H} = -0.446\,\vec{a}_z$ A/m. □

EXAMPLE 4.7

A wire is formed into a square loop and placed in the xy-plane with its center at the origin and each of its sides parallel to either of the x or y-axes. Each side is 40 cm in length and the wire carries a current of 10 A whose direction is clockwise when the loop is viewed from above. Calculate the magnetic field intensity at the center of the loop.

SOLUTION

Figure E4.7 shows a square loop of wire placed in the xy-plane. Since the given direction of current I is clockwise, the magnetic field intensity $\vec{H}$ will be along negative z-direction according to the right-hand rule. Each side segment of the square wire will contribute the same amount of magnetic field.

Replacing $\vec{a}_\phi$ with $-\vec{a}_z$ in Eq. (4.9), the magnetic field intensity due to a straight conductor is

$$\vec{H} = \frac{Il}{2\pi\rho\sqrt{4\rho^2 + l^2}}(-\vec{a}_z)$$

Here $\rho = l/2$. Hence, the magnetic field intensity due to a single side of square wire is

$$\vec{H}_1 = \frac{-Il}{2\pi\left(\dfrac{l}{2}\right)\sqrt{4\left(\dfrac{l}{2}\right)^2 + l^2}}\vec{a}_z = \frac{-I}{\pi l\sqrt{2}}\vec{a}_z$$

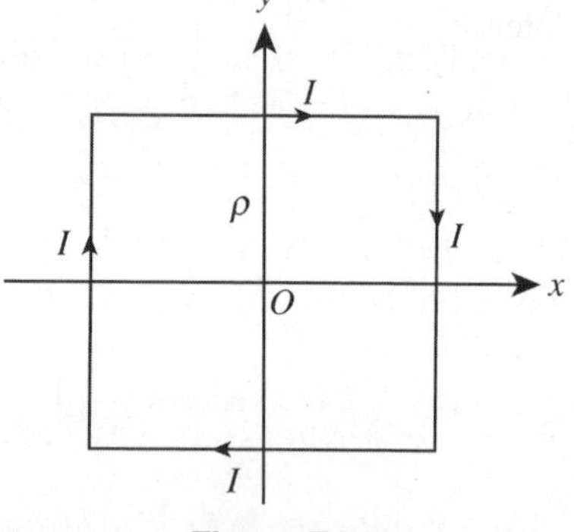

Figure E4.7

Therefore, the magnetic field intensity at the center of the square loop due to four segments of the wire can be written as

$$\vec{H} = 4\vec{H}_1 = \frac{-4I}{\pi l\sqrt{2}}\vec{a}_z$$

$$= \frac{-4\times10}{\pi\times0.4\times\sqrt{2}}\vec{a}_z = -22.52\vec{a}_z \text{ A/m}$$

When the current is in anti-clockwise direction, the magnetic field intensity $\vec{H}$ will be along positive z-direction. ◻

EXAMPLE 4.8

Determine the magnetic field intensity $\vec{H}$ at the center of a square current loop of side l.

SOLUTION

Consider a square loop located in xy-plane carrying current I in anti-clockwise direction, as shown in Figure E4.8.

Due to symmetry, each half side contributes same amount of magnetic field $\vec{H}$ at the center. Using Biot–Savart's law, the differential magnetic field at the origin for a half side $0 \le x \le l/2$ and $y = -l/2$ is

$$d\vec{H} = \frac{Id\vec{l}\times\vec{a}_R}{4\pi R^2} = \frac{Id\vec{l}\times\vec{R}}{4\pi R^3}$$

where the current element $Id\vec{l} = I\,dx\,\vec{a}_x$ and the distance vector $\vec{R} = -x\vec{a}_x + (l/2)\vec{a}_y$. Hence,

$$d\vec{H} = \frac{\left(I\,dx\,\vec{a}_x\right)\times\left(-x\vec{a}_x + (l/2)\vec{a}_y\right)}{4\pi\left[x^2 + (l/2)^2\right]^{3/2}}$$

$$= \frac{I\,dx\,(l/2)\vec{a}_z}{4\pi\left[x^2 + (l/2)^2\right]^{3/2}}$$

$$\text{(since } \vec{a}_x\times\vec{a}_x = 0 \text{ and } \vec{a}_x\times\vec{a}_y = \vec{a}_z\text{)}$$

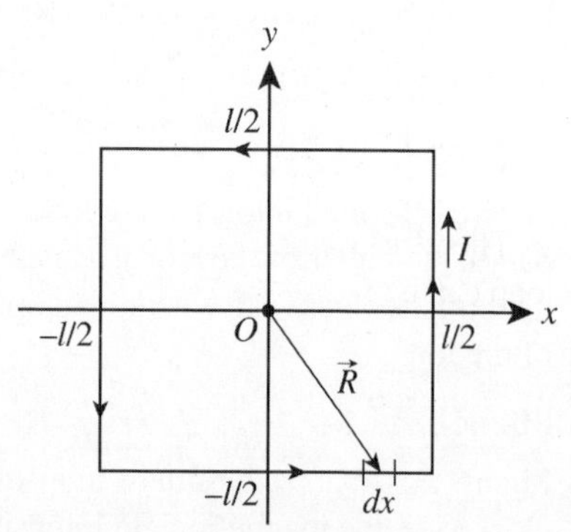

Figure E4.8

There are eight half sides and all contribute to $\vec{H}$ in the same direction. Therefore, the total magnetic field intensity at the origin is

$$\vec{H} = 8\int_0^{l/2} \frac{I\,dx\,(l/2)\vec{a}_z}{4\pi\left[x^2+(l/2)^2\right]^{3/2}} = \frac{Il\vec{a}_z}{\pi}\int_0^{l/2}\frac{dx}{\left[x^2+(l/2)^2\right]^{3/2}}$$

$$= \frac{Il\vec{a}_z}{\pi}\left[\frac{4x}{l^2\sqrt{x^2+(l/2)^2}}\right]_0^{l/2} = \frac{I\,\vec{a}_z}{\pi l}\left[\frac{2l}{\sqrt{(l/2)^2+(l/2)^2}}\right]$$

$$= \frac{2\sqrt{2}I}{\pi l}\vec{a}_z = \frac{2\sqrt{2}I}{\pi l}\vec{a}_n \text{ A/m}$$

where $\vec{a}_n$ is the unit normal to the plane of the loop as given by the right-hand rule. If the current flows in clockwise direction, the magnetic field intensity will be in $-\vec{a}_z$ direction i.e., in negative z-direction. ☐

EXAMPLE 4.9

Determine the magnetic field intensity at the center of a square-shaped wire of sides equal to 5 m placed in xy-plane and carrying a current of 10 A.

SOLUTION

Figure E4.9 shows a square conductor carrying current in anti-clockwise direction in xy-plane. Each side segment of the square is of finite length and will contribute the same amount of magnetic field.

From Eq. (4.9), the magnetic field due to a straight conductor along positive z-direction is

$$\vec{H} = \frac{Il}{2\pi\rho\sqrt{4\rho^2+l^2}}(\vec{a}_z)$$

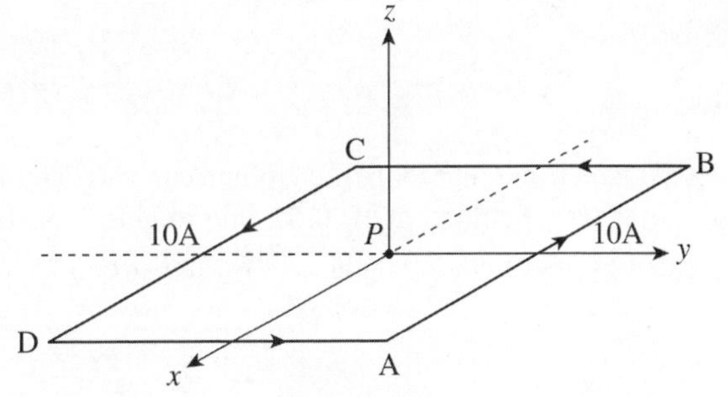

Figure E4.9

Here, $\rho = l/2$. Hence, the magnetic field due to a single side segment of square is

$$\vec{H}_1 = \frac{Il}{2\pi\left(\dfrac{l}{2}\right)\sqrt{4\left(\dfrac{l}{2}\right)^2+l^2}}\vec{a}_z = \frac{I}{\pi l\sqrt{2}}\vec{a}_z$$

Therefore, the magnetic field intensity due to four segments of the square-shaped wire at the center of the loop can be written as

$$\vec{H} = 4\vec{H}_1 = \frac{4I}{\pi l\sqrt{2}}\vec{a}_z$$

$$= \frac{4\times10}{\pi\times5\times\sqrt{2}}\vec{a}_z = 1.8\vec{a}_z \text{ A/m}$$

If the current is assumed to be flowing in clockwise direction, then the magnetic field intensity $\vec{H}$ will be along negative z-direction.

Alternate method

From Example 4.8, the magnetic field intensity at the center of the square-shaped wire is

$$\vec{H} = \frac{2\sqrt{2}I}{\pi l}\,\vec{a}_z = \frac{2\sqrt{2}(10)}{\pi(5)}\,\vec{a}_z = 1.8\,\vec{a}_z \text{ A/m} \qquad \square$$

EXAMPLE 4.10

A triangular wire loop of each side 4 m in length carries a current of 20 A as shown in Figure E4.10(a). Determine the magnetic field intensity $\vec{H}$ at $(0,0,5)$ due to side 1 and side 3.

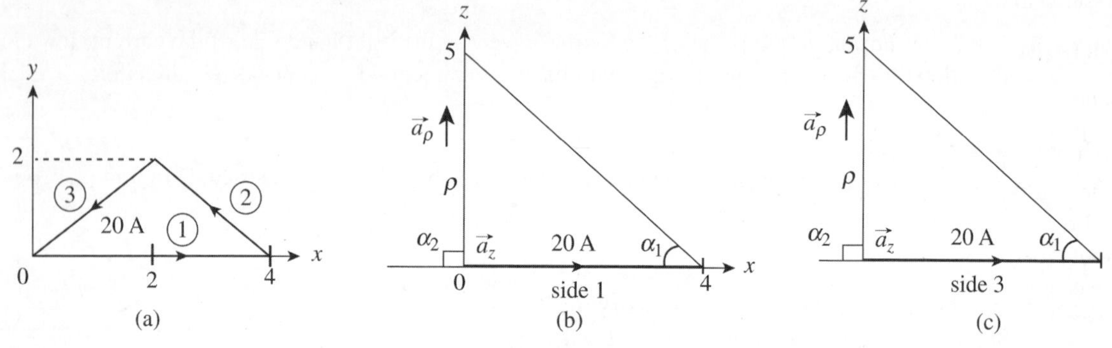

Figure E4.10

SOLUTION

Consider a triangular loop on xy-plane carrying a current of 20 A, as shown in Figure E4.10(a). To determine the magnetic field $\vec{H}$ at $(0,0,5)$ due to side 1 of the loop, assume Figure E4.10(b) in which the side 1 is treated as a straight conductor. For a linear conductor extending from $x = 0$ and $x = 4$, $\cos\alpha_2 = \cos\dfrac{\pi}{2} = 0$ and $\cos\alpha_1 = \dfrac{4}{\sqrt{41}}$.

From Figure E4.10(b), it is seen that $\rho = 5$, $\vec{a}_l = \vec{a}_x$ and $\vec{a}_\rho = \vec{a}_z$. Hence, $\vec{a}_\phi = \vec{a}_x \times \vec{a}_z = -\vec{a}_y$ which shows that the magnetic field induced will be along negative y-direction due to the current flowing in the x-direction.

From Eq. (4.8a), the magnetic field $\vec{H}$ due to a current carrying conductor of length l is

$$\vec{H} = \frac{I}{4\pi\rho}\left(\cos\alpha_1 - \cos\alpha_2\right)\vec{a}_\phi$$

$$= \frac{20}{4\pi \times 5}\left[\frac{4}{\sqrt{41}} - 0\right](-\vec{a}_y) = -198.9\,\vec{a}_y \text{ mA/m}$$

To determine the magnetic field $\vec{H}$ at $(0,0,5)$ due to side 3 of the loop, assume Figure E4.10(c) in which the side 1 is treated as a straight conductor. From Figure E4.10(b), it is seen that $\rho = 5$, $\vec{a}_l = \dfrac{-\vec{a}_x - \vec{a}_y}{\sqrt{2}}$ and $\vec{a}_\rho = \vec{a}_z$. Therefore,

$$\vec{a}_\phi = \vec{a}_l \times \vec{a}_\rho = \left(\frac{-\vec{a}_x - \vec{a}_y}{\sqrt{2}}\right) \times \vec{a}_z = \frac{-\vec{a}_x + \vec{a}_y}{\sqrt{2}}$$

Hence, the magnetic field $\vec{H}$ at $(0,0,5)$ due to side 3 of the loop is

$$\vec{H} = \frac{I}{4\pi\rho}\left(\cos\alpha_1 - \cos\alpha_2\right)\vec{a}_\phi$$

$$= \frac{20}{4\pi\times 5}\left[\frac{4}{\sqrt{41}} - 0\right]\left(\frac{-\vec{a}_x + \vec{a}_y}{\sqrt{2}}\right)$$

$$= -140.7\vec{a}_x + 140.7\vec{a}_y \ \text{mA/m}$$

EXAMPLE 4.11

Determine the magnetic field $\vec{H}$ at the center of a n sided polygon shaped wire, carrying a steady current I. Assume that R is the distance from the center to any side. Also, find the value of $\vec{H}$ when n tends to infinity.

SOLUTION

Consider a loop wire carrying a current of I amperes which is shaped like a regular polygon of n sides, as shown in Figure E4.11. Assume that R is the distance from the center to any side and the side corners make an angle α with the center.

Let d be the distance of side 1 and center of the polygon. For a polygon of n sides, $\alpha = 2\pi / n$. The magnetic field intensity at the center due to the conductor side 1 is

$$\vec{H}_1 = \frac{I}{4\pi d}\left(\cos\alpha_1 + \cos\alpha_2\right)\vec{a}_\phi$$

Here, $\alpha_1 = \alpha_2 = 90° - \dfrac{\alpha}{2}$.

Therefore, $\vec{H}_1 = \dfrac{2I}{4\pi d}\left[\cos\left(90° - \dfrac{\alpha}{2}\right)\right]\vec{a}_\phi = \dfrac{I}{2\pi d}\sin\left(\dfrac{\alpha}{2}\right)\vec{a}_\phi$

For a total of n sides, the magnetic field becomes

$$\vec{H} = \frac{nI}{2\pi d}\sin\left(\pi / n\right)\vec{a}_\phi$$

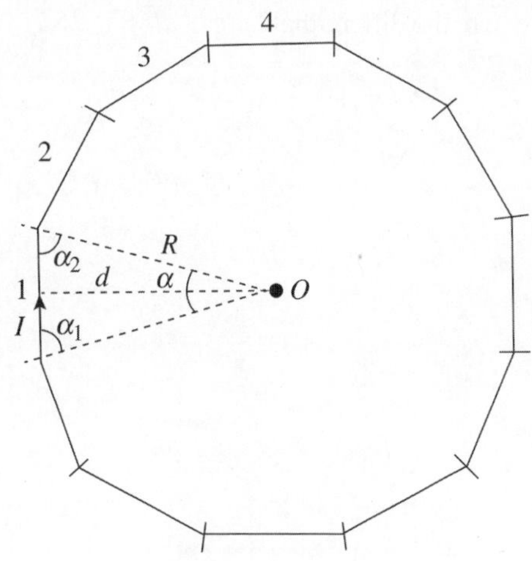

Figure E4.11

Substituting $d = R\cos\left(\pi / n\right)$ in the above equation, we get

$$\vec{H} = \frac{nI}{2\pi}\frac{\sin\left(\pi / n\right)}{R\cos\left(\pi / n\right)}\vec{a}_\phi = \frac{nI}{2\pi R}\tan\left(\pi / n\right)\vec{a}_\phi$$

When n tends to infinity, the regular polygon becomes a circle. Applying the limit to the above magnetic field expression due to n sided polygon, we have

$$\vec{H} = \underset{n\to\infty}{Lt}\ \frac{nI}{2\pi R}\tan\left(\frac{\pi}{n}\right)\vec{a}_\phi = \frac{I\,\vec{a}_\phi}{2R}\ \underset{n\to\infty}{Lt}\ \frac{\sin(\pi / n)}{\pi / n}\ \frac{1}{\cos(\pi / n)}$$

As $n \to \infty$, $\pi / n = 0$. Therefore, $\underset{n\to\infty}{Lt}\ \cos(\pi / n) = 1$ and $\underset{n\to\infty}{Lt}\ \dfrac{\sin(\pi / n)}{\pi / n} = 1$.

Hence, the magnetic field becomes

$$\vec{H} = \frac{I}{2R}\vec{a}_\phi \text{ A/m}$$

This field equation is the same as that of the magnetic field equation due to a circular conductor of radius R, carrying current I. Therefore, the n sided polygon becomes a circle as n tends to infinity. ☐

4.2.2 Magnetic Field due to a Circular Conductor

Consider a circular loop of radius ρ in the xy-plane carrying a steady current I, as shown in Figure 4.5. The magnetic field intensity is to be determined at a point $P(0,0,h)$ on the axis of the loop. Using Biot–Savart's law, the differential magnetic field intensity $d\vec{H}$ at a point P due to a current element $Id\vec{l}$ is given by

$$d\vec{H} = \frac{Id\vec{l} \times \vec{R}}{4\pi R^3} \tag{4.11}$$

where the differential length $d\vec{l} = \rho\, d\phi\, \vec{a}_\phi$ on the circular loop and the distance vector $\vec{R} = (0,0,h) - (x,y,0) = -\rho\vec{a}_\rho + h\vec{a}_z$.

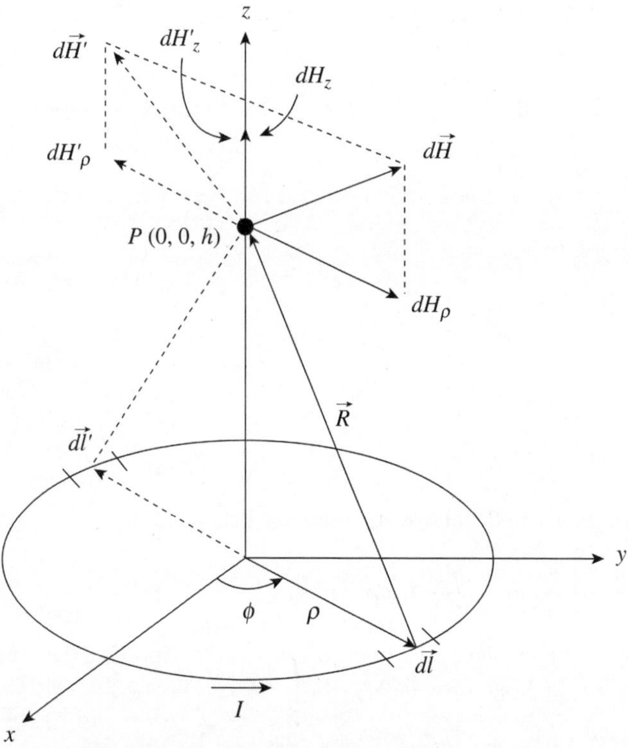

Figure 4.5 *Magnetic field due to a circular loop*

Here, any element $d\vec{l}$ on the circular loop is perpendicular to the distance vector $\vec{R}$ and all elements around the loop are at the same distance R from P with $R = \sqrt{\rho^2 + h^2}$.

The cross product of $d\vec{l}$ and $\vec{R}$ in Eq. (4.11) is given by

$$d\vec{l} \times \vec{R} = \left(\rho\, d\phi\, \vec{a}_\phi\right) \times \left(-\rho\vec{a}_\rho + h\vec{a}_z\right) = \rho\, h\, d\phi\, \vec{a}_\rho + \rho^2 d\phi\, \vec{a}_z \tag{4.12}$$

since $\vec{a}_\phi \times \vec{a}_\rho = -\vec{a}_z$ and $\vec{a}_\phi \times \vec{a}_z = \vec{a}_\rho$.

Substituting Eq. (4.12) in Eq. (4.11), we get

$$d\vec{H} = \frac{I}{4\pi(\rho^2 + h^2)^{3/2}}\left(\rho\, h\, d\phi\, \vec{a}_\rho + \rho^2 d\phi\, \vec{a}_z\right)$$

$$= dH_\rho \vec{a}_\rho + dH_z \vec{a}_z \tag{4.13}$$

Therefore, the magnetic field has components dH_ρ and dH_z in the ρz-plane. For a differential element $d\vec{l}$ in the circular loop, the diametrically opposite element is $d\vec{l}'$ due to symmetry.

From Figure 4.5, it is seen that the field components due to $d\vec{l}$ and $d\vec{l}'$ along $\vec{a}_\rho$ get cancelled because they are in opposite directions and the field components along $\vec{a}_z$ are added to form the total magnetic field. Hence, the net magnetic field is along z-direction only. Since $H_\rho = 0$, Eq. (4.13) can be integrated over ϕ as

$$\vec{H} = \int_{\phi=0}^{\phi=2\pi} dH_z \vec{a}_z = \frac{I}{4\pi} \int_{\phi=0}^{\phi=2\pi} \frac{\rho^2 d\phi}{(\rho^2 + h^2)^{3/2}} \vec{a}_z$$

$$= \frac{I\rho^2 \vec{a}_z}{4\pi(\rho^2 + h^2)^{3/2}} \int_{\phi=0}^{\phi=2\pi} d\phi$$

$$= \frac{I\rho^2 2\pi}{4\pi(\rho^2 + h^2)^{3/2}} \vec{a}_z$$

Therefore, $\quad \vec{H} = \dfrac{I\rho^2}{2(\rho^2 + h^2)^{3/2}} \vec{a}_z \tag{4.14}$

The above equation is the expression for the magnetic field intensity at point P on the axis of the circular loop carrying current I. At the center of the loop, i.e., $h = 0$, Eq. (4.14) reduces to

$$\vec{H} = \frac{I}{2\rho} \vec{a}_z \tag{4.15}$$

The magnetic field intensity at the center of the circular loop can be determined by Eq. (4.15). When the point of observation is far away from the loop such that $h^2 >> \rho^2$, the size of the loop becomes very small compared to distance h. Hence, Eq. (4.14) becomes

$$\vec{H} = \frac{I\rho^2}{2h^3} \vec{a}_z \tag{4.16}$$

In this case, the current carrying loop can be considered as a magnetic dipole. The magnetic dipole moment for a circular loop is given by

$$\vec{m} = IA\vec{a}_z = I\pi\rho^2 \vec{a}_z$$

where the area of the circular loop $A = \pi\rho^2$. Substituting the magnetic moment expression in Eq. (4.16), the magnetic field intensity becomes

$$\vec{H} = \frac{\vec{m}}{2\pi h^3} \qquad (\text{for } h >> \rho) \tag{4.17}$$

Equation (4.17) is applicable mainly for points far away from the loop but on the axis of the loop. A current loop with dimensions much smaller than the distance between the loop and the point of observation, i.e., $\rho \ll R$ is called a magnetic dipole. This is because the magnetic field line pattern of the loop or dipole is similar to that of a permanent magnet.

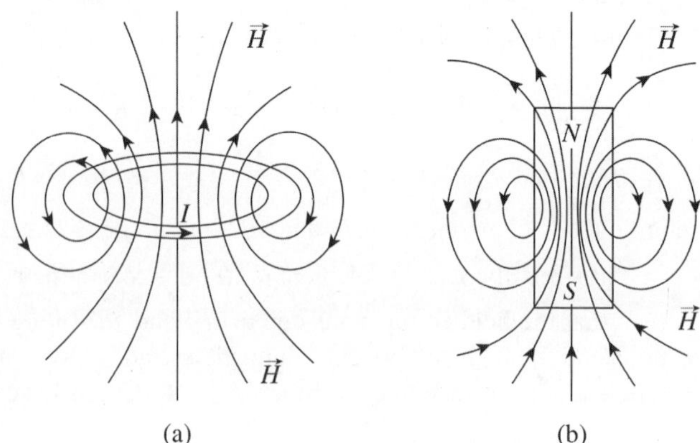

Figure 4.6 *Magnetic field pattern due to (a) current loop or magnetic dipole and (b) permanent magnet*

Figures 4.6(a) and (b) show the magnetic field patterns due to a current carrying loop and a permanent magnet. From the direction of magnetic field lines, it is seen that the region above the loop acts like a north pole and the region below the loop acts like a south pole. Therefore, a current carrying coil acts as an electromagnet as their magnetic field patterns are similar.

EXAMPLE 4.12

A wire carrying a current of 8 A is formed into a circular loop. If the magnetic field intensity at the center of the loop is 40 A/m, what is the radius of the loop if the loop has (i) only one turn and (ii) 10 turns?

SOLUTION

From Eq. (4.15), the magnetic field $\vec{H}$ at the center of the circular loop carrying current I is

$$\vec{H} = \frac{I}{2\rho}\vec{a}_z$$

For N turns, the magnitude of magnetic field is

$$H = \frac{NI}{2\rho}$$

(*i*) The radius of the loop for $N = 1$ turn is

$$\rho = \frac{I}{2H} = \frac{8}{2 \times 40} = 0.1 \text{ m}$$

(*ii*)   The radius of the loop for $N = 10$ turns is

$$\rho = \frac{NI}{2H} = \frac{10 \times 8}{2 \times 40} = 1 \text{ m}$$

EXAMPLE 4.13

A circular loop located on $x^2 + y^2 = 4, z = 0$ carries a direct current of 7 A along $\vec{a}_\phi$. Determine the magnetic field intensity $\vec{H}$ at $(0,0,5)$ and $(0,0,-5)$.

SOLUTION

Given $\rho = 2, I = 7\,\text{A}$ and $h = 5$.

From Eq. (4.14), the magnetic field $\vec{H}$ at $(0,0,5)$ due to the circular loop carrying current I is

$$\vec{H} = \frac{I\rho^2}{2(\rho^2 + h^2)^{3/2}}\,\vec{a}_z$$

$$= \frac{7 \times (2)^2}{2(4 + 25)^{3/2}}\,\vec{a}_z = 0.09\vec{a}_z = 90\vec{a}_z \text{ mA/m}$$

If h is replaced with $-h$, the z-component of magnetic field intensity $\vec{H}$ remains the same and the ρ-component gets cancelled due to the axial symmetry of the loop. Therefore, the magnetic field intensity at $(0, 0, -5)$ is

$$\vec{H} \text{ at } (0,0,-5) = \vec{H} \text{ at } (0,0,5) = 0.09\vec{a}_z = 90\vec{a}_z \text{ mA/m} \qquad \Box$$

EXAMPLE 4.14

A thin ring of radius 5 cm is placed on a plane $z = 1$ cm so that its center is at $(0, 0, 1)$ cm. If the ring carries 50 mA along $\vec{a}_\phi$, determine the magnetic field at (i) $(0, 0, -1)$ cm and (ii) $(0, 0, 10)$ cm.

SOLUTION

The magnetic field due to a thin ring of radius $\rho = 5$ cm carrying current I is

$$\vec{H} = \frac{I\rho^2}{2(\rho^2 + h^2)^{3/2}}\,\vec{a}_z$$

(*i*) Since the thin ring is placed on $z = 1$ cm plane and its center is at $(0, 0, 1)$ cm, the point of observation $(0, 0, -1)$ cm is at a distance $h = 2$ cm. Hence, the magnetic field is

$$\vec{H} = \frac{50 \times 10^{-3} \times 25 \times 10^{-4}}{2(5^2 + 2^2)^{3/2} \times 10^{-6}}\,\vec{a}_z = 400.23\,\vec{a}_z \text{ mA/m}$$

(*ii*)   At $(0, 0, 10$ cm$)$, $h = 9$ cm. Therefore, the magnetic field is

$$\vec{H} = \frac{50 \times 10^{-3} \times 25 \times 10^{-4}}{2(5^2 + 9^2)^{3/2} \times 10^{-6}}\,\vec{a}_z = 57.26\,\vec{a}_z \text{ mA/m} \qquad \Box$$

EXAMPLE 4.15

Consider that two identical circular current loops of radius 3 m and current 20 A are in parallel planes, separated on their common axis by 10 m. Find the magnetic field intensity at a point midway between the two loops.

SOLUTION

Given $I = 20$A, radius $\rho = 3$ m and distance $2h = 10$ m, i.e., $h = 5$ m.

The magnetic field intensity due to top current loop is along $-\vec{a}_z$ direction. Hence,

$$\vec{H}_1 = \frac{I\rho^2}{2(\rho^2 + h^2)^{3/2}}(-\vec{a}_z)$$

$$= \frac{20 \times 3^2}{2\left(3^2 + 5^2\right)^{3/2}}(-\vec{a}_z)$$

$$= -0.454\,\vec{a}_z\ \text{A/m}$$

The magnetic field intensity due to bottom current loop is along $\vec{a}_z$ direction. Hence,

$$\vec{H}_2 = \frac{I\,\rho^2}{2(\rho^2 + h^2)^{3/2}}\,\vec{a}_z$$

$$= \frac{20 \times 3^2}{2\left(3^2 + 5^2\right)^{3/2}}\,\vec{a}_z$$

$$= 0.454\,\vec{a}_z\ \text{A/m}$$

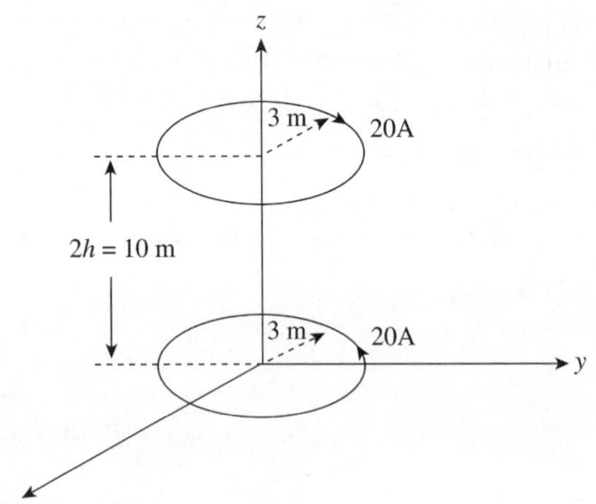

Figure E4.15

Hence, the magnetic field intensity at a point midway between the two loops as shown Figure E4.15 is

$$\vec{H} = \vec{H}_1 + \vec{H}_2 = -0.454\,\vec{a}_z + 0.454\,\vec{a}_z = 0 \qquad \square$$

EXAMPLE 4.16

Derive the magnetic field strength due to a solenoid of length l and radius a with N turns carrying current I. Also, show that if $l \gg a$ at the center of the solenoid, $\vec{H} = \dfrac{NI}{l}\vec{a}_z$.

SOLUTION

Figure E4.16 shows the cross-section of the solenoid of length l and radius a with N turns carrying current I.

The magnetic field strength $\vec{H}$ is to be determined at a point P located on the axis of the solenoid. Since the solenoid consists of circular loops, the expression for magnetic field strength due to a circular conductor is

$$\vec{H} = \frac{Ia^2}{2(a^2 + z^2)^{3/2}}\vec{a}_z$$

where I is the current carried by the loop and z is the distance along the axis of a circular loop of radius a.

Hence, the contribution to the field at point P along z-direction due to an elemental length dz of the solenoid can be written as

$$dH_z = \frac{Ia^2\,dl}{2(a^2 + z^2)^{3/2}} = \frac{Ia^2 n\,dz}{2(a^2 + z^2)^{3/2}}$$

Here, n is the total number of turns per unit length and $dl = n\,dz$. The total field at point P is determined by integrating the contributions from the entire length of the solenoid. This is obtained by expressing the variable z in terms of angle α. From Figure E4.16, it is seen that,

$$z = a\tan\alpha$$

$$a^2 + z^2 = a^2 + a^2\tan^2\alpha = a^2\sec^2\alpha$$

$$dz = a\sec^2\alpha\,d\alpha$$

Therefore, $\quad dH_z = \dfrac{nIa^2\,(a\sec^2\alpha\,d\alpha)}{2(a^2\sec^2\alpha)^{3/2}} = \dfrac{nId\alpha}{2\sec\alpha}$

Integrating the above equation from α_1 to α_2, we get the magnetic field strength due to the entire length of the solenoid as

$$H_z = \frac{nI}{2}\int_{\alpha_1}^{\alpha_2}\frac{d\alpha}{\sec\alpha} = \frac{nI}{2}(\sin\alpha_2 - \sin\alpha_1)$$

Hence, $\quad \vec{H} = H_z\vec{a}_z = \dfrac{nI}{2}(\sin\alpha_2 - \sin\alpha_1)\vec{a}_z$

where α_1 and α_2 are the angles subtended at P by the end turns and $N = nl$ is the total number of turns over the length l. Substituting $n = \dfrac{N}{l}$, we get

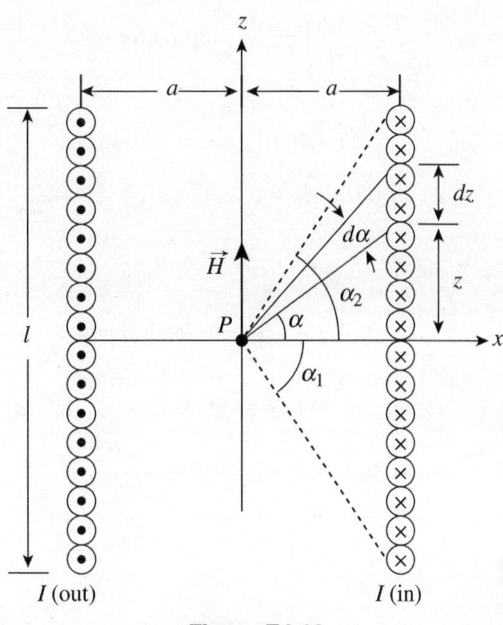

Figure E4.16

$$\vec{H} = \frac{NI}{2l}(\sin\alpha_2 - \sin\alpha_1)\vec{a}_z$$

If the length of solenoid l is much greater than its radius a, i.e., $l \gg a$, then $\alpha_1 = -\pi/2$ and $\alpha_2 = \pi/2$. Hence, the magnetic field strength $\vec{H}$ at the center of the solenoid is

$$\vec{H} = nI\,\vec{a}_z = \frac{NI}{l}\vec{a}_z$$

The above equation is derived for $\vec{H}$ at the midpoint of the solenoid and is approximately valid at all points in the interior of the solenoid, except near the ends. But for point P situated at the end points of solenoid, with $\alpha_1 = 0$ and $\alpha_2 = \pi/2$, the magnetic field strength becomes

$$\vec{H} = \frac{NI}{2l}\vec{a}_z$$

The above equation is derived for $\vec{H}$ at the end points of the solenoid and it is half as large as $\vec{H}$ at the midpoint of the solenoid. ❑

EXAMPLE 4.17

Determine the magnetic field intensity at $(0,0,0),(0,0,75)\,$cm and $(0,0,50)$ cm due to a solenoid (Refer to Figure E4.16 of previous example) having a length 75 cm and a radius of 5 cm with 2000 turns carrying current of 50 mA along $\vec{a}_\phi$.

SOLUTION

Given $N = 2000$ turns, $l = 75$ cm, $a = 5$ cm and $I = 50$ mA.

The magnetic field intensity due to a solenoid is

$$\vec{H} = \frac{NI}{2l}(\sin\alpha_2 - \sin\alpha_1)\vec{a}_z = \frac{2000 \times 50 \times 10^{-3} \times (\sin\alpha_2 - \sin\alpha_1)}{2 \times 0.75}\vec{a}_z$$

$$= 66.67(\sin\alpha_2 - \sin\alpha_1)\vec{a}_z \ \text{A/m}$$

Refer to Figure E4.16 of previous example.

(i) At $(0,0,0)$, $\alpha_2 = 0°$ and $\sin\alpha_1 = \dfrac{-0.75}{\sqrt{0.75^2 + 0.05^2}} = -0.998$

Hence, $\vec{H} = 66.67(0 + 0.998)\vec{a}_z = 66.54\vec{a}_z$ A/m

(ii) At $(0,0,75)$, $\alpha_1 = 0°$ and $\sin\alpha_2 = \dfrac{0.75}{\sqrt{0.75^2 + 0.05^2}} = 0.998$

Hence, $\vec{H} = 66.67(0.998 - 0)\vec{a}_z = 66.54\vec{a}_z$ A/m

(iii) At $(0,0,50)$, $\sin\alpha_1 = \dfrac{-0.25}{\sqrt{0.25^2 + 0.05^2}} = -0.9806$ and $\sin\alpha_2 = \dfrac{0.50}{\sqrt{0.50^2 + 0.05^2}} = 0.995$

Hence, $\vec{H} = 66.67(0.995 + 0.9806)\vec{a}_z = 131.71\vec{a}_z$ A/m   ❑

4.3   STOKES'S THEOREM

Stokes's theorem states that the line integral (circulation) of any vector around a closed path l or contour c is equal to the surface integral of the curl of that vector over the open surface s bounded by l. For the magnetic field vector $\vec{H}$, Stokes's theorem is expressed as

$$\oint_l \vec{H} \cdot d\vec{l} = \int_s (\nabla \times \vec{H}) \cdot d\vec{s} \tag{4.18}$$

Stokes's theorem is applicable to time varying fields as well as static fields in any coordinate systems. The theorem is mostly used in derivations where a conversion from closed line integration to surface integration is required. It can also be used to convert the surface integral of the curl of a vector field into a closed line integral. The proof for this theorem has already been explained in section 1.11 of Chapter 1.

EXAMPLE 4.18

Evaluate both sides of the Stokes's theorem for the field $\vec{H} = 6xy\vec{a}_x - 3y^2\vec{a}_y$ A/m and the rectangular path around the region, $2 \le x \le 5$, $-1 \le y \le 1$, and $z = 0$. Let the positive direction of $d\vec{s}$ be $\vec{a}_z$.

SOLUTION

According to Stokes's theorem,

$$\oint_l \vec{H} \cdot d\vec{l} = \int_s (\nabla \times \vec{H}) \cdot d\vec{s}$$

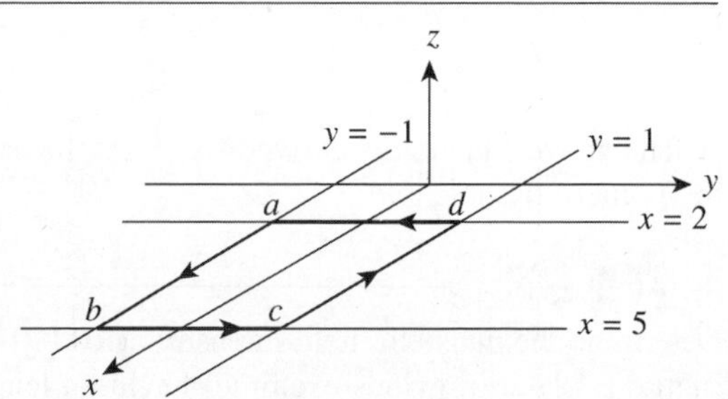

Figure E4.18

Let us first evaluate the left hand side (LHS) of Stokes's theorem. The integral to be evaluated on a perimeter of a closed path is shown in Figure E4.18.

The direction is *a-b-c-d-a* such that its normal is in positive $\vec{a}_z$ direction according to right-hand rule. Therefore,

$$\oint_l \vec{H} \cdot d\vec{l} = \int_a^b \vec{H} \cdot d\vec{l} + \int_b^c \vec{H} \cdot d\vec{l} + \int_c^d \vec{H} \cdot d\vec{l} + \int_d^a \vec{H} \cdot d\vec{l}$$

Here, $\quad \int_a^b \vec{H} \cdot d\vec{l} = \int\limits_{x=2}^{5} \left(6xy\vec{a}_x - 3y^2\vec{a}_y\right) \cdot dx\vec{a}_x = \int\limits_{x=2}^{5} 6xy\,dx = 6y\left[\dfrac{x^2}{2}\right]_2^5$

$$= \frac{6y}{2}\left[25-4\right] = 63y$$

For path *ab*, $y = -1$. Therefore, $\int_a^b \vec{H} \cdot d\vec{l} = 63(-1) = -63$.

Similarly, $\int_b^c \vec{H} \cdot d\vec{l} = \int\limits_{y=-1}^{1} -3y^2\,dy = -3\left[\dfrac{y^3}{3}\right]_{-1}^{1} = -\left[y^3\right]_{-1}^{1} = -\left[1-(-1)\right] = -2$

$$\int_c^d \vec{H} \cdot d\vec{l} = \int\limits_{x=5}^{2} 6xy\,dx = 6y\left[\dfrac{x^2}{2}\right]_5^2 = \frac{6y}{2}\left[4-25\right] = -63y$$

For path *cd*, $y = 1$. Therefore, $\int_c^d \vec{H} \cdot d\vec{l} = -63$.

$$\int_d^a \vec{H} \cdot d\vec{l} = \int\limits_{y=1}^{-1} -3y^2\,dy = -\left[y^3\right]_1^{-1} = -\left[-1-1\right] = 2$$

$$\text{LHS} = \oint_l \vec{H} \cdot d\vec{l} = -63-2-63+2 = -126\,\text{A}$$

Now, evaluating right hand side (RHS) of Stokes's theorem,

$$\nabla \times \vec{H} = \begin{vmatrix} \vec{a}_x & \vec{a}_y & \vec{a}_z \\ \dfrac{\partial}{\partial x} & \dfrac{\partial}{\partial y} & \dfrac{\partial}{\partial z} \\ 6xy & -3y^2 & 0 \end{vmatrix} = \vec{a}_x\left[0-0\right] + \vec{a}_y\left[0-0\right] + \vec{a}_z\left[0-6x\right] = -6x\,\vec{a}_z$$

$$\int_s (\nabla \times \vec{H}) \cdot d\vec{s} = \int_s \left(-6x\vec{a}_z\right) \cdot \left(dx\,dy\vec{a}_z\right)$$

where the surface area normal to $\vec{a}_z$ direction is $d\vec{s} = dx\,dy\vec{a}_z$.

Therefore, $\text{RHS} = \int_s (\nabla \times \vec{H}) \cdot d\vec{s} = \int\limits_{y=-1}^{1} \int\limits_{x=2}^{5} -6x\,dx\,dy = -6\left[\dfrac{x^2}{2}\right]_2^5 \left[y\right]_{-1}^{1}$

$$= -\frac{6}{2}\times\left[25-4\right]\times\left[1-(-1)\right] = -3\times21\times2 = -126\,\text{A}$$

Thus, both LHS and RHS are same and hence, Stokes's theorem is verified. ❑

EXAMPLE 4.19

Given a field $\vec{H} = \rho^2 \sin^2 \phi\, \vec{a}_\rho + \rho^2 \cos^2 \phi\, \vec{a}_\phi + 2z^2 \vec{a}_z$ A/m. Evaluate both sides of Stokes's theorem for the path formed by the intersection of the cylinder $\rho = 2$ and plane $z = 1$ and for the surface defined by $\rho = 2, 1 \le z \le 3$ and $z = 3, 0 \le \rho \le 2$.

SOLUTION

According to Stokes's theorem,

$$\oint_l \vec{H} \cdot d\vec{l} = \int_s (\nabla \times \vec{H}) \cdot d\vec{s}$$

Let us first evaluate L.H.S $= \oint_l \vec{H} \cdot d\vec{l}$ on the periphery of the cylinder in which the differential length $d\vec{l} = \rho\, d\phi\, \vec{a}_\phi$ is on the intersection of the cylinder $\rho = 2$ and plane $z = 1$.

$$\oint_l \vec{H} \cdot d\vec{l} = \oint_l (\rho^2 \sin^2 \phi\, \vec{a}_\rho + \rho^2 \cos^2 \phi\, \vec{a}_\phi + 2z^2 \vec{a}_z) \cdot (\rho\, d\phi\, \vec{a}_\phi)$$

$$= \int_0^{2\pi} \rho^3 \cos^2 \phi\, d\phi \quad (\text{since } \vec{a}_\rho \cdot \vec{a}_\phi = 0, \vec{a}_\phi \cdot \vec{a}_\phi = 1 \text{ and } \vec{a}_z \cdot \vec{a}_\phi = 0)$$

$$= \rho^3 \int_0^{2\pi} \frac{(1 + \cos 2\phi)}{2} d\phi = \frac{\rho^3}{2} \left[\int_0^{2\pi} d\phi + \int_0^{2\pi} \cos 2\phi\, d\phi \right]$$

$$= \frac{2^3}{2} \times 2\pi = 8\pi \text{ A} \quad (\text{since } \rho = 2)$$

Let us evaluate RHS of Stokes's theorem. In cylindrical coordinates,

$$\nabla \times \vec{H} = \frac{1}{\rho} \begin{vmatrix} \vec{a}_\rho & \rho \vec{a}_\phi & \vec{a}_z \\ \dfrac{\partial}{\partial \rho} & \dfrac{\partial}{\partial \phi} & \dfrac{\partial}{\partial z} \\ H_\rho & \rho H_\phi & H_z \end{vmatrix} = \left(\frac{1}{\rho} \frac{\partial H_z}{\partial \phi} - \frac{\partial H_\phi}{\partial z} \right) \vec{a}_\rho + \left(\frac{\partial H_\rho}{\partial z} - \frac{\partial H_z}{\partial \rho} \right) \vec{a}_\phi + \frac{1}{\rho} \left(\frac{\partial (\rho H_\phi)}{\partial \rho} - \frac{\partial H_\rho}{\partial \phi} \right) \vec{a}_z$$

$$= 0 \vec{a}_\rho + 0 \vec{a}_\phi + \frac{1}{\rho} \left(\frac{\partial (\rho^3 \cos^2 \phi)}{\partial \rho} - \frac{\partial (\rho^2 \sin^2 \phi)}{\partial \phi} \right) \vec{a}_z$$

$$= \frac{1}{\rho} \left(3\rho^2 \cos^2 \phi - \rho^2 \sin 2\phi \right) \vec{a}_z = \left(3\rho \cos^2 \phi - \rho \sin 2\phi \right) \vec{a}_z$$

Here, the surface area in $\vec{a}_z$ direction is $d\vec{s} = \rho\, d\rho\, d\phi\, \vec{a}_z$.

$$\int_s (\nabla \times \vec{H}) \cdot d\vec{s} = \int_s \left(3\rho \cos^2 \phi - \rho \sin 2\phi \right) \vec{a}_z \cdot \rho\, d\rho\, d\phi\, \vec{a}_z$$

$$= \int_0^{2\pi} \int_0^2 (3\rho \cos^2 \phi - \rho \sin 2\phi) \rho\, d\rho\, d\phi \quad (\text{since } \vec{a}_z \cdot \vec{a}_z = 1)$$

$$= \int_0^{2\pi} \left[\frac{3\rho^3}{3} \cos^2 \phi - \frac{\rho^3}{3} \sin 2\phi \right]_0^2 d\phi = \int_0^{2\pi} \left[8 \cos^2 \phi - \frac{8}{3} \sin 2\phi \right] d\phi$$

$$= \int_0^{2\pi} \left[4 + 4 \cos 2\phi - \frac{8}{3} \sin 2\phi \right] d\phi = 8\pi \text{ A}$$

Hence, both LHS and RHS are same and thus, the Stokes's theorem is verified. $\qquad\square$

EXAMPLE 4.20

Evaluate both sides of Stokes's theorem for the magnetic field $\vec{H} = 10\sin\theta\, \vec{a}_\phi$ A/m and the surface $r = 3, 0 \le \theta \le 90°, 0 \le \phi \le 90°$. Assume that the surface has $\vec{a}_r$ direction.

SOLUTION

According to Stokes's theorem,

$$\oint_l \vec{H} \cdot d\vec{l} = \int_s (\nabla \times \vec{H}) \cdot d\vec{s}$$

where the differential length is $d\vec{l} = dr\vec{a}_r + rd\theta\, \vec{a}_\theta + r\sin\theta\, d\phi\, \vec{a}_\phi$ in spherical system. The closed path forming its perimeter is composed of three circular arcs.

From Figure E4.20, it is seen that the path 1 is $\phi = 0, 0 \le \theta \le 90°$, the path 2 is $r = 3, \theta = 90°, 0 \le \phi \le 90°$ and the path 3 is $r = 3, \phi = 90°, 0 \le \theta \le 90°$. For all three paths, $r = 3$ m.

Let us first evaluate LHS $= \oint \vec{H} \cdot d\vec{l}$ over these three paths.

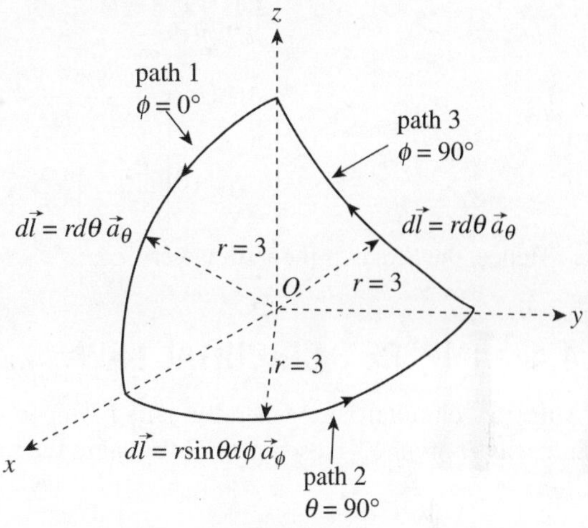

Figure E4.20

$$\oint \vec{H} \cdot d\vec{l} = \int H_r\, dr + \int H_\theta\, r\, d\theta + \int H_\phi\, r\sin\theta\, d\phi$$

From the given field, $H_r = 0$, $H_\theta = 0$, $H_\phi = 10\sin\theta$. Therefore, only the third line integral exists.

Hence, $\displaystyle\oint_l \vec{H} \cdot d\vec{l} = \int_{\phi=0}^{\pi/2} 10\sin\theta\, r\sin\theta\, d\phi = 10r\times\sin^2\theta\times[\phi]_0^{\pi/2}$

$$= 10\times3\times[\sin 90°]^2\times\frac{\pi}{2} = 47.1\,\text{A}$$

Let us evaluate RHS of Stokes's theorem. In spherical coordinates,

$$\nabla\times\vec{H} = \frac{1}{r\sin\theta}\left[\frac{\partial(H_\phi\sin\theta)}{\partial\theta} - \frac{\partial H_\phi}{\partial\phi}\right]\vec{a}_r + \frac{1}{r}\left[\frac{1}{\sin\theta}\frac{\partial H_r}{\partial\phi} - \frac{\partial(rH_\phi)}{\partial r}\right]\vec{a}_\theta + \frac{1}{r}\left[\frac{\partial(rH_\theta)}{\partial r} - \frac{\partial H_r}{\partial\theta}\right]\vec{a}_\phi$$

Since $H_r = 0$, $H_\theta = 0$ and $H_\phi = 10\sin\theta$, we have

$$\nabla\times\vec{H} = \frac{1}{r\sin\theta}\left[10\frac{\partial\sin^2\theta}{\partial\theta} - 0\right]\vec{a}_r + \frac{1}{r}\left[0 - \frac{\partial(r\times10\sin\theta)}{\partial r}\right]\vec{a}_\theta + \frac{1}{r}[0-0]\vec{a}_\phi$$

$$= \frac{1}{r\sin\theta}[10\times2\sin\theta\cos\theta]\vec{a}_r + \frac{1}{r}[-10\sin\theta]\vec{a}_\theta$$

$$= \frac{10}{r\sin\theta}\sin 2\theta\, \vec{a}_r - \frac{10}{r}\sin\theta\, \vec{a}_\theta$$

Here, the surface area in $\vec{a}_r$ direction is $d\vec{s} = r^2\sin\theta\, d\theta\, d\phi\, \vec{a}_r$.

Therefore, $(\nabla \times \vec{H}) \cdot d\vec{s} = \left(\dfrac{10}{r \sin \theta} \sin 2\theta \right) \cdot \left(r^2 \sin \theta \, d\theta \, d\phi \right)$ (since $\vec{a}_r \cdot \vec{a}_r = 1$)

$$\int_s (\nabla \times \vec{H}) \cdot d\vec{s} = \int_{\phi=0}^{\pi/2} \int_{\theta=0}^{\pi/2} 10r \sin 2\theta \, d\theta \, d\phi = 10r \left[\dfrac{-\cos 2\theta}{2} \right]_0^{\pi/2} [\phi]_0^{\pi/2}$$

$$= 10 \times r \times \left[\dfrac{-\cos \pi}{2} - \dfrac{(-\cos 0)}{2} \right] \times \left[\dfrac{\pi}{2} \right], \quad \text{where } r = 3 \text{ m}$$

$$= 10 \times 3 \times \left[\dfrac{1}{2} + \dfrac{1}{2} \right] \times \dfrac{\pi}{2} = 47.1 \, \text{A}$$

Hence, the Stokes's theorem is verified.

4.4   AMPERE'S CIRCUITAL LAW

Ampere's circuital law, generally called Ampere's law, states that the line integral of the magnetic field intensity $\vec{H}$ around a closed path l is equal to the total current enclosed by the path as given by

$$\oint_l \vec{H} \cdot d\vec{l} = I \tag{4.19}$$

where I is the total current enclosed by the path. The above equation is called the *integral form of Ampere's law*. The current can be carried by a conductor of any shape.

The direction of path l is considered such that the current I and magnetic field $\vec{H}$ satisfy the right-hand rule defined by Biot–Savart's law. The direction of current is along the direction of the right thumb and direction of path l is chosen along the direction of the remaining four fingers as shown in Figure 4.7.

When the current I is enclosed by the path l, the line integral of $\vec{H}$ is equal to current I as shown in Figure 4.7(a). The line integral of $\vec{H}$ is equal to zero when the path l does not enclose the current I as shown in Figure 4.7(b). The current I denoted by the symbol $\odot$ in Figure 4.7 shows that the direction of current is out of the page.

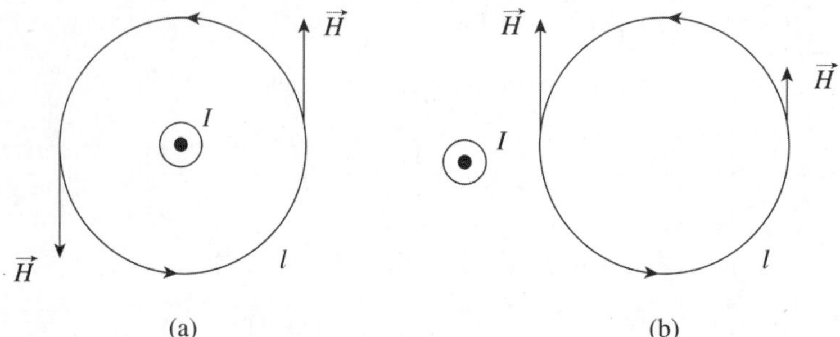

Figure 4.7   *Illustration of Ampere's law: (a) line integral of $\vec{H}$ equals to I and (b) line integral of $\vec{H}$ equals to zero*

4.4.1   Point Form of Ampere's Circuital Law

In electrostatics, Gauss's law is used to determine the electric field intensity and flux density in a region having symmetrical charge distribution. The determination of field depends on the proper choice of the Gaussian surface enclosing the charges. Similarly, in magnetostatics, Ampere's law is used to determine the magnetic field when the current distribution is symmetrical. Ampere's law is a special case of Biot–Savart's law from which it can also be derived. The point form of Ampere's circuital law can be obtained by using Stokes's theorem.

The current can be expressed in terms of current density $\vec{J}$ as

$$I = \int_s \vec{J} \cdot d\vec{s} \tag{4.20}$$

Comparing Eq. (4.19) and Eq. (4.20), we get

$$\oint_l \vec{H} \cdot d\vec{l} = \int_s \vec{J} \cdot d\vec{s} \tag{4.21}$$

The line integral on the left hand side of the above equation can be converted to surface integral by making use of Eq. (4.18) of Stokes's theorem. Therefore,

$$\int_s (\nabla \times \vec{H}) \cdot d\vec{s} = \int_s \vec{J} \cdot d\vec{s} \tag{4.22}$$

Comparing the surface integrals on both sides of the above equation, we obtain

$$\nabla \times \vec{H} = \vec{J} \tag{4.23}$$

The above equation is one of the Maxwell's equations applicable to static magnetic fields and it is known as the *point form or differential form of Ampere's law.*

The differential form of Ampere's circuital law states that the curl of the magnetic field intensity $\vec{H}$ is equal to the conduction current density $\vec{J}$ i.e., $\nabla \times \vec{H} = \vec{J}$.

Proof: Consider a differential rectangular path of lengths $\Delta x, \Delta y$ in the xy-plane centered at point P as shown in Figure 4.8. Let current I with current density $\vec{J}$ A/m^2 flows through the enclosed path along the z-direction. Consider the magnetic field intensity at point P in rectangular coordinates is

$$\vec{H}_0 = H_{x_0}\, \vec{a}_x + H_{y_0}\, \vec{a}_y + H_{z_0}\, \vec{a}_z$$

The total current density is represented by

$$\vec{J} = J_x\, \vec{a}_x + J_y\, \vec{a}_y + J_z\, \vec{a}_z$$

From Ampere's circuital law, we have

$$\oint_l \vec{H} \cdot d\vec{l} = I_{encl}$$

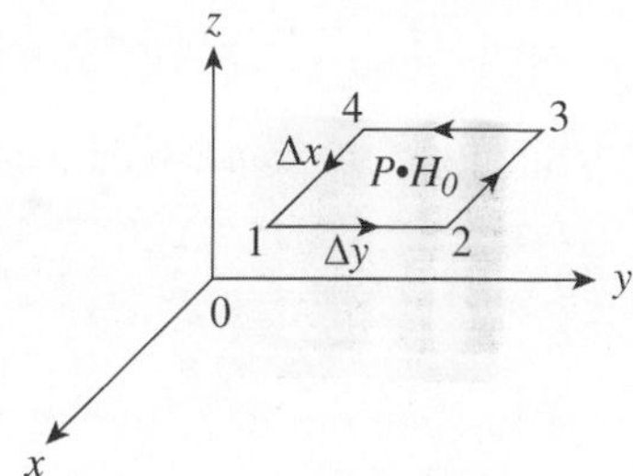

Figure 4.8 *An incremental rectangular closed path*

where I_{encl} is the net current flowing in the closed path 1-2-3-4-1, as shown in Figure 4.8.

The field along the path 1 to 2 is

$$\left(\vec{H} \cdot d\vec{l} \right)_{1.2} = H_y \Delta y \approx \left(H_{y_0} + \frac{\Delta x}{2} \frac{\partial H_y}{\partial x} \right) \Delta y$$

The field along the path 2 to 3 is

$$\left(\vec{H} \cdot d\vec{l} \right)_{2.3} = H_x \Delta x \approx -\left[H_{x_0} + \frac{\Delta y}{2} \frac{\partial H_x}{\partial y} \right] \Delta x$$

The field along the path 3 to 4 is

$$\left(\vec{H} \cdot d\vec{l} \right)_{3.4} = H_y \Delta y \approx -\left[H_{y_0} - \frac{\Delta x}{2} \frac{\partial H_y}{\partial x} \right] \Delta y$$

The field along the path 4 to 1 is

$$\left(\vec{H}\cdot d\vec{l}\right)_{4.1} = H_x \Delta x = \left[H_{x_0} - \frac{\Delta y}{2}\frac{\partial H_x}{\partial y} \right]\Delta x$$

Hence, the total magnetic field intensity along the closed path is obtained by combining the above field equations as

$$\oint_l \vec{H}\cdot d\vec{l} = H_{y_0}\Delta y + \frac{\Delta x \Delta y}{2}\frac{\partial H_y}{\partial x} - H_{x_0}\Delta x - \frac{\Delta x \Delta y}{2}\frac{\partial H_x}{\partial y}$$

$$-H_{y_0}\Delta y + \frac{\Delta x \Delta y}{2}\frac{\partial H_y}{\partial x} + H_{x_0}\Delta x - \frac{\Delta x \Delta y}{2}\frac{\partial H_x}{\partial y}$$

$$= \left(\frac{\partial H_y}{\partial x} - \frac{\partial H_x}{\partial y} \right)\Delta x \Delta y = I_{encl}$$

where the current enclosed through the surface area $\Delta x \Delta y$ is $I_{encl} = J_z \Delta x \Delta y$ and the z-component of current density is written as

$$\frac{\partial H_y}{\partial x} - \frac{\partial H_x}{\partial y} = J_z$$

Similarly, the x and y-components of the current densities are

$$\frac{\partial H_x}{\partial z} - \frac{\partial H_z}{\partial x} = J_y \quad \text{and} \quad \frac{\partial H_z}{\partial y} - \frac{\partial H_y}{\partial z} = J_x$$

Since $\vec{J} = J_x \vec{a}_x + J_y \vec{a}_y + J_z \vec{a}_z$, we can write

$$\left(\frac{\partial H_z}{\partial y} - \frac{\partial H_y}{\partial z} \right)\vec{a}_x + \left(\frac{\partial H_x}{\partial z} - \frac{\partial H_z}{\partial x} \right)\vec{a}_y + \left(\frac{\partial H_y}{\partial x} - \frac{\partial H_x}{\partial y} \right)\vec{a}_z = \vec{J}$$

Representing in matrix form, we have $\vec{J} = \begin{vmatrix} \vec{a}_x & \vec{a}_y & \vec{a}_z \\ \dfrac{\partial}{\partial x} & \dfrac{\partial}{\partial y} & \dfrac{\partial}{\partial z} \\ H_x & H_y & H_z \end{vmatrix}$ (rectangular coordinates)

The above determinant is known as curl $\vec{H}$, represented by $\nabla \times \vec{H}$ i.e., the cross product of del operator and $\vec{H}$. Therefore, $\nabla \times \vec{H} = \vec{J}$.

Note: (*i*) Curl of $\vec{H}$ in cylindrical coordinate system is

$$\nabla \times \vec{H} = \frac{1}{\rho}\begin{vmatrix} \vec{a}_\rho & \rho\vec{a}_\phi & \vec{a}_z \\ \dfrac{\partial}{\partial \rho} & \dfrac{\partial}{\partial \phi} & \dfrac{\partial}{\partial z} \\ H_\rho & \rho H_\phi & H_z \end{vmatrix}$$

(*ii*) Curl of $\vec{H}$ in spherical coordinate system is

$$\nabla \times \vec{H} = \frac{1}{r^2 \sin\theta} \begin{vmatrix} \vec{a}_r & r\vec{a}_\theta & r\sin\theta\,\vec{a}_\phi \\ \dfrac{\partial}{\partial r} & \dfrac{\partial}{\partial \theta} & \dfrac{\partial}{\partial \phi} \\ H_r & rH_\theta & r\sin\theta\,H_\phi \end{vmatrix}$$

4.4.2   Physical Interpretation of the Curl

When a current is flowing through a conductor, the magnetic field lines seem to swirl in concentric circles around the conductor with any radius. The direction of curl of the magnetic field intensity is along the axis about which rotation of the vector field exists, i.e., along the current direction. Its direction can be obtained from the right-hand thumb rule. The curl of a vector usually exists for rotational field. If the curl is zero, it is called irrotational.

EXAMPLE 4.21

Determine the current density for a magnetic field intensity of $\vec{H} = 28\sin x\,\vec{a}_y$ A/m.

SOLUTION

From point form of Ampere's circuital law, we have

$$\vec{J} = \nabla \times \vec{H} = \begin{vmatrix} \vec{a}_x & \vec{a}_y & \vec{a}_z \\ \dfrac{\partial}{\partial x} & \dfrac{\partial}{\partial y} & \dfrac{\partial}{\partial z} \\ 0 & 28\sin x & 0 \end{vmatrix} = \frac{\partial}{\partial x}(28\sin x)\vec{a}_z$$

$$= 28\cos x\,\vec{a}_z \text{ A/m}^2 \qquad \qquad \square$$

EXAMPLE 4.22

In cylindrical coordinates, the magnetic field intensity is given by $\vec{H} = \left(2\rho - \rho^2\right)\vec{a}_\phi$ A/m for $0 < \rho < 1$. (*i*) Determine the current density as a function of ρ within this cylinder. (*ii*) What is the total current passing through the surface $z = 0, 0 < \rho < 1$ in $\vec{a}_z$ direction? and (*iii*) Verify the same using Stokes's theorem.

SOLUTION

Given the magnetic field intensity $\vec{H} = \left(2\rho - \rho^2\right)\vec{a}_\phi$ A/m for $0 < \rho < 1$.

(*i*) The current density is

$$\vec{J} = \nabla \times \vec{H} = \frac{1}{\rho} \begin{vmatrix} \vec{a}_\rho & \rho\vec{a}_\phi & \vec{a}_z \\ \dfrac{\partial}{\partial \rho} & \dfrac{\partial}{\partial \phi} & \dfrac{\partial}{\partial z} \\ 0 & \rho\left(2\rho - \rho^2\right) & 0 \end{vmatrix}$$

$$= 0\vec{a}_\rho + 0\vec{a}_\phi + \frac{1}{\rho}\left(\frac{\partial\left(2\rho^2 - \rho^3\right)}{\partial\rho}\right)\vec{a}_z = (4 - 3\rho)\vec{a}_z$$

(*ii*) The total current passing through the surface $z = 0$, $0 < \rho < 1$ in the $\vec{a}_z$ direction is

$$I = \int_s \vec{J}\cdot d\vec{s} = \int_0^{2\pi}\int_0^1 J_z\,\rho\,d\rho\,d\phi \qquad\qquad (\text{since } d\vec{s} = \rho\,d\rho\,d\phi\,\vec{a}_z)$$

$$= \int_0^{2\pi}\int_0^1 (4 - 3\rho)\,\rho\,d\rho\,d\phi = \int_0^{2\pi}\left(\frac{4\rho^2}{2} - \frac{3\rho^3}{3}\right)\Bigg|_0^1 d\phi$$

$$= 2\pi\,(2 - 1) = 2\pi = 6.28\,\text{A}$$

(*iii*) Using Stokes's theorem, we get

$$\oint_l \vec{H}\cdot d\vec{l} = \int_0^{2\pi}\left(2\rho - \rho^2\right)\vec{a}_\phi\cdot\rho\,d\phi\,\vec{a}_\phi \qquad\qquad (\text{since } \rho = 1)$$

$$= 2\pi\,(2 - 1) = 2\pi = 6.28\,\text{A} = I$$

Hence, the Stokes's theorem is verified.   ☐

EXAMPLE 4.23

The magnetic field $\vec{H}$ due to a current source is given by $\vec{H} = \left[y\cos(\alpha x)\right]\vec{a}_x + \left(y + e^x\right)\vec{a}_z$ A/m. Determine the current density over the *yz*-plane.

SOLUTION

From point form of Ampere's circuital law, we have

$$\vec{J} = \nabla\times\vec{H} = \begin{vmatrix} \vec{a}_x & \vec{a}_y & \vec{a}_z \\ \dfrac{\partial}{\partial x} & \dfrac{\partial}{\partial y} & \dfrac{\partial}{\partial z} \\ y\cos(\alpha x) & 0 & y + e^x \end{vmatrix} \qquad (\text{in Cartesian form})$$

$$= \left[\frac{\partial}{\partial y}\left(y + e^x\right)\right]\vec{a}_x + \left[\frac{\partial\{y\cos(\alpha x)\}}{\partial z} - \frac{\partial\left(y + e^x\right)}{\partial x}\right]\vec{a}_y + \left[-\frac{\partial}{\partial y}\{y\cos(\alpha x)\}\right]\vec{a}_z$$

$$= (1)\vec{a}_x + \left(0 - e^x\right)\vec{a}_y + (-\cos\alpha x)\vec{a}_z$$

Since $x = 0$ on *yz*-plane, the current density over the *yz*-plane is

$$\vec{J} = \vec{a}_x - e^0\vec{a}_y - \cos 0\,\vec{a}_z$$

$$= \vec{a}_x - \vec{a}_y - \vec{a}_z \ \text{A/m}^2$$

    ☐

EXAMPLE 4.24

A flat perfectly conducting surface in *xy*-plane is situated in a magnetic field,

$$\vec{H} = \begin{cases} 3\cos x\,\vec{a}_x + z\cos x\,\vec{a}_y \ \text{A/m} & z \geq 0 \\ 0 & z < 0 \end{cases}$$

Find the current density on the conductor surface.

SOLUTION

From point form of Ampere's circuit law, the current density is given by

$$\vec{J} = \nabla \times \vec{H}$$

$$= \begin{vmatrix} \vec{a}_x & \vec{a}_y & \vec{a}_z \\ \dfrac{\partial}{\partial x} & \dfrac{\partial}{\partial y} & \dfrac{\partial}{\partial z} \\ H_x & H_y & H_z \end{vmatrix} = \begin{vmatrix} \vec{a}_x & \vec{a}_y & \vec{a}_z \\ \dfrac{\partial}{\partial x} & \dfrac{\partial}{\partial y} & \dfrac{\partial}{\partial z} \\ 3\cos x & z\cos x & 0 \end{vmatrix}$$

From the given magnetic field $\vec{H}$, it is seen that $H_x = 3\cos x$, $H_y = z\cos x$ and $H_z = 0$.
Therefore,

$$\vec{J} = \left[0 - \frac{\partial(z\cos x)}{\partial z}\right]\vec{a}_x + \left[\frac{\partial(3\cos x)}{\partial z} - 0\right]\vec{a}_y + \left[\frac{\partial(z\cos x)}{\partial x} - \frac{\partial(3\cos x)}{\partial y}\right]\vec{a}_z$$

$$= -\cos x\,\vec{a}_x - z\sin x\,\vec{a}_z \ \text{A/m}^2$$

Hence, $\vec{J} = \begin{cases} -\cos x\,\vec{a}_x - z\sin x\,\vec{a}_z \ \text{A/m}^2, & z \geq 0 \\ 0, & z < 0 \end{cases}$

EXAMPLE 4.25

If $\vec{H} = y\vec{a}_x - x\vec{a}_y$ A/m on plane $z = 0$, then (*i*) determine the current density and (*ii*) verify Ampere's law by taking the circulation of $\vec{H}$ around the rectangular path with $z = 0$, $0 < x < 5$ and $-2 < y < 6$.

SOLUTION

Given $\vec{H} = y\vec{a}_x - x\vec{a}_y$ A/m on plane $z = 0$.

(*i*) From differential or point form of Ampere's law, the current density is

$$\vec{J} = \nabla \times \vec{H} = \begin{vmatrix} \vec{a}_x & \vec{a}_y & \vec{a}_z \\ \dfrac{\partial}{\partial x} & \dfrac{\partial}{\partial y} & \dfrac{\partial}{\partial z} \\ y & -x & 0 \end{vmatrix} = (-1-1)\vec{a}_z = -2\vec{a}_z \ \text{A/m}^2$$

(*ii*) The circulation of $\vec{H}$ around the rectangular path shown in Figure E4.25 can be obtained from the integral form of Ampere's law i.e., $\oint_l \vec{H} \cdot d\vec{l} = I$

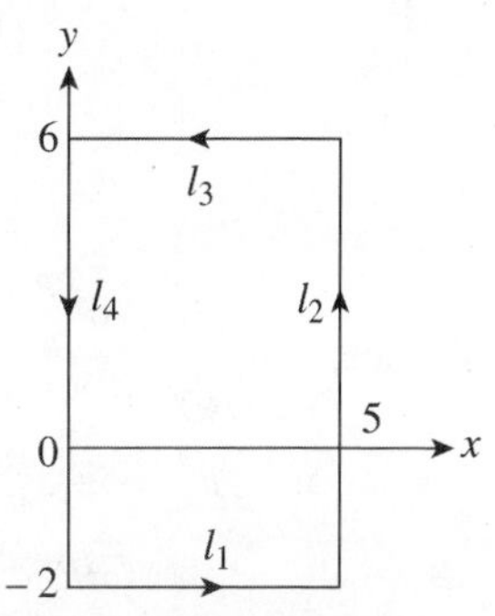

Figure E4.25

LHS of Ampere's law:

$$\oint_l \vec{H} \cdot d\vec{l} = \left(\int_{l_1} + \int_{l_2} + \int_{l_3} + \int_{l_4} \right) \vec{H} \cdot d\vec{l}$$

where

$$\int_{l_1} \vec{H} \cdot d\vec{l} = \int_0^5 \left(y\vec{a}_x - x\vec{a}_y \right) \cdot \left(dx\vec{a}_z \right) = \int_0^5 y\, dx \Big|_{y=-2} = (-2)(5) = -10$$

$$\int_{l_2} \vec{H} \cdot d\vec{l} = \int_{-2}^6 \left(y\vec{a}_x - x\vec{a}_y \right) \cdot \left(dy\vec{a}_y \right) = \int_{-2}^6 -x\, dy \Big|_{x=5} = (-5)(8) = -40$$

$$\int_{l_3} \vec{H} \cdot d\vec{l} = \int_5^0 \left(y\vec{a}_x - x\vec{a}_y \right) \cdot \left(dx\vec{a}_x \right) = \int_5^0 y\, dx \Big|_{y=6} = (6)(-5) = -30$$

and

$$\int_{l_4} \vec{H} \cdot d\vec{l} = \int_6^{-2} \left(y\vec{a}_x - x\vec{a}_y \right) \cdot \left(dy\vec{a}_y \right) = \int_6^{-2} -x\, dy \Big|_{x=0} = 0$$

Therefore, $\oint_l \vec{H} \cdot d\vec{l} = -10 - 40 - 30 + 0 = -80\text{A}$

RHS of Ampere's law:

$$I = \int_s \vec{J} \cdot d\vec{s} = \int_{y=-2}^6 \int_{x=0}^5 \left(-2\vec{a}_z \right) \cdot \left(dx\, dy\, \vec{a}_z \right)$$

$$= -2\int_{-2}^6 \int_0^5 dx\, dy = (-2)(5)(8) = -80\text{A}$$

Hence, Ampere's law is verified.

EXAMPLE 4.26

If an irrotational field is given by $\vec{F} = (x + 2y + lz)\vec{a}_x + (mx - 3y - z)\vec{a}_y + (4x + ny + 2z)\vec{a}_z$, determine the constants l, m and n for the above field.

SOLUTION

Since the vector field is irrotational, its curl is zero.

Therefore, $\nabla \times \vec{F} = 0$

$$\nabla \times \vec{F} = \begin{vmatrix} \vec{a}_x & \vec{a}_y & \vec{a}_z \\ \dfrac{\partial}{\partial x} & \dfrac{\partial}{\partial y} & \dfrac{\partial}{\partial z} \\ F_x & F_y & F_z \end{vmatrix}$$

$$= \left[\frac{\partial F_z}{\partial y} - \frac{\partial F_y}{\partial z} \right] \vec{a}_x + \left[\frac{\partial F_x}{\partial z} - \frac{\partial F_z}{\partial x} \right] \vec{a}_y + \left[\frac{\partial F_y}{\partial x} - \frac{\partial F_x}{\partial y} \right] \vec{a}_z = 0$$

Hence,

$$\frac{\partial F_z}{\partial y} - \frac{\partial F_y}{\partial z} = \frac{\partial F_x}{\partial z} - \frac{\partial F_z}{\partial x} = \frac{\partial F_y}{\partial x} - \frac{\partial F_x}{\partial y} = 0$$

Given $F_x = x + 2y + lz$, $\quad F_y = mx - 3y - z$, $\quad F_z = 4x + ny + 2z$

$$\frac{\partial F_z}{\partial y} - \frac{\partial F_y}{\partial z} = n + 1 = 0 \qquad \text{i.e., } n = -1$$

$$\frac{\partial F_x}{\partial z} - \frac{\partial F_z}{\partial x} = l - 4 = 0 \qquad\qquad \text{i.e., } l = 4$$

$$\frac{\partial F_y}{\partial x} - \frac{\partial F_x}{\partial y} = m - 2 = 0 \qquad\qquad \text{i.e., } m = 2$$

Hence, the constants $l = 4$, $m = 2$ and $n = -1$ make the given field irrotational. ❏

EXAMPLE 4.27

The magnetic field intensity is given in a region of space as,

$$\vec{H} = \frac{x + 2y}{z^2}\,\vec{a}_y + \frac{2}{z}\,\vec{a}_z \text{ A/m}$$

(*i*) Find $\nabla \times \vec{H}$.

(*ii*) Find $\vec{J}$.

(*iii*) Find the total current passing through the surface $z = 4$, $1 < x < 2$, and $3 < y < 5$ in the $\vec{a}_z$ direction using $\vec{J}$.

SOLUTION

(*i*) $\nabla \times \vec{H}$ in Cartesian coordinates is

$$\nabla \times \vec{H} = \begin{vmatrix} \vec{a}_x & \vec{a}_y & \vec{a}_z \\ \dfrac{\partial}{\partial x} & \dfrac{\partial}{\partial y} & \dfrac{\partial}{\partial z} \\ H_x & H_y & H_z \end{vmatrix}$$

$$= \left[\frac{\partial H_z}{\partial y} - \frac{\partial H_y}{\partial z}\right]\vec{a}_x + \left[\frac{\partial H_x}{\partial z} - \frac{\partial H_z}{\partial x}\right]\vec{a}_y + \left[\frac{\partial H_y}{\partial x} - \frac{\partial H_x}{\partial y}\right]\vec{a}_z$$

From the given field $\vec{H}$, we find that $H_x = 0$, $H_y = \dfrac{x + 2y}{z^2}$ and $H_z = \dfrac{2}{z}$

$$\nabla \times \vec{H} = \left[\frac{\partial\left(\frac{2}{z}\right)}{\partial y} - \frac{\partial\left(\frac{x+2y}{z^2}\right)}{\partial z}\right]\vec{a}_x + \left[0 - \frac{\partial\left(\frac{2}{z}\right)}{\partial x}\right]\vec{a}_y + \left[\frac{\partial\left(\frac{x+2y}{z^2}\right)}{\partial x} - 0\right]\vec{a}_z$$

$$= \left[0 - \left\{\frac{z^2(0) - (x + 2y)(2z)}{\left(z^2\right)^2}\right\}\right]\vec{a}_x + [0 - 0]\vec{a}_y + \left[\frac{1}{z^2} - 0\right]\vec{a}_z$$

$$= \frac{2(x + 2y)}{z^3}\,\vec{a}_x + \frac{1}{z^2}\,\vec{a}_z$$

(*ii*) From point form of Ampere's circuit law,

$$\nabla \times \vec{H} = \vec{J}$$

Therefore, $\vec{J} = \dfrac{2(x+2y)}{z^3}\,\vec{a}_x + \dfrac{1}{z^2}\,\vec{a}_z$ A/m^2

(*iii*) The current is

$$I = \int_s \vec{J} \cdot d\vec{s}$$

where the surface area in $\vec{a}_z$ direction is $d\vec{s} = dx\,dy\,\vec{a}_z$.

$$I = \int\limits_{y=3}^{5} \int\limits_{x=1}^{2} \frac{1}{z^2}\,dx\,dy \qquad\qquad (\text{since } \vec{a}_z \cdot \vec{a}_z = 1 \text{ and } z = 4)$$

$$= \frac{1}{(4)^2} \times [x]_1^2 \times [y]_3^5 = \frac{1}{16} \times (2-1) \times (5-3) = \frac{1}{8}$$

Hence, the total current passing through the surface is $I = \dfrac{1}{8}$ A   ❑

EXAMPLE 4.28

If the magnetic field intensity is $\vec{H} = x^2\vec{a}_x + 2yz\,\vec{a}_y + \left(-x^2\right)\vec{a}_z$ A/m, find the current density at point (*i*) $(2,3,4)$ (*ii*) $\rho = 6$, $\phi = 45°$, $z = 3$ and (*iii*) $r = 3.6$, $\theta = 60°$, $\phi = 90°$.

SOLUTION

Given $\vec{H} = x^2\vec{a}_x + 2yz\,\vec{a}_y + \left(-x^2\right)\vec{a}_z$ A/m.

(*i*) *To find the current density at point $(2,3,4)$ in rectangular coordinates:*

From Ampere's law in differential form, $\vec{J} = \nabla \times \vec{H}$. The current density, in Cartesian coordinate system, is

$$\vec{J} = \nabla \times \vec{H} = \begin{vmatrix} \vec{a}_x & \vec{a}_y & \vec{a}_z \\ \dfrac{\partial}{\partial x} & \dfrac{\partial}{\partial y} & \dfrac{\partial}{\partial z} \\ H_x & H_y & H_z \end{vmatrix} = \begin{vmatrix} \vec{a}_x & \vec{a}_y & \vec{a}_z \\ \dfrac{\partial}{\partial x} & \dfrac{\partial}{\partial y} & \dfrac{\partial}{\partial z} \\ x^2 & 2yz & -x^2 \end{vmatrix}$$

$$= \left(\frac{\partial}{\partial y}\left(-x^2\right) - \frac{\partial}{\partial z}(2yz) \right)\vec{a}_x - \left(\frac{\partial}{\partial x}\left(-x^2\right) - \frac{\partial}{\partial z}\left(x^2\right) \right)\vec{a}_y + \left(\frac{\partial}{\partial x}(2yz) - \frac{\partial}{\partial y}\left(x^2\right) \right)\vec{a}_z$$

$$= \left(0-(2y)\right)\vec{a}_x - \left((-2x)-0\right)\vec{a}_y + (0-0)\vec{a}_z$$

$$= -2y\vec{a}_x + 2x\vec{a}_y$$

At $P\,(2,3,4)$, $\vec{J} = -6\vec{a}_x + 4\vec{a}_y$ A/m^2

(*ii*) *To find the current density at point $(6, 45°, 3)$ in cylindrical coordinates:*

Transforming the cylindrical coordinates (ρ, ϕ, z) into rectangular coordinates (x, y, z) using the relations,

$$x = \rho\cos\phi = 6\times\cos 45° = 4.242$$
$$y = \rho\sin\phi = 6\times\sin 45° = 4.242$$
$$z = z = 3$$

Now, the point $(6, 45°, 3)$ is converted into $(4.242, 4.242, 3)$.

Here $\nabla\times\vec{H} = -2y\vec{a}_x + 2x\vec{a}_y$.

At point $(4.242, 4.242, 3)$, $\vec{J} = \nabla\times\vec{H} = -8.484\vec{a}_x + 8.484\vec{a}_y$ A/m^2

(iii) To find the current density at point $(3.6, 60°, 90°)$ in spherical coordinates:

Transforming the spherical coordinates (r, θ, ϕ) into rectangular coordinates (x, y, z) using the relations,

$$x = r\sin\theta\cos\phi = 3.6\sin 60°\times\cos 90° = 0$$
$$y = r\sin\theta\sin\phi = 3.6\sin 60°\times\sin 90° = 3.117$$
$$z = r\cos\theta = 3.6\times\cos 60° = 1.8$$

Now, the point $(3.6, 60°, 90°)$ is converted into $(0, 3.117, 1.8)$.

Here $\vec{J} = \nabla\times\vec{H} = -2y\vec{a}_x + 2x\vec{a}_y$

At point $(0, 3.117, 1.8)$, $\vec{J} = \nabla\times\vec{H} = -2\times3.117\vec{a}_x + 0 = -6.234x\,\vec{a}_x$ A/m^2 $\qquad\square$

EXAMPLE 4.29

The magnetic field intensity $\vec{H}$ is given by $\vec{H} = -y\left(x^2 + y^2\right)\vec{a}_x + x\left(x^2 + y^2\right)\vec{a}_y$ A/m in the $z = 0$ plane for the region $-5 < x, y < 5$. Calculate the current passing through the $z = 0$ plane and through the region $-1 < x < 1$ and $-2 < y < 2$.

SOLUTION

Given $\vec{H} = -y\left(x^2 + y^2\right)\vec{a}_x + x\left(x^2 + y^2\right)\vec{a}_y$ A/m . The total current passing through the surface or region $z = 0$ is

$$I = \int_s \vec{J}\cdot d\vec{s}$$

From Ampere's circuital law

$$\vec{J} = \nabla\times\vec{H} = \begin{vmatrix} \vec{a}_x & \vec{a}_y & \vec{a}_z \\ \dfrac{\partial}{\partial x} & \dfrac{\partial}{\partial y} & \dfrac{\partial}{\partial z} \\ -y\left(x^2 + y^2\right) & x\left(x^2 + y^2\right) & 0 \end{vmatrix}$$

$$= \left[-\frac{\partial}{\partial z}x\left(x^2 + y^2\right)\right]\vec{a}_x + \left[\frac{\partial}{\partial z}\left(-y\left(x^2 + y^2\right)\right)\right]\vec{a}_y + \left[\frac{\partial}{\partial x}x\left(x^2 + y^2\right) - \frac{\partial}{\partial x}\left(-y\left(x^2 + y^2\right)\right)\right]\vec{a}_z$$

$$= 0 + 0 + \left[\frac{\partial}{\partial x}\left(x^3 + xy^2\right) - \frac{\partial}{\partial y}\left(-yx^2 - y^3\right)\right]\vec{a}_z$$

$$= \left(3x^2 + y^2 + x^2 + 3y^2\right)\vec{a}_z = \left(4x^2 + 4y^2\right)\vec{a}_z = 4\left(x^2 + y^2\right)\vec{a}_z \text{ A/m}^2$$

Since the magnetic field has xy-distribution, the current density has z-component only. The current flowing in z-direction is obtained by integrating $\vec{J}$ over the region $x < 1$ and $y < 2$.

From Stokes's theorem, we have

$$I = \int_s \left(\nabla \times \vec{H} \right) \cdot d\vec{s} = \int_s \vec{J} \cdot d\vec{s}$$

$$= \int_{-2}^{2} \int_{-1}^{1} 4 \left(x^2 + y^2 \right) dx\, dy$$

$$= 4 \int_{-2}^{2} \left[\frac{x^3}{3} + xy^2 \right]_{-1}^{1} dy = 4 \int_{-2}^{2} \left[\left(\frac{1}{3} + y^2 \right) - \left(\frac{-1}{3} - y^2 \right) \right] dy$$

$$= 4 \int_{-2}^{2} \left[\left(\frac{1}{3} + y^2 \right) + \left(\frac{1}{3} + y^2 \right) \right] dy = 8 \int_{-2}^{2} \left[\frac{1}{3} + y^2 \right] dy$$

$$= 8 \left[\frac{y}{3} + \frac{y^3}{3} \right]_{-2}^{2} = 8 \left[\left(\frac{2}{3} + \frac{8}{3} \right) - \left(\frac{-2}{3} - \frac{8}{3} \right) \right]$$

$$= 53.33 \, \text{A}$$

EXAMPLE 4.30

Consider the portion of a sphere specified by $r = 4, 0 \leq \theta \leq 0.1\pi, 0 \leq \phi \leq 0.3\pi$.

Given $\vec{H} = 6r \sin \phi\, \vec{a}_r + 18r \sin \theta \cos \phi\, \vec{a}_\phi$ A/m, determine the current flowing through the surface.

SOLUTION

Given $\vec{H} = 6r \sin \phi\, \vec{a}_r + 18r \sin \theta \cos \phi\, \vec{a}_\phi$ A/m in spherical coordinates. Since the surface is directed along $\vec{a}_r$, $d\vec{s} = r^2 \sin \theta\, d\theta\, d\phi\, \vec{a}_r$.

We know that, $I = \int_s \vec{J} \cdot d\vec{s} = \int_s \left(\nabla \times \vec{H} \right) \cdot d\vec{s}$

where

$$\nabla \times \vec{H} = \frac{1}{r^2 \sin \theta} \begin{vmatrix} \vec{a}_r & r\vec{a}_\theta & r \sin \theta\, \vec{a}_\phi \\ \dfrac{\partial}{\partial r} & \dfrac{\partial}{\partial \theta} & \dfrac{\partial}{\partial \phi} \\ H_r & rH_\theta & r \sin \theta H_\phi \end{vmatrix} \qquad \text{(in spherical coordinates)}$$

The radial component of $\nabla \times \vec{H}$ is

$$\nabla \times \vec{H} = \frac{1}{r^2 \sin \theta} \left[\frac{\partial}{\partial \theta} \left(r \sin \theta H_\phi \right) - \frac{\partial}{\partial \phi} r(0) \right] \vec{a}_r \qquad \text{(since } H_\theta = 0\text{)}$$

$$= \frac{1}{r^2 \sin \theta} \left[\frac{\partial}{\partial \theta} \left(r \sin \theta \left(18r \sin \theta \cos \phi \right) \right) \right] \vec{a}_r$$

$$= \frac{18r^2 \cos \phi}{r^2 \sin \theta} \left[\frac{\partial}{\partial \theta} \left(\sin^2 \theta \right) \right] \vec{a}_r$$

$$= \frac{18\cos\phi}{\sin\theta}\left[2\sin\theta\cos\theta\right]\vec{a}_r = 36\cos\theta\cos\phi\,\vec{a}_r$$

Now, the current flowing through the surface is

$$I = \int_{\theta=0}^{0.1\pi}\int_{\phi=0}^{0.3\pi}(36\cos\theta\cos\phi\,\vec{a}_r)\cdot(r^2\sin\theta\,d\theta\,d\phi\,\vec{a}_r)$$

At $r=4$, $I = 576\times\int_0^{0.1\pi}\sin\theta\cos\theta\,d\theta\times\int_0^{0.3\pi}\cos\phi\,d\phi$

$$= \frac{576}{2}\times\left[-\frac{\cos 2\theta}{2}\right]_0^{0.1\pi}\times\left[\sin\phi\right]_0^{0.3\pi} \qquad (\text{since } \sin 2\theta = \sin\theta\cos\theta)$$

$$= 288\times 0.095\times 0.809 = 22.1\,\text{A}$$

EXAMPLE 4.31

Given $\vec{J} = 10^3\sin\theta\,\vec{a}_r$ A/m^2 , find the current passing through spherical shell of $r = 0.2$ m.

SOLUTION

Given $\vec{J} = 10^3\sin\theta\,\vec{a}_r$ A/m^2 and $r = 0.2$ m.

We know that, $I = \int_s \vec{J}\cdot d\vec{s}$ where $d\vec{s} = r^2\sin\theta\,d\phi\,d\theta\,\vec{a}_r$ in spherical coordinates.

Therefore, the current is

$$I = \int_{\phi=0}^{2\pi}\int_{\theta=0}^{\pi}\left(10^3\sin\theta\,\vec{a}_r\right)\cdot\left(r^2\sin\theta\,d\phi\,d\theta\,\vec{a}_r\right)$$

$$= r^2\int_0^{2\pi}\int_0^{\pi}10^3\sin^2\theta\,d\theta\,d\phi$$

$$= 0.2^2\times 10^3\times\int_{\theta=0}^{\pi}\sin^2\theta\,d\theta\times\int_{\phi=0}^{2\pi}d\phi$$

$$= 40\times\int_{\theta=0}^{\pi}\sin^2\theta\,d\theta\times(2\pi) = 80\pi\int_{\theta=0}^{\pi}\left[\frac{1-\cos 2\theta}{2}\right]d\theta$$

$$= 80\pi\left\{\frac{1}{2}\int_0^{\pi}d\theta - \frac{1}{2}\int_0^{\pi}\cos 2\theta\,d\theta\right\}$$

$$= 80\pi\left\{\frac{1}{2}\times\pi - \frac{1}{4}\left[\sin 2\theta\right]_0^{\pi}\right\}$$

$$= 80\pi\left[\frac{\pi}{2} - 0\right] = 40\pi^2 = 394.78\,\text{A}$$

EXAMPLE 4.32

A circular conductor of 1 cm radius has an internal magnetic field of $\vec{H} = \dfrac{1}{\rho}\left(\dfrac{1}{a^2}\sin a\rho - \dfrac{\rho}{a}\cos a\rho\right)\vec{a}_\phi$ A/m ,

where $a = \dfrac{\pi}{2\rho_0}$, ρ_0 being the radius of the conductor. Calculate the total current in the conductor.

SOLUTION

Given $\vec{H} = \dfrac{1}{\rho}\left(\dfrac{1}{a^2}\sin a\rho - \dfrac{\rho}{a}\cos a\rho \right)\vec{a}_\phi$ A/m.

$$H_\phi = \frac{1}{\rho}\left(\frac{1}{a^2}\sin a\rho - \frac{\rho}{a}\cos a\rho \right) = \left(\frac{1}{\rho a^2}\sin a\rho - \frac{1}{a}\cos a\rho \right) \text{ A/m}$$

Since the given field is in cylindrical coordinates, we have

$$\vec{J} = \nabla \times \vec{H} = \frac{1}{\rho}\begin{vmatrix} \vec{a}_\rho & \rho\vec{a}_\phi & \vec{a}_z \\ \dfrac{\partial}{\partial \rho} & \dfrac{\partial}{\partial \phi} & \dfrac{\partial}{\partial z} \\ 0 & \rho H_\phi & 0 \end{vmatrix} = \frac{1}{\rho}\left[\frac{-\partial}{\partial z}\left(\rho H_\phi \right)\vec{a}_\rho + \frac{\partial}{\partial \rho}\left(\rho H_\phi \right)\vec{a}_z \right]$$

$$= \frac{1}{\rho}\left[0 + \frac{\partial}{\partial \rho}\left(\rho H_\phi \right)\vec{a}_z \right] = \frac{1}{\rho}\frac{\partial}{\partial \rho}\left(\rho H_\phi \right)\vec{a}_z$$

$$= \frac{1}{\rho}\frac{\partial}{\partial \rho}\left[\frac{\rho}{\rho a^2}\sin a\rho - \frac{\rho}{a}\cos a\rho \right]\vec{a}_z$$

$$= \left(\frac{1}{\rho a^2}\frac{\partial}{\partial \rho}\left(\sin a\rho \right) - \frac{1}{a\rho}\left(\frac{\partial}{\partial \rho}\rho\cos a\rho \right) \right)\vec{a}_z$$

$$= \left(\frac{1}{\rho a^2}\left[a\cos a\rho \right] - \frac{1}{a\rho}\left[\cos a\rho - a\rho\sin a\rho \right] \right)\vec{a}_z$$

$$= \sin a\rho\, \vec{a}_z \text{ A/m}^2$$

Hence, the total current I enclosed by the conductor is

$$I_{encl} = \int_s \vec{J}\cdot d\vec{s} \quad \text{where } ds = \rho\, d\rho\, d\phi\, \vec{a}_z$$

Therefore, $I_{encl} = \displaystyle\int_0^1\int_0^{2\pi} (\sin a\rho\, \vec{a}_z)\cdot(\rho\, d\rho\, d\phi\, \vec{a}_z) = \int_0^1 \rho\sin a\rho\, d\rho \int_0^{2\pi} d\phi$

$$= 2\pi\int_0^1 \rho\sin a\rho\, d\rho = 2\pi\left[\frac{\rho\cos a\rho}{a} + \frac{\sin a\rho}{a^2} \right]_0^1$$

$$= 2\pi\left[\frac{\cos a}{a} + \frac{\sin a}{a^2} - \frac{\cos 0}{a} \right]$$

Given $a = \dfrac{\pi}{2\rho_0}$ and $\rho_0 = 10^{-2}$ m. Therefore, $a = 50\pi$.

Hence, $I_{encl} = 2\pi\left[\dfrac{\cos 50\pi}{50\pi} + \dfrac{\sin 50\pi}{\left(50\pi\right)^2} - \dfrac{1}{50\pi} \right]$

$$= 2\pi\left[\frac{1}{50\pi} - \frac{1}{50\pi} \right] = 0$$

4.5   APPLICATIONS OF AMPERE'S LAW

Ampere's law is used to determine the magnetic field intensity $\vec{H}$ for the symmetric current distributions by proper choice of Amperian contour or path around it. The determination of magnetic field intensity corresponding to an infinite line current, infinite sheet current, infinitely long coaxial line and toroidal coil using Ampere's law are discussed in this section.

4.5.1   Magnetic Field due to an Infinite Line Current

Figure 4.9 shows an infinitely long straight wire, carrying current I, placed along the z-axis. The magnetic field intensity can be determined at any point P in free space by constructing an Amperian path through P around the wire carrying current. The symmetrical current distribution requires that the magnetic field lines must be concentric circles and these circles form an Amperian path.

The magnetic field intensity will have a constant magnitude along the closed path and this path encloses the current I.

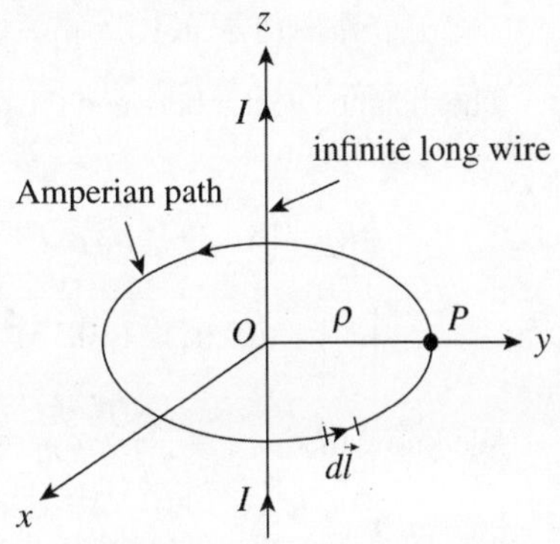

Figure 4.9   *Infinitely long wire carrying current*

By Ampere's law, $\displaystyle\oint_l \vec{H} \cdot d\vec{l} = I = \int_0^{2\pi} (H_\phi \vec{a}_\phi) \cdot (\rho \, d\phi \, \vec{a}_\phi)$

where $\vec{H} = H_\phi \vec{a}_\phi$ and $d\vec{l} = \rho \, d\phi \, \vec{a}_\phi$ in cylindrical coordinates.

Therefore, the enclosed current is

$$I = H_\phi \int_0^{2\pi} \rho \, d\phi$$

$$= H_\phi (2\pi\rho) \tag{4.24}$$

Therefore, the magnitude of magnetic field intensity in ϕ direction is given by

$$H_\phi = \frac{I}{2\pi\rho} \tag{4.25}$$

Representing the above equation in vector form, we obtain

$$\vec{H} = \frac{I}{2\pi\rho} \vec{a}_\phi \tag{4.26}$$

Hence, the magnetic field intensity is inversely proportional to the radius ρ of the circular path. The above expression derived using Ampere's law is same as the one derived using Biot–Savart's law for an infinitely long current carrying wire.

EXAMPLE 4.33

Given that two infinitely long and parallel wires carry currents $I_1 = I_2 = I$A in opposite directions. They are separated by a distance of 15 cm. If the magnetic field intensity at a point 8 cm from one wire and at 17 cm from the other is 17.554 A/m, determine the value of current I.

SOLUTION

Given $I_1 = I_2 = I$A and separation between the conductors is 15 cm. Let H_1 and H_2 be the fields at point P located at 8 cm and 17 cm away from the conductors respectively and the total field is

$$H = H_1 + H_2 = 17.554 \text{ A/m}$$

Assume the conductors A and B are normal to the xy-plane as shown in Figure E4.33.

The distance vector between the point $P\,(8, 0, 0)$ cm and the conductor A at $(0, 0, 0)$ is

$$\vec{R}_1 = \left(8\,\vec{a}_x\right)\times10^{-2}\ \text{m} = 0.08\,\vec{a}_x \ \text{ and } \ \left|\vec{R}_1\right| = 0.08$$

The distance vector between the point $P\,(8, 0, 0)$ cm and the conductor B at $(0, 15, 0)$ cm is

$$\vec{R}_2 = \left(8\,\vec{a}_x - 15\vec{a}_y\right)\times10^{-2}\,\text{m} = 0.08\,\vec{a}_x - 0.15\,\vec{a}_y$$

and $\qquad \left|\vec{R}_2\right| = \sqrt{(0.08)^2 + (0.15)^2} = 0.17$

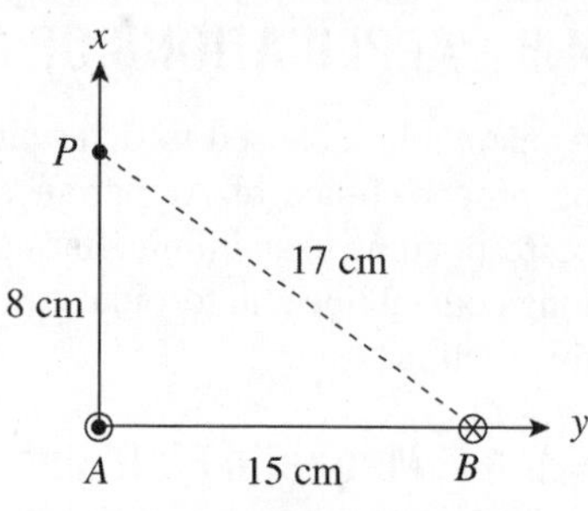

Figure E4.33

We know that, $\vec{H}_1 = \dfrac{-I}{2\pi R_1}\,\vec{a}_{R1} = \dfrac{-I}{2\pi\,(0.08)}\left(\vec{a}_x\right) = -1.989 I\,\vec{a}_x$ A/m $\qquad \left(\text{since } \vec{a}_{R1} = \dfrac{\vec{R}_1}{\left|\vec{R}_1\right|}\right)$

and $\qquad \vec{H}_2 = \dfrac{I}{2\pi R_2}\,\vec{a}_{R2} = \dfrac{I}{2\pi\,(0.17)}\left(0.47\vec{a}_x - 0.882\vec{a}_y\right)$ $\qquad \left(\text{since } \vec{a}_{R2} = \dfrac{\vec{R}_2}{\left|\vec{R}_2\right|}\right)$

$$= I\left(0.44\vec{a}_x - 0.826\vec{a}_y\right)\ \text{A/m}$$

Therefore, the total magnetic field intensity is

$$\vec{H} = \vec{H}_1 + \vec{H}_2$$

$$= \left(-1.989\vec{a}_x\right)I + \left(0.44\vec{a}_x - 0.826\vec{a}_y\right)I = \left(-1.549\vec{a}_x - 0.826\vec{a}_y\right)I$$

$$H = \left|\vec{H}\right| = \sqrt{(-1.549)^2 + (-0.826)^2} = 1.7554\,I$$

$$17.554 = 1.7554\,I$$

Hence, $I = 10$ A

EXAMPLE 4.34

A single-phase circuit comprises two parallel conductors, A and B, each 1 cm in diameter and spaced 1 m apart. The conductors carry currents of +100 A and –100 A, respectively. Determine the magnetic field intensity at the surface of each conductor and also in the space exactly midway between A and B.

SOLUTION

Consider that two current carrying conductors separated by 1 m are shown in Figure E4.34 and the two currents are seen flowing in opposite directions.

According to right-hand thumb rule, the field produced at P is in same direction due to both the conductors as shown in the Figure E4.34. The magnetic field intensity at any point P midway between A and B is equal to the sum of fields due to both conductors. Therefore,

$$\vec{H} = \vec{H}_1 + \vec{H}_2 = \dfrac{I_1}{2\pi\rho_1}\,\vec{a}_\phi + \dfrac{I_2}{2\pi\rho_2}\,\vec{a}_\phi$$

where $\rho_1 = \rho_2 = 0.5\,\text{m}$, $I_1 = I_2 = 100\text{A}$.

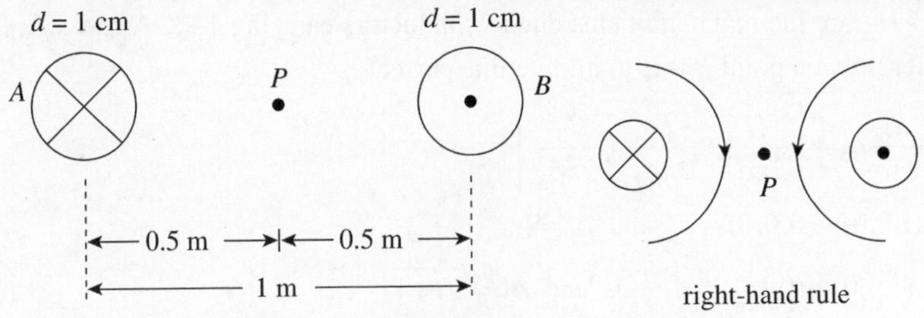

Figure E4.34

Therefore, $\vec{H}$ at $P = \dfrac{2\times100}{2\pi\times0.5}\vec{a}_\phi = 63.69\vec{a}_\phi$ A/m

At the surface of conductor A, the magnetic field intensity is

$$\vec{H}_1 = \frac{I}{2\pi\rho_1}\vec{a}_\phi = \frac{I}{2\pi\times0.5\times10^{-2}}\vec{a}_\phi$$

where the radius of the conductor A at $\rho_1 = \dfrac{d}{2} = 0.5\times10^{-2}$ m.

The magnetic field intensity at the surface of other conductor A due to conductor B is

$$\vec{H}_2 = \frac{I}{2\pi\times\left(1-0.5\times10^{-2}\right)}\vec{a}_\phi$$

Therefore, the total field intensity at the surface of the conductor A is $\vec{H}_A = \vec{H}_1 + \vec{H}_2$.

$$\vec{H}_A = \left[\frac{100}{2\pi\times0.5\times10^{-2}} + \frac{100}{2\pi\times0.995}\right]\vec{a}_\phi = 3200\vec{a}_\phi \text{ A/m}$$

The magnetic field intensity $\vec{H}_B$ on the surface of conductor B is same as that on conductor A but in opposite direction. Therefore, $\vec{H}_B = -3200\vec{a}_\phi$ A/m

EXAMPLE 4.35

Consider that three infinite conductors are carrying currents of 1A, 2A, and 3A, respectively in the same direction. The conductors are arranged in a straight line at a distance of 1 m. The conductor carrying current 1A is leftmost and that carrying 3A is rightmost. Find the magnetic field intensity $\vec{H}$ at a point 1 m exactly above the conductor carrying a current of 1A.

SOLUTION

Figure E4.35 shows three infinite conductors carrying currents 1A, 2A and 3A, respectively on the $x = 0$ plane.

The magnetic field intensity $\vec{H}$ at point $P(1, 0, 0)$ due to the three conductors is the sum of magnetic field intensities of individual conductors. Therefore

$$\vec{H} = \vec{H}_1 + \vec{H}_2 + \vec{H}_3$$

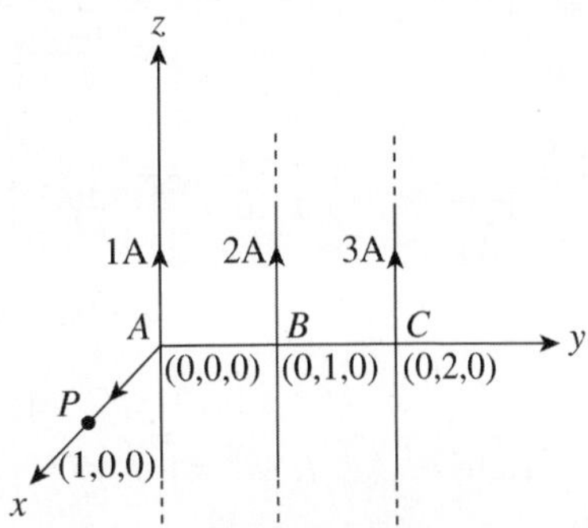

Figure E4.35

where $\vec{H}_1, \vec{H}_2$ and $\vec{H}_3$ are the magnetic fields due to conductors carrying 1A, 2A and 3 A, respectively. The magnetic field intensity at a point P due to infinite line current is

$$\vec{H} = \frac{I}{2\pi\rho}\vec{a}_\phi = \left[\frac{I_1}{2\pi\rho_1} + \frac{I_2}{2\pi\rho_2} + \frac{I_3}{2\pi\rho_3}\right]\vec{a}_\phi$$

where

$$\vec{\rho}_1 = (1,0,0) - (0,0,0) = \vec{a}_x \text{ and } \rho_1 = 1$$

$$\vec{\rho}_2 = (1,0,0) - (0,1,0) = \vec{a}_x - \vec{a}_y \text{ and } \rho_2 = \sqrt{1+1} = \sqrt{2}$$

$$\vec{\rho}_3 = (1,0,0) - (0,2,0) = \vec{a}_x - 2\vec{a}_y \text{ and } \rho_3 = \sqrt{1+2^2} = \sqrt{5}$$

Therefore, $\vec{H} = \left[\dfrac{1}{2\pi} + \dfrac{2}{2\pi\sqrt{2}} + \dfrac{3}{2\pi\sqrt{5}}\right]\vec{a}_\phi = \dfrac{1}{2\pi}\left[1 + \sqrt{2} + \dfrac{3}{\sqrt{5}}\right]\vec{a}_\phi = 0.6\vec{a}_\phi$ A/m

EXAMPLE 4.36

In a cylindrical region $0 < \rho < 0.8\,\text{m}$, $\vec{J} = 3e^{-5\rho}\vec{a}_z$ A/m^2. Determine $\vec{H} = H_\phi \vec{a}_\phi$.

SOLUTION

Given $\vec{J} = 3e^{-5\rho}\vec{a}_z$ A/m^2 for $0 < \rho < 0.8$ m.

From Stokes's theorem, we have

$$\oint_l \vec{H} \cdot d\vec{l} = \oint_s (\nabla \times \vec{H}) \cdot d\vec{s} = \oint_s \vec{J} \cdot d\vec{s}$$

where $d\vec{s} = \rho\, d\rho\, d\phi\, \vec{a}_z$ in cylindrical coordinates.

Therefore, $\oint_s \vec{J} \cdot d\vec{s} = \int_{\phi=0}^{2\pi} \int_0^\rho \left(3e^{-5\rho}\vec{a}_z\right) \cdot \left(\rho\, d\rho\, d\phi\, \vec{a}_z\right) = \int_{\phi=0}^{2\pi} \int_0^\rho 3\rho\, e^{-5\rho} d\rho\, d\phi$

$$= \int_{\phi=0}^{2\pi} d\phi \int_0^\rho 3\rho\, e^{-5\rho} d\rho = 6\pi \int_0^\rho \rho e^{-5\rho} d\rho$$

Integrating by parts, we get

$$= 6\pi\left[\left[\frac{\rho e^{-5\rho}}{(-5)}\right]_0^\rho - \int_0^\rho \left[\frac{e^{-5\rho}}{(-5)}\right] d\rho\right]$$

$$= 6\pi\left[\frac{\rho e^{-5\rho}}{(-5)} - \frac{e^{-5\rho}}{25}\right]_0^\rho$$

Hence, $\oint_s \vec{J} \cdot d\vec{s} = \dfrac{6\pi}{5}\left(-\rho e^{-5\rho} - \dfrac{e^{-5\rho}}{5}\right) + \dfrac{6\pi}{25} = I_{encl}$

From the cylindrical cross-section, the line integral along path l is $2\pi\rho$.

Therefore $\oint_l \vec{H} \cdot d\vec{l} = H_\phi(2\pi\rho)$

Here, $\oint_l \vec{H} \cdot d\vec{l} = \int_s \vec{J} \cdot d\vec{s}$

$$H_\phi(2\pi\rho) = I_{encl}$$

For $0 \le \rho \le 0.8$, $\quad H_\phi = \dfrac{1}{2\pi\rho}\left[\dfrac{6\pi}{5}\left(-\rho e^{-5\rho} - \dfrac{e^{-5\rho}}{5} \right) + \dfrac{6\pi}{25} \right]$

$$= \dfrac{3}{5\rho}\left(-\rho e^{-5\rho} - \dfrac{e^{-5\rho}}{5} \right) + \dfrac{3}{25\rho} \ \text{A/m}$$

At $\rho = 0.8$, $\quad H_\phi = 0.75\left(-0.8e^{-4} - \dfrac{e^{-4}}{5} \right) + 0.15$

$$= -0.75e^{-4} + 0.15 = 0.136 \ \text{A/m}$$

For $\rho > 0.8$ $\quad I_{encl} = \dfrac{6\pi}{5}\left(-0.8e^{-4} - \dfrac{e^{-4}}{5} \right) + \dfrac{6\pi}{25}$

$$= -0.069 + 0.754 = 0.685 \ \text{A}$$

Therefore, $\quad H_\phi\left(2\pi\rho\right) = I_{encl} = 0.685 \ \text{A}$

$$H_\phi = \dfrac{0.685}{2\pi\rho} = \dfrac{0.109}{\rho} \ \text{A/m}$$

Hence, $\quad \vec{H} = \begin{cases} \left[\dfrac{3}{5\rho}\left(-\rho e^{-5\rho} - \dfrac{e^{-5\rho}}{5} \right) + \dfrac{3}{25\rho} \right] \vec{a}_\phi, & 0 < \rho < 0.8 \\[4mm] 0.136\,\vec{a}_\phi, & \rho = 0.8 \\[4mm] \dfrac{0.109}{\rho}\,\vec{a}_\phi, & \rho > 0.8 \end{cases}$

EXAMPLE 4.37

Given $\vec{H} = \dfrac{y^2 z}{x}\,\vec{a}_x + \dfrac{y^2 z^2}{2x^2}\,\vec{a}_z$ A/m , find the current crossing the square surface at $y = 2$ bounded by $x = z = 1$ and $x = z = 2$.

SOLUTION

Given $\vec{H} = \dfrac{y^2 z}{x}\,\vec{a}_x + \dfrac{y^2 z^2}{2x^2}\,\vec{a}_z$ A/m

Using Stokes's theorem, we get

$$I = \int_s \left(\nabla \times \vec{H} \right) \cdot d\vec{s}, \qquad \text{where } d\vec{s} = dx\,dz\,\vec{a}_y$$

Now, $\nabla \times \vec{H} = \begin{vmatrix} \vec{a}_x & \vec{a}_y & \vec{a}_z \\[2mm] \dfrac{\partial}{\partial x} & \dfrac{\partial}{\partial y} & \dfrac{\partial}{\partial z} \\[3mm] \dfrac{y^2 z}{x} & 0 & \dfrac{y^2 z^2}{2x^2} \end{vmatrix}$

Since $d\vec{s}$ is in xz-plane, $\nabla \times \vec{H}$ can have $\vec{a}_y$ component only. Therefore,

$$\left(\nabla \times \vec{H}\right)_y = \left[\frac{-\partial}{\partial x}\left[\frac{y^2 z^2}{2x^2}\right] + \frac{\partial}{\partial z}\left(\frac{y^2 z}{x}\right)\right]\vec{a}_y = \left(\frac{-y^2 z^2}{2}\left(\frac{-2}{x^3}\right) + \frac{y^2}{x}\right)\vec{a}_y$$

$$= \left(\frac{y^2 z^2}{x^3} + \frac{y^2}{x}\right)\vec{a}_y$$

Hence, $\quad I = \int_1^2 \int_1^2 \left(\frac{y^2 z^2}{x^3} + \frac{y^2}{x}\right)\vec{a}_y \cdot dx\,dz\,\vec{a}_y = \int_1^2 \int_1^2 \left(\frac{y^2 z^2}{x^3} + \frac{y^2}{x}\right)dx\,dz$

At $y = 2$, $\quad I = \int_1^2 \int_1^2 \left(\frac{4z^2}{x^3} + \frac{4}{x}\right)dx\,dz = 4\int_1^2 \left[\frac{1}{x^3}\cdot\frac{z^3}{3} + \frac{z}{x}\right]_1^2 dx$

$$= 4\int_1^2\left(\frac{1}{3x^3}\left[2^3 - 1^3\right] + \frac{1}{x}(2-1)\right)dx = 4\int_1^2\left(\frac{7}{3}\frac{1}{x^3} + \frac{1}{x}\right)dx$$

$$= 4\left[\frac{7}{3}\left[\frac{-1}{2x^2}\right]_1^2 + \left[\ln x\right]_1^2\right] = 4\left[\frac{-7}{3}\left(\frac{1}{8} - \frac{1}{2}\right) + \ln 2 - \ln 1\right]$$

$$= 4\left[\frac{7}{8} + \ln 2\right] = 6.27\,\text{A} \qquad \Box$$

4.5.2 Magnetic Field due to an Infinite Current Sheet

Consider an infinite sheet of current flowing in the positive y-direction and located in $z = 0$ plane as shown in Figure 4.10. The sheet has a uniform surface current density of $\vec{K} = K_y \vec{a}_y$. Using symmetry considerations and the right-hand rule, the direction of magnetic field intensity $\vec{H}$ is shown in Figure 4.10.

The magnetic field intensity in x-direction for an infinite current sheet is given by

$$\vec{H} = \begin{cases} H_0 \vec{a}_x, & z > 0 \\ -H_0 \vec{a}_x, & z < 0 \end{cases} \tag{4.27}$$

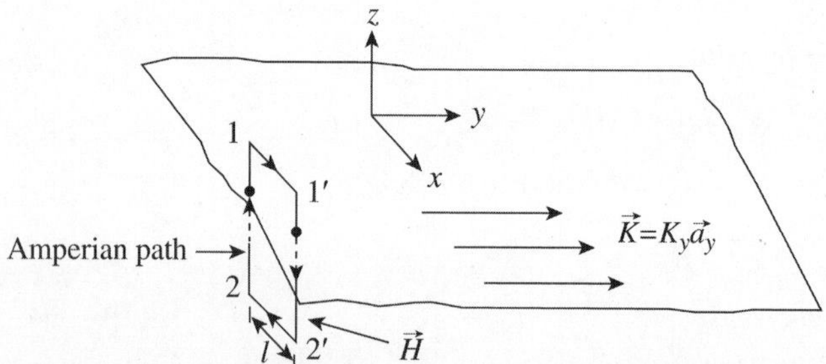

Figure 4.10 *Uniform sheet of surface current density*

The rectangular closed path $1\text{-}1'\text{-}2'\text{-}2\text{-}1$ around the sheet forms an Amperian path and it is used to determine the line integral of Ampere's law. This rectangular path consists of straight line segments which are either parallel or perpendicular to H_x. Since $\vec{K}$ represents current per unit length along the y-direction, the total current crossing the surface of the rectangular loop of length l is $I = K_y l$. Since the magnetic field intensity $\vec{H}$ is zero along the path $1'$ - $2'$ and 2-1, applying Ampere's law, we have

$$\oint_l \vec{H} \cdot d\vec{l} = 2H_0 l = I = K_y l$$

$$H_0 = \frac{K_y}{2} \tag{4.28}$$

Substituting Eq. (4.28) in Eq. (4.27), we get

$$\vec{H} = \begin{cases} \dfrac{K_y}{2}\vec{a}_x, & z > 0 \text{ (above the sheet)} \\[2mm] -\dfrac{K_y}{2}\vec{a}_x, & z < 0 \text{ (below the sheet)} \end{cases} \tag{4.29}$$

The above equation shows that the magnetic field intensity is positive on one side of the current sheet and negative on the other side of the sheet.

Defining $\vec{a}_n$ as the unit normal vector directed outward to the current sheet, Eq. (4.29) can be written as

$$\vec{H} = \frac{\vec{K}}{2} \times \vec{a}_n \tag{4.30}$$

The above equation is the general expression for magnetic field intensity due to an infinite sheet of surface current density $\vec{K}$ A/m .

EXAMPLE 4.38

Consider that a plane $y = 0$ carries a uniform current of $30\vec{a}_z$ mA/m. Calculate magnetic field intensity at $(1, 10, -2)$ m in rectangular coordinate system.

SOLUTION

From Eq. (4.30), the magnetic field due to an infinite sheet of surface current density $\vec{K}$ is

$$\vec{H} = \frac{\vec{K}}{2} \times \vec{a}_n$$

where $\vec{K} = 30\vec{a}_z$ mA/m and $\vec{a}_n$ is the unit normal vector directed from the current sheet to the point of interest. For plane $y = 0$, $\vec{H}$ cannot have any component in z-direction. Point $(1, 10, -2)$ is at the right of plane $y = 0$ and hence, $\vec{a}_n = \vec{a}_y$. Therefore, the field intensity becomes

$$\vec{H} = \frac{1}{2}\left[30\vec{a}_z \times \vec{a}_y\right]$$

$$\vec{H} \text{ at } (1,10,-2) = -15\vec{a}_x \text{ mA/m} \qquad (\text{since } \vec{a}_z \times \vec{a}_y = -\vec{a}_x) \qquad \square$$

EXAMPLE 4.39

Plane $y = 1$ carries current $\vec{K} = 50\vec{a}_z$ mA/m as shown in Figure E4.39. Determine the magnetic field intensity $\vec{H}$ at (*i*) $(0,0,0)$ and (*ii*) $(1, 5, -3)$

SOLUTION

For an infinite current sheet, the magnetic field intensity is

$$\vec{H} = \frac{\vec{K}}{2} \times \vec{a}_n$$

where $\vec{a}_n$ is the unit normal vector directed from the current sheet to the point of interest.

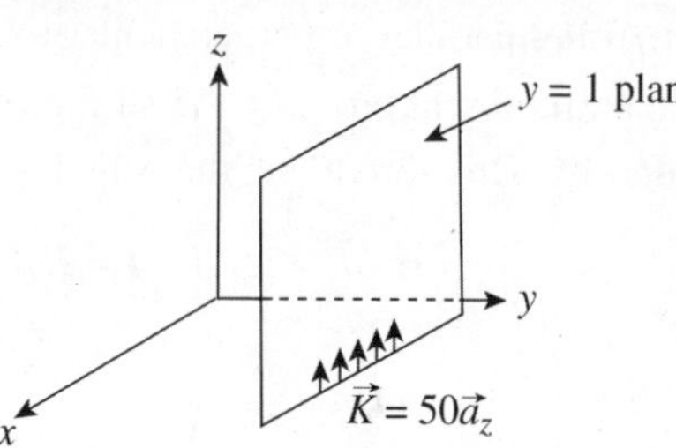

Figure E4.39

(*i*) Since $P\,(0,0,0)$ lies to the left of plane $y = 1$, $\vec{a}_n = -\vec{a}_y$. Therefore, the magnetic field is

$$\vec{H} = \frac{50\vec{a}_z}{2} \times (-\vec{a}_y) = 25\vec{a}_x \text{ mA/m}$$

(*ii*) Since $P\,(1, 5, -3)$ lies to the right of plane $y = 1$, $\vec{a}_n = \vec{a}_y$. Therefore, the magnetic field is

$$\vec{H} = \frac{50\vec{a}_z}{2} \times (\vec{a}_y) = -25\vec{a}_x \text{ mA/m} \qquad \square$$

EXAMPLE 4.40

Determine the magnetic field intensity $\vec{H}$ at (*i*) $(1,1,1)$ and (*ii*) $(0,-3,10)$ for the plane $z = 0$ and $z = 5$ carrying current $\vec{K} = -20\vec{a}_x$ mA/m and $\vec{K} = 20\vec{a}_x$ mA/m, respectively.

SOLUTION

Consider the parallel current sheets $z = 0$ and $z = 5$ as shown in Figure E4.40. The net magnetic field intensity is the sum of contributions due to the current sheets $z = 0$ and $z = 5$.

Therefore, $\vec{H} = \vec{H}_0 + \vec{H}_5$

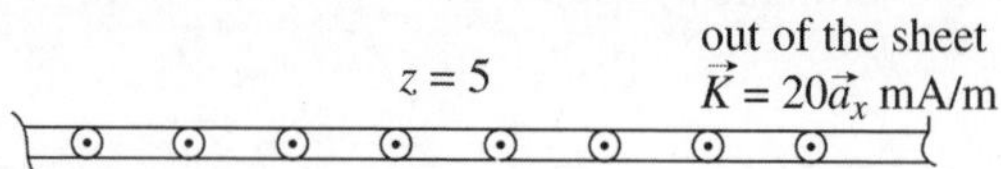

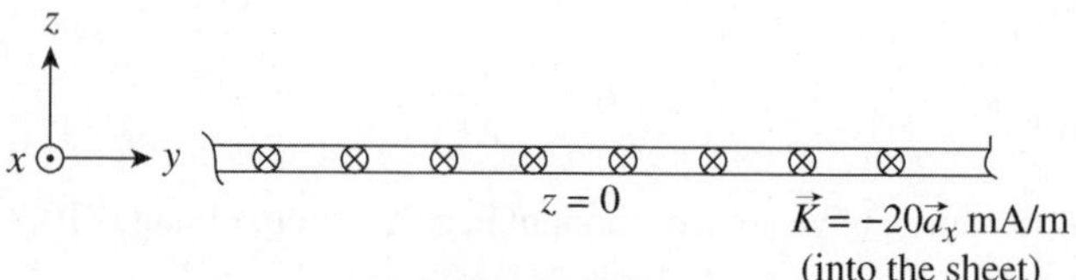

Figure E4.40

(*i*) Point $(1,1,1)$ is in between the current sheets $z = 0$ and $z = 5$. Hence, the magnetic field intensity at $(1,1,1)$ is

$$\vec{H}_0 = \frac{\vec{K}}{2} \times \vec{a}_n = \frac{-20\vec{a}_x}{2} \times \vec{a}_z = 10\vec{a}_y \text{ A/m}$$

$$\vec{H}_5 = \frac{\vec{K}}{2} \times \vec{a}_n = \frac{20\vec{a}_x}{2} \times (-\vec{a}_z) = 10\vec{a}_y \text{ A/m}$$

Therefore, $\vec{H} = \vec{H}_0 + \vec{H}_5 = 20\vec{a}_y$ A/m (*ii*) Point $(0,-3,10)$ is above the current sheets $z = 5$ and $z = 0$. Hence, the magnetic field intensity at $(0,-3,10)$ is

$$\vec{H}_0 = \frac{\vec{K}}{2} \times \vec{a}_n = \frac{-20\vec{a}_x}{2} \times \vec{a}_z = 10\vec{a}_y \text{ A/m}$$

$$\vec{H}_5 = \frac{\vec{K}}{2} \times \vec{a}_n = \frac{20\vec{a}_x}{2} \times \vec{a}_z = -10\vec{a}_y \text{ A/m}$$

Therefore, $\vec{H} = \vec{H}_0 + \vec{H}_5 = 0$ A/m

4.5.3 Magnetic Field due to an Infinitely Long Coaxial Cable

Figure 4.11 shows the cross-section of an infinitely long coaxial cable consisting of two concentric cylinders placed along the z-axis, represented out of page. The cable carries a uniformly distributed current $+I$ in the inner conductor of radius a and the return current $-I$ in the outer conductor of radius b and thickness t. Since the current distribution is symmetrical, Ampere's law can be applied along the Amperian path or contour for each of the four possible regions such as $0 \le \rho \le a, a \le \rho \le b, b \le \rho \le b+t$ and $\rho \ge b+t$.

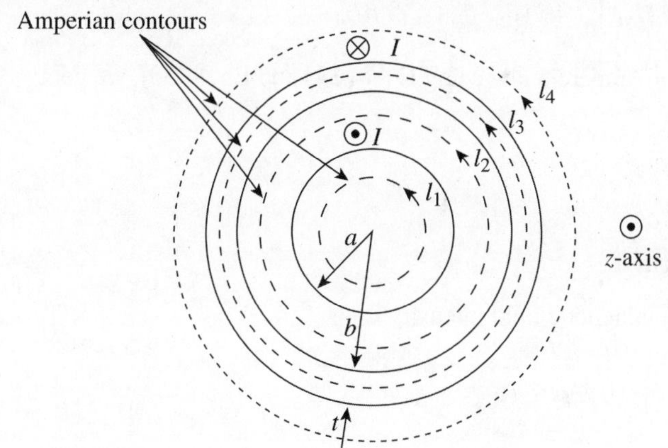

Figure 4.11 *Cross-section of a coaxial cable (with z-axis shown as out of page)*

Region 1: $0 \le \rho \le a$

Applying Ampere's law to path l_1, we obtain

$$\oint_{l_1} \vec{H}_1 \cdot d\vec{l} = I_{encl} = \int \vec{J} \cdot d\vec{s} \tag{4.31}$$

Since there is uniform distribution of current along z-direction, the current density is

$$\vec{J} = \frac{I}{\pi a^2} \vec{a}_z$$

Here, the differential surface area along z-direction is $d\vec{s} = \rho \, d\phi \, d\rho \, \vec{a}_z$.
Therefore, Eq. (4.31) becomes

$$I_{encl} = \int \vec{J} \cdot d\vec{s} = \int \left(\frac{I}{\pi a^2} \vec{a}_z \right) \cdot \left(\rho \, d\phi \, d\rho \, \vec{a}_z \right)$$

$$= \frac{I}{\pi a^2} \int_0^{2\pi} d\phi \int \rho\, d\rho = \frac{I}{\pi a^2} \times 2\pi \times \frac{\rho^2}{2} \qquad\qquad \left(\text{since } \vec{a}_z \cdot \vec{a}_z = 1\right)$$

$$= \frac{I\rho^2}{a^2} \tag{4.32}$$

Substituting Eq. (4.32) in Eq. (4.31), we get

$$\oint_{l_1} \vec{H}_1 \cdot d\vec{l}_1 = \frac{I\rho^2}{a^2} \tag{4.33}$$

Since the current is along z-direction, the magnetic field $\vec{H}_1$ will be along ϕ direction in the cylindrical coordinate system. Hence, $\vec{H}_1 = H_1 \vec{a}_\phi$ and $d\vec{l}_1 = \rho\, d\phi\, \vec{a}_\phi$. Now, the left hand side of Ampere's law in Eq. (4.33) becomes

$$\oint_{l_1} \vec{H}_1 \cdot d\vec{l}_1 = \int_0^{2\pi} \left(H_1 \vec{a}_\phi\right) \cdot \left(\rho\, d\phi\, \vec{a}_\phi\right)$$

$$= H_1 \rho \int_0^{2\pi} d\phi \left(\vec{a}_\phi \cdot \vec{a}_\phi\right) = 2\pi\rho H_1 \tag{4.34}$$

Equating both sides of Ampere's law using Eq. (4.34) and Eq. (4.33), we get

$$2\pi\rho H_1 = \frac{I\rho^2}{a^2}$$

$$H_1 = \frac{I\rho}{2\pi a^2}$$

Since $\vec{H}_1 = H_1 \vec{a}_\phi$, the magnetic field intensity is

$$\vec{H}_1 = \frac{I\rho}{2\pi a^2}\, \vec{a}_\phi, \left(0 \le \rho \le a\right) \tag{4.35}$$

Region 2: $a \le \rho \le b$

Applying Ampere's law to path l_2, we obtain

$$\oint_{l_2} \vec{H}_2 \cdot d\vec{l}_2 = I_{encl} = I$$

$$H_2(2\pi\rho) = I$$

$$H_2 = \frac{I}{2\pi\rho}$$

Since $\vec{H}_2 = H_2 \vec{a}_\phi$, the magnetic field intensity is

$$\vec{H}_2 = \frac{I}{2\pi\rho}\, \vec{a}_\phi, \qquad \left(a \le \rho \le b\right) \tag{4.36}$$

The above equation shows that the whole current is enclosed in the path l_2 and the magnetic field intensity is independent of the radius a of inner conductor. Equation (4.36) obtained using Ampere's law is same as the one obtained in Eq. (4.10) using Biot–Savart's law.

Region 3: $b \leq \rho \leq b+t$

Applying Ampere's law to path l_3, we get

$$\oint_{l_3} \vec{H}_3 \cdot d\vec{l}_3 = H_3(2\pi\rho) = I_{encl} \tag{4.37}$$

where $I_{encl} = I + \int \vec{J} \cdot d\vec{s}$ is the enclosed current.

The current density $\vec{J}$ of the outer conductor along $-z$-direction is

$$\vec{J} = -\frac{I}{\pi[(b+t)^2 - b^2]} \vec{a}_z$$

Hence, the enclosed current in Eq. (4.37) is written as

$$I_{encl} = I - \frac{I}{\pi[(b+t)^2 - b^2]} \int_0^{2\pi} \int_{\rho=b}^{\rho} \rho \, d\rho \, d\phi$$

$$= I\left(1 - \frac{\rho^2 - b^2}{t^2 + 2bt}\right) \tag{4.38}$$

Substituting Eq. (4.38) in Eq. (4.37), we get

$$H_3(2\pi\rho) = I_{encl} = I\left(1 - \frac{\rho^2 - b^2}{t^2 + 2bt}\right)$$

$$H_3 = \frac{I}{2\pi\rho}\left(1 - \frac{\rho^2 - b^2}{t^2 + 2bt}\right)$$

Since $\vec{H}_3 = H_3 \vec{a}_\phi$, the magnetic field intensity is

$$\vec{H}_3 = \frac{I}{2\pi\rho}\left(1 - \frac{\rho^2 - b^2}{t^2 + 2bt}\right)\vec{a}_\phi, \, (b \leq \rho \leq b+t) \tag{4.39}$$

Region 4: $\rho \geq b+t$

Applying Ampere's law to path l_4, we get

$$\oint_{l_4} \vec{H}_4 \cdot d\vec{l}_4 = I_{encl} = 0 \tag{4.40}$$

Here, if the radius ρ is larger than the outer radius of the outer conductor, then no current is enclosed and hence, the magnetic field is zero. Therefore,

$$\vec{H}_4 = H_4 \vec{a}_\phi = 0 \tag{4.41}$$

The magnitude of $\vec{H}$ is shown in Figure 4.12.

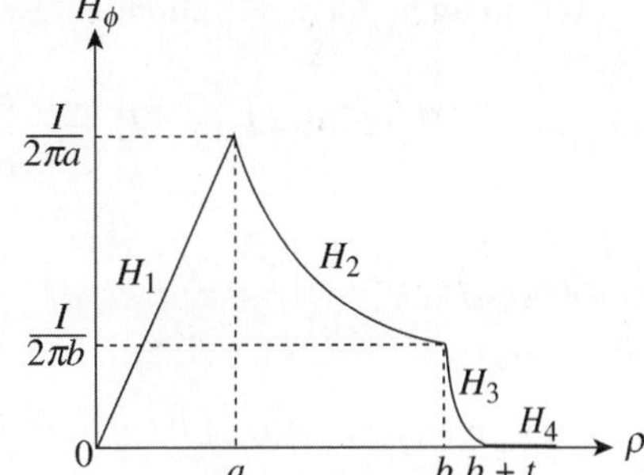

Figure 4.12 *Plot of H_ϕ vs ρ*

Therefore, the magnetic field intensity $\vec{H}_1, \vec{H}_2, \vec{H}_3$ and $\vec{H}_4$ for all four regions derived in Eqns. (4.35), (4.36), (4.39) and (4.41) can be summarized as follows:

$$\vec{H} = \begin{cases} \dfrac{I\rho}{2\pi a^2}\,\vec{a}_\phi, & 0 \le \rho \le a \\[2ex] \dfrac{I}{2\pi\rho}\,\vec{a}_\phi, & a \le \rho \le b \\[2ex] \dfrac{I}{2\pi\rho}\left(1 - \dfrac{\rho^2 - b^2}{t^2 + 2bt}\right)\vec{a}_\phi, & b \le \rho \le b+t \\[2ex] 0, & \rho \ge b+t \end{cases}$$

EXAMPLE 4.41

Determine the magnetic field intensity at a point $P(0.01, 0, 0)$ m if current through a coaxial cable is 6A, which is along the z-axis and $a = 3$ mm, $b = 9$ mm, and $c = 11$ mm.

SOLUTION

Consider a coaxial cable as shown in Figure E4.41. The inner conductor has radius a. The outer conductor has a thickness defined by the inner radius b and outer radius c.

Let the inner conductor carry a current of $+I$ A and the outer conductor carry a current of $-I$ A along the z-axis. The space between the inner and outer conductor is filled with air.

If the circular path of radius ρ is within $b \le \rho \le c$, then the current enclosed by the path is

$$I_{encl} = I + I'$$

where $I' = -I\left(\dfrac{\rho^2 - b^2}{c^2 - b^2}\right).$

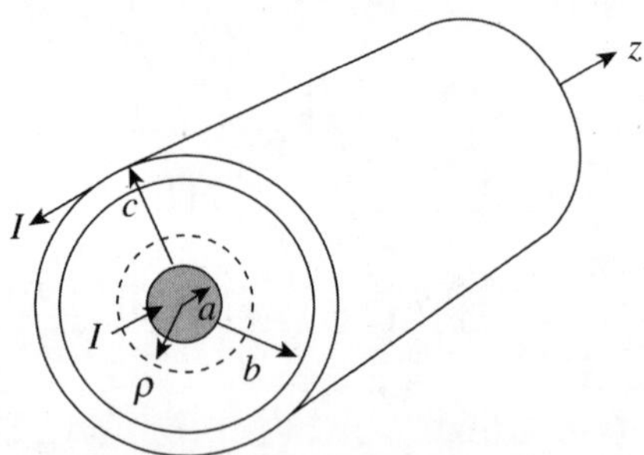

Figure E4.41   *Coaxial cable*

Therefore, $I_{encl} = I - I\left(\dfrac{\rho^2 - b^2}{c^2 - b^2}\right) = I\left(\dfrac{c^2 - \rho^2}{c^2 - b^2}\right)$

According to Ampere's circuital law, we have

$$H_\phi(2\pi\rho) = I_{encl} = I\left(\dfrac{c^2 - \rho^2}{c^2 - b^2}\right)$$

Hence, $H_\phi = \dfrac{I}{2\pi\rho}\left(\dfrac{c^2 - \rho^2}{c^2 - b^2}\right)$

For a given point $P(0.01, 0, 0)$, $\rho = \sqrt{(0.01)^2 + (0)^2} = 0.01\ \text{m} = 10\ \text{mm}$

Since P is in the region, $b < \rho < c$, the magnetic field intensity is

$$\vec{H} = \dfrac{I}{2\pi\rho}\left[\dfrac{c^2 - \rho^2}{c^2 - b^2}\right]\vec{a}_\phi$$

Substituting the given values in this equation, we get

$$\vec{H} = \frac{6}{2\pi \times 0.01}\left[\frac{(0.011)^2 - (0.01)^2}{(0.011)^2 - (0.009)^2}\right] = 50.11\,\vec{a}_\phi \text{ A/m}$$

4.5.4 Magnetic Field inside a Toroidal Coil

Figure 4.13(a) shows a toroidal coil with closed spaced winding wrapped around the core in the form of a ring. The inner and outer radii of the ring are a and b respectively. The magnetic field intensity for a toroid with N turns carrying current I can be determined for three regions such as $\rho < a$, $a < \rho < b$, and $\rho > b$ respectively.

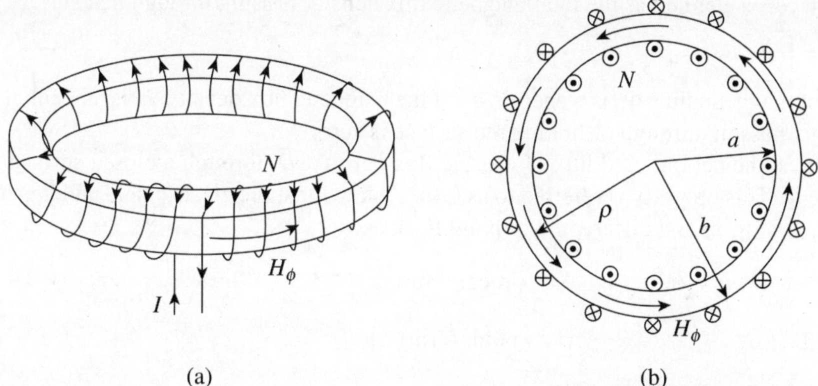

Figure 4.13 *Toroidal coil: (a) with N turns and (b) cross-sectional view of enclosed current*

From symmetry, it is clear that the magnetic field intensity $\vec{H}$ is in the ϕ direction and its magnitude is constant. If a circular Amperian path or contour is constructed with center at the origin and radius $\rho < a$, there will be no current flowing through the surface of the contour and hence, $\vec{H} = 0$ in the region interior to the toroidal coil for $\rho < a$.

Similarly, for an Amperian path with $\rho > b$, the total current flowing through its surface is zero since equal number of current coils cross the surface in both directions. Therefore, $\vec{H} = 0$ in the region exterior to the toroidal coil for $\rho > b$.

The application of Ampere's law shows that the magnetic field exists only inside the ring. An Amperian path of radius ρ is constructed for the region inside the core. Since N turns cut through this path each carrying current I, the net current crossing the surface of the Amperian path with radius ρ is NI and its direction is into the page as shown in Figure 4.13(b). Applying Ampere's law in the region, $a < \rho < b$, we get

$$\oint_c \vec{H} \cdot d\vec{l} = \int_0^{2\pi} (H_\phi \vec{a}_\phi) \cdot (\rho\, d\phi\, \vec{a}_\phi) = 2\pi\rho H_\phi = NI$$

$$H_\phi = \frac{NI}{2\pi\rho}$$

Therefore, the magnetic field intensity along ϕ direction inside the ring is given by

$$\vec{H} = \frac{NI}{2\pi\rho}\,\vec{a}_\phi \text{ for } a < \rho < b \tag{4.42}$$

4.6 MAGNETIC FLUX AND MAGNETIC FLUX DENSITY

The magnetic flux density $\vec{B}$ in static magnetic field is similar to the electric flux density $\vec{D}$ in static electric field. Since $\vec{D} = \varepsilon_0 \vec{E}$ in free space, the magnetic flux density $\vec{B}$ is related to magnetic field intensity $\vec{H}$ in the same way as given by

$$\vec{B} = \mu_0 \vec{H} \tag{4.43}$$

where μ_0 is a constant known as the *permeability of free space* and it is measured in H/m. The value of μ_0 in free space is given by

$$\mu_0 = 4\pi \times 10^{-7} \ \text{H/m}$$

The unit of magnetic flux density is weber per square metre (Wb/m^2) or tesla (T). The *magnetic flux* Φ linking any surface s is defined as the total magnetic flux density passing through that surface s. Therefore,

$$\Phi = \int_s \vec{B} \cdot d\vec{s} \tag{4.44}$$

where the unit of magnetic flux Φ is weber (Wb). If the magnetic flux density $\vec{B}$ is tangential to the surface, then the total flux passing through or linking the surface is zero.

In electrostatics, the net outward flux of electric flux density $\vec{D}$ through a closed surface is equal to the enclosed charge Q. This property is referred to as Gauss's law for static electric field and it is mathematically expressed in integral form and differential or point form as

$$\psi = \oint_s \vec{D} \cdot d\vec{s} = Q \qquad \text{(integral form)}$$

$$\nabla \cdot \vec{D} = \rho_v \qquad \text{(point form)}$$

where ρ_v is the volume charge density.

The charge Q is the source of electric flux lines and these lines originate on +ve charge and terminate on –ve charge. Therefore, it is possible to have an isolated charge as shown in Figure 4.14(a). Similarly, in electric dipole shown in Figure 4.14(b), the electric flux through a closed surface surrounding one of the charges is equal to the charge enclosed and it is not zero. This shows that the electric flux lines are not necessarily closed.

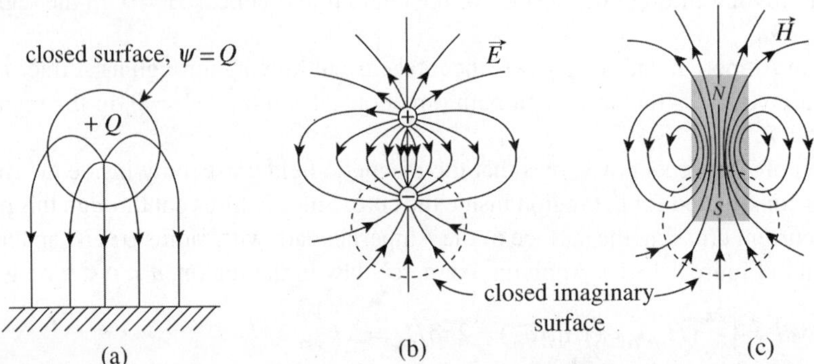

Figure 4.14 *Flux through a closed surface for (a) isolated electric charge, (b) electric dipole, and (c) bar magnet*

The magnetic equivalent to a point charge is a magnetic pole and such poles always occur in pairs. The number of magnetic flux lines leaving the north pole is exactly equal to the number of magnetic flux lines entering the south pole. This shows that the magnetic flux lines always form closed paths and there is no possibility of isolated magnetic poles or magnetic charges.

Suppose, if a permanent magnet is divided any number of times, each new piece will always have a north pole and south pole. It is impossible to separate the north pole and south pole; thus, magnetic monopole does not exist. For a bar magnet shown in Figure 4.14(c), the total magnetic flux through a closed surface surrounding the south pole of the magnet is always zero. In addition, the magnetic flux lines due to currents do not begin or end at any point but they form concentric circles around an infinitely long current carrying conductor. These observations lead to the fact that magnetic flux lines always form continuous closed loops.

Since an isolated magnetic pole does not exist, the net flux passing through a closed surface must be zero, which is given by

$$\oint_s \vec{B} \cdot d\vec{s} = 0 \qquad \text{(integral form)} \qquad (4.45)$$

which is called the *integral form of Gauss's law for static magnetic fields*. This property is also known as the law of conservation of magnetic flux or law of non-existence of isolated magnetic monopoles. The closed surface integral in the above equation can be converted into a volume integral by the application of divergence theorem as given by

$$\oint_s \vec{B} \cdot d\vec{s} = \int_v (\nabla \cdot \vec{B}) dv = 0 \qquad (4.46)$$

where v is the volume bounded by the closed surface s. Since the volume under consideration is not zero, the above equation indicates that

$$\nabla \cdot \vec{B} = 0 \qquad \text{(point form)} \qquad (4.47)$$

which is one of the Maxwell's equations applicable to static magnetic fields and it shows that the magnetic flux lines are always continuous. This is called the *point form or differential form of Gauss's law for static magnetic fields*. Since the divergence of $\vec{B}$ is always zero, the magnetic field intensity is solenoidal or continous.

EXAMPLE 4.42

If the magnetic field, $\vec{H} = r \sin\phi\, \vec{a}_r + 2.5r \sin\theta \cos\phi\, \vec{a}_\phi$ A/m, exists in a medium with $\mu_r = 3$, determine the magnetic flux density.

SOLUTION

Given $\vec{H} = r \sin\phi\, \vec{a}_r + 2.5r \sin\theta \cos\phi\, \vec{a}_\phi$ A/m and $\mu_r = 3$.

The magnetic flux density is

$$\vec{B} = \mu\vec{H} = \mu_0\mu_r\vec{H} = 4\pi \times 10^{-7} \times 3 \times \left(r \sin\phi\, \vec{a}_r + 2.5r \sin\theta \cos\phi\, \vec{a}_\phi \right)$$

$$= 3.77r \sin\phi\, \vec{a}_r + 9.42r \sin\theta \cos\phi\, \vec{a}_\phi \ \ \mu\text{Wb/m}^2 \qquad \square$$

EXAMPLE 4.43

A circular coil of radius 2 cm is in a magnetic flux density of 10 Wb/m². If the plane of the coil is perpendicular to the field, determine the total flux around the coil.

SOLUTION

Given flux density = 10 Wb/m² and area of the coil = $\pi r^2 = \pi \times \left(2 \times 10^{-2}\right)^2 = 4\pi \times 10^{-4}$.

The total flux around the coil is

$$\Phi = \text{flux density} \times \text{Area}$$

$$= 10 \times 4\pi \times 10^{-4} = 12.56 \ \text{mWb} \qquad \square$$

EXAMPLE 4.44

Given $\vec{B} = 2.5\sin\left(\dfrac{\pi x}{2}\right)e^{-2y}\vec{a}_z$ Wb/m^2, find the total magnetic flux crossing the strip for $z = 0$, $y \geq 0$ and $0 \leq x \leq 2$m.

SOLUTION

The magnetic flux crossing the strip is

$$\Phi = \int_s \vec{B}\cdot d\vec{s}, \quad \text{where } d\vec{s} = dx\,dy\,\vec{a}_z \text{ in rectangular coordinates}$$

$$= \int_s \left[2.5\sin\frac{\pi x}{2}e^{-2y}\vec{a}_z\right]\cdot\left(dx\,dy\,\vec{a}_z\right)$$

$$= \int_{x=0}^{2}\int_{y=0}^{\infty} 2.5\sin\frac{\pi x}{2}e^{-2y}\,dx\,dy$$

$$= 2.5\left[\frac{-\cos\dfrac{\pi x}{2}}{\dfrac{\pi}{2}}\right]_0^2 \left[\frac{e^{-2y}}{-2}\right]_0^{\infty} = 2.5\left[\frac{-\cos\pi-(-\cos 0)}{\dfrac{\pi}{2}}\right]\left[\frac{e^{-\infty}}{-2}-\frac{e^0}{-2}\right]$$

$$= \frac{2.5\times 2}{\pi}\times 2\times\frac{1}{2} = 1.592 \text{ Wb}$$

EXAMPLE 4.45

A radial magnetic field, $\vec{H} = \dfrac{2.39\times 10^6}{\rho}\cos\phi\,\vec{a}_\rho$ A/m. Determine the magnetic flux crossing the surface defined by $0 \leq \phi \leq \pi/4$ and $0 \leq z \leq 2$m.

SOLUTION

The portion of the cylinder is shown in Figure E4.45. The flux crossing the given surface is

$$\Phi = \int_s \vec{B}\cdot d\vec{s}$$

where the surface area $d\vec{s}$ normal to $\vec{a}_\rho$ direction is $d\vec{s} = \rho\,d\phi\,dz\,\vec{a}_\rho$.

Since $\vec{B} = \mu_0\vec{H}$, the magnetic flux crossing the surface is

$$\Phi = \int_s \mu_0\vec{H}\cdot d\vec{s}$$

$$= \mu_0\int_s\left(\frac{2.39\times 10^6}{\rho}\cos\phi\,\vec{a}_\rho\right)\cdot(\rho\,d\phi\,dz\,\vec{a}_\rho)$$

$$= \mu_0\int_{z=0}^{2}\int_{\phi=0}^{\pi/4} 2.39\times 10^6\cos\phi\,d\phi\,dz = 2.39\times 10^6\,\mu_0\left[\sin\phi\right]_0^{\pi/4}\left[z\right]_0^2$$

$$= 2.39\times 10^6\times 4\pi\times 10^{-7}\times\left[\sin\frac{\pi}{4}-\sin 0\right]\times[2-0] = 4.24 \text{ Wb}$$

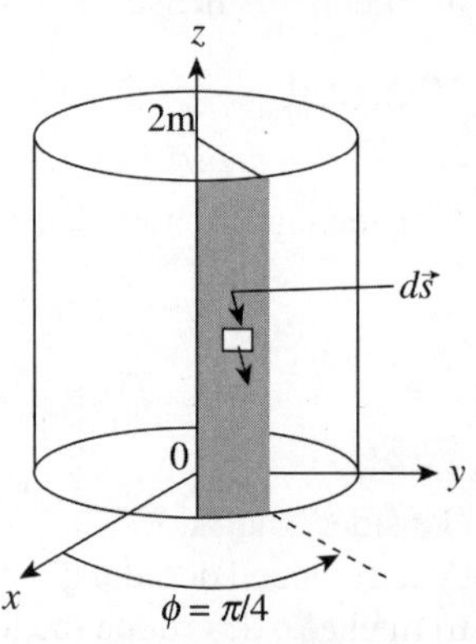

Figure E4.45

EXAMPLE 4.46

An iron ring has a mean circumference of 1.2 m and a cross-sectional area of 8 cm^2. It is wound with 480 turns. When it is carrying a current of 2A, the flux is found to be 1Wb. What is the permeability of iron?

SOLUTION

Given the mean circumference $l = 1.2$ m, $A = 8$ cm^2, $I = 2$A, $N = 480$ turns and $\Phi = 1\,\text{Wb}$.

The magnetic flux density is

$$B = \frac{\text{Flux}}{\text{Area}} = \frac{\Phi}{A} = \frac{1}{8\times10^{-4}} = 1250 \ \text{Wb/m}^2$$

Also, $B = \mu H = \mu_0\,\mu_r\,H$.

Here,
$$H = \frac{NI}{l} = \frac{480\times2}{1.2} = 800 \ \text{ampere-turns/m}$$

Therefore,
$$\mu_r = \frac{B}{\mu_0 H} = \frac{1250}{4\pi\times10^{-7}\times800} = 0.124\times10^7$$

❑

EXAMPLE 4.47

Calculate the magnetic flux density due to a coil of 1000 ampere-turns and area of 100 cm^2 on the axis of coil at a distance of 10 m from the center.

SOLUTION

Given $NI = 1000$ ampere-turns, $h = 10$ m and area $= 100$ cm^2.

Therefore, $\pi a^2 = 100\times10^{-4}$ m^2 i.e., $a = 5.64\,\text{cm}$.

The magnitude of magnetic field intensity due to a coil of N turns carrying current I is

$$H = \frac{NIa^2}{2(h^2 + a^2)^{3/2}}$$

Since $B = \mu H$, the magnitude of flux density due to a coil is

$$B = \frac{\mu NIa^2}{2(h^2 + a^2)^{3/2}} = \frac{\mu\times1000\times(5.64\times10^{-2})^2}{2\left(10^2 + (5.64\times10^{-2})^2\right)^{3/2}} = 1.59\mu\times10^{-3}\,\text{T}$$

where μ is the permeability.

❑

EXAMPLE 4.48

Consider that the currents $I_1 = I_2 = 10A$ flow in opposite directions through two long parallel wires separated by a distance of 20 cm. Find the magnitude and the direction of magnetic flux density at a point 20 cm away from each conductor.

SOLUTION

Given the current through wire 1 is $I_1 = 10$A, current through wire 2 is $I_2 = -10$A, the distance between two wires is $d = 20$ cm and $\rho_1 = \rho_2 = 20$ cm $= 0.2$ m. The magnitude of magnetic field intensity produced by the wire 1 is

$$H_1 = \frac{I_1}{2\pi\rho_1}$$

Since $B = \mu H$, the magnitude of flux density due to wire 1 is $B_1 = \dfrac{\mu I_1}{2\pi \rho_1}$

Similarly, the magnitude of flux density due to wire 2 is $B_2 = \dfrac{\mu I_2}{2\pi \rho_2}$

Therefore, the required magnitude of magnetic flux density is

$$B = B_1 + B_2 = \frac{\mu}{2\pi}\left(\frac{I_1}{\rho_1} + \frac{I_2}{\rho_2} \right)$$

Substituting the given values, we get

$$B = \frac{\mu}{2\pi}\left(\frac{10}{0.2} - \frac{10}{0.2} \right) = 0$$

EXAMPLE 4.49

Consider that two long, identical and parallel conductors carrying a current of 500 A in opposite directions are strung on poles 50 m apart. If the radius of each conductor is 4 cm and the separation between their axes is 2 m, determine the flux passing through the region bounded by the conductors and the two consecutive poles.

SOLUTION

Figure E4.49 shows two parallel conductors, each of radius a, separated by a distance b, carrying currents in opposite directions. Let l be the distance between two consecutive poles. The magnetic flux density at a point y in the plane of the conductors is

$$\vec{B} = -\frac{\mu_0 I}{2\pi}\left[\frac{1}{y} + \frac{1}{b-y} \right]\vec{a}_x$$

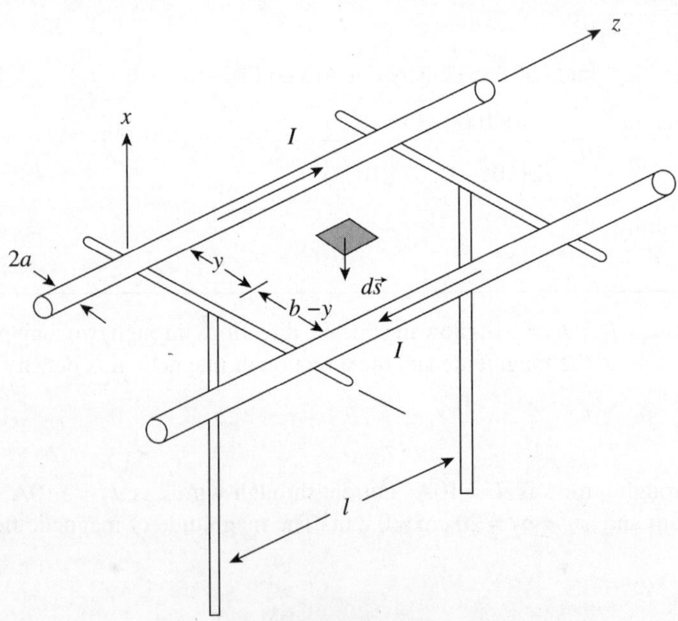

Figure E4.49

Here, the elementary surface is $d\vec{s} = -dy\,dz\,\vec{a}_x$. Therefore, the required flux is

$$\Phi = \int_s \vec{B} \cdot d\vec{s} = \int_s \frac{\mu_0 I}{2\pi}\left[\frac{1}{y} + \frac{1}{b-y}\right] dy\,dz$$

$$= \frac{\mu_0 I}{2\pi}\int_a^{b-a}\left[\frac{1}{y} + \frac{1}{b-y}\right] dy \int_0^l dz$$

$$= \frac{\mu_0 I l}{2\pi}\ln\left[\frac{b-a}{a}\right]\text{ Wb}$$

Substituting the given values of $a = 0.04\,\text{m}$, $b = 2\,\text{m}$, $l = 50\,\text{m}$ and $I = 500\,\text{A}$ in the above equation, we get

$$\Phi = \frac{4\pi\times 10^{-7}\times 500\times 50}{2\pi}\ln\left[\frac{2-0.04}{0.04}\right] = 38.92\,\text{mWb} \qquad \square$$

 4.50

A solid non-magnetic conductor of radius $\rho = 2\,\text{cm}$ carries a total current of 60A in $\vec{a}_z$ direction. The conductor is non-homogeneous having a conductivity that varies with ρ as $\sigma = 10^5\left(1+2.5\times 10^5\rho^2\right)$ S/m. Find the total flux crossing the radial plane defined by $\phi = 0$, $0 < z < 1\,\text{m}$ and $0 < \rho < 1\,\text{cm}$.

SOLUTION

Given $\rho = 2\,\text{cm} = 2\times 10^{-2}\,\text{m}$ and $I = 60\,\text{A}$ along $\vec{a}_z$ direction. Consider the plane defined by $\phi = 0$, $0 < z < 1$ and $1 < \rho < 0.01$.

The current density is

$$\vec{J} = \sigma\vec{E} = \sigma E\,\vec{a}_z\text{ A/m}^2$$

$$= 10^5\left(1+2.5\times 10^5\rho^2\right)E\,\vec{a}_z\text{ A/m}^2$$

Therefore, the total current is

$$I = \int \vec{J}\cdot d\vec{s} = \int \vec{J}\cdot\left(\rho\,d\rho\,d\phi\,\vec{a}_z\right), \qquad \text{where } d\vec{s} = \rho\,d\rho\,d\phi\,\vec{a}_z$$

$$= \int_0^{2\pi}\int_0^{\rho}\left[10^5\left(1+2.5\times 10^5\rho^2\right)E\vec{a}_z\right]\cdot\left[\rho\,d\rho\,d\phi\,\vec{a}_z\right]$$

$$= \int_0^{2\pi}\int_0^{0.02}10^5\left(1+2.5\times 10^5\rho^2\right)E\,\rho\,d\rho\,d\phi$$

$$= 10^5 E\int_0^{2\pi}\int_0^{0.02}\left(\rho+2.5\times 10^5\rho^3\right)d\rho\,d\phi$$

Substituting $I = 60\,\text{A}$, we get

$$60 = 10^5 E\left[\frac{\rho^2}{2} + 2.5\times 10^5\frac{\rho^4}{4}\right]_0^{0.02}[\phi]_0^{2\pi}$$

$$= 10^5 E\left[\frac{(0.02)^2}{2} + 2.5\times 10^5\times\frac{(0.02)^4}{4}\right]\times(2\pi)$$

$$= 10^5 E\left[0.0002 + 0.01\right]\times 2\pi$$

Hence, $\qquad E = \dfrac{60}{10^5 \times 0.0102 \times 2\pi} = 9.36 \ \text{mV/m}$

Therefore, the current density is

$$\vec{J} = \sigma E \vec{a}_z = 936\left(1 + 2.5 \times 10^5 \rho^2\right)\vec{a}_z \ \text{A/m}^2$$

From Ampere's circuital law,

$$\oint_l \vec{H} \cdot d\vec{l} = I_{encl}$$

$$= 2\pi\rho \, H_\phi = \int_s \vec{J} \cdot d\vec{s}$$

Therefore, $\ 2\pi\rho \, H_\phi = \displaystyle\int_0^{2\pi}\int_0^{\rho} 936\left[1 + 2.5 \times 10^5 \rho^2\right]\rho \, d\rho \, d\phi$

$$= 936\left[\frac{\rho^2}{2} + \frac{2.5 \times 10^5 \rho^4}{4}\right]_0^{\rho} [\phi]_0^{2\pi}$$

$$= 936\left[\frac{\rho^2}{2} + \frac{2.5 \times 10^5 \rho^4}{4}\right] \times (2\pi)$$

Therefore, $\qquad \vec{H}_\phi = 936\left[\dfrac{\rho}{2} + \dfrac{2.5 \times 10^5 \rho^3}{4}\right]\vec{a}_\phi \ \text{A/m}$

Since $\vec{B} = \mu_0 \vec{H}_\phi$, the flux density is

$$\vec{B} = 936\mu_0\left[\frac{\rho}{2} + \frac{2.5 \times 10^5 \rho^3}{4}\right]\vec{a}_\phi \ \text{Wb/m}^2$$

The total flux Φ in the region $0 < z < 1$, $0 < \rho < 0.01$ is

$$\Phi = \int_s \vec{B} \cdot d\vec{s}, \ \text{where} \ d\vec{s} = d\rho \, dz \, \vec{a}_\phi$$

$$= \int_{z=0}^{1}\int_{\rho=0}^{0.01} 936\mu_0\left[\frac{\rho}{2} + \frac{2.5 \times 10^5 \rho^3}{4}\right] d\rho \, dz$$

$$= 936\mu_0 \times \int_0^{0.01}\left[\frac{\rho}{2} + \frac{2.5 \times 10^5 \rho^3}{4}\right] d\rho \times [z]_0^1$$

$$= 936\mu_0\left[\frac{\rho^2}{4} + \frac{2.5 \times 10^5 \rho^4}{16}\right]_0^{0.01}$$

$$= 936\mu_0\left[\frac{(0.01)^2}{4} + \frac{2.5 \times 10^5 (0.01)^4}{16}\right] = 0.169\mu_0 \ \text{Wb} \qquad \Box$$

4.7 SCALAR AND VECTOR MAGNETIC POTENTIALS

In electrostatics, the determination of electric field intensity $\vec{E}$ is simplified by making use of the relation, $\vec{E} = -\nabla V$ where V is the scalar electric potential. Similarly, in magnetostatics, a potential can be defined as magnetic potential and it can be either a scalar V_m or a vector $\vec{A}$.

The negative gradient of scalar magnetic potential V_m gives the magnetic field intensity as represented by

$$\vec{H} = -\nabla V_m \tag{4.48}$$

The unit of scalar magnetic potential is ampere. From point form of Ampere's law,

$$\vec{J} = \nabla \times \vec{H} \tag{4.49}$$

Substituting Eq. (4.48) in Eq. (4.49), we get

$$\vec{J} = \nabla \times (-\nabla V_m) \tag{4.50}$$

However, as per vector identity rules, the curl of the gradient of any scalar field should be zero, i.e., $\nabla \times (\nabla V) = 0$. Since the above equation involves curl of the gradient of the scalar magnetic potential, the current density will be zero throughout the region in which the scalar potential is defined. Therefore, the scalar magnetic potential V_m given in Eq. (4.48) is applicable only if $\vec{J} = 0$, i.e., V_m is defined only in a region where $\vec{J} = 0$.

For a source free region where $\vec{J} = 0$, Eq. (4.49) becomes $\nabla \times \vec{H} = 0$ which also shows that $\oint_l \vec{H} \cdot d\vec{l} = 0$ using Stokes's theorem, i.e., the closed path l does not enclose any current. Since $\vec{E} = -\nabla V$ in electrostatics, the electric potential V at point a with respect to point b is given by

$$V_{ab} = -\int_b^a \vec{E} \cdot d\vec{l}$$

Similarly, in magnetostatics, the scalar magnetic potential of point a with respect to point b is given by

$$V_m = -\int_b^a \vec{H} \cdot d\vec{l}$$

The magnetic potential difference between any two points is commonly referred to as the magnetomotive force or mmf. The scalar potential V_m also satisfies Laplace's equation similar to $\nabla^2 V = 0$ in electrostatic fields and by law of non-existence of magnetic monopoles, $\nabla \cdot \vec{B} = 0$ and in free space, it can be written as

$$\nabla \cdot \vec{B} = \mu_0 \nabla \cdot \vec{H} = 0 \tag{4.51}$$

Substituting Eq. (4.48) in Eq. (4.51), we get

$$\mu_0 \nabla \cdot (-\nabla V_m) = 0$$

$$\nabla^2 V_m = 0 \qquad \text{(when } \vec{J} = 0) \tag{4.52}$$

The above equation shows that the Laplace's equation in static magnetic fields is applicable only in a current free region where $\vec{J} = 0$ similar to scalar magnetic potential V_m.

As the divergence of $\vec{B}$ is zero, the magnetic flux density is always solenoidal (continuous). A vector whose divergence is zero can be expressed in terms of curl of another vector quantity as

$$\vec{B} = \nabla \times \vec{A} \tag{4.53}$$

where $\vec{A}$ is called the vector magnetic potential and is expressed in weber per metre (Wb/m). The vector identity rule which is used to define $\vec{A}$ states that the divergence of the curl of any vector field is zero, i.e., $\nabla \cdot (\nabla \times \vec{A}) = 0$.

In addition, the vector magnetic potential $\vec{A}$ can be obtained by making use of the Biot–Savart's law. The magnetic flux density $\vec{B}$ at any point $P(x, y, z)$ produced by a current carrying conductor is given by

$$\vec{B} = \frac{\mu_0 I}{4\pi} \int_l \frac{d\vec{l}' \times \vec{R}}{R^3}$$

where $\vec{R}$ is the distance vector from the line element dl' at the source coordinates (x', y', z') to the field coordinates (x, y, z) as shown in Figure 4.15 and its magnitude is represented by

$$R = \left|\vec{R}\right| = \left|\vec{r} - \vec{r}'\right| = \left[(x - x')^2 + (y - y')^2 + (z - z')^2\right]^{1/2} \tag{4.54}$$

Referring to Example 4.68, we can write

$$\nabla\left(\frac{1}{R}\right) = -\frac{(x - x')\vec{a}_x + (y - y')\vec{a}_y + (z - z')\vec{a}_z}{\left[(x - x')^2 + (y - y')^2 + (z - z')^2\right]^{3/2}} = -\frac{\vec{R}}{R^3}$$

The magnetic flux density can also be written as

$$\vec{B} = \frac{\mu_0 I}{4\pi}\int_{l'}\nabla\left(\frac{1}{R}\right)\times d\vec{l}' \tag{4.55}$$

Here, the $-$ve sign is removed by interchanging the terms in the vector product.

Consider the vector identity,

$$\nabla\times(f\vec{F}) = f(\nabla\times\vec{F}) + (\nabla f)\times\vec{F} \tag{4.56}$$

where f is the scalar field and $\vec{F}$ is the vector field. Taking $\vec{F} = d\vec{l}'$ and $f = \frac{1}{R}$, the integrand of Eq. (4.55) can be expressed as

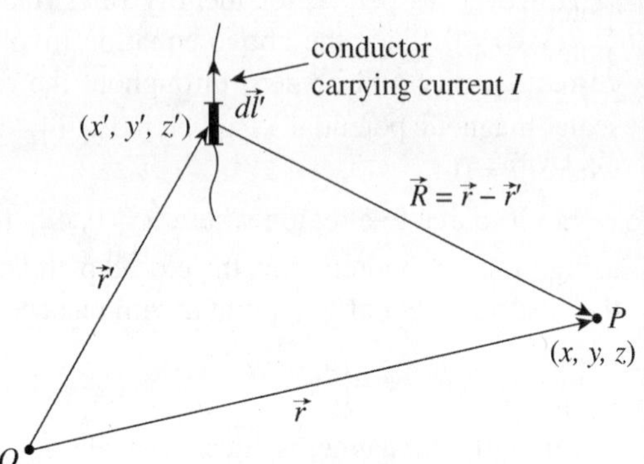

Figure 4.15 *Representation of field point (x, y, z) and source point (x', y', z')*

$$\nabla\left(\frac{1}{R}\right)\times d\vec{l}' = \nabla\times\left(\frac{d\vec{l}'}{R}\right) - \frac{1}{R}\left(\nabla\times d\vec{l}'\right)$$

Since the curl operation is with respect to field point $P(x, y, z)$, $\nabla\times d\vec{l}' = 0$. Substituting the above equation in Eq. (4.55), we have

$$\vec{B} = \frac{\mu_0 I}{4\pi}\int_{l'}\nabla\times\left(\frac{d\vec{l}'}{R}\right) \tag{4.57}$$

Rearranging the above equation, we get

$$\vec{B} = \nabla\times\left[\frac{\mu_0 I}{4\pi}\int_{l'}\frac{d\vec{l}'}{R}\right] \tag{4.58}$$

Since $\vec{B} = \nabla\times\vec{A}$, the expression for vector magnetic potential due to line current is obtained as

$$\vec{A} = \frac{\mu_0}{4\pi}\int_{l'}\frac{I d\vec{l}'}{R} \tag{4.59}$$

If the current carrying conductor forms a closed loop, the above equation becomes

$$\vec{A} = \frac{\mu_0}{4\pi}\oint_{l'}\frac{I d\vec{l}'}{R} \tag{4.60}$$

Equation (4.59) can be generalized by expressing vector magnetic potential in terms of surface current density as

$$\vec{A} = \frac{\mu_0}{4\pi}\int_{s'}\frac{\vec{K}ds'}{R} \qquad \left(\sin ce\ d\vec{l}' = \vec{K}ds'\right) \tag{4.61}$$

Similarly, the vector magnetic potential can be written in terms of volume current density as

$$\vec{A} = \frac{\mu_0}{4\pi} \int_{v'} \frac{\vec{J}dv'}{R} \tag{4.62}$$

Substituting Eq. (4.53) in Eq. (4.44), we obtain

$$\Phi = \int_s \vec{B} \cdot d\vec{s} = \int_s (\nabla \times \vec{A}) \cdot d\vec{s} \tag{4.63}$$

Applying Stokes's theorem, we get

$$\Phi = \oint_l \vec{A} \cdot d\vec{l} \tag{4.64}$$

Therefore, the magnetic flux Φ can be obtained by using magnetic flux density $\vec{B}$ or vector magnetic potential $\vec{A}$. Similarly, the magnetic field intensity $\vec{H}$ can be determined either by using scalar magnetic potential V_m or vector magnetic potential $\vec{A}$, except that V_m can be defined only in a source free region $(\vec{J} = 0)$.

Using $\vec{B} = \mu_0 \vec{H}$ in the differential form of Ampere's law $\nabla \times \vec{H} = \vec{J}$, we get

$$\nabla \times \vec{B} = \mu_0 \vec{J} \tag{4.65}$$

Substituting Eq. (4.53) in Eq. (4.65), we obtain

$$\nabla \times (\nabla \times \vec{A}) = \mu_0 \vec{J} \tag{4.66}$$

For any vector $\vec{A}$, the Laplacian of $\vec{A}$ obeys the vector identity as given by

$$\nabla^2 \vec{A} = \nabla(\nabla \cdot \vec{A}) - \nabla \times (\nabla \times \vec{A}) \tag{4.67}$$

In Cartesian coordinates,

$$\nabla^2 \vec{A} = \left(\frac{\partial^2}{\partial x^2} + \frac{\partial^2}{\partial y^2} + \frac{\partial^2}{\partial z^2} \right) \left(A_x \vec{a}_x + A_y \vec{a}_y + A_z \vec{a}_z \right)$$
$$= \nabla^2 A_x \vec{a}_x + \nabla^2 A_y \vec{a}_y + \nabla^2 A_z \vec{a}_z$$

Substituting Eq. (4.66) in Eq. (4.67) and rearranging, we get

$$\nabla(\nabla \cdot \vec{A}) - \nabla^2 \vec{A} = \mu_0 \vec{J} \tag{4.68}$$

Since $\nabla \cdot \vec{B} = 0$, we can also define $\nabla \cdot \vec{A} = 0$ in magnetic fields. Therefore, the above equation can be written as

$$\nabla^2 \vec{A} = -\mu_0 \vec{J} \tag{4.69}$$

which is called the vector Poisson's equation in magnetostatics.

The use of vector magnetic potential is a powerful approach to solve electromagnetic field problems. In addition to Biot–Savart's law and Ampere's circuital law, the vector magnetic potential provides a third approach for determining the magnetic field intensity. It is particularly useful to compute the radiation fields in antenna problems.

EXAMPLE 4.51

Given $\vec{A} = (y\cos ax)\vec{a}_x + (y + e^x)\vec{a}_z$, determine $\nabla \times \vec{A}$ at the origin.

SOLUTION

In rectangular coordinates,

$$\nabla \times \vec{A} = \begin{vmatrix} \vec{a}_x & \vec{a}_y & \vec{a}_z \\ \dfrac{\partial}{\partial x} & \dfrac{\partial}{\partial y} & \dfrac{\partial}{\partial z} \\ A_x & A_y & A_z \end{vmatrix} = \begin{vmatrix} \vec{a}_x & \vec{a}_y & \vec{a}_z \\ \dfrac{\partial}{\partial x} & \dfrac{\partial}{\partial y} & \dfrac{\partial}{\partial z} \\ y\cos ax & 0 & y+e^x \end{vmatrix}$$

$$= \vec{a}_x - e^x \vec{a}_y - \cos ax\, \vec{a}_z$$

At $(0,0,0)$, $\nabla \times \vec{A} = \vec{a}_x - \vec{a}_y - \vec{a}_z$ ☐

EXAMPLE 4.52

The magnetic field intensity in a current free region is $\vec{H} = \dfrac{1}{\rho}\vec{a}_\phi$ A/m. The region is defined by $1 \le \rho \le 2$m, $0 \le \phi \le 2\pi$ and $0 \le z \le 2$m. Determine the scalar magnetic potential at $(4,50°,2)$.

SOLUTION

Given $\vec{H} = \dfrac{1}{\rho}\vec{a}_\phi$ A/m.

The scalar magnetic potential is

$$V_m = -\int \vec{H} \cdot d\vec{l} \quad \text{where} \quad d\vec{l} = d\rho\,\vec{a}_\rho + \rho\,d\phi\,\vec{a}_\phi + dz\vec{a}_z$$

Hence, $\quad V_m = -\int \left(\dfrac{1}{\rho}\vec{a}_\phi \right) \cdot \left(d\rho\,\vec{a}_\rho + \rho\,d\phi\,\vec{a}_\phi + dz\vec{a}_z \right)$

$$= -\int \frac{1}{\rho}\rho\,d\phi = -\phi$$

At $(4,50°,2)$, $V_m = -50° \times \dfrac{\pi}{180°} = -0.87$ A ☐

EXAMPLE 4.53

A very long, straight conductor lies along the z-axis. It carries a uniform current I in the z-direction. Obtain an expression for the magnetic potential difference between two points in space.

SOLUTION

Figure E4.53 shows a straight conductor carrying current I placed along the z-axis. From Eq. (4.26), the magnetic field intensity due to this conductor using Ampere's law is

$$\vec{H} = \frac{I}{2\pi\rho}\vec{a}_\phi$$

If $P(\rho_2,\phi_2,z_2)$ and $Q(\rho_1,\phi_1,z_1)$ are the two points in free space as shown in Figure E4.53, then the scalar magnetic potential at point P with respect to Q is

$$V_m = -\int_Q^P \vec{H} \cdot d\vec{l}$$

where $\vec{H} \cdot d\vec{l} = \left(H_\phi \vec{a}_\phi \right) \cdot \left(d\rho\,\vec{a}_\rho + \rho\,d\phi\,\vec{a}_\phi + dz\,\vec{a}_z \right) = \rho\, H_\phi d\phi.$

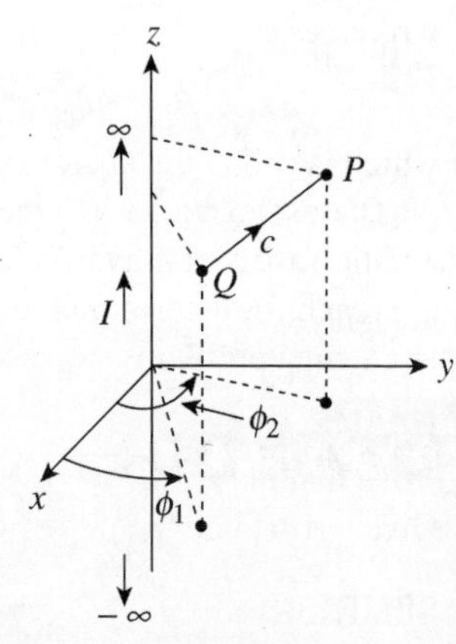

Figure E4.53

Hence, $\quad V_m = -\int_{\phi_1}^{\phi_2} \rho\, H_\phi\, d\phi = -\int_{\phi_1}^{\phi_2} \rho\, \dfrac{I}{2\pi\rho}\, d\phi$

$$= -\int_{\phi_1}^{\phi_2} \dfrac{I}{2\pi}\, d\phi = -\dfrac{I}{2\pi}\left[\phi_2 - \phi_1\right]$$

$$= \dfrac{I}{2\pi}\left[\phi_1 - \phi_2\right]\ \text{A}$$

Here, $\phi_2 > \phi_1$. Therefore, the above equation provides the mmf drop in traversing the path from point Q to point P. $\qquad\square$

EXAMPLE 4.54

A coaxial cable has inner and outer radii a and b, respectively. The inner cable carries a current I. Find the scalar magnetic potential at a radius ρ inside the cable $(a < \rho < b)$.

SOLUTION

From Eq. (4.36), the magnetic field intensity inside the coaxial cable of radius ρ is

$$\vec{H} = \dfrac{I}{2\pi\rho}\,\vec{a}_\phi \qquad\qquad \text{for } (a < \rho < b) \qquad\qquad (1)$$

From the definition of vector magnetic potential, we have

$$\vec{H} = -\nabla V_m = -\left(\dfrac{\partial V_m}{\partial \rho}\,\vec{a}_\rho + \dfrac{1}{\rho}\dfrac{\partial V_m}{\partial \phi}\,\vec{a}_\phi + \dfrac{\partial V_m}{\partial z}\,\vec{a}_z\right)$$

$$= -\dfrac{1}{\rho}\dfrac{\partial V_m}{\partial \phi}\,\vec{a}_\phi \qquad\qquad (\text{since } \vec{H} \text{ is a function of } \phi \text{ only}) \qquad\qquad (2)$$

By equating the $\vec{a}_\phi$ components of $\vec{H}$ in Eq. (1) and Eq. (2), we obtain

$$\dfrac{I}{2\pi\rho}\,\vec{a}_\phi = -\dfrac{1}{\rho}\dfrac{\partial V_m}{\partial \phi}\,\vec{a}_\phi$$

Therefore, $\dfrac{\partial V_m}{\partial \phi} = -\dfrac{I}{2\pi}$

Integrating the above equation, we get

$$V_m = -\dfrac{I}{2\pi}\phi + c$$

where c is the integration constant.

Applying the boundary condition that at $\phi = 0$, $V_m = 0$ i.e., zero current enclosed, we have $c = 0$.

Hence, the scalar magnetic potential inside the coaxial cable is $V_m = -\dfrac{I}{2\pi}\phi\ \text{A}$. $\qquad\square$

EXAMPLE 4.55

Prove that the scalar magnetic potential at $(0, 0, z)$ due to a circular loop of radius ρ is

$$V_m = \dfrac{I}{2}\left[1 - \dfrac{z}{\sqrt{\rho^2 + z^2}}\right]$$

SOLUTION

From Eq. (4.14), the magnetic field at $(0,0,z)$ due to a circular loop of radius ρ is

$$\vec{H} = \frac{I\rho^2}{2\left[\rho^2 + z^2\right]^{\frac{3}{2}}} \, \vec{a}_z \tag{1}$$

From the definition of scalar magnetic potential, we have

$$\vec{H} = -\nabla V_m = -\left(\frac{\partial V_m}{\partial \rho}\vec{a}_\rho + \frac{1}{\rho}\frac{\partial V_m}{\partial \phi}\vec{a}_\phi + \frac{\partial V_m}{\partial z}\vec{a}_z\right)$$

$$= -\frac{\partial V_m}{\partial z}\vec{a}_z \qquad \text{(since } \vec{H} \text{ is a function of } z \text{ only)} \tag{2}$$

Equating the $\vec{a}_z$ components of $\vec{H}$ in Eq. (1) and Eq. (2), we obtain

$$\frac{\partial V_m}{\partial z} = -\frac{I\rho^2}{2\left[\rho^2 + z^2\right]^{3/2}} \tag{3}$$

Integrating the above equation, we get

$$V_m = -\int_\infty^z \frac{I\rho^2}{2\left[\rho^2 + z^2\right]^{3/2}}\, dz = -\frac{I\rho^2}{2}\int_\infty^z \frac{dz}{\left[\rho^2 + z^2\right]^{3/2}}$$

$$= -\frac{I\rho^2}{2}\left(\frac{z/\rho^2}{\sqrt{\rho^2 + z^2}}\right) + c = -\frac{Iz}{2\sqrt{\rho^2 + z^2}} + c \tag{4}$$

where c is the integration constant.

As $z \to \infty$, $V_m = 0$ i.e., $0 = -\dfrac{I}{2} + c$

Therefore, $c = \dfrac{I}{2}$

Substituting the constant c in Eq. (4), we get

$$V_m = \frac{I}{2}\left[1 - \frac{z}{\sqrt{\rho^2 + z^2}}\right] \text{A} \qquad \qquad \square$$

EXAMPLE 4.56

Given the vector magnetic potential, $\vec{A} = -\dfrac{\rho^2}{2}\vec{a}_z$ Wb/m. Calculate the total magnetic flux crossing the surface $1 \le \rho \le 5$m, $\phi = \pi/4$ and $0 \le z \le 2$m.

SOLUTION

Given $\vec{A} = -\dfrac{\rho^2}{2}\vec{a}_z$ Wb/m in cylindrical coordinates.

We know that, $\vec{B} = \nabla \times \vec{A}$.

Therefore, $\vec{B} = \dfrac{1}{\rho}\begin{vmatrix} \vec{a}_\rho & \rho\,\vec{a}_\phi & \vec{a}_z \\ \dfrac{\partial}{\partial\rho} & \dfrac{\partial}{\partial\phi} & \dfrac{\partial}{\partial z} \\ A_\rho & \rho A_\phi & A_z \end{vmatrix} = \dfrac{1}{\rho}\begin{vmatrix} \vec{a}_\rho & \rho\,\vec{a}_\phi & \vec{a}_z \\ \dfrac{\partial}{\partial\rho} & \dfrac{\partial}{\partial\phi} & \dfrac{\partial}{\partial z} \\ 0 & 0 & -\dfrac{\rho^2}{2} \end{vmatrix}$ (in cylindrical coordinates)

$$= -\frac{\partial A_z}{\partial \rho}\,\vec{a}_\phi = \rho\,\vec{a}_\phi \ \text{Wb/m}^2$$

Hence, the total magnetic flux crossing the area is

$$\Phi = \int_s \vec{B}\cdot d\vec{s} = \int_s (\rho\,\vec{a}_\phi)\cdot(d\rho\,dz\,\vec{a}_\phi)$$

$$= \int_{z=0}^{2}\int_{\rho=1}^{5}\rho\,d\rho\,dz = \frac{1}{2}\Big[\rho^2\Big]_1^5\Big[z\Big]_0^2 = \frac{1}{2}\times 24\times 2$$

$$= 24 \ \text{Wb}$$

EXAMPLE 4.57

A current distribution gives rise to the vector magnetic potential, $\vec{A} = x^2 y\vec{a}_x + y^2 x\vec{a}_y - 4xyz\vec{a}_z$ Wb/m. Calculate the total magnetic flux density $\vec{B}$ at $(-1,2,5)$ and the flux crossing through the surface defined by $0 \le x \le 1$, $-1 \le y \le 4$ and $z = 1$.

SOLUTION

Given $\vec{A} = x^2 y\vec{a}_x + y^2 x\vec{a}_y - 4xyz\vec{a}_z$ Wb/m in rectangular coordinates.

We know that, $\vec{B} = \nabla\times\vec{A}$.

Therefore, $\vec{B} = \begin{vmatrix} \vec{a}_x & \vec{a}_y & \vec{a}_z \\ \dfrac{\partial}{\partial x} & \dfrac{\partial}{\partial y} & \dfrac{\partial}{\partial z} \\ A_x & A_y & A_z \end{vmatrix} = \begin{vmatrix} \vec{a}_x & \vec{a}_y & \vec{a}_z \\ \dfrac{\partial}{\partial x} & \dfrac{\partial}{\partial y} & \dfrac{\partial}{\partial z} \\ x^2 y & y^2 x & -4xyz \end{vmatrix}$ (in rectangular coordinates)

$$= (-4xz - 0)\vec{a}_x - (-4yz - 0)\vec{a}_y + (y^2 - x^2)\vec{a}_z$$

$$= -4xz\vec{a}_x + 4yz\vec{a}_y + (y^2 - x^2)\vec{a}_z$$

At $(-1,2,5)$, $\vec{B} = 20\vec{a}_x + 40\vec{a}_y + 3\vec{a}_z$ Wb/m^2

The magnetic flux crossing the surface is

$$\Phi = \int_s \vec{B}\cdot d\vec{s} = \int_s (B_z\vec{a}_z)\cdot(dx\,dy\,\vec{a}_z)$$

$$= \int_{y=-1}^{4}\int_{x=0}^{1}(y^2 - x^2)dx\,dy = \int_{-1}^{4}y^2\,dy - 5\int_0^1 x^2\,dx$$

$$= \frac{1}{3}(64+1) - \frac{5}{3} = \frac{65-5}{3} = 20 \ \text{Wb}$$

EXAMPLE 4.58

In cylindrical coordinates, $\vec{A} = 50\rho^2 \vec{a}_z$ Wb/m is a vector magnetic potential, in a certain region of free space. Determine $\vec{H}, \vec{B}, \vec{J}$ and using $\vec{J}$, find the total current I crossing the surface $0 \le \rho \le 1, 0 \le \phi \le 2\pi$ and $z = 0$.

SOLUTION

Given $\vec{A} = 50\rho^2 \vec{a}_z$ Wb/m, in cylindrical coordinates. The magnetic flux density in cylindrical coordinates can be written as

$$\vec{B} = \nabla \times \vec{A} = -\frac{\partial A_z}{\partial \rho}\vec{a}_\phi \qquad \left(\text{since } \frac{\partial A_z}{\partial \phi} = 0\right)$$

$$= -\frac{\partial(50\rho^2)}{\partial \rho}\vec{a}_\phi = -100\rho\,\vec{a}_\phi \text{ Wb/m}^2$$

Since $\vec{B} = \mu_0 \vec{H}$, the magnetic field intensity is

$$\vec{H} = \frac{\vec{B}}{\mu_0} = \frac{-100\rho}{\mu_0}\vec{a}_\phi \text{ A/m}$$

Here, the magnetic field intensity $\vec{H}$ has only $\vec{a}_\phi$ component and the other components are zero.

Therefore, $H_\rho = 0$, $H_\phi = \dfrac{-100\rho}{\mu_0}$ and $H_z = 0$

Hence, using Ampere's law, we get

$$\vec{J} = \nabla \times \vec{H} = \frac{1}{\rho}\begin{vmatrix} \vec{a}_\rho & \rho\vec{a}_\phi & \vec{a}_z \\ \dfrac{\partial}{\partial \rho} & \dfrac{\partial}{\partial \phi} & \dfrac{\partial}{\partial z} \\ H_\rho & \rho H_\phi & H_z \end{vmatrix} = \frac{1}{\rho}\begin{vmatrix} \vec{a}_\rho & \rho\vec{a}_\phi & \vec{a}_z \\ \dfrac{\partial}{\partial \rho} & \dfrac{\partial}{\partial \phi} & \dfrac{\partial}{\partial z} \\ 0 & \dfrac{-100\rho^2}{\mu_0} & 0 \end{vmatrix} \qquad \text{(in cylindrical coordinates)}$$

$$= \frac{1}{\rho}\frac{\partial}{\partial \rho}\left(\frac{-100\rho^2}{\mu_0}\right)\vec{a}_z = -\frac{100}{\rho\mu_0}[2\rho]\vec{a}_z = -\frac{200}{\mu_0}\vec{a}_z \text{ A/m}^2$$

Now, the current is

$$I = \int_s \vec{J}\cdot d\vec{s}, \qquad \text{where } d\vec{s} = \rho\,d\rho\,d\phi\,\vec{a}_z$$

$$= \int_{\phi=0}^{2\pi}\int_{\rho=0}^{1}\left(-\frac{200}{\mu_0}\vec{a}_z\right)\cdot(\rho\,d\rho\,d\phi\,\vec{a}_z) = \int_{\phi=0}^{2\pi}\int_{\rho=0}^{1}-\frac{200}{\mu_0}\rho\,d\rho\,d\phi$$

$$= -\frac{200}{\mu_0}\times\left[\frac{\rho^2}{2}\right]_0^1\times[\phi]_0^{2\pi} = \frac{-200}{\mu_0}\times\left[\frac{1}{2}\right]\times[2\pi]$$

$$= -500\times10^6 \text{ A}$$

Hence, the current is 500 MA and the negative sign indicates the direction of current flow in negative z-direction. ◻

EXAMPLE 4.59

Let $\vec{A} = (3y - z)\vec{a}_x + 2xz\vec{a}_y$ Wb/m in a certain region of free space.

  (i) Show that $\nabla \cdot \vec{A} = 0$

  (ii) At $P(2, -1, 3)$ determine $\vec{A}, \vec{B}, \vec{H}$ and $\vec{J}$

SOLUTION

Given $\vec{A} = (3y - z)\vec{a}_x + 2xz\vec{a}_y$ Wb/m.

(i) $\nabla \cdot \vec{A} = \dfrac{\partial A_x}{\partial x} + \dfrac{\partial A_y}{\partial y} + \dfrac{\partial A_z}{\partial z}$

$$= \frac{\partial}{\partial x}[3y - z] + \frac{\partial}{\partial y}[2xz] + \frac{\partial}{\partial z}[0] = 0$$

Hence, $\nabla \cdot \vec{A} = 0$ is proved.

(ii) At $P(2, -1, 3)$, $\vec{A} = [3(-1) - 3]\vec{a}_x + 2(2)(3)\vec{a}_y = -6\vec{a}_x + 12\vec{a}_y$ Wb/m.

We know that, $\vec{B} = \nabla \times \vec{A}$

Therefore, $\vec{B} = \begin{vmatrix} \vec{a}_x & \vec{a}_y & \vec{a}_z \\ \dfrac{\partial}{\partial x} & \dfrac{\partial}{\partial y} & \dfrac{\partial}{\partial z} \\ 3y - z & 2xz & 0 \end{vmatrix} = \vec{a}_x[0 - 2x] + \vec{a}_y[-1 + 0] + \vec{a}_z[2z - 3]$

$$= -2x\vec{a}_x - \vec{a}_y + (2z - 3)\vec{a}_z$$

At $P(2, -1, 3)$, $\vec{B} = -4\vec{a}_x - \vec{a}_y + 3\vec{a}_z$ Wb/m^2

Since $\vec{B} = \mu_0 \vec{H}$, the magnetic field intensity is $\vec{H} = \dfrac{\vec{B}}{\mu_0} = \dfrac{1}{\mu_0}\left[-4\vec{a}_x - \vec{a}_y + 3\vec{a}_z\right]$ A/m

From Ampere's law, $\vec{J} = \nabla \times \vec{H}$

Therefore, $\vec{J} = \dfrac{1}{\mu_0}\begin{vmatrix} \vec{a}_x & \vec{a}_y & \vec{a}_z \\ \dfrac{\partial}{\partial x} & \dfrac{\partial}{\partial y} & \dfrac{\partial}{\partial z} \\ -2x & -1 & 2z - 3 \end{vmatrix}$, where $\vec{H} = \dfrac{1}{\mu_0}\left[-2x\vec{a}_x - \vec{a}_y + (2z - 3)\vec{a}_z\right]$

$$= \frac{1}{\mu_0}\left[(0 - 0)\vec{a}_x + (0 - 0)\vec{a}_y + (0 - 0)\vec{a}_z\right] = 0$$

◻

EXAMPLE 4.60

At $P(x, y, z)$, the components of vector magnetic potential $\vec{A}$ are $A_x = 4x + 3y + 2z$, $A_y = 5x + 6y + 3z$ and $A_z = 2x + 3y + 5z$. Show that $\vec{B}$ is a conservative field.

SOLUTION

We know that, $\vec{B} = \nabla \times \vec{A}$.

Therefore,
$$\vec{B} = \begin{vmatrix} \vec{a}_x & \vec{a}_y & \vec{a}_z \\ \dfrac{\partial}{\partial x} & \dfrac{\partial}{\partial y} & \dfrac{\partial}{\partial z} \\ A_x & A_y & A_z \end{vmatrix} = \begin{vmatrix} \vec{a}_x & \vec{a}_y & \vec{a}_z \\ \dfrac{\partial}{\partial x} & \dfrac{\partial}{\partial y} & \dfrac{\partial}{\partial z} \\ 4x+3y+2z & 5x+6y+3z & 2x+3y+5z \end{vmatrix}$$

$$= \vec{a}_x[3-3] + \vec{a}_y[2-2] + \vec{a}_z[5-3] = 2\vec{a}_z$$

Therefore, $\vec{B} = 2\vec{a}_z\,\text{Wb/m}^2$. Since the components of $\vec{B}$ are constants, $\nabla \times \vec{B} = 0$. Hence, $\vec{B}$ is a conservative field. ◻

EXAMPLE 4.61

Obtain the vector magnetic potential $\vec{A}$ for the current sheet placed in xy-plane having surface current density $\vec{K} = K_y\vec{a}_y$ A/m.

SOLUTION

Consider an infinite current sheet in xy-plane with $\vec{K} = K_y\vec{a}_y$ as shown in Figure E4.61. Therefore, for a current sheet of current density $\vec{K}$, the magnetic field intensity is

$$\vec{H} = \frac{\vec{K}}{2} \times \vec{a}_n$$

For the given sheet, $\vec{a}_n = \vec{a}_z$ and $\vec{K} = K_y\vec{a}_y$. Hence,

$$\vec{K} \times \vec{a}_n = \begin{vmatrix} \vec{a}_x & \vec{a}_y & \vec{a}_z \\ 0 & K_y & 0 \\ 0 & 0 & 1 \end{vmatrix} = K_y\vec{a}_x$$

Therefore, $\vec{H} = \dfrac{1}{2}K_y\vec{a}_x$ A/m.

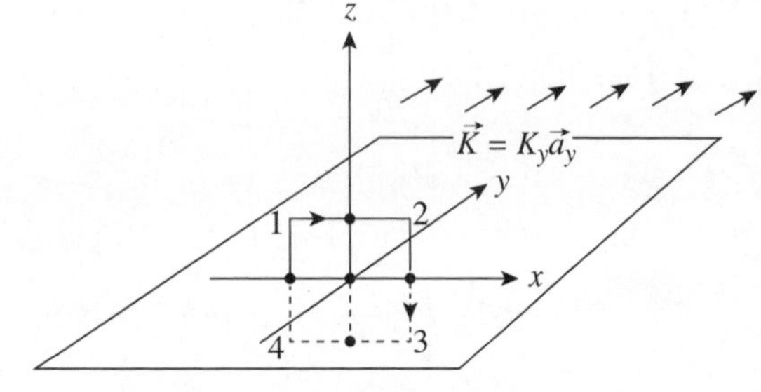

Figure E4.61

The magnetic flux density is

$$\vec{B} = \mu_0\vec{H} = \frac{\mu_0}{2}K_y\vec{a}_x \ \text{Wb/m}^2$$

The vector magnetic potential can be obtained from the expression, $\vec{B} = \nabla \times \vec{A} = \begin{vmatrix} \vec{a}_x & \vec{a}_y & \vec{a}_z \\ \dfrac{\partial}{\partial x} & \dfrac{\partial}{\partial y} & \dfrac{\partial}{\partial z} \\ A_x & A_y & A_z \end{vmatrix}$

Since $\vec{B}$ has only $\vec{a}_x$ component, consider $\vec{a}_x$ of $\nabla \times \vec{A}$ and by equating, we get

$$\vec{a}_x\left[\frac{\partial A_z}{\partial y} - \frac{\partial A_y}{\partial z}\right] = \frac{\mu_0}{2}K_y\vec{a}_x$$

Therefore, $\dfrac{\partial A_z}{\partial y} - \dfrac{\partial A_y}{\partial z} = \dfrac{\mu_0}{2}K_y$

The vector magnetic potential $\vec{A}$ must be independent of x and y. Therefore,

$$\frac{\partial A_z}{\partial y} = 0 \quad \text{and} \quad -\frac{\partial A_y}{\partial z} = \frac{\mu_0}{2} K_y$$

Integrating the above equation, we get

$$A_y = \int -\frac{\mu_0}{2} K_y \, dz = -\frac{\mu_0}{2} K_y \, z + c_1$$

where c_1 is the constant of integration.

Let $A_y = 0$ at $z = z_0$. Therefore,

$$0 = -\frac{\mu_0}{2} K_y z_0 + c_1$$

Hence, $\quad c_1 = \frac{\mu_0}{2} K_y z_0$

Therefore, $\quad A_y = \frac{\mu_0}{2} K_y \left(z_0 - z \right)$, for $z > 0$

Hence, the vector magnetic potential is

$$\vec{A} = \frac{\mu_0}{2} K_y \left(z_0 - z \right) \vec{a}_y \text{ Wb/m}$$

Since $\vec{K} = K_y \vec{a}_y$, the vector magnetic potential can be written as

$$\vec{A} = -\frac{\mu_0}{2} \vec{K} \left(z - z_0 \right) \text{ Wb/m}$$

For $z < 0$, the vector magnetic potential is $\vec{A} = \frac{\mu_0}{2} \vec{K} \left(z - z_0 \right)$ Wb/m.

EXAMPLE 4.62

If $\vec{A} = 10\rho^{1.5} \, \vec{a}_z$ Wb/m in free space, find (i) $\vec{H}$ and (ii) $\vec{J}$ (iii) Show that $\oint_l \vec{H} \cdot d\vec{l} = I$ for a circular path with $\rho = 1$.

SOLUTION

Since vector magnetic potential is $\vec{A} = 10\rho^{1.5}\vec{a}_z$ Wb/m, the magnetic flux density is

$$\vec{B} = \nabla \times \vec{A} = \frac{1}{\rho} \begin{vmatrix} \vec{a}_\rho & \rho\vec{a}_\phi & \vec{a}_z \\ \dfrac{\partial}{\partial \rho} & \dfrac{\partial}{\partial \phi} & \dfrac{\partial}{\partial z} \\ A_\rho & \rho A_\phi & A_z \end{vmatrix} = \frac{1}{\rho} \begin{vmatrix} \vec{a}_\rho & \rho\vec{a}_\phi & \vec{a}_z \\ \dfrac{\partial}{\partial \rho} & \dfrac{\partial}{\partial \phi} & \dfrac{\partial}{\partial z} \\ 0 & 0 & 10\rho^{1.5} \end{vmatrix}$$

$$= -\frac{\partial}{\partial \rho}\left(10\rho^{1.5} \right) \vec{a}_\phi = -15\rho^{0.5} \vec{a}_\phi \text{ Wb/m}^2$$

(i) The magnetic field intensity is

$$\vec{H} = \frac{\vec{B}}{\mu_0} = \frac{-15\rho^{0.5}}{\mu_0} \vec{a}_\phi \text{ A/m}$$

(*ii*) The current density is

$$
\vec{J} = \nabla \times \vec{H} = \frac{1}{\rho}
\begin{vmatrix}
\vec{a}_\rho & \rho\vec{a}_\phi & \vec{a}_z \\
\dfrac{\partial}{\partial \rho} & \dfrac{\partial}{\partial \phi} & \dfrac{\partial}{\partial z} \\
H_\rho & \rho H\phi & H_z
\end{vmatrix}
= \frac{1}{\rho}
\begin{vmatrix}
\vec{a}_\rho & \rho\vec{a}_\phi & \vec{a}_z \\
\dfrac{\partial}{\partial \rho} & \dfrac{\partial}{\partial \phi} & \dfrac{\partial}{\partial z} \\
0 & \dfrac{-15\rho^{1.5}}{\mu_0} & 0
\end{vmatrix}
$$

$$
= \frac{1}{\rho}\frac{\partial}{\partial \rho}\left(\frac{-15\rho^{1.5}}{\mu_0}\right)\vec{a}_z
= \frac{-15}{\rho\mu_0}\left(1.5\rho^{0.5}\right)\vec{a}_z
= \frac{-22.5}{\mu_0\sqrt{\rho}}\,\vec{a}_z\,\mathrm{A/m}^2
$$

(*iii*) We know that, $I = \int_s \vec{J}\cdot d\vec{s}$

$$
= \int_0^{2\pi}\int_0^1\left(\frac{-22.5}{\mu_0\sqrt{\rho}}\,\vec{a}_z\right)\cdot\left(\rho\,d\rho\,d\phi\,\vec{a}_z\right)
= \frac{-22.5}{\mu_0}\int_0^{2\pi}\int_0^1\sqrt{\rho}\,d\rho\,d\phi
$$

$$
= \frac{-22.5}{\mu_0}[2\pi]\left[\frac{\rho^{1.5}}{1.5}\right]_0^1
= \frac{-30\pi}{\mu_0}\,\mathrm{A} \quad (\text{given } \rho = 1)
$$

$$
\oint_l \vec{H}\cdot d\vec{l} = \int_{\phi=0}^{2\pi}\left(H_\phi\vec{a}_\phi\right)\cdot\left(\rho\,d\phi\,\vec{a}_\phi\right)
= \int_0^{2\pi}\left(\frac{-15\rho^{0.5}}{\mu_0}\right)\left(\rho\,d\phi\right)
$$

$$
= \frac{-15\rho^{0.5}}{\mu_0}\bigg|_{\rho=1}\int_0^{2\pi}d\phi = \frac{-15}{\mu_0}(2\pi) = \frac{-30\pi}{\mu_0}\,\mathrm{A}
$$

Hence, $\oint_l \vec{H}\cdot d\vec{l} = I$ is proved.

EXAMPLE 4.63

A long, straight conductor located along the z-axis carries a current I in the z- direction. Obtain an expression for the vector magnetic potential at a point in the bisecting plane of the conductor. What is the magnetic flux density and magnetic field intensity at that point?

SOLUTION

Figure E4.63 shows a current carrying conductor placed along z- axis extending from $z = -l$ to $z = l$. Let P be the point at which the vector magnetic potential, flux density and field intensity are to be determined.

From Eq. (4.59), the expression for vector magnetic potential due to line current is

$$
\vec{A} = \frac{\mu_0}{4\pi}\int_{l'}\frac{I\,d\vec{l'}}{R}
$$

where the current element $I\,d\vec{l'} = I\,dz\,\vec{a}_z$ and the distance vector of point P from the current element is written as $\vec{R} = \rho\vec{a}_\rho - z\vec{a}_z$.

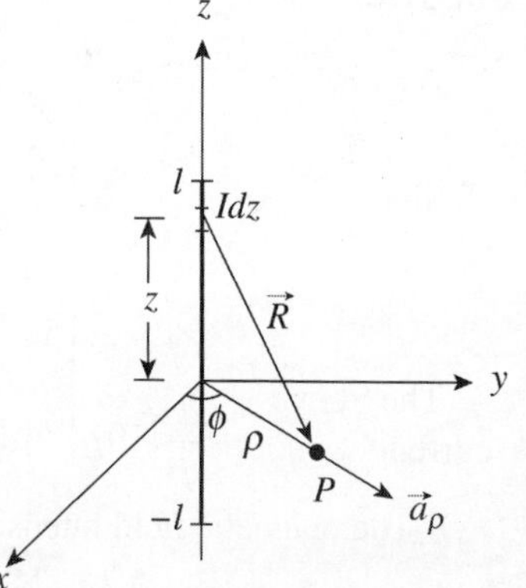

Figure E4.63

Therefore, the vector magnetic potential is

$$\vec{A} = \frac{\mu_0 I}{4\pi} \int_{-l}^{l} \frac{dz}{\sqrt{\rho^2 + z^2}} \vec{a}_z$$

$$= \frac{\mu_0 I}{4\pi} \left[\ln\left(z + \sqrt{\rho^2 + z^2}\right) \right]_{-l}^{l} \vec{a}_z$$

$$= \frac{\mu_0 I}{4\pi} \left[\ln\left(l + \sqrt{\rho^2 + l^2}\right) - \ln\left(-l + \sqrt{\rho^2 + l^2}\right) \right] \vec{a}_z$$

The above equation is an exact expression for the vector magnetic potential at a point P in the bisecting plane of the current carrying conductor. For a very long conductor, $l > \rho$, the following approximations can be used to obtain a simplified expression for magnetic potential.

$$l + \sqrt{\rho^2 + l^2} \approx l + l\left[1 + \left(\frac{\rho}{2l}\right)^2\right] \approx 2l$$

and

$$-l + \sqrt{\rho^2 + l^2} \approx -l + l\left[1 + \left(\frac{\rho}{2l}\right)^2\right] \approx \frac{\rho^2}{2l}$$

Using the above approximations, the vector magnetic potential becomes

$$\vec{A} = \frac{\mu_0 I}{4\pi} \left[\ln(2l) - \ln\left(\frac{\rho^2}{2l}\right) \right] \vec{a}_z$$

Hence,

$$\vec{A} = \frac{\mu_0 I}{2\pi} \ln\left(\frac{2l}{\rho}\right) \vec{a}_z \ \text{Wb/m}$$

The magnetic flux density at point P is

$$\vec{B} = \nabla \times \vec{A} = -\frac{\partial A_z}{\partial \rho} \vec{a}_\phi = -\frac{\mu_0 I}{2\pi} \frac{\partial}{\partial \rho} \left[\ln\left(\frac{2l}{\rho}\right) \right] \vec{a}_\phi$$

$$= -\frac{\mu_0 I}{2\pi} \times \frac{\rho}{2l} \times \left(-\frac{2l}{\rho^2}\right) \vec{a}_\phi = \frac{\mu_0 I}{2\pi\rho} \vec{a}_\phi \ \text{Wb/m}^2$$

Since $\vec{B} = \mu_0 \vec{H}$, the magnetic field intensity is

$$\vec{H} = \frac{I}{2\pi\rho} \vec{a}_\phi \ \text{A/m}$$

The above expression is identical with the one derived using Biot–Savart's law for an infinitely long, current carrying conductor. ❑

EXAMPLE 4.64

Show that the vector magnetic potential at a distant point $P(x, y, z)$ due to a finite line current flowing through $-l \le z \le l$ along $\vec{a}_z$ is

$$\vec{A} = \frac{\mu_0 Il}{2\pi \left[x^2 + y^2 + z^2 \right]^{1/2}} \vec{a}_z$$

SOLUTION

From Example 4.63, the vector magnetic potential due to finite line current is

$$\vec{A} = \frac{\mu_0 I}{2\pi} \int_{-l}^{l} \frac{dz}{\sqrt{\rho^2 + z^2}} \vec{a}_z = \frac{\mu_0 I}{2\pi} \int_{0}^{l} \frac{dz}{\sqrt{\rho^2 + z^2}} \vec{a}_z$$

$$= \frac{\mu_0 I}{2\pi} \int_{0}^{l} \frac{dl}{\sqrt{x^2 + y^2 + z^2}} \vec{a}_z$$

where $dl = dz$ and $\rho^2 = x^2 + y^2$.

Hence, $\vec{A} = \dfrac{\mu_0 I}{2\pi \left[x^2 + y^2 + z^2 \right]^{1/2}} \vec{a}_z \times [l]_0^l = \dfrac{\mu_0 Il}{2\pi \left[x^2 + y^2 + z^2 \right]^{1/2}} \vec{a}_z$ Wb/m   ❑

EXAMPLE 4.65

Show that the vector potential due to moving charge Q at a distance R is given by $\vec{A} = \dfrac{\mu_0 Q \vec{u}}{4\pi R}$, where $\vec{u}$ is the velocity of charge.

SOLUTION

The vector magnetic potential due to line current is

$$\vec{A} = \frac{\mu_0}{4\pi} \int \frac{I d\vec{l}}{R} = \frac{\mu_0}{4\pi R} \int I d\vec{l}$$

$$= \frac{\mu_0}{4\pi R} \int \frac{dQ}{dt} \vec{u} dt \qquad \left(\text{since } I = \frac{dQ}{dt} \text{ and } \vec{u} = \frac{d\vec{l}}{dt} \right)$$

$$= \frac{\mu_0 \vec{u}}{4\pi R} \int dQ = \frac{\mu_0 Q \vec{u}}{4\pi R} \text{ Wb/m} \qquad\qquad ❑$$

EXAMPLE 4.66

An infinitely long conductor of radius a is placed such that its axis is along the z-axis. The vector magnetic potential, due to a direct current I_0 flowing along $\vec{a}_z$ in the conductor is given by $\vec{A} = -\dfrac{I_0}{4\pi a^2} \mu_0 (x^2 + y^2) \vec{a}_z$ Wb/m. Find the magnetic field intensity $\vec{H}$. Also, confirm the result using Ampere's law.

SOLUTION

Given $\vec{A} = -\dfrac{I_0}{4\pi a^2} \mu_0 \left(x^2 + y^2 \right) \vec{a}_z$ Wb/m.

Since $\rho^2 = x^2 + y^2$, the vector magnetic potential can be written in cylindrical coordinates as

$$\vec{A} = -\frac{I_0}{4\pi a^2} \mu_0 \rho^2 \vec{a}_z$$

The magnetic flux density is

$$\vec{B} = \nabla \times \vec{A} = \frac{1}{\rho} \begin{vmatrix} \vec{a}_\rho & \rho\,\vec{a}_\phi & \vec{a}_z \\ \dfrac{\partial}{\partial \rho} & \dfrac{\partial}{\partial \phi} & \dfrac{\partial}{\partial z} \\ 0 & 0 & -\dfrac{I_0}{4\pi a^2}\mu_0\rho^2 \end{vmatrix} = \frac{I_0\mu_0\rho}{2\pi a^2}\vec{a}_\phi$$

Since $\vec{B} = \mu_0\vec{H}$, the magnetic field intensity is

$$\vec{H} = \frac{I_0\rho}{2\pi a^2}\vec{a}_\phi \ \text{A/m}$$

By Ampere's law, $\oint \vec{H}\cdot d\vec{l} = I_{enc}$, where I_{enc} is the enclosed current.

i.e., $\quad H_\phi \cdot 2\pi\rho = I_0 \cdot \dfrac{\rho^2}{a^2}$

$$H_\phi = \frac{I_0\rho}{2\pi a^2}$$

$$\vec{H} = \frac{I_0\rho}{2\pi a^2}\vec{a}_\phi \ \text{A/m}$$

Thus, the magnetic field intensity is confirmed using Ampere's law. $\qquad\square$

EXAMPLE 4.67

The inner conductor of a 50 m long coaxial cable has a radius of 1 cm and carries a current of 100 A in the z-direction as shown in Figure E4.67. The outer conductor is very thin and has a radius of 10 cm. Calculate the total flux enclosed within the conductors.

SOLUTION

From Eq. (4.64), the magnetic flux in terms of vector magnetic potential is

$$\Phi = \oint_l \vec{A}\cdot d\vec{l}$$

The vector magnetic potential at any point within the cable is

$$\vec{A} = \frac{\mu_0 I}{2\pi}\ln\left(\frac{2l}{\rho}\right)\vec{a}_z$$

Let a and b be the radius of the inner and the outer conductors of the coaxial cable. Therefore, the total flux enclosed is

$$\Phi = \oint_{l_1}\vec{A}\cdot d\vec{l}_1 + \oint_{l_2}\vec{A}\cdot d\vec{l}_2 + \oint_{l_3}\vec{A}\cdot d\vec{l}_3 + \oint_{l_4}\vec{A}\cdot d\vec{l}_4$$

From Figure E4.67, it is seen that the vector magnetic potential has z-component only and the integration along l_2 and l_4 paths will be zero.

Hence, the total flux within the coaxial cable is $\Phi = \oint_{l_1}\vec{A}\cdot d\vec{l}_1 + \oint_{l_3}\vec{A}\cdot d\vec{l}_3$

$\left(\text{since } d\vec{l}_1 = dz\,\vec{a}_z \text{ and } d\vec{l}_3 = -dz\,\vec{a}_z\right)$

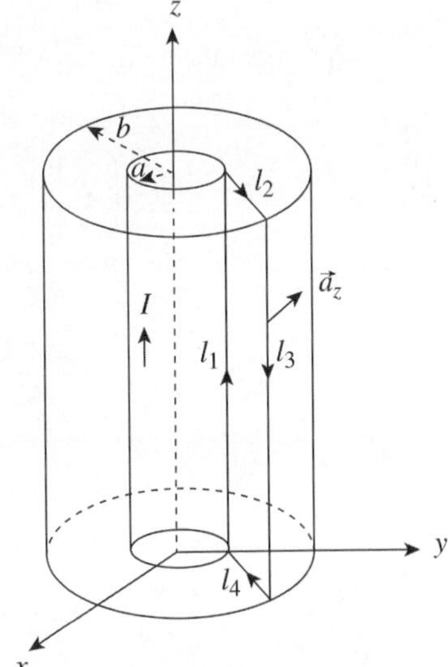

Figure E4.67

$$= \frac{\mu_0 I}{2\pi} \ln\left(\frac{2l}{a}\right)\int_{-l}^{l} dz - \frac{\mu_0 I}{2\pi}\ln\left(\frac{2l}{b}\right)\int_{-l}^{l} dz$$

$$= \frac{\mu_0 Il}{\pi}\ln\left(\frac{b}{a}\right)\text{Wb}$$

Substituting the given values of $I = 100$A, $l = 50$m, $a = 1$cm and $b = 10$cm in the above expression, we get

$$\Phi = \frac{4\pi\times 10^{-7}\times 100\times 50}{\pi}\ln\left(\frac{10}{1}\right) = 4.6 \text{ mWb}$$

4.8   DERIVATION OF STEADY MAGNETIC FIELD LAWS

Biot–Savart's law and Ampere's law are the two most important laws used in static magnetic fields. Both these laws can be derived using the concept of vector magnetic potential as discussed in this section.

From Eq. (4.60), the expression for vector magnetic potential $\vec{A}$ due to line current is given by

$$\vec{A} = \frac{\mu_0}{4\pi}\oint_{l'}\frac{Id\vec{l}'}{R}$$

Since $\vec{B} = \nabla\times\vec{A}$, the magnetic flux density $\vec{B}$ can be written as

$$\vec{B} = \nabla\times\left[\frac{\mu_0}{4\pi}\oint_{l'}\frac{Id\vec{l}'}{R}\right] = \frac{\mu_0 I}{4\pi}\left[\oint_{l'}\nabla\times\frac{1}{R}d\vec{l}'\right]\tag{4.70}$$

Considering the vector identity given in Eq. (4.56),

$$\nabla\times(f\vec{F}) = f(\nabla\times\vec{F}) + (\nabla f)\times\vec{F}$$

Taking $\vec{F} = d\vec{l}'$ and $f = \dfrac{1}{R}$, Eq. (4.70) can be changed to

$$\vec{B} = \frac{\mu_0 I}{4\pi}\oint_{l'}\left[\frac{1}{R}\left(\nabla\times d\vec{l}'\right) + \left(\nabla\frac{1}{R}\right)\times d\vec{l}'\right]\tag{4.71}$$

Since ∇ operates with respect to (x, y, z) and $d\vec{l}'$ is a function of (x', y', z'), the curl of $d\vec{l}'$ will be zero, i.e., $\nabla\times d\vec{l}' = 0$. Therefore, the above equation becomes

$$\vec{B} = \frac{\mu_0 I}{4\pi}\oint_{l'}\left[\left(\nabla\frac{1}{R}\right)\times d\vec{l}'\right]\tag{4.72}$$

The magnitude of distance vector is defined in Eq. (4.54) and its inverse can be written as

$$\frac{1}{R} = \left[(x-x')^2 + (y-y')^2 + (z-z')^2\right]^{-1/2}$$

Therefore, $\nabla\left(\dfrac{1}{R}\right) = -\dfrac{(x-x')\vec{a}_x + (y-y')\vec{a}_y + (z-z')\vec{a}_z}{\left[(x-x')^2 + (y-y')^2 + (z-z')^2\right]^{3/2}} = -\dfrac{\vec{R}}{R^3} = -\dfrac{\vec{a}_R}{R^2}$ (4.73)

where $\vec{a}_R$ is a unit vector from the source point to field point. Using Eq. (4.73) in Eq. (4.72) and removing the prime in $d\vec{l}'$, we get

$$\vec{B} = \frac{\mu_0 I}{4\pi}\oint_{l}\left[\left(-\frac{\vec{a}_R}{R^2}\right)\times d\vec{l}\right]\tag{4.74}$$

The negative sign in Eq. (4.74) can be removed by interchanging the terms of the vector product. Therefore, the magnetic flux density $\vec{B}$ becomes

$$\vec{B} = \frac{\mu_0 I}{4\pi} \oint_l \left[\frac{d\vec{l} \times \vec{a}_R}{R^2} \right]$$

Since $\vec{B} = \mu_0 \vec{H}$, the magnetic field intensity is written as

$$\vec{H} = \frac{I}{4\pi} \oint_l \frac{d\vec{l} \times \vec{a}_R}{R^2} \tag{4.75}$$

Here, the current I flows along the closed path l. Hence, the magnetic field intensity derived in the above equation using the vector magnetic potential is known as Biot–Savart's law and it is same as the one defined in section 4.2.

Similarly, Ampere's circuital law can also be derived using the vector magnetic potential. From Eq. (4.18), Stokes's theorem is given by

$$\oint_l \vec{H} \cdot d\vec{l} = \int_s \left(\nabla \times \vec{H} \right) \cdot d\vec{s}$$

$$= \frac{1}{\mu_0} \int_s \left(\nabla \times \vec{B} \right) \cdot d\vec{s} \quad (\text{since } \vec{B} = \mu_0 \vec{H})$$

$$= \frac{1}{\mu_0} \int_s \left(\nabla \times \nabla \times \vec{A} \right) \cdot d\vec{s} \quad (\text{since } \vec{B} = \nabla \times \vec{A}) \tag{4.76}$$

From Eq. (4.67), the vector identity is given by

$$\nabla^2 \vec{A} = \nabla(\nabla \cdot \vec{A}) - \nabla \times (\nabla \times \vec{A}) \tag{4.77}$$

Since $\nabla \cdot \vec{A} = 0$, the above equation becomes

$$\nabla^2 \vec{A} = -\nabla \times (\nabla \times \vec{A}) \tag{4.78}$$

Substituting Eq. (4.78) in Eq. (4.76), we get

$$\oint_l \vec{H} \cdot d\vec{l} = \frac{1}{\mu_0} \int_s \left(-\nabla^2 \vec{A} \right) \cdot d\vec{s}$$

$$= \int_s \vec{J} \cdot d\vec{s} \qquad (\text{since } \nabla^2 \vec{A} = -\mu_0 \vec{J})$$

$$\oint_l \vec{H} \cdot d\vec{l} = I \tag{4.79}$$

where $I = \int_s \vec{J} \cdot d\vec{s}$. The above equation is the integral form of Ampere's circuital law, derived from vector magnetic potential. Making use of Stokes's theorem, we get the point form of Ampere's law as discussed in section 4.4.1.

EXAMPLE 4.68

Show that $\nabla_2 \left(\dfrac{1}{R_{12}} \right) = -\nabla_1 \left(\dfrac{1}{R_{12}} \right) = \dfrac{\vec{R}_{21}}{\left| \vec{R}_{12} \right|^3}$

SOLUTION

If the points $\left(x_1, y_1, z_1 \right)$ and $\left(x_2, y_2, z_2 \right)$ are in Cartesian coordinate system, the distance vectors are expressed as

$$\vec{R}_{12} = (x_2 - x_1)\vec{a}_x + (y_2 - y_1)\vec{a}_y + (z_2 - z_1)\vec{a}_z$$

$$\vec{R}_{21} = (x_1 - x_2)\vec{a}_x + (y_1 - y_2)\vec{a}_y + (z_1 - z_2)\vec{a}_z$$

and their magnitudes are given by

$$R_{12} = |\vec{R}_{12}| = \sqrt{(x_2 - x_1)^2 + (y_2 - y_1)^2 + (z_2 - z_1)^2}$$

$$R_{21} = |\vec{R}_{21}| = \sqrt{(x_1 - x_2)^2 + (y_1 - y_2)^2 + (z_1 - z_2)^2}$$

The unit vectors are written as

$$\vec{a}_{12} = \frac{\vec{R}_{12}}{|\vec{R}_{12}|} = \frac{\vec{R}_{12}}{R_{12}} = \frac{(x_2 - x_1)}{R_{12}}\vec{a}_x + \frac{(y_2 - y_1)}{R_{12}}\vec{a}_y + \frac{(z_2 - z_1)}{R_{12}}\vec{a}_z$$

$$\vec{a}_{21} = \frac{\vec{R}_{21}}{|\vec{R}_{21}|} = \frac{\vec{R}_{21}}{R_{21}} = \frac{(x_1 - x_2)}{R_{21}}\vec{a}_x + \frac{(y_1 - y_2)}{R_{21}}\vec{a}_y + \frac{(z_1 - z_2)}{R_{21}}\vec{a}_z$$

Therefore,
$$\nabla_2\left(\frac{1}{R_{12}}\right) = \nabla_2\left(\frac{1}{\sqrt{(x_2 - x_1)^2 + (y_2 - y_1)^2 + (z_2 - z_1)^2}}\right)$$

$$= \frac{\partial}{\partial x_2}\left(\frac{1}{\sqrt{(x_2 - x_1)^2 + (y_2 - y_1)^2 + (z_2 - z_1)^2}}\right)\vec{a}_x$$

$$+ \frac{\partial}{\partial y_2}\left(\frac{1}{\sqrt{(x_2 - x_1)^2 + (y_2 - y_1)^2 + (z_2 - z_1)^2}}\right)\vec{a}_y$$

$$+ \frac{\partial}{\partial z_2}\left(\frac{1}{\sqrt{(x_2 - x_1)^2 + (y_2 - y_1)^2 + (z_2 - z_1)^2}}\right)\vec{a}_z$$

Let $t = (x_2 - x_1)^2 + (y_2 - y_1)^2 + (z_2 - z_1)^2$

Hence, $dt = 2(x_2 - x_1)\,dx_2$

$$\frac{\partial}{\partial x_2}\left(\frac{1}{\sqrt{(x_2 - x_1)^2 + (y_2 - y_1)^2 + (z_2 - z_1)^2}}\right) = -\frac{(x_2 - x_1)}{|\vec{R}_{12}|^3}$$

Using $\dfrac{\partial}{\partial y_2}$ and $\dfrac{\partial}{\partial z_2}$ terms, we have

$$\nabla_2\left(\frac{1}{R_{12}}\right) = -\frac{(x_2 - x_1)}{R_{12}^3}\vec{a}_x - \frac{(y_2 - y_1)}{R_{12}^3}\vec{a}_y - \frac{(z_2 - z_1)}{R_{12}^3}\vec{a}_z = -\frac{\vec{R}_{12}}{R_{12}^3}$$

Similarly,
$$\nabla_1\left(\frac{1}{R_{12}}\right) = \frac{(x_2 - x_1)}{R_{12}^3}\vec{a}_x + \frac{(y_2 - y_1)}{R_{12}^3}\vec{a}_y + \frac{(z_2 - z_1)}{R_{12}^3}\vec{a}_z = \frac{\vec{R}_{12}}{R_{12}^3}$$

From these two expressions, we have

$$\nabla_2\left(\frac{1}{R_{12}}\right) = -\nabla_1\left(\frac{1}{R_{12}}\right) = -\frac{\vec{R}_{12}}{R_{12}^3} = \frac{\vec{R}_{21}}{\left|\vec{R}_{12}\right|^3} \qquad \left(\text{since } \vec{R}_{12} = -\vec{R}_{21}\right) \qquad \square$$

REVIEW QUESTIONS

1. State right-hand thumb rule.

2. Define magnetic field intensity and state its unit.

3. State and explain Biot–Savart's law.

4. How Biot–Savart's law can be applied to distributed sources?

5. Derive an expression for magnetic field intensity due to a linear conductor of infinite length carrying current I at a distant point P. Assume R to be the distance between conductor and point P. Use Biot–Savart's law.

6. Find the magnetic field intensity and flux density at a point P which is at a distance h from a straight-line conductor carrying a current I ampere.

7. Using Biot–Savart's law, find $\vec{H}$ due to conductor of finite length.

8. Show by means of Biot–Savart's law that the flux density produced by an infinitely long straight wire, carrying a current I, in a point at a distance normal to the wire is given by $\mu_0\mu_r\,\dfrac{I}{2\pi a}$.

9. Find the magnetic field density $\vec{H}$ and magnetic flux density $\vec{B}$ at the center of a square loop of side l in xy-plane at the origin as center, carrying current I.

10. A square conducting loop of side $2a$ lies in the $z = 0$ plane and carries a current I in the counter clockwise direction. Show that at the center of the loop, $\vec{H} = \dfrac{\sqrt{2}I}{\pi a}\,\vec{a}_z$.

11. A circular loop of wire of radius a, lying in the xy-plane with its center at the origin, carries a current I in the $\vec{a}_\phi$ direction. Using Biot–Savart's law, find $H(0,0,0)$ and $H(0,0,0)$.

12. Sketch the magnetic field pattern due to a circular loop carrying current.

13. A circuit carrying a direct current of 5A forms a regular hexagon inscribed in a circle of radius 1 m. Calculate the magnetic flux density at the center of the hexagon. Assume the medium to be the free space.

14. A conductor is bent in the form of a regular polygon of n sides inscribed in a circle of radius R. Derive the expression for flux density $\vec{B}$ at the center when it carries a current of I ampere. Also, find the value of $\vec{B}$ when n tends to infinity.

15. Using Biot–Savart's law, find $\vec{H}$ on axis of a current loop.

16. Using Biot–Savart's law, derive the magnetic field intensity on the axis of a circular loop carrying a steady current I.

17. A circular loop located on $x^2 + y^2 = 9$, $z = 0$ carries a direct current of 10A along $\vec{a}_\phi$. Determine $\vec{H}$ at point $(0,0,5)$ and $(0,0,-5)$.

18. Find the magnetic field intensity at a point on the axis, 5 m from the center of a circular loop carrying current of 50A with area 100 cm^2.

19. Derive the magnetic field intensity due to a solenoid of length l and radius a with N turns carrying current I.

20. A current carrying conductor is in the form $x^2 + y^2 = r^2$ at $z = 0$ plane carrying current I in $\vec{a}_\phi$ direction. Find the expression for $\vec{H}$ at (i) $(0,0,0)$ (ii) $(0,0,h)$ and (iii) $(0,0,-h)$.

21. Find an expression for magnetic field intensity at the center of a circular wire carrying a current I in the anti-clockwise direction. The radius of circle is r and the wire is in the xy-plane.

22. Using Biot–Savart's law, find $\vec{H}$ inside a long solenoid carrying a current of I ampere and show that $\vec{H}$ at the ends of such a solenoid is half of that in the middle.

23. A long solenoid has 2 turns per mm. Determine the current in its windings needed to produce a magnetic flux density of 0.5 T in its interior.

24. A solenoid has a radius of 2 mm and a length of 1.2 cm. If the number of turns per unit length is 200 and the current is 12 A, calculate the magnetic flux density at (i) the center and (ii) at the ends of the solenoid.

25. Can a static magnetic field exist in a good conductor? Explain.

26. State and prove the Stokes's theorem.

27. Evaluate both sides of the Stokes's theorem for the field $\vec{H} = 6xy\,\vec{a}_x - 3y^2\vec{a}_y$ A/m and the rectangular path around the strip, $1 \le x \le 3$, $-2 \le y \le z$, $z = 0$. Let the positive direction of $d\vec{s}$ be $\vec{a}_z$.

28. Given that the field $\vec{H} = 6r\sin\phi\,\vec{a}_r + 18r\sin\theta\cos\phi\,\vec{a}_\phi$ A/m. Evaluate both sides of the Stokes's theorem for the portion of a sphere specified by $r = 4$, $0 \le \theta \le 0.1\pi$ and $0 \le \phi \le 0.3\pi$. Assume $d\vec{s}$ in the direction of $\vec{a}_r$.

29. State and explain Ampere's circuital law.

30. Give some applications of Ampere's circuital law.

31. Describe the application of Ampere's circuital law to an unsymmetrical field.

32. Define and establish Ampere's circuital law for electromagnetic field.

33. Using Ampere's circuital law, find $\vec{H}$ due to infinite long straight conductor.

34. Describe any two applications of Ampere's circuital law.

35. Using Ampere's circuital law, find $\vec{H}$ due to an infinite sheet of current.

36. A very long and thin, straight wire located along the z-axis carries a current I in the z-direction. Find the magnetic field intensity at any point in free space using Ampere's law.

37. Using Ampere's circuital law, find $\vec{H}$ due to a coaxial cable carrying current I.

38. Using Ampere's circuital law, find $\vec{H}$ and $\vec{B}$ inside a long, straight non-magnetic conductor of 9 mm radius carrying a uniform current density of 200 kA/m^2.

39. The plane $z = 0$ and $z = 6$ carry current $\vec{K} = -20\vec{a}_x$ A/m and $\vec{K} = 20\vec{a}_x$ A/m, respectively. Determine $\vec{H}$ at (i) $(1,1,1)$ and (ii) $(0,-3,10)$.

40. Deduce and sketch the variation of magnetic field intensity as a function of radial distance in a coaxial transmission line with an inner radius of the outer conductor and an outer radius of the outer conductor 3 and 4 times the radius of the solid inner conductor, respectively. Bearing in mind that the cable carries a uniformly distributed current $+I$ in the inner conductor and $-I$ in the outer annular conductor.

41. Enumerate Ampere's circuital law and render a simple proof for the same.

42. Using Ampere's circuital law, obtain an expression for the magnetic field intensity at any point due to concentric cylindrical conductors, the inner and outer conductors carrying equal and opposite currents.

43. Derive the expression for a curl, applying Ampere's circuital law to an incremental surface element.

44. Show that $\nabla \times \vec{H} = \vec{J}$.

45. Obtain the expression for $\vec{H}$ in all the regions if a cylindrical conductor carries a direct current I with its radius being R. Plot the variation of $\vec{H}$ against the distance R from the center of the conductor.

46. Derive the magnetic field intensity inside the toroid using Ampere's circuital law.

47. Using Stokes's theorem, derive and write down Ampere's law in differential or point form.

48. State the point form of Ampere's circuital law and explain it.

49. Explain the physical significance of a curl.

50. Sketch variation of $\vec{H}$ against ρ in coaxial cable.

51. What is $\vec{H}$ at point due to current sheet of density $\vec{K}$ A/m ?

52. Plot the variation of $\vec{H}$ inside and outside a circular conductor with uniform current density.

53. Plane $y = 0$ carries a uniform current of $15\,\vec{a}_z$ mA/m. Calculate the magnetic field intensity at $(1,10,-2)\,\text{m}$ in rectangular coordinate system.

54. What should be the direction of currents of same magnitude in two identical co-axial cylindrical coils to have maximum magnitude of $\vec{B}$ at a point on the axis?

55. Draw the magnetic field pattern in and around a solenoid.

56. In a certain conducting region, $\vec{H} = yz(x^2 + y^2)\vec{a}_x - y^2 xz\vec{a}_y + 4x^2 y^2 \vec{a}_z$ A/m. (*i*) Determine $\vec{J}$ at $(5,2,-3)$ (*ii*) Find the current passing through $x = -1, 0 < y, z < 2$ and (*iii*) Show that $\nabla \cdot \vec{B} = 0$

57. Define magnetic flux and state its unit.

58. Define magnetic flux density and state its unit.

59. What is the significance of $\nabla \cdot \vec{B} = 0$?

60. What is permeability? State its unit.

61. State the relation between magnetic flux and flux density.

62. Derive the expression for Maxwell's equation, $\nabla \times \vec{B} = 0$.

63. Derive Maxwell's equation connected with Ampere's circuital law.

64. Explain Gauss's law in integral and differential form for the magnetic fields.

65. Derive the expression for the flux in a coaxial cable.

66. State Gauss's law for magnetic fields.

67. A square loop 10 cm on a side has 500 turns that are closely and tightly wound and carries a current of 120 A. Determine the magnetic flux density at the center of the loop.

68. The magnetic field intensity is given by $\vec{H} = -y\left(x^2 + y^2\right)\vec{a}_x + x\left(x^2 + y^2\right)\vec{a}_y$ A/m in $z = 0$ plane for $-5 \leq x \leq 5$ and $-5 \leq y \leq 5\text{m}$. Calculate the current passing through the $z = 0$ plane in the $\vec{a}_z$ direction inside the rectangle $-1 < x < 1$ and $-2 < y < 2$.

69. Find I at $(3,2,1)$ if $\vec{H} = xy\vec{a}_x + xyz\vec{a}_y$ A/m.

70. Given that $\vec{H} = 0.1y^3\vec{a}_x + 0.4x\vec{a}_z$ A/m in a region. Determine the current flow through the path a-b-c-d when $a(5,4,1), b(5,6,1), c(0,6,1)$ and $d(0,4,1)$.

71. Find the total current in a circular conductor of radium 4 mm if the current density varies according to
$$J = \left(\frac{10^4}{r}\right) \text{A/m}^2.$$

72. The magnetic field intensity around a perfect cylindrical conductor of radius 10 cm is $\dfrac{10}{\rho}\vec{a}_\phi$ A/m. What is the surface current density on the surface of the conductor? Also, compute the current on the surface of the conductor.

73. A long straight wire carries a current of 100A. Calculate the total flux passing through a plane bounded by $\rho = 1\,\text{cm}, \rho = 10\,\text{cm}, z = 5\,\text{cm}$ and $z = 50\,\text{cm}$.

74. The current density in a very long, cylindrical conductor of radius 10 cm is given as $\vec{J} = 200e^{-0.5\rho}\vec{a}_z$ A/m^2. Calculate the magnetic field intensity at any point in space.

75. Find the flux crossing the plane surface defined by $0.5 \le \rho \le 2\,\text{m}$ and $0 \le z \le 3\,\text{m}$ if $\vec{B} = \left(\dfrac{4}{\rho}\vec{a}_\phi\right)$T .

76. Compute the magnetic flux density at $(0,1,2)$ if the vector magnetic potential distribution is given by
$$5\left(x^2 + y^2 + z^2\right)^{-1}\vec{a}_x \text{Wb/m}.$$

77. Determine the magnetic flux through a rectangular loop $(a \times b)$ due to an infinitely long conductor carrying current *I*. The loop and the straight conductors are separated by distance *d*.

78. Explain the concept of scalar and vector magnetic potentials.

79. Derive the Laplace's and Poisson's equations for the magnetic fields.

80. Consider that a plane $z = -2$ carries a uniform current of $50\vec{a}_y$ A/m. If scalar magnetic potential, $V_m = 0$ at the origin, find V_m at (*i*) $(-2,0,5)$ and (*ii*) $(10,3,1)$.

81. A very long, straight conductor is located along the *z*-direction. Obtain an expression for the vector magnetic potential at a point in the bisecting plane of the conductor. What is the magnetic flux density at that point?

82. Given the vector magnetic potential as $\vec{A} = -\dfrac{\rho^2}{4}\vec{a}_z$ Wb/m in cylindrical system. Calculate the flux crossing the surface $\phi = \dfrac{\pi}{2}, 1 \le \rho \le 2\,\text{m}, 0 \le z \le 5\,\text{m}$.

83. If the vector magnetic potential is given by $\vec{A} = \dfrac{20}{(x^2 + y^2 + z^2)}\vec{a}_x$ Wb/m. Determine $\vec{B}$.

84. If $\vec{A} = r\phi z\vec{a}_z$ Wb/m, calculate curl of $\vec{A}$ at the point $(2, 30°, 3)$.

85. Find the current density $\vec{J}$ when $\vec{A} = \dfrac{10}{\rho^2}\vec{a}_z$ Wb/m in free space.

86. Distinguish scalar and vector magnetic potential as applied to magnetic fields.

87. What is a scalar magnetic potential? Also, derive an expression for vector magnetic potential.

88. State Laplace's equation for scalar magnetic potential.

89. Define vector magnetic potential and state its unit.

90. Derive the static magnetic field laws from the vector magnetic potential.

91. State the Poisson's equation for magnetostatic fields.

MAGNETIC FORCES AND MATERIALS

5.1 INTRODUCTION

The fundamental concepts such as the force exerted by the magnetic field on moving charges, current elements and loops are covered in this chapter, which are important to understand the working principle of ammeters, voltmeters, galvanometers, plasmas, cyclotrons, motors and generators. The concept of boundary conditions for magnetostatics at the interface of two different mediums is also discussed.

This chapter starts with the explanation of force exerted on moving point charge, current element, forces and torques on current carrying conductors with a known current density distribution. The various types of magnetic materials, concept of magnetic moments and dipoles are also discussed. Further, discussions are carried out on inductors, inductances of solenoid, toroid, co-axial cable and parallel-wire transmission line, magnetic circuits, magnetic energy and applications of static magnetic field.

5.2 FORCE ON A MOVING CHARGE

According to Coulomb's law, a stationary or a moving charge Q experiences an electric force $\vec{F}_e$ in an electric field. The force on a charged particle is related to electric field intensity $\vec{E}$ as

$$\vec{F}_e = Q\vec{E} \tag{5.1}$$

For a positive charge, the force is in the same direction as the electric field intensity and is equal to the product of charge Q and electric field $\vec{E}$.

Suppose if the charge is placed in a steady magnetic field, it experiences a force only when the charge is in motion. The *magnetic force* $\vec{F}_m$ exerted on a charge Q moving with a velocity $\vec{u}$ in a magnetic field of flux density $\vec{B}$ is

$$\vec{F}_m = Q\vec{u} \times \vec{B} \tag{5.2}$$

Using cross product definition, the magnitude of $\vec{F}_m$ can be written a

$$F_m = QuB\sin\theta \tag{5.3}$$

The unit of force is newton (N). Here, the magnitude of magnetic force $\vec{F}_m$ is equal to the product of magnitudes of the charge Q, its velocity $\vec{u}$, the flux density $\vec{B}$ and the sine of the angle θ between $\vec{u}$ and $\vec{B}$.

For a positive charge, the direction of force $\vec{F}_m$ is in the direction of the cross product $\vec{u} \times \vec{B}$ and it is perpendicular to the plane containing $\vec{u}$ and $\vec{B}$ according to right-hand rule as shown in Figure 5.1.

The direction of magnetic force $\vec{F}_m$ for a negative charge is in a direction opposite to that of a positive charge. From Eq. (5.3), it is noted that the magnitude of $\vec{F}_m$ is maximum when $\vec{u}$ is perpendicular to $\vec{B}$ i.e., $\theta = 90°$ and it is zero when $\vec{u}$ is parallel to $\vec{B}$ i.e., $\theta = 0°$.

If a moving charge Q is in the presence of both the electric and magnetic fields, then the electromagnetic force acting on the charge is given by

$$\vec{F} = \vec{F}_e + \vec{F}_m = Q(\vec{E} + \vec{u} \times \vec{B}) \tag{5.4}$$

Figure 5.1 *Magnetic force $\vec{F}_m$ on a moving charge in magnetic field with flux density $\vec{B}$*

This equation is known as the *Lorentz force equation* which relates mechanical force and electrical force. If m is the mass of the charged particle moving in both $\vec{E}$ and $\vec{B}$ fields, then by Newton's second law of motion, we can write

$$\vec{F} = m\frac{d\vec{u}}{dt} = Q(\vec{E} + \vec{u} \times \vec{B}) \tag{5.5}$$

The solution of Lorentz force equation is useful in determining the motion of charged particles in electric and magnetic fields. Table 5.1 gives the summary of the force exerted on a charged particle.

Table 5.1 *Conditions of force on a charged particle*

State of Particle	$\vec{E}$ field	$\vec{B}$ field	Combined Fields $\vec{E}$ and $\vec{B}$
Stationary	$\vec{F}_e = Q\vec{E}$	--	$\vec{F} = Q\vec{E}$
Moving	$\vec{F}_e = Q\vec{E}$	$\vec{F}_m = Q\vec{u} \times \vec{B}$	$\vec{F} = Q\left(\vec{E} + \vec{u} \times \vec{B}\right)$

From Eqs (5.1) and (5.2), the differences between the electric force and magnetic force are summarized as follows:

(*i*) The electric force is always in the direction of the electric field whereas the magnetic force is always perpendicular to the magnetic field.

(*ii*) The electric force acts on a stationary or a moving charge whereas the magnetic force acts on it only when the charge is in motion.

(*iii*) The electric force displaces a point charge at the cost of energy whereas no work is done by the magnetic force when a point charge is displaced, i.e., the kinetic energy of the charge remains unchanged.

EXAMPLE 5.1

A charged particle with velocity $\vec{u}$ is moving in a medium containing uniform fields $\vec{E} = E\vec{a}_x$ V/m and $\vec{B} = B\vec{a}_y$ Wb/m^2. What should $\vec{u}$ be so that the particle experiences no net force on it?

SOLUTION

Given $\vec{E} = E\vec{a}_x$ V/m and $\vec{B} = B\vec{a}_y$ Wb/m^2.

The force exerted on a charged particle by the electric field is

$$\vec{F}_e = Q\vec{E} = QE\vec{a}_x$$

The force exerted on a charged particle by the magnetic field is

$$\vec{F}_m = Q\vec{u} \times \vec{B} = Q\left(\vec{u} \times B\vec{a}_y\right)$$

For net force to be zero, $\vec{F}_m$ has to be along $-\vec{a}_x$, which requires $\vec{u}$ to be along $+\vec{a}_z$.

Hence, $\qquad QE = QuB$

$$u = \frac{E}{B}$$

Therefore, $\qquad \vec{u} = \frac{E}{B}\vec{a}_z$ m/s

EXAMPLE 5.2

Find the force on a particle of mass 1.7×10^{-27} kg and charge 1.602×10^{-19} C if it enters a field of magnetic flux density $B = 10$ mWb/m^2 with an initial velocity of 90 km/s.

SOLUTION

Given $B = 10$ mWb/m^2, $Q = 1.602 \times 10^{-19}$ C and $u = 90$ km/s. Assume $\vec{B}$ and $\vec{u}$ are perpendicular to each other. Therefore, the magnitude of magnetic force is

$$F_m = QuB = (1.602 \times 10^{-19})(90 \times 10^3)(10 \times 10^{-3})$$

$$= 14.42 \times 10^{-17}\, \text{N}$$

EXAMPLE 5.3

If the magnetic field intensity is $\vec{H} = \left(\dfrac{0.01}{\mu_0}\right)\vec{a}_x$ A/m, what is the force on a charge of 1 pC moving with a velocity of $10^6\,\vec{a}_y$ m/s?

SOLUTION

Given $\vec{H} = \left(\dfrac{0.01}{\mu_0}\right)\vec{a}_x$ A/m, $Q = 1\,\text{pC} = 10^{-12}$ C and $\vec{u} = 10^6\,\vec{a}_y$ m/s.

The magnetic force $\vec{F}_m$ exerted on a charge Q moving with a velocity $\vec{u}$ in a magnetic field of flux density $\vec{B}$ is

$$\vec{F}_m = Q\vec{u} \times \vec{B}$$

where $\vec{B} = \mu_0 \vec{H} = \mu_0 \left(\dfrac{0.01}{\mu_0} \right) \vec{a}_x = 0.01 \vec{a}_x$ T.

Now, $\qquad \vec{u} \times \vec{B} = 10^6 \vec{a}_y \times 0.01 \vec{a}_x = -10^4 \vec{a}_z \qquad\qquad$ (since $\vec{a}_y \times \vec{a}_x = -\vec{a}_z$)

Therefore, $\qquad \vec{F}_m = 10^{-12} \left(-10^4 \vec{a}_z \right) = -10^{-8} \vec{a}_z$ N $\qquad\qquad\qquad\qquad$ ◻

EXAMPLE 5.4

Compute the centripetal force necessary to hold an electron of mass $m = 9.107 \times 10^{-31}$ kg in a circular orbit of radius 0.5×10^{-10} m with an angular velocity of 3×10^{16} rad/s.

SOLUTION

Given $m = 9.107 \times 10^{-31}$ kg, $\omega = 3 \times 10^{16}$ rad/s and $r = 0.5 \times 10^{-10}$ m.

The centripetal force necessary to hold an electron in a circular orbit is

$$F = \frac{mv^2}{r} = m\omega^2 r, \qquad \text{where} \quad v = \omega r$$

$$= \left(9.107 \times 10^{-31} \right) \left(3 \times 10^{16} \right)^2 \left(0.5 \times 10^{-10} \right) = 4.1 \times 10^{-8} \text{ N} \qquad\qquad ◻$$

EXAMPLE 5.5

If a proton is fixed in position and an electron revolves about it in a circular path of radius 0.5×10^{-10} m, what is the magnetic flux density at the proton?

SOLUTION

The coulomb force of attraction that exist between proton and electron is

$$F = \frac{Q^2}{4\pi\varepsilon_0 r^2} \tag{1}$$

The centripetal force needed for the circular motion of electron is

$$F = m\omega^2 r \tag{2}$$

Equating Eqs. (1) and (2), we get

$$\frac{Q^2}{4\pi\varepsilon_0 r^2} = m\omega^2 r$$

Hence, $\qquad \omega^2 = \dfrac{Q^2}{4\pi\varepsilon_0 m r^3}$

Since the electron is equivalent to a current loop $I = (\omega / 2\pi) Q$, the magnetic flux density at the center of such a loop is

$$B = \mu_0 H = \frac{\mu_0 I}{2\rho} = \frac{\mu_0 \omega Q}{4\pi r}, \qquad \text{where} \quad \rho = r$$

Substituting the value of ω in this equation, we have

$$B = \frac{\left(\dfrac{\mu_0}{4\pi}\right)Q^2}{r^2\sqrt{4\pi\varepsilon_0 m r}}$$

Here, the charge of an electron, $Q = 1.602\times10^{-19}\,\text{C}$ and the mass of an electron, $m = 9.107\times10^{-31}\,\text{kg}$.

Therefore, $\qquad B = \dfrac{\left(10^{-7}\right)\left(1.602\times10^{-19}\right)^2}{\left(0.5\times10^{-10}\right)^2\sqrt{\left(\dfrac{1}{9}\times10^{-9}\right)\left(9.107\times10^{-31}\right)\left(0.5\times10^{-10}\right)}} = 9\,\text{T}$ ❑

EXAMPLE 5.6

A point charge of $4\,\text{C}$ moves with a velocity of $5\vec{a}_x + 6\vec{a}_y - 7\vec{a}_z\,\text{m/s}$. Find the force exerted if the magnetic flux density is $5\vec{a}_x + 7\vec{a}_y + 9\vec{a}_z\,\text{Wb/m}^2$.

SOLUTION

Given $Q = 4\,\text{C}$, $\vec{u} = 5\vec{a}_x + 6\vec{a}_y - 7\vec{a}_z\,\text{m/s}$ and $\vec{B} = 5\vec{a}_x + 7\vec{a}_y + 9\vec{a}_z\,\text{Wb/m}^2$.

The force acting on a point charge in the presence of magnetic field is

$$\vec{F}_m = Q\left(\vec{u}\times\vec{B}\right)$$

Here, $\qquad \vec{u}\times\vec{B} = \begin{vmatrix} \vec{a}_x & \vec{a}_y & \vec{a}_z \\ 5 & 6 & -7 \\ 5 & 7 & 9 \end{vmatrix}$

$$= \vec{a}_x\left[(6\times9)-(-7\times7)\right] - \vec{a}_y\left[(5\times9)-(-7\times5)\right] + \vec{a}_z\left[(5\times7)-(6\times5)\right]$$

$$= \vec{a}_x\left(54+49\right) - \vec{a}_y\left(45+35\right) + \vec{a}_z\left(35-30\right)$$

$$= 103\vec{a}_x - 80\vec{a}_y + 5\vec{a}_z$$

Therefore, $\qquad \vec{F}_m = Q\left(\vec{u}\times\vec{B}\right) = 4\left(103\vec{a}_x - 80\vec{a}_y + 5\vec{a}_z\right)$

$$= 412\vec{a}_x - 320\vec{a}_y + 20\vec{a}_z\,\text{N}$$

Then, the magnitude of force is

$$\left|\vec{F}_m\right| = \sqrt{(412)^2 + (-320)^2 + (20)^2} = 522.05\,\text{N}$$ ❑

5.3 FORCE ON A DIFFERENTIAL CURRENT ELEMENT

The current density $\vec{J}$ can be expressed in terms of velocity $\vec{u}$ and volume charge density ρ_v as

$$\vec{J} = \rho_v\vec{u} \tag{5.6}$$

The differential amount of charge dQ can also be expressed in terms of volume charge density ρ_v as

$$dQ = \rho_v\,dv \tag{5.7}$$

The force on a differential current element $Id\vec{l}$ of a conductor carrying current due to the magnetic field of flux density $\vec{B}$ can be determined using Eq. (5.6) and Eq. (5.7) as given below. Now, the differential force exerted on differential amount of charge moving in a steady magnetic field is given by

$$d\vec{F} = dQ\vec{u} \times \vec{B} \tag{5.8}$$

Substituting Eq. (5.7) in Eq. (5.8), we get

$$d\vec{F} = \rho_v dv\,\vec{u} \times \vec{B}$$

Using Eq. (5.6), we can express $d\vec{F}$ in terms of $\vec{J}$ as

$$d\vec{F} = \vec{J}dv \times \vec{B} \tag{5.9}$$

Recalling the relationship between current elements discussed in previous chapter, we have

$$\vec{J}dv = \vec{K}ds = Id\vec{l}$$

Then, the differential force exerted on a surface current density is

$$d\vec{F} = \vec{K}ds \times \vec{B} \tag{5.10}$$

Similarly, the differential force exerted on a differential current element is

$$d\vec{F} = Id\vec{l} \times \vec{B} \tag{5.11}$$

Integrating Eq. (5.9) over a volume v, the force becomes

$$\vec{F} = \int_v \vec{J}dv \times \vec{B} \tag{5.12}$$

Integrating Eq. (5.10) over either open or closed surface s, we have

$$\vec{F} = \int_s \vec{K}ds \times \vec{B} \tag{5.13}$$

Similarly, integrating Eq. (5.11) over a closed path, we get

$$\vec{F} = \oint_l Id\vec{l} \times \vec{B} \tag{5.14}$$

Here, the magnetic field developed by the current element $Id\vec{l}$ does not exert force on the element itself similar to a point charge which does not exert a force in itself. In other words, the magnetic flux density $\vec{B}$ is always external to the current element $Id\vec{l}$.

For a straight conductor in a uniform magnetic field, the simplified expression for force is given by

$$\vec{F} = I\vec{l} \times \vec{B} \tag{5.15}$$

Hence, the magnitude of force on a current element is

$$F = BIl\sin\theta$$

where θ is the angle between the direction of current element and the direction of magnetic flux density.

EXAMPLE 5.7

A wire of length $1\,\text{m}$ carries a current of $10\,\text{A}$ and makes an angle of $30°$ with uniform magnetic field of flux density $B = 1.5\,\text{Wb/m}^2$. Calculate the magnitude of the force on the wire.

SOLUTION

Given $I = 10\,\text{A}$, $B = 1.5\,\text{Wb/m}^2$, $l = 1$ m and $\theta = 30°$.

The magnitude of force on a current element is

$$F = BIl\sin\theta$$

$$= 1.5\times10\times1\times\sin 30° = 7.5\,\text{N}$$

EXAMPLE 5.8

A current element $4\,\text{m}$ in length lies along y-axis centered at origin. The current is $10\,\text{A}$ in $\vec{a}_y$ direction. If

it experiences a force of $15\left(\dfrac{\vec{a}_x + \vec{a}_z}{\sqrt{2}}\right)\text{N}$ due to a uniform magnetic field, determine $\vec{B}$ and $\vec{H}$ in free space.

SOLUTION

The force exerted on a straight current element in uniform magnetic field is

$$\vec{F} = I\vec{l}\times\vec{B}$$

Hence, $\dfrac{15}{\sqrt{2}}\left(\vec{a}_x + \vec{a}_z\right) = \left[(10)(4\vec{a}_y)\times\left(B_x\vec{a}_x + B_y\vec{a}_y + B_z\vec{a}_z\right)\right]$

$$\frac{15}{\sqrt{2}}\left(\vec{a}_x + \vec{a}_z\right) = \begin{vmatrix} \vec{a}_x & \vec{a}_y & \vec{a}_z \\ 0 & 40 & 0 \\ B_x & B_y & B_z \end{vmatrix}$$

$$10.61\left(\vec{a}_x + \vec{a}_z\right) = \left(40B_z\right)\vec{a}_x - \left(40B_x\right)\vec{a}_z$$

Comparing the coefficients of unit vectors, we get

$$-40B_x = 10.61 \quad \text{i.e.,} \quad B_x = -0.265$$

and $\qquad 40B_z = 10.61 \quad \text{i.e.,} \quad B_z = 0.265$

Hence, the uniform magnetic flux density is

$$\vec{B} = B_x\vec{a}_x + B_z\vec{a}_z = 0.265\left(-\vec{a}_x + \vec{a}_z\right)\text{T}$$

Therefore, $\vec{H} = \dfrac{\vec{B}}{\mu_0} = \dfrac{0.265\left(-\vec{a}_x + \vec{a}_z\right)}{4\pi\times10^{-7}} = 0.211\times10^6\left(-\vec{a}_x + \vec{a}_z\right)\text{A/m}$

EXAMPLE 5.9

Calculate the force on a straight conductor of length $30\,\text{cm}$ carrying a current of $5\,\text{A}$ in a magnetic field along the z-axis. The magnetic flux density is $\vec{B} = 3.5\times10^{-3}\left(\vec{a}_x - \vec{a}_y\right)\text{Wb/m}^2$, where $\vec{a}_x$ and $\vec{a}_y$ are unit vectors.

SOLUTION

Given $\vec{l} = 0.3\vec{a}_z$, $I = 5\,\text{A}$ and $\vec{B} = 3.5\times10^{-3}\left(\vec{a}_x - \vec{a}_y\right)\text{Wb/m}^2$.

The force on the conductor is

$$\vec{F} = I\vec{l}\times\vec{B} = 5\left[0.3\vec{a}_z\times3.5\times10^{-3}\left(\vec{a}_x - \vec{a}_y\right)\right]$$

$$= 5.25 \times 10^{-3}\, \vec{a}_x + 5.25 \times 10^{-3}\, \vec{a}_y \qquad (\text{since } \vec{a}_z \times \vec{a}_x = \vec{a}_y \text{ and } \vec{a}_z \times \vec{a}_y = -\vec{a}_x)$$

$$= 5.25 \vec{a}_x + 5.25 \vec{a}_y\, \text{mN}$$

The magnitude of force is

$$F = 5.25 \times 10^{-3}\sqrt{2} = 7.42\,\text{mN}$$

EXAMPLE 5.10

A conductor of length $5\,\text{m}$ located at $z = 0$, $x = 4\,\text{m}$ carries a current of $10\,\text{A}$ in the $-\vec{a}_y$ direction. Find the components of $\vec{B}$ in the region if the force on the conductor is $1.2 \times 10^{-2}\,\text{N}$ in the direction $\dfrac{(-\vec{a}_x + \vec{a}_z)}{\sqrt{2}}$.

SOLUTION

Given $\vec{F} = \left(1.2 \times 10^{-2}\right)\dfrac{\left(-\vec{a}_x + \vec{a}_z\right)}{\sqrt{2}}$, $\vec{l} = -5\vec{a}_y$ and $I = 10\,\text{A}$.

The magnetic force is

$$\vec{F} = I\vec{l} \times \vec{B}$$

$$\left(1.2 \times 10^{-2}\right)\left(\frac{-\vec{a}_x + \vec{a}_z}{\sqrt{2}}\right) = \begin{vmatrix} \vec{a}_x & \vec{a}_y & \vec{a}_z \\ 0 & (10)(-5) & 0 \\ B_x & B_y & B_z \end{vmatrix}$$

$$= -50 B_z \vec{a}_x + 50 B_x \vec{a}_z = 50\left(-B_z \vec{a}_x + B_x \vec{a}_z\right)$$

Comparing the coefficients of unit vectors, we get

$$B_z = B_x = \frac{1.2 \times 10^{-2}}{50 \times \sqrt{2}} = 1.7 \times 10^{-4}\,\text{Wb/m}^2$$

EXAMPLE 5.11

A conductor of length $0.25\,\text{m}$ lies along the y-axis and carries a current of $25\,\text{A}$ in the $\vec{a}_y$ direction. Find the power needed for parallel translation of the conductor to $x = 5\,\text{m}$ at a constant speed in 3 seconds if the uniform field is $\vec{B} = 0.06\vec{a}_z$ T.

SOLUTION

Given $\vec{l} = 0.25\vec{a}_y$, $t = 3s$, $I = 25\,\text{A}$ and $\vec{B} = 0.06\vec{a}_z$ T.

Here, $\qquad \vec{F} = I\vec{l} \times \vec{B} = 25\left(0.25\vec{a}_y \times 0.06\vec{a}_z\right)$

$$= 0.375\vec{a}_x \qquad (\text{since } \vec{a}_y \times \vec{a}_z = \vec{a}_x)$$

Therefore, the work done by the force along x-direction is

$$W = \int_{\text{initial}}^{\text{final}} \vec{F} \cdot d\vec{l} = \int_0^5 \left(0.375\vec{a}_x\right) \cdot \left(dx\vec{a}_x\right)$$

$$= 0.375 \int_0^5 dx = 0.375\left(x\right)_0^5 = 1.875\,\text{J}$$

Hence, the power required for parallel translation is

$$P = \frac{W}{t} = \frac{1.875}{3} = 0.625\,\text{W}$$

EXAMPLE 5.12

A conductor of length $10\,\text{m}$ carrying current $4\,\text{A}$ is placed on the y-axis between $y = \pm 3\,\text{m}$. If the magnetic flux density is $\vec{B} = 0.05\vec{a}_x\,\text{T}$, determine the work done in moving the conductor at constant speed parallel to $x = z = 3\,\text{m}$.

SOLUTION

Given $\vec{l} = 10\vec{a}_y$, $I = 4\,\text{A}$, $\vec{B} = 0.05\vec{a}_x\,\text{T}$ and the conductor is located between $y = \pm 3\,\text{m}$.

Here, $\vec{F} = I\vec{l} \times \vec{B} = 4\left(10\vec{a}_y\right) \times 0.05\vec{a}_x = -2\vec{a}_z$

But the applied force is equal and opposite. Hence, $\vec{F}_a = 2\vec{a}_z$.

Since this force is constant, the conductor may be moved first along z-direction and then in the x-direction as shown in Figure E5.12. Here, $\vec{F}_a$ is completely in the z-direction and no work is done in moving along x-direction. Therefore, the work done by the force along z-direction is

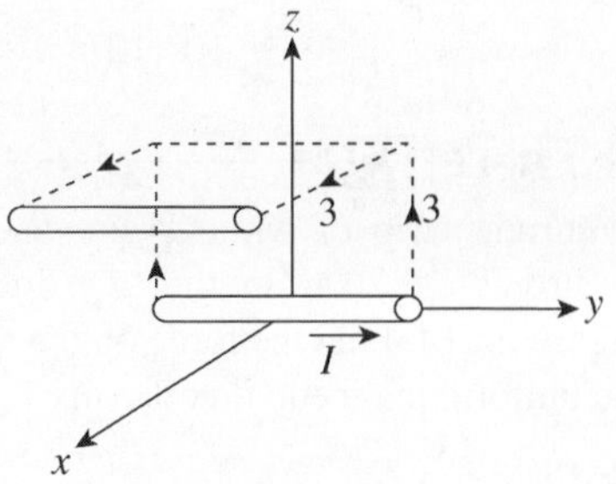

$$W = \int_{\text{initial}}^{\text{final}} \vec{F} \cdot d\vec{l}$$

$$= \int_0^3 \left(2\vec{a}_z\right) \cdot \left(dz\vec{a}_z\right) = 2\left[z\right]_0^3 = 6\,\text{J}$$

Figure E5.12

EXAMPLE 5.13

A conductor is placed on the z-axis at $-2.5\,\text{m} \le z \le 2.5\,\text{m}$ carrying a fixed current of $10\,\text{A}$ in the $-\vec{a}_z$ direction as shown in Figure E5.13. For a magnetic field of the flux density $\vec{B} = 5 \times 10^{-4} e^{-0.2x}\vec{a}_y\,\text{Wb/m}^2$, determine the work and power required to move the conductor at constant speed to $x = 4\,\text{m}$ and $y = 0$ in $10\,\text{ms}$.

SOLUTION

Given $\vec{l} = -5\vec{a}_z$, $I = 10\,\text{A}$, $t = 10\,\text{ms}$ and

$\vec{B} = 5 \times 10^{-4} e^{-0.2x}\vec{a}_y\,\text{Wb/m}^2$.

Assuming the motion of the conductor is parallel to the x-axis, the force is

$$\vec{F} = I\vec{l} \times \vec{B} = 10\left(-5\vec{a}_z\right) \times 5 \times 10^{-4} e^{-0.2x}\vec{a}_y$$

$$= 25 \times 10^{-3} e^{-0.2x}\vec{a}_x \qquad \text{(since } \vec{a}_z \times \vec{a}_y = -\vec{a}_x\text{)}$$

But the applied force is equal and opposite. Hence, $\vec{F}_a = -25 \times 10^{-3} e^{-0.2x}\vec{a}_x$.

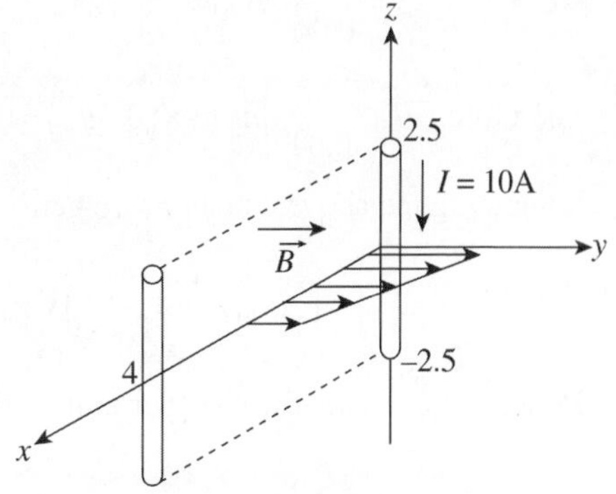

Figure E5.13

Therefore, the work done by the force along x-direction is

$$W = \int_0^4 \left(-25\times10^{-3}e^{-0.2x}\vec{a}_x\right)\cdot\left(dx\vec{a}_x\right)$$

$$= -25\times10^{-3}\left[\frac{e^{-0.2x}}{-0.2}\right]_0^4 = -6.89\times10^{-2}\,\text{J}$$

Since the conductor is moved by the magnetic field, the work done is negative. Then, the power is

$$P = \frac{W}{t} = \frac{-6.89\times10^{-2}}{10\times10^{-3}} = -6.89\,\text{W}$$

$\square$

EXAMPLE 5.14

A current strip of width 4 cm and of length l carries a current of 20A in the $\vec{a}_x$ direction, as shown in Figure E5.14. Find the force on the strip per unit length if the uniform magnetic flux density is $\vec{B} = 0.4\vec{a}_y\,\text{Wb/m}^2$.

SOLUTION

Given $\vec{B} = 0.4\vec{a}_y\,\text{Wb/m}^2$, $I = 20\,\text{A}$ and $b = 0.04\,\text{m}$.

The differential force exerted on a differential current element is

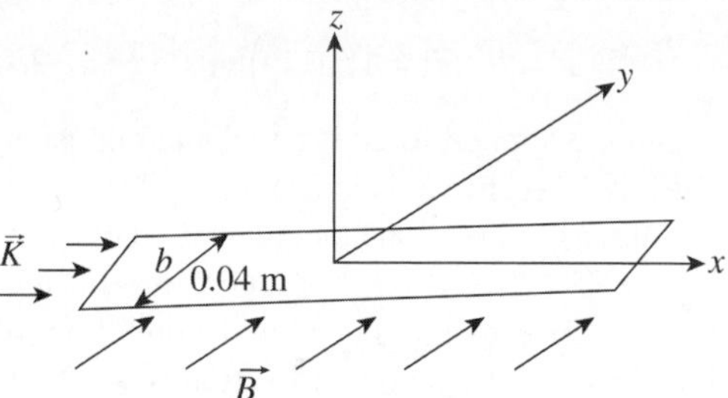

Figure E5.14

$$d\vec{F} = Id\vec{l}\times\vec{B}$$

The expression for $d\vec{F}$ can be written in terms of surface current density K as

$$d\vec{F} = \vec{K}ds\times\vec{B}$$

where $\vec{K} = \dfrac{I}{b}\vec{a}_x = \dfrac{20\vec{a}_x}{0.04}$ and $ds = dxdy$.

Therefore, $d\vec{F}\left(\dfrac{20\vec{a}_x}{0.04}\right)dx\,dy\times\left(0.4\vec{a}_y\right) = 200dx\,dy\vec{a}_z$

Integrating the above equation, we get,

$$\vec{F} = \int\limits_{-0.02}^{0.02}\int\limits_{0}^{l} 200dx\,dy\,\vec{a}_z = \int\limits_{-0.02}^{0.02}\left(200l\right)dy\,\vec{a}_z = 200l\left[y\right]_{-0.02}^{0.02} = 8l\,\vec{a}_z$$

Hence, the force on the strip per unit length is

$$\frac{\vec{F}}{l} = 8\,\vec{a}_z\,\text{N/m}$$

$\square$

5.4 FORCE BETWEEN CURRENT ELEMENTS

In electrostatic fields, a point charge exerts a force on another point charge, separated by a small distance. If these charges are of the same type, then the force between the two charges is repulsive. But when the two charges are of opposite type, the force between the two is an attractive one.

When a current carrying conductor is placed in an external magnetic field, the magnetic force $\vec{F}_m$ will act on the conductor. However, the current in the conductor also generates its own magnetic field. Hence, if there are two current carrying conductors, then each conductor will exert a magnetic force on the other.

Consider two current elements $I_1\,d\vec{l}_1$ and $I_2\,d\vec{l}_2$ as shown in Figure 5.2. Assume the directions of I_1 and I_2 are same with respect to the source. Both current elements produce their own magnetic fields. As the current flow is in the same direction in both the elements, the differential amount of differential force $d\left(d\vec{F}_1\right)$ exerted on element $I_1\,d\vec{l}_1$ due to the field $d\vec{B}_2$ which is generated by other element $I_2\,d\vec{l}_2$ is an attractive force.

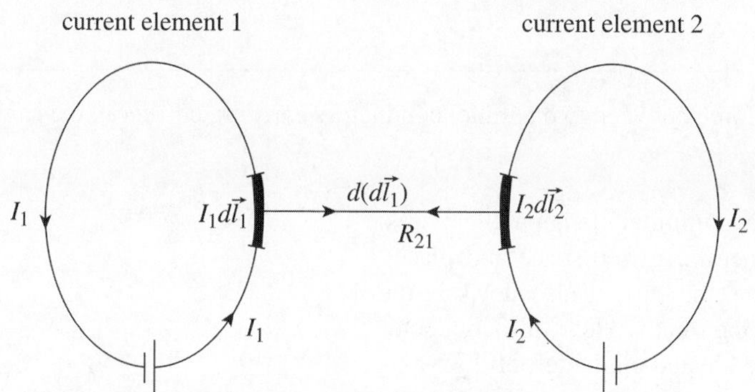

Figure 5.2 *Force between two current elements*

From Eq. (5.11), the differential force exerted on a differential current element is

$$d\left(d\vec{F}_1\right) = I_1\,d\vec{l}_1 \times d\vec{B}_2 \tag{5.16}$$

According to Biot–Savart's law, the magnetic field produced by current element $I_2\,d\vec{l}_2$ in free space is

$$d\vec{B}_2 = \mu_0 d\vec{H}_2 = \mu_0\left[\frac{I_2 d\vec{l}_2 \times \vec{a}_{R21}}{4\pi R_{21}^2}\right] \tag{5.17}$$

Substituting Eq. (5.17) in Eq. (5.16), we get

$$d\left(d\vec{F}_1\right) = \frac{\mu_0 I_1 d\vec{l}_1 \times \left(I_2 d\vec{l}_2 \times \vec{a}_{R21}\right)}{4\pi R_{21}^2} \tag{5.18}$$

This equation represents the ampere's law of force between two current elements and is similar to Coulomb's law, which represents the force between two stationary charges in electric field.

Integrating Eq. (5.18) twice, the total force $\vec{F}_1$ exerted on current element 1 due to the magnetic flux density $\vec{B}_2$ produced by the current element 2 is given by

$$\vec{F}_1 = \frac{\mu_0 I_1 I_2}{4\pi} \oint_{l_1} \oint_{l_2} \frac{d\vec{l}_1 \times \left(d\vec{l}_2 \times \vec{a}_{R21}\right)}{R_{21}^2} \tag{5.19}$$

Similarly, the force $\vec{F}_2$ exerted on the current element 2 due to the magnetic flux density $\vec{B}_1$ produced by the current element 1 is given by

$$\vec{F}_2 = \frac{\mu_0 I_2 I_1}{4\pi} \oint_{l_2} \oint_{l_1} \frac{d\vec{l}_2 \times \left(d\vec{l}_1 \times \vec{a}_{R12}\right)}{R_{12}^2} \tag{5.20}$$

Using bac-cab rule of vector triple product to Eq. (5.19) and Eq. (5.20), it is found that

$$\vec{F}_2 = -\vec{F}_1 \qquad (\text{since } \vec{a}_{R12} = -\vec{a}_{R21}) \qquad\qquad (5.21)$$

This equation shows that both the forces $\vec{F}_1$ and $\vec{F}_2$ obey Newton's third law, which states that for every action, there is an equal and opposite reaction.

Equation (5.21) also shows that the two elements carrying current in same direction attract each other with equal forces. If the currents are in opposite directions, the current elements will repel each other with equal forces.

EXAMPLE 5.15

Derive the magnetic force between two parallel conductors carrying current in the same direction.

SOLUTION

Figure E5.15 shows two infinitely long parallel wires, separated by a distance d, in free space and placed along z-axis. Assume, the current also flows in the positive direction along z-axis. Here, the conductor carrying current I_1 is located on the left of the z-axis and the other conductor carrying current I_2 is placed on the right of the z-axis.

The magnetic flux density $\vec{B}_1$ due to current I_1 is defined at the location of the conductor carrying current I_2 i.e., along $-\vec{a}_x$ direction. Conversely, the field $\vec{B}_2$ due to I_2 can be defined at the location of the conductor carrying current I_1.

The magnetic flux density due to an infinitely long conductor carrying current I_1 is

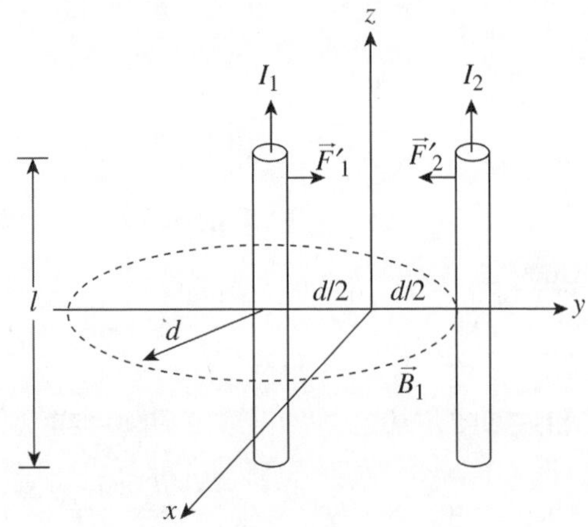

Figure E5.15

$$\vec{B}_1 = \frac{\mu_0 I_1}{2\pi\rho}\vec{a}_\phi = \frac{\mu_0 I_1}{2\pi d}\left(-\vec{a}_x\right)$$

Therefore, the force $\vec{F}_2$ exerted on a length l of conductor carrying current I_2 due to flux density $\vec{B}_1$ is

$$\vec{F}_2 = I_2\left(l\vec{a}_z \times \vec{B}_1\right) = I_2 l\vec{a}_z \times \frac{\mu_0 I_1}{2\pi d}\left(-\vec{a}_x\right)$$

$$= \frac{\mu_0 I_1 I_2 l}{2\pi d}\left(-\vec{a}_y\right) \qquad (\text{since } \vec{a}_z \times \vec{a}_x = \vec{a}_y)$$

Therefore, the force per unit length is

$$\vec{F}'_2 = \frac{\vec{F}_2}{l} = -\frac{\mu_0 I_1 I_2}{2\pi d}\vec{a}_y$$

Similarly, the force $\vec{F}_1$ exerted on the conductor carrying current I_1 due to flux density $\vec{B}_2$ is

$$\vec{F}_1 = I_1\left(l\vec{a}_z \times \vec{B}_2\right) = I_1 l\vec{a}_z \times \frac{\mu_0 I_2}{2\pi d}\vec{a}_x = \frac{\mu_0 I_1 I_2 l}{2\pi d}\vec{a}_y$$

Therefore, the force per unit length is

$$\vec{F}_1' = \frac{\vec{F}_1}{l} = \frac{\mu_0 I_1 I_2}{2\pi d}\, \vec{a}_y$$

Hence, $\vec{F}_1' = -\vec{F}_2'$. This shows that the two conductors carrying current in same direction attract each other with equal forces. If the currents are in opposite direction, the wires will repel each other with equal forces. ❑

EXAMPLE 5.16

Consider that two long parallel conductors $2\,\text{m}$ apart carry currents of $50\,\text{A}$ and $100\,\text{A}$, respectively in the same direction. Determine the magnitude and direction of the force between them per unit length.

SOLUTION

Given $I_1 = 50\,\text{A}$, $I_2 = 100\,\text{A}$ and $d = 2\,\text{m}$.

The force between two parallel conductors per unit length is

$$\frac{\vec{F}}{l} = \frac{\mu_0 I_1 I_2}{2\pi d}\, \vec{a}_n = \frac{4\pi \times 10^{-7}\,(50)(100)}{(2\pi)(2)} = 5\times 10^{-4}\,\vec{a}_n = 0.5\vec{a}_n \text{ mN/m}$$

Since the conductors are in same direction, the force is attractive. The direction of the force is normal to the plane of the conductors. ❑

EXAMPLE 5.17

Consider that two long parallel conductors carry $80\,\text{A}$. If the conductors are separated by $3\,\text{mm}$, find the force per metre of each conductor if the current flowing through them is in the opposite directions.

SOLUTION

Given $I_1 = I_2 = 80\,\text{A}$ and $d = 3\,\text{mm} = 3\times 10^{-3}\,\text{m}$.

The magnitude of force per metre of each conductor is

$$\frac{F}{l} = \frac{\mu_0 I_1 I_2}{2\pi d}$$

$$= \frac{4\pi \times 10^{-7} \times 80 \times 80}{2\pi \times 3 \times 10^{-3}} = 0.427\,\text{N/m}$$

As the currents are in opposite direction, the two conductors will repel each other with equal forces. ❑

EXAMPLE 5.18

Consider that two wires, carrying current $3\,\text{A}$ and $6\,\text{A}$ in the same direction, are placed with their axes $5\,\text{cm}$ apart, and free space permeability, $\mu_0 = 4\pi \times 10^{-7}$ H/m. Calculate the force per unit length between them.

SOLUTION

Given $I_1 = 3\,\text{A}$, $I_2 = 6\,\text{A}$ and $d = 5\,\text{cm}$.

The magnitude of force between two parallel conducting wires is

$$F = \frac{\mu I_1 I_2 l}{2\pi d}$$

Therefore, the magnitude of force per unit length is

$$\frac{F}{l} = \frac{\mu_0 \mu_r I_1 I_2}{2\pi d}$$

$$= \frac{4\pi \times 10^{-7} \times 3 \times 6}{2\pi \times 5 \times 10^{-2}} = 72 \ \mu\text{N/m}$$

Since the two wires carry current in same direction, the force experienced between them is attractive. ☐

EXAMPLE 5.19

A distribution line consists of two straight parallel conductors supported on the cross arms of wooden poles spaced 100 m apart. The normal spacing between the two conductors is 20 cm. Suppose a current of 10,000 A flows down in one conductor and returns to the other conductor during a fault, determine the force on each 100 m section of the conductor.

SOLUTION

Given two straight parallel conductors with separation, $d = 20\,\text{cm}$ and $I_1 = I_2 = 10^4\,\text{A}$.

$$\text{Therefore,} \quad \frac{F}{l} = \frac{\mu_0 I_1 I_2}{2\pi d} = \frac{4\pi \times 10^{-7} \times 10^4 \times 10^4}{2\pi \times 0.2} = 100\,\text{N/m} \qquad ☐$$

EXAMPLE 5.20

Consider that a rectangular loop carrying current I_2 is placed parallel to an infinitely long filamentary wire carrying current I_1 as shown in Figure E5.20(a). Show that the force experienced by the loop is given by

$$\vec{F}_l = -\frac{\mu_0 I_1 I_2 b}{2\pi} \left[\frac{1}{\rho_0} - \frac{1}{\rho_0 + a} \right] \vec{a}_\rho \ \text{N}.$$

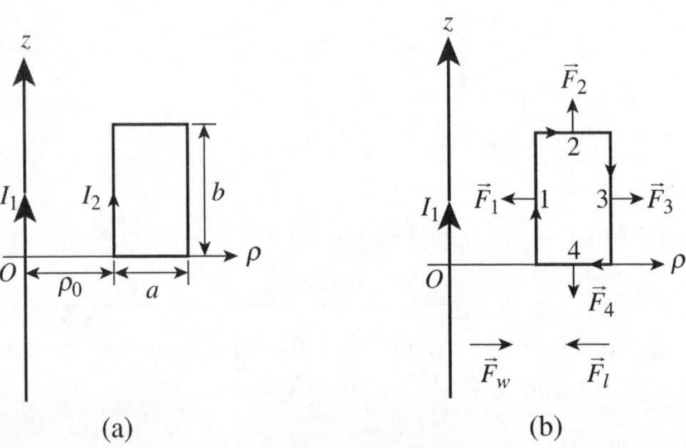

Figure E5.20

SOLUTION

Figure E5.20(a) shows a rectangular loop placed inside the field produced by an infinitely long wire carrying current I_1 on z-axis.

The total force acting on the loop is

$$\vec{F}_l = \vec{F}_1 + \vec{F}_2 + \vec{F}_3 + \vec{F}_4 = I_2 \oint d\vec{l}_2 \times \vec{B}_1$$

where $\vec{F}_1, \vec{F}_2, \vec{F}_3$ and $\vec{F}_4$ are the forces exerted on sides of the loop $1, 2, 3$ and 4 as shown in Figure E5.20(b). The magnetic flux density due to the infinitely long wire carrying current I_1 is

$$\vec{B}_1 = \frac{\mu_0 I_1}{2\pi\rho_0}\vec{a}_\phi$$

Therefore, the force acting on the side of loop 1 is

$$\vec{F}_1 = I_2 \int d\vec{l}_2 \times \vec{B}_1 = I_2 \int_{z=0}^{b} dz\,\vec{a}_z \times \frac{\mu_0 I_1}{2\pi\rho_0}\vec{a}_\phi$$

$$= -\frac{\mu_0 I_1 I_2 b}{2\pi\rho_0}\vec{a}_\rho \qquad (\text{since } \vec{a}_z \times \vec{a}_\phi = -\vec{a}_\rho) \tag{1}$$

As shown in Figure E5.20(b), the force $\vec{F}_1$ is attractive and it is directed towards the long wire. The force $\vec{F}_1$ is along $-\vec{a}_\rho$ direction due to the fact that the side of loop 1 and the long wire carry current along the same direction.

Similarly, the force acting on the side of loop 3 is

$$\vec{F}_3 = I_2 \int d\vec{l}_2 \times \vec{B}_1 = I_2 \int_{z=b}^{0} dz\vec{a}_z \times \frac{\mu_0 I_1}{2\pi\left(\rho_0 + a\right)}\vec{a}_\phi$$

$$= \frac{\mu_0 I_1 I_2 b}{2\pi\left(\rho_0 + a\right)}\vec{a}_\rho \tag{2}$$

The force $\vec{F}_3$ is repulsive as the side of loop 3 and the long wire carry current in opposite direction as shown in Figure E5.20(b).

The force acting on the side of loop 2 is

$$\vec{F}_2 = I_2 \int_{\rho_0}^{\rho_0 + a} d\rho\vec{a}_\rho \times \frac{\mu_0 I_1 \vec{a}_\phi}{2\pi\rho}$$

$$= \frac{\mu_0 I_1 I_2}{2\pi}\ln\left(\frac{\rho_0 + a}{\rho_0}\right)\vec{a}_z \qquad (\text{since } \vec{a}_\rho \times \vec{a}_\phi = \vec{a}_z) \tag{3}$$

As shown in Figure E5.20(b), the force $\vec{F}_2$ is parallel to z-axis.
The force acting on the side of loop 4 is

$$\vec{F}_4 = I_2 \int_{\rho_0 + a}^{\rho_0} d\rho\,\vec{a}_\rho \times \frac{\mu_0 I_1 \vec{a}_\phi}{2\pi\rho}$$

$$= -\frac{\mu_0 I_1 I_2}{2\pi}\ln\left(\frac{\rho_0 + a}{\rho_0}\right)\vec{a}_z \tag{4}$$

As shown in Figure E5.20(b), the force $\vec{F}_4$ is also parallel to z-axis. Adding Eqs. (1), (2), (3) and (4), the total force $\vec{F}_l$ on the loop is

$$\vec{F}_l = \vec{F}_1 + \vec{F}_2 + \vec{F}_3 + \vec{F}_4$$

$$= \frac{\mu_0 I_1 I_2 b}{2\pi} \left[\frac{1}{\rho_0 + a} - \frac{1}{\rho_0} \right] \vec{a}_\rho$$

$$= -\frac{\mu_0 I_1 I_2 b}{2\pi} \left[\frac{1}{\rho_0} - \frac{1}{\rho_0 + a} \right] \vec{a}_\rho$$

The total force $\vec{F}_l$ acting on the loop is an attractive force which tries to draw the loop towards the wire carrying current I_1. By Newton's third law, the force $\vec{F}_w$ acting on the wire is opposite to that of $\vec{F}_l$. □

EXAMPLE 5.21

A triangular loop of wire in free space join points, $A(1,0,1), B(3,0,1)$ and $C(3,0,4)$. The wire carries a current of $6\,\text{mA}$ flowing in the $\vec{a}_z$ direction from B *to* C. A filamentary current of $15\,\text{A}$ flows along the entire z-axis in the $\vec{a}_z$ direction. Find the total force on the loop.

SOLUTION

Given points $A(1,0,1), B(3,0,1)$ and $C(3,0,4)$ forming a triangle loop with sides AB, BC and CA as shown in Figure E5.21. The total force on the loop is equal to the sum of the forces due to currents along sides AB, BC and CA.

i.e.,
$$\vec{F} = \vec{F}_{AB} + \vec{F}_{BC} + \vec{F}_{CA}$$

Given the current flowing through the loop is $I = 6\,\text{mA}$ and the current flowing through the z-axis is $I_1 = 15\,\text{A}$.

The magnetic flux density is $\vec{B} = \mu_0 H = \mu_0 \dfrac{I_1}{2\pi\rho} \vec{a}_\phi$

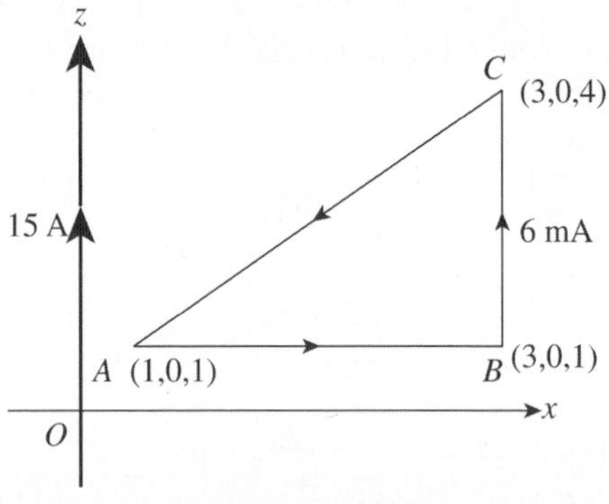

Figure E5.21

In rectangular coordinates,

$$\vec{B} = \mu_0 \frac{I_1}{2\pi x}\left(-\vec{a}_y\right) = \frac{-15\mu_0}{2\pi x} \vec{a}_y = \frac{-15 \times 4\pi \times 10^{-7}}{2\pi x} \vec{a}_y = \frac{-3 \times 10^{-6}}{x} \vec{a}_y$$

The differential force along the side AB is

$$d\vec{F}_{AB} = I d\vec{l}_{AB} \times \vec{B}, \qquad \text{where } d\vec{l}_{AB} = dx\vec{a}_x$$

Therefore, $\quad d\vec{F}_{AB} = I dx\vec{a}_x \times \left(\dfrac{-3 \times 10^{-6}}{x} \vec{a}_y \right)$

$$= \frac{\left(6 \times 10^{-3}\right)\left(-3 \times 10^{-6}\right) dx}{x} \left(\vec{a}_x \times \vec{a}_y\right) = -\frac{18 dx}{x} \vec{a}_z \times 10^{-9}$$

Integrating the above equation, we get

$$\vec{F}_{AB} = -18 \int_1^3 \frac{dx}{x} \times 10^{-9} \vec{a}_z = -18\left[\ln(3) - \ln(1)\right] \times 10^{-9} \vec{a}_z = -19.77 \vec{a}_z \text{ nN}$$

The differential force along the side BC is

$$d\vec{F}_{BC} = I d\vec{l}_{BC} \times \vec{B}, \qquad \text{where } d\vec{l}_{BC} = dz\vec{a}_z$$

Therefore, $d\vec{F}_{BC} = 6\times10^{-3}\,dz\vec{a}_z \times \left(\dfrac{-3\times10^{-6}}{x}\right)\vec{a}_y$, where $x = 3$ and $\vec{a}_z \times \vec{a}_y = -\vec{a}_x$

$$= 6\times10^{-3}\left(10^{-6}\right)\left(\vec{a}_x\right)dz = 6\times10^{-9}\,dz\vec{a}_x$$

Integrating the above equation, we get

$$\vec{F}_{BC} = 6\times10^{-9}\int_1^4 dz\vec{a}_x = 6\times10^{-9}\left[z\right]_1^4\vec{a}_x = 18\times10^{-9}\vec{a}_x$$

The differential force along the side CA is

$$d\vec{F}_{CA} = Id\vec{l}_{CA} \times \vec{B}, \qquad \text{where} \quad d\vec{l}_{CA} = -dx\vec{a}_x - dz\vec{a}_z$$

Therefore, $d\vec{F}_{CA} = 6\times10^{-3}\left(-dx\vec{a}_x - dz\vec{a}_z\right)\times\left(\dfrac{-3\times10^{-6}}{x}\vec{a}_y\right) = \dfrac{18\times10^{-9}}{x}\left(dx\vec{a}_z - dz\vec{a}_x\right)$

Integrating the above equation, we get

$$\vec{F}_{CA} = 18\times10^{-9}\int_3^1 \frac{dx}{x}\vec{a}_z - \int_4^1 \frac{18\times10^{-9}}{3}dz\vec{a}_x$$

$$= 18\times10^{-9}\left[\ln x\right]_3^1\vec{a}_z - 6\times10^{-9}[z]_4^1\vec{a}_x$$

$$= -19.77\times10^{-9}\vec{a}_z + 18\times10^{-9}\vec{a}_x$$

Hence, the total force is

$$\vec{F} = \vec{F}_{AB} + \vec{F}_{BC} + \vec{F}_{CA}$$

$$= -19.77\times10^{-9}\vec{a}_z + 18\times10^{-9}\vec{a}_x - 19.77\times10^{-9}\vec{a}_z + 18\times10^{-9}\vec{a}_x$$

$$= 36\vec{a}_x - 39.54\vec{a}_z \ \text{nN} \qquad\qquad \square$$

5.5 FORCE AND TORQUE ON A CLOSED CIRCUIT

The force $\vec{F}$ exerted on the a filamentary closed circuit by the magnetic field is

$$\vec{F} = \oint_l Id\vec{l} \times \vec{B} = -I\oint_l \vec{B} \times d\vec{l} \tag{5.22}$$

For a uniform magnetic flux density $\vec{B}$, the above equation can be represented as

$$\vec{F} = -I\vec{B}\times\oint_l d\vec{l} \tag{5.23}$$

Since, the line integral over a closed path is zero i.e., $\oint_l d\vec{l} = 0$, the force on a closed circuit in a uniform magnetic field is zero. If the field is not uniform, the force is not zero. For uniform fields, this result is applicable not only to current element circuits but also to surface current and volume current density circuits. Therefore, any closed circuit carrying direct current does not experience any force in a uniform magnetic field.

The torque on a closed circuit can be determined by considering the force on closed circuit or current loop. Though the force is zero for uniform magnetic fields, the torque is not equal to zero. The *torque* $\vec{T}$ is defined as the mechanical moment of force on the loop and is equal to the vector product of moment $\vec{d}$ and force $\vec{F}$. It is given by

$$\vec{T} = \vec{d} \times \vec{F} \qquad (5.24)$$

The unit of torque is newton-metre (N · m).

Figure 5.3(a) shows a rectangular loop of length l and width w placed in a uniform magnetic field of flux density $\vec{B}$. The sides ab and cd of the loop carrying current I are parallel to the magnetic field as shown in Figure 5.3(a) and hence, no force is exerted on these sides. Therefore, the force experienced on sides bc and da is given by

$$\vec{F} = I \int_{b}^{c} d\vec{l} \times \vec{B} + I \int_{d}^{a} d\vec{l} \times \vec{B}$$

$$= I \int_{0}^{l} dz \vec{a}_{z} \times \vec{B} + I \int_{l}^{0} dz \vec{a}_{z} \times \vec{B} = \vec{F}_{0} - \vec{F}_{0} = 0$$

Since the magnetic flux density $\vec{B}$ is uniform, the magnitude of $\vec{F}_{0}$ is $\left|\vec{F}_{0}\right| = IBl$. Since the force experienced on side bc is equal and opposite to that on side da, the net force will be zero. Hence, no force is exerted on the current loop as a whole.

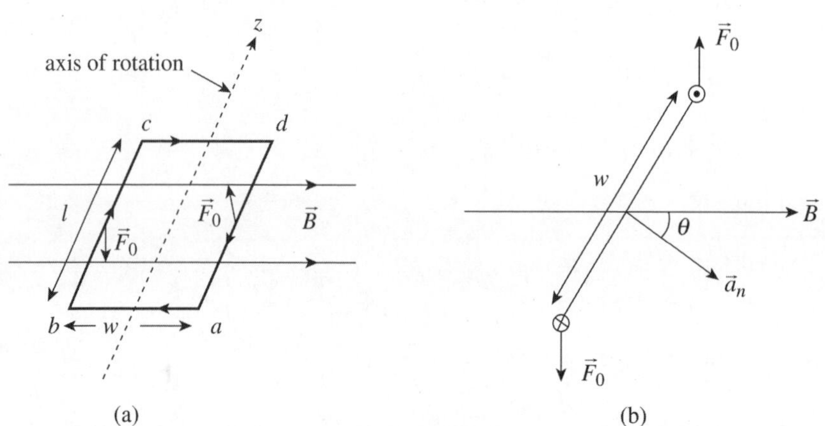

Figure 5.3 *Closed circuit in a uniform magnetic field: (a) rectangular current loop and (b) cross-sectional view of the loop*

Figure 5.3(b) shows the cross-sectional view of the current loop in which $\vec{F}_{0}$ and $-\vec{F}_{0}$ act at different points on the loop. If the normal unit vectors to the plane of the loop makes an angle θ with the field $\vec{B}$, then the torque on the loop becomes

$$\left|\vec{T}\right| = \left|\vec{F}_{0}\right| w \sin \theta = BI\,l\,w \sin \theta$$

or
$$T = BIA \sin \theta \qquad (5.25)$$

where $A = lw$ is the area of the loop.

The magnetic dipole moment $(\vec{m})$ of the loop is defined as the product of current and area of the loop with its direction normal to the loop. It is given by

$$\vec{m} = IA \vec{a}_{n} \qquad (5.26)$$

where $\vec{a}_n$ is a unit vector normal to the plane of the loop and its direction is determined by the right-hand rule i.e., the direction of four fingers of the right-hand is in the direction of current I and the direction of thumb is along $\vec{a}_n$. The unit of magnetic dipole moment is ampere-square metre $(\text{A} \cdot \text{m}^2)$.

The torque can be expressed in terms of magnetic dipole moment as

$$\vec{T} = \vec{m} \times \vec{B} \tag{5.27}$$

This equation determines the torque for the rectangular loop carrying current I and it can also be used to determine the torque on a loop of any shape. The torque is in the direction of the axis of rotation i.e., z-axis as shown in Figure 5.3(a). The torque is maximum when the magnetic field is parallel to the plane of the loop $(\theta = 90°)$ and it is zero when the field is perpendicular to the plane of the loop $(\theta = 0°)$.

EXAMPLE 5.22

A conductor located at, $x = 0.6\,\text{m}$, $y = 0$ and $0 < z < 2\,\text{m}$ carries a current of $10\,\text{A}$ in the $\vec{a}_z$ direction. The magnetic flux density is $\vec{B} = 5\vec{a}_x\,\text{T}$ along the length of the conductor. Find the torque about the z-axis.

SOLUTION

Given $\vec{d} = 0.6\vec{a}_x, l = 2\vec{a}_z, \vec{B} = 5\vec{a}_z\,\text{T}$ and $I = 10\,\text{A}$.

The magnetic force is

$$\vec{F} = I\vec{l} \times \vec{B} = 10\left(2\vec{a}_z \times 5\vec{a}_x\right) = 100\vec{a}_y\,\text{N}$$

Also, the magnetic torque is

$$\vec{T} = \vec{d} \times \vec{F} = 0.6\vec{a}_x \times 100\vec{a}_y = 60\vec{a}_z\,\text{N} \cdot \text{m}$$

EXAMPLE 5.23

Find the maximum torque on an 75-turn, rectangular coil, $0.5\,\text{m}$ by $0.6\,\text{m}$, carrying a current of 4A in magnetic field of flux density $B = 5\,\text{T}$.

SOLUTION

Given $l = 0.5\,\text{m}$, $w = 0.6\,\text{m}$, $I = 4\text{A}$, $N = 75$ and $B = 5\,\text{T}$.

For a rectangular coil of N turns, the torque is $T = NBIA\sin\theta$. The maximum torque is obtained when $\theta = 90°$.

Hence, $\vec{T}_{\text{max}} = NBIlw$, where $A = lw$

$$= 75(5)(4)(0.5)(0.6) = 450\,\text{N} \cdot \text{m}$$

EXAMPLE 5.24

A 200-turn, rectangular coil, $30\text{ cm} \times 15\text{ cm}$ with a current of $5\,\text{A}$ is placed in an uniform magnetic field of flux density $B = 0.2\,\text{T}$. Determine the magnetic moment m and the maximum torque.

SOLUTION

Given $l = 30$ cm, $w = 15$ cm, $I = 5$ A, $N = 200$ and $B = 0.2\,\text{T}$.

Area of the rectangular coil is $A = lw = \left(30 \times 10^{-2}\right)\left(15 \times 10^{-2}\right) = 0.045\,\text{m}^2$

The magnitude of dipole moment for N turns is

$$m = NIA = 200 \times 5 \times 0.045 = 45 \, \text{A} \cdot \text{m}^2$$

The maximum torque on a rectangular loop is

$$T_{\text{max}} = mB = (45)(0.2) = 9 \text{N} \cdot \text{m}$$

EXAMPLE 5.25

A square coil of 200 turns and 0.5 m long sides is in a region with a uniform magnetic flux density of 0.2 T. If the maximum magnetic torque exerted on the coil is $4 \times 10^{-2} \, \text{N} \cdot \text{m}$, what is the current flowing in the coil?

SOLUTION

Given area, $A = a^2 = (0.5)^2 = 0.25 \, \text{m}^2$, $N = 200$, $B = 0.2 \, \text{T}$ and $T_{\text{max}} = 4 \times 10^{-2} \, \text{N}$.

The maximum torque exerted on a square coil is

$$T_{\text{max}} = NIAB$$

Therefore, the current flowing in the coil is

$$I = \frac{T_{\text{max}}}{NAB} = \frac{4 \times 10^{-2}}{200 \times 0.25 \times 0.2} = 4 \, \text{mA}$$

EXAMPLE 5.26

A rectangular coil of area $10 \, \text{cm}^2$ surrounded by a uniform magnetic flux density of $\vec{B} = 0.6\vec{a}_x + 0.4\vec{a}_y + 0.5\vec{a}_z \, \text{Wb/m}^2$ carrying current of $50 \, \text{A}$ lies on plane $2x + 6y - 3z = 7$ such that the magnetic moment of the coil is directed away from the origin. Determine (i) magnetic moment (ii) torque on the coil and (iii) the value of the maximum torque.

SOLUTION

Given area, $A = 10 \, \text{cm}^2$, $\vec{B} = 0.6\vec{a}_x + 0.4\vec{a}_y + 0.5\vec{a}_z \, \text{Wb/m}^2$ and $I = 50 \, \text{A}$.

(*i*) The magnetic moment is

$$\vec{m} = IA\vec{a}_n = (50)\left(10 \times 10^{-4}\right)\left(\frac{2\vec{a}_x + 6\vec{a}_y - 3\vec{a}_z}{\sqrt{49}}\right)$$

$$= \left(14.29\vec{a}_x + 42.86\vec{a}_y - 21.43\vec{a}_z\right) \times 10^{-3} \, \text{A} \cdot \text{m}^2$$

(*ii*) The torque on the coil is

$$\vec{T} = \vec{m} \times \vec{B} = \left[\frac{(50)\left(10 \times 10^{-4}\right)}{7}\left(2\vec{a}_x + 6\vec{a}_y - 3\vec{a}_z\right)\right] \times \left[0.6\vec{a}_x + 0.4\vec{a}_y + 0.5\vec{a}z\right]$$

$$= \frac{(50)\left(10 \times 10^{-4}\right)}{7 \times 10} \begin{vmatrix} \vec{a}_x & \vec{a}_y & \vec{a}_z \\ 2 & 6 & -3 \\ 6 & 4 & 5 \end{vmatrix}$$

$$= 7.143 \times 10^{-4}\left[42\vec{a}_x - 28\vec{a}_y - 4\vec{a}_z\right] = 0.03\vec{a}_x - 0.02\vec{a}_y - 0.025\vec{a}_z \, \text{N} \cdot \text{m}$$

(*iii*) The maximum torque is

$$T_{\text{max}} = |\vec{T}| = |\vec{m} \times \vec{B}| = \sqrt{\left(0.03^2\right) + \left(0.02\right)^2 + \left(0.025\right)^2} = 43.87 \times 10^{-3}\,\text{N} \cdot \text{m}$$

or

$$T_{\text{max}} = BIA = \left|0.6\vec{a}_x + 0.4\vec{a}_y + 0.5\vec{a}_z\right|(50)\left(10 \times 10^{-4}\right)$$

$$= \sqrt{\left(30\right)^2 + \left(20\right)^2 + \left(25\right)^2} \times 10^{-3} = 43.87 \times 10^{-3}\,\text{N} \cdot \text{m} \qquad \square$$

EXAMPLE 5.27

A square coil shown in Figure E5.27 is placed in the magnetic field of flux density $\vec{B} = 0.05\dfrac{\vec{a}_x + \vec{a}_y}{\sqrt{3}}\,\text{Wb/m}^2$.

Determine the torque about *z*-axis when the coil is in the position shown and carries a current of 5A.

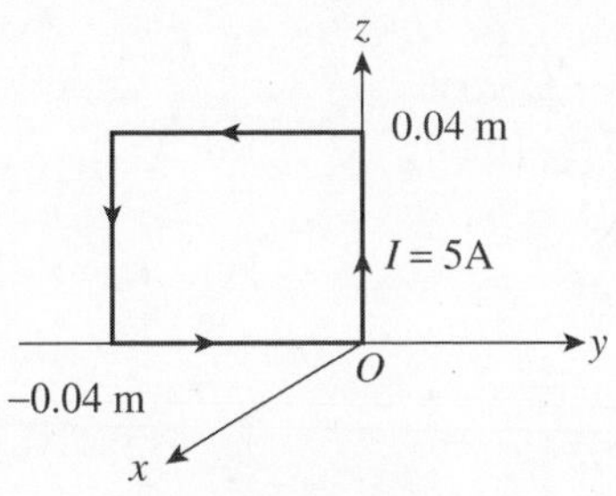

Figure E5.27

SOLUTION

Given $I = 5\text{A}$ and $\vec{B} = 0.05\dfrac{\vec{a}_x + \vec{a}_y}{\sqrt{2}}\,\text{Wb/m}^2$.

The magnetic dipole moment is

$$\vec{m} = IA\vec{a}_n$$

where area of coil, $A = 0.04 \times 0.04 = 1.6 \times 10^{-3}\,\text{m}^2$ and $\vec{a}_n$ is the unit vector normal to the plane of a square coil.

As shown in Figure E5.27, the coil is placed in *yz*-plane. Hence, a unit vector normal to *yz*-plane is in positive *x*-direction i.e., along $\vec{a}_x$.

Therefore,

$$\vec{m} = (5)\left(1.6 \times 10^{-3}\right)\vec{a}_x$$

$$= 8 \times 10^{-3}\,\vec{a}_x\,\text{A} \cdot \text{m}^2$$

Hence, the magnetic torque is

$$\vec{T} = \vec{m} \times \vec{B} = \left(8 \times 10^{-3}\,\vec{a}_x\right) \times \left(0.05\dfrac{\vec{a}_x + \vec{a}_y}{\sqrt{3}}\right)$$

$$= 2.31 \times 10^{-4}\,\vec{a}_z \qquad \text{(since } \vec{a}_x \times \vec{a}_x = 0 \text{ and } \vec{a}_x \times \vec{a}_y = \vec{a}_z\text{)}$$

$$= 0.231\,\vec{a}_z\,\text{mN} \cdot \text{m} \qquad \square$$

EXAMPLE 5.28

A loop wire is bent in the form of triangle as shown in the Figure E5.28. A current of $100\,mA$ flows in $\vec{a}_x$ direction in the segment AB. If the uniform magnetic field has flux density $\vec{B} = 0.2\vec{a}_x - 0.1\vec{a}_y + 0.2\vec{a}_z$ T, then determine the (i) force on segment AB and (ii) torque on the loop if origin is at $A(0,0,0)$.

SOLUTION

Given $I = 100\,mA = 100 \times 10^{-3}$ A and $\vec{B} = 0.2\vec{a}_x - 0.1\vec{a}_y + 0.2\vec{a}_z$ T.

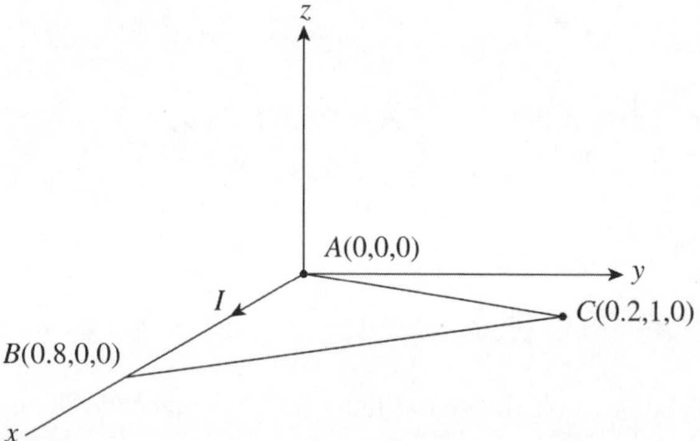

Figure E5.28

(*i*) The force exerted on segment AB shown in Figure E5.28 is

$$\vec{F}_{AB} = I d\vec{l} \times \vec{B}$$

where $d\vec{l} = 0.8\vec{a}_x$.

Therefore, $\vec{F}_{AB} = 100 \times 10^{-3}\left(0.8\vec{a}_x\right) \times \left(0.2\vec{a}_x - 0.1\vec{a}_y + 0.2\vec{a}_z\right)$

$$= -16\vec{a}_y - 8\vec{a}_z \text{ mN}$$

(*ii*) The torque on a loop is

$$\vec{T} = \vec{m} \times \vec{B} = I\vec{A} \times \vec{B}$$

Here, the area of triangle shaped loop placed in xy-plane, can be written in vector form as

$$\vec{A} = \frac{1}{2}\left[0.8\vec{a}_x \times \left(0.2\vec{a}_x + \vec{a}_y\right)\right] = 0.4\vec{a}_z$$

Therefore, $\vec{T} = 100 \times 10^{-3}\left(0.4\vec{a}_z\right) \times \left(0.2\vec{a}_x - 0.1\vec{a}_y + 0.2\vec{a}_z\right)$

$$= 4\vec{a}_x + 8\vec{a}_y \text{ mN·m}$$

EXAMPLE 5.29

A solenoid $25\,cm$ long and of $1\,cm$ mean diameter of the coil-turns has a uniform distributed winding of 2000 turns. If the solenoid is placed in a uniform field of flux density 2 Wb/m^2 and a current of $5\,A$ is passed through the solenoid winding, determine (i) the maximum force on the solenoid and (ii) torque on the solenoid?

SOLUTION

Given $l = 25\,cm = 0.25\,cm$, $d = 1\,cm = 0.01\,m$, $I = 5\,A$, $N = 2000$ and $B = 2$ Wb/m^2.

Area of solenoidal loop, $A = \pi r^2 = \dfrac{\pi d^2}{4} = 0.25\pi \times 10^{-4}\,m^2$

(*i*) The force on the solenoid is

$$\vec{F} = I\vec{l} \times \vec{B}$$

Hence, the maximum force per turn is

$$F = BIl = 2\times5\times0.25 = 2.5 \text{ newton per turn}$$

For 2000 turns, we have

$$F = 2.5\times2000 = 5000\,\text{N}$$

(*ii*) The torque on the solenoid is

$$T = BIA$$

$$= 2\times5\times\pi\times0.25\times10^{-4} = 7.85\times10^{-4}\,\text{N}\cdot\text{m}$$

For 2000 turns, $T = 7.85\times10^{-4}\times2000 = 1.57\,\text{N}\cdot\text{m}$

EXAMPLE 5.30

What is the maximum torque on a square loop of 1000 turns in a field of uniform magnetic flux density $B = 1\,\text{Wb/m}^2$? The loop has $10\,\text{cm}$ side and carries a current of 3A. What is the magnetic moment of the loop?

SOLUTION

Given $a = 10\,\text{cm} = 0.1\,\text{m}$, $I = 3\,\text{A}$, $N = 1000$ and $B = 1\,\text{Wb/m}^2$.

The maximum torque on a single square loop is

$$T_{\text{max}} = BIA$$

where the area of square loop, $A = a^2 = 0.1^2 = 0.01$.

Therefore, $T_{\text{max}} = 1\times3\times0.01 = 0.03\,\text{N}\cdot\text{m/turns}$

For 1000 turns, $T_{\text{max}} = 0.03\times1000 = 30\,\text{N}\cdot\text{m}$

The magnetic moment of the loop is

$$m = IA = 3\times0.01 = 0.03\,\text{A}\cdot\text{m}^2$$

EXAMPLE 5.31

A galvanometer has a rectangular coil suspended in a radial magnetic field so that the magnetic field always acts across the plane of the coil. If the coil is $10\,\text{mm}\times10\,\text{mm}$ side and has 1000 turns and the magnet provides a constant flux density of 0.3 T, find the torque on the coil for a current of $10\,\text{mA}$.

SOLUTION

Given $a = b = 10\,\text{mm} = 10^{-2}\,\text{m}$, $I = 10\times10^{-3}\,\text{A}$, $N = 1000$ and $B = 0.3$ T.

Area of the rectangular coil is $A = a\times b = 10^{-4}\,\text{m}^2$.

The dipole moment for N turns is

$$m = NIA = 1000\times10^{-2}\times10^{-4} = 10^{-3}\,\text{A}\cdot\text{m}^2$$

The magnitude of torque on a rectangular loop is

$$T = mB = 0.3\times10^{-3} = 0.3\,\text{mN}\cdot\text{m}$$

EXAMPLE 5.32

Find the maximum torque on an orbiting charged particle if the charge is 1.602×10^{-19} C, the circular path has a radius of 1×10^{-10} m, the angular velocity is 2×10^{16} rad/s and $B = 0.4 \times 10^{-3}$ T.

SOLUTION

Given $Q = 1.602 \times 10^{-19}$ C, $\rho = 1 \times 10^{-10}$ m, $\omega = 2 \times 10^{16}$ rad/s and $B = 0.4 \times 10^{-3}$ T.

The orbiting charge has a magnetic moment

$$\vec{m} = \frac{\omega}{2\pi} Q A \vec{a}_n = \frac{2 \times 10^{16}}{2\pi} \left(1.602 \times 10^{-19}\right) \pi \left(1 \times 10^{-10}\right)^2 \vec{a}_n$$

$$= 1.602 \times 10^{-23} \vec{a}_n \, \text{A} \cdot \text{m}^2$$

The torque will be maximum when $\vec{a}_n$ is normal to $\vec{B}$.

Therefore, $T_{\text{max}} = mB = \left(1.602 \times 10^{-23}\right)\left(0.4 \times 10^{-3}\right) = 6.41 \times 10^{-27} \, \text{N} \cdot \text{m}$

EXAMPLE 5.33

A rectangular coil carrying a current of 5 A is placed in the magnetic field of flux density $\vec{B} = 0.3\left(\vec{a}_x + \vec{a}_y\right)$ Wb/m^2. The coil is lying in the yz-plane and has dimensions 0.8 m $\times 0.4$ m. Find the torque on the coil.

SOLUTION

Given $I = 5$ A, $\vec{B} = 0.3\left(\vec{a}_x + \vec{a}_y\right)$ Wb/m^2 and area, $\vec{A} = \left(0.8 \times 0.4\right)\vec{a}_x = 0.32\vec{a}_x \, \text{m}^2$.

The torque on the coil is

$$\vec{T} = \vec{m} \times \vec{B} = I\vec{A} \times \vec{B}$$

$$= 5\left(0.32\vec{a}_x\right) \times 0.3\left(\vec{a}_x + \vec{a}_y\right)$$

$$= 5\left(0.32\right)\left(0.3\right)\vec{a}_z = 0.48\vec{a}_z \, \text{N} \cdot \text{m}$$

EXAMPLE 5.34

A loop with dimensions 3 m $\times 4$ m lies in the xy-plane with a uniform field $\vec{B} = -0.6\vec{a}_y + 0.8\vec{a}_z$ T. The loop current is 12 mA. Find the torque on the loop.

SOLUTION

Given $\vec{B} = -0.6\vec{a}_y + 0.8\vec{a}_z$ T, area $\vec{A} = \left(3 \times 4\right)\vec{a}_z = 12\vec{a}_z \, \text{m}^2$ and $I = 12 \times 10^{-3}$ A.

The torque on the loop is

$$\vec{T} = I\vec{A} \times \vec{B} = 12 \times 10^{-3}\left(12\vec{a}_z\right) \times \left(-0.6\vec{a}_y + 0.8\vec{a}_z\right)$$

$$= 144\left(-0.6\right)\left(-\vec{a}_x\right) \times 10^{-3} = 86.4\vec{a}_x \, \text{mN} \cdot \text{m}$$

EXAMPLE 5.35

A rectangular current loop in the $z = 0$ plane has corners at $(0,0,0)$, $(1,0,0)$, $(1,2,0)$ and $(0,2,0)$. The loop carries a current of 5 A. Find the total force on the loop produced by the magnetic field of flux density $\vec{B} = 5\vec{a}_x + 2\vec{a}_y - 4\vec{a}_z$ Wb/m^2.

SOLUTION

Given magnetic flux density $\vec{B} = 5\vec{a}_x + 2\vec{a}_y - 4\vec{a}_z\,\mathrm{Wb/m^2}$ and $I = 5\,\mathrm{A}$. Figure E5.35 shows a rectangular current loop carrying a current.

Here, the force on side 1 is

$$\vec{F}_1 = \int I d\vec{l} \times \vec{B} = 5\int_0^1 (dx\vec{a}_x) \times (5\vec{a}_x + 2\vec{a}_y - 4\vec{a}_z)$$

$$= 5\int_0^1 (2\vec{a}_z + 4\vec{a}_y)\,dx = (20\vec{a}_y + 10\vec{a}_z)\ \mathrm{N}$$

Similarly, the force on side 3 is

$$\vec{F}_3 = -(20\vec{a}_y + 10\vec{a}_z)\ \mathrm{N}$$

Then, the force on side 2 is

$$\vec{F}_2 = 5\int_0^2 (dy\vec{a}_y) \times (5\vec{a}_x + 2\vec{a}_y - 4\vec{a}_z)$$

$$= 5\int_0^2 (-5\vec{a}_z - 4\vec{a}_x)\,dy = -(50\vec{a}_z + 40\vec{a}_x)\ \mathrm{N}$$

Similarly, the force on side 4 is

$$\vec{F}_4 = (50\vec{a}_z + 40\vec{a}_x)\ \mathrm{N}$$

Therefore, the total force is

$$\vec{F} = \vec{F}_1 + \vec{F}_2 + \vec{F}_3 + \vec{F}_4 = 0$$

The torque on the loop is

$$\vec{T} = \vec{m} \times \vec{B}$$

Here, the dipole moment $\vec{m} = IA = 5\,(1)\,(2)\vec{a}_z = 10\vec{a}_z\,\mathrm{A\cdot m^2}$.

Hence, $\quad \vec{T} = 10\vec{a}_z \times (5\vec{a}_x + 2\vec{a}_y - 4\vec{a}_z) = 50\vec{a}_y - 20\vec{a}_x\ \mathrm{N\cdot m}$

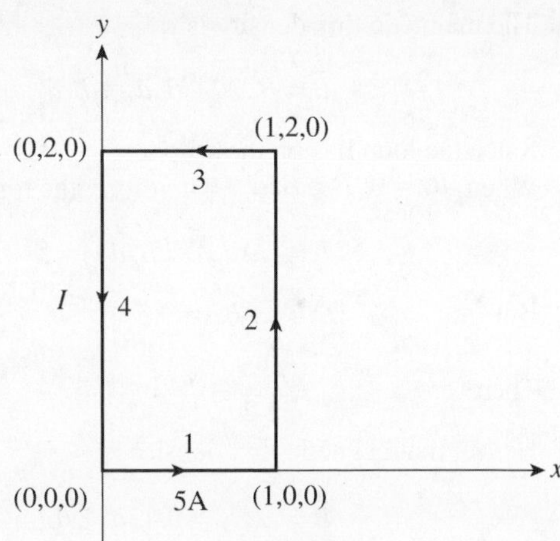

Figure E5.35

EXAMPLE 5.36

A current filament carrying $5\,\mathrm{A}$ is located along a rectangular path given by $x = \pm 0.2\,\mathrm{m}$, $y = \pm 0.3\,\mathrm{m}$. If uniform magnetic field of flux density $\vec{B}$ causes a torque on the loop of magnitude of $0.5\,\mathrm{N\cdot m}$, find $\vec{B}$ when $B_y = 0$.

SOLUTION

Given $I = 5\,\mathrm{A}$, $x = \pm 0.2\,\mathrm{m}$, $y = \pm 0.3\,\mathrm{m}$ and $T = 0.5\,\mathrm{N\cdot m}$.

The torque on a closed rectangular path is

$$\vec{T} = \vec{m} \times \vec{B}$$

where the magnetic moment $\vec{m} = IA\vec{a}_z\,\mathrm{A\cdot m^2}$ is along the z-axis.

Area of the loop is $A = 0.4 \times 0.6 = 0.24\,\mathrm{m^2}$

The magnetic flux density is

$$\vec{B} = B_x \vec{a}_x + B_y \vec{a}_y + B_z \vec{a}_z$$

Since the loop lies on the xy-plane, $B_z = 0$.
When $B_y = 0$, $\vec{B} = B_x \vec{a}_x$. Therefore, the torque is

$$\vec{T} = \left(IA\vec{a}_z\right) \times \left(B_x \vec{a}_x\right) = 5\left(0.24\vec{a}_z\right) \times B_x \vec{a}_x = 1.2 B_x \vec{a}_y$$

But

$$|T| = 1.2 B_x = 0.5$$

Therefore,

$$B_x = \frac{0.5}{1.2} = 0.42$$

Hence, the magnetic flux density is

$$\vec{B} = B_x \vec{a}_x = 0.42\vec{a}_x \ \text{Wb/m}^2$$

EXAMPLE 5.37

Prove that the force on a closed filamentary circuit in a uniform magnetic field is zero.

SOLUTION

The force exerted on a closed current element in a magnetic flux density $\vec{B}$ is

$$\vec{F} = \oint_l I \, d\vec{l} \times \vec{B} = -\oint_l \vec{B} \times I \, d\vec{l}$$

Assume that the magnetic flux intensity is uniform throughout the field. Then, the force is

$$\vec{F} = -I\vec{B} \times \oint_l d\vec{l}$$

Since the closed line integral in a uniform field is zero, i.e., $\oint_l d\vec{l} = 0$, the force becomes

$$\vec{F} = -I\vec{B} \times 0 = 0$$

Therefore, the force on a closed current circuit in a uniform magnetic field is zero.

EXAMPLE 5.38

Determine the torque about the y-axis for the two conductors of length l, separated by a fixed distance w, in the uniform field of flux density $\vec{B}$ shown in Figure E5.38.

SOLUTION

As shown in Figure E5.38, the conductor 1 experiences the force of

$$\vec{F}_1 = I\vec{l} \times \vec{B} = Il\vec{a}_y \times B\vec{a}_x = BIl\left(-\vec{a}_z\right)$$

Therefore, the torque is

$$\vec{T}_1 = \vec{d} \times \vec{F} = \frac{w}{2}\left(-\vec{a}_x\right) \times BIl\left(-\vec{a}_z\right) = BIl\frac{w}{2}\left(-\vec{a}_y\right)$$

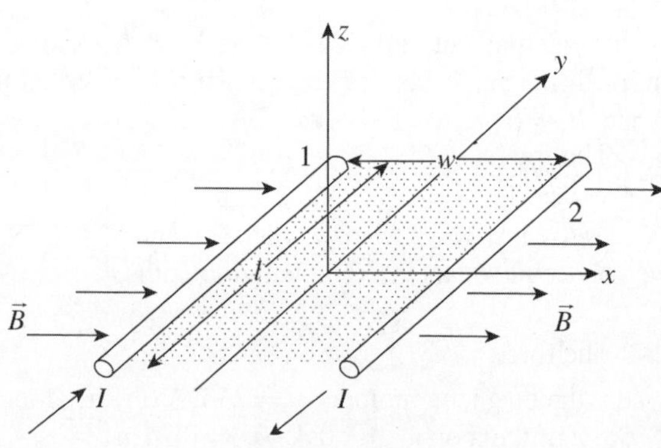

Figure E5.38

Similarly, the force on conductor 2 also results in same torque i.e., $\vec{T}_2 = BIl\dfrac{w}{2}\left(-\vec{a}_y\right)$.

Therefore, $\vec{T} = \vec{T}_1 + \vec{T}_2 = BIlw\left(-\vec{a}_y\right)\,\text{N}\cdot\text{m}$ ☐

EXAMPLE 5.39

A rectangular loop in the xy-plane with sides b_1 and b_2 carrying a current I lies in a uniform magnetic field of flux density $\vec{B} = B_x\vec{a}_x + B_y\vec{a}_y + B_z\vec{a}_z$ Wb/m^2. Determine the force and torque on the loop.

SOLUTION

Assume a rectangular loop is placed in the xy-plane with sides b_1 and b_2 as shown in Figure E5.39.

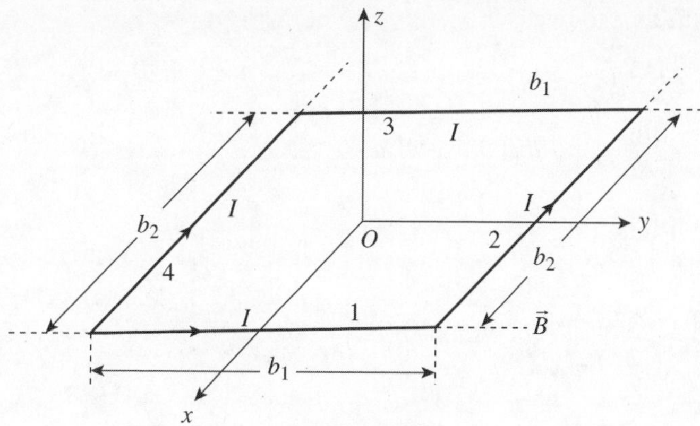

Figure E5.39

Here, the length of sides 1 and 3 is b_1 and both these sides are parallel to y-axis. The length of sides 2 and 4 is b_2 and both these sides are parallel to x-axis. The origin is at the center of the loop.

The force acting on side 1 is

$$\vec{F}_1 = Id\vec{l}_1 \times \vec{B} = I\left(b_1\vec{a}_y\right)\times\left(B_x\vec{a}_x + B_y\vec{a}_y + B_z\vec{a}_z\right)$$

$$= Ib_1\left(-B_x\vec{a}_z + B_z\vec{a}_x\right)$$

$$= Ib_1\left(B_z\vec{a}_x - B_x\vec{a}_z\right) \tag{1}$$

The force acting on side 2 is

$$\vec{F}_2 = Id\vec{l}_2 \times \vec{B} = I\left(-b_2\vec{a}_x\right)\times\left(B_x\vec{a}_x + B_y\vec{a}_y + B_z\vec{a}_z\right)$$

$$= Ib_2\left(B_z\vec{a}_y - B_y\vec{a}_z\right) \tag{2}$$

The force acting on side 3 is

$$\vec{F}_3 = Id\vec{l}_3 \times \vec{B} = I\left(-b_1\vec{a}_y\right)\times\left(B_x\vec{a}_x + B_y\vec{a}_y + B_z\vec{a}_z\right)$$

$$= Ib_1\left(-B_z\vec{a}_x + B_x\vec{a}_z\right) = -\vec{F}_1 \tag{3}$$

The force acting on side 4 is

$$\vec{F}_4 = Id\vec{l}_4 \times \vec{B} = I\left(b_2\vec{a}_x\right) \times \left(B_x\vec{a}_x + B_y\vec{a}_y + B_z\vec{a}_z\right)$$

$$= Ib_2\left(-B_z\vec{a}_y + B_y\vec{a}_z\right) = -\vec{F}_2 \tag{4}$$

Adding Eqs $(1),(2),(3)$ and (4), we get the total force on the loop of sides b_1 and b_2 is

$$\vec{F} = \vec{F}_1 + \vec{F}_2 + \vec{F}_3 + \vec{F}_4$$

$$= \vec{F}_1 + \vec{F}_2 - \vec{F}_1 - \vec{F}_2$$

$$= 0$$

The total torque on the rectangular loop can be obtained by choosing the origin of the torque at the center of the loop. Therefore, the total torque is

$$\vec{T} = \vec{T}_1 + \vec{T}_2 + \vec{T}_3 + \vec{T}_4$$

$$\vec{T}_1 = \vec{d}_1 \times \vec{F}_1 = \left(\frac{b_2}{2}\vec{a}_x\right) \times \left[Ib_1\left(B_z\vec{a}_x - B_x\vec{a}_z\right)\right]$$

$$= I\left(\frac{b_1b_2}{2}\right)\left(B_x\vec{a}_y\right) \tag{5}$$

$$\vec{T}_2 = \vec{d}_2 \times \vec{F}_2 = \left(\frac{b_1}{2}\vec{a}_y\right) \times \left[Ib_2\left(B_z\vec{a}_y - B_y\vec{a}_z\right)\right]$$

$$= I\left(\frac{b_1b_2}{2}\right)\left(-B_y\vec{a}_x\right) \tag{6}$$

$$\vec{T}_3 = \vec{d}_3 \times \vec{F}_3 = \left(-\frac{b_2}{2}\vec{a}_x\right) \times \left[Ib_1\left(-B_z\vec{a}_x + B_x\vec{a}_z\right)\right]$$

$$= I\left(\frac{b_1b_2}{2}\right)\left(B_x\vec{a}_y\right) = \vec{T}_1 \tag{7}$$

$$\vec{T}_4 = \vec{d}_4 \times \vec{F}_4 = \left(-\frac{b_1}{2}\vec{a}_y\right) \times \left[Ib_2\left(-B_z\vec{a}_y + B_y\vec{a}_z\right)\right]$$

$$= I\left(\frac{b_1b_2}{2}\right)\left(-B_y\vec{a}_x\right) = \vec{T}_2 \tag{8}$$

Adding Eqs. $(5),(6),(7)$ and (8), we get the total torque as

$$\vec{T} = \vec{T}_1 + \vec{T}_2 + \vec{T}_3 + \vec{T}_4$$

$$= \vec{T}_1 + \vec{T}_2 + \vec{T}_1 + \vec{T}_2 = 2\left(\vec{T}_1 + \vec{T}_2\right)$$

$$= 2\left[I\left(\frac{b_1b_2}{2}\right)\left(B_x\vec{a}_y\right) + I\left(\frac{b_1b_2}{2}\right)\left(-B_y\vec{a}_x\right)\right]$$

$$= Ib_1b_2\left(-B_y\vec{a}_x + B_x\vec{a}_y\right)\text{N}\cdot\text{m}$$

The total torque can also be obtained by

$$\vec{T} = I\left(d\vec{s}\right) \times \vec{B}$$

Since the loop is in xy-plane with dimensions of sides as b_1 and b_2, the differential surface area of the loop is $d\vec{s} = \left(b_1 b_2\right)\vec{a}_z$.

Therefore,
$$\vec{T} = I\left(b_1 b_2 \vec{a}_z\right) \times \left(B_x \vec{a}_x + B_y \vec{a}_y + B_z \vec{a}_z\right)$$
$$= I b_1 b_2 \left(-B_y \vec{a}_x + B_x \vec{a}_y\right) \mathrm{N \cdot m}$$

5.6 MAGNETIC DIPOLE

A small filamentary loop carrying a current I or a permanent bar magnet is known as a magnetic dipole. The magnetic field strength $\vec{H}$ produced by a magnetic dipole is determined by considering a circular loop of radius a carrying current I as shown in Figure 5.4.

The magnetic vector potential at $P\left(r,\theta,\phi\right)$ is

$$\vec{A} = \frac{\mu I}{4\pi} \oint_l \frac{d\vec{l}}{R}$$

Here, for a circular loop, $d\vec{l} = a\,d\phi\,\vec{a}_\phi$, and $\vec{a}_\phi$ at $d\vec{l}$ is not the same as $\vec{a}_\phi$ at point $P(r,\theta,\phi)$. Since $\vec{a}_\phi = -\sin\phi\,\vec{a}_x + \cos\phi\,\vec{a}_y$ in spherical coordinates, we can write $d\vec{l} = a\,d\phi\left(-\sin\phi\,\vec{a}_x + \cos\phi\,\vec{a}_y\right)$. For every current element $I d\vec{l}$, there is a corresponding differential current element located diametrically opposite on the y-axis. The contribution of $I d\vec{l}$ to vector magnetic potential $\vec{A}$ will be only in the $-\vec{a}_x$

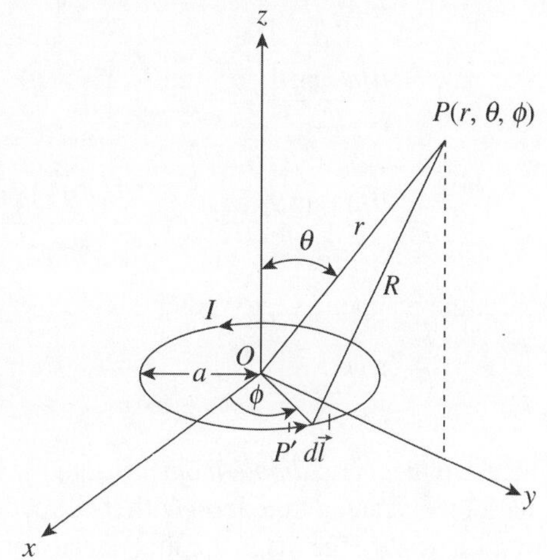

Figure 5.4 *Magnetic field due to circular loop*

direction. However, the contribution of $I d\vec{l}$ to $\vec{A}$ in the $\vec{a}_y$ direction gets cancelled. Therefore, the vector magnetic potential is

$$\vec{A} = \frac{\mu I}{4\pi} \int_0^{2\pi} \frac{a\sin\phi}{R}\,d\phi\left(-\vec{a}_x\right)$$

The above equation can also be written along $\vec{a}_\phi$ direction as

$$\vec{A} = \frac{\mu I}{2\pi} \int_{-\pi/2}^{\pi/2} \frac{a\sin\phi}{R}\,d\phi\,\vec{a}_\phi \tag{5.28}$$

Applying law of cosines to the triangle OPP', we have

$$R^2 = r^2 + a^2 - 2ar\sin\theta\sin\phi$$

or
$$R = \left[r^2 + a^2 - 2ar\sin\theta\sin\phi\right]^{1/2}$$

If the point P is far away from the radius of the loop, i.e., $r \gg a$, then

$$\frac{1}{R} = \left[r^2 + a^2 - 2ar\sin\theta\sin\phi \right]^{-1/2} \approx \frac{1}{r}\left(1 - \frac{2a\sin\theta\sin\phi}{r} \right)^{-1/2} \approx \frac{1}{r}\left(1 + \frac{a\sin\theta\sin\phi}{r} \right)$$

Substituting the above expression in Eq. (5.28), we get

$$\vec{A} = \frac{\mu I a}{2\pi r} \int_{-\pi/2}^{\pi/2} \left(1 + \frac{a\sin\theta\sin\phi}{r} \right) \sin\phi\, d\phi\, \vec{a}_\phi$$

$$= \frac{\mu I a}{2\pi r}\left[\int_{-\pi/2}^{\pi/2} \sin\phi\, d\phi + \int_{-\pi/2}^{\pi/2} \frac{a\sin\theta\sin^2\phi}{r}\, d\phi \right] \vec{a}_\phi$$

$$= \frac{\mu I a^2 \sin\theta}{2\pi r^2}\left[\int_{-\pi/2}^{\pi/2} \sin^2\phi\, d\phi \right] \vec{a}_\phi$$

$$= \frac{\mu I a^2 \sin\theta}{2\pi r^2}\left[\frac{\phi}{2} - \frac{\sin 2\phi}{4} \right]_{-\pi/2}^{\pi/2} \vec{a}_\phi \qquad \left(\text{since } \int \sin^2\phi\, d\phi = \frac{\phi}{2} - \frac{\sin 2\phi}{4} \right)$$

$$= \frac{\mu I a^2 \sin\theta}{2\pi r^2} \times \frac{\pi}{2}\, \vec{a}_\phi = \frac{\mu I \left(\pi a^2 \right) \sin\theta}{4\pi r^2}\, \vec{a}_\phi$$

Hence, the magnetic vector potential is

$$\vec{A} = \frac{\mu\left(\vec{m} \times \vec{a}_r \right)}{4\pi r^2} \tag{5.29}$$

where the *magnetic dipole moment* is $\vec{m} = IA\vec{a}_n = I\left(\pi a^2 \right)\vec{a}_z$. It is the product of current flowing in the circular loop and area of the loop with its direction normal to the loop.

From Eq. (5.29), the magnetic flux density produced by the magnetic dipole can be obtained as

$$\vec{B} = \nabla \times \vec{A} = \frac{1}{r^2\sin\theta}\begin{vmatrix} \vec{a}_r & r\vec{a}_\theta & r\sin\theta\,\vec{a}_\phi \\ \dfrac{\partial}{\partial r} & \dfrac{\partial}{\partial \theta} & \dfrac{\partial}{\partial \phi} \\ 0 & 0 & r\sin\theta\left[\dfrac{\mu I\left(\pi a^2 \right)\sin\theta}{4\pi r^2} \right] \end{vmatrix}$$

$$= \left(\frac{1}{r\sin\theta} \right)\frac{\partial}{\partial \theta}\left(\sin\theta\, \frac{\mu I\left(\pi a^2 \right)\sin\theta}{4\pi r^2} \right)\vec{a}_r - \left(\frac{1}{r} \right)\frac{\partial}{\partial r}\left(r\, \frac{\mu I\left(\pi a^2 \right)\sin\theta}{4\pi r^2} \right)\vec{a}_\theta$$

$$= \frac{\mu I\left(\pi a^2 \right)\cos\theta}{2\pi r^3}\vec{a}_r + \frac{\mu I\left(\pi a^2 \right)\sin\theta}{4\pi r^3}\vec{a}_\theta$$

Therefore, the magnetic flux density is

$$\vec{B} = \frac{\mu I\left(\pi a^2\right)}{4\pi r^3}\left(2\cos\theta\,\vec{a}_r + \sin\theta\,\vec{a}_\theta\right) = \frac{\mu m}{4\pi r^3}\left(2\cos\theta\,\vec{a}_r + \sin\theta\,\vec{a}_\theta\right)$$

Since $\vec{B} = \mu\vec{H}$, the magnetic field strength $\vec{H}$ is

$$\vec{H} = \frac{m}{4\pi r^3}\left(2\cos\theta\,\vec{a}_r + \sin\theta\,\vec{a}_\theta\right) \tag{5.30}$$

The magnetic field lines of a magnetic dipole are similar to the magnetic field pattern of a filamentary conductor carrying current I and bar magnet shown in Figures 5.5(a) and (b).

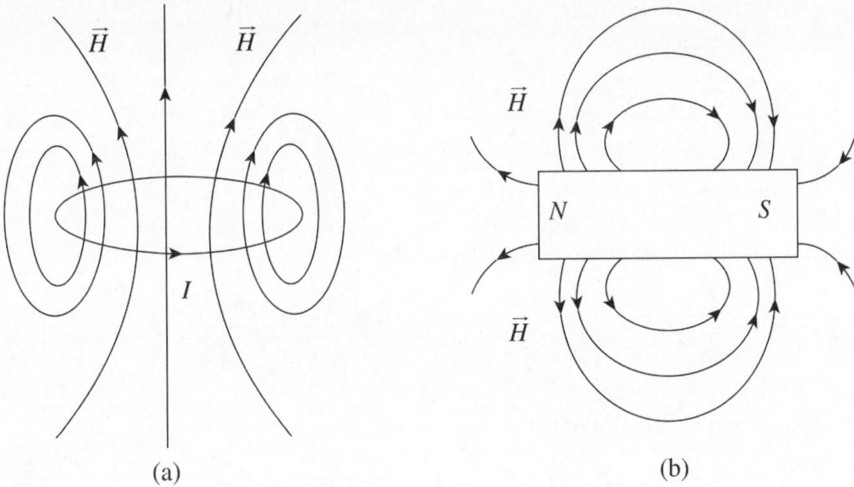

Figure 5.5 *Magnetic field lines in (a) filamentary conductor and (b) bar magnet*

EXAMPLE 5.40

A small circular loop of radius $10\,\text{cm}$ is centered at the origin and placed on the $z = 0$ plane. If the loop carries a current of $1\,\text{A}$ along $\vec{a}_\phi$, calculate (i) the magnetic moment of the loop (ii) the magnetic field strength at $(2,2,2)$ and (iii) the magnetic flux density at $(-6,8,10)$.

SOLUTION

Given $I = 1\,\text{A}$ and $\rho = 10\,\text{cm}$.

(i) The magnetic moment is

$$\vec{m} = IA\vec{a}_n = \pi\rho^2\vec{a}_n = \pi\left(0.1\right)^2\vec{a}_n = 0.01\pi\vec{a}_n\,\text{A}\cdot\text{m}^2$$

(ii) Transforming the point $(2,2,2)$ from rectangular coordinates into spherical coordinates, we have

$$r = \sqrt{2^2 + 2^2 + 2^2} = 2\sqrt{3}$$

$$\theta = \tan^{-1}\left(\frac{\sqrt{2^2 + 2^2}}{2}\right) = \tan^{-1}\left(\sqrt{2}\right) = 54.736°$$

Here, $\cos\theta = \dfrac{1}{\sqrt{3}}$ and $\sin\theta = \sqrt{\dfrac{2}{3}}$

From Eq. (5.30), the magnetic field strength due to a circular loop is

$$\vec{H} = \frac{m}{4\pi\, r^3}\left(2\cos\theta\,\vec{a}_r + \sin\theta\,\vec{a}_\theta\right) = \frac{0.01\pi}{4\pi\left(2\sqrt{3}\right)^3}\left(\frac{2}{\sqrt{3}}\,\vec{a}_r + \sqrt{\frac{2}{3}}\,\vec{a}_\theta\right)$$

$$= \left(6.9\vec{a}_r + 4.89\vec{a}_\theta\right)\times 10^{-5}\,\text{A/m}$$

(*iii*) Transforming the point $\left(-6,8,10\right)$ from rectangular coordinates to spherical coordinates, we have

$$r = \sqrt{6^2 + 8^2 + 10^2} = 10\sqrt{2}$$

$$\theta = \tan^{-1}\left(\frac{\sqrt{6^2 + 8^2}}{10}\right) = \tan^{-1}\left(1\right) = 45°$$

Here, $\cos\theta = \sin\theta = \dfrac{1}{\sqrt{2}}$

The magnetic flux density at point $\left(-6,8,10\right)$ is

$$\vec{B} = \mu\vec{H} = \frac{m\mu_0\mu_r}{4\pi r^3}\left(2\cos\theta\,\vec{a}_r + \sin\theta\,\vec{a}_\theta\right) = \frac{0.01\pi\times 4\pi\times 10^{-7}}{4\pi\left(10\sqrt{2}\right)^3}\left(\frac{2}{\sqrt{2}}\,\vec{a}_r + \frac{1}{\sqrt{2}}\,\vec{a}_\theta\right)$$

$$= \left(1.57\,\vec{a}_r + 0.79\,\vec{a}_\theta\right)\,\text{pWb/m}^2$$

5.7 NATURE AND CLASSIFICATION OF MAGNETIC MATERIALS

The magnetic materials are classified as either magnetic or non-magnetic based on their strong magnetic properties. However, the magnetic materials with weak magnetic properties are also widely used in some applications. Hence, an exact nature and classification of magnetic materials are essential as given in the following six groups.

(i) Diamagnetic Materials

These include Bismuth, Antimony, Copper, Zinc, Silicon, Germanium, Graphite, Sulphar, Diamond, Sodium Chloride, Hydrogen, Helium, Gold, Silver, Mercury and Lead. In diamagnetic material, the permanent magnetic moment of each atom is zero. The relative permeability is less than 1. The susceptibility χ_m is independent of temperature and negative, and is of the order of -10^{-5} for most diamagnetic materials. They become weakly magnetized but in the opposite direction from the magnetizing field. Perfect diamagnetism occurs ($\chi_m = -1$ or $\mu_r = 0$ and $B = 0$) in some materials called superconductors at temperatures nearer to absolute zero and hence, superconductors will not have magnetic fields.

Diamagnetism occurs in those substances whose atoms consist of an even number of electrons. The electrons of such atoms are paired. The electrons in each pair have orbital motions as well as spin motions in opposite sense. The resultant magnetic dipole moment of the atom is thus zero. Hence, when such a substance is placed in a magnetic field, the field does not tend to align the atoms (dipoles) of the substance. The magnetic field, however, modifies the motion of the electron in orbits that are equivalent to tiny current-loops. The electron moves in a direction so as to produce a magnetic field in same direction as the external field is slowed down, while the other is accelerated. The electron pair and hence, the atoms acquire an effective magnetic dipole moment which is opposite to the applied field. Hence, for diamagnetic materials, the magnetic moment is opposite to H. Hence, the susceptibility χ_m of diamagnetic substance is negative and is very small.

(ii) Paramagnetic Materials

In paramagnetic materials, the magnetic fields associated with orbiting and spinning electrons do not cancel out. There is a net intrinsic moment in it. The molecules in it behave like little magnets. When such a substance is placed in an external field, it will turn and line up with its axis parallel to the external field. The magnetic moment m and the magnetic field H are in same direction and hence, the susceptibility χ_m is positive.

When a paramagnetic substance is heated, the thermal agitation of its atoms increases and hence, the alignment of the dipole becomes disturbed. Hence, the magnetization of paramagnetic substances decreases as the temperature increases. In this case, susceptibility is inversely proportional to temperature i.e., $\chi_m \alpha \dfrac{1}{T}$. For most paramagnetic materials like air, oxygen, platinum, tungsten, potassium, erbium chloride, neodymium oxide and yttrium oxide χ_m is of the order of 10^{-5} to 10^{-3}. The diamagnetic and paramagnetic materials with $\mu_r \approx 1$ are linear and non-magnetic.

(iii) Ferromagnetic Materials

The other four classes of magnetic materials are ferromagnetic, anti-ferromagnetic, ferrimagnetic and super paramagnetic which have strong atomic moments. Ferromagnetic materials like Iron, Cobalt, Nickel and their alloys are very strongly magnetic. A ferromagnet has a spontaneous large magnetic moment i.e., a magnetic moment even in zero applied fields. The atoms (or molecules) of ferromagnetic materials have a net intrinsic magnetic dipole moment, which is primarily due to the spin of the electrons.

The interaction between the neighbouring atomic magnetic dipoles is very strong. It is called spin exchange interaction and is present even in the absence of an external magnetic field. The exchange interaction aligns the neighboring magnetic dipole moments parallel to one another and this spreads over a small finite volume of the bulk. This small volume of the bulk is called domain. All magnetic moments within a domain will point in the same direction, resulting in a large magnetic moment. Thus, a bulk material consists of many domains. The domains are oriented in different directions. The total magnetic moment of a sample of the substances is the vector sum of the magnetic moments of different domains.

In an unmagnetized piece of ferromagnetic material, the magnetic moment of the domains themselves is not aligned. When an external field is applied to ferromagnetic material, the domains aligned with the field increases in size at the expense of the others. In a very strong field, all the domains are lined up in the direction of the field and provide the highly observed magnetism.

If a ferromagnetic material is heated to a high temperature, thermal vibrations may become strong enough to offset the alignment within a domain. At such temperature, the material loses its ferromagnetic property and behaves like a paramagnetic material. The critical temperature above which a ferromagnetic material looses it ferromagnetic characteristics and becomes paramagnet is called curie temperature.

Ferromagnetic materials are always non-linear and magnetic except when their temperatures are above curie temperature. Some alloys of non-ferromagnetic metals are ferromagnetic, such as bismuth-manganese and copper-manganese-tin.

(iv) Antiferromagnetic Materials

These materials include manganese oxide (MnO), nickel oxide (NiO), ferrous sulfide (FeS) and cobalt chloride ($CoCl_2$). Anti-ferromagnetism is present at low temperatures i.e., below room temperature. In these materials, the forces between adjacent atoms cause the atomic moments to line up in an anti-parallel fashion and the net magnetic moment is zero. These materials will be affected slightly by the presence of an external magnetic field.

(v) Ferrimagnetic Materials

These materials are ferrites such as iron oxide magnetite (Fe_3O_4), Nickel-Zinc ferrite ($Ni_{0.5}\,Zn_{0.5}\,Fe_2O_4$) and Nickel ferrite ($NiFe_2O_4$) in which the conductivity is low. They have greater resistance than the ferromagnetic materials. Ferrimagnetism disappears above the Curie temperature. The ferrimagnetic materials show an anti-parallel alignment of adjacent atomic moments, but the moments are not equal and hence, there will be a good response to an external magnetic field.

(vi) Superparamagnetic materials

They include magnetic tape used in audio or video tape recorders. An assembly of ferromagnetic substances in a non-ferromagnetic matrix results in superparamagnetic materials. There exist domains within the individual particles of superparamagnetic materials. But these domain walls cannot penetrate the intervening matrix material to the adjacent particle.

5.7.1 Hysteresis Loop

The ferromagnetic material can be tested by applying increasing values of H and measuring the corresponding values of magnetic flux density B. The $B-H$ curves or magnetization curves for a few ferromagnetic materials are shown in Figures 5.6(a) and (b). Using these $B-H$ curves and the relation $\mu_r = \dfrac{B}{\mu_0 H}$, the relative permeability μ_r can be determined. For silicon steel, μ_r vs H is extremely non-linear as shown in Figure 5.6(c).

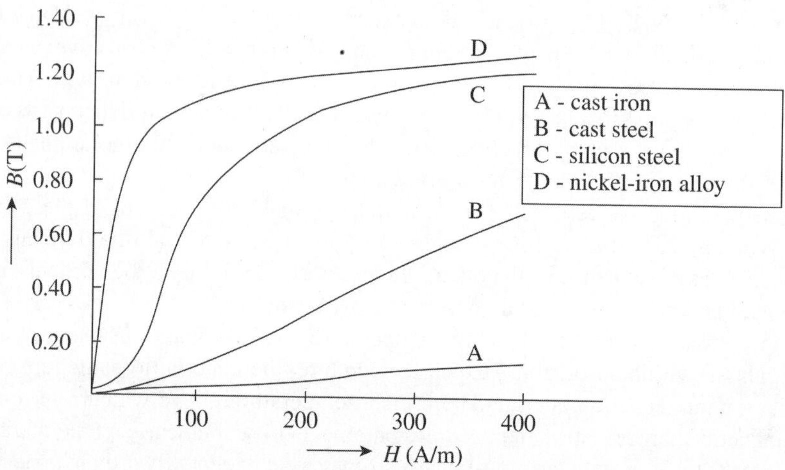

Figure 5.6 *(a) Magnetization (B-H) curve*

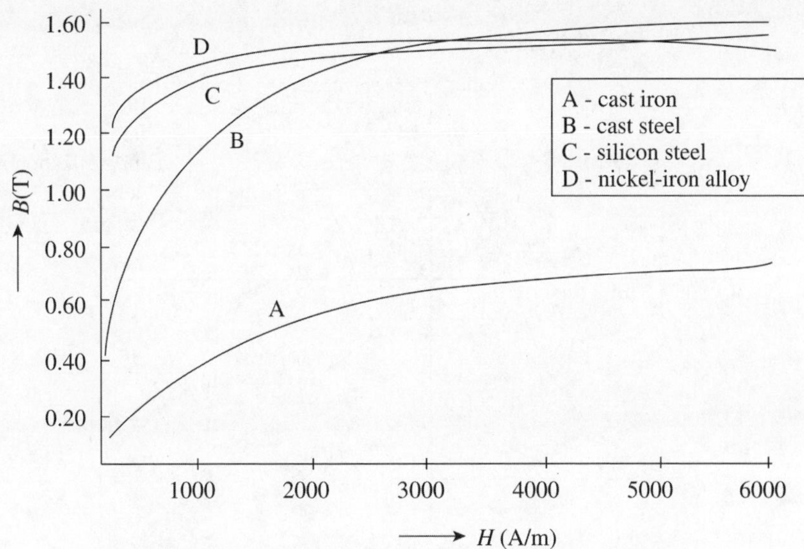

Figure 5.6 *(b) Magnetization (B-H) curve as a function of H*

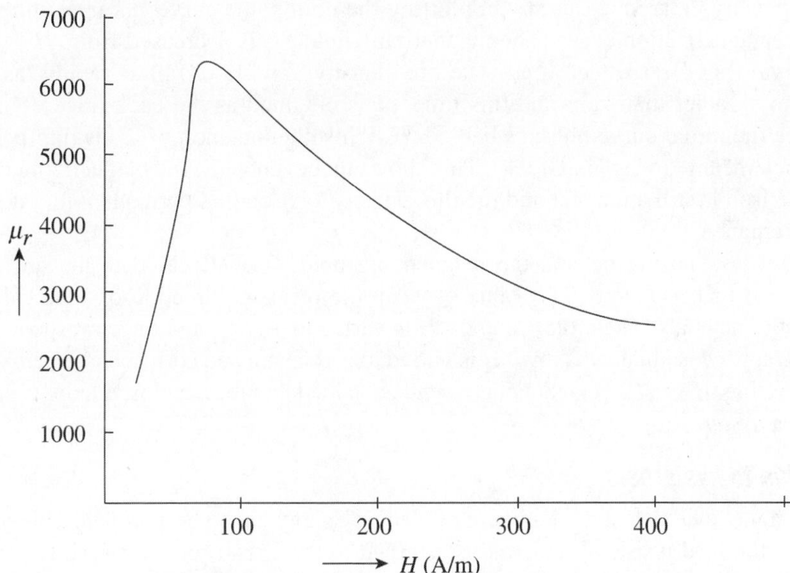

Figure 5.6 *(c) μ_r vs H for silicon steel*

If a ferromagnetic material is in completely demagnetized state, it is made to undergo through a cycle of magnetization in which H is increased from zero to a maximum, then decreases to zero, then reversed and again taken to $-H_{max}$ and finally brought back to zero. The variation of magnetic flux density B with respect to magnetic field intensity H can be represented by a closed Hysteresis loop as shown in Figure 5.7.

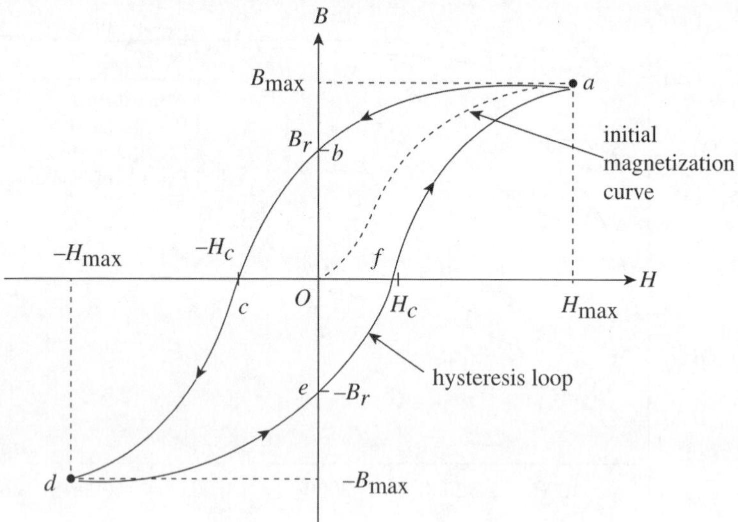

Figure 5.7 *Hysteresis Loop*

When the magnetizing field H is increased from zero to maximum, the corresponding values of magnetic flux density B are measured. On plotting the points, the curve oa is obtained and this is the virgin or initial magnetization curve. The magnetizing field H is decreased from H_{max} to zero and the corresponding values of B are measured. The flux density B will not fall as rapidly as it increases and will fall back to b rather than zero and this time ab is obtained as the back trace of oa i.e., the curve does not retrace the initial curve but lags behind H. This phenomenon of B lagging behind H is called hysteresis (which means "to lag" in Greek). This shows that even when the magnetizing field is made zero or removed, the iron is still a magnet and the flux density ob is called permanent flux density or residual magnetism or remanence.

To reduce the residual magnetism, the magnetizing field H is increased in the negative direction to reach a point c to make B zero. The value of oc in the reversed direction of H is called coercivity of the ferromagnetic materials. Then, the value of H is varied to $-H_{max}$ and the corresponding value of B is measured and graph cd is obtained. Now, H is varied to zero again and corresponding curve de is obtained. By further increasing H to H_{max}, again curve efa is obtained and thus, a closed loop $abcdefa$ is obtained, which is called a *hysteresis loop.*

Energy loss due to hysteresis

To produce a magnetic field, a certain amount of electric energy has to be supplied. The energy is stored in free space when the field is established, and is returned to the circuit producing the energy when the field collapses. However, in ferromagnetic materials, all the energy supplied cannot be returned and a part of it is lost in the form of heat. If the magnetization is carried through a complete cycle, the energy lost can be shown to be proportional to the area of the hysteresis loop. The shape of $B-H$ curve depends upon the nature of the ferromagnetic materials.

Use of Hysteresis loop

The magnetic properties of different magnetic materials can be studied using Hysteresis loop. The shape of the hysteresis loops varies from one material to another. Some ferrites have an almost rectangular hysteresis loop and are used in digital computers as magnetic information storage devices. The hysteresis curves for soft iron and steel are shown in Figure 5.8.

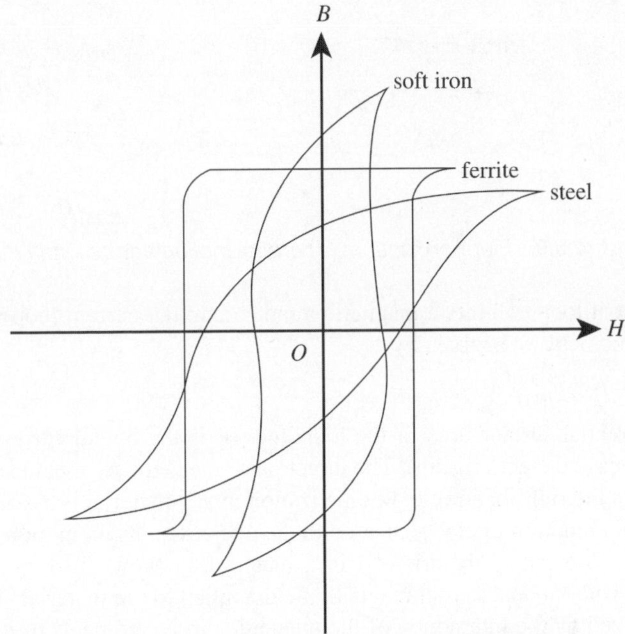

Figure 5.8　*Hysteresis curve for soft iron, ferrite and steel*

The materials used in electric generators, motors and transformers must have tall but narrow hysteresis loops so that the hysteresis losses are minimal. From the hysteresis loop, the following results are obtained.

(*i*)　The soft iron is characterized by high magnetic induction, high residual magnetism and small coercive field density. But the residual magnetism is removed by small reverse magnetic field. Materials like soft iron have narrow hysteresis loops.

(*ii*)　The steel has a lower magnetic induction, greater coercivity and small residual magnetism. Though the residual magnetism is small in steel, but is more permanent due to the large coercive field density. Hence, steel is said to possess higher retentivity than soft iron. Materials like steel have wide hysteresis loops.

(*iii*)　The area of the hysteresis loop for soft iron is smaller than that for steel. Hence, the energy lost per cycle is correspondingly less. Hence, soft iron is preferred to steel for cores of dynamos, transformers, etc., which are subjected to a large number of cycles so that the loss of energy may be minimum.

5.8　MAGNETIZATION AND PERMEABILITY

Any material is made up of atoms in which the electrons revolve in orbits around the nucleus as in Figure 5.9(a) and also rotates (spins) about their own axes as in Figure 5.9(b). The phenomenon of orbiting and spinning of electrons produce an internal magnetic field. This field is similar to the magnetic field produced by a current loop.

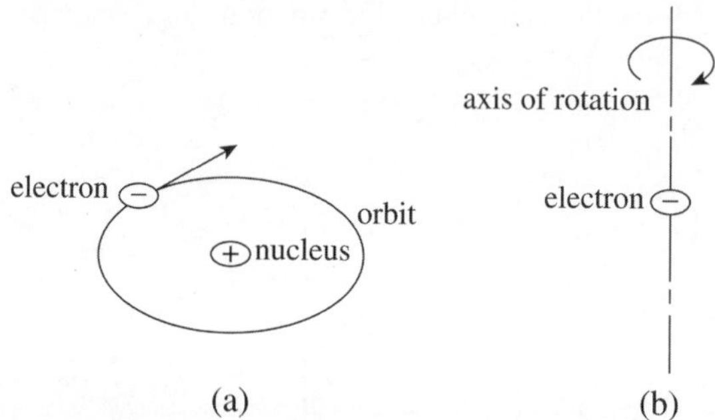

Figure 5.9 *Electron motion: (a) orbital motion and (b) spin motion*

The equivalent current loop exhibits a magnetic moment and the current loop is regarded as a magnetic dipole. The magnetic moment $\vec{m}$ is given by

$$\vec{m} = I_b \vec{ds} = I_b ds \vec{a}_n \tag{5.31}$$

where $\vec{ds}$ is the differential surface area of the loop and I_b is the bound current produced by the bound charges (orbital electrons and electron spin). The direction of magnetic moment is normal to the plane of the loop in accordance with the right-hand rule. Magnetization in any material is associated with atomic current loops generated by orbital motion of electrons around the nucleus and spin motion of electrons.

The dipole moments are randomly oriented in a material as shown in Figure 5.10(a). The magnetic dipole moment is zero without an external magnetic field applied to the material. The magnetic behavior of a material is characterized by the interaction of the magnetic dipole moments of its atoms with the external magnetic field. However, when such a material is kept in an external magnetic field shown in Figure 5.10(b), the random orientation of dipole moments disappears and they tend to align themselves in the direction of the applied field. As a result, the net magnetic moment is not zero.

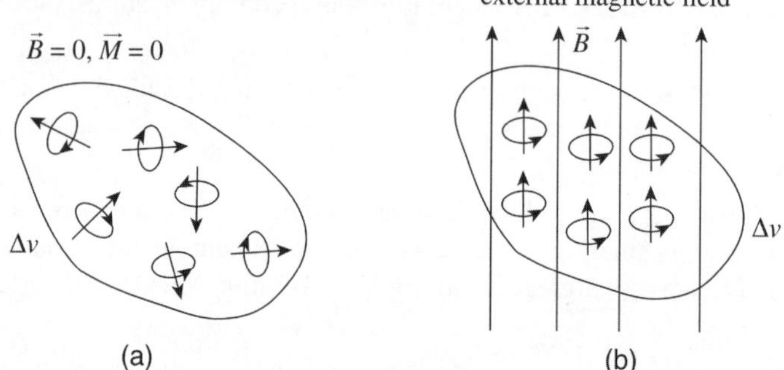

Figure 5.10 *Magnetic dipole moment in a differential volume Δv: (a) with no external field $\vec{B} = 0$ and (b) with external field applied*

If there are n magnetic dipoles in a given volume Δv, then the total magnetic dipole moment $\vec{m}_t$ is obtained by the vector sum as

$$\vec{m}_t = \sum_{k=1}^{n\Delta v} \vec{m}_k$$

The *magnetization* is defined as the magnetic dipole moment per unit volume as given by

$$\vec{M} = \underset{\Delta v \to 0}{Lt} \frac{1}{\Delta v} \sum_{k=1}^{n\Delta v} \vec{m}_k \tag{5.32}$$

Its unit is A/m.

Figure 5.11 shows an alignment of a magnetic dipole along a closed path and it is seen that the magnetic moment makes an angle θ with the element of path $\vec{dl}$. The magnetic moment $\vec{m}$ consists of a bound current I_b circulating about an area $\vec{ds}$.

To obtain magnetic moment making angle θ with $\vec{dl}$, it is necessary to define the differential volume in terms of differential surface area $\vec{ds}$ and differential length $\vec{dl}$. Therefore, the differential volume can be defined as $\vec{ds} \cdot \vec{dl}$ and there are $n\vec{ds} \cdot \vec{dl}$ magnetic dipoles in this small volume.

Under the influence of external magnetic field, random orientation changes to partial alignment of magnetic moments. The bound current, crossing the differential surface enclosed by the path, increases by I_b for each magnetic dipole. Therefore,

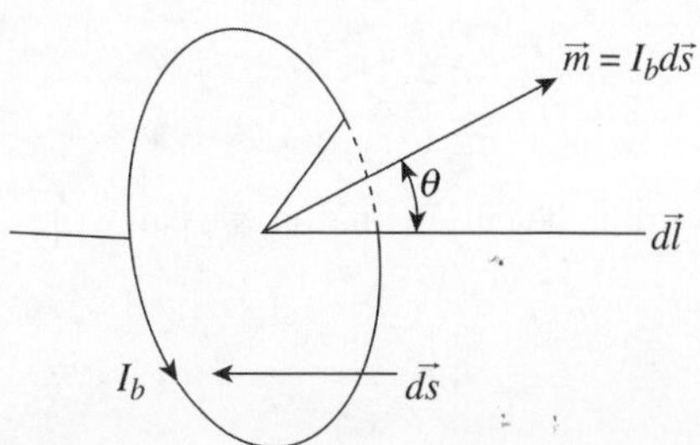

Figure 5.11 *Alignment of magnetic dipole moment due to external magnetic field*

$$dI_b = nI_b \vec{ds} \cdot \vec{dl} = \vec{M} \cdot \vec{dl}$$

where the magnetization is $\vec{M} = n\vec{m} = nI_b\vec{ds}$.

The total increase in bound current can be obtained by integrating the above equation over a closed path as given by

$$I_b = \oint \vec{M} \cdot \vec{dl} \tag{5.33}$$

The total current is the summation of bound current and free current. Representing Ampere's circuital law in terms of the total current, we have

$$I_T = I_b + I = \oint \vec{H} \cdot \vec{dl} \tag{5.34}$$

where I is the free current due to the free electrons. Since $\vec{B} = \mu_0 \vec{H}$ in free space, the total current becomes

$$I_T = \oint \frac{\vec{B}}{\mu_0} \cdot \vec{dl} \tag{5.35}$$

Using Eq. (5.33), Eq. (5.34) and Eq. (5.35), the free current enclosed by the path is

$$I = I_T - I_b = \oint \left(\frac{\vec{B}}{\mu_0} - \vec{M} \right) \cdot \vec{dl}$$

Comparing the above equation with Ampere's circuital law i.e., $I = \oint \vec{H} \cdot \vec{dl}$, we get

$$\vec{H} = \frac{\vec{B}}{\mu_0} - \vec{M}$$

or $\qquad \vec{B} = \mu_0 \left(\vec{H} + \vec{M} \right) \tag{5.36}$

Since, $\vec{B} = \mu_0 \vec{H}$ in free space, the magnetization $\vec{M}$ is zero. The relationship given in Eq. (5.36) is true for all the materials irrespective of the nature of the material whether it is linear or not.

The expressions for currents can also be defined in terms of current densities. Let $\vec{J}_T$ be the total current density, $\vec{J}_b$ be the bound current density and $\vec{J}$ be the free current density. Then, we can write the expressions for currents as

$$I_b = \int_s \vec{J}_b \cdot d\vec{s}$$

$$I_T = \int_s \vec{J}_T \cdot d\vec{s}$$

and $\qquad I = \int_s \vec{J} \cdot d\vec{s}$

From the curl definition, we can write

$$\nabla \times \vec{M} = \vec{J}_b$$

$$\nabla \times \frac{\vec{B}}{\mu_0} = \vec{J}_T$$

and $\qquad \nabla \times \vec{H} = \vec{J}$

For linear isotropic magnetic materials, $\vec{M}$ depends linearly on $\vec{H}$ such that

$$\vec{M} = \chi_m \vec{H} \tag{5.37}$$

where. χ_m is dimensionless quantity and is known as *magnetic susceptibility* of the medium. It is a measure of susceptibility or sensitivity of the material to a magnetic field. Substituting Eq. (5.37) in Eq. (5.36), we get

$$\vec{B} = \mu_0 \left(\vec{H} + \chi_m \vec{H} \right) = \mu_0 \left(1 + \chi_m \right) \vec{H} \tag{5.38}$$

For any magnetic material,

$$\vec{B} = \mu \vec{H} = \mu_0 \mu_r \vec{H} \tag{5.39}$$

Comparing Eq. (5.38) and Eq. (5.39), the relative permeability $\left(\mu_r \right)$ can be expressed in terms of magnetic susceptibility as

$$\mu_r = 1 + \chi_m = \frac{\mu}{\mu_0} \tag{5.40}$$

The quantity $\mu = \mu_0 \mu_r$ is called the *permeability* of the material. It is measured in henry/metre. But the relative permeability is a dimensionless quantity similar to the magnetic susceptibility. The ratio of the permeability of a given material to that of free space is known as the relative permeability of the material.

EXAMPLE 5.41

Find the permeability of the material whose magnetic susceptibility is 49.

SOLUTION

The relative permeability can be expressed in terms of magnetic susceptibility as

$$\mu_r = 1 + \chi_m = 1 + 49 = 50$$

Hence, the permeability of a material is

$$\mu = \mu_0 \mu_r = 4\pi \times 10^{-7} \times 50 = 62.8 \times 10^{-6} \text{ H/m}$$

EXAMPLE 5.42

Region $0 \leq z \leq 4\,\text{m}$ is occupied by an infinite slab of permeable material $\mu_r = 2.5$. If $\vec{B} = 20y\vec{a}_x - 10x\vec{a}_y\ \text{mWb/m}^2$ within the slab, determine (i) $\vec{J}$ (ii) $\vec{J}_b$ (iii) $\vec{M}$ and (iv) $\vec{K}_b$ on $z = 0$.

SOLUTION

Given $\vec{B} = 20y\vec{a}_x - 10x\vec{a}_y\ \text{mWb/m}^2$ and $\mu_r = 2.5$.

(*i*) From Ampere's law,

$$\vec{J} = \nabla \times \vec{H}$$

$$= \nabla \times \frac{\vec{B}}{\mu_0 \mu_r} = \frac{1}{4\pi \times 10^{-7} \times 2.5}\left(\frac{\partial B_y}{\partial x} - \frac{\partial B_x}{\partial y}\right)\vec{a}_z$$

$$= \frac{10^6}{\pi}\left(-10 - 20\right) \times 10^{-3}\,\vec{a}_z = -9.55\vec{a}_z\ \text{kA/m}^2$$

(*ii*) The bound volume current density is

$$\vec{J}_b = \chi_m \vec{J} = \left(\mu_r - 1\right)\vec{J} = 1.5\left(-9.55\vec{a}_z\right) \times 10^3$$

$$= -14.325\vec{a}_z\ \text{kA/m}^2$$

(*iii*) The magnetization is

$$\vec{M} = \chi_m \vec{H} = \chi_m \frac{\vec{B}}{\mu_0 \mu_r} = \frac{1.5\left(20y\vec{a}_x - 10x\vec{a}_y\right) \times 10^{-3}}{4\pi \times 10^{-7} \times 2.5}$$

$$= 9.55y\,\vec{a}_x - 4.78x\,\vec{a}_y\ \text{kA/m}$$

(*iv*) The bound surface current density is

$$\vec{K}_b = \vec{M} \times \vec{a}_n$$

Since $z = 0$ is the lower side of the slab occupying $0 \leq z \leq 2$, $\vec{a}_n = -\vec{a}_z$.

Therefore, $\vec{K}_b = \left(9.55y\vec{a}_x - 4.78x\vec{a}_y\right) \times \left(-\vec{a}_z\right)10^3$

$$= 4.78x\vec{a}_x + 9.55y\vec{a}_y\ \text{kA/m}$$

EXAMPLE 5.43

The magnetic field strength $H = 1200$ A/m is in a material when the magnetic flux density is $B = 2\ \text{Wb/m}^2$. When H is reduced to 400 A/m, $B = 1.4\ \text{Wb/m}^2$. Calculate the change in magnetization M.

SOLUTION

Case (i):

Given $H = 1200$ A/m and $B = 2\ \text{Wb/m}^2$. Since $B = \mu H$, the permeability is

$$\mu = \frac{B}{H} = \frac{2}{1200} = \frac{1}{600}$$

The relative permeability, $\mu_r = \dfrac{\mu}{\mu_0} = \dfrac{1}{600} \times \dfrac{1}{4\pi \times 10^{-7}} = 1326.96$ (Since $\mu = \mu_0 \mu_r$)

The magnetic susceptibility is $\chi_m = \mu_r - 1 = 1325.96$

The magnetization, $M_1 = \chi_m H = 1325.96 \times 1200 = 1592.152 \times 10^3$ A/m

Case (ii):

Given $H = 400$ A/m and $B = 1.4$ Wb/m^2.

The permeability, $\mu = \dfrac{B}{H} = \dfrac{1.4}{400}$

The relative permeability, $\mu_r = \dfrac{\mu}{\mu_0} = \dfrac{1.4}{400} \times \dfrac{1}{4\pi \times 10^{-7}} = 2786.6$

The magnetic susceptibility is $\chi_m = \mu_r - 1 = 2785.6$

The magnetization, $M_2 = \chi_m H = 2785.6 \times 400 = 1114.24 \times 10^3$ A/m

Hence, the change in magnetization is

$$\Delta M = M_1 - M_2 = \left(1591.152 - 1114.24\right) \times 10^3 = 476.9 \text{ kA/m}$$

EXAMPLE 5.44

Find the magnetic field strength within a magnetic material where

(*i*) $M = 300$ A/m and $\mu = 1.5 \times 10^{-5}$ H/m

(*ii*) $B = 150\,\mu$T and $\chi_m = 15$

(*iii*) There are 4.1×10^{28} atoms/m^3, each atom has a dipole moment of 2.5×10^{-27} A·m^2 and $\mu_r = 30$.

SOLUTION

(*i*) Given $M = 300$ A/m and $\mu = 1.5 \times 10^{-5}$ H/m.

Since $\mu = \mu_0 \mu_r$, the relative permeability μ_r is

$$\mu_r = \frac{\mu}{\mu_0} = \frac{1.5 \times 10^{-5}}{4\pi \times 10^{-7}} = 11.94$$

The magnetic field strength and the magnetization are related to each other by

$$M = \chi_m H = \left(\mu_r - 1\right) H$$

Hence, the magnetic field strength is

$$H = \frac{M}{\mu_r - 1} = \frac{300}{\left(11.94 - 1\right)} = 27.42 \text{ A/m}$$

(*ii*) Given $B = 150\,\mu$T and $\chi_m = 15$.

The magnetic flux density, $B = \mu H = \mu_0 \mu_r H$.

Hence, the magnetic field strength is

$$H = \frac{B}{\mu_0 \mu_r} = \frac{B}{\mu_0 \left(1 + \chi_m\right)} \qquad \text{(since } \mu_r = 1 + \chi_m\text{)}$$

$$= \frac{150\times10^{-6}}{4\pi\times10^{-7}\times(1+15)} = 7.46\,\text{A/m}$$

(*iii*) Given $n = 4.1\times10^{28}$ atoms/m^3, $m = 2.5\times10^{-27}$ A$\cdot$m^2 and $\mu_r = 30$.

The magnetization is

$$M = nm = 4.1\times10^{28}\times2.5\times10^{-27} = 102.5\,\text{A/m}$$

Hence, the magnetic field strength is

$$H = \frac{M}{\mu_r - 1} = \frac{102.5}{30-1} = 3.53\,\text{A/m}$$

EXAMPLE 5.45

If $\vec{B} = 0.15x\vec{a}_y$ Wb/m^2 in a material for which $\chi_m = 3.5$, determine (i) μ_r (ii) μ (iii) $\vec{H}$ (iv) $\vec{M}$ (v) $\vec{J}$ and (vi) $\vec{J}_b$.

SOLUTION

Given $\vec{B} = 0.15x\vec{a}_y$ Wb/m^2 and magnetic susceptibility $\chi_m = 3.5$.

(*i*) The relative permeability is

$$\mu_r = \chi_m + 1 = 3.5 + 1 = 4.5$$

(*ii*) The permeability of the material is $\mu = \mu_0\mu_r$.

Therefore, $\mu = 4\pi\times10^{-7}\times4.5 = 5.652\times10^{-6}$ H/m

(*iii*) Since $\vec{B} = \mu\vec{H}$, the magnetic field strength is

$$\vec{H} = \frac{\vec{B}}{\mu} = \frac{(0.15x)\vec{a}_y}{5.652\times10^{-6}} = \left(26.54\times10^3\,x\right)\vec{a}_y\,\text{A/m}$$

(*iv*) The magnetization is

$$\vec{M} = \chi_m\vec{H} = 3.5\left(26.54\times10^3\,x\right)\vec{a}_y$$

$$= \left(92.89\times10^3\,x\right)\vec{a}_y\,\text{A/m}$$

(*v*) According to Ampere's law, $\vec{J} = \nabla\times\vec{H}$.

$$\text{Therefore, } \vec{J} = \begin{vmatrix} \vec{a}_x & \vec{a}_y & \vec{a}_z \\ \dfrac{\partial}{\partial x} & \dfrac{\partial}{\partial y} & \dfrac{\partial}{\partial z} \\ 0 & 26.54\times10^3\,x & 0 \end{vmatrix} = \frac{\partial}{\partial x}\left[26.54\times10^3\,x\right]\vec{a}_z$$

$$= 26.54\times10^3\,\vec{a}_z\,\text{A/m}^2$$

(*vi*) The bound current density, $\vec{J}_b = \nabla\times\vec{M}$

$$
\text{Hence, } \vec{J}_b = \begin{vmatrix} \vec{a}_x & \vec{a}_y & \vec{a}_z \\ \dfrac{\partial}{\partial x} & \dfrac{\partial}{\partial y} & \dfrac{\partial}{\partial z} \\ 0 & 92.89\times10^3\,x & 0 \end{vmatrix} = \dfrac{\partial}{\partial x}\left[92.89\times10^3\,x\right]\vec{a}_z
$$

$$
= 92.89\times10^3\,\vec{a}_z \ \text{A/m}^2
$$

EXAMPLE 5.46

In certain region, the magnetic flux density in a magnetic material with $\chi_m = 9$ is given as $\vec{B} = 0.005y^2\vec{a}_x$ T. At $y = 0.8\,\text{m}$, determine the magnitude of (i) $\vec{J}$ (ii) $\vec{J}_b$ and (iii) $\vec{J}_T$.

SOLUTION

(i) The current density is

$$
\vec{J} = \nabla \times \vec{H} \tag{1}
$$

But $\quad \vec{H} = \dfrac{\vec{B}}{\mu} = \dfrac{\vec{B}}{\mu_0\mu_r} = \dfrac{\vec{B}}{\mu_0\left(\chi_m+1\right)}$

Substituting $\vec{H}$ in Eq. (1), we get

$$
\vec{J} = \nabla \times \dfrac{\vec{B}}{\mu_0\left(\chi_m+1\right)} = \dfrac{1}{\mu_0\left(\chi_m+1\right)}\left(\nabla\times\vec{B}\right)
$$

$$
\text{where} \quad \nabla\times\vec{B} = \begin{vmatrix} \vec{a}_x & \vec{a}_y & \vec{a}_z \\ \dfrac{\partial}{\partial x} & \dfrac{\partial}{\partial y} & \dfrac{\partial}{\partial z} \\ 0.005y^2 & 0 & 0 \end{vmatrix}
$$

$$
= \left[0-0\right]\vec{a}_x - \left[0-\dfrac{\partial}{\partial z}\left(0.005y^2\right)\right]\vec{a}_y + \left[0-\dfrac{\partial}{\partial y}\left(0.005y^2\right)\right]\vec{a}_z = -0.01y\vec{a}_z
$$

Hence, $\quad \vec{J} = \dfrac{1}{\mu_0\left(\chi_m+1\right)}\left(-0.01y\vec{a}_z\right)$

$$
= \dfrac{-0.01y}{4\pi\times10^{-7}\left(9+1\right)}\vec{a}_z = -796.18y\vec{a}_z
$$

At $y = 0.8\,\text{m}, \vec{J} = -796.18\times0.8\,\vec{a}_z = -636.94\vec{a}_z$ A/m^2

The magnitude of $\vec{J}$ is $636.94\,\text{A/m}^2$.

(ii) The bound current density is

$$
\vec{J}_b = \nabla\times\vec{M} \tag{2}
$$

But $\quad \vec{M} = \chi_m\vec{H} = \dfrac{\chi_m\vec{B}}{\mu} = \dfrac{\chi_m\vec{B}}{\mu_0\mu_r} = \dfrac{\chi_m\vec{B}}{\mu_0\left(\chi_m+1\right)}$

Substituting $\vec{M}$ in Eq. (2), we get

$$\vec{J}_b = \nabla \times \frac{\chi_m \vec{B}}{\mu_0(\chi_m+1)} = \frac{\chi_m}{\mu_0(\chi_m+1)}\left(\nabla \times \vec{B}\right)$$

where $\qquad \nabla \times \vec{B} = -0.01y\,\vec{a}_z$

Hence, $\vec{J}_b = \dfrac{9}{4\pi \times 10^{-7} \times 10}\left(-0.01y\vec{a}_z\right) = -7165.6y\vec{a}_z$

At $y = 0.8\,\text{m}$, $\vec{J}_b = -7165.6 \times 0.8\,\vec{a}_z = -5732.48\,\vec{a}_z$ A/m^2

The magnitude of $\vec{J}_b$ is 5732.48 A/m^2.

(*iii*) The total current density is

$$\vec{J}_T = \nabla \times \frac{\vec{B}}{\mu_0}$$

$$= \frac{1}{\mu_0}\left(\nabla \times \vec{B}\right) = \frac{1}{4\pi \times 10^{-7}}\left(-0.01y\vec{a}_z\right)$$

$$= -7961.78y\vec{a}_z \ \text{A/m}^2$$

At $y = 0.8\,\text{m}$, $\vec{J}_T = -7961.78 \times 0.8\,\vec{a}_z = -6369.42\,\vec{a}_z$ A/m^2

Hence, the magnitude of $\vec{J}_T$ is 6369.42 A/m^2.

Alternative method

The total current density can also be written as

$$\vec{J}_T = \vec{J}_b + \vec{J}$$

$$= \left(-5732.48\,\vec{a}_z\right) + \left(-636.94\,\vec{a}_z\right) = -6369.42\vec{a}_z\,\text{A/m}^2$$

The magnitude of $\vec{J}_T$ is 6369.42 A/m^2. $\qquad\qquad\qquad\qquad\qquad\quad\Box$

5.9   BOUNDARY CONDITIONS FOR MAGNETIC FIELDS

For solving problems related to magnetic fields in regions having medium with different physical properties, $\vec{H}$ and $\vec{B}$ vectors are examined at the interface to obtain the magnetic boundary conditions.

5.9.1   Boundary Conditions on Tangential Components

In Figure 5.12(a), there is an interface between material 1 with permeability μ_1 and material 2 with permeability μ_2. Consider a closed rectangular path *abcda* as shown in Figure 5.12(a).

By applying Ampere's law around this closed path, i.e., $\oint_l \vec{H} \cdot d\vec{l} = I$, the variation of $\vec{H}$ across an interface is obtained. Allowing the rectangle shrink to zero, i.e., $bc = da = \Delta h$ approach zero, we have

$$\oint_l \vec{H} \cdot d\vec{l} = \vec{H}_1 \cdot \Delta w - \vec{H}_2 \cdot \Delta w = \vec{K}\,\Delta w$$

or $\qquad H_{t1} - H_{t2} = K \qquad\qquad\qquad\qquad\qquad\qquad\qquad\qquad\qquad\qquad\qquad$ (5.41) where $\vec{K}$ is the surface current density on the interface normal to the contour c.

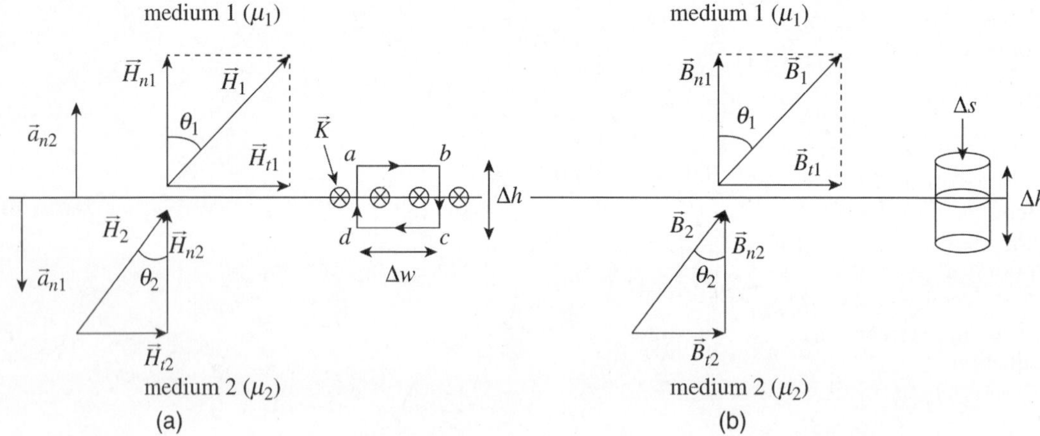

Figure 5.12 *Boundary conditions between two magnetic media (a) for $\vec{H}$ and (b) for $\vec{B}$*

Therefore, the Eq. (5.41) can be represented in vector form as

$$\left(\vec{H}_1 - \vec{H}_2\right) \times \vec{a}_{n1} = \vec{K} \tag{5.42}$$

where $\vec{a}_{n1}$ is the outward unit normal at the interface directed from medium 1 to medium 2. If $\vec{a}_{n2}$ is the unit normal vector at the boundary directed from medium 2 to medium 1, then the above equation becomes

$$\vec{a}_{n2} \times \left(\vec{H}_1 - \vec{H}_2\right) = \vec{K} \tag{5.43}$$

Hence, the tangential component of $\vec{H}$ is discontinuous across an interface where a free surface current density exists, and the amount of discontinuity is determined by the above equations. Surface currents can exist only on the surfaces of perfect conductors and superconductors. If there is no current flowing at the interface i.e., $K = 0$, then Eq. (5.41) becomes

$$\vec{H}_{t1} = \vec{H}_{t2} \text{ or } \frac{\vec{B}_{t1}}{\mu_1} = \frac{\vec{B}_{t2}}{\mu_2} \tag{5.44}$$

From the above equation, it is evident that the tangential component of $\vec{H}$ is continuous and $\vec{B}$ is discontinuous across the boundary.

5.9.2 Boundary Conditions on Normal Components

By using a small "pillbox" positioned across the interface as shown in Figure 5.12(b), the behavior of $\vec{B}$ can be determined. Applying Gauss's law for magnetic field to the pill box, we have

$$\oint_s \vec{B} \cdot d\vec{s} = \int_{top} \vec{B}_1 \cdot d\vec{s}_1 + \int_{cylinder} \vec{B} \cdot d\vec{s} + \int_{bottom} \vec{B}_2 \cdot d\vec{s}_2 = 0$$

By allowing the cylinder height $\Delta h \to 0$, we obtain

$$\int_{top} \vec{B}_1 \cdot d\vec{s}_1 + \int_{bottom} \vec{B}_2 \cdot d\vec{s}_2 = 0$$

i.e., $$\vec{B}_{n1} \Delta \vec{s} - \vec{B}_{n2} \Delta \vec{s} = 0$$

Therefore, $B_{n1} = B_{n2}$ (5.45)

Hence, the normal component of $\vec{B}$ is continuous across the boundary between two adjacent media. For homogeneous mediums, $\vec{B}_1 = \mu_1 \vec{H}_1$ and $\vec{B}_2 = \mu_2 \vec{H}_2$. Then, the above equation becomes

$$\mu_1 H_{n1} = \mu_2 H_{n2}$$

$$\frac{H_{n1}}{H_{n2}} = \frac{\mu_2}{\mu_1} \tag{5.46}$$

Here, the normal component of $\vec{H}$ is discontinuous across the interface and it undergoes some change at the boundary.

If the fields make an angle θ with the normal to the boundary, Eq. (5.45) can be written as

$$B_1 \cos\theta_1 = B_{n1} = B_{n2} = B_2 \cos\theta_2 \tag{5.47}$$

Equation (5.44) can also be written as

$$\frac{B_1}{\mu_1}\sin\theta_1 = H_{t1} = H_{t2} = \frac{B_2}{\mu_2}\sin\theta_2 \tag{5.48}$$

Dividing Eq. (5.48) by Eq. (5.47), we get

$$\frac{\tan\theta_1}{\tan\theta_2} = \frac{\mu_1}{\mu_2} \tag{5.49}$$

The above equation is similar to Eq. (3.29) and it is called the *law of refraction* for magnetic flux lines at a boundary with no surface current.

EXAMPLE 5.47

The magnetic flux density is given by $\vec{B}_1 = 1.2\vec{a}_x + 0.8\vec{a}_y + 0.4\vec{a}_z \text{ Wb/m}^2$ for the medium 1 as shown in Figure E5.47. Determine $\vec{B}_2$ and $\vec{H}_2$ in the medium 2 and also calculate the angles made by the fields with the normal.

SOLUTION

Given $\vec{B}_1 = 1.2\vec{a}_x + 0.8\vec{a}_y + 0.4\vec{a}_z \text{ Wb/m}^2$ in medium 1 and $\mu_{r1} = 10$. Assume that the boundary is current free.

Since $\vec{B}_1 = \mu \vec{H}_1$, the magnetic field strength in medium 1 is

$$\vec{H}_1 = \frac{\vec{B}_1}{\mu_1} = \frac{\vec{B}_1}{\mu_0 \mu_{r1}} = \frac{1}{\mu_0}\left[\frac{1.2\vec{a}_x + 0.8\vec{a}_y + 0.4\vec{a}_z}{10}\right]$$

$$= \frac{1}{\mu_0}\left[0.12\vec{a}_x + 0.08\vec{a}_y + 0.04\vec{a}_z\right] \text{ A/m} \tag{1}$$

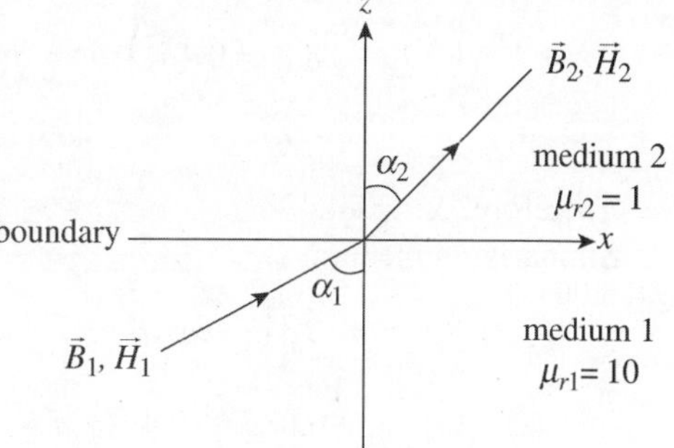

Figure E5.47

As shown in Figure E5.47, the x and y-components are tangential at the boundary and z-component is normal to the boundary. For a current free interface, the tangential components for $\vec{H}_1$ and $\vec{H}_2$ remain same. From Eq. (5.46), the normal component of magnetic field strength is

$$\frac{H_{n1}}{H_{n2}} = \frac{\mu_2}{\mu_1} = \frac{\mu_{r2}}{\mu_{r1}}$$

Therefore, $H_{n2} = \dfrac{\mu_{r1}}{\mu_{r2}} H_{n1}$ (2)

Here, the normal component of $\vec{H}_1$ is in z-direction and it is given by $H_{n1} = \dfrac{0.04}{\mu_0}$ A/m. Substituting the value of H_{n1} in Eq. (2), we get

$$H_{n2} = \frac{10}{1} \times \frac{0.04}{\mu_0} = \frac{0.4}{\mu_0} \text{ A/m} \tag{3}$$

Therefore, the magnetic field strength in the medium 2 is calculated as

$$H_{t2x} = H_{t1x} = \frac{0.12}{\mu_0}, \qquad H_{t2y} = H_{t1y} = \frac{0.08}{\mu_0}$$

$$H_{n2} = \frac{0.4}{\mu_0}$$

Hence, $\quad \vec{H}_2 = H_{t2x}\vec{a}_x + H_{t2y}\vec{a}_y + H_{n2}\vec{a}_z$

$$= \frac{1}{\mu_0}\left[0.12\vec{a}_x + 0.08\vec{a}_y + 0.4\vec{a}_z\right] \text{ A/m} \tag{4}$$

Then, the magnetic flux density in medium 2 is

$$\vec{B}_2 = \mu_2\vec{H}_2 = \left(\mu_0\mu_{r2}\right)\vec{H}_2$$

$$= \mu_0\left[\frac{1}{\mu_0}\left(0.12\vec{a}_x + 0.08\vec{a}_y + 0.4\vec{a}_z\right)\right]$$

$$= 0.12\vec{a}_x + 0.08\vec{a}_y + 0.4\vec{a}_z \text{ Wb/m}^2 \tag{5}$$

As z-direction is perpendicular to boundary, in medium 1, we can write

$$\vec{B}_1 \cdot \vec{a}_z = \left|\vec{B}_1\right|\left|\vec{a}_z\right|\cos\alpha_1$$

$$\left(1.2\vec{a}_x + 0.8\vec{a}_y = 0.4\vec{a}_z\right)\cdot\vec{a}_z = \sqrt{(1.2)^2 + (0.8)^2 + (0.4)^2}\,(1)\,(\cos\alpha_1)$$

$$0.4 = (1.4966)\,(\cos\alpha_1) \qquad (\text{since } \vec{a}_x \cdot \vec{a}_z = \vec{a}_y \cdot \vec{a}_z = 0)$$

Therefore, $\quad \alpha_1 = 74.49° \tag{6}$

Similarly, in medium 2,

$$\vec{B}_2 \cdot \vec{a}_z = \left|\vec{B}_2\right|\left|\vec{a}_z\right|\cos\alpha_2$$

$$\left(0.12\vec{a}_x + 0.08\vec{a}_y + 0.4\vec{a}_z\right)\cdot\vec{a}_z = \sqrt{(0.12)^2 + (0.08)^2 + (0.4)^2}\,(1)\,(\cos\alpha_2)$$

$$0.4 = (0.425)(\cos\alpha_2)$$

Therefore, $\quad \alpha_2 = 19.75° \tag{7}$

Hence, the fields make angle $74.49°$ in medium 1 and $19.75°$ in medium 2. ❑

EXAMPLE 5.48

A current sheet $\vec{K} = 10\,\vec{a}_y$ A/m is located at $z = 0$. The region 1 at $z < 0$ has $\mu_{r1} = 10$ and region 2 at $z > 0$ has $\mu_{r2} = 6$. Given $\vec{H}_2 = 15\vec{a}_x + 10\vec{a}_z$ A/m, find $\vec{H}_1$.

SOLUTION

From the given data, it is seen that z-axis is normal to the boundary. The normal component of $\vec{H}_2$ is along $\vec{a}_z$ i.e., $H_{n2} = 10\,\text{A/m}$. Similarly, the tangential component of $\vec{H}_2$ is along $\vec{a}_x$ i.e., $H_{t2} = 15\,\text{A/m}$. Therefore, $\vec{H}_2 = \vec{H}_{t2}\vec{a}_x + \vec{H}_{n2}\vec{a}_z = 15\vec{a}_x + 10\vec{a}_z$.

Since the current sheet is located at $z = 0$, the tangential component of $\vec{H}$ is discontinuous at the boundary. From the boundary conditions on tangential components of magnetic field, we can write

$$(\vec{H}_1 - \vec{H}_2) \times \vec{a}_{n1} = \vec{K}$$

where $\vec{a}_{n1}$ is the unit vector normal to the boundary drawn from medium 1 to medium 2.

Here, $\vec{a}_{n1} = \vec{a}_z$

Therefore, $(\vec{H}_1 - \vec{H}_2) \times \vec{a}_z = \vec{K} = 10\vec{a}_y$ (1)

Also, normal component of $\vec{H}$ is discontinuous for the boundary having a current sheet. From boundary conditions on normal components of magnetic field, we can write

$$\frac{H_{n1}}{H_{n2}} = \frac{\mu_2}{\mu_1} = \frac{\mu_0 \mu_{r2}}{\mu_0 \mu_{r1}} = \frac{\mu_{r2}}{\mu_{r1}}$$

Therefore, $H_{n1} = H_{n2} \dfrac{\mu_{r2}}{\mu_{r1}} = 10\left(\dfrac{6}{10}\right) = 6$ (2)

Similar to $\vec{H}_2$, the normal component of $\vec{H}_1$ is along $\vec{a}_z$. Hence, we can write

$$\vec{H}_1 = H_{t1}\vec{a}_x + H_{n1}\vec{a}_z = H_{t1}\vec{a}_x + 6\vec{a}_z \tag{3}$$

$$\vec{H}_1 - \vec{H}_2 = \left[H_{t1}\vec{a}_x + 6\vec{a}_z\right] - \left[15\vec{a}_x + 10\vec{a}_z\right]$$

$$= \left(H_{t1} - 15\right)\vec{a}_x - 4\vec{a}_z$$

Substituting the value of $\left(\vec{H}_1 - \vec{H}_2\right)$ in Eq. (1), we get

$$\left[\left(H_{t1} - 15\right)\vec{a}_x - 4\vec{a}_z\right] \times \vec{a}_z = 10\vec{a}_y$$

$$-\left(H_{t1} - 15\right)\vec{a}_y = 10\vec{a}_y \ \left(\text{since } \vec{a}_x \times \vec{a}_z = -\vec{a}_y \text{ and } \vec{a}_z \times \vec{a}_z = 0\right) \tag{4}$$

Comparing both the sides of the above equation, we have

$$-H_{t1} + 15 = 10$$

i.e., $\qquad\qquad H_{t1} = 5$ (5)

Substituting Eq. (5) in Eq. (3), we obtain the magnetic field in region 1 as

$$\vec{H}_1 = 5\vec{a}_x + 6\vec{a}_z \ \text{A/m}$$

EXAMPLE 5.49

In region 1, $\mu_{r1} = 10$ and in region 2, $\mu_{r2} = 2$. Also, $B_1 = 10\vec{a}_x + 20\vec{a}_y + 30\vec{a}_z$ mT, everywhere in region 1. Find (i) the angle θ_1 that B_1 makes with the normal to the boundary and (ii) the angle θ_2 that B_2 makes with the normal to the boundary.

SOLUTION

Given $\mu_{r1} = 10$, $\mu_{r2} = 2$ and $\vec{B}_1 = 0.01\vec{a}_x + 0.02\vec{a}_y + 0.03\vec{a}_z$ T.

Here, $\vec{H}_1 = \dfrac{\vec{B}_1}{\mu_1} = \dfrac{1}{10\mu_0}\left(0.01\vec{a}_x + 0.02\vec{a}_y + 0.03\vec{a}_z\right)$ A/m $\qquad$ (1)

Let us assume z-axis be the normal to the boundary. If H_{n1} and H_{n2} are the normal components of $\vec{H}_1$ and $\vec{H}_2$, then

$$\frac{H_{n1}}{H_{n2}} = \frac{\mu_{r2}}{\mu_{r1}}$$

From Eq. (1), $H_{n1} = \dfrac{0.03}{10\mu_0}$

Therefore, $H_{n2} = \dfrac{H_{n1}\mu_{r1}}{\mu_{r2}} = \dfrac{0.03}{10\mu_0} \times \dfrac{10}{2} = \dfrac{0.015}{\mu_0}$

At the boundary,

$$\vec{H}_{t1} = \vec{H}_{t2} = \frac{1}{\mu_0}\left(0.01\,\vec{a}_x + 0.02\,\vec{a}_y\right) \qquad (2)$$

Hence, $\quad \vec{H}_2 = \vec{H}_{t2} + \vec{H}_{n2} = \dfrac{1}{\mu_0}\left(0.001\vec{a}_x + 0.002\vec{a}_y + 0.015\vec{a}_z\right)$ A/m

and $\qquad \vec{B}_2 = \dfrac{\mu}{\mu_0}\left(0.001\vec{a}_x + 0.002\vec{a}_y + 0.015\vec{a}_z\right) = 2\left(0.001\vec{a}_x + 0.002\vec{a}_y + 0.015\vec{a}_z\right)$

$$= 0.002\vec{a}_x + 0.004\vec{a}_y + 0.03\vec{a}_z \text{ T}$$

Also, at the boundary,

$$B_1 \cdot \vec{a}_z = |B_1|\,|\vec{a}_z|\cos\theta_1$$

$$\cos\theta_1 = \frac{\vec{B}_1 \cdot \vec{a}_z}{B_1} = \frac{0.03}{\sqrt{0.01^2 + 0.002^2 + 0.03^2}} = \frac{0.03}{0.0374} = 0.8021$$

Therefore, $\quad \theta_1 = \cos^{-1}(0.8021) = 36.66°$

Similarly, $\cos\theta_2 = \dfrac{\vec{B}_2 \cdot \vec{a}_z}{B_2} = \dfrac{0.03}{\sqrt{0.002^2 + 0.004^2 + 0.03^2}} = \dfrac{0.03}{0.0303} = 0.99$

$$\theta_2 = \cos^{-1}(0.99) = 8.1° \qquad \square$$

EXAMPLE 5.50

Consider that two magnetic mediums with permeabilities μ_1 and μ_2 are separated by a common boundary as shown in Figure E5.50. The magnetic field intensity in medium 1 at the point P_1 has a magnitude H_1 and makes an angle θ_1 with normal. Find the magnitude and direction of magnetic field intensity at point P_2 in medium 2.

SOLUTION

Let $\vec{B}_1$ (and $\vec{H}_1$) make an angle θ_1 with a normal to the surface as shown in Figure E5.50. Since the normal components of $\vec{B}$ are continuous,

$$B_{n1} = B_1 \cos\theta_1 = B_2 \cos\theta_2 = B_{n2}$$

i.e., $\mu_2 H_2 \cos\theta_2 = \mu_1 H_1 \cos\theta_1 \qquad$ (1)

As there are no perfect conductors in both the mediums, the tangential component of $\vec{H}$ is continuous. Therefore,

$$H_2 \sin\theta_2 = H_1 \sin\theta_1 \qquad (2)$$

Dividing Eq. (2) by Eq. (1), we get

$$\frac{\tan\theta_2}{\mu_2} = \frac{\tan\theta_1}{\mu_1}$$

or

$$\frac{\tan\theta_2}{\tan\theta_1} = \frac{\mu_2}{\mu_1}$$

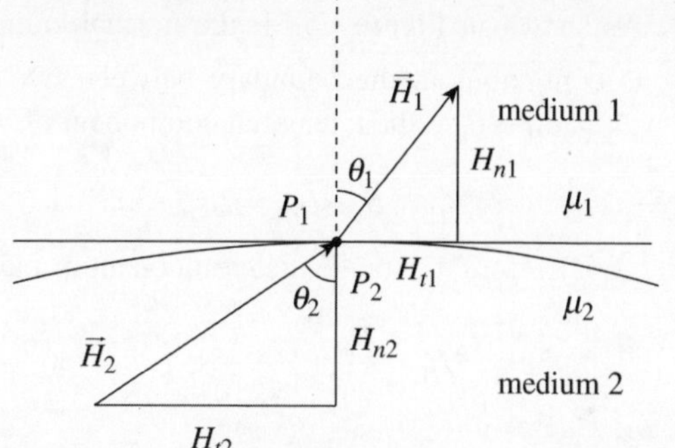

Therefore, $\theta_2 = \tan^{-1}\left(\dfrac{\mu_2}{\mu_1}\tan\theta_1\right) \qquad (3)$

Figure E5.50

Equation (3) describes the refraction property of the magnetic field. From Eq. (1) and Eq. (2), we get

$$\cos^2\theta_2 + \sin^2\theta_2 = 1 = \left(\frac{\mu_1}{\mu_2}\frac{H_1}{H_2}\right)^2\cos^2\theta_1 + \left(\frac{H_1}{H_2}\right)^2\sin^2\theta_1$$

Solving the above equation, the magnitude of $\vec{H}_2$ is

$$H_2 = H_1\sqrt{\sin^2\theta_1 + \left(\frac{\mu_1}{\mu_2}\right)^3\cos^2\theta_1}\ \text{A/m} \qquad (4)$$

If $\mu_2 \gg \mu_1$, then θ_2 will be nearly $90°$ and if $\mu_1 \gg \mu_2$, then θ_2 will be approximately zero. ❐

EXAMPLE 5.51

An interface is explained with the following details.

$\mu_1 = 4\ \mu\text{H/m}$ in region 1 where $z > 0$

$\mu_2 = 7\ \mu\text{H/m}$ in region 2 where $z < 0$

$\vec{K} = 80\vec{a}_x\ \text{A/m}$ on $z = 0$

If $\vec{B}_1 = 2\vec{a}_x - 3\vec{a}_y + \vec{a}_z\ \text{mT}$ is applied in region 1, find $\vec{B}_2$ in region 2.

SOLUTION

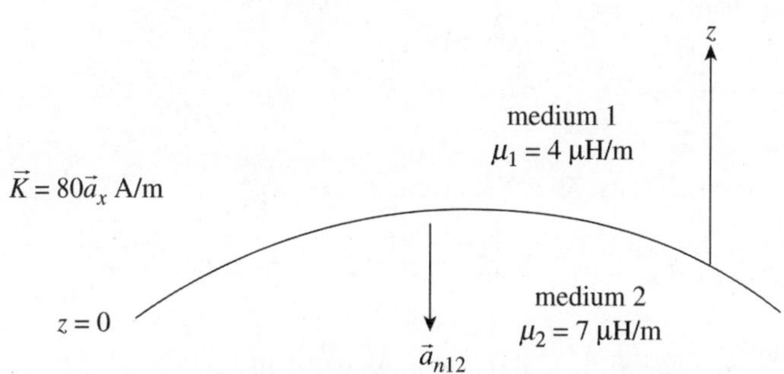

Figure E5.51

As shown in Figure E5.51, the normal component of $\vec{B}_1$ is $\vec{B}_{n1} = \vec{a}_z$ mT. The normal component of $\vec{B}$ is continuous at the boundary between two mediums i.e., $\vec{B}_{n2} = \vec{B}_{n1}$. Hence, $\vec{B}_{n2} = \vec{B}_{n1} = \vec{a}_z$ mT. Since $\vec{B}_1 = \vec{B}_{t1} + \vec{B}_{n1}$, the tangential component of $\vec{B}_1$ is

$$\vec{B}_{t1} = \vec{B}_1 - \vec{B}_{n1} = 2\vec{a}_x - 3\vec{a}_y \text{ mT}$$

Therefore, the tangential component of magnetic field intensity $\vec{H}_1$ is

$$\vec{H}_{t1} = \frac{\vec{B}_{t1}}{\mu_1} = \frac{1}{4 \times 10^{-6}}\left(2\vec{a}_x - 3\vec{a}_y\right) \times 10^{-3} = 500\vec{a}_x - 750\vec{a}_y \text{ A/m}$$

The tangential component of magnetic field intensity at the boundary of two magnetic mediums is $\left(\vec{H}_1 - \vec{H}_2\right) \times \vec{a}_{n1} = \vec{K}$

$$\vec{H}_{t1} - \vec{H}_{t2} = \vec{a}_{n1} \times \vec{K}$$

i.e., $\qquad \vec{H}_{t2} = \vec{H}_{t1} - \left(\vec{a}_{n1} \times \vec{K}\right)$

where $\qquad \vec{a}_{n1} = -\vec{a}_z$ and $\vec{a}_{n1} \times \vec{K} = -\vec{a}_z \times 80\vec{a}_x = -80\vec{a}_y$

Therefore, $\quad \vec{H}_{t2} = 500\vec{a}_x - 750\vec{a}_y + 80\vec{a}_y = 500\vec{a}_x - 670\vec{a}_y \text{ A/m}$

Here, $\qquad\qquad \vec{B}_{t2} = \mu_2 \vec{H}_{t2}$

Therefore, $\qquad \vec{B}_{t2} = 7 \times 10^{-6} \times \left(500\vec{a}_x - 670\vec{a}_y\right) = 3.5\vec{a}_x - 4.69\vec{a}_y \text{ mT}$

Hence, $\qquad\qquad \vec{B}_2 = \vec{B}_{t2} + \vec{B}_{n2} = 3.5\vec{a}_x - 4.69\vec{a}_y + \vec{a}_z \text{ mT}$ $\qquad\qquad\qquad$ ❑

EXAMPLE 5.52

In medium 1, $\mu_{r1} = 1.5$ when $z < 0$ and in medium 2, $\mu_{r2} = 5$ when $z > 0$. Near the origin, $\vec{B}_1 = 2.4\vec{a}_x + 10\vec{a}_z$ T and $\vec{B}_2 = 25.75\vec{a}_x - 17.7\vec{a}_y + 10\vec{a}_z$ T. If the interface carries a sheet current, what is its density at the origin?

SOLUTION

Near the origin,

$$\vec{H}_1 = \frac{\vec{B}_1}{\mu_1} = \frac{\vec{B}_1}{\mu_0 \mu_{r1}} = \frac{1}{1.5\mu_0}\left(2.4\vec{a}_x + 10\vec{a}_z\right) = \frac{1}{\mu_0}\left(1.6\vec{a}_x + 6.67\vec{a}_z\right) \text{ A/m}$$

and $\qquad \vec{H}_2 = \frac{\vec{B}_2}{\mu_2} = \frac{\vec{B}_2}{\mu_0 \mu_{r2}} = \frac{1}{5\mu_0}\left(25.75\vec{a}_x - 17.7\vec{a}_y + 10\vec{a}_z\right) = \frac{1}{\mu_0}\left(5.15\vec{a}_x - 3.55\vec{a}_y + 2\vec{a}_z\right) \text{ A/m}$

Then, the surface current density $\vec{K}$ at the origin is

$$\vec{K} = \left(\vec{H}_1 - \vec{H}_2\right) \times \vec{a}_{n1} = \frac{1}{\mu_0}\left(-3.55\vec{a}_x + 3.55\vec{a}_y + 4.67\vec{a}_z\right) \times \vec{a}_z$$

$$= \frac{3.55}{4\pi \times 10^{-7}}\left(\vec{a}_x + \vec{a}_y\right) = 2.83\left(\vec{a}_x + \vec{a}_y\right) \times 10^6 \text{ A/m} \qquad\qquad ❑$$

5.10 MAGNETIC CIRCUIT

Magnetic circuit is the path traced by magnetic flux. Magnetic flux usually traces a complete loop i.e., coming back to its starting point. In any magnet, magnetic flux leaves its north pole, passing through air, enters the magnet at its south pole and finally reaches point of start.

It is possible to establish magnetic flux in a definite path by using a magnetic material of high permeability. By this way, the magnetic flux forms a closed circuit exactly as an electric current does in an electric circuit.

Magnetic circuits can be classified into simple and composite circuits. A simple magnetic circuit is made up of a single magnetic material. Thus, a simple magnetic circuit reflects the magnetic properties of the material used. But, a composite magnetic circuit will have at least two different materials of different magnetic properties i.e., one of the materials may be magnetic and the other one may be non-magnetic (such as air).

5.10.1 Fundamentals of Magnetic Circuits

Magnetic flux (Φ): It is defined as the magnetic lines of force produced by a magnet. It is represented by Φ and its unit is weber (Wb).

Magnetomotive force (V_m): It is defined as the driving force which produces magnetic flux in the magnetic circuit. It is represented by V_m and its unit is ampere-turn $(A \cdot t)$. The scalar magnetic potential is referred to as magnetomotive force (*mmf*) in magnetic circuits.

Reluctance $(\Re)$: It is defined as the property of a magnetic circuit which opposes the magnetic flux. It is represented by $\Re$ and its unit is ampere-turn per weber $(A \cdot t/Wb)$.

Permeance (P): It is defined as the property of a magnetic circuit which admits the magnetic flux. It is the reciprocal of reluctance. It is represented by P and its unit is weber per ampere-turn $(Wb/A \cdot t)$.

5.10.2 Analysis of Simple Magnetic Circuit

Magnetic devices such as solenoids, toroids, transformers, motors, generators and relays can be considered as magnetic circuits. Consider a circular solenoid or a toroidal iron ring having a magnetic path of length l, area of cross-section a and a coil of N turns carrying current I as shown in Figure 5.13.

The *mmf* produced is

$$V_m = NI = \oint \vec{H} \cdot d\vec{l} \tag{5.50}$$

According to the definition of H, the magnitude of field intensity inside the solenoid is

$$H = \frac{NI}{l} \tag{5.51}$$

The magnetic flux density is

$$B = \mu H, \qquad \text{where } \mu = \mu_0 \mu_r \tag{5.52}$$

Substituting Eq. (5.51) in Eq. (5.52), we get

$$B = \frac{\mu_0 \mu_r NI}{l} \tag{5.53}$$

But, the total flux produced, $\Phi = BA = \dfrac{\mu_0 \mu_r A NI}{l}$ (5.54)

Therefore, $\quad \Phi = \dfrac{NI}{l\,/\,\mu_0 \mu_r A} = \dfrac{NI}{\Re}$

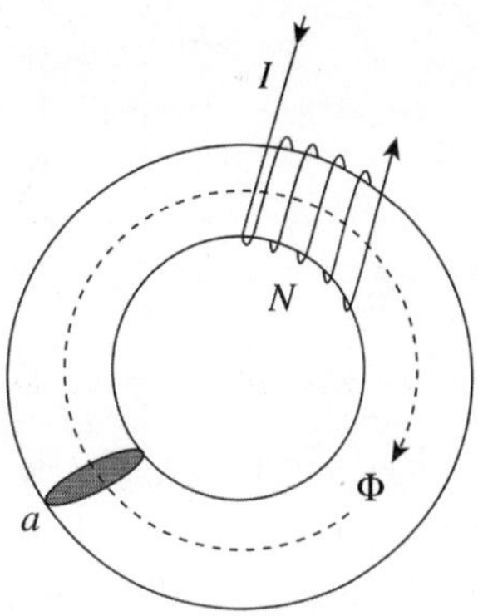

Figure 5.13 *Toroidal iron ring*

Thus, reluctance is $\mathfrak{R} = \dfrac{l}{\mu_0 \mu_r A}$ $\hspace{2cm}$ (5.55)

Mathematically, mmf = reluctance × flux

The above equation is also known as *Ohm's law of magnetic circuit* because it resembles a similar expression in electric circuits.

i.e., $\hspace{1cm}$ emf = resistance × current

Therefore, it is evident that reluctance is analogous to resistance in an electric circuit. Since reluctance is inversely proportional to permeability, its value is very high for air and non-magnetic materials. For ferromagnetic materials such as steel or iron, the reluctance is small.

The ampere turns to produce a given flux (Φ) or flux density (B) in a magnetic circuit can be determined by using the steps given below:

(*i*) Determine the flux density, $B = \dfrac{\Phi}{A}$

(*ii*) Determine the field intensity, $H = \dfrac{B}{\mu_0 \mu_r}$

(*iii*) Obtain mmf using the formula, mmf = $H\,l$, i.e., ampere turns for any part of magnetic circuit = magnetic field intensity in that part × length of that part

5.10.3 Analysis of Series Magnetic Circuits

Consider a composite circuit shown in Figure 5.14(a) consisting of three different magnetic materials of different relative permeabilities along with an air gap.

Let l_1, l_2 and l_3 be the lengths of the various magnetic materials used in the circuit, A_1, A_2 and A_3 be the areas of the cross-section of the respective part of circuit, l_g be the length of the air gap and A_g be the area of cross-section at the air gap.

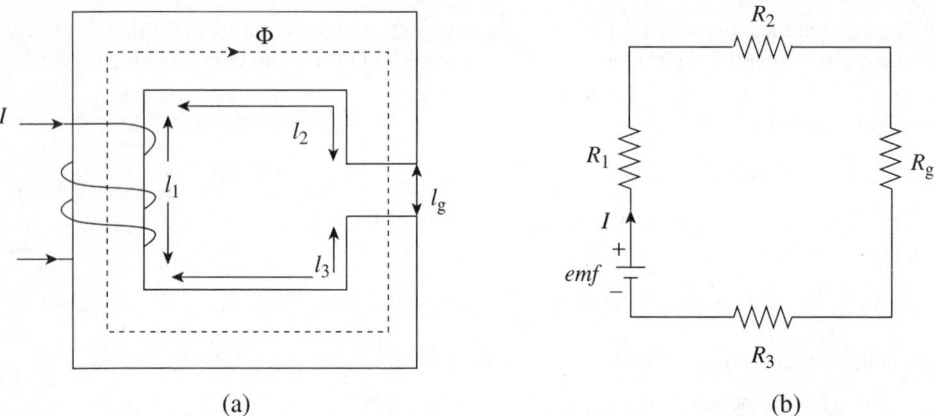

Figure 5.14 *Composite magnetic circuit: (a) series magnetic circuit and (b) equivalent electric circuit*

The equivalent electrical circuit for the series composite magnetic circuit is shown in Figure 5.14(b). Each part of the series circuit will offer reluctance to the magnetic flux (Φ). The amount of reluctance will depend upon the dimensions and relative permeability of that part. Since the different parts of the circuit are in series, the total reluctance $(\mathfrak{R})$ is equal to the sum of reluctances of individual parts.

Therefore, total reluctance, $\mathfrak{R} = \mathfrak{R}_1 + \mathfrak{R}_2 + \mathfrak{R}_3 + \mathfrak{R}_g$

Substituting for the reluctance components, we get

$$\Re = \frac{l_1}{\mu_0 \mu_{r1} A_1} + \frac{l_2}{\mu_0 \mu_{r2} A_2} + \frac{l_3}{\mu_0 \mu_{r3} A_3} + \frac{l_g}{\mu_0 \mu_{rg} A_g}$$

Therefore, the mmf in the circuit is,

$$V_m = \text{Flux} \times \text{Reluctance} = \Phi\Re_1 + \Phi\Re_2 + \Phi\Re_3 + \Phi\Re_g$$

$$= \left[\frac{\Phi l_1}{\mu_0 \mu_{r1} A_1} + \frac{\Phi l_2}{\mu_0 \mu_{r2} A_2} + \frac{\Phi l_3}{\mu_0 \mu_{r3} A_3} + \frac{\Phi l_g}{\mu_0 \mu_{rg} A_g} \right]$$

$$= \frac{B_1}{\mu_0 \mu_{r1}} l_1 + \frac{B_2}{\mu_0 \mu_{r2}} l_2 + \frac{B_3}{\mu_0 \mu_{r3}} l_3 + \frac{B_g}{\mu_0} l_g \qquad \left(\text{since } B = \frac{\Phi}{A} \text{ and } \mu_{rg} = 1 \text{ for air} \right)$$

Hence, the total mmf can be represented in terms of magnetic field intensity and length as

$$\text{Total mmf} = V_m = H_1 l_1 + H_2 l_2 + H_3 l_3 + H_g l_g \qquad \left(\text{since } H = \frac{B}{\mu_0 \mu_r} \right)$$

This equation is similar to the *emf* equation in the electrical equivalent circuit i.e., from the equivalent electrical circuit shown in Figure 5.13(b).

The total resistance of the circuit is equal to the sum of various individual resistance values,

i.e., $\quad R = R_1 + R_2 + R_3 + R_g$

Therefore, total $\text{emf} = V = IR_1 + IR_2 + IR_3 + IR_g = \text{Current} \times \text{Total resistance}$

Thus, by analogy with electric circuit, we have

Total mmf required $= A \cdot t$ for series paths $+ A \cdot t$ for air gap

5.10.4 Analysis of Parallel Magnetic Circuits

In a magnetic circuit, if the flux has more than one path, then it is known as a parallel magnetic circuit and it is shown in Figure 5.15(a). Parallel magnetic circuits exist in electrical machines. The equivalent electrical circuit for the parallel composite magnetic circuit is shown in Figure 5.15(b).

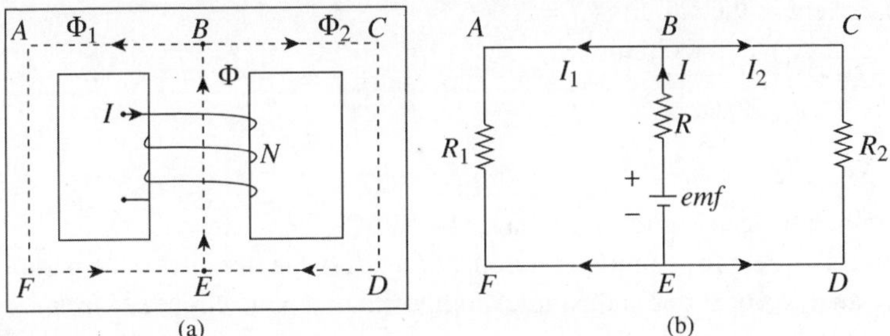

Figure 5.15 *Composite magnetic circuit: (a) parallel magnetic circuit and (b) equivalent electric circuit*

In a parallel magnetic circuit, the total flux exists in a common section of the magnetic circuit which contains the exciting coil. It divides into two parts and each part follows the different paths and recombines at the other end of the common section. The parameters referring to the magnetic circuit shown in Figure 5.15(a) are tabulated in Table 5.2.

Table 5.2 *Parallel Magnetic circuit parameters*

Part of circuit	Flux	Length	Cross-sectional area	Magnetic field intensity	Reluctance
$B - A - F - E$	Φ_1	l_1	A_1	H_1	$\mathfrak{R}_1$
$B - C - D - A$	Φ_2	l_2	A_2	H_2	$\mathfrak{R}_2$
$B - E$	Φ	l_3	A_3	H_3	$\mathfrak{R}$

Here, the total flux in the circuit is $\Phi = \Phi_1 + \Phi_2$.
Therefore, the mmf in the circuit is

$$V_m = \Phi\mathfrak{R} + \Phi_1\mathfrak{R}_1$$

or $\qquad V_m = \Phi\mathfrak{R} + \Phi_2\mathfrak{R}_2$

Using the relations $\Phi = \mu HA$ and $\mathfrak{R} = l\,/\,\mu A$, the mmf can be represented in terms of magnetic field and length as

$$V_m = H_3 l_3 + H_1 l_1$$

or $\qquad V_m = H_3 l_3 + H_2 l_2$

This equation is similar to the emf equation in the electrical equivalent circuit shown in Figure 5.15(b). The parameters referring to the equivalent electric circuit shown in Figure 5.15(b) are tabulated in Table 5.3.

Table 5.3 *Equivalent electric circuit parameters*

Part of circuit	Current	Resistance
$B - A - F - E$	I_1	R_1
$B - C - D - A$	I_2	R_2
$B - E$	I	R

Here, the total current in the circuit is $I = I_1 + I_2$
Therefore, the emf (V) in the circuit is

$$V = IR + I_1 R_1$$

or $\qquad V = IR + I_2 R_2$

Thus, by analogy with electric circuit, we have
Total mmf required $= \text{A}\cdot\text{t}$ for common section $(BE) + \text{A}\cdot\text{t}$ for any one of the parallel paths $(AF$ or $CD)$
From the above analysis of series and parallel composite magnetic circuits, *Kirchhoff's laws for Magnetic Circuits* can be stated as follows:
First Law The total flux towards a node is equal to the total flux away from the node in any magnetic circuit. It can also be stated that the sum of all magnetic fluxes at a single node is zero. Hence, Σ magnetic flux $= 0$.
Second Law In any magnetic circuit, the sum of the product of the magnetic flux and the reluctance in each part of the magnetic circuit is equal to the summation of individual mmf produced in each part of the magnetic circuit.

i.e., $\qquad \Sigma\text{mmf} = \Sigma\left(\text{reluctance} \times \text{magnetic flux}\right)$

The comparison between magnetic circuit and electric circuit is discussed in Table 5.4.

Table 5.4 *Comparison between magnetic circuit and electric circuit*

S. No.	Magnetic Circuit	Electric Circuit
1	The closed path traced by magnetic flux is known as magnetic circuit.	The closed path traced by electric current is known as electric circuit.
2	The driving force to produce flux in magnetic circuit is magnetomotive force (*mmf*) and its unit is ampere-turn $(A \cdot t)$.	The driving force to generate current in electric circuit is electromotive force (*emf*) and its unit is volt (V).
3	Magnetic flux is opposed by reluctance $(\mathfrak{R})$. The reluctance is $\mathfrak{R} = \dfrac{l}{\mu A}$, where μ is the permeability. Its unit is $A \cdot t/Wb$.	Electric current is opposed by resistance (R). The resistance is $R = \dfrac{\rho l}{A}$, where ρ is the resistivity. Its unit is ohm.
4	Magnetic flux, $\Phi = \dfrac{mmf}{reluctance}$ Wb	Electric current, $I = \dfrac{emf}{resistance}$ A
5	Ohm's law is given by $mmf = reluctance \times magnetic\ flux$ i.e., $V_m = \mathfrak{R}\Phi$	Ohm's law is given by $emf = resistance \times electric\ current$ i.e., $V = RI$
6	Kirchhoff's laws are given by Σ magnetic flux $= 0$ and $\Sigma\ mmf = \Sigma (reluctance \times magnetic\ flux)$	Kirchhoff's laws are given by Σ electric current $= 0$ and $\Sigma\ emf = \Sigma (resistance \times electric\ current)$
7	Permeance is given by $P = \dfrac{1}{\mathfrak{R}}$ Wb/A $\cdot$ t	Conductance is given by $G = \dfrac{1}{R}\Omega^{-1}$
8	Magnetic flux is established in a circuit and does not actually flow.	Electric current flows in a circuit due to the movement of electrons
9	Energy is required to establish the magnetic flux, not to maintain it.	Energy is required to maintain the flow of electric current.

EXAMPLE 5.53

Determine the reluctance of an air gap in a dc machine where the apparent area is $A_a = 2 \times 10^{-2}\ m^2$ and the gap length $l_a = 5\ mm$.

SOLUTION

Given $l_a = 5\ mm$ and $A_a = 2 \times 10^{-2}\ m^2$.

The reluctance of an air gap is

$$\mathfrak{R} = \frac{l_a}{\mu_0 A_a} = \frac{5 \times 10^{-3}}{\left(4\pi \times 10^{-7}\right)\left(2 \times 10^{-2}\right)} = 1.99 \times 10^5\ A \cdot t/Wb$$

EXAMPLE 5.54

A magnetic circuit employs an air core toroid with 500 turns, cross sectional area of $6\,\text{cm}^2$, mean radius of $15\,\text{cm}$ and coil current of 4 A. Determine reluctance of the circuit, flux density and magnetic field intensity.

SOLUTION

Given $A = 6\,\text{cm}^2$, $N = 500$, $\rho = 15\,\text{cm}$ and $I = 4\,\text{A}$.

The reluctance is
$$\Re = \frac{l}{\mu A} = \frac{2\pi\rho}{\mu_0\mu_r A}$$
where $l = 2\pi\rho$ is the circumference of the toroid.

Hence,
$$\Re = \frac{2\pi \times 15 \times 10^{-2}}{4\pi \times 10^{-7} \times 1 \times 6 \times 10^{-4}} \qquad (\text{since } \mu_r = 1 \text{ for air})$$
$$= 1.25 \times 10^9 \text{ A}\cdot\text{t/Wb}$$

The total magnetic flux is
$$\Phi = \frac{\text{mmf}}{\text{reluctance}} = \frac{NI}{\Re}$$
$$= \frac{500 \times 4}{1.25 \times 10^9} = 1.6 \times 10^{-6} \text{ Wb}$$

Therefore, the magnetic flux density is
$$B = \frac{\Phi}{A} = \frac{1.6 \times 10^{-6}}{6 \times 10^{-4}} = 2.667 \times 10^{-3} \text{ Wb/m}^2$$

Since $B = \mu H$, the magnetic field intensity is
$$H = \frac{B}{\mu} = \frac{2.667 \times 10^{-3}}{4\pi \times 10^{-7}} = 2123.4 \text{ A/m}$$

EXAMPLE 5.55

A cobalt ring $\left(\mu_r = 600\right)$ has a mean radius of $30\,\text{cm}$. If a coil wound on the ring carries a current of $12\,\text{A}$, calculate the number of turns required to establish an average magnetic flux density of 1.5 Wb/m in the ring.

SOLUTION

Given $B = 1.5\,\text{Wb/m}$, $\rho = 30\,\text{cm}$ and $I = 12\,\text{A}$.

For the cobalt ring, $\mu_r = 600$.

The ampere turns is $NI = Hl = \dfrac{Bl}{\mu}$, where $l = 2\pi\rho = 0.6\pi$.

Hence, the number of turns required to establish an average magnetic flux is
$$N = \frac{Bl}{\mu_0\mu_r I} = \frac{1.5 \times 0.6\pi}{4\pi \times 10^{-7} \times 600 \times 12} = 312.5$$

Therefore, $N \approx 313$ turns

EXAMPLE 5.56

For the magnetic circuit shown in Figure E5.56(a), calculate the current in the coil that will produce a magnetic flux density of 2.5 Wb/m^2 in the air gap assuming that $\mu = 100\mu_0$ and that all branches have same cross-sectional area of $20\,\text{cm}^2$. Draw the equivalent circuit of Figure E5.56(a).

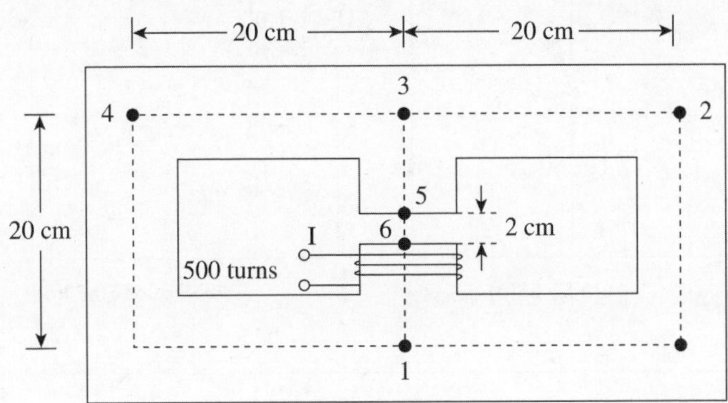

Figure E5.56(a)

SOLUTION

Given $B_a = 2.5\,\text{Wb/m}^2$ and $A = 20\,\text{cm}^2$. Figure E5.56(a) shows the magnetic circuit in which $\mathfrak{R}_1, \mathfrak{R}_2, \mathfrak{R}_3$ and $\mathfrak{R}_a$ are the reluctances in paths 1-4-3, 1-2-3, 3-5 and 1-6, and 5-6 (air gap), respectively. The reluctance is $\mathfrak{R} = l\,/\,\mu A$.

Therefore, $\mathfrak{R}_1 = \mathfrak{R}_2 = \dfrac{l}{\mu_0 \mu_r A} = \dfrac{60 \times 10^{-2}}{\left(4\pi \times 10^{-7}\right)(100)\left(20 \times 10^{-4}\right)} = 2.39 \times 10^6\,\text{A} \cdot \text{t/Wb}$

$$\mathfrak{R}_3 = \dfrac{18 \times 10^{-2}}{\left(4\pi \times 10^{-7}\right)(100)\left(20 \times 10^{-4}\right)} = 0.72 \times 10^6\,\text{A} \cdot \text{t/Wb}$$

$$\mathfrak{R}_a = \dfrac{2 \times 10^{-2}}{\left(4\pi \times 10^{-7}\right)(1)\left(20 \times 10^{-4}\right)} = 7.96 \times 10^6\,\text{A} \cdot \text{t/Wb}$$

The magnetic circuit reluctances $\mathfrak{R}_1$ and $\mathfrak{R}_2$ can be treated as parallel resistors as in electric circuit.

Therefore, $\mathfrak{R}_1 \parallel \mathfrak{R}_2 = \dfrac{\mathfrak{R}_1 \mathfrak{R}_2}{\mathfrak{R}_1 + \mathfrak{R}_2} = \dfrac{\mathfrak{R}_1}{2} = 1.195 \times 10^6\,\text{A} \cdot \text{t/Wb}$

Hence, the total reluctance is

$$\mathfrak{R}_T = \mathfrak{R}_a + \mathfrak{R}_3 + \mathfrak{R}_1 \parallel \mathfrak{R}_2 = \left(7.96 + 0.72 + 1.195\right) \times 10^6$$

$$= 9.875 \times 10^6\,\text{A} \cdot \text{t/Wb}$$

Hence, the magnetomotive force, $\text{mmf} = NI = \Phi_a \mathfrak{R}_T = B_a A \mathfrak{R}_T$

Therefore, $\quad I = \dfrac{B_a A \mathfrak{R}_T}{N} = \dfrac{2.5 \times 20 \times 10^{-4} \times 9.875 \times 10^6}{500} = 98.75\,\text{A}$

Figure E5.56 (b)shows the magnetic equivalent circuit of Figure E5.56 (a). Its simplified circuit is shown in Figure E5.56(c).

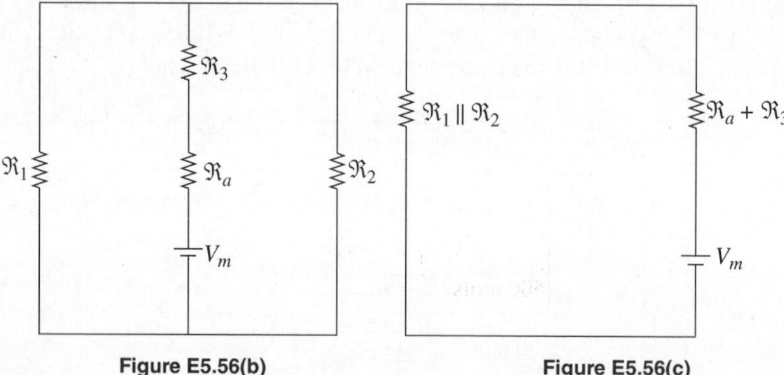

Figure E5.56(b)   Figure E5.56(c)

EXAMPLE 5.57

An iron toroid with a circular cross-section of radius 20 mm has a mean length of 280 mm and a flux of $\Phi = 2\,\text{mWb}$. Find the mmf required for the silicon steel core with relative permeability, $\mu_r = 1000$. Find the mmf required to establish the same flux if there is an air gap of 1 mm thickness in the core of the toroid.

SOLUTION

Given $l = 0.28\,\text{m}$, $l_a = 1\times10^{-3}\,\text{m}$, $\Phi = 2\,\text{mWb}$, $\rho = 20\,\text{mm}$ and $\mu_r = 1000$.

(*i*)   The reluctance of iron core is

$$\mathfrak{R}_c = \frac{l}{\mu_0 \mu_r A} = \frac{0.28}{4\pi\times10^{-7}\times1000\times\pi\times\left(20\times10^{-3}\right)^2}$$

$$= \frac{0.28\times10^7}{4\pi\times1.256} = 177.4\times10^3\,\text{A}\cdot\text{t/Wb}$$

Therefore, the mmf required for the silicon steel core is

$$V_m = \mathfrak{R}_c\Phi = 177.4\times10^3\times2\times10^{-3} = 354.8\,\text{A}\cdot\text{t}$$

(*ii*)   The reluctance of the air gap is

$$\mathfrak{R}_a = \frac{l_a}{\mu_0 \mu_r A} = \frac{1\times10^{-3}}{4\pi\times10^{-7}\times1\times\pi\times\left(20\times10^{-3}\right)^2} = 633.71\times10^3\,\text{A}\cdot\text{t/Wb}$$

Hence, the total reluctance is

$$\mathfrak{R}_t = \mathfrak{R}_c + \mathfrak{R}_a = 177.4\times10^3 + 633.71\times10^3 = 811.11\times10^3\,\text{A}\cdot\text{t/Wb}$$

Therefore, the mmf required to establish the same flux is

$$V_m = \mathfrak{R}_t\Phi$$

$$= 811.11\times10^3\times2\times10^{-3} = 1622\,\text{A}\cdot\text{t}$$

EXAMPLE 5.58

The toroidal core shown in Figure E5.58(a) has $\rho_0 = 5\,\text{cm}$ and a circular cross-section with $a = 2\,\text{cm}$. If the core is made of steel $(\mu = 1000\mu_0)$ and has a coil with 100 turns, calculate the amount of current that will produce a flux of 1 mWb in the core. Draw its equivalent circuit.

SOLUTION

Given $\rho_0 = 5\,\text{cm}$, $a = 2\,\text{cm}$, $N = 100$ and $\Phi = 1\,\text{mWb}$.

Magnetic Field Method

For a toroid, $B = \dfrac{\mu NI}{l} = \dfrac{\mu_0 \mu_r NI}{2\pi\rho_0}$

Therefore, the magnetic flux is

$$\Phi = BA = \frac{\mu_0 \mu_r NI\pi a^2}{2\pi\rho_0}$$

Hence, $I = \dfrac{2\rho_0\Phi}{\mu_0\mu_r Na^2} = \dfrac{2\left(5\times10^{-2}\right)\left(1\times10^{-3}\right)}{4\pi\times10^{-7}\,(1000)(100)\left(4\times10^{-4}\right)}$

$$= \frac{100}{16\pi} = 1.99\,\text{A}$$

Electric Circuit Method

The magnetomotive force is $V_m = NI = \Phi\mathfrak{R} = \Phi\,\dfrac{l}{\mu A} = \Phi\,\dfrac{2\pi\rho_0}{\mu_0\mu_r\pi a^2}$

Hence, $I = \dfrac{2\rho_0\Phi}{\mu_0\mu_r Na^2} = 1.99\,\text{A}$

The equivalent circuit is shown in Figure E5.58(b).

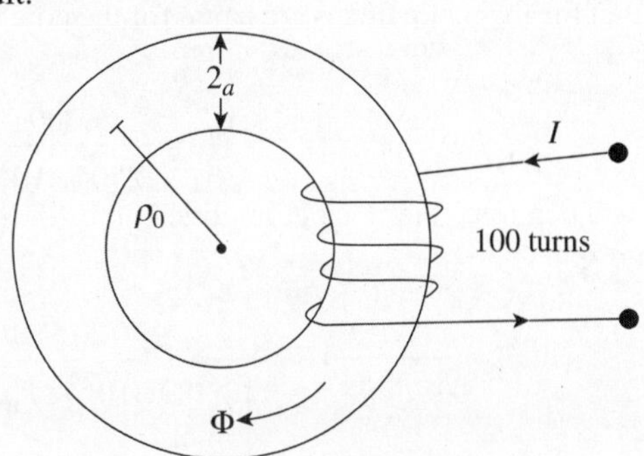

Figure E5.58(a)

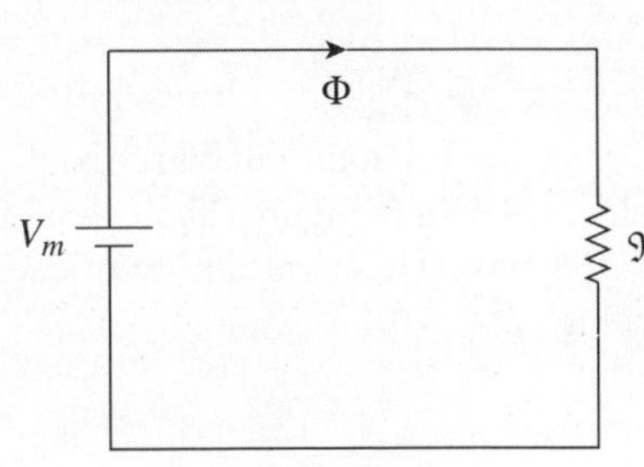

Figure E5.58(b)

EXAMPLE 5.59

The magnetic circuit of Figure E5.59(a) has current 20 A in the coil of 1000 turns. Assume that all branches have same cross-section of $2\,\text{cm}^2$ and that the material of the core is iron with $\mu_r = 1500$. Calculate $\mathfrak{R}$, Φ and V_m for (i) the core and (ii) the air gap. Draw the equivalent circuit of Figure E5.59(a).

SOLUTION

Given $\mu_r = 1500$, $A = 2\,\text{cm}^2$, $I = 20\,\text{A}$ and $N = 1000\,\text{turns}$.

The magnetomotive force is $V_m = NI = 1000\times20 = 20000\,\text{A}\cdot\text{t}$
The reluctance for the core is

$$\mathfrak{R}_c = \frac{l_c}{\mu_0\mu_r A} = \frac{(24+20-0.6)\times10^{-2}}{4\pi\times10^{-7}\times1500\times2\times10^{-4}} = 0.115\times10^7\,\text{A}\cdot\text{t/m}$$

The reluctance for the air gap is

$$\mathfrak{R}_a = \frac{l_a}{\mu_0\mu_r A} = \frac{0.6\times10^{-2}}{4\pi\times10^{-7}\times1\times2\times10^{-4}} = 2.389\times10^7\,\text{A}\cdot\text{t/m}$$

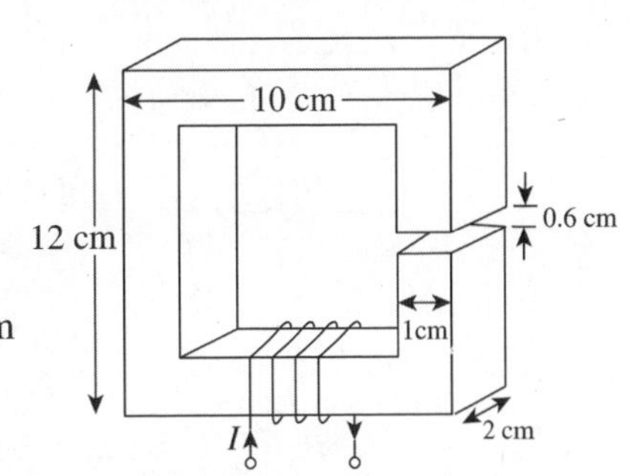

Figure E5.59(a)

Hence, the total reluctance for the magnetic circuit is

$$\Re = \Re_a + \Re_c = 2.504 \times 10^7 \, \text{A} \cdot \text{t/m}$$

From the equivalent circuit shown in Figure E5.59(b), it is seen that the magnetic fluxes are equal for the core and the air gap as given by

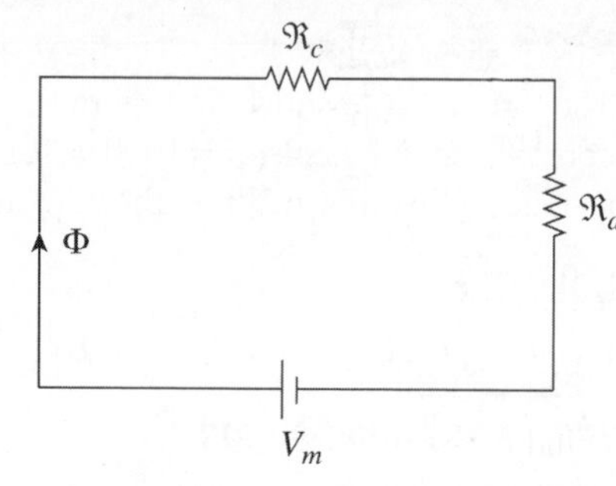

Figure E5.59(b)

$$\Phi = \Phi_c = \Phi_a = \frac{V_m}{\Re} = \frac{20000}{2.504 \times 10^7} = 7.98 \times 10^{-4} \, \text{Wb}$$

Therefore, the magnetomotive force (mmf) for the core and the air gap is

$$V_{mc} = \frac{\Re_c}{\Re_a + \Re_c} V_m = \frac{0.115 \times 10^7}{\left(2.389 \times 10^7\right) + \left(0.115 \times 10^7\right)} \times 20000 = 919 \, \text{A} \cdot \text{t}$$

$$V_{ma} = \frac{\Re_a}{\Re_a + \Re_c} V_m = \frac{2.389 \times 10^7}{\left(2.389 \times 10^7\right) + \left(0.115 \times 10^7\right)} \times 20000 = 19,081 \, \text{A} \cdot \text{t} \qquad \square$$

EXAMPLE 5.60

Determine the total reluctance and permeance between the ends of the series-connected rectangular iron blocks shown in Figure E5.60, assuming that the flux density B is uniform throughout the blocks and normal to the ends. The permeability of each block is uniform, the value of block 1 being $\mu_{r1} = 500$ and block 2 being, $\mu_{r2} = 2000$.

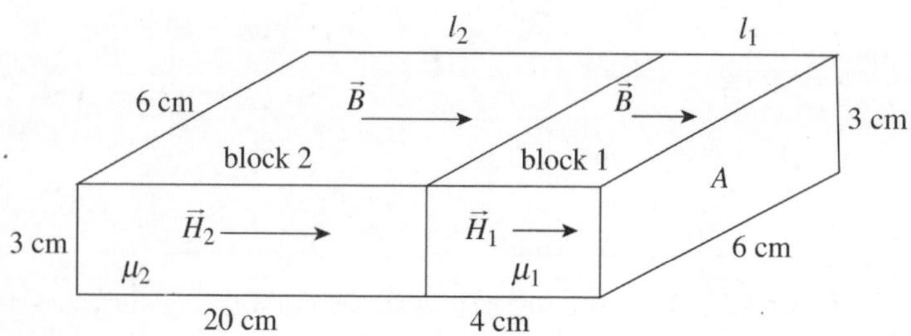

Figure E5.60

SOLUTION

The reluctance, $\Re_1$ of block 1 is

$$\Re_1 = \frac{l_1}{\mu_1 A} = \frac{4 \times 10^{-2}}{4\pi \times 10^{-7} \times 500 \times 3 \times 6 \times 10^{-4}} = 0.354 \times 10^5 \, \text{A} \cdot \text{t/Wb}$$

The reluctance $\Re_2$ of block 2 is

$$\Re_2 = \frac{l_2}{\mu_2 A} = \frac{20 \times 10^{-2}}{4\pi \times 10^{-7} \times 2000 \times 3 \times 6 \times 10^{-4}} = 0.422 \times 10^5 \, \text{A} \cdot \text{t/Wb}$$

Since the total reluctance $\Re_T$ is equal to the sum of the individual reluctances,

$$\mathcal{R}_T = \mathcal{R}_1 + \mathcal{R}_2 = (0.354 + 0.422) \times 10^5 = 0.796 \times 10^5 \, \text{A} \cdot \text{t/Wb}$$

Therefore, the total permeance is

$$P_T = \frac{1}{\mathcal{R}_T} = \frac{1}{0.796 \times 10^5} = 12.56 \, \mu\text{Wb/A} \cdot \text{t}$$

EXAMPLE 5.61

Find the total reluctance and permeance between the ends of the parallel connected rectangular iron block shown in Figure E5.61, assuming that B is uniform in each block and normal to the ends. The permeability of each block is uniform with the value in block 1, $\mu_{r1} = 500$ and in block 2, $\mu_{r2} = 2000$.

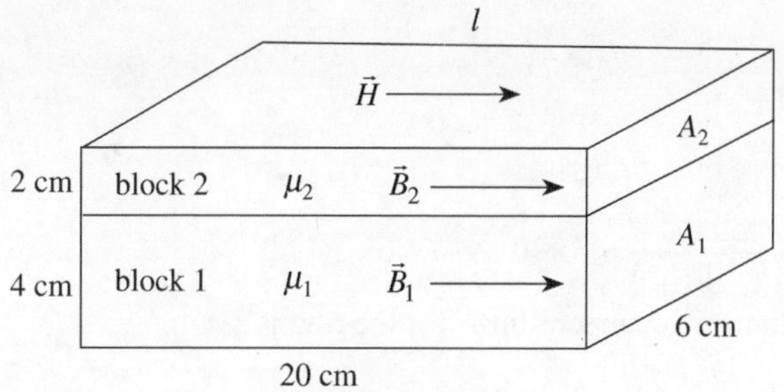

Figure E5.61

SOLUTION

Since the blocks are in parallel, it is more convenient to calculate the total permeance first. The permeance P_1 of block 1 is

$$P_1 = \frac{\mu_1 A_1}{l} = \frac{4\pi \times 10^{-7} \times 500 \times 24 \times 10^{-4}}{0.2} = 7.536 \times 10^{-6} \, \text{Wb/A} \cdot \text{t}$$

The permeance P_2 of block 2 is

$$P_2 = \frac{\mu_2 A_2}{l} = \frac{4\pi \times 10^{-7} \times 2000 \times 12 \times 10^{-4}}{0.2} = 15.12 \times 10^{-6} \, \text{Wb/A} \cdot \text{t}$$

Since, the total permeance P_T is equal to the sum of the individual permeances,

$$P_T = P_1 + P_2 = (7.536 + 15.12) \times 10^{-6} = 22.656 \, \mu\text{Wb/A} \cdot \text{t}$$

Then, the total reluctance is

$$\mathcal{R}_T = \frac{1}{P_T} = \frac{1}{22.656 \times 10^{-6}} = 44.2 \times 10^3 \, \text{A} \cdot \text{t/Wb}$$

EXAMPLE 5.62

An iron ring has a cross-sectional area $= 10\,\text{cm}^2$ and a mean length $l = 60\,\text{cm}$. Calculate the number of ampere-turns required for the ring for $B = 1\,\text{Wb/m}^2$ by first evaluating the reluctance of the ring. For the iron, $H = 1000\,\text{A/m}$ at $B = 1\,\text{Wb/m}^2$.

SOLUTION

Given $l = 60\,\text{cm}$, $A = 10\,\text{cm}^2$ and $H = 1000\,\text{A/m}$ at $B = 1\,\text{Wb/m}^2$ for iron.

The reluctance is

$$\Re = \frac{V_m}{\Phi} = \frac{NI}{BA}$$

Hence, $NI = \Re BA$

Since $H = 1000\,\text{A/m}$ at $B = 1\,\text{Wb/m}^2$,

$$\mu = \frac{B}{H} = \frac{1}{1000} = 10^{-3}\,\text{H/m}$$

Hence, the relative permeability is

$$\mu_r = \frac{\mu}{\mu_0} = \frac{10^{-3}}{4\pi \times 10^{-7}} = 795.77$$

Therefore, the reluctance of the ring is

$$\Re = \frac{l}{\mu A} = \frac{0.6}{10^{-3} \times 10^{-3}} = 6 \times 10^5\,\text{A} \cdot \text{t/Wb}$$

Hence, the required number of ampere-turns for the ring is

$$NI = \Re BA = 6 \times 10^5 \times 1 \times 10^{-3} = 600\ \text{ampere-turns}$$

or $\qquad NI = Hl = 1000 \times 0.6 = 600\ \text{ampere-turns}$

5.11 INDUCTANCE

An inductor is the magnetic equivalent of an electrical capacitor. It can store magnetic energy in the magnetic field like a capacitor storing electric energy in the electric field. A typical example of an inductor is a coil consisting of multiple turns of wire wound in a helical manner around a cylindrical iron core. Such a structure is called a *solenoid.*

Consider a coil with N turns carrying current I, produces a magnetic field as shown in Figure 5.16. The magnetic field causes a flux $\Phi = \int_s \vec{B} \cdot d\vec{s}$ which links each turn of the coil. Therefore, the flux linkage λ is defined as the product of the number of turns N and the flux Φ linking each turn of the coil. It is given by

$$\lambda = N\Phi \tag{5.56}$$

For a coil having a single turn, the flux linkage is equal to the total flux. If the medium surrounding the coil is linear, then the flux linkage λ is proportional to the current I producing it.

i.e., $\qquad \lambda \ \alpha \ I$

$$\lambda = LI \tag{5.57}$$

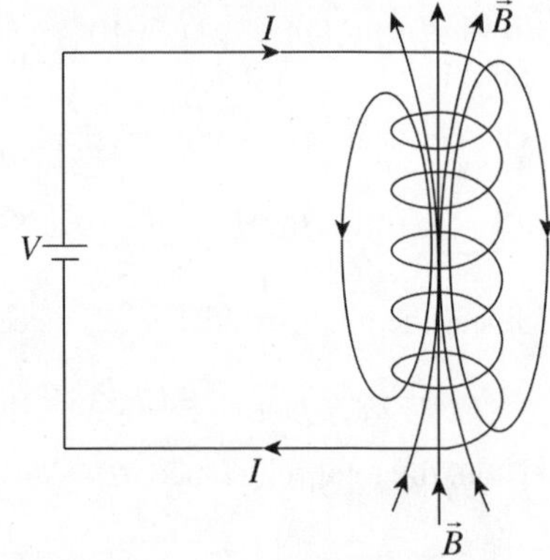

Figure 5.16 *Magnetic field produced by a coil carrying current I*

where the constant of proportionality L is called the inductance of the coil. Any coil or a circuit that has inductance is said to be an inductor.

5.11.1 Self Inductance

The inductance of a coil or an inductor is defined as the ratio of the total magnetic flux linkage λ to the current I flowing through the coil or inductor as given by

$$L = \frac{\lambda}{I} = \frac{N\Phi}{I} \tag{5.58}$$

The unit for inductance is henry (H) or weber per ampere (Wb/A). The inductance defined by the above equation is commonly called *self inductance* as the flux linkages are produced by the inductor itself.

The inductance can be regarded as a measure of magnetic energy stored in an inductor like the capacitance is regarded as a measure of electric energy stored in a capacitor. From circuit theory, the magnetic energy stored in an inductor is given by

$$W_m = \frac{1}{2}LI^2 \tag{5.59}$$

Therefore, the self inductance can be calculated from magnetic energy a

$$L = \frac{2W_m}{I^2}$$

5.11.2 Mutual Inductance

Consider two coils carrying currents I_1 and I_2 as shown in Figure 5.17, in which magnetic coupling takes place between the two coils. This coupling result in four flux linkages such as $\Phi_{11}, \Phi_{22}, \Phi_{12}$ and Φ_{21}. The current I_1 in coil 1 produces a flux Φ_{11} while coil 2 is open. Therefore, the self inductance of coil 1 is

$$L_{11} = \frac{\lambda_{11}}{I_1} = \frac{N_1\Phi_{11}}{I_1}$$

Similarly, the current I_2 in coil 2 establishes a flux Φ_{22} while coil 1 is open. Therefore, the self inductance of coil 2 is

$$L_{22} = \frac{\lambda_{22}}{I_2} = \frac{N_2\Phi_{22}}{I_2}$$

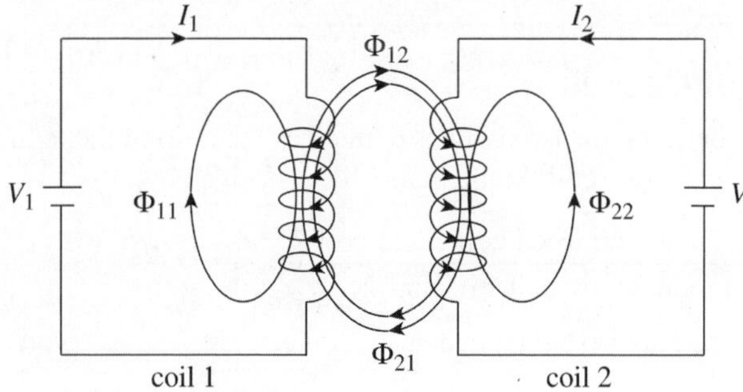

Figure 5.17 *Magnetic coupling between two coils*

The flux produced in coil 1 also links with coil 2 and produces another flux represented by Φ_{12}. The total flux linkage of the second coil due to the flux produced by current I_1 in the first coil is $\lambda_{12} = N_2\Phi_{12}$.

Similarly, the flux in coil 2 also links with coil 1 producing a flux represented by Φ_{21}. The flux linkage of the first coil due to the flux produced by current I_2 in the second coil is $\lambda_{21} = N_1\Phi_{21}$. The inductance defined in terms of flux linkages is called mutual inductance.

The *mutual inductance* between two coils is defined as the ratio of flux linkage of one coil to the current in other coil. Therefore, the mutual inductance M_{12} between coil 1 and coil 2 is given by

$$M_{12} = \frac{\lambda_{12}}{I_1} = \frac{N_2\Phi_{12}}{I_1} \tag{5.60}$$

where Φ_{12} is the flux produced by current I_1 which links the second coil carrying current I_2. Similarly, the mutual inductance M_{21} between coil 2 and coil 1 is given by

$$M_{21} = \frac{\lambda_{21}}{I_2} = \frac{N_1\Phi_{21}}{I_2} \tag{5.61}$$

where Φ_{21} is the flux produced by current I_2 which links the first coil carrying current I_1. If the medium surrounding the two coils is linear, then

$$M_{12} = M_{21} \tag{5.62}$$

The mutual inductance depends on the magnetic interaction between the two current carrying coils. Mutual inductance is important in transformers in which the primary and secondary windings share a common magnetic core. Similar to self inductance, the mutual inductance M_{12} or M_{21} is also measured in henry or weber per ampere.

Mutual inductance can also be defined as the ratio of the voltage generated in one circuit to the rate of change of current in the other circuit.

i.e., $$M = \frac{V_2}{dI_1 \, / \, dt}$$

where V_2 is the voltage induced in coil 2 due to the current in coil 1. Therefore,

$$V_2 = M_{21}\frac{dI_1}{dt}$$

Similarly, $$V_1 = M_{12}\frac{dI_2}{dt}$$

5.11.3   Coefficient of Coupling

The coefficient of coupling between the two coils is defined as the ratio of the total flux linkage between the two coils to the flux produced by one coil. Mathematically, it is given by

$$k = \frac{\text{Total flux linkage between coil 1 and coil 2}}{\text{Flux produced by coil 1 or coil 2}} = \frac{\lambda_{12}}{\Phi_1} = \frac{\lambda_{21}}{\Phi_2}$$

The coefficient of coupling can also be defined as

$$k = \frac{M}{\sqrt{L_1 L_2}} \tag{5.63}$$

where M is the mutual inductance between the two coils, i.e., $M = M_{12} = M_{21}$. The range of k is $0 \le k \le 1$ in which $k = 0$ denotes no coupling and $k = 1$ denotes perfect coupling.

A comparison between self inductance and mutual inductance is listed in Table 5.5.

Table 5.5 *Comparison of self inductance and mutual inductance*

S. No.	Self inductance	Mutual inductance
1.	Self inductance is the ratio of flux linkage to the current flowing through the same coil.	Mutual inductance of a coil is defined as the ratio of flux linkage in one coil due to the current in other coil.
2.	It is associated with only one coil.	It is associated with more than one coil.
3.	Self inductance is the actual value of an inductor element	It is not the actual value of an inductance but only a property associated with it.
4.	It is given by $$L_1 = \frac{N_1\Phi_1}{I_1} \text{ or } L_2 = \frac{N_2\Phi_2}{I_2}$$	It is given by $$M_{12} = \frac{N_2\Phi_{12}}{I_1} \text{ or } M_{21} = \frac{N_1\Phi_{21}}{I_2}$$
5.	The self inductance of a coil can be increased by increasing the number of turns (N), area of cross-section (A) and by selecting the material of high permeability (μ).	The mutual inductance of a coil can be increased by increasing the relative permeability (μ_r) and by maintaining low spacing between the two coils.
6.	It depends on the current I passing through its own coil.	It depends on current passing through its neighbouring coil.

EXAMPLE 5.63

A current of 2 A is flowing through an inductor of 100 mH. What is the energy stored in the inductor?

SOLUTION

Given $I = 2\,\text{A}$ and $L = 100\,\text{mH}$.

The energy stored in the inductor is

$$W_m = \frac{1}{2}LI^2 = \frac{1}{2}\times 100\times 10^{-3}\times (2)^2 = 0.2\,\text{J}$$

EXAMPLE 5.64

A coil has a self-inductance of 1 H and a resistance of 4 Ω. If it is connected to a 40 volt dc supply, estimate the energy stored in the magnetic field when the current has attained its final steady value.

SOLUTION

The inductor acts as short circuit in the steady state. Hence, the steady state current through the inductor shown in Figure E5.64 is

$$I = \frac{V}{R} = \frac{40}{4} = 10\,\text{A}$$

Therefore, the energy stored by the inductor is

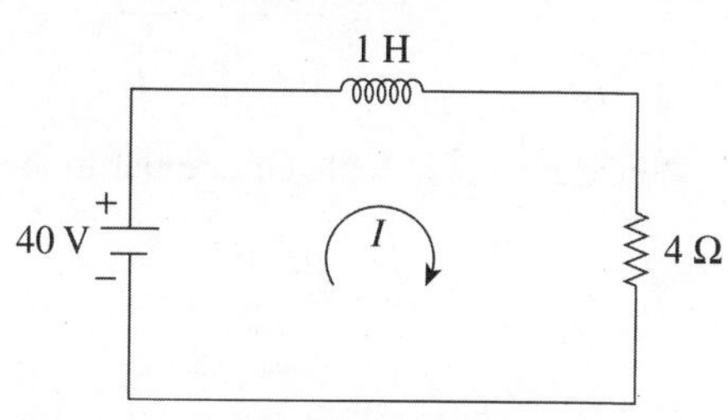

Figure E5.64

$$W_m = \frac{1}{2}LI^2 = \frac{1}{2}(1)(10^2) = 50\,\text{J}$$

EXAMPLE 5.65

Consider that two coaxial circular wires of radii a and b are separated by distance h, where $h \gg a, b$ and $b > a$ as shown in Figure E5.65. Find the mutual inductance between the wires.

SOLUTION

Let I_1 be the current flowing in wire 1. The magnetic vector potential due to wire 1 at any point P on wire 2 is

$$\vec{A}_1 = \frac{\mu I_1 a^2 \sin\theta}{4r^2} \vec{a}_\phi = \frac{\mu I_1 a^2 b}{4\left[h^2 + b^2\right]^{3/2}} \vec{a}_\phi$$

where $\sin\theta = \dfrac{b}{r}$ and $r = \left(h^2 + b^2\right)^{1/2}$.

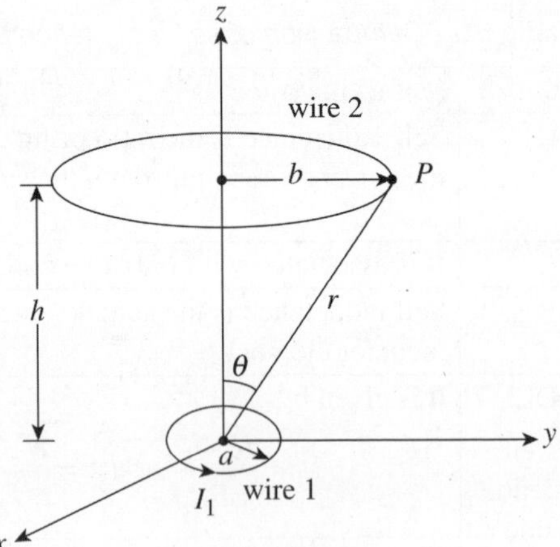

Figure E5.65

If $h \gg b$, then the magnetic vector potential becomes

$$\vec{A}_1 \approx \frac{\mu I_1 a^2 b}{4h^3} \vec{a}_\phi$$

Therefore,

$$\Phi_{12} = \oint \vec{A}_1 \cdot d\vec{l}_2 = \left(\frac{\mu I_1 a^2 b}{4h^3}\right)(2\pi b) = \frac{\mu \pi I_1 a^2 b^2}{2h^3}$$

Hence, the mutual inductance is

$$M_{12} = \frac{\Phi_{12}}{I_1} = \frac{\mu \pi a^2 b^2}{2h^3}$$

EXAMPLE 5.66

Find the mutual inductance of two coplanar concentric circular loops of radii $2\,\text{m}$ and $3\,\text{m}$.

SOLUTION

Given $a = 2\,\text{m}$ and $b = 3\,\text{m}$. The magnetic vector potential due to circular loop 1 at any point P on loop 2 is

$$\vec{A}_1 = \frac{\mu I_1 a^2 b}{4\left[h^2 + b^2\right]^{3/2}} \vec{a}_\phi$$

Since $h = 0$, for coplanar circular loops, the magnetic vector potential is

$$\vec{A}_1 = \frac{\mu I_1 a^2}{4b^2} \vec{a}_\phi$$

Therefore,

$$\Phi_{12} = \oint \vec{A}_1 \cdot d\vec{l}_2 = \left(\frac{\mu I_1 a^2}{4b^2}\right)(2\pi b) = \frac{\mu \pi I_1 a^2}{2b}$$

Hence, the mutual inductance is

$$M_{12} = \frac{\Phi_{12}}{I_1} = \frac{\mu \pi a^2}{2b}$$

$$= \frac{4\pi \times 10^{-7} \times \pi \times 4}{6} = 2.63\,\mu\text{H}$$

EXAMPLE 5.67

A solenoid with $N_1 = 2000$, $\rho_1 = 1\,\text{cm}$ and $l_1 = 200\,\text{cm}$ is concentric within a second coil of $N_2 = 6000$, $\rho_2 = 2\,\text{cm}$ and $l_2 = 200\,\text{cm}$. Find the mutual inductance assuming free space conditions.

SOLUTION

Given $N_1 = 2000$, $\rho_1 = 1\,\text{cm}$, $l_1 = 200\,\text{cm}$ (for solenoid 1) and $N_2 = 6000$, $\rho_2 = 2\,\text{cm}$, $l_2 = 200\,\text{cm}$ (for solenoid 2). For a solenoid with large length as compared to small cross-section, the magnetic field intensity inside the coil is assumed to be constant and it is zero for points just outside the solenoid. Assume the current flowing through the solenoid 1 as I_1.

The magnetic field intensity is

$$H_1 = \frac{N_1 I_1}{l_1} = \frac{2000 I_1}{200 \times 10^{-2}} = 1000 I_1 \text{ A/m}$$

Then, the magnetic flux density is

$$B_1 = \mu H_1 = \mu_0 \mu_r H_1$$

$$= 4\pi \times 10^{-7} \times 1000 I_1 = 1.256 \times 10^{-3} I_1 \text{Wb/m}^2$$

Therefore, the magnetic flux produced is

$$\Phi_1 = B_1 A_1 = \left(1.256 \times 10^{-3} I_1\right) [\pi \left(1 \times 10^{-2}\right)^2]$$

$$= 0.394 \times 10^{-6} I_1 \text{ Wb}$$

Since H_1 and B_1 are zero outside the solenoid 1, the flux determined above can link only with the solenoid 2. Therefore, the mutual inductance between two solenoids is

$$M_{12} = \frac{N_2 \Phi_1}{I_1} = \frac{6000 \times 0.394 \times 10^{-6} I_1}{I_1} = 2.364 \text{ mH}$$

EXAMPLE 5.68

A toroidal coil of 1000 turns is wound over a magnetic ring with inner radius of 15 mm, outer radius 20 mm, height 10 mm and relative permeability of 250. A very long, straight conductor passing through the center of the toroid carries a steady current. Determine the mutual inductance between the toroid and the straight conductor.

SOLUTION

Given $N_1 = 1000$, $h = 10\,\text{mm}$, $a = 15\,\text{mm}$, $b = 20\,\text{mm}$ and $\mu_r = 250$.

The magnetic flux density at any radius ρ within the toroid is

$$\vec{B} = \frac{\mu I}{2\pi\rho}\,\vec{a}_\phi$$

Hence, the flux linking the toroid is

$$\Phi_{21} = \int_s \vec{B}\cdot d\vec{s} = \left(\frac{\mu I}{2\pi\rho}\,\vec{a}_\phi\right)\cdot\left(d\rho\,dz\,\vec{a}_\phi\right) \qquad (\text{since } d\vec{s} = d\rho\,dz\,\vec{a}_\phi)$$

$$= \frac{\mu I}{2\pi}\int_a^b \frac{1}{\rho}\,d\rho\int_0^h dz$$

$$= \frac{\mu I h}{2\pi}\ln\left(\frac{b}{a}\right)$$

Therefore, the mutual inductance is

$$M_{21} = \frac{N_1 \Phi_{21}}{I} = \frac{\mu N_1 h}{2\pi}\ln\left(\frac{b}{a}\right)$$

$$= \frac{4\pi\times10^{-7}\times250\times1000\times10\times10^{-3}}{2\pi}\ln\left(\frac{20}{15}\right) = 0.145\,\text{mH}.$$

EXAMPLE 5.69

For two coils with negligible resistance and of self inductance of $0.2\,\text{H}$ and $0.1\,\text{H}$, determine the effective inductance of their combination in each case, if mutual inductance is $0.1\,\text{H}$.

SOLUTION

Given $L_1 = 0.2\,\text{H}$, $L_2 = 0.1\,\text{H}$ and $M = 0.1\,\text{H}$.

If the two coils are connected in series aiding, then their effective inductance is

$$L_{eff} = L_1 + L_2 + 2M$$

$$= 0.2 + 0.1 + 2(0.1) = 0.5\,\text{H}$$

If the two coils are connected in series opposition, then their effective inductance is

$$L_{eff} = L_1 + L_2 - 2M$$

$$= 0.2 + 0.1 - 2(0.1) = 0.1\,\text{H}$$

If the two coils are connected in parallel aiding, then their effective inductance is

$$L_{eff} = \frac{L_1 L_2 - M^2}{L_1 + L_2 - 2M} = \frac{(0.2)(0.1) - (0.1)^2}{(0.2) + (0.1) - 2(0.1)} = 0.1\,\text{H}$$

If the two coils are connected in parallel opposition, then their effective inductance is

$$L_{eff} = \frac{L_1 L_2 - M^2}{L_1 + L_2 + 2M} = \frac{(0.2)(0.1) - (0.1)^2}{(0.2) + (0.1) + 2(0.1)} = 0.02\,\text{H}$$

EXAMPLE 5.70

The effective inductance when two coils are connected in series aiding and series opposing are $3.48\,\text{H}$ and $2.12\,\text{H}$, respectively. If the inductance of one coil is 14 times the inductance of the other, determine the inductance of each coil, the mutual inductance and the coefficient of coupling between them.

SOLUTION

For series aiding, $L_1 + L_2 + 2M = 3.48$
For series opposing, $L_1 + L_2 - 2M = 2.12$
  Therefore, $L_1 + L_2 = 2.8$ and $M = 0.34$
  If $L_1 = 14L_2$, we get

$$L_2 = 0.187\,\text{H}$$

$$L_1 = 2.613\text{H}$$

Therefore, the coefficient of coupling between the two coils is

$$k = \frac{M}{\sqrt{L_1 L_2}} = \frac{0.34}{\sqrt{2.613 \times 0.187}} = 0.486$$

EXAMPLE 5.71

The self inductances of two coils are 600 mH and 400 mH. The coefficient of coupling is 0.7. Calculate the effective inductance when the coils are connected in (i) parallel aiding and (ii) parallel opposing.

SOLUTION

Given $k = 0.7$, $L_1 = 600\,\text{mH}$ and $L_2 = 400\,\text{mH}$.
  The mutual inductance is

$$M = k\sqrt{L_1 L_2} = 0.7\sqrt{0.6 \times 0.4} = 0.343 \text{ H}$$

(*i*) For parallel aiding, the effective inductance is

$$L = \frac{L_1 L_2 - M^2}{L_1 + L_2 - 2M} = \frac{0.6 \times 0.4 - (0.343)^2}{0.6 + 0.4 - (2 \times 0.343)} = 389.65 \text{ mH}$$

(*ii*) For parallel opposing, the effective inductance is

$$L = \frac{L_1 L_2 - M^2}{L_1 + L_2 + 2M} = \frac{0.6 \times 0.4 - (0.343)^2}{0.6 + 0.4 + (2 \times 0.343)} = 72.57 \text{ mH}$$

5.12 DETERMINATION OF INDUCTANCE

An inductor is a coil or conductor of any shape suitable to store magnetic energy. Typical examples of inductors are solenoid, toroid, coaxial cable and parallel-wire transmission line. The self inductance L of the above inductors can be evaluated using the following steps.

(*i*) Choose a suitable coordinate system based on the shape of the inductor material.

(*ii*) Assume the inductor carries current I through it.

(*iii*) Obtain the magnetic field intensity $\vec{H}$ from Biot–Savart's law or Ampere's law (only if symmetry exists).

(*iv*) Determine the magnetic flux density $\vec{B}$ using the formula $\vec{B} = \mu\vec{H}$.

(*v*) Calculate the flux Φ from $\Phi = \int_s \vec{B} \cdot d\vec{s}$

(*vi*) Determine the self inductance L using $L = \dfrac{\lambda}{I} = \dfrac{N\Phi}{I}$

5.12.1   Inductance of a Solenoid

A *solenoid* is a coil consisting of multiple turns of wire wound in a helical manner around a cylindrical iron core, as shown in Figure 5.18. Figure 5.18(a) shows that the wire turns of a solenoid are loosely wounded whereas its wire turns are tightly wounded in Figure 5.18(b). If the wire carries a current I, an uniform magnetic field is produced within the interior region of the solenoid. The magnetic field pattern of the tightly wounded solenoid is similar to that of a permanent magnet.

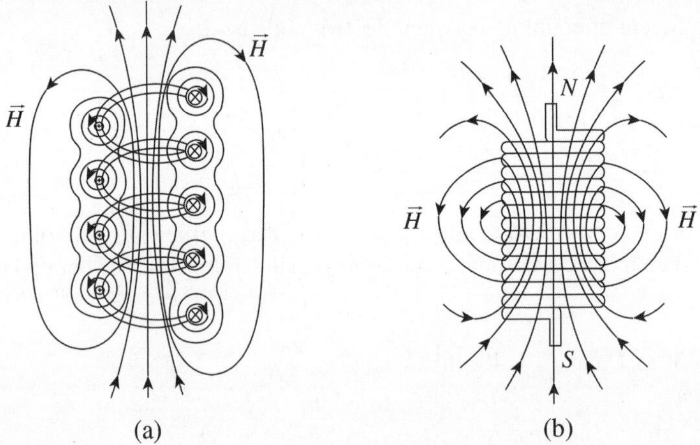

Figure 5.18   *Solenoid: (a) loosely wounded and (b) tightly wounded*

For a solenoid of length l with N turns carrying current I, the magnitude of magnetic field intensity H at the center of the solenoid is

$$H = nI$$

where the number of turns per unit length is $n = \dfrac{N}{l}$.

Since $B = \mu H$, the magnetic flux density of the solenoid is $B = \mu n I$. If A is the cross sectional area of the solenoid, the total flux linkage λ through the cross-section is given by

$$\lambda = N\Phi = NBA \qquad (\text{since } \Phi = BA)$$

$$= N\mu nIA = N\mu\left[\frac{N}{l}\right]IA = \frac{\mu N^2 IA}{l}$$

Hence, the inductance of the solenoid is given by

$$L = \frac{\lambda}{I} = \frac{\text{Total Flux Linkage}}{\text{Total current}}$$

$$= \frac{\mu N^2 A}{l} \, \text{H} \tag{5.64}$$

Therefore, the inductance per unit length of the solenoid is

$$L' = \frac{L}{l} = \mu n^2 A \ \text{H/m} \tag{5.65}$$

EXAMPLE 5.72

Calculate the inductance of a solenoid of 200 turns wound tightly on a cylindrical tube of 10 cm diameter. The length of the tube is 50 cm and the solenoid is in air.

SOLUTION

Given $l = 50\,\text{cm} = 50\times10^{-2}\,\text{m}$, $d = 10\,\text{cm} = 10\times10^{-2}\,\text{m}$ and $N = 200$.

For a given solenoid in air, $\mu_r = 1$ and $\mu_0 = 4\pi\times10^{-7}\,\text{H/m}$.

The inductance of a solenoid is

$$L = \frac{\mu N^2 A}{l} = \frac{\mu_0 \mu_r N^2 \left(\pi\rho^2\right)}{l}, \qquad \text{where } \rho = \frac{d}{2} = 5\times10^{-2}\,\text{m}$$

Therefore, $\quad L = \dfrac{4\pi\times10^{-7}\times(200)^2 \times \pi\times\left(5\times10^{-2}\right)^2}{50\times10^{-2}} = 0.79\,\text{mH}$ ☐

EXAMPLE 5.73

A solenoid is 0.3 m long and has a radius of 0.005 m. If it is closely wound and contains 1000 turns and the current flowing through it is 3 A, find the inductance per unit length of the solenoid.

SOLUTION

Given $l = 0.3\,\text{m}$, $\rho = 0.005\,\text{m}$, $N = 1000$ and $I = 3\text{A}$.

The magnetic flux density is $B = \mu_0 H$.

Therefore, $\quad B = \mu_0 \dfrac{NI}{l} = 4\pi\times10^{-7}\times\dfrac{1000\times3}{0.3} = 4\pi\times10^{-3}\ \text{Wb/m}^2$

Then, the inductance per unit length of the solenoid is

$$L' = \frac{L}{l} = \frac{N\Phi}{I} = \frac{NBA}{I} \qquad (\text{since } \Phi = BA)$$

$$= \frac{1000\times4\pi\times10^{-3}\times\pi\left(5\times10^{-3}\right)^2}{3} = 329\ \mu\text{H/m}$$ ☐

EXAMPLE 5.74

A solenoid with 2000 turns is 300 mm long and in 20 mm diameter. If the current is 600 mA, find the inductance of the solenoid and energy stored in solenoid.

SOLUTION

Given $N = 2000$ turns, $l = 0.3\,$m, $I = 0.6\,$A and $\rho = 0.01\,$m.

The inductance of the solenoid, $L = \dfrac{\mu_0 N^2 A}{l} = \dfrac{4\pi \times 10^{-7} \times (2000)^2 \times \pi (0.01)^2}{0.3} = 5.26\,$mH

Therefore, the energy stored, $W_m = \dfrac{1}{2} L I^2 = \dfrac{1}{2} \times 5.26 \times 10^{-3} \times (0.6)^2 = 0.9468\,$mJ $\square$

EXAMPLE 5.75

A solenoid has an inductance of 120 mH. If the length of the solenoid is increased by two times and the radius is decreased to half of its original value, find the new inductance.

SOLUTION

Given $L = 20\,$mH.

The inductance of the solenoid is

$$L = \frac{\mu N^2 A}{l} = 20\,\text{mH}$$

where $l =$ length of the solenoid, Area $A = \pi \rho^2$ and $N =$ Number of turns.

If length is made $2l$ and the radius is made $\dfrac{\rho}{2}$, then the inductance becomes

$$L_{new} = \frac{\mu N^2 \left[\pi (\rho/2)^2 \right]}{(2l)} = \frac{\mu N^2 (\pi \rho^2)}{8l} = \frac{1}{8} \left(\frac{\mu N^2 A}{l} \right)$$

$$= \frac{1}{8} \left(20 \times 10^{-3} \right) = 2.5\,\text{mH}$$ $\square$

EXAMPLE 5.76

A solenoid is 50 cm long, 2 cm in diameter and contains 1500 turns. The cylindrical core has a diameter of 2 cm and a relative permeability of 75. This coil is co-axial with a second solenoid of 50 cm long, 3 cm diameter and 1200 turns. Calculate L_{in} for the inner solenoid and L_{out} for the outer solenoid.

SOLUTION

(*i*) Given $\mu_r = 75$, $d = 2\,$cm, $l = 50\,$cm and $N = 1500$ (for inner solenoid).

The inductance of inner solenoid is

$$L_{in} = \frac{\mu N^2 A}{l} = \frac{\mu_0 \mu_r N^2 (\pi \rho^2)}{l}, \qquad \text{where } \rho = \frac{d}{2} = 1 \times 10^{-2}\,\text{m}$$

$$= \frac{4\pi \times 10^{-7} \times 75 \times (1500)^2 \times \pi \times (1 \times 10^{-2})^2}{50 \times 10^{-2}}$$

$$= 133.1\,\text{mH}$$

(*ii*) Given $\mu_r = 1$ (for air), $d = 3\,$cm, $l = 50\,$cm and $N = 1200$ (for outer solenoid).

The inductance of outer solenoid is

$$L_{out} = \frac{\mu_0 \mu_r N^2 \left(\pi \rho^2\right)}{l}, \qquad \text{where } \rho = \frac{d}{2} = 1.5 \times 10^{-2}\,\text{m}$$

$$= \frac{4\pi \times 10^{-7} \times (1200)^2 \times \pi \times \left(1.5 \times 10^{-2}\right)^2}{50 \times 10^{-2}}$$

$$= 2.56\,\text{mH}$$

EXAMPLE 5.77

A solenoid (air core) of 1 m length and 4 cm diameter is wound with 2000 turns of copper wire. It is placed coaxially within another solenoid with same length and number of turns but with a diameter of 7 cm. Determine the mutual inductance between the two solenoids and also the coupling coefficient of the arrangement.

SOLUTION

Given $N = 2000$, $l = 1\,\text{m}$, $d_1 = 4\,\text{cm}$ and $d_2 = 7\text{cm}$.

The self inductance of the solenoid 1 is

$$L_1 = \frac{\mu N^2 A}{l} = \mu_0 N_1^2 \left(\pi r_1^2\right) = 4\pi \times 10^{-7} \times (2000)^2 \times \pi (0.02)^2 = 6.3165\text{mH}$$

The self inductance of the solenoid 2 is

$$L_2 = \mu_0 N_2^2 \left(\pi r_2^2\right) = 4\pi \times 10^{-7} \times (2000)^2 \times \pi (0.035)^2 = 19.35\,\text{mH}$$

The mutual inductance is

$$M_{12} = \mu_0 N_1 N_2 \pi r_1^2 = 4\pi \times 10^{-7} \times 2000 \times 2000 \times \pi (0.02)^2 = 6.3165\,\text{mH}$$

Therefore, the coupling coefficient is

$$k = \frac{M_{12}}{\sqrt{L_1 L_2}} = \frac{6.3165 \times 10^{-3}}{\sqrt{6.3165 \times 10^{-3} \times 19.35 \times 10^{-3}}} = 0.5713$$

EXAMPLE 5.78

A very long solenoid with $2\,\text{cm} \times 2\,\text{cm}$ cross-section has an iron core with $\mu_r = 2000$ and 4000 turns/metre. If it carries a current of 500 mA, determine (i) its self inductance per metre and (ii) the energy per metre stored in field.

SOLUTION

Given area of solenoid $A = 2\,\text{cm} \times 2\,\text{cm}$, number of turns per unit length $n = 4000$ turns/metre, $\mu_r = 2000$ and $I = 500$ mA.

(*i*) The inductance per unit length of a solenoid is

$$L' = \frac{L}{l} = \mu n^2 A = \mu_0 \mu_r n^2 A$$

$$= \left(4\pi \times 10^{-7} \times 2000\right)\left(4000\right)^2\left(2 \times 10^{-2} \times 2 \times 10^{-2}\right)$$

$$= 16.07 \, \text{H/m}$$

(*ii*) The energy per metre stored by inductor is

$$W_m = \frac{1}{2}L'I^2 = \frac{1}{2}(16.07)\left(500 \times 10^{-3}\right)^2 = 2 \, \text{J/m} \qquad \square$$

5.12.2 Inductance of a Toroid

A *toroid* is a coil with closely spaced turns of wire wrapped around the core in the form of a ring as shown in Figure 5.19. The inner and outer radii of the toroidal ring are a and b, respectively.

The magnitude of magnetic field intensity for a toroid with N turns carrying current I in the region $a < \rho < b$ is

$$H = \frac{NI}{2\pi\rho}$$

Since $B = \mu H$, the magnetic flux density of the solenoid is

$$B = \mu \frac{NI}{2\pi\rho}$$

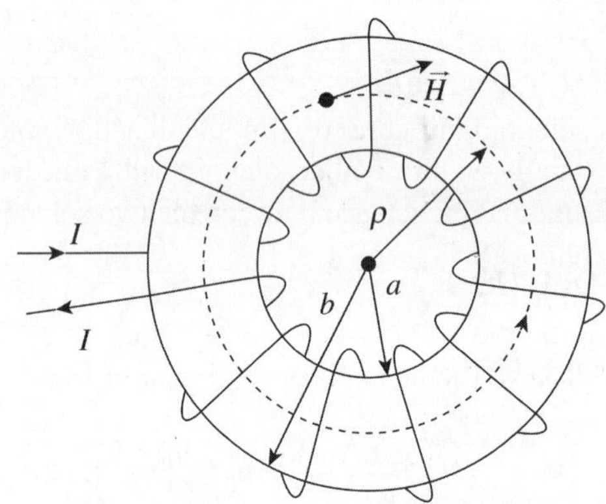

Figure 5.19 *Toroidal ring*

If A is the cross-sectional area of the toroid, then the total flux linkage λ through the cross-section is given by

$$\lambda = N\Phi = NBA \qquad (\text{since } \Phi = BA)$$

$$= N \times \frac{\mu NI}{2\pi\rho} \times A = \frac{\mu N^2 IA}{2\pi\rho}$$

Hence, the inductance of the toroid is

$$L = \frac{\lambda}{I} = \frac{\text{Total Flux Linkage}}{\text{Total current}}$$

$$= \frac{\mu N^2 A}{2\pi\rho} \, \text{H} \qquad\qquad\qquad (5.66)$$

where $A = \pi\rho^2$ is the cross-sectional area of a toroidal ring.

For a toroid with N number of turns, h as the height, ρ_1 as inner radius and ρ_2 as outer radius, the inductance is given by

$$L = \frac{\mu N^2 h}{2\pi} \ln\left(\frac{\rho_2}{\rho_1}\right) \text{H}$$

EXAMPLE 5.79

An air core toroid has circular cross-section of 4 mm radius. Find its inductance if there are 2500 turns and the mean radius is 20 mm.

SOLUTION

Given mean radius $\rho = 20\,\text{mm}$, $N = 2500$ and radius of cross-section $r = 4\,\text{mm}$.

The inductance of toroid is

$$L = \frac{\mu N^2 A}{2\pi\rho} = \frac{\mu_0 \mu_r N^2 \left(\pi r^2\right)}{2\pi\rho}$$

$$= \frac{\left(4\pi \times 10^{-7} \times 1\right)\left(2500\right)^2 \left(\pi\left(4 \times 10^{-3}\right)^2\right)}{2\pi \times 20 \times 10^{-3}} \qquad \text{(since } \mu_r = 1 \text{ for air)}$$

$$= 3.14\,\text{mH} \qquad\qquad\qquad \square$$

EXAMPLE 5.80

A coil of 500 turns is wound on a closed iron ring of mean radius 10 cm and cross-section area of $4\,\text{cm}^2$. Find the self inductance of the winding if the relative permeability of iron is 400.

SOLUTION

Given $A = 4\,\text{cm}^2 = 4 \times 10^{-4}\,\text{m}^2$, $\rho = 10\,\text{cm} = 10 \times 10^{-2}\,\text{m}$ and $N = 500$.

For a toroidal ring of iron, $\mu_r = 400$.

The inductance of an iron toroid is

$$L = \frac{\mu N^2 A}{2\pi\rho} = \frac{\left(\mu_0 \mu_r\right) N^2 A}{2\pi\rho}$$

$$= \frac{\left(4\pi \times 10^{-7} \times 400\right)\left(500\right)^2 \left(4 \times 10^{-4}\right)}{\left(2\pi \times 10 \times 10^{-2}\right)} = 80\,\text{mH} \qquad\qquad \square$$

EXAMPLE 5.81

Calculate the inductance of a toroid formed by surfaces $\rho_1 = 3\,\text{cm}$ and $\rho_2 = 6\,\text{cm}$, $z = 0$ and $z = 2\,\text{cm}$ wrapped with 1000 turns of wire and filled with a magnetic material with $\mu_r = 5$.

SOLUTION

Given outer radius, $\rho_2 = 6\,\text{cm}$, inner radius, $\rho_1 = 3\,\text{cm}$, height, $h = z = 2\,\text{cm}$, $\mu_r = 5$ and $N = 1000$.

The inductance of a toroid is

$$L = \frac{\mu N^2 h}{2\pi} \ln\left(\frac{\rho_2}{\rho_1}\right), \qquad \text{where } \mu = \mu_0 \mu_r$$

$$\text{Therefore, } L = \frac{\left(4\pi \times 10^{-7} \times 5\right)\left(1000\right)^2 \left(2 \times 10^{-2}\right)}{2\pi} \ln\left(\frac{6 \times 10^{-2}}{3 \times 10^{-2}}\right) = 13.9\,\text{mH} \qquad \square$$

EXAMPLE 5.82

A 200-turn coil wound on an iron ring having mean radius $\rho = 0.25\,\text{m}$. If the relative permeability of iron is 500, calculate the coil current to establish a 0.8 T average flux density in the ring.

SOLUTION

Given $\mu_r = 500$, $N = 200$ turns, $B = 0.8\,\text{T}$ and $\rho = 0.25\,\text{m}$.

Here,
$$H = \frac{B}{\mu_0 \mu_r} = \frac{NI}{2\pi\rho}$$

Therefore,
$$I = \frac{2\pi\rho B}{\mu_0 \mu_r N} = \frac{2\pi \times 0.25 \times 0.8}{4\pi \times 10^{-7} \times 500 \times 200} = 10\,\text{A}$$

EXAMPLE 5.83

A toroidal coil of 500 turns is wound on a steel ring of 0.5 m mean diameter and $2 \times 10^{-3}\,\text{m}^2$ cross-sectional area. An excitation of 4000 A/m produces a flux density of 1T. Find the inductance of the coil. If an air gap of 2mm width is cut in it, determine the current required to maintain the same flux density.

SOLUTION

Given $B = 1\text{T}$, $H = 4000\,\text{A/m}$, $N = 500\,\text{turns}$, $d = 0.5\,\text{m}$, $w_{ag} = 2\,\text{mm}$ and $A = 2 \times 10^{-3}\,\text{m}^2$.

The inductance of the coil is

$$L = \frac{\mu_0 N^2 A}{l}, \qquad \text{where } l = 2\pi\rho \text{ and } \rho = \frac{d}{2}$$

Therefore,
$$L = \frac{4\pi \times 10^{-7} \times 500 \times 500 \times 2 \times 10^{-3}}{2\pi \times 0.25} = 0.4\,\text{mH}$$

The magnetic flux density is
$$B = \frac{\mu_0 NI}{2\pi\left(\rho - w_{ag}\right)}$$

$$1 = \frac{4\pi \times 10^{-7} \times 500 \times I}{2\pi\left(0.25 - 2 \times 10^{-3}\right)}$$

Therefore,
$$I = \frac{2\pi \times 0.248}{4\pi \times 10^{-7} \times 500} = 2480\,\text{A}$$

EXAMPLE 5.84

A toroid core of 500 turns has a mean radius of 0.5 m and a radius of the winding section with 15 mm. Find the average self inductance (i) with air core and (ii) with iron core $\mu_r = 750$.

SOLUTION

Given $N = 500\,\text{turns}$, mean radius $\rho = 0.5\,\text{m}$ and radius of winding $r = 15\,\text{mm}$.

(i)
$$L_{air} = \frac{\mu_0 N^2 A}{2\pi\rho} = \frac{\mu_0 N^2 \left(\pi r^2\right)}{2\pi\rho} = \frac{4\pi \times 10^{-7} \times (500)^2 \times \pi \left(15 \times 10^{-3}\right)^2}{2\pi \times 0.5} = 70.65\,\mu\text{H}$$

(ii) $L_{iron} = L_{air} \times \mu_r = 70.65 \times 10^{-6} \times 750 = 52.98\,\text{mH}$

EXAMPLE 5.85

An iron ring of toroid, 0.2 m in diameter and 10 sq.cm sectional area of the core, is uniformly wound with 250 turns of wire. If the flux density in the core is to be 1Tesla and relative permeability of iron $\mu_r = 500$, what is the exciting current required to be passed in the winding? Also, determine the value of self-inductance and the energy stored.

SOLUTION

Given $d = 0.2\,\text{m}$, $A = 10\,\text{cm}^2$, $N = 250\,\text{turns}$, $\mu_r = 500$ and $B = 1\,\text{T}$.

Here, $B = \mu_0 \mu_r H$ and $H = \dfrac{NI}{l_m} = \dfrac{NI}{2\pi\rho}$, where $\rho = d/2$.

Therefore, $B = \mu_0 \mu_r \left(\dfrac{NI}{\pi d} \right)$

$$1 = \left(4\pi \times 10^{-7} \right)(500) \left(\dfrac{250I}{0.2\pi} \right)$$

Upon solving, we get $I = 4\,\text{A}$.
The inductance is

$$L = \frac{\mu_0 \mu_r N^2 A}{l_m} = \frac{\left(4\pi \times 10^{-7} \right)}{\left(0.2\pi \right)}(500)(250)^2 \times 10^{-3} = 0.0625\,\text{H} = 62.5\,\text{mH}$$

The energy stored in the inductor is

$$W_m = \frac{1}{2}LI^2 = \frac{1}{2}\times 62.5 \times 10^{-3} \times 4^2 = 0.5\,\text{J}$$

EXAMPLE 5.86

A toroid has a core of square cross section, $2500\,\text{mm}^2$ in area, and a mean diameter of 250 mm. The core material is of relative permeability 1000. Calculate (i) the reluctance of the flux path and (ii) the number of turns to be wound on the core to obtain an inductance of 1H.

SOLUTION

Given $d = 250\,\text{mm}$, $A = 2500\,\text{mm}^2$, $\mu_r = 1000$ and $L = 1\text{H}$.

(*i*) The reluctance of the flux path is

$$\Re = \frac{l}{\mu A} = \frac{\pi \times 250 \times 10^{-3}}{4\pi \times 10^{-7} \times 1000 \times 2500 \times 10^{-6}} \qquad (\text{since } l = 2\pi\rho = \pi d)$$

$$= 250 \times 10^3 \,\text{A} \cdot \text{t/Wb}$$

(*ii*) The inductance of a toroid is

$$L = \frac{\mu N^2 A}{l} = \frac{N^2}{\Re}$$

$$N^2 = L\Re = 1 \times 250 \times 10^3$$

Therefore, $N = 500\,\text{turns}$

EXAMPLE 5.87

An air-core toroid has a mean radius of 40 mm and is wound with 400 turns of wire. The circular cross-section of the toroid has a radius of 4 mm. A current of 10 A is passed in the wire. Find the inductance and the energy stored.

SOLUTION

Given mean radius $\rho = 40\,$mm, $N = 400$, $I = 10$A and radius of cross-section $r = 4\,$mm.

The inductance of toroid is

$$L = \frac{\mu N^2 A}{2\pi\rho} = \frac{\mu_0 \mu_r N^2 \left(\pi r^2\right)}{2\pi\rho}$$

$$= \frac{\left(4\pi \times 10^{-7} \times 1\right)\left(400\right)^2 \left[\pi \times \left(4 \times 10^{-3}\right)^2\right]}{2\pi \times 40 \times 10^{-3}} \qquad \text{(since } \mu_r = 1 \text{ for air)}$$

$$= 40.192\,\mu\text{H}$$

Therefore, the energy stored by toroid is

$$W_m = \frac{1}{2}LI^2 = \frac{1}{2}\left(40.192 \times 10^{-6}\right)\left(10\right)^2 = 2.009\,\text{mJ} \qquad \square$$

EXAMPLE 5.88

The core of a toroid is $12\,\text{cm}^2$ and is made of material with $\mu_r = 200$. If the mean radius of the toroid is $50\,$cm, calculate the number of turns needed to obtain an inductance of $2.5\,$H.

SOLUTION

Given $A = 12\,\text{cm}^2$, $\rho = 50\,$cm and $L = 2.5\,$H. For a toroidal core, $\mu_r = 200$. The inductance of a toroid is

$$L = \frac{\mu N^2 A}{2\pi\rho}$$

Hence, $$N^2 = \frac{2\pi\rho L}{\mu_0 \mu_r A} = \frac{2\pi \times 50 \times 10^{-2} \times 2.5}{4\pi \times 10^{-7} \times 200 \times 12 \times 10^{-4}} = 0.02604 \times 10^9$$

Therefore, $$N = 5103 \text{ turns} \qquad \square$$

EXAMPLE 5.89

An air-core toroid with rectangular cross-section, has 700 turns, with inner radius of 1 cm and outer radius of 2 cm and height is 1.5 cm. Find the inductance using (i) the formula for square cross-section of toroids (ii) the approximate formula for toroid, which assumes a uniform H at mean radius.

SOLUTION

Given inner radius, $\rho_1 = 1\,$cm, outer radius, $\rho_2 = 2\,$cm, height, $h = 1.5\,$cm and $N = 700$.

(*i*) The inductance of toroid of square cross-section is

$$L = \frac{\mu_0 \mu_r N^2 h}{2\pi} \ln\left(\frac{\rho_2}{\rho_1}\right)$$

$$= \frac{4\pi \times 10^{-7} \times 1 \times (700)^2 \times 1.5 \times 10^{-2}}{2\pi} \ln\left(\frac{2 \times 10^{-2}}{1 \times 10^{-2}}\right) = 1.02 \, \text{mH}$$

(*ii*) By approximate formula for toroid, the inductance is

$$L = \frac{\mu_0 N^2 A}{2\pi \rho}$$

where the area of square cross-section, $A = (1\text{cm})(1.5\text{cm}) = 1.5 \times 10^{-4} \, \text{m}^2$ and the mean radius, $\rho = 1.5\,\text{cm} = 1.5 \times 10^{-2}\,\text{m}$.

Hence, $L = \dfrac{4\pi \times 10^{-7} \times (700)^2 \times \left(1.5 \times 10^{-4}\right)}{2\pi \times 1.5 \times 10^{-2}} = 0.98 \, \text{mH}$

Therefore, the inductance obtained by both formulae is approximately same for toroid, even when the radius is larger than the cross-section. ❏

EXAMPLE 5.90

An iron ring of relative permeability 100 is wound uniformly with two coils of 100 turns and 400 turns of wire. The cross-section of the ring is $4\,\text{cm}^2$ and the mean circumference is 50 cm. Calculate (i) the self inductance of the each of the two coils and the mutual inductance, (ii) the total self-inductance of the coils when connected in series in the same sense and (iii) the total inductance of the coils when connected in series opposition. Ignore leakage flux.

SOLUTION

Given $\mu_r = 100$, $N_1 = 100$, $N_2 = 400$, $A = 4\,\text{cm}^2$ and $l = 50\,\text{cm}$.

(*i*) The self inductance of coil 1 is

$$L_1 = \frac{\mu_0 \mu_r N_1^2 A}{l} = \frac{4\pi \times 10^{-7} \times 100 \times 100^2 \times 4 \times 10^{-4}}{0.50} = 1.005 \, \text{mH}$$

The self inductance of coil 2 is

$$L_2 = \frac{\mu_0 \mu_r N_2^2 A}{l} = \frac{4\pi \times 10^{-7} \times 100 \times 400^2 \times 4 \times 10^{-4}}{0.50} = 16.08 \, \text{mH}$$

The mutual inductance is

$$M_{12} = M_{21} = \frac{\mu_0 \mu_r N_1 N_2 A}{l}$$

$$= \frac{4\pi \times 10^{-7} \times 100 \times 100 \times 400 \times 4 \times 10^{-4}}{0.50} = 4.02 \, \text{mH}$$

(*ii*) The total self-inductance of the coils when connected in series in the same sense is

$$L_{eff} = L_1 + L_2 + 2M$$

$$= 1.005 + 16.085 + 2(4.02)$$

$$= 25.13 \, \text{mH}$$

(*iii*) The total inductance of the coils when connected in series opposition is

$$L_{eff} = L_1 + L_2 - 2M$$

$$= 1.005 + 16.085 - 2(4.02)$$

$$= 9.05\,\text{mH}$$

5.12.3 Inductance of a Coaxial Cable

Consider a coaxial cable of length l with inner conductor of radius a and outer conductor of radius b as shown in Figure 5.20. Assume the current through the coaxial cable is I.

Since the coaxial cable is a two-conductor transmission line separated by a dielectric, its total inductance is the sum of internal inductance and external inductance as given by

$$L = L_{in} + L_{ex} \tag{5.67}$$

where L_{in} is the internal inductance produced by the flux due to the inner conductor in the region $0 < \rho < a$ and L_{ex} is the external inductance produced by the flux between the inner and the outer conductor in the region $a < \rho < b$.

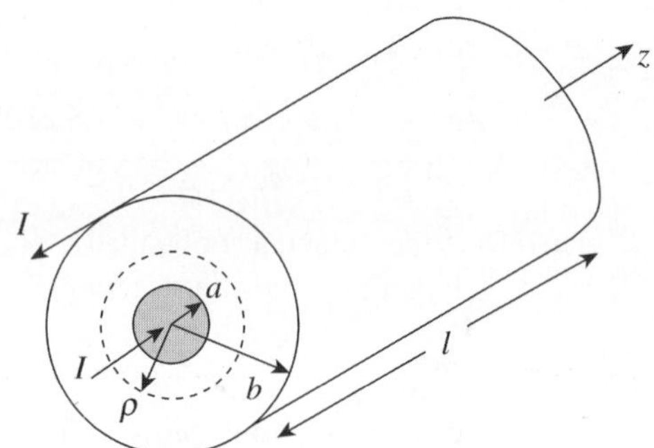

Figure 5.20 *Coaxial cable*

Let ρ be the radius of a Gaussian surface inside the cable. From Ampere's law, the magnetic flux density for the region $0 < \rho < a$ is

$$\vec{B}_1 = \frac{\mu I \rho}{2\pi a^2}\,\vec{a}_\phi$$

For the region $a < \rho < b$, the magnetic flux density is

$$\vec{B}_2 = \frac{\mu I}{2\pi \rho}\,\vec{a}_\phi$$

Let us first determine the internal inductance L_{in} by considering the flux linkages due to the inner conductor in the region $0 < \rho < a$. The flux linkage due to inner conductor is

$$\Phi_1 = \int_s \vec{B}_1 \cdot d\vec{s}_1$$

where $d\vec{s}_1$ is the differential area through which the flux leaves the region $0 < \rho < a$ as given by

$$d\vec{s}_1 = \left(\frac{\pi \rho^2}{\pi a^2}\right) d\rho\, dz\, \vec{a}_\phi = \frac{\rho^2}{a^2} d\rho\, dz\, \vec{a}_\phi$$

Therefore, $\Phi_1 = \displaystyle\int_{\rho=0}^{a}\int_{z=0}^{l} \left(\frac{\mu I \rho}{2\pi a^2}\,\vec{a}_\phi\right)\cdot\left(\frac{\rho^2}{a^2} d\rho\, dz\, \vec{a}_\phi\right)$

$$= \int_0^a \int_0^l \frac{\mu I}{2\pi a^4}\rho^3 d\rho\, dz = \frac{\mu I l}{2\pi a^4}\left[\frac{\rho^4}{4}\right]_0^a = \frac{\mu I l}{8\pi}\,\text{Wb}$$

The internal inductance L_{in} due to the inner conductor of the coaxial cable in the region $0 < \rho < a$ is

$$L_{in} = \frac{\Phi_1}{I} = \frac{\mu l}{8\pi} \, \text{H} \tag{5.68}$$

When a current flows through a long conductor, a magnetic flux is produced around the conductor which leads to internal inductance. Here, the internal inductance is independent of the radius of the inner conductor.

Let us now determine the external inductance L_{ex} by considering the flux linkages between the inner and outer conductors in the region $a < \rho < b$. Therefore, the flux linkage in the region $a < \rho < b$ is

$$\Phi_2 = \int_s \vec{B}_2 \cdot d\vec{s}_2 = \int_{\rho=a}^{b} \int_{z=0}^{l} \left(\frac{\mu I}{2\pi\rho} \, \vec{a}_\phi \right) \cdot \left(d\rho \, dz \, \vec{a}_\phi \right)$$

$$= \frac{\mu I l}{2\pi} \left[\ln \rho \right]_a^b = \frac{\mu I l}{2\pi} \ln \left[\frac{b}{a} \right] \text{Wb}$$

The external inductance L_{ex} in the region $a < \rho < b$ is

$$L_{ex} = \frac{\Phi_2}{I} = \frac{\mu l}{2\pi} \ln \left[\frac{b}{a} \right] \text{H} \tag{5.69}$$

Therefore, the total inductance of the coaxial cable is

$$L = L_{in} + L_{ex} = \frac{\mu l}{8\pi} + \frac{\mu l}{2\pi} \ln \left[\frac{b}{a} \right] \tag{5.70}$$

$$= \frac{\mu l}{2\pi} \left[\frac{1}{4} + \ln \left(\frac{b}{a} \right) \right] = \frac{\mu l}{2\pi} \left[\ln \left(\frac{b}{a} \right) \right] \text{H}$$

Hence, the inductance per unit length is

$$L' = \frac{L}{l} = \frac{\mu}{2\pi} \left[\ln \left(\frac{b}{a} \right) \right] \text{H/m} \tag{5.71}$$

At low frequencies, the internal inductance is significant while at high frequencies, the internal inductance is negligible as the current in the conductor will concentrate near the surface and the enclosed current becomes very small in the region $0 < \rho < a$.

EXAMPLE 5.91

Find inductance per unit length of a co-axial cable if radius of inner and outer conductors are 2 mm and 6 mm respectively. Assume relative permeability as unity.

SOLUTION

Given $a = 2\,\text{mm}$ and $b = 6\,\text{mm}$.

For a co-axial cable, the inductance per unit length is

$$L' = \frac{L}{l} = \frac{\mu}{2\pi} \ln \left(\frac{b}{a} \right) = \frac{\mu_0 \mu_r}{2\pi} \ln \left(\frac{b}{a} \right)$$

$$= \frac{4\pi \times 10^{-7} \times 1}{2\pi} \times \ln \left(\frac{6 \times 10^{-3}}{2 \times 10^{-3}} \right) = 0.2197 \, \mu\text{H/m}$$

EXAMPLE 5.92

Calculate the inductance of a 20 m length of co-axial cable filled with a material for which $\mu_r = 40$ and radii of inner and outer conductors are 2 mrm and 8 mm respectively.

SOLUTION

Given $\mu_r = 40$, $l = 20\,\text{m}$, $a = 2\,\text{mm} = 2\times10^{-3}\,\text{m}$ and $b = 8\,\text{mm} = 8\times10^{-3}\,\text{m}$.

The inductance of a co-axial cable is

$$L = \frac{\mu l}{2\pi}\ln\left(\frac{b}{a}\right) = \frac{(\mu_0\mu_r)(l)}{2\pi}\ln\left(\frac{b}{a}\right)$$

$$= \frac{4\pi\times10^{-7}\times40\times20}{2\pi}\ln\left(\frac{8\times10^{-3}}{2\times10^{-3}}\right)$$

$$= 221.8\times10^{-6} = 221.8\,\mu\text{H}$$

5.12.4 Inductance of a Parallel-Wire Transmission Line

Consider a parallel-wire or two-wire transmission line separated by a distance d carrying currents in opposite directions and each wire having radius a as shown in Figure 5.21. Let I be the current flowing through wire 1 and $-I$ be the current flowing through wire 2.

Let ρ be the radius of a Gaussian surface in the wire. From Ampere's law, the magnetic flux density for the region $\rho < a$ is

$$\vec{B}_1 = \frac{\mu I \rho}{2\pi a^2}\vec{a}_\phi$$

Let us first determine the inductance L_1 by considering the flux linkages due to wire 1 in the region $0 < \rho < a$. The flux linkage in the wire 1 is

$$\Phi_1 = \int_s \vec{B}_1 \cdot d\vec{s}_1$$

where $d\vec{s}_1$ is the differential area through which the flux leaves the region $0 < \rho < a$ as given by

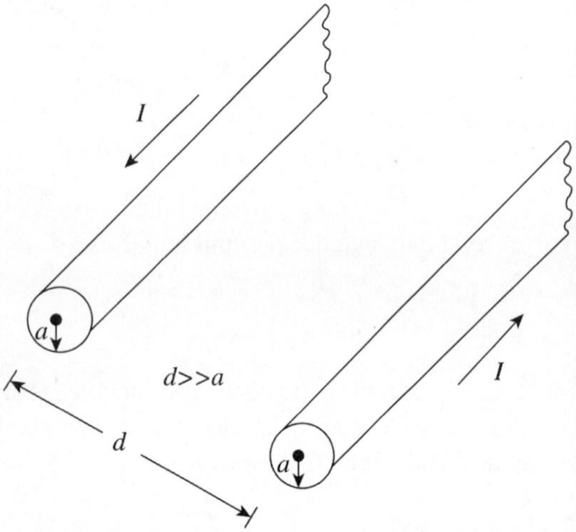

Figure 5.21 *Parallel-wire transmission line*

$$d\vec{s}_1 = \left(\frac{\pi\rho^2}{\pi a^2}\right)d\rho\,dz\,\vec{a}_\phi = \frac{\rho^2}{a^2}d\rho\,dz\,\vec{a}_\phi$$

Therefore, $\displaystyle \Phi_1 = \int_{\rho=0}^{a}\int_{z=0}^{l}\left(\frac{\mu I \rho}{2\pi a^2}\vec{a}_\phi\right)\cdot\left(\frac{\rho^2}{a^2}d\rho\,dz\,\vec{a}_\phi\right)$

$$= \int_0^a\int_0^l\frac{\mu I}{2\pi a^4}\rho^3\,d\rho\,dz = \frac{\mu I l}{2\pi a^4}\left[\frac{\rho^4}{4}\right]_0^a = \frac{\mu I l}{8\pi}\,\text{Wb}$$

Since wire 2 is kept at a distance from wire 1, the flux linkage between the wires due to the flux density in the region $a < \rho < (d-a)$ is

$$\Phi_2 = \int_s \vec{B}_2 \cdot d\vec{s}_2, \text{ where } \vec{B}_2 = \frac{\mu I}{2\pi\rho}\vec{a}_\phi$$

$$= \int_{\rho=a}^{d-a}\int_{z=0}^{l}\left(\frac{\mu I}{2\pi\rho}\vec{a}_\phi\right)\cdot\left(d\rho\,dz\,\vec{a}_\phi\right) = \frac{\mu Il}{2\pi}\left[\ln\rho\right]_a^{d-a}$$

$$= \frac{\mu Il}{2\pi}\ln\left(\frac{d-a}{a}\right)\text{Wb}$$

Hence, the total flux linkage between the wires produced by wire 1 is

$$\Phi_1 + \Phi_2 = \frac{\mu Il}{8\pi} + \frac{\mu Il}{2\pi}\ln\left(\frac{d-a}{a}\right)$$

By symmetry, the same amount of flux will be produced by the current $-I$ in wire 2. Therefore, the total flux linkage produced between the two-wire line is

$$\Phi = 2\left(\Phi_1 + \Phi_2\right) = \frac{\mu Il}{4\pi} + \frac{\mu Il}{\pi}\ln\left(\frac{d-a}{a}\right)$$

$$= \frac{\mu Il}{\pi}\left[\frac{1}{4} + \ln\left(\frac{d-a}{a}\right)\right]\text{Wb} \tag{5.72}$$

Therefore, the total inductance of the parallel-wire transmission line is given by

$$L = \frac{\Phi}{I} = \frac{\mu l}{\pi}\left[\frac{1}{4} + \ln\left(\frac{d-a}{a}\right)\right]\text{H} \tag{5.73}$$

The inductance per unit length is

$$L' = \frac{L}{l} = \frac{\mu}{\pi}\left[\frac{1}{4} + \ln\left(\frac{d-a}{a}\right)\right]\text{H/m}$$

If $d \gg a$, the inductance per unit length is

$$L' = \frac{\mu}{\pi}\left[\frac{1}{4} + \ln\frac{d}{a}\right]\text{H/m} \tag{5.74}$$

EXAMPLE 5.93

Calculate the loop inductance per unit length and the loop inductance per kilometre of two parallel wires spaced 100 cm apart having a conductor diameter of 2 cm.

SOLUTION

The loop inductance per unit length of two parallel wires is

$$L' = \frac{L}{l} = \frac{\mu_0}{\pi}\left[\frac{1}{4} + \ln\left(\frac{d}{a}\right)\right] \qquad (\text{since } d \gg a)$$

where radius of the wire, $a = 1\,\text{cm}$ and distance between the two parallel wires, $d = 100\,\text{cm}$.

Therefore, $L' = \dfrac{4\pi \times 10^{-7}}{\pi}\left[0.25 + \ln(100)\right] = 1.942\,\mu\text{H/m}$

The loop inductance is $L' = 1.942$ mH/km $\qquad\qquad\qquad\qquad\qquad\square$

5.13 ENERGY STORED IN MAGNETIC FIELDS

Similar to the capacitor, discussed in Chapter 4, the inductor is also an energy storing element. The capacitor stores energy in electrostatic field, while the inductor stores energy in magnetic field. From Eq. (5.59), the energy stored in an inductor is given by

$$W_m = \frac{1}{2}LI^2$$

This expression can also be derived in terms of $\vec{B}$ and $\vec{H}$ as follows:

Figure 5.22 shows a differential volume in a magnetic field. Assume that the conducting sheets with current ΔI are present at the top and bottom surfaces of the differential volume. Assume the whole region is filled with such differential volumes.

From the definition of inductance, the inductance (ΔL) of a differential volume can be written as

$$\Delta L = \frac{\Delta \Phi}{\Delta I} = \frac{B\Delta s}{\Delta I} \qquad (\text{since } \Phi = BA)$$

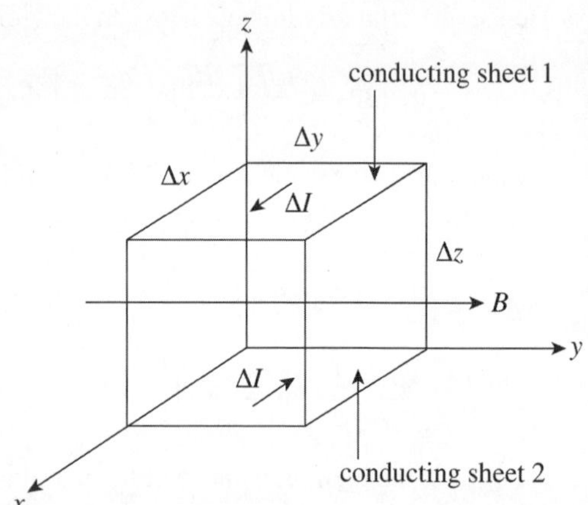

Figure 5.22 *Differential volume in magnetic field*

where the differential surface area $\Delta s = \Delta x \Delta z$. Since $B = \mu H$, the inductance is given by

$$\Delta L = \frac{\mu H \Delta x \Delta z}{\Delta I}$$

Now the differential current ΔI can be expressed in terms of the magnetic field intensity H. The current flowing through the conducting sheets present at the top and bottom is in y-direction as given by $\Delta I = H \Delta y$. The energy stored in the inductor of a differential volume is

$$\Delta W_m = \frac{1}{2}\Delta L\, \Delta I^2 \qquad\qquad\qquad\qquad (5.75)$$

Substituting values of ΔL and ΔI in the above equation, we have

$$\Delta W_m = \frac{1}{2}\left(\frac{\mu H \Delta x \Delta z}{H \Delta y}\right)(H \Delta y)^2 = \frac{1}{2}\mu H^2 \left(\Delta x\, \Delta y\, \Delta z\right)$$

$$= \frac{1}{2}\mu H^2 \Delta v$$

where the differential volume $\Delta v = \Delta x\, \Delta y\, \Delta z$.

The magnetostatic energy density is defined as the ratio of energy stored per unit volume as given by

$$w_m = \underset{\Delta v \to 0}{Lt} \frac{\Delta W_m}{\Delta v} = \frac{1}{2}\mu H^2 \tag{5.76}$$

The unit of energy density is J/m^3.

The magnetostatic energy density can be expressed in another form as

$$w_m = \frac{1}{2}(\mu H)H = \frac{1}{2}B \cdot H = \frac{B^2}{2\mu} \tag{5.77}$$

Therefore, the energy stored in a magnetostatic field in a linear medium is

$$W_m = \int w_m dv$$

$$W_m = \frac{1}{2}\int(\vec{B}\cdot\vec{H})dv = \frac{1}{2}\int(\mu H^2)dv = \frac{1}{2}\int\left(\frac{B^2}{\mu}\right)dv \tag{5.78}$$

Hence, the above equation represents the magnetostatic energy in terms of magnetic field intensity and flux density.

5.14 POTENTIAL ENERGY AND FORCES ON MAGNETIC MATERIALS

The energy stored in a magnetic field in a linear medium is given by

$$W_m = \frac{1}{2}\int(\vec{B}\cdot\vec{H})dv = \frac{1}{2}\int(\mu H^2)dv = \frac{1}{2}\int\left(\frac{B^2}{\mu}\right)dv$$

The above expression is similar to the potential energy stored in an electric field as given by

$$W_e = \frac{1}{2}\int(\vec{D}\cdot\vec{E})dv = \frac{1}{2}\int(\varepsilon E^2)dv = \frac{1}{2}\int\left(\frac{D^2}{\varepsilon}\right)dv$$

Any electromechanical system requires the determination of force exerted by a magnetic field on a magnetic material. Some of the common electromechanical systems are relays, rotating machines, electromagnets and magnetic levitation.

Consider an electromagnet made of iron with constant relative permeability as shown in Figure 5.23. The coil wounded on the iron core has N turns and carries a current I. Let the magnetic field in the air gap be same as that in iron. i.e., $B_{n1} = B_{n2}$. The two magnetic circuits are separated by differential element represented by dl. This differential displacement is equal to the change in the energy in the air gap.

The force exerted between the two pieces of iron can be calculated by the change in total energy. The work needed to make the displacement is equal to the change in energy stored in the air gap as given by

$$-Fdl = dW_m = 2\left[\frac{1}{2}\frac{B^2}{\mu_0}A\,dl\right] \tag{5.79}$$

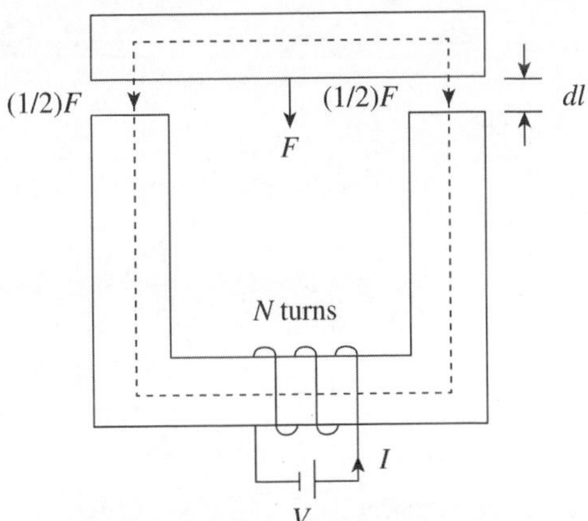

Figure 5.23 *Electromagnet*

where A is the cross-sectional area of air gap. As there are two air gaps, factor 2 is used to determine total energy. The negative sign indicates that there is a force of attraction and this force acts to reduce the air gap.

Therefore, $\quad F = -\dfrac{B^2 A}{\mu_0}$

Here, the force is exerted on the lower iron piece and not on the current carrying upper piece which gives rise to the magnetic field. The tractive force across a single gap is

$$F = -\frac{B^2 A}{2\mu_0}$$

The *tractive pressure* is defined as the ratio of force on a magnetic surface per area as given by

$$p = \frac{F}{A} = -\frac{B^2}{2\mu_0} = \frac{1}{2} BH = \frac{1}{2} \mu_0 H^2 \tag{5.80}$$

This equation is same as the energy density w_m in the air gap. The knowledge on tractive pressure is important for many applications in electromechanical systems.

EXAMPLE 5.94

If $\mu_1 = 5\mu_0$ for region $1 (0 < \phi < \pi)$ and $\mu_2 = 2\mu_0$ for region $2 (\pi < \phi < 2\pi)$ and $\vec{B}_2 = 10\vec{a}_\rho + 15\vec{a}_\phi - 20\vec{a}_z$ mWb/m^2, determine (i) $\vec{B}_1$ and (ii) the energy densities in the two mediums.

SOLUTION

(*i*) Given $\mu_1 = 5\mu_0$ for region 1 and $\mu_2 = 2\mu_0$, $\vec{B}_2 = 10\vec{a}_\rho + 15\vec{a}_\phi - 20\vec{a}_z$ mWb/m^2 for region 2.

Using magnetic boundary conditions for normal and tangential components, we have

$$\vec{B}_{n1} = \vec{B}_{n2} = 15\vec{a}_\phi$$

$$\vec{H}_{t1} = \vec{H}_{t2} \text{ and } \frac{\vec{B}_{t1}}{\mu_1} = \frac{\vec{B}_{t2}}{\mu_2}$$

Therefore, $\vec{B}_{t1} = \dfrac{\mu_1}{\mu_2} \vec{B}_{t2} = \dfrac{5\mu_0}{2\mu_0} \left(10\vec{a}_\rho - 20\vec{a}_z\right) = 25\vec{a}_\rho - 50\vec{a}_z$

Thus, $\vec{B}_1 = \vec{B}_{t1} + \vec{B}_{n1} = 25\vec{a}_\rho + 15\vec{a}_\phi - 50\vec{a}_z$ mWb/m^2

(*ii*) The energy densities in the two mediums are

$$w_{m1} = \frac{1}{2}\vec{B}_1 \cdot \vec{H}_1 = \frac{B_1^2}{2\mu_1} = \frac{\left(25^2 + 15^2 + 50^2\right) \times 10^{-6}}{2 \times 5 \times 4\pi \times 10^{-7}} = 266.72 \text{ J/m}^3$$

$$w_{m2} = \frac{1}{2}\vec{B}_2 \cdot \vec{H}_2 = \frac{B_2^2}{2\mu_2} = \frac{\left(10^2 + 15^2 + 20^2\right) \times 10^{-6}}{2 \times 2 \times 4\pi \times 10^{-7}} = 144.31 \text{J/m}^3$$

EXAMPLE 5.95

A long solenoid with length l and radius ρ consists of N turns of wire and a current I passes through the coil. Find the energy stored in the system.

SOLUTION

The magnetic field inside the solenoid is

$$\vec{H} = \frac{NI}{l}\,\vec{a}_z$$

The magnetic energy density within the solenoid is

$$w_m = \frac{1}{2}\mu_0 H^2 = \frac{1}{2}\mu_0\left(\frac{NI}{l}\right)^2$$

The total magnetic energy stored inside the solenoid is

$$W_m = \int_v w_m\,dv = \frac{1}{2}\int_v \mu_0\left(\frac{NI}{l}\right)^2 (\rho\,d\rho\,d\phi\,dz)$$

$$= \frac{1}{2}\mu_0\left(\frac{NI}{l}\right)^2 \int_0^\rho \rho\,d\rho \int_0^{2\pi} d\phi \int_0^l dz$$

$$= \frac{1}{2}\mu_0\left(\frac{NI}{l}\right)^2 \left(\pi\rho^2 l\right) = \frac{1}{2}\frac{\pi\mu_0\rho^2 N^2 I^2}{l}$$

$$= \frac{1}{2\mu_0}\left(\frac{\mu_0 NI}{l}\right)^2 \left(\pi\rho^2 l\right) = \frac{B^2}{2\mu_0}\left(\pi\rho^2 l\right)$$

where $\pi\rho^2 l$ is the volume within the solenoid.

EXAMPLE 5.96

Calculate the energy stored in the magnetic field of the toroidal winding.

SOLUTION

The magnetic field intensity inside the toroid is

$$\vec{H} = \frac{NI}{2\pi\rho}\,\vec{a}_\varphi, \ a \le \rho \le b$$

where a and b are the inner and outer radii of the toroid.

The magnetic energy density in the toroid is

$$w_m = \frac{1}{2}\mu_0 H^2 = \frac{1}{2}\mu_0\left(\frac{NI}{2\pi\rho}\right)^2 = \frac{1}{8}\mu_0\left(\frac{NI}{\pi\rho}\right)^2$$

Hence, the total magnetic energy within the toroid is

$$W_m = \int w_m\,dv = \frac{1}{8}\int \mu_0\left(\frac{NI}{\pi\rho}\right)^2 (\rho\,d\rho\,d\phi\,dz)$$

$$= \frac{N^2 I^2}{8\pi^2}\mu_0 \int_a^b \frac{1}{\rho}\,d\rho \int_0^{2\pi} d\phi \int_0^h dz$$

$$= \frac{\mu_0}{4\pi} N^2 I^2 h \,\ln\!\left(\frac{b}{a}\right)$$

EXAMPLE 5.97

Derive an expression for the magnetic energy stored in a coaxial cable of length l with inner and outer radii a and b. The insulation material has permeability μ.

SOLUTION

The magnetic field in the insulating material i.e., in the region between a and b for a coaxial cable is

$$H = \frac{I}{2\pi\rho}$$

where ρ is the radial distance from the inner conductor to the outer conductor.

The magnetic energy stored in the coaxial cable is

$$W_m = \frac{1}{2}\int_v \left(\mu H^2\right) dv = \frac{\mu I^2}{8\pi^2}\int_v \left(\frac{1}{\rho^2}\right) dv$$

$$= \frac{\mu I^2}{8\pi^2}\int_v \left(\frac{1}{\rho^2}\right)(\rho\,d\rho\,d\phi\,dz)$$

$$= \frac{\mu I^2}{8\pi^2}\int_a^b \frac{1}{\rho}d\rho\int_0^{2\pi} d\phi\int_0^l dz$$

$$= \frac{\mu I^2 l}{4\pi}\ln\left(\frac{b}{a}\right)$$

5.15   APPLICATIONS OF STATIC MAGNETIC FIELDS

The applications of static magnetic fields are mainly based on fundamental concepts studied in magnetostatics. Here, the circular motion of an electron in the magnetic field is described first and it is followed by some applications of static magnetic fields.

5.15.1   Motion of Electron in Magnetic Field

The magnetic force acting on a charged particle in a uniform magnetic field is

$$\vec{F}_m = Q\vec{u}\times\vec{B}$$

i.e.,
$$F_m = QuB\sin\theta \tag{5.81}$$

where θ is the angle between the direction of the magnetic field and the direction of motion of the particle with drift velocity $\vec{u}$. Here, it is seen that the magnitude of the magnetic force is proportional to the charge of the particle Q, the magnetic flux density B, the speed of the charged particle u and the angle θ between the directions of motion of the charged particle and the magnetic flux density.

If an electron is placed in a uniform magnetic field with zero initial velocity, then the magnetic force on the electron is zero, in accordance with Eq. (5.81). If the electron moves along the direction of magnetic flux density, then the angle is zero and the magnetic force is zero. A particle whose initial velocity has no component normal to a uniform magnetic field will continue to move with constant velocity along the lines of flux since the magnetic force on the particle is zero.

The magnetic force acting on an electron moving perpendicularly to the direction of the magnetic flux density is illustrated in Figure 5.24. The magnetic field is perpendicular to the plane of paper and directed towards the reader.

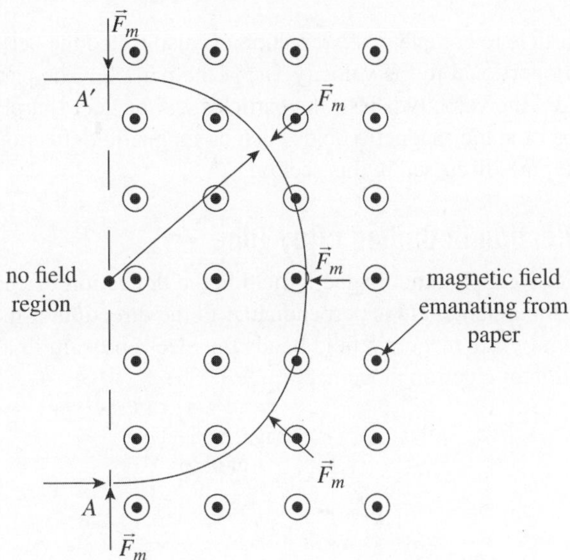

Figure 5.24 *Motion of an electron in a magnetic field*

Figure 5.24 shows that the electron is entering the magnetic field from no-field region with an initial velocity u_0. The direction of the current is opposite to that of the motion. Hence, the magnetic force is upwards and the electron will have a change in its direction of motion. At every point in the magnetic field, force acts on the electron and the resultant direction will be perpendicular to both the magnetic field and the direction of motion of electron at that point.

At every instant, the direction of force $\vec{F}_m$ is perpendicular to the direction of the particle and no work is done on the electron. This means that the kinetic energy is unaltered and the speed remains the same. This type of force makes an electron to move in a circular path with uniform speed. As shown in Figure 5.24, the direction of the magnetic force is always towards the centre O of the circle. This force is same as the centripetal force which always tries to push the electron towards the centre. Therefore,

$$\frac{mu^2}{r} = QBu \tag{5.82}$$

where r is the radius of circular path of the electron.

From Eq. (5.82), the radius of the electron path is given by

$$r = \frac{mu^2}{QBu} = \frac{mu}{QB} \tag{5.83}$$

The angular velocity of the electron in radians per second is given by

$$\omega = \frac{u}{r} = \frac{QB}{m} \tag{5.84}$$

The time for one revolution is

$$T = \frac{2\pi}{\omega} = \frac{2\pi m}{QB} \text{ seconds} \tag{5.85}$$

The time taken by the particle to complete one revolution is also called the period. We see from Eq. (5.83) that the radius is directly proportional to the velocity (u) of the particle. The particles that move faster will traverse in larger circles and if the velocity is less, the particles will be bent sharply in smaller circular paths.

Some of the applications of static magnetic fields such as magnetic deflection in cathode ray tube, Hall effect and mass spectrometer are discussed in this section.

5.15.2 Magnetic Deflection in Cathode Ray Tube

One of the important applications of static magnetic field is the deflection of charged particle in a cathode ray tube (CRT). The applied magnetic field is perpendicular to the direction of the electron beam. The force exerted on the electron beam by the magnetic field bends the electron beam in a direction perpendicular to both the field and the direction of electron movement.

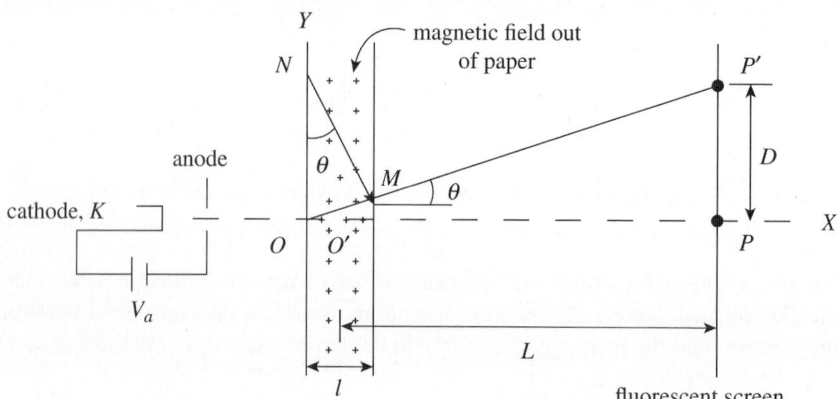

Figure 5.25 *Magnetic deflection system in a CRT*

Figure 5.25 shows the magnetic deflection system in a CRT. In the region of the uniform magnetic field, the electron experiences a force QBu, where u is the velocity. The path OM is the arc of a circle whose center is at N. The velocity of the charged particles remains constant before entering into the field as given by

$$u = \sqrt{\frac{2QV_a}{m}} \tag{5.86}$$

The small angle of deflection θ is equal to the length of the arc OM divided by r, the radius of the circle. Therefore,

$$\theta \approx \frac{l}{r} \tag{5.87}$$

The magnetic field continues to deflect the electron beam at right angles to its movement and hence, the path taken by the electron beam within the magnetic field is a part of a circle whose radius r is given by

$$r = \frac{mu}{QB} \tag{5.88}$$

where B is the magnetic flux density in Wb/m^2, u is velocity of the electron beam in m/s, m is the mass of an electron in kg, and Q is the charge of an electron in C.

Usually, L is far greater than l so that small error will be made in assuming that the straight line MP', if projected backward, will pass through the center O' of the region of the magnetic field. Therefore,

$$D = L \tan \theta = L\theta \tag{5.89}$$

Using Eqs. (5.86) to (5.88), the above equation becomes

$$D \approx L\theta = \frac{lL}{r} = \frac{lLQB}{mu} = \frac{lLB}{\sqrt{V_a}} \sqrt{\frac{Q}{2m}}$$

The magnetic deflection sensitivity of a CRT is defined as the ratio of the deflection to the magnetic field density. The magnetic deflection sensitivity D is

$$\frac{D}{B} = \frac{lL}{\sqrt{V_a}} \sqrt{\frac{Q}{2m}} \text{ mm/Wb/m}^2 \tag{5.90}$$

The magnetostatic deflection sensitivity is also defined as the amount of deflection of the spot caused by a current of 1 mA through the deflection of coil. Thus, magnetostatic deflection sensitivity can also be expressed in cm/mA.

The magnetostatic deflection sensitivity is independent of magnetic flux density B. The electrostatic deflection sensitivity varies inversely with the anode voltage, whereas the magnetic deflection sensitivity varies inversely with the square root of the anode voltage. The sensitivity increases with L and hence, for maximum sensitivity, the deflecting coils are placed as far down the neck of the cathode ray tube as possible. Here, the deflection of the charged particle is mainly due to the magnetic field in cathode ray tube.

5.15.3 Hall Effect

When a transverse magnetic field of flux density $\vec{B}$ is applied to a specimen (thin strip of metal or semiconductor) carrying current I, an electric field intensity $\vec{E}$ is induced in the direction perpendicular to both I and $\vec{B}$. This phenomenon is known as the *Hall effect*.

A Hall effect measurement experimentally confirms the validity of the concept that it is possible for two independent types of charge carriers, electrons and holes, to exist in a semiconductor.

The schematic arrangement of the semiconductor, the magnetic field and the current flow pertaining to the Hall effect are shown in Figure 5.26. Under the equilibrium condition, the electric field intensity $\vec{E}$ due to the Hall effect must exert a force on the carrier of charge Q, which just balances the magnetic force.

i.e., $\qquad Q\vec{E} = Q\vec{u} \times \vec{B}$ $\tag{5.91}$

where $\vec{u}$ is the drift velocity of the charge perpendicular to the magnetic field $\vec{B}$. Therefore, the magnitude of electric field intensity is

$$E = Bu \tag{5.92}$$

Also, the magnitude of electric field intensity due to Hall effect is

$$E = \frac{V_H}{d} \tag{5.93}$$

where d is the distance between surfaces 1 and 2, and V_H is the Hall effect voltage appearing between surfaces 1 and 2. In an N-type semiconductor, the current is carried by electrons and these electrons will be forced downward towards side 2 which becomes negatively charged with respect to side 1.

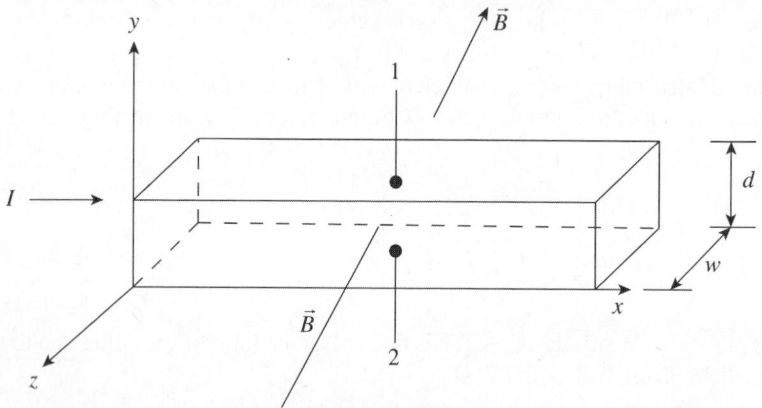

Figure 5.26 *Schematic arrangement to observe the Hall effect*

The current density $\vec{J}$ is related to volume charge density ρ_v and velocity $\vec{u}$ by

$$\vec{J} = \rho_v \vec{u} \tag{5.94}$$

Further, the magnitude of current density is related to current I by

$$J = \frac{I}{A} = \frac{I}{w \times d} \tag{5.95}$$

where w is the width of the specimen in the direction of magnetic field $\vec{B}$.

Combining the above relations, we get

$$V_H = Ed = Bud = \frac{BJd}{\rho_v} = \frac{BI}{\rho_v w} \tag{5.96}$$

The Hall coefficient R_H is defined by

$$R_H = \frac{1}{\rho_v} \tag{5.97}$$

Therefore, $V_H = \dfrac{R_H BI}{w}$ \qquad (5.98)

This potential difference between the two surfaces is called the Hall effect voltage. A measurement of the Hall coefficient R_H determines not only the sign of the charge carriers but also their concentration. The Hall coefficient for a P-type semiconductor is positive, whereas it is negative for an N-type semiconductor. This is true because the Hall voltage in a P-type semiconductor is of opposite polarity to that in an N-type semiconductor.

The advantage of Hall effect transducers is that they are non-contact devices with high resolution and small size.

The Hall effect is mainly used to find whether a semiconductor is N-or P-type and also to determine the density of free electrons in a metal. Since V_H is proportional to B for a given current I, Hall effect can be used to measure the ac power and the strength of magnetic field and sense the angular position of static magnetic fields in a magnetic field meter. It is also used in an instrument called Hall effect multiplier which gives the output proportional to the product of two input signals. Hall effect devices for such applications are made from a thin wafer or film of indium antimonide (InSb) or indium arsenide. Some of the other applications of Hall effect are in measurement of velocity, rpm, sorting, limit sensing and non-contact current measurements.

5.15.4 Mass Spectrometer

The separation of ions based on their masses can be done using mass spectrometer. Figure 5.27 shows a mass spectrometer and it consists of four basic components. They are (i) an ion source, (ii) a velocity selector, (iii) a deflection region with uniform magnetic field and (iv) an ion detector such as an electron multimeter. The mass spectrometer is mainly used in the study of isotopes.

The ion source ionizes the atom by knocking one or more electrons off to produce positive ions. Mass spectrometers always work with positive ions. These positive ions are accelerated by the velocity selector so that they all have the same kinetic energy. These ions now enter into a region with uniform magnetic field of flux density $\vec{B}'$ perpendicular to their motion.

The speed of the positive ion in the velocity selector is given by

$$u_0 = \frac{E}{B} \qquad (5.99)$$

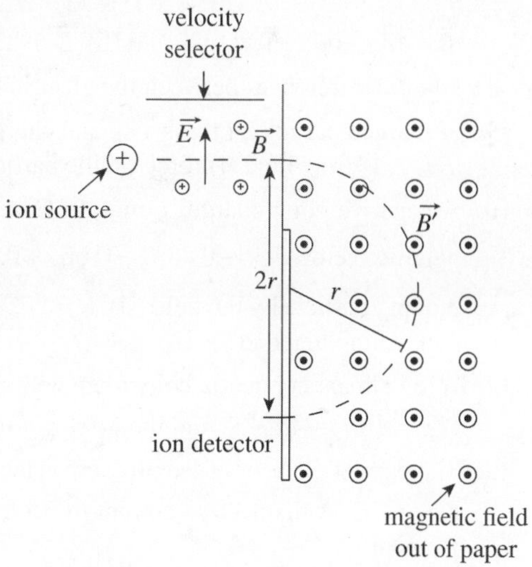

Figure 5.27 *Components of mass spectrometer*

Each ion is then deflected by a magnetic field of flux density $\vec{B}'$ according to their masses and each will take a semicircular path before being detected by the ion detector. Here, ions with lighter mass get deflected more. The amount of deflection also depends on the number of positive charges on the ion. The more the ion is charged, the more it gets deflected. The beam of ions passing through the ion detector is detected electrically.

The radius of the circular path taken by the charged particle in a magnetic field $\vec{B}'$ is

$$r = \frac{mu_0}{Q|\vec{B}'|} \qquad (5.100)$$

Here, the radius of the orbit depends on the mass of each ion. Therefore, the mass of a charged particle m can be determined by knowing the radius. From Eqs. (5.99) and (5.100), we get

$$m = \frac{QB'r}{u_0} = \frac{QB'rB}{E}$$

REVIEW QUESTIONS

1. Write the expression for force on a moving charge in a magnetic field.

2. Give the conditions of force on a charged particle in electric field and magnetic field.

3. Derive Lorentz force equation.

4. Mention the importance of Lorentz force equation.

5. Find the force exerted on a 5 m long conductor lying along z-direction with a current of 5 A in $\vec{a}_z$ direction and the magnetic flux density $\vec{B} = 0.08\vec{a}_x$ T.

6. A current element $2\,\text{m}$ in length carries $5\,\text{A}$ current along the y-axis, centered at the origin. If it experiences a force $\dfrac{1.5\left(\vec{a}_x + \vec{a}_z\right)}{\sqrt{2}}\,\text{N}$ due to a uniform magnetic field, determine magnetic flux density $\vec{B}$.

7. A point charge of value $-60\,\text{nC}$ is moving with a velocity of $4000\,\text{km/s}$ in a direction specified by the unit vector $\vec{a}_u = -0.48\vec{a}_x - 0.6\vec{a}_y + 0.64\vec{a}_z$. Using Lorentz force equation, find the force $\vec{F}$ if (a) $\vec{B} = 4\vec{a}_x - 6\vec{a}_y + 10\vec{a}_z\,\text{mT}$ and (b) $\vec{E} = 4\vec{a}_x - 6\vec{a}_y + 10\vec{a}_z\,\text{kV/m}$.

8. List the differences between the electric force and magnetic force.

9. A charged particle of mass $1\,\text{kg}$ and charge $2\,\text{C}$ starts at orgin with zero initial velocity in region where $\vec{E} = 3\vec{a}_z\,\text{V/m}$. Find (i) force on the particle and (ii) the time it takes to reach the point $P(0,0,12)\,\text{m}$.

10. A negative point charge, $Q = -40\,\text{nC}$ is moving with a velocity of $6\times10^6\,\text{m/s}$ in a direction specified by unit vector $\vec{a}_u = -0.48\vec{a}_x - 0.6\vec{a}_y + 0.64\vec{a}_z$. Find the magnitude of the vector force exerted on the moving particle by the field: (i) $\vec{B} = 2\vec{a}_x - 3\vec{a}_y + 5\vec{a}_z\,\text{mT}$, (ii) $\vec{E} = 2\vec{a}_x - 3\vec{a}_y + 5\vec{a}_z\,\text{kV/m}$, (iii) $\vec{B}$ and $\vec{E}$ both acting together.

11. A long linear conductor coincident with z-axis carries $10\,\text{A}$ current. The current flows in $+\vec{a}_z$ direction. If $\vec{B} = \left(3\vec{a}_x + 4\vec{a}_y\right)\text{T}$, find the force per unit length of conductor.

12. The current element of length $2\,\text{cm}$ is located at the origin in free space and carries a current of $12\,\text{mA}$ along $\vec{a}_x$. A filamentary current of $15\vec{a}_z\,\text{A}$ is located along $x = 3$, $y = 4$. Find the force on a current filament.

13. Derive the expression for force on a differential current element in a magnetic field.

14. Derive an expression for force between two current elements.

15. A conducting current strip carrying current of density $\vec{K} = 12\vec{a}_z\,\text{A/m}$ lies in the $x = 0$ plane between $y = 0.5$ and $y = 1.5\,\text{m}$. There is also a current filament of $I = 5\,\text{A}$ in the $\vec{a}_z$ direction along the z-axis. Find the force exerted on the filament by the current strip.

16. Consider that two circular loops of radii 1 m carrying currents 10 A and 5 A are situated in the $z = 0$ and $z = 1\,\text{m}$ planes, respectively and with their centers lying on the z-axis. Find the force experienced by current elements $\vec{dl_1}$ and $\vec{dl_2}$ located at $(1,0,0)$ and $(0,1,0)$ respectively.

17. Derive an expression for the force between two parallel wires carrying currents in the same direction.

18. Determine the force per metre length between two long parallel wires A and B separated by 10 mm in air and each carry current of 100 A in the same direction.

19. Two straight long parallel wires with their axes 10 mm apart are carrying currents of $10\,\text{kA}$ each in opposite direction. Calculate the force between them in N/m length. Indicate the direction of force on a neat diagram.

20. Consider that two infinite parallel conductors carry parallel currents of 10 A each. Find the magnitude and direction of the force between the conductors per metre length if the distance between them is 20 cm.

21. Derive the expression for force on a straight current carrying conductor placed in a magnetic field.

22. Two infinite and parallel conductor sheets carry surface currents $\vec{J}_s$ in opposite directions. If $\vec{J}_s = 10^{-2}\,\text{A/m}$ and the separation $d = 0.01\,\text{m}$, then find the force of translation per square metre.

23. Consider that two wires carry currents of 2 A and 3 A in opposite direction with 5 cm apart from each other in free space. Calculate force between them and state the nature of force.

24. Derive an expression for the torque developed in a current loop placed in a magnetic field.

25. Write an expression for torque in vector form.

26. Find an expression for torque acting on a square loop carrying a current I.

27. Find the torque that will be produced on a rectangular current loop if it is placed in a magnetic field of flux density $\vec{B}$. Show that $\vec{T} = \vec{m} \times \vec{B}$ also holds for the system.

28. A loop with magnetic dipole moment $8 \times 10^{-3}\, \vec{a}_z\, \text{A} \cdot \text{m}^2$ lies in a uniform magnetic field of flux density $\vec{B} = 0.2\vec{a}_x + 0.4\vec{a}_z\, \text{Wb/m}^2$. Calculate torque.

29. Derive an expression for the torque developed in a current loop placed in a magnetic field.

30. A differential current loop is placed in the $z = 0$ plane having a magnetic flux density $\vec{B}$. Find the total torque on the loop about the origin located at the center of the loop.

31. A rectangular loop in the xy-plane with sides b_1 and b_2 carry a current I in a uniform magnetic flux density $\vec{B} = B_x\vec{a}_x + B_y\vec{a}_y + B_z\vec{a}_z$. Determine the force and torque on the loop.

32. What is magnetic moment?

33. Derive the expression for the magnetic moment of a planar coil.

34. Write a short note on magnetic dipole moment.

35. For 500 turn rectangular coil, 15 cm in dimension, current of 5 A flows through it. It is placed in uniform field of $B = 0.1\,\text{T}$. Determine magnetic dipole moment and maximum torque.

36. Discuss how a differential current loop behaves like a magnetic dipole.

37. Define magnetic dipole.

38. Derive an expression for magnetic field intensity produced by a magnetic dipole.

39. Sketch the field due to magnetic dipole.

40. Classify different magnetic materials with suitable examples.

41. Briefly describe the nature and classification of magnetic materials.

42. Define diamagnetic, paramagnetic and ferromagnetic material.

43. What is meant by hysteresis? Draw hysteresis curve.

44. Explain the phenomenon of hysteresis with reference to ferromagnetic materials.

45. What is meant by soft and hard magnetic materials?

46. Explain ferrimagnetic and super magnetic material.

47. What is meant by ferromagnetic materials and ferrites?

48. Define magnetization.

49. Define magnetic susceptibility and magnetic permeability.

50. What is relative permeability of material?

51. Give the relationship between μ_r and χ_m.

52. What is the relationship between magnetic flux density, magnetic field intensity and magnetization?

53. Write notes on (i) diamagnetic (ii) paramagnetic (iii) ferromagnetic and (iv) antiferromagnetic materials.

54. Mention the uses of hysteresis loop.

55. Draw the $B - H$ curve for classifying magnetic materials.

56. Explain the phenomenon of hysteresis with reference to ferromagnetic material.

57. Define law of refraction for magnetic field.

58. State the magnetic boundary conditions between two mediums.

59. Derive the magnetic boundary condition at the interface between two magnetic mediums.

60. The interface $4x - 5z = 0$ between the magnetic mediums carries current $35\vec{a}_y$ A/m. If $\vec{H}_1 = 25\vec{a}_x - 30\vec{a}_y + 45\vec{a}_z$ A/m in region $4x - 5z \leq 0$ where $\mu_{r1} = 5$, calculate $\vec{H}_2$ in region $4x - 5z \geq 0$ where $\mu_{r2} = 10$.

61. Define a magnetic circuit with a sketch and hence, obtain the expression for its reluctance.

62. Write a note on magnetic circuits.

63. Briefly analyze composite magnetic circuits.

64. Tabulate the similarities and dissimilarities between electric and magnetic circuits.

65. Derive the expression for the reluctance in a magnetic circuit.

66. A magnetic circuit has four elements in series having reluctances $\Re_1, \Re_2 \Re_3$ and $\Re_4$. The flux flowing in each element is Φ weber. Determine the mmf equivalent of each element in the magnetic circuit. If the magnetic circuit is closed, determine the total mmf in the closed magnetic circuit.

67. Discuss the relation between field theory and circuit theory.

68. Define self inductance and mutual inductance.

69. What is meant by coefficient of coupling?

70. An iron ring of relative permittivity 200 wound uniformly with two coils of 100 and 400 turns of wire. The cross-section of the ring is $4\,\text{cm}^2$ and the mean length is 50 cm. Calculate the self inductance for each of the two coils and the mutual inductance.

71. Consider that two coils are connected in series and the total self inductance is 4.4 mH. When one coil is reversed, the total self inductance is 1.6 mH. All the flux due to the first coil links the second coil. But only 40% of the flux due to the second coil links the first coil. Find the self inductance of each coil and mutual inductance.

72. Write notes on self inductance and mutual inductance.

73. Give the comparison between self inductance and mutual inductance.

74. A small loop of wire with radius a lies at a distance z above the center of a large loop with radius b. The planes of the two loops are parallel and perpendicular to the common axis. Suppose current I flows in the big loop. Find the flux through the little loop. Find the mutual inductance.

75. The effective inductances when two coupled coils are connected in series aiding and series opposing are 3.28 mH and 0.72 mH, respectively. If the self inductance of one coil is four times the self inductance of the other, determine (i) the self inductance of each coil (ii) the mutual inductance and (iii) the coefficient of coupling.

76. What is a solenoid?

77. Give the expression for inductance and flux density inside the solenoid.

78. Derive an expression for inductance of a solenoid with N turns and length l carrying a current of I amperes.

79. A 4000 turns solenoid is 2 m long and has diameter 10 cm. Calculate the inductance of the solenoid and energy stored when a current of 8 A flowing through the coil.

80. Explain the constructional features of solenoid.

81. A solenoid with length 10 cm and radius 1 cm has 450 turns. Calculate its inductance.

82. Calculate the inductance of a long solenoid of length 80 cm and diameter 5 cm, having 2000 turns and relative permeability unity.

83. Calculate the inductance of a solenoid of 200 turns wound on a cylindrical tube 6 cm diameter. The length of the tube is 60 cm, and the medium is air.

84. Derive the expression for the magnetic flux density and inductance of a long solenoid.

85. A solenoid of length 30 cm is wound on a wooden core, the external and internal diameter of which are 4.0 cm and 3.5 cm respectively. If the current in the coil is 0.12 A, find the number of turns required to produce a magnetizing force of $750\,\text{A}\cdot\text{t/m}$ at the center of the coil.

86. Derive the formula for inductance of a coil with iron core.

87. Obtain the expression for the self inductance of a toroid of circular section with N closely spaced turns.

88. The core of a toroid is $12\,\text{cm}^2$. Calculate the number of turns required to obtain an inductance of 2.5 H.

89. A toroidal coil of 500 turns has a mean radius of 0.5 m and a radius of the winding section 15 mm. What is the average self-inductance (i) with air-core and (ii) with an iron core of relative permeability $\mu_r = 750$?

90. A toroidal core is composed of a material with $\mu_r = 25$. The surface forming toroid are $z = 0$, $z = 0.025\,\text{m}$, $\rho_1 = 0.025\,\text{m}$ and $\rho_2 = 0.04\,\text{m}$. The core is wound symmetrically with 12000 turns of wire such that $\vec{H}$ is in the $\vec{a}_\phi$ direction. Find inductance.

91. A 1000 turn closely and tightly wound toroid has an inductance of 20mH when the current in the coil is 2.5 A. What is the magnetic flux in the toroid?

92. Derive the expression for internal and external inductance of a coaxial cable.

93. An air coaxial transmission line has a solid inner conductor of radius a and a very thin outer conductor of inner radius b. Determine the inductance per unit length of the line.

94. Show that the inductance of the coaxial cable is $L = \dfrac{\mu l}{2\pi}\ln\left(\dfrac{b}{a}\right)$.

95. Using energy method, find the internal inductance of conductors with uniform current distribution in a coaxial transmission line.

96. Find the flux between the conductors of a coaxial line, carrying a uniformly distributed current I in the inner conductor and $-I$ in the outer conductor.

97. The inner and outer conductors of a coaxial cable are having radii a and b, respectively. If the inner conductor is carrying current I and outer conductor is carrying the return current I in the opposite direction. Derive the expressions for (i) the internal inductance and (ii) the external inductance.

98. Calculate the internal and external inductances per unit length of a transmission line consisting of two long parallel conducting wire of radius a that carry currents in opposite directions. The axes of the wires are separated by a distance d, which is much larger than a.

99. Write short notes on self and mutual inductance.

100. Determine the inductance per unit length of a parallel-wire transmission line with the wires having radius a and are separated by a distance d. Neglect any contribution to inductance, an account of flux inside the wires.

101. Derive the expressions for energy stored and energy density in the magnetic field.

102. Determine the energy density stored in the free space by fields, (i) $\vec{H}_A = 10^3\,\vec{a}_x\,\text{A/m}$, (ii) $\vec{H}_B = 10^3\,\vec{a}_y\,\text{A/m}$ and (iii) $\vec{H}_C = 10^3\,\vec{a}_x - 10^3\,\vec{a}_y\,\text{A/m}$.

103. In a certain material for which $\mu = 6.5\mu_0$, $\vec{H} = 10\vec{a}_x + 25\vec{a}_y - 40\vec{a}_z$ A/m, find (i) magnetic susceptibility (ii) magnetic flux density (iii) magnetization and (iv) magnetic energy density.

104. Derive an expression for the energy stored in the magnetic field of a coil possessing an inductance of L henry when the current in the coil is I ampere.

105. Show that energy produced per unit volume per second is equal to sum of energy stored per unit volume per second and the energy dissipated per unit volume per second.

106. Derive the energy density in magnetic field for the case of long solenoid of length l.

107. Prove that the energy stored in a magnetic field in the static case is given by $\int_v \frac{1}{2} \vec{B} \cdot \vec{H} \, dv$.

108. A coil has a self-inductance of 1H and a resistance of 2Ω. If it is connected to a 20 volt dc supply, estimate the energy stored in the magnetic field when the current has attained its final steady value.

109. A 500 turn toroid of square cross-section has an inner radius of 10 cm and an outer radius of 15 cm. The relative permeability of the core is 1000. For a current of 10 A in the coil, calculate (i) the energy density, (ii) the stored energy and (iii) the inductance of the toroid.

110. Write a note on potential energy and forces on magnetic materials.

111. Write notes on the applications of static magnetic fields.

112. Describe the motion of electron in a magnetic field.

113. Explain how magnetic deflection takes place in a cathode ray tube.

114. Discuss the operation of Hall effect and its applications.

115. Explain the construction and working principle of mass spectrometer.

CHAPTER 6

TIME-VARYING FIELDS AND MAXWELL'S EQUATIONS

6.1 INTRODUCTION

As we have seen in the previous chapters, it was thought that electric fields can only be produced by the presence of charges. However, in 1831, Michael Faraday performed numerous experiments and found that there was a flow of current when he moved a magnet inside a coil. From his experiments, it was proved that electric fields can be produced not only by charges, but also by changing magnetic fields.

A static electric field intensity $\vec{E}$ can exist without a magnetic field $\vec{H}$. This can be illustrated by the presence of electric field in a capacitor with a static charge Q. Similarly, a conductor with a steady current I has a magnetic field intensity $\vec{H}$ in the absence of electric field $\vec{E}$. Electric charges induce electric fields, and electric currents induce magnetic fields. As long as the charge and current distributions remain constant in time, there will not be any change in the fields that they induce. When the charge and current sources are varying with time, the fields will also vary with time. These time-varying fields are also known as dynamic fields. Hence, the electric and magnetic fields become interconnected and the coupling between them produces electromagnetic waves (EM waves) that are capable of travelling through free space and also in any other medium.

In 1873, James Clerk Maxwell established the first unified theory of electricity and magnetism. Modern electromagnetism is based on a set of four fundamental relations called Maxwell's equations. These equations hold good for any material, including free space (vacuum) and at any location (x, y, z). In general, all the quantities in these equations may be a function of time t. The Maxwell's equations are used to study time-varying electromagnetic phenomena.

In this chapter, the concepts of electromotive force based on Faraday's law and displacement current based on Maxwell's equations are discussed. Further, the boundary conditions for static electric and magnetic fields modified for time-varying fields are presented. The time-varying electromagnetic (EM) fields constitute EM waves, which are carriers of information, mainly in free space between the transmitter and receiver. The problems related to antennas can be solved with the help of Maxwell's equations and boundary conditions. The applications of Maxwell's equations in time-varying conditions are also discussed.

6.2 FUNDAMENTAL RELATIONS FOR ELECTROSTATIC AND MAGNETOSTATIC FIELDS

Electrostatics and magnetostatics are special cases of EM fields. Electrostatics corresponds to stationary charges, whereas magnetostatics corresponds to steady currents. The two important quantities that define static electric fields are electric field intensity $\vec{E}$ and electric flux density $\vec{D}$. For linear and isotropic medium,

$\vec{D}$ and $\vec{E}$ are interrelated by $\vec{D} = \varepsilon\,\vec{E}$, where ε is the permittivity of the medium. The fundamental differential equations that govern the static electric fields are

$$\nabla \times \vec{E} = 0 \qquad \text{(Conservative property of electrostatics)}$$

and $\qquad \nabla \cdot \vec{D} = \rho_v \qquad$ (Gauss's law for electrostatics)

where ρ_v is the volume charge density.

Similarly, the two important quantities that define static magnetic fields are magnetic field intensity $\vec{H}$ and magnetic flux density $\vec{B}$. For linear and isotropic medium, $\vec{B}$ and $\vec{H}$ are interrelated by $\vec{B} = \mu\,\vec{H}$, where μ is the permeability of the medium. The fundamental differential equations that govern the static magnetic fields are

$$\nabla \cdot \vec{B} = 0 \qquad \text{(Gauss's law for magnetostatics)}$$

and $\qquad \nabla \times \vec{H} = \vec{J} \qquad$ (Ampere's circuital law)

where $\vec{J}$ is the volume current density.

Hence, it is observed that the electric field vectors ($\vec{E}$ and $\vec{D}$) and magnetic field vectors ($\vec{H}$ and $\vec{B}$) form separate and independent pairs. They are not related to each other under static conditions. The fundamental relations for electrostatic and magnetostatic fields are listed in Table 6.1.

Table 6.1 *Fundamental relations for electrostatic and magnetostatic fields*

Fundamental relations	Electrostatics	Magnetostatics
Sources	Stationary charges	Steady currents
Static field condition	$\dfrac{\partial Q}{\partial t} = 0$	$\dfrac{\partial I}{\partial t} = 0$
Field quantities	$\vec{E}$ and $\vec{D}$	$\vec{H}$ and $\vec{B}$
Constitutive parameters	ε and σ	μ
Constitutive relations	$\vec{D} = \varepsilon\,\vec{E}$	$\vec{B} = \mu\,\vec{H}$
Field equations in differential or point form	$\nabla \cdot \vec{D} = \rho_v$ $\nabla \times \vec{E} = 0$	$\nabla \cdot \vec{B} = 0$ $\nabla \times \vec{H} = \vec{J}$
Field equations in integral form	$\oint_s \vec{D} \cdot d\vec{s} = Q$ $\oint_l \vec{E} \cdot d\vec{l} = 0$	$\oint_s \vec{B} \cdot d\vec{s} = 0$ $\oint_l \vec{H} \cdot d\vec{l} = I$
Force on charge Q	$\vec{F}_e = Q\vec{E}$	$\vec{F}_m = Q\vec{u} \times \vec{B}$
Flux	$\psi = \displaystyle\int_s \vec{D} \cdot d\vec{s}$ $\psi = Q = CV$	$\Phi = \displaystyle\int_s \vec{B} \cdot d\vec{s}$ $\Phi = LI$
Potential	$\vec{E} = -\nabla V$	$\vec{H} = -\nabla V_m$ (if $\vec{J} = 0$)

Fundamental relations	Electrostatics	Magnetostatics
Energy density	$w_e = \dfrac{1}{2}\varepsilon E^2$	$w_m = \dfrac{1}{2}\mu H^2$
Poisson's equation	$\nabla^2 V = -\dfrac{\rho_v}{\varepsilon}$	$\nabla^2 \vec{A} = -\mu \vec{J}$
Circuit elements	R and C	L

6.3 FARADAY'S LAW FOR ELECTROMAGNETIC INDUCTION

When a wire or conductor moves through a magnetic field by cutting its flux, a voltage is induced in the wire. Similarly, when the magnetic flux, Φ, cuts across a stationary conductor, a voltage is induced. This induced voltage is called *electromotive force* or simply emf. In either case, the induced emf and the rate of change of the magnetic flux are related in differential form as

$$V_{emf} = -\frac{d\Phi}{dt} \tag{6.1}$$

where V_{emf} is the total electromotive force in volt, Φ is the total magnetic flux in weber and t is the time in second.

The process of inducing an emf in a coil in the presence of time-varying magnetic field is known as *electromagnetic induction*. The negative sign in Eq. (6.1) indicates that the induced emf opposes the flux producing it. This is known as *Lenz's law*, which states that the current produced by the change of magnetic flux in the loop always opposes the change of magnetic flux Φ. Hence, Faraday's law states that the total emf induced in a coil or closed loop is equal to the negative rate of change of the total magnetic flux linking the circuit.

Equation (6.1) applies to a single-turn loop. For a multi-turn loop, where all turns are associated with the same flux Φ, Faraday's law may be expressed as

$$V_{emf} = -N\frac{d\Phi}{dt} \tag{6.2}$$

where N is the number of turns of the loop. If every turn is not associated with the same value of flux, then the Faraday's law may be expressed as

$$V_{emf} = -\frac{d\lambda}{dt} \tag{6.3}$$

where λ is the total flux linkage in weber-turns. Hence, for N turns, the flux linkage is

$$\lambda = \Phi_{m1} + \Phi_{m2} + \ldots + \Phi_{mN}$$

where Φ_{m1} is the flux associated with the first turn, Φ_{m2} is the flux associated with the second turn, and Φ_{mN} is the flux associated with the Nth turn.

The magnetic flux Φ passing through a loop is defined as the surface integral of normal component of magnetic flux density $\vec{B}$ over the surface area of the loop as given by

$$\Phi = \int_s \vec{B} \cdot d\vec{s} \tag{6.4}$$

The induced emf can be defined in terms of electric field intensity $\vec{E}$ as

$$V_{emf} = \oint_l \vec{E} \cdot d\vec{l} \tag{6.5}$$

where l is the closed path of integration. Using Eqs (6.1), (6.4) and (6.5), the induced emf can be expressed in terms of $\vec{E}$ and $\vec{B}$ as

$$V_{emf} = \oint_l \vec{E} \cdot d\vec{l} = -\frac{d}{dt} \int_s \vec{B} \cdot d\vec{s} = -\int_s \frac{\partial \vec{B}}{\partial t} \cdot d\vec{s} \tag{6.6}$$

Here, the direction of closed path l and the direction of surface area $d\vec{s}$ are related by the right-hand rule. Equation (6.6) is known as the *integral form of Faraday's law*.

EXAMPLE 6.1

A circular loop conductor of radius 0.1 m lies in the $z = 0$ plane and has a resistance of 5Ω. Given $B = 0.2 \sin 10^3 t\, \vec{a}_z$ T, find the induced emf and the current.

SOLUTION

Given $B = 0.2 \sin 10^3 t\, \vec{a}_z$ T, $\rho = 0.1\,\text{m}, R = 5\Omega$, and area, $A = \pi\rho^2 = \pi \times (0.1)^2\,\text{m}^2$.

The magnetic flux, $\Phi = BA = \pi \times 0.01 \times 0.2 \sin 10^3 t = 2\pi \sin 10^3 t$ mWb

The induced emf, $V_{emf} = -\dfrac{d\Phi}{dt} = -2\pi \times 10^{-3} \times 10^3 \cos 10^3 t = -2\pi \cos 10^3 t$ V

Hence, the current, $I = \dfrac{V}{R} = -\dfrac{2\pi}{5} \cos 10^3 t = -0.4\pi \cos 10^3 t$ A

Here, the negative sign shows that the current flows in the opposite direction.

EXAMPLE 6.2

A 30 cm × 40 cm rectangular loop rotates at 150 rad/s in a magnetic field of 0.06 Wb/m^2 normal to the axis of rotation. If the loop has 50 turns, determine the induced voltage in the loop.

SOLUTION

Given area $A = 0.3\,\text{m} \times 0.4\,\text{m}, N = 50, \omega = 150\,\text{rad/s}$ and $B = 0.06$ Wb/m^2.

We know that, $\Phi = \int_s \vec{B} \cdot d\vec{s} = \int_s B\,ds \cos\theta = B\cos\theta \int_s ds = BA\cos\theta$

According to Faraday's law,

$$V_{emf} = -N\frac{d\Phi}{dt} = -N\frac{d}{dt}\left(BA\cos\omega t\right), \text{where } \theta = \omega t = 90°$$

$$= NBA\omega \sin\omega t = 50 \times 0.06 \times 0.3 \times 0.4 \times 150 = 54 \text{ V}$$

6.4 TRANSFORMER AND MOTIONAL EMFs

The electric and magnetic fields are interrelated in time-varying case as evident from Eq. (6.6). It is also clear that the time derivate operates on the magnetic field of flux density $\vec{B}$ as well as the differential surface area $d\vec{s}$. Therefore, an emf can be produced in closed conducting circuit by the following three ways:

  (*i*) By placing a stationary conductor in a time-varying magnetic field (the induced emf in this case is called transformer emf)

 (*ii*) By placing a moving conductor in a static magnetic field (the induced emf in this case is called motional emf)

(*iii*) By placing a moving conductor in a time-varying field.

6.4.1 Stationary Conductor in Time-Varying Magnetic Field (Transformer emf)

A stationary conductor with current I is placed in a time-varying magnetic field of flux density $\vec{B}$ as shown in Figure 6.1. The induced current flows in such a way to satisfy Lenz's law, so that a magnetic field is produced which opposes a change in value of $\vec{B}$.

From Faraday's law,

$$V_{emf} = \oint_l \vec{E} \cdot d\vec{l} = -\int_s \frac{\partial \vec{B}}{\partial t} \cdot d\vec{s} \qquad (6.7)$$

The emf given by the above equation is termed as transformer emf, which is due to the time-varying current caused by the time-varying magnetic field in a stationary loop. This effect mainly occurs due to transformer action.

Using Stoke's theorem, we get

$$\int_s (\nabla \times \vec{E}) \cdot d\vec{s} = -\int_s \frac{\partial \vec{B}}{\partial t} \cdot d\vec{s} \qquad (6.8)$$

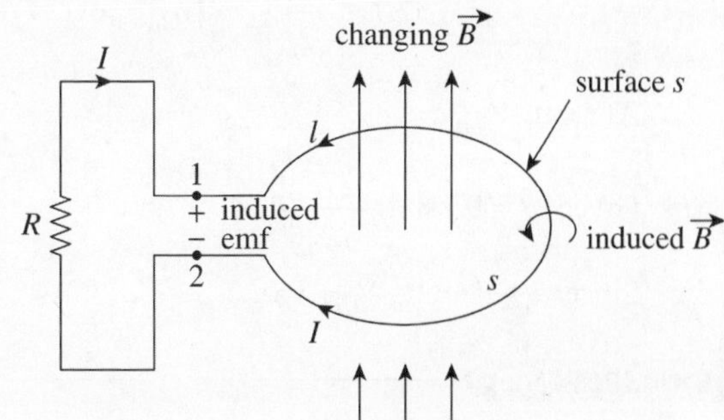

Figure 6.1 *Stationary conducting loop placed in time-varying magnetic field*

Comparing the surface integrals on both sides, we get

$$\nabla \times \vec{E} = -\frac{\partial \vec{B}}{\partial t} \qquad (6.9)$$

The above equation is in a differential form, which relates the field quantities at any point in space, whether or not a physical circuit exists at that point. This equation is known as the *differential form of Faraday's law*, which states that a time-varying magnetic field induces an electric field $\vec{E}$ whose curl is equal to the negative of the time derivative of $\vec{B}$.

Equation (6.9) is one of the Maxwell's equations for time-varying fields, and it also shows that the time-varying electric field is not conservative in nature, i.e., $\nabla \times \vec{E} \neq 0$. Since the work done in moving a charge on a closed path in a time-varying electric field is due to energy from the time-varying magnetic field, laws of energy conservation are thus satisfied. Suppose if $\vec{B}$ is time independent, i.e., $\dfrac{\partial \vec{B}}{\partial t} = 0$, then Eqs. (6.9) and (6.7) reduces to the electrostatic equations.

That is, $\nabla \times \vec{E} = 0$ and $\oint_l \vec{E} \cdot d\vec{l} = 0$.

EXAMPLE 6.3

Determine the emf developed around a circular path at $t = 0$ with radius $\rho = 0.5$ m in the plane $z = 0$, if

(*i*) $\vec{B} = 0.1 \sin(377t)\, \vec{a}_z$ T and (*ii*) $\vec{B} = 0.1 \sin\left(\dfrac{377t}{\rho}\right)\vec{a}_\rho$ T.

SOLUTION

Given $\rho = 0.5$ m in $z = 0$ plane (cylindrical coordinates). The emf induced in a time-varying field is

$$V_{emf} = -\int_s \frac{\partial \vec{B}}{\partial t} \cdot d\vec{s}, \quad \text{where } d\vec{s} = \rho\, d\rho\, d\phi\, \vec{a}_z$$

(*i*) Given $\vec{B} = 0.1 \sin(377t)\, \vec{a}_z$ T.

$$V_{emf} = -\int_s 0.1 \times \left[377 \cos(377t)\vec{a}_z\right] \cdot \left[\rho\, d\rho\, d\phi\, \vec{a}_z\right]$$

$$= -37.7\cos(377t)\int_0^{0.5} \rho\, d\rho \int_0^{2\pi} d\phi$$

$$= -37.7 \times \left[\frac{\rho^2}{2}\right]_0^{0.5} \times [\phi]_0^{2\pi} \cos(377t) = -29.59\cos(377t)$$

At $t = 0$, $V_{emf} = -29.59$ V

(*ii*) Given $\vec{B} = 0.1\sin\left(\dfrac{377t}{\rho}\right)\vec{a}_\rho$ T.

Since $\vec{a}_\rho \cdot \vec{a}_z = 0$, $V_{emf} = 0$. □

EXAMPLE 6.4

A magnetic core of uniform cross-section 4 cm^2 is connected to a 120 V, 60 Hz generator as shown in Figure E6.4. Determine the induced emf V_2 in the secondary coil.

SOLUTION

Given $V_1 = 120$ V, $N_1 = 800$, and $N_2 = 400$.

According to Faraday's law, the voltages in the primary and secondary coils are

$$V_1 = -N_1 \frac{d\Phi}{dt} \qquad (1)$$

and

$$V_2 = -N_2 \frac{d\Phi}{dt} \qquad (2)$$

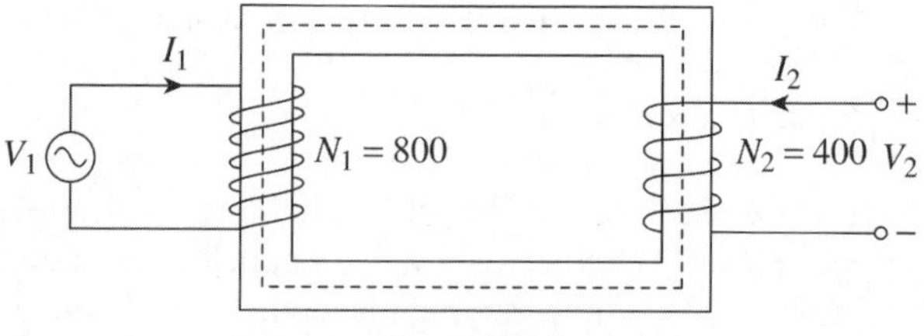

Figure E6.4

Dividing Eq. (2) by Eq. (1), we get

$$\frac{V_2}{V_1} = \frac{N_2}{N_1}$$

Hence, the induced emf V_2 in the secondary coil is

$$V_2 = \frac{N_2}{N_1} V_1 = \frac{400 \times 120}{800} = 60 \text{ V} \qquad □$$

EXAMPLE 6.5

An area of 0.5 m^2 in the $z = 0$ plane is enclosed by a filamentary conductor. Find the induced voltage, given that, $\vec{B} = 0.65\cos 10^3 t\left(\dfrac{\vec{a}_y + \vec{a}_z}{\sqrt{2}}\right)$ T.

SOLUTION

Given area $A = 0.5\,\text{m}^2$ and $\vec{B} = 0.65\cos 10^3 t\left(\dfrac{\vec{a}_y + \vec{a}_z}{\sqrt{2}}\right)$ T.

For a stationary conductor in a time-varying field, the induced emf is

$$V_{emf} = -\int_s \frac{\partial \vec{B}}{\partial t}\cdot d\vec{s}\,, \quad \text{where } d\vec{s} = ds\,\vec{a}_z$$

$$= \int_s 0.65\times10^3 \sin 10^3 t \left(\frac{\vec{a}_y + \vec{a}_z}{\sqrt{2}} \right) \cdot (ds\, \vec{a}_z)$$

$$= \frac{650}{\sqrt{2}} \sin 10^3 t \int_s ds = \frac{650}{\sqrt{2}} \sin 10^3 t \times 0.5 = 229.81 \sin 10^3 t \text{ V} \qquad \square$$

EXAMPLE 6.6

A stationary 10 turn square coil of side 1 m is situated with its lower left corner coincident with the origin and with sides x_1 and y_1 along x-axis and y-axis, respectively. If the magnetic flux density $\vec{B}$ is normal to the plane of the coil and has its amplitude given by $B_0 = \sin\left(\dfrac{\pi x}{x_1}\right) \sin\left(\dfrac{\pi y}{y_1}\right)$ T, determine the r.m.s value of emf induced in the coil if B_0 varies harmonically at a frequency of 1 kHz.

SOLUTION

Given $N = 10, f = 1$ kHz, and $B_0 = \sin\left(\dfrac{\pi x}{x_1}\right) \sin\left(\dfrac{\pi y}{y_1}\right) T.$

Since the side of the given square coil $a = 1$ m, $x_1 = y_1 = 1$ m. For a stationary conductor in a time-varying field, the induced emf is

$$V_{emf} = -N \int_s \frac{\partial \vec{B}}{\partial t} \cdot d\vec{s}$$

Given that B varies with time as $B = B_0 \cos \omega t$.

Hence, $\dfrac{\partial B}{\partial t} = -\omega B_0 \sin \omega t$

which has maximum value at $\omega t = -\dfrac{\pi}{2}$

That is, $\left. \dfrac{\partial B}{\partial t} \right|_{\max} = \omega B_0$

Therefore, $V_{\max} = -N\omega \int_s B_0 ds = \left| -N\omega \int_0^1 \int_0^1 \sin(\pi x) \sin(\pi y)\, dx\, dy \right|$ \qquad (since $ds = dx\, dy$)

$$= N\omega \int_0^1 \int_0^1 \sin(\pi x) \sin(\pi y)\, dx\, dy = N\omega \left. \frac{\cos \pi x}{\pi} \right|_0^1 \left. \frac{\cos \pi y}{\pi} \right|_0^1$$

$$= \frac{N\omega}{\pi^2} (\cos \pi - \cos 0)(\cos \pi - \cos 0)$$

$$= \frac{N\omega}{\pi^2} (2\times 2) = \frac{4N\omega}{\pi^2}$$

$$\frac{4\times 10 \times 2 \ \times 10}{} \qquad \text{(since } \omega = 2\pi f)$$

$$= 25.465 \text{ kV}$$

$$V_{rms} = \frac{V_{max}}{\sqrt{2}} = 18 \text{ kV}$$

6.4.2 Moving Conductor in Static Magnetic Field (Motional emf)

When a moving conductor carrying current is placed in a static magnetic field, an emf is induced in the loop as shown in Figure 6.2. The force $\vec{F}_m$ on a charge Q moving with a uniform velocity $\vec{u}$ placed in a magnetic field of flux density $\vec{B}$ is

$$\vec{F}_m = Q\vec{u} \times \vec{B} \tag{6.10}$$

Therefore, the electric field intensity is represented by

$$\vec{E}_m = \frac{\vec{F}_m}{Q} = \vec{u} \times \vec{B} \tag{6.11}$$

The field produced by the motion of the charged particle is known as motional electric field and its direction is normal to the plane containing $\vec{u}$ and $\vec{B}$.

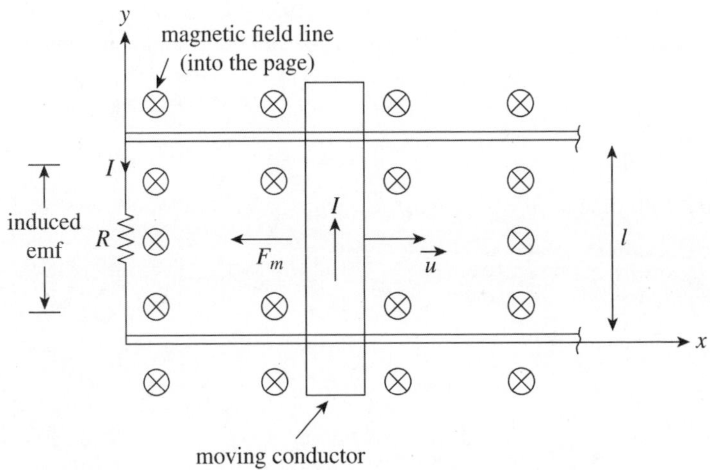

Figure 6.2 *Moving conductor in a static magnetic field*

If we assume that a large number of free electrons moving with a uniform velocity $\vec{u}$ is present in a conducting loop, then the emf induced in the loop is given by

$$V_{emf} = \oint_l \vec{E}_m \cdot d\vec{l} = \oint_l (\vec{u} \times \vec{B}) \cdot d\vec{l} \tag{6.12}$$

The emf given in the above equation is termed as motional emf or flux cutting emf, as it is caused by motional effect. The motional emf is present in dc/ac motors, dc/ac generators, induction generators and alternators.

Applying Stokes's theorem to the above equation, we get

$$\int_s (\nabla \times \vec{E}_m) \cdot d\vec{s} = \int_s \nabla \times (\vec{u} \times \vec{B}) \cdot d\vec{s} \tag{6.13}$$

Comparing the surface integrals on both sides, we get

$$\nabla \times \vec{E}_m = \nabla \times (\vec{u} \times \vec{B}) \tag{6.14}$$

EXAMPLE 6.7

A conductor of length 100 cm moves at right angles to a uniform field of strength 10,000 lines/cm^2, with a velocity of 50 m/s. Determine the induced emf when the conductor moves at an angle of 30° to the direction of the field.

SOLUTION

Given $l = 100$ cm $= 1$ m, $B = 10,000$ lines/cm$^2 = 1$ Wb/m^2, $u = 50$ m/s and $\theta = 30°$.

For a moving conductor in a stationary magnetic field, the induced emf is

$$V_{emf} = \oint_l (\vec{u} \times \vec{B}) \cdot d\vec{l}$$
$$= Blu \sin\theta = 1 \times 1 \times 50 \times \sin 30° = 25 \text{ V}$$

EXAMPLE 6.8

Calculate the maximum emf induced in a coil of 4,000 turns and radius of 12 cm rotating at 30 rps in a magnetic field of flux density 500 Gauss.

SOLUTION

Given radius $\rho = 0.12$ m, $B = 500$ Gauss $= 0.05$ Wb/m^2 and $N = 4000$.

Here, $\omega = 2\pi \times$ rps $= 2\pi \times 30 = 60\pi$ rad/s

For a moving coil in a stationary magnetic field, the induced emf is

$$V_{emf} = \oint_l (\vec{u} \times \vec{B}) \cdot d\vec{l}$$
$$= Blu \sin\theta$$

For maximum emf, $\theta = 90°$. Therefore, the maximum induced emf per unit length is

$$\frac{V_{emf}}{l} = Bu = B\rho\omega \qquad \text{(since } u = \rho\omega\text{)}$$
$$= 0.05 \times 0.12 \times 60\pi = 1.131 \text{ V/m}$$

Therefore, for N turns, the maximum induced emf per unit length is

$$\left(\frac{V_{emf}}{l} \right)_{max} = \frac{V_{emf}}{l} \times N = 4000 \times 1.131 = 4524 \text{ V/m}$$

EXAMPLE 6.9

A conductor 1 cm in length is parallel to z-axis and rotates at radius of 25 cm at 1200 rpm. Find the induced voltage, if the radial field is given by $\vec{B} = 0.5\vec{a}_\rho$ T.

SOLUTION

Given length $l = 0.01$ m, radius $\rho = 0.25$ m, velocity $= 1200$ rpm, and $\vec{B} = 0.5\vec{a}_\rho$ T.

Here, $\omega = \dfrac{2\pi \times \text{rpm}}{60} = \dfrac{2\pi \times 1200}{60} = 40\pi$ rad/s

For a rotating conductor in a stationary magnetic field, the induced emf is

$$V_{emf} = \int (\vec{u} \times \vec{B}) \cdot d\vec{l}$$

Since the conductor is parallel to z-axis, the differential length is $d\vec{l} = dz\,\vec{a}_z$.

Therefore, $V_{emf} = \displaystyle\int_{\rho=0}^{l} (\rho\omega\,\vec{a}_\phi \times 0.5\vec{a}_\rho) \cdot dz\,\vec{a}_z$ (since $\vec{a}_\phi \times \vec{a}_\rho = -\vec{a}_z$)

$$= -40\pi \times 0.25 \times 0.5 \int_0^{0.01} dz = -5\pi \left[z\right]_0^{0.01} = -0.157$$

That is, $V_{emf} = -157$ mV

The negative sign indicates that upper end of the conductor is positive, while the lower end is negative. Therefore, the magnitude of the induced voltage is 157 mV. $\qquad\square$

EXAMPLE 6.10

A rod of length l rotates about the z-axis with an angular velocity ω. If $\vec{B} = B_0\vec{a}_z$ T, calculate the voltage induced on the conductor.

SOLUTION

For a rotating rod in a stationary magnetic field, the induced emf is

$$V_{emf} = \int (\vec{u} \times \vec{B}) \cdot d\vec{l}$$

$$= \int_{\rho=0}^{l} (\rho\omega\,\vec{a}_\phi \times B_0\vec{a}_z) \cdot d\rho\,\vec{a}_\rho$$

$$= \int_0^l B_0\rho\omega\,\vec{a}_\rho \cdot d\rho\,\vec{a}_\rho \quad (\text{since } \vec{a}_\phi \times \vec{a}_z = \vec{a}_\rho)$$

$$= B_0\omega \left[\frac{\rho^2}{2}\right]_0^l = \frac{1}{2} B_0\omega l^2 \text{ V} \qquad\square$$

EXAMPLE 6.11

A square loop of side 4 cm with a resistor of 10Ω on one side is placed in a uniform magnetic field of 50 mT in the direction of x-axis. Calculate (*i*) the induced current at time $t = 1$ ms and (*ii*) the induced emf at $t = 3$ ms. It is given that the square loop cuts the flux lines at a frequency of 10 Hz and the axis of loop rotation is perpendicular to the field. Also, the loop lies in the yz-plane at time $t = 0$.

SOLUTION

Given side of a square loop $a = 4$ cm $= 0.04$ m, $B = 50 \times 10^{-3}$ T, $\theta = 90°$, $R = 10\Omega$, $f = 10$Hz and $\omega = 2\pi f = 20\pi$ rad/s.

For a moving conductor in a stationary magnetic field, the induced emf is

$$V_{emf} = \oint_l (\vec{u} \times \vec{B}) \cdot d\vec{l}$$

For a square loop with side $a = 0.04$ m, the linear velocity is $u = \dfrac{a\omega}{2}$ m/s.

Therefore, $V_{emf} = uBl\sin\theta$, where $\theta = \omega t$ and $l = 2a$

$$= \left(\frac{a\omega}{2}\right)B(2a)\sin\theta = a^2\omega B\sin\omega t$$

$$= (0.04)^2 \times 20\pi \times 50 \times 10^{-3}\sin(20\pi\, t)$$

$$= 5.03\sin(20\pi t)\ \text{mV}$$

The induced emf at $t = 1$ ms is

$$V_{emf} = 5.03\times 10^{-3}\times\sin\left(20\pi\times 10^{-3}\right) = 5.52\ \mu\text{V}$$

(*i*) The induced current is

$$i = \frac{V_{emf}}{R} = \frac{5.52\times 10^{-6}}{10} = 0.552\ \mu\text{A}$$

(*ii*) The induced emf at $t = 3$ ms is

$$V_{emf} = 5.03\times 10^{-3}\sin\left(20\pi\times 3\times 10^{-3}\right) = 16.55\,\mu\text{V}$$

EXAMPLE 6.12

The conductor moves with a velocity $\vec{u} = 4.5\sin 10^6 t\,\vec{a}_z$ m/s as shown in Figure E6.12. Find the induced voltage in the conductor if (i) $\vec{B} = 0.08\,\vec{a}_y$ T and $\vec{B} = 0.08\,\vec{a}_x$ T.

SOLUTION

(*i*) Given $\vec{u} = 4.5\sin 10^6 t\,\vec{a}_z$ m/s and $\vec{B} = 0.08\,\vec{a}_y$ T.

For a conductor moving with velocity $\vec{u}$ in a stationary magnetic field, the induced emf is represented by

$$V_{emf} = \int(\vec{u}\times\vec{B})\cdot d\vec{l}$$

$$= 4.5\sin 10^6 t\int(\vec{a}_z\times 0.08\,\vec{a}_y)\cdot(dx\,\vec{a}_x)$$

$$= 0.36\sin 10^6 t\int_0^{0.4}(-\vec{a}_x)\cdot(dx\vec{a}_x)$$

$$= -0.144\sin 10^6 t\ \text{V}$$

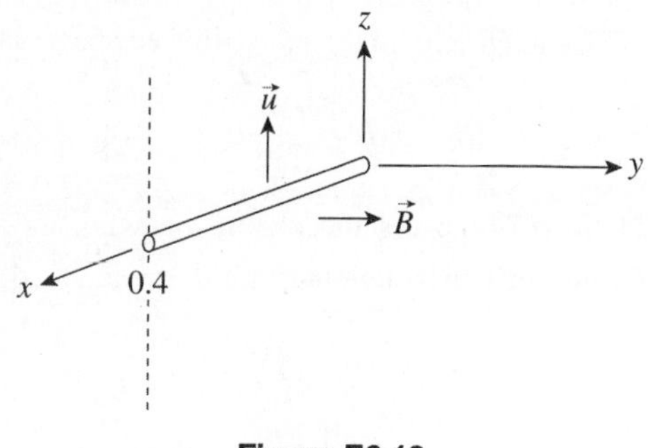

Figure E6.12

(*ii*) Since $\vec{B} = 0.08\,\vec{a}_x$ T, the conductor placed along x-axis is parallel to the magnetic field and it does not cut any field lines. Hence, the induced voltage must be zero.

EXAMPLE 6.13

The wire shown in Figure E6.13 is in free space and carries a current of $I = 20$A. A 50 cm long metal rod moves at a constant velocity of $\vec{u} = 5\vec{a}_z$ m/s. Find V_{12}.

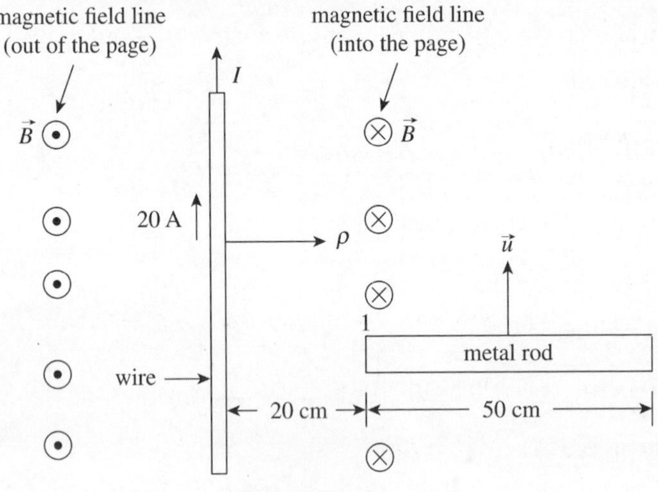

Figure E6.13

SOLUTION

Given $\vec{u} = 5\vec{a}_z$ m/s and $I = 20$ A.

The magnetic field intensity induced by the current carrying wire is

$$\vec{H} = \frac{I}{2\pi\rho}\vec{a}_\phi$$

Here, the direction of the magnetic field is in ϕ direction and it is directed into the page at the metal rod side of the wire as shown in Figure E6.13.

The magnetic flux density, in free space, is

$$\vec{B} = \mu_0\vec{H} = \frac{\mu_0 I}{2\pi\rho}\vec{a}_\phi$$

where ρ is the distance from the wire and the metal rod. Since the metal rod is moving with velocity $\vec{u} = 5\vec{a}_z$ m/s in a stationary field, the induced motional emf is

$$V_{12} = V_{emf} = \int(\vec{u}\times\vec{B})\cdot d\vec{l}$$

$$= \int_{70\text{ cm}}^{20\text{ cm}}\left(5\vec{a}_z\times\frac{\mu_0 I}{2\pi\rho}\vec{a}_\phi\right)\cdot(d\rho\,\vec{a}_\rho)$$

$$= -\frac{5\mu_0 I}{2\pi}\int_{70\text{ cm}}^{20\text{ cm}}\frac{d\rho}{\rho} \qquad (\text{since } \vec{a}_z\times\vec{a}_\phi = -\vec{a}_\rho)$$

$$= -\frac{5\times 4\pi\times 10^{-7}\times 20}{2\pi}\times\ln\left(\frac{20}{70}\right)$$

$$= 25.06\,\mu V$$

EXAMPLE 6.14

The Faraday disc generator consists of a thin circular metal disc of radius b rotating with a constant angular velocity ω rad/s in a uniform and constant magnetic field of flux density $\vec{B} = B_0 \vec{a}_z$ Wb/m^2 that is parallel to the axis of rotation. The brush contacts are provided at the axis and on the rim of the disc as shown in Figure E6.14. Determine the open circuit voltage of the generator.

SOLUTION

Consider the path *1-2-3-4-5-6-1* shown in Figure E6.14, in which the part *3-4-5* moves with the disc and only the straight portion *4-5* cuts the magnetic flux.

The induced V_{emf} is

$$V_{emf} = \oint_l (\vec{u} \times \vec{B}) \cdot d\vec{l}$$

$$= \int_{\text{path 4}}^{\text{path 5}} \left[(\rho \omega \, \vec{a}_\phi) \times B_0 \vec{a}_z \right] \cdot (d\rho \, \vec{a}_\rho)$$

where ρ is the radius in cylindrical coordinates, $\vec{u}$ is the linear velocity along ϕ direction, i.e., $\vec{u} = \rho \omega \, \vec{a}_\phi$, and ω is the angular velocity.

Therefore, the open circuit voltage or the induced emf of the Faraday disc generator is

$$V_o = V_{emf} = \omega B_0 \int_b^0 \rho \, d\rho = -\frac{\omega B_0 b^2}{2} \text{ V} \qquad \text{(since } \vec{a}_\phi \times \vec{a}_z = \vec{a}_\rho)$$

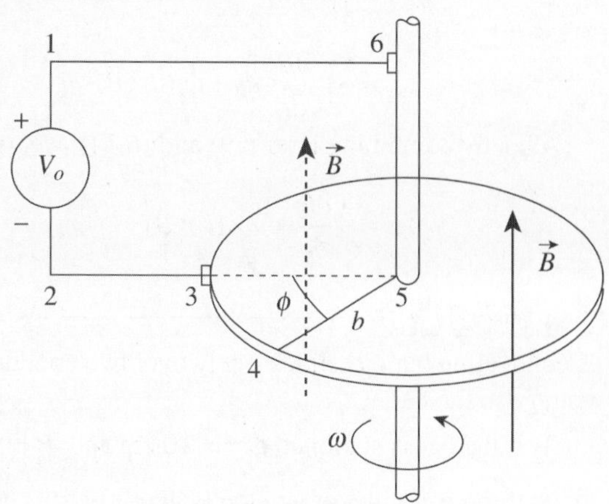

Figure E6.14

EXAMPLE 6.15

A Faraday's copper disc, 0.5 m in diameter, is rotated at 1000 rpm on a horizontal axis perpendicular to and through the center of the disc, the axis lying in a horizontal field of 10 mT. Determine the emf measured between the brushes.

SOLUTION

Given diameter $d = 0.5$ m, disc velocity = 1000 rpm, and $B = 10 \times 10^{-3}$ T.

$$\text{Here, } \omega = \frac{2\pi \times \text{rpm}}{60} = \frac{2\pi \times 1000}{60} = 104.72 \text{ rad/s}$$

The induced emf in a Faraday's disc is

$$V_{emf} = -\frac{\omega B b^2}{2}$$

$$= -\frac{104.72 \times 10 \times 10^{-3} \times (0.25)^2}{2}, \text{ where radius } b = \frac{d}{2} = \frac{0.5}{2} = 0.25 \text{ m}$$

$$= -32.72 \text{ mV}$$

6.4.3   Moving Conductor in Time-Varying Magnetic Field

If a moving conductor carrying a current is placed in a time-varying magnetic field, then the induced emf is the sum of both transformer and motional emf.

Therefore, combining Eq. (6.7) and Eq. (6.12), we get

$$V_{emf} = \oint_l \vec{E} \cdot d\vec{l} = \text{Transformer emf} + \text{motional emf}$$

$$= -\int_s \frac{\partial \vec{B}}{\partial t} \cdot d\vec{s} + \oint_l (\vec{u} \times \vec{B}) \cdot d\vec{l} \tag{6.15}$$

Also, by combining Eqs (6.9) and (6.14), we get

$$\nabla \times \vec{E} = -\frac{\partial \vec{B}}{\partial t} + \nabla \times (\vec{u} \times \vec{B}) \tag{6.16}$$

EXAMPLE 6.16

A conducting bar *CD* slides freely over two conducting rails as shown in Figure E6.16. Calculate the induced voltage in the bar.

  (*i*) If the bar is stationed at $y = 10$ cm and $\vec{B} = 5\cos 10^6 t\, \vec{a}_z$ mWb/m^2

 (*ii*) If the bar slides at a velocity $\vec{u} = 30\vec{a}_y$ m/s and $\vec{B} = 5\vec{a}_z$ mWb/m^2

(*iii*) If the bar slides at a velocity $\vec{u} = 30\vec{a}_y$ m/s and $\vec{B} = 5\cos(10^6 t - y)\vec{a}_z$ mWb/m^2

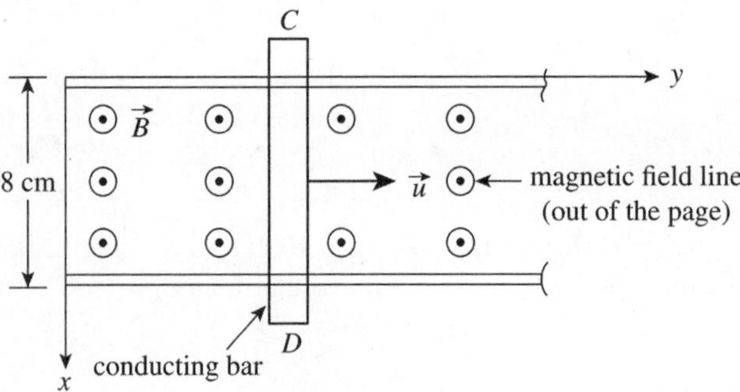

Figure E6.16

SOLUTION

  (*i*) For a stationary bar in a time-varying magnetic field, the transformer emf is

$$V_{emf} = -\int \frac{\partial \vec{B}}{\partial t} \cdot d\vec{s}$$

$$= \int_{y=0}^{0.1} \int_{x=0}^{0.08} 5 \times 10^{-3} \times 10^6 \sin 10^6 t\, dx\, dy$$

$$= 5 \times 10^3 \times 0.08 \times 0.1 \sin 10^6 t$$

$$= 40 \sin 10^6 t \text{ V}$$

Here, the polarity of induced voltage is based on Lenz's law and the point C on the bar is at a lower potential than point D when $\vec{B}$ is increasing.

(*ii*) For a sliding bar in a stationary magnetic field, the motional emf is

$$V_{emf} = \int (\vec{u} \times \vec{B}) \cdot d\vec{l}$$

$$= \int_{x=l}^{0} (u\vec{a}_y \times B\vec{a}_z) \cdot dx\,\vec{a}_x$$

$$= -uBl = -30 \times 5 \times 10^{-3} \times 0.08$$

$$= -12 \text{ mV}$$

(*iii*) For sliding bar in a time-varying magnetic field, both transformer emf and motional emf are present. Therefore, the induced emf is

$$V_{emf} = -\int \frac{\partial \vec{B}}{\partial t} \cdot d\vec{s} + \int (\vec{u} \times \vec{B}) \cdot d\vec{l}$$

$$= \int_{x=0}^{0.08} \int_{0}^{y} 5 \times 10^{-3} \times (10^6) \sin(10^6 t - y')\, dy'\, dx'$$

$$+ \int_{0.08}^{0} \left[30\vec{a}_y \times 5 \times 10^{-3} \cos(10^6 t - y)\vec{a}_z \right] \cdot dx\,\vec{a}_x$$

$$= 400 \cos(10^6 t - y')\Big|_{0}^{y} - 150 \times 10^{-3} \times 0.08 \cos\left(10^6 t - y\right)$$

$$= 400 \cos(10^6 t - y) - 400 \cos 10^6 t - 12 \times 10^{-3} \cos\left(10^6 t - y\right)$$

$$\approx 400 \cos(10^6 t - y) - 400 \cos 10^6 t \text{ V}$$

Here, the motional emf is negligible compared to the transformer emf. ❑

6.5 DISPLACEMENT CURRENT

Faraday's experimental law has been used to obtain one of the Maxwell's equations in differential (point) form as

$$\nabla \times \vec{E} = -\frac{\partial \vec{B}}{\partial t}$$

which shows that a time-varying magnetic field generates an electric field.

For static magnetic fields, Ampere's circuital law in point form is represented by

$$\nabla \times \vec{H} = \vec{J} \tag{6.17}$$

As this current density $\vec{J}$ is due to the movement of actual charges such as electrons, protons, and ions, it is called conduction current density. Ampere's law in differential form is not valid for open circuits i.e., it can only be used to solve the closed-circuit problems. In order to remove this inconsistency, Maxwell proposed the concept of displacement current, and also inferred that every electric current that include conduction and displacement currents should form a closed circuit. To demonstrate this concept, the analysis of a simple circuit model shown in Figure 6.3 is considered.

A current is generally defined as the movement of charge, and charge is a conservative one, i.e., it can neither be generated nor destroyed. Therefore, the continuity equation that is satisfied by both charge density ρ_v and the current density J is given by

$$\nabla \cdot \vec{J} = -\frac{\partial \rho_v}{\partial t} \tag{6.18}$$

Further, to proceed with this formulation, taking divergence on both sides of the Eq. (6.17) and also employing vector identity, we get

$$\nabla \cdot (\nabla \times \vec{H}) = \nabla \cdot \vec{J} = 0$$

Hence, it is clear that Eq. (6.17) can be true only if $\dfrac{\partial \rho_v}{\partial t} = 0$ and it cannot be applicable for time-varying conditions. Therefore, Ampere's original law holds good only for steady current distributions for which $\vec{J}$ is constant in time. But for time-varying charge distributions, i.e., $\dfrac{\partial \rho_v}{\partial t} \neq 0$ in a charging or discharging capacitor, Ampere's law does not hold good.

Therefore, Eq. (6.17) becomes

$$\nabla \times \vec{H} = \vec{J} + \vec{J}_d \tag{6.19}$$

Again using the vector identity, we have

$$\nabla \cdot (\nabla \times \vec{H}) = 0 = \nabla \cdot \vec{J} + \nabla \cdot \vec{J}_d$$

$$\nabla \cdot \vec{J}_d = -\nabla \cdot \vec{J} = \frac{\partial \rho_v}{\partial t}$$

$$= \frac{\partial}{\partial t}(\nabla \cdot \vec{D}) = \nabla \cdot \frac{\partial \vec{D}}{\partial t} \qquad (\text{since } \rho_v = \nabla \cdot \vec{D})$$

Therefore, $\vec{J}_d = \dfrac{\partial \vec{D}}{\partial t}$ $\qquad\qquad\qquad\qquad\qquad\qquad\qquad\qquad$ (6.20)

Substituting Eq. (6.20) in Eq. (6.19), we get

$$\nabla \times \vec{H} = \vec{J} + \frac{\partial \vec{D}}{\partial t} \tag{6.21}$$

The above equation is the modified form of Ampere's law, called *Ampere–Maxwell law*, which is consistent with the continuity equation. Further, Maxwell called the term $\dfrac{\partial \vec{D}}{\partial t}$ as displacement current density $\vec{J}_d$. It has the dimensions of current density, i.e., ampere per square metre.

If the surface integral is taken on both sides of the above equation over an arbitrary open surface s with closed path l, we get

$$\int_s (\nabla \times \vec{H}) \cdot d\vec{s} = \int_s \vec{J} \cdot d\vec{s} + \int_s \frac{\partial \vec{D}}{\partial t} \cdot d\vec{s} \tag{6.22}$$

The Ampere's law in integral form for the time-varying case can be obtained by applying Stokes's theorem to the left-hand side (LHS) of the above equation.

Therefore, $\oint_l \vec{H} \cdot d\vec{l} = I_c + \int_s \dfrac{\partial \vec{D}}{\partial t} \cdot d\vec{s}$ $\qquad\qquad\qquad\qquad\qquad\qquad$ (6.23) where $I_c = \int_s \vec{J} \cdot d\vec{s}$ is the conduction current. Since the second term on the right-hand side (RHS) of the above equation is proportional to the time derivative of the electric flux density or displacement density $\vec{D}$, it is called the displacement current I_d. The unit of displacement current is ampere.

That is,

$$I_d = \int_s \vec{J}_d \cdot d\vec{s} = \int_s \frac{\partial \vec{D}}{\partial t} \cdot d\vec{s} \tag{6.24}$$

Substituting Eq. (6.24) in Eq. (6.23), we can write

$$\oint_l \vec{H} \cdot d\vec{l} = I_c + I_d = I \tag{6.25}$$

Here, the displacement current I_d is associated with time-varying electric fields, and it is present in all imperfect conductors and dielectrics along with time-varying conduction current.

The concept of displacement current was one of the major contributions of Maxwell and it helps in providing relationship between electric and magnetic fields under time-varying conditions. The propagation of EM wave is not possible without considering displacement current.

The concept of displacement current is best understood by the flow of current in the dielectric medium between the two plates of a capacitor. Consider a circuit shown in Figure 6.3 in which an ac voltage is applied across the parallel plates of capacitor. The applied ac voltage $v_s(t)$ is given by

$$v_s(t) = V_1 \sin \omega t$$

where V_1 is the magnitude of the applied voltage. In general, the total current flow through any surface is the sum of conduction current I_c and displacement current I_d. Let us assume the cross-section of the conducting wire as s_1 and cross-section of the dielectric between the parallel plates as s_2 to find I_c and I_d.

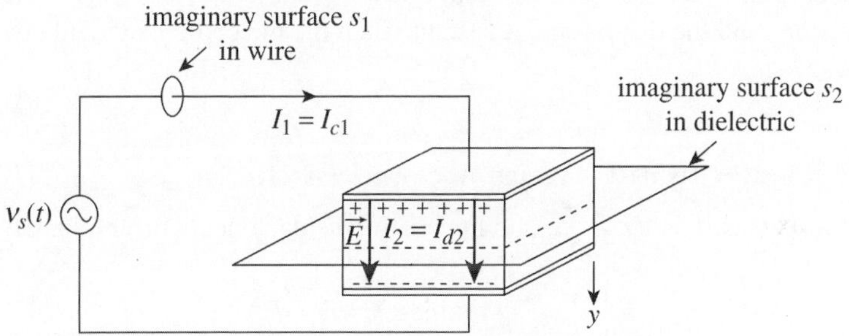

Figure 6.3 *Illustration of displacement current concept in a capacitor*

Let I_{c1} and I_{d1} be the conduction current and displacement current, respectively in the wire surface. Since $\vec{D} = \vec{E} = 0$ in a perfect conductor, it is seen that from Eq. (6.24), the displacement current in the wire conductor is zero, i.e., $I_{d1} = 0$. Hence, the total current flowing through the wire conductor is the conduction current.

That is,

$$I_1 = I_{c1} = C \frac{dv_c}{dt} = C \frac{d}{dt}(V_1 \sin \omega t) = CV_1 \omega \cos \omega t \tag{6.26}$$

where the voltage across the capacitor $v_c = v_s(t)$.

Let I_{c2} and I_{d2} be the conduction current and displacement current, respectively in the dielectric surface of the capacitor. Since charges cannot flow through the perfect dielectric medium, conduction does not take place. Therefore, the conduction current is zero inside the dielectric medium between the plates of the capacitor, i.e., $I_{c2} = 0$.

Due to the applied voltage, there will be an electric field between the parallel plates along y-direction from higher potential to lower potential. Therefore,

$$\vec{E} = \frac{v_c}{d}\vec{a}_y = \frac{V_1 \sin \omega t}{d}\vec{a}_y$$

where d is the distance between the parallel plates. Since $I_{c2} = 0$, the total current flowing through the dielectric medium between the parallel plates of the capacitor is the displacement current.

That is, $I_2 = I_{d2} = \int_s \frac{\partial \vec{D}}{\partial t} \cdot d\vec{s} = \int_s \frac{\partial}{\partial t}\left(\frac{\varepsilon V_1 \sin \omega t}{d}\vec{a}_y \right) \cdot \left(ds\, \vec{a}_y \right)$ (since $\vec{D} = \varepsilon \vec{E}$)

$$= \frac{\varepsilon A}{d} V_1 \omega \cos \omega t$$

Therefore, $I_2 = CV_1 \omega \cos \omega t$ (6.27)

where $C = \dfrac{\varepsilon A}{d}$ is the capacitance of the parallel-plate capacitor.

From Eq. (6.26) and Eq. (6.27), it is evident that the current in the wire surface (conduction current) I_1 and the current in the dielectric surface (displacement current) I_2 are identical. Since both the currents are equal, it results in continuous flow of current through the circuit.

EXAMPLE 6.17

The parallel plates in a capacitor have an area of 5 cm^2 and are separated by 0.5 cm. A voltage of $10 \sin 10^3 t$ V is applied to the capacitor. Find the displacement current when the dielectric material between the plates has a relative permittivity of 5.

SOLUTION

Given $d = 0.5$ cm, $\varepsilon_r = 5$, $V = 10 \sin 10^3 t$ V, and $A = 5 \,\mathrm{cm}^2 = 5 \times 10^{-4} \,\mathrm{m}^2$.

The magnitude of flux density is $D = \varepsilon E$ and hence, the displacement current density is

$$J_d = \frac{\partial D}{\partial t} = \frac{\partial (\varepsilon E)}{\partial t} = \frac{\partial}{\partial t}\left(\varepsilon \frac{V}{d} \right) \qquad \text{(since } E = V/d)$$

$$= \frac{\varepsilon}{d}\frac{dV}{dt} = \frac{\varepsilon_0 \varepsilon_r}{d}\frac{dV}{dt}$$

The displacement current is

$$I_d = J_d \times A = \frac{\varepsilon_0 \varepsilon_r A}{d}\frac{dV}{dt}$$

$$= \frac{8.854 \times 10^{-12} \times 5 \times 5 \times 10^{-4}}{0.5 \times 10^{-2}} \times \frac{dV}{dt}$$

$$= 442.7 \times 10^{-14} \times \frac{dV}{dt} = 442.7 \times 10^{-14} \times \frac{d}{dt} \left(10 \sin 10^3 t \right)$$

$$= 442.7 \times 10^{-14} \times 10 \times 10^3 \cos 10^3 t = 44.27 \times 10^{-9} \cos 10^3 t$$

Therefore, $I_d = 44.27 \cos 10^3 t$ nA

EXAMPLE 6.18

Find the displacement current density within a parallel-plate capacitor having a dielectric with $\varepsilon_r = 10$, area of the plates $A = 0.01$ m^2, distance of separation $d = 0.05$ mm, and applied voltage $V = 200 \sin 200t$.

SOLUTION

Given $A = 0.01$ m^2, $d = 0.05 \times 10^{-3}$ m, $\varepsilon_r = 10$, and $V = 200 \sin 200t$.

The magnitude of displacement current density is

$$J_d = \frac{\partial D}{\partial t} = \frac{\partial (\varepsilon E)}{\partial t}, \text{ where } E = \frac{V}{d}$$

$$= \frac{d}{dt} \left(\frac{\varepsilon V}{d} \right) = \frac{\varepsilon}{d} \frac{dV}{dt} = \frac{\varepsilon_0 \varepsilon_r}{d} \frac{dV}{dt}$$

$$= \frac{8.854 \times 10^{-12} \times 10}{0.05 \times 10^{-3}} \times \frac{d}{dt} \left(200 \sin 200t \right)$$

$$= 1.77 \times 10^{-6} \times 200^2 \cos 200t = 0.07 \cos 200t \text{ A/m}^2$$

EXAMPLE 6.19

A copper wire carries a conduction current of 1 A. Determine the displacement current in the wire at 1 MHz. For copper $\varepsilon = \varepsilon_0$ and $\sigma = 5.8 \times 10^7$ S/m.

SOLUTION

Given $I_c = 1$ A, $f = 1$ MHz $= 10^6$ Hz, $\varepsilon = \varepsilon_0$, and $\sigma = 5.8 \times 10^7$ S/m.

The conduction current is

$$I_c = J_c \times A = \sigma E \times A, \text{ where } J_c = \sigma E \text{ and } A \text{ is the area}$$

Hence,

$$E = \frac{I_c}{\sigma A}$$

The magnitude of displacement current density is

$$J_d = \frac{\partial D}{\partial t} = \frac{\partial (\varepsilon E)}{\partial t} \qquad \left(\text{since } \frac{\partial}{\partial t} = j\omega \right)$$

$$= \omega \varepsilon E = \omega \varepsilon_0 \frac{I_c}{\sigma A}, \text{ where } \omega = 2\pi f = 2\pi \times 10^6 = 6.28 \times 10^6 \text{ rad/s}$$

$$= 6.28 \times 10^6 \times 8.854 \times 10^{-12} \times \frac{1.724 \times 10^{-8}}{A}$$

$$= \frac{9.585 \times 10^{-13}}{A}$$

Therefore, the displacement current is

$$I_d = J_d A = \frac{9.585 \times 10^{-13} \times A}{A}$$

$$= 9.58 \times 10^{-13}\, \text{A}$$

EXAMPLE 6.20

Find the displacement current density within a parallel-plate capacitor, where $\varepsilon = 100\varepsilon_0$, $A = 0.01$ m^2, $d = 0.05$ mm, and the voltage applied across the capacitor is $100 \sin 200\pi t$ V.

SOLUTION

Given $\varepsilon = 100\varepsilon_0$, $A = 0.01$ m^2, $d = 0.05$ mm, and $V = 100 \sin 200\pi t$.

The capacitance of parallel-plate capacitor is

$$C = \frac{\varepsilon A}{d} = \frac{100 \times 8.854 \times 10^{-12} \times 0.01}{0.05 \times 10^{-3}} = 0.1771\,\mu\text{F}$$

The displacement current is

$$I_d = C\frac{dV}{dt} = 0.1771 \times 10^{-6} \times \frac{d}{dt}\left(100 \sin 200\pi t\right)$$

$$= 0.1771 \times 10^{-6} \times 100 \times 200\pi \times \left(\cos 200\pi t\right)$$

$$= 11.13 \cos\left(200\pi t\right)\, \text{mA}$$

The displacement current density is

$$J_d = \frac{I_d}{A} = \frac{11.13 \times 10^{-3} \cos 200\pi t}{0.01}$$

$$= 1.11 \cos\left(200\pi t\right)\, \text{A/m}^2$$

Alternate method

The magnitude of displacement current density is

$$J_d = \frac{\partial D}{\partial t} = \frac{\partial(\varepsilon E)}{\partial t}$$

$$= \varepsilon \frac{\partial}{\partial t}\left(\frac{V}{d}\right), \text{ where } E = \frac{V}{d}$$

$$= \frac{\varepsilon}{d}\frac{\partial V}{\partial t} = \frac{100\varepsilon_0}{0.05 \times 10^{-3}} \times \frac{\partial}{\partial t}(100\sin 200\pi\, t)$$

$$= \frac{100 \times 8.854 \times 10^{-12}}{0.05 \times 10^{-3}} \times 100 \times 200\pi \times \cos(200\pi t)$$

$$= 1.113\cos(200\pi\, t) \text{ A/m}^2$$

EXAMPLE 6.21

Find the amplitude of the displacement current density (i) in air near the car antenna where the field strength of the FM signal is $\vec{E} = 80\cos\left(6.277 \times 10^8\, t - 2.092\, y\right)\vec{a}_z$ V/m and (ii) inside a capacitor where $\varepsilon_r = 600$ and $\vec{D} = 3 \times 10^{-6}\sin\left(6 \times 10^6\, t - 0.3464\, x\right)\vec{a}_z$ C/m^2.

SOLUTION

(*i*) Given $\vec{E} = 80\cos\left(6.277 \times 10^8\, t - 2.092\, y\right)\vec{a}_z$ V/m.

The displacement current density is

$$\vec{J}_d = \frac{\partial \vec{D}}{\partial t} = \frac{\partial}{\partial t}\left(\varepsilon_0 \varepsilon_r \vec{E}\right) \text{ (for air, } \varepsilon_r = 1)$$

$$= \varepsilon_0 \frac{\partial}{\partial t}\left[80\cos\left(6.277 \times 10^8\, t - 2.092\, y\right)\vec{a}_z\right]$$

$$= 8.854 \times 10^{-12} \times 80 \times \left(-6.277 \times 10^8\right)\sin\left(6.277 \times 10^8\, t - 2.092\, y\right)\vec{a}_z$$

$$= -0.4446\sin\left(6.277 \times 10^8\, t - 2.092\, y\right)\vec{a}_z \text{ A/m}^2$$

Hence, the magnitude of the displacement current density is

$$\left|\vec{J}_d\right| = 0.4446 \text{ A/m}^2$$

(*ii*) Given $\vec{D} = 3 \times 10^{-6}\sin\left(6 \times 10^6\, t - 0.3464\, x\right)\vec{a}_z$ C/m^2 and inside the capacitor $\varepsilon_r = 600$.

The displacement current density is

$$\vec{J}_d = \frac{\partial \vec{D}}{\partial t} = \frac{\partial}{\partial t}\left[3 \times 10^{-6}\sin\left(6 \times 10^6\, t - 0.3464\, x\right)\vec{a}_z\right]$$

$$= 3 \times 10^{-6} \times 6 \times 10^6 \times \cos\left(6 \times 10^6\, t - 0.3464\, x\right)\vec{a}_z$$

$$= 18\cos\left(6 \times 10^6\, t - 0.3464\, x\right)\vec{a}_z \text{ A/m}^2$$

Hence, the magnitude of the displacement current density is

$$\left|\vec{J}_d\right| = 18 \text{ A/m}^2$$

EXAMPLE 6.22

Find the conduction and displacement current densities in a material having conductivity of 10^{-3} S/m and $\varepsilon_r = 2.5$ if the electric field in the material is $E = 5.8 \times 10^{-6} \sin\left(9 \times 10^9 t\right)$ V/m.

SOLUTION

Given $\sigma = 10^{-3}$ S/m, $\varepsilon_r = 2.5$, and $E = 5.8 \times 10^{-6} \sin\left(9 \times 10^9 t\right)$ V/m.

The conduction current density is

$$J_c = \sigma E = 10^{-3} \times 5.8 \times 10^{-6} \sin\left(9 \times 10^9 t\right)$$

$$= 5.8 \sin\left(9 \times 10^9 t\right) \text{ nA/m}^2$$

The displacement current density is

$$J_d = \frac{\partial D}{\partial t} = \frac{\partial}{\partial t}(\varepsilon E)$$

$$= \varepsilon \frac{\partial E}{\partial t} = \varepsilon_0 \varepsilon_r \frac{\partial}{\partial t}\left[5.8 \times 10^{-6} \sin\left(9 \times 10^9 t\right)\right]$$

$$= 8.85 \times 10^{-12} \times 2.5 \times 5.8 \times 10^{-6} \times 9 \times 10^9 \cos\left(9 \times 10^9 t\right)$$

$$= 1.155 \times 10^{-6} \cos\left(9 \times 10^9 t\right) = 1.155 \cos\left(9 \times 10^9 t\right) \text{ μA/m}^2$$

EXAMPLE 6.23

Find the electric flux density and volume charge density if the electric field intensity is given by $\vec{E} = 2x^2 \vec{a}_x + 4y^2 \vec{a}_y + 2z^2 \vec{a}_z$ V/m in a medium whose $\varepsilon_r = 4$.

SOLUTION

Given $\vec{E} = 2x^2 \vec{a}_x + 4y^2 \vec{a}_y + 2z^2 \vec{a}_z$ V/m.

The electric flux density is

$$\vec{D} = \varepsilon \vec{E} = \varepsilon_0 \varepsilon_r \vec{E} = 8.854 \times 10^{-12} \times 4 \times \left(2x^2 \vec{a}_x + 4y^2 \vec{a}_y + 2z^2 \vec{a}_z\right)$$

$$= 70.83 x^2 \vec{a}_x + 141.66 y^2 \vec{a}_y + 70.83 z^2 \vec{a}_z \text{ pC/m}^2$$

From Maxwell's equation, we have

$$\nabla \cdot \vec{D} = \frac{\partial D_x}{\partial x} + \frac{\partial D_y}{\partial y} + \frac{\partial D_z}{\partial z} = \rho_v$$

Hence, $\rho_v = 141.66x + 283.32y + 141.66z \text{ pC/m}^3$

EXAMPLE 6.24

In a certain region, $\vec{J} = (2y\vec{a}_x + xz\vec{a}_y + z^3\vec{a}_z)\sin 10^4 t$ A/m^2. Determine the volume charge density ρ_v if $\rho_v = (x, y, 0, t) = 0$.

SOLUTION

Given $\vec{J} = (2y\vec{a}_x + xz\vec{a}_y + z^3\vec{a}_z)\sin 10^4 t$ A/m^2.

The continuity equation is

$$\nabla \cdot \vec{J} = -\frac{\partial \rho_v}{\partial t}$$

Integrating the above equation, we get

$$\rho_v = -\int (\nabla \cdot \vec{J})\, dt$$

$$= -\int (0 + 0 + 3z^2)\sin 10^4 t\, dt \qquad \left(\text{since } \nabla \cdot \vec{J} = \frac{\partial J_x}{\partial x} + \frac{\partial J_y}{\partial y} + \frac{\partial J_z}{\partial z}\right)$$

$$= \frac{3z^2}{10^4}\cos 10^4 t + c_0$$

Given $\rho_v = 0$ at $z = 0$. Substituting this condition in the above equation, we get $c_0 = 0$.

Therefore, $\rho_v = 0.3z^2 \cos 10^4 t$ mC/m^3 ☐

EXAMPLE 6.25

If the electric field strength of a radio broadcast signal at a TV receiver is given by $\vec{E} = 10\cos(\omega t - \beta y)\vec{a}_z$ V/m, determine the displacement current density. If the same field exists in a medium whose conductivity is given by 5×10^3 Ω^{-1} /cm , find the conduction current density.

SOLUTION

Given the field strength $\vec{E}$ at a TV receiver in free space is $\vec{E} = 10\cos(\omega t - \beta y)\vec{a}_z$ V/m.

The electric flux density is

$$\vec{D} = \varepsilon_0 \vec{E} = 10\varepsilon_0 \cos(\omega t - \beta y)\vec{a}_z \text{ C/m}^2$$

The displacement current density is

$$\vec{J}_d = \frac{\partial \vec{D}}{\partial t} = \frac{\partial}{\partial t}\left[10\varepsilon_0 \cos(\omega t - \beta y)\vec{a}_z\right]$$

$$= -10\varepsilon_0 \omega \sin(\omega t - \beta y)\vec{a}_z \text{ A/m}^2$$

$$= -88.54\omega \sin(\omega t - \beta y)\vec{a}_z \text{ pA/m}^2$$

The conduction current density is

$$\vec{J}_c = \sigma \vec{E}$$

where $\sigma = 5 \times 10^3$ Ω^{-1} /cm $= 5 \times 10^5$ Ω^{-1}/m.

Hence, $\vec{J}_c = 5 \times 10^5 \times 10\cos(\omega t - \beta y)\vec{a}_z = 5 \times 10^6 \cos(\omega t - \beta y)\vec{a}_z$ A/m^2 ☐

EXAMPLE 6.26

A coaxial capacitor has the parameters $a = 5$ mm, $b = 30$ mm, $l = 20$ cm, $\varepsilon_r = 8$, and $\sigma = 10^{-6}$ S/m. If the conduction current density in the capacitor is $\left(\dfrac{2}{\rho}\right)\sin(10^6 t)\,\vec{a}_\rho$ A/m^2, determine (i) the total conduction current through the capacitor, (ii) the maximum value of the displacement current density, and (iii) the total displacement current.

SOLUTION

Given $\vec{J}_c = \dfrac{2}{\rho}\sin(10^6 t)\vec{a}_\rho$ A/m^2, $a = 5\times10^{-3}$ m, $b = 0.03$ m, $l = 0.2$ m, $\varepsilon_r = 8$, and $\sigma = 10^{-6}$ S/m.

(*i*) The total conduction current is

$$I_c = \int_s \vec{J}_c \cdot d\vec{s}, \text{ where } d\vec{s} = \rho\, d\phi\, dz\, \vec{a}_\rho$$

$$= \int_s \left(\frac{2}{\rho}\sin(10^6 t)\vec{a}_\rho \cdot \rho\, d\phi\, dz\, \vec{a}_\rho\right)$$

$$= \int_0^{2\pi}\int_0^{0.2} 2\sin(10^6 t)\, d\phi\, dz = 2\sin(10^6 t)(2\pi)(0.2) = 2.512\sin(10^6 t)\text{ A}$$

(*ii*) The displacement current density is

$$\vec{J}_d = \frac{\partial \vec{D}}{\partial t} = \frac{\partial \varepsilon \vec{E}}{\partial t}$$

$$= \frac{\partial}{\partial t}\left(\frac{\varepsilon \vec{J}_c}{\sigma}\right) = \frac{\varepsilon_r \varepsilon_0}{\sigma}\frac{\partial \vec{J}_c}{\partial t}$$

$$= \frac{8\varepsilon_0}{\sigma}\frac{\partial}{\partial t}\left(\frac{2}{\rho}\sin(10^6 t)\right)\vec{a}_\rho = \frac{8\varepsilon_0}{\sigma}\left(\frac{2}{\rho}\right)10^6\cos(10^6 t)\,\vec{a}_\rho$$

$$= \frac{16\times8.854\times10^{-12}\times10^6}{10^{-6}\times\rho}\cos(10^6 t)\,\vec{a}_\rho$$

$$= \frac{141.664}{\rho}\cos(10^6 t)\,\vec{a}_\rho\text{A/m}^2$$

The maximum value of displacement current density at $\rho = 5$ mm is

$$J_{d(\max)} = \frac{141.664}{5\times10^{-3}} = 28.33\times10^3\text{ A/m}^2$$

(*iii*) The total displacement current is

$$I_d = \int_s \vec{J}_d \cdot d\vec{s}$$

$$= \int_s \frac{141.664}{\rho}\cos(10^6 t)\,\vec{a}_\rho \cdot \rho\, d\phi\, dz\, \vec{a}_\rho$$

$$= 141.664\int_0^{0.2}\int_0^{2\pi}\cos(10^6 t)\, d\phi\, dz$$

$$= 141.664 \cos(10^6 t) \, (0.2) \, (2\pi)$$

$$= 178.02 \cos(10^6 t) \, \text{A}$$

EXAMPLE 6.27

In a cylindrical conductor of radius 2 mm, the current density varies with the distance from the axis according to $\vec{J} = 10^3 e^{-400\rho} \vec{a}_z$ A/m^2. Find the conduction current.

SOLUTION

Given $\vec{J} = 10^3 e^{-400\rho} \vec{a}_z$ A/m^2 and radius $\rho = 0.002$ m.

The conduction current is

$$I_c = \int_s \vec{J} \cdot d\vec{s} = \int_0^{2\pi} \int_0^{0.002} \left(10^3 e^{-400\rho} \vec{a}_z \right) \cdot \left(\rho \, d\rho \, d\phi \, \vec{a}_z \right)$$

$$= 2\pi \times 10^3 \int_0^{0.002} e^{-400\rho} \rho \, d\rho = 2\pi \times 10^3 \left[\frac{-\rho}{400} e^{-400\rho} - \frac{e^{-400\rho}}{(-400)^2} \right]_0^{0.002}$$

$$= 2\pi \times 10^3 \left[\frac{e^{-400\rho}}{(-400)^2} (-400\rho - 1) \right]_0^{0.002}$$

$$= \frac{2\pi \times 10^3}{16 \times 10^4} \left[-e^{-400\rho} (400\rho + 1) \right]_0^{0.002}$$

$$= 39.26 \times 10^{-3} [-e^{-0.8} (0.8 + 1) + 1]$$

$$= 39.26 \times 10^{-3} (-0.8088 + 1) = 7.51 \text{ mA}$$

EXAMPLE 6.28

Consider that two parallel conducting plates of area 0.05 m^2 are separated by 2 mm of a lossy dielectric for which $\varepsilon_r = 5$ and $\sigma = 5 \times 10^{-4}$ S/m. Given an applied voltage $V = 5 \sin 10^7 t$ V, find total r.m.s. current.

SOLUTION

Given $d = 2 \times 10^{-3}$, Area $A = 0.05$ m^2, $\varepsilon_r = 5$, $\sigma = 5 \times 10^{-4}$ S/m, and $V = 5 \sin 10^7 t$ V.

The electric field produced due to the applied voltage is

$$E = \frac{V}{d} = \frac{5 \sin 10^7 t}{2 \times 10^{-3}} = 2500 \sin 10^7 t \text{ V/m}$$

The conduction current density is

$$J_c = \sigma E = \left(5 \times 10^{-4} \right) \left(2500 \sin 10^7 t \right) = 1.25 \sin 10^7 t \text{ A/m}^2$$

The displacement current density is

$$J_d = \varepsilon \frac{dE}{dt} = \varepsilon_0 \varepsilon_r \frac{dE}{dt} = 8.854 \times 10^{-12} \times 5 \times \frac{d}{dt} \left(2500 \sin 10^7 t \right)$$

$$= 8.854 \times 10^{-12} \times 5 \times 2500 \times 10^7 \times \cos 10^7 t$$

$$= 1.11 \cos 10^7 t \ \text{A/m}^2$$

The conduction current is

$$I_c = J_c A = 1.25 \sin 10^7 t \times 0.05 = 0.06 \sin 10^7 t \ \text{A}$$

The displacement current is

$$I_d = J_d A = 1.11 \cos 10^7 t \times 0.05 = 0.056 \cos 10^7 t \ \text{A}$$

Both the currents are at right angles to each other and the total current is

$$I_T = \sqrt{I_c^2 + I_d^2} = \sqrt{(0.06)^2 + (0.056)^2} = 0.08 \text{A}$$

Hence, the r.m.s. current is

$$I_{rms} = \frac{I_T}{\sqrt{2}} = \frac{0.08}{\sqrt{2}} = 0.057 \ \text{A}$$

EXAMPLE 6.29

A coaxial capacitor of length $l = 6$ cm uses an insulating dielectric material with $\varepsilon_r = 9$. The radii of the cylindrical conductors are 1 and 2 cm. If the voltage applied across the capacitor is $V = 100 \sin(120\pi t)$ V, what is the displacement current?

SOLUTION

Given $V = 100 \sin(120\pi t)$ V, $l = 6$ cm, $\varepsilon_r = 9$, a = 1 cm, and b = 2 cm.

The displacement current between the cylindrical conductors is

$$I_d = \int_s \frac{\partial \vec{D}}{\partial t} \cdot d\vec{s} = \int_s \frac{\partial (\varepsilon \vec{E})}{\partial t} \cdot d\vec{s}$$

$$= \int_s \frac{\partial}{\partial t} \left(\frac{\varepsilon V}{\rho \ln\left(\frac{b}{a}\right)} \vec{a}_\rho \right) \cdot \left(\rho \, d\phi \, dz \, \vec{a}_\rho \right)$$

where $\vec{E} = \dfrac{V}{\rho \ln\left(\frac{b}{a}\right)} \vec{a}_\rho$ V/m and $d\vec{s} = \rho \, d\phi \, dz \, \vec{a}_\rho$ in cylindrical coordinates.

Therefore, $I_d = \dfrac{\partial}{\partial t} \left(\dfrac{\varepsilon V}{\rho \ln\left(\frac{b}{a}\right)} \right) \int_s \rho \, dz \, d\phi$

$$= \left(\frac{\varepsilon_0 \varepsilon_r \times 100 \times 120\pi \times \cos(120\pi\, t)}{\ln\left(\dfrac{b}{a}\right)} \right) \int_0^l dz \int_0^{2\pi} d\phi$$

$$= \frac{2\pi\varepsilon_0\varepsilon_r l}{\ln\left(\dfrac{b}{a}\right)} \times 100 \times 120\pi \times \cos(120\pi\, t)$$

Here, the capacitance of a coaxial capacitor is

$$C = \frac{2\pi\varepsilon_0\varepsilon_r l}{\ln\left(\dfrac{b}{a}\right)} = \frac{2\pi \times \dfrac{1}{36\pi} \times 10^{-9} \times 9 \times 0.06}{\ln\left(\dfrac{0.02}{0.01}\right)} = 0.043 \times 10^{-9}\,\text{F}$$

Hence, $I_d = 0.043 \times 10^{-9} \times 100 \times 120\pi \times \cos(120\pi\, t) = 1.62\cos(120\pi\, t)\ \mu\text{A}$

6.6 MAXWELL'S EQUATIONS

When the charge and current source vary with time, i.e., under time-varying conditions, the electric and magnetic fields are interconnected and the coupling between them results in EM waves. These waves are capable of travelling through free space and any material medium. The study of time-varying electromagnetic phenomena can be best carried out using the four Maxwell's equations. Maxwell unified the theory of electricity and magnetism using Gauss's law, Faraday's law, and Ampere's law.

The two divergence equations in Maxwell's equations remain the same as in static case for electric and magnetic fields (Gauss's law). The two curl equations for electric and magnetic field in static case have been modified under time-varying conditions, i.e., a time-varying magnetic field generates an electric field (Faraday's law) and conversely, a time-varying electric field produces a magnetic field (Ampere's law). Maxwell modified the Ampere's law by introducing the concept of displacement current.

6.6.1 Maxwell's Equation from Gauss's law for Electrostatic fields

According to Gauss's law for electrostatic fields, the total electric flux Ψ passing through a closed surface is equal to the total charge Q enclosed by that surface, i.e., $\Psi = Q$. We know that, $\psi = \oint_s \vec{D} \cdot d\vec{s}$.

For a volume change density ρ_v, the total charge enclosed is given by

$$Q = \int_v \rho_v dv \tag{6.28}$$

Equating the above two equations, we get

$$\oint_s \vec{D} \cdot d\vec{s} = \int_v \rho_v dv \qquad \text{(Integral form)} \tag{6.29}$$

By divergence theorem,

$$\oint_s \vec{D} \cdot d\vec{s} = \int_v (\nabla \cdot \vec{D}) dv \tag{6.30}$$

Substituting Eq. (6.30) in Eq. (6.29), we have

$$\int_v (\nabla \cdot \vec{D}) dv = \int_v \rho_v dv \tag{6.31}$$

Comparing the volume integrals on both sides in the above equation, we get

$$\nabla \cdot \vec{D} = \rho_v \qquad \text{(Differential or point form)} \qquad (6.32)$$

This equation states that the total electric flux density passing through a closed surface (Gaussian surface) is equal to the total charge inside the surface.

6.6.2 Maxwell's Equation from Gauss's Law for Magnetostatic Fields

According to Gauss's law for magnetostatic fields, the total magnetic flux Φ passing through any closed surface in a magnetic field is equal to zero. The inference from the above law is that an isolated magnetic pole or magnetic charge does not exist in magnetism.

$$\text{Hence,} \quad \Phi = \oint_s \vec{B} \cdot d\vec{s} = 0 \qquad \text{(Integral form)} \qquad (6.33)$$

By divergence theorem,

$$\oint_s \vec{B} \cdot d\vec{s} = \int_v (\nabla \cdot \vec{B}) \, dv \qquad (6.34)$$

Substituting Eq. (6.34) in Eq. (6.33), we get

$$\int_v (\nabla \cdot \vec{B}) \, dv = 0 \qquad (6.35)$$

Since dv cannot be zero, we have

$$\nabla \cdot \vec{B} = 0 \qquad \text{(Differential or point form)} \qquad (6.36)$$

This equation states that the total magnetic flux passing through any closed surface is zero.

6.6.3 Maxwell's Equation from Faraday's Law

According to Faraday's law, the induced emf in any closed circuit or path is equal to the negative time rate of change of magnetic flux linkage by the circuit or the path, i.e., $V_{emf} = -\dfrac{d\Phi}{dt}$. This statement is valid only for time-varying fields. However, if the field is static, the induced emf is zero.

For time-varying fields

By Faraday's law,

$$\oint_l \vec{E} \cdot d\vec{l} = -\int_s \frac{\partial \vec{B}}{\partial t} \cdot d\vec{s} \qquad \text{(Integral form)} \qquad (6.37)$$

By Stokes's theorem,

$$\oint_l \vec{E} \cdot d\vec{l} = \int_s (\nabla \times \vec{E}) \cdot d\vec{s} \qquad (6.38)$$

Substituting Eq. (6.38) in Eq. (6.37), we have

$$\int_s (\nabla \times \vec{E}) \cdot d\vec{s} = -\int_s \frac{\partial \vec{B}}{\partial t} \cdot d\vec{s} \qquad (6.39)$$

Comparing the surface integrals on both sides of the above equation, we get

$$\nabla \times \vec{E} = -\frac{\partial \vec{B}}{\partial t} \qquad \text{(Differential form or point form)} \qquad (6.40)$$

This equation states that the electromotive force around a closed path is equal to the negative of the time derivative of the magnetic flux density flowing through any surface bounded by the path.

6.6.4 Maxwell's Equation from Ampere's Circuital Law

According to Ampere's circuital law, the line integral of magnetic field around a closed path is equal to the net current I enclosed by the same closed path. Here, the net current is equal to the surface integral of both conduction and displacement current densities over the surface bounded by the same closed path. This statement is valid only for time-varying fields. However, if the field is static, only conduction current exists.

For time-varying fields

By Ampere's circuit law,

$$\oint_l \vec{H} \cdot d\vec{l} = I \tag{6.41}$$

We know that, $I = I_c + I_d = \int_s \left(\vec{J} + \frac{\partial \vec{D}}{\partial t} \right) \cdot d\vec{s}$ $\tag{6.42}$

Substituting Eq. (6.36) in Eq. (6.35), we get

$$\oint_l \vec{H} \cdot d\vec{l} = \int_s \left(\vec{J} + \frac{\partial \vec{D}}{\partial t} \right) \cdot d\vec{s} \qquad \text{(Integral form)} \tag{6.43}$$

Also, by Stokes's theorem,

$$\oint_l \vec{H} \cdot d\vec{l} = \int_s (\nabla \times \vec{H}) \cdot d\vec{s} \tag{6.44}$$

Substituting Eq. (6.44) in Eq. (6.43), we get

$$\int_s (\nabla \times \vec{H}) \cdot d\vec{s} = \int_s \left(\vec{J} + \frac{\partial \vec{D}}{\partial t} \right) \cdot d\vec{s} \tag{6.45}$$

Comparing the surface integrals on both sides of the above equation, we get

$$\nabla \times \vec{H} = \vec{J} + \frac{\partial \vec{D}}{\partial t} \qquad \text{(Differential or point form)} \tag{6.46}$$

This equation states that the magnetomotive force around a closed path is equal to the sum of electric displacement and conduction currents through any surface bounded by the path.

Therefore, the four Maxwell's equations in general form, for free space and for good conductors are summarized in Tables 6.2–6.4.

(*i*) **General form:** The Maxwell's equations in general form are given in Table 6.2.

Table 6.2 *Maxwell's equations in general form*

Reference	Point form	Integral form
Gauss's law	$\nabla \cdot \vec{D} = \rho_v$	$\oint_s \vec{D} \cdot d\vec{s} = \int_v \rho_v \, dv$
Gauss's law for magnetism	$\nabla \cdot \vec{B} = 0$	$\oint_s \vec{B} \cdot d\vec{s} = 0$

Reference	Point form	Integral form
Faraday's law	$\nabla \times \vec{E} = -\dfrac{\partial \vec{B}}{\partial t}$	$\oint_l \vec{E} \cdot d\vec{l} = -\int_s \dfrac{\partial \vec{B}}{\partial t} \cdot d\vec{s}$
Ampere's law	$\nabla \times \vec{H} = \vec{J} + \dfrac{\partial \vec{D}}{\partial t}$	$\oint_l \vec{H} \cdot d\vec{l} = \int_s \left(\vec{J} + \dfrac{\partial \vec{D}}{\partial t} \right) \cdot d\vec{s}$

(*ii*) **For free space:** The Maxwell's equations in free space are listed in Table 6.3. In free space, the charge density $\rho_v = 0$ and conduction current density $\vec{J} = 0$.

Table 6.3 *Maxwell's equations for free space*

Reference	Point form	Integral form
Gauss's law	$\nabla \cdot \vec{D} = 0$	$\oint_s \vec{D} \cdot d\vec{s} = 0$
Gauss's law for magnetism	$\nabla \cdot \vec{B} = 0$	$\oint_s \vec{B} \cdot d\vec{s} = 0$
Faraday's law	$\nabla \times \vec{E} = -\dfrac{\partial \vec{B}}{\partial t}$	$\oint_l \vec{E} \cdot d\vec{l} = -\int_s \dfrac{\partial \vec{B}}{\partial t} \cdot d\vec{s}$
Ampere's law	$\nabla \times \vec{H} = \dfrac{\partial \vec{D}}{\partial t}$	$\oint_l \vec{H} \cdot d\vec{l} = \int_s \dfrac{\partial \vec{D}}{\partial t} \cdot d\vec{s}$

(*iii*) **For a good conductor:** The Maxwell's equations for good conductors are given in Table 6.4. For good conductors, the charge density $\rho_v = 0$ and the displacement current density $\dfrac{\partial \vec{D}}{\partial t} = 0$.

Table 6.4 *Maxwell's equations for good conductor*

Reference	Point form	Integral form
Gauss's law	$\nabla \cdot \vec{D} = 0$	$\oint_s \vec{D} \cdot d\vec{s} = 0$
Gauss's law for magnetism	$\nabla \cdot \vec{B} = 0$	$\oint_s \vec{B} \cdot d\vec{s} = 0$
Faraday's law	$\nabla \times \vec{E} = -\dfrac{\partial \vec{B}}{\partial t}$	$\oint_l \vec{E} \cdot d\vec{l} = -\int_s \dfrac{\partial \vec{B}}{\partial t} \cdot d\vec{s}$
Ampere's law	$\nabla \times \vec{H} = \vec{J}$	$\oint_l \vec{H} \cdot d\vec{l} = \int_s \vec{J} \cdot d\vec{s} = I$

EXAMPLE 6.30

If $\vec{D} = 20x\vec{a}_x - 15y\vec{a}_y + kz\vec{a}_z \ \mu C/m^2$ and $\vec{B} = 2\vec{a}_y$ mT, find the value of k to satisfy the Maxwell's equations for region $\sigma = 0$, $\rho_v = 0$.

SOLUTION

Since $\sigma = 0$ and $\rho_v = 0$, the medium is free space. Therefore, the Maxwell's equation obtained from Gauss's law is

$$\nabla \cdot \vec{D} = \rho_v = 0$$

$$\frac{\partial \vec{D}_x}{\partial x} + \frac{\partial \vec{D}_y}{\partial y} + \frac{\partial \vec{D}_z}{\partial z} = 0$$

$$\frac{\partial}{\partial x}(20x) + \frac{\partial}{\partial y}(-15y) + \frac{\partial}{\partial z}(kz) = 0$$

$$20 - 15 + k = 0$$

Therefore, $$k = -5$$

EXAMPLE 6.31

A two-dimensional electric field is given by $\vec{E} = x^2 \vec{a}_x + x\vec{a}_y$ V/m. Show that this electric field cannot arise from a static distribution of charge.

SOLUTION

For static electric fields, $\nabla \times \vec{E} = 0$

For the given field, $\vec{E} = x^2 \vec{a}_x + x\vec{a}_y$,

$$\nabla \times \vec{E} = \begin{vmatrix} \vec{a}_x & \vec{a}_y & \vec{a}_z \\ \dfrac{\partial}{\partial x} & \dfrac{\partial}{\partial y} & \dfrac{\partial}{\partial z} \\ x^2 & x & 0 \end{vmatrix} = \left[-\frac{\partial}{\partial z}(x) \right]\vec{a}_x - \left[-\frac{\partial}{\partial z}(x^2) \right]\vec{a}_y + \left[\frac{\partial}{\partial x}(x) - \frac{\partial}{\partial y}(x^2) \right]\vec{a}_z$$

$$= \vec{a}_z \neq 0$$

Since $\nabla \times \vec{E} \neq 0$, the given electric field $\vec{E}$ is not static. Hence, it is clear that this electric field cannot arise from a static distribution of charge.

EXAMPLE 6.32

Select the value of k so that the following pair of fields satisfies Maxwell's equations in region where $\sigma = 0$, $\rho_v = 0$.

$$\vec{E} = 60 \sin 10^6 t \, \sin 0.01z \, \vec{a}_x \text{ V/m}$$

and

$$\vec{H} = 0.6 \cos 10^6 t \cos 0.01z \, \vec{a}_y \text{ A/m},$$

$$\mu = k$$

SOLUTION

Since the pair of fields satisfies Maxwell's equation, we can write

$$\nabla \times \vec{E} = -\frac{\partial \vec{B}}{\partial t}$$

$$\text{LHS} = \nabla \times \vec{E} = \begin{vmatrix} \vec{a}_x & \vec{a}_y & \vec{a}_z \\ \dfrac{\partial}{\partial x} & \dfrac{\partial}{\partial y} & \dfrac{\partial}{\partial z} \\ E_x & 0 & 0 \end{vmatrix} = \frac{\partial E_x}{\partial z}\vec{a}_y - \frac{\partial E_x}{\partial y}\vec{a}_z$$

$$= \frac{\partial}{\partial z}\left(60\sin 10^6 t \sin 0.01z\right)\vec{a}_y \qquad \left(\text{since } \frac{\partial E_x}{\partial y} = 0\right)$$

$$= 60\times 0.01\times \sin 10^6 t \cos 0.01z\ \vec{a}_y$$

$$= 0.6\left(\sin 10^6 t \cos 0.01z\right)\vec{a}_y$$

$$\text{RHS} = -\frac{\partial \vec{B}}{\partial t} = -\mu\frac{\partial \vec{H}}{\partial t}, \ \left(\text{given } \mu = k\right)$$

$$= -k\frac{\partial}{\partial t}\left(0.6\cos 10^6 t \cos 0.01z\ \vec{a}_y\right) = k\times 0.6\times 10^6 \sin 10^6 t \cos 0.01z\ \vec{a}_y$$

Equating LHS with RHS, we have

$$0.6\left(\sin 10^6 t \cos 0.01z\right)\vec{a}_y = k\left(6\times 10^5\right)\sin 10^6 t \cos 0.01z\ \vec{a}_y$$

Comparing $\vec{a}_y$ components on both sides of the above equation, we get

$$0.6 = k\left(6\times 10^5\right)$$

Therefore,

$$k = 1\times 10^{-6}\,\text{H/m} = 1\ \mu\text{H/m}$$

EXAMPLE 6.33

If the magnetic field intensity $\vec{H} = \left(3x\cos \beta + 6y\sin \alpha\right)\vec{a}_z$ A/m, find current density $\vec{J}$ if the fields are invariant with time.

SOLUTION

For time-varying fields, the Ampere's law is

$$\nabla \times \vec{H} = \vec{J} + \frac{\partial \vec{D}}{\partial t}$$

Since the given fields are time-invariant, $\dfrac{\partial \vec{D}}{\partial t} = 0.$

Therefore, $\nabla \times \vec{H} = \vec{J} = \begin{vmatrix} \vec{a}_x & \vec{a}_y & \vec{a}_z \\ \dfrac{\partial}{\partial x} & \dfrac{\partial}{\partial y} & \dfrac{\partial}{\partial z} \\ 0 & 0 & H_z \end{vmatrix} = \frac{\partial H_z}{\partial y}\vec{a}_x - \frac{\partial H_z}{\partial x}\vec{a}_y$

$$= \frac{\partial}{\partial y}(3x\cos\beta + 6y\sin\alpha)\vec{a}_x - \frac{\partial}{\partial x}(3x\cos\beta + 6y\sin\alpha)\vec{a}_y$$

$$= 6\sin\alpha\,\vec{a}_x - 3\cos\beta\,\vec{a}_y \text{ A/m}^2 \qquad \square$$

EXAMPLE 6.34

Given $\vec{E} = 5\sin(\omega t - \beta z)\vec{a}_y$ V/m in free space, determine $\vec{D}$, $\vec{B}$ and $\vec{H}$.

SOLUTION

Given $\vec{E} = 5\sin(\omega t - \beta z)\vec{a}_y$ V/m. Here, the electric field has only y-component and its variation is in the z-direction. Therefore, the magnetic field has x-component only.

We know that, $\vec{D} = \varepsilon_0\vec{E} = 5\varepsilon_0\sin(\omega t - \beta z)\vec{a}_y$ C/m^2.

From Faraday's law, we have

$$\nabla \times \vec{E} = -\frac{\partial \vec{B}}{\partial t}$$

$$\text{LHS} = \nabla \times \vec{E} = \begin{vmatrix} \vec{a}_x & \vec{a}_y & \vec{a}_z \\ \dfrac{\partial}{\partial x} & \dfrac{\partial}{\partial y} & \dfrac{\partial}{\partial z} \\ 0 & E_y & 0 \end{vmatrix} = \left[-\frac{\partial E_y}{\partial z}\right]\vec{a}_x - (0)\vec{a}_y + \left[\frac{\partial E_y}{\partial x}\right]\vec{a}_z$$

$$= \left[-\frac{\partial}{\partial z}5\sin(\omega t - \beta z)\right]\vec{a}_x \qquad \left(\text{since } \frac{\partial E_y}{\partial x} = 0\right)$$

$$= 5\beta\cos(\omega t - \beta z)\vec{a}_x$$

$$\text{RHS} = -\frac{\partial \vec{B}}{\partial t} = 5\beta\cos(\omega t - \beta z)\vec{a}_x$$

Integrating above equation, we get

$$\vec{B} = -5\int \beta\cos(\omega t - \beta z)dt\,\vec{a}_x = -\frac{5\beta}{\omega}\sin(\omega t - \beta z)\vec{a}_x \text{ Wb/m}^2$$

Since $\vec{B} = \mu_0\vec{H}$, the magnetic field is

$$\vec{H} = \frac{\vec{B}}{\mu_0} = -\frac{5\beta}{\mu_0\omega}\sin(\omega t - \beta z)\vec{a}_x \text{ A/m} \qquad \square$$

EXAMPLE 6.35

If electric field intensity in free space is given by $\vec{E} = \dfrac{50}{\rho}\cos\left(10^8 t - 10z\right)\vec{a}_\rho$ V/m. Find the magnetic flux density $\vec{B}$.

SOLUTION

Given $\vec{E} = \dfrac{50}{\rho}\cos\left(10^8 t - 10z\right)\vec{a}_\rho$ V/m in cylindrical coordinates.

For time-varying fields, the Faraday's law is

$$\nabla \times \vec{E} = -\frac{\partial \vec{B}}{\partial t}$$

$$\text{LHS} = \nabla \times \vec{E} = \frac{1}{\rho}\begin{vmatrix} \vec{a}_\rho & \rho\,\vec{a}_\phi & \vec{a}_z \\ \dfrac{\partial}{\partial \rho} & \dfrac{\partial}{\partial \phi} & \dfrac{\partial}{\partial z} \\ \vec{E}_\rho & 0 & 0 \end{vmatrix}$$

$$= \frac{1}{\rho}\left\{ -\left[0 - \frac{\partial}{\partial z}\left\{ \frac{50}{\rho}\cos\left(10^8 t - 10z\right)\right\} \right]\rho\,\vec{a}_\phi + \left[0 - \frac{\partial}{\partial \phi}\left\{ \frac{50}{\rho}\cos\left(10^8 t - 10z\right)\right\} \right]\vec{a}_z \right\}$$

$$= \frac{1}{\rho}\left\{ \frac{50}{\rho}\frac{\partial}{\partial z}\cos\left(10^8 t - 10z\right) \right\}\rho\,\vec{a}_\phi = \frac{50}{\rho}\times(-10)\times\left[-\sin\left(10^8 t - 10z\right)\right]\vec{a}_\phi$$

$$= \frac{500}{\rho}\sin\left(10^8 t - 10z\right)\vec{a}_\phi$$

$$\text{RHS} = -\frac{\partial \vec{B}}{\partial t} = \frac{500}{\rho}\sin\left(10^8 t - 10z\right)\vec{a}_\phi$$

Therefore, $\dfrac{\partial \vec{B}}{\partial t} = -\dfrac{500}{\rho}\sin\left(10^8 t - 10z\right)\vec{a}_\phi$

Integrating the above equation, we get

$$\vec{B} = \frac{500}{\rho}\times\frac{1}{10^8}\times\cos\left(10^8 t - 10z\right)\vec{a}_\phi$$

$$= \frac{5}{\rho}\cos\left(10^8 t - 10z\right)\vec{a}_\phi \ \mu\text{Wb/m}^2 \qquad\qquad\square$$

EXAMPLE 6.36

If the electric field strength $\vec{E}$ of an EM wave in free space is given by $\vec{E} = 4\cos\omega\left(t - \dfrac{z}{v_0}\right)\vec{a}_y$ V/m, find the magnetic field strength $\vec{H}$.

SOLUTION

Given $\vec{E} = 4\cos\omega\left(t - \dfrac{z}{v_0}\right)\vec{a}_y$ V/m.

$$\frac{\partial \vec{B}}{\partial t} = -\nabla \times \vec{E} = \begin{vmatrix} \vec{a}_x & \vec{a}_y & \vec{a}_z \\ \dfrac{\partial}{\partial x} & \dfrac{\partial}{\partial y} & \dfrac{\partial}{\partial z} \\ 0 & E_y & 0 \end{vmatrix} = -\left[\left(-\frac{\partial E_y}{\partial z}\right)\vec{a}_x - (0)\vec{a}_y + \left(\frac{\partial E_y}{\partial x}\right)\vec{a}_z \right]$$

$$= \frac{\partial}{\partial z}\left[4\cos\omega\left(t - \frac{z}{v_0}\right)\right]\vec{a}_x = \frac{4\omega}{v_0}\sin\omega\left(t - \frac{z}{v_0}\right)\vec{a}_x \qquad \left(\text{since } \frac{\partial E_y}{\partial x} = 0 \right)$$

Integrating this equation, we get

$$\vec{B} = \frac{4\omega}{v_0} \int \sin \omega \left(t - \frac{z}{v_0} \right) dt \, \vec{a}_x = \frac{-4\omega}{v_0 \omega} \cos \omega \left(t - \frac{z}{v_0} \right) \vec{a}_x$$

$$\vec{H} = \frac{\vec{B}}{\mu_0} = \frac{-4}{v_0 \mu_0} \cos \omega \left(t - \frac{z}{v_0} \right) \vec{a}_x$$

$$= \frac{-4}{\eta_0} \cos \omega \left(t - \frac{z}{v_0} \right) \vec{a}_x \qquad \left[\text{since } v_0 = \frac{1}{\sqrt{\mu_0 \varepsilon_0}} \right]$$

where $\eta_0 = \sqrt{\dfrac{\mu_0}{\varepsilon_0}} = 120\pi \ \Omega$.

Therefore,

$$\vec{H} = -\frac{1}{30\pi} \cos \omega \left(t - \frac{z}{v_0} \right) \vec{a}_x \ \text{A/m} \qquad \qquad \square$$

EXAMPLE 6.37

In free space, the magnetic field of an EM wave is given by $\vec{H} = 0.5\omega\varepsilon_0 \cos(\omega t - 50x)\vec{a}_z$ A/m. Find the electric field and displacement current density.

SOLUTION

Given $\vec{H} = 0.5\omega\varepsilon_0 \cos(\omega t - 50x)\vec{a}_z$ A/m.

The Ampere – Maxwell law is,

$$\nabla \times \vec{H} = \vec{J} + \frac{\partial \vec{D}}{\partial t}$$

Since $\vec{J} = 0$ for free space,

$$\nabla \times \vec{H} = \frac{\partial \vec{D}}{\partial t} = \varepsilon_0 \frac{\partial \vec{E}}{\partial t} = \begin{vmatrix} \vec{a}_x & \vec{a}_y & \vec{a}_z \\ \dfrac{\partial}{\partial x} & \dfrac{\partial}{\partial y} & \dfrac{\partial}{\partial z} \\ 0 & 0 & H_z \end{vmatrix} = \left(\frac{\partial H_z}{\partial y} \right) \vec{a}_x - \left(\frac{\partial H_z}{\partial x} \right) \vec{a}_y + (0)\vec{a}_z$$

$$\varepsilon_0 \frac{\partial \vec{E}}{\partial t} = -\frac{\partial H_z}{\partial x} \vec{a}_y \qquad \left(\text{since } \frac{\partial H_z}{\partial y} = 0 \right)$$

$$= -\frac{\partial}{\partial x} \left[0.5\omega\varepsilon_0 \cos(\omega t - 50x) \right] \vec{a}_y = -0.5\omega\varepsilon_0 \times 50 \times \sin(\omega t - 50x)\vec{a}_y$$

$$= -25\varepsilon_0 \omega \sin(\omega t - 50x)\vec{a}_y$$

$$\frac{\partial \vec{E}}{\partial t} = -25\omega \sin(\omega t - 50x)\vec{a}_y$$

Integrating this equation, we have

$$\vec{E} = -25\omega \int \sin(\omega t - 50x)\, dt\, \vec{a}_y$$

$$= \frac{25\omega}{\omega}\cos(\omega t - 50x)\vec{a}_y = 25\cos(\omega t - 50x)\vec{a}_y \ \text{V/m}$$

The displacement current density $\vec{J}_d$ is

$$\vec{J}_d = \frac{\partial \vec{D}}{\partial t} = \varepsilon_0 \frac{\partial \vec{E}}{\partial t} = \varepsilon_0 \frac{\partial}{\partial t}\Big[25\cos(\omega t - 50x)\Big]\vec{a}_y$$

$$= -25\varepsilon_0 \omega \sin(\omega t - 50x)\vec{a}_y \ \text{A/m}^2$$

EXAMPLE 6.38

If there is a magnetic field represented by

$$\vec{B} = 10\sin(\omega t - \beta x)\vec{a}_x + 10y\cos(\omega t - \beta x)\vec{a}_y \ \text{Wb/m}^2$$

in a medium where $\rho_v = 0$, $\sigma = 0$ and, and $J = 0$. Determine the electric field. Assume $\varepsilon_r = 1$ and $\mu_r = 1$.

SOLUTION

Given $\vec{B} = 10\sin(\omega t - \beta x)\vec{a}_x + 10y\cos(\omega t - \beta x)\vec{a}_y \ \text{Wb/m}^2$.

We know that, the Ampere–Maxwell law is,

$$\nabla \times \vec{H} = \vec{J} + \frac{\partial \vec{D}}{\partial t}$$

Since $\vec{J} = 0$ in free space, $\vec{D} = \varepsilon_0 \vec{E}$ and $\vec{B} = \mu_0 \vec{H}$.

Therefore, $\nabla \times \vec{H} = \dfrac{1}{\mu_0}(\nabla \times \vec{B}) = \varepsilon_0 \dfrac{\partial \vec{E}}{\partial t}$

$$\nabla \times \vec{B} = \mu_0 \varepsilon_0 \frac{\partial \vec{E}}{\partial t} \tag{1}$$

LHS of Eq. (1) is

$$\nabla \times \vec{B} = \begin{vmatrix} \vec{a}_x & \vec{a}_y & \vec{a}_z \\ \dfrac{\partial}{\partial x} & \dfrac{\partial}{\partial y} & \dfrac{\partial}{\partial z} \\ B_x & B_y & 0 \end{vmatrix} = \left[-\frac{\partial B_y}{\partial z}\right]\vec{a}_x + \left[\frac{\partial B_x}{\partial z}\right]\vec{a}_y + \left[\frac{\partial B_y}{\partial x} - \frac{\partial B_x}{\partial y}\right]\vec{a}_z$$

Since B_x and B_y are independent of y and z, $\dfrac{\partial B_y}{\partial z} = 0$, $\dfrac{\partial B_x}{\partial y} = 0$ and $\dfrac{\partial B_x}{\partial z} = 0$.

$$\nabla \times \vec{B} = \left[\frac{\partial B_y}{\partial x}\right]\vec{a}_z = \frac{\partial}{\partial x}\Big[10y\cos(\omega t - \beta x)\Big]\vec{a}_z$$

$$= 10\beta\, y \sin(\omega t - \beta x)\vec{a}_z$$

But

$$\nabla \times \vec{B} = \mu_0 \varepsilon_0 \frac{\partial \vec{E}}{\partial t}$$

Therefore,

$$\frac{\partial \vec{E}}{\partial t} = \frac{1}{\mu_0 \varepsilon_0} \left(\nabla \times \vec{B} \right) = \frac{1}{\mu_0 \varepsilon_0} \left[10\beta\, y \sin\left(\omega t - \beta x \right) \right] \vec{a}_z$$

Integrating the above equation, we obtain

$$\vec{E} = \frac{10\beta\, y}{\mu_0 \varepsilon_0} \int \sin\left(\omega t - \beta x \right) dt\, \vec{a}_z = -\frac{10\beta\, y}{\omega \mu_0 \varepsilon_0} \cos\left(\omega t - \beta x \right) \vec{a}_z \ \text{V/m} \qquad \square$$

EXAMPLE 6.39

An electric field intensity in free space is given by $\vec{E} = 5\cos\left(10^8 t - \beta z\right)\vec{a}_x$ V/m, where E_m is the amplitude of $\vec{E}$, ω is the angular frequency, and β is the phase constant. Determine $\vec{B}, \vec{H}$ and $\vec{D}$. Assume $\varepsilon_r = 1, \mu_r = 1,$ and $\sigma = 0$.

SOLUTION

Given $\vec{E} = 5\cos\left(10^8 t - \beta z\right)\vec{a}_x$ V/m.

From the Faraday's law, we have

$$\nabla \times \vec{E} = -\frac{\partial \vec{B}}{\partial t}$$

Therefore, $\nabla \times \vec{E} = \begin{vmatrix} \vec{a}_x & \vec{a}_y & \vec{a}_z \\ \dfrac{\partial}{\partial x} & \dfrac{\partial}{\partial y} & \dfrac{\partial}{\partial z} \\ E_x & 0 & 0 \end{vmatrix} = [0]\vec{a}_x + \left[\frac{\partial E_x}{\partial z} \right] \vec{a}_y - \left[\frac{\partial E_x}{\partial y} \right] \vec{a}_z$

$$= \left[\frac{\partial}{\partial z} 5\cos\left(10^8 t - \beta z\right) \right]\vec{a}_y \qquad \left(\text{since } \frac{\partial E_x}{\partial y} = 0 \right)$$

$$= 5\beta \sin\left(10^8 t - \beta z\right)\vec{a}_y$$

Hence,

$$-\frac{\partial \vec{B}}{\partial t} = 5\beta \sin\left(10^8 t - \beta z\right)\vec{a}_y$$

Integrating the above equation, we obtain

$$\vec{B} = -\int 5\beta \sin\left(10^8 t - \beta z\right) dt\, \vec{a}_y$$

$$= \frac{5\beta}{10^8} \cos\left(10^8 t - \beta z\right)\vec{a}_y \ \text{Wb/m}^2$$

Since $\vec{B} = \mu \vec{H}$, the magnetic field intensity is

$$\vec{H} = \frac{\vec{B}}{\mu} = \frac{\vec{B}}{\mu_0 \mu_r} = \frac{5\beta \cos\left(10^8 t - \beta z\right)\vec{a}_y}{10^8 \times 4\pi \times 10^{-7} \times 1} = 39.8\beta \cos\left(10^8 t - \beta z\right)\vec{a}_y \text{ mA/m}$$

Since $\vec{D} = \varepsilon \vec{E}$, the electric flux density is

$$\vec{D} = \varepsilon_0 \varepsilon_r \vec{E} = 8.854 \times 10^{-12} \times 1 \times 5 \cos\left(10^8 t - \beta z\right)\vec{a}_x$$

$$= 44.27 \cos\left(10^8 t - \beta z\right)\vec{a}_x \text{ pC/m}^2 \qquad \qquad \square$$

EXAMPLE 6.40

Verify whether the following fields $\vec{E} = 10\sin x \sin t\, \vec{a}_y$ V/m and $\vec{H} = \dfrac{10}{\mu_0}\cos x \cos t\, \vec{a}_z$ A/m satisfy Maxwell's equations in free space.

SOLUTION

In free space, $\vec{J} = 0$ and $\nabla \times \vec{H} = \dfrac{\partial \vec{D}}{\partial t}$

That is,

$$\begin{vmatrix} \vec{a}_x & \vec{a}_y & \vec{a}_z \\ \dfrac{\partial}{\partial x} & \dfrac{\partial}{\partial y} & \dfrac{\partial}{\partial z} \\ 0 & 0 & H_z \end{vmatrix} = \frac{\partial \vec{D}}{\partial t}$$

Therefore, $\dfrac{-\partial H_z}{\partial x}\vec{a}_y = \varepsilon_0 \dfrac{\partial E_y}{\partial t}\vec{a}_y \qquad \left(\text{since } \dfrac{\partial H_z}{\partial y} = 0\right)$

$$\frac{10}{\mu_0}\sin x \cos t = 10\varepsilon_0 \sin x \cos t$$

$$\frac{10}{\mu_0} = 10\varepsilon_0$$

or

$$\mu_0 \varepsilon_0 = 1$$

Since $\mu_0 \varepsilon_0 = 4\pi \times 10^{-7} \times \dfrac{10^{-9}}{36\pi} = \dfrac{10^{-16}}{9} \neq 1$, the given fields do not satisfy Maxwell's equations in free space. $\qquad \square$

EXAMPLE 6.41

Find the displacement current density next to your radio in air, where the local FM station provides a carrier having $\vec{H} = 0.4\cos\left[210\left(3 \times 10^8 t - x\right)\right]\vec{a}_z$ A/m.

SOLUTION

Given $\vec{H} = 0.4\cos[210(3 \times 10^8 t - x)]\vec{a}_z = 0.4\cos[6.3 \times 10^{10} t - 210x]\vec{a}_z$ A/m.

The displacement current density is

$$\vec{J}_d = \frac{\partial \vec{D}}{\partial t} = \frac{\partial}{\partial t}\left(\varepsilon\,\vec{E}\right) = \varepsilon_0 \frac{\partial \vec{E}}{\partial t} \qquad \text{(for air, } \varepsilon_r = 1)$$

Also, we know that

$$\nabla \times \vec{E} = \frac{-\partial \vec{B}}{\partial t} = \frac{-\partial}{\partial t}\left(\mu_0 \vec{H}\right) = -\mu_0 \frac{\partial \vec{H}}{\partial t} \qquad \text{(for air, } \mu_r = 1)$$

$$= -\mu_0 \times 0.4\left(-6.3\times10^{10}\right)\sin\left(6.3\times10^{10}\,t - 210x\right)\vec{a}_z$$

$$= 4\pi\times10^{-7} \times 2.52\times10^{10}\,\sin\left(6.3\times10^{10}\,t - 210x\right)\vec{a}_z$$

$$\nabla \times \vec{E} = 31.65\times10^{3}\,\sin\left(6.3\times10^{10}\,t - 210x\right)\vec{a}_z$$

But for $\vec{a}_z$ component,

$$\nabla \times \vec{E} = \begin{vmatrix} 0 & 0 & \vec{a}_z \\ \dfrac{\partial}{\partial x} & \dfrac{\partial}{\partial y} & \dfrac{\partial}{\partial z} \\ E_x & E_y & E_z \end{vmatrix}$$

$$\left[\frac{\partial E_y}{\partial x} - \frac{\partial E_x}{\partial y}\right]\vec{a}_z = 31.65\times10^{3}\,\sin\left(6.3\times10^{10}\,t - 210x\right)\vec{a}_z$$

$$\frac{-\partial E_x}{\partial y} + \frac{\partial E_y}{\partial x} = 31.65\times10^{3}\,\sin\left(6.3\times10^{10}\,t - 210x\right)$$

Since the field is varying in the x-direction

$$\frac{-\partial E_x}{\partial y} = 0$$

and $\dfrac{\partial E_y}{\partial x} = 31.65\times10^{3}\,\sin\left(6.3\times10^{10}\,t - 210x\right)$

Integrating the above equation, we get

$$E_y = 31.65\times10^{3}\left[\frac{-\cos\left(6.3\times10^{10}\,t - 210x\right)}{-210}\right]$$

$$\vec{E} = 150.71\cos\left(6.3\times10^{10}\,t - 210x\right)\vec{a}_y\,\text{V/m}$$

Therefore, the displacement current density is

$$\vec{J}_d = \varepsilon_0 \frac{\partial \vec{E}}{\partial t} = \varepsilon_0\left(150.71\right)\times\left(-6.3\times10^{10}\right)\times\sin\left(6.3\times10^{10}\,t - 210x\right)\vec{a}_y$$

$$= -8.854 \times 10^{-12} \times 9.49 \times 10^{12} \sin\left(6.3 \times 10^{10} t - 210x\right) \vec{a}_y$$

$$= -84.02 \sin\left(6.3 \times 10^{10} t - 210x\right) \vec{a}_y \ \text{A/m}^2$$

EXAMPLE 6.42

In free space, $\vec{E} = 20\cos(\omega t - 50x)\vec{a}_y$ V/m. Determine (*i*) $\vec{J}_d$, (*ii*) $\vec{H}$, and (*iii*) ω.

SOLUTION

Given $\vec{E} = 20\cos(\omega t - 50x)\vec{a}_y$ V/m in free space. Here, $\varepsilon_r = 1$.

(*i*) The displacement current density is

$$\vec{J}_d = \frac{\partial \vec{D}}{\partial t} = \frac{\partial}{\partial t}(\varepsilon \vec{E}) = \varepsilon_0 \frac{\partial \vec{E}}{\partial t} = -20\omega\varepsilon_0 \sin(\omega t - 50x)\vec{a}_y \ \text{A/m}^2$$

(*ii*) For time-varying fields, the Ampere's law is

$$\nabla \times \vec{H} = \vec{J}_c + \vec{J}_d \quad \text{(for free space, } \vec{J}_c = 0)$$

Since the electric field has y-component and its variation is in x-direction, the magnetic field has z-component only, i.e., $H_x = H_y = 0$.

Therefore, $\vec{J}_d = \nabla \times \vec{H} = \begin{vmatrix} \vec{a}_x & \vec{a}_y & \vec{a}_z \\ \dfrac{\partial}{\partial x} & \dfrac{\partial}{\partial y} & \dfrac{\partial}{\partial z} \\ 0 & 0 & H_z \end{vmatrix} = -\frac{\partial H_z}{\partial x}\vec{a}_y$

That is,

$$-\frac{\partial H_z}{\partial x}\vec{a}_y = -20\omega\varepsilon_0 \sin(\omega t - 50x)\vec{a}_y$$

Integrating the above equation, we get

$$H_z = \frac{-20\omega\varepsilon_0}{-50}\cos(\omega t - 50x) = 0.4\omega\varepsilon_0 \cos(\omega t - 50x)$$

$$\vec{H} = 0.4\omega\varepsilon_0 \cos(\omega t - 50x)\vec{a}_z \ \text{A/m}$$

(*iii*) From Faraday's law,

$$\nabla \times \vec{E} = -\mu\frac{\partial \vec{H}}{\partial t} = -\mu_0\frac{\partial \vec{H}}{\partial t} \qquad \text{(for free space, } \mu_r = 1)$$

But $\nabla \times \vec{E} = \begin{vmatrix} \vec{a}_x & \vec{a}_y & \vec{a}_z \\ \dfrac{\partial}{\partial x} & \dfrac{\partial}{\partial y} & \dfrac{\partial}{\partial z} \\ 0 & E_y & 0 \end{vmatrix} = -\frac{\partial E_y}{\partial z}\vec{a}_x + \frac{\partial E_y}{\partial x}\vec{a}_z$

Therefore, $-\dfrac{\partial E_y}{\partial z}\vec{a}_x + \dfrac{\partial E_y}{\partial x}\vec{a}_z = -\mu_0\dfrac{\partial \vec{H}}{\partial t} = 0.4\omega^2\mu_0\varepsilon_0 \sin(\omega t - 50x)\vec{a}_z$

Equating the z-components on both sides of this equation, we get

$$\frac{\partial E_y}{\partial x} = 0.4\omega^2 \mu_0 \varepsilon_0 \sin(\omega t - 50x)$$

$$1000\sin(\omega t - 50x) = 0.4\omega^2 \mu_0 \varepsilon_0 \sin(\omega t - 50x)$$

$$1000 = 0.4\omega^2 \mu_0 \varepsilon_0 = \frac{0.4\omega^2}{c^2} \qquad \left(\text{since } c = \frac{1}{\sqrt{\mu_0 \varepsilon_0}} \right)$$

$$\omega^2 = \frac{1000 \times \left(3 \times 10^8\right)^2}{0.4}$$

Hence, $\omega = 1.5 \times 10^{10}$ rad/s

EXAMPLE 6.43

A medium is characterized by $\sigma = 0$, $\mu = 2\mu_0$, and $\varepsilon = 5\varepsilon_0$. If the magnetic field $\vec{H} = 2\cos(\omega t - 3y)\vec{a}_z$ A/m, determine ω and $\vec{E}$.

SOLUTION

Given $\sigma = 0$, $\mu = 2\mu_0$, $\varepsilon = 5\varepsilon_0$, and $\vec{H} = 2\cos(\omega t - 3y)\vec{a}_z$ A/m.

Since $\beta = \omega\sqrt{\mu\varepsilon}$, the angular velocity is

$$\omega = \frac{\beta}{\sqrt{\mu\varepsilon}} = \frac{3}{\sqrt{2\mu_0 \times 5\varepsilon_0}}, \text{ where } \beta = 3$$

$$= \frac{3c}{\sqrt{10}} = \frac{3 \times 3 \times 10^8}{\sqrt{10}} = 2.846 \times 10^8 \text{ rad/s} \qquad \left(\text{since } c = \frac{1}{\sqrt{\mu_0 \varepsilon_0}} = 3 \times 10^8 \text{ m/s} \right)$$

We know that,

$$\nabla \times \vec{H} = \sigma \vec{E} + \varepsilon \frac{\partial \vec{E}}{\partial t}, \text{ where } \sigma = 0 \text{ in free space.}$$

Integrating the above equation, we get

$$\vec{E} = \frac{1}{\varepsilon} \int (\nabla \times \vec{H}) \, dt$$

$$\text{where } \nabla \times \vec{H} = \begin{vmatrix} \vec{a}_x & \vec{a}_y & \vec{a}_z \\ \dfrac{\partial}{\partial x} & \dfrac{\partial}{\partial y} & \dfrac{\partial}{\partial z} \\ 0 & 0 & H_z \end{vmatrix} = \frac{\partial H_z}{\partial y}\vec{a}_x - \frac{\partial H_z}{\partial x}\vec{a}_y = 6\sin(\omega t - 3y)\vec{a}_x$$

Therefore, $\vec{E} = \dfrac{6}{\varepsilon}\displaystyle\int \sin(\omega t - 3y)\vec{a}_x \, dt = -\dfrac{6}{\omega\varepsilon}\cos(\omega t - 3y)\vec{a}_x$

$$= -\frac{6}{2.846\times10^8 \times 5\times 8.854\times10^{-12}}\cos(\omega t - 3y)\,\vec{a}_x$$

$$= -476.2\cos(2.846\times10^8\, t - 3y)\,\vec{a}_x \text{ V/m} \qquad \Box$$

EXAMPLE 6.44

The magnetic field intensity in free space is given as $\vec{H} = H_0 \sin\theta\,\vec{a}_y$ A/m , where $\theta = \omega t - \beta z$ and β is a constant quantity. Determine the displacement current density.

SOLUTION

Given $\vec{H} = H_0 \sin\theta\,\vec{a}_y = H_0 \sin(\omega t - \beta z)\,\vec{a}_y$ A/m.

For time-varying fields, $\nabla\times\vec{H} = \vec{J}_c + \vec{J}_d,$ where $\vec{J}_c = 0$ in free space.

Therefore,

$$\vec{J}_d = \nabla\times\vec{H} = \begin{vmatrix} \vec{a}_x & \vec{a}_y & \vec{a}_z \\ \dfrac{\partial}{\partial x} & \dfrac{\partial}{\partial y} & \dfrac{\partial}{\partial z} \\ 0 & H_0\sin\theta & 0 \end{vmatrix}$$

$$= \left[-\frac{\partial}{\partial z}\left(H_0\sin\theta\right)\right]\vec{a}_x + [0]\vec{a}_y + \left[\frac{\partial}{\partial x}\left(H_0\sin\theta\right)\right]\vec{a}_z$$

$$= -\frac{\partial}{\partial z}\left[H_0\sin(\omega t - \beta z)\right]\vec{a}_x + \frac{\partial}{\partial x}\left[H_0\left(\sin\omega t - \beta z\right)\right]\vec{a}_z$$

$$= -(-\beta)H_0\cos(\omega t - \beta z)\,\vec{a}_x + [0]\vec{a}_y$$

$$= \beta H_0\cos(\omega t - \beta z)\,\vec{a}_x \text{ A/m}^2 \qquad \Box$$

EXAMPLE 6.45

An antenna radiates in free space and $\vec{H} = H_\theta\vec{a}_\theta = \dfrac{12\sin\theta}{r}\cos(2\pi\times10^8 t - \beta r)\vec{a}_\theta$ mA/m. Determine the corresponding $\vec{E}$ in terms of β.

SOLUTION

For time-varying fields, the Ampere's law is

$$\nabla\times\vec{H} = \vec{J}_c + \vec{J}_d = \sigma\vec{E} + \varepsilon_0\frac{\partial\vec{E}}{\partial t} \quad \text{(for free space, } \sigma = 0 \text{ and } \varepsilon = \varepsilon_0)$$

Integrating the above equation, we get

$$\vec{E} = \frac{1}{\varepsilon}\int(\nabla\times\vec{H})\,dt \qquad\qquad (1)$$

where $\nabla \times \vec{H} = \dfrac{1}{r^2 \sin\theta} \begin{vmatrix} \vec{a}_r & r\vec{a}_\theta & r\sin\theta\,\vec{a}_\phi \\ \dfrac{\partial}{\partial r} & \dfrac{\partial}{\partial \theta} & \dfrac{\partial}{\partial \phi} \\ 0 & rH_\theta & 0 \end{vmatrix}$, in spherical coordinates

$$= -\frac{1}{r\sin\theta}\frac{\partial H_\theta}{\partial \phi}\vec{a}_r + \frac{1}{r}\frac{\partial (rH_\theta)}{\partial r}\vec{a}_\phi \tag{2}$$

Since the given magnetic field $\vec{H}$ does not depend on ϕ, the first term in the above equation is zero.

Therefore, $\nabla \times \vec{H} = \dfrac{12\sin\theta}{r}\beta \sin(2\pi \times 10^8 t - \beta r)\vec{a}_\phi$ $\tag{3}$

Substituting Eq. (3) in Eq. (1), we get

$$\vec{E} = \frac{12\sin\theta}{\varepsilon_0 r}\beta \int \sin(2\pi \times 10^8 t - \beta r)\vec{a}_\phi\, dt$$

$$= -\frac{12\sin\theta}{2\pi \times 10^8 \varepsilon_0 r}\beta \cos(2\pi \times 10^8\, t - \beta r)\vec{a}_\phi = -\frac{6.67\sin\theta}{r}\beta \cos(2\pi \times 10^8\, t - \beta r)\vec{a}_\phi\ \text{V/m} \qquad \square$$

EXAMPLE 6.46

Find the displacement current density $\vec{J}_d$ in air within a large power distribution transformer where $\vec{B} = 1.1 \cos\left[1.257 \times 10^{-6}\left(3 \times 10^8 t - y\right)\right]\vec{a}_x$ T.

SOLUTION

Given $\vec{B} = 1.1 \cos\left[1.257 \times 10^{-6}\left(3 \times 10^8 t - y\right)\right]\vec{a}_x = 1.1\cos\left(377t - 1.257 \times 10^{-6} y\right)\vec{a}_x$ T

The displacement current density is

$$\vec{J}_d = \frac{\partial \vec{D}}{\partial t} = \varepsilon_0 \frac{\partial \vec{E}}{\partial t}$$

We know that, $\vec{\nabla} \times \vec{E} = -\dfrac{\partial \vec{B}}{\partial t} = -\dfrac{\partial}{\partial t}\left[1.1 \cos\left(377t - 1.257 \times 10^{-6} y\right)\vec{a}_x\right]$

$$= -1.1(-377)\sin\left(377t - 1.257 \times 10^{-6} y\right)\vec{a}_x$$

$$= 414.7\sin\left(377t - 1.257 \times 10^{-6} y\right)\vec{a}_x$$

The cross product for x-component is

$$\nabla \times \vec{E} = \begin{vmatrix} \vec{a}_x & 0 & 0 \\ \dfrac{\partial}{\partial x} & \dfrac{\partial}{\partial y} & \dfrac{\partial}{\partial z} \\ E_x & E_y & E_z \end{vmatrix}$$

$$\left[\frac{\partial E_z}{\partial y} - \frac{\partial E_y}{\partial z}\right]\vec{a}_x = 414.7\sin\left(377t - 1.257 \times 10^{-6}\, y\right)\vec{a}_x$$

$$\frac{\partial E_z}{\partial y} - \frac{\partial E_y}{\partial z} = 414.7\sin\left(377t - 1.257 \times 10^{-6}\, y\right)$$

Since the field is varying in the y-direction, $\dfrac{\partial E_y}{\partial z} = 0$. Therefore, $\vec{E}$ has z-component only.

$$\frac{\partial E_z}{\partial y} = 414.7\sin\left(377t - 1.257 \times 10^{-6}\, y\right)$$

Integrating above equation, we get

$$E_z = 414.7\left[\frac{-\cos\left(377t - 1.257 \times 10^{-6}\, y\right)}{-1.257 \times 10^{-6}}\right]$$

$$\vec{E} = 329.91 \times 10^6 \cos\left(377t - 1.257 \times 10^6\, y\right)\vec{a}_z \, \text{V/m}$$

Substituting the value of $\vec{E}$ in Eq. (1), we get

$$\vec{J}_d = \varepsilon_0 \frac{\partial \vec{E}}{\partial t}$$

$$= \varepsilon_0 \times 329.91 \times 10^6 \times (-377) \times \sin\left(377t - 1.257 \times 10^{-6}\, y\right)\vec{a}_z$$

$$= -8.854 \times 10^{-12} \times 1.243 \times 10^{11} \times \sin\left(377t - 1.257 \times 10^{-6}\, y\right)\vec{a}_z$$

$$= -1.1\sin\left(377t - 1.257 \times 10^{-6}\, y\right)\vec{a}_z \, \text{A/m}^2 \qquad \square$$

EXAMPLE 6.47

In a medium characterized by $\sigma = 0$, $\mu = \mu_0$, $\varepsilon = 9\varepsilon_0$, and $\vec{E} = 30\sin(10^8 t - \beta z)\vec{a}_y$ V/m. Determine β and $\vec{H}$.

SOLUTION

Given $\vec{E} = 30\sin(10^8 t - \beta z)\vec{a}_y$ V/m.

The given field satisfies the Gauss's law for electric field.
That is,

$$\nabla \cdot \vec{E} = \frac{\partial E_y}{\partial y} = 0 \qquad\qquad \text{(since } \vec{E} \text{ has only } y\text{-component)}$$

According to Faraday's law,

$$\nabla \times \vec{E} = -\mu \frac{\partial \vec{H}}{\partial t}$$

Integrating this equation, we get

$$\vec{H} = -\frac{1}{\mu}\int(\nabla\times\vec{E})\,dt$$

But

$$\nabla\times\vec{E} = \begin{vmatrix} \vec{a}_x & \vec{a}_y & \vec{a}_z \\ \dfrac{\partial}{\partial x} & \dfrac{\partial}{\partial y} & \dfrac{\partial}{\partial z} \\ 0 & E_y & 0 \end{vmatrix} = -\frac{\partial E_y}{\partial z}\vec{a}_x + \frac{\partial E_y}{\partial x}\vec{a}_z$$

$$= 30\beta\cos(10^8 t - \beta z)\vec{a}_x + 0$$

Hence,

$$\vec{H} = -\frac{30\beta}{\mu}\int\cos(10^8 t - \beta z)\vec{a}_x\,dt$$

$$= -\frac{30\beta}{10^8\,\mu}\sin(10^8 t - \beta z)\,\vec{a}_x\,\text{A/m}$$

$$\nabla\cdot\vec{H} = \frac{\partial H_x}{\partial x} = 0$$

The above equation shows that the Gauss's law for magnetic field is also satisfied.

We know that, $\nabla\times\vec{H} = \sigma\vec{E} + \varepsilon\dfrac{\partial\vec{E}}{\partial t}$, where $\sigma = 0$ in free space.

Integrating the above equation, we get

$$\vec{E} = \frac{1}{\varepsilon}\int(\nabla\times\vec{H})\,dt$$

But

$$\nabla\times\vec{H} = \begin{vmatrix} \vec{a}_x & \vec{a}_y & \vec{a}_z \\ \dfrac{\partial}{\partial x} & \dfrac{\partial}{\partial y} & \dfrac{\partial}{\partial z} \\ H_x & 0 & 0 \end{vmatrix} = \frac{\partial H_x}{\partial z}\vec{a}_y - \frac{\partial H_x}{\partial y}\vec{a}_z$$

$$= \frac{30\beta^2}{10^8\,\mu}\cos(10^8 t - \beta z)\vec{a}_y$$

Hence,

$$\vec{E} = \frac{30\beta^2}{10^8\,\mu\varepsilon}\int\cos(10^8 t - \beta z)\vec{a}_y\,dt$$

$$= \frac{30\beta^2}{10^{16}\,\mu\varepsilon}\sin(10^8 t - \beta z)\vec{a}_y\,\text{V/m}$$

Comparing this equation with the given $\vec{E}$, we get

$$\frac{30\beta^2}{\mu\varepsilon 10^{16}} = 30$$

$$\beta = \pm 10^8 \sqrt{\mu\varepsilon} = \pm 10^8 \sqrt{\mu_0 \times 9\varepsilon_0}$$

$$= \pm \frac{10^8 \times 3}{c} = \pm \frac{10^8 \times 3}{3 \times 10^8} = \pm 1, \qquad \left(\text{since } c = \frac{1}{\sqrt{\mu_0 \varepsilon_0}} = 3 \times 10^8 \text{ m/s} \right)$$

Substituting the above β value in $\vec{H}$ equation, we get

$$\vec{H} = \mp \frac{30}{10^8 \times 4\pi \times 10^{-7}} \sin(10^8 t \mp z)\,\vec{a}_x$$

$$= \mp \frac{3}{4\pi} \sin(10^8 t \mp z)\,\vec{a}_x \text{ A/m}$$

EXAMPLE 6.48

Check whether the following fields are genuine EM fields, i.e., they satisfy Maxwell's equations.

(i) $\vec{A} = 40\sin(\omega t + 10x)\vec{a}_z$ Wb/m

(ii) $\vec{D} = \dfrac{1}{r}\sin\theta \sin(\omega t - 5r)\vec{a}_\theta$ C/m^2

Assume that the fields exist in charge-free regions.

SOLUTION

(i) Given $\vec{A} = 40\sin(\omega t + 10x)\vec{a}_z$ in rectangular coordinates.

For possible EM fields, Maxwell's equations have to be satisfied.

That is, $\nabla \cdot \vec{A} = 0$ and $\nabla \times \vec{A} \neq 0$.

Hence, for the given field $\vec{A}$,

$$\nabla \cdot \vec{A} = \frac{\partial A_x}{\partial x} + \frac{\partial A_y}{\partial y} + \frac{\partial A_z}{\partial z} = 0$$

and $\nabla \times \vec{A} = \begin{vmatrix} \vec{a}_x & \vec{a}_y & \vec{a}_z \\ \dfrac{\partial}{\partial x} & \dfrac{\partial}{\partial y} & \dfrac{\partial}{\partial z} \\ 0 & 0 & A_z \end{vmatrix}$, where $A_z = 40\sin(\omega t + 10x)$

$$= \frac{\partial A_z}{\partial y}\vec{a}_x - \frac{\partial A_z}{\partial x}\vec{a}_y = -400\cos(\omega t + 10x)\vec{a}_y \neq 0$$

Hence, the given field $\vec{A}$ is a possible EM field.

(ii) Given $\vec{D} = \dfrac{1}{r}\sin\theta \sin(\omega t - 5r)\vec{a}_\theta$ in spherical coordinates.

Here, $\nabla \cdot \vec{D} = \dfrac{1}{r^2}\dfrac{\partial}{\partial r}(r^2 D_r) + \dfrac{1}{r\sin\theta}\dfrac{\partial}{\partial \theta}(D_\theta \sin\theta) + \dfrac{1}{r\sin\theta}\dfrac{\partial D_\phi}{\partial \phi}$

$$= \dfrac{1}{r^2\sin\theta}\sin(\omega t - 5r)\dfrac{\partial}{\partial\theta}(\sin^2\theta) \neq 0$$

and $\nabla\times\vec{D} = \dfrac{1}{r^2\sin\theta}\begin{vmatrix} \vec{a}_r & r\vec{a}_\theta & r\sin\theta\,\vec{a}_\phi \\ \dfrac{\partial}{\partial r} & \dfrac{\partial}{\partial\theta} & \dfrac{\partial}{\partial\phi} \\ 0 & rD_\theta & 0 \end{vmatrix} = -\dfrac{1}{r\sin\theta}\dfrac{\partial D_\theta}{\partial\phi}\vec{a}_r + \dfrac{1}{r}\dfrac{\partial}{\partial r}(rD_\theta)\vec{a}_\phi$

$$= -\dfrac{5}{r}\sin\theta\cos(\omega t - 5r)\vec{a}_\phi \neq 0$$

Hence, the given field $\vec{D}$ is not an EM field. $\qquad\square$

EXAMPLE 6.49

Do the fields $\vec{E} = E_m \sin x \sin t\, \vec{a}_y$ V/m and $\vec{H} = \dfrac{E_m}{\mu_0}\cos x \cos t\, \vec{a}_z$ A/m satisfy Maxwell's equations?

SOLUTION

Considering the Maxwell's equation derived from Faraday's law,

$$\nabla\times\vec{E} = -\dfrac{\partial\vec{B}}{\partial t} = -\mu_0\dfrac{\partial\vec{H}}{\partial t} \qquad \text{(Assuming } \mu_r = 1)$$

$$\text{LHS} = \nabla\times\vec{E} = \begin{vmatrix} \vec{a}_x & \vec{a}_y & \vec{a}_z \\ \dfrac{\partial}{\partial x} & \dfrac{\partial}{\partial y} & \dfrac{\partial}{\partial z} \\ 0 & E_y & 0 \end{vmatrix} = -\dfrac{\partial E_y}{\partial z}\vec{a}_x + \dfrac{\partial E_y}{\partial x}\vec{a}_z$$

$$= -\left[\dfrac{\partial}{\partial z}E_m \sin x \sin t\right]\vec{a}_x + \left[\dfrac{\partial}{\partial x}E_m \sin x \sin t\right]\vec{a}_z$$

$$= E_m \sin t \cos x\, \vec{a}_z$$

$$\text{RHS} = -\mu_0\dfrac{\partial\vec{H}}{\partial t} = -\mu_0\dfrac{\partial}{\partial t}\left[\dfrac{E_m}{\mu_0}\cos x \cos t\right]\vec{a}_z$$

$$= -\mu_0\left(\dfrac{E_m}{\mu_0}\right)\times\cos x\dfrac{\partial}{\partial t}(\cos t)\vec{a}_z$$

$$= E_m \sin t \cos x\, \vec{a}_z$$

Both LHS and RHS are equal, i.e., $\nabla\times\vec{E} = -\dfrac{\partial\vec{B}}{\partial t}$.

Hence, the given fields $\vec{E}$ and $\vec{H}$ satisfy the Maxwell's equations. $\qquad\square$

EXAMPLE 6.50

Given magnetic field intensity $\vec{H} = H_m e^{j(\omega t + \beta z)} \vec{a}_x$ A/m in free space, find $\vec{E}$.

SOLUTION

From Maxwell's equation, $\nabla \times \vec{H} = \vec{J} + \dfrac{\partial \vec{D}}{\partial t}$

For free space, $\vec{J} = 0$.

$$\text{Therefore, } \nabla \times \vec{H} = \frac{\partial \vec{D}}{\partial t} = \varepsilon_0 \frac{\partial \vec{E}}{\partial t} = \begin{vmatrix} \vec{a}_x & \vec{a}_y & \vec{a}_z \\ \dfrac{\partial}{\partial x} & \dfrac{\partial}{\partial y} & \dfrac{\partial}{\partial z} \\ H_x & 0 & 0 \end{vmatrix}$$

$$= (0)\vec{a}_x + \left(\frac{\partial H_x}{\partial z}\right)\vec{a}_y - \left(\frac{\partial H_x}{\partial y}\right)\vec{a}_z$$

$$\text{Hence, } \varepsilon_0 \frac{\partial \vec{E}}{\partial t} = \frac{\partial H_x}{\partial z}\vec{a}_y \qquad \left(\text{since } \frac{\partial H_x}{\partial y} = 0\right)$$

$$= j\beta H_m e^{j(\omega t + \beta z)} \vec{a}_y$$

$$\frac{\partial \vec{E}}{\partial t} = j\frac{\beta}{\varepsilon_0} H_m e^{j(\omega t + \beta z)} \vec{a}_y$$

Integrating the above equation, we have

$$\vec{E} = j\frac{\beta}{\varepsilon_0} H_m \int e^{j(\omega t + \beta z)} \vec{a}_y \, \partial t = j\frac{\beta}{\varepsilon_0} \times \frac{H_m}{j\omega} e^{j(\omega t + \beta z)} \vec{a}_y$$

$$= \frac{\beta H_m}{\omega \varepsilon_0} e^{j(\omega t + \beta z)} \vec{a}_y \text{ V/m}$$

EXAMPLE 6.51

Given $\vec{E} = 30\pi e^{j(10^8 t + \beta z)} \vec{a}_x$ V/m and $\vec{H} = H_m e^{j(10^8 t + \beta z)} \vec{a}_y$ A/m in free space, find H_m and $\vec{B}$ ($\beta > 0$).

SOLUTION

Given $\vec{E} = 30\pi e^{j(10^8 t + \beta z)} \vec{a}_x$ V/m and $\vec{H} = H_m e^{j(10^8 t + \beta z)} \vec{a}_y$ A/m.

We know that the velocity of the wave in free space is

$$c = \frac{\omega}{\beta} = \frac{1}{\sqrt{\varepsilon_0 \mu_0}} = 3 \times 10^8 \text{ m/s}$$

Therefore, $\beta = \dfrac{10^8}{3 \times 10^8} = \dfrac{1}{3}$ rad/m (given $\omega = 10^8$)

The ratio of magnitude of electric and magnetic field is

$$\frac{E_m}{H_m} = \sqrt{\frac{\mu_0}{\varepsilon_0}} = 120\pi \ \Omega$$

Hence, $H_m = \pm \dfrac{30\pi}{120\pi} = \pm \dfrac{1}{4}$ A/m (given $E_m = 30\pi$)

To find the sign of H_m, apply $\nabla \times \vec{E} = -\dfrac{\partial \vec{B}}{\partial t}$

$$\text{LHS} = \nabla \times \vec{E} = \begin{vmatrix} \vec{a}_x & \vec{a}_y & \vec{a}_z \\ \dfrac{\partial}{\partial x} & \dfrac{\partial}{\partial y} & \dfrac{\partial}{\partial z} \\ E_x & 0 & 0 \end{vmatrix} = \dfrac{\partial E_x}{\partial z}\vec{a}_y - \dfrac{\partial E_x}{\partial y}\vec{a}_z$$

$$= j\beta 30\pi e^{j(10^8 t + \beta z)}\vec{a}_y \qquad \left(\text{since } \dfrac{\partial E_x}{\partial y} = 0 \right)$$

$$\text{RHS} = -\dfrac{\partial \vec{B}}{\partial t} = -\mu_0 \dfrac{\partial \vec{H}}{\partial t} = -j10^8 \mu_0 H_m e^{j(10^8 t + \beta z)}\vec{a}_y$$

Equating LHS and RHS, we get $H_m = -\dfrac{1}{4}$

Therefore, the magnetic flux density is

$$\vec{B} = \mu_0 \vec{H} = -\dfrac{\mu_0}{4} e^{j\left(10^8 t + \beta z\right)}\vec{a}_y \text{ Wb/m}^2$$

EXAMPLE 6.52

In a homogenous non-conducting region where $\mu_r = 1$, find ε_r and ω if $\vec{E} = 30\pi e^{j\left(\omega t - (4/3)y\right)}\vec{a}_z$ V/m and $\vec{H} = 2e^{j\left(\omega t - (4/3)y\right)}\vec{a}_x$ A/m.

SOLUTION

The ratio of magnitude of electric and magnetic field is

$$\dfrac{E_m}{H_m} = \sqrt{\dfrac{\mu}{\varepsilon}} = 120\pi \sqrt{\dfrac{\mu_r}{\varepsilon_r}}$$

$$\dfrac{30\pi}{2} = 120\pi \sqrt{\dfrac{1}{\varepsilon_r}} \qquad (\text{since } \mu_r = 1)$$

Therefore, $\varepsilon_r = 64$

From the given $\vec{E}$ and $\vec{H}$ fields, $\beta = \dfrac{4}{3}$. Hence, the velocity in a homogenous non-conducting region is

$$c = \dfrac{\omega}{\beta} = \dfrac{1}{\sqrt{\varepsilon\mu}} = \dfrac{3\times10^8}{\sqrt{\varepsilon_r \mu_r}} \text{ m/s}$$

$$\omega = \dfrac{3\times10^8}{\sqrt{\varepsilon_r}} \times \beta = \dfrac{3\times10^8}{\sqrt{64}} \times \dfrac{4}{3} = 0.5\times10^8 \text{ rad/s}$$

EXAMPLE 6.53

Given $\vec{E} = E_0 z^2 e^{-t} \vec{a}_x$ in free space. Determine the magnetic field using Faraday's law and verify the Ampere's law.

SOLUTION

Given $\vec{E} = E_0 z^2 e^{-t} \vec{a}_x$ V/m in free space. The Faraday's law in free space is

$$\nabla \times \vec{E} = \frac{-\partial \vec{B}}{\partial t}$$

$$\text{LHS} = \nabla \times \vec{E} = \nabla \times \left(E_0 z^2 e^{-t} \vec{a}_x \right) = E_0 e^{-t} \left[\nabla \times \left(z^2 \right) \vec{a}_x \right]$$

$$= E_0 e^{-t} \begin{vmatrix} \vec{a}_x & \vec{a}_y & \vec{a}_z \\ \dfrac{\partial}{\partial x} & \dfrac{\partial}{\partial y} & \dfrac{\partial}{\partial z} \\ z^2 & 0 & 0 \end{vmatrix} = E_0 e^{-t} \left\{ \left[\frac{\partial}{\partial z} z^2 \right] \vec{a}_y + \left[-\frac{\partial}{\partial y} z^2 \right] \vec{a}_z \right\}$$

$$= E_0 e^{-t} (2z) \vec{a}_y = 2 E_0 z e^{-t} \vec{a}_y$$

Therefore,

$$\nabla \times \vec{E} = -\frac{\partial \vec{B}}{\partial t} = 2 E_0 z e^{-t} \vec{a}_y$$

Integrating the above equation, we get,

$$\vec{B} = 2 E_0 z e^{-t} \vec{a}_y \ \text{Wb/m}^2$$

The above equation shows that a magnetic field exists.

Similarly, Ampere's law in free space is

$$\nabla \times \vec{H} = \frac{\partial \vec{D}}{\partial t} \ \text{(for free space, } \vec{J} = 0)$$

Since $\vec{H} = \dfrac{\vec{B}}{\mu_0}$ and $\vec{D} = \varepsilon_0 \vec{E}$,

$$\nabla \times \frac{\vec{B}}{\mu_0} = \frac{\partial}{\partial t} (\varepsilon_0 \vec{E})$$

$$\frac{1}{\mu_0} (\nabla \times \vec{B}) = \varepsilon_0 \frac{\partial \vec{E}}{\partial t}$$

$$\text{LHS} = \frac{1}{\mu_0} \left(\nabla \times \vec{B} \right) = \frac{1}{\mu_0} \left[\nabla \times \left(2 E_0 z e^{-t} \vec{a}_y \right) \right] = \frac{2 E_0 e^{-t}}{\mu_0} \left[\nabla \times \left(z \vec{a}_y \right) \right]$$

$$= \frac{2E_0 e^{-t}}{\mu_0} \begin{vmatrix} \vec{a}_x & \vec{a}_y & \vec{a}_z \\ \dfrac{\partial}{\partial x} & \dfrac{\partial}{\partial y} & \dfrac{\partial}{\partial z} \\ 0 & z & 0 \end{vmatrix} = \frac{2E_0 e^{-t}}{\mu_0} \left\{ \left[-\frac{\partial}{\partial z} z \right] \vec{a}_x + \left[\frac{\partial}{\partial x} z \right] \vec{a}_z \right\}$$

$$= \frac{-2E_0 e^{-t}}{\mu_0} \vec{a}_x$$

$$\text{RHS} = \varepsilon_0 \frac{\partial \vec{E}}{\partial t} = \varepsilon_0 \frac{\partial}{\partial t} \left(E_0 z^2 e^{-t} \vec{a}_x \right) = E_0 \varepsilon_0 z^2 \left(-e^{-t} \right) \vec{a}_x$$

$$= -\varepsilon_0 E_0 z^2 e^{-t} \vec{a}_x$$

Here, LHS $\neq$ RHS, which shows that the Ampere's law is not satisfied.

6.7 RELATION BETWEEN FIELD THEORY AND CIRCUIT THEORY

The differential and integral forms of Maxwell's equations are usually referred to as *field equations* and the quantities associated with them are called *field quantities*. If the Maxwell's equations can be written in terms of *circuit quantities* with then the corresponding forms are known as *circuit equations*. The circuit equations are considered from circuit theory and they are special cases of the general field equations. The relation between field theory and circuit theory is listed in Table 6.5.

Table 6.5 *Relation between field theory and circuit theory*

S. No.	Field theory	Circuit theory
1.	Electric field intensity $\vec{E}$	Voltage V
2.	Magnetic field intensity $\vec{H}$	Current I
3.	Electric flux density $\vec{D}$	Electric charge density ρ_{ev}
4.	Magnetic flux density $\vec{B}$	Magnetic charge density ρ_{mv}
5.	Electric displacement current density $\vec{J}_d = \varepsilon \dfrac{\partial \vec{E}}{\partial t}$	Current through a capacitor $I = C \dfrac{dV}{dt}$
6.	Magnetic displacement current density $\vec{M}_d = \mu \dfrac{\partial \vec{H}}{\partial t}$	Voltage across an inductor $V = L \dfrac{dI}{dt}$
7.	*Constitutive relations* (i) Conduction current density, $\vec{J} = \sigma \vec{E}$ (ii) Dielectric material, $\vec{D} = \varepsilon \vec{E}$ (iii) Magnetic material, $\vec{B} = \mu \vec{H}$	*Element laws* (i) Ohm's law, $V = RI$ (ii) Charge in a capacitor, $Q = CV$ (iii) Flux of an inductor, $\Phi = LI$

S. No.	Field theory	Circuit theory
8.	Faraday's law $$\oint_l \vec{E}\cdot d\vec{l} = -\int_s \frac{\partial \vec{B}}{\partial t}\cdot d\vec{s}$$	Kirchhoff's voltage law $$\sum V = -L\frac{\partial I}{\partial t}\approx 0$$
9.	Continuity equation $$\oint_s \vec{J}\cdot d\vec{s} = -\int_v \frac{\partial \rho_v}{\partial t}\, dv$$	Kirchhoff's current law $$\sum I = -C\frac{\partial V}{\partial t}\approx 0$$
10.	*Power and energy densities* (i) Instantaneous power, $$P = \oint_s (\vec{E}\times\vec{H})\cdot d\vec{s}$$ (ii) Dissipated power, $$P = \int_v \sigma E^2 dv$$ (iii) Energy density in electric field, $$w_e = \frac{1}{2}\varepsilon E^2$$ (iv) Energy density in magnetic field, $$w_m = \frac{1}{2}\mu H^2$$	*Power and energy* (i) Power–voltage–current relation, $$P = VI$$ (ii) Power dissipated in a resistor, $$P = \frac{V^2}{R}$$ (iii) Energy stored in a capacitor, $$W_e = \frac{1}{2}CV^2$$ (iv) Energy stored in an inductor, $$W_m = \frac{1}{2}LI^2$$

Series RLC Circuit for comparison

The total electric field intensity $\vec{E}_t$ in any circuit is given by the sum of the electric field related to electromotive force $\vec{E}_{emf}$ and the electric field due to charges and currents $\vec{E}$.

Therefore,

$$\vec{E}_t = \vec{E}_{emf} + \vec{E}$$

That is,

$$\vec{E}_{emf} = \vec{E}_t - \vec{E} \tag{6.47}$$

The total electric field intensity is also represented by

$$\vec{E}_t = \frac{\vec{J}}{\sigma} \tag{6.48}$$

where $\vec{J}$ is the current density and σ is the conductivity.

Also, for time-varying fields, the electric field intensity is given by

$$\vec{E} = -\nabla V - \frac{\partial \vec{A}}{\partial t} \tag{6.49}$$

where V is the scalar electric potential and $\vec{A}$ is the vector magnetic potential.

Substituting Eq. (6.48) and Eq. (6.49) in Eq. (6.47), we get

$$\vec{E}_{emf} = \frac{\vec{J}}{\sigma} - \left[-\nabla V - \frac{\partial \vec{A}}{\partial t} \right]$$

That is, $\vec{E}_{emf} = \dfrac{\vec{J}}{\sigma} + \nabla V + \dfrac{\partial \vec{A}}{\partial t}$ \hfill (6.50)

Consider a series RLC circuit with an applied voltage V as shown in Figure 6.4(a). The equivalent representation by field theory is shown in Figure 6.4(b)

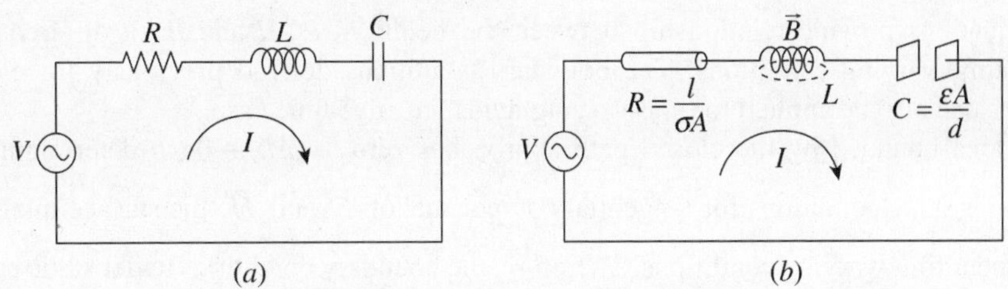

Figure 6.4 *Example for comparison between field and circuit theory: (a) series RLC circuit and (b) equivalent representation by field theory*

Applying Kirchhoff's Voltage Law (KVL) to the circuit shown in Figure 6.4(b) and integrating all the terms in Eq. (6.50), we get

$$\oint_l \vec{E}_{emf} \cdot d\vec{l} = \oint_l \frac{\vec{J}}{\sigma} \cdot d\vec{l} + \oint_l \nabla V \cdot d\vec{l} + \oint_l \frac{\partial \vec{A}}{\partial t} \cdot d\vec{l}$$ \hfill (6.51)

Since $\oint_l \vec{E}_{emf} \cdot d\vec{l}$ is applied voltage V, the above equation becomes

$$V = \frac{Jl}{\sigma} + Ed + \frac{d}{dt} \oint_l \vec{A} \cdot d\vec{l}$$ \hfill (6.52)

The last term of the above equation can be simplified using Stokes's theorem as follows:

$$\frac{d}{dt} \oint_l \vec{A} \cdot d\vec{l} = \frac{d}{dt} \int_s \left(\nabla \times \vec{A} \right) \cdot d\vec{s} = \frac{d}{dt} \int_s \vec{B} \cdot d\vec{s} = \frac{d\Phi}{dt} = L \frac{dI}{dt}$$

where $\nabla \times \vec{A} = \vec{B}$ and $\Phi = LI = \int_s \vec{B} \cdot d\vec{s}$

Hence, Eq. (6.52) becomes

$$V = \frac{I}{A} \left(\frac{l}{\sigma} \right) + \frac{Dd}{\varepsilon} + L \frac{dI}{dt}$$ \hfill (6.53)

where $J = \dfrac{I}{A}$ and $E = \dfrac{D}{\varepsilon}$.

Substituting $R = \dfrac{l}{\sigma A}$ and $D = \dfrac{Q}{A}$ in Eq. (6.53), we get

$$V = RI + \frac{Q}{\varepsilon A / d} + L \frac{dI}{dt}$$ \hfill (6.54)

As $C = \dfrac{\varepsilon A}{d}$ and $Q = \int I dt$, Eq. (6.54) becomes

$$V = RI + L\frac{dI}{dt} + \frac{1}{C}\int I\, dt$$

Thus, the relation between field theory and circuit theory is discussed using series RLC circuit.

6.8 ELECTROMAGNETIC BOUNDARY CONDITIONS

Maxwell's equations provide relationship between the fields $\vec{E}, \vec{D}, \vec{H}$ and $\vec{B}$ in differential and integral forms under time-varying conditions. The boundary conditions derived previously for electrostatics and magnetostatics can also be applied to time-varying fields, i.e., dynamic case.

Since the area bounded by the closed path approaches zero as $\Delta h \rightarrow 0$ in determining the boundary conditions under static conditions for tangential components of $\vec{E}$ and $\vec{H}$, the surface integrals of $\dfrac{\partial \vec{B}}{\partial t}$ and $\dfrac{\partial \vec{D}}{\partial t}$ vanish under time-varying conditions. Therefore, the boundary conditions under static case remain valid for time-varying fields also.

The solution of any EM field problems obtained by using Maxwell's equations should also satisfy the boundary conditions at the interface between different mediums. The boundary conditions for EM fields between different mediums in scalar form and vector form are summarized in Table 6.6.

Table 6.6 *Boundary conditions for EM fields*

Field components	Scalar form	Vector form
Tangential $\vec{E}$	$E_{t1} = E_{t2}$	$\vec{a}_n \times (\vec{E}_1 - \vec{E}_2) = 0$
Normal $\vec{D}$	$D_{n1} - D_{n2} = \rho_s$	$\vec{a}_n \cdot (\vec{D}_1 - \vec{D}_2) = \rho_s$
Tangential $\vec{H}$	$H_{t1} - H_{t2} = K$	$\vec{a}_n \times (\vec{H}_1 - \vec{H}_2) = \vec{K}$
Normal $\vec{B}$	$B_{n1} = B_{n2}$	$\vec{a}_n \cdot (\vec{B}_1 - \vec{B}_2) = 0$

In Table 6.6, $\vec{a}_n$ denotes the unit vector at the interface pointing from medium 2 to medium 1, ρ_s is the surface charge density, and $\vec{K}$ is the surface current density. The electromagnetic boundary conditions show that the tangential components of $\vec{E}_1$ and $\vec{E}_2$ are continuous at the boundary. However, the tangential components of $\vec{H}_1$ and $\vec{H}_2$ at any point on the boundary are discontinuous by an amount equal to the surface current density $\vec{K}$ at that point.

Similarly, the electromagnetic boundary conditions also show that the normal components of $\vec{B}_1$ and $\vec{B}_2$ are continuous at the boundary. However, the normal components of $\vec{D}_1$ and $\vec{D}_2$ at any point on the boundary are discontinuous by an amount equal to the surface charge density ρ_s at that point.

For a perfect conductor, the conductivity is infinite, i.e., $\sigma = \infty$ and the EM fields ($\vec{E}$ and $\vec{H}$) are zero inside the conductor. But the surface charge density ρ_s and surface current density $\vec{K}$ can exist on the surface of a perfect conductor. The boundary conditions between a dielectric and a perfect conductor are listed in Table 6.7.

Table 6.7 *Boundary conditions between a dielectric and a perfect conductor*

Field components	Medium 1 (Dielectric)	Medium 2 (Perfect conductor)
Tangential $\vec{E}$	$E_{t1} = 0$	$E_{t2} = 0$
Normal $\vec{D}$	$D_{n1} = \rho_s$	$D_{n2} = 0$
Tangential $\vec{H}$	$H_{t1} = K$	$H_{t2} = 0$
Normal $\vec{B}$	$B_{n1} = 0$	$B_{n2} = 0$

Therefore, if medium 2 is a perfect conductor, then the tangential and normal components of the fields at the boundary are

$$E_{t1} = 0,\ D_{n1} = \rho_s,\ H_{t1} = K,\ \text{and}\ B_{n1} = 0$$

For a perfect dielectric, the conductivity is zero, i.e., $\sigma = 0$ and there are no free charges and no surface currents at the interface between two dielectrics, i.e., $\rho_s = 0$ and $\vec{K} = 0$. Table 6.8 lists the boundary conditions between two perfect dielectrics (lossless mediums).

Table 6.8 *Boundary conditions between two perfect dielectrics*

Field components	Mediums 1 and 2 (Dielectric)
Tangential $\vec{E}$	$E_{t1} = E_{t2}$
Normal $\vec{D}$	$D_{n1} = D_{n2}$
Tangential $\vec{H}$	$H_{t1} = H_{t2}$
Normal $\vec{B}$	$B_{n1} = B_{n2}$

Therefore, EM fields existing in any medium under time-varying conditions should satisfy Maxwell's equations.

EXAMPLE 6.54

Region 1 is defined by $x < 0$ and characterized by $\mu_{r1} = 4$, whereas region 2 is defined by $x > 0$ and characterized by $\mu_{r2} = 8$. If the magnetic field in region 1 is given by $\vec{H}_1 = 8\vec{a}_x + 3\vec{a}_y - 6\vec{a}_z$ A/m for a source-free boundary, determine $\vec{H}_2$ and its magnitude.

SOLUTION

Given $\vec{H}_1 = 8\vec{a}_x + 3\vec{a}_y - 6\vec{a}_z$ A/m. Here, the normal component of the field is in x-direction.

For region 1 $(x < 0)$, the tangential and normal components of the magnetic field are

$$\vec{H}_{t1} = 3\vec{a}_y - 6\vec{a}_z \quad \text{and} \quad \vec{H}_{n1} = 8\vec{a}_x$$

For a source-free interface, $\vec{H}_{t1} = \vec{H}_{t2}$ and $\vec{B}_{n1} = \vec{B}_{n2}$. Therefore, the tangential and normal components of the magnetic field in region 2 $(x > 0)$, are

$$\vec{H}_{t2} = 3\vec{a}_y - 6\vec{a}_z$$

and
$$\vec{H}_{n2} = \frac{\mu_{r1}}{\mu_{r2}} \vec{H}_{n1} = \frac{4}{8}\left(8\vec{a}_x\right) = 4\vec{a}_x$$

Therefore, $\vec{H}_2 = \vec{H}_{t2} + \vec{H}_{n2}$

$$= 4\vec{a}_x + 3\vec{a}_y - 6\vec{a}_z \;\; \text{A/m}$$

Hence, the magnitude of $\vec{H}_2$ is

$$\left|\vec{H}_2\right| = \sqrt{4^2 + 3^2 + (-6)^2} = 7.81 \;\text{A/m} \qquad \square$$

EXAMPLE 6.55

A three-dimensional space is divided into region $1(x < 0)$ and region $2(x > 0)$ where $\sigma_1 = \sigma_2 = 0$ and $\vec{E}_1 = 2\vec{a}_x + 4\vec{a}_y + 6\vec{a}_z$ V/m. Find $\vec{E}_2$ and $\vec{D}_2$. Assume $\varepsilon_{r1} = 2$ and $\varepsilon_{r2} = 4$.

SOLUTION

Given $\vec{E}_1 = 2\vec{a}_x + 4\vec{a}_y + 6\vec{a}_z$ V/m.

For region 1 $(x < 0)$, the tangential and normal components of the electric field are

$$\vec{E}_{t1} = 4\vec{a}_y + 6\vec{a}_z \;\; \text{and} \;\; \vec{E}_{n1} = 2\vec{a}_x$$

Since $\vec{D} = \varepsilon \vec{E}$, the tangential component of the electric flux density is

$$\vec{D}_{t1} = \varepsilon_0 \varepsilon_{r1} \vec{E}_{t1} = 2\varepsilon_0 \left(4\vec{a}_y + 6\vec{a}_z\right), \;\text{where}\; \varepsilon_{r1} = 2$$

For a source-free interface, $\vec{E}_{t1} = \vec{E}_{t2}$ and $\vec{D}_{n1} = \vec{D}_{n2}$. The tangential and normal components of the electric field in region 2 are

$$\vec{E}_{t2} = 4\vec{a}_y + 6\vec{a}_z$$

and

$$\vec{E}_{n2} = \frac{\varepsilon_{r1}}{\varepsilon_{r2}} \vec{E}_{n1} = \frac{2}{4}\vec{a}_x = 0.5\vec{a}_x$$

Therefore,

$$\vec{E}_2 = \vec{E}_{t2} + \vec{E}_{n2}$$

$$= 0.5\vec{a}_x + 4\vec{a}_y + 6\vec{a}_z \,\text{V/m}$$

$$\vec{D}_2 = \varepsilon_2 \vec{E}_2 = \varepsilon_0 \varepsilon_{r2} \vec{E}_2 = 4\varepsilon_0 (0.5\vec{a}_x + 4\vec{a}_y + 6\vec{a}_z)$$

$$= \varepsilon_0 \left(2\vec{a}_x + 16\vec{a}_y + 24\vec{a}_z\right) \;\text{C/m}^2 \qquad \square$$

EXAMPLE 6.56

A current sheet, $\vec{K} = 8.5\vec{a}_z$ A/m, at $x = 0$ separates region 1, $x < 0$, where $\vec{H}_1 = 20\vec{a}_y$ A/m and region 2, $x > 0$. Find $\vec{H}_2$ at $x = 0$.

SOLUTION

Given $\vec{H}_1 = 20\vec{a}_y$ A/m in region 1. Here, the normal component of the field is in x-direction. From the given field, it is seen that $H_{n1} = H_{n2} = 0$ and $B_{n1} = B_{n2} = 0$.

For a current sheet $\vec{K} = 8.5\vec{a}_z$ A/m at $x = 0$, the tangential component is

$$(\vec{H}_1 - \vec{H}_2) \times \vec{a}_{n12} = \vec{K} \qquad \text{(Refer to Table 6.6)}$$

where $\vec{a}_{n12}$ is the unit vector at the interface pointing from region 1 to region 2.

$$(20\vec{a}_y - H_{y2}\vec{a}_y) \times \vec{a}_x = 8.5\vec{a}_z$$

$$(20 - H_{y2})\vec{a}_y \times \vec{a}_x = 8.5\vec{a}_z$$

$$(20 - H_{y2})(-\vec{a}_z) = 8.5\vec{a}_z$$

$$H_{y2} = 28.5$$

Therefore,

$$\vec{H}_2 = 28.5\vec{a}_y \text{ A/m} \qquad \square$$

EXAMPLE 6.57

Region 1, $z < 0$, has $\mu_{r1} = 3.5$, while region 2, $z > 0$, has $\mu_{r2} = 10$. Near the origin, $\vec{B}_1 = 2.4\vec{a}_x + 10\vec{a}_y$ T and $\vec{B}_2 = 25\vec{a}_x - 17\vec{a}_y + 10\vec{a}_z$ T. If the interface carries a sheet current, determine its density at the origin.

SOLUTION

Given $\mu_{r1} = 3.5$, $\vec{B}_1 = 2.4\vec{a}_x + 10\vec{a}_y$ T in region 1 and $\mu_{r2} = 10$, $\vec{B}_2 = 25\vec{a}_x - 17\vec{a}_y + 10\vec{a}_z$ T in region 2.

The magnetic field intensity near the origin in region 1 is

$$\vec{H}_1 = \frac{1}{\mu_0 \mu_{r1}} \vec{B}_1 = \frac{1}{3.5\mu_0}(2.4\vec{a}_x + 10\vec{a}_y) = \frac{1}{\mu_0}\left(0.69\vec{a}_x + 2.86\vec{a}_y\right) \text{A/m}$$

Similarly, in region 2, the magnetic field intensity is

$$\vec{H}_2 = \frac{1}{\mu_0 \mu_{r2}} \vec{B}_2 = \frac{1}{10\mu_0}(25\vec{a}_x - 17\vec{a}_y + 10\vec{a}_z) = \frac{1}{\mu_0}\left(2.5\vec{a}_x - 1.7\vec{a}_y + \vec{a}_z\right) \text{A/m}$$

According to magnetic boundary conditions,

$$\vec{K} = (\vec{H}_1 - \vec{H}_2) \times \vec{a}_{n12} \qquad \text{(Refer to Table 6.6)}$$

Hence, $\vec{K} = \dfrac{1}{\mu_0}(-1.81\vec{a}_x + 1.7\vec{a}_y + 1.86\vec{a}_z) \times \vec{a}_z = \dfrac{1}{\mu_0}\left(1.7\vec{a}_x + 1.81\vec{a}_y\right)$ A/m

where $\vec{a}_x \times \vec{a}_z = -\vec{a}_y$, $\vec{a}_y \times \vec{a}_z = \vec{a}_x$ and $\vec{a}_z \times \vec{a}_z = 0$. $\qquad \square$

6.9 POTENTIAL FUNCTIONS

Under time-varying conditions, there exists an interconnection between electric and magnetic fields. This interconnection leads to the relationship between scalar electric potential V and vector magnetic potential $\vec{A}$. The electric and magnetic fields can be related in terms of their sources, i.e., volume charge density and volume current density. However, it is more convenient to relate the potentials in terms of sources and the fields in terms of potentials.

For static electric fields, the scalar electric potential is expressed in terms of volume charge density as

$$V = \frac{1}{4\pi\varepsilon_0} \int_v \frac{\rho_v \, dv}{R}$$

For static magnetic fields, the vector magnetic potential is expressed in terms of volume current density as

$$\vec{A} = \frac{\mu_0}{4\pi} \int_v \frac{\vec{J} \, dv}{R}$$

For time-varying case, the scalar electric potential and vector magnetic potential are expressed as

$$V(R,t) = \frac{1}{4\pi\varepsilon_0} \int_v \frac{\rho_v(R,t)}{R} dv$$

and

$$\vec{A}(R,t) = \frac{\mu_0}{4\pi} \int_v \frac{\vec{J}(R,t)}{R} dv$$

These time-varying potentials are due to time-varying charge and current distributions. These expressions do not take care of propagation delay.

Since $\nabla \times \vec{E} = 0$ in electrostatics, the static electric field intensity $\vec{E}$ is conservative. If a vector field $\vec{E}$ is said to be conservative, then it can be expressed as the gradient of a scalar V. Hence, the electric field intensity $\vec{E}$ can be defined as

$$\vec{E} = -\nabla V \qquad \text{(static case)}$$

Under time-varying conditions, Faraday's law is given by

$$\nabla \times \vec{E} = -\frac{\partial \vec{B}}{\partial t} \tag{6.55}$$

The curl of $\vec{A}$ is written

$$\nabla \times \vec{A} = \vec{B} \tag{6.56}$$

Substituting Eq. (6.56) in (6.55), we obtain

$$\nabla \times \vec{E} = -\frac{\partial}{\partial t}(\nabla \times \vec{A})$$

That is, $\quad \nabla \times \left(\vec{E} + \frac{\partial \vec{A}}{\partial t} \right) = 0$

Since the curl of the gradient of a scalar is zero, the solution to the above equation under time-varying case is

$$\vec{E} + \frac{\partial \vec{A}}{\partial t} = -\nabla V$$

Therefore, $\quad \vec{E} = -\nabla V - \dfrac{\partial \vec{A}}{\partial t} \quad$ (dynamic case) $\tag{6.57}$

If the scalar electric potential $\dot{V}$ and vector magnetic potential $\vec{A}$ are known, then the electric field intensity $\vec{E}$ can be obtained from Eq. (6.57) and the magnetic flux density $\vec{B}$ can be found from Eq. (6.56).

From Maxwell's equations, we know that, $\nabla \cdot \vec{D} = \rho_v$ is also valid for time-varying conditions. Taking divergence of Eq. (6.57), we get

$$\nabla \cdot \vec{E} = -\nabla^2 V - \frac{\partial}{\partial t}(\nabla \cdot \vec{A}) = \frac{\rho_v}{\varepsilon} \qquad \text{(since } \vec{D} = \varepsilon \vec{E})$$

That is, $\nabla^2 V + \dfrac{\partial}{\partial t}(\nabla \cdot \vec{A}) = -\dfrac{\rho_v}{\varepsilon}$ \hfill (6.58)

Under time-varying conditions, we know that,

$$\nabla \times \vec{H} = \vec{J} + \frac{\partial \vec{D}}{\partial t} \tag{6.59}$$

Taking the curl on Eq. (6.56), we get

$$\nabla \times \nabla \times \vec{A} = \nabla \times \vec{B} = \nabla \times \mu \vec{H} \tag{6.60}$$

Substituting Eq. (6.59) in Eq. (6.60), we have

$$\nabla \times \nabla \times \vec{A} = \mu\left(\vec{J} + \frac{\partial \vec{D}}{\partial t} \right) = \mu\left(\vec{J} + \frac{\partial(\varepsilon \vec{E})}{\partial t} \right) \tag{6.61}$$

Substituting Eq. (6.57) in Eq. (6.61), we get

$$\nabla \times \nabla \times \vec{A} = \mu \vec{J} - \mu \varepsilon \nabla\left(\frac{\partial V}{\partial t} \right) - \mu \varepsilon \frac{\partial^2 \vec{A}}{\partial t^2}$$

Applying vector identity, i.e., $\nabla \times \nabla \times \vec{A} = \nabla(\nabla \cdot \vec{A}) - \nabla^2 \vec{A}$ to the above equation, we get

$$\nabla^2 \vec{A} - \nabla(\nabla \cdot \vec{A}) = -\mu \vec{J} + \mu \varepsilon \nabla\left(\frac{\partial V}{\partial t} \right) + \mu \varepsilon \frac{\partial^2 \vec{A}}{\partial t^2} \tag{6.62}$$

A vector field $\vec{A}$ is defined completely when its curl and divergence are known. The curl of $\vec{A}$ is given by $\nabla \times \vec{A} = \vec{B}$ and the divergence of $\vec{A}$ can be chosen as

$$\nabla \cdot \vec{A} = -\mu \varepsilon\left(\frac{\partial V}{\partial t} \right) \tag{6.63}$$

This equation is known as the *Lorentz condition or Lorentz gauge for potentials*, which provides the relation between V and $\vec{A}$. For static magnetic fields, the time derivative of voltage is zero, i.e., $\dfrac{\partial V}{\partial t} = 0$ and the above equation reduces to $\nabla \cdot \vec{A} = 0$. Substituting Eq. (6.63) in Eq. (6.62), we get

$$\nabla^2 \vec{A} - \mu \varepsilon \frac{\partial^2 \vec{A}}{\partial t^2} = -\mu \vec{J} \tag{6.64}$$

Substituting Eq. (6.63) in Eq. (6.58), we get

$$\nabla^2 V - \mu \varepsilon \frac{\partial^2 V}{\partial t^2} = -\frac{\rho_v}{\varepsilon} \tag{6.65}$$

The above two equations are known as *non-homogeneous wave equations* which relate the vector magnetic potential $\vec{A}$ with volume current density $\vec{J}$ and the scalar electric potential V with volume charge density ρ_v. The above non-homogeneous wave equations reduce to Poisson's equations for static fields.

6.10 WAVE EQUATIONS AND THEIR SOLUTIONS

The relationship between EM fields and source distributions (charge and current) can be obtained from Maxwell's equations. All EM field problems can be solved by using Maxwell's equations. From the knowledge of charge and current distributions (ρ_v and $\vec{J}$), the non-homogeneous wave equations in Eqs. (6.64) and (6.65) are first solved for vector magnetic potential $\vec{A}$ and scalar electric potential V. By knowing $\vec{A}$ and V, the fields $\vec{E}$ and $\vec{B}$ can be obtained from Eqs. (6.57) and (6.56), respectively.

6.10.1 Solution of Wave Equations for Potentials

Consider an elemental point charge $Q = \rho_v(t)\Delta v$ at time t, is located at the origin in spherical coordinate system. Due to spherical symmetry, the scalar electric potential V depends only on r and t. It does not depend on θ and ϕ. To obtain far field expressions, r should be replaced with R. The scalar potential V, in spherical coordinate system, satisfies the following homogeneous equation:

$$\frac{1}{R^2}\frac{\partial}{\partial R}\left(R^2\frac{\partial V}{\partial R}\right) - \mu\varepsilon\frac{\partial^2 V}{\partial t^2} = 0 \tag{6.66}$$

Letting the scalar function $V(R,t) = \frac{1}{R}U(R,t)$ and substituting $V(R,t)$ in Eq. (6.66), we get

$$\frac{\partial^2 U}{\partial R^2} - \mu\varepsilon\frac{\partial^2 U}{\partial t^2} = 0$$

Upon solving, we have

$$U(R,t) = f(t - R\sqrt{\mu\varepsilon})$$

The above equation indicates that the wave is travelling in positive R direction with velocity $\dfrac{1}{\sqrt{\mu\varepsilon}}$. Then, the function U at $R+\Delta R$ at a later time $t+\Delta t$ is

$$U(R+\Delta R, t+\Delta t) = f\left(t + \Delta t - (R+\Delta R)\sqrt{\mu\varepsilon}\right) = f(t - R\sqrt{\mu\varepsilon})$$

Here, the function retains its form if $\Delta t = \Delta R\sqrt{\mu\varepsilon} = \dfrac{\Delta R}{u}$, where $u = \dfrac{1}{\sqrt{\mu\varepsilon}}$ is the velocity of wave propagation. Therefore, the scalar function $V(R,t)$ can be written as

$$V(R,t) = \frac{1}{R}U(R,t) = \frac{1}{R}f\left(t - \frac{R}{u}\right) \tag{6.67}$$

and

$$\Delta V(R,t) = \frac{1}{R}\Delta f\left(t - \frac{R}{u}\right) \tag{6.68}$$

For a point charge $Q = \rho_v(t)\Delta v$ at the origin, the scalar potential is represented by

$$\Delta V(R) = \frac{Q}{4\pi\varepsilon_0 R} = \frac{\rho_v(t)\Delta v}{4\pi\varepsilon_0 R} \tag{6.69}$$

Comparing Eq. (6.68) and Eq. (6.69), we get

$$\Delta f\left(t - \frac{R}{u}\right) = \frac{\rho_v\left(t - \dfrac{R}{u}\right)\Delta v}{4\pi\varepsilon_0} \tag{6.70}$$

Substituting Eq. (6.70) in Eq. (6.68), we obtain

$$\Delta V(R,t) = \frac{\rho_v\left(t - \dfrac{R}{u}\right)\Delta v}{4\pi\varepsilon_0 R} \tag{6.71}$$

The effects of all the charges can be obtained by integrating Eq. (6.71) over a volume v as given by

$$V(R,t) = \frac{1}{4\pi\varepsilon_0}\int_v \frac{\rho_v\left(t - \dfrac{R}{u}\right)}{R}\,dv \tag{6.72}$$

The above equation shows that the scalar potential at a distance R from the source at time t depends on the charge density at an earlier time $\left(t - \dfrac{R}{u}\right)$. But to obtain far field expressions, this delay time should be taken into account. The potentials in which the delay time or retarded time is taken into account are known as *retarded potentials* and Eq. (6.72) is called the retarded scalar potential.

Similarly, the solution of non-homogeneous wave equations for vector magnetic potential in Eq. (6.64) is given by

$$\vec{A}(R,t) = \frac{\mu_0}{4\pi}\int_v \frac{\vec{J}\left(t - \dfrac{R}{u}\right)}{R}\,dv \tag{6.73}$$

This equation is called the retarded vector potential. The electric field intensity and magnetic field intensity can be obtained from $\vec{A}$ and V by differentiation. Both the fields are also retarded in time. Therefore, the EM wave takes some time to travel and the effect of time-varying charges and currents is experienced only at distant points after some delay.

This delay time or retarded time is given by

$$t' = t - \frac{R}{u}$$

where $R = |r - r'|$ is the distance between the source point r and the observation point r' and $u = 1/\sqrt{\mu\varepsilon}$ is the velocity of wave propagation. In the case of free space, this velocity becomes the velocity of light and it is equivalent to 3×10^8 m/s.

EXAMPLE 6.58

If the retarded scalar electric potential $V = (x - v_0 t)$ and the vector magnetic potential $\vec{A} = \left(\dfrac{x}{v_0} - t\right)\vec{a}_x$, where v_0 is the velocity of propagation, then determine (*i*) $\nabla\cdot\vec{A}$ (*ii*) $\vec{B}, \vec{H}, \vec{E}$, and $\vec{D}$ (*iii*) also, show that $\nabla\cdot\vec{A} = -\mu_0\varepsilon_0\dfrac{\partial V}{\partial t}$ in free space.

SOLUTION

Given $V = x - v_0 t$ and $\vec{A} = \left(\dfrac{x}{v_0} - t\right)\vec{a}_x$.

(*i*) $\quad \nabla\cdot\vec{A} = \dfrac{\partial A_x}{\partial x} + \dfrac{\partial A_y}{\partial y} + \dfrac{\partial A_z}{\partial z}$

The given vector magnetic potential has only x-component, i.e., $A_y = 0$ and $A_z = 0$.

Therefore, $\nabla \cdot \vec{A} = \dfrac{\partial A_x}{\partial x} = \dfrac{\partial}{\partial x}\left(\dfrac{x}{v_0} - t\right) = \dfrac{1}{v_0}$ \hfill (1)

(*ii*) The magnetic flux density can be written in terms vector magnetic potential as

$$\vec{B} = \nabla \times \vec{A}$$

$$= \begin{vmatrix} \vec{a}_x & \vec{a}_y & \vec{a}_z \\ \dfrac{\partial}{\partial x} & \dfrac{\partial}{\partial y} & \dfrac{\partial}{\partial z} \\ A_x & 0 & 0 \end{vmatrix} = (0)\vec{a}_x + \left(\dfrac{\partial A_x}{\partial z}\right)\vec{a}_y + \left(-\dfrac{\partial A_x}{\partial y}\right)\vec{a}_z$$

Since A_x is independent of y and z, $\dfrac{\partial A_x}{\partial z} = \dfrac{\partial A_x}{\partial y} = 0$ and $\nabla \times \vec{A} = 0$.

Therefore, $\vec{B} = 0$ and $\vec{H} = 0$ \hfill (since $\vec{B} = \mu_0 \vec{H}$)

The electric field intensity under time-varying condition is

$$\vec{E} = -\nabla V - \dfrac{\partial \vec{A}}{\partial t}$$

where $\nabla V = \dfrac{\partial V}{\partial x}\vec{a}_x + \dfrac{\partial V}{\partial y}\vec{a}_y + \dfrac{\partial V}{\partial z}\vec{a}_z$. Since V is independent of y and z, $\dfrac{\partial V}{\partial y} = \dfrac{\partial V}{\partial z} = 0$.

Therefore, $\vec{E} = -\dfrac{\partial V}{\partial x}\vec{a}_x - \dfrac{\partial}{\partial t}\left(\dfrac{x}{v_0} - t\right)\vec{a}_x$

$$= -\vec{a}_x + \vec{a}_x = 0$$

and $\vec{D} = \varepsilon_0 \vec{E} = 0$

(*iii*) Given $V = x - v_0 t$ \hfill (2)

Differentiating Eq. (2), we get

$$\dfrac{\partial V}{\partial t} = \dfrac{\partial}{\partial t}(x - v_0 t) = -v_0$$ \hfill (3)

Multiplying by $\mu_0 \varepsilon_0$ on both sides of Eq. (3), we have

$$\mu_0 \varepsilon_0 \dfrac{\partial V}{\partial t} = -v_0 \times \mu_0 \varepsilon_0 = -v_0 \times \dfrac{1}{v_0^2} \qquad \text{(since } v_0 = c = \dfrac{1}{\sqrt{\mu_0 \varepsilon_0}}\text{)}$$

$$= -\dfrac{1}{v_0}$$ \hfill (4)

Comparing Eq. (1) and Eq. (4), we get

$$\nabla \cdot \vec{A} = -\mu_0 \varepsilon_0 \dfrac{\partial V}{\partial t}$$

Hence, it is proved. \hfill ❑

6.10.2 Source-Free Wave Equations

In a source-free region, the charge density ρ_v and current density $\vec{J}$ are both zero. Consider an EM wave is propagating in a linear, isotropic, and homogeneous non-conducting medium ($\sigma = 0$) characterized by ε and μ. Since $\vec{D} = \varepsilon \vec{E}$ and $\vec{D} = \mu \vec{H}$, Maxwell's equations derived in Eqs. (6.32), (6.36), (6.40), and (6.46) reduce to

$$\nabla \cdot \vec{E} = 0 \tag{6.74a}$$

$$\nabla \cdot \vec{H} = 0 \tag{6.74b}$$

$$\nabla \times \vec{E} = -\mu \frac{\partial \vec{H}}{\partial t} \tag{6.74c}$$

$$\nabla \times \vec{H} = \varepsilon \frac{\partial \vec{E}}{\partial t} \tag{6.74d}$$

The first-order differential equations are called Maxwell's equations in source-free region with only two variables ($\vec{E}$ and $\vec{H}$).

Taking curl on both sides of Eq. (6.74c), we obtain

$$\nabla \times (\nabla \times \vec{E}) = -\mu \frac{\partial}{\partial t}(\nabla \times \vec{H}) \tag{6.75}$$

Substituting Eq. (6.74d) in Eq. (6.75), we have

$$\nabla \times (\nabla \times \vec{E}) = -\mu\varepsilon \frac{\partial^2 \vec{E}}{\partial t^2} \tag{6.76}$$

The curl of curl of $\vec{E}$ is

$$\nabla \times (\nabla \times \vec{E}) = \nabla(\nabla \cdot \vec{E}) - \nabla^2 \vec{E}$$

$$= -\nabla^2 \vec{E} \qquad \text{(since } \nabla \cdot \vec{E} = 0) \tag{6.77}$$

Substituting Eq. (6.77) in Eq. (6.76), we get

$$\nabla^2 \vec{E} - \mu\varepsilon \frac{\partial^2 \vec{E}}{\partial t^2} = 0 \tag{6.78}$$

Since the velocity of wave propagation $u = \dfrac{1}{\sqrt{\mu\varepsilon}}$, the above equation becomes

$$\nabla^2 \vec{E} - \frac{1}{u^2} \frac{\partial^2 \vec{E}}{\partial t^2} = 0 \tag{6.79}$$

Similarly, the equation for magnetic field can be written as

$$\nabla^2 \vec{H} - \frac{1}{u^2} \frac{\partial^2 \vec{H}}{\partial t^2} = 0 \tag{6.80}$$

The above two equations are known as *homogeneous wave equations* in a lossless source-free medium.

6.11 TIME-HARMONIC FIELDS

Under time-varying conditions, the electric and magnetic fields, $\vec{E}$, $\vec{D}$, $\vec{H}$ and $\vec{B}$ and their sources, the charge density ρ_v and current density $\vec{J}$, are represented as functions of the spatial coordinates (x, y, z) and the time variable t. If this variation of time is a sinusoidal function with angular frequency ω, then the above quantities can be represented by a time-independent phasor that depends on (x, y, z) only. A time-harmonic field is one that varies sinusoidally or periodically with time and it is one of the important cases of time-varying EM fields.

Phasor analysis is an important mathematical tool for solving linear system problems in which the excitation is time periodic function. Since sinusoids can be easily expressed in terms of phasors, the phasor notation is generally employed in time harmonic fields.

A complex number z can be written in rectangular form as

$$z = x + jy$$

where x and y are the real and imaginary parts of z, respectively and $j = \sqrt{-1}$.

Alternately, z may also be written in polar form as

$$z = r\angle\phi = re^{j\phi} = r(\cos\phi + j\sin\phi)$$

where r is the magnitude of z, given by $r = |z| = \sqrt{x^2 + y^2}$ and ϕ is the phase of z, given by $\phi = \tan^{-1}\dfrac{y}{x}$.

Consider a phasor z represented in rectangular form as $z = x + jy$ and in polar form as $z = r\angle\phi = re^{j\phi}$. The phasor representation is shown in Figure 6.5, which involves both forms of z.

For example, a sinusoidal time-varying voltage source is represented by

$$v_s(t) = V_0 \sin(\omega t + \phi) \tag{6.81}$$

where $\sin\theta = \cos\left(\dfrac{\pi}{2} - \theta\right)$ and $\cos(-\theta) = \cos\theta$, the above equation can be written in cosine form as

$$v_s(t) = V_0 \cos\left(\frac{\pi}{2} - \omega t - \phi\right)$$

$$= V_0 \cos\left(\omega t + \phi - \frac{\pi}{2}\right) \tag{6.82}$$

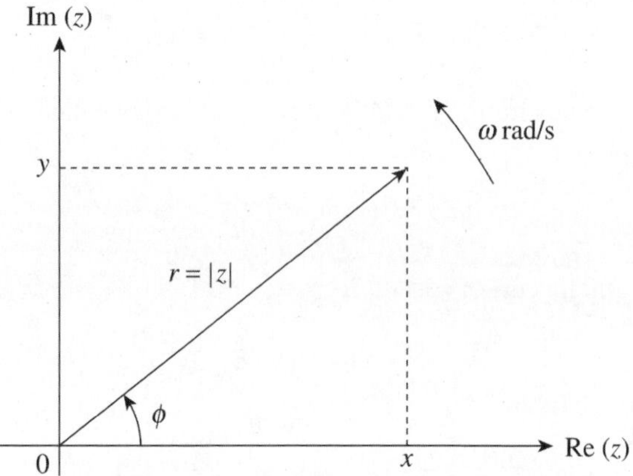

Figure 6.5 *Representation of phasor*

Since the real part of $v_s(t)$ is the cosine term, Eq. (6.82) can be written in phasor form as

$$v_s(t) = \mathrm{Re}\left[V_0 e^{j\left(\omega t + \phi - \frac{\pi}{2}\right)}\right] = \mathrm{Re}\left[V_0 e^{j\left(\phi - \frac{\pi}{2}\right)} e^{j\omega t}\right] = \mathrm{Re}\left[\tilde{V}_s e^{j\omega t}\right]$$

where $\tilde{V}_s = V_0 e^{j\left(\phi - \frac{\pi}{2}\right)}$ is a time-independent function called the phasor of the instantaneous time function $v_s(t)$.

A phasor is a complex quantity and it is denoted by a tilde over the letter. The phasor $\tilde{V}_s$ relating to the time function $v_s(t)$ consists of magnitude and phase information but is independent of time t. Phasor quantities are not functions of time t, and it is important to note that any quantity with j term must be a phasor.

Similarly, an unknown variable $i(t)$ can be defined in phasor form as

$$i(t) = \text{Re}\left[\tilde{I}e^{j\omega t} \right] \tag{6.83}$$

Differentiating the above equation, we get

$$\frac{di}{dt} = \frac{d}{dt}\left[\text{Re}(\tilde{I}e^{j\omega t}) \right] = \text{Re}\left[\frac{d}{dt}(\tilde{I}e^{j\omega t}) \right]$$

$$= \text{Re}\left[j\omega \tilde{I}e^{j\omega t} \right] \tag{6.84}$$

The above equation shows that differentiation in time domain is equivalent to multiplication by $j\omega$ in phasor domain.

Similarly, integrating Eq. (6.83), we get

$$\int i\, dt = \int \text{Re}(\tilde{I}e^{j\omega t})\, dt = \text{Re}\int \tilde{I}e^{j\omega t}\, dt$$

$$= \text{Re}\left[\frac{\tilde{I}}{j\omega} e^{j\omega t} \right] \tag{6.85}$$

The above equation shows that integration in time domain is equivalent to division by $j\omega$ in phasor domain. The above two properties of phasors are useful in writing the time-dependent field equations in phasor form.

Using phasor notation, a time-harmonic electric field intensity $\vec{E}$ can be represented as

$$\vec{E}(x,y,z,t) = \text{Re}\left[\tilde{E}(x,y,z)e^{j\omega t} \right] \tag{6.86}$$

where $\tilde{E}(x,y,z)$ is a vector phasor, which contains information on magnitude, direction, and phase. Similarly, other field and source quantities can also be represented in phasor form, which is independent of time.

The Maxwell's equations derived earlier, can be written in terms of vector field phasors ($\tilde{E}, \tilde{D}, \tilde{H}$ and $\tilde{B}$) and source phasors ($\tilde{\rho}_v, \tilde{J}$) in a linear, isotropic, and homogeneous medium. Table 6.9 shows the time-harmonic Maxwell's equation in phasor domain. Here, $\partial/\partial t = j\omega$.

Table 6.9 *Maxwell's equations for harmonically varying fields in phasor form*

Reference laws	Point form	Integral form
Gauss's law	$\nabla \cdot \tilde{D} = \tilde{\rho}_v$	$\oint_s \tilde{D} \cdot d\vec{s} = \int_v \tilde{\rho}_v dv$
Gauss's law for magnetism	$\nabla \cdot \tilde{B} = 0$	$\oint_s \tilde{B} \cdot d\vec{s} = 0$
Faraday's law	$\nabla \times \tilde{E} = -j\omega \tilde{B}$	$\oint_l \tilde{E} \cdot d\vec{l} = -j\omega \int_s \tilde{B} \cdot d\vec{s}$
Ampere's law	$\nabla \times \tilde{H} = \tilde{J} + j\omega \tilde{D}$	$\oint_l \tilde{H} \cdot d\vec{l} = \int_s (\tilde{J} + j\omega \tilde{D}) \cdot d\vec{s}$

The constitutive relationships in the phasor form are

$$\tilde{D} = \varepsilon \tilde{E} \tag{6.87}$$

and $\qquad \tilde{B} = \mu \tilde{H} \tag{6.88}$

where ε μ, and σ are the permittivity, permeability, and conductivity of the medium. Using Eqs. (6.87) and (6.88), the point form of Maxwell's equations given in Table 6.9 can also be simplified as

$$\nabla \cdot \tilde{E} = \tilde{\rho}_v / \varepsilon \tag{6.89a}$$

$$\nabla \cdot \tilde{H} = 0 \tag{6.89b}$$

$$\nabla \times \tilde{E} = -j\omega \mu \tilde{H} \tag{6.89c}$$

$$\nabla \times \tilde{H} = \tilde{J} + j\omega \varepsilon \tilde{E} \tag{6.89d}$$

Similarly, the non-homogeneous wave equations given in Eqs. (6.64) and (6.65) can also be written in phasor form as

$$\nabla^2 \tilde{A} + k^2 \tilde{A} = -\mu \tilde{J} \tag{6.90}$$

$$\nabla^2 \tilde{V} + k^2 \tilde{V} = -\frac{\tilde{\rho}_v}{\varepsilon} \tag{6.91}$$

where $k = \omega\sqrt{\mu\varepsilon} = \dfrac{\omega}{u}$ is called the wave number. The above two equations are also known as *non-homogeneous Helmholtz's equations*. The phasor solutions of Eqs. (6.90) and (6.91) are obtained from Eqs. (6.72) and (6.73) and they are represented by

$$\tilde{A}(R) = \frac{\mu_0}{4\pi} \int_v \frac{\tilde{J}\, e^{-jkR}}{R} dv \tag{6.92}$$

and

$$\tilde{V}(R) = \frac{1}{4\pi\varepsilon_0} \int_v \frac{\tilde{\rho}_v e^{-jkR}}{R} dv \tag{6.93}$$

Here, the wave number k can be expressed in terms of wavelength λ in the medium as given by

$$k = \frac{2\pi f}{u} = \frac{2\pi}{\lambda} \qquad (\text{since } \lambda = u / f)$$

Equations (6.92) and (6.93) are the retarded vector magnetic and scalar electric potentials due to time-harmonic sources.

EXAMPLE 6.59

Given $\vec{A} = 20\cos(10^8 t - 20x + 30°)\vec{a}_z$ and $\tilde{B} = -j10\,\vec{a}_x + 20e^{j2\pi x/3}\vec{a}_y$. Express (i) $\vec{A}$ in phasor form and (ii) $\tilde{B}$ in instantaneous form.

SOLUTION

(*i*) Given $\vec{A}$ in instantaneous form as

$$\vec{A} = 20\cos(10^8 t - 20x + 30°)\vec{a}_z$$

The phasor form of $\vec{A}$ can be obtained from its real part as given by

$$\vec{A} = \text{Re}[20e^{j(\omega t - 20x + 30°)}\vec{a}_z], \quad \text{where } \omega = 10^8$$

This equation can be simplified to

$$\vec{A} = \text{Re}[20e^{j(30°-20x)}\vec{a}_z e^{j\omega t}] = \text{Re}\left(\tilde{A}e^{j\omega t}\right)$$

Hence, $\vec{A}$ in phasor form is

$$\tilde{A} = 20e^{j(30°-20x)}\vec{a}_z$$

(*ii*) Given $\tilde{B}$ in phasor form as

$$\tilde{B} = -j10\vec{a}_x + 20e^{j\frac{2\pi x}{3}}\vec{a}_y = 10e^{-j\frac{\pi}{2}}\vec{a}_x + 20e^{j\frac{2\pi x}{3}}\vec{a}_y$$

The above equation can be simplified to instantaneous form as

$$\vec{B} = \text{Re}(\tilde{B}e^{j\omega t})$$

$$= \text{Re}\left[10e^{j\left(\omega t - \frac{\pi}{2}\right)}\vec{a}_x + 20e^{j\left(\omega t + \frac{2\pi x}{3}\right)}\vec{a}_y\right]$$

$$= 10\cos\left(\omega t - \frac{\pi}{2}\right)\vec{a}_x + 20\cos\left(\omega t + \frac{2\pi x}{3}\right)\vec{a}_y$$

Hence, $\vec{B}$ in instantaneous form is

$$\vec{B} = 10\sin\omega t\,\vec{a}_x + 20\cos\left(\omega t + \frac{2\pi x}{3}\right)\vec{a}_y \qquad \square$$

EXAMPLE 6.60

Given $\vec{P} = 2\sin\left(10t + x - \frac{\pi}{4}\right)\vec{a}_y$ and $\tilde{Q} = e^{jx}(\vec{a}_x - \vec{a}_z)\sin\pi y$. Determine (i) $\vec{P}$ in phasor form and (ii) $\tilde{Q}$ in instantaneous form.

SOLUTION

(*i*) Given $\vec{P}$ in instantaneous form as

$$\vec{P} = 2\sin\left(10t + x - \frac{\pi}{4}\right)\vec{a}_y$$

Changing the above expression to cosine form, we can write

$$\vec{P} = 2\cos\left(10t + x - \frac{\pi}{4} - \frac{\pi}{2}\right)\vec{a}_y$$

The phasor form of $\vec{P}$ can be obtained from its real part as given by

$$\vec{P} = \text{Re}[2e^{j\left(\omega t + x - \frac{\pi}{4} - \frac{\pi}{2}\right)}\vec{a}_y], \text{ where } \omega = 10$$

Simplifying this equation, we get

$$\vec{P} = \text{Re}[2e^{j\left(x-\frac{\pi}{4}-\frac{\pi}{2}\right)}\vec{a}_y e^{j\omega t}] = \text{Re}[2e^{j\left(x-\frac{3\pi}{4}\right)}\vec{a}_y e^{j\omega t}]$$

$$= \text{Re}\left(\tilde{P}e^{j\omega t}\right)$$

Hence, $\vec{P}$ in phasor form is

$$\tilde{P} = 2e^{j\left(x-\frac{3\pi}{4}\right)}\vec{a}_y$$

(*ii*) Given $\tilde{Q}$ in phasor form as

$$\tilde{Q} = e^{jx}(\vec{a}_x - \vec{a}_z)\sin \pi y$$

Simplifying the above equation to instantaneous form, we get

$$\vec{Q} = \text{Re}(\tilde{Q}e^{j\omega t}) = \text{Re}\left[e^{jx}(\vec{a}_x - \vec{a}_z)\sin(\pi y)e^{j\omega t}\right]$$

$$= \text{Re}\left[e^{j(\omega t + x)}(\vec{a}_x - \vec{a}_z)\sin(\pi y)\right]$$

$$= \sin(\pi y)\cos(\omega t + x)(\vec{a}_x - \vec{a}_z)$$

Hence, $\vec{Q}$ in instantaneous form is

$$\vec{Q} = \sin(\pi y)\cos(\omega t + x)(\vec{a}_x - \vec{a}_z)$$

EXAMPLE 6.61

A series RL circuit shown in Figure E6.61 is connected to a voltage source given by $v_s(t) = 5\cos(\omega t - 120°)$ V. For $R = 500\ \Omega$, $L = 3$ mH and $\omega = 10^5$ rad/s, determine (i) the phasor current $\tilde{I}$ and (ii) the instantaneous current $i(t)$.

SOLUTION

Figure E6.61 shows a series RL circuit connected to a given voltage source $v_s(t) = 5\cos(\omega t - 120°)$ V. The voltage phasor corresponding to $v_s(t)$ is

$$\tilde{v}_s = 5e^{-j120°}\ \text{V}$$

The voltage loop of the RL circuit is

$$Ri(t) + L\frac{di}{dt} = v_s(t)$$

and the corresponding phasor equation is

$$R\tilde{I} + j\omega L\tilde{I} = \tilde{v}_s$$

(*i*) The phasor current is

$$\tilde{I} = \frac{\tilde{v}_s}{R + j\omega L}$$

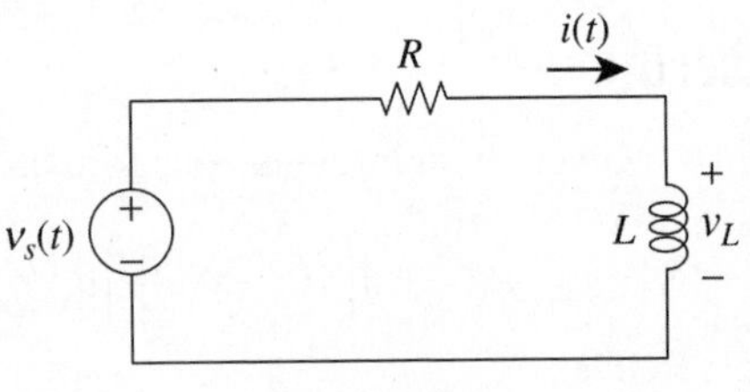

Figure E6.61

$$= \frac{5e^{-j120°}}{500 + j \times 10^5 \times 3 \times 10^{-3}}$$

$$= \frac{5e^{-j120°}}{500 + j300} = \frac{5e^{-j120°}}{583e^{j30.96°}}$$

$$= 8.58 \times 10^{-3} e^{-j150.96°}$$

$$= 8.58\angle -150.96°\ \text{mA}$$

(*ii*) The instantaneous current is

$$i(t) = \text{Re}(\tilde{I}e^{j\omega t}) = \text{Re}\left[8.58 \times 10^{-3} e^{-j150.96°}\, e^{j\omega t} \right]$$

$$= 8.58 \cos(\omega t - 150.96°)\ \text{mA} \qquad \square$$

EXAMPLE 6.62

Given $\vec{E} = 200e^{(4y-\omega t)}\vec{a}_x$ V/m in free space. Using Maxwell's equation, determine $\vec{H}$. Assume that all fields vary harmonically for which $\nabla \times \vec{E} = -j\omega\mu\vec{H}$.

SOLUTION

Given $\vec{E} = 200e^{(4y-\omega t)}\vec{a}_x$ V/m and $\nabla \times \vec{E} = -j\omega\mu\vec{H}$.

In free space, $\mu = \mu_0$ and $\vec{H} = \dfrac{-1}{j\omega\mu_0}\left(\nabla \times \vec{E}\right)$

In rectangular coordinates,

$$\nabla \times \vec{E} = \begin{vmatrix} \vec{a}_x & \vec{a}_y & \vec{a}_z \\ \dfrac{\partial}{\partial x} & \dfrac{\partial}{\partial y} & \dfrac{\partial}{\partial z} \\ E_x & E_y & E_z \end{vmatrix} = \begin{vmatrix} \vec{a}_x & \vec{a}_y & \vec{a}_z \\ \dfrac{\partial}{\partial x} & \dfrac{\partial}{\partial y} & \dfrac{\partial}{\partial z} \\ 200e^{(4y-\omega t)} & 0 & 0 \end{vmatrix}$$

$$= -\left[\frac{-\partial}{\partial z}(200e^{(4y-\omega t)}) \right]\vec{a}_y + \left[\frac{-\partial}{\partial y}(200e^{(4y-\omega t)}) \right]\vec{a}_z$$

$$= -800e^{(4y-\omega t)}\vec{a}_z$$

Given, $\nabla \times \vec{E} = -j\omega\mu\vec{H}$

Therefore, $\vec{H} = \dfrac{-1}{j\omega\mu_0}\left(-800e^{(4y-\omega t)} \right)\vec{a}_z$

$$= \frac{800}{j\omega\mu_0}e^{(4y-\omega t)}\vec{a}_z\ \text{A/m} \qquad \square$$

EXAMPLE 6.63

The electric and magnetic field intensities in free space are given by

$$\vec{E} = \frac{100}{\rho}\cos(10^8 t + \beta z)\,\vec{a}_\phi \ \text{V/m}$$

and

$$\vec{H} = \frac{H_0}{\rho}\cos(10^8 t + \beta z)\vec{a}_\rho \ \text{A/m}$$

Express the above fields in phasor form and determine the constants H_0 and β such that the fields satisfy Maxwell's equations.

SOLUTION

The instantaneous forms of $\vec{E}$ and $\vec{H}$ are represented by

$$\vec{E} = \text{Re}(\tilde{E}e^{j\omega t}) \quad \text{and} \quad \vec{H} = \text{Re}(\tilde{H}e^{j\omega t}) \tag{1}$$

where $\omega = 10^8$ and the corresponding phasors $\tilde{E}$ and $\tilde{H}$ are written as

$$\tilde{E} = \frac{100}{\rho}e^{j\beta z}\vec{a}_\phi \tag{2}$$

and

$$\tilde{H} = \frac{H_0}{\rho}e^{j\beta z}\vec{a}_\rho \tag{3}$$

For free space, $\rho_v = 0$, $\sigma = 0$, $\varepsilon = \varepsilon_0$, and $\mu = \mu_0$. So, Maxwell's equations in phasor form are

$$\nabla \cdot \vec{D} = \varepsilon_0 \nabla \cdot \vec{E} = 0 \quad \text{i.e., } \nabla \cdot \tilde{E} = 0 \tag{4}$$

$$\nabla \cdot \vec{B} = \mu_0 \nabla \cdot \vec{H} = 0 \quad \text{i.e., } \nabla \cdot \tilde{H} = 0 \tag{5}$$

$$\nabla \times \vec{H} = \sigma \vec{E} + \varepsilon_0 \frac{\partial \vec{E}}{\partial t} \quad \text{i.e., } \nabla \times \tilde{H} = j\omega\varepsilon_0 \tilde{E} \tag{6}$$

$$\nabla \times \vec{E} = -\mu_0 \frac{\partial \vec{H}}{\partial t} \quad \text{i.e., } \nabla \times \tilde{E} = -j\omega\mu_0 \tilde{H} \tag{7}$$

Substituting Eq. (2) in Eq. (4), we get

$$\nabla \cdot \tilde{E} = \frac{1}{\rho}\frac{\partial}{\partial \phi}(\tilde{E}_\phi) = 0$$

The above equation shows that the given electric field satisfies the Maxwell's equations. Substituting Eq. (3) in Eq. (5), we get

$$\nabla \cdot \tilde{H} = \frac{1}{\rho}\frac{\partial}{\partial \rho}(\rho\tilde{H}_\rho) = 0$$

This shows that the given magnetic field also satisfies the Maxwell's equations.

Now, $\nabla \times \tilde{H} = \nabla \times \left(\dfrac{H_0}{\rho} e^{j\beta z} \vec{a}_\rho \right) = \dfrac{1}{\rho} \begin{vmatrix} \vec{a}_\rho & \rho\,\vec{a}_\phi & \vec{a}_z \\ \dfrac{\partial}{\partial \rho} & \dfrac{\partial}{\partial \phi} & \dfrac{\partial}{\partial z} \\ \dfrac{H_o}{\rho} e^{j\beta z} & 0 & 0 \end{vmatrix} = \dfrac{jH_0\beta}{\rho} e^{j\beta z} \vec{a}_\phi \qquad (8)$

Substituting Eqs. (8) and (2) in Eq. (6), we get

$$\frac{jH_0\beta}{\rho} e^{j\beta z} \vec{a}_\phi = j\omega\varepsilon_0 \frac{100}{\rho} e^{j\beta z} \vec{a}_\phi$$

$$H_0\beta = 100\omega\varepsilon_0 \qquad (9)$$

Similarly, substituting Eqs. (2) and (3) in Eq. (7), we have

$$-j\beta \frac{100}{\rho} e^{j\beta z} \vec{a}_\rho = -j\omega\mu_0 \frac{H_0}{\rho} e^{j\beta z} \vec{a}_\rho$$

$$\frac{H_0}{\beta} = \frac{100}{\omega\mu_0} \qquad (10)$$

Multiplying Eq. (9) with Eq. (10), we get

$$H_0^2 = (100)^2 \frac{\varepsilon_0}{\mu_0}$$

$$H_0 = \pm 100 \sqrt{\frac{\varepsilon_0}{\mu_0}} \ , \ \text{where} \ \sqrt{\frac{\mu_0}{\varepsilon_0}} = 120\pi$$

$$= \pm \frac{100}{120\pi} = \pm 0.2654$$

Dividing Eq. (9) by Eq. (10), we get

$$\beta^2 = \omega^2 \mu_0 \varepsilon_0$$

$$\beta = \pm\omega\sqrt{\mu_0\varepsilon_0} = \pm\frac{\omega}{c} = \pm\frac{10^8}{3\times10^8} \ \left(\text{since} \ c = \frac{1}{\sqrt{\mu_0\varepsilon_0}} = 3\times10^8 \ \text{m/s} \right)$$

$$= \pm 0.333$$

All the four Maxwell's equations are satisfied by either $H_0 = 0.2654$, $\beta = 0.333$ or $H_0 = -0.2654$, $\beta = -0.333$. $\qquad\square$

EXAMPLE 6.64

In a medium characterized by $\sigma = 0$, $\mu = \mu_0$, $\varepsilon = 9\varepsilon_0$ and $\vec{E} = 30\sin(10^8 t - \beta z)\vec{a}_y$ V/m. Determine β and $\vec{H}$ using phasor method.

SOLUTION

The instantaneous form of $\vec{E}$ is written in phasor form as

$$\vec{E} = \mathrm{Im}(\tilde{E}e^{j\omega t}), \qquad \text{where } \omega = 10^8$$

Hence, $\quad \tilde{E} = 30e^{-j\beta z}\vec{a}_y \qquad\qquad (1)$

$$\nabla \cdot \tilde{E} = \frac{\partial \tilde{E}_y}{\partial y} = 0$$

The above equation shows that the given field satisfies the Gauss's law for electric field in phasor domain. Faraday's law in phasor form is

$$\nabla \times \tilde{E} = -j\omega\mu\, \tilde{H}$$

$$\tilde{H} = \frac{\nabla \times \tilde{E}}{-j\omega\mu} = \frac{1}{-j\omega\mu}\left[-\frac{\partial \tilde{E}_y}{\partial z}\vec{a}_x \right] \qquad\qquad (2)$$

Substituting Eq. (1) in Eq. (2), we get

$$\tilde{H} = -\frac{30\beta}{\omega\mu}e^{-j\beta z}\vec{a}_x \qquad\qquad (3)$$

Here, Gauss's law for magnetic field is also satisfied, i.e., $\nabla \cdot \tilde{H} = 0$.

$$\nabla \times \tilde{H} = j\omega\varepsilon\, \tilde{E}$$

$$\tilde{E} = \frac{\nabla \times \tilde{H}}{j\omega\varepsilon} = \frac{1}{j\omega\varepsilon}\frac{\partial \tilde{H}_x}{\partial z}\vec{a}_y \qquad\qquad (4)$$

Substituting Eq. (3) in Eq. (4), we get

$$\tilde{E} = \frac{30\beta^2 e^{-j\beta z}}{\omega^2 \mu\varepsilon}\vec{a}_y \qquad\qquad (5)$$

Comparing Eq. (5) and Eq. (1), we get

$$30 = \frac{30\beta^2}{\omega^2 \mu\varepsilon}$$

$$\beta = \pm\omega\sqrt{\mu\varepsilon} = \pm 10^8 \sqrt{\mu_0 \times 9\varepsilon_0}$$

$$= \pm\frac{10^8 \times 3}{c} = \pm\frac{10^8 \times 3}{3\times 10^8} = \pm 1 \qquad \left(\text{since } c = \frac{1}{\sqrt{\mu_0\varepsilon_0}} 3\times 10^8 \text{ m/s}\right)$$

Substituting $\beta = \pm 1$ in Eq. (3), we get

$$\tilde{H} = \mp\frac{30}{\omega\mu}e^{\mp j\beta z}\vec{a}_x = \mp\frac{30}{10^8 \times 4\pi \times 10^{-7}}e^{\mp j\beta z}\vec{a}_x$$

$$= \mp\frac{3}{4\pi}e^{\mp j\beta z}\vec{a}_x$$

From phasor form of $\widetilde{H}$, the instantaneous form can be written as

$$\vec{H} = \text{Im}(\widetilde{H}e^{j\omega t}) = \mp \frac{3}{4\pi}\sin(10^8 t \mp z)\,\vec{a}_x \text{ A/m}$$

The above solution obtained using phasor domain is same as the one obtained using time domain in Example 6.47. ∎

6.11.1 Ratio between Conduction Current Density and Displacement Current Density

Some materials are neither good conductors nor perfect dielectrics and hence, both conduction current and displacement current exist. Assuming the time dependence $e^{j\omega t}$ for $\vec{E}$, the total current density is

$$\vec{J}_t = \vec{J}_c + \vec{J}_d = \sigma \vec{E} + \frac{\partial}{\partial t}(\varepsilon \vec{E}) = \sigma \widetilde{E} + j\omega\varepsilon \widetilde{E}$$

where $\dfrac{\partial}{\partial t} = j\omega$ and $\widetilde{E}$ is a phasor vector field.

The magnitude of conduction current density is $\left|\vec{J}_c\right| = \sigma\left|\widetilde{E}\right|$ and the magnitude of displacement current density is $\left|\vec{J}_d\right| = \omega\varepsilon\left|\widetilde{E}\right|$. Hence, it is evident that displacement current density increases as the frequency increases. Therefore, the ratio of $\left|\vec{J}_c\right|$ to $\left|\vec{J}_d\right|$ becomes

$$\frac{\left|\vec{J}_c\right|}{\left|\vec{J}_d\right|} = \frac{\sigma}{\omega\varepsilon}$$

At low frequencies, the displacement current density $\vec{J}_d$ is usually negligible compared to conduction current density $\vec{J}_c$. But at high frequencies (radio frequencies), the value of $\vec{J}_d$ becomes comparable with $\vec{J}_c$ in wave propagation. Therefore, a conducting material at very low frequency may become dielectric at very high frequency.

6.11.2 Comparison of Different Types of Currents and Their Current Densities

The summary of different types of currents and their current densities are summarized in Tables 6.10 and 6.11, respectively.

Table 6.10 *Comparison of conduction, convection, and displacement currents*

S. No.	Conduction current	Convection current	Displacement current
1.	Conduction current is defined as the current due to the flow of electrons in a conducting medium.	Convection current is defined as the current due to the flow of electrons in a non-conducting medium.	Displacement current is the flow of charge which results due to time-varying electric field.
2.	It is the current passing through the resistors and wires.	It is the leakage current passing through the dielectric medium.	It is the rate of flow of charge between the capacitor plates in a capacitor circuit.
3.	It is independent of frequency.	It is directly proportional to frequency.	It is directly proportional to frequency.

S. No.	Conduction current	Convection current	Displacement current
4.	It obeys Ohm's law and hence, it has linear charge characteristics.	It does not obey Ohm's law and its characteristics are non-linear.	It does not obey Ohm's law and so it has non-linear characteristics.
5.	It exists both in time-variant and invariant case.	It also exists both in time-variant and invariant cases.	It exists only in time-varying case.
6.	Typical examples are current flowing through conductors, resistors, etc.	Typical examples are electron beam moving through CRT, liquids, vacuum, etc.	Typical examples are current flowing between capacitor plates and all imperfect conductors carrying a time-varying conduction current.

Table 6.11 *Comparison of displacement current density and conduction current density*

S. No.	Displacement current density	Conduction current density
1.	It is defined as the displacement current at a given point, passing through a unit surface area, which is normal to the direction of the displacement current.	It is defined as the conduction current at a given point, passing through a unit surface area, which is normal to the direction of the conduction current.
2.	Displacement current results when a time-varying voltage is applied across the dielectric material.	The flow of current in conducting material results in conduction current.
3.	Displacement current density is given by $\vec{J}_d = \dfrac{\partial \vec{D}}{\partial t}$.	Conduction current density is given by $\vec{J}_c = \sigma \vec{E}$.
4.	Displacement current density exists only in a dielectric medium.	Conduction current density exists only in conductors.
5.	Displacement current density exists only in time-varying fields.	Conduction current density exists both in static and time-varying (dynamic) fields.

EXAMPLE 6.65

Find the frequency at which conduction current density and displacement current density are equal in a medium with $\sigma = 4 \times 10^{-4} \ \Omega^{-1} / \text{m}$ and $\varepsilon_r = 80$.

SOLUTION

Given $\sigma = 4 \times 10^{-4} \ \Omega^{-1} / \text{m}$ and $\varepsilon_r = 80$.

The relation between conduction current density and displacement current density is

$$\frac{\left| \vec{J}_c \right|}{\left| \vec{J}_d \right|} = \frac{\sigma}{\omega \varepsilon} \text{, where } \omega = 2\pi f$$

When $\left| J_c \right| = \left| J_d \right|$, $\sigma = \omega \varepsilon$.

That is, $\omega = \dfrac{\sigma}{\varepsilon}$ or $2\pi f = \dfrac{\sigma}{\varepsilon}$

Therefore,

$$f = \frac{\sigma}{2\pi \varepsilon_0 \varepsilon_r} = \frac{4 \times 10^{-4}}{2\pi \times 8.854 \times 10^{-12} \times 80} = 89.92 \times 10^3 \ \text{Hz}$$

EXAMPLE 6.66

In a material for which $\sigma = 5$ S/m and $\varepsilon_r = 1$, the electric field intensity is $E = 250\sin\left(10^{10} t\right)$ V/m. Find the conduction and displacement current densities and the frequency at which they have equal magnitudes.

SOLUTION

Given $\sigma = 5$ S/m, $\varepsilon_r = 1$ and $E = 250\sin(10^{10} t)$ V/m.

The conduction current density is

$$J_c = \sigma E = 5 \times 250 \sin(10^{10} t) = 1250 \sin(10^{10} t) \text{ A/m}^2$$

The displacement current density is

$$J_d = \frac{\partial D}{\partial t} = \frac{\partial(\varepsilon E)}{\partial t} = \varepsilon_0 \varepsilon_r \frac{\partial E}{\partial t}$$

$$= 8.854 \times 10^{-12} \times 250 \times 10^{10} \cos(10^{10} t)$$

$$= 22.135 \cos(10^{10} t) \text{ A/m}^2$$

When $\left|J_c\right| = \left|J_d\right|$, $\sigma = \omega\varepsilon$.

That is,

$$\omega = \frac{\sigma}{\varepsilon} \text{ or } 2\pi f = \frac{\sigma}{\varepsilon}$$

Therefore,

$$f = \frac{\sigma}{2\pi\varepsilon_0\varepsilon_r} = \frac{5}{2\pi \times 8.854 \times 10^{-12} \times 1} = 89.87 \times 10^9 \text{ Hz}$$

EXAMPLE 6.67

(i) Show that the ratio of the amplitudes of the conduction current density and displacement current density is $\dfrac{\sigma}{\omega\varepsilon}$, for the applied field $\vec{E} = \vec{E}_m \cos\omega t$. Assume $\mu = \mu_0$.

(ii) What is this amplitude ratio if the applied field intensity is $\vec{E} = \vec{E}_m e^{-t/\tau}$ where τ is real?

SOLUTION

(i) The conduction current density is

$$\vec{J}_c = \sigma \vec{E} = \sigma \vec{E}_m \cos\omega t$$

The displacement current density is

$$\vec{J}_d = \frac{\partial \vec{D}}{\partial t} = \frac{\partial(\varepsilon \vec{E})}{\partial t} = \varepsilon \frac{\partial}{\partial t}\left[\vec{E}_m \cos\omega t\right]$$

$$= -\omega\varepsilon \vec{E}_m \sin\omega t$$

The ratio of the amplitudes of the two current densities is

$$\frac{\left|\vec{J}_c\right|}{\left|\vec{J}_d\right|} = \frac{\sigma\,\vec{E}_m}{\omega\varepsilon\,\vec{E}_m} = \frac{\sigma}{\omega\varepsilon}$$

(*ii*) Given $\vec{E} = \vec{E}_m e^{-t/\tau}$

$$\vec{J}_c = \sigma\,\vec{E} = \sigma\,\vec{E}_m e^{-t/\tau}$$

Also,

$$\vec{J}_d = \varepsilon\frac{\partial\vec{E}}{\partial t} = \varepsilon\,\vec{E}_m\left(-\frac{1}{\tau}\right)e^{-t/\tau} = -\frac{\varepsilon\,\vec{E}_m}{\tau}e^{-t/\tau}$$

Therefore, the ratio of the amplitudes of the two current densities is

$$\frac{\left|\vec{J}_c\right|}{\left|\vec{J}_d\right|} = \frac{\sigma\,E_m}{\varepsilon\,E_m/\tau} = \frac{\sigma\tau}{\varepsilon}$$

EXAMPLE 6.68

A 50 V voltage generator at 20 MHz is connected to the plates of an air dielectric parallel-plate capacitor with plate are 2.8 cm^2 and separation distance 0.2 mm. Find the maximum value of displacement current density and displacement current.

SOLUTION

Given $V_s = 50$ V, $d = 0.2$ mm, $A = 2.8$ cm^2 and $f = 20$ MHz.

The displacement current density can be written in phasor form as

$$\tilde{J}_d = j\omega\tilde{D}$$

The maximum value of displacement current density is

$$\left.\left|\tilde{J}_d\right|\right|_{\max} = \omega\varepsilon\,\vec{E} = \omega\varepsilon_0\frac{V_s}{d} \qquad \text{(for air dielectric, } \varepsilon_r = 1 \text{ and } \varepsilon = \varepsilon_0\text{)}$$

$$= 2\pi\times20\times10^6\times\frac{10^{-9}}{36\pi}\times\frac{50}{0.2\times10^{-3}} \qquad \text{(since } \omega = 2\pi f\text{)}$$

$$= 277.78 \text{ A/m}^2$$

Therefore, the displacement current is

$$\tilde{I} = \left|\tilde{J}_d\right|A = 277.8\times2.8\times10^{-4} = 77.78 \text{ mA}$$

EXAMPLE 6.69

Determine the ratio of conduction current density to displacement current density at 1 GHz for (*i*) distilled water ($\mu = \mu_0$, $\varepsilon = 81\varepsilon_0$ and $\sigma = 2\times10^{-3}$ S/m) and (*ii*) sea water ($\mu = \mu_0$, $\varepsilon = 81\varepsilon_0$ and $\sigma = 25$ S/m).

SOLUTION

(*i*) For distilled water ($\mu = \mu_0$, $\varepsilon = 81\varepsilon_0$ and $\sigma = 2\times10^{-3}$ S/m), the ratio of conduction current density to displacement current density in phasor form is

$$\frac{\left|\tilde{J}_c\right|}{\left|\tilde{J}_d\right|} = \frac{\sigma}{\omega\varepsilon}, \text{ where } \varepsilon = 81\varepsilon_0 \text{ and } \varepsilon_0 = 8.854\times10^{-12}$$

$$= \frac{2\times10^{-3}}{2\pi\times10^9\times81\times8.854\times10^{-12}} = 0.44$$

(*ii*) For sea water ($\mu = \mu_0$, $\varepsilon = 81\varepsilon_0$ and $\sigma = 25$ S/m), the ratio of conduction current density to displacement current density is

$$\frac{\left|\tilde{J}_c\right|}{\left|\tilde{J}_d\right|} = \frac{\sigma}{\omega\varepsilon} = \frac{25}{2\pi\times10^9\times81\times8.854\times10^{-12}} = 5.56 \qquad \square$$

EXAMPLE 6.70

Assuming that sea water has $\mu = \mu_0$, $\varepsilon = 81\varepsilon_0$ and $\sigma = 20$ S/m, determine the frequency at which the conduction current density is 10 times the displacement current density in magnitude.

SOLUTION

Given $\mu = \mu_0$, $\varepsilon = 81\varepsilon_0$, $\sigma = 20$ S/m for sea water and $\left|\tilde{J}_c\right| = 10\left|\tilde{J}_d\right|$.

We know that,

$$\frac{\left|\tilde{J}_c\right|}{\left|\tilde{J}_d\right|} = \frac{\sigma}{\omega\varepsilon} = 10$$

Therefore, $\omega = \dfrac{\sigma}{10\varepsilon}$

That is, $f = \dfrac{\sigma}{2\pi\times10\varepsilon} = \dfrac{20}{20\pi\times81\times8.854\times10^{-12}} = 0.44$ GHz $\qquad \square$

EXAMPLE 6.71

A circular cross-section conductor of radius 2.5 mm carries a current of $I_c = 6.5\sin(4\times10^{10}t)$ μA. What is the amplitude of the displacement current density, if $\sigma = 25$ MS/m and $\varepsilon_r = 1$?

SOLUTION

Given $\sigma = 25$ MS/m, $\varepsilon_r = 1$ and $I_c = 6.5\sin\left(4\times10^{10}t\right)$ μA.

Here, $\omega = 4\times10^{10}$ rad/s. The ratio of amplitude of current densities is

$$\frac{J_c}{J_d} = \frac{\sigma}{\omega\varepsilon} = \frac{25\times10^6}{4\times10^{10}\times8.854\times10^{-12}} = 7.05\times10^7$$

Therefore, the amplitude of displacement current density is

$$J_d = \frac{J_c}{7.05\times10^7}, \qquad \text{where } J_c = \frac{I_c}{A}$$

$$= \frac{6.5\times10^{-6}}{\pi\times\left(2.5\times10^{-3}\right)^2 \times 7.05\times10^7} = 4.7\,\text{nA/m}^2$$

EXAMPLE `6.72`

A coaxial capacitor with inner radius 5 mm, outer radius 6 mm and length 500 mm has a dielectric for which $\varepsilon_r = 10$ and an applied voltage $250\sin 377t$ V. Determine the displacement current I_d and compare with the conduction current I_c.

SOLUTION

Given $a = 5\,\text{mm}$, $b = 6\,\text{mm}$, $l = 500\,\text{mm}$, $\varepsilon_r = 10$ and an applied voltage $V_0 = 250\sin 377t$ V. Assume the outer conductor is connected to ground. Referring to Example 3.70, the potential between the inner and the outer conductors of a coaxial capacitor is

$$V = \frac{V_0 \ln(\rho)}{\ln\left(\dfrac{a}{b}\right)} - \frac{V_0 \ln(b)}{\ln\left(\dfrac{a}{b}\right)}\,\text{V}$$

where ρ is the radius of the coaxial capacitor. The electric field intensity is related to scalar electric potential by

$$\vec{E} = -\nabla V = -\frac{\partial V}{\partial \rho}\vec{a}_\rho \ \text{(in cylindrical coordinates)}$$

$$= \frac{V_0}{\rho \ln\left(\dfrac{b}{a}\right)}\vec{a}_\rho = \frac{250\sin 377t}{\rho \ln\left(\dfrac{6\times10^{-3}}{5\times10^{-3}}\right)}\vec{a}_\rho = \frac{1.37\times10^3}{\rho}\sin 377t\,\vec{a}_\rho\,\text{V/m}$$

The electric field intensity is related to electric flux density as

$$\vec{D} = \varepsilon_0\varepsilon_r\vec{E} = 8.854\times10^{-12}\times10\times\frac{1.37\times10^3}{\rho}\sin 377t\,\vec{a}_\rho = \frac{12.1\times10^{-8}}{\rho}\sin 377t\,\vec{a}_\rho\,\text{C/m}^2$$

The displacement current density is

$$\vec{J}_d = \frac{\partial \vec{D}}{\partial t} = \frac{4.56\times10^{-5}}{\rho}\cos 377t\,\vec{a}_\rho\,\text{A/m}^2$$

The displacement current is

$$I_d = J_d\times\text{Area} = J_d\times 2\pi\rho l = \frac{4.56\times10^{-5}}{\rho}\times 2\pi\,\rho\times 0.5 = 143.2\cos 377t\,\mu\text{A}$$

The capacitance of a coaxial capacitor is

$$C = \frac{2\pi\varepsilon_0\varepsilon_r l}{\ln\left(\dfrac{b}{a}\right)} = \frac{2\pi\times8.854\times10^{-12}\times10\times0.5}{\ln\left(\dfrac{6}{5}\right)} = 1.52\,\text{nF}$$

The conduction current is

$$I_c = C\frac{dV_0}{dt} = 1.52\times10^{-9}\times\frac{d}{dt}\left(250\sin 377t\right)$$

$$= 1.52\times10^{-9}\times250\times377\times\cos 377t = 143.2\cos 377t\ \mu A$$

It is seen that the displacement current and conduction current are equal, i.e., $I_C = I_d$.

6.12 ELECTROMAGNETIC SPECTRUM

Electromagnetic spectrum is a family of waves which extends from very low frequency range to ultra-high frequency range exceeding 10^{24} Hz. These include radio waves (RF), microwaves, infrared (IR), visible light, ultraviolet (UV), X-rays, and gamma (γ) rays. EM waves consist of electric and magnetic fields which oscillate at the same frequency f and travel at the velocity of light $u = c = 3\times10^8$ m/s.

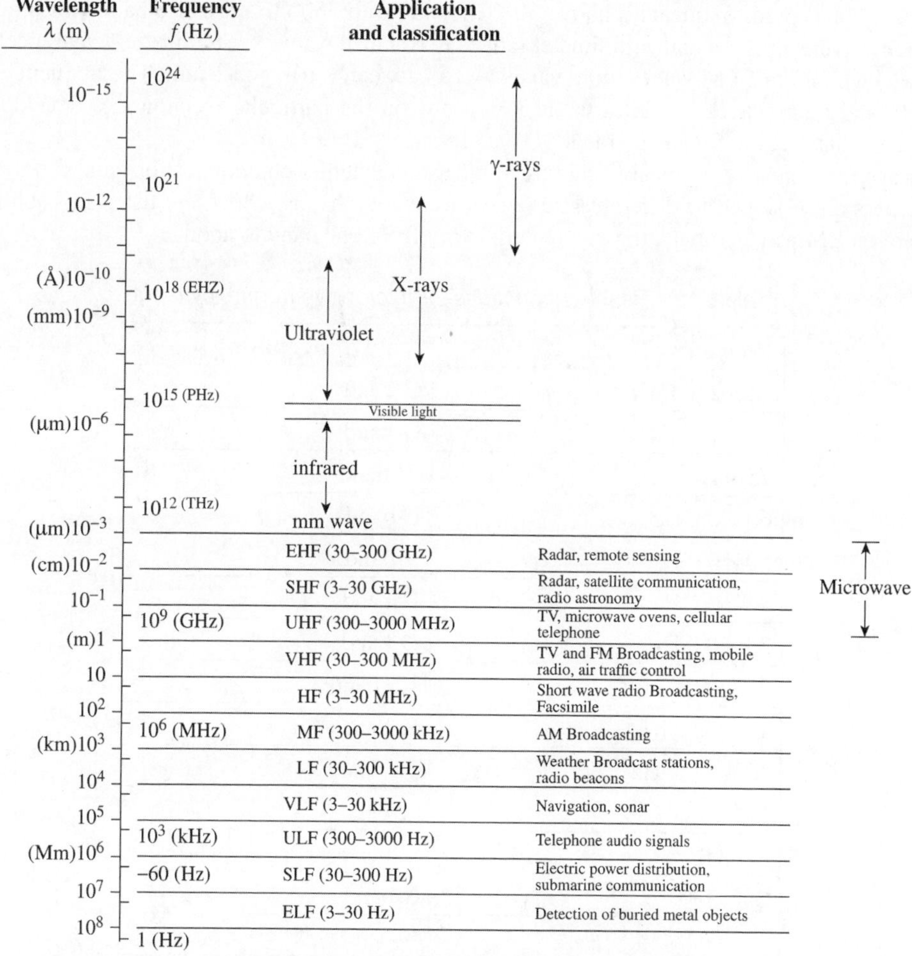

Figure 6.6 *Electromagnetic spectrum*

If the sources of the fields are time-harmonic, then the resultant EM wave generated is also time-harmonic. The solution to wave equations represents propagation of waves. Both Maxwell's equations and Helmholtz's equations do not impose any limit on the frequency of the waves. The wavelength of an EM wave is related to its oscillation frequency f by $\lambda = \dfrac{c}{f}$.

Electromagnetic spectrum is divided into frequency and wavelength ranges on logarithmic scales based on their applications and is shown in Figure 6.6. Different frequencies have different applications based on their excitation mechanisms. The visible part of the EM spectrum covers a very narrow wavelength from violet ($\lambda = 0.38$ μm) to red ($\lambda = 0.72$ μm).

The frequency range of visible light is from 4.2×10^{14} Hz to 7.9×10^{14} Hz. The UV band lie on the shorter wavelength (higher frequency) side of the visible spectrum. The infrared and the radio band lie on the larger wavelength (lower frequency) side of the visible spectrum. Each spectral range can be specified in terms of its wavelength or frequency range.

Microwaves lie in the region between radio waves and infrared and are used to describe EM waves with frequencies ranging from 300 MHz to 300 GHz, which corresponds to wavelengths in free space from 1 m to 1 mm. EM waves with frequencies above 30 GHz and up to 300 GHz are also called millimeter waves because their wavelengths are in the millimeter range (1–10 mm). Above the millimeter wave spectrum is the infrared, which consist of EM waves with wavelengths between 1 μm and 1 mm. The frequency boundary between RF and microwaves is arbitrary and it depends on the particular technologies developed for the exploitation of that specific frequency range.

Microwave frequencies find its applications in radar and satellite communications and for convenience, alphabet letters are assigned to different microwave frequency bands, which are listed in Table 6.12. The properties of an EM wave propagating in a material vary from one band to another.

Table 6.12 *Band designations for microwave frequency range*

Frequency Range	Band designation
140–220 GHz	G-band
110–170 GHz	D-band
75–110 GHz	W-band
60–90 GHz	E-band
50–70 GHz	V-band
40–60 GHz	U-band
33–50 GHz	Q-band
26.5–40 GHz	Ka-band
18–26.5 GHz	K-band
12.4–18 GHz	Ku-band
8–12.4 GHz	X-band
4–8 GHz	C-band
2–4 GHz	S-band
1–2 GHz	L-band
300–3,000 MHz	UHF-band

6.13   APPLICATIONS OF EM (DYNAMIC) FIELDS

The existence of EM fields is based on Maxwell's equations under various boundary conditions. Here, two applications of Maxwell's equations in time-varying conditions are discussed. They are (*i*) transformer and (*ii*) betatron.

6.13.1   Transformer

A transformer is a static device used for coupling two or more electric circuits. It is working on the principle of mutual induction and it transfers an electric energy from one circuit to another when there is no electrical connection between the two circuits. The principle of mutual induction states that, when two coils are inductively coupled and if current in one coil is changed uniformly, then an emf gets induced in the other coil.

The basic transformer is shown in Figure 6.7. It consists of two inductive coils which are electrically separated but are wound on a high-permeability laminated steel magnetic core to maximize the coupling. The two coils have high mutual inductance. It is used to transfer electric energy from one voltage level to another.

One of the two coils is connected to a source of alternating voltage. This coil in which electrical energy is fed with the help of source is called primary winding. The second coil which is connected to a load Z_L is called secondary winding. The electrical energy transformed to this winding is drawn out by the load. The primary winding has N_1 turns while the secondary winding has N_2 turns.

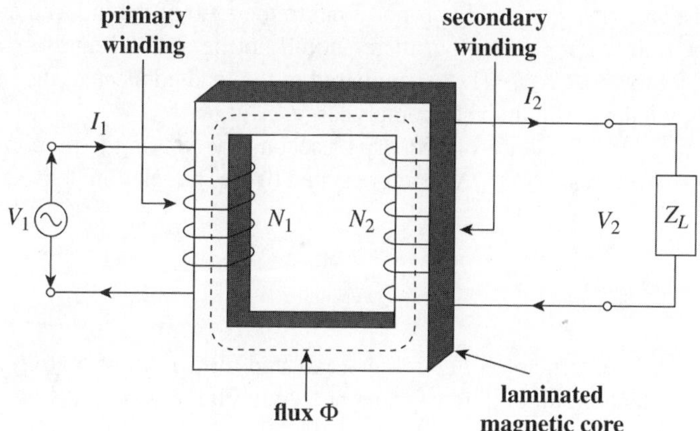

Figure 6.7   *Basic transformer*

When primary winding is excited by an alternating voltage, it circulates an alternating current. This time-varying current produces time-varying flux Φ which completes its path through common magnetic core as shown by dotted lines in Figure 6.7. Thus, an alternating flux links with the secondary winding and mutually induced emf gets developed in the secondary winding. If the load is connected to the secondary winding, this emf drives a current through it.

Ideal transformer

In an ideal transformer, there is no loss as the primary and secondary windings have zero resistance, and the core has infinite permeability. Under ideal conditions, the emf gets induced in the primary winding and secondary winding. According to Faraday's law, the flux Φ and V_1 are related on the primary side by

$$V_1 = -N_1 \frac{d\Phi}{dt} \tag{6.94}$$

Similarly, on the secondary side, the flux Φ and V_2 are related by

$$V_2 = -N_2 \frac{d\Phi}{dt} \tag{6.95}$$

Combining Eqs. (6.94) and (6.95), we get

$$\frac{V_1}{V_2} = \frac{N_1}{N_2} \tag{6.96}$$

This equation shows that the ratio of the induced emf in the two windings is equal to the ratio of their turns. In case of ideal transformer, the entire power supplied by the source connected to the primary winding is delivered to the load on the secondary winding. Therefore, no power is lost in the core.

That is, $P_1 = P_2$ $\tag{6.97}$

Since $P_1 = V_1 I_1$ and $P_2 = V_2 I_2$, we have

$$\frac{V_2}{V_1} = \frac{I_1}{I_2} = \frac{N_2}{N_1} = a \tag{6.98}$$

Here, the ratio of the currents is inversely proportional to the ratio of the induced emfs.

The coils should be tightly coupled so that there should not be any leakage flux and the coefficient of coupling should be equal to one, i.e., $k = 1$. As compared to the load connected, the inductive reactances of primary and secondary windings should be extremely large.

For a transformer, the self-inductance of primary or secondary winding is proportional to the square of number of turns of coil. The turns ratio N_1/N_2 is represented by a. The relation between self-inductances and number of turns is given by

$$\frac{L_2}{L_1} = \frac{N_2^2}{N_1^2} = a^2 \tag{6.99}$$

An ideal transformer with coefficient of coupling $k = 1$ and turns ratio of N_1 to N_2 is represented by the symbol $1 : a$, in the equivalent circuit of a transformer shown in Figure 6.8.

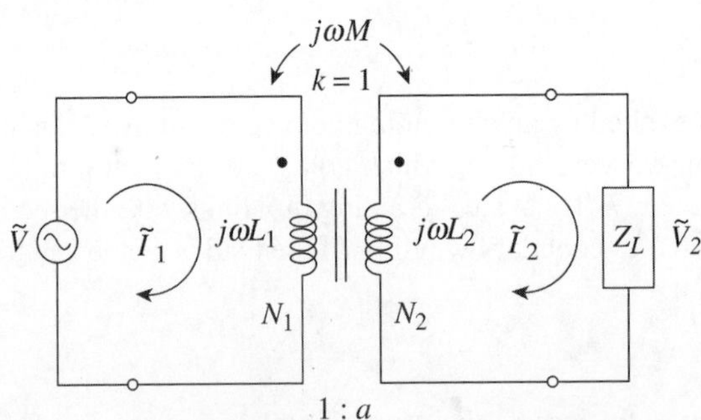

Figure 6.8 *Equivalent circuit of a transformer*

The two mesh equations are represented by

$$\tilde{V}_1 = \left(j\omega L_1\right)\tilde{I}_1 - \left(j\omega M\right)\tilde{I}_2 \tag{6.100}$$

$$0 = -\left(j\omega M\right)\tilde{I}_1 + \left(Z_L + j\omega L_2\right)\tilde{I}_2 \tag{6.101}$$

From Eq. (6.101), the current $\tilde{I}_2$ can be expressed in terms of current $\tilde{I}_1$ as

$$\tilde{I}_2 = \frac{j\omega M}{Z_L + j\omega L_2}\tilde{I}_1 \tag{6.102}$$

Substituting Eq. (6.102) in Eq. (6.100), we get

$$\tilde{V}_1 = \left(j\omega L_1\right)\tilde{I}_1 - \left(j\omega M\right)\left[\frac{j\omega M}{Z_L + j\omega L_2}\right]\tilde{I}_1$$

$$= \left(j\omega L_1\right)\tilde{I}_1 + \frac{\omega^2 M^2}{Z_L + j\omega L_2}\tilde{I}_1$$

$$= \left[j\omega L_1 + \frac{\omega^2 M^2}{Z_L + j\omega L_2}\right]\tilde{I}_1 \tag{6.103}$$

The input impedance of an ideal transformer is given by

$$Z_{in} = \frac{\tilde{V}_1}{\tilde{I}_1}$$

Therefore, $\quad Z_{in} = j\omega L_1 + \dfrac{\omega^2 M^2}{Z_L + j\omega L_2} \tag{6.104}$

According to the standard assumptions of an ideal transformer, the coefficient of coupling, $k = 1$.

Therefore, $\quad M = \sqrt{L_1 L_2}$ (or) $\quad M^2 = L_1 L_2$

Substituting the value of M^2 in Eq. (6.104), we get

$$Z_{in} = j\omega L_1 + \frac{\omega^2 L_1 L_2}{Z_L + j\omega L_2} = \frac{j\omega L_1\left(Z_L + j\omega L_2\right) + \omega^2 L_1 L_2}{Z_L + j\omega L_2}$$

$$= \frac{jZ_L \omega L_1 - \omega^2 L_1 L_2 + \omega^2 L_1 L_2}{Z_L + j\omega L_2}$$

$$= \frac{\left(j\omega L_1\right)Z_L}{Z_L + j\omega L_2} \tag{6.105}$$

We know that, $\dfrac{L_2}{L_1} = a^2$ (or) $\quad L_2 = a^2 L_1$

Substituting the value of L_2 in Eq. (6.105), we get

$$Z_{in} = \frac{\left(j\omega L_1\right)Z_L}{Z_L + j\omega a^2 L_1} \tag{6.106}$$

Assume that, L_1 is very large when compared to Z_L. Hence, neglecting Z_L in the denominator term of the above expression, we have

$$Z_{in} = \frac{j\omega L_1}{j\omega a^2 L_1} Z_L$$

Therefore, $$Z_{in} = \left(\frac{1}{a^2}\right) Z_L = \left(\frac{N_1}{N_2}\right)^2 Z_L \tag{6.107}$$

and $$Z_L = \left(\frac{N_2}{N_1}\right)^2 Z_{in} \tag{6.108}$$

Thus, an ideal transformer transforms only the magnitude of the impedance and not the phase angle. The efficiency of the transformer is simply the ratio of the power output to the power input.

6.13.2 Betatron

Betatron is a type of particle accelerator which makes use of the electric field induced by a time-varying magnetic field in order to accelerate the electrons, i.e., beta particles to high speeds in a circular orbit. Modern betatron designs are compact and are used to produce high-energy X-ray beams for a variety of applications.

Figure 6.9 (a) shows the schematic of a betatron consists of a vacuum glass tube formed into a circular loop and embedded in an electromagnet in which the windings are parallel to the loop. An alternating electric current in these windings produces a time-varying magnetic field that periodically changes in direction. During one quarter of the alternating current cycle, the direction and magnetic flux density $\vec{B}$ as well as the rate of change of the field inside the orbit have values appropriate for accelerating electrons in one direction.

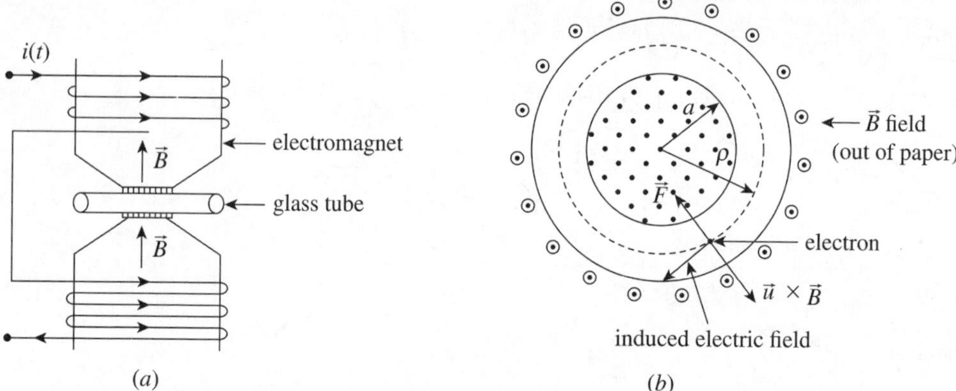

Figure 6.9 *Betatron: (a) schematic and (b) force experienced by an electron in a betatron with velocity $\vec{u}$*

From Maxwell's equations, we have

$$\oint_l \vec{E} \cdot d\vec{l} = -\int_s \frac{\partial \vec{B}}{\partial t} \cdot d\vec{s} \tag{6.109}$$

The acceleration of electrons is controlled by two forces, one acting in the direction of the motion of the electrons and the other at right angles to that direction. The force in the direction of electron motion is exerted by the electric field produced through induction by the strengthening of the magnetic field within the circle. This force will accelerate the electrons. The second perpendicular force arises as the electrons move through the magnetic field and it maintains the electrons in a circular orbit within the closed loop as shown in Figure 6.9(b).

For a circular loop of constant radius a, Eq. (6.109) becomes

$$E_\phi = -\frac{1}{2\pi a}\frac{d\Phi}{dt} \qquad \left(\text{since } \Phi = \int_s \vec{B}\cdot d\vec{s} = B\int_0^a \rho\, d\rho \int_0^{2\pi} d\phi\right)$$

Here, the electric field is along the azimuthal (ϕ) direction and Φ is the total flux passing through the surface bounded by the circular loop.

The force exerted on the electron by the electric field intensity $\vec{E}$ is

$$F_\phi = -QE_\phi = \frac{Q}{2\pi a}\frac{d\Phi}{dt} \tag{6.110}$$

where Q is the magnitude of the charge on the electron. From Newton's second law of motion, the rate of change of momentum p is equal to the force exerted on the electron.

That is, $\quad \dfrac{dp}{dt} = \dfrac{Q}{2\pi a}\dfrac{d\Phi}{dt}$

The gain in momentum at any time t is given by

$$p = \frac{Q\Phi}{2\pi a} \tag{6.111}$$

To maintain a circular orbit for electron at a constant radius a, the centripetal force acting on the electron must be equal in magnitude and opposite in direction to the Lorentz force.

That is, $\quad \dfrac{mu^2}{a} = QBu$

or $\qquad\qquad mu = QBa \tag{6.112}$

where m is the mass of the electron.

Since the momentum of electron $p = mu$, equating Eqs. (6.111) and (6.112), we get

$$mu = \frac{Q\Phi}{2\pi a} = QBa$$

That is, $\quad B = \dfrac{\Phi}{2\pi a^2} \tag{6.113}$

The average magnetic flux density in free space is

$$B_0 = \frac{\Phi}{\pi a^2} \tag{6.114}$$

Comparing Eqs. (6.113) and (6.114), we get

$$B = \frac{1}{2}B_0 \tag{6.115}$$

Here, the magnetic flux density at a radius a is equal to one half of its average value. This is known as *betatron condition*.

At the beginning of the appropriate quarter-cycle, electrons are injected into the betatron, where they make lakhs of orbits and they gain energy in moving through the orbits. At the end of the quarter-cycle, the electrons are deflected onto a target to produce X-rays or other high-energy phenomena. Large betatron can impart electron beams with energies greater than 400 mega electron volts (MeV) for use in particle-physics research.

REVIEW QUESTIONS

1. Describe the fundamental relations between electrostatic and magnetostatic fields.

2. State Faraday's law for induced emf.

3. State Lenz's law.

4. Derive an expression for emf induced in terms of electric field and magnetic flux density.

5. Explain Faraday's law of electromagnetic induction and derive the expression for induced emf.

6. Define transformer emf and motional emf.

7. Explain about stationary loop in time-varying magnetic field and moving loop in static magnetic field.

8. Write an expression for an induced emf when a moving closed path is placed in a time-varying magnetic field.

9. The sides of a square loop in the $z = 0$ plane are located at $x = \pm 0.5\,\text{m}$ and $y = \pm 5\,\text{m}$. There exists a uniform time-varying magnetic field given by $\vec{B} = \left(0.2\vec{a}_x - 0.4\vec{a}_y + 0.8\vec{a}_z\right)\cos 3000t\ \text{Wb/m}^2$. If the total resistance of square loop is $1\,\text{k}\Omega$, find the current through the loop.

10. A rectangular loop of length $a = 1$ m and width $b = 80$ cm is placed in a uniform magnetic field. Calculate the maximum value of induced emf if the magnetic flux density $B = 0.1\,\text{Wb/m}^2$ is constant and the loop rotates with a frequency of 50 Hz.

11. Explain induced emf and derive the expressions for statically and dynamically induced emfs.

12. A conductor of 1 m length moving with a velocity of 100 m/s is perpendicular to a magnetic flux density of 1 T. What is the value of emf induced?

13. A straight conductor of 0.4 m lies on the x-axis with one end at the origin. The conductor is subjected to a magnetic flux density $\vec{B} = 0.05\,\vec{a}_y\,\text{T}$ and the velocity $\vec{u} = 4.5\sin^3 t\,\vec{a}_z$ m/s. Calculate the motional electric field intensity and emf induced in the conductor.

14. Explain the terms (*i*) motional emf and (*ii*) static emf.

15. A square coil with a loop area 0.02 m^2 and 100 turns is rotated about its axis at right angle to a uniform magnetic field, $B = 2$ T. Calculate the instantaneous value of emf induced in the coil when its plane is (*i*) at right angle to the field, (*ii*) in the plane of the field, and (*iii*) when the plane of the coil is 45° to the field.

16. Calculate the emf induced across a solenoid of 1 mH when a current increasing at the rate of 2 ampere per second flows through the solenoid.

17. Explain Faraday's law and Ampere's law.

18. What is displacement current? Obtain an expression for the same.

19. Give the relationship between conduction current density and displacement current density.

20. Explain the significance of displacement current with an example.

21. Give the expressions for conduction and displacement current densities.

22. Explain the concept of displacement current and obtain an expression for the displacement current density.

23. Show that, for a capacitor, the conduction current in the wire equals the displacement current in the dielectric if subjected to a time-varying field.

24. A voltage of $v(t) = 0.1\sin 120\pi t$ V is applied to a capacitor of 1 pF. Find the displacement current at $t = 0$.

25. A capacitor has a capacitance of 1.5 pF. Find the displacement current at $t = 0$, if a voltage of $5\sin 100\pi t$ is applied to it.

26. In a time-varying field, how do you define a good conductor and a lossy dielectric material?

27. What are the general statements about electromagnetic boundary conditions?

28. Write down the boundary conditions for fields between a dielectric (medium 1) and a perfect conductor (medium 2) in time-varying case.

29. Derive the boundary conditions for electric and magnetic fields in the time-varying case for two different dielectrics separated by a sharp boundary.

30. Show that the normal components of $\vec{B}$ is continuous for conductors.

31. Show that the tangential component of $\vec{H}$ is discontinuous for conductors.

32. Derive the boundary conditions for $\vec{D}$ and $\vec{H}$ in the time-varying case for two different dielectric media having distinct values of μ and ε and separated by a sharp boundary.

33. Derive the boundary conditions at the boundary between two magnetic materials.

34. Write down the boundary conditions at the interface between different medium in both scalar and vector forms.

35. What are the salient points to be noted when the boundary conditions are applied?

36. Show that for the time-varying case,

$$\vec{E} = -\nabla V - \frac{\partial \vec{A}}{\partial t}$$

where V is the scalar potential and $\vec{A}$ is the magnetic vector potential.

37. Derive Maxwell's equations in point form and integral form using Ampere's law, Faraday's law, and Gauss's law.

38. Explain the physical significance of each of the Maxwell's equations in the time-varying case and briefly indicate how the equations were arrived at.

39. From the fundamental laws, derive Maxwell's equations and the need for Maxwell's contribution to electromagnetic theory. State the equations in both differential and integral forms.

40. Derive general field relations for time-varying electric and magnetic fields using Maxwell's equations.

41. Explain Ampere's law for time-varying fields.

42. Prove that $\nabla \times \vec{E} = \dfrac{-\partial \vec{B}}{\partial t}$.

43. Derive the expression for one of the Maxwell's equations, $\nabla \times \vec{E}$ for time-varying fields.

44. State and explain Maxwell's hypothesis.

45. Prove that modified Ampere's law is consistent with time-varying field.

46. Discuss the physical interpretation of Maxwell's equations.

47. State and explain Maxwell's equations in integral and point form in free space.

48. State Maxwell's equations for static fields. Explain how they are modified for time-varying electric and magnetic fields.

49. Write down Maxwell's curl equations.

50. Write the generalized Ampere's law and explain the significance of displacement current. Can a displacement current produce heating effect and also magnetic field around it?

51. In a copper rod of 1 mm × 1 mm cross-section, a conduction current of 1 A is flowing at a frequency of 50 Hz. Find the displacement current in the rod assuming that for copper, $\varepsilon = \varepsilon_0, \mu = \mu_0$, and $\sigma = 5.8 \times 10^7$ S/m.

52. Furnish Maxwell's equations in differential form and in integral form and explain the importance of the equations in field theory.

53. Compare field theory and circuit theory.

54. A circular loop of 10 cm radius located in the *xy*-plane is in a magnetic field. Find out the induced emf if $\vec{B} = \left(3\vec{a}_y + 4\vec{a}_z\right) \cos 377t$ T.

55. In free space, $\vec{E} = 0.5 \cos\left(10^3 t - 50x\right)\vec{a}_y$ V/m. Calculate $\vec{J}_d$ and $\vec{H}$.

56. Given $\vec{H} = 2\cos\left(\omega t - 3y\right)\vec{a}_z$ A/m in a medium characterized by $\sigma = 0, \mu = 4\mu_0$ and $\varepsilon = 10\varepsilon_0$. Determine $\vec{E}$.

57. For a medium with $\sigma = 5 \times 10^3$ S/m and $\varepsilon_r = 40$, determine the frequency at which the conduction current density is equal to the displacement current density.

58. Determine the amplitude of the displacement current density in air space within a large power transformer where $\vec{H} = 10^6 \cos\left(377t + 1.2566 \times 10^{-6} z\right)\vec{a}_y$ A/m.

59. Find the amplitude of the displacement current density inside a typical metallic conductor where $\sigma = 6 \times 10^7$ S/m, $f = 1$kHz, and $\varepsilon_r = 1$.

60. Find the displacement current within a parallel-plate capacitor, where $\varepsilon_r = 100$, $A = 0.1\,\text{m}^2$, $d = 0.05\,\text{mm}$ and the capacitor voltage is $20\sin 500\pi t$ volts.

61. In a conducting medium, $\vec{H} = y^2 z\vec{a}_x + 2(x+1)yz\,\vec{a}_y - (x+1)z^2\vec{a}_z$ A/m. Find the current density at $(1,0,-3)$ and calculate the current passing through the $y = 1$ plane, $0 \le x \le 1$, and $0 \le z \le 1$.

62. In free space, $\vec{D} = D_m \sin\left(\omega t + \beta t\right)\vec{a}_x$ C/m^2. Determine magnetic flux density and displacement current density.

63. The magnetic field intensity in free space is given as $\vec{H} = H_0 \cos\theta\,\vec{a}_y$ A/m where $\theta = \omega t - \beta z$ and β is a constant quantity. Determine the displacement current density.

64. A moist soil has a conductivity of 10^{-3} S/m and $\varepsilon_r = 4.5$. Find J_c and J_d, where the electric field intensity is $E = 9 \times 10^{-6} \sin\left(6 \times 10^6 t\right)$ V/m.

65. A magnetic field, $\vec{H} = 3\cos x \vec{a}_x + z \cos x \vec{a}_y$ A/m, for $z \geq 0$ is applied to a perfectly conducting surface in the xy-plane. Find the current density on the conductor surface.

66. An electric field in a medium which is source-free is given by $\vec{E} = 3.5\cos\left(10^8 t - \beta z\right)\vec{a}_x$ V/m. Determine $\vec{B}$, $\vec{H}$, and $\vec{D}$. Assume $\varepsilon_r = 1$, $\mu_r = 1$, and $\sigma = 0$.

67. A conduction current in a copper conductor is 20 A. Find the displacement current in the conductor at 100 MHz. For copper, $\varepsilon_r = 1, \mu_r = 1$, and $\sigma = 5.8 \times 10^7$ S/m.

68. Derive the Lorentz's condition for potentials.

69. Derive the non-homogeneous wave equations, which relate the vector magnetic potential $\vec{A}$ with volume current density $\vec{J}$.

70. Give the relationship between scalar potential V and volume charge density ρ_v.

71. Define retarded scalar potential and derive the expression for it.

72. Derive the expression for retarded vector potential.

73. Define retarded time.

74. Explain the concept of retarded potential.

75. What is meant by time-varying field? How are they different than static fields?

76. Give the Maxwell's equations in source-free region.

77. Write notes on time-harmonic fields.

78. Derive Maxwell's curl equations from Ampere's law and Faraday's law. Express the equations in phasor form for time-varying harmonic fields.

79. State and explain the differential and integral forms of Maxwell's equations for fields varying hormonally with time.

80. Write Maxwell's equation in point form using phasor notation and derive the wave equation from them for free space condition.

81. Starting from Maxwell's equations, derive the partial differential equations of $\vec{E}$ and $\vec{H}$ in a homogenous medium containing both charges and currents.

82. Write Helmholtz's equations in non-homogeneous medium.

83. Derive the ratio between conduction current density and displacement current density.

84. Find the frequency such that conduction current density equals the magnitude of displacement current density in a medium with $\sigma = 4 \times 10^{-3}$ S/m and $\varepsilon_r = 30$.

85. Calculate the ratio of the amplitudes of conduction current density to displacement current density for the electric field $E = E_0 \cos \omega t$ V/m in (*i*) copper $\varepsilon = \varepsilon_0$, $\sigma = 5.8 \times 10^7$ S/m, $\omega = 1000$ rad/s and (*ii*) in polystyrene $\varepsilon_r = 2.53$, $\sigma = 10^{-16}$ S/m, and $\omega = 1000$ rad/s.

86. What is the significance behind the ratio of magnitudes of the conduction current density to the displacement current density?

87. Discuss the condition under which conduction current is equal to displacement current.

88. Distinguish between conduction, convection, and displacement currents.

89. Distinguish between displacement current density and conduction current density.

90. Show that the ratio of the amplitudes of the conduction current density and displacement current density is $\dfrac{\sigma}{\omega\varepsilon}$ for the applied field $E = E_m \cos \omega t$. Assume $\mu = \mu_0$.

91. Discuss in detail about electromagnetic spectrum.

92. Write notes on the applications of time-varying fields.

93. Discuss the operation of a transformer.

94. What is ideal transformer? Describe briefly.

95. Distinguish between ideal transformer and practical transformer.

96. Explain the construction and working principle of betatron.

ELECTROMAGNETIC WAVES

7.1 INTRODUCTION

In general, the electromagnetic wave (EM wave) is a carrier of energy or information and a function of both space and time. The existence of EM waves was predicted by Maxwell, and it was formulated through his well-known Maxwell's equations. Later, Heinrich Hertz proved experimentally that Maxwell's prediction of EM wave was true and also succeeded in the generation and detection of radio waves.

The study of wave behaviour is the major concern and it begins with the derivation of wave equations. The EM wave propagation in different mediums can be best understood by applying Maxwell's equations. The wave parameters such as wavelength and velocity, the medium parameters such as propagation constant and intrinsic impedance, the concept of Poynting vector and Poynting's theorem, and the laws governing the reflection and refraction of plane waves incident normally and obliquely on a plane boundary are discussed in this chapter.

7.2 ELECTROMAGNETIC WAVE EQUATIONS

Maxwell's equations can be used to obtain wave equations considering the variations of electric and magnetic fields with respect to space and time. The generalized wave equations are obtained with the assumptions that the electric and magnetic fields are present in a linear, homogenous, isotropic, and charge-free ($\rho_v = 0$) medium with permeability μ, permittivity ε, and conductivity σ. Also, assuming that the medium obeys the Ohm's law, i.e., $\vec{J} = \sigma \vec{E}$, the Maxwell's equations are given by

$$\nabla \times \vec{E} = -\mu \frac{\partial \vec{H}}{\partial t} \tag{7.1}$$

$$\nabla \times \vec{H} = \sigma \vec{E} + \varepsilon \frac{\partial \vec{E}}{\partial t} \tag{7.2}$$

$$\nabla \cdot \vec{B} = 0 \text{ , i.e., } \nabla \cdot \vec{H} = 0 \tag{7.3}$$

$$\nabla \cdot \vec{D} = 0 \text{ , i.e., } \nabla \cdot \vec{E} = 0 \tag{7.4}$$

Taking curl on both the sides of Eq. (7.1), we get

$$\nabla \times \left(\nabla \times \vec{E} \right) = -\mu \left(\nabla \times \frac{\partial \vec{H}}{\partial t} \right) \tag{7.5}$$

Rewriting Eq. (7.5), we get

$$\nabla \times \nabla \times \vec{E} = -\mu \frac{\partial}{\partial t}\left(\nabla \times \vec{H}\right) \tag{7.6}$$

The validity of the above equation is confirmed as ∇ operator indicates differentiation with respect to space, while $\dfrac{\partial}{\partial t}$ operator indicates differentiation with respect to time. Since both the operators are independent of each other, they can be interchanged.

Substituting Eq. (7.2) in Eq. (7.6), we get

$$\nabla \times \nabla \times \vec{E} = -\mu \frac{\partial}{\partial t}\left(\sigma \vec{E} + \varepsilon \frac{\partial \vec{E}}{\partial t}\right) \tag{7.7}$$

$$\nabla \times \nabla \times \vec{E} = -\mu\sigma \frac{\partial \vec{E}}{\partial t} - \mu\varepsilon \frac{\partial^2 \vec{E}}{\partial t^2} \tag{7.8}$$

According to the vector identity, we have

$$\nabla \times \nabla \times \vec{E} = \nabla\left(\nabla \cdot \vec{E}\right) - \nabla^2 \vec{E}$$

Since $\nabla \cdot \vec{E} = 0$, the above equation can be written as

$$\nabla \times \nabla \times \vec{E} = -\nabla^2 \vec{E} \tag{7.9}$$

where $\nabla^2 \vec{E}$ is the Laplacian of $\vec{E}$ and it is defined in the rectangular coordinates as

$$\nabla^2 \vec{E} = \left(\frac{\partial^2}{\partial x^2} + \frac{\partial^2}{\partial y^2} + \frac{\partial^2}{\partial z^2}\right)\vec{E}$$

Substituting Eq. (7.9) in Eq. (7.8), we get

$$-\nabla^2 \vec{E} = -\mu\sigma \frac{\partial \vec{E}}{\partial t} - \mu\varepsilon \frac{\partial^2 \vec{E}}{\partial t^2}$$

That is,

$$\nabla^2 \vec{E} = \mu\sigma \frac{\partial \vec{E}}{\partial t} + \mu\varepsilon \frac{\partial^2 \vec{E}}{\partial t^2} \tag{7.10}$$

The above equation is the general wave equation for the electric field $\vec{E}$. It can be decomposed into three one-dimensional, homogeneous, scalar wave equations and the solution of each component of $\vec{E}$ represents waves. Replacing $\dfrac{\partial}{\partial t}$ by $j\omega$, the above equation can be written in phasor domain as

$$\nabla^2 \tilde{E} = \mu\sigma\left(j\omega\right)\tilde{E} + \mu\varepsilon\left(j\omega\right)^2 \tilde{E}$$

$$= j\omega\mu\left(\sigma + j\omega\varepsilon\right)\tilde{E}$$

That is,

$$\nabla^2 \tilde{E} - \gamma^2 \tilde{E} = 0 \tag{7.11}$$

where $\gamma^2 = j\omega\mu\left(\sigma + j\omega\varepsilon\right)$ and γ is called the propagation constant (in m^{-1}) of the medium.

Similarly, the wave equation for $\vec{H}$ can be obtained by taking curl on both the sides of Eq. (7.2), we get

$$\nabla \times \left(\nabla \times \vec{H} \right) = \nabla \times \left(\sigma \vec{E} \right) + \varepsilon \left(\nabla \times \frac{\partial \vec{E}}{\partial t} \right) \tag{7.12}$$

Rearranging the above equation, we have

$$\nabla \times \nabla \times \vec{H} = \sigma \left(\nabla \times \vec{E} \right) + \varepsilon \frac{\partial}{\partial t} \left(\nabla \times \vec{E} \right) \tag{7.13}$$

Substituting Eq. (7.1) in Eq. (7.13) and rearranging, we get

$$\nabla \times \nabla \times \vec{H} = \sigma \left(-\mu \frac{\partial \vec{H}}{\partial t} \right) + \varepsilon \left(-\mu \frac{\partial^2 \vec{H}}{\partial t^2} \right)$$

Therefore,

$$\nabla \times \nabla \times \vec{H} = -\mu\sigma \frac{\partial \vec{H}}{\partial t} - \mu\varepsilon \frac{\partial^2 \vec{H}}{\partial t^2} \tag{7.14}$$

According to the vector identity, we have

$$\nabla \times \nabla \times \vec{H} = \nabla \left(\nabla \cdot \vec{H} \right) - \nabla^2 \vec{H}$$

Since $\nabla \cdot \vec{H} = 0$, the above equation can be written as

$$\nabla \times \nabla \times \vec{H} = -\nabla^2 \vec{H} \tag{7.15}$$

Substituting Eq. (7.15) in Eq. (7.14), we get

$$-\nabla^2 \vec{H} = -\mu\sigma \frac{\partial \vec{H}}{\partial t} - \mu\varepsilon \frac{\partial^2 \vec{H}}{\partial t^2}$$

That is,

$$\nabla^2 \vec{H} = \mu\sigma \frac{\partial \vec{H}}{\partial t} + \mu\varepsilon \frac{\partial^2 \vec{H}}{\partial t^2} \tag{7.16}$$

The above equation is the general wave equation for the magnetic field $\vec{H}$. It can also be decomposed into three one-dimensional, homogeneous, scalar wave equations and the solution of each component of $\vec{H}$ represents waves. Replacing $\frac{\partial}{\partial t}$ by $j\omega$, the above equation in phasor domain is

$$\nabla^2 \tilde{H} = j\omega\mu \left(\sigma + j\omega\varepsilon \right) \tilde{H}$$

That is,

$$\nabla^2 \tilde{H} - \gamma^2 \tilde{H} = 0 \tag{7.17}$$

where $\gamma^2 = j\omega\mu \left(\sigma + j\omega\varepsilon \right)$ and γ is called the propagation constant (in m^{-1}) of the medium. Equations (7.11) and (7.17) are also known as *homogeneous vector Helmholtz's equations or wave equations* in phasor form.

7.3 WAVE PARAMETERS

The electric field of a plane wave travelling in "+z"-direction in time domain is represented by

$$\vec{E}(z,t) = E_0 e^{-\alpha z} \cos(\omega t - \beta z)\vec{a}_x \tag{7.18}$$

where E_0 is the amplitude of the wave, $(\omega t - \beta z)$ is the phase of the wave in radian, ω is the angular frequency in rad/s and β is the phase constant or wave number in rad/m. The phase of the wave depends on time t and space variable z.

For a general medium, the *propagation constant* γ is defined per unit length of the medium and is a complex value given by

$$\gamma = \alpha + j\beta$$

where α is the attenuation constant of the medium in neper per metre (Np/m) and β is the phase constant in rad/m. This phase constant is also referred as the wave number k.

For a wave travelling in "+z"-direction, the phase of the wave is

$$\omega t - \beta z = \text{constant} \tag{7.19}$$

Differentiating the above equation with respect to time, we get

$$\omega - \beta \frac{\partial z}{\partial t} = 0 \tag{7.20}$$

Hence,

$$\frac{\partial z}{\partial t} = \frac{\omega}{\beta} = u_p \tag{7.21}$$

where u_p represents the *phase velocity* or the *velocity of propagation* of the wave in the medium in metre/second (m/s). Since $\omega = 2\pi f$, the phase constant can be written as

$$\beta = \frac{\omega}{u_p} = \frac{2\pi}{\lambda} \tag{7.22}$$

where λ is called wavelength and it is defined as the distance travelled by the wave along the medium while the phase angle is changing through 2π radian. Substituting Eq. (7.22) in Eq. (7.21), we get

$$u_p = f\lambda \tag{7.23}$$

The phase velocity is also determined by the constitutive parameters μ and ε of the medium. If the medium is free space or vacuum, $\mu = \mu_0$ and $\varepsilon = \varepsilon_0$, then the phase velocity is given by

$$u_p = c = \frac{1}{\sqrt{\mu_0 \varepsilon_0}} = 3 \times 10^8 \, \text{m/s}$$

where c is the velocity of light.

The *intrinsic impedance* η of the medium is defined as the ratio of magnitude of electric field $\vec{E}$ to magnetic field $\vec{H}$ in the medium. Its unit is ohm (Ω).

That is,

$$\eta = \frac{|\vec{E}|}{|\vec{H}|} \tag{7.24}$$

Using Eqs. (7.18) and (7.24), the magnetic field of a plane wave travelling in "+z"-direction can be written in time domain as

$$\vec{H}(z,t) = H_0 e^{-\alpha z} \cos(\omega t - \beta z)\vec{a}_y \tag{7.25}$$

where

$$H_0 = \frac{E_0}{|\eta|}$$

For free space, the intrinsic impedance η_0 is

$$\eta_0 = \sqrt{\frac{\mu_0}{\varepsilon_0}} = 120\pi = 377\,\Omega$$

EXAMPLE 7.1

A uniform plane wave with $\vec{E} = E_x \vec{a}_x$ propagates in a lossless simple $(\varepsilon_r = 16, \mu_r = 1 \text{ and } \sigma = 0)$ in the "+z"-direction. Assume E_x is sinusoidal with a frequency of 100 MHz and has a maximum value of 10^{-8} V/m at $t = 0$ and $z = \frac{1}{4}$ m .

  (*i*) Write the instantaneous expression for $\vec{E}$ for any t and z .

  (*ii*) Write the instantaneous expression for $\vec{H}$.

  (*iii*) Sketch the $\vec{E}$ and $\vec{H}$ fields of a uniform plane wave at $t = 0$.

SOLUTION

Given $\vec{E} = E_x \vec{a}_x$, $\varepsilon_r = 16$, $\mu_r = 1$, $f = 100\,\text{MHz}$, $\alpha = 0$ and $\sigma = 0$ in a lossless medium.

The phase constant is

$$\beta = \omega\sqrt{\mu\varepsilon} = \omega\sqrt{\mu_0\varepsilon_0}\sqrt{\mu_r\varepsilon_r} = \frac{\omega}{c}\sqrt{\mu_r\varepsilon_r}$$

$$= \frac{2\pi \times 10^8}{3 \times 10^8}\sqrt{16} = \frac{8\pi}{3}\,\text{rad/m}$$

where $c = \dfrac{1}{\sqrt{\mu_0\varepsilon_0}} = 3 \times 10^8\,\text{m/s}$

  (*i*) Using $\cos\omega t$ as the reference, the instantaneous expression for $\vec{E}$ can be written as

$$\vec{E}(z,t) = E_x \cos(\omega t - \beta z + \phi)\vec{a}_x$$

$$= 10^{-8}\cos\left(2\pi \times 10^8 t - \beta z + \phi\right)\vec{a}_z$$

When the argument of the above cosine function becomes zero, the electric field will be maximum, i.e., $E_x = 10^{-8}$.

Therefore,

$$2\pi \times 10^8 t - \beta z + \phi = 0$$

At $t = 0$ and $z = \dfrac{1}{4}$, we have

$$\phi = \beta z = \left(\frac{8\pi}{3}\right)\left(\frac{1}{4}\right) = \frac{2\pi}{3}\ \text{rad}$$

Therefore, the instantaneous expression for electric field is

$$\vec{E}(z,t) = 10^{-8} \cos\left(2\pi \times 10^8 t - \frac{8\pi}{3}z + \frac{2\pi}{3}\right)\vec{a}_x$$

$$= 10^{-8} \cos\left[2\pi \times 10^8 t - \frac{8\pi}{3}\left(z - \frac{1}{4}\right)\right]\vec{a}_x\ \text{V/m}$$

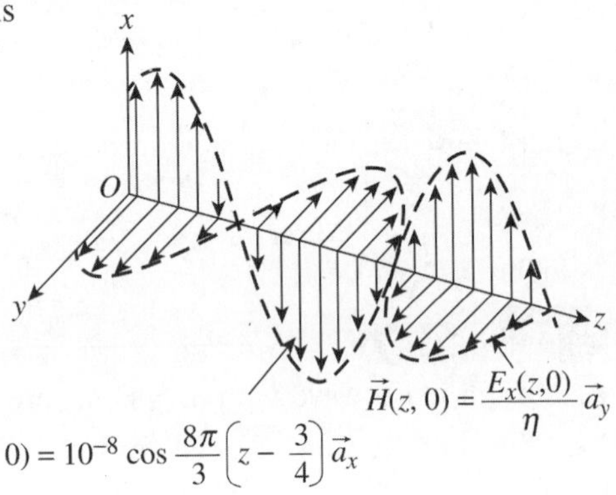

(*ii*) The magnetic field $\vec{H}$ is

$$\vec{H} = H_y \vec{a}_y = \frac{E_x}{\eta}\vec{a}_y$$

where

$$\eta = \sqrt{\frac{\mu}{\varepsilon}} = \sqrt{\frac{\mu_0}{\varepsilon_0}}\sqrt{\frac{\mu_r}{\varepsilon_r}} = \frac{\eta_0}{\sqrt{\varepsilon_r}} = \frac{120\pi}{\sqrt{16}} = 30\pi\ \Omega$$

Hence, $\vec{H}(z,t) = \dfrac{10^{-8}}{30\pi}\cos\left[2\pi \times 10^8 t - \dfrac{8\pi}{3}\left(z - \dfrac{1}{4}\right)\right]\vec{a}_y\ \text{A/m}$

Figure E7.1

(*iii*) Figure E7.1 shows the electric field $\vec{E}$ and magnetic field $\vec{H}$ of a uniform plane wave propagating in a lossless medium. $\square$

<hr>

EXAMPLE 7.2

The electric field in free space is given by $\vec{E} = 100 \cos\left(10^8 t + \beta x\right)\vec{a}_y\ \text{V/m}$. (*i*) Find the direction of wave propagation. (*ii*) Calculate β, λ and the time taken to travel a distance of $\lambda / 2$. (*iii*) Sketch the wave at $t = 0$, $T / 4$ and $T / 2$.

SOLUTION

Given $\vec{E} = 100 \cos\left(10^8 t + \beta x\right)\vec{a}_y\ \text{V/m}$.

(*i*) Here, the positive sign in $\left(\omega t + \beta x\right)$ shows that the wave is propagating in $-$ve x-direction.

(*ii*) The phase constant and the wavelength are

$$\beta = \frac{\omega}{u} = \frac{\omega}{c} = \frac{10^8}{3 \times 10^8} = \frac{1}{3}\ \text{rad/m}$$

$$\lambda = \frac{2\pi}{\beta} = 6\pi\ \text{m}$$

where $u = c$ in free space.

If T is the period of the wave, it takes T sec to travel a distance λ at the speed of c.

Therefore, the time taken to travel a distance of $\lambda / 2$ is

$$t_1 = \frac{T}{2} = \frac{1}{2}\frac{2\pi}{\omega} = \frac{\pi}{10^8} = 31.42\ \text{ns}$$

where

$$T = \frac{1}{f} = \frac{2\pi}{\omega}$$

(*iii*) At $t = 0$, $E_y = 100\cos\beta x$

$$\text{At } t = \frac{T}{4}, \ E_y = 100\cos\left(\omega \cdot \frac{2\pi}{4\omega} + \beta x\right) = 100\cos\left(\beta x + \frac{\pi}{2}\right) = -100\sin\beta x$$

$$\text{At } t = \frac{T}{2}, \ E_y = 100\cos\left(\omega \cdot \frac{2\pi}{2\omega} + \beta x\right) = 100\cos\left(\beta x + \pi\right) = -100\cos\beta x$$

Figure E7.2 shows that E_y is plotted against x at $t = 0$, $T/4$ and $T/2$. Note that a point P on the wave moves along $-x$ as t increases with time, i.e., the wave travels along negative x-direction.

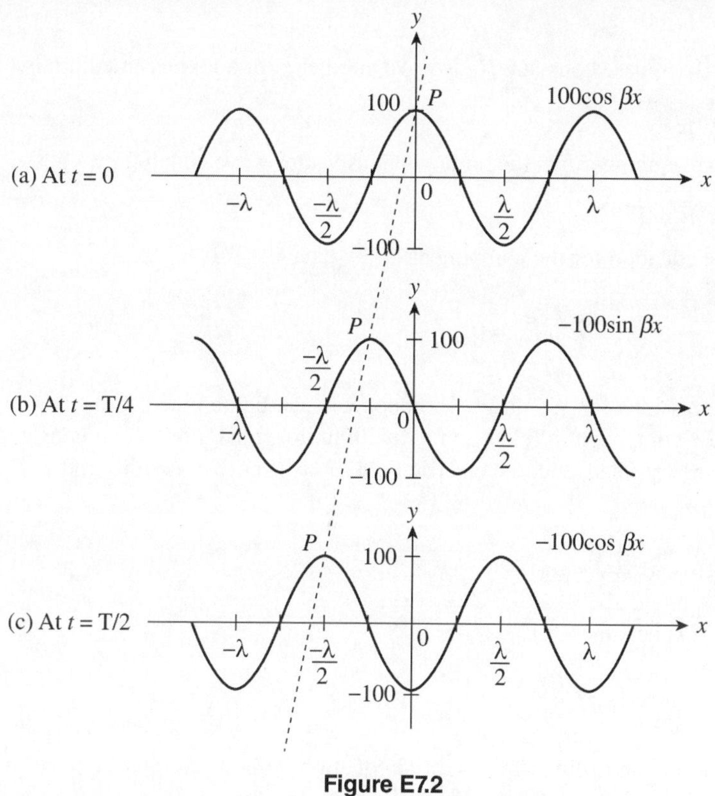

Figure E7.2

7.4 PLANE WAVE PROPAGATION

One of the important applications of Maxwell's equations is mainly related to the problem of EM wave propagation. A uniform plane wave, an important fundamental phenomenon of electromagnetics, represents the simplest case and it is a particular solution of Maxwell's equations with electric and magnetic fields having uniform properties at all points in a plane.

The propagation properties of an EM wave, i.e., velocity and wavelength are generally characterized by the constitutive parameters μ, ε and σ of the medium and the angular velocity ω. The EM wave propagation can be obtained by solving the Maxwell's equations in the following mediums:

(i) Lossless dielectrics,

(ii) Lossy dielectrics,

(iii) Free space, and

(iv) Good conductors

7.4.1 Wave Propagation in Lossless Dielectrics

For a lossless dielectric medium, the wave propagates without any attenuation as the conductivity is zero in the medium, i.e., $\sigma = 0$. From Eq. (7.11), the phasor form of homogeneous vector wave equation in a lossless medium is represented by

$$\nabla^2 \tilde{E} - \gamma^2 \tilde{E} = 0$$

where $\gamma^2 = -\omega^2 \mu\varepsilon$. The phase constant β or wave number k for a lossless medium is

$$\beta = k = \omega\sqrt{\mu\varepsilon}$$

Substituting the wave number k in the homogeneous vector wave equation, we get

$$\nabla^2 \tilde{E} + k^2 \tilde{E} = 0 \tag{7.26}$$

Writing the above equation for the component $\tilde{E}_x$, we have

$$\left(\frac{\partial^2}{\partial x^2} + \frac{\partial^2}{\partial y^2} + \frac{\partial^2}{\partial z^2} + k^2 \right) \tilde{E}_x = 0 \tag{7.27}$$

Similarly, the expressions for $\tilde{E}_y$ and $\tilde{E}_z$ components can be obtained. Consider a uniform plane wave characterized by the x-component of electric field with uniform magnitude and constant phase over a plane surface perpendicular to z. Therefore, the electric field $\tilde{E}$ does not vary with x and y.

That is,

$$\frac{\partial^2 \tilde{E}_x}{\partial x^2} = 0 \ \text{ and } \ \frac{\partial^2 \tilde{E}_x}{\partial y^2} = 0$$

Therefore, Eq. (7.27) becomes

$$\frac{\partial^2 \tilde{E}_x}{\partial z^2} + k^2 \tilde{E}_x = 0 \tag{7.28}$$

The above equation is an ordinary differential equation with $\tilde{E}_x$ in phasor form, depending only on z. Therefore, the general solution for the above equation is given by

$$\tilde{E}_x(z) = \tilde{E}_x^+(z) + \tilde{E}_x^-(z) = E_{x0}^+ e^{-jkz} + E_{x0}^- e^{jkz} \tag{7.29}$$

where E_{x0}^+ and E_{x0}^- are arbitrary constants that can be determined by boundary conditions. The solution given by Eq. (7.29) consists of negative exponential component with e^{-jkz}, which represents a wave with amplitude E_{x0}^+ travelling in the positive z-direction. The second term with e^{jkz} represents a wave with amplitude E_{x0}^- travelling in the negative z-direction.

The first phasor term on the right-hand side of Eq. (7.29) can be represented in time domain as

$$E_x^+(z,t) = \text{Re}\left[\tilde{E}_x^+(z)e^{j\omega t}\right] = \text{Re}\left[E_{x0}^+ e^{j(\omega t - kz)}\right]$$

$$= E_{x0}^+ \cos(\omega t - kz) \tag{7.30}$$

Figure 7.1 represents the electric field waveform for different values of t and $E_{x0}^+ \cos kz$ is a cosine curve with amplitude E_{x0}^+ at $t = 0$. The wave travelling in the positive z-direction at successive times is called a travelling wave.

For a wave travelling in the "$+z$"- direction, the phase of the wave is

$$\omega t - kz = \text{constant} \tag{7.31}$$

Differentiating the above equation with respect to time, we get

$$\omega - k\frac{\partial z}{\partial t} = 0$$

Therefore,

$$u_p = \frac{\partial z}{\partial t} = \frac{\omega}{k} \tag{7.32}$$

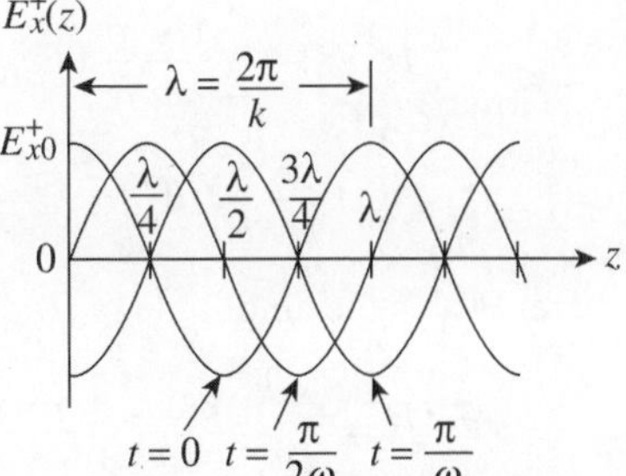

Figure 7.1 *Electric field wave propagating in "+z"-direction*

where u_p represents the phase velocity of the wave in the lossless medium. Since $\omega = 2\pi f$, the wave number can be written as

$$k = \frac{\omega}{u_p} = \frac{2\pi f}{f\lambda} = \frac{2\pi}{\lambda} \text{ or } \lambda = \frac{2\pi}{k}$$

where λ is called wavelength. Similarly, the second term on the right side of Eq. (7.29) represents a cosine wave travelling in the negative z-direction with the same velocity.

Let us consider that the wave travels only in the positive z-direction, i.e., $E_{x0}^- = 0$. Therefore, the electric field can be written as

$$\tilde{E}(z) = \tilde{E}_x^+(z)\vec{a}_x = E_{x0}^+ e^{-jkz}\vec{a}_x \tag{7.33}$$

With $\tilde{E}_y = \tilde{E}_z = 0$, the associated magnetic field can be obtained from Faraday's law as

$$\nabla \times \vec{E} = -j\omega\mu\tilde{H}$$

That is,

$$\nabla \times \vec{E} = \begin{vmatrix} \vec{a}_x & \vec{a}_y & \vec{a}_z \\ \dfrac{\partial}{\partial x} & \dfrac{\partial}{\partial y} & \dfrac{\partial}{\partial z} \\ \tilde{E}_x^+(z) & 0 & 0 \end{vmatrix} = -j\omega\mu\left(\tilde{H}_x\vec{a}_x + \tilde{H}_y\vec{a}_y + \tilde{H}_z\vec{a}_z\right)$$

$$(0)\vec{a}_x + \frac{\partial \tilde{E}_x^+(z)}{\partial z}\vec{a}_y - \frac{\partial \tilde{E}_x^+(z)}{\partial y}\vec{a}_z = -j\omega\mu\left(\tilde{H}_x\vec{a}_x + \tilde{H}_y\vec{a}_y + \tilde{H}_z\vec{a}_z\right) \tag{7.34}$$

Equating the x, y, and z-components of the fields on both sides of the above equation, we get

$$\tilde{H}_x = 0 \tag{7.35a}$$

$$\tilde{H}_y = \frac{1}{-j\omega\mu} \frac{\partial \tilde{E}_x^+(z)}{\partial z} \tag{7.35b}$$

$$\tilde{H}_z = \frac{1}{j\omega\mu} \frac{\partial \tilde{E}_x^+(z)}{\partial y} = 0 \tag{7.35c}$$

Therefore, $\tilde{H}_y$ is the only non-zero component of magnetic field.

Substituting Eq. (7.33) in Eq. (7.35b), we get

$$\tilde{H}_y(z) = \frac{1}{-j\omega\mu} \frac{\partial}{\partial z}\left(E_{x0}^+ e^{-jkz}\right) = \frac{E_{x0}^+}{-j\omega\mu}(-jk)\left(e^{-jkz}\right)$$

$$= \frac{k}{\omega\mu} E_{x0}^+ e^{-jkz} = H_{y0}^+ e^{-jkz} \tag{7.36}$$

where H_{y0}^+ is the amplitude of $\tilde{H}_y(z)$. Therefore,

$$H_{y0}^+ = \frac{k}{\omega\mu} E_{x0}^+ = \frac{1}{\eta} E_{x0}^+ \tag{7.37}$$

where η is the intrinsic impedance of a lossless medium as defined by

$$\eta = \frac{E_{x0}^+}{H_{y0}^+} = \frac{\omega\mu}{k} = \frac{\omega\mu}{\omega\sqrt{\mu\varepsilon}} = \sqrt{\frac{\mu}{\varepsilon}} \qquad \left(\text{since } k = \omega\sqrt{\mu\varepsilon}\right)$$

Hence, for a uniform plane wave, the ratio of the amplitudes of electric field to magnetic field represents the intrinsic impedance of the medium in ohm (Ω).

Therefore, the electric and magnetic fields in phasor form are summarized as

$$\tilde{E}(z) = \tilde{E}_x^+(z)\vec{a}_x = E_{x0}^+ e^{-jkz}\vec{a}_x \tag{7.38}$$

$$\tilde{H}(z) = \tilde{H}_y^+(z)\vec{a}_y = \frac{\tilde{E}_x^+(z)}{\eta}\vec{a}_y = \frac{E_{x0}^+}{\eta} e^{-jkz}\vec{a}_y \tag{7.39}$$

The electric and magnetic fields in time domain are given by

$$\vec{E}(z,t) = \text{Re}\left[\tilde{E}(z)e^{j\omega t}\right] = E_{x0}^+ \cos(\omega t - kz)\vec{a}_x \tag{7.40}$$

$$\vec{H}(z,t) = \text{Re}\left[\tilde{H}(z)e^{j\omega t}\right] = \frac{E_{x0}^+}{\eta} \cos(\omega t - kz)\vec{a}_y \tag{7.41}$$

If the fields are represented by amplitude E_{x0}^+ and phase angle ϕ, the instantaneous form of fields given in Eqs. (7.40) and (7.41) can also be written as

$$\vec{E}(z,t) = E_{x0}^+ \cos(\omega t - kz + \phi)\vec{a}_x \tag{7.42}$$

$$\vec{H}(z,t) = \frac{E_{x0}^+}{\eta} \cos(\omega t - kz + \phi)\vec{a}_y \tag{7.43}$$

From the above two equations, it is evident that the electric and magnetic fields are perpendicular to each other and both are transverse to the direction of wave propagation. Such directional properties result in a

Transverse Electro Magnetic (TEM) wave. The waves travelling along coaxial cables and waves radiated by antennas are examples of TEM waves. The above equations show that both $\vec{E}$ and $\vec{H}$ depend on z and t and they are said to be in phase. This in-phase property is the characteristic of waves propagating in lossless medium.

The electric field intensity for a uniform plane wave propagating in the positive z-direction can be written in phasor form as

$$\tilde{E}(z) = \vec{E}_0 e^{-jkz}$$

where $\vec{E}_0 = E_{x0}\vec{a}_x$ is a vector with magnitude E_{x0} and direction along x.

In general,

$$\tilde{E}(x,y,z) = \vec{E}_0 e^{-jk_x x - jk_y y - jk_z z} \tag{7.44}$$

The above equation satisfies the homogeneous Helmholtz's equation, provided that

$$k_x^2 + k_y^2 + k_z^2 = \omega^2 \mu\varepsilon$$

If the wave number vector is defined as

$$\vec{k} = k_x\vec{a}_x + k_y\vec{a}_y + k_z\vec{a}_z \tag{7.45}$$

and the radius vector as

$$\vec{r} = x\vec{a}_x + y\vec{a}_y + z\vec{a}_z \tag{7.46}$$

then Eq. (7.44) can be written as

$$\tilde{E}(r) = \vec{E}_0 e^{-j(\vec{k}\cdot\vec{r})} = \vec{E}_0 e^{-j(k\vec{a}_n\cdot\vec{r})} \; \text{V/m} \tag{7.47}$$

where $\vec{a}_n$ is the unit vector in the direction of propagation. Since $\nabla\cdot\tilde{E} = 0$ in a charge-free region, the divergence of the above electric field also becomes zero.

That is,

$$\nabla\cdot\left(\vec{E}_0 e^{-jk\vec{a}_n\cdot\vec{r}}\right) = 0$$

$$\vec{E}_0 \cdot \nabla\left(e^{-jk\vec{a}_n\cdot\vec{r}}\right) = 0 \tag{7.48}$$

But

$$\nabla\left(e^{-jk\vec{a}_n\cdot\vec{r}}\right) = \left(\vec{a}_x\frac{\partial}{\partial x} + \vec{a}_y\frac{\partial}{\partial y} + \vec{a}_z\frac{\partial}{\partial z}\right)e^{-j(k_x x + k_y y + k_z z)}$$

$$= -j\left(k_x\vec{a}_x + k_y\vec{a}_y + k_z\vec{a}_z\right)e^{-j(k_x x + k_y y + k_z z)}$$

$$= -jk\vec{a}_n e^{-j(k\vec{a}_n\cdot\vec{r})} \tag{7.49}$$

Hence, Eq. (7.48) can be written as

$$\vec{E}_0 \cdot \left[-jk\vec{a}_n e^{-j(k\vec{a}_n\cdot\vec{r})}\right] = 0$$

$$-jk\left(\vec{a}_n\cdot\vec{E}_0\right)\left[e^{-j(k\vec{a}_n\cdot\vec{r})}\right] = 0$$

which requires $\vec{E}_0 \cdot \vec{a}_n = 0$. Therefore, the plane wave solution in Eq. (7.47) shows that $\vec{E}_0$ is transverse to the direction of propagation. The magnetic field associated with the electric field $\tilde{E}(r)$ in Eq. (7.47) can be obtained from the time-harmonic Maxwell's equation given by the curl of $\tilde{E}$.

That is,

$$\nabla \times \tilde{E}(r) = -j\omega\mu\tilde{H}(r)$$

Therefore,

$$\tilde{H}(r) = \frac{1}{-j\omega\mu}\nabla \times \tilde{E}(r) = \frac{-jk}{-j\omega\mu}\vec{a}_n \times \tilde{E}(r)$$

or

$$\tilde{H}(r) = \frac{1}{\eta}\vec{a}_n \times \tilde{E}(r) \tag{7.50}$$

where $\eta = \dfrac{\omega\mu}{k} = \sqrt{\dfrac{\mu}{\varepsilon}}$ is the intrinsic impedance of the lossless medium. Equation (7.50) relates the magnetic field phasor $\tilde{H}$ in terms of electric field phasor $\tilde{E}$.

Substituting Eq. (7.47) in Eq. (7.50), the magnetic field phasor is represented by

$$\tilde{H}(r) = \frac{1}{\eta}\left(\vec{a}_n \times \tilde{E}_0\right)e^{-j\left(k\vec{a}_n \cdot \vec{r}\right)}\,\text{A/m} \tag{7.51}$$

Hence, any uniform plane wave travelling in an arbitrary direction denoted by the unit vector, $\vec{a}_n$, is a TEM wave with $\tilde{E}$ and $\tilde{H}$ perpendicular to each other and both are normal to $\vec{a}_n$.

Similarly, the electric field phasor can be related in terms of the magnetic field phasor by assuming $\tilde{H}(r) = \vec{H}_0 e^{-j\left(k\vec{a}_n \cdot \vec{r}\right)}$. The time-harmonic Maxwell's equation given by the curl of $\tilde{H}$ is

$$\nabla \times \tilde{H}(r) = j\omega\varepsilon\,\tilde{E}(r)$$

Therefore,

$$\tilde{E}(r) = \frac{1}{j\omega\varepsilon}\nabla \times \tilde{H}(r) = \frac{-jk}{j\omega\varepsilon}\vec{a}_n \times \tilde{H}(r)$$

or

$$\tilde{E}(r) = -\eta\vec{a}_n \times \tilde{H}(r) \tag{7.52}$$

The above equation relates the electric field phasor $\tilde{E}$ in terms of magnetic field phasor $\tilde{H}$.

7.4.2 Wave Propagation in Lossy Dielectrics

The homogeneous vector wave equation in a source-free lossy medium for electric field is given by

$$\nabla^2\tilde{E} - \gamma^2\tilde{E} = 0 \tag{7.53}$$

Similarly, for magnetic field, the wave equation is

$$\nabla^2\tilde{H} - \gamma^2\tilde{H} = 0 \tag{7.54}$$

where

$$\gamma^2 = j\omega\mu\left(\sigma + j\omega\varepsilon\right) \qquad (7.54a)$$

The propagation constant γ is a complex quantity in a lossy dielectric medium and it is defined by

$$\gamma = \alpha + j\beta$$

where α is the attenuation constant and β is the phase constant. Therefore, Eq. (7.54a) becomes

$$\left(\alpha + j\beta\right)^2 = j\omega\mu\left(\sigma + j\omega\varepsilon\right)$$

Hence,

$$\left(\alpha^2 - \beta^2\right) + j2\alpha\beta = j\omega\mu\left(\sigma + j\omega\varepsilon\right) = j\omega\mu \times j\omega\left(\varepsilon + \frac{\sigma}{j\omega}\right)$$

$$= -\omega^2\mu\left(\varepsilon - j\frac{\sigma}{\omega}\right) = -\omega^2\mu\varepsilon_c$$

where the complex permittivity, $\varepsilon_c = \varepsilon - j\dfrac{\sigma}{\omega}$.

Equating the real and imaginary parts on both sides of the above equation, we get

$$\alpha^2 - \beta^2 = -\omega^2\mu\varepsilon \qquad (7.55)$$

and

$$2\alpha\beta = \omega\mu\sigma \qquad (7.56)$$

Solving Eqs. (7.55) and (7.56) for α and β, we get

$$\alpha = \omega\sqrt{\frac{\mu\varepsilon}{2}\left[\sqrt{1 + \left(\frac{\sigma}{\omega\varepsilon}\right)^2} - 1\right]} \text{ Np/m} \qquad (7.57)$$

and

$$\beta = \omega\sqrt{\frac{\mu\varepsilon}{2}\left[\sqrt{1 + \left(\frac{\sigma}{\omega\varepsilon}\right)^2} + 1\right]} \text{ rad/m} \qquad (7.58)$$

The above equations define the attenuation constant and phase constant in a lossy dielectric medium and both are valid for any linear, isotropic, and homogeneous medium.

Consider an electric field phasor $\tilde{E} = \tilde{E}_x\left(z\right)\vec{a}_z$ travelling in the positive z-direction. Therefore, Eq. (7.53) becomes

$$\left(\nabla^2 - \gamma^2\right)\tilde{E}_x\left(z\right) = 0 \qquad (7.59)$$

or

$$\left(\frac{\partial^2}{\partial z^2} - \gamma^2\right)\tilde{E}_x\left(z\right) = 0$$

Therefore, the solution of this wave equation is

$$\tilde{E}(z) = \tilde{E}_x(z)\vec{a}_x = E_{x0}e^{-\gamma z}\vec{a}_x$$

$$= E_{x0}e^{-\alpha z}e^{-j\beta z}\vec{a}_x \tag{7.60}$$

and the magnitude of $\tilde{E}_x(z)$ is

$$\left|\tilde{E}_x(z)\right| = \left|E_{x0}e^{-\alpha z}e^{-j\beta z}\right| = \left|E_{x0}\right|e^{-\alpha z} \tag{7.61}$$

The above equation shows that the magnitude of electric field decreases exponentially by a factor $e^{-\alpha z}$ in a lossy medium. The instantaneous form of x-component of the electric field can be written as

$$\vec{E}(z,t) = \text{Re}\left[\tilde{E}_x(z)e^{j\omega t}\vec{a}_x\right] = \text{Re}\left[E_{x0}e^{-\alpha z}e^{j(\omega t - \beta z)}\vec{a}_x\right]$$

$$= E_{x0}e^{-\alpha z}\cos(\omega t - \beta z)\vec{a}_x \tag{7.62}$$

The above solution shows that the electric field has only an x-component and it is propagating in the positive z-direction. Figure 7.2 shows the attenuation suffered by the electric field travelling along positive z-direction at $t = 0$ and $t = \Delta t$. The arrows indicate the instantaneous values of electric field.

Similarly, the associated magnetic field in a lossy medium can be obtained from Eq. (7.50) as

$$\tilde{H} = \frac{1}{\eta_c}\vec{a}_n \times \tilde{E}$$

Therefore,

$$\tilde{H}(z) = \tilde{H}_y(z)\vec{a}_y = \frac{E_{x0}}{\eta_c}e^{-\alpha z}e^{-j\beta z}\vec{a}_y$$

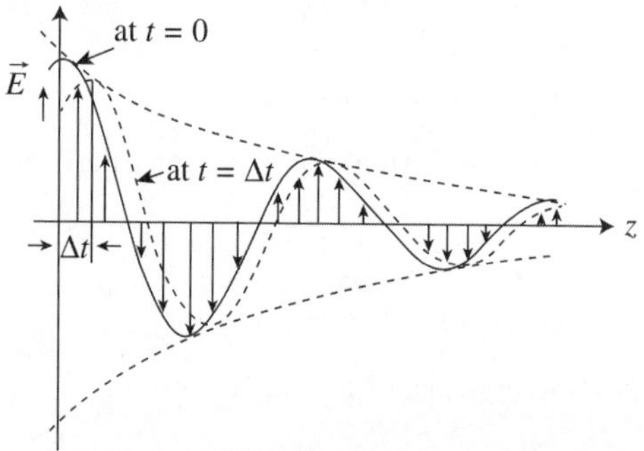

Figure 7.2 *Attenuation in the electric field*

where $\eta_c = \sqrt{\dfrac{\mu}{\varepsilon_c}} = \sqrt{\dfrac{\mu}{\varepsilon}}\left(1 - j\dfrac{\sigma}{\omega\varepsilon}\right)^{-1/2} = |\eta|\angle\theta_\eta$ is the complex intrinsic impedance of the lossy dielectric

medium and $\varepsilon_c = \varepsilon - j\dfrac{\sigma}{\omega}$. This expression for intrinsic impedance is also valid for any linear, isotropic, and

homogeneous medium. Here, $|\eta|$ is the magnitude of the intrinsic impedance and θ_η is its phase angle.

Therefore, the instantaneous form of *y-component* of the magnetic field can be written as

$$\vec{H}(z,t) = \text{Re}\left[\tilde{H}_y(z)e^{j\omega t}\vec{a}_y\right] = \text{Re}\left(\frac{E_{x0}}{\eta_c}e^{-\alpha z}e^{j(\omega t - \beta z)}\vec{a}_y\right)$$

$$= \text{Re}\left(\frac{E_{x0}}{|\eta|e^{j\theta_\eta}}e^{-\alpha z}e^{j(\omega t - \beta z)}\vec{a}_y\right)$$

$$= \frac{E_{x0}}{|\eta|}e^{-\alpha z}\cos(\omega t - \beta z - \theta_\eta)\vec{a}_y \tag{7.63}$$

Since η_c is a complex quantity, the electric and magnetic field intensities in a lossy dielectric are not in phase. Similar to the electric field, the magnitude of magnetic field also decreases exponentially by a factor $e^{-\alpha z}$ in a lossy dielectric medium.

The attenuation constant α is a measure of rate of decrease in field amplitude when the wave propagates in the lossy medium and it is measured in neper per metre (Np/m) or in decibel per metre (dB/m). In the case of lossless medium, $\alpha = 0$. The phase constant β or wave number k is a measure of the phase shift per length in the medium and it is measured in radians per metre (rad/m).

In a lossy medium,

$$\beta = \omega\sqrt{\mu\varepsilon_c} = \omega\sqrt{\mu\varepsilon\left(1 - j\frac{\sigma}{\omega\varepsilon}\right)} \tag{7.64}$$

The ratio $\dfrac{\sigma}{\omega\varepsilon}$ is known as a loss tangent and it is a measure of power loss in the medium. It is represented by

$$\tan\delta_c = \frac{\sigma}{\omega\varepsilon}$$

where δ_c is called the loss angle. A medium is said to be a perfect conductor if $\tan\delta_c$ is very large $\left(\text{i.e.}, \sigma \gg \omega\varepsilon\right)$, and a perfect dielectric if $\tan\delta_c$ is very small $\left(\sigma \ll \omega\varepsilon\right)$. The propagation properties of the wave in the medium depend not only on the constitutive parameters μ, ε and σ but also on the frequency of operation. Hence, a medium can be considered as a good conductor at low frequencies but can have the properties of a lossy dielectric at very high frequencies.

If $\dfrac{\sigma}{\omega\varepsilon} \gg 1$, then the medium is called a *good conductor*. If $\dfrac{\sigma}{\omega\varepsilon} \ll 1$, then the medium is called a *low-loss dielectric*. A low-loss dielectric is a good but imperfect insulator with non-zero conductivity $\left(\text{i.e.}, \sigma \gg \omega\varepsilon\right)$. The general expression for propagation constant γ is given by

$$\gamma = j\omega\sqrt{\mu\varepsilon_c} = j\omega\sqrt{\mu\varepsilon}\left(1 - j\frac{\sigma}{\omega\varepsilon}\right)^{1/2} \tag{7.65}$$

Applying binomial approximation $(1-x)^{1/2} \approx 1 - \dfrac{x}{2}$ to the above equation, we get

$$\gamma \cong j\omega\sqrt{\mu\varepsilon}\left(1 - j\frac{\sigma}{2\omega\varepsilon}\right) \tag{7.66}$$

Therefore, the real part of Eq. (7.66) gives the attenuation constant as

$$\alpha = \frac{\sigma}{2}\sqrt{\frac{\mu}{\varepsilon}} \tag{7.67}$$

and the imaginary part of Eq. (7.66) gives the phase constant as

$$\beta = \omega\sqrt{\mu\varepsilon} \tag{7.68}$$

The above expression for β is same as that of wave number k of the lossless medium. The complex intrinsic impedance η_c of a low-loss dielectric medium is represented by

$$\eta_c = \sqrt{\frac{\mu}{\varepsilon_c}} = \sqrt{\frac{\mu}{\varepsilon}}\left(1 - j\frac{\sigma}{\omega\varepsilon}\right)^{-1/2}$$

Applying binomial approximation $(1-x)^{-1/2} = 1 + \dfrac{x}{2}$, we get

$$\eta_c = \sqrt{\frac{\mu}{\varepsilon}}\left(1 + j\frac{\sigma}{2\omega\varepsilon}\right) \tag{7.69}$$

From Eq. (7.68), the phase velocity of the wave in the low-loss dielectric medium is given by

$$u_p = \frac{\omega}{\beta} = \frac{1}{\sqrt{\mu\varepsilon}} \tag{7.70}$$

7.4.3 Wave Propagation in Free Space

If the medium is vacuum or free space in which $\mu = \mu_0$, $\varepsilon = \varepsilon_0$ and $\sigma = 0$, the phase velocity and intrinsic impedance are given by

$$u_p = c \cong \frac{1}{\sqrt{\mu_0\varepsilon_0}} = 3\times10^8\,\text{m/s}$$

and

$$\eta = \eta_0 = \sqrt{\frac{\mu_0}{\varepsilon_0}} = 120\pi = 377\,\Omega$$

where c is the velocity of light in vacuum and η_0 is the intrinsic impedance of free space. Hence, in free space, the EM wave travels at the speed of light and it is evident that light is an EM wave.

Also, in free space, the attenuation and phase constants are given by

$$\alpha = 0 \quad \text{and} \quad \beta = \omega\sqrt{\mu_0\varepsilon_0} = \frac{\omega}{c}$$

In addition, the electric field and magnetic field intensities in free space are represented by

$$\vec{E}(z,t) = E_0 \cos(\omega t - \beta z)\vec{a}_x \tag{7.71}$$

and

$$\vec{H}(z,t) = H_0 \cos(\omega t - \beta z)\vec{a}_y = \frac{E_0}{\eta_0}\cos(\omega t - \beta z)\vec{a}_y \tag{7.72}$$

The above equations show that the electric field is along x-direction, the magnetic field is along y-direction and the direction of propagation of both the fields is along z-direction. Both the fields are orthogonal to each other and also normal to the direction of wave propagation, $\vec{a}_z$, i.e., the fields lie in an xy-plane that is transverse to the direction of propagation. Such type of wave is called a TEM wave and it is shown in Figure 7.3.

In general, if $\vec{a}_E$, $\vec{a}_H$ and $\vec{a}_k$ the unit vectors along $\vec{E}$, $\vec{H}$ and the direction of wave propagation, respectively, then their cross products are represented by

$$\vec{a}_k \times \vec{a}_E = \vec{a}_H$$

$$\vec{a}_k \times \vec{a}_H = -\vec{a}_E$$

$$\vec{a}_E \times \vec{a}_H = \vec{a}_k$$

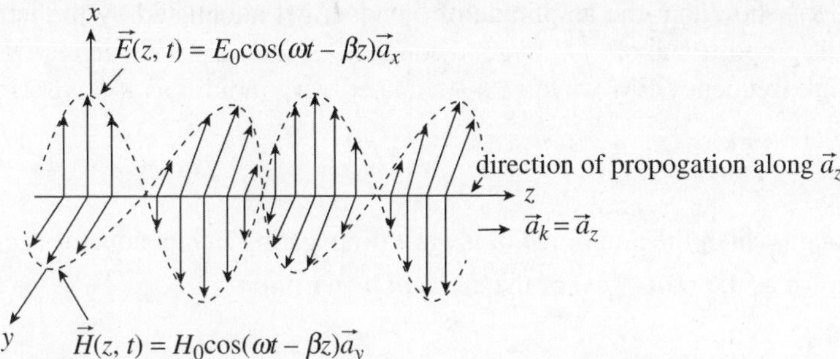

Figure 7.3 *TEM wave in free space with plot of $\vec{E}$ and $\vec{H}$ at $t = 0$*

7.4.4 Wave Propagation in Good Conductors

A medium is called a good conductor in which $\sigma \gg \omega\varepsilon$ or $\dfrac{\sigma}{\omega\varepsilon} \gg 1$. Under this condition, Eqs. (7.57) and (7.58) for attenuation constant and phase constant can be approximated as

$$\alpha = \omega\sqrt{\frac{\mu\sigma}{2\omega}} = \sqrt{\pi f \mu\sigma} = \beta$$

The above equation shows that both α and β are equal in a good conductor and both are directly proportional to the square root of frequency f and conductivity σ. The complex intrinsic impedance of a good conductor is represented by

$$\eta_c = \sqrt{\frac{\mu}{\varepsilon_c}} = \sqrt{\frac{j\omega\mu}{\sigma}} \tag{7.73}$$

where $\varepsilon_c = \varepsilon - j\dfrac{\sigma}{\omega} \cong -j\dfrac{\sigma}{\omega}$. Simplifying the above equation, we get

$$\eta_c = (1+j)\sqrt{\frac{\pi f \mu}{\sigma}} = (1+j)\frac{\alpha}{\sigma} \qquad \left(\text{since } \sqrt{j} = 1\angle 45° = \frac{1+j}{\sqrt{2}}\right)$$

The intrinsic impedance has a phase angle of $45°$, which shows that the electric field leads the magnetic field by $45°$. The phase velocity in a good conductor is

$$u_p = \frac{\omega}{\beta} = \sqrt{\frac{2\omega}{\mu\sigma}} = \sqrt{\frac{4\pi f}{\mu\sigma}} \qquad (\text{since } \omega = 2\pi f)$$

Also, the wavelength of a plane wave in a good conductor is

$$\lambda = \frac{2\pi}{\beta} = \frac{u_p}{f} = \frac{1}{f}\sqrt{\frac{4\pi f}{\mu\sigma}} = 2\sqrt{\frac{\pi}{f\mu\sigma}}$$

In addition, the electric field and magnetic field intensities in a good conductor are represented by

$$\vec{E}(z,t) = E_0 e^{-\alpha z}\cos(\omega t - \beta z)\vec{a}_x$$

$$\vec{H}(z,t) = \frac{E_0}{|\eta_c|\angle 45°}\cos(\omega t - \beta z)\vec{a}_y = \frac{E_0}{\sqrt{\omega\mu/\sigma}}e^{-\alpha z}\cos(\omega t - \beta z - 45°)\vec{a}_y$$

The above equations show that the amplitude of $\vec{E}$ and $\vec{H}$ get attenuated by the factor $e^{-\alpha z}$. Since the attenuation constant is proportional of $\sqrt{f}$ in good conductors, it tends to be large at very high frequencies. This shows that a high frequency EM wave gets attenuated very rapidly as it travels in a good conducting medium.

Skin depth

The distance δ through which the amplitude of a wave propagating in a conductor decreases by a factor of e^{-1} or 36.8% is known as the *skin depth* or the *depth of penetration.*

That is,

$$E_0 e^{-\alpha\delta} = E_0 e^{-1}$$

Hence,

$$\delta = \frac{1}{\alpha} = \frac{1}{\sqrt{\pi f \mu\sigma}} \tag{7.74}$$

Since $\alpha = \beta$ in a good conductor, the skin depth can also be written as

$$\delta = \frac{1}{\beta} = \frac{\lambda}{2\pi}$$

The skin depth is a measure of the depth to which an EM wave can penetrate into a conducting medium. The phenomenon by which the fields in a conducting medium decrease rapidly is called *skin effect.*

Equation (7.74) shows that the skin depth decreases with increase in frequency. At very high or microwave frequencies, the skin depth in a good conductor is so small such that the fields and associated currents are confined in a very thin layer of conducting surface. Hence, the electric and magnetic fields can hardly propagate through any conducting medium. Table 7.1 summarizes the expressions for the propagation properties of wave in different types of medium.

Table 7.1 *Wave propagation properties in different types of medium*

Propagation parameters	Lossy medium	Lossless medium	Free space	Good conductor	Units
Attenuation constant (α)	$\omega\sqrt{\dfrac{\mu\varepsilon}{2}\left[\sqrt{1+\left(\dfrac{\sigma}{\omega\varepsilon}\right)^2}-1\right]}$	0	0	$\sqrt{\pi f \mu\sigma}$	Np/m or dB/m
Phase constant (β)	$\omega\sqrt{\dfrac{\mu\varepsilon}{2}\left[\sqrt{1+\left(\dfrac{\sigma}{\omega\varepsilon}\right)^2}+1\right]}$	$\omega\sqrt{\mu\varepsilon}$	$\omega\sqrt{\mu_0\varepsilon_0}$	$\sqrt{\pi f \mu\sigma}$	rad/m
Complex intrinsic impedance (η_c)	$\sqrt{\dfrac{\mu}{\varepsilon}}\left(1-j\dfrac{\sigma}{\omega\varepsilon}\right)^{-1/2}$	$\sqrt{\dfrac{\mu}{\varepsilon}}$	$\sqrt{\dfrac{\mu_0}{\varepsilon_0}}$	$(1+j)\dfrac{\alpha}{\sigma}$	Ω
Phase velocity (u_p)	$\dfrac{\omega}{\beta}\cong\dfrac{1}{\sqrt{\mu\varepsilon}}$	$\dfrac{1}{\sqrt{\mu\varepsilon}}$	$\dfrac{1}{\sqrt{\mu_0\varepsilon_0}}$	$\sqrt{\dfrac{4\pi f}{\mu\sigma}}$	m/s

EXAMPLE 7.3

In a perfect dielectric, $\vec{E}(z,t) = 10^3 \sin(\omega t - \beta z)\vec{a}_y$ V/m. Determine $\vec{H}(z,t)$.

SOLUTION

Given $\vec{E}(z,t) = 10^3 \sin(\omega t - \beta z)\vec{a}_y$ V/m. For a perfect dielectric, $\mu_r = \varepsilon_r = 1$.

Here, the electric field is directed in positive y-direction. The uniform plane wave is propagating in positive z-direction as indicated by $-\beta z$ term in the expression of $\vec{E}$. Therefore, the direction of magnetic field can be obtained by

$$\vec{a}_k \times \vec{a}_E = \vec{a}_H$$

That is,

$$\vec{a}_z \times \vec{a}_y = -\vec{a}_x$$

Here, the magnetic field is directed in negative x-direction.

The amplitudes of $\vec{E}$ and $\vec{H}$ are related to each other as

$$\eta_0 = \frac{E_m}{H_m}$$

where $\eta_0 = 377\,\Omega$ and $E_m = 10^3$.

Therefore,

$$H_m = \frac{E_m}{\eta_0} = \frac{10^3}{377} = 2.65 \text{A/m}$$

Hence, the magnetic field $\vec{H}$ is

$$\vec{H}(z,t) = -2.65\sin(\omega t - \beta z)\vec{a}_x \text{ A/m}$$

EXAMPLE 7.4

Determine the propagation constant γ for a material having $\mu_r = 1$, $\varepsilon_r = 4$ and $\sigma = 0.35\text{pS/m}$, if the wave frequency is 2.6 MHz.

SOLUTION

Given $\mu_r = 1$, $\varepsilon_r = 4$ and $\sigma = 0.35\text{pS/m}$ for a material with the wave frequency $f = 2.6\,\text{MHz}$. To determine whether the material is a conductor or dielectric, we can make use of the displacement current concept. For the given medium, the ratio of amplitudes of conduction current density to the displacement current density is

$$\left|\frac{\vec{J}_c}{\vec{J}_d}\right| = \frac{\sigma}{\omega\varepsilon} = \frac{\sigma}{\omega(\varepsilon_0\varepsilon_r)}$$

Here, $\dfrac{\sigma}{\omega\varepsilon} = \dfrac{0.35\times10^{-12}}{2\pi\times2.6\times10^6\times4\times\left(10^{-9}/36\pi\right)} = 0.2\times10^{-9} \approx 0$

Therefore, from the value of the ratio of amplitudes of the current densities, it is clear that

$$\left|\frac{\vec{J}_c}{\vec{J}_d}\right| \ll 1 \text{ or } \left|\vec{J}_c\right| \ll \left|\vec{J}_d\right|$$

The above equation indicates that the conduction current density is very small compared to the displacement current density. Hence, the material is almost a lossless dielectric material.

For a perfect dielectric, $\sigma = 0$ and

$$\alpha = 0, \ \beta = \omega\sqrt{\mu\varepsilon} = 2\pi f \frac{\sqrt{\mu_r \varepsilon_r}}{c} = 10.89 \times 10^{-2} \,\text{rad/m}$$

Therefore, the propagation constant is

$$\gamma = \alpha + j\beta = j10.89 \times 10^{-2} \,\text{m}^{-1}$$

Here, the material behaves like a perfect dielectric at the given frequency.

EXAMPLE 7.5

Determine the depth of penetration for copper at 2 MHz.

SOLUTION

Since copper is a good conductor, its depth of penetration is

$$\delta = \frac{1}{\sqrt{\pi f \mu \sigma}} = \frac{1}{\sqrt{\pi f \left(\mu_0 \mu_r\right)\sigma}}$$

We know that, for copper, $\mu_r = 1$ and $\sigma = 5.8 \times 10^7 \,\text{S/m}$.
Therefore,

$$\delta = \frac{1}{\sqrt{\pi \times 2 \times 10^6 \times 4\pi \times 10^{-7} \times 1 \times 5.8 \times 10^7}} = 46.75 \,\mu\text{m}$$

EXAMPLE 7.6

Determine the skin depth at a frequency of 2.6 MHz in aluminum, where $\sigma = 28.2 \,\text{MS/m}$ and $\mu_r = 1$. Also, find the propagation constant and wave velocity.

SOLUTION

Given $f = 2.6 \,\text{MHz}$, $\sigma = 28.2 \,\text{MS/m}$ and $\mu_r = 1$.

The skin depth is

$$\delta = \frac{1}{\sqrt{\pi f \mu \sigma}} = \frac{1}{\sqrt{\pi \times 2.6 \times 10^6 \times 4\pi \times 10^{-7} \times 28.2 \times 10^6}}$$

$$= 5.88 \times 10^{-5} \,\text{m} = 58.8 \,\mu\text{m}$$

We know that, $\alpha = \beta = \dfrac{1}{\delta}$

Therefore, the propagation constant is

$$\gamma = \alpha + j\beta = 1.7 \times 10^4 + j1.7 \times 10^4 = 2.40 \times 10^4 \,\angle 45^\circ \,\text{m}^{-1}$$

and the wave velocity is

$$u_p = \frac{\omega}{\beta} = \omega\delta = 2\pi \times 2.6 \times 10^6 \times 58.8 \times 10^{-6} = 960 \,\text{m/s}$$

EXAMPLE 7.7

In a homogeneous region where $\mu_r = 1$ and $\varepsilon_r = 50$, the fields are given as $\vec{E} = 40\pi e^{j(\omega t - \beta z)}\vec{a}_x$ V/m and $\vec{B} = \mu_0 H_m e^{j(\omega t - \beta z)}\vec{a}_y$ Wb/m^2. Determine ω and $\vec{H}_m$ if the wavelength is 1.75 m.

SOLUTION

Assume lossless medium in which $\sigma = 0$. The wavelength is

$$\lambda = \frac{2\pi}{\beta}$$

Therefore, the phase constant is

$$\beta = \frac{2\pi}{\lambda} = \frac{2\pi}{1.75} = 3.59 \,\text{rad/m}$$

But for a lossless medium,

$$\beta = \omega\sqrt{\mu\varepsilon} = 3.59$$

Therefore, $\omega = \dfrac{3.59}{\sqrt{\mu\varepsilon}} = \dfrac{3.59}{\sqrt{(\mu_0\mu_r)(\varepsilon_0\varepsilon_r)}} = \dfrac{3.59}{\sqrt{(4\pi\times10^{-7})(1)(8.854\times10^{-12})(50)}}$

$$= 1.522\times10^8 \,\text{rad/s}$$

The intrinsic impedance is

$$\eta = \sqrt{\frac{\mu}{\varepsilon}} = \sqrt{\frac{\mu_0\mu_r}{\varepsilon_0\varepsilon_r}} = 120\pi\sqrt{\frac{1}{50}} = 53.278\,\Omega$$

But intrinsic impedance can also be expressed in of the magnitudes of electric and magnetic fields as,

$$\eta = \frac{E_m}{H_m}$$

Hence, the magnitude of the magnetic field is

$$H_m = \frac{E_m}{\eta}, \text{ where } E_m = 40\pi \text{ (given)}$$

$$= \frac{40\pi}{53.278} = 2.36 \,\text{A/m}$$

EXAMPLE 7.8

An EM wave travels in free space with the electric field component $\tilde{E} = 50 e^{j(0.5y + 0.866z)}\vec{a}_x$ V/m. Determine *(i)* ω, *(ii)* λ and *(iii)* the magnetic field component in the wave.

SOLUTION

Given $\tilde{E} = 50 e^{j(0.5y + 0.866z)}\vec{a}_x$ V/m.

(*i*) Comparing the given $\tilde{E}$ with $\tilde{E} = E_0 e^{j\left(k_x x + k_y y + k_z z\right)} \vec{a}_x$, it is found that $k_x = 0$, $k_y = 0.5$ and $k_z = 0.866$.

Here, $\vec{k} = k_x \vec{a}_x + k_y \vec{a}_y + k_z \vec{a}_z$.

Therefore,

$$k = \sqrt{k_x^2 + k_y^2 + k_z^2} = \sqrt{(0.5)^2 + (0.866)^2} = 1$$

But in free space, $\quad k = \beta = \omega\sqrt{\mu_0 \varepsilon_0} = \dfrac{\omega}{c} = \dfrac{2\pi}{\lambda}$

Thus,

$$\omega = kc = 3 \times 10^8 \,\text{rad/s}$$

(*ii*) The wavelength, $\lambda = \dfrac{2\pi}{k} = 2\pi = 6.28\text{m}$

(*iii*) From Eq. (7.50), the corresponding magnetic field in free space is

$$\tilde{H} = \frac{1}{\eta}\vec{a}_n \times \tilde{E} = \frac{k}{\omega\mu_0}\vec{a}_n \times \tilde{E}$$

where $\eta = \dfrac{\omega\mu_0}{k}$ and $\vec{a}_n = 0.5\vec{a}_y + 0.866\vec{a}_z$.

Therefore,

$$\tilde{H} = \frac{\left(0.5\vec{a}_y + 0.866\vec{a}_z\right)}{4\pi \times 10^{-7} \times 3 \times 10^8} \times 50 e^{j(0.5y + 0.866z)}\vec{a}_x$$

$$= \left(114.9\vec{a}_y - 66.3\vec{a}_z\right) e^{j(0.5y + 0.866z)} \,\text{mA/m} \qquad\qquad \square$$

EXAMPLE 7.9

A lossy dielectric has an intrinsic impedance of $100\angle 30°\,\Omega$ at a particular frequency. The plane wave propagating through the dielectric, at that frequency, has the magnetic field component, given by

$$\vec{H} = 20 e^{-\alpha x} \cos\left(\omega t - \frac{1}{2}x\right)\vec{a}_y \,\text{A/m}$$

Find $\vec{E}$ and α. Determine the skin depth and wave polarization.

SOLUTION

Given $\eta = 100\angle 30°\,\Omega$ and $\vec{H} = 20 e^{-\alpha x} \cos\left(\omega t - \frac{1}{2}x\right)\vec{a}_y \,\text{A/m}$.

Here, the negative sign in $\left(\omega t - \beta x\right)$ shows that the wave is propagating in "$+x$"-direction.

The given wave travels along $\vec{a}_x$ so that $\vec{a}_k = \vec{a}_x$ and $\vec{a}_H = \vec{a}_y$.

Therefore,

$$-\vec{a}_E = \vec{a}_k \times \vec{a}_H = \vec{a}_x \times \vec{a}_y = \vec{a}_z$$

That is,

$$\vec{a}_E = -\vec{a}_z$$

The above equation shows that the electric field is along $-\vec{a}_z$ direction.

The intrinsic impedance is

$$\eta = \frac{E_0}{H_0} = 100\angle 30° = 100e^{j\pi/6}$$

Therefore,

$$E_0 = \eta H_0 = 2000e^{j\pi/6} \qquad \left(\text{since } H_0 = 20\right)$$

The electric field $\vec{E}$ and magnetic field $\vec{H}$ always have the same form except for the amplitude and phase difference. Hence,

$$\vec{E} = \text{Re}\left(2000e^{j\pi/6}e^{-\gamma x}e^{j\omega t}\vec{a}_E\right)$$

That is,

$$\vec{E} = -2e^{-\alpha x}\cos\left(\omega t - \frac{x}{2} + \frac{\pi}{6}\right)\vec{a}_z \text{ kV/m}$$

where $\gamma = \alpha + j\beta$ and $\beta = \dfrac{1}{2}$.

Since

$$\alpha = \omega\sqrt{\frac{\mu\varepsilon}{2}\left[\sqrt{1+\left(\frac{\sigma}{\omega\varepsilon}\right)^2}-1\right]}$$

and

$$\beta = \omega\sqrt{\frac{\mu\varepsilon}{2}\left[\sqrt{1+\left(\frac{\sigma}{\omega\varepsilon}\right)^2}+1\right]}$$

Hence,

$$\frac{\alpha}{\beta} = \left[\frac{\sqrt{1+\left(\frac{\sigma}{\omega\varepsilon}\right)^2}-1}{\sqrt{1+\left(\frac{\sigma}{\omega\varepsilon}\right)^2}+1}\right]^{\frac{1}{2}}$$

But $\dfrac{\sigma}{\omega\varepsilon} = \tan 2\theta_\eta = \tan 60° = \sqrt{3}$. Therefore,

$$\frac{\alpha}{\beta} = \left[\frac{2-1}{2+1}\right]^{\frac{1}{2}} = \frac{1}{\sqrt{3}}$$

Therefore, the attenuation constant,

$$\alpha = \frac{\beta}{\sqrt{3}} = \frac{1}{2\sqrt{3}} = 0.2887\,\text{Np/m}$$

and the skin depth,

$$\delta = \frac{1}{\alpha} = 2\sqrt{3} = 3.464\ \text{m}$$

Since the electric field has z-component, the wave polarization is along the z-direction. ◻

EXAMPLE 7.10

A 300 MHz uniform plane wave propagates through fresh water for which $\sigma = 0$, $\mu_r = 1$, and $\varepsilon_r = 78$. Determine (*i*) attenuation constant, (*ii*) phase constant, (*iii*) wavelength and (*iv*) intrinsic impedance.

SOLUTION

(*i*) For the given medium, i.e., fresh water, the conductivity is $\sigma = 0$. Assuming medium to be lossless, we can write

Attenuation constant, $\alpha = 0$

(*ii*) The phase constant is

$$\beta = \omega\sqrt{\mu\varepsilon} = \omega\sqrt{\left(\mu_0\mu_r\right)\left(\varepsilon_0\varepsilon_r\right)}$$

$$= \left(2\pi \times 300 \times 10^6\right)\sqrt{\left(4\pi \times 10^{-7} \times 1\right)\left(8.854 \times 10^{-12} \times 78\right)}$$

$$= 55.53\,\text{rad/m}$$

(*iii*) The wavelength is

$$\lambda = \frac{2\pi}{\beta} = \frac{2\pi}{55.53} = 0.113\ \text{m}$$

(*iv*) The intrinsic impedance is

$$\eta = \sqrt{\frac{\mu}{\varepsilon}} = \sqrt{\frac{\mu_0\mu_r}{\varepsilon_0\varepsilon_r}} = \frac{120\pi}{\sqrt{\varepsilon_r}} = \frac{120\pi}{\sqrt{78}} = 42.65\ \Omega$$ ◻

EXAMPLE 7.11

Determine α, β, γ and η for damp soil at a frequency of 1 MHz given that $\varepsilon_r = 12$, $\mu_r = 1$ and $\sigma = 20\,\text{mS/m}$.

SOLUTION

Given $f = 1\,\text{MHz}$, $\varepsilon_r = 12$, $\mu_r = 1$ and $\sigma = 20\,\text{mS/m}$.

To determine the type of medium, let us first find ratio of $\dfrac{\sigma}{\omega\varepsilon}$.

Here,

$$\frac{\sigma}{\omega\varepsilon} = \frac{\sigma}{\left(2\pi f\right)\left(\varepsilon_0\varepsilon_r\right)} = \frac{20 \times 10^{-3}}{\left(2 \times \pi \times 10^6\right)\left(8.854 \times 10^{-12} \times 12\right)} = 29.96$$

Since $\dfrac{\sigma}{\omega\varepsilon} \gg 1$, damp soil acts as quasi-conductor at a frequency of 1 MHz. For such a medium, the propagation constant is

$$\gamma = \sqrt{j\omega\mu(\sigma + j\omega\varepsilon)}$$

$$= \sqrt{j\left(2\pi \times 1 \times 10^6\right)\left(4\pi \times 10^{-7} \times 1\right)\left[20 \times 10^{-3} + j\left(2\pi \times 1 \times 10^6\right)\left(8.854 \times 10^{-12} \times 12\right)\right]}$$

$$= \sqrt{j(7.8956)\left[20 \times 10^{-3} + j6.6757 \times 10^{-4}\right]}$$

$$= \sqrt{\left[7.8956\angle 90°\right]\left[0.02\angle 1.911°\right]}$$

$$= 0.3973\angle 45°\,\mathrm{m}^{-1}$$

The propagation constant is

$$\gamma = \alpha + j\beta = 0.2809 + j0.2809\,\mathrm{m}^{-1}$$

Comparing the real and imaginary terms, we get

$$\alpha = 0.2809\,\mathrm{Np/m}$$

$$\beta = 0.2809\,\mathrm{rad/m}$$

The velocity of propagation is

$$u = \frac{\omega}{\beta} = \frac{2\pi f}{\beta} = \frac{2\pi \times 1 \times 10^6}{0.2809} = 22.36 \times 10^6\,\mathrm{m/s}$$

The wavelength is

$$\lambda = \frac{2\pi}{\beta} = \frac{2\pi}{0.2809} = 22.368\,\mathrm{m}$$

The intrinsic impedance is

$$\eta = \sqrt{\frac{j\omega\mu}{\sigma + j\omega\varepsilon}} = \sqrt{\frac{j(2\pi f)(\mu_0\mu_r)}{\sigma + j(2\pi f)(\varepsilon_0\varepsilon_r)}}$$

$$= 19.869\angle 45.05°\,\Omega$$

EXAMPLE 7.12

A 3 GHz wave is propagating through a material that has a dielectric constant of 2.4 and loss tangent of 0.005. Find α, β and the wavelength of the material.

SOLUTION

Given $f = 3\,\mathrm{GHz}$, loss tangent, $\tan\delta_c = 0.005$ and $\varepsilon_r = 2.4$.

The loss tangent for a dielectric is

$$\tan\delta_c = \frac{\sigma}{\omega\varepsilon} = \frac{\sigma}{\omega\varepsilon_0\varepsilon_r}$$

$$0.005 = \frac{\sigma}{\left(2\pi\times3\times10^9\right)\left(8.854\times10^{-12}\times2.4\right)}$$

Therefore,

$$\sigma = 2\times10^{-3} = 2\,\text{mS/m}$$

Since $\dfrac{\sigma}{\omega\varepsilon} \ll 1$, the material is considered as a practical dielectric material. Therefore,

$$\alpha = \frac{\sigma}{2}\sqrt{\frac{\mu}{\varepsilon}} = \frac{\sigma}{2}\sqrt{\frac{\mu_0\mu_r}{\varepsilon_0\varepsilon_r}}$$

$$= \frac{2\times10^{-3}}{2}120\pi\sqrt{\frac{1}{2.4}} = 0.243\,\text{Np/m}$$

The propagation constant is

$$\beta = \omega\sqrt{\mu\varepsilon} = 2\pi f\times\sqrt{\mu_0\mu_r\varepsilon_0\varepsilon_r}$$

$$= 2\pi\times3\times10^9\times\sqrt{\left(4\pi\times10^{-7}\right)\left(2.4\times8.854\times10^{-12}\right)}$$

$$= 97.33\,\text{rad/m}$$

The wavelength is

$$\lambda = \frac{2\pi}{\beta} = \frac{2\pi}{97.33} = 0.065\,\text{m}$$

EXAMPLE 7.13

The wet and marshy soil is characterized by $\sigma = 10^{-2}\,\text{S/m}$, $\varepsilon_r = 15$ and $\mu_r = 1$. Show that at 60Hz, it can be considered as good conductor. Also at 60 Hz, calculate (*i*) skin depth, (*ii*) intrinsic impedance and (*iii*) propagation constant.

SOLUTION

If $\dfrac{\sigma}{\omega\varepsilon} \gg 1$, then the medium is said to be a good conductor.

$$\text{Therefore,}\quad \frac{\sigma}{\omega\varepsilon} = \frac{10^{-2}}{2\pi\times60\times8.854\times10^{-12}\times15} = 0.1997\times10^5$$

Here, $\dfrac{\sigma}{\omega\varepsilon} \gg 1$. Hence, the wet and marshy soil can be considered as a good conductor at 60Hz.

(*i*) For a good conductor, the propagation constant is

$$\gamma = \sqrt{j\omega\mu\sigma} = \sqrt{\omega\mu\sigma}\angle 45° \qquad\qquad \left(\text{since } \sqrt{j} = 1\angle 45°\right)$$

$$= \sqrt{\left(2\pi\times 60\right)\left(4\pi\times 10^{-7}\times 1\right)\left(10^{-2}\right)}\angle 45° = 2.18\times 10^{-3}\angle 45°$$

Also, $\gamma = \alpha + j\beta = \left(1.54 + j1.54\right)\times 10^{-3}\,\text{m}^{-1}$

Comparing real and imaginary terms, we get

$$\alpha = 1.54\times 10^{-3}\,\text{Np/m}$$

$$\beta = 1.54\times 10^{-3}\,\text{rad/m}$$

(*ii*) The skin depth is

$$\delta = \frac{1}{\alpha} = \frac{1}{1.54\times 10^{-3}} = 649.35\,\text{m}$$

(*iii*) The intrinsic impedance η is

$$\eta = \sqrt{\frac{\omega\mu}{\sigma}}\angle 45° = \sqrt{\frac{\left(2\pi\times 60\right)\left(4\pi\times 10^{-7}\times 1\right)}{10^{-2}}}\angle 45° = 0.218\angle 45°\,\Omega \qquad \square$$

EXAMPLE 7.14

A plane wave travelling in a positive x-direction in a lossless unbounded medium having permeability 4.5 times that of free space and a permittivity twice that of free space. (i) Find the phase velocity of wave. (ii) If the electric field $\vec{E}$ has only y-component with amplitude of 30 V/m, find the amplitude and direction of magnetic field $\vec{H}$.

SOLUTION

Given that, for a lossless unbounded medium, $\mu = 4.5\mu_0$ and $\varepsilon = 2\varepsilon_0$.

The phase velocity of the wave is

$$u_p = \frac{1}{\sqrt{\mu\varepsilon}} = \frac{1}{\sqrt{\mu_0\varepsilon_0}}\frac{1}{\sqrt{\mu_r\varepsilon_r}} = \frac{c}{\sqrt{\mu_r\varepsilon_r}}$$

$$= \frac{3\times 10^8}{\sqrt{4.5\times 2}} = 1\times 10^8\,\text{m/s}$$

Since the plane wave is travelling in x-direction and the electric field $\vec{E}$ has only y-component, the direction of magnetic field can be obtained by

$$\vec{a}_k \times \vec{a}_E = \vec{a}_H$$

That is,

$$\vec{a}_x \times \vec{a}_y = \vec{a}_z$$

Here, the magnetic field is directed in positive z-direction.

The intrinsic impedance η is

$$\eta = \sqrt{\frac{\mu}{\varepsilon}} = \sqrt{\frac{\mu_0}{\varepsilon_0}}\sqrt{\frac{\mu_r}{\varepsilon_r}} = 120\pi\sqrt{\frac{4.5}{2}} = 565.1\,\Omega$$

The intrinsic impedance can also be represented in terms of the amplitudes of $\vec{E}$ and $\vec{H}$ as

$$\eta = \frac{E_m}{H_m}$$

The amplitude of magnetic field is

$$H_m = \frac{E_m}{\eta}, \qquad \text{where } E_m = 30\,\text{V/m (given)}$$

$$= \frac{30}{565.1} = 0.053\,\text{A/m}$$

EXAMPLE 7.15

The electric field intensity of a linearly polarized uniform plane wave propagating in the "$+z$"-direction in seawater is $\vec{E} = 200\cos 10^7\,\pi t\,\vec{a}_x$ V/m at $z = 0$. The constitutive parameters of seawater are $\varepsilon_r = 36$, $\mu_r = 1$ and $\sigma = 4\,\text{S/m}$.

  (i) Determine the attenuation constant, phase constant, intrinsic impedance, phase velocity, wavelength and skin depth.

  (ii) Find the distance at which the amplitude of $\vec{E}$ is 1% of its value at $z = 0$.

  (iii) Write the expressions for $\vec{E}(z,t)$ and $\vec{H}(z,t)$ at $z = 0.9\,$m as functions of t.

SOLUTION

Given $\vec{E} = 200\cos 10^7\,\pi t\,\vec{a}_x$ V/m. Here, $\omega = 10^7\,\pi\,\text{rad/s}$

Hence, the frequency of the plane wave is

$$f = \frac{\omega}{2\pi} = \frac{10^7\,\pi}{2\pi} = 5\times10^6\,\text{Hz}$$

Now,

$$\frac{\sigma}{\omega\varepsilon} = \frac{\sigma}{\omega\varepsilon_0\varepsilon_r} = \frac{4}{10^7\,\pi\left(\dfrac{1}{36\pi}\times10^{-9}\right)36} = 400$$

Since $\dfrac{\sigma}{\omega\varepsilon} \gg 1$, formulae for good conductors can be used.

  (i) The attenuation constant, $\alpha = \sqrt{\pi f\,\mu\sigma} = \sqrt{\pi\left(5\times10^6\right)\left(4\pi\times10^{-7}\right)4} = 8.89\,\text{Np/m}$

      The phase constant, $\beta = \alpha = \sqrt{\pi f\,\mu\sigma} = 8.89\,\text{rad/m}$

The intrinsic impedance, $\eta_c = (1+j)\sqrt{\dfrac{\pi f \mu}{\sigma}}$

$$= (1+j)\sqrt{\dfrac{\pi\left(5\times10^6\right)\left(4\pi\times10^{-7}\right)}{4}} = \pi e^{j\pi/4}\,\Omega$$

The phase velocity, $u_p = \dfrac{\omega}{\beta} = \dfrac{10^7\pi}{8.89} = 3.53\times10^6$ m/s

The wavelength, $\lambda = \dfrac{2\pi}{\beta} = \dfrac{2\pi}{8.89} = 0.707\,\text{m}$

The skin depth, $\delta = \dfrac{1}{\alpha} = \dfrac{1}{8.89} = 0.112\,\text{m}$

(*ii*) Let z_1 be the distance at which the amplitude of wave decreases to 1% of its value at $z = 0$. That is,

$$e^{-\alpha z_1} = 0.01$$

or

$$e^{\alpha z_1} = \dfrac{1}{0.01} = 100$$

Hence,

$$z_1 = \dfrac{1}{\alpha}\ln\left(100\right) = \dfrac{4.605}{8.89} = 0.518\,\text{m}$$

(*iii*) The electric field in phasor form is

$$\tilde{E}(z) = 200 e^{-\alpha z} e^{-j\beta z}\,\vec{a}_x$$

The instantaneous expression for $\vec{E}$ is

$$\vec{E}(z,t) = \text{Re}\left[\tilde{E}(z)e^{j\omega t}\right]$$

$$= \text{Re}\left[200 e^{-\alpha z}e^{j(\omega t - \beta z)}\vec{a}_x\right] = 200 e^{-\alpha z}\cos\left(\omega t - \beta z\right)\vec{a}_x$$

At $z = 0.9$m, we have

$$\vec{E}(0.9,t) = 200 e^{-0.9\alpha}\cos\left(10^7\pi t - 0.9\beta\right)\vec{a}_x$$

$$= 0.067\cos\left(10^7\pi t - 8\right)\vec{a}_x \text{ V/m}$$

We know that a uniform plane wave is a TEM wave with electric and magnetic fields perpendicular to each other and both are normal to the direction of wave propagation $\vec{a}_z$. Therefore, $\vec{H} = H_y\vec{a}_y$. Now, the magnetic field in phasor form is represented by

$$\tilde{H}_y(z) = \dfrac{\tilde{E}_x(z)}{\eta_c}$$

At $z = 0.9\,\text{m}$, $\tilde{H}_y(0.9) = \dfrac{200e^{-0.9\alpha}e^{-j0.9\beta}}{\pi e^{j\pi/4}} = \dfrac{0.067e^{-j8}}{\pi e^{j\pi/4}} = 0.021e^{-j2.5}$

The instantaneous expression for the magnetic field is

$$H_y(z,t) = \text{Re}\left[\frac{\tilde{E}_x(z)}{\eta_c}e^{j\omega t}\right] = \text{Re}\left[0.021e^{-j2.5}e^{j\omega t}\right]$$

At $z = 0.9\,\text{m}$, the magnetic field is

$$\vec{H}(0.9,t) = 0.021\cos\left(10^7\pi t - 2.5\right)\vec{a}_y\,\text{A/m}$$

EXAMPLE 7.16

A uniform plane wave propagating in medium has $\vec{E} = 4e^{-\alpha z}\sin\left(10^8 t - \beta z\right)\vec{a}_y$ V/m. If the medium is characterized by $\varepsilon_r = 1$, $\mu_r = 10$ and $\sigma = 6\,\text{S/m}$, find α, β and $\vec{H}$.

SOLUTION

Given $\vec{E} = 4e^{-\alpha z}\sin\left(10^8 t - \beta z\right)\vec{a}_y$ V/m, $\varepsilon_r = 1$, $\mu_r = 10$ and $\sigma = 6\,\text{S/m}$.

To identify whether the medium is a lossy dielectric or a good conductor, loss tangent has to be determined. The loss tangent is

$$\frac{\sigma}{\omega\varepsilon} = \frac{6}{10^8 \times 1 \times 8.854 \times 10^{-12}} = 6777 \qquad \left(\text{since } \varepsilon = \varepsilon_0\varepsilon_r\right)$$

Since $\dfrac{\sigma}{\omega\varepsilon} \gg 1$, the medium is considered as a good conductor at the given frequency of operation. In a good conductor, the attenuation constant and phase constant are equal.

Therefore,

$$\alpha = \beta = \sqrt{\frac{\mu\omega\sigma}{2}} = \left[\frac{4\pi \times 10^{-7} \times 10 \times 10^8 \times 6}{2}\right]^{1/2} \qquad \left(\text{since } \mu = \mu_0\mu_r\right)$$

$$= 61.38$$

That is,

$$\alpha = 61.38\,\text{Np/m}, \quad \beta = 61.38\,\text{rad/m}$$

The intrinsic impedance,

$$|\eta| = \sqrt{\frac{\mu\omega}{\sigma}} = \left[\frac{4\pi \times 10^{-7} \times 10 \times 10^8}{6}\right]^{1/2} = 14.47\,\Omega$$

$$\tan 2\theta_\eta = \frac{\sigma}{\omega\varepsilon} = 6777$$

$$\theta_\eta = 45° = \frac{\pi}{4}$$

Therefore, $\vec{H}$ lags $\vec{E}$ by $45°$ or $\dfrac{\pi}{4}$ in case of good conductors.
That is,

$$\vec{H} = H_0 e^{-\alpha z} \sin\left(\omega t - \beta z - \frac{\pi}{4}\right)\vec{a}_H$$

Here,

$$\vec{a}_H = \vec{a}_k \times \vec{a}_E = \vec{a}_z \times \vec{a}_y = -\vec{a}_x$$

and

$$H_0 = \frac{E_0}{|\eta|} = \frac{4}{14.47} = 0.28$$

Hence,

$$\vec{H} = -0.28 e^{-61.38z} \sin\left(10^8 t - 61.38z - \frac{\pi}{4}\right)\vec{a}_x \ \text{A/m}$$

EXAMPLE 7.17

Calculate the intrinsic impedance η, the propagation constant γ and the wave velocity u for a conducting medium in which $\sigma = 58\,\text{MS/m}$ and $\mu_r = 1$ at a frequency $f = 100\,\text{MHz}$.

SOLUTION

For a conducting medium, $\sigma = 58\,\text{MS/m}$ and $\mu_r = 1$ at a frequency $f = 100\,\text{MHz}$.

The intrinsic impedance,

$$\eta = \sqrt{\frac{j\omega\mu}{\sigma}} = \sqrt{\frac{2\pi \times 100 \times 10^6 \times 4\pi \times 10^{-7}}{58 \times 10^6}}\angle 45° = 3.69 \times 10^{-3} \angle 45°\,\Omega$$

The propagation constant,

$$\gamma = \alpha + j\beta = \sqrt{j\omega\mu\sigma} = \sqrt{\omega\mu\sigma}\angle 45°$$

$$= \sqrt{2\pi \times 100 \times 10^6 \times 4\pi \times 10^{-7} \times 58 \times 10^6}\angle 45° = 2.14 \times 10^5 \angle 45°\text{m}^{-1}$$

$$\gamma = \alpha + j\beta = 1.53 \times 10^5 + j1.53 \times 10^5\,\text{m}^{-1}$$

Comparing the real and imaginary parts, we get

The attenuation constant, $\alpha = 1.53 \times 10^5\,\text{Np/m}$

The phase constant, $\beta = 1.53 \times 10^5\,\text{rad/m}$

The skin depth, $\delta = \dfrac{1}{\alpha} = \dfrac{1}{1.53 \times 10^5} = 6.61\,\mu\text{m}$

The wave velocity, $u = \omega\delta = 2\pi \times 100 \times 10^6 \times 6.61 \times 10^{-6} = 4.15 \times 10^3\,\text{m/s}$

EXAMPLE 7.18

The magnetic field is given by $\vec{H} = -0.5\cos(\omega t - z)\vec{a}_x + 0.1\sin(\omega t - z)\vec{a}_y\,\text{A/m}$ in a lossless medium for which $\eta = 30\pi$ and $\mu_r = 1$. Calculate ε_r, ω and $\vec{E}$.

SOLUTION

Given $\eta = 30\pi$, $\beta = 1$, $\mu_r = 1$ and $\vec{H} = -0.5\cos(\omega t - z)\vec{a}_x + 0.1\sin(\omega t - z)\vec{a}_y\,\text{A/m}$.

Since the given medium is a lossless one, $\sigma = 0$ and $\alpha = 0$. The intrinsic impedance is

$$\eta = \sqrt{\frac{\mu}{\varepsilon}} = \sqrt{\frac{\mu_0\mu_r}{\varepsilon_0\varepsilon_r}} = \frac{120\pi}{\sqrt{\varepsilon_r}}$$

That is,

$$\sqrt{\varepsilon_r} = \frac{120\pi}{\eta} = \frac{120\pi}{30\pi} = 4$$

Squaring both the sides of the above equation, we get

$$\varepsilon_r = 16$$

The phase constant is

$$\beta = \omega\sqrt{\mu\varepsilon} = \omega\sqrt{\mu_0\varepsilon_0}\sqrt{\mu_r\varepsilon_r} = \frac{\omega}{c}\sqrt{16} = \frac{4\omega}{c}$$

or

$$\omega = \frac{\beta c}{4} = \frac{1\times 3\times 10^8}{4}$$

$$= 0.75\times 10^8\,\text{rad/s}$$

From the given magnetic field $\vec{H}$, the electric field $\vec{E}$ can be determined by using Maxwell's equations. Applying Maxwell's equations,

$$\nabla\times\vec{H} = \sigma\vec{E} + \varepsilon\frac{\partial\vec{E}}{\partial t}$$

The first term on the right-hand side of the above equation is zero because $\sigma = 0$. Thus, the electric field is $\vec{E} = \dfrac{1}{\varepsilon}\int(\nabla\times\vec{H})\,dt$.

Here,

$$\nabla\times\vec{H} = \begin{vmatrix} \vec{a}_x & \vec{a}_y & \vec{a}_z \\ \dfrac{\partial}{\partial x} & \dfrac{\partial}{\partial y} & \dfrac{\partial}{\partial z} \\ H_x & H_y & 0 \end{vmatrix} = -\frac{\partial H_y}{\partial z}\vec{a}_x + \frac{\partial H_x}{\partial z}\vec{a}_y + \frac{\partial H_y}{\partial x}\vec{a}_z - \frac{\partial H_x}{\partial y}\vec{a}_z$$

where, $H_x = -0.5\cos(\omega t - z)$ and $H_y = -0.1\sin(\omega t - z)$.

Hence, $\nabla \times \vec{H} = 0.1\cos(\omega t - z)\vec{a}_x - 0.5\sin(\omega t - z)\vec{a}_y$

Therefore, $\vec{E} = \dfrac{1}{\varepsilon}\int(\nabla \times \vec{H})\,dt = \dfrac{0.1}{\varepsilon\omega}\sin(\omega t - z)\vec{a}_x + \dfrac{0.5}{\varepsilon\omega}\cos(\omega t - z)\vec{a}_y$

Substituting $\varepsilon = \varepsilon_0\varepsilon_r = 8.854\times10^{-12}\times16 = 141.664\times10^{-12}$ and $\omega = 0.75\times10^8$ rad/s in the above equation, we get

$$\vec{E} = 9.41\sin(\omega t - z)\vec{a}_x + 47.06\cos(\omega t - z)\vec{a}_y \text{ V/m}$$

EXAMPLE 7.19

A narrow-band signal propagates in a lossy dielectric medium which has a loss tangent 0.3 at a carrier frequency of 650 kHz. The dielectric constant of the medium is 3.5. Determine *(i)* α, *(ii)* β, *(iii)* u_p and *(iv)* u_g.

SOLUTION

(i) Since the given loss tangent $\dfrac{\sigma}{\omega\varepsilon} = 0.3,$ the expressions of α and β derived for low-loss dielectric in Eqs. (7.67) and (7.68) can be used.

Here, $\sigma = 0.3\omega\varepsilon = 0.3\times2\pi f\times\varepsilon_0\varepsilon_r = 3.794\times10^{-5}$

(ii) The attenuation and phase constants are

$$\alpha = \frac{\sigma}{2}\sqrt{\frac{\mu}{\varepsilon}} = \frac{3.794\times10^{-5}}{2}\times\frac{120\pi}{\sqrt{3.5}} = 3.82\times10^{-3}\,\text{Np/m}$$

$$\beta = \omega\sqrt{\mu\varepsilon} = 2\pi\left(650\times10^3\right)\times\frac{\sqrt{3.5}}{3\times10^8} = 0.0254\,\text{rad/m}$$

(iii) From Eq. (7.70), the phase velocity is

$$u_p = \frac{\omega}{\beta} = \frac{\omega}{\omega\sqrt{\mu\varepsilon}} = \frac{3\times10^8}{\sqrt{3.5}} = 1.604\times10^8\,\text{m/s}$$

(iv) Since $\beta = \omega\sqrt{\mu\varepsilon}$, the group velocity is

$$u_g = \frac{1}{(d\beta/d\omega)}, \text{ where } \frac{d\beta}{d\omega} = \sqrt{\mu\varepsilon}$$

$$= \frac{1}{\sqrt{\mu\varepsilon}} \cong u_p = 1.604\times10^8\ \text{m/s}$$

EXAMPLE 7.20

A 100 MHz uniform plane wave is travelling in a non-magnetic medium with $\mu = \mu_0$ and $\varepsilon_r = 4$. Determine *(i)* phase velocity, *(ii)* wave number, *(iii)* the wavelength in the medium and *(iv)* the intrinsic impedance of the medium.

SOLUTION

(*i*) The phase velocity is

$$u_p = \frac{1}{\sqrt{\mu\varepsilon}} = \frac{1}{\sqrt{\mu_0\varepsilon_0}\sqrt{\varepsilon_r}} = \frac{c}{\sqrt{\varepsilon_r}}$$

$$= \frac{3\times10^8}{\sqrt{4}} = 1.5\times10^8\,\text{m/s}$$

(*ii*) The wave number is

$$k = \beta = \frac{\omega}{u_p} = \frac{2\pi\times10^8}{1.5\times10^8} = 1.33\pi\ \text{rad/m}$$

(*iii*) The wavelength in the medium is

$$\lambda = \frac{2\pi}{\beta} = \frac{2\pi}{1.33\pi} = 1.5\,\text{m}$$

(*iv*) The intrinsic impedance is

$$\eta = \sqrt{\frac{\mu}{\varepsilon}} = \sqrt{\frac{\mu_0}{\varepsilon_0}}\cdot\frac{1}{\sqrt{\varepsilon_r}} = \frac{377}{2} = 188.5\,\Omega \qquad \square$$

EXAMPLE 7.21

If the magnetic field phasor of a plane wave travelling in a medium with intrinsic impedance $\eta = 100\,\Omega$ is given by $\tilde{H} = \left(20\vec{a}_y + 30\vec{a}_z\right)e^{-j4x}\text{mA/m}$, determine the associated electric field phasor.

SOLUTION

Given $\tilde{H} = \left(20\vec{a}_y + 30\vec{a}_z\right)e^{-j4x}\text{mA/m}$.

The associated electric field phasor is

$$\tilde{E} = -\eta\vec{a}_k \times \tilde{H}, \text{ where } \vec{a}_k = \vec{a}_x$$

$$= -100\left[\vec{a}_x \times \left(20\vec{a}_y + 30\vec{a}_z\right)\right]e^{-j4x}\times10^{-3}$$

$$= \left(-2\vec{a}_z + 3\vec{a}_y\right)e^{-j4x}\text{V/m} \qquad \square$$

EXAMPLE 7.22

The constitutive parameters of copper are $\sigma = 5.8\times10^7\,\text{S/m}$, $\mu = \mu_0 = 4\pi\times10^{-7}\,\text{H/m}$ and $\varepsilon = \varepsilon_0 = \left(1/36\pi\right)\times10^{-9}\,\text{F/m}$. Assuming that these parameters are frequency independent, over what frequency range of the electromagnetic spectrum is copper, a good conductor?

SOLUTION

For good conductors, $\sigma \gg \omega\varepsilon$. Therefore, let us assume that,

$$\frac{\sigma}{\omega\varepsilon} > 100$$

We know that, $\omega = 2\pi f$.

Therefore, $\dfrac{\sigma}{100\varepsilon} > \omega$ (or) $\omega < \dfrac{\sigma}{100\varepsilon}$

Then, $2\pi f < \dfrac{\sigma}{100\varepsilon_0}$

$$f < \frac{\sigma}{200\pi\varepsilon_0} = \frac{5.8\times10^7}{200\pi\times(1/36\pi)\times10^{-9}} = 1.04\times10^{16}\,\text{Hz}$$

So, copper is a good conductor for frequencies less than $1.04\times10^{16}\,\text{Hz}$. ❑

EXAMPLE 7.23

A certain signal generator produces a uniform plane wave in free space having a wavelength of 15 cm. When this wave travels through a lossless material of unknown characteristics, its wavelength changes to 7 cm. In this material, the amplitude of an electric field is 100 V/m and of a magnetic field is 0.2 A/m. Determine *(i)* the frequency of generator, *(ii)* μ_r and *(iii)* ε_r.

SOLUTION

Given $\lambda_1 = 15\,\text{cm}$, $\lambda_2 = 7\,\text{cm}$, $E_m = 100\,\text{V/m}$ and $H_m = 0.2\,\text{A/m}$.

The velocity of propagation in free space is

$$u_1 = c = f\lambda_1 = 3\times10^8\,\text{m/s}$$

The frequency of generator is

$$f = \frac{c}{\lambda_1} = \frac{3\times10^8}{15\times10^{-2}} = 2\times10^9\,\text{Hz} \tag{1}$$

Now, the wave travels through the lossless medium with wavelength $\lambda_2 = 7\,\text{cm} = 7\times10^{-2}\,\text{m}$ but the frequency f remains same. Therefore, the velocity of a wave in the lossless material is

$$u_2 = f\lambda_2 = \left(2\times10^9\right)\left(7\times10^{-2}\right) = 1.4\times10^8\,\text{m/s} \tag{2}$$

The velocity of the signal in the lossless material can also be written as

$$u_2 = \frac{1}{\sqrt{\mu\varepsilon}} = \frac{1}{\sqrt{(\mu_0\mu_r)(\varepsilon_0\varepsilon_r)}}$$

$$1.4\times10^8 = \frac{c}{\sqrt{\mu_r\varepsilon_r}} = \frac{3\times10^8}{\sqrt{\mu_r\varepsilon_r}}$$

Hence, $\mu_r\varepsilon_r = 4.587$ $\tag{3}$

The intrinsic impedance in the lossless material is

$$\eta = \sqrt{\frac{\mu}{\varepsilon}} = \sqrt{\frac{\mu_0\mu_r}{\varepsilon_0\varepsilon_r}}$$

This intrinsic impedance η can also be expressed in terms of the amplitudes of the fields as

$$\eta = \frac{E_m}{H_m} = \frac{100}{0.2} = 500\,\Omega$$

Comparing the above two expressions for η, we get

$$500 = 120\pi\sqrt{\frac{\mu_r}{\varepsilon_r}}$$

$$\frac{\mu_r}{\varepsilon_r} = 1.762 \qquad\qquad (4)$$

Solving Eqs. (3) and (4), we get

$$\mu_r = 2.843$$

$$\varepsilon_r = 1.613 \qquad\qquad \square$$

EXAMPLE 7.24

A plane wave $\vec{E} = E_0 \cos\left(\omega t - \beta z\right)\vec{a}_x$ V/m is incident on a good conductor at $z = 0$. Determine the current density in the conductor.

SOLUTION

Since the current density $\vec{J} = \sigma\vec{E}$, it is expected that $\vec{J}$ has to satisfy the wave equation.

That is,

$$\nabla^2\tilde{J} - \gamma^2\tilde{J} = 0$$

Here, the given electric field $\vec{E}$ has only an x-component and it varies with z.

Therefore, $\vec{J} = J_x\left(z,t\right)\vec{a}_x$ and $\dfrac{d^2}{dz^2}\tilde{J}_x - \gamma^2\tilde{J}_x = 0$

The above equation is an ordinary second-order differential equation and its solution is

$$\tilde{J}_x = Ae^{-\gamma z} + Be^{+\gamma z}$$

As z tends to infinity, $\tilde{J}_x$ will have finite value and the constant B will be zero. We know that, for a good conductor, $\sigma \gg \omega\varepsilon$ and $\alpha = \beta = 1/\delta$.

Hence,

$$\gamma = \alpha + j\beta = \alpha\left(1 + j\right) = \frac{\left(1 + j\right)}{\delta}$$

Therefore, the current density in the conductor is

$$\tilde{J}_x = Ae^{-z(1+j)/\delta}$$

or

$$\tilde{J}_x = \tilde{J}_x\left(0\right)e^{-z(1+j)/\delta}$$

where $\tilde{J}_x(0)$ is the phasor form of current density on the conductor surface.

Hence,

$$\vec{J} = J_x \vec{a}_x = Ae^{-z(1+j)/\delta}\vec{a}_x \ \text{A/m}^2 \qquad \square$$

EXAMPLE 7.25

A uniform plane wave is travelling at a velocity of 2.5×10^5 m/s having wavelength $\lambda = 0.25\,$mm in a non-magnetic good conductor. Calculate the frequency of wave and the conductivity of a medium.

SOLUTION

Given $u_p = 2.5\times10^5\,$m/s and $\lambda = 0.25\,$mm.

The velocity of propagation is

$$u_p = \lambda f$$

Therefore, the frequency of the wave is

$$f = \frac{u_p}{\lambda} = \frac{2.5\times10^5}{0.25\times10^{-3}} = 1\times10^9\,\text{Hz} = 1\,\text{GHz}$$

But the velocity of propagation can also be written as

$$u_p = \frac{\omega}{\beta} = \frac{2\pi f}{\beta}$$

The phase constant is

$$\beta = \frac{2\pi f}{u_p} = \frac{2\pi\times1\times10^9}{2.5\times10^5} = 25.13\times10^3\,\text{rad/m}$$

For good conductor, $\beta = \sqrt{\pi f u \sigma} = \sqrt{\pi f \left(\mu_0 \mu_r\right)\sigma}$

Since $\mu_r = 1$ for a non-magnetic material,

$$\beta = 25.13\times10^3 = \sqrt{\pi\times1\times10^9\times\left(4\pi\times10^{-7}\right)\times\sigma}$$

Solving for the conductivity, σ, of the medium, we get

$$\sigma = \frac{\left(25.13\times10^3\right)^2}{3943.84} = 1.6\times10^5\,\text{S/m} \qquad \square$$

EXAMPLE 7.26

A uniform plane in a medium with $\sigma = 10^{-3}\,$S/m, $\varepsilon = 80\varepsilon_0$ and $\mu = \mu_0$ is having a frequency of 10 kHz. Calculate different parameters of the wave.

SOLUTION

Given $f = 10\,$kHz, $\sigma = 10^{-3}\,$S/m, $\varepsilon = 80\varepsilon_0$ and $\mu = \mu_0$.

In order to determine the type of medium, let us first find the ratio of $\dfrac{\sigma}{\omega\varepsilon}$.

$$\frac{\sigma}{\omega\varepsilon} = \frac{\sigma}{(2\pi f)(80\varepsilon_0)} = \frac{10^{-3}}{2\pi\times10\times10^3\times80\times8.854\times10^{-12}} = 22.47$$

As the ratio of $\dfrac{\sigma}{\omega\varepsilon}$ is greater than 1, the medium can be assumed to be a conducting medium at frequency of $10\,\text{kHz}$. Therefore, for the conducting medium, the different parameters can be obtained as follows:

(*i*) The attenuation constant,

$$\alpha = \sqrt{\pi f\,\mu\sigma} = \sqrt{\pi f\,\mu_0\sigma} = \sqrt{\pi\times10\times10^3\times4\pi\times10^{-7}\times10^{-3}}$$

$$= 6.28\times10^{-3}\,\text{Np/m}$$

(*ii*) The phase constant,

$$\beta = \alpha = 6.28\times10^{-3}\,\text{rad/m}$$

(*iii*) The propagation constant,

$$\gamma = \alpha + j\beta = 6.28\times10^{-3} + j6.28\times10^{-3}$$

$$= 8.88\times10^{-3}\angle45°\text{m}^{-1}$$

(*iv*) The complex intrinsic impedance,

$$\eta_c = \sqrt{\frac{j\omega\mu}{\sigma + j\omega\varepsilon}} = \sqrt{\frac{j(2\pi f)\mu_0}{\sigma + j(2\pi f)(80\varepsilon_0)}}$$

$$= \sqrt{\frac{j\left(2\pi\times10\times10^3\right)\left(4\pi\times10^{-7}\right)}{10^{-3} + j\left(2\pi\times10\times10^3\right)\left(80\times8.854\times10^{-12}\right)}}$$

$$= \sqrt{\frac{j0.079}{0.001 + j4.45\times10^{-5}}} = \sqrt{\frac{0.079\angle90°}{1\times10^{-3}\angle2.548°}} = 8.89\angle43.73°\,\Omega$$

(*v*) The wavelength,

$$\lambda = \frac{2\pi}{\beta} = \frac{2\pi}{6.28\times10^{-3}} = 1000\,\text{m}$$

(*vi*) The velocity of propagation,

$$u_p = \frac{1}{\sqrt{\mu\varepsilon}} = \frac{1}{\sqrt{\mu_0\left(80\varepsilon_0\right)}} = \frac{3\times10^8}{\sqrt{80}}$$

$$= 0.335\times10^8\,\text{m/s}$$

EXAMPLE 7.27

The electric field associated with a plane wave travelling in a perfect dielectric medium is given by $E_x(z,t) = 10\cos\left(2\pi \times 10^7 t - 0.1\pi z\right)$ V/m. Find the velocity of propagation and intrinsic impedance. Assume $\mu = \mu_0$.

SOLUTION

Given $E_x(z,t) = 10\cos\left(2\pi \times 10^7 t - 0.1\pi z\right)$ V/m.

The general expression for electric field is $E_x(z,t) = E_{x0}\cos\left(\omega t - \beta z\right)$ V/m.

Comparing the given field with the general expression, we get $E_{x0} = 10$, $\omega = 2\pi \times 10^7$ rad/s and $\beta = 0.1\pi$ rad/m.

(*i*) The velocity of wave propagation in a perfect dielectric medium is

$$u = \frac{1}{\sqrt{\mu\varepsilon}} = \frac{c}{\sqrt{\mu_r \varepsilon_r}}$$

It is given that $\mu = \mu_0$. Therefore, $\mu_r = 1$ for the given medium.

The phase constant is given by

$$\beta = \omega\sqrt{\mu\varepsilon} = \omega\sqrt{\mu_0\left(\varepsilon_0\varepsilon_r\right)}$$

$$0.1\pi = \left(2\pi \times 10^7\right)\sqrt{\left(4\pi \times 10^{-7}\right)\left(8.854 \times 10^{-12} \times \varepsilon_r\right)}$$

Solving for ε_r, we get

$$\varepsilon_r = 2.2469$$

Hence, the velocity of wave propagation is

$$u_p = \frac{c}{\sqrt{\mu_r \varepsilon_r}} = \frac{3 \times 10^8}{\sqrt{1 \times 2.2469}} = 2 \times 10^8 \text{ m/s}$$

(*ii*) The intrinsic impedance of a dielectric medium is

$$\eta = \eta_0\sqrt{\frac{\mu_r}{\varepsilon_r}}, \text{ where } \eta_0 = 377\Omega \text{ (for free space)}$$

$$= 377\sqrt{\frac{1}{2.2469}} = 251.33\Omega$$

7.5 POYNTING VECTOR AND POYNTING'S THEOREM

The energy is transferred from the transmitter to the receiver by means of an EM wave in free space. The power flow in any medium can be obtained using Poynting's theorem. This theorem was developed in 1884 by an English Physicist John H. Poynting. The rate of energy transfer and the electric and magnetic field intensities of the travelling EM wave are related by Poynting's theorem. This relation can be obtained from Maxwell's curl equations.

The Maxwell's curl equation of $\vec{H}$ is given by

$$\nabla \times \vec{H} = \vec{J} + \frac{\partial \vec{D}}{\partial t} \tag{7.75}$$

Taking the scalar product on both sides of the above equation with $\vec{E}$, we have

$$\vec{E} \cdot \left(\nabla \times \vec{H} \right) = \vec{E} \cdot \vec{J} + \vec{E} \cdot \frac{\partial \vec{D}}{\partial t} \tag{7.76}$$

Using the vector identity $\nabla \cdot \left(\vec{E} \times \vec{H} \right) = \vec{H} \cdot \left(\nabla \times \vec{E} \right) - \vec{E} \cdot \left(\nabla \times \vec{H} \right)$ in the above equation, we get

$$\vec{H} \cdot \left(\nabla \times \vec{E} \right) - \nabla \cdot \left(\vec{E} \times \vec{H} \right) = \vec{J} \cdot \vec{E} + \vec{E} \cdot \frac{\partial \vec{D}}{\partial t} \tag{7.77}$$

Since $\nabla \times \vec{E} = -\frac{\partial \vec{B}}{\partial t}$ is the Maxwell's curl equation of $\vec{E}$, the above equation becomes

$$\nabla \cdot \left(\vec{E} \times \vec{H} \right) = -\vec{E} \cdot \frac{\partial \vec{D}}{\partial t} - \vec{H} \cdot \frac{\partial \vec{B}}{\partial t} - \vec{J} \cdot \vec{E} \tag{7.78}$$

For time-varying fields in a linear, homogeneous and isotropic medium, $\vec{D} = \varepsilon \vec{E}$ and $\vec{B} = \mu \vec{H}$. Since the constitutive parameters ε, μ and σ do not change with time in a simple medium, we have

$$\vec{E} \cdot \frac{\partial \vec{D}}{\partial t} = \vec{E} \cdot \frac{\partial \left(\varepsilon \vec{E} \right)}{\partial t} = \frac{1}{2} \frac{\partial \left(\varepsilon \vec{E} \cdot \vec{E} \right)}{\partial t} = \frac{\partial}{\partial t} \left(\frac{1}{2} \varepsilon E^2 \right)$$

$$\vec{H} \cdot \frac{\partial \vec{B}}{\partial t} = \vec{H} \cdot \frac{\partial \left(\mu \vec{H} \right)}{\partial t} = \frac{1}{2} \frac{\partial \left(\mu \vec{H} \cdot \vec{H} \right)}{\partial t} = \frac{\partial}{\partial t} \left(\frac{1}{2} \mu H^2 \right)$$

$$\vec{J} \cdot \vec{E} = \left(\sigma \vec{E} \right) \cdot \vec{E} = \sigma E^2$$

Substituting the above equations in Eq. (7.78), we get

$$\nabla \cdot \left(\vec{E} \times \vec{H} \right) = -\frac{\partial}{\partial t} \left[\frac{1}{2} \varepsilon E^2 + \frac{1}{2} \mu H^2 \right] - \sigma E^2 \tag{7.79}$$

Taking volume integral on both the sides of Eq. (7.79), we get

$$\int_v \nabla \cdot \left(\vec{E} \times \vec{H} \right) dv = -\frac{\partial}{\partial t} \int_v \left[\frac{1}{2} \varepsilon E^2 + \frac{1}{2} \mu H^2 \right] dv - \int_v \sigma E^2 dv \tag{7.80}$$

Applying divergence theorem to the left-hand side of the above equation, we get

$$\oint_s \left(\vec{E} \times \vec{H} \right) \cdot d\vec{s} = -\frac{\partial}{\partial t} \int_v \left[\frac{1}{2} \varepsilon E^2 + \frac{1}{2} \mu H^2 \right] dv - \int_v \sigma E^2 dv \tag{7.81}$$

The above equation is called the *Poynting's theorem*. The first and second term on the right-hand side of Eq. (7.81) represents the rate of decrease in energy stored in the electric and magnetic fields, respectively. The last term is the ohmic power dissipated in the volume due to the flow of conduction current density. The left-hand side of Eq. (7.81) represents the total power flowing out of the volume through its surface.

Poynting's theorem states that the net power leaving the volume v is equal to the difference between the rate of decrease of the electric and magnetic energies stored within v and the ohmic power dissipation. Here, the quantity $\vec{E} \times \vec{H}$ is known as the *Poynting vector* and it represents the total power flow per unit area.

That is,

$$\vec{S} = \vec{E} \times \vec{H} \tag{7.82}$$

The unit of Poynting vector is watt per square metre (W/m^2). This Poynting vector $\vec{S}$ is an instantaneous power density vector associated with an electromagnetic field at a given point. Therefore, the surface integral of Poynting vector $\vec{S}$ over a closed surface in Eq. (7.81) equals the power leaving the enclosed volume.

Equation (7.81) can also be written as

$$-\oint_S \left(\vec{E} \times \vec{H}\right) \cdot d\vec{s} = \frac{\partial}{\partial t} \int_V \left(w_e + w_m\right) dv + \int_v p_\sigma \, dv \tag{7.83}$$

where $p_\sigma = \sigma E^2$ is the ohmic power density, $w_e = \frac{1}{2} \varepsilon E^2$ is the energy density in electric field and $w_m = \frac{1}{2} \mu H^2$ is the energy density in magnetic field. It is evident from Eq. (7.83) that the total power flowing into a closed surface is equal to the sum of the rate of increase in energy stored in the electric and magnetic fields and the ohmic power dissipated in the enclosed volume.

For static fields, $\frac{\partial}{\partial t} = 0$. Therefore, the first two terms on the right side of Eq. (7.83) vanishes and the total power flowing into a closed surface is equal to the ohmic power dissipated in the enclosed volume. For lossless medium, $\sigma = 0$. Hence, the last term of Eq. (7.83) vanishes and the total power flowing into a closed surface is equal to the sum of the rate of increase in energy stored in the electric and magnetic fields in the enclosed volume.

7.5.1 Instantaneous and Average Power Densities

Since the Poynting vector $\vec{S}$ is the cross product of $\vec{E}$ and $\vec{H}$, the direction of power flow at any point is normal to both $\vec{E}$ and $\vec{H}$. Therefore, for a uniform plane wave, with E_x and H_y component, the wave propagation is in the "$+z$"-direction. The instantaneous power density of the wave along z-direction can be written as

$$\vec{S} = S_z \vec{a}_z = E_x \vec{a}_x \times H_y \vec{a}_y = E_x H_y \vec{a}_z$$

That is,

$$S_z = E_x H_y \tag{7.84}$$

Considering the wave propagation in "$+z$"-direction, the amplitudes of electric and magnetic fields in a perfect dielectric are

$$E_x = E_{x0} \cos\left(\omega t - \beta z\right) \tag{7.85}$$

$$H_y = \frac{E_{x0}}{\eta} \cos\left(\omega t - \beta z\right) \tag{7.86}$$

where η is the intrinsic impedance of the medium.

Substituting Eq. (7.85) and Eq. (7.86) in Eq. (7.84), we get

$$S_z = \frac{E_{x0}^2}{\eta} \cos^2\left(\omega t - \beta z\right) \tag{7.87}$$

For lossy dielectric, E_x and H_y are not in time phase and it is associated with an attenuation constant α. Hence,

$$E_x = E_{x0}e^{-\alpha z}\cos(\omega t - \beta z)$$

and

$$H_y = \frac{E_{x0}}{\eta}e^{-\alpha z}\cos(\omega t - \beta z) == \frac{E_{x0}}{|\eta|}e^{-\alpha z}\cos(\omega t - \beta z - \theta_\eta)$$

where $\eta = |\eta|\angle\theta_\eta = |\eta|e^{j\theta_\eta}$ and θ_η is the phase angle of the intrinsic impedance.

Therefore,

$$S_z = E_x H_y = \frac{E_{x0}^2}{|\eta|}e^{-2\alpha z}\cos(\omega t - \beta z)\cos(\omega t - \beta z - \theta_\eta)$$

Since $\cos A\cos B = \dfrac{1}{2}\big[\cos(A+B) + \cos(A-B)\big]$,

$$S_z = \frac{E_{x0}^2}{2|\eta|}e^{-2\alpha z}\big[\cos(2\omega t - 2\beta z - \theta_\eta) + \cos\theta_\eta\big] \tag{7.88}$$

For the power transmitted by an EM wave, the average power density is a more significant quantity than the instantaneous power density. The time-average power density can be obtained by integrating Eq. (7.88) over one cycle and dividing it by the fundamental period, $T = \dfrac{1}{f} = \dfrac{2\pi}{\omega}$.

Hence,

$$S_{z(avg)} = \frac{1}{T}\int_0^T S_z\, dt$$

$$= \frac{1}{T}\int_0^T \frac{E_{x0}^2}{2|\eta|}e^{-2\alpha z}\big[\cos(2\omega t - 2\beta z - \theta_\eta) + \cos\theta_\eta\big]\, dt \tag{7.89}$$

The integration of second harmonic component, i.e., $\cos(2\omega t - 2\beta z - \theta_\eta)$ in the above equation is zero and the time-average power density is represented by

$$S_{z(avg)} = \frac{E_{x0}^2}{2|\eta|}e^{-2\alpha z}\cos\theta_\eta \; \text{W/m}^2$$

The instantaneous Poynting vector or power density of the wave can be written in phasor form as

$$\vec{S}_z = \mathrm{Re}\big[\tilde{E}e^{j\omega t}\big]\times\mathrm{Re}\big[\tilde{H}e^{j\omega t}\big]$$

$$= \frac{1}{2}\mathrm{Re}\big[\tilde{E}\times\tilde{H}^* + \tilde{E}\times\tilde{H}e^{j2\omega t}\big] \tag{7.90}$$

where $\tilde{H}^*$ denotes the complex conjugate of $\tilde{H}$. The average power density can also be obtained in phasor form by integrating the above equation over one cycle and dividing it by the fundamental period, $T = \dfrac{1}{f} = \dfrac{2\pi}{\omega}$.

$$\vec{S}_{z(avg)} = \frac{1}{T}\int_0^T S_z\, dt = \frac{1}{T}\int_0^T \frac{1}{2}\mathrm{Re}\big[\tilde{E}\times\tilde{H}^* + \tilde{E}\times\tilde{H}e^{j2\omega t}\big]\, dt \tag{7.91}$$

The second harmonic component in the equation integrates to zero and the time-average power density or Poynting vector is represented by

$$\vec{S}_{z(avg)} = \frac{1}{2}\mathrm{Re}\left[\tilde{E}\times\tilde{H}^*\right]\text{W/m}^2 \qquad (7.92)$$

The above equation is a general formula for determining the average power density of an EM wave propagating in the "$+z$"-direction. It is applicable to both lossless and lossy mediums.

The electric and magnetic fields in Eqs. (7.85) and (7.86) can be expressed in phasor form as

$$\tilde{E} = E_{x0}e^{-j\beta z}\vec{a}_x \qquad (7.93)$$

$$\tilde{H}^* = \frac{E_{x0}}{\eta^*}e^{j\beta z}\vec{a}_y = \frac{E_{x0}}{|\eta|}e^{j\theta_\eta}e^{j\beta z}\vec{a}_y \qquad (7.94)$$

where E_{x0} is a real value.

Substituting Eq. (7.93) and Eq. (7.94) in Eq. (7.92), we get the average power density in phasor domain as

$$\vec{S}_{z(avg)} = \frac{1}{2}\mathrm{Re}\left[E_{x0}e^{-j\beta z}\vec{a}_x \times \frac{E_{x0}}{|\eta|}e^{j\theta_\eta}e^{j\beta z}\vec{a}_y\right]$$

$$= \frac{\left|E_{x0}^2\right|}{2\eta}\vec{a}_z \qquad \text{(since } \vec{a}_x\times\vec{a}_y = \vec{a}_z\text{)}$$

The average power density is generally expressed as $\vec{S}_{(avg)}$.

EXAMPLE 7.28

A plane TEM wave has a power density of 2 W/m^2 in a medium with $\varepsilon_r = 3$ and $\mu_r = 1$. Find $\vec{E}$ and $\vec{H}$.

SOLUTION

The intrinsic impedance for the given medium is

$$\eta = \sqrt{\frac{\mu}{\varepsilon}} = \sqrt{\frac{\mu_0\mu_r}{\varepsilon_0\varepsilon_r}} = 120\pi\sqrt{\frac{1}{3}} = 217.51\,\Omega$$

The magnitude of average power density is

$$S_{avg} = \frac{1}{2}\frac{E_m^2}{\eta}$$

That is,

$$E_m^2 = 2P_{avg}\eta = 2(2)(217.5076) = 870$$

Hence,

$$E_m = \sqrt{870} = 29.5\,\text{V/m}$$

Here, the magnetic field is

$$H_m = \frac{E_m}{\eta} = \frac{29.5}{217.51} = 0.135\,\text{A/m}$$

If the electric field intensity is assumed to be in x-direction, then for a TEM wave, $\vec{H}$ will be perpendicular to $\vec{E}$ and its direction will be in y-direction. The direction of power flow will be in z-direction. Therefore, the electric and magnetic fields are

$$\vec{E} = E_m \cos(\omega t - \beta z)\vec{a}_x = 29.5\cos(\omega t - \beta z)\vec{a}_x\,\text{V/m}$$

and
$$\vec{H} = H_m \cos(\omega t - \beta z)\vec{a}_y = 0.135\cos(\omega t - \beta z)\vec{a}_y\,\text{A/m} \qquad\square$$

EXAMPLE 7.29

A radio station transmits power radially around a spherical region. The desired electrical field intensity at a distance of $10\,\text{km}$ from the station is $2\,\mu\text{V/m}$. Calculate the corresponding magnetic field, power density, and power transmitted by station.

SOLUTION

Given $E_m = 2\,\mu\text{V/m}$ and distance, $r = 10\text{km} = 10\times10^3\,\text{m}$ from the station.
The magnitude of the magnetic field is

$$H_m = \frac{E_m}{\eta_0} = \frac{2\times10^{-6}}{120\pi} = 5.3\times10^{-9}\,\text{A/m}$$

The magnitude of the power density is

$$S = E_m H_m = \left(2\times10^{-6}\right)\left(5.3\times10^{-9}\right) = 10.6\times10^{-15}\,\text{W/m}^2$$

The power is transmitted in radial direction at a distance 10 km from the station over a spherical region. The area of the spherical region is

$$\text{Area} = 4\pi r^2 = 4\pi\left(10^4\right)^2 = 12.56\times10^8\,\text{m}^2$$

Hence, the total power radiated over the spherical region is

$$P = \text{Power density}\times\text{Area}$$

$$= 10.6\times10^{-15}\times12.56\times10^8 = 13.3\,\mu\text{W} \qquad\square$$

EXAMPLE 7.30

The electric field intensity of a uniform plane wave in free space is given by $\vec{E} = 100\cos(\omega t + 8z)\vec{a}_x\,\text{V/m}$. Determine (*i*) the velocity of propagation, (*ii*) the wave frequency, (*iii*) the wavelength, (*iv*) the magnetic field intensity and (*v*) the average power density in the medium.

SOLUTION

Given $\vec{E} = 100\cos(\omega t + 8z)\vec{a}_x\,\text{V/m}$.

(*i*) The wave propagates in free space with the velocity of light. The given electric field shows that the wave is travelling in the negative z-direction. Therefore, the phase velocity is

$$\vec{u}_p = -3\times10^8\,\vec{a}_z\,\text{m/s}$$

(*ii*) The wave frequency is

$$\omega = \beta\left|\vec{u}_p\right| = 8\times3\times10^8 = 2.4\times10^9\,\text{rad/s}$$

(*iii*) The wavelength of the wave in free space is

$$\lambda = \frac{2\pi}{\beta} = \frac{2\pi}{8} = 0.785\,\text{m}$$

(*iv*) The electric field intensity in phasor form is

$$\tilde{E} = 100e^{j8z}\vec{a}_x\,\text{V/m}$$

Hence, the corresponding magnetic field intensity in phasor form is written as

$$\tilde{H} = \frac{1}{\eta_0}\vec{a}_k\times\tilde{E} = \frac{1}{\eta_0}\left(-\vec{a}_z\right)\times100e^{j8z}\vec{a}_x$$

where $\vec{a}_k = -\vec{a}_z$ and $\eta_0 = 377\,\Omega$.

Therefore, the magnetic field intensity is

$$\tilde{H} = -\frac{100}{377}e^{j8z}\vec{a}_y = -0.265e^{j8z}\vec{a}_y\,\text{A/m}$$

The instantaneous form of magnetic field intensity is

$$\tilde{H} = -0.265\cos\left(2.4\times10^9 t + 8z\right)\vec{a}_y\,\text{A/m}$$

(*v*) The average power density in the medium is

$$\vec{S}_{avg} = \frac{1}{2}\text{Re}\left(\tilde{E}\times\tilde{H}^*\right) = -\frac{1}{2}\left(100\vec{a}_x\times0.265\vec{a}_y\right)$$

$$= -13.25\vec{a}_z\,\text{W/m}^2 \qquad (\text{since }\vec{a}_x\times\vec{a}_y = \vec{a}_z)$$

EXAMPLE 7.31

In a non-magnetic medium $\vec{E} = 2\sin\left(4\pi\times10^7 t - 0.6x\right)\vec{a}_z\,\text{V/m}$. Find (*i*) ε_r, η, (*ii*) the time-average power carried by the wave and (*iii*) the total power crossing $200\,\text{cm}^2$ of plane $2x + y = 5$.

SOLUTION

Given $\vec{E} = 2\sin\left(4\pi\times10^7 t - 0.6x\right)\vec{a}_z\,\text{V/m}$. Here, the wave is propagating in positive x-direction.

(*i*) From the given electric field expression, $\alpha = 0$ and $\beta \neq \omega/c$. Hence, the medium is not free space, but it is a lossless medium.

Here, $\beta = 0.6$, $\omega = 4\pi\times10^7$, $\mu = \mu_0$ and $\varepsilon = \varepsilon_0\varepsilon_r$.

Therefore, $\beta = \omega\sqrt{\mu\varepsilon} = \omega\sqrt{\mu_0\varepsilon_0\varepsilon_r} = \frac{\omega}{c}\sqrt{\varepsilon_r}$ $\qquad (\text{since } c = \frac{1}{\sqrt{\mu_0\varepsilon_0}})$

That is,

$$\sqrt{\varepsilon_r} = \frac{\beta c}{\omega} = \frac{0.6\left(3\times10^8\right)}{4\pi\times10^7} = \frac{4.5}{\pi}$$

$$\varepsilon_r = 2.053$$

The intrinsic impedance is

$$\eta = \sqrt{\frac{\mu}{\varepsilon}} = \sqrt{\frac{\mu_0}{\varepsilon_0}}\sqrt{\frac{\mu_r}{\varepsilon_r}} = 120\pi\sqrt{\frac{1}{2.053}} = 262.98\,\Omega$$

(*ii*) The Poynting vector or power density vector $\vec{S}$ is

$$\vec{S} = \vec{E}\times\vec{H} = \frac{E_0^2}{\eta}\sin^2\left(\omega t - \beta x\right)\vec{a}_x$$

$$\vec{S}_{avg} = \vec{S}_{x(avg)} = \frac{1}{T}\int_0^T S\,dt = \frac{E_0^2}{2\eta}\vec{a}_x = \frac{4}{2\times262.98}\vec{a}_x = 7.6\,\vec{a}_x\ \text{mW/m}^2$$

(*iii*) The unit normal vector on plane $2x + y = 5$ is $\vec{a}_n = \dfrac{2\vec{a}_x + \vec{a}_y}{\sqrt{5}}$

Hence, the total power crossing the surface is

$$P = \vec{S}_{avg}\cdot s\vec{a}_n \quad \text{where area}\ s = 200\,\text{cm}^2 = 200\times10^{-4}\,\text{m}^2$$

$$= \left(7.6\times10^{-3}\,\vec{a}_x\right)\cdot\left(200\times10^{-4}\right)\left[\frac{2\vec{a}_x + \vec{a}_y}{\sqrt{5}}\right]$$

$$= \frac{30.4\times10^{-5}}{\sqrt{5}} = 135.95\,\mu\text{W}$$

EXAMPLE `7.32`

In free space $\vec{E}(z,t) = 60\cos\left(\omega t - \beta z\right)\vec{a}_x\ (\text{V/m})$. Find the average power crossing a circular area of radius 4 m in the plane $z =$ constant.

SOLUTION

Given $\vec{E}(z,t) = 60\cos\left(\omega t - \beta z\right)\vec{a}_x$ in free space.

The electric field can be written in complex form as

$$\vec{E} = 60e^{j(\omega t - \beta z)}\vec{a}_x\ (\text{V/m})$$

Here, the term $\left(\omega t - \beta z\right)$ shows that the wave is propagating in "$+z$"-direction. Since $\eta = 120\pi\,\Omega$ in free space, the magnetic field is

$$\vec{H} = \frac{1}{\eta_0}\vec{a}_k\times\vec{E} = \frac{60}{120\pi}\left(\vec{a}_z\right)\times e^{j(\omega t - \beta z)}\vec{a}_x$$

$$= \frac{1}{2\pi}e^{j(\omega t - \beta z)}\vec{a}_y\,\text{A/m} \qquad (\text{since } \vec{a}_z\times\vec{a}_x = \vec{a}_y)$$

Hence, the average power density is

$$\vec{S}_{avg} = \vec{S}_{z(avg)} = \frac{1}{2}\text{Re}\left(\tilde{E}\times\tilde{H}^{*}\right)$$

$$= \frac{1}{2}(60)\left(\frac{1}{2\pi}\right)\vec{a}_{z} = \frac{15}{\pi}\vec{a}_{z}\ \text{W/m}^{2}$$

The average power flow P_{avg} normal to the area is

$$\text{Average power} = \text{Average power density} \times \text{Area}$$

Hence, $$P_{avg} = \left(\frac{15}{\pi}\right)\times\pi\times(2)^{2} = 60\,\text{W}$$

EXAMPLE 7.33

When a plane wave travels in free space, it has an average power density of $40\ \text{W/m}^{2}$. Calculate the amplitudes of $\vec{E}$ and $\vec{B}$ fields.

SOLUTION

The magnitude of average power density is

$$\left|\vec{S}_{avg}\right| = \frac{\left|\vec{E}\right|^{2}}{2\eta_{0}}$$

$$40 = \frac{\left|\vec{E}\right|^{2}}{2\times 120\pi}$$

Therefore, the amplitude of electric field is $\left|\vec{E}\right| = 173.62\ \text{V/m}$
The amplitude of magnetic field is

$$\left|\vec{B}\right| = \mu_{0}\left|\vec{H}\right| = \mu_{0}\cdot\frac{\left|\vec{E}\right|}{\eta_{0}} = \frac{4\pi\times 10^{-7}\times 173.62}{120\pi} = 0.58\ \mu\text{Wb/m}^{2}$$

EXAMPLE 7.34

A forward travelling plane wave in free space is $E_{x} = \cos\left(4\pi\times 10^{7}t - \beta z\right)\text{V/m}$. Calculate the instantaneous and time-average Poynting vectors.

SOLUTION

Given $E_{x} = \cos\left(4\pi\times 10^{7}t - \beta z\right)\text{V/m}$.

Therefore,

$$H_{y} = \frac{E_{x}}{\eta_{0}} = \frac{1}{120\pi}\cos\left(4\pi\times 10^{7}t - \beta z\right)\text{A/m}$$

Here, $\omega = 4\pi\times 10^{7}\ \text{rad/s}$ and $\beta = \frac{\omega}{c} = \frac{4\pi\times 10^{7}}{3\times 10^{8}} = 0.42\ \text{rad/m}$

The instantaneous Poynting vector is

$$\vec{S} = \vec{E} \times \vec{H} = E_x \vec{a}_x \times E_y \vec{a}_y = \frac{1}{120\pi} \cos^2 \left(4\pi \times 10^7 t - 0.42z\right) \vec{a}_z$$

$$= \frac{1}{2} \times \frac{1}{120\pi} \left[1 + \cos 2\left(4\pi \times 10^7 t - 0.42z\right)\right] \vec{a}_z \ \text{W/m}^2$$

The time-average Poynting vector is

$$\vec{S}_{avg} = \vec{S}_{z(avg)} = \frac{1}{2} \times \frac{1}{120\pi} \vec{a}_z = 1.326 \vec{a}_z \ \text{mW/m}^2 \qquad \square$$

EXAMPLE 7.35

If free space, $\vec{E} = 100 \sin\left(\omega t - \beta z\right)\vec{a}_x$ V/m. Calculate the total power passing through a rectangular area of sides 30mm$\times$10mm in $z = 0$ plane. Assume $\eta_0 = \dfrac{E_m}{H_m}$ and $\eta_0 = 120\pi \ \Omega$.

SOLUTION

Given $\vec{E} = 100 \sin\left(\omega t - \beta z\right)\vec{a}_x$ V/m. Here, the electric field in along x-direction and the wave is propagating in z-direction. The direction of magnetic field can be obtained by

$$\vec{a}_k \times \vec{a}_E = \vec{a}_H$$

That is,

$$\vec{a}_z \times \vec{a}_x = \vec{a}_y$$

Therefore, the magnetic field can be written as

$$\vec{H} = \frac{100}{\eta_0} \sin\left(\omega t - \beta z\right)\vec{a}_y \ \text{A/m}$$

Converting both the sinusoidal functions of the fields to co-sinusoidal functions, the electric and magnetic fields are

$$\vec{E} = 100 \cos\left(\omega t - \beta z - \frac{\pi}{2}\right)\vec{a}_x$$

$$\vec{H} = \frac{100}{\eta_0} \cos\left(\omega t - \beta z - \frac{\pi}{2}\right)\vec{a}_y$$

Writing the above equations in phasor form, we get

$$\tilde{E} = 100 e^{j\left(-\beta z - \frac{\pi}{2}\right)}\vec{a}_x$$

$$\tilde{H} = \frac{100}{\eta_0} e^{j\left(-\beta z - \frac{\pi}{2}\right)}\vec{a}_y$$

Thus, the complex conjugate of $\vec{H}$ is

$$\tilde{H}^* = \frac{100}{\eta_0} e^{j\left(\beta z + \frac{\pi}{2}\right)}\vec{a}_y$$

Hence, the average power density is

$$\vec{S}_{avg} = \frac{1}{2}\text{Re}\left(\vec{E}\times\vec{H}^*\right)$$

$$= \frac{1}{2}(100)\left(\frac{100}{\eta_0}\right)\text{Re}\left[e^{j\left(-\beta z-\frac{\pi}{2}\right)}\vec{a}_x \times e^{j\left(\beta z+\frac{\pi}{2}\right)}\vec{a}_y\right] = \frac{1}{2}\frac{(100)^2}{120\pi}\vec{a}_z$$

$$= 13.27\,\vec{a}_z\,\text{W/m}^2$$

The total power crossing area is

$$P = \left|\vec{S}_{avg}\right| \times \text{Area} = 13.27\times10\times10^{-3}\times30\times10^{-3}$$

$$= 3.98\,\text{mW}$$

Here, the flow of power is normal to the area. Since the area is in $z=0$ plane, the direction normal to this plane is $\vec{a}_z$. $\square$

EXAMPLE 7.36

If the field vectors of a wave in free space are given by

$$\vec{E} = 50\cos\left(\omega t + \frac{4\pi}{3}x\right)\vec{a}_z\,\text{V/m}$$

$$\vec{H} = \frac{50}{120\pi}\cos\left(\omega t + \frac{4\pi}{3}x\right)\vec{a}_y\,\text{V/m}$$

Determine the Poynting vector and power crossing 10m^2 patch of the yz-plane.

SOLUTION

The given electric and magnetic fields can be expressed in phasor form as

$$\tilde{E} = 50e^{j\left(\frac{4\pi}{3}\right)x}\vec{a}_z$$

$$\tilde{H} = \frac{50}{120\pi}e^{j\left(\frac{4\pi}{3}\right)x}\vec{a}_y$$

Here, the term $\left(\omega t + \beta x\right)$ shows that the wave is propagating in negative x-direction.

The complex conjugate of the magnetic field $\vec{H}$ is

$$\tilde{H}^* = \frac{50}{120\pi}e^{-j\left(\frac{4\pi}{3}\right)x}\vec{a}_y$$

Hence, the Poynting vector or the average power density in

$$\vec{S}_{avg} = \frac{1}{2}\operatorname{Re}\left(\tilde{E}\times\tilde{H}^{*}\right) = \frac{1}{2}\operatorname{Re}\left[50e^{j\left(\frac{4\pi}{3}\right)x}\vec{a}_{z}\times\frac{50}{120\pi}e^{-j\left(\frac{4\pi}{3}\right)x}\vec{a}_{y}\right]$$

$$= \frac{1}{2}\frac{(50)^{2}}{120\pi}\left(-\vec{a}_{x}\right) = -3.31\vec{a}_{x}\,\text{W/m}^{2} \qquad \text{(since } \vec{a}_{z}\times\vec{a}_{y} = -\vec{a}_{x}\text{)}$$

The total power crossing area of 10m^{2} of the *yz*-plane is

$$P = \left|\vec{S}_{avg}\right|\times\text{Area} = 3.31\times10 = 33.1\,\text{W}$$

Hence, the Poynting vector is $\vec{S}_{avg} = -3.31\vec{a}_{x}\,\text{W/m}^{2}$ and the total power crossing the area is 33.1 W.   ❑

EXAMPLE 7.37

A uniform plane wave 10 MHz frequency has average Poynting vector 4W/m^{2}. If the medium is perfect dielectric with $\mu_{r} = 2$ and $\varepsilon_{r} = 3$, determine (*i*) velocity, (*ii*) wavelength, (*iii*) intrinsic impedance and (*iv*) rms value of electric field.

SOLUTION

Given $\vec{S}_{avg} = 4\text{W/m}^{2}$ and $f = 10\times10^{6}\,\text{Hz}$.

For a perfect dielectric, $\sigma = 0$, $\mu_{r} = 2$ and $\varepsilon_{r} = 3$.

(*i*) The attenuation constant and phase constant are

$$\alpha = 0$$

$$\beta = \omega\sqrt{\mu\varepsilon} = \omega\sqrt{\left(\mu_{0}\mu_{r}\right)\left(\varepsilon_{0}\varepsilon_{r}\right)}$$

$$= \left(2\pi\times10\times10^{6}\right)\sqrt{\left(4\pi\times10^{-7}\times2\right)\left(8.854\times10^{-12}\times3\right)}$$

$$= 0.5133\,\text{rad/m}$$

The velocity of propagation is

$$u_{p} = \frac{\omega}{\beta} = \frac{2\pi f}{\beta} = \frac{2\pi\times10\times10^{6}}{0.5133} = 122.4\times10^{6}\,\text{m/s}$$

(*ii*) The wavelength is

$$\lambda = \frac{2\pi}{\beta} = \frac{2\pi}{0.5133} = 12.24\,\text{m}$$

(*iii*) The intrinsic impedance of the medium is

$$\eta = \sqrt{\frac{\mu}{\varepsilon}} = \sqrt{\frac{\mu_{0}\mu_{r}}{\varepsilon_{0}\varepsilon_{r}}} = \sqrt{\frac{\mu_{0}}{\varepsilon_{0}}}\sqrt{\frac{\mu_{r}}{\varepsilon_{r}}} = 120\pi\sqrt{\frac{2}{3}} = 307.6\,\Omega$$

(*iv*) From Poynting's theorem,

$$S_{avg} = \frac{1}{2}\frac{E_m^2}{\eta}$$

The magnitude of the electric field is

$$E_m = \sqrt{(2\eta)(S_{avg})} = \sqrt{2\times307.6\times4} = 49.6\,\text{V/m}$$

Hence, the rms value of electric field is

$$E_{rms} = \frac{E_m}{\sqrt{2}} = \frac{49.6}{\sqrt{2}} = 35.07\,\text{V/m}$$

EXAMPLE 7.38

Find the Poynting vector on the surface of a long, straight conducting wire of radius, b and conductivity, σ that carries a direct current of I. Verify Poynting's theorem.

SOLUTION

Figure E7.38 shows a segment of length l of the long wire. The current in the wire is uniformly distributed over its cross-sectional area in the case of dc condition. Assume that the axis of the wire coincides with the z-axis.

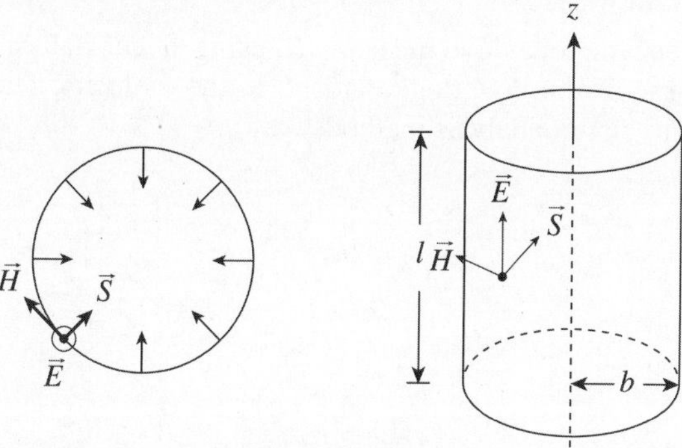

Figure E7.38

Therefore, the current density is

$$\vec{J} = \frac{I}{A}\vec{a}_z = \frac{I}{\pi b^2}\vec{a}_z$$

where $A = \pi b^2$. The electric field intensity is

$$\vec{E} = \frac{\vec{J}}{\sigma} = \frac{I}{\sigma\pi b^2}\vec{a}_z$$

The magnetic field intensity on the surface of the wire is

$$\vec{H} = \frac{I}{2\pi\rho}\vec{a}_\phi = \frac{I}{2\pi b}\vec{a}_\phi$$

where ρ is the radius in cylindrical coordinate system. Hence, the Poynting vector at the surface of the wire is

$$\vec{S} = \vec{E} \times \vec{H} = \frac{I^2}{2\sigma\pi^2 b^3} \left(\vec{a}_z \times \vec{a}_\phi \right)$$

$$= -\frac{I^2}{2\sigma\pi^2 b^3} \vec{a}_\rho \qquad \text{(since } \vec{a}_z \times \vec{a}_\phi = -\vec{a}_\rho)$$

Here, the power density is directed radially everywhere into the wire surface.

Poynting's theorem can be verified by integrating $\vec{S}$ over the wall of the wire segment shown in Figure E7.38. Therefore,

$$-\oint_s \vec{S} \cdot d\vec{s} = -\oint_s \left(S\vec{a}_\rho \right) \cdot \left(ds\vec{a}_\rho \right) = \left(\frac{I^2}{2\sigma\pi^2 b^3} \right) 2\pi b l$$

$$= I^2 \left(\frac{l}{\sigma\pi b^2} \right) = I^2 \left(\frac{l}{\sigma A} \right) = I^2 R$$

where $R = l / \sigma A$. The above result shows that the negative surface integral of the Poynting vector is exactly equal to the $I^2 R$ power loss in the conducting wire. Hence, Poynting's theorem is verified. $\qquad \square$

EXAMPLE 7.39

A voltage source V is connected to a load resistor R using a coaxial cable of length l as shown in Figure E7.39(a). Show that use of the Poynting vector $\vec{S}$ in the dielectric leads to the same instantaneous power in the resistor, similar to circuit analysis method.

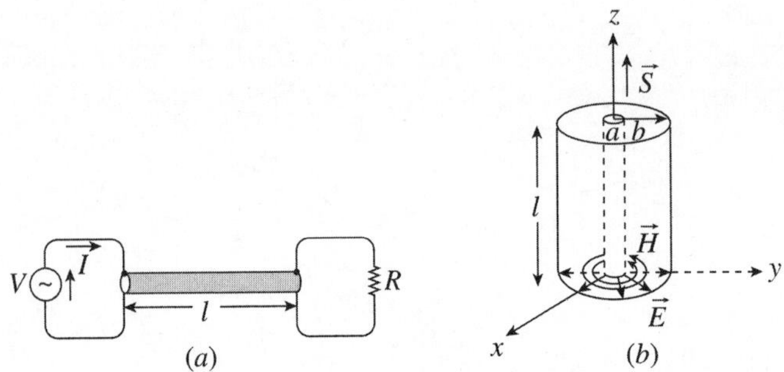

Figure E7.39

SOLUTION

Figure E7.39(a) shows a coaxial cable of length l in which the power is transferred from the source to the load resistance R by applying an ac voltage between the inner and outer conductors.

The magnetic field intensity $\vec{H}$ will be directed in the circuit path about the axis as shown in Figure E7.39(b). Here, the radii of the inner and outer conductors of the coaxial cable are a and b, respectively.

By Ampere's law, the enclosed current in the region between the two conductions is equal to the magnetomotive force around any of these circles of $\vec{H}$.

$$\oint_l \vec{H} \cdot d\vec{l} = I$$

The magnetic field $\vec{H}$ is constant along any of the circular path. Let ρ be the radius of the circle being considered. Then, the magnetomotive force is

$$\oint_l \vec{H} \cdot d\vec{l} = 2\pi\rho\, H = I$$

Hence, the magnitude of magnetic field intensity is

$$H = \frac{I}{2\pi\rho} \tag{1}$$

The potential difference between the inner and outer conductors of a coaxial cable of length l is represented by

$$V = \frac{Q}{2\pi\varepsilon\, l} \ln\left(\frac{b}{a}\right) \tag{2}$$

The electric field intensity for a finite line charge with uniform charge density ρ_l is

$$\vec{E} = \frac{\rho_l}{2\pi\varepsilon\rho}\, \vec{a}_\rho = \frac{Q}{2\pi\varepsilon\rho\, l}\, \vec{a}_\rho \qquad \left(\text{where } \rho_l = \frac{Q}{l}\right) \tag{3}$$

From Eqs. (2) and (3), the electric field vector along the radial direction can be written as

$$\vec{E} = \frac{V}{\rho \ln\left(\dfrac{b}{a}\right)}\, \vec{a}_\rho \tag{4}$$

According to Poynting's theorem, the Poynting vector $\vec{S}$ in the dielectric between the two conductors of the coaxial cable is

$$\vec{S} = \vec{E} \times \vec{H} = \frac{VI}{2\pi\rho^2 \ln\left(\dfrac{b}{a}\right)}\, \vec{a}_z \qquad \left(\text{since } \vec{a}_\rho \times \vec{a}_\phi = \vec{a}_z\right)$$

The above equation represents the instantaneous power density. The total instantaneous power flowing over a cross-section of the dielectric is

$$P(t) = \int_s \vec{S} \cdot d\vec{s}, \text{ where } d\vec{s} \text{ is the differential surface area along } \vec{a}_z$$

$$= \int_0^{2\pi} \int_a^b \left[\frac{VI}{2\pi\rho^2 \ln\left(\dfrac{b}{a}\right)}\, \vec{a}_z \right] \cdot \left[\rho\, d\rho\, d\phi\, \vec{a}_z \right]$$

$$= \frac{VI}{\ln\left(\dfrac{b}{a}\right)} \int_a^b \frac{d\rho}{\rho} = \frac{VI}{\ln\left(\dfrac{b}{a}\right)} \times \left[\ln \rho\right]_a^b$$

Hence,

$$P = VI$$

The above equation shows that the power flow in a coaxial cable is the product of voltage and current. It is same as the circuit theory analysis for the instantaneous power loss in the resistor. ❏

7.6 WAVE POLARIZATION

The *polarization* of a uniform plane wave is defined as the orientation of the electric field at a given point in space as a function of time. It describes the time varying behaviour and direction of the electric field strength. The polarization of a wave depends on the transmitting source such as an antenna. There are three types of uniform plane wave polarization, namely,

(*i*) linear polarization,

(*ii*) circular polarization, and

(*iii*) elliptical polarization

7.6.1 Linear Polarization

A wave is said to be linearly polarized if the electric field oscillates along a straight line as a function of time at some point in the medium. Consider a uniform plane wave travelling in the z-direction with the electric field phasor $\tilde{E}$ lying in the xy-plane. The wave is said to be *x-polarized* or *horizontally polarized* if $\tilde{E}_y = 0$ and only $\tilde{E}_x$ is present. If $\tilde{E}_x = 0$ and only $\tilde{E}_y$ is present, then the wave is said to be *y-polarized* or *vertically polarized*. If both $\tilde{E}_x$ and $\tilde{E}_y$ are in the same phase, then the direction of electric field depends on the magnitudes of $\tilde{E}_x$ and $\tilde{E}_y$. The instantaneous angle $\tan^{-1} \dfrac{\tilde{E}_y}{\tilde{E}_x}$ that the electric field makes with the x-axis is constant with time. As the direction of the resultant electric field is constant with time in all these three cases, the wave is said to be linearly polarized.

7.6.2 Circular Polarization

A wave is said to be circularly polarized if the locus of the electric field vector is a circle. When the fields $\tilde{E}_x$ and $\tilde{E}_y$ have equal magnitudes and phase difference of $\pm 90°$, the locus of the electric field traces a circle and the wave is circularly polarized.

In phasor form, the electric field of a uniform plane wave travelling in the z-direction is represented by

$$\tilde{E}(z) = E_0 e^{-j\beta z}$$

The time-varying x- and y-components of the electric field are given by

$$E_x(z,t) = \mathrm{Re}\left[\tilde{E}_x(z) e^{j\omega t}\right] = \mathrm{Re}\left[E_0 e^{-j\beta z} e^{j\omega t}\right]$$

$$= \mathrm{Re}\left[E_0 e^{j(\omega t - \beta z)}\right] = E_0 \cos(\omega t - \beta z) \tag{7.95}$$

$$E_y(z,t) = \mathrm{Im}\left[\tilde{E}_y(z) e^{j\omega t}\right] = E_0 \sin(\omega t - \beta z) \tag{7.96}$$

Since the plane wave travels in the z-direction, the electric field lies in the xy-plane $(z = 0)$. Therefore, the x- and y-components of the electric field become

$$E_x = E_0 \cos \omega t$$

$$E_y = E_0 \sin \omega t$$

Squaring and adding the above two equations, we get

$$E_x^2 + E_y^2 = E_0^2 \tag{7.97}$$

Equation (7.97) represents a circle. The wave polarization is called left circular polarization if the phase difference is $+90°$. It is called right circular polarization if the phase difference is $-90°$.

7.6.3 Elliptical Polarization

A wave is said to be elliptically polarized if $\tilde{E}_x$ and $\tilde{E}_y$ are not equal in magnitude and they differ by $90°$ phase. Here, the locus of the tip of $\tilde{E}$ traces an ellipse. Since the x- and y-components of the electric field differ in amplitude and the y-component leads the x-component by $90°$, the electric field can be represented by the complex vector as

$$E_0 = a\,\vec{a}_x + jb\vec{a}_y$$

where a and b are positive real constants. The resultant electric field is represented by

$$\vec{E}_z(0,t) = a\cos\omega t\,\vec{a}_x - b\sin\omega t\,\vec{a}_y \tag{7.98}$$

From the above equation, the x and y-components of the electric field are

$$E_x = a\cos\omega t$$

$$E_y = -b\sin\omega t$$

Therefore,

$$\frac{E_x^2}{a^2} + \frac{E_y^2}{b^2} = 1 \tag{7.99}$$

The above equation represents an ellipse and hence, the wave is said to be elliptically polarized.

7.7 REFLECTION AND REFRACTION OF PLANE WAVES

The propagation of uniform plane waves in an unbounded, homogeneous medium has been discussed so far. When EM waves propagate from one medium to another medium with different constitutive parameters, they are partially reflected and partially transmitted. The behaviour of a plane wave having normal incidence and oblique incidence with a perfect conductor boundary is explained in this section. Similarly, the wave behaviour between two dielectric mediums for normal incidence and oblique incidence is also discussed.

7.7.1 Normal Incidence at Perfect Conducting Boundary

Consider an EM wave travelling in a perfect dielectric (medium1, $\sigma_1 = 0$) strikes an interface with a perfect conductor (medium 2, $\sigma_2 = \infty$) as shown in Figure 7.4. When the incident wave $\left(\tilde{E}_i \text{ and } \tilde{H}_i\right)$ is normal to the surface of a perfect conductor, the wave is entirely reflected. For time-varying fields, the EM wave energy cannot be transmitted into the perfect conductor. Since there can be no loss within a perfect conductor, none of the energy is absorbed. Hence, the amplitudes of reflected wave of electric and magnetic fields remain the same as that of the incident wave. The only difference is the direction of power flow.

The incident electric and magnetic field intensity phasors are represented by

$$\tilde{E}_i(z) = E_{i0}e^{-j\beta_1 z}\vec{a}_x$$

$$\tilde{H}_i(z) = \frac{E_{i0}}{\eta_1}e^{-j\beta_1 z}\vec{a}_y$$

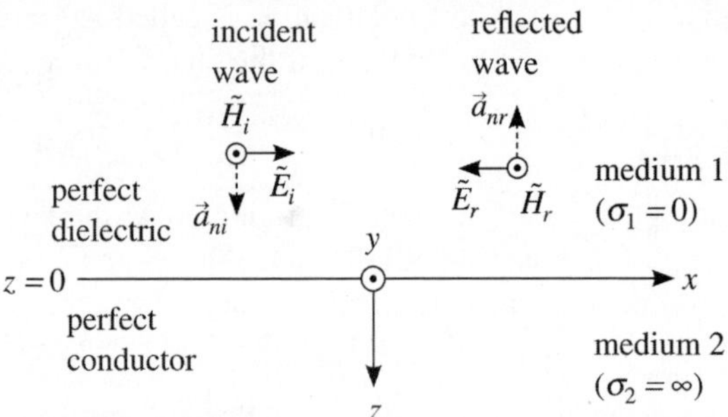

Figure 7.4 *Normal incidence on a plane conductor boundary*

where E_{i0} is the magnitude of $\tilde{E}_i$ at $z = 0$, β_1 and η_1 are the phase constant and the intrinsic impedance of medium 1, respectively. The boundary surface is the plane $z = 0$ as shown in Figure 7.4. Here, the incident electric field is along x-direction, the incident magnetic field is along y-direction and the wave travels in the "$+z$"-direction.

Both the electric and magnetic fields vanish, i.e., $\tilde{E}_2 = 0$ and $\tilde{H}_2 = 0$ inside a perfect conductor (medium 2) and therefore, no wave is transmitted across the boundary into the conductor medium $(z > 0)$. The incident wave gets reflected at the conductor boundary and gives rise to a reflected wave $\left(\tilde{E}_r \text{ and } \tilde{H}_r\right)$ Hence, the reflected electric field intensity phasor is represented by

$$\tilde{E}_r(z) = E_{r0}e^{j\beta_1 z}\vec{a}_x$$

The above equation shows that the reflected wave travels in the negative z-direction. Therefore, the total electric field in medium 1 is the sum of incident wave and reflected wave. Therefore,

$$\tilde{E}_1(z) = \tilde{E}_i(z) + \tilde{E}_r(z) = \left(E_{i0}e^{-j\beta_1 z} + E_{r0}e^{j\beta_1 z}\right)\vec{a}_x \tag{7.100}$$

We know that, the tangential component of electric field is continuous at the boundary $z = 0$.
That is,

$$\tilde{E}_1(0) = E_{i0} + E_{r0} = \tilde{E}_2(0) = 0$$

Hence,

$$E_{r0} = -E_{i0} \tag{7.101}$$

This means that the incident and reflected electric fields have equal amplitude but opposite phase on reflection from the conductor boundary. Substituting Eq. (7.101) in Eq. (7.100), we get

$$\tilde{E}_1(z) = E_{i0}\left(e^{-j\beta_1 z} - e^{j\beta_1 z}\right)\vec{a}_x$$

$$= -2jE_{i0}\sin\beta_1 z\,\vec{a}_x \qquad \left(\text{since } \sin\beta_1 z = \frac{e^{j\beta_1 z} - e^{-j\beta_1 z}}{2j}\right)$$

The instantaneous time domain expression corresponding to the electric field phasor is given by

$$\vec{E}_1(z,t) = \text{Re}\left[\tilde{E}_1(z)e^{j\omega t}\right] = \text{Re}\left[-2jE_{i0}\sin\beta_1 z\,\vec{a}_x\left(e^{j\omega t}\right)\right]$$

$$= 2E_{i0}\sin\beta_1 z\sin\omega t\,\vec{a}_x \tag{7.102}$$

From Eq. (7.102), it is seen that the incident and reflected waves combine to form a *standing wave*. For a given time t, the electric field varies sinusoidally with the distance measured from the conductor boundary.

Figure 7.5 shows the standing waves of electric field $\vec{E}_1$ for different values of ωt. From Figure 7.5, it is seen that the electric field vanishes at the conductor boundary $z = 0$ and also at multiples of half wavelength points from the conductor surface. The maximum value of electric field occurs at odd multiples of a quarter wavelength from the conductor surface.

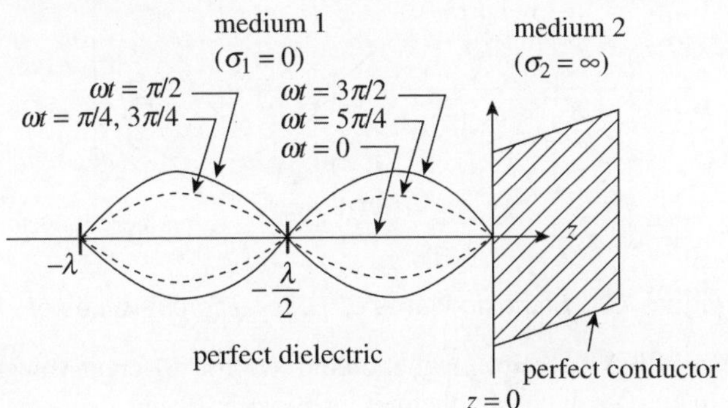

Figure 7.5 *Standing waves of $\vec{E}_1$ for different values of ωt*

Since $\tilde{H}(z) = \dfrac{1}{\eta}\vec{a}_n \times \tilde{E}(z)$, the reflected magnetic field intensity phasor is represented by

$$\tilde{H}_r(z) = \frac{1}{\eta_1}\vec{a}_{nr} \times \tilde{E}_r(z) = \frac{1}{\eta_1}\left(-\vec{a}_z\right) \times \tilde{E}_r(z)$$

$$= \frac{1}{\eta_1}\left(-\vec{a}_z\right) \times \left(E_{r0}e^{j\beta_1 z}\vec{a}_x\right) = -\frac{1}{\eta_1}E_{r0}e^{j\beta_1 z}\vec{a}_y$$

$$= \frac{E_{i0}}{\eta_1}e^{j\beta_1 z}\vec{a}_y \qquad \left(\text{since } E_{r0} = -E_{i0}\right)$$

The total magnetic field in medium 1 is the sum of incident wave and reflected wave as given by

$$\tilde{H}_1(z) = \tilde{H}_i(z) + \tilde{H}_r(z) = \frac{E_{i0}}{\eta_1}\left(e^{-j\beta_1 z} + e^{j\beta_1 z}\right)\vec{a}_y \tag{7.103}$$

$$= \frac{2E_{i0}}{\eta_1}\cos\beta_1 z\,\vec{a}_y \qquad \left(\text{since }\cos\beta_1 z = \frac{e^{j\beta_1 z} + e^{-j\beta_1 z}}{2}\right)$$

From the electric and magnetic field expressions, it is seen that no average power is associated with the total EM wave in medium 1. Both $\tilde{E}_1(z)$ and $\tilde{H}_1(z)$ are in phase quadrature, i.e., $90°$ degree phase difference. The instantaneous time domain expression corresponding to the magnetic field phasor is given by

$$\vec{H}_1(z,t) = \text{Re}\left[\tilde{H}_1(z)e^{j\omega t}\right] = \text{Re}\left[\frac{2E_{i0}}{\eta_1}\cos\beta_1 z\,\vec{a}_y\left(e^{j\omega t}\right)\right]$$

$$= \frac{2E_{i0}}{\eta_1}\cos\beta_1 z\cos\omega t\,\vec{a}_y \tag{7.104}$$

Hence, the resultant magnetic field also has a standing wave distribution. For a given time t, the magnetic field varies co-sinusoidally with the distance measured from the conductor boundary.

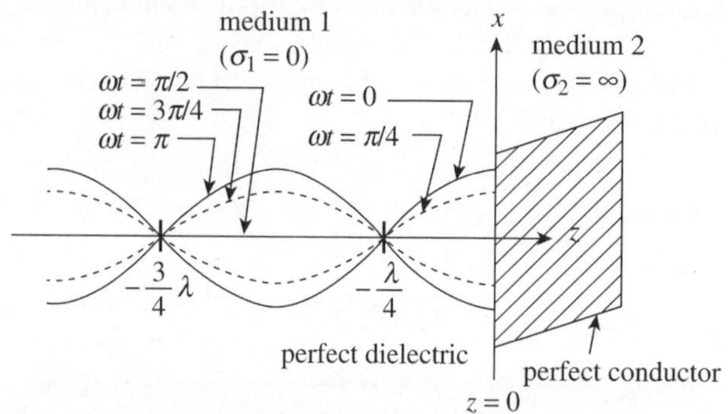

Figure 7.6 *Standing waves of $\vec{H}_1$ for different values of ωt*

Figure 7.6 shows the standing waves of magnetic field $\vec{H}_1$ for different values of ωt. Here, it is noted that the magnetic field is maximum at the conductor boundary $z = 0$ and also at multiples of half wavelength points from the conductor surface. The zero points of magnetic field occur at odd multiples of a quarter wavelength from the conductor surface.

7.7.2 Oblique Incidence at Perfect Conducting Boundary

When an EM wave is incident obliquely on a perfect conductor boundary with some arbitrary angle, the behaviour of the reflected wave is characterized by the polarization of the incident wave. This type of oblique incidence leads to three well-known laws in optics: (*i*) Snell's law of reflection, (*ii*) Snell's law of refraction, and (*iii*) Brewster's law making polarization by reflection.

There are two cases for the oblique incidence, namely, perpendicular polarization and parallel polarization. When the incident electric field is perpendicular to the plane of incidence, it is called a *perpendicular polarized wave*. When the electric field is parallel to the plane of incidence, it is called a *parallel polarized wave*. The plane which contains the vector indicating the unit normal to the boundary and the direction of propagation of the incident wave is called the *plane of incidence*.

Case (i): Perpendicular Polarization

Consider an EM wave travelling in a perfect dielectric $\left(\text{medium } 1, \sigma_1 = 0\right)$ strikes an interface with a perfect conductor $\left(\text{medium } 2, \sigma_2 = \infty\right)$ as shown in Figure 7.7. When the plane wave $\left(\tilde{E}_i \text{ and } \tilde{H}_i\right)$ is incident obliquely at the surface of a perfect conductor, the wave is entirely reflected. If the electric field phasor $\tilde{E}_i$ is perpendicular to the plane of incidence, this type of polarization is called *perpendicular polarization* or *horizontal polarization* or E-*polarization*.

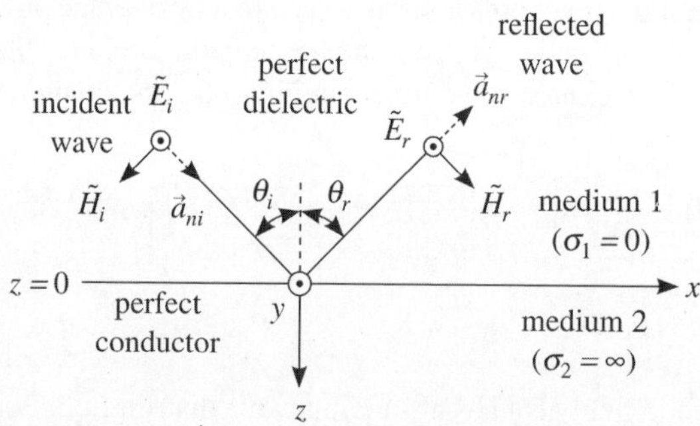

Figure 7.7 *Oblique incidence of a plane conductor boundary with perpendicular polarization*

From Figure 7.7, the unit normal vector in the direction of the incident wave is given by

$$\vec{a}_{ni} = \sin\theta_i\,\vec{a}_x + \cos\theta_i\,\vec{a}_z \tag{7.105}$$

where θ_i is the angle of incidence measured from the normal to the boundary surface.

Therefore, the incident electric field intensity phasor is represented by

$$\tilde{E}_i\left(x,z\right) = E_{i0}e^{-j\beta_1\left(\vec{a}_{ni}\cdot\vec{r}\right)}\vec{a}_y = E_{i0}e^{-j\beta_1\left[\sin\theta_i\,\vec{a}_x + \cos\theta_i\,\vec{a}_z\right]\cdot\left[x\vec{a}_x + y\vec{a}_y + z\vec{a}_z\right]}\vec{a}_y$$

$$= E_{i0}e^{-j\beta_1\left[x\sin\theta_i + z\cos\theta_1\right]}\vec{a}_y \tag{7.106}$$

where $\vec{r} = x\vec{a}_x + y\vec{a}_y + z\vec{a}_z$.

The incident magnetic field intensity phasor is represented by

$$\tilde{H}_i\left(x,z\right) = \frac{1}{\eta_1}\left[\vec{a}_{ni}\times\tilde{E}_i\left(x,z\right)\right]$$

$$= \frac{1}{\eta_1}\left[\left(\sin\theta_i\,\vec{a}_x + \cos\theta_i\,\vec{a}_z\right)\times\left(E_{i0}e^{-j\beta_1\left[x\sin\theta_i + z\cos\theta_i\right]}\vec{a}_y\right)\right]$$

$$= \frac{E_{i0}}{\eta_1}\left(\sin\theta_i\,\vec{a}_z - \cos\theta_i\,\vec{a}_x\right)e^{-j\beta_1\left(x\sin\theta_i + z\cos\theta_i\right)} \tag{7.107}$$

where η_1 is the intrinsic impedance of medium 1.

Referring to Figure 7.7, the unit normal vector in the direction of the reflected wave is given by

$$\vec{a}_{nr} = \sin\theta_r\,\vec{a}_x - \cos\theta_r\,\vec{a}_z \tag{7.108}$$

where θ_r is the angle of incidence.

Similar to the relation given in Eq. (7.106), the reflected electric field intensity phasor is

$$\tilde{E}_r\left(x,z\right) = E_{r0}e^{-j\beta_1\left[x\sin\theta_r - z\cos\theta_r\right]}\vec{a}_y \tag{7.109}$$

Since the medium 2 is a perfect conductor, the wave gets completely reflected and there will be no transmission into the conductor. Hence, according to boundary condition, the tangential component of electric field must be equal to zero at the interface $z = 0$.

Therefore, at $z = 0$, we have

$$\tilde{E}_1\left(x,0\right) = \tilde{E}_i\left(x,0\right) + \tilde{E}_r\left(x,0\right) = 0$$

That is,

$$\left\{E_{i0}e^{-j\beta_1\left[x\sin\theta_i\right]} + E_{r0}e^{-j\beta_1\left[x\sin\theta_r\right]}\right\}\vec{a}_y = 0 \tag{7.110}$$

The above equation is valid for all values of x and it is seen that, $E_{i0} = -E_{r0}$ and $\theta_i = \theta_r$. If the angle of incidence is equals to the angle of reflection, then it is known as *Snell's law of reflection*. Hence, the reflected electric field wave represented in Eq. (7.109) can also be written as

$$\tilde{E}_r\left(x,z\right) = -E_{i0}e^{-j\beta_1\left[x\sin\theta_i - z\cos\theta_i\right]}\vec{a}_y \tag{7.111}$$

The total electric field intensity phasor in medium 1 is the sum of incident and reflected electric field phasors. Therefore, using Eqs. (7.106) and (7.111), we have

$$\tilde{E}_1(x,z) = \tilde{E}_i(x,z) + \tilde{E}_r(x,z)$$

$$= E_{i0}e^{-j\beta_1[x\sin\theta_i + z\cos\theta_i]}\vec{a}_y - E_{i0}e^{-j\beta_1[x\sin\theta_i - z\cos\theta_i]}\vec{a}_y$$

$$= E_{i0}e^{-j\beta_1 x\sin\theta_i}\left(e^{-j\beta_1 z\cos\theta_i} - e^{j\beta_1 z\cos\theta_i}\right)\vec{a}_y$$

$$= -2jE_{i0}\sin(\beta_1 z\cos\theta_i)e^{-j\beta_1 x\sin\theta_i}\vec{a}_y \qquad \left(\text{since } \sin\theta = \frac{e^{j\theta} - e^{-j\theta}}{2j}\right) \qquad (7.112)$$

The reflected magnetic field intensity phasor is represented by

$$\tilde{H}_r(x,z) = \frac{1}{\eta_1}\left[\vec{a}_{nr} \times \vec{E}_r(x,z)\right]$$

Using Eqs. (7.108) and (7.111), we get

$$\tilde{H}_r(x,z) = \frac{1}{\eta_1}\left[(\sin\theta_r\vec{a}_x - \cos\theta_r\vec{a}_z) \times \left(-E_{i0}e^{-j\beta_1[x\sin\theta_i - z\cos\theta_i]}\vec{a}_y\right)\right]$$

$$= \frac{E_{i0}}{\eta_1}\left(-\sin\theta_i\vec{a}_z - \cos\theta_i\vec{a}_x\right)e^{-j\beta_1[x\sin\theta_i - z\cos\theta_i]} \qquad (7.113)$$

The total magnetic field intensity phasor in medium 1 is the sum of incident and reflected magnetic field phasors. Therefore, using Eqs. (7.107) and (7.113), we have

$$\tilde{H}_1(x,z) = \tilde{H}_i(x,z) + \tilde{H}_r(x,z)$$

$$= -\frac{2E_{i0}}{\eta_1}\left\{\begin{matrix}\cos\theta_i\cos(\beta_1 z\cos\theta_i)e^{-j\beta_1 x\sin\theta_i}\vec{a}_x \\ + j\sin\theta_i\sin(\beta_1 z\cos\theta_i)e^{-j\beta_1 x\sin\theta_i}\vec{a}_z\end{matrix}\right\} \qquad (7.114)$$

From Eqs. (7.112) and (7.114), the following observations can be made for oblique incidence of a uniform plane wave with perpendicular polarization.

(*i*) The *y*-component of electric field intensity phasor, i.e., $\tilde{E}_{1y}$ and the *x*-component of magnetic field intensity phasor, i.e., $\tilde{H}_{1x}$ form a standing wave pattern due to the presence of $\sin\beta_1 z$ and $\cos\beta_1 z$ terms, respectively. Therefore, the average power is not propagated in the direction normal to the boundary, i.e., *z*-direction.

(*ii*) In the direction parallel to the conductor boundary, i.e., in *x*-direction, both $\tilde{E}_{1y}$ and $\tilde{H}_{1z}$ are in phase with respect to time and space. Therefore, the phase velocity and the wavelength of the wave propagating in the *x*-direction are given by

$$u_{1x} = \frac{\omega}{\beta_{1x}} = \frac{\omega}{\beta_1\sin\theta_i} = \frac{u_1}{\sin\theta_i}, \text{ where } u_1 = \frac{\omega}{\beta_1}$$

$$\lambda_{1x} = \frac{2\pi}{\beta_{1x}} = \frac{2\pi}{\beta_1\sin\theta_i} = \frac{\lambda_1}{\sin\theta_i}, \text{ where } \lambda_1 = \frac{2\pi}{\beta_1}$$

(iii) Since the amplitude of the wave varies with z in the x-direction, the wave propagating in the x-direction is known as non-uniform plane wave.

Case (ii): Parallel Polarization

Consider that an EM wave travelling in a perfect dielectric $\left(\text{medium 1, } \sigma_1 = 0\right)$ strikes an interface with a perfect conductor $\left(\text{medium 2, } \sigma_2 = \infty\right)$ as shown in Figure 7.8. When the plane wave $\left(\tilde{E}_i \text{ and } \tilde{H}_i\right)$ is incident obliquely at the surface of a perfect conductor, the wave is entirely reflected. If the electric field phasor $\tilde{E}_i$ is parallel to the plane of incidence, this type of polarization is called *parallel polarization* or *vertical polarization* or H-*polarization*.

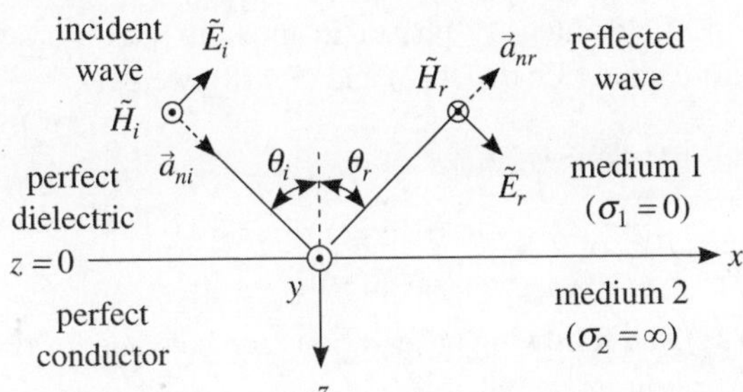

Figure 7.8 *Oblique incidence on a plane conductor boundary with parallel polarization*

From Figure 7.8, it is evident that the incident and reflected electric fields will have components in x- and z-directions. But the incident and reflected magnetic fields will have components only in y-direction. Here, the unit vectors $\vec{a}_{ni}$ and $\vec{a}_{nr}$ represent the direction of propagation of incident and reflected waves.

The incident electric and magnetic field intensity phasors are represented by

$$\tilde{E}_i(x,z) = E_{i0}\left(\cos\theta_i \vec{a}_x - \sin\theta_i \vec{a}_z\right)e^{-j\beta_1[x\sin\theta_i + z\cos\theta_i]} \tag{7.115}$$

$$\tilde{H}_i(x,z) = \frac{E_{i0}}{\eta_1}e^{-j\beta_1[x\sin\theta_i + z\cos\theta_i]}\vec{a}_y \tag{7.116}$$

Similarly, the reflected electric and magnetic field intensity phasors are represented by

$$\tilde{E}_r(x,z) = E_{r0}\left(\cos\theta_r \vec{a}_x + \sin\theta_r \vec{a}_z\right)e^{-j\beta_1[x\sin\theta_r - z\cos\theta_r]} \tag{7.117}$$

$$\tilde{H}_r(x,z) = -\frac{E_{r0}}{\eta_1}e^{-j\beta_1[x\sin\theta_r - z\cos\theta_r]}\vec{a}_y \tag{7.118}$$

According to boundary condition, the tangential component of electric field must be equal to zero at the interface $z = 0$. Hence, the total electric field vanishes for all values of x.

That is,

$$\tilde{E}_1(x,0) = \tilde{E}_i(x,0) + \tilde{E}_r(x,0) = 0$$

$$E_{i0}\cos\theta_i \vec{a}_x e^{-j\beta_1 x\sin\theta_i} + E_{r0}\cos\theta_r \vec{a}_x e^{-j\beta_1 x\sin\theta_r} = 0$$

The above equation is valid for all values of x only if $E_{i0} = -E_{r0}$ and $\theta_i = \theta_r$. Thus, the reflected electric field represented in Eq. (7.117) can also be written as

$$\tilde{E}_r(x,z) = -E_{i0}\left(\cos\theta_i \vec{a}_x + \sin\theta_i \vec{a}_z\right)e^{-j\beta_1[x\sin\theta_i - z\cos\theta_i]} \tag{7.119}$$

The total electric field intensity phasor in medium 1 is the sum of incident and reflected electric field phasors. Therefore, using Eqs. (7.115) and (7.119), we get

$$\tilde{E}_1(x,z) = \tilde{E}_i(x,z) + \tilde{E}_r(x,z)$$

$$= E_{i0}\cos\theta_i \left(e^{-j\beta_1 z\cos\theta_i} - e^{j\beta_1 z\cos\theta_i}\right)e^{-j\beta_1 x\sin\theta_i}\,\vec{a}_x$$

$$- E_{i0}\sin\theta_i \left(e^{-j\beta_1 z\cos\theta_i} + e^{j\beta_1 z\cos\theta_i}\right)e^{-j\beta_1 x\sin\theta_i}\,\vec{a}_z$$

$$= -2E_{i0}\{j\cos\theta_i \sin\left(\beta_1 z\cos\theta_i\right)\vec{a}_x + \sin\theta_i \cos\left(\beta_1 z\cos\theta_i\right)\vec{a}_z\}e^{-j\beta_1 x\sin\theta_i} \tag{7.120}$$

Similarly, the total magnetic field intensity phasor in medium 1 is the sum of incident and reflected magnetic field phasors. Therefore, using Eqs. (7.116) and (7.118), we get

$$\tilde{H}_1(x,z) = \tilde{H}_i(x,z) + \tilde{H}_r(x,z)$$

$$= \frac{2E_{i0}}{\eta_1}\cos\left(\beta_1 z\cos\theta_i\right)e^{-j\beta_1 x\sin\theta_i}\,\vec{a}_y \tag{7.121}$$

From Eqs. (7.120) and (7.121), the following observations can be made for oblique incidence of a uniform plane wave with parallel polarization.

(*i*) The x-component of electric field, i.e., $\tilde{E}_{1x}$ and the y-component of magnetic field, i.e., $\tilde{H}_{1y}$ form a standing wave pattern due to the presence of $\sin\beta_1 z$ and $\cos\beta_1 z$ terms. Therefore, no average power is propagated in the direction normal to the boundary, i.e., z-direction.

(*ii*) In the direction parallel to the conductor boundary, i.e., in x-direction, both $\tilde{E}_{1z}$ and $\tilde{H}_{1y}$ are in phase with time and space. Therefore, the phase velocity and the wavelength of the wave propagating in the x-direction are given by

$$u_{1x} = \frac{u_1}{\sin\theta_i}$$

and

$$\lambda_{1x} = \frac{\lambda_1}{\sin\theta_i}$$

(*iii*) As in the case of perpendicular polarization, the wave propagating in the x-direction is known as non-uniform plane wave.

7.7.3 Normal Incidence at Perfect Dielectric Boundary

When an EM wave is incident normally on the surface of a perfect dielectric, part of the incident energy is transmitted and part of it is reflected. Figure 7.9 shows a uniform plane wave on a dielectric boundary in which medium 1 and medium 2 have different values of permeability and permittivity. Both mediums are assumed to be dissipation less $(\sigma_1 = \sigma_2 = 0)$.

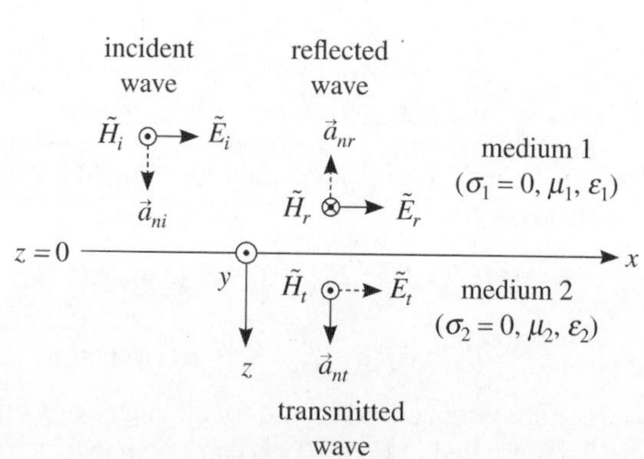

Figure 7.9 *Normal incidence on a plane dielectric boundary*

Consider a plane wave travelling in the "$+z$"-direction as shown in Figure 7.9 and the boundary surface is the plane $z = 0$. The incident electric and magnetic field intensity phasors are given by

$$\tilde{E}_i(z) = E_{i0}e^{-j\beta_1 z}\vec{a}_x$$

$$\tilde{H}_i(z) = \frac{E_{i0}}{\eta_1}e^{-j\beta_1 z}\vec{a}_y$$

where E_{i0} is the magnitude of $\tilde{E}_i$ at $z = 0$, β_1, and η_1 are the phase constant and the intrinsic impedance of medium 1, respectively. Since there is medium discontinuity at $z = 0$, the incident wave is partly reflected back to medium 1 and partly transmitted to medium 2. Therefore, the reflected electric field and magnetic field phasors are represented by

$$\tilde{E}_r(z) = E_{r0}e^{j\beta_1 z}\vec{a}_x$$

$$\tilde{H}_r(z) = \frac{1}{\eta_1}\vec{a}_{nr}\times\tilde{E}_r(z) = \frac{1}{\eta_1}\left(-\vec{a}_z\right)\times\tilde{E}_r(z)$$

$$= \frac{1}{\eta_1}\left(-\vec{a}_z\right)\times\left(E_{r0}e^{j\beta_1 z}\vec{a}_x\right) = -\frac{E_{r0}}{\eta_1}e^{j\beta_1 z}\vec{a}_y$$

Also, the transmitted electric field and magnetic field phasors are represented by

$$\tilde{E}_t(z) = E_{t0}e^{-j\beta_2 z}\vec{a}_x$$

$$\tilde{H}_t(z) = \frac{1}{\eta_2}\vec{a}_{nt}\times\tilde{E}_t(z) = \frac{1}{\eta_2}\left(\vec{a}_z\right)\times\tilde{E}_t(z)$$

$$= \frac{1}{\eta_2}\left(\vec{a}_z\right)\times\left(E_{t0}e^{-j\beta_2 z}\vec{a}_x\right) = \frac{E_{t0}}{\eta_2}e^{-j\beta_2 z}\vec{a}_y$$

where E_{t0} is the magnitude of $\tilde{E}_t$ at $z = 0$, β_2, and η_2 are the phase constant and the intrinsic impedance of medium 2, respectively. Since the tangential components of the electric and magnetic field intensities must be continuous at the dielectric interface $z = 0$, we have

$$\tilde{E}_i(0) + \tilde{E}_r(0) = \tilde{E}_t(0) \text{ or } E_{i0} + E_{r0} = E_{t0} \tag{7.122}$$

and $\quad \tilde{H}_i(0) + \tilde{H}_r(0) = \tilde{H}_t(0) \text{ or } \dfrac{1}{\eta_1}\left(E_{i0} - E_{r0}\right) = \dfrac{E_{t0}}{\eta_2} \tag{7.123}$

Substituting Eq. (7.122) in Eq. (7.123), we get

$$\eta_2\left(E_{i0} - E_{r0}\right) = \eta_1\left(E_{i0} + E_{r0}\right)$$

$$\left(\eta_2 - \eta_1\right)E_{i0} = \left(\eta_2 + \eta_1\right)E_{r0}$$

Therefore,

$$\Gamma = \frac{E_{r0}}{E_{i0}} = \frac{\eta_2 - \eta_1}{\eta_2 + \eta_1} \tag{7.124}$$

where Γ is the *reflection coefficient*, and it is defined as the ratio of magnitude of reflected wave to incident wave.

Rearranging Eq. (7.122), we have

$$\frac{E_{t0}}{E_{i0}} = 1 + \frac{E_{r0}}{E_{i0}} \tag{7.125}$$

Substituting Eq. (7.124) in Eq. (7.125), we get

$$\frac{E_{t0}}{E_{i0}} = 1 + \frac{\eta_2 - \eta_1}{\eta_2 + \eta_1} = \frac{\eta_2 + \eta_1 + \eta_2 - \eta_1}{\eta_2 + \eta_1} = \frac{2\eta_2}{\eta_2 + \eta_1}$$

Therefore,

$$\tau = \frac{2\eta_2}{\eta_2 + \eta_1} \tag{7.126}$$

where τ is the *transmission coefficient*, and it is defined as the ratio of magnitude of transmitted wave to incident wave. The relation between the reflection coefficient and the transmission coefficient is given by

$$\tau = 1 + \Gamma \tag{7.127}$$

For the magnetic fields, we have

$$\frac{H_{r0}}{H_{i0}} = -\frac{E_{r0}}{E_{i0}} = \frac{\eta_1 - \eta_2}{\eta_1 + \eta_2}$$

$$\frac{H_{t0}}{H_{i0}} = \frac{\eta_1}{\eta_2} \frac{E_{t0}}{E_{i0}} = \frac{2\eta_1}{\eta_1 + \eta_2}$$

If medium 2 is a perfect conductor $(\eta_2 = 0)$, then $E_{r0} = -E_{i0}$ and $E_{t0} = 0$. Hence, the incident wave will be totally reflected and a standing wave is formed. Such a standing wave will have zero and maximum points. If medium 2 is not a perfect conductor, partial reflection will be produced at the boundary. The total electric field intensity phasor in medium 1 can be written as

$$\tilde{E}_1(z) = \tilde{E}_i(z) + \tilde{E}_r(z) = E_{i0}\left(e^{-j\beta_1 z} + \Gamma e^{j\beta_1 z}\right)\vec{a}_x \qquad \left(\text{since } \Gamma = \frac{E_{r0}}{E_{i0}}\right)$$

$$= E_{i0}\left[(1+\Gamma)e^{-j\beta_1 z} + \Gamma\left(e^{j\beta_1 z} - e^{-j\beta_1 z}\right)\right]\vec{a}_x$$

$$= E_{i0}\left[(1+\Gamma)e^{-j\beta_1 z} + \Gamma(2j\sin\beta_1 z)\right]\vec{a}_x$$

$$= E_{i0}\left[\tau e^{-j\beta_1 z} + \Gamma(2j\sin\beta_1 z)\right]\vec{a}_x \tag{7.128}$$

The above equation shows that the electric field $\tilde{E}_1(z)$ consists of two parts: (i) a travelling wave with amplitude τE_{i0} and (ii) a standing wave with amplitude $2\Gamma E_{i0}$. Due to the existence of the travelling wave, $\tilde{E}_1(z)$ will not be zero at fixed distances from the boundary and it has definite locations of maximum and minimum electric field values.

Standing Wave Ratio

The ratio of the maximum to the minimum values of the electric field of a standing wave is called the *standing wave ratio* (SWR) or S. It is given by

$$S = \frac{|E|_{max}}{|E|_{min}} = \frac{E_{i0} + E_{r0}}{E_{i0} - E_{r0}}$$

$$= \frac{E_{i0}\left(1 + \dfrac{E_{r0}}{E_{i0}}\right)}{E_{i0}\left(1 - \dfrac{E_{r0}}{E_{i0}}\right)} = \frac{1 + |\Gamma|}{1 - |\Gamma|} \tag{7.129}$$

Rearranging the above equation, the reflection coefficient can also be written in terms of standing wave ratio as

$$|\Gamma| = \frac{S - 1}{S + 1} \tag{7.130}$$

Here, the value of reflection coefficient Γ ranges from -1 to $+1$ and the value of standing wave ratio S ranges from 1 to ∞.

7.7.4 Oblique Incidence at Perfect Dielectric Boundary

Consider a uniform plane wave incident obliquely at the interface between two dielectric mediums with some arbitrary angle of incidence θ_i. The two dielectric mediums are assumed to be lossless with different constitutive parameters (μ_1, ε_1) and (μ_2, ε_2) as shown in Figure 7.10. Due to these different parameters, there exists a discontinuity at the interface. Therefore, a part of the incident wave is reflected and a part of the wave is transmitted into the dielectric medium.

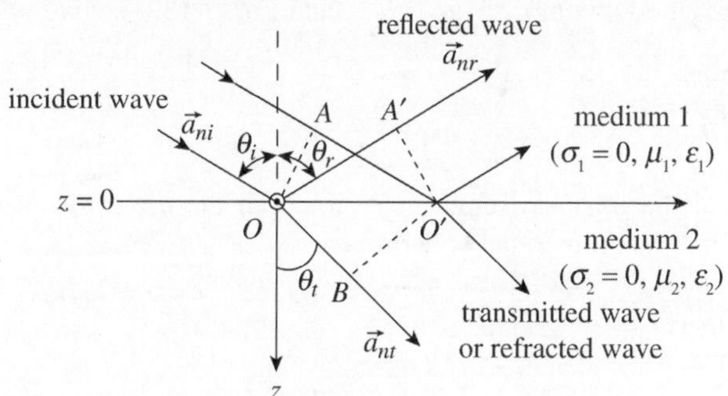

Figure 7.10 *Oblique incidence on a plane dielectric boundary*

Assume that the lines $OA, O'A', O'B$ make intersections of the plane of incidence with equiphase surfaces of the incident, reflected and transmitted waves, respectively. The incident and reflected waves travel in medium 1 with phase velocity u_{p1}. Figure 7.10 shows that the distances OA' and AO' are equal in medium 1. Therefore,

$$OO' \sin\theta_r = OO' \sin\theta_i$$

That is,

$$\theta_r = \theta_i \tag{7.131}$$

Therefore, the angle of incidence is equal to the angle of reflection. This is called *Snell's law of reflection.*

From Figure 7.10, it is seen that the transmitted wave propagates in medium 2 with phase velocity u_{p2}. The time taken by the incident wave to travel from A to O' in medium 1 is equal to the time taken by the transmitted wave to travel from O to B in medium 2. Therefore, we can write

$$\frac{OB}{u_{p2}} = \frac{AO'}{u_{p1}}$$

$$\frac{OB}{AO'} = \frac{OO' \sin\theta_t}{OO' \sin\theta_i} = \frac{u_{p2}}{u_{p1}}$$

Simplifying the above equation and phase velocity relation, we have

$$\frac{\sin\theta_t}{\sin\theta_i} = \frac{u_{p2}}{u_{p1}} = \frac{\omega/\beta_2}{\omega/\beta_1} = \frac{\beta_1}{\beta_2} \tag{7.132}$$

For any medium, the ratio of the speed of light in free space to that in the medium is called the index of refraction, n, i.e., $n = c/u_p$. Hence, for medium 1, the refractive index is $n_1 = c/u_{p1}$ and for medium 2, the refractive index is $n_2 = c/u_{p2}$. Using refractive index, Eq. (7.132) can also be written as

$$\frac{\sin\theta_t}{\sin\theta_i} = \frac{n_1}{n_2} \tag{7.133}$$

The above equation is called *Snell's law of refraction*, which states that the ratio of the sine of angle of transmission (refraction) in medium 2 to the sine of angle of incidence in medium 1 is equal to the ratio of refractive indices n_1/n_2 at an interface between the two dielectric mediums.

If the medium is non-magnetic with $\mu_1 = \mu_2 = \mu_0$. then Eq. (7.132) is given by

$$\frac{\sin\theta_t}{\sin\theta_i} = \frac{1/\sqrt{\mu_0 \varepsilon_2}}{1/\sqrt{\mu_0 \varepsilon_1}} = \sqrt{\frac{\varepsilon_1}{\varepsilon_2}} \tag{7.134}$$

where $u_p = 1/\sqrt{\mu\varepsilon}$. Since the intrinsic impedances for both the dielectric mediums are different, these impedances in medium 1 and medium 2 can be written as

$$\eta_1 = \sqrt{\frac{\mu_1}{\varepsilon_1}} = \sqrt{\frac{\mu_0}{\varepsilon_1}} \quad \text{and} \quad \eta_2 = \sqrt{\frac{\mu_2}{\varepsilon_2}} = \sqrt{\frac{\mu_0}{\varepsilon_2}}$$

Using the above relations, we get

$$\frac{\sin\theta_t}{\sin\theta_i} = \frac{\eta_2}{\eta_1} \tag{7.135}$$

Combining the Eqs. (7.132), (7.133), (7.134), and (7.135), we get

$$\frac{\sin\theta_t}{\sin\theta_i} = \frac{u_{p2}}{u_{p1}} = \frac{\beta_1}{\beta_2} = \frac{n_1}{n_2} = \sqrt{\frac{\varepsilon_1}{\varepsilon_2}} = \frac{\eta_2}{\eta_1} \tag{7.136}$$

Assume that the medium 1 is denser compared to medium 2, i.e., $\varepsilon_1 > \varepsilon_2$. Under this condition, the angle of transmission θ_t becomes greater than the angle of incidence θ_i. Also, the angle of transmission increases with angle of incidence. Here, the transmitted wave will be aligned along the interface when $\theta_t = \dfrac{\pi}{2}$ as shown in Figure 7.11.

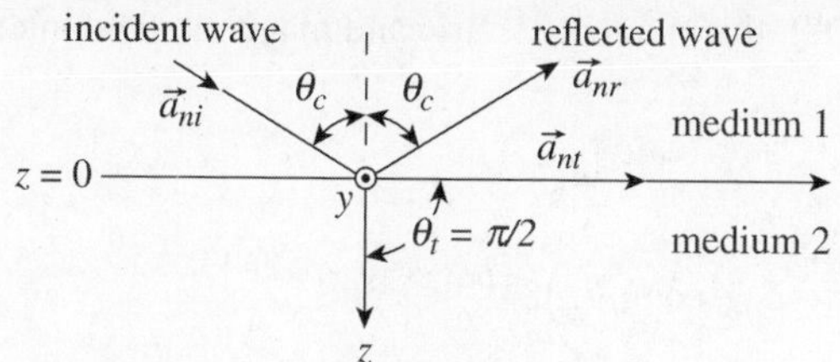

Figure 7.11 *Total reflection at* $\theta_t = \pi / 2$

If θ_t increases further, then there will be no transmitted wave (refracted wave) in medium 2 and the entire incident wave is said to be *totally reflected*. Hence, total reflection takes place at the condition of $\theta_t = \dfrac{\pi}{2}$. The angle of incidence at which the total reflection takes place is called *critical angle* θ_c. Substituting $\theta_t = \dfrac{\pi}{2}$ and $\theta_i = \theta_c$ in Eq. (7.134), we get

$$\frac{\sin \pi / 2}{\sin \theta_c} = \sqrt{\frac{\varepsilon_1}{\varepsilon_2}}$$

That is,

$$\sin \theta_c = \sqrt{\frac{\varepsilon_2}{\varepsilon_1}}$$

Hence,

$$\theta_c = \sin^{-1} \sqrt{\frac{\varepsilon_2}{\varepsilon_1}} = \sin^{-1} \left(\frac{n_2}{n_1} \right) \tag{7.137}$$

The Snell's law of reflection and Snell's law of refraction derived in this section are independent of wave polarization. These laws can also be derived in the cases of perpendicular polarization and parallel polarization by matching the phase of the propagating waves at the interface $z = 0$.

Case (i): Perpendicular Polarization

Consider a uniform plane wave travelling in a perfect dielectric $\left(\text{medium 1}, \sigma_1 = 0 \right)$, which strikes an interface obliquely with another dielectric $\left(\text{medium 2}, \sigma_2 = 0 \right)$ as shown in Figure 7.12. If the electric field phasor $\tilde{E}_i$ is perpendicular to the plane of incidence, then this type of polarization is called *perpendicular polarization*.

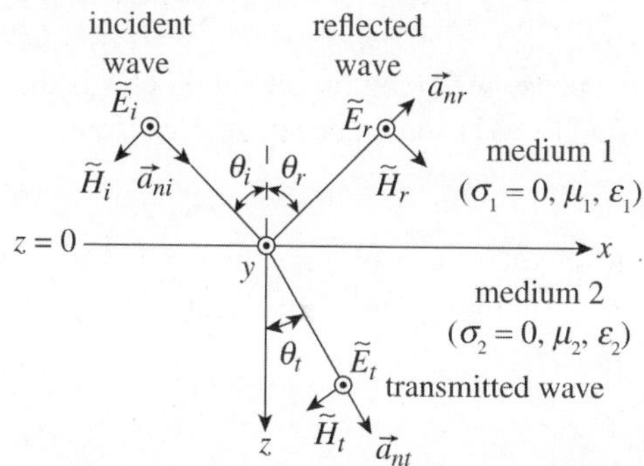

Figure 7.12 *Oblique incidence on a plane dielectric boundary with perpendicular polarization*

From Eqs. (7.106) and (7.107), the incident electric and magnetic field intensity phasors in medium 1 are represented by

$$\tilde{E}_i\left(x,z\right) = E_{i0}e^{-j\beta_1\left[x\sin\theta_i + z\cos\theta_i\right]}\vec{a}_y \tag{7.138}$$

$$\tilde{H}_i\left(x,z\right) = \frac{E_{i0}}{\eta_1}\left(\sin\theta_i\vec{a}_z - \cos\theta_i\vec{a}_x\right)e^{-j\beta_1\left[x\sin\theta_i + z\cos\theta_i\right]} \tag{7.139}$$

where η_1 is the intrinsic impedance of medium 1.

In a dielectric–dielectric interface, $E_{r0} \neq E_{i0}$. From Eqs. (7.109) and (7.113), the reflected electric and magnetic field intensity phasors in medium 1 are represented by

$$\tilde{E}_r\left(x,z\right) = E_{r0}e^{-j\beta_1\left[x\sin\theta_r - z\cos\theta_r\right]}\vec{a}_y \tag{7.140}$$

$$\tilde{H}_r\left(x,z\right) = \frac{E_{r0}}{\eta_1}\left(\sin\theta_r\vec{a}_z + \cos\theta_r\vec{a}_x\right)e^{-j\beta_1\left[x\sin\theta_r - z\cos\theta_r\right]} \tag{7.141}$$

From Figure 7.12, it is seen that a wave is transmitted in medium 2. The transmitted electric and magnetic field intensity phasors in medium 2 can be written as

$$\tilde{E}_t\left(x,z\right) = E_{t0}e^{-j\beta_2\left[x\sin\theta_t + z\cos\theta_t\right]}\vec{a}_y \tag{7.142}$$

$$\tilde{H}_t\left(x,z\right) = \frac{E_{t0}}{\eta_2}\left(\sin\theta_t\vec{a}_z - \cos\theta_t\vec{a}_x\right)e^{-j\beta_2\left[x\sin\theta_t + z\cos\theta_t\right]} \tag{7.143}$$

where η_2 is the intrinsic impedance of medium 2. According to boundary conditions, the tangential components of $\tilde{E}$ and $\tilde{H}$ must be continuous at the interface $z = 0$. Therefore, at $z = 0$, we have

$$\tilde{E}_i\left(x,0\right) + \tilde{E}_r\left(x,0\right) = \tilde{E}_t\left(x,0\right)$$

That is,

$$E_{i0}e^{-j\beta_1 x\sin\theta_i} + E_{r0}e^{-j\beta_1 x\sin\theta_r} = E_{t0}e^{-j\beta_2 x\sin\theta_t} \tag{7.144}$$

Similarly, the magnetic field intensity phasor $\tilde{H}$ at $z = 0$ along x-direction is given by

$$\tilde{H}_i\left(x,0\right) + \tilde{H}_r\left(x,0\right) = \tilde{H}_t\left(x,0\right)$$

That is,

$$\frac{1}{\eta_1}\left(-E_{i0}\cos\theta_i e^{-j\beta_1 x\sin\theta_i} + E_{r0}\cos\theta_r e^{-j\beta_1 x\sin\theta_r}\right) = -\frac{E_{t0}}{\eta_2}\cos\theta_t e^{-j\beta_1 x\sin\theta_t} \tag{7.145}$$

The necessary condition to have phase matching for all values of x is that the exponential factors, which are functions of x in Eqs. (7.144) and (7.145) should be equal. Therefore,

$$\beta_1 x\sin\theta_i = \beta_1 x\sin\theta_r = \beta_2 x\sin\theta_t$$

The above condition leads to Snell's law of reflection $\left(\theta_i = \theta_r\right)$ and Snell's law of refraction $\left(\sin\theta_t / \sin\theta_i = \beta_1 / \beta_2\right)$. Using this condition, Eqs. (7.144) and (7.145) can be simplified as

$$E_{i0} + E_{r0} = E_{t0} \qquad \text{(for electric field)}$$

$$\frac{1}{\eta_1}\left(E_{i0} - E_{r0}\right)\cos\theta_i = \frac{E_{t0}}{\eta_2}\cos\theta_t \qquad \text{(for magnetic field)}$$

Using these two equations, the reflection coefficient and transmission coefficient with perpendicular polarization are represented by

$$\Gamma_\perp = \frac{E_{r0}}{E_{i0}} = \frac{\eta_2 \cos\theta_i - \eta_1 \cos\theta_t}{\eta_2 \cos\theta_i + \eta_1 \cos\theta_t} \tag{7.146}$$

and

$$\tau_\perp = \frac{E_{t0}}{E_{i0}} = \frac{2\eta_2 \cos\theta_i}{\eta_2 \cos\theta_i + \eta_1 \cos\theta_t} \tag{7.147}$$

Both reflection coefficient $\Gamma_\perp$ and transmission coefficient $\tau_\perp$ for oblique incidence with perpendicular polarization are related by $1 + \Gamma_\perp = \tau_\perp$, and it is similar to Eq. (7.127) for normal incidence. Suppose if medium 2 is a perfect conductor $(\eta_2 = 0)$, then Eqs. (7.146) and (7.147) reduce to $\Gamma_\perp = -1$ and $\tau_\perp = 0$ which show that the incident wave gets totally reflected by the conductor boundary.

Brewster Angle $\theta_{B\perp}$

When there is no reflection, i.e., $E_{r0} = 0$, the reflection coefficient also becomes zero, i.e., $\Gamma_\perp = 0$. Therefore, Eq. (7.146) becomes

$$\eta_2 \cos\theta_i = \eta_1 \cos\theta_t \tag{7.148}$$

According to Snell's law of refraction,

$$\frac{\sin\theta_t}{\sin\theta_i} = \frac{n_1}{n_2}$$

But,

$$\cos\theta_t = \sqrt{1 - \sin^2\theta_t} = \sqrt{1 - \left(\frac{n_1}{n_2}\right)^2 \sin^2\theta_i} \tag{7.149}$$

Substituting Eq. (7.149) in Eq. (7.148) and making use of Eq. (7.136) by replacing θ_i with $\theta_{B\perp}$, we get

$$\sin^2\theta_{B\perp} = \frac{1 - (\mu_1 \varepsilon_2 / \mu_2 \varepsilon_1)}{1 - (\mu_1 / \mu_2)^2} \tag{7.150}$$

Here, the angle $\theta_{B\perp}$ is called the Brewster angle, and it is defined as the angle of incidence θ_i at which the reflection coefficient $\Gamma_\perp = 0$.

For a non-magnetic material with $\mu_1 = \mu_2$, the Brewster angle $\theta_{B\perp}$ does not exist as the denominator of Eq. (7.150) becomes zero. Also if $\varepsilon_1 = \varepsilon_2$ and $\mu_1 \neq \mu_2$, Eq. (7.150) reduces to

$$\sin^2\theta_{B\perp} = \frac{\mu_2}{\mu_1 + \mu_2}$$

That is,

$$\sin\theta_{B\perp} = \sqrt{\frac{\mu_2}{\mu_1 + \mu_2}} \quad \text{or} \quad \tan\theta_{B\perp} = \sqrt{\frac{\mu_2}{\mu_1}}$$

The possibility of two mediums having same permittivity but different permeabilities is a very rare situation in electromagnetics.

Case (ii): Parallel Polarization

Consider that a uniform plane wave is incident obliquely on the dielectric–dielectric interface with the electric field phasor $\tilde{E}_i$ parallel to the plane of incidence as shown in Figure 7.13. If $\tilde{E}_i$ is parallel to the plane of incidence, this type of polarization is called parallel *polarization.*

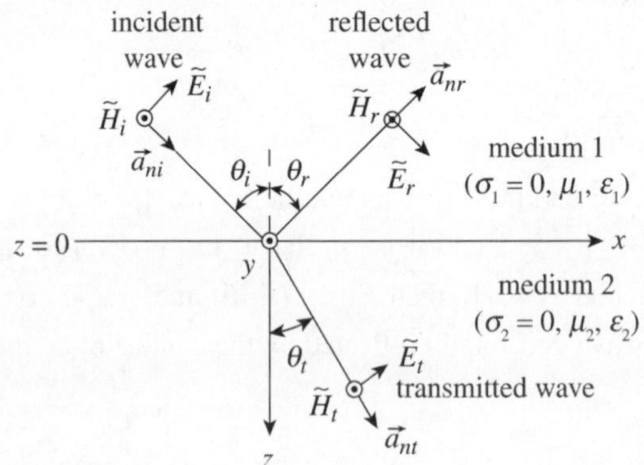

Figure 7.13 *Oblique incidence on a plane dielectric boundary with parallel polarization*

From Eqs. (7.115) and (7.116), the incident electric and magnetic field intensity phasors in medium 1 are represented by

$$\tilde{E}_i(x,z) = E_{i0}\left(\cos\theta_i\,\vec{a}_x - \sin\theta_i\,\vec{a}_z\right)e^{-j\beta_1[x\sin\theta_i + z\cos\theta_i]} \tag{7.151}$$

$$\tilde{H}_i(x,z) = \frac{E_{i0}}{\eta_1}e^{-j\beta_1[x\sin\theta_i + z\cos\theta_i]}\vec{a}_y \tag{7.152}$$

Similarly, the reflected electric and magnetic field intensity phasors in medium 1 are given by

$$\tilde{E}_r(x,z) = E_{r0}\left(\cos\theta_r\,\vec{a}_x + \sin\theta_r\,\vec{a}_z\right)e^{-j\beta_1[x\sin\theta_r - z\cos\theta_r]} \tag{7.153}$$

$$\tilde{H}_r(x,z) = -\frac{E_{r0}}{\eta_1}e^{-j\beta_1[x\sin\theta_r - z\cos\theta_r]}\vec{a}_y \tag{7.154}$$

Now in medium 2, the transmitted electric and magnetic field intensity phasors in medium 2 are represented by

$$\tilde{E}_t(x,z) = E_{t0}\left(\cos\theta_t\,\vec{a}_x - \sin\theta_t\,\vec{a}_z\right)e^{-j\beta_2[x\sin\theta_t + z\cos\theta_t]} \tag{7.155}$$

$$\tilde{H}_t(x,z) = \frac{E_{t0}}{\eta_2}e^{-j\beta_2[x\sin\theta_t + z\cos\theta_t]}\vec{a}_y \tag{7.156}$$

Similar to perpendicular polarization, using boundary conditions, the tangential component of electric field is continuous at the boundary $z = 0$. Therefore,

$$(E_{i0} + E_{r0})\cos\theta_i = E_{t0}\cos\theta_t \qquad \text{(for electric field)}$$

$$\frac{1}{\eta_1}\left(E_{i0} - E_{r0}\right) = \frac{E_{t0}}{\eta_2} \qquad \text{(for magnetic field)}$$

Solving E_{r0} and E_{t0} in terms of E_{i0}, the reflection coefficient in parallel polarization is given by

$$\Gamma_{\parallel} = \frac{E_{r0}}{E_{i0}} = \frac{\eta_2 \cos\theta_t - \eta_1 \cos\theta_i}{\eta_2 \cos\theta_t + \eta_1 \cos\theta_i} \tag{7.157}$$

Similarly, the transmission coefficient in parallel polarization is given by

$$\tau_{\parallel} = \frac{E_{t0}}{E_{i0}} = \frac{2\eta_2 \cos\theta_i}{\eta_2 \cos\theta_t + \eta_1 \cos\theta_i} \tag{7.158}$$

The reflection and transmission coefficients in parallel polarization are related by

$$1 + \Gamma_{\parallel} = \tau_{\parallel} \left(\frac{\cos\theta_t}{\cos\theta_i} \right) \tag{7.159}$$

If the medium 2 is a perfect conductor with $\eta_2 = 0$, the incident wave gets totally reflected by the conducting medium. Substituting $\eta_2 = 0$ in Eqs. (7.157) and (7.158), we get $\Gamma_{\parallel} = -1$ and $\tau_{\parallel} = 0$.

Brewster Angle $\theta_{B\parallel}$

When there is no reflection, i.e., $E_{r0} = 0$, the reflection coefficient also becomes zero, i.e., $\Gamma_{\parallel} = 0$. Therefore, Eq. (7.157) becomes

$$\eta_2 \cos\theta_i = \eta_1 \cos\theta_t \tag{7.160}$$

According to Snell's law of refraction,

$$\frac{\sin\theta_t}{\sin\theta_i} = \frac{n_1}{n_2}$$

But,

$$\cos\theta_t = \sqrt{1 - \sin^2\theta_t} = \sqrt{1 - \left(\frac{n_1}{n_2}\right)^2 \sin^2\theta_t} \tag{7.161}$$

Substituting Eq. (7.161) in Eq. (7.160) and making use of Eq. (7.136) by replacing θ_i with $\theta_{B\parallel}$, we get

$$\sin^2\theta_{B\parallel} = \frac{1 - (\mu_2\varepsilon_1 / \mu_1\varepsilon_2)}{1 - (\varepsilon_1 / \varepsilon_2)^2} \tag{7.162}$$

Here, the angle $\theta_{B\parallel}$ is called the Brewster angle of no reflection $\left(\Gamma_{\parallel} = 0\right)$ for the case of parallel polarization. For a non-magnetic material with $\mu_1 = \mu_2$,

$$\sin\theta_{B\parallel} = \sqrt{\frac{1}{1 + (\varepsilon_1 / \varepsilon_2)}} \tag{7.163}$$

or

$$\tan\theta_{B\parallel} = \sqrt{\frac{\varepsilon_2}{\varepsilon_1}} \tag{7.164}$$

Therefore, the Brewster angle exists only for parallel polarization in a non-magnetic medium and its value depends on the ratio of permittivities of the mediums.

If a wave composed of both perpendicular and parallel polarization components is incident on a non-magnetic boundary at the Brewster angle $\theta_{B\parallel}$, the parallel polarized component is totally transmitted into medium 2 and only the component with perpendicular polarization will be reflected. Hence, the Brewster angle is also known as a *polarizing angle*.

EXAMPLE 7.40

Determine the critical angle for wave propagation from Teflon $\left(\varepsilon_r = 2.1\right)$ into free space.

SOLUTION

Given $\varepsilon_{r1} = 2.1$ for Teflon medium 1 and $\varepsilon_{r2} = 1$ for free space medium 2.

From Eq. (7.137), the critical angle is

$$\theta_c = \sin^{-1}\sqrt{\frac{\varepsilon_2}{\varepsilon_1}} = \sin^{-1}\sqrt{\frac{\varepsilon_0 \varepsilon_{r2}}{\varepsilon_0 \varepsilon_{r1}}} = \sin^{-1}\sqrt{\frac{\varepsilon_{r2}}{\varepsilon_{r1}}}$$

$$= \sin^{-1}\frac{1}{\sqrt{2.1}} = 43.64°$$

EXAMPLE 7.41

Determine the critical angle for the EM wave passing through glass to air if ε_r for glass is 9.

SOLUTION

Given that, medium 1 is glass $\left(\varepsilon_{r1} = 9\right)$ and medium 2 is air $\left(\varepsilon_{r2} = 1\right)$.

The critical angle is

$$\theta_c = \sin^{-1}\sqrt{\frac{\varepsilon_2}{\varepsilon_1}} = \sin^{-1}\sqrt{\frac{\varepsilon_{r2}}{\varepsilon_{r1}}} = \sin^{-1}\frac{1}{\sqrt{9}} = 19.47°$$

EXAMPLE 7.42

A light beam is incident from air to a medium with a dielectric constant 4 and relative permeability 100. If the angle of incidence is $30°$, find the angle of reflection and angle of refraction.

SOLUTION

Given $\mu_{r2} = 4$, $\varepsilon_{r2} = 100$ and $\theta_i = 30°$. For air, $\mu_{r1} = 1$ and $\varepsilon_{r1} = 1$.

Here, angle of reflection θ_r = angle of incidence $\theta_i = 30°$.

Using Snell's law of refraction, we get

$$\sqrt{\mu_1 \varepsilon_1}\, \sin\theta_i = \sqrt{\mu_2 \varepsilon_2}\, \sin\theta_t$$

$$\sqrt{\mu_0 \varepsilon_0}\, \sin 30° = \sqrt{\mu_0 \left(100\right)\varepsilon_0 \left(4\right)}\, \sin\theta_t$$

$$\sin\theta_t = \frac{\sin 30°}{20} = 0.025$$

$$\theta_t = \sin^{-1}\left(0.025\right) = 1.43°$$

Therefore, the angle of refraction, $\theta_t = 1.43°$.

EXAMPLE 7.43

A wave is incident at an angle of $60°$ from air to Teflon, $\varepsilon_r = 2.1$. Determine the angle of transmission.

SOLUTION

From Snell's law refraction,

$$\frac{\sin\theta_t}{\sin\theta_i} = \sqrt{\frac{\varepsilon_{r1}}{\varepsilon_{r2}}} = \sqrt{\frac{1}{2.1}}$$

That is,

$$\sin\theta_t = \sin 60° \frac{1}{\sqrt{2.1}}$$

Therefore, the angle of transmission is

$$\theta_t = \sin^{-1}(0.598) = 36.7°$$

EXAMPLE 7.44

Determine the Brewster angle for a parallel-polarized wave travelling from air into glass for which $\varepsilon_r = 5$.

SOLUTION

From Eq. (7.164), the critical angle is

$$\theta_{B\parallel} = \tan^{-1}\sqrt{\frac{\varepsilon_2}{\varepsilon_1}} = \tan^{-1}\sqrt{5} = 65.91°$$

EXAMPLE 7.45

A perpendicular polarized wave propagates from medium 1 $\left(\varepsilon_{r1} = 9, \mu_{r1} = 1 \text{ and } \sigma_1 = 0\right)$ to medium 2 (free space) with an angle of incidence of $15°$. Given $E_{i0} = 2\,\mu\text{V/m}$, determine $E_{r0}, E_{t0}, H_{i0}, H_{r0}$ and H_{t0}.

SOLUTION

Given $E_{i0} = 2\,\mu\text{V/m}$ and $\theta = 15°$.

Here, the constitutive parameters in medium 1 are $\varepsilon_{r1} = 9$, $\mu_{r1} = 1$ and $\sigma_1 = 0$ and in medium 2 (free space) are $\varepsilon_{r2} = 9$, $\mu_{r2} = 1$ and $\sigma_2 = 0$. The intrinsic impedances in medium 1 and medium 2 are

$$\eta_1 = \frac{\eta_0}{\sqrt{\varepsilon_{r1}}} = \frac{377}{\sqrt{9}} = 125.67\,\Omega \quad \text{and} \quad \eta_2 = \eta_0 = 377\,\Omega \text{ (free space)}$$

From Snell's law of refraction,

$$\frac{\sin\theta_t}{\sin\theta_i} = \sqrt{\frac{\varepsilon_1}{\varepsilon_2}}$$

That is,

$$\sin\theta_t = \sin\theta_i\sqrt{\frac{\varepsilon_1}{\varepsilon_2}} = \sin 15°\sqrt{\frac{9\varepsilon_0}{\varepsilon_{r2}\varepsilon_0}} = 0.776$$

Hence, the angle of transmission is

$$\theta_t = \sin^{-1}(0.776) = 50.9°$$

Now, the reflected and transmitted electric fields are

$$\frac{E_{r0}}{E_{i0}} = \frac{\eta_2\cos\theta_i - \eta_1\cos\theta_t}{\eta_2\cos\theta_i + \eta_1\cos\theta_t} = \frac{377\cos 15° - 125.67\cos 50.9°}{377\cos 15° + 125.67\cos 50.9°} = 0.643$$

Therefore,

$$E_{r0} = 0.643E_{i0} = 0.643 \times 2 \times 10^{-6} = 1.286\,\mu V/m$$

$$\frac{E_{t0}}{E_{i0}} = \frac{2\eta_2\cos\theta_i}{\eta_2\cos\theta_i + \eta_1\cos\theta_t} = \frac{2(377)\cos 15°}{377\cos 15° + 125.67\cos 50.9°} = 1.643$$

Therefore,

$$E_{t0} = 1.643E_{i0} = 1.643 \times 2 \times 10^{-6} = 3.286\,\mu V/m$$

Hence, the incident, reflected and transmitted magnetic fields are

$$H_{i0} = E_{i0}/\eta_1 = 15.9\,nA/m$$

$$H_{r0} = E_{r0}/\eta_1 = 10.23\,nA/m$$

and $\qquad H_{t0} = E_{t0}/\eta_2 = 8.72\,nA/m$

EXAMPLE 7.46

A uniform plane wave with 25 V/m electric field is normally incident on an infinitely thick slab of a material of dielectric constant 4. Find the electric and magnetic fields just inside the slab surface. How much power penetrates the material slab?

SOLUTION

Given $E_i = 25\,V/m$ and $\varepsilon_{r2} = 4$.

Here, the wave is incident from air to the dielectric slab.

Therefore,

$$\eta_1 = \eta_0 \quad \text{and} \quad \eta_2 = \frac{\eta_0}{\sqrt{\varepsilon_{r2}}} = \frac{\eta_0}{\sqrt{4}} = \frac{\eta_0}{2}$$

where $\eta_0 = 377\,\Omega$.

The transmission coefficient is

$$\tau = \frac{E_t}{E_i} = \frac{2\eta_2}{\eta_2 + \eta_1} = \frac{2\left(\dfrac{\eta_0}{2}\right)}{\dfrac{\eta_0}{2} + \eta_0} = \frac{1}{0.5 + 1} = 0.667$$

Hence, the electric field transmitted inside the slab is

$$E_t = \tau E_i = 0.667 \times 25 = 16.675 \, \text{V/m}$$

Therefore, the magnetic field transmitted inside the slab is

$$H_t = \frac{E_t}{\eta_2} = \frac{16.675}{\eta_0/2} = \frac{33.35}{377} = 0.088 \, \text{A/m}$$

Hence, the power transferred to the slab is

$$P = E_t H_t = 1.467 \, \text{W/m}^2$$

□

<hr>

EXAMPLE 7.47

A 2 GHz uniform plane wave $\tilde{E}_i = 20e^{-j\beta z}\vec{a}_x$ V/m in free space is incident normally on a large plane, lossless dielectric slab $(z > 0)$ having $\mu = \mu_0$ and $\varepsilon = 9\varepsilon_0$. Determine the reflected wave $\tilde{E}_r$ and the transmitted wave $\tilde{E}_t$.

SOLUTION

Given $\tilde{E}_i = 20e^{-j\beta z}\vec{a}_x$ V/m.

The reflected electric field in phasor form is

$$\tilde{E}_r = E_{r0}e^{j\beta_1 z}\vec{a}_x$$

Here,

$$\frac{E_{r0}}{E_{i0}} = \Gamma = \frac{\eta_2 - \eta_1}{\eta_2 + \eta_1} = \frac{\dfrac{\eta_0}{3} - \eta_0}{\dfrac{\eta_0}{3} + \eta_0} = -\frac{1}{2}$$

$$E_{r0} = \left(-\frac{1}{2}\right)20 = -10$$

Hence, the reflected electric field wave in medium 1 is

$$\tilde{E}_r = -10e^{j\beta_1 z}\vec{a}_x \, \text{V/m}$$

where

$$\beta_1 = \frac{\omega}{c} = \frac{2\pi \times 2 \times 10^9}{3 \times 10^8} = \frac{40\pi}{3}$$

The transmitted electric field in phasor form is

$$\tilde{E}_t = E_{t0}e^{-j\beta_2 z}\vec{a}_x$$

Here,

$$\frac{E_{t0}}{E_{i0}} = \tau = 1 + \Gamma = 1 - \frac{1}{2} = \frac{1}{2}$$

$$E_{t0} = \left(\frac{1}{2}\right)20 = 10$$

Hence, the transmitted electric field wave in medium 2 is

$$\tilde{E}_t = 10e^{-j\beta_2 z}\vec{a}_x$$

where

$$\beta_2 = \frac{\omega\sqrt{\varepsilon_r}}{c} = \frac{2\pi\times 2\times 10^9\times\sqrt{9}}{3\times 10^8} = \frac{120\pi}{3} \qquad \square$$

EXAMPLE 7.48

A normally incident $\vec{E}$ field has amplitude 1 V/m in free space just outside of seawater in which $\varepsilon_r = 80$, $\mu_r = 1$ and $\sigma = 2.5\,\text{S/m}$. For a frequency of 30 MHz, at what depth will the amplitude of $\vec{E}$ be 1 mV/m?

SOLUTION

Given $\vec{E}_1 = 1\,\text{V/m}$ in free space and the constitutive parameter of seawater are $\varepsilon_r = 80$, $\mu_r = 1$ and $\sigma = 2.5\,\text{S/m}$.

Assume the free space as medium 1 and the seawater as medium 2. The intrinsic impedance of medium 1 (free space) is

$$\eta_1 = \eta_0 = 377\,\Omega$$

The intrinsic impedance of medium 2 (seawater) is

$$\eta_2 = \sqrt{\frac{j\omega\mu}{\sigma + j\omega\varepsilon}} = \sqrt{\frac{j\omega\mu_0\mu_r}{\sigma + j\omega\varepsilon_0\varepsilon_r}}$$

$$= \sqrt{\frac{j\left(2\pi\times 30\times 10^6\right)\left(4\pi\times 10^{-7}\times 1\right)}{2.5 + \left(2\pi\times 30\times 10^6\right)\left(8.854\times 10^{-12}\times 80\right)}} = \sqrt{\frac{j236.87}{\left(2.5 + j0.1335\right)}}$$

$$= \sqrt{\frac{236.87\angle 90°}{2.503\angle 3.056°}}$$

$$= 9.728\angle 43.47°\,\Omega = \left(7.06 + j6.69\right)\Omega$$

Here, the amplitude of $\vec{E}$ outside the sea water is $E_{i0} = 1\,\text{V/m}$ and the amplitude of $\vec{E}$ inside the sea water is E_{t0}.

From Eq. (7.126), we have

$$\frac{E_{t0}}{E_{i0}} = \frac{2\eta_2}{\eta_1 + \eta_2}$$

Here,

$$E_{t0} = \frac{2\eta_2}{\eta_1 + \eta_2}E_{i0} = \left[\frac{2\left(9.728\angle 43.47°\right)}{377 + \left(7.06 + j6.69\right)}\right]\times 1$$

$$= \frac{19.456\angle 43.47°}{384.06 + j6.69} = \frac{19.456\angle 43.47°}{384.12\angle 1°}$$

$$= 0.051\angle 42.47°\,\text{V/m}$$

In the lossy dielectric, the amplitude of the wave travelling exponentially decreases due to factor $e^{-\alpha z}$. The propagation constant in medium 2 is

$$\gamma = \alpha + j\beta = \sqrt{j\omega\mu\left(\sigma + j\omega\varepsilon\right)}$$

$$= \sqrt{j\left(2\pi \times 30 \times 10^6\right)\left(4\pi \times 10^{-7} \times 1\right)\left[2.5 + j\left(2\pi \times 30 \times 10^6\right)\left(80 \times 8.854 \times 10^{-12}\right)\right]}$$

$$= \sqrt{\left(j236.63\right)\left(2.5 + j0.133\right)}$$

$$= \sqrt{\left(236.36\angle 90°\right)\left(2.503\angle 3.045°\right)}$$

$$= 24.34\angle 46.52°\,\text{m}^{-1} = \left(16.75 + j17.66\right)\text{m}^{-1}$$

Hence, the attenuation constant α is

$$\alpha = 16.75\,\text{Np/m}$$

Let z be the depth from the surface of the sea water of which the amplitude of $\vec{E}$ is 1 mV/m. Hence, we can write

$$\left|\vec{E}\right| \text{ at } z = \vec{E}_t e^{-\alpha z}$$

$$1 \times 10^{-3} = 0.051 e^{-16.75z}$$

$$e^{-16.75z} = \frac{10^{-3}}{0.051} = 19.61 \times 10^{-3}$$

Taking natural logarithm on both side of the above equation, we get

$$-16.75z = \ln\left(19.61 \times 10^{-3}\right) = -3.93$$

Hence, $\qquad z = 0.235\,\text{m}$

EXAMPLE 7.49

A uniform plane wave in a lossless medium with intrinsic impedance η_1 is incident normally onto another lossless medium with intrinsic impedance η_2 through a plane boundary. Obtain the expressions for the time-average power densities in both the mediums in terms of reflection coefficient and transmission coefficient.

SOLUTION

The time-average power density or Poynting vector is

$$\vec{S}_{avg} = \frac{1}{2}\text{Re}\left[\vec{E} \times \vec{H}^*\right]\text{W/m}^2$$

The electric and magnetic fields in lossless medium 1 in terms of reflection coefficient are

$$\vec{E}_1\left(z\right) = E_{i0}e^{-j\beta_1 z}\left(1 + \Gamma e^{j2\beta_1 z}\right)\vec{a}_x$$

$$\vec{H}_1\left(z\right) = \frac{E_{i0}}{\eta_1}e^{-j\beta_1 z}\left(1 - \Gamma e^{j2\beta_1 z}\right)\vec{a}_y$$

Hence,

$$\vec{S}_{1avg} = \frac{E_{i0}^2}{2\eta_1} \text{Re}\left[\left(1 + \Gamma e^{j2\beta_1 z}\right)\left(1 - \Gamma e^{-j2\beta_1 z}\right)\right]\vec{a}_z$$

$$= \frac{E_{i0}^2}{2\eta_1} \text{Re}\left[\left(1 - \Gamma^2\right) + \Gamma\left(e^{j2\beta_1 z} - e^{-j2\beta_1 z}\right)\right]\vec{a}_z$$

$$= \frac{E_{i0}^2}{2\eta_1} \text{Re}\left[\left(1 - \Gamma^2\right) + j2\Gamma \sin 2\beta_1 z\right]\vec{a}_z$$

$$= \frac{E_{i0}^2}{2\eta_1}\left(1 - \Gamma^2\right)\vec{a}_z$$

where the reflection coefficient Γ is a real number because both the mediums are lossless. The electric and magnetic fields in lossless medium 2 in terms of transmission coefficient are

$$\vec{E}_2(z) = \tau\, E_{i0} e^{-j\beta_2 z}\vec{a}_x$$

$$\vec{H}_2(z) = \frac{\tau}{\eta_2} E_{i0} e^{-j\beta_2 z}\vec{a}_y$$

Hence,

$$\vec{S}_{2avg} = \frac{E_{i0}^2}{2\eta_2}\tau^2\vec{a}_z$$

For a lossless medium, the power flow in medium 1 must be equal to that in medium 2. Therefore,

$$\vec{S}_{1avg} = \vec{S}_{2avg}$$

That is,

$$1 - \Gamma^2 = \frac{\eta_1}{\eta_2}\tau^2 \qquad \qquad \square$$

<hr>

EXAMPLE 7.50

An electromagnetic wave travelling in free space is incident on dielectric medium with $\varepsilon_r = 4$ at an angle of $45°$. Find the angle by which $\vec{E}$ tilts as the wave crosses the boundary.

SOLUTION

Given that, the electromagnetic wave from free space (medium 1) is incident obliquely at an angle of $45°$ with a dielectric (medium 2). The angle of tilt of $\vec{E}$ in medium 2 is nothing but the angle of transmission θ_t.

For free space, $\varepsilon_1 = \varepsilon_{r1}\varepsilon_0 = \varepsilon_0$ and for dielectric, $\varepsilon_2 = \varepsilon_{r2}\varepsilon_0 = 4\varepsilon_0$.

From Snell's law of refraction,

$$\frac{\sin\theta_t}{\sin\theta_i} = \sqrt{\frac{\varepsilon_1}{\varepsilon_2}}$$

That is,

$$\frac{\sin\theta_t}{\sin 45°} = \sqrt{\frac{\varepsilon_0}{4\varepsilon_0}}$$

$$\sin\theta_t = 0.353$$

Hence, the angle of transmission is

$$\theta_t = \sin^{-1}(0.353) = 20.7°$$

❐

EXAMPLE 7.51

Determine the ratio of $\dfrac{E_{r0}}{E_{i0}}$ and $\dfrac{E_{t0}}{E_{i0}}$ at the boundary for the normal incidence and for oblique incidence at $\theta_i = 10°$. For region 1, $\varepsilon_{r1} = 16$, $\mu_{r1} = 1$ and $\sigma_1 = 0$, region 2 is free space. Assume perpendicular polarization.

SOLUTION

For region 1, $\varepsilon_{r1} = 16$, $\mu_{r1} = 1$ and $\sigma_1 = 0$ means perfect dielectric.

Therefore,

$$\eta_1 = \sqrt{\frac{\mu_1}{\varepsilon_1}} = \sqrt{\frac{\mu_0\mu_{r1}}{\varepsilon_0\varepsilon_{r1}}} = 120\pi\sqrt{\frac{1}{16}} = 94.16\,\Omega$$

For region 2 (free space), $\varepsilon_{r2} = 1$ and $\mu_{r2} = 1$.
Therefore,

$$\eta_2 = \eta_0 = 120\pi = 377\,\Omega$$

(*i*) *For normal incidence:*

The reflection coefficient is given by

$$\Gamma = \frac{E_{r0}}{E_{i0}} = \frac{\eta_2 - \eta_1}{\eta_2 + \eta_1} = \frac{377 - 94.16}{377 + 94.16} = 0.6$$

The transmission coefficient is given by

$$\tau = \frac{E_{t0}}{E_{i0}} = \frac{2\eta_2}{\eta_2 + \eta_1} = \frac{2(377)}{377 + 94.16} = 1.6$$

(*ii*) *For oblique incidence:*

From Snell's law of refraction,

$$\frac{\sin\theta_t}{\sin\theta_i} = \sqrt{\frac{\varepsilon_1}{\varepsilon_2}} = \sqrt{\frac{\varepsilon_{r1}\varepsilon_0}{\varepsilon_{r2}\varepsilon_0}} = \sqrt{\frac{16}{1}} = 4$$

That is,

$$\sin\theta_t = 4\times\sin(10) = 0.694$$

$$\theta_t = \sin^{-1}(0.694) = 44°$$

For perpendicular polarization, the reflection coefficient is

$$\Gamma = \frac{E_{r0}}{E_{i0}} = \frac{\eta_2 \cos\theta_i - \eta_1 \cos\theta_t}{\eta_2 \cos\theta_i + \eta_1 \cos\theta_t}$$

$$= \frac{377\cos 10° - 94.16\cos 44°}{377\cos 10° + 94.16\cos 44°} = 0.691$$

The transmission coefficient is

$$\tau = \frac{E_{t0}}{E_{i0}} = \frac{2\eta_2 \cos\theta_i}{\eta_2 \cos\theta_i + \eta_1 \cos\theta_t}$$

$$= \frac{2(377)(\cos 10°)}{377\cos 10° + 94.16\cos 44°} = 1.69 \qquad\qquad \square$$

EXAMPLE 7.52

The dielectric constant of glycerol is 40. (i) Determine the Brewster angle for parallel polarization $\theta_{B\|}$ and the corresponding angle of transmission. (ii) A plane wave with perpendicular polarization is incident from air on water surface at $\theta_i = \theta_{B\|}$. Find the reflection and transmission coefficients.

SOLUTION

Given $\varepsilon_{r2} = 40$ for glycerol (medium 2).

(i) From Eq. (7.163), the Brewster angle of no reflection for parallel polarization is

$$\theta_{B\|} = \sin^{-1}\frac{1}{\sqrt{1 + (\varepsilon_{r1}/\varepsilon_{r2})}}$$

$$= \sin^{-1}\frac{1}{\sqrt{1 + (1/40)}} = 81.02°$$

where $\varepsilon_{r1} = 1$ for air (medium 1).

From Snell's law of refraction,

$$\frac{\sin\theta_t}{\sin\theta_i} = \frac{\sin\theta_t}{\sin\theta_{B\|}} = \sqrt{\frac{\varepsilon_1}{\varepsilon_2}} = \frac{1}{\sqrt{\varepsilon_{r2}}} \qquad \text{(since } \theta_i = \theta_{B\|})$$

Hence, the corresponding angle of transmission is

$$\theta_t = \sin^{-1}\left(\frac{\sin\theta_{B\|}}{\sqrt{\varepsilon_{r2}}}\right) = \sin^{-1}\left(\frac{1}{\sqrt{\varepsilon_{r2} + 1}}\right)$$

$$= \sin^{-1}\left(\frac{1}{\sqrt{41}}\right) = 8.98°$$

(ii) Using Eqs. (7.146) and (7.147), the reflection coefficient and transmission coefficient for an incident wave with perpendicular polarization are

$$\Gamma_\perp = \frac{\eta_2 \cos\theta_i - \eta_1 \cos\theta_t}{\eta_2 \cos\theta_i + \eta_1 \cos\theta_t}$$

$$\tau_\perp = \frac{2\eta_2 \cos\theta_i}{\eta_2 \cos\theta_i + \eta_1 \cos\theta_t}$$

In medium 1 (air), $\eta_1 = 377\,\Omega$

In medium 2 (glycerol), $\eta_2 = \dfrac{377}{\sqrt{\varepsilon_{r2}}} = 59.61\,\Omega$

Hence,

$$\Gamma_\perp = \frac{59.61\cos 81.02^\circ - 377\cos 8.98^\circ}{59.61\cos 81.02^\circ + 377\cos 8.98^\circ} = \frac{9.3 - 372.38}{9.3 + 372.38} = -0.951$$

and

$$\tau_\perp = \frac{2(59.61)\cos 81.02^\circ}{59.61\cos 81.02^\circ + 377\cos 8.98^\circ} = 0.049$$

EXAMPLE 7.53

A uniform plane wave of 200 MHz travelling in a free space impinges normally on a large block of material having $\varepsilon_r = 4$, $\mu_r = 9$ and $\sigma = 0$. Calculate transmission and reflection coefficients at the interface.

SOLUTION

For medium 1 (free space),

$$\eta_1 = 120\pi = 377\,\Omega$$

For medium 2, $\varepsilon_{r2} = 4$, $\mu_{r2} = 9$ and $\sigma = 0$ indicates that it is a lossless dielectric. For lossless dielectric, the intrinsic impedance is

$$\eta_2 = \sqrt{\frac{\mu}{\varepsilon}} = \sqrt{\frac{\mu_0 \mu_{r2}}{\varepsilon_0 \varepsilon_{r2}}} = 120\pi\sqrt{\frac{9}{4}} = 565.1\,\Omega$$

Therefore, the transmission coefficient is

$$\tau = \frac{2\eta_2}{\eta_1 + \eta_2} = \frac{2(565.1)}{377 + 565.1} = 1.1996$$

and the reflection coefficient is

$$\Gamma = \frac{\eta_2 - \eta_1}{\eta_2 + \eta_1} = \frac{565.1 - 377}{565.1 + 377} = 0.1996$$

EXAMPLE 7.54

In free space $(z \le 0)$, a plane wave with $\vec{H} = 20\cos\left(10^8 t - \beta z\right)\vec{a}_x\,\text{A/m}$ is incident normally on a lossless medium $\left(\varepsilon = 2\varepsilon_0, \mu = 18\mu_0\right)$ in region $z \ge 0$. Determine the reflected wave $\vec{H}_r$, $\vec{E}_r$ and the transmitted wave $\vec{H}_t$ and $\vec{E}_t$.

SOLUTION

Given $\vec{H} = 20\cos\left(10^8 t - \beta z\right)\vec{a}_x$ A/m.

For medium 1 (free space),

$$\beta_1 = \frac{\omega}{c} = \frac{10^8}{3\times10^8} = \frac{1}{3}$$

$$\eta_1 = \eta_0 = 120\pi$$

For medium 2 (lossless dielectric medium),

$$\beta_2 = \omega\sqrt{\mu\varepsilon} = \omega\sqrt{\mu_0\varepsilon_0}\sqrt{\mu_r\varepsilon_r} = \frac{\omega}{c}(6) = 6\beta_1 = 2$$

$$\eta_2 = \sqrt{\frac{\mu}{\varepsilon}} = \sqrt{\frac{\mu_0}{\varepsilon_0}}\sqrt{\frac{\mu_r}{\varepsilon_r}} = 3\eta_0$$

Since $\vec{H} = 20\cos\left(10^8 t - \beta z\right)\vec{a}_x$ A/m, the electric field is

$$\vec{E}_i = E_{i0}\cos\left(10^8 t - \beta_1 z\right)\vec{a}_{E_i}$$

where

$$\vec{a}_{E_i} = \vec{a}_{H_i} \times \vec{a}_{k_i} = \vec{a}_x \times \vec{a}_z = -\vec{a}_y \text{ and } E_{i0} = \eta_1 H_{i0} = 20\eta_0$$

Therefore,

$$\vec{E}_i = -20\eta_0\cos\left(10^8 t - \beta_1 z\right)\vec{a}_y \text{ V/m}$$

Now

$$\frac{E_{r0}}{E_{i0}} = \Gamma = \frac{\eta_2 - \eta_1}{\eta_2 + \eta_1} = \frac{3\eta_0 - \eta_0}{3\eta_0 + \eta_0} = \frac{1}{2}$$

$$E_{r0} = \frac{1}{2}E_{i0}$$

Hence, the reflected electric field wave is

$$\vec{E}_r = -E_{r0}\cos\left(10^8 t + \beta_1 z\right)\vec{a}_y = -10\eta_0\cos\left(10^8 t + \frac{1}{3}z\right)\vec{a}_y \text{ V/m}$$

and the reflected magnetic field wave is

$$\vec{H}_r = -H_{r0}\cos\left(10^8 t + \beta_1 z\right)\vec{a}_x = -10\cos\left(10^8 t + \frac{1}{3}z\right)\vec{a}_x \text{ V/m}$$

Similarly,

$$\frac{E_{t0}}{E_{i0}} = \tau = 1 + \Gamma = \frac{3}{2}$$

$$E_{t0} = \frac{3}{2}E_{i0}$$

Hence, the transmitted electric field wave is

$$\vec{E}_t = E_{t0}\cos\left(10^8 t - \frac{4}{3}z\right)\vec{a}_{E_t}, \qquad \text{where } \vec{a}_{E_t} = \vec{a}_{E_i} = -\vec{a}_y$$

$$= -3\eta_0\cos\left(10^8 t - \frac{4}{3}z\right)\vec{a}_y \text{ V/m}$$

and the transmitted magnetic field wave is

$$\vec{H}_t = 10\cos\left(10^8 t - \frac{4}{3}z\right)\vec{a}_x \text{ A/m}$$

EXAMPLE 7.55

Consider $\vec{E}$ and $\vec{H}$ waves, travelling in free space, are normally incident on the interface with a perfect dielectric with $\varepsilon_r = 3$. Compute the magnitudes of incident, reflected and transmitted $\vec{E}$ and $\vec{H}$ waves at the interface.

SOLUTION

Let us assume the magnitude of incident electric filed wave as E_{i0}.

For medium 1 (free space),

$$\eta_1 = 120\pi = 377\,\Omega$$

For medium 2 (perfect dielectric),

$$\eta_2 = \sqrt{\frac{\mu}{\varepsilon}} = \sqrt{\frac{\mu_0\mu_r}{\varepsilon_0\varepsilon_{r2}}} = 120\pi\sqrt{\frac{1}{3}} = 217.507\,\Omega$$

The transmission coefficient is

$$\tau = \frac{E_{t0}}{E_{i0}} = \frac{2\eta_2}{\eta_1 + \eta_2} = \frac{2(217.507)}{377 + 217.507} = 0.7317$$

Hence, the magnitude of reflected wave is $E_{t0} = 0.7317 E_{i0}$ V/m

The reflection coefficient is

$$\Gamma = \frac{E_{r0}}{E_{i0}} = \frac{\eta_2 - \eta_1}{\eta_2 + \eta_1} = \frac{217.507 - 377}{217.507 + 377} = -0.2683$$

The negative sign indicates that the wave is in opposite direction.

Hence, the magnitude of reflected wave is $E_{r0} = 0.2683 E_{i0}$ V/m

The ratio of magnitudes of magnetic field is

$$\frac{H_{t0}}{H_{i0}} = \frac{E_{r0}/\eta_2}{E_{i0}/\eta_1} = \frac{\eta_1}{\eta_2}\left(\frac{E_{t0}}{E_{i0}}\right) = \frac{377}{217.507}(0.7317) = 1.2682$$

Hence, the magnitude of transmitted magnetic field wave is

$$H_{t0} = 1.2682 H_{i0} \text{ A/m}$$

But the magnitude of incident magnetic field wave is

$$H_{i0} = \frac{E_{i0}}{\eta_1} = \frac{E_{i0}}{377} = \left(2.62525 \times 10^{-3}\right) E_{i0}$$

Therefore,

$$H_{t0} = \left(1.2682\right)\left(2.6525 \times 10^{-3} E_{i0}\right) = 3.3639 E_{i0} \text{mA/m}$$

Similarly,

$$\frac{H_{r0}}{H_{i0}} = \frac{-E_{r0}/\eta_1}{E_{i0}/\eta_1} = -\frac{E_{r0}}{E_{i0}} = -\left(-0.2683\right) = 0.2683$$

Hence, the magnitude of reflected magnetic field wave is

$$H_{r0} = \left(0.2683\right) H_{i0} = \left(0.2683\right)\left(2.6525 \times 10^{-3} E_{i0}\right)$$

$$= 0.7116 E_{i0} \text{ mA/m}$$

EXAMPLE 7.56

Given a uniform plane wave in air as

$$\vec{E}_i = 20\cos\left(\omega t - \beta z\right)\vec{a}_x + 60\sin\left(\omega t - \beta z\right)\vec{a}_y \text{V/m}$$

(*i*) Find $\vec{H}_i$.

(*ii*) If the wave encounters a perfectly conducting plate normal to the z-axis at $z = 0$, find the reflected wave $\vec{E}_r$ and $\vec{H}_r$.

(*iii*) What are the total $\vec{E}$ and $\vec{H}$ fields for $z \le 0$?

(*iv*) Calculate the time-average Poynting vectors for $z \le 0$ and $z \ge 0$.

SOLUTION

Given $\vec{E}_i = 20\cos\left(\omega t - \beta z\right)\vec{a}_x + 60\sin\left(\omega t - \beta z\right)\vec{a}_y \text{V/m}$ in air.

(*i*) The incident electric field consists of x and y-components and it can be written as

$$\vec{E}_i = \vec{E}_{i1} + E_{i2}$$

where $\vec{E}_{i1} = 20\cos\left(\omega t - \beta z\right)\vec{a}_x$ and $\vec{E}_{i2} = 60\cos\left(\omega t - \beta z\right)\vec{a}_y$

Since the medium 1 is air (free space), its relative permittivity $\varepsilon_r \approx 1$.

Assume $\vec{H}_i = \vec{H}_{i1} + \vec{H}_{i2}$

Here,

$$\vec{H}_{i1} = \vec{H}_{i10}\cos\left(\omega t - \beta z\right)\vec{a}_{H1}$$

where $H_{i10} = \dfrac{E_{i10}}{\eta_0} = \dfrac{20}{120\pi} = \dfrac{1}{6\pi}$ and $\vec{a}_{H_1} = \vec{a}_k \times \vec{a}_{E_1} = \vec{a}_z \times \vec{a}_x = \vec{a}_y$

Therefore,

$$\vec{H}_{i1} = \frac{1}{6\pi}\cos(\omega t - \beta z)\vec{a}_y$$

Similarly, we can write

$$\vec{H}_{i2} = H_{i20}\sin(\omega t - \beta z)\vec{a}_{H2}$$

where $\vec{H}_{i20} = \dfrac{E_{i20}}{\eta_0} = \dfrac{60}{120\pi} = \dfrac{1}{2\pi}$ and $\vec{a}_{H_2} = \vec{a}_k \times \vec{a}_{E_2} = \vec{a}_z \times \vec{a}_y = -\vec{a}_x$

Therefore,

$$\vec{H}_{i2} = -\frac{1}{2\pi}\sin(\omega t - \beta z)\vec{a}_x$$

Hence, the incident magnetic field can be written as

$$\vec{H}_i = \vec{H}_{i1} + \vec{H}_{i2}$$

$$= \frac{1}{6\pi}\cos(\omega t - \beta z)\vec{a}_y - \frac{1}{2\pi}\sin(\omega t - \beta z)\vec{a}_x \, \text{A/m}$$

(*ii*) Since medium 2 is a perfect conductor, $\sigma_2 / \omega\varepsilon_2 \gg 1$. This shows that $\eta_2 \ll \eta_1$.

That is, $\Gamma = -1$ and $\tau = 0$

Here, the incident $\vec{E}$ and $\vec{H}$ fields are totally reflected.

Therefore,

$$E_{r0} = \Gamma E_{i0} = -E_{i0}$$

If the wave strikes a perfectly conducting plate (medium 2) normal to the z-axis at $z = 0$, then the reflected electric field travelling in –ve z-direction is

$$\vec{E}_r = -20\cos(\omega t + \beta z)\vec{a}_x - 60\sin(\omega t + \beta z)\vec{a}_y \, \text{V/m}$$

Assume

$$\vec{H}_r = \vec{H}_{r1} + \vec{H}_{r2}$$

Here,

$$\vec{H}_{r1} = H_{r10}\cos(\omega t + \beta z)\vec{a}_{H1}$$

where $H_{r10} = \dfrac{E_{r10}}{\eta_0} = \dfrac{-20}{120\pi} = -\dfrac{1}{6\pi}$ and $\vec{a}_{H_1} = \vec{a}_k \times \vec{a}_{E_1} = (-\vec{a}_z) \times \vec{a}_x = -\vec{a}_y$

Therefore,

$$\vec{H}_{r1} = \frac{1}{6\pi}\cos(\omega t + \beta z)\vec{a}_y$$

Similarly, we can write

$$\vec{H}_{r2} = \vec{H}_{r20}\sin(\omega t + \beta z)\vec{a}_{H2}$$

where $\vec{H}_{r20} = \dfrac{E_{r20}}{\eta_0} = \dfrac{-60}{120\pi} = -\dfrac{1}{2\pi}$ and $\vec{a}_{H_2} = \vec{a}_k \times \vec{a}_{E_2} = \left(-\vec{a}_z\right) \times \vec{a}_y = \vec{a}_x$

Therefore,

$$\vec{H}_{r2} = -\frac{1}{2\pi} \sin\left(\omega t + \beta z\right) \vec{a}_x$$

Hence, the reflected magnetic field can be written as

$$\vec{H}_r = \vec{H}_{r1} + \vec{H}_{r2}$$

$$= \frac{1}{6\pi} \cos\left(\omega t + \beta z\right) \vec{a}_y - \frac{1}{2\pi} \sin\left(\omega t + \beta z\right) \vec{a}_x \, \text{A/m}$$

(*iii*) For $z \le 0$, the total fields in air are

$$\vec{E}_1 = \vec{E}_i + \vec{E}_r \text{ and } \vec{H}_1 = \vec{H}_i + \vec{H}_r$$

The incident and reflected fields in medium 1 (air) represent standing waves. The total fields in medium 2 (conductor) are

$$\vec{E}_2 = \vec{E}_t = 0 \text{ and } \vec{H}_2 = \vec{H}_t = 0$$

(*iv*) For $z \le 0$, the time-average Poynting vector in medium 1 is

$$\vec{S}_{1avg} = \frac{\left|\vec{E}_1\right|^2}{2\eta_1} \vec{a}_k = \frac{1}{2\eta_0}\left(E_{i0}^2 \vec{a}_z - E_{r0}^2 \vec{a}_z\right)$$

$$= \frac{1}{240\pi}\left[\left(20^2 + 60^2\right)\vec{a}_z - \left(20^2 + 60^2\right)\vec{a}_z\right] = 0$$

For $z \ge 0$, the time-average Poynting vector in medium 2 is

$$\vec{S}_{2avg} = \frac{\left|\vec{E}_2\right|^2}{2\eta_2} \vec{a}_k = \frac{E_{t0}^2}{2\eta_2} \vec{a}_z = 0$$

This shows that the entire incident power is reflected in medium 1 itself and no power is transmitted in medium 2. $\qquad\qquad\qquad\square$

7.8   SURFACE CURRENT, SURFACE IMPEDANCE AND POWER LOSS IN A CONDUCTOR

7.8.1   Surface Current

From boundary conditions, we know that the tangential component of the electric field is zero at the surface of an ideal conductor. The tangential component of magnetic field is equal to the surface current density $\vec{J}_s$ on the conductor as given by

$$\vec{H}_t = \vec{a}_n \times \vec{H} = \vec{J}_s$$

where $\vec{a}_n$ is the outward normal unit vector to the conductor surface, $\vec{H}$ is the total magnetic field at the surface and $\vec{H}_t$ is the tangential component of the magnetic field. The surface current density can be represented either by $\vec{J}_s$ or $\vec{K}$ and its unit is A/m. The surface current concept is useful in analyzing the good conductors.

Consider an electric field $\vec{E}$ tangential to the conducting surface along x-direction, which exists only at the surface. For good conductors, the magnetic field $\vec{H}$ is almost tangential to the surface along y-axis. The intrinsic impedance of the conductor η_c is given by the ratio of the amplitude of the electric field to the magnetic field, i.e., $\dfrac{|\vec{E}|}{|\vec{H}|}$. The fields $\vec{E}$ and $\vec{H}$ constitute a wave propagating inside the conductor as shown in Figure 7.14.

The propagation constant of the wave inside the conductor is

$$\gamma = \alpha + j\beta = \sqrt{\frac{\omega\mu\sigma}{2}} + j\sqrt{\frac{\omega\mu\sigma}{2}} \tag{7.165}$$

Here, the amplitude of electric field decreases exponentially inside the conductor and the field at a depth z from the surface of the conductor is represented by

$$\vec{E}(z) = E_0{}^{-\gamma z}\vec{a}_x = E_0{}^{-\alpha z}e^{-j\beta z}\vec{a}_x$$

The conduction current flows in the same direction as the electric field $\vec{E}$ and it is mainly due to conductivity σ of the conductor. The conduction current density at a depth z is given by

$$\vec{J}(z) = \sigma\vec{E} = \sigma E_0 e^{-\alpha z}e^{-j\beta z}\vec{a}_x$$

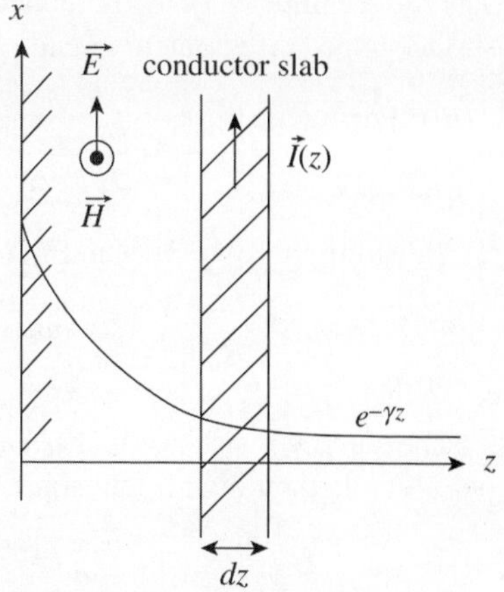

Figure 7.14 *Field variation inside a conductor*

Consider a conductor slab parallel to the surface having unit width along y-direction and thickness dz. Here, the sheet is located at a distance of z from the surface. The current in the sheet is given by

$$\vec{I}(z) = \vec{J}(z)dz = \sigma E_0 e^{-\gamma z}dz\,\vec{a}_x \tag{7.166}$$

Since the current is flowing along x-direction, the integration of $\vec{I}(z)$ along z gives the total current flow per unit width (surface current density) of the conductor surface. It is given by

$$\vec{J}_s = \int_0^\infty \vec{J}\,dz = \int_0^\infty \sigma E_0 e^{-\gamma z}dz\,\vec{a}_x$$

$$= \sigma E_0 \left[-\frac{e^{-\gamma z}}{\gamma} \right]_0^\infty \vec{a}_x = \frac{\sigma E_0}{\gamma}$$

The field decays very rapidly inside the conductor and the current $\vec{J}_s$ flows close to the surface and it can be treated as the surface current. In order to justify that $\vec{J}_s$ is equivalent to the surface current, it should be related to the tangential magnetic field $\vec{H}$. For a good conductor, the intrinsic impedance is represented by

$$\eta_c = \sqrt{\frac{j\omega\mu}{\sigma}} = \frac{\gamma}{\sigma} \tag{7.167}$$

where $\gamma = \sqrt{j\omega\mu\sigma}$ is the propagation constant. The magnetic field at the surface of the conductor is given by

$$\left|\vec{H}\right| = \frac{\left|\vec{E}\right|}{\left|\eta_c\right|} = \frac{\left|\vec{E}\right|}{\left|\gamma\right|}\sigma = \left|\vec{J}_s\right| \tag{7.168}$$

For a non-ideal conductor, there is only a volume current density $\vec{J}$ and there is no surface current. However, the total integrated current $\vec{J}_s$ can be treated like the surface current. Therefore, it is observed that for an ideal conductor $(\sigma = \infty)$, the skin depth reaches to zero and the current $\vec{J}_s$ is the surface current. This surface current is confined entirely to the surface of the conductor at high frequencies.

7.8.2   Surface Impedance

The surface impedance Z_s is defined as the ratio of the tangential electric field E_0 to the surface current $\vec{J}_s$. The surface impedance is an important parameter mainly used to determine the conductor losses. It is represented by

$$Z_s = \frac{\left|\vec{E}_{\tan}\right|}{\left|\vec{J}_s\right|} = \frac{E_0}{J_s} = \frac{\gamma}{\sigma} = \eta_c \tag{7.169}$$

Substituting Eq. (7.165) in Eq. (7.169) and separating the real and imaginary parts, we get

$$Z_s = R_s + jX_s = \sqrt{\frac{\omega\mu}{2\sigma}} + j\sqrt{\frac{\omega\mu}{2\sigma}} \tag{7.170}$$

The surface resistance is the real part of surface impedance and it is defined as the skin effect resistance per unit length at high frequencies. The depth of penetration in a conductor is

$$\delta = \sqrt{\frac{2}{\omega\mu\sigma}} \tag{7.171}$$

From Eqs. (7.170) and (7.171), we get

$$R_s = \frac{1}{\sigma\delta}$$

The surface resistance of a plane conductor at any frequency is equivalent to the dc resistance of a thickness δ of the same conductor. This thickness δ is also called the depth of penetration or skin depth.

7.8.3   Power Loss in a Conductor

Consider a thin conductor slab with unit length and unit width as shown in Figure 7.15. The differential resistance of the conductor slab is represented by

$$dR = \frac{\rho l}{A} = \frac{1}{\sigma\,dz} \tag{7.172}$$

where the resistivity $\rho = 1/\sigma$ and the cross-sectional area of the resistor, $A = l \times dz = dz$ (by considering the length of the resistor as $l = 1\,\text{m}$).

The ohmic loss in the conductor slab is written as

$$dW = \frac{1}{2}\left|I\left(z\right)\right|^2 dR \tag{7.173}$$

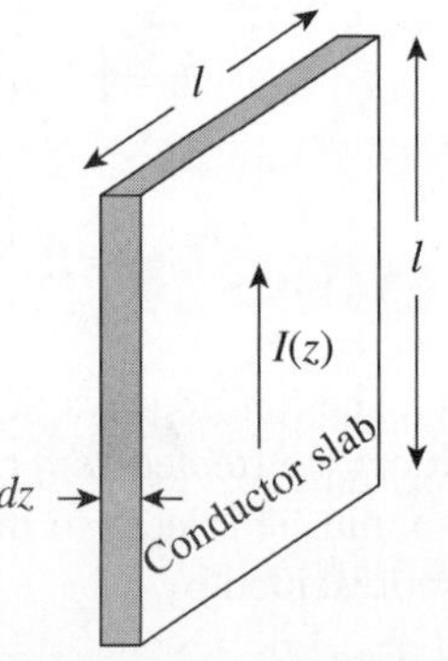

Figure 7.15   *Power loss in a thin conductor sheet*

Substituting Eqs. (7.166) and (7.172) in Eq. (7.173), we get

$$dW = \frac{1}{2}\left|\sigma E_0 e^{-\gamma z} dz\right|^2 \frac{1}{\sigma \, dz} = \frac{1}{2}\sigma \left|E_0\right|^2 e^{-2\alpha z} dz \tag{7.174}$$

Here, the total loss per unit area of the conductor surface can be obtained by integrating the above equation from $z = 0$ to $z = \infty$.

Therefore,

$$W = \frac{1}{2}\int_0^\infty \sigma \left|E_0\right|^2 e^{-2\alpha z} dz = \frac{1}{2}\sigma \left|E_0\right|^2 \left[\frac{e^{-2\alpha z}}{-2\alpha}\right]_0^\infty$$

Since $\left|E_0\right| = \dfrac{|\gamma|\left|\vec{J}_s\right|}{\sigma}$, the power loss in a conductor is given by

$$W = \frac{1}{2}\frac{\sigma \left|E_0\right|^2}{2\alpha} = \frac{1}{2}\frac{\sigma}{2\alpha}\frac{|\gamma|^2}{\sigma^2}\left|\vec{J}_s\right|^2 \tag{7.175}$$

Substituting Eq. (7.165) in Eq. (7.175), we get

$$W = \frac{1}{2}\frac{\left|\vec{J}_s\right|^2 \omega\mu\sigma}{2\sigma\sqrt{\omega\mu\sigma/2}} \qquad (\text{since } |\gamma| = \sqrt{\omega\mu\sigma})$$

$$= \frac{1}{2}\left|\vec{J}_s\right|^2 \sqrt{\frac{\omega\mu}{2\sigma}} = \frac{1}{2}R_s\left|\vec{J}_s\right|^2 \tag{7.176}$$

where $R_s = \sqrt{\dfrac{\omega\mu}{2\sigma}}$.

The above equation shows that the power loss in a conductor sheet is proportional to the surface resistance R_s and square of the surface current density. The surface resistance increases with frequency and decreases with the conductivity.

As the conductivity increases, the wave attenuates rapidly inside the conductor. This attenuation is not due to the ohmic loss and the energy finds it difficult to enter the conducting surface. For an ideal conductor, i.e., $\sigma = \infty$, there is no penetration of the wave. The current concentrates and flows only on the surface of the conductor and there is no power loss in the conductor sheet.

EXAMPLE 7.57

The magnetic field at the surface of a good conductor is 4 A/m. The frequency of the field is 600 MHz. If the conductivity of the conductor is 10^7 S/m, determine the skin depth, surface impedance and the power loss per unit area of the conductor.

SOLUTION

Given $f = 600\,\text{MHz}$, $\sigma = 10^7\,\text{S/m}$ and $H = 4\,\text{A/m}$.

Here, $\omega = 2\pi f = 2\pi \times 600 \times 10^6 = 3.77 \times 10^9\,\text{rad/s}$

The skin depth is

$$\delta = \frac{1}{\sqrt{\pi f \mu_0 \sigma}} = \frac{1}{\sqrt{\pi \times 600 \times 10^6 \times 4\pi \times 10^{-7} \times 10^7}} = 6.5 \ \mu\text{m}$$

The surface impedance is

$$Z_s = \sqrt{\frac{j\omega\mu_0}{\sigma}} = \frac{1+j}{\sqrt{2}} \sqrt{\frac{2\pi \times 600 \times 10^6 \times 4\pi \times 10^{-7}}{10^7}} \qquad \left(\text{since } \sqrt{j} = \frac{1+j}{\sqrt{2}} \right)$$

$$= (15.3 + j15.3) \times 10^{-3} \ \Omega$$

The surface r.m.s current density $\left| \vec{J}_s \right| = \left| \vec{H} \right| = 4$ A/m. Therefore, the power loss per unit area is

$$W = R_s \left| J_s \right|^2 = 15.3 \times 10^{-3} \times (4)^2 = 244.8 \ \text{mW/m}^2$$

where $R_s = 15.3 \ \Omega$. Here, it is noted that the factor $\dfrac{1}{2}$ is not used since the surface current has the r.m.s value of 4 A/m.　　　　◻

REVIEW QUESTIONS

1. What is electromagnetic wave?
2. Give typical examples of electromagnetic wave.
3. Write a general wave equation in terms of electric and magnetic fields.
4. What do you mean by uniforwm plane wave?
5. What are the characteristics of uniform plane wave?
6. What is meant by transverse electromagnetic wave?
7. Define phase velocity. Write its mathematical expression.
8. Define intrinsic impedance of a medium.
9. What is the intrinsic impedance of free space? What is its value?
10. Define propagation constant.
11. Define attenuation constant and phase constant.
12. Define wave number. How is wave number related to wavelength?
13. Define wavelength.
14. Determine the wavelength of an electromagnetic wave travelling in the free space at 30 GHz.
15. Write down the general equations for velocity, propagation constant, intrinsic impedance and wavelength.
16. Derive the expression for the attenuation constant, phase constant and intrinsic impedance for a uniform plane wave in a good conductor.
17. Derive the Helmholtz equations in time domain for a source-free, linear, homogeneous and isotropic dielectric medium.
18. Derive the general wave equation.

19. Write down wave equations in phasor form.

20. From Maxwell's curl equations, derive the wave equation in $\vec{H}$ for a plane wave travelling in the positive x-direction in a medium with constants, $\mu = \mu_0$, $\varepsilon = \varepsilon_0$ and $\sigma = 0$. The electric field is in the y-direction.

21. A lossless medium has a relative dielectric constant of 64 and a relative permeability of unity. Find the intrinsic impedance of the medium.

22. Show that, for good conductors, $\nabla^2 \vec{J} = \sigma\mu \dfrac{\partial \vec{J}}{\partial t}$, whereas $\nabla^2 \vec{A} - \mu\varepsilon \dfrac{\partial^2 \vec{A}}{\partial t^2} = -\mu\vec{J}$ applies to both good and poor conductors.

23. Derive wave equations in phasor form and also derive for α, β, γ and η.

24. From Maxwell's equations, derive the electromagnetic wave equation in conducting medium for $\vec{E}$ and $\vec{H}$ fields.

25. Derive the wave equation starting from Maxwell's equations for free space.

26. Obtain the solution for a uniform plane wave in an isotropic homogeneous dielectric medium.

27. Obtain the wave equation for a conducting medium.

28. Discuss about the plane waves in lossy dielectrics.

29. Discuss about the propagation of plane waves in free space and in a homogeneous material.

30. A 10 GHz plane wave travelling in a free space has an amplitude $E_x = 10\text{V/m}$. Determine the (*i*) velocity of propagation, (*ii*) wavelength, (*iii*) intrinsic impedance and (*iv*) amplitude and direction of $\vec{H}$.

31. Explain clearly the intrinsic impedance of the medium. Derive the expression for intrinsic impedance of the dielectric medium.

32. Derive the equation for plane waves in (*i*) free space, (*ii*) homogeneous material and (*iii*) conducting medium.

33. Explain the propagation of EM waves in good conductor.

34. Derive the wave equation for uniform plane waves.

35. Obtain the wave equation for plane waves in lossy dielectrics.

36. Explain the plane wave propagation in low-loss dielectrics.

37. Explain the wave propagation in perfect dielectric.

38. Discuss in detail about wave propagation in lossy dielectric and good conductors.

39. Write the equations for velocity, propagation constant, intrinsic impedance, attenuation constant, phase constant and wavelength for an electromagnetic wave in free space.

40. What is meant by perfect dielectric?

41. Write down the expression for velocity, attenuation constant, phase constant and intrinsic impedance if the wave propagates in a perfect dielectric.

42. Give the expressions for propagation constant and intrinsic impedance if the wave propagates in a lossy dielectric.

43. Derive the expression describing propagation of uniform plane wave in good conductor.

44. A uniform plane wave with $\vec{E} = E_x \vec{a}_x$ propagates in a lossless medium $\left(\varepsilon_r = 4, \mu_r = 1, \sigma = 0\right)$ in positive z-direction. If the electric field is sinusoidal with a frequency of $100\,\text{MHz}$ with amplitude $10^{-4}\,\text{V/m}$ at $t = 0$, then (*i*) write the expression for $\vec{E}$ for any t value and (*ii*) write the instantaneous expression for $\vec{H}$.

45. Give the significance of intrinsic impedance. What is meant by lossy dielectric?

46. A 9 GHz uniform plane wave travels in a lossless unbounded medium having $\mu = \mu_0$ and $\varepsilon_r = 4\varepsilon_0$. Determine *(i)* velocity of propagation, *(ii)* wavelength, *(iii)* intrinsic impedance, *(iv)* attenuation constant and *(v)* phase constant.

47. A uniform plane wave at a frequency of 1 GHz is travelling in a large block of Teflon $\left(\mu_r = 1, \varepsilon_r = 2.1 \text{ and } \sigma = 0\right)$. Determine μ, η, β and λ.

48. In a medium characterized by $\varepsilon_r = 9$, $\mu_r = 1$ and $\sigma = 0.1 \text{S/m}$, determine the phase angle by which the magnetic field leads the electric field at 100 MHz.

49. What is loss tangent?

50. What is the significance of loss tangent?

51. A signal in a lossy dielectric medium has a loss tangent of 0.2 at 550 kHz. The dielectric constant of a medium is 2.5. Determine α and β.

52. Define depth of penetration.

53. Explain skin effect.

54. The attenuation constant of a plane wave propagation through the dielectric is 0.2887 Np/m. Find the skin depth.

55. Derive the expression for depth of penetration of a plane wave in conducting medium.

56. Write expression for intrinsic impedance, attenuation constant and phase constant for good conducting medium.

57. What is skin effect? Discuss the depth of penetration in dielectric and conductor.

58. Calculate the skin depth of copper at 60 Hz and at 6 GHz.

59. Starting from Maxwell's equations, obtain the expression for Poynting vector and give the physical interpretation of the equation. Discuss with practical examples.

60. Define Poynting vector and prove that the electromagnetic power flow is the product of the electric and magnetic field intensities.

61. Discuss about Poynting vector and power flow.

62. Obtain the expression for instantaneous power flow per unit area.

63. Discuss Poynting vector and Poynting's theorem and their significance.

64. In free space, $\vec{H} = 0.2 \cos\left(\omega t - \beta z\right)\vec{a}_x \text{V/m}$. Find the total power passing through a circular disc of radium 5 cm.

65. Give the unit of Poynting vector.

66. Explain about instantaneous, average and complex Poynting vector.

67. If $\vec{E} = E_m \cos\left(\omega t - \beta z\right)\vec{a}_x \text{V/m}$ is the electric field propagating in free space, calculate the Poynting vector.

68. Justify that, in a plane wave propagating in a dielectric medium, the average energy stored is equally divided between the electric and magnetic fields.

69. A plane wave in a dielectric medium has $\vec{E} = E_0 \sin\left(\beta x - \omega t\right)\vec{a}_z \text{V/m}$. Derive expressions for the associated $\vec{H}$ field and the instantaneous Poynting vector $\vec{S}$. What is the average power density in the medium?

70. State and prove Poynting's theorem. A plane wave travelling in free space has an average Poynting vector of 5W/m^2. Find the average energy density.

71. Prove that the average Poynting vector of a circularly polarized wave is twice that of linearly polarized wave if the maximum field intensity is the same for both waves.

72. Prove that the instantaneous Poynting vector of a plane travelling wave is a constant when the wave is circularly polarized.

73. In a free space, $\vec{E} = 200\cos(\omega t - \beta z)\vec{a}_x$ V/m. Find the total power passing through a rectangular area of sides 10 mm and 25 mm in the $z = 0$ plane.

74. In a free space, $\vec{E} = 10\cos(\omega t - \beta z)\vec{a}_x$ V/m. Show that the average power crossing a circular disc of radius 15.5 m in $z = $ constant plane is 1 W.

75. Derive the point from and integral form of Poynting's theorem.

76. Derive the expression for power flow in a coaxial cable. Write the significance of the expression derived.

77. In a free space, $\vec{E} = 50\cos(\omega t - \beta z)\vec{a}_x$ V/m. Determine the average power crossing a circular area of radius 5 m in the plane $z = $ constant.

78. Show that the power loss in a conductor is given by *VI* using Poynting theorem.

79. A plane TEM wave has power density of $2.4\,\text{W/m}^2$ in a medium with $\varepsilon_r = 4$ and $\mu_r = 1$. Find $\vec{E}$ and $\vec{H}$.

80. Write the expression for average density in terms of the amplitude of electric field.

81. What is meant by power loss in plane conductor?

82. A wave travelling in a lossless, non-magnetic medium has an electric field amplitude of 24.56 V/m and an average power density of $4\,\text{W/m}^2$. Determine the phase velocity of the wave.

83. What is meant by polarization of a uniform plane wave?

84. Classify polarization.

85. What is linear polarization?

86. What are the conditions to be satisfied for a linearly polarized uniform plane wave?

87. What is meant by circular polarization?

88. Explain the various types of wave polarization.

89. What is the condition to be satisfied for a circularly polarized uniform plane wave?

90. What is meant by elliptical polarization?

91. What is the condition to be satisfied for an elliptically polarized uniform plane wave?

92. Explain the different types of polarization of uniform plane waves and express them in terms of mathematical models.

93. Define plane of incidence.

94. What is meant by normal incidence and oblique incidence?

95. Explain the polarizations with reference to oblique incidence.

96. What do you mean by perpendicular polarization and parallel polarization?

97. What is the difference between a perpendicular polarized wave and a parallel polarized wave?

98. Explain Snell's law of reflection and Snell's law of refraction.

99. Define transmission coefficient and reflection coefficient. What is the relationship between them?

100. What is total reflection in case of oblique incidence at a plane dielectric boundary? What is critical angle θ_c? Derive its expression.

101. Give the transmission and reflection coefficients for wave incident at plane dielectric boundary.

102. Derive the expression for reflection coefficient and transmission coefficient for a obliquely incident wave having (*i*) perpendicular polarization and (*ii*) parallel polarization.

103. Explain what is meant by refraction index.

104. Describe about reflection of plane waves by a perfect dielectric.

105. Write important results about transmission and reflection coefficients for wave incident at plane dielectric boundary.

106. For normal incidence at plane conducting boundary, write the expressions for transmission and reflection coefficients.

107. Discuss about the reflection of plane waves from a conductor for normal and oblique incidences.

108. Explain reflection of uniform plane waves with normal incidence at a plane dielectric boundary.

109. A plane wave is incident normally on a perfect conductor. Derive the expression for standing wave. Find the location of nodes and antinodes in electric and magnetic fields. Sketch the standing wave pattern.

110. A plane wave is incident at an angle of $\theta_1 = 30°$ from air into polystyrene. Calculate the angle of transmission θ_i if $\varepsilon_r = 2.7$ for polystyrene.

111. Explain in detail the oblique incidence of plane waves on a free space interface with the polarization parallel to the plane of incidence.

112. Consider that travelling $\vec{E}$ and $\vec{H}$ waves in free space are normally incident on the interface with a perfect dielectric for which $\varepsilon_r = 3$. Determine the magnitudes of incident, reflected and transmitted $\vec{E}$ and $\vec{H}$ waves at interface.

113. Consider an electromagnetic wave with oblique incidence on a dielectric interface and derive an expression for reflection and transmission coefficients in case of perpendicular and parallel polarizations.

114. A plane wave is incident upon a boundary surface that is not parallel to the plane containing electric field and magnetic field (oblique incidence). Derive the transmission and reflection coefficients.

115. A plane wave in free space $(z \le 0)$ is incident normally on a large block of material with $\varepsilon_r = 12$, $\mu_r = 3$, $\sigma = 0$, which occupies $z \ge 0$. If the incident electric field is given by $\vec{E} = 30\cos(\omega t - z)\vec{a}_y\,\text{V/m}$, determine (*i*) ω, (*ii*) the standing wave ratio, (*iii*) the reflected magnetic field and (*iv*) the average power density of the transmitted wave.

116. What do you mean by standing waves?

117. Define standing wave ratio. What is its relationship with the reflection coefficient?

118. A uniform plane wave in air with $\vec{H} = 4\sin(\omega t - 5x)\vec{a}_y\,\text{A/m}$ is normally incident on a dielectric medium with the parameters $\mu = \mu_0$, $\varepsilon = 4\varepsilon_0$, and $\sigma = 0$. (*i*) Obtain the total electric field in air, (*ii*) calculate the time-average power density in the dielectric medium and (*iii*) find the standing wave ratio.

119. What is meant critical angle of reflection? What is its significance?

120. What is Brewster angle?

121. Give the significance of Brewster angle.

122. Is the Brewster angle possible for a perpendicularly polarized wave? Justify your answer mathematically.

123. What is the difference between Brewster angle and critical angle? Why is the Brewster angle also called a polarizing angle?

124. A polarized wave is incident from air to polystyrene with $\mu = \mu_0$, $\varepsilon = 2.6\varepsilon_0$ at Brewster angle. Determine the transmission angle.

125. If η_1 and η_2 are both real and positive, show that the standing wave in region 1 equals $\dfrac{\eta_2}{\eta_1}$ if $\eta_2 > \eta_1$, and is equal to $\dfrac{\eta_1}{\eta_2}$ if $\eta_1 > \eta_2$.

126. The plane wave $\vec{E} = 30\cos(\omega t - z)\vec{a}_x\,$V/m in air normally hits a lossless medium $\left(\mu = \mu_0, \varepsilon = 4\varepsilon_0\right)$ at $z = 0$. (i) Determine Γ, τ and S. (ii) Calculate the reflected electric and magnetic fields.

127. Briefly explain the wave incident (i) normally on a perfect conductor and (ii) obliquely to the surface of perfect conductor.

128. Briefly explain the wave incident (i) normally on a perfect dielectric and (ii) obliquely to the surface of perfect dielectric.

129. A 10 MHz uniform plane wave $\vec{H} = 30\sin(\omega t + \beta x)\vec{a}_z\,$mA/m exists in region $x \geq 0$ having $\sigma = 0$, $\mu = 4\mu_0$, $\varepsilon = 9\varepsilon_0$. At $x = 0$, the wave encounters free space. Determine (i) the polarization of the wave, (ii) the phase constant, (iii) the displacement current density in region $x \geq 0$, (iv) the reflected and transmitted magnetic fields and (v) the average power density in each region.

130. Evaluate the reflection and transmission coefficients for the case of an EM wave in air ($\mu_1 = \mu_0$, $\varepsilon_1 = \varepsilon_0$ and $\sigma_1 = 0$) incident normally upon a copper sheet ($\mu_2 = \mu_0$, $\varepsilon_2 = \varepsilon_0$ and $\sigma_2 = 5.8 \times 10^7$ S/m) at a frequency of 1 MHz.

131. What do you mean by surface current and surface impedance?

132. Explain the difference between the intrinsic impedance and the surface impedance of a conductor. Staring from the wave equation, show that for a good conductor, the surface impedance is equal to the intrinsic impedance.

133. Write short notes on (i) Reflection by a perfect dielectric medium, (ii) Brewster angle and (iii) surface impedance.

134. Show that the time-average power loss per unit volume in a good conductor is given by $\dfrac{1}{2}\sigma E_{x0}^2 e^{-2z/\delta}$.

135. Describe the power loss in a plane conductor and furnish the details of its evaluation.

TRANSMISSION LINES-I (TRANSMISSION LINE THEORY)

8.1 INTRODUCTION

Transmission lines are a means of conveying information and power from one point to another. The size and separation of conducting wires become significant. The two-conductor transmission lines usually take the form of parallel-wire (balanced) line, coaxial (unbalanced) line or parallel-plate transmission line (strip line) as illustrated in Fig. 8.1.

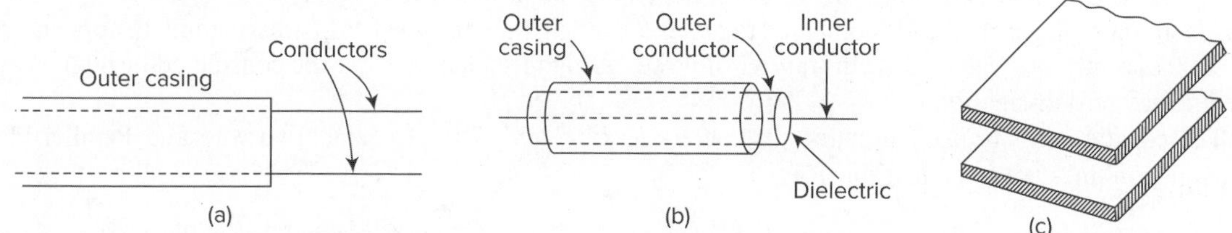

Figure 8.1 *Transmission lines (a) parallel-wire (balanced) line, (b) coaxial (unbalanced) line, and (c) parallel-plate transmission line (strip line)*

If the separation of conducting wires approaches a half-wavelength at the operating frequency, the radiation is likely to occur in a parallel-wire transmission line than in a coaxial line. Hence for the transverse electromagnetic (TEM) wave, a certain minimum separation (in wave length) between the conductors is required for the possible wave propagation. The TEM mode is considered below radio frequencies of 300 MHz. Here, the electric field and magnetic field are perpendicular to each other and both are transverse to the direction of propagation along the guiding line. Transmission lines consist of at least two separate conductors and a voltage can exist between them.

In a transmission line, a system of conductors guides this low-frequency type TEM wave, whereas wave guide supports transverse electric (TE) or transverse magnetic (TM) waves.

In this chapter, parallel-wire transmission line parameters, line equations, primary and secondary constants, phase and group velocities, concepts of infinite line, lossless or low loss characterization, types of distortion and types of loading are discussed in detail.

8.2 TRANSMISSION LINE PARAMETERS

The circuits discussed in the previous chapters deal with *lumped parameters* wherein resistance, inductance and capacitance are individually concentrated are lumped at discrete points in the circuit.

A transmission line having resistance (R), inductance (L), capacitance (C) and conductance (G) distributed uniformly along its length is specified as per-unit-length parameters called *distributed parameters*. These parameters are also called primary constants of the transmission line. The characteristic impedance, Z_0 and propagation constant, γ corresponds to secondary constants of the line.

For example, the electric line used for transmission of telephone messages or for the transmission of power is an electric circuit with distributed parameters. Here, the resistance, inductance, capacitance and conductance are distributed along the length of the circuit. Each elemental length of the circuit has its own values and concentration of the individual parameters is not possible.

Transmission line at radio frequencies:

When a line, either open-wire or coaxial used in the frequency range of MHz or more, contains approximations and its assumptions may be made as listed below.

(i) Due to skin effect, internal inductance becomes zero because the current may be flowing on the surface of the conductor.

(ii) While computing Z, assume $\omega L \gg R$. This assumption is justifiable because it is found that the resistance increases with $\sqrt{f}$ $\left[\text{since } \dfrac{R_{ac}}{R_{dc}} = 7.53a\sqrt{f} \text{ for copper}\right]$ while the line reactance increases directly with f, [since $\omega L = 2\pi f L$] due to skin effect.

(iii) The lines are well constructed that G may be considered zero.

The analysis is made in either of two ways, depending on whether R is small with respect to ωL or R is considered completely negligible compared to ωL. If R is small, then the line has low dissipation. In applications where losses may be neglected, as in transfer of power at high frequency, R may be considered negligible, and the line has zero dissipation.

The equations for transmission-line parameters R, L, C and G for Coaxial, Two wire and Parallel Plate transmission lines are given in Table 8.1.

Table 8.1 *Transmission-line Parameters R, L, C and G for Coaxial, Two Wire and Parallel Plate Transmission Lines*

Parameters	Coaxial line	Two wire line	Parallel Plate line	Unit
R	$\dfrac{R_s}{2\pi}\left(\dfrac{1}{a}+\dfrac{1}{b}\right)$	$\dfrac{R_s}{\pi a}$	$\dfrac{2R_s}{w}$	Ω/m
L	$\dfrac{\mu}{2\pi}\ln(b/a)$	$\dfrac{\mu}{\pi}\ln[(d/2a)+\sqrt{(d+2a)^2-1}]$	$\dfrac{\mu d}{w}$	H/m
G	$\dfrac{2\pi\sigma}{\ln(b/a)}$	$\dfrac{\pi\sigma}{\ln[(d/2a)+\sqrt{(d/2a)^2-1}]}$	$\dfrac{\sigma w}{d}$	S/m
C	$\dfrac{2\pi\varepsilon}{\ln(b/a)}$	$\dfrac{\pi\varepsilon}{\ln[(d/2a)+\sqrt{(d/2a)^2-1}]}$	$\dfrac{\varepsilon w}{d}$	F/m

Coaxial line:　　a = outer radius of inner conductor in meters

　　　　　　　　b = inner radius of inner conductor in meters

Two-wire line:　　a = radius of each wire in meters

　　　　　　　　d = space between wires' centers in meters

Parallel-plate line: w = width of each plate in meters

$\qquad d$ = thickness of insulation between plates in meters

Here ε, μ and σ are the parameters of the insulating materials between the conductors. Surface resistance, $R_s = \sqrt{\pi f \mu_C / \sigma_C}$, where μ_c and σ_c are the constitutive parameters of the conductors.

If $(d/2a)^2 \gg 1$, then $\ln[(d/2a) + \sqrt{(d/2a)^2 - 1}] \cong \ln(d/a)]$.

8.3 TRANSMISSION LINE THEORY

From the distributed parameters (continuous distribution of R, L, C and G along the line), a new circuit concept is developed for the analysis of long transmission lines carrying the TEM wave. Consider a symmetrical T-network terminated in its characteristic impedance Z_0 as shown in Fig. 8.2. Here, the series arm has two series impedances $Z_1/2$ so that the total impedance of the series arm is equal to Z_1, and the impedance of the shunt arm is equal to Z_2.

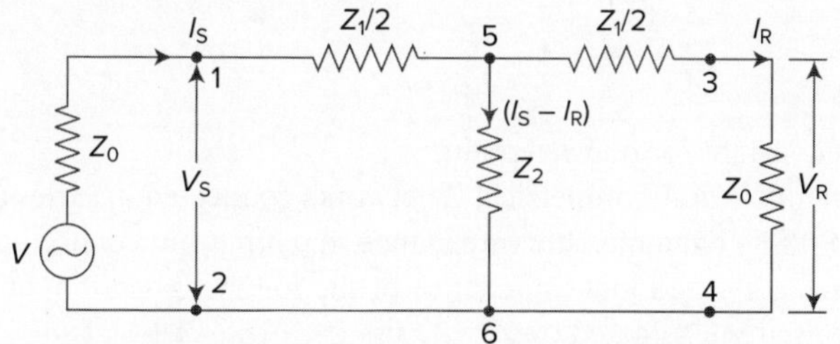

Figure 8.2 *A symmetrical T-network*

To determine the characteristic impedance:

The characteristic impedance of a symmetrical network is defined as the input impedance of the network when its terminating impedance is equal to Z_0. The Z_0 of the T-network can be determined in terms of its series and shunt impedances. Therefore, its characteristic impedance is equal to the input impedance.

$$Z_0 = Z_{\text{in}} = \frac{Z_1}{2} + \frac{\left(Z_0 + \dfrac{Z_1}{2}\right) Z_2}{\left(Z_0 + Z_2 + \dfrac{Z_1}{2}\right)}$$

$$= \frac{\dfrac{Z_1}{2}\left(Z_0 + Z_2 + \dfrac{Z_1}{2}\right) + Z_2\left(Z_0 + \dfrac{Z_1}{2}\right)}{Z_0 + Z_2 + \dfrac{Z_1}{2}}$$

i.e.,

$$Z_0\left(Z_0 + Z_2 + \frac{Z_1}{2}\right) = \frac{Z_1}{2}\left(Z_0 + Z_2 + \frac{Z_1}{2}\right) + Z_2\left(Z_0 + \frac{Z_1}{2}\right)$$

$$Z_0^2 + Z_0 Z_2 + \frac{Z_1 Z_0}{2} = \frac{Z_1 Z_0}{2} + \frac{Z_1 Z_2}{2} + \frac{Z_1^2}{4} + Z_0 Z_2 + \frac{Z_1 Z_2}{2}$$

$$Z_0^2 = \frac{Z_1^2}{4} + Z_1 Z_2$$

Therefore,

$$Z_0 = \sqrt{\frac{Z_1^2}{4} + Z_1 Z_2}$$

i.e.,

$$Z_0 = \sqrt{Z_1 Z_2 \left(1 + \frac{Z_1}{4Z_2}\right)} \tag{8.1}$$

To determine the propagation constant:
Applying KVL to the symmetrical *T*-network, we get

$$V_S = I_S \left(\frac{Z_1}{2} + Z_2\right) - I_R Z_2$$

The second arm gives

$$0 = -I_S Z_2 + I_R \left(\frac{Z_1}{2} + Z_2 + Z_0\right)$$

Therefore,

$$e^{\gamma} = \frac{I_S}{I_R} = \frac{\dfrac{Z_1}{2} + Z_2 + Z_0}{Z_2} = 1 + \frac{Z_1}{2Z_2} + \frac{Z_0}{Z_2} \tag{8.2}$$

where γ is the propagation constant for one *T*-section.

Consider a number of identical and symmetrical *T* networks connected in series as shown in Fig. 8.3. If the last section is terminated with its characteristic impedance, the input impedance at the first section becomes Z_0. Each section is terminated by the input impedance of the following section, and since the last section is terminated by Z_0, all sections are terminated by Z_0.

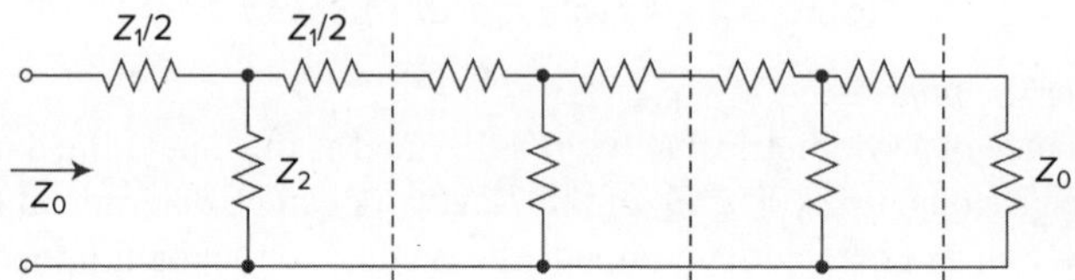

Figure 8.3 *A transmission line of cascaded symmetrical sections of impedances*

If there are n such terminated sections where the input and output currents are I_S and I_R, respectively, then

$$\frac{I_S}{I_R} = e^{n\gamma}$$

Substituting Eqn. (8.1) in Eqn. (8.2), for one symmetrical *T*-section, we get

$$e^{\gamma} = e^{\alpha + j\beta} = 1 + \frac{Z_1}{2Z_2} + \sqrt{\frac{Z_1}{Z_2} + \left(\frac{Z_1}{2Z_2}\right)^2}$$

$$= 1 + \frac{Z_1}{2Z_2} + \sqrt{\frac{Z_1}{Z_2}\left(1 + \frac{Z_1}{4Z_2}\right)} \tag{8.3}$$

A uniform transmission line can be considered with infinite number of T sections, each of infinitesimal size. Since each conductor has a certain length and diameter, it will have resistance and inductance. Since both the conducting wires are close to each other, there will be capacitance between them. Also, since the medium between the conducting wires is not perfectly insulated, there will be a leakage of current represented by shunt conductance.

The constants of an incremented length Δx of transmission line are indicated in Fig. 8.4. The series constants $Z = R + j\omega L$ are in Ω per unit length of line. The constants for an incremental length of transmission line are:

$R =$ Loop resistance (conductor loss) per unit length
$L =$ Loop inductance per unit length
$C =$ Short capacitance per unit length
$G =$ Short conductance (dielectric loss) per unit length

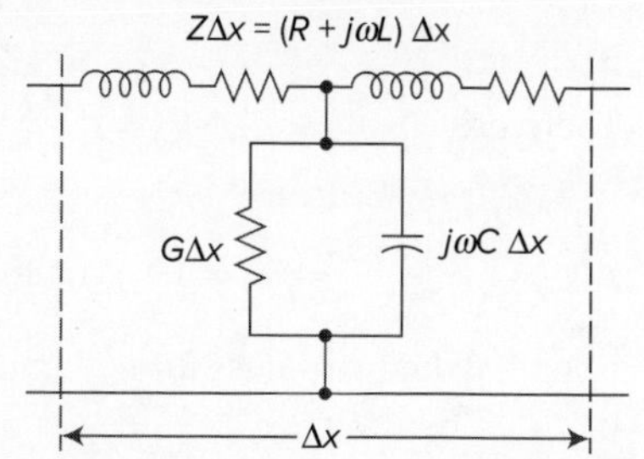

Figure 8.4 *The primary constants for an incremental length of transmission line*

where R, L, C and G are the primary constants of the transmission lines and $Y = G + j\omega C$ are in $\mho$ per unit length of line. Thus one T section, representing an incremental length Δx of the line, has a series impedance $Z\Delta x$ and a shunt admittance $Y\Delta x$.

The characteristic impedance (Z_0) of any small section is considered as that of the whole line. The Z_0 of a line of distributed constants can then be obtained by substituting $Z_1 = Z\Delta x$ and $Z_2 = \dfrac{1}{Y\Delta x}$ in Eqn. (8.1) for one section as

$$Z_0 = \sqrt{\frac{Z\Delta x}{Y\Delta x}\left(1 + \frac{Z\Delta x Y\Delta x}{4}\right)}$$

$$= \sqrt{\frac{Z}{Y}\left(1 + \frac{ZY(\Delta x)^2}{4}\right)} \tag{8.4}$$

If Δx tends to zero, the value of Z_0 for the line of distributed constants is obtained as

$$Z_0 = \sqrt{\frac{Z}{Y}} \tag{8.5}$$

Therefore, $\qquad Z_0 = \sqrt{\dfrac{R + j\omega L}{G + j\omega C}}$

From Binomial theorem, we have

$$(1 + x)^n = 1 + nx + \frac{n(n-1)}{1\cdot 2}x^2 + \cdots + \frac{n(n-1)(n-2)\cdots(n-r+1)}{1\cdot 2\cdot 3\cdots r}x^r + \cdots$$

Then, the radical in Eqn. (8.3) may be expanded as

$$\sqrt{\frac{Z_1}{Z_2}\left(1 + \frac{Z_1}{4Z_2}\right)} = \sqrt{\frac{Z_1}{Z_2}}\left[1 + \frac{Z_1}{4Z_2}\right]^{\frac{1}{2}} = \sqrt{\frac{Z_1}{Z_2}}\left[1 + \frac{1}{2}\left(\frac{Z_1}{4Z_2}\right) - \frac{1}{8}\left(\frac{Z_1}{4Z_2}\right)^2 + \cdots\right]$$

Therefore, using the above equation, Eqn. (8.3) becomes

$$e^{\gamma} = 1 + \sqrt{\frac{Z_1}{Z_2}} + \frac{1}{2}\left(\sqrt{\frac{Z_1}{Z_2}}\right)^2 + \frac{1}{8}\left(\sqrt{\frac{Z_1}{Z_2}}\right)^3 - \frac{1}{128}\left(\sqrt{\frac{Z_1}{Z_2}}\right)^5 + \cdots$$

For the incremental length Δx, $Z_1 = Z\Delta x$, $Z_2 = \dfrac{1}{Y\Delta x}$, and the propagation constant is $\gamma\Delta x$.

Therefore,
$$e^{\gamma\Delta x} = 1 + \sqrt{ZY}\,\Delta x + \frac{1}{2}(\sqrt{ZY})^2(\Delta x)^2 + \frac{1}{8}(\sqrt{ZY})^3(\Delta x)^3 - \frac{1}{128}(\sqrt{ZY})^5(\Delta x)^5 + \cdots \tag{8.6}$$

Also,
$$e^{\gamma\Delta x} = 1 + \gamma\Delta x + \frac{\gamma^2\Delta x^2}{2!} + \frac{\gamma^3\Delta x^3}{3!} + \cdots \tag{8.7}$$

Equating the two values for $e^{\gamma\Delta x}$ and cancelling the unity terms, we get

$$\gamma\Delta x + \frac{\gamma^2\Delta x^2}{2} + \frac{\gamma^3\Delta x^3}{6} + \cdots = \sqrt{ZY}\,\Delta x + \frac{(\sqrt{ZY})^2\Delta x^2}{2} + \frac{(\sqrt{ZY})^3\Delta x^3}{8} + \cdots$$

Dividing the above equation by Δx, we have

$$\gamma + \frac{\gamma^2\Delta x}{2} + \frac{\gamma^3(\Delta x)^2}{6} + \cdots = \sqrt{ZY} + \frac{(\sqrt{ZY})^2\Delta x}{2} + \frac{(\sqrt{ZY})^3(\Delta x)^2}{8} + \cdots$$

If Δx tends to zero, then $\gamma = \sqrt{ZY}$ $\tag{8.8}$

Therefore, $\gamma = \sqrt{(R + j\omega L)(G + j\omega C)}$ is the value of propagation constant for the line of distributed constants with identical elemental lengths. Since Z and Y are in terms of unit length, γ is also expressed in terms of per unit length value.

8.4   TRANSMISSION LINE EQUATIONS

The general circuit equations to determine the values of voltage and current at any point on a transmission line are discussed below:

A circuit with distributed parameters requires a new method of analysis which is different from that of the circuit with lumped constants, since a voltage drop occurs across each series increment of line, the voltages applied to each increment of shunt admittance is a variable and thus the shunted current is a variable along the line. In lumped constant circuits, the current around the loop is assumed constant, whereas in transmission line, the current varies from point to point along the line. Differential equations describing this action can be formed for the steady state, from which general circuit equation can be obtained.

The notations used are as follows:

> R = Series resistance, Ω per unit length of line (includes both wires)
> L = Series inductance, Henry per unit length of line
> C = Capacitance between conductors, farad per unit length of line
> G = Shunt leakage conductance between conductors, $\mho$ per unit length of line
> ωL = Series reactance, Ω per unit length of line
> $Z = R + j\omega L$ = Series impedance, Ω per unit length of line
> ωC = Shunt susceptance, $\mho$ per unit length of line
> $Y = G + j\omega C$ = Shunt admittance, $\mho$ per unit length of line
> s = Distance between point of observation and receiving end of the line.
> I = Current in the line at any point
> V = Voltage between conductors at any point
> l = length of the transmission line

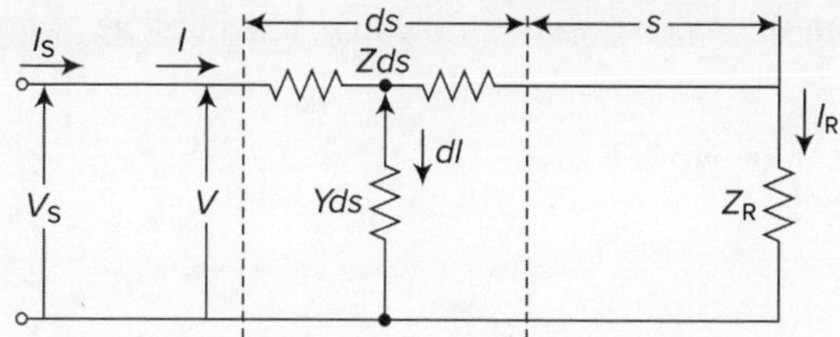

Figure 8.5 *A long line with the elements of one of the infinitesimal T-sections shown*

As shown in Fig. 8.5, the elemental *T*-section is of length ds and carries a current I. The series line impedance is Z per unit length of line, the series impedance of the element is $Z\,ds$, and the voltage drop in the length ds is

$$dV = IZ\,ds$$

Therefore,
$$\frac{dV}{ds} = IZ \tag{8.9}$$

The shunt admittance per unit length of line is Y, and the admittance of the element of line is $Y\,ds$. The current dI that flows through the line or from one conductor to the other conductor is

$$dI = VY\,ds$$

Therefore,
$$\frac{dI}{ds} = VY \tag{8.10}$$

Differentiating Eqns. (8.9) and (8.10), with respect to "s", we have

$$\frac{d^2V}{ds^2} = Z\frac{dI}{ds}, \quad \frac{d^2I}{ds^2} = Y\frac{dV}{ds}$$

Then,
$$\frac{d^2V}{ds^2} = ZYV \tag{8.11}$$

Similarly,
$$\frac{d^2I}{ds^2} = ZYI \tag{8.12}$$

The Eqns. (8.11) and (8.12) correspond to differential equations of the transmission line in terms of distributed circuit constants. If $V = V_o e^{j\omega x}$ and $I = I_o e^{j\omega x}$, they are similar to the forms of the wave equation.

Equation (8.11) can be written as

$$\frac{d^2V}{ds^2} - ZYV = 0$$

i.e.,
$$(m^2 - ZY)V = 0$$

Therefore,
$$m = \pm\sqrt{ZY} \tag{8.13}$$

Hence,
$$V = Ae^{\sqrt{ZY}\,s} + Be^{-\sqrt{ZY}\,s} \tag{8.14}$$

Similarly, from Eqn. (8.12), we have

$$I = Ce^{\sqrt{ZY}\,s} + De^{-\sqrt{ZY}\,s} \tag{8.15}$$

where A, B, C and D are arbitrary constants of integration.

Since distance is measured from the receiving end of the line, it is possible to assign conditions such that

$$s = 0, I = I_R, V = V_R$$

Then Eqns. (8.14) and (8.15) can be written as

$$V_R = A + B$$

$$I_R = C + D \tag{8.16}$$

Differentiating Eqns. (8.14) and (8.15), we get

$$\frac{dV}{ds} = A\sqrt{ZY}\,e^{\sqrt{EY}\,s} - B\sqrt{ZY}\,e^{-\sqrt{ZY}}$$

Substituting $\dfrac{dV}{ds} = IZ$ of Eqn.(8.19), we have

$$IZ = A\sqrt{ZY}\,e^{\sqrt{ZY}\,s} - B\sqrt{ZY}\,e^{-\sqrt{ZY}s}$$

Therefore, $\qquad I = A\sqrt{\dfrac{Y}{Z}}\,e^{\sqrt{ZY}\,s} - B\sqrt{\dfrac{Y}{Z}}\,e^{-\sqrt{ZY}\,s}$ $\tag{8.17}$

Similarly, $\qquad \dfrac{dI}{ds} = C\sqrt{ZY}\,e^{\sqrt{ZY}\,s} - D\sqrt{ZY}\,e^{-\sqrt{ZY}\,s}$

Therefore, $\qquad V = C\sqrt{\dfrac{Z}{Y}}\,e^{\sqrt{ZY}\,s} - D\sqrt{\dfrac{Z}{Y}}\,e^{-\sqrt{ZY}\,s} \quad \left(\text{since } \dfrac{dI}{ds} = VY\right)$ $\tag{8.18}$

At $s = 0$, Eqns. (8.17) and (8.18) become

$$I_R = A\sqrt{\frac{Y}{Z}} - B\sqrt{\frac{Y}{Z}} \tag{8.19}$$

$$V_R = C\sqrt{\frac{Z}{Y}} - D\sqrt{\frac{Z}{Y}} \tag{8.20}$$

Upon solving Eqns. (8.16), (8.19) and (8.20) and using the relation of $V_R = I_R Z_R$ and $Z_o = \sqrt{\dfrac{Z}{Y}}$ of the lines, we get

$$A = \frac{V_R}{2} + \frac{I_R}{2}\sqrt{\frac{Z}{Y}} = \frac{V_R}{2}\left(1 + \frac{Z_0}{Z_R}\right)$$

$$B = \frac{V_R}{2} - \frac{I_R}{2}\sqrt{\frac{Z}{Y}} = \frac{V_R}{2}\left(1 - \frac{Z_0}{Z_R}\right)$$

$$C = \frac{I_R}{2} + \frac{V_R}{2}\sqrt{\frac{Y}{Z}} = \frac{I_R}{2}\left(1 + \frac{Z_R}{Z_0}\right)$$

$$D = \frac{I_R}{2} - \frac{V_R}{2}\sqrt{\frac{Y}{Z}} = \frac{I_R}{2}\left(1 - \frac{Z_R}{Z_0}\right)$$

Hence, Eqns. (8.14) and (8.15) can be written as

$$V = \frac{V_R}{2}\left[\left(1 + \frac{Z_0}{Z_R}\right)e^{\sqrt{ZY}\,s} + \left(1 + \frac{Z_0}{Z_R}\right)e^{-\sqrt{ZY}\,s}\right] \tag{8.21}$$

$$I = \frac{I_R}{2}\left[\left(1 + \frac{Z_R}{Z_0}\right)e^{\sqrt{ZY}\,s} + \left(1 - \frac{Z_R}{Z_0}\right)e^{-\sqrt{ZY}\,s}\right] \tag{8.22}$$

Then

$$V = \frac{V_R(Z_R + Z_0)}{2Z_R}\left[e^{\sqrt{ZY}\,s} + \left(\frac{Z_R - Z_0}{Z_R + Z_0}\right)e^{-\sqrt{ZY}\,s}\right] \tag{8.23}$$

$$I = \frac{I_R(Z_R + Z_0)}{2Z_R}\left[e^{\sqrt{ZY}\,s} - \left(\frac{Z_R - Z_0}{Z_R + Z_0}\right)e^{-\sqrt{ZY}\,s}\right] \tag{8.24}$$

These are useful form of the equations for voltage and current at any point on a transmission line, and are solutions to wave equation.

Rearranging Eqns. (8.21) and (8.22), we get

$$V = V_R\left(\frac{e^{\sqrt{ZY}\,s} + e^{-\sqrt{ZY}\,s}}{2}\right) + I_R Z_0\left(\frac{e^{\sqrt{ZY}\,s} - e^{-\sqrt{ZY}\,s}}{2}\right)$$

$$I = I_R\left(\frac{e^{\sqrt{ZY}\,s} + e^{-\sqrt{ZY}\,s}}{2}\right) + \frac{E_R}{Z_0}\left(\frac{e^{\sqrt{ZY}\,s} - e^{-\sqrt{ZY}\,s}}{2}\right)$$

Therefore,

$$V = V_R \cosh \sqrt{ZY}\,s + I_R Z_0 \sinh \sqrt{ZY}\,s \tag{8.25}$$

$$I = I_R \cosh \sqrt{ZY}\,s + \frac{E_R}{Z_0} \sinh \sqrt{ZY}\,s \tag{8.26}$$

The above equations constitute another useful form for the voltage and current values at any point on a transmission line.

8.5 CONCEPTS OF INFINITE LINE

To determine sending end current I_s for a finite line:
Equation (8.26) may be written for the sending end current I_s of a line of length l as

$$I_S = I_R \cosh \sqrt{ZY}\,\ell + \frac{V_R}{Z_0} \sinh \sqrt{ZY}\,\ell$$

If the line is terminated in $Z_R = Z_0$, then

$$I_S = I_R(\cosh \sqrt{ZY}\,\ell + \sinh \sqrt{ZY}\,\ell)$$

Therefore,

$$\frac{I_S}{I_R} = e^{\sqrt{ZY}\,\ell} = e^{\gamma \ell} \tag{8.27}$$

where,

$$\gamma = \sqrt{ZY} \quad \text{and} \quad \gamma = \alpha + j\beta$$

To determine sending end input impedance Z_s:

Dividing Eqn. (8.25) by Eqn. (8.26), we get the input impedance of the line of length ℓ as

$$Z_S = \frac{V_S}{I_S} = Z_0 \left[\frac{Z_R \cosh \gamma\ell + Z_0 \sinh \gamma\ell}{Z_0 \cosh \gamma\ell + Z_R \sinh \gamma\ell} \right] \tag{8.28}$$

Dividing Eqn. (8.23) by Eqn. (8.24), we get the sending end input impedance as

$$Z_S = \frac{V_S}{I_S} = Z_0 \left[\frac{e^{\gamma\ell} + \left(\dfrac{Z_R - Z_0}{Z_R + Z_0} \right) e^{-\gamma\ell}}{-e^{\gamma\ell} - \left(\dfrac{Z_R - Z_0}{Z_R + Z_0} \right) e^{-\gamma\ell}} \right] \tag{8.29}$$

When the line is terminated in its characteristic impedance i.e., $Z_R = Z_0$, Eqn. (8.29) becomes

$$Z_s = Z_0 \tag{8.30}$$

Then input impedance of an infinite line may be found by letting ℓ approach infinity in Eqn. (8.28) or (8.29).

The result is $\qquad Z_s = Z_0 \tag{8.31}$

Thus by comparison of the results shown in Eqns. (8.30) and (8.31), a line of finite length shown in Fig. 8.6, terminated in a load equivalent to its characteristic impedance, appears to the sending end generator as an infinite line. A finite line terminated in Z_0 and an infinite line is indistinguishable by measurements at the source.

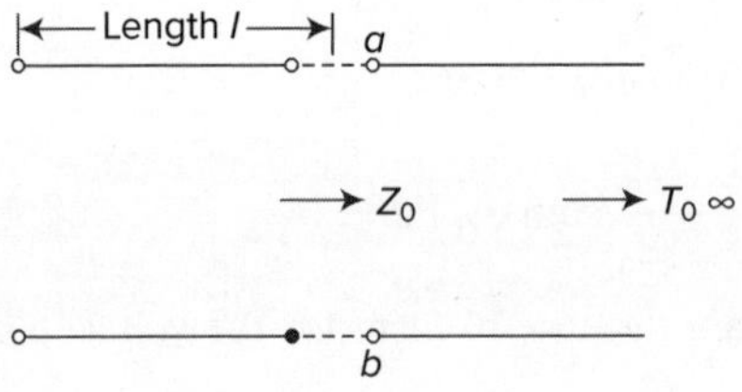

Figure 8.6 *A length ℓ taken from an infinite line*

$$V = \frac{V_R(Z_R + Z_0)}{2Z_R} \left[e^{\gamma s} + \left(\frac{Z_R - Z_0}{Z_R + Z_0} \right) e^{-\gamma s} \right] \tag{8.32}$$

$$I = \frac{I_R(Z_R + Z_0)}{2Z_R} \left[e^{\gamma s} - \left(\frac{Z_R - Z_0}{Z_R + Z_0} \right) e^{-\gamma s} \right] \tag{8.33}$$

For a portion of an infinite line, or a finite line terminated in its characteristic impedance,

$$Z_R = Z_0$$

Therefore, Eqns. (8.32) and (8.34) can be written as

$$V = V_R e^{\gamma s}$$

$$I = I_R e^{\gamma s}$$

It is apparent that the voltage and current values change with distance and from the receiving end because of the factor $e^{\gamma s}$.

Using Fig. 8.7, these expressions may be readily written for distance voltage and current values at that point, giving

$$V_R = V_S e^{-\gamma s}, \quad I_R = I_S e^{-\gamma s}$$

If the terminals a, b are considered at any point on the infinite line, then E and I at any point are expressed in terms of V_S and I_S as

$$V = V_S e^{-\gamma s} \tag{8.34}$$

$$I = I_S e^{-\gamma s} \tag{8.35}$$

Since $r = \alpha + j\beta$, then

$$V = V_S e^{-\alpha s} e^{-j\beta s} \tag{8.36}$$

and

$$I = I_S e^{-\gamma s} e^{-j\beta s} \tag{8.37}$$

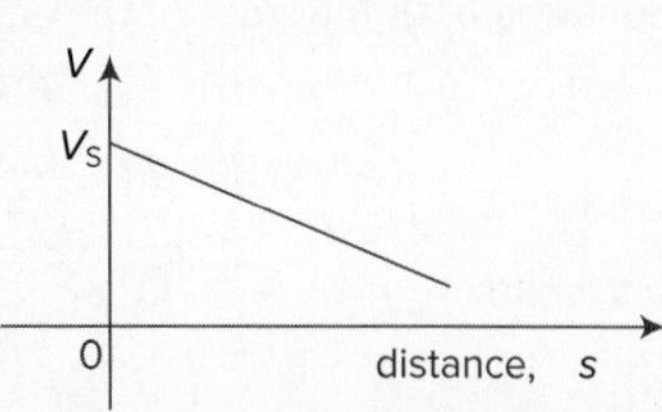

Figure 8.7 *Voltage along a point line as measured by an effective reading meter*

Since the sending end values will be functions of time as $V_S = V_{S_o} e^{j\omega t}$ and $I_S = I_{S_o} e^{j\omega t}$, it is seen that Eqns. (8.36) and (8.37) are functions of both distance and time. This is a property of any solution to the wave eqn.

$$V = V_S e^{-\alpha s}$$

$$I = I_S e^{-\alpha s}$$

Although the analysis has been given here in terms of current and voltage, it should be remembered that actually energy is being propagated along the line in the form of electric and magnetic fields. The waves of current and voltage are merely convenient by means of observation of the fields present.

8.6 PHASE AND GROUP VELOCITIES

8.6.1 Phase Velocity or Velocity of Propagation

The distance that a wave travels along the line while the phase angle is changing through 2π radians is called a wavelength (λ). Therefore,

$$\lambda = \frac{2\pi}{\beta} \tag{8.38}$$

and

$$\lambda = \frac{v_p}{f} \tag{8.39}$$

where v_p is the velocity of propagation along the line

Therefore,

$$v_p = \lambda f = \frac{2\pi f}{\beta} = \frac{\omega}{\beta}$$

Therefore,

$$v_p = \frac{\omega}{\beta} \tag{8.40}$$

We know that $Z = R + j\omega L$ and $Y = G + j\omega C$

$$\gamma = \alpha + j\beta = \sqrt{ZY} = \sqrt{(R + j\omega L)(G + j\omega C)} = \sqrt{RG - \omega^2 LC + j\omega(LG + CR)}$$

Squaring both sides,

$$\alpha^2 + j2\alpha\beta - \beta^2 = RG - \omega^2 LC + j\omega(LG + CR) \tag{8.41}$$

Equating the real part of Eqn. (8.41), we have

$$\alpha^2 - \beta^2 = RG - \omega^2 LC$$

Equating the imaginary part of Eqn. (8.41), we have

$$2\alpha\beta = \omega(LG + CR)$$

Squaring both the sides of the above equations, we get

$$4\alpha^2\beta^2 = \omega^2(LG + CR)^2$$

$$4(\beta^2 + RG - \omega^2 LC)\beta^2 = \omega^2(LG + CR)$$

$$\beta = \sqrt{\frac{\omega^2 LC - RG + \sqrt{(RG - \omega^2 LC)^2 + \omega^2(LG + CR)^2}}{2}}$$

$$\alpha = \sqrt{\frac{RG - \omega^2 LC + \sqrt{(RG - \omega^2 LC)^2 + \omega^2(LG + CR)^2}}{2}}$$

For a perfect line at radio frequencies, $R = 0$ and $G = 0$, then

$$\beta = \omega\sqrt{LC}$$

Therefore, $\qquad v_p = \dfrac{\omega}{\beta} = \dfrac{1}{\sqrt{LC}}$ m/s

The above equation shows that the line parameters L and C determine the velocity of propagation of the wave.

i.e., $\qquad v_p = \dfrac{1}{\sqrt{\mu\varepsilon}}$ m/s

8.6.2 Group Velocity

If the transmission line or transmission medium is such that different frequencies travel with different velocities, then the line or the medium is said to be dispersive. In that case, signals are propagated with a velocity known as group velocity (v_g). Normally, phase velocity is slightly greater than the group velocity. Thus, group velocity is defined as the velocity of the envelope of a complex signal. Assuming that ω_1 and ω_2 are two close angular frequencies being transmitted and β_1 and β_2 are the corresponding phase constants, the group velocity v_g is defined by

$$v_g = \frac{\omega_2 - \omega_1}{\beta_2 - \beta_1} = \frac{d\omega}{d\beta}$$

For a propagating wave in free space, $\beta = \omega\sqrt{\mu\varepsilon}$

Taking its derivative, we get

$$\frac{d\beta}{d\omega} = \sqrt{\mu\varepsilon}$$

Therefore, the group velocity in such a wave becomes $v_g = \dfrac{d\omega}{d\beta} = \dfrac{1}{\sqrt{\mu\varepsilon}}$

The phase velocity in this case is equal to velocity of light for propagation in space without reflection.

Hence, $v_p = \dfrac{1}{\sqrt{\mu\varepsilon}} = v_g$

Therefore, since group velocity is equal to the phase velocity, the group velocity is equal to the velocity of light in the medium for a freely propagating wave. In this case, the product of phase velocity and group velocity is equal to the square of velocity of light. That is,

$$v_p v_g = c^2$$

In space, $v_p = 3 \times 10^8$ m/s, i.e., the velocity of light in free space, c.

8.7 TYPES OF DISTORTION

A signal is said to be distorted if the received signal is not the exact replica of the transmitted signal. There are three types of distortions in the wave transmitted along the transmission line. They are

(i) Distortion due to variation of characteristic impedance Z_0 with frequency
(ii) Frequency distortion due to the variation of attenuation constant, α with frequency
(iii) Phase distortion due to the variation of phase constant, β with frequency

8.7.1 Distortion Due to Z_0 Varying with Frequency

The characteristic impedance Z_0 of the line varies with the frequency while the line is terminated in impedance which does not vary with frequency in similar fashion as that of Z_0. This causes the distortion. The power is absorbed at certain frequencies while it gets reflected for certain frequencies. So there exists the selective power absorption due to this type of distortion.

$$Z_0 = \sqrt{\frac{R + j\omega L}{G + j\omega C}} = \sqrt{\frac{R\left(1 + j\omega \dfrac{L}{R}\right)}{G\left(1 + j\omega \dfrac{C}{G}\right)}}$$

If the condition $LG = CR$ is satisfied, then $\dfrac{L}{R} = \dfrac{C}{G}$. Therefore,

$$\left(1 + j\omega \frac{L}{R}\right) = \left(1 + j\omega \frac{C}{G}\right)$$

Therefore, $$Z_0 = \sqrt{\frac{R}{G}} \angle 0° = \sqrt{\frac{L}{C}} \angle 0°$$

For such a line, Z_0 does not vary with frequency, ω and it is purely resistive in nature. This line can be easily and correctly terminated in an impedance matching with Z_0 at all the frequencies. Here, $Z_R = \sqrt{\dfrac{R}{G}} = \sqrt{\dfrac{L}{C}}$. This eliminates the selective power absorption and hence, the distortion.

8.7.2 Frequency Distortion

The attenuation constant is

$$\alpha = \sqrt{\frac{RG - \omega^2 LC + \sqrt{(RG - \omega^2 LC)^2 + \omega^2(LG + CR)^2}}{2}}$$

Here, in general, α is a function of frequency. All frequencies of the wave transmitted on a line will not be attenuated equally. Hence, the received waveform will not be identical with the input waveform. This variation is known as *frequency distortion*.

8.7.3 Phase or Delay Distortion

The phase constant β is

$$\beta = \sqrt{\frac{\omega^2 LC - RG + \sqrt{(RG - \omega^2 LC)^2 + \omega^2(LG + CR)^2}}{2}}$$

and it is a complicated function of frequency. Hence, the line will introduce delay or phase distortion.

Since the velocity of propagation is $v_p = \dfrac{\omega}{\beta}$, it is apparent that ω and β do not involve frequency in the same manner and the velocity of propagation will be a function of frequency. All frequencies applied to a transmission line will not have the same time of transmission. Since some frequency components will be delayed more than those of other frequency components, for an applied voice-voltage wave, the received waveform will not be identical with the input waveform. This phenomenon is known as phase or delay distortion. Equalizers are used at the line terminals to reduce these distortions.

8.8 CONDITIONS FOR DISTORTIONLESS LINE

If a transmission line has no frequency distortion and delay distortion, then α and the velocity of propagation must not be functions of frequency.

$$v_p = \frac{\omega}{\beta}$$

Then β must be a direct function of frequency.

$$\beta = \sqrt{\frac{\omega^2 LC - RG + \sqrt{(RG - \omega^2 LC)^2 + \omega^2(LG + CR)^2}}{2}}$$

If the term under the second radical is to be reduced to equal $(RG + \omega^2 LC)^2$, then

$$\beta = \omega\sqrt{LC}$$

Therefore, $v_p = \dfrac{\omega}{\beta} = \dfrac{1}{\sqrt{LC}}$ is same for all frequencies and eliminate delay distortion.

Expanding the terms under the internal radical and equating to $(RG + \omega^2 LC)^2$, we get

$$R^2 G^2 - 2\omega^2 LCRG + \omega^4 L^2 C^2 + \omega^2 L^2 G^2 + 2\omega^2 LCRG + \omega^2 C^2 R^2 = (RG + \omega^2 LC)^2$$

Simplifying, we get

$$\omega^2 L^2 G^2 - 2\omega^2 LCRG + \omega^2 C^2 R^2 = 0$$

$$(LG - CR)^2 = 0$$

Therefore, $LG = CR$

The above condition makes β a direct function of frequency.

We know that, $\quad \alpha = \sqrt{\dfrac{RG - \omega^2 LC + \sqrt{(RG - \omega^2 LC)^2 + \omega^2 (LG + CR)^2}}{2}}$

This may be made independent of frequency, if the term under the internal radical is reduced to

$$(RG + \omega^2 LC)^2$$

Therefore $\qquad LG = CR$

Therefore, $\qquad \alpha = \sqrt{RG}$

This condition is independent of frequency, thus eliminating frequency distortion. Unfortunately, such a hypothetical line is not practical with distributed parameters

$$LG = CR$$

Therefore, $\qquad \dfrac{L}{C} = \dfrac{R}{G}$

Here, smaller value of G requires a varying value of L. For increasing G values, α gets increased leading to poor line efficiency. For lowering the value of R, the size and cost of the conductors are increased. Hence, it is difficult to achieve the hypothetical results.

8.9 CONSTANTS FOR THE LINE OF ZERO DISSIPATION AND MINIMUM ATTENUATION

Here, $\qquad R = G = 0$

The line parameters for the line of zero dissipation are

$$Z = j\omega L \quad \text{and} \quad Y = j\omega C$$

Characteristic impedance, $Z_0 = \sqrt{\dfrac{Z}{Y}} = \sqrt{\dfrac{j\omega L}{j\omega C}} = \sqrt{\dfrac{L}{C}}\ \Omega$

Since this value is resistive,

$$Z_0 = R_0 = \sqrt{\dfrac{L}{C}}\ \Omega$$

The value of characteristic impedance (at high frequency) of the open wire line can be found directly from the line dimensions as

$$R_0 = 120 \ln \dfrac{d}{a}\ \Omega$$

$$R_0 = 276 \log \dfrac{d}{a}\ \Omega$$

The characteristic impedance of the coaxial line is

$$R_0 = \frac{60}{\sqrt{\varepsilon_r}} \ln \frac{b}{a} \; \Omega$$

$$R_0 = \frac{138}{\sqrt{\varepsilon_r}} \ln \frac{b}{a} \; \Omega$$

where $\varepsilon_r = 1$ for air-spaced lines.
The propagation constant γ is

$$\gamma = \sqrt{ZY} = \sqrt{j\omega L \times j\omega C} = j\omega\sqrt{LC}$$

Here $\alpha = 0$ and $\beta = \omega\sqrt{LC}$ radians/m
The velocity of propagation is

$$v = \frac{\omega}{\beta} = \frac{1}{\sqrt{LC}} \text{ m/s}$$

For air-spaced open-wire line,

$$v = 3 \times 10^8 \text{ m/s}$$

which is the velocity of light in space.
For coaxial line,

$$v = \frac{3 \times 10^8}{\sqrt{\varepsilon_r}} \text{ m/s}$$

8.10 TYPES OF LOADING

Increase in the inductance of the transmission line by lumped inductors spaced at intervals along the transmission line is termed as loading. Figure 8.8 shows the types of loading based on attenuation. Loading is classified as,

(i) Lumped loading
(ii) Continuous loading
(iii) Patch loading

Lumped Loading The inductance of a transmission line can be increased by the introduction of loading coil at uniform intervals is called lumped loading. It acts as a low pass filter. So it is applicable only for a limited range of frequencies. The loading coils have a certain resistance and hence, increasing total effective inductance increases R. Further, hysteresis and eddy current losses that occur in the loading coils result in increase in R.

However, there is a practical limit to the amount by which the inductance of the line can be increased for the reduction of attenuation. Thus, loading coil should be carefully designed so that it will not introduce any distortion.

Continuous Loading A type of iron or some other magnetic material is wound on the transmission line to increase the permeability of the surrounding medium to increase the inductance. The advantages of continuous loading over lumped loading is that attenuation factor increases uniformly with increase in frequency. Minimum attenuation is obtained in this loading method.

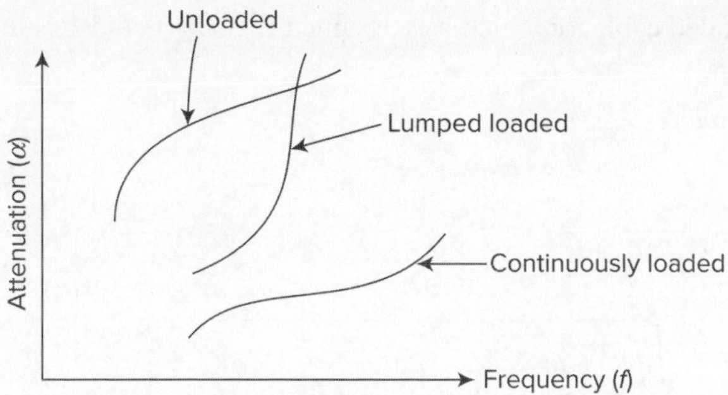

Figure 8.8 *Loading of lines*

Patch Loading Patch loading utilizes section of continuously loaded cable separated by sections of unloaded cable. The length of each section is normally a quarter kilometer. This method provides the advantage of continuous loading with considerable reduction in cost.

Telephone Cable In the ordinary telephone cable, the wires are insulated with paper and twisted in pairs, which results in negligible values of inductance and conductance in the audio range of frequencies. Therefore,

$$Z = R \quad \text{and} \quad Y = j\omega C, \ \gamma = \sqrt{ZY}$$

We know that, $\gamma = \sqrt{RG - \omega^2 LC + j\omega(LG + CR)}$

Since $L = G = 0$, $\gamma = \sqrt{j\omega CR}$

$$= \sqrt{\omega CR} \ \angle 45°$$

$$= \sqrt{\omega CR} \ [\cos 45° + j \sin 45°]$$

$$= \sqrt{\omega CR} \left[\frac{1}{\sqrt{2}} + j\frac{1}{\sqrt{2}} \right]$$

$$= \sqrt{\frac{\omega CR}{2}} (1 + j1)$$

Therefore, $\alpha = \sqrt{\dfrac{\omega CR}{2}}$ and $\beta = \sqrt{\dfrac{\omega CR}{2}}$

Hence, $v = \dfrac{\omega}{\beta} = \sqrt{\dfrac{2\omega}{CR}}$

Here, both the attenuation α and the velocity of propagation v are functions of frequency. At higher frequencies, the attenuation will be more and the wave travels faster than the lower frequencies, resulting in frequency and delay distortions on telephone cable.

Inductance Loading of Telephone Cables The distortionless conditions can be achieved either by increasing L/C ratio i.e., increasing the values of inductance L with lumped loading inductors spaced at intervals along the line, called lumped loading line, or by winding the cable with a high-permeability steel tape such as permalloy to obtain distributed or uniform loading especially in under-water applications where design of lumped loading coils is practically difficult.

Consider a uniformly loaded cable for which it is assumed that $G = 0$ and L is increased in such a way that ωL is large with respect to R.

Then,
$$Z = R + j\omega L$$

$$Y = j\omega C$$

Here
$$Z = \sqrt{R^2 + \omega^2 L^2} \ \angle \ \frac{\pi}{2} - \tan^{-1}\frac{R}{\omega L}$$

Then
$$\gamma = \sqrt{ZY} = \sqrt{\sqrt{R^2 + \omega^2 L^2} \ \angle \ \frac{\pi}{2} - \tan^{-1}\frac{R}{\omega L} \times \omega C \ \angle \ \frac{\pi}{2}}$$

$$= \omega\sqrt{LC}\sqrt{1 + \frac{R^2}{\omega^2 L^2}} \ \angle \ \frac{\pi}{2} - \frac{1}{2}\tan^{-1}\frac{R}{\omega L}$$

Since $R \ll \omega L$, the term $\dfrac{R^2}{\omega^2 L^2}$ is neglected.

Therefore,
$$\gamma = \omega\sqrt{LC} \ \angle \ \frac{\pi}{2} - \frac{1}{2}\tan^{-1}\frac{R}{\omega L}$$

If $\theta = \dfrac{\pi}{2} - \dfrac{1}{2}\tan^{-1}\dfrac{R}{\omega L}$, then $\cos\theta = \cos\left(\dfrac{\pi}{2} - \dfrac{1}{2}\tan^{-1}\dfrac{R}{\omega L}\right) = \sin\left(\dfrac{1}{2}\tan^{-1}\dfrac{R}{\omega L}\right).$

For a small angle, $\sin\theta = \tan\theta = \theta$

Therefore, $\cos\theta = \dfrac{R}{2\omega L}$

Similarly,
$$\sin\theta = \sin\left(\frac{\pi}{2} - \frac{1}{2}\tan^{-1}\frac{R}{\omega L}\right) = 1$$

Therefore,
$$\gamma = \omega\sqrt{LC}\,[\cos\theta + j\sin\theta] = \omega\sqrt{LC}\left[\frac{R}{2\omega L} + j\right]$$

For the uniformly loaded cable,

$$\alpha = \frac{R}{2}\sqrt{\frac{C}{L}}, \ \beta = \omega\sqrt{LC} \text{ and } v = \frac{\omega}{\beta} = \frac{1}{\sqrt{LC}}$$

From the above equations, it is seen that both the attenuation and velocity of propagation are independent of frequency, and the loaded cable will be distortionless. Also, the attenuation α can be reduced by increasing L, provided that R is not greatly increased.

Since uniform loading is costly and there will be a small increase in L per unit length, lumped loading is generally used as a means of transmission improvement for cables.

Campbell's Equation The performance of a line loaded at uniform intervals can be analysed by considering a symmetrical section of line from the center of one loading coil to the center of the next, where the loading coil impedance is Z_C. The section of line may be replaced with an equivalent T section having symmetrical series arms, as shown in Fig. 8.9.

As in filter circuits, one of the series arms is called $\dfrac{Z_1}{2}$ as given by

$$\frac{Z_1}{2} = Z_0 \tanh \frac{\gamma \ell}{2}$$

where ℓ is the number of kms between loading coils and γ is the propagation constant per km.

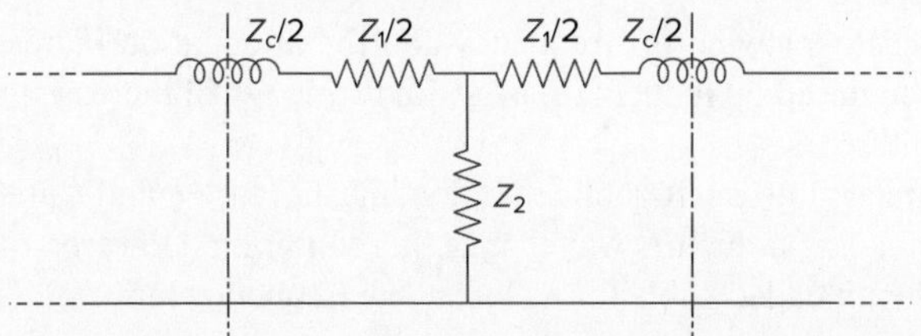

Figure 8.9 *Equivalent T-section for part of a line between two lumped loading coils of impedance, Z_C*

Upon including half a loading coil, the equivalent series arm of the loaded section becomes

$$\frac{Z_1'}{2} = \frac{Z_C}{2} + \frac{Z_1}{2} = \frac{Z_C}{2} + Z_0 \tanh \frac{\gamma \ell}{2}$$

and the shunt Z_2 arm of the equivalent *T*-section is

$$Z_2 = \frac{Z_0}{\sinh r\ell}$$

We know that, $\cosh \gamma \ell = 1 + \dfrac{Z_1}{2Z_2}$

Therefore, $\cosh \gamma' \ell = 1 + \dfrac{Z_1}{2Z_2}$

$$= 1 + \frac{\dfrac{Z_C}{2} + Z_0 \tanh \dfrac{\gamma \ell}{2}}{\dfrac{Z_0}{\sinh \gamma \ell}}$$

$$\sinh \gamma \ell = \frac{e^{\gamma \ell} - e^{-\gamma \ell}}{2}$$

$$\cosh \gamma \ell = \frac{e^{\gamma \ell} + e^{-\gamma \ell}}{2}$$

$$\tanh \gamma \ell = \frac{e^{\gamma \ell} - e^{-\gamma \ell}}{e^{\gamma \ell} + e^{-\gamma \ell}}$$

The above equation can be written as

$$\tanh \frac{\gamma \ell}{2} = \frac{\cosh \gamma \ell - 1}{\sinh \gamma \ell}$$

Therefore, $\qquad \cosh \gamma \ell = \dfrac{Z_C}{2Z_0} \sinh \gamma \ell + \cosh \gamma \ell$

This equation is called Campbell's equation and is used to determine the values of γ and the effects of loading that reduces attenuation and distortion on lines.

As shown in Fig. 8.9 for a cable, Z_2 is capacitive and the cable capacitance plus lumped inductances will act as a low pass filter. Therefore,

$$f_c = \frac{1}{\pi\sqrt{LC}}$$

The attenuation is reduced below cutoff frequency and the attenuation increases above cutoff frequency. The cutoff frequency can be raised by reducing L or C. Reducing L will increase the attenuation and reducing C will increase the expenditure.

Practically, the distortionless line is not obtained by loading, because R and L are functions of frequency. The eddy current losses in the loading inductors will change this condition. However, there will be an improvement in the loaded cable over the unloaded cable for a reasonable frequency range.

Example 8.1

Find the characteristic impedance in a low-loss transmission line with

$$L = 0.1\ \mu H/m \quad and \quad C = 100\ pF/m$$

Solution   The characteristic impedance is

$$Z_0 = \sqrt{L/C} = \sqrt{0.1 \times 10^{-6}/(100 \times 10^{-12})} = 31.62\ \Omega$$

Example 8.2

A transmission line has a characteristic impedance of $710\angle-16°\Omega$ at 1 kHz. At this frequency, attenuation and phase shift is found to be 0.01 Np and 0.035 radians per km respectively. Calculate the primary constants of the line.

Solution $Z_0 = 710\angle-16°\ \Omega,\ \alpha = 0.01\ \text{Np},\ \beta = 0.035\ \text{rad}, f = 1\ \text{kHz},$

$$\gamma = 0.01 + j0.035 = \sqrt{(10^2 + 35^2)10^{-3}}\ \angle\tan^{-1}3.5 = 36.4 \times 10^{-3}\ \angle74°3'$$

We know that, $Z_0 = \sqrt{\dfrac{R + j\omega L}{G + j\omega C}}$ and $\gamma = \sqrt{(R + j\omega L)(G + j\omega C)}$

Therefore, $Z_0\gamma = R + j\omega L$

or
$$\begin{aligned}
R + j\omega L = Z_0\gamma &= (710\angle-16°) \times (36.4 \times 10^{-3}\ \angle74°3') \\
&= 25.84\angle58°3' \\
&= 25.84\cos(58°3') + j25.84\sin(58°3') \\
&= 13.68 + j21.89
\end{aligned}$$

Therefore, $R = 13.68\ \Omega/km$

$\omega L = 21.89$

or $2\pi \times 10^3\ L = 21.89$

$$L = \frac{21.89}{2000\pi} = 3.484\ \text{mH/km}$$

Dividing γ by Z_0 gives

$$\frac{\sqrt{(R+j\omega L)(G+j\omega C)}}{\sqrt{(R+j\omega L)/(G+j\omega C)}} = G + j\omega C = \frac{36.4 \times 10^{-3} \angle 74°3'}{710 \angle -16°}$$

Therefore, $\quad G + j\omega C = 0.05127 \times 10^{-3} \angle 90°3'$
$$= [0.05127 \cos (90°3') + j0.05127 \sin (90°3')]10^{-3}$$
$$= j0.51279 \times 10^{-3}$$

Here, $G = 0$ and $\omega C = 0.051269 \times 10^{-3}$

Hence, $\quad C = \dfrac{0.051269 \times 10^{-3}}{2 \times \pi \times 1000} = 0.00812 \ \mu\text{F/km}$

Example 8.3

A transmission line of 2 km long operates at 10 kHz and has parameters $R = 30 \ \Omega/km$, $C = 80 \ nF/km$, $L = 2.2$ mH/km and $G = 20 \ nV/km$. Find the characteristic impedance, propagation constant, attenuation and phase shift per km.

Solution Given $l = 2$ km, $R = 30 \ \Omega/\text{km}$, $L = 2.2 \ \text{mH/km}$, $G = 20 \ \text{n}\Omega/\text{km}$, $C = 80 \ \text{nF/km}$ and $f = 10$ kHz
Therefore, $R + j\omega L = 30 + j(2 \times \pi \times 10 \times 10^{-3}) \times 2.2 \times 10^{-3} = 141.4479 \angle 77.75°$
$$G = j\omega C = 20 \times 10^{-9} + j2 \times \pi \ 10 \times 10^{3} \times 80 \times 10^{-9} = 5.0265 \times 10^{-3} \angle 89.99°$$

The characteristic impedance Z_0 is

$$Z_0 = \sqrt{\frac{R+j\omega L}{G+j\omega C}}$$

$$= \sqrt{\frac{141.4479 \angle 77.75°}{5.0265 \times 10^{-3} \angle 89.99°}} = 167.7511 \angle -6.12 \ \Omega$$

$$\gamma = \sqrt{ZY} = \sqrt{(R+j\omega L)(G+j\omega C)}$$

$$= \sqrt{141.4479 \angle 77.75° \times 5.0265 \times 10^{-3} \angle 89.99°}$$

$$\gamma = \alpha + j\beta = 0.09 + j0.8383$$

Hence, attenuation constant, $\alpha = 0.09$ neper/km
and phase constant, $\beta = 0.8383$ rad/km

Example 8.4

A generator of 1 V, 1 kHz supplies power to a 1000 km open wire line terminated in Z_0 having the following parameters: $R = 10.4 \ \Omega/km$, $L = 0.00367 \ H/km$, $G = 0.8 \times 10^{-6} \ \Omega/km$, $C = 0.00835 \ \mu F/km$. Calculate the power delivered at the receiving end.

Solution

$$Z = R + j\omega L = 10.4 + j(2 \times \pi \times 1000) \times 3.67 \times 10^{-3} = 10.4 + j23.0592$$
$$= 25.2959 \angle 65.72°$$
$$Y = G + j\omega C = 0.8 \times 10^{-6} + j(2 \times \pi \times 1000) \times 0.00835 \times 10^{-6} = 0.8 \times 10^{-6} + j5.2464 \times 10^{-5}$$
$$= 5.247 \times 10^{-5} \angle 89.12°$$

The characteristic impedance is

$$Z_0 = \sqrt{\frac{Z}{Y}} = \sqrt{\frac{R + j\omega L}{G + j\omega C}} = \sqrt{\frac{25.2959 \angle 65.72°}{5.247 \times 10^{-5} \angle 89.12°}} = 694.3342 \angle -11.7° \ \Omega$$

The propagation constant is

$$\gamma = \sqrt{ZY} = \sqrt{(R + j\omega L)(G + j\omega C)}$$

$$= \sqrt{(25.2959 \angle 65.72°)(5.247 \times 10^{-5} \angle 89.12°)} = 0.03643 \angle 77.42°$$

Therefore, $\gamma = \alpha + j\beta = 0.007934 + j0.03555$

Then, $\alpha = 0.007934$ neper/km

$\beta = 0.03555$ rad/km

For 1000 km long transmission line, the propagation constant can be written as,

$$e^{-\gamma t} = e^{-(\alpha + j\beta)t} = e^{-\alpha t} \angle -\beta l$$

$$= e^{-(0.007934)(1000)} \angle -(0.03553)(1000)$$

$$= 3.5835 \times 10^{-4} \angle -35.53°$$

The transmission line is terminated in Z_0 at the load side and the line is connected to a generator of 1 V. Since the internal impedance is not mentioned, it is assumed that the generator is ideal. The set up is as shown in the Fig. 8.10.

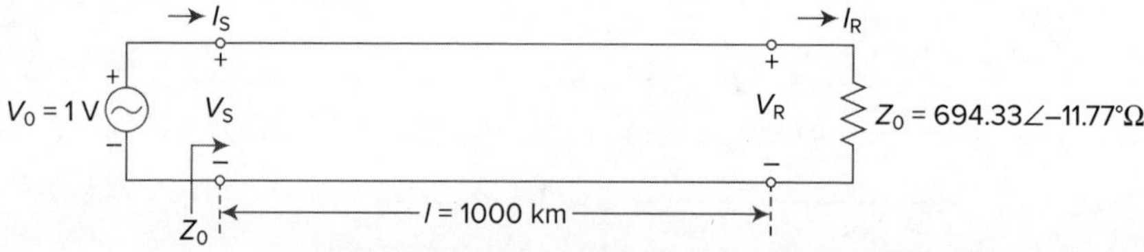

Figure 8.10

At input side, $V_s = V_g = 1\angle 0°$ V

Thus $$I_S = \frac{V_S}{Z_0} = \frac{1\angle 0°}{694.3342 \angle -11.7°} = 1.442 \times 10^{-3} \angle +11.7° \ \text{A}$$

Hence current at the receiving end is given by

$$I_R = I_S \cdot e^{-\gamma t}$$

$$= [1.4402 \times 10^{-3} \angle 11.7°][e^{-(0.007934)(1000)} \angle -(0.03553)(1000)]$$

$$= [1.4402 \times 10^{-3} \angle 11.7°][3.5835 \times 10^{-4} \angle -35.53 \ \text{rad}]$$

$$= [1.4402 \times 10^{-3} \angle 11.7°][3.5835 \angle 10^{-4} \angle -235.72°]$$

$$= 0.516 \times 10^{-6} \angle 224.02° \ A = 0.5161 \angle -224.02 \ \mu A$$

The receiving end voltage is

$$V_R = I_R Z_0 = (0.5161 \times 10^{-6} \angle -224.02)(694.33 \angle -11.7°)$$

$$= 0.3583 \times 10^{-3} \angle -235.72° \ \text{V}$$

Hence received power is

$$P_R = V_R I_R \cos \theta \qquad \text{where } \theta = \angle V_R - \angle I_R$$

$$= 0.3583 \times 10^{-3} \times 0.5161 \times 10^{-6} \cos (11.7) = 0.181 \ n\text{W}$$

Example 8.5

The primary constants of a 10 km open wire transmission line are:

$$R = 14 \ \Omega/km, \ L = 4.6 \ mH/km, \ C = 0.01 \ \mu F/km \ and \ G = 0.3 \ \mu\Omega/km$$

Also, the sending end has a generator of e.m.f of $10\angle 0°$ V at 1 kHz and the internal resistance of 600 Ω. Its receiving end is terminated by an impedance equal to the characteristic impedance of the line. Find the (i) characteristic impedance (ii) attenuation constant and phase constant (iii) sending-end current (iv) sending-end voltage (v) sending-end power (vi) receiving-end current (vii) receiving-end voltage (viii) receiving-end power (ix) line power loss in dB (x) wavelength of the signal and (xi) length of the line in wavelengths.

Solution   Given $R = 14 \ \Omega/km$, $L = 4.6 \ mH/km$, $C = 0.01 \ \mu F/km$ and $G = 0.3 \ \mu\Omega/km$, $V_G = 10$ V, $Z_0 = 600 \ \Omega$, $l = 10$ km and $f = 1$ kHz

Therefore, $R + j\omega L = R + j2\pi f L = 14 + j2\pi \times 10^3 \times 4.6 \times 10^{-3} = 14 + j28.9 = 32.1\angle 64.2°$

and $G + j\omega C = G + j2\pi f C = 0.3 \times 10^{-6} + j2\pi \times 10^3 \times 0.01 \times 10^{-6}$

$$= 0.3 \times 10^{-6} + j62.8 \times 10^{-6} = 62.8 \times 10^{-6} \ \angle 89.7°$$

(i)   The characteristic impedance is

$$Z_0 = \sqrt{\frac{Z}{Y}} = \sqrt{\frac{R + j\omega L}{G + j\omega C}} = \sqrt{\frac{32.1\angle 64.2°}{62.8 \times 10^{-6} \ \angle 89.7°}} = 715\angle -12.8°$$

$$= (697 - j158) \ \Omega$$

(ii)   The propagation constant is

$$\gamma = \sqrt{ZY} = \sqrt{(R + j\omega L)(G + j\omega C)} = \sqrt{(32.1\angle 64.2°)(62.8 \times 10^{-6} \ \angle 89.7°)}$$

$$= 0.0449\angle 77° = (0.01 + j0.0438) = (\alpha + j\beta)$$

Hence, the attenuation constant, $\alpha = 0.01$ neper/km and the phase constant, $\beta = 0.0438$ rad/km.

(iii)   The sending end current is

$$I_S = \frac{V_G}{(Z_S + Z_0)} = \frac{10\angle 0°}{(600 + 697 - j158)}$$

$$= \frac{10\angle 0°}{1307\angle -6.96°} = 7.65\angle 6.96° \ mA$$

(iv)   The sending end voltage is

$$V_S = I_S Z_S$$
$$= 7.65\angle 6.96° \times 10^{-2} \times 715\angle -12.8°$$
$$= 5.47\angle -5.8° \text{V}$$

(v)   The sending end power is

$$P_S = |V_S| \, |I_S| \times \text{power factor}$$
$$= 5.47 \times 7.65 \times 10^{-3} \times \cos (6.96° + 5.8°)$$
$$= 41.8 \cos 12.76° = 40.8 \ mW$$

Alternatively, $P_S = |I_S|^2 R_r = (7.65 \times 10^{-3})^2 \times 697 \ W = 40.8 \ mW$

(vi)   The receiving-end current is

$$I_R = \frac{V_R}{Z_R} = \frac{2.02\angle -257°}{715\angle -12.8°} = 2.83\angle -244° \ mA$$

(vii) The receiving-end voltage while $l = 100$ km is

$$V_R = V_s e^{-\alpha t} e^{-j\beta t}$$
$$= 5.47\angle{-5.8°}\ e^{-0.01 \times 100} e^{-j0.0438 \times 100}$$
$$= 5.47\ e^{-1.0} \angle(-5.8° - 4.38\ \text{rad})$$
$$= 5.47 \times 0.368 \angle(-5.8° - 25.1°)$$
$$= 2.02\angle{-257°}\ \text{V}$$

(viii) The receiving-end power is

$$P_R = |I_R|^2 R_R = (2.83 \times 10^{-3})^2 \times 697 = 5.58\ \text{mW}$$

(ix) The transmission line loss is $10 \log_{10}\left[\dfrac{40.8}{5.58}\right] = 8.7\ \text{dB}$

(x) The signal wavelength is $\lambda = \left(\dfrac{2\pi}{\beta}\right) = \left(\dfrac{2\pi}{0.0438}\right) = 143.5\ \text{km}$

(xi) Length of the line in wavelength is, l in wavelength $= \left(\dfrac{100}{143.5}\right) = 0.697\,\lambda$

Example 8.6

The primary constants for transmission line per loop-km are:

$$R = 6\ \Omega,\ L = 2.2\ mH,\ C = 0.005\ \mu H\ \text{and}\ G = 0.25\ \mu\mho$$

If the applied signal frequency is 1 kHz, then determine

(i) The terminating impedance to have no reflected waves in the line,

(ii) The line attenuation in a distance of 100 km, with proper termination, and

(iii) The phase velocity of the transmitted wave.

Solution If the line is terminated by its characteristic impedance, there will be no reflection.

(i) The total series impedance is
$$Z = R + j\omega L = 6 + j2\pi \times 10^3 \times 2.2 \times 10^{-3} = 15.04\angle 66.5°$$
The total shunt admittance is
$$Y = G + j\omega C = 0.25 \times 10^{-6} + j^2 \pi \times 10^3 \times 0.005 \times 10^{-6}$$
$$= (0.25 + j3.14)10^{-6} = 31.42 \times 10^{-6}\angle 89.5°$$

Therefore, $Z_0 = \sqrt{\dfrac{Z}{Y}} = \sqrt{\dfrac{15.04\angle 66.5°}{31.4 \times 10^{-6}\ \angle 89.5°}} = 692\angle{-12.5°}\ \Omega = Z_R.$

(ii) The propagation constant is
$$\gamma = \sqrt{ZY}$$
$$= \sqrt{(15.04\angle 66.5°)(31.4 \times 10^{-6}\ \angle 89.5°)}$$
$$= \sqrt{(15.04 \times 31.4 \times 10^{-6})}\ \angle 78°$$
$$= 21.73 \times 10^{-3}\angle 78°$$
$$= 21.73 \times 10^{-3}\ (\cos 78° + j \sin 78°)$$
$$= 0.022(0.2079 + j0.9/81)$$
$$= 0.0046 + j0.0215$$

Since $\gamma = \alpha + j\beta$, we have $\alpha = 0.0046$ neper/km and $\beta = 0.0215$ rad/km

Therefore, the total attenuation in 100 km is $\alpha = 100 \times 0.0046 = 0.46$ neper

or $\qquad 0.46 \times 8.686 = 3.99$ dB

(iii) The phase velocity of the wave is

$$v_p = \left(\frac{\omega}{\beta}\right) = \left(\frac{6.28 \times 10^3}{0.0215}\right) = 2.9 \times 10^5 \text{ km/sec}$$

Example 8.7

A 12 km open wire line is terminated in its characteristic impedance. At a certain frequency, the signal voltage measured at a distance of 1 km reduces to 90% of the sending end voltage. Determine voltage at the receiving end in terms of the sending end voltage V_S.

Solution Signal voltage at the sending end $= V_S$

Signal voltage v at 1 km $= 0.9\, V_S$

Therefore $\qquad V = V_S e^{-\gamma}$

or $\qquad 0.9 V_S = V_S e^{-\gamma}$

$\qquad\qquad e^{-\gamma} = 0.9$

When $L = 12$ km, the voltage V is given by

$$V_R = V_S e^{\gamma \times 12}$$
$$= V_S e^{(-\gamma)12}$$
$$= V_S (0.9)^{12} = 0.282\, V_S$$

or $\qquad V_R = 28.2\%$ of V_S

Example 8.8

A telephone line has primary constants per km as $R = 20\ \Omega$, $L = 10$ mH, $C = 0.1\ \mu F$ and insulation resistance between conductors is $0.1\ M\Omega$. Find the input impedance if the line length is very long and signal has an angular velocity of 5000 rad/sec.

Solution Given $R = 20\ \Omega$, $L = 10$ mH $= 10^{-2}$ H, $G = \dfrac{1}{0.1 \times 10^6} = 10^{-5}$ S, $C = 0.1\ \mu F = 10^{-7}\ F$ and $\omega = 500$ rad/sec.

Since the line length is large, it may be treated as an infinite length and its input impedance equals characteristic impedance Z_0.

Therefore, $\qquad Z_m = Z_0 = \sqrt{\dfrac{R + \omega L}{G + j\omega C}} = \dfrac{\sqrt{20 + j5000 \times 10^{-2}}}{10^{-5} + j5000 \times 10^{-7}}$

$$= \dfrac{\sqrt{20 + j50}}{(10 + j500)10^{-6}} = 10^3 \times \dfrac{\sqrt{2 + j5}}{1 + j50}$$

$$= 10^3 \times \dfrac{\sqrt{53.85 \angle 68.2°}}{50.01 \angle 88.85°} = 328 \angle -10.33°\ \Omega$$

Example 8.9

The primary constants of a 20-km telephone line per loop-km are: $R = 50\ \Omega$, $L = 30$ mH, $C = 0.05\ \mu F$ and $G = 0$. If the line is terminated in an impedance equal to its characteristic impedance at 5000 rad/sec and e.m.f of 10 V, at this angular frequency, is maintained across the sending end. Find the (i) value of the receiving-end current as well as its phase with respect to the sending-end voltage, and (ii) attenuation of the line is dB.

Solution With the line terminated in its characteristic impedance, it behaves as a 20-km action of an infinitely long line.

Here, $\qquad V_R = V_S e^{-\gamma}$

where $\qquad \gamma = \sqrt{(R + j\omega L)(G + j\omega C)}$

$$= \sqrt{(50 + j150) + (0 + j2.5 \times 10^{-4})}$$

$$= 0.199\angle 80°47'$$

So that $\qquad \alpha = 0.032$ neper/km

and $\qquad \beta = 0.197$ rad/km or $11.2°$ per/km

Here, $\qquad |V_R| = 10e^{(-20 \times 0.033)} = 5.27$

and $\qquad \angle\theta = -20 \times 11.2 = -224°$

Then $\qquad Z_0 = \sqrt{\dfrac{(R + j\omega L)}{(G + j\omega C)}}$

$$= 10^2 \sqrt{(50 + j150)/j2.5}$$

$$= 795\angle -9°12'\ \Omega$$

Also, $\qquad I_R = \left(\dfrac{5.27\angle -224°}{795\angle -9°12'}\right) A$

$$= 6.6\angle -215°\ \text{mA}$$

Here the attenuation is $20\log_{10}\left(\dfrac{10}{5.27}\right) = 5.6$ dB

Example 8.10

If a cable pair is short-circuited at 10 km from one end, find the input impedance measured at the free end under the following conditions:

> *Attenuation constant, $\alpha = 0.616$ dB/km,*
> *Phase constant, $\beta = 1.400$ rad/km, and*
> *Characteristic impedance, $Z_0 = 52.55\angle -3.1°\ \Omega$*

Solution Under short-circuit conditions, the input impedance is

$$Z_{\text{in}} = Z_0 \tanh^{(\gamma l)}$$

$$= Z_0 \tanh (e^{xl}e^{j\beta t})$$

$$= Z_0 \frac{[e^{\alpha l}e^{j\beta l} - e^{-\alpha l}]}{[e^{\alpha l}e^{j\beta l} + e^{-\alpha l}e^{-j\beta l}]}$$

Here $20 \log_{10}\left(\dfrac{V_S}{V_R}\right) = 6.16$, with $l = 1 - 10$ km,

or $\qquad\qquad \log_{10}\left(\dfrac{V_S}{V_R}\right) = 0.308,$

or $\qquad\qquad \left(\dfrac{V_S}{V_R}\right) = e^{\alpha l} = 2.032$

With a phase change of 14 rad over a distance of 10 km, we have $e^{j\beta t} = 1\angle 14$ rad

Hence, $\qquad Z_{\text{in}} = Z_0 \dfrac{(2.032\angle 14 \text{ rad} - 0.492\angle -14 \text{ rad})}{(2.032\angle 14 \text{ rad} + 0.492\angle -14 \text{ rad})}$

Now $\qquad 1\angle 14 \text{ rad} = 1\angle(4\pi + 1.433) \text{ rad} = 1\angle 82.1° = (0.137 + j0.991)$

and $\qquad 1\angle -14 \text{ rad} = 1 - 82.1°$

$\qquad\qquad\qquad = (0.137 - j0.991)$

when $\qquad (0.137 + j0.991) = (0.2784 + j2.014)$

and $\qquad 0.492(0.137 - j0.991) = (0.0674 - j0.488)$

So, $\qquad Z_{\text{in}} = Z_0 \dfrac{[(0.2784 - 0.0674) + j(2.014 - 0.488)]}{[(0.2784 + 0.0674) + j(2.014 - 0.488)]}$

$\qquad\qquad\quad = Z_0[(0.2110 + j2.504)]/[0.3458 + j1.526]$

$\qquad\qquad\quad = 52.5\angle -3.1°[(2.51\angle 85.2°/1.56\angle 77.1°)] = 84.5\angle 5° \ \Omega$

Example 8.11

The primary constants of an open-wire telephone line at 796 kHz are $R = 4\ \Omega/km$, $L = 3\ mH/km$, $C = 0.015\ \mu F/km$, and $G = 1\ \mu\Omega^{-1}/km$.

(i) Find the attenuation and phase constants, phase velocity and characteristic impedance.

(ii) Also, find the voltage at a distance of 100 km, if the line is terminated in its characteristic impedance and if 1 V (r.m.s) is applied at the input end.

Solution

(i) $\qquad\qquad Z = (R + j\omega L)$

or $\qquad\qquad Z = (4 + j15)$

or $\qquad\qquad\quad = 15.53\angle 75.1°$

$\qquad\qquad\quad Y = (G + j\omega C)$

$\qquad\qquad\qquad = (1 + j75)10^{-6}$

$\qquad\qquad\qquad = 75 \times 10^{-6}\angle 89.2°$

$\qquad\qquad\quad \gamma = \sqrt{ZY}$

$\qquad\qquad\qquad = \sqrt{.001164\angle 164.3°}$

$\qquad\qquad\qquad = 0.03415\angle 82.15°$

$\qquad\qquad\quad \alpha = 0.00466 \text{ neper/km}$

$\qquad\qquad\quad \beta = 0.0338 \text{ rad/km}$

$$v_p = \left(\frac{\omega}{\beta}\right) = \left(\frac{5000}{0.0338}\right) = 148000 \text{ km/sec}$$

$$Z_0 = 455\angle{-7.1°} = (452 - j56.1)\ \Omega$$

$$I_S = \left(\frac{V_S}{Z_0}\right)$$

$$= [1\angle 0°/455\angle{-7.1°}]$$
$$= 0.022\angle 7.1°\ \text{A}$$

$$v = \sqrt{2}e^{-0.00466z}\sin(5000t - 0.0338z)$$

where $z = 100$

Hence, $v_{100} = 0.627\angle{-194°}\ \text{V}$

Example 8.12

In a 100 km telephone transmission line, at 1000 Hz, $Z_0 = (685 - j92)\ \Omega$, $\alpha = 0.00497$ neper/km and $\beta = 0.352$ rad/km. With the line terminated in $Z_R = (2000 + j0)\ \Omega$, the line is supplied by a generator with an e.m.f. of 700 Ω (r.m.s) and an internal resistance of 700 Ω. Estimate the values of (i) sending end impedance, (ii) sending-end voltage, current as well as power, and (iii) receiving-end voltage, current and power.

Solution

Given $\qquad \beta l = 3.52\ \text{rad} = 202°$

Hence $\qquad e^{\gamma l} = e^{(0.497 + j3.52)}$

$$= e^{0.497}\angle 202°$$
$$= 1.64(\cos 202° + j\sin 202°)$$
$$= -1.52 - j0.615$$

$$e^{-\gamma l} = e^{-(0.497)}\angle{-202°} = (-0.566 + j0.229)$$

The sending-end impedance is given by

$$Z_S = Z_0\left[\frac{(Z_R + Z_0)e^{\gamma d} + (Z_R - Z_0)e^{-\gamma d}}{(Z_R + Z_0)e^{\gamma d} - (Z_R - Z_0)e^{-\gamma d}}\right]$$

where $d = l$.

Hence, $\qquad Z_S = (685 - j92) \times \left[\dfrac{(2685 - j92)e^{\gamma l} + (1315 + j92)e^{-\gamma l}}{(2685 - j92)e^{\gamma l} - (1315 + j92)e^{-\gamma l}}\right]$

$$= 691\angle{-7.65°} \times \frac{(5060\angle 14.4°)}{(3810\angle 27.45°)} = 919\angle{-20.7°} = (861 - j325)\ \Omega$$

$$|I_S| = |E_g/(Z_g + Z_S)| = |10/(700 + 861 - j325)| = 6.26\ \text{mA (r.m.s.)}$$

$$|E_S| = |I_S||Z_S| = 6.26 \times 10^{-3} \times 919 = 5.75\ \text{V (r.m.s.)}$$

$$|P_S| = (6.26 \times 10^{-3})^2 \times 861\ \text{W} = 33.8\ \text{mW}$$

$$[6.26 \times 10^{-3}/|I_R|] = (3810/2 \times 691)$$

So,
$$|I_R| = 2.28 \text{ mA}$$
$$|E_R| = |I_R| \, |Z_R| = 2.28 \times 10^{-3} \times 2000 = 4.56 \text{ V}$$

$$P_R = \frac{|E_R|}{\sqrt{2}} \times \frac{|I_R|}{\sqrt{2}} = 5.2 \text{ mW}$$

Example 8.13

A lossless transmission line of length l = 30 m at 20 MHz with air as dielectric. Find the voltage at a distance of 20, if the line has a characteristic impedance of (50 + j0) Ω and terminated by a load impedance of (25 + j0) Ω with a sending-end voltage of 100 V.

Solution Here,
$$(1 - x) = (30 - 20) = 10 \text{ m}$$

$$\lambda = \left(\frac{c}{f} \right) = \left(\frac{3 \times 10^3}{20 \times 10^6} \right) = 15 \text{ m}$$

$$\beta(l - x) = \left(\frac{2\pi}{\lambda} \right)(10)\left(\frac{2\pi}{15} \right)(10) = \pi + \left(\frac{\pi}{3} \right)$$

$$\cos\left[\pi + \left(\frac{\pi}{3} \right) \right] = -\cos\left(\frac{\pi}{3} \right) = -0.500$$

$$\sin\left[\pi + \left(\frac{\pi}{3} \right) \right] = -\sin\left(\frac{\pi}{3} \right) = -0.866$$

$$\cos \beta(l) = \cos\left(\frac{2\pi}{15} \right)(30) = \cos(4\pi) = 1$$

$$\sin \beta(l) = \sin(4p) = 0$$

Here,
$$V_x = V_s \left[\frac{\{Z_L \cos \beta(l - x) + jZ_0 \sin \beta(l - x)\}}{\{Z_L \cos \beta l + jZ_0 \sin \beta l\}} \right]$$

Substituting $x = 20$, we have

$$V_{20} = 100 \left[\frac{\{25(-0.5) + j50(-0.866)\}}{\{(25)(1) + j(50)(0)\}} \right] = (-50 - j173.2) \text{ V}$$

i.e.,
$$|V_{20}| = \sqrt{(-50)^2 + (-173.2)^2} = 180.3 \text{ V}$$

$$\phi = \tan^{-1}\left[\frac{(-173.2)}{(-50)} \right] = 252°54'$$

Example 8.14

In a parallel-wire line, parameters at a frequency of 4 MHz are: $R = 0.025\ \Omega/m$, $L = 2\ \mu H/m$, $C = 5.56\ pF/m$ and $G = 0$. Find the efficiency of power transmission, if the line is 100 m long and is terminated in a resistance of 300 Ω.

Solution

$$Z_0 = \sqrt{\frac{L}{C}\left[1+\left(\frac{j}{2\omega}\right)\left\{\left(\frac{G}{C}\right)-\left(\frac{R}{L}\right)\right\}\right]}$$

$$= \sqrt{\frac{L}{C}} = \sqrt{\frac{2\times10^{-6}}{5.56\times10^{-12}}} = 600\ \Omega$$

$$\alpha = \left(\frac{1}{2}\right)\left[R\sqrt{\frac{C}{L}}+G\sqrt{\frac{L}{C}}\right] = \left(\frac{1}{2}\right)\left[R\sqrt{\frac{C}{L}}\right]$$

$$= \left(\frac{1}{2}\right)\left[0.025\times\sqrt{\frac{5.56\times10^{-12}}{2\times10^{-6}}}\right] = 21\times10^{-6}$$

$$e^{-\alpha l} = 0.998, \text{ with } l = 100\ m$$

The power dissipated, is given by

$$P_d = I_r^2 R\int_0^{100}\left[\left(\cos^2\beta y+\left(\frac{1}{4}\right)\sin^2\beta y\right)\right]dy$$

Since $\qquad I = I_r\cos\beta y + j\left(\frac{V_R}{R_0}\right)\sin\beta y$

and $\qquad V_R = I_r R_0$

Here, $\qquad R = 0.025$ and $\beta = \omega\sqrt{LC} = 0.0838$.

Also, $\qquad \left(\frac{R_r}{R_0}\right)^2 = \left(\frac{1}{4}\right)$

So, $\qquad P_d = 1.51 I_r^2$

Hence, the power supplied to the load is

$$P_{\text{load}} = 300 I_r^2$$

Hence, $\qquad \eta = \left(\frac{P_{\text{load}}}{P_{\text{load}}+P_d}\right) = 3\frac{00 I_r^2}{(300+1.51)}I_r^2 = 99.5\%$

Example 8.15

A high-frequency transmission line of zero leakage has a small but finite attenuation, with $R = 0.01\,\Omega$, $L = 7 \times 10^{-9}$ H, $C = 0.15$ pF all per cm length of line. Compute the receiving-end voltage for an input of 1 V and a frequency of 200 MHz.

Solution

Now
$$\gamma = j\beta = j\omega\sqrt{LC} = j2\pi \times 200 \times 10^6 \sqrt{7 \times 10^{-9} \times 0.15 \times 10^{-12}} = j0.04072$$

$$v = \left(\frac{2\pi f}{\beta}\right) - \left(\frac{2\pi \times 200 \times 10^6}{0.04072}\right) = 3.09 \times 10^{10} \text{ cm/sec}$$

$$\lambda = \left(\frac{c}{f}\right) = \left(\frac{3.09 \times 10^{10}}{200 \times 10^6}\right) = 154.5 \text{ cm}$$

Here, $\left(\dfrac{\lambda}{4}\right) = 38.6$ cm is the length of the line.

Also,
$$Z_1 = \left(\frac{1}{2}\right)Rl = \left(\frac{1}{2}\right)(0.01 \times 38.6) = 0.193\,\Omega$$

$$I_S = \left(\frac{V_S}{Z_i}\right) = \left(\frac{1}{0.193}\right) = 5.18 \text{ A}$$

$$Z_0 = \sqrt{\left(\frac{L}{C}\right)} = \sqrt{\left(\frac{7 \times 10^{-9}}{0.15 \times 10^{-12}}\right)} = 216\,\Omega$$

$$V_R = jZ_0 I_S = -j216 \times 5.18 = -j1120 \text{ V}$$

Example 8.16

A particular telephone cable has following primary constants. $R = 44\,\Omega$/km R, $G = 1\,\mu\text{℧}$/km, $L = 0.001$ H/km, $C = 0.065\,\mu$F/km. It is loading with 88 mH loading coils of resistance 3.7 Ω with 1.5 km spacing. Find the approximate value of the Z_0, α and β for the cable at 1600 Hz. Also find the cut-off frequency.

Solution   Let us find the values of constants including loading coils.
Inductance per unit length of coil added

$$L = \frac{88}{1.5} = 58.667 \text{ mH/km}$$

Therefore, $L = $ Total inductance/km
$$= 0.001 + 58.667 \times 10^{-3} = 0.05967 \text{ H/km}$$
Resistance per unit length of coil added

$$R = \frac{37}{1.5} = 2.4667\,\Omega\text{/km}$$

Therefore, $R = $ Total resistance/km $= 44 + 2.4667 = 46.4667\,\Omega$/km

The approximate values for the cable are

$$Z_0 = \sqrt{\frac{L'}{C}} = \sqrt{\frac{0.05967}{0.065 \times 10^{-6}}} = 958.123 \,\Omega$$

$$\alpha = \frac{R'}{2}\sqrt{\frac{C}{L'}} + \frac{G}{2}\sqrt{\frac{L'}{C}} = \frac{46.4667}{2}\sqrt{\frac{0.065 \times 10^{-6}}{0.05967}} + \frac{1 \times 10^{-6}}{2}\sqrt{\frac{0.05967}{0.065 \times 10^{-6}}}$$

$$= 0.0247 \text{ nepers/km}$$

$$\beta = \omega\sqrt{L'C} = 1600 \times 2\pi\sqrt{0.05967 \times 0.065 \times 10^{-6}} = 0.626 \text{ rad/km}$$

The cut-off frequency is given by

$$f_C = \frac{1}{\pi\sqrt{L'C}} = \frac{1}{\pi\sqrt{0.05967 \times 0.065 \times 10^{-6}}} = 5.111 \text{ kHz}$$

Example 8.17

For a cable it is decided to provide lumped loading. The primary constant of the cable are $R = 40\,\Omega/km$, $L = 1\, mH/km$, $G = 1\,\mu\mho/km$, $C = 0.05\,\mu F/km$. Find the new value of inductance required to achieve the distortionless condition. By what factor, the inductance is required to be raised?

Solution

The distortionless condition is

$$RC = LG$$

$$L' = \frac{RC}{G} = \frac{40 \times 0.05 \times 10^{-6}}{1 \times 10^{-6}} = 2\text{H/km}$$

The factor by which inductance to be increased $= \dfrac{L'}{L} = \dfrac{2}{1 \times 10^{-3}} = 2000$

Example 8.18

How much inducting loading is required to make a 16 gauge cable distortionless? Assume the line parameters are distortionless. The line parameters are $R = 42.1\,\Omega/km$, $G = 1.5\,\mu\mho/km$, $C = 0.062\,\mu F/km$ and $L = 1\, mH/km$.

Solution

According to the condition for distortionless line, the total inductance required by

$$RC = LG$$

where L' is the total inductance including additional inductance (L_{add}) along with original inductance.

$$L' = \frac{RC}{G} = \frac{42.1 \times 0.062 \times 10^{-6}}{1 \times 10^{-3}} = 2.6102 \text{ mH}$$

But $L' = L_{add} + L$

Therefore, $\qquad 2.1602 \times 10^{-3} = L_{add} + 1 \times 10^{-3}$

Hence, $L_{add} = 1.6102$ mH.

REVIEW QUESTIONS

1. What are the applications of transmission lines?
2. What is TEM wave propagation?
3. Do parallel-plane transmission lines satisfy TEM wave propagation?
4. Express the voltage and current waves in a transmission line in terms of the forward and backward-travelling waves.
5. Why are the boundary conditions required for the voltage and current in a transmission line?
6. Express the propagation constant and the characteristic impedance of a transmission line in terms of the parameters R, L, C and G.
7. Express the delay in a transmission line.
8. Define a perfectly matched transmission line?
9. What is the difference between a perfect conductor and an imperfect conductor?
10. What is the propagation constant in an imperfect transmission line?
11. How distortion can be reduced in a transmission line?
12. What is meant by loading?
13. What is meant by inductance loading of telephone cables?
14. Define and differentiate phase and group velocity of a transmission line.
15. Define the term characteristic impedance of a transmission line.
16. What is the relationship between group velocity and group velocity?
17. Write the Campbell's equation.
18. Differentiate lump parameters from distributed parameters of a transmission line.
19. The constants per km of a certain cable are: $R = 42.9\ \Omega$, $L = 0.07$ mH, $C = 0.01\ \mu$F and $G = 2.5\ \mu\mho$. Calculate α, Z_0 and v_p at $\omega = 5000$ radians per second.
20. A telephone line of 20 km long has the following constants per km resistance 90 Ω; capacitance 0.063 mF, inductance 0.1 mH and leakage conductance 1.5 $\mu\mho$. The line is terminated in its characteristic impedance. Calculate: (i) the characteristic impedance, (ii) wavelength, and (iii) the velocity of propagation when of 1 kHz is applied at the sending end.
21. The propagation constant at 1 kHz for a certain line is $\gamma = 0.008 + j0.0029$. The absolute value of the characteristic impedance is 700 Ω. Assuming that $G = 0$, find R, L and C.
22. The primary constants of a cable are $R = 80\ \Omega$/km, $L = 2$ mH/km, $G = 0.3\ \mu\mho$/km and $C = 0.07\ \mu$F/km. Calculate the secondary constants at frequency of 1 kHz.
23. At 8 MHz, the characteristic impedance of a transmission line is $(40 - j2)$ and the propagation constant is $(0.01 + j0.18)$ per meter. Find the primary constants.
24. A telephone line, 10 km long has the following constants: $Z_0 = 300\angle 0°\Omega$, $\beta = 0.1$ neper/km and $\alpha = 0.05$ radians km. Determine the receiving end current when 20 mA is sent at the transmitting end and when the receiving end is short circuited.
25. A telephone cable has a resistance of 20 Ω/km and a capacitance of 0.05 μF/km the inductance and leakage being negligible. The loading coils having an inductance of 80 mH and a resistance of 10 Ω are inserted at intervals of 0.7 km. Calculate the attenuation constant for frequency 5 kHz and the approximate value of cut-off frequency.

26. A certain cable has the following constants: $R = 42.9$ Ω/km, $L = 0.7$ mH/km, $C = 0.1$ μF/km and $G = 2.5$ μmho/km. It is loaded with coils having an inductance of 18 mH and a resistance of 1.4 Ω. The coils are spaced 1.135 km apart. Assuming the inductance of the load coils to be uniformly distributed, calculate α, Z_0 and v_p at $\omega = 5000$ radians per second.

27. A transmission line of characteristic impedance $620\angle{-44°}$ and propagation constant $\gamma = 0.0085 + j0.0062$ at frequency 500 Hz is loaded by coil of 50 mH and 1 Ω at intervals of 1.5 km. Calculate the value of Z_0, P, v_p and λ of the loaded cable.

28. A transmission line has the following primary constants at angular frequency of 0.4 rad/sec, $R = 40$ Ω/km, $L = 1$ mH/km, $C = 0.065$ μF/km and $G = 1.2 \times 10^{-6}$ mho/km. If loading coil of inductance 0.32 mH and resistance 2.5 Ω are added at regular intervals of 1.45 km, calculate the secondary constants of the loaded lines.

TRANSMISSION LINES–II (IMPEDANCE MATCHING IN HIGH FREQUENCY LINES)

9.1 INTRODUCTION

Transmission lines operating at Ultra High Frequencies (UHF) ranging from 300–3000 MHz or wavelengths from 100 cm to 10 cm have conductor and dielectric losses which can be neglected when the physical length of the transmission line is small. In this case, the total attenuation is nearly zero and the loss is primarily due to the phase shift. Hence, a UHF line is considered to be lossless if and only if the line length is assumed to be small. The UHF lines can become resonant at particular frequencies when the line is terminated with extreme impedances like the open or short circuit.

When a voltage is applied to a transmission line, it produces an incident wave. There is no reflected wave if the line is infinitely long or if it is a terminated by its characteristic impedance. However, when a line is terminated with impedances other than Z_R, a portion of the energy will be absorbed and remaining will be reflected back. Therefore, the line with any termination is a case of partial reflection whereas a line terminated with open and short-circuit condition is the case of total reflection.

In this chapter, methods of transforming impedance are developed whereby load and generator impedances may be matched for maximum power transfer. Also, the use of Smith chart and its applications are discussed.

9.2 INPUT IMPEDANCE RELATIONS

The input impedance (Z_{in}) of the transmission line is defined as the impedance measured across the input terminals of the transmission line. In other words, input impedance of a transmission line is the impedance seen looking into the sending end or input terminals. It is the impedance into which the source must work when the line is connected.

Thus,
$$Z_{in} = \frac{V_s}{I_s}$$

Referring to Fig 8.5 of the previous chapter, at the sending end, $x = 0$, $V_R = V_s$ and $I = I_s$. Applying the conditions above to Eqns. (8.25) and (8.26), we get

$$I_s = \frac{V_s}{Z_0}\sinh \gamma l + I_R \cosh \gamma l$$

Therefore,
$$Z_{\text{in}} = \frac{V_s}{I_s} = \frac{V_s \cosh \gamma l + I_R Z_0 \sinh \gamma l}{\dfrac{V_s}{Z_0} \sinh \gamma l + I_R \cosh \gamma l} \tag{9.1}$$

Multiplying numerator and denominator by $\dfrac{Z_0}{I_R}$, we get

$$Z_{\text{in}} = Z_0 \frac{\dfrac{V_R}{I_R} \cosh \gamma l + Z_0 \sinh \gamma l}{\dfrac{V_R}{I_R} \sinh \gamma l + Z_0 \cosh \gamma l} \tag{9.2}$$

But
$$Z_R = \frac{V_R}{I_R}$$

Therefore,
$$Z_{\text{in}} = Z_0 \frac{Z_R \cosh \gamma l + Z_0 \sinh \gamma l}{Z_R \sinh \gamma l + Z_0 \cosh \gamma l} \tag{9.3}$$

This can be further simplified by dividing the numerator and the denominator with $\cosh \gamma l$ and substituting

$$\frac{\sinh \gamma l}{\cosh \gamma l} = \tanh \gamma l$$

Therefore,
$$Z_{\text{in}} = Z_0 \frac{Z_R + Z_0 \tanh \gamma l}{Z_0 + Z_R \tanh \gamma l} \tag{9.4}$$

In an open-circuit line, $Z_{\text{in}} = Z_{oc}$ and $Z_R = \infty$. Then, Eqn. (9.4) will become

$$Z_{oc} = Z_0 \frac{1 + \dfrac{Z_0}{Z_R} \tanh \gamma l}{\dfrac{Z_0}{Z_R} + \tanh \gamma l} = Z_0 \coth \gamma l \tag{9.5}$$

Similarly, in a short-circuited line $Z_{\text{in}} = Z_{sc}$ and $Z_R = 0$. Then, Eqn. (9.4) will become

$$Z_{sc} = Z_0 \frac{0 + Z_0 \tanh \gamma l}{Z_0 + 0} = Z_0 \tanh \gamma l \tag{9.6}$$

A transmission line said to be properly terminated when it is terminated by its characteristic impedance. For such lines, the input impedance is the characteristic impedance of the line itself. However, if $Z_R \neq Z_0$, the input impedance will have a values between zero and infinity.

9.3 SHORT CIRCUIT AND OPEN CIRCUIT LINES

The input impedance of a line of length l is

$$Z_S = Z_0 \left[\frac{Z_R \cosh \gamma l + Z_0 \sinh \gamma l}{Z_0 \cosh \gamma l + Z_R \sinh \gamma l} \right] \tag{9.7}$$

(i) For the short circuit case, $Z_R = 0$
Therefore, $Z_{SC} = Z_0 \tanh \gamma l$

The input impedance Z_S is

$$Z_S = Z_0 \left[\frac{\cosh \gamma l + \left(\dfrac{Z_0}{Z_R} \right) \sinh \gamma l}{\left(\dfrac{Z_0}{Z_R} \right) \cosh \gamma l + \sinh \gamma l} \right] \qquad (9.8)$$

(ii) For the open circuit case, $Z_R = \infty$.

Therefore, substituting $Z_R = \infty$ in Eqn. (9.8), the input impedance of the open-circuit line of length l becomes

$$Z_{OC} = Z_0 \coth \gamma l \qquad (9.9)$$

Therefore, $Z_0 = \sqrt{Z_{OC} Z_{SC}}$ $\qquad (9.10)$

From the above two equations, $\tanh \gamma l = \sqrt{\dfrac{Z_{SC}}{Z_{OC}}}$ $\qquad (9.11)$

T and π sections equivalent to lines:

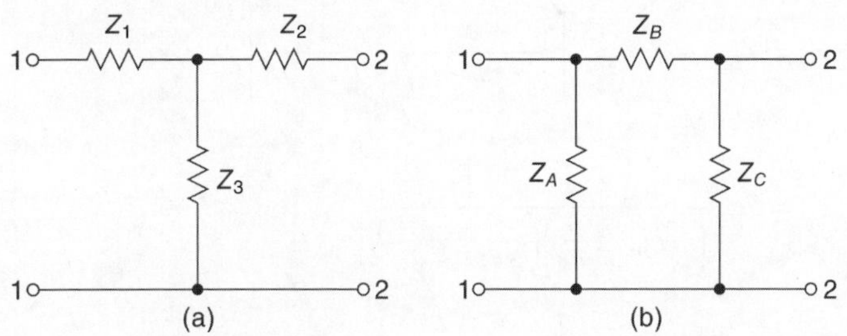

Figure 9.1 *(a) T-network and (b) π-network*

For T-section:

For the T-section shown in Fig. 9.1(a) to be equivalent, the open and short-circuit measurements should be identical. Therefore,

$$Z_{1oc} = Z_1 + Z_3 \qquad (9.12)$$

$$Z_{1sc} = Z_1 + \frac{Z_2 Z_3}{Z_2 + Z_3} \qquad (9.13)$$

$$Z_{2oc} = Z_2 + Z_3 \qquad (9.14)$$

$$Z_{2sc} = Z_2 + \frac{Z_1 Z_3}{Z_1 + Z_3} \qquad (9.15)$$

Subtracting Eqn. (9.13) from Eqn. (9.12),

$$Z_{1oc} - Z_{sc} = Z_3 - \frac{Z_2 Z_3}{Z_2 + Z_3} = \frac{Z_3^2}{Z_2 + Z_3} = \frac{Z_3^2}{Z_{2oc}}$$

$$Z_3 = \sqrt{Z_{2oc}(Z_{1oc} - Z_{1sc})}$$

Using Eqns. (9.12) and (9.14), we get

$$Z_1 = Z_{1oc} - Z_3 \qquad (9.16)$$

$$Z_2 = Z_{2oc} - Z_3 \tag{9.17}$$

$$Z_3 = \sqrt{Z_{2oc}(Z_{1oc} - Z_{1sc})} \tag{9.18}$$

Also,

$$Z_{1OC} = \frac{Z_0}{\tanh \gamma l} = Z_o \left(\frac{e^{\gamma l} + e^{-\gamma l}}{e^{\gamma l} - e^{-\gamma l}} \right) \tag{9.19}$$

$$Z_{1SC} = Z_0 \tanh \gamma l = Z_0 \left(\frac{e^{\gamma l} - e^{-\gamma l}}{e^{\gamma l} + e^{-\gamma l}} \right) \tag{9.20}$$

Since the line is symmetric, $Z_{1OC} = Z_{2OC}$.

Therefore, substituting Eqn. (9.19) and (9.20) in Eqn. (9.18), we get the shunt element of the T-section as

$$Z_3 = \sqrt{\frac{Z_0}{\tanh \gamma l} \left(\frac{Z_0}{\tanh \gamma l} - Z_0 \tanh \gamma l \right)} = \frac{Z_0}{\sinh \gamma l} \tag{9.21}$$

Substituting Eqn. (9.19) and (9.20) in Eqn. (9.16) and (9.17), we get the series elements for the equivalent section as

$$Z_1 = Z_2 = Z_{1OC} - Z_3 = Z_o \left[\frac{e^{\gamma l} + e^{-\gamma l}}{e^{\gamma l} - e^{-\gamma l}} - \frac{2}{e^{\gamma l} - e^{-\gamma l}} \right]$$

$$= Z_0 \left[\frac{\left(e^{\frac{\gamma l}{2}} - e^{\frac{-\gamma l}{2}} \right)^2}{\left(e^{\frac{\gamma l}{2}} - e^{\frac{-\gamma l}{2}} \right)\left(e^{\frac{\gamma l}{2}} + e^{\frac{-\gamma l}{2}} \right)} \right]$$

$$= Z_0 \left[\frac{e^{\frac{\gamma l}{2}} - e^{\frac{-\gamma l}{2}}}{e^{\frac{\gamma l}{2}} + e^{\frac{-\gamma l}{2}}} \right] = Z_0 \tanh \frac{\gamma l}{2} \tag{9.22}$$

For π–section:

From π-network of Fig. 9.1(b), the open circuit and short circuit measurements are

$$Z_{1oc} = \frac{Z_A(Z_B + Z_C)}{Z_A + Z_B + Z_C} \tag{9.23}$$

$$Z_{2oc} = \frac{Z_C(Z_A + Z_B)}{Z_A + Z_B + Z_C} \tag{9.24}$$

$$Z_{1sc} = \frac{Z_A Z_B}{Z_A + Z_B} \tag{9.25}$$

Multiplying Eqns. (9.24) and (9.25), we get

$$Z_{2oc} Z_{1sc} = \frac{Z_A Z_B Z_C}{Z_A + Z_B + Z_C} \tag{9.26}$$

Subtracting Eqn. (9.25) from Eqn. (9.23), we get

$$Z_{1oc} - Z_{1sc} = \frac{Z_C Z_A^2}{(Z_A + Z_B + Z_C)(Z_A + Z_B)} \tag{9.27}$$

Multiplying the above equation with Eqn. (9.24), we get

$$Z_{2oc}(Z_{1oc} - Z_{1sc}) = \frac{Z_A^2 Z_C^2}{(Z_A + Z_B + Z_C)^2} \tag{9.28}$$

The values for the three π section branches are

$$Z_A = \frac{Z_{2oc} Z_{1sc}}{Z_{2oc} - \sqrt{Z_{2oc}(Z_{1oc} - Z_{1sc})}} \tag{9.29}$$

$$Z_B = \frac{Z_{2oc} Z_{1sc}}{\sqrt{Z_{2oc}(Z_{1oc} - Z_{1sc})}} \tag{9.30}$$

$$Z_C = \frac{Z_{2oc} Z_{1sc}}{Z_{1oc} - \sqrt{Z_{2oc}(Z_{1oc} - Z_{1sc})}} \tag{9.31}$$

The π network equivalent to any complicated network is designed by using the above three equations. For a symmetrical π network,

$$Z_A = Z_C = \frac{Z_{2OC} Z_{1SC}}{Z_{2OC} - \sqrt{Z_{2OC}(Z_{1OC} - Z_{1SC})}} \tag{9.32}$$

Substituting Eqn. (9.19) and (9.20) in Eqn. (9.32), we get

$$Z_A = Z_C = \frac{Z_0^2}{Z_0\left(\dfrac{e^{\gamma l} + e^{-\gamma l}}{e^{\gamma l} - e^{-\gamma l}}\right) - \dfrac{2Z_0}{e^{\gamma l} - e^{-\gamma l}}}$$

$$= \frac{Z_0\left(e^{\frac{\gamma l}{2}} - e^{\frac{-\gamma l}{2}}\right)\left(e^{\frac{\gamma l}{2}} + e^{\frac{-\gamma l}{2}}\right)}{\left(e^{\frac{\gamma l}{2}} - e^{\frac{-\gamma l}{2}}\right)^2} = \frac{Z_0}{\tanh\left(\dfrac{\gamma l}{2}\right)} \tag{9.33}$$

$$Z_B = \frac{Z_{2OC} Z_{1SC}}{\sqrt{Z_{2OC}(Z_{1OC} - Z_{1SC})}} \tag{9.34}$$

$$= \frac{Z_0^2}{Z_0 / \sinh \gamma l} = Z_0 \sinh \gamma l \tag{9.35}$$

The T-section and π–section equivalent circuits for a transmission line are shown in Fig 9.2(a) and (b) respectively.

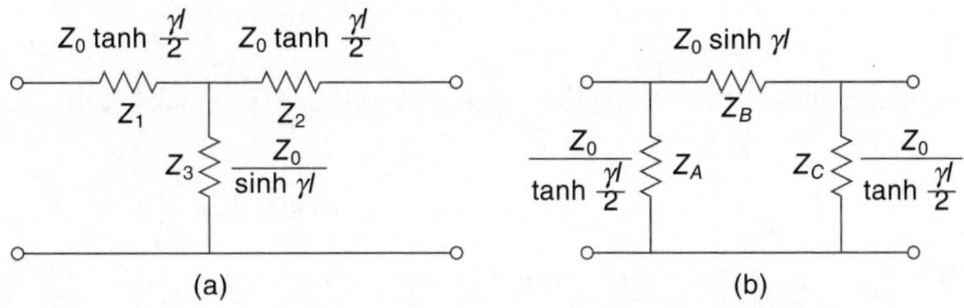

Figure 9.2 *Equivalent circuits for a transmission line (a) T-section and (b) π–section*

9.3.1 Open and Short Circuit Impedances for a Dissipation Line

The input impedance of a line with length $s = l$ and small dissipation can be written from Eqn. (9.3) by substituting $\gamma = \alpha + j\beta$.

$$Z_s = \frac{E_s}{I_s} = Z_0 \left[\frac{(Z_R + \alpha l Z_0)\cos \beta l + j(Z_R \alpha l + Z_0)\sin \beta l}{(Z_R c + Z_0)\cos \beta l + j(Z_R + \alpha l Z_0 \sin \beta l)} \right] \tag{9.36}$$

For a line terminated in a short circuit, $Z_R = 0$, and the input impedance becomes

$$Z_{SC} = Z_0 \left(\frac{\alpha l \cos \beta l + j \sin \beta l}{\cos \beta l + j \alpha l \sin \beta l} \right) \tag{9.37}$$

Assuming $Z_0 = R_0$ and rationalizing the above equation, we get

$$Z_{SC} = R_0 \left(\frac{\alpha l \cos \beta l + j \sin \beta l}{\cos \beta l + j \alpha l \sin \beta l} \right) \times \left(\frac{\cos \beta l - j \alpha l \sin \beta l}{\cos \beta l - j \alpha l \sin \beta l} \right)$$

$$= R_0 \left(\frac{\alpha l [\cos^2 \beta l + \sin^2 \beta l] + j(1 - \alpha^2 l^2)\sin \beta l \cos \beta l}{\cos^2 \beta l + \alpha l \sin^2 \beta l} \right)$$

$$= R_0 \left[\frac{\alpha l + j(1 - \alpha^2 l^2)\sin \beta l \cos \beta l}{1 - (1 - \alpha^2 l^2)\sin^2 \beta l} \right]$$

Substituting $\beta l = \dfrac{2\pi l}{\lambda}$, we get

$$Z_{SC} = R_0 \left[\frac{\alpha l + j(1 - \alpha^2 l^2)\sin(2\pi l / \lambda)\cos(2\pi l / \lambda)}{1 - (1 - \alpha^2 l^2)\sin^2(2\pi l / \lambda)} \right] \tag{9.38}$$

The real and imaginary parts of the above equation are

$$R_{SC} = \frac{R_0 \alpha l}{1 - (1 - \alpha^2 l^2)\sin^2(2\pi l / \lambda)} \tag{9.39}$$

$$X_{SC} = \frac{R_0(1 - \alpha^2 l^2)\sin(2\pi l / \lambda)\cos(2\pi l / \lambda)}{1 - (1 - \alpha^2 l^2)\sin^2(2\pi l / \lambda)} \tag{9.40}$$

For values of l from 0 to $\lambda/4$, the reactance is positive and hence inductive in nature; for values of l between $\lambda/4$ and $\lambda/2$ the line exhibits capacitive property with negative reactance and is seen to oscillate in sign for every quarter wavelength. This performance is similar to that of the dissipationless line except that the above expression for reactance reaches a maximum but does not become infinite.

For certain applications, it is convenient to have the admittance of the short-circuited line of small dissipation. It can be obtained by rationalizing the reciprocal of Eqn. (9.37), giving

$$Y_{SC} = G_0 \left(\frac{\cos \beta l + j \alpha l \sin \beta l}{\alpha l \cos \beta l + j \sin \beta l} \right) \times \left(\frac{\alpha l \cos \beta l - j \sin \beta l}{\alpha l \cos \beta l - j \sin \beta l} \right)$$

$$= G_0 \left(\frac{\alpha l(\cos^2 \beta l + \sin^2 \beta l) - j(1 - \alpha^2 l^2)\cos \beta l \sin \beta l}{\alpha^2 l^2 \cos^2 \beta l + \sin^2 \beta l} \right)$$

$$Y_{SC} = G_0 \left[\frac{\alpha l - j(1 - \alpha^2 l^2)\sin(\beta l)\cos(\beta l)}{1 - (1 - \alpha^2 l^2)\cos^2(\beta l)} \right] \tag{9.41}$$

Substituting $\beta l = \dfrac{2\pi l}{\lambda}$, we get

$$Y_{SC} = G_0 \left[\frac{\alpha l - j(1 - \alpha^2 l^2)\sin(2\pi l/\lambda)\cos(2\pi l/\lambda)}{1 - (1 - \alpha^2 l^2)\cos^2(2\pi l/\lambda)} \right] \tag{9.42}$$

After the numerator and denominator of Eqn. (9.36) are divided by Z_R and after Z_R has been set equal to ∞, an expression for the input impedance of an open-circuited line is obtained as

$$Z_{OC} = Z_0 \left(\frac{\cos \beta l + j\alpha l \sin \beta l}{\alpha l \cos \beta l + j \sin \beta l} \right) \tag{9.43}$$

Upon rationalizing and substituting $R_0 = Z_0$ and $\beta = 2\pi/\lambda$, this becomes

$$Z_{OC} = R_0 \left[\frac{\alpha l - j(1 - \alpha^2 l^2)\sin(2\pi l/\lambda)\cos(2\pi l/\lambda)}{1 - (1 - \alpha^2 l^2)\cos^2(2\pi l/\lambda)} \right] \tag{9.44}$$

The open-circuit impedance has components

$$R_{OC} = \frac{R_0 \alpha l}{1 - (1 - \alpha^2 l^2)\cos^2(2\pi l/\lambda)} \tag{9.45}$$

$$X_{OC} = \frac{-R_0(1 - \alpha^2 l^2)\sin(2\pi l/\lambda)\cos(2\pi l/\lambda)}{1 - (1 - \alpha^2 l^2)\cos^2(2\pi l/\lambda)} \tag{9.46}$$

For value of l between 0 and $\lambda/4$ this reactance is capacitive; for values of l between $\lambda/4$ and $\lambda/2$, it is inductive and can be seen to oscillate in sign every quarter wavelength, always being opposite in sign to the reactance of the short-circuited line.

The input admittance of the open-circuited line is

$$Y_{OC} = G_0 \left[\frac{\alpha l + j(1 - \alpha^2 l^2)\sin(2\pi l/\lambda)\cos(2\pi l/\lambda)}{1 - (1 - \alpha^2 l^2)\sin^2(2\pi l/\lambda)} \right] \tag{9.47}$$

At very high frequencies, the distributed inductive reactance of the leads of a capacitor may be greater than the actual capacitive reactance, so that the capacitor may appear to be an inductor. The inductor may have so much distributed shunting capacitance that it becomes a parallel-resonant circuit or even behaves like a capacitor. Lines may be used as efficient impedance matching sections and as reactive elements in wave filters.

9.4 REFLECTION ON A LINE NOT TERMINATED WITH Z_0

Referring to Eqns. (8.32) and (8.33) of previous chapter, the voltage and current on the line, with s measured as positive from the receiving end are,

$$V = \frac{V_R(Z_R + Z_0)}{2Z_R} \left[e^{\gamma s} + \left(\frac{Z_R - Z_0}{Z_R + Z_0} \right) e^{-\gamma s} \right] \tag{9.48}$$

$$I = \frac{I_R(Z_R + Z_0)}{2Z_0}\left[e^{\gamma s} - \left(\frac{Z_R - Z_0}{Z_R + Z_0}\right)e^{-\gamma s}\right] \qquad (9.49)$$

The Eqns. (9.48) and (9.49) have two terms viz., one that varies exponentially with $+s$ and the other with $-s$. With Z_R is not equal to Z_0, the wave travelling from the sender end to the receiver end is identified as the component varying with $e^{\gamma s}$. This wave of voltage or current is called as *incident wave*. The second term, varying with $e^{-\gamma s}$, represents the voltage or current wave progressing from the receiver end toward the sender end, and decreasing in amplitude with increased distance from the load. Such voltage or current wave is called as *reflected wave*. Figure 9.3 illustrates the incident and reflected waveforms under extreme impedance mismatch.

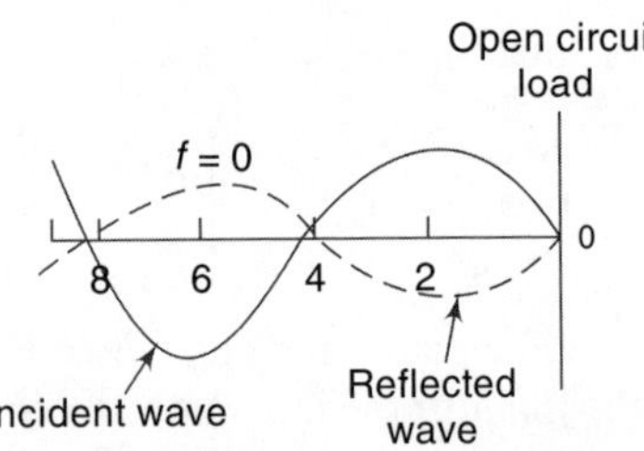

Figure 9.3 *Incident and reflected waveforms under open-circuit condition*

The relative phase angles of the incident and reflected waves at the load are determined using the component $\left(\dfrac{Z_R - Z_0}{Z_R + Z_0}\right)$. Therefore, both angle and magnitude of Z_R and Z_0 enter into the determination of the phase angle between the two waves.

In case of an infinite line ($s = \infty$), or for $Z_R = Z_0$, the second term within the brackets of Eqn. (9.48) and (9.49) becomes zero and hence the reflected wave is absent. The line terminated in Z_0 behaves in exactly similar fashion, the waves traveling smoothly down the line and the energy being absorbed in Z_0 load without setting up a reflected wave. Such a line is frequently called as a *smooth line*.

At a load where $Z_R \neq Z_0$, $Z_R = \dfrac{V_R}{I_R}$

Reflection is considered as an undesirable effect on a transmission line. If the attenuation is not large; the returning wave appears as an echo at the sender end. Also, if reflections are present, then there is a reduction in the power efficiency since the portion of the received energy is rejected by the load. In travelling down the transmission line as a reflected wave, the energy is further reduced due to the R and G components of the transmission line. If the impedance of the generator is not Z_0, the reflected wave is reflected again at the sending end, becoming a new incident wave. Energy is thus transmitted back and forth on the line until fully dissipated by the line losses. Thus, a termination of load with Z_0 is desirable for no reflection.

9.5 REFLECTION COEFFICIENT

The reflection coefficient is defined as the ratio of the amplitude of the reflected voltage wave to the amplitude of the incident voltage wave at the receiving end of the line.

Substituting $K = \dfrac{Z_R - Z_0}{Z_R + Z_0}$ in Eqns. (9.48) and (9.49), we get

$$V = \frac{V_R(Z_R + Z_0)}{2Z_R}(e^{\gamma l} + Ke^{-\gamma l}) \qquad (9.50)$$

$$I = \frac{I_R(Z_R + Z_0)}{2Z_0}(e^{\gamma l} - Ke^{-\gamma s}) \qquad (9.51)$$

From Eqn. (9.50) with $l = 0$, this ratio becomes

$$K = \frac{\text{reflected voltage at load}}{\text{incident voltage at load}} = \frac{Z_R - Z_0}{Z_R + Z_0}, \text{ where } 0 \leq |K| \leq 1$$

Rearranging the above equation, we get

$$\frac{Z_R}{Z_0} = \frac{1 + K}{1 - K}$$

(i) For an open circuit line, $Z_R = \infty$. Therefore,

$$K = \frac{1 - \dfrac{Z_0}{Z_R}}{1 + \dfrac{Z_0}{Z_R}} = 1$$

(ii) For a short circuit line, $Z_R = 0$. Therefore, $K = -1$ and there is a phase reversal of voltage.

(iii) For a matched line, $Z_R = Z_0$. Therefore, $K = 0$ and there is no reflected wave.

The sign of K, and hence the polarity of the reflected wave, is dependent on the angles and magnitudes of Z_R and Z_0. For a termination of Z_0, the reflection coefficient is zero.

9.5.1 Input Impedance in Terms of Reflection Coefficient

The input impedance Z_{in} of a line terminated in impedance Z_R as per Eqn. (9.3) is given by

$$Z_{in} = Z_0 \frac{Z_R \cosh \gamma l + Z_0 \sinh \gamma l}{Z_0 \cosh \gamma l + Z_R \sinh \gamma l}$$

Changing hyperbolic functions to exponential form, we get

$$Z_{in} = Z_0 \frac{Z_R \left(\dfrac{e^{\gamma l} + e^{-\gamma l}}{2} \right) + Z_0 \left(\dfrac{e^{\gamma l} + e^{-\gamma l}}{2} \right)}{Z_0 \left(\dfrac{e^{\gamma l} + e^{-\gamma l}}{2} \right) + Z_R \left(\dfrac{e^{\gamma l} + e^{-\gamma l}}{2} \right)}$$

$$= Z_0 \frac{\dfrac{e^{\gamma l}}{2}(Z_R + Z_0) + \dfrac{e^{-\gamma l}}{2}(Z_R - Z_0)}{\dfrac{e^{\gamma l}}{2}(Z_R + Z_0) - \dfrac{e^{-\gamma l}}{2}(Z_R - Z_0)}$$

Dividing numerator and denominator by $\dfrac{e^{\gamma l}}{2}(Z_R + Z_0)$, we get

$$Z_{in} = Z_0 \frac{1 + \dfrac{e^{-2\gamma l}}{2} \left(\dfrac{Z_R - Z_0}{Z_R + Z_0} \right)}{1 - \dfrac{e^{-2\gamma l}}{2} \left(\dfrac{Z_R - Z_0}{Z_R + Z_0} \right)}$$

Using $K = \dfrac{Z_R - Z_0}{Z_R + Z_0}$ in the above equation, we get

$$Z_{\text{in}} = Z_0 \frac{1 + Ke^{-2\gamma l}}{1 - Ke^{-2\gamma l}} \tag{9.52}$$

Thus, input impedance Z_{in} of a line of length l can be calculated if the secondary constant of a line P and Z_0 reflection coefficient K is given.

9.6 VOLTAGE STANDING WAVE RATIO (VsWr)

As discussed in the previous section, the reflection occurs when the line is not properly terminated with its characteristic impedance. Hence, an improper line termination may result in the reflection of waves. The vector sum of the incident and the reflected waves give rise to voltage and current standing waves with definite maxima and minima along the length of the line as indicated in Fig. 9.4. In fact, when reflection takes place in the line, at some points, the incident and reflected signals are in phase and hence both components add together. On the other hand, at some other point, the two components may oppose each other. The resultant graphical profile of both these incident and reflected wave is called as standing waves. The points where the resultant signal (voltage or current) is maximum are known as voltage or current maxima. On the other hand, the points where the resultant signal (voltage or current) is minimum are called voltage or current minima.

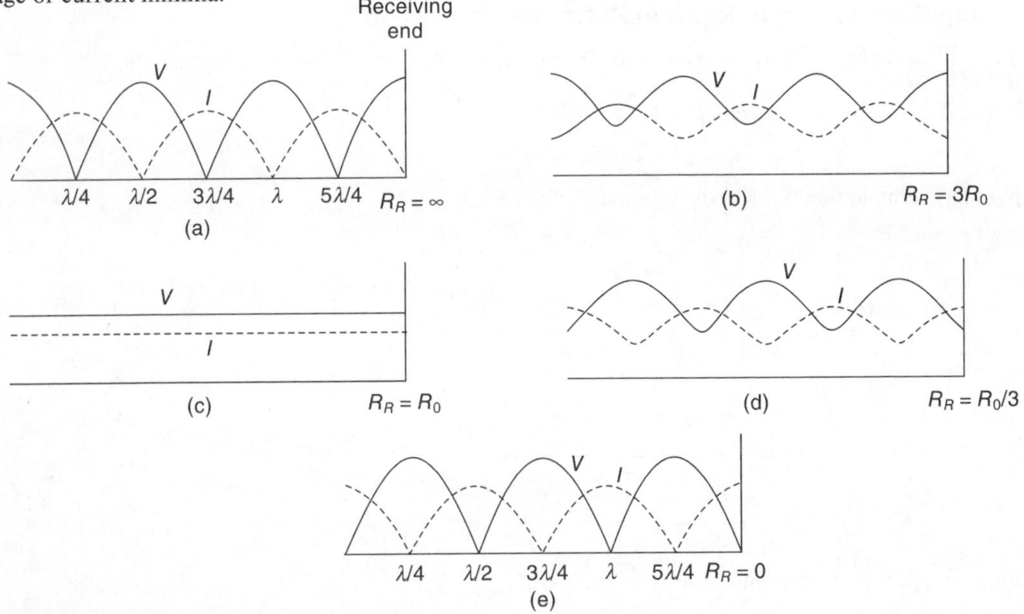

Figure 9.4 *Voltages and currents for dissipationless line (a) when $R_R = \infty$ or open circuit (b) when $R_R = 3R$ (c) when $R_R = R_0$ (d) $R_R = R_0/3$ and (e) $R_R = 0$ or short circuit*

Thus it is evident that,

$$|V_{\text{max}}| = |V_i| + |V_r|$$
$$|V_{\text{min}}| = |V_i| - |V_r|$$
$$|I_{\text{max}}| = |I_i| + |I_r|$$
$$|I_{\text{min}}| = |I_i| - |I_r|$$

The magnitude of standing waves provides an idea of the amount of reflection.

The ratio of the maximum and minimum magnitude of current or voltage on a line having standing waves is called *standing wave ratio* (SWR) or denoted by S.

Therefore,
$$\text{VSWR} = S = \frac{|V_{\max}|}{|V_{\min}|} = \frac{|V_i| + |V_r|}{|V_i| - |V_r|} = \frac{1 + \left|\dfrac{V_i}{V_r}\right|}{1 - \left|\dfrac{V_i}{V_r}\right|}$$

In terms of reflection coefficient K, the standing wave ratio becomes

$$S = \frac{1 + |K|}{1 - |K|}, \text{ where } K = \frac{V_r}{V_i} \tag{9.53}$$

In terms of Standing Wave Ratio (S), the reflection coefficient K can be written as

$$|K| = \frac{S - 1}{S + 1} = \frac{|V_{\max}| - |V_{\min}|}{|V_{\max}| + |V_{\min}|}$$

The Current Standing Wave Ratio ($CSWR$) is defined as

$$\text{CSWR} = \frac{1 - |K|}{1 + |K|} \tag{9.54}$$

It is significant that VSWR is always greater than 1, and when it is equal to 1, the line it properly terminated and there is no reflection. VSWR is more popular since it is easy to measure at different points of the line by using a voltmeter. However for the measurement of current, an ammeter that is connected in series to predict the maxima and minima points which makes the measurement process cumbersome.

9.6.1 Travelling Waves

Input and transfer impedances
The input impedance of the transmission line is given by Eqn. (9.3) or Eqn. (9.52) as

$$Z_S = Z_0 \left[\frac{Z_R \cosh \gamma l + Z_0 \sinh \gamma l}{Z_0 \cosh \gamma l + Z_R \sinh \gamma l} \right]$$

or
$$Z_S = Z_0 \left[\frac{e^{\gamma l} + K e^{-\gamma l}}{e^{\gamma l} - K e^{-\gamma l}} \right]$$

The sending end voltage V_S is given by

$$V_S = \frac{V_R(Z_R + Z_0)}{2 Z_R}[e^{\gamma l} + K e^{-\gamma l}]$$

$$= \frac{I_R(Z_R + Z_0)}{2}[e^{\gamma l} + K e^{-\gamma l}]$$

Therefore, the transfer impedance Z_T is

$$Z_T = \frac{V_S}{I_S} = \frac{(Z_R + Z_0)}{2}[e^{\gamma l} + K e^{-\gamma l}]$$

Substituting $K = \dfrac{Z_R - Z_0}{Z_R + Z_0}$, we get

$$Z_T = Z_R\left[\frac{e^{\gamma l} + e^{-\gamma l}}{2}\right] + Z_0\left[\frac{e^{\gamma l} - e^{-\gamma l}}{2}\right]$$

Therefore, $\qquad Z_T = Z_R \cosh \gamma l + Z_0 \sinh \gamma l$ $\hfill$ (9.55)

9.6.2 Input Impedance of the Dissipationless Transmission Line

The sending end voltage and current at a distance from the receiving end for a line of length l are expressed by

$$V_S = V_R \cos \beta l + jI_R R_0 \sin \beta l$$

and $\qquad I_S = I_R \cos \beta l + j\dfrac{V_R}{R_0}\sin \beta l$

Consider a line of length l and terminated in Z_R as shown in the Fig. 9.5. The input impedance is

$$Z_{\text{in}} = \frac{V_S}{I_S} = \frac{V_R \cos \beta l + jI_R R_0 \sin \beta l}{I_R \cos \beta l + j\dfrac{V_R}{R_0}\sin \beta l} = R_0\left[\frac{V_R \cos \beta l + jI_R R_0 \sin \beta l}{I_R \cos \beta l + jV_R \sin \beta l}\right]$$

$$= R_0\left[\frac{V_R + jI_R R_0 \tan \beta l}{I_R R_0 + jV_R \tan \beta l}\right] = R_0\left[\frac{\dfrac{V_R}{I_R} + jR_0 \tan \beta l}{R_0 + j\dfrac{V_R}{I_R}\tan \beta l}\right]$$

Therefore, $\qquad Z_{\text{in}} = R_0\left[\dfrac{Z_R + jR_0 \tan \beta l}{R_0 + jZ_R \tan \beta l}\right]$

$$= R_0\left[\frac{Z_R \cos \beta l + jR_0 \sin \beta l}{R_0 \cos \beta l + jZ_R \sin \beta l}\right]$$

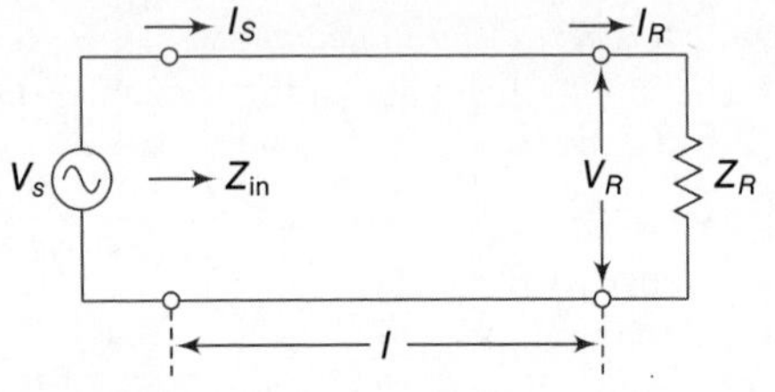

Writing numerator and denominator in exponential forms and rearranging, we get

$$Z_{\text{in}} = R_0\left[\frac{1 + \dfrac{Z_R - Z_0}{Z_R + Z_0}e^{-j2\beta l}}{1 - \dfrac{Z_R - Z_0}{Z_R + Z_0}e^{-j2\beta l}}\right]$$

Figure 9.5 *A line of length l and terminated in Z_R*

Substituting the reflection coefficient, $K = \dfrac{Z_R - Z_0}{Z_R + Z_0}$, we have

$$Z_{\text{in}} = Z_S = R_0\left[\frac{1 + |K|\angle\phi e^{-2\beta l}}{1 - |K|\angle\phi e^{-j2\beta l}}\right]$$

$$= R_0\left[\frac{1 + |K|\angle\phi - 2\beta l}{1 - |K|\angle\phi - 2\beta l}\right]$$

The input impedance will be maximum at a distance, s,

Therefore, $\qquad \phi = 2\beta l \quad$ or $\quad \phi - 2\beta l = 0$,

or $\qquad l = \dfrac{\phi}{2\beta}$

Then $\qquad Z_{S(\max)} = R_0 \left[\dfrac{1 + |K|}{1 - |K|} \right] = SR_0$

where S is standing wave ratio and $Z_{S\,(\max)}$ becomes resistive.

At a distance of $\dfrac{\lambda}{4}$ from the point where the impedance is maximum, we get a point of minimum impedance.

Hence the input impedance will be minimum if

$$dV_{\min} = l = \frac{\phi}{2\beta} \pm \frac{\lambda}{4} = \left[\frac{\phi}{2\left(\dfrac{2\pi}{\lambda}\right)} + \frac{\lambda}{4} \right] = \frac{\lambda}{4}\left[\frac{\phi}{\pi} + 1 \right]$$

i.e., $\qquad l = \dfrac{\phi}{2\beta} + \dfrac{1}{4}\left(\dfrac{2\pi}{\beta} \right) \qquad \left(\text{since } \lambda = \dfrac{2\pi}{\beta} \right)$

i.e., $\qquad l = \dfrac{\phi + \pi}{2\beta}$

or $\qquad 2\beta l = \phi + \pi$

Then

$$Z_{S(\max)} = R_0 \left[\frac{1 + |K|\angle\phi - (\phi + \pi)}{1 - |K|\angle\phi - (\phi + \pi)} \right] = R_0 \left[\frac{1 + |K|\angle -\pi}{1 - |K|\angle -\pi} \right] = R_0 \left[\frac{1 - |K|}{1 + |K|} \right] = \frac{R_0}{S}$$

where S is standing wave ratio and $Z_{S\,(\min)}$ is also resistive.

9.6.3 Reflection Factor and Reflection Loss (Mismatching Loss)

If $Z_2 \neq Z_1$ as in Fig. 9.6, the impedance mismatch will create a change in the ratio of the energy transmitted by the electric field to that transmitted by the magnetic field or ratio of voltage to current. Hence, a portion of energy is reflected by the load. The energy delivered to the load may be less than that of energy delivered if impedances Z_1 and Z_2 are matched, resulting in a reflection loss.

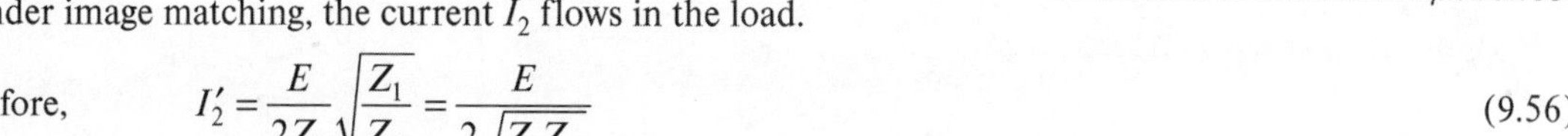

Figure 9.6 *Transmission line connected to the source and load impedances*

Under image matching, the current I_2 flows in the load.

Therefore, $\qquad I_2' = \dfrac{E}{2Z_1} \sqrt{\dfrac{Z_1}{Z_2}} = \dfrac{E}{2\sqrt{Z_1 Z_2}}$ $\qquad\qquad$ (9.56)

Without image matching, this current is

$$|I_2| = \frac{|E|}{|Z_1 + Z_2|}$$

$\qquad\qquad$ (9.57)

Therefore, reflection factor,

$$k = \left|\frac{I_2}{I_2'}\right| = \left|\frac{2\sqrt{Z_1 Z_2}}{Z_1 + Z_2}\right| \tag{9.58}$$

The reflection loss is the reciprocal of k,

$$\text{Reflection loss} = \ln\frac{1}{|k|} = \ln\left|\frac{Z_1 + Z_2}{2\sqrt{Z_1 Z_2}}\right| \text{ nepers} \tag{9.59}$$

$$\text{Reflection loss} = 20\log\frac{1}{|k|} = 20\log\left|\frac{Z_1 + Z_2}{2\sqrt{Z_1 Z_2}}\right| \text{ dB} \tag{9.60}$$

9.6.4 Insertion Loss

The insertion of a four-terminal network or a line between a generator and a load will vary the impedance matching between the source and load. As a result, the corresponding change in power delivered to the load will result in a +ve or −ve insertion loss. Here, the insertion loss of a line or network is defined as the number of nepers or decibels.

The insertion loss is considered to be the resultant of several individual losses. In Fig. 9.7, it is seen that, if Z_S is not equal to Z_g at port 1, 1, then a reflection loss occurs at that point. If the impedances are not matched at port 2, 2, then a second reflection loss occurs at the receiving end. The total insertion loss due to insertion of a line or network between a generator and a load is obtained from the ratio of the load current flowing when the load is directly connected to the generator to the current actually flowing in the load.

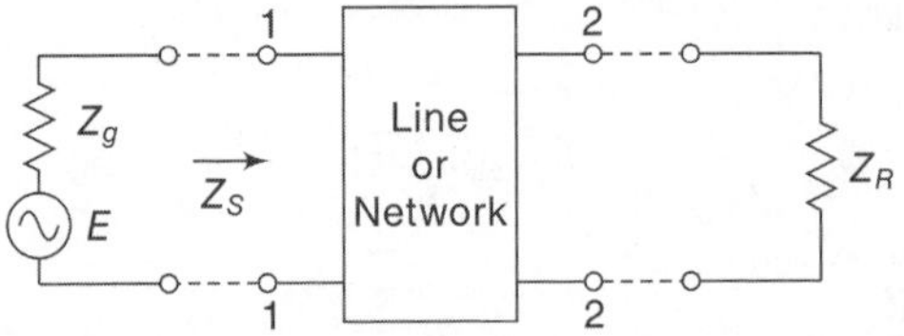

Figure 9.7 *Illustration of the insertion loss*

Due to the introduction of the line between source and load as in Fig. 9.6, the insertion loss can be calculated. The sending current I_S is

$$I_S = \frac{I_R(Z_R + Z_0)}{2Z_0}(e^{\gamma l} - Ke^{-\gamma l}) \tag{9.61}$$

or

$$I_S = \frac{V}{Z_g + Z_S} \tag{9.62}$$

The input impedance, $Z_S = Z_0\left[\dfrac{e^{\gamma l} + Ke^{-\gamma l}}{e^{\gamma l} - Ke^{-\gamma l}}\right] \tag{9.63}$

Substituting (9.63) into (9.62), we get

$$I_S = \frac{V}{Z_g + Z_0\left(\dfrac{e^{\gamma l} + Ke^{-\gamma l}}{e^{\gamma l} - Ke^{-\gamma l}}\right)}$$

Therefore,

$$I_S = \frac{E}{Z_g + Z_0\left(\dfrac{e^{\gamma l} + Ke^{-\gamma l}}{e^{\gamma l} - Ke^{-\gamma l}}\right)}$$

Therefore,
$$I_S = \frac{E(e^{\gamma l} - Ke^{-\gamma l})}{Z_g(e^{\gamma l} - Ke^{-\gamma l}) + Z_0(e^{\gamma l} + Ke^{-\gamma l})} \tag{9.64}$$

Substituting (9.64) into (9.61), we get

$$I_R = \frac{2Z_0 E}{(Z_R + Z_0)[Z_g(e^{\gamma l} - Ke^{-\gamma l}) + Z_0(e^{\gamma l} + Ke^{-\gamma l})]}$$

Substituting
$$K = \frac{Z_R - Z_0}{Z_R + Z_0}$$

$$I_R = \frac{2Z_0 E}{(Z_R + Z_0)(Z_g + Z_0)e^{\gamma l} + (Z_0 - Z_g)(Z_R - Z_0)e^{-\gamma l}}$$

which is the value of current actually flowing in the load Z_R.

In the absence of the insertion of the network, the current I_R' flowing in the load is

$$I_R' = \frac{E}{Z_g + Z_R}$$

Therefore,
$$\frac{I_R'}{I_R} = \frac{(Z_R + Z_0)(Z_g + Z_0)e^{\alpha l}e^{j\beta l} + (Z_0 - Z_g)(Z_R - Z_0)e^{-\alpha l}e^{-j\beta l}}{2Z_0(Z_g + Z_R)} \tag{9.65}$$

If α is large or the line is sufficiently long, the second form in the numerator of Eqn. (9.65) may be neglected w.r.t the first, leaving

$$\frac{I_R'}{I_R} = \frac{(Z_R + Z_0)(Z_g + Z_0)e^{\alpha l}e^{j\beta l}}{2Z_0(Z_g + Z_R)} \tag{9.66}$$

Multiplying both numerator and denominator by $2\sqrt{Z_g Z_R}$ in Eqn. (9.66), we get

$$\frac{I_R'}{I_R} = \frac{2\sqrt{Z_g Z_R}(Z_R + Z_0)(Z_g + Z_0)e^{\alpha l}e^{j\beta l}}{4\sqrt{Z_g Z_R}Z_0(Z_g + Z_R)} \tag{9.67}$$

The insertion loss is determined as a function of current magnitudes only. Rearranging the above expression, we get

$$\left|\frac{I_R'}{I_R}\right| = \frac{|Z_g + Z_0|}{2\sqrt{Z_g Z_0}} \cdot \frac{|Z_R + Z_0|}{2\sqrt{Z_R Z_0}} \cdot \frac{2\sqrt{Z_g Z_R}}{|Z_g + Z_R|} \cdot e^{\alpha l} \tag{9.68}$$

The coefficients on the R.H.S may be recognized as reflection factors.

(i) $K_S = \dfrac{2\sqrt{Z_g Z_0}}{(Z_g + Z_0)}$, where K_S is the reflection factor at the 1, 1 terminals

(ii) $K_R = \dfrac{2\sqrt{Z_R Z_0}}{|Z_R + Z_0|}$ where K_R is the reflection factor at the 2, 2 terminals

(iii) $K_{SR} = \dfrac{2\sqrt{Z_g Z_R}}{|Z_g + Z_R|}$, where K_{SR} is the reflection factor if the generator where directly connected to the load.

(iv) The fourth term is $e^{\alpha l}$, the loss in the line. Therefore, The current ratio is

$$\left|\frac{I_R'}{I_R}\right| = \frac{K_{RS}}{K_S K_R} e^{\alpha l}$$

Therefore, insertion loss in neper $= \ln\dfrac{1}{K_S} + \ln\dfrac{1}{K_R} - \ln\dfrac{1}{K_{SR}} + \alpha l$

$$\text{Insertion loss in dB} = 20\left[\log\frac{1}{K_S} + \log\frac{1}{K_R} - \log\frac{1}{K_{SR}} + 0.4343\alpha l\right] \tag{9.69}$$

It is to be noted that the term $\ln\dfrac{1}{K_{SR}}$ indicates the presence of reflection loss that would occur if the source

is directly connected to the load. Since it is not due to insertion of the line, the equation shows this loss as

subtracted.

9.7 IMPEDANCE MATCHING AND IMPEDANCE TRANSFORMATION

The transmission lines of different wavelengths can be used as impedance matching and impedance transformation, and their properties are discussed below.

9.7.1 The Eighth-Wave ($\lambda/8$) Line

Consider a transmission line of length $\dfrac{\lambda}{8}$ as shown in the Fig. 9.8.
Here, λ is the wavelength of the transmitted frequency f.

The input impedance is expressed as

$$Z_{\text{in}} = R_0\left[\frac{Z_R + jR_0\tan(\beta s)}{R_0 + jZ_R\tan(\beta s)}\right] \tag{9.70}$$

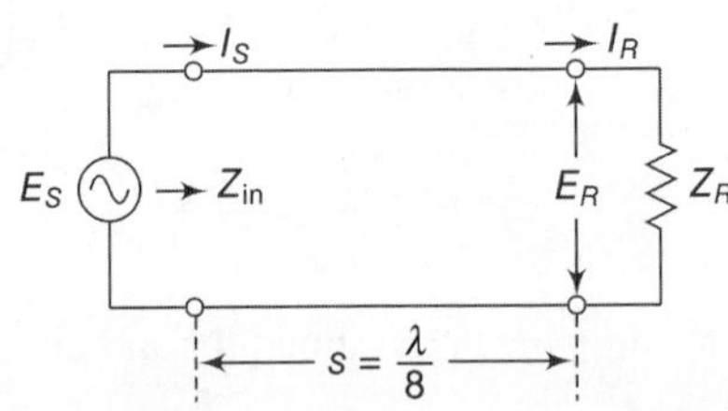

Figure 9.8 *The eighth-wave ($\lambda/8$) Line*

Substituting $\beta = \dfrac{2\pi}{\lambda}$ and $s = \dfrac{\lambda}{8}$ in Eqn. (9.70), we get

$$Z_{\text{in}} = R_0\left[\frac{Z_R + jR_0\tan\left(\dfrac{2\pi}{\lambda}\cdot\dfrac{\lambda}{8}\right)}{R_0 + jZ_R\tan\left(\dfrac{2\pi}{\lambda}\cdot\dfrac{\lambda}{8}\right)}\right] = R_0\left[\frac{Z_R + jR_0\tan\left(\dfrac{\pi}{4}\right)}{R_0 + jZ_R\tan\left(\dfrac{\pi}{4}\right)}\right] \tag{9.71}$$

Therefore,
$$Z_{\text{in}} = R_0\left[\frac{Z_R + jR_0}{R_0 + jZ_R}\right] \tag{9.72}$$

If a line is terminated in pure resistance $Z_R = R_R$, then Eqn.(9.72) becomes

$$Z_{\text{in}} = R_0\left[\frac{R_R + jR_0}{R_0 + jR_R}\right] \tag{9.73}$$

Thus the magnitude of the input impedance in Eqn. (9.73) is given by

$$|Z_{\text{in}}| = R_0\left[\frac{\sqrt{R_R^2 + R_0^2}}{\sqrt{R_0^2 + R_R^2}}\right] = R_0$$

Thus, the eight-wave line is generally used to transform any resistance R_R to impedance Z_{in} having its magnitude equal to the characteristic resistance R_0 of the line.

9.7.2 The Quarter-Wave ($\lambda/4$) Line-Impedance Matching

The input impedance in Eqn. (9.70) is given as

$$Z_{\text{in}} = R_0 \left[\frac{Z_R + jR_0 \tan(\beta s)}{R_0 + jZ_R \tan(\beta s)} \right]$$

Substituting $\beta = \dfrac{2\pi}{\lambda}$ and $s = \dfrac{\lambda}{4}$ in Eqn. (9.70) for the line in Fig. 9.8, we get

$$Z_{\text{in}} = R_0 \left[\frac{\dfrac{Z_R}{\tan\left(\dfrac{2\pi}{\lambda} \cdot \dfrac{\lambda}{4} \right)} + jR_0}{\dfrac{R_0}{\tan\left(\dfrac{2\pi}{\lambda} \cdot \dfrac{\lambda}{4} \right)} + jZ_R} \right] = R_0 \left[\frac{\dfrac{Z_R}{\tan\left(\dfrac{\pi}{2} \right)} + jR_0}{\dfrac{R_0}{\tan\left(\dfrac{\pi}{2} \right)} + jZ_R} \right] = R_0 \left[\frac{jR_0}{jZ_R} \right]$$

Therefore,
$$Z_{\text{in}} = \frac{R_0^2}{Z_R} \tag{9.74}$$

Thus, the above equation is similar to the equation for impedance matching using transformer.

Thus a quarter-wave line shown in Fig. 9.9 may be used as a transformer for impedance matching of Load Z_R with input impedance $Z_{\text{in}} = Z_R$.

For matching impedances Z_R and Z_{in} the line with characteristic impedance R_0 may be selected such that $R_0 = |\sqrt{Z_R \cdot Z_{\text{in}}}|$

Low impedance is transformed into high impedance by using a quarter-wave line and vice versa. Quarter wave line can be used as an impedance inverter. Therefore, a short circuited $\lambda/4$ line provides infinite input impedance whereas, an open circuited $\lambda/4$ line offers zero input impedance i.e., a short circuit quarter-wave line acts as an open circuit at the other end while an open circuit quarter-wave line acts as a short circuit at the other end.

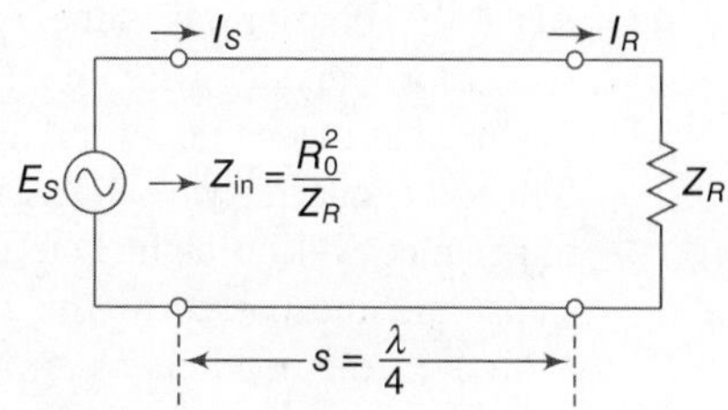

Figure 9.9 *The quarter-wave ($\lambda/4$) line*

Applications of quarter-wave line:

(a) Consider R_A the antenna resistance and R_0 the characteristic impedance of the line. A quarter-wave impedance matching section shown in Fig. 9.10 is designed such that its characteristic impedance R_0' transforms antenna resistance R_A to the characteristic impedance of line R_0 given by $R_0' = \sqrt{R_A \cdot R_0}$.

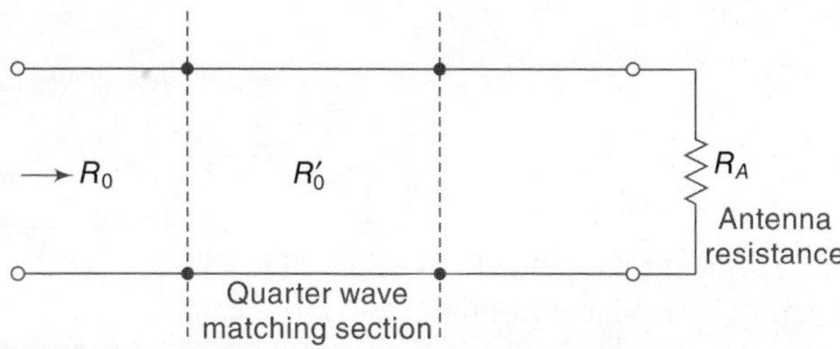

Figure 9.10 *Application of quarter-wave line to couple transmission line to the antenna*

The condition for critical coupling between two impedances is provided by the characteristics impedance of quarter-wave line R_0'. This shows that maximum power can be transferred from the line to the load. Suppose if the distance between the line and antenna is greater than the quarter-wave section of the line, the same transformation can be achieved by using a line with any odd number of quarter-wave sections in length. However, with line of odd multiples of $\lambda/4$ in length, the line losses increase with increase in length, thereby reducing the efficiency.

(b) When a quarter- wave section is in the line with the load being not purely resistive, the impedance of the line is either SR_0 or $\dfrac{R_0}{S}$ at points where voltage is minimum ($E_{\min}$) or current is maximum ($I_{\max}$). Hence, for decrease in impedance from R_0, the characteristic impedance of the quarter-wave matching section R_0' is

$$R_0' = \sqrt{R_0 \left(\frac{R_0}{S} \right)} = R_0 \sqrt{\frac{1}{S}}$$

For increase in impedance from R_0, the characteristic impedance of the quarter-wave matching section is

$$R_0' = \sqrt{R_0 (SR_0)} = R_0 \sqrt{S}$$

(c) Also, the quarter-wave line is deployed to give mechanical support to the open wire line. Figure 9.11 shows a quarter-wave line used as mechanical support being shorted at ground.

Since the quarter-wave line is shorted at ground, the input impedance will be high. Due to this mechanical support, any signal on line passes to the receiving end without any loss. Moreover, the line acts as an insulator at this point, and such quarter-wave lines are called copper insulators.

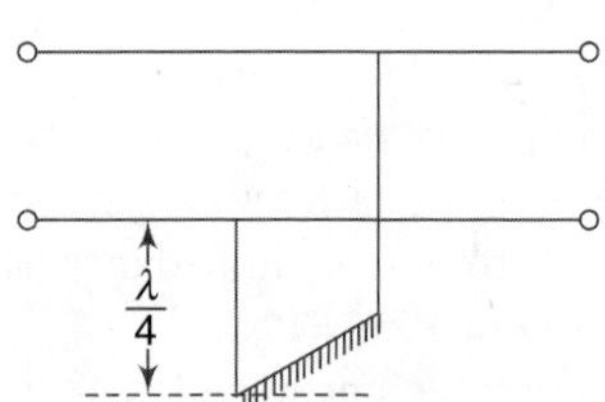

Figure 9.11 *Quarter-wave line used as mechanical support to open wire line*

9.7.3 The Half-Wave ($\lambda/2$) Line

The input impedance of a line is expressed by

$$Z_{\text{in}} = R_0 \left[\frac{Z_R + jR_0 \tan(\beta s)}{R_0 + jZ_R \tan(\beta s)} \right]$$

Substituting $\quad \beta = \dfrac{2\pi}{\lambda}$ and $s = \dfrac{\lambda}{2}$, we get

$$Z_{\text{in}} = R_0 \left[\frac{Z_R + jR_0 \tan\left(\frac{2\pi}{\lambda} \cdot \frac{\lambda}{2} \right)}{R_0 + jZ_R \tan\left(\frac{2\pi}{\lambda} \cdot \frac{\lambda}{2} \right)} \right]$$

$$= R_0 \left[\frac{Z_R + jR_0 \tan(\pi)}{R_0 + jZ_R \tan(\pi)} \right] = R_0 \left[\frac{Z_R}{R_0} \right] = Z_R \quad (9.75)$$

From the above equation, it is evident that the half-wave line, shown in Fig. 9.12, repeats its terminating impedance. In other words, the half-wave line may be considered as one transformer.

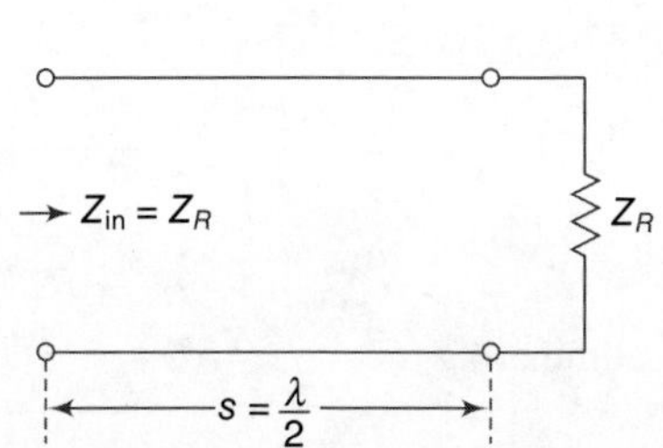

Figure 9.12 *A half-wave line*

9.8 SMITH CHART–CONFIGURATION AND APPLICATIONS

9.8.1 The Smith Circle Diagram

A modified form of circle diagram for a dissipation-less line has been developed by P.H. Smith as shown in Fig. 9.13. The input impedance for a dissipation-less line is

$$\frac{Z_s}{R_0} = \frac{1 + |K| \angle \phi - 2\beta s}{1 - |K| \angle \phi - 2\beta s} \qquad (9.76)$$

Since $\dfrac{Z_s}{R_0}$ is complex, the above equation can be written as

$$\frac{Z_s}{R_0} = r_a + jx_a, \qquad (9.77)$$

where r_a and x_a are the values of resistance and reactance per unit of R_0,

Then, $$r_a + jx_a = \frac{1 + |K| \angle \phi - 2\beta s}{1 - |K| \angle \phi - 2\beta s} \qquad (9.78)$$

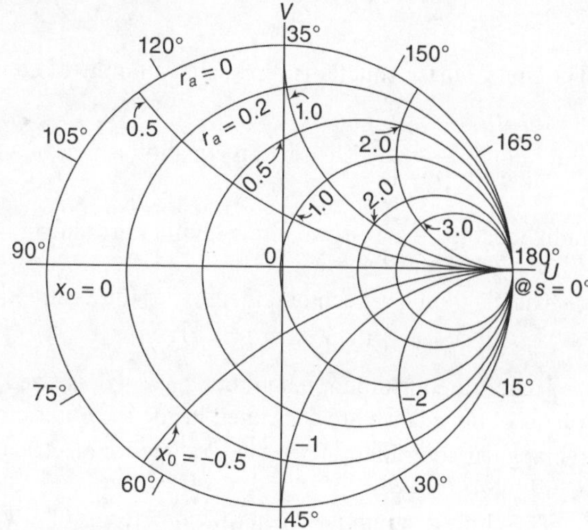

Figure 9.13   *Basis of the Smith circle diagram*

Replacing $|K|$ by its equivalent in terms of standing wave ratio, S, we get

$$(r_a + 1 + jx_a)\left(\frac{S-1}{S+1}\right)\angle \phi - 2\beta s = (r_a - 1 + jx_a)$$

Therefore, $$\left(\frac{S-1}{S+1}\right)\angle \phi - 2\beta s = \frac{(r_a - 1 + jx_a)}{(r_a + 1 + jx_a)} \qquad (9.79)$$

Multiplying and dividing by $(r_a + 1 - jx_a)$ in Eqn. (9.79) and simplifying, we get

$$\left(\frac{S-1}{S+1}\right)\angle \phi - 2\beta s = |K|\angle \phi - 2\beta s = \frac{r_a^2 - 1 + x_a^2 + j2x_a}{(r_a + 1)^2 + x_a^2} \qquad (9.80)$$

The above equation can be written as

$$U + jV = \frac{r_a^2 - 1 + x_a^2}{(r_a + 1)^2 + x_a^2} + \frac{j2x_a}{(r_a + 1)^2 + x_a^2} \qquad (9.81)$$

Equating real and imaginary parts of Eqn. (9.81), we get

$$U = \frac{r_a^2 - 1 + x_a^2}{(r_a + 1)^2 + x_a^2} \qquad (9.82)$$

$$V = \frac{2x_a}{(r_a + 1)^2 + x_a^2} \qquad (9.83)$$

Eliminating the first of x_a and then of r_a from Eqns. (9.82) and (9.83), we get

$$\left[U - \left(\frac{r_a}{r_a + 1}\right)\right]^2 + V^2 = \frac{1}{(r_a + 1)^2} \qquad (9.84)$$

$$(U-1)^2 + \left(V - \frac{1}{x_a}\right)^2 = \frac{1}{x_a^2} \tag{9.85}$$

The first of these equations represents a family of constant-r_a circles having centers on the U axis at $\dfrac{r_a}{(r_a+1)}$ and radii of $\dfrac{1}{(r_a+1)}$. The second equation is that of a family of constant-x_a circles with centers at $1 + \dfrac{j}{x_a}$ and radii equal to $\dfrac{1}{x_a}$. The two circle families are shown in Fig. 9.13.

The diagram has been obtained under the assumption that

$$|K| \angle \phi - 2\beta s = U + jV$$

Hence, the maximum magnitude of $U + jV$ is fixed at unity by the maximum value of K. Thus, all possible values of impedance are contained inside the outer circle of unit radius. The same relation between polar and rectangular coordinates fixes the βs angles or electrical-line-length coordinates at equal increments around the $K = 1$ circle ($S = \infty$).

The circle diagram has been drawn in terms of S with values from zero to infinity, all lying outside the unit circle, that appeared as a point at $(1, 0)$. The Smith diagram is essentially an inversion of the other diagram mapping all points or S values inside a unit circle. This diagram has achieved considerable popularity.

In a commercially available format of the Smith chart, the βs increments are indicated around the outer edge of the chart in terms of wavelengths, as depicted in Fig. 9.14. A transparent straightedge is fixed at the center to serve as a distance coordinate to any point on the chart. This straightedge is marked in terms of K or S, giving the effect of adding constant-S circles to the chart without complicating the figure with additional lines.

The impedance of a line may be read at any point on the appropriate standing-wave ratio or S circle. The point at the center of the chart represents the impedance of a line which is terminated in its characteristic impedance, where $\dfrac{Z}{R_0} = 1$ for all distances. In the chart, the point at the extreme left of the resistance or τ_a axis represents zero impedance or short circuit, the point at the extreme right represents infinite impedance or open circuit and the outer circle represents $S = \infty$.

The purpose of this chart is for admittance as well as for impedance. The r_a and x_a axes become g_a and b_a axes with the usual implication where capacitive susceptance is positive or above and inductive susceptance below, the U or real axis. The point at the left of the conductance or g_a axis represents zero conductance or an open circuit, and the infinite conductance or a short circuit is represented by the point at the extreme right of the conductance g_a.

9.8.2 Applications of the Smith Chart

The use of the Smith chart is similar to that of the previously discussed circle diagram and it is used to:

(i)   Determine input impedance of a line.
(ii) Convert impedance into admittance.
(iii) Determine input impedance and admittance of a short-circuited line.
(iv) Determine input impedance and admittance of an open-circuited line.
(v)   Utilize as an admittance diagram.

They are clearly explained in examples given at the end of this chapter.

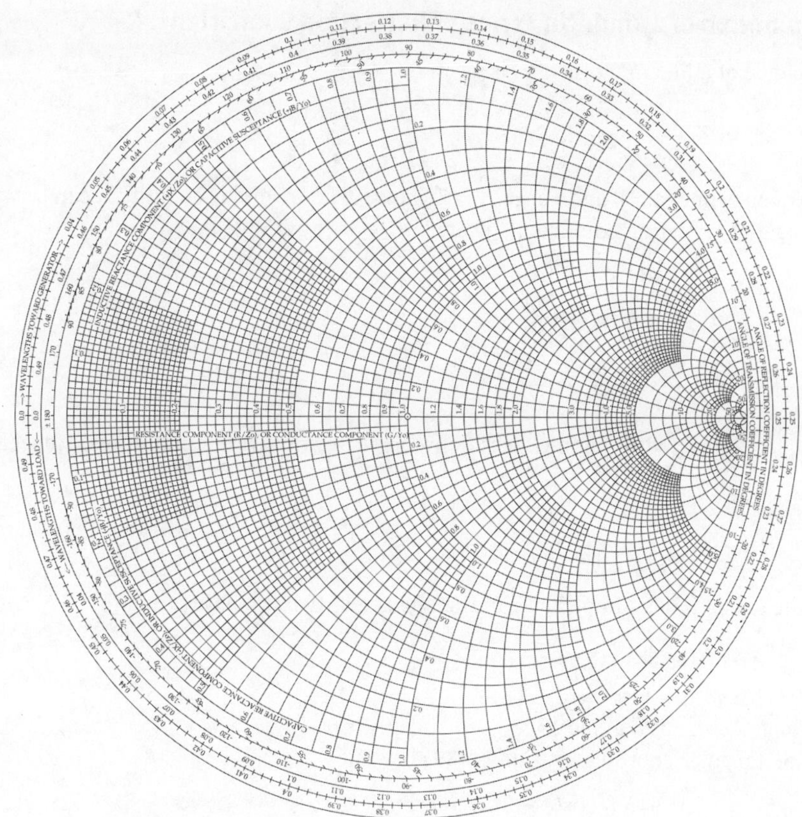

Figure 9.14 *The Smith transmission-line chart.*

9.9 SINGLE STUB MATCHING

It is known that a section of transmission line can be incorporated as matching section between load and the source. It is also possible to connect sections of open or short circuited line called stub in shunt with the main line at some point or points to obtain effective impedance matching. This process is called stub matching. Its advantages are (i) the length and characteristic impedance of the line remain unaltered and (ii) adjustable susceptance is added in shunt with the line. Stub matching can be classified into two basic types, viz., Single stub matching and Double stub matching.

Consider a transmission line that has a characteristic admittance Y_0 terminated in a conductance Y_R as depicted in Fig. 9.15.

When Y_R differs from Y_o, the standing waves are set up. If the line is traversed from the point of maximum (or minimum) conductance to that of minimum (or maximum) conductance, obviously, there will be a point at which the real part of the admittance is equal to the characteristic admittance. The values of susceptance of the stub and the line will be conjugate if an appropriate susceptance is added in shunt so as to achieve impedance matching.

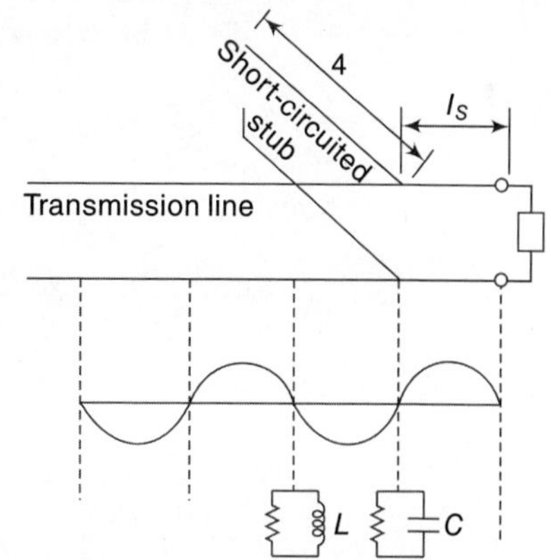

Figure 9.15 *Single Stub matching*

9.9.1 Determination of l_s and l_t in Terms of Reflection Coefficient, *K*

The input impedance of a line in terms of K is given by

$$Z_{\text{in}} = Z_0 \frac{1 + Ke^{-2\gamma l}}{1 - Ke^{-2\gamma l}} \tag{9.86}$$

For a high frequency line, $\alpha = 0$ and hence, $\gamma = j\beta$. Since K is a complex quantity, it can be written as $|K|e^{j\phi}$, where ϕ is the angle of reflection coefficient. Therefore,

$$Z_{\text{in}} = Z_0 \frac{1 + |K|e^{j\phi}e^{-2j\beta l}}{1 - |K|e^{j\phi}e^{-2j\beta l}} \tag{9.87}$$

$$= Z_0 \frac{1 + |K|e^{j(\phi - 2\beta l)}}{1 - |K|e^{j(\phi - 2\beta l)}} \tag{9.88}$$

Since the stub is connected in parallel, it is convenient to work with admittances. Hence, the input Y_{in} is given by,

$$Y_{\text{in}} = G_0 \frac{1 - |K|e^{j(\phi - 2\beta l)}}{1 + |K|e^{j(\phi - 2\beta l)}} \tag{9.89}$$

Assuming that the characteristic impedance of the line is resistive, we have

$$Z_0 = R_0 = \frac{1}{G_0}$$

where G_0 is the characteristics conductance.

Changing to rectangular coordinates, Eqn. (9.89) becomes,

$$Y_{\text{in}} = G_0 \frac{1 - |K|\{\cos(\phi - 2\beta l) + j\sin(\phi - 2\beta l)\}}{1 + |K|\{\cos(\phi - 2\beta l) + j\sin(\phi - 2\beta l)\}}$$

$$= G_0 \frac{1 - |K|\cos(\phi - 2\beta l) - j|K|\sin(\phi - 2\beta l)}{1 + |K|\cos(\phi - 2\beta l) + j|K|\sin(\phi - 2\beta l)} \tag{9.90}$$

Multiplying the numerator and denominator by $1 + |K|\cos(\phi - 2\beta l) - j|K|\sin(\phi - 2\beta l)$ we get,

$$Y_{\text{in}} = G_0 \frac{1 - |K|^2 - 2j|K|\sin(\phi - 2\beta l)}{1 + |K|^2 + 2|K|\cos(\phi - 2\beta l)}$$

$$G_{\text{in}} + jB_{\text{in}} = G_0 \frac{1 - |K|^2 - 2j|K|\sin(\phi - 2\beta l)}{1 + |K|^2 + 2|K|\cos(\phi - 2\beta l)} \tag{9.91}$$

Changing to normalized form, we have

$$\frac{G_{\text{in}}}{G_0} + j\frac{B_{\text{in}}}{G_0} = \frac{1 - |K|^2 - 2j|K|\sin(\phi - 2\beta l)}{1 + |K|^2 + 2|K|\cos(\phi - 2\beta l)}$$

Separating the real and imaginary parts, we get

$$\frac{G_{\text{in}}}{G_0} = \frac{1 - |K|^2}{1 + |K|^2 + 2|K|\cos(\phi - 2\beta l)} \tag{9.92}$$

$$\frac{B_{\text{in}}}{G_0} = \frac{-2|K|\sin(\phi - 2\beta l)}{1 + |K|^2 + 2|K|\cos(\phi - 2\beta l)} \tag{9.93}$$

At point of attachment of stub, $Z_{\text{in}} = Z_0$ for no reflection and $l = l_s$. Hence, $G_{\text{in}} = G_0$ or $\dfrac{G_{\text{in}}}{G_0} = 1$. Hence, Eqn. (9.92) becomes

$$1 = \frac{1 - |K^2|}{1 + |K|^2 + 2|K|\cos(\phi - 2\beta l_s)}$$

$$1 + |K|^2 + 2|K|\cos(\phi - 2\beta l_s) = 1 - |K|^2$$

$$\cos(\phi - 2\beta l_s) = -|K| \tag{9.94}$$

$$\phi - 2\beta l_s = \cos^{-1}\{-|K|\}$$

But $\qquad \cos^{-1}\{-|K|\} = -\pi + \cos^{-1}|K|$

Therefore, $\qquad \phi - 2\beta l_s = -\pi + \cos^{-1}|K| \tag{9.95}$

$$2\beta l_s = \phi + \pi - \cos^{-1}|K|$$

$$l_s = \frac{\phi + \pi - \cos^{-1}|K|}{2\beta}$$

$$l_s = \frac{\lambda}{4\pi}(\phi + \pi - \cos^{-1}|K|) \qquad \text{since,} \quad \beta = \frac{2\pi}{\lambda} \tag{9.96}$$

Normalized susceptance given by Eq. (9.93) is simplified by using Eqn. (9.94). Substituting $l = l_s$, we get

$$\frac{B_{\text{in}}}{G_0} = \frac{-2|K|\sin(\phi - 2\beta l_s)}{1 + |K| + 2|K|\cos(\phi - 2\beta l_s)}$$

$$B_{\text{in}} = G_0 \frac{-2|K|\sin(-\pi + \cos^{-1}|K|)}{1 + |K|^2 + 2|K| \times \{-|K|\}} = G_0 \frac{-2K \sin(\cos^{-1}|K|)}{1 + |K|^2 - 2|K|^2}$$

Letting $\cos^{-1}|K| = \theta$ i.e., $\cos\theta = |K|$. Therefore,

$$\sin(\cos^{-1}|K|) = \sin\theta = \sqrt{1 - \cos^2\theta} = \sqrt{1 - |K|^2}$$

Therefore, $\qquad B_{\text{in}} = G_0 \dfrac{-2|K|\sqrt{1 - |K|^2}}{1 - |K|^2} = G_0 \dfrac{-2|K|}{\sqrt{1 - |K|^2}}$

The susceptance of the stub required to cancel the line susceptance must be negative of B_{in}. The susceptance of the lossless short-circuited stub is $-G_0 \cot \beta l_t$. Therefore,

$$G_0 \cot \beta l_t = G_0 \frac{2|K|}{\sqrt{1 - |K|^2}}$$

$$\frac{1}{\tan \beta l_t} = \frac{2|K|}{\sqrt{1 - |K|^2}}$$

i.e., $\qquad \tan \beta l_t = \dfrac{\sqrt{1 - |K|^2}}{2|K|}$

Therefore,
$$\beta l_t = \tan^{-1} \frac{\sqrt{1-|K|^2}}{2|K|}$$

$$l_t = \frac{1}{\beta} \tan^{-1} \frac{\sqrt{1-|K|^2}}{2|K|} = \frac{\lambda}{2\pi} \tan^{-1} \frac{\sqrt{1-|K|^2}}{2|K|} \quad \text{since } \beta = \frac{2\pi}{\lambda} \tag{9.97}$$

Thus, l_s and l_t can be computed using the Eqns. (9.96) and (9.97) when the reflection coefficient K and frequency of operation are known.

9.9.2 Determination of l_s and l_t by Smith Chart

If the load and the characteristic impedances of the line are given, then the length of the stub l_t and its location from the load l_s can be determined with the help of Smith chart.

For example, assume that the given load is $26 - j16$ and the characteristic impedance of the line and stub is 100 Ω.

Hence,
$$\frac{Z_R}{Z_0} = \frac{26 - j16}{100} = 0.26 - j0.16$$

Diametrically opposite point $2.75 + j1.75$ of the line will give the normalized load admittance. It is rather necessary to deal with admittances since the stub is to be connected in parallel to the line.

By locating the point $A(2.75 + j1.75)$ on the Smith Chart shown in Fig. 9.15 and having coordinates $2.75+ j1.75$ with O as centre and OP as radius S–circle is drawn. Hence, the standing wave ratio of the stub is 4.0.

The circle $\dfrac{R}{R_0 = 1}$ or $\dfrac{Y}{Y_0} = 1$ is the locus of all points for which the load impedance is equal to the characteristic impedance. This is the desired condition for no reflection, which is apparently the point of stub connection. Accordingly, the stub is located by the intersection of the S–circle and $\dfrac{Y}{Y_0} = 1$ circle as indicated by Q. In fact, there will be two points where S–circle will cut $\dfrac{Y}{Y_0} = 1$ circle. But the point nearer to the load will be considered. In this case, B is nearer to the load while moving clockwise towards the generator. The point Q is $(0.324\lambda - 0.222\lambda) = 0.102\lambda$ away from P as measured by the outer circle. Thence, the stub should be located 0.102λ from the load or $l_s = 0.102\lambda$. The l_s is also expressed in terms of its distance from $V_{\min}$. Here,
$$0.324 - 0.25\lambda = 0.074\lambda$$

The b_s value of Q represents the susceptance of the line at the stub connection which is read as 1.5 that indicates inductive susceptance. This value of line susceptance must be neutralized by short-circuited (or open circuited) stub having the same characteristic impedance as the line. Along these lines, the input susceptance of the short circuited stub should be +1.5, and the input admittance of a short-circuited stub line having capacitive susceptance of $\dfrac{b_s}{Y_0} = +1.5$ would plot at the intersection of the +1.5 susceptance circle and the $K = 1$ i.e., outermost circle at point R. This intersection occurs at 0.156λ or $0.156\lambda + 0.25\lambda = 0.406$ from short-circuited end point B. Then a short-circuited stub line 0.406λ in length will have the required capacitive susceptance. Hence, $l_t = 0.406\lambda$. In Fig. 9.16, B will be the short circuited end as the Smith chart is now being used as admittance chart.

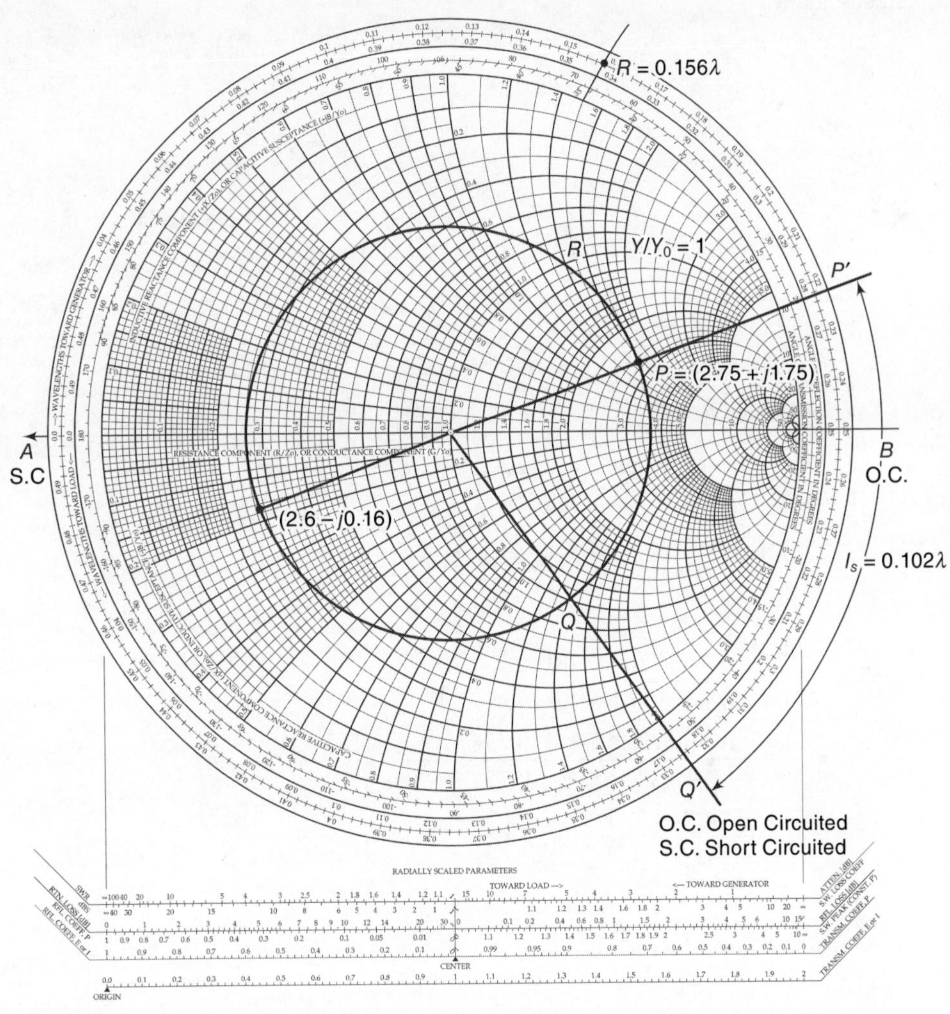

Figure 9.16 *Determination of stub length and its location*

Example 9.1

A generator of 1 V, 1 kHz supplies power to a 100 km open wire line terminated in 200 Ω resistance. The line parameters are R = 10 Ω/km, L = 3.8 mH/km, G = 1 μ℧/km and C = 0.0085 μF/km. Determine the characteristic impedance, attenuation constant, phase constant, reflection coefficient, input impedance, input power, output power and transmission efficiency.

Solution Given $R = 10\ \Omega/\text{km}$, $L = 3.8\ \text{mH/km}$, $G = 1\ \mu\text{℧/km}$ and $C = 0.0085\ \mu\text{F/km}$. Therefore,
The total series impedance is

$$Z = R + j\omega L = 10 + j(2\pi \times 1 \times 10^3)3.8 \times 10^{-3} = 10 + j23.876 = 25.885\angle 67.27°$$

The total shunt admittance is

$$Y = G + j\omega C = 1 \times 10^{-6} + j(2\pi \times 1 \times 10^3)0.0085 \times 10^{-6} + j5.34 \times 10^{-5}$$

$$= 5.34 \times 10^{-5} \angle 88.92°$$

(i) The characteristic impedance is

$$Z_0 = \sqrt{\frac{Z}{Y}} = \sqrt{\frac{R + j\omega L}{G + j\omega C}} = \sqrt{\frac{25.885\angle 67.27°}{5.34 \times 10^{-5} \angle 88.92°}} = 696.204\angle -10.825° \, \Omega$$

(ii) The propagation constant is

$$\gamma = \sqrt{ZY} = \sqrt{(R + j\omega L)(G + j\omega C)} = \sqrt{25.885\angle 67.27° \times 5.34 \times 10^{-5} \angle 88.92°}$$

$$= 0.03717\angle 78.095° = 0.0076 + j0.03637$$

The attenuation constant, $\alpha = 0.00766$ neper/km and phase constant, $\beta = 0.03637$ rad/km.

(iii) The reflection coefficient is

$$K = \frac{Z_R - Z_0}{Z_R + Z_0} \text{ where } Z_R = 200\angle 0° \, \Omega$$

Therefore, $K = \dfrac{200\angle 0° - 696.204\angle -10.825°}{200\angle 0° + 696.204\angle -10.825°}$

$$= \frac{200 + j0 - 683.8152 + j130.754}{200 + j0 + 683.8153 - j130.754} = \frac{-483.8153 + j130.754}{883.8153 - j130.754}$$

$$= \frac{501.1724\angle 164.876°}{893.435\angle -8.415°} = 0.5609\angle 173.291°$$

(iv) The input impedance, $Z_S = Z_0 \left\{ \dfrac{e^{\gamma l} + Ke^{-\gamma l}}{e^{\gamma l} - Ke^{-\gamma l}} \right\}$

Here, $e^{\gamma l} = e^{\alpha l}\angle \beta l \text{ rad} = e^{0.00766 \times 100} \angle 0.03637 \times 100 \text{ rad}$

$$= 2.1511\angle 3.637 \text{ rad} = 2.1511\angle 208.4°$$

$e^{-\gamma l} = e^{-\alpha l} \angle -\beta l \text{ rad} = e^{-0.0766 \times 100} \angle -0.03637 \times 100 \text{ rad} = 0.4676 \angle -208.4°$

Therefore,

$$Z_S = 696.204\angle -10.825° \left\{ \frac{2.1511\angle 208.4° + 0.5609\angle 173.29° \times 0.4676\angle -208.4°}{2.1511\angle 208.4° - 0.5609\angle 173.29° \times 0.4676\angle -208.4°} \right\}$$

$$= 696.204\angle -10.85° \left\{ \frac{2.1511\angle 208.4° + 0.2607\angle -35.11°}{2.1511\angle 208.4° - 0.2607\angle -35.11°} \right\}$$

$$= 696.204\angle -10.85° \left\{ \frac{-1.8922 - j1.023 + 0.2132 - j0.1499}{-1.8922 - j1.023 - 0.2132 + j0.1499} \right\}$$

$$= 696.204\angle -10.85° \left\{ \frac{-1.679 - j1.1729}{-2.1054 - j0.8731} \right\}$$

$$= 696.204\angle -10.85° \left\{ \frac{2.0481\angle -145.062°}{2.2792\angle -157.476°} \right\}$$

$$= 625.6122\angle +1.564° \ \Omega$$

(v) We know that, $I_S = \dfrac{I_R(Z_R + Z_0)}{2Z_0}\left[e^{\gamma s} - \dfrac{Z_R - Z_0}{Z_R + Z_0}e^{-\gamma s} \right]$

At sending end, $s = l$ as s is measured from the receiving end.

Therefore, $I_S = \dfrac{I_R(Z_R + Z_0)}{2Z_0}[e^{\gamma l} - Ke^{-\gamma l}]$

Now, $\quad Z_S = \dfrac{V_S}{I_S}$ and $V_S = 1\angle 0°$ V

Hence, $\quad I_S = \dfrac{V_S}{Z_S} = \dfrac{1\angle 0°}{625.6122\angle 1.564°} = 1.5984 \times 10^{-3}\angle -1.1564°$ A

Then, $\quad Z_R + Z_0 = 200\angle 0° + 696.204\angle -10.825° = 883.81\angle -8.415°$

$\qquad\qquad Ke^{-\gamma l} = 0.5609\angle 173.291° \times 0.4676\angle -208.4° = 0.2627\ \angle -35.11°$

i.e., $\quad 1.5984 \times 10^{-3}\ \angle -1.1564° = \dfrac{I_R \times 883.81\angle -8.415°}{2 \times 696.204\angle -10.825°}\ [2.1511\angle 208.4° - 0.2627\angle -35.11°]$

$\qquad 1.5984 \times 10^{-3}\ \angle -1.1564° = I_R 0.6347\angle +2.41°\ [2.28\angle -157.52°]$

Therefore, $I_R = 1.0932 \times 10^{-3}\ \angle 153.909°$ A

(vi) $\qquad V_R = I_R Z_R = 1.0932 \times 10^{-3}\ \angle 153.909° \times 200\angle 0° = 0.2186\angle 153.909°$ V

Here, $\quad P_R = E_R I_R = \cos\theta = 0.2186 \times 1.0932 \times 10^{-3} \times \cos[0°] = 2.3897 \times 10^{-4}$ W

Therefore, $P_R = I_R^2 \times R = (1.0932 \times 10^{-3})^2 \times 200 = 2.3897 \times 10^{-4}$ W

(vii) $P_S = E_S I_S \cos\theta = 1\angle 0° \times 1.5984 \times 10^{-3} \times \cos(-1.1564°) = 1.598 \times 10^{-3}$ W

(viii) Transmission efficiency, $\eta = \dfrac{P_R}{P_S} \times 100 = \dfrac{2.3897 \times 10^{-4}}{1.598 \times 10^{-3}} \times 100 = 14.954\%$

Example 9.2

Find the sending end impedance of the line having $Z_0 = 710\angle 14°$, $\gamma = 0.007 + j0.028/km$, $Z_R = 300\ \Omega$ *and* $l = 100$ *km.*

Solution Given $Z_0 = 710\angle 14°$, $\gamma = 0.007 + j0.028/km$, $Z_R = 300\ \Omega$ and $l = 100$ km.

The input impedance of a line having characteristic impedance Z_0 and terminated in Z_R is

$$Z_S = Z_0 \left[\frac{Z_R \cosh \gamma l + Z_0 \sinh \gamma l}{Z_0 \cosh \gamma l + Z_R \sinh \gamma l} \right] \qquad\qquad (1)$$

Both cosh γl and sinh γl can be determined separately as

$$\cosh \gamma l = \cosh(\alpha + j\beta)l = \cosh(\alpha l + j\beta l)$$
$$= \cosh[(0.007 \times 100) + j(0.028 \times 100)]$$
$$= \cosh[0.7 + j2.8]$$

Since $\cosh(\alpha + j\beta) = \cosh \alpha \cos \beta + j \sin \alpha \sin \beta$,

$$\cosh(0.7 + j2.8) = \cosh(0.7)\cos(2.8) + j \sinh(0.7)\sin(2.8) = -1.1826 + j0.2541$$

Similarly, sinh $\gamma l = \sinh(\alpha l + j\beta l) = \sinh(0.7 + j2.8)$

We know that, $\sinh(\alpha + j\beta) = \sinh \alpha \cos \beta + j \cosh \alpha \sin \beta$

Therefore, $\sinh(0.7 + j2.8) = \sinh(0.7)\cos(2.8) + j \cosh(0.7)\sin(2.8) = -0.7147 + j0.42$

Substituting the values of Z_0, Z_R sinh γl and cosh γl in equation (1), we get

$$Z_S = 710\angle 14° \left[\frac{300(-1.1826 + j0.2541) + 710\angle 14°(-0.7147 + j0.42)}{710\angle 14°(-1.1826 + j0.2541) + 300(-0.7147 + j0.42)} \right]$$

$$= 710\angle 14° \left[\frac{(300\angle 0°)(1.2095\angle 167.87°) + (710\angle 14°)(0.8289\angle 149.55°)}{(710\angle 14°)(1.2095\angle 167.87°) + (300\angle 0°)(0.8289\angle 149.55°)} \right]$$

$$= 710\angle 14° \left[\frac{(362.85\angle 167.87°) + (588.519\angle 163.55°)}{(858.745\angle 181.87°) + (248.67\angle 149.55°)} \right]$$

$$= 710\angle 14° \left[\frac{(-354.748 + j76.2458) + (-564.4292 + j166.6559)}{(-858.2876 - j28.0224) + (-214.3713 + j126.0225)} \right]$$

$$= 710\angle 14° \left[\frac{-919.1772 + j242.9017}{-1072.6589 + j98} \right]$$

$$= 710\angle 14° \left[\frac{950.7302\angle 165.19°}{1077.1263\angle 174.77°} \right]$$

$$= 626.68\angle 4.42° \ \Omega$$

Example 9.3

A transmission line of 100 Ω characteristic impedance is $(3/8)\lambda$ long and is terminated by a 50 Ω impedance. Determine the line input impedance at 10 MHz, if the dielectric is air.

Solution   Given $Z_0 = 100 \ \Omega$ and $Z_L = 50 \ \Omega$

The input impedance is

$$Z_S = Z_0 \left[\frac{\{(Z_L/Z_0) + j \tan \beta l\}}{\{1 + j(Z_L/Z_0)\tan \beta l\}} \right]$$

Here,
$$\lambda = \frac{c}{f} = \frac{3 \times 10^8}{10 \times 10^6} = 30 \text{ m}$$

$$l = \frac{3\lambda}{8} = \frac{3 \times 30}{8} = 11.25 \text{ m}$$

$$\beta l = \frac{360 \times 11.25}{30} = 135°$$

$$\tan(\beta l) = \tan 135° = -1$$

Therefore, the input impedance is

$$Z_s = Z_0\left[\frac{0.5 - j}{1 - j0.5}\right] = Z_0 \frac{(0.5 - j)(1 + 0.5j)}{1.25}$$

$$= Z_0(0.8 - j0.6) = 100(0.8 - j0.6) = (80 - j60)\,\Omega$$

Example 9.4

It is desired to match a load of impedance $(100 + j100)\,\Omega$ to a generator of internal impedance $(600 + j0)\,\Omega$ at 10 MHz by means of a quarter wavelength line and a reactive stub connected across the load terminals. Determine the required characteristic impedance of the quarter-wavelength line and the length of the stub, if the length of the stub has the same characteristic impedance as the quarter wavelength line.

Solution Given $Z_{in} = 600\,\Omega$ and $Z_R = Z_L = (100 + j100) = 141.4\angle 45°$

i.e. $$Y_L = \frac{1}{141.4}\angle -45° = (5 \times 10^{-3}) - (j5 \times 10^{-3})$$

The shunt stub neutralizes the reactance part of Y_L. In the case of an open-circuited stub, we have

$$Z_{OC} = -jZ_0\cos(\beta l) \quad \text{and} \quad Y_{OC} = (j/Z_0)\tan(\beta l)$$

Also, for a short-circuited stub,

$$Z_{SC} = jZ_0\tan(\beta l) \quad \text{and} \quad Y_{SC} = (-j/Z_0)\cot(\beta l)$$

Here, an open-circuited stub is required to neutralize $(-j5 \times 10^{-3})$. Therefore,

$$(1/Z_0)\tan \beta l = 5 \times 10^{-3}$$

where $Z_0 = \sqrt{Z_{in}Z_R} = \sqrt{600 \times 141.4} = 291.27\,\Omega$

Therefore, $\tan \beta l = 291.27 \times 5 \times 10^{-3} = 1.4564$

i.e., $$\beta l = \left(\frac{2\pi}{\lambda}\right)l = \tan^{-1}(1.4564) = 55.53°$$

where $\lambda = \dfrac{c}{f} = \dfrac{3 \times 10^8}{10^7} = 30$ m

Therefore, the length of the stub, $l = \dfrac{\lambda}{2\pi} \times 55.53° = \dfrac{30}{360°} \times 55.53° = 4.63$ m

Example 9.5

Find the reflection coefficient in the case of a transmission line with a VSWR value of 2.5.

Solution Given VSWR, $S = 2.5$

The reflection coefficient, $K = \dfrac{S - 1}{S + 1} = \dfrac{2.5 - 1}{2.5 + 1} = 0.4286$

Example 9.6

Find the SWR value in the case of a transmission line with a reflection coefficient of 0.6.

Solution   The reflection coefficient is given by

$$K = \frac{S-1}{S+1}$$

Here, $$S = \frac{1+|K|}{1-|K|} = \frac{1+0.6}{1-0.6} = 4$$

Example 9.7

Determine the value of VSWR in the case of (i) $Z_R = 0$, (ii) $Z_R = \infty$, (iii) $Z_R = Z_0$ and (iv) $Z_R = 2Z_0$, if Z_0 represents the characteristic impedance of a line and Z_0 represents the load impedance.

Solution   We know that the voltage reflection coefficient is $K = \dfrac{Z_R - Z_0}{Z_R + Z_0}$

(i) When $Z_R = 0$, $K = \dfrac{Z_R - Z_0}{Z_R + Z_0} = \dfrac{0 - Z_0}{0 + Z_0} = -1$

$$\text{VSWR} = \frac{1+|K|}{1-|K|} = \frac{1+1}{1-1} = \infty$$

(ii) When $Z_R = \infty$, $K = \dfrac{\infty - Z_0}{\infty + Z_0} = 1$

$$\text{VSWR} = \frac{1+|K|}{1-|K|} = \frac{1+1}{1-1} = \infty$$

(iii) When $Z_R = Z_0$, $K = \dfrac{Z_0 - Z_0}{Z_0 + Z_0} = 0$

$$\text{VSWR} = \frac{1+|K|}{1-|K|} = \frac{1+0}{1-0} = 1$$

(iv) When $Z_R = 2Z_0$, $K = \dfrac{2Z_0 - Z_0}{2Z_0 + Z_0} = \dfrac{Z_0}{3Z_0} = \dfrac{1}{3}$

$$\text{VSWR} = \frac{1+|K|}{1-|K|} = \frac{1+\dfrac{1}{3}}{1-\dfrac{1}{3}} = 2$$

Example 9.8

A short-wave 4 W transmitter, operating at 27 MHz, is connected through a 10-m 50 Ω cable to an aerial with a load resistance of 300 Ω. Assume that the velocity of propagation is 2.07×10^8 m/sec.
Determine

(i) The reflection coefficient,
(ii) The electrical length of the cable in wavelength,

(iii) The VSWR value, and

(iv) The amount of the transmitter output power absorbed by the aerial.

Solution   Given $Z_L = 300\ \Omega$, $Z_0 = 50\ \Omega$, $v = 2.07 \times 10^8$ m/sec, $f = 27$ MHz, aerial length = 10 m and Transmitter power = 4 W.

(i) $K = \dfrac{Z_L - Z_0}{Z_L + Z_0} = \dfrac{300 - 50}{300 + 50} = 0.71$

(ii) $\lambda = (v/f) = (2.07 \times 10^8 / 27 \times 10^6) = 7.67$ m.

Here v is the assumed velocity of propagation in the cable. The electrical length is $(10/7.67)\lambda = 1.3\lambda$.

(iii) With a resistive load, VSWR $= \dfrac{R_L}{Z_0} = \dfrac{300}{50} = 6$

Alternatively, VSWR $= \dfrac{1 + |K|}{1 - |K|} = \dfrac{1 + 0.71}{1 - 0.71} = 6$

(iv) Sine the fraction (0.71) of the voltage travelling towards the load is reflected, the fraction (0.29) of the voltage is absorbed by the aerial.

$$P_{\text{aerial}} = (0.29)^2 \times 4 = 0.33 \text{ W}$$

Example 9.9

A line with characteristic impedance of 50 Ω is terminated in an impedance of (75 + j75) Ω. Determine the reflection coefficient and voltage standing wave ratio.

Solution   Given $Z_0 = 50\ \Omega$ and $Z_R = 75 + j75\ \Omega$

Here, $K = \dfrac{Z_R - Z_0}{Z_R + Z_0} = \dfrac{75 + j75 - 50}{75 + j75 + 50} = \dfrac{25 + j75}{125 + j75}$

$$= \dfrac{79.0569\angle 71.56°}{145.7737\angle 30.96°} = 0.54\angle 40.6° = |K|\ \angle\phi$$

The voltage standing wave ratio is

$$S = \dfrac{1 + |K|}{1 + |K|} = \dfrac{1 + 0.54}{1 - 0.54} = 3.35$$

Example 9.10

A lossless line has a standing wave ratio of 4. The characteristic impedance R_0 is 150 Ω and the maximum, voltage measured on the line is 135 V. Determine the power being delivered to the load.

Solution   Given $R_0 = 150\ \Omega$, $S = 4$ and $V_{\max} = 135$ V

At voltage maxima, the impedance is maximum. Therefore,

$$R_{\max} = SR_0 = 4(150) = 600\ \Omega$$

Then the power delivered to the load is

$$P = \dfrac{V_{\max}^2}{R_{\max}} = \dfrac{(135)^2}{600} = 30.375 \text{ W}$$

Example 9.11

A loss-free radio frequency transmission line has a characteristic impedance Z_0 of 600 Ω and is connected to a resistive load of 75 Ω. Determine the position and length of a short-circuited stub, or the same construction as the line, which would enable the main length of the line to be correctly terminated at 150 MHz.

Solution The input impedance, looking into the parallel connection of stub and loaded termination, must be (1/600) Ω. Looking into a length of the line measured from the loaded end, the input admittance is

$$Y_{\text{in}} = \frac{\left[600 + j75 \tan\left(\dfrac{2\pi l}{\lambda}\right)\right]}{600\left(75 + j600 \tan\left(\dfrac{2\pi l}{\lambda}\right)\right)}$$

The length of the stub and the position of its connection are to be arranged in such a way that the real part of Y_{in} is (1/600) Ω, and the imaginary part is neutralized by the admittance of the stub.

Here,

$$Y_{\text{in}}(\text{real part}) = \frac{(600 \times 75) + (600 \times 75) \tan^2\left(\dfrac{2\pi l}{\lambda}\right)}{600\left[75^2 + 600^2 \tan^2\left(\dfrac{2\pi l}{\lambda}\right)\right]}$$

$$= \frac{0.125 + 0.125 \tan^2\left(\dfrac{2\pi l}{\lambda}\right)}{600\left[0.0156 + \tan^2\left(\dfrac{2\pi l}{\lambda}\right)\right]}$$

Hence $\qquad 0.875 \tan^2(2\pi l/\lambda) = 0.109$,

$\qquad\qquad\quad \tan(2\pi l/\lambda) = 0.353$,

Therefore, $\qquad (2\pi l/\lambda) = 19.50°$

i.e., $\qquad\qquad (l/\gamma) = (19.50\pi/180 \times 2\pi) = 0.054$,

Substituting $\qquad \lambda = 200$ cm, we get

$\qquad\qquad\quad l = 10.8$ cm.

If the length of the stub is l_s, then $\phi = \dfrac{2\pi l_s}{\lambda}$ so that the susceptance of the stub is $(2\pi l/600) \cot \phi$.

Here $\qquad Y_{\text{in}}$ (imaginary part) $= [\{(75)^2 - (600)^2\}]/[600\{(75)^2 + (600)^2 \tan^2(2\pi l/\lambda)\}]$

$\qquad\qquad\qquad\qquad = [0.0156 - 1]/[600(0.0156 + 0.1245)]$

$\qquad\qquad\qquad\qquad = -0.9844/600 \times 0.14 = -7.03/600$

For neutralization of susceptance, we have

$\qquad\qquad\quad \cot \phi = -7.03$

i.e., $\qquad\qquad \phi = 172°$

Therefore, $\qquad l_s = (172/360)200 = 95.5$ cm

Example 9.12

A low pass transmission line has characteristic impedance of 70 Ω and is terminated by another impedance of $(115 - j50)$ Ω. The wavelength on the line is 2.5 m. Find the standing wave ratio, maximum and minimum line impedances. Also, determine the distance between the load and the first voltage minimum.

Solution   Given $Z_0 = 70$ Ω, $Z_R = (115 - j80)$ $\Omega = 140\angle -34.8°$ Ω and $\lambda = 2.5$ m.

The reflection coefficient is $K = \dfrac{Z_R - Z_0}{Z_R + Z_0} = \dfrac{(115 - j80) - 70}{(115 - j80) + 70} = \dfrac{45 - j80}{185 - j80} = 0.46\angle -37.22°$

Therefore, $|K| = 0.46$

Then, the standing wave ratio, $S = \dfrac{1 + |K|}{1 - |K|} = \dfrac{1.46}{0.54} = 2.7$

The maximum line impedance $= SZ_0 = 2.7 \times 70 = 189$ Ω

The minimum line impedance $= \dfrac{Z_0}{S} = \dfrac{70}{2.7} = 25.9$ Ω

The distance between the load and the first voltage minimum is

$$d = \frac{\lambda}{4} + \frac{Z_0}{Z_R} = \frac{2.5}{4} + \frac{70}{140} = 1.125 \text{ m}$$

Example 9.13

Design a quarter wave transformer to match a load of 200 Ω to a source resistance of 500 Ω. The operating frequency is 200 MHz.

Solution   Given $Z_R = 200$ Ω, and $Z_{in} = 500$ Ω
The characteristic impedance of quarter wave transmission line is

$$R_0 = \sqrt{Z_R \cdot Z_{in}} = \sqrt{(200)(500)} = 316.22 \text{ } \Omega$$

The wavelength, $\lambda = \dfrac{c}{f} = \dfrac{3 \times 10^8}{200 \times 0^6} = 1.5$ m

Therefore, the length of the quarter wave line, $l_s = \dfrac{\lambda}{4} = \dfrac{1.5}{4} = 0.375$ m

Example 9.14

It is required to match 200 Ω load to a 300 Ω transmission line to reduce the SWR along line to 1. What must be the characteristic impedance of a quarter waver transformer used for this purpose if it is directly connected to the load?

Solution   Given $Z_R = 200$ Ω and $R_0 = 300$ Ω
When SWR is of value 1 it means that the line is perfectly matched without any reflection.

By definition, $R'_0 = \sqrt{R_0 \cdot Z_R} = \sqrt{(200)(300)} = 244.95$ Ω

Example 9.15

An ideal lossless quarter wave line of characteristic impedance 60 Ω is terminated in a load impedance Z_L. Give the value of input impedance of the line when $Z_L = 0$ and 60 Ω.

Solution   Given $R_0 = 60$ Ω.

For a quarter wave line, $Z_{in} = \dfrac{R_0^2}{Z_L}$

(i) If $Z_L = 0$, then $Z_{in} = \dfrac{(60)^2}{0} = \infty$ i.e., open circuit.

(ii) If $Z_L = \infty$, then $Z_{in} = \dfrac{(60)^2}{\infty} = 0$ i.e, short circuit.

(iii) If $Z_L = 60$ Ω, then $Z_{in} = \dfrac{(60)^2}{60} = 60$ Ω

Example 9.16

Determine the input impedance of the transmission line of electrical length 28° with terminated load impedance of $\dfrac{Z_R}{R_0} = 2.6 + j1$. Use Smith chart.

Solution   Given the normalized load impedance $z_R = 2.6 + j1$ and electrical length of line = 28°.

(i) In the Smith chart, the intersection of $r = 26$ circle and $x = +j1$ circle represents load impedance point and it is represented as point A.

(ii) With point $O(1, 0)$ as the centre and distance OA as the radius, draw a line from O to A and extend the line upto point A' on outer scale as shown in Fig. E9.16.

(iii) As the given electrical length 28° corresponds to length expressed in wavelength, then $\dfrac{28°}{360°}$ $\lambda = 0.7777\lambda = 0.078\lambda$.

(iv) Moving 0.078λ distance form A' to locate point B' along βs scale on the outer periphery result in $(0.227 + 0.078)\lambda = 0.305\lambda$. This point is marked as B'.

(v) Further, from center point O to B', draw a line which intersects constant S-circle at point B forming the source or input point.

(vi) The coordinates of point B is the intersection of $r = 1.58$ circle and $x = -j1.4$ circle. Since the Smith chart is used as impedance chart, the imaginary part or reactive part of input impedance is negative capacitive reactance. Therefore, the value of normalized input impedance is

$$z_s = \frac{Z_S}{R_0} = (1.58 - j1.4)\,\Omega$$

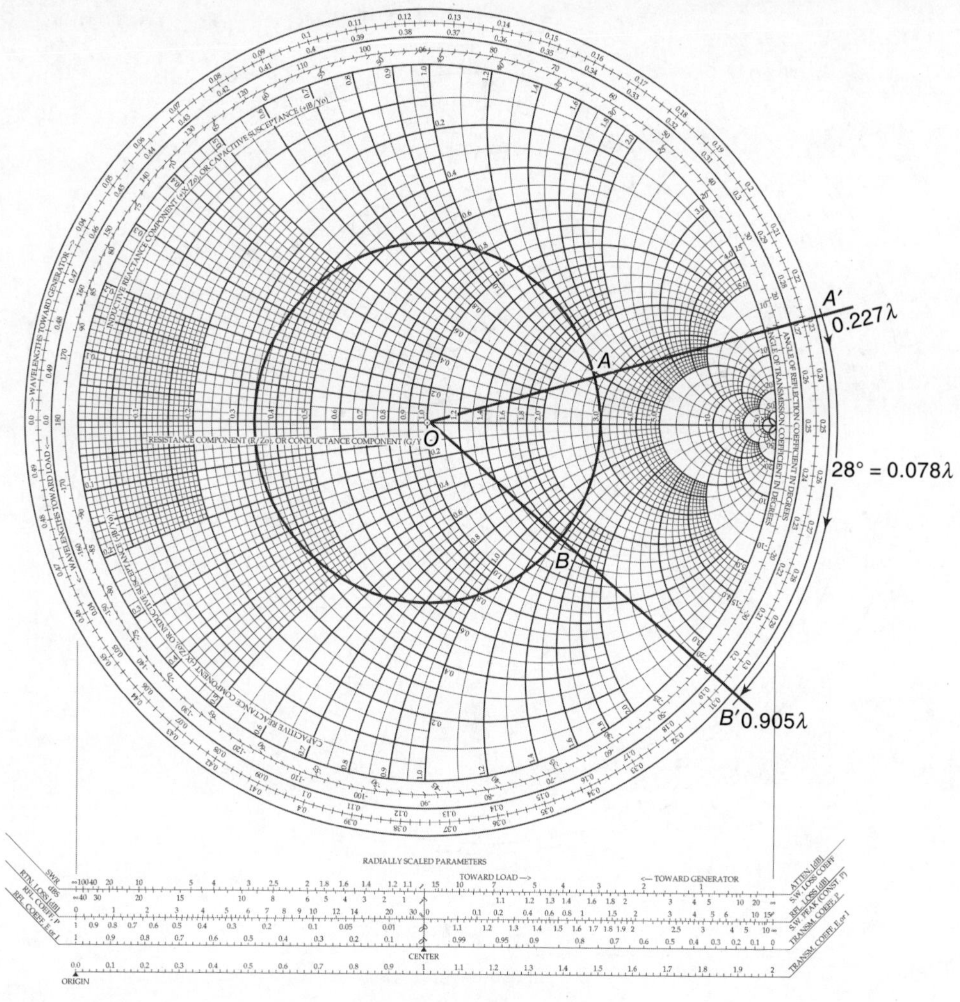

Figure E9.16

Example 9.17

The transmission line has standing wave ratio S = 2.5 and voltage minima exists at 0.15λ from the load. Find the load and input impedance for a line of 0.35λ length. Use Smith chart.

Solution   Given $S = 2.5$, $V_{\min}$ at 0.15λ from load and l = length of the line = 0.35λ.

(i) With $O(1, 0)$ as center of the Smith chart shown in Fig. E9.17, draw a constant S-circle through point 2.5 on the real axis.

(ii) For impedance chart, the voltage minima occurs at a point on the real axis to the left end of the origin at which the constant S-circle ($S = 2.5$) cuts. It is denoted by point A' which represents voltage minima at 0.4 $\left(\text{i.e., } \dfrac{1}{S} = \dfrac{1}{2.5} = 0.4\right)$.

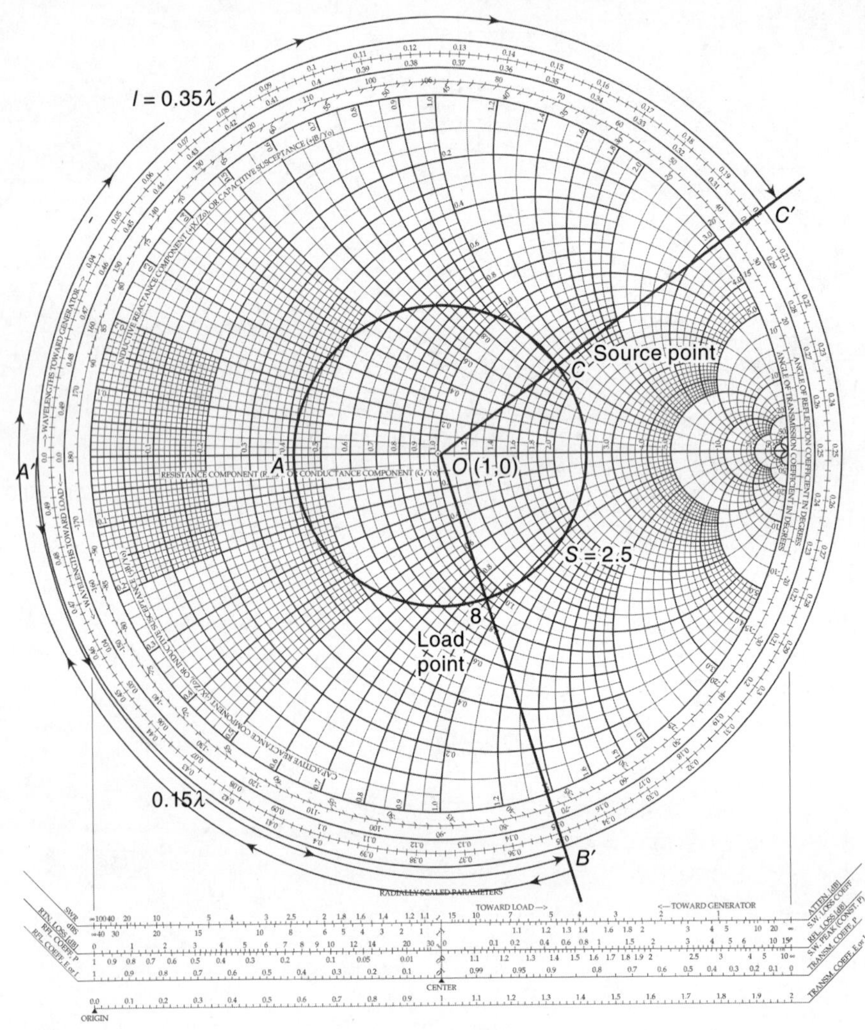

Figure E9.17

(iii) As the voltage minima is at a distance of 0.15λ from the load, we need to travel towards load with a distance of 0.15λ in anticlockwise direction to obtain load point B' from the voltage minima point A'.

(iv) From center point O to B' draw a line such that it intersects constant S circle at the load point B. Here, the point B is the intersection of $r = 0.89$ circle and $x = -j0.9$ circle. Since the Smith chart is used as impedance chart, the imaginary part or reactive part of input impedance is negative capacitive reactance. Hence, the normalized load impedance is

$$z_R = \frac{Z_R}{R_0} = (0.89 - j0.9)\ \Omega$$

(v) Since the total length of the line is 0.35λ, we have to travel 0.35λ towards generator from B' to point C' on the outer periphery in clockwise direction to obtain source or generator point. Draw a line from the center O to point C'. The intersection of this line with the constant S-circle ($S = 2.5$) at point C forms the source or generator point.

(vi) The point C is the intersection of $r = 1.68$ circle and $x = +j1$ circle. Since the Smith chart is used as impedance chart, the imaginary part or reactive part of input impedance is positive inductive reactance. So, the normalized input impedance will be

$$z_S = \frac{Z_S}{R_0} = (1.68 + j1.0)\,\Omega$$

Example 9.18

A transmission line has a characteristic impedance of 300 Ω and terminated in a load $Z_L = (150 + j150)$ Ω. Find the following using Smith chart. (i) VSWR (ii) Reflection coefficient (iii) input impedance at distance 0.1λ from the load (iv) input admittance from 0.1λ from load and (v) position of first voltage minimum and maximum from the load.

Solution   Given $Z_0 = R_0 = 300\,\Omega$ and $Z_L = (150 + j150)\Omega$.

(i) The normalized load impedance is given by

$$z_L = \frac{Z_L}{R_0} = \frac{150 + j150}{300} = 0.5 + j0.5\,\Omega$$

The intersection of $r = 0.5$ circle and $x = +j0.5$ circle is marked as load point A as shown in Fig. E9.18.

(ii) With point $O(1, 0)$ as center and OA as radius, draw a constant S-circle which cuts the real axis at 2.6. This will give the value of VSWR as $S = 2.6$.

(iii) Make a line OA and extend it upto point A' on the outer periphery of the chart. This line will intersect the angle of reflection coefficient scale at $118°$ which represents the angle of reflection coefficient. To obtain the magnitude of K, the linear scale is shown at the bottom of the chart. The distance OA is equivalent to magnitude of K shown at the bottom of the chart i.e., $|K| = 0.42$. So, the reflection coefficient is $K = 0.42\angle 118°$.

(iv) As the input impedance is at a distance of 0.1λ from load, moving in clockwise direction from point $A'(0.086\lambda)$ to reach point B' results in $(0.086 + 0.1)\lambda = 0.186\lambda$. Now a line OB' is drawn such that it cuts S-circle ($S = 2.6$) at input impedance point B. This point B is the intersection of $r = 1.38$ circle and $x = +j1.12$ circle. Therefore, the input impedance at a distance of 0.1λ from the load is $z_d = \dfrac{Z_d}{R_0} = (1.38$

$+ j1.12)\Omega$. Hence, the actual impedance is $Z_d = R_0(1.38 + j1.12) = 300(1.38 + j1.12) = (414 + j336)\Omega$.

(v) As the input admittance is at a distance of 0.1λ away from load, draw a diameter through O and B. This line will cut constant $-S$ circle in the opposite side at point C. This point is the intersection of $g = 0.44$ circle and $b = -j0.38$ circle. Therefore, the input admittance is

$$y_d = \frac{Y_d}{G_0} = 0.44 - j0.38$$

and the actual admittance is

$$Y_d = G_0(0.44 - j0.38) = \frac{1}{R_0}(0.44 - j0.38) = \frac{0.44 - j0.38}{300}$$

i.e., $Y_d = (1.4667 - j1.2667) \times 10^{-3}\,\Omega^{-1}$

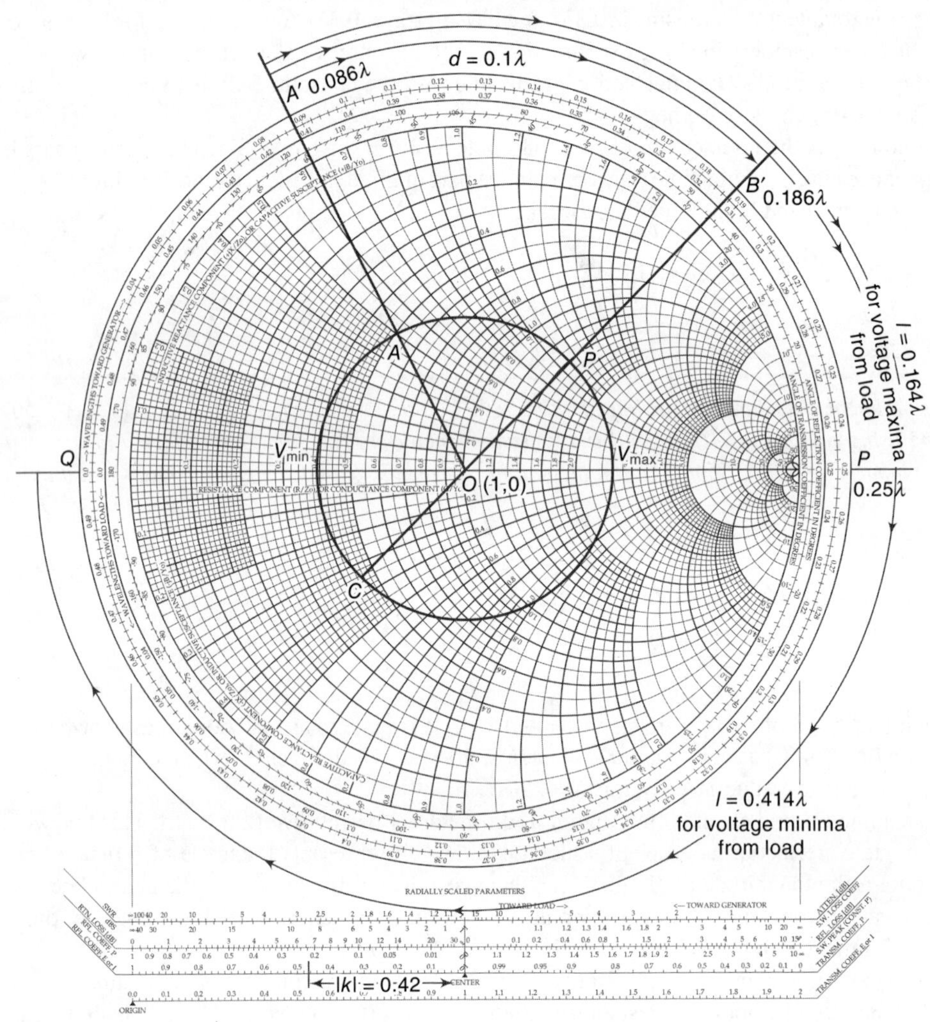

Figure E9.18

(vi) To the left of center on real axis, the voltage minima occurs at $S = 0.39$ and to the right of center on real axis, the voltage maxima occurs at $S = 2.6$. To obtain the position of the voltage maxima from load, moving in clockwise direction from point A' (load point) to point P (voltage maxima point) leads to $0.25\lambda - 0.086\lambda = 0.164\lambda$. So, the first voltage maxima is located at a distance of 0.164λ from the load.

(vii) Now to obtain the position of voltage minima from load, moving in clockwise direction from point A' (load point) to point Q (voltage minima point) leads to $0.25\lambda + 0.164\lambda = 0.414\lambda$. So, the first voltage minima is located at a distance of 0.414λ from the load.

Example 5.19

A transmission line of 100 m long is terminated in load of $(100 - j200)\Omega$. Determine the line impedance at 25 m from the load end at a frequency of 10 MHz. Assume line impedance as $Z_0 = 100\ \Omega$. Determine the input impedance and admittance using Smith chart.

Solution

(a) To obtain input impedance:

(i) First determine the normalized load impedance.

i.e., $\qquad z_R = \dfrac{Z_R}{R_0} = \dfrac{100 - j200}{100} = (1 - j2)\ \Omega$

Here, the intersection of $r = 1$ circle and $x = -j2$ circle is marked as load point A in the chart as shown in Fig. E9.19(a).

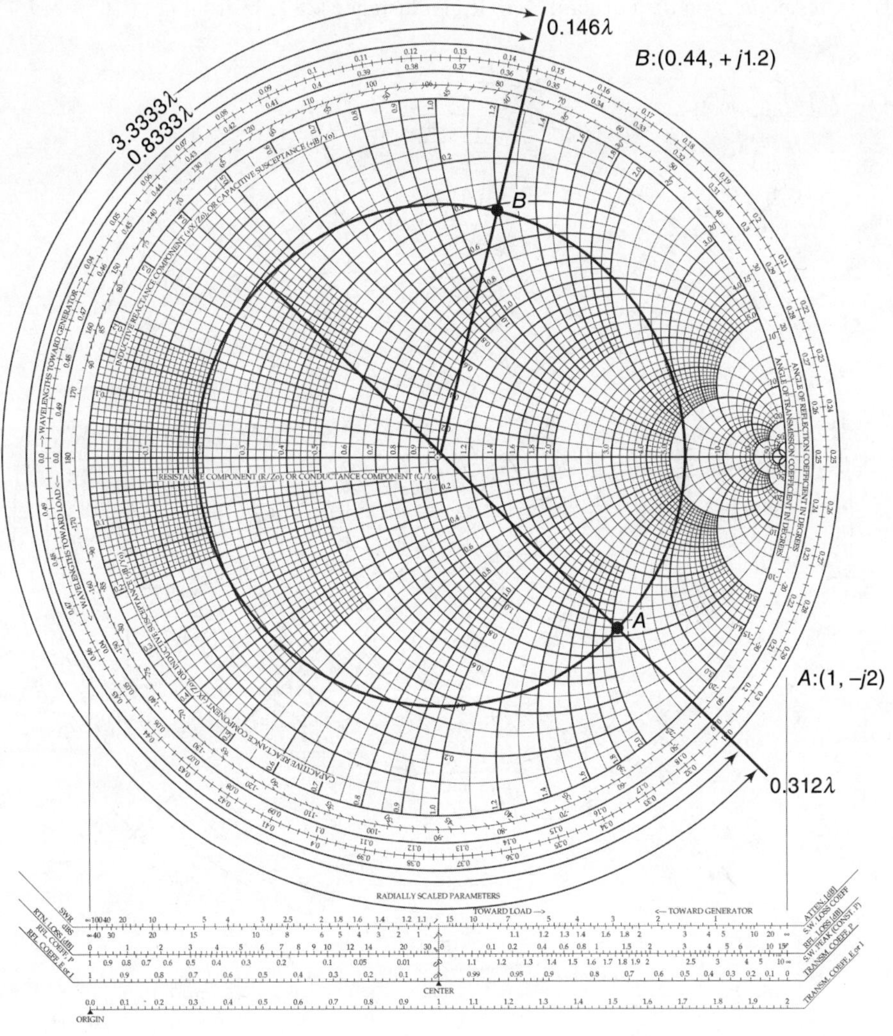

Figure E9.19(a)

(ii) With *OA* as radius, draw a circle representing constant *S*-circle.

Also, for given line, $\lambda = \dfrac{c}{f} = \dfrac{3 \times 10^8}{10 \times 10^6} = 30$ m

(iii) From the above load point *A*, move towards the generator in clockwise direction on the chart resulting in

$$s_1 = 25 \text{ m} = \frac{25}{30}\lambda = 0.8333\lambda$$

This locates point *B* on the constant *S*-circle at a distance 0.8333λ from point *A*.

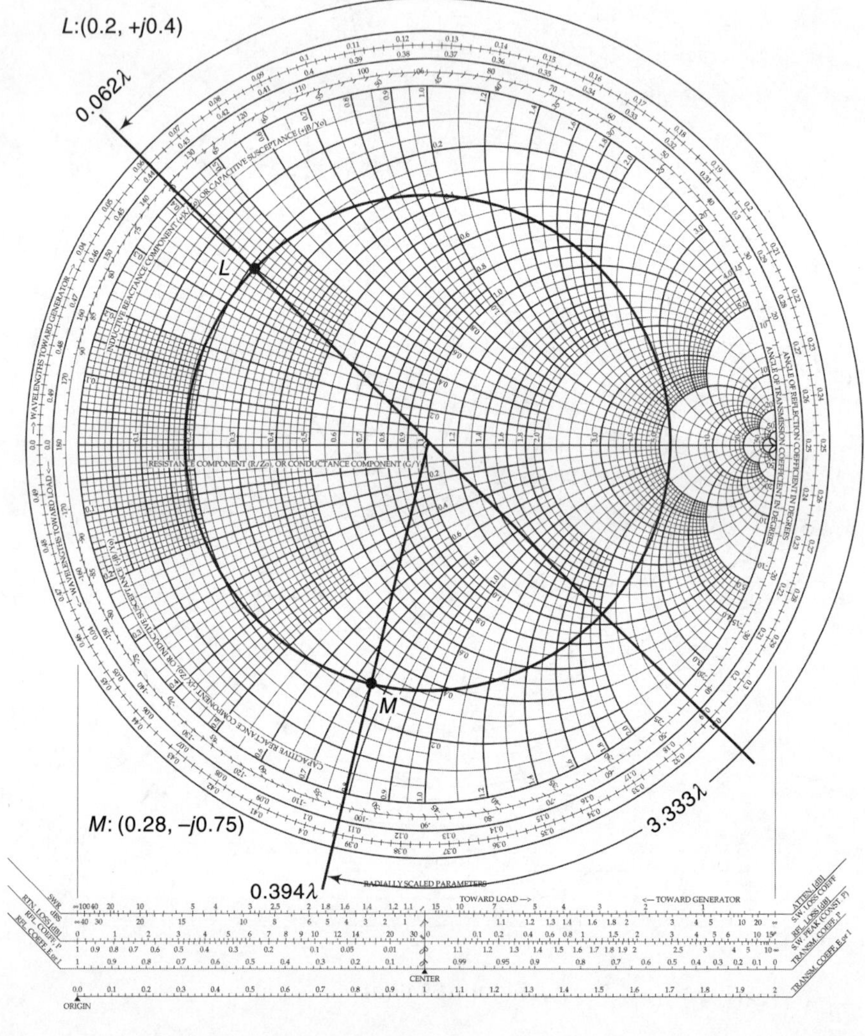

Figure E9.19(b)

(iv) At point B, the resistance is 0.44 and the susceptance is 1.2. Here, the impedance of line at a distance 25 m from the load is given by

$$Z_S = R_0(0.44 + j1.2) = 100(0.44 + j1.2)$$

i.e., $\qquad Z_S = (44 + j120)\,\Omega$

(v) Further to obtain input impedance, moving a line length of 100 m i.e., 3.3333λ distance from load point A, it is noticed that the same point is reached as shown in Fig. E9.19(a). Hence, the input impedance will also be the same i.e. $Z_{\text{in}} = (44 + j120)\,\Omega$.

(b) To obtain input admittance:

  (i) First calculate the normalized admittance.

i.e., $\qquad y_R = \dfrac{Y_R}{G_0} = \dfrac{1/Z_R}{1/Z_0} = \dfrac{Z_0}{Z_R} = \dfrac{100}{100 - j200} = \dfrac{1}{1 - j2} = \dfrac{1 + j2}{5} = 0.2 + j0.4$

  (ii) As shown in Fig. E9.19(b), mark the load point as L on the Smith chart. Moving a length of 100 m i.e. 3.3333λ from load point L, we reach the input admittance point M. At this point M, the conductance is 0.28 and susceptance is $-j0.75$. Therefore, the input admittance is

$$Y_{\text{in}} = G_0(0.28 - j0.75) = \dfrac{(0.28 - j0.75)}{100} = (2.8 \times 10^{-3} - j7.5 \times 10^{-3})\,\Omega^{-1}$$

Example 9.20

A load $(50 - j100)\,\Omega$ is connected across a 50 Ω line. Design a short circuited stub to provide matching between the load and line at a signal frequency of 30 MHz using Smith chart.

Solution Given $Z_R = 50 - j100\ \Omega$ and $Z_0 = R_0 = 50\ \Omega$.

  (i) First determine the normalized load admittance. Here, the Smith chart is used as admittance chart.

$$\dfrac{Y_R}{G_0} = \dfrac{1/Z_R}{1/Z_0} = \dfrac{Z_0}{Z_R} = \dfrac{50}{50 - j100} = \dfrac{1}{1 - j2} = \dfrac{1 + j2}{5} = 0.2 + j0.4$$

  (ii) This normalized admittance is marked as load point A on the chart as shown in Fig. E9.20.

  (iii) Through point A, draw a constant S circle that cuts the real axis at 5.8 indicating the SWR as 5.8 before the use of stub.

  (iv) The intersection of S circle and unity conductance circle is marked as point B. As point B is nearest to the load, the susceptance at this point is $+j2$ (capacitive nature). This is the location where the stub is to be connected.

  (v) Extending the line OA and OB to the outer periphery of the chart, we obtain $\beta s = 0.062\lambda$ for point A and $\beta s = 0.188\lambda$ for point B. Moving from the load to generator end in clockwise direction, the distance from the load to the point at which stub is to be connected is $s_1 = (0.188\lambda - 0.062\lambda) = 0.126\lambda$

  (vi) As the line susceptance is capacitive, the stub susceptance should be opposite i.e., $-j2$. The intersection of $-j2$ susceptance circle with the outer periphery of the chart is marked as C. So at point C, $\beta s = 0.322\lambda$. As the given stub is a short circuited one, measuring the distance from the extreme right hand side on the real axis forms the short circuit point ($\beta s = 0.25\lambda$). Hence, the length of the short circuited stub is given by

$$L = 0.322\lambda - 0.25\lambda = 0.272\lambda$$

Here, a short circuited stub of length 0.072λ should be located at a distance of 0.126λ from the load of $(50 - j100)\,\Omega$ with 50 Ω line.

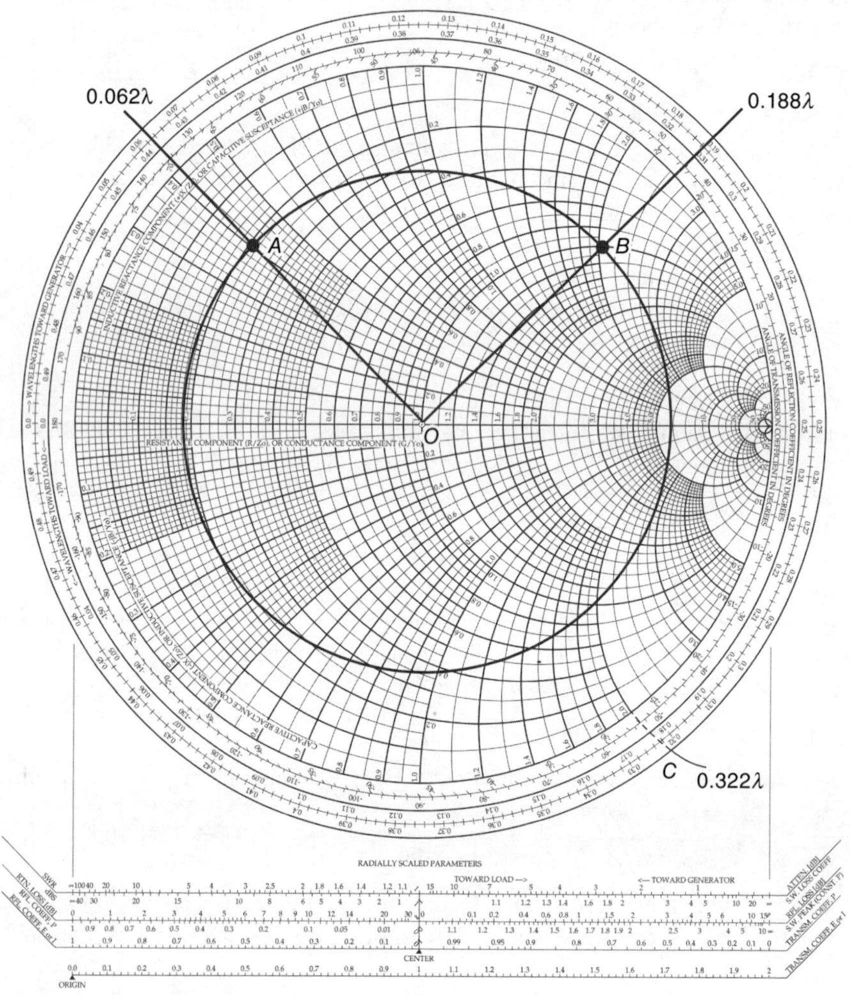

Figure E9.20

Example 9.21

An RF transmission line with a characteristic impedance of $300\angle 0°$ Ω is terminated in an impedance of $100\angle -45°$ Ω. The load is to be matched to the transmission line by using a short circuited stub. With the help of Smith chart, determine the length of the stub and the distance from the load.

Solution   Given $Z_R = 100\angle -45°$ $\Omega = (70.71 - j70.71)$ Ω and $Z_0 = R_0 = 300$ Ω.

(i) First determine the normalized load impedance

i.e., $$z_R = \frac{Z_R}{R_0} = \frac{70.71 - j70.71}{300} = (0.2357 - j0.2357)\ \Omega$$

(ii) This normalized impedance is marked as load point A at the intersection of $r = 0.2357$ circle and $x = -j0.2357$ circle on the chart as shown in Fig. E9.21. As the imaginary component i.e., reactive component of the impedance is negative, the point A is located below the horizontal axis.

(iii) Through point A, draw a constant S circle with center point O as origin and OA as radius that cuts the real axis at 4.6 indicating the SWR as 4.6 before the use of stub.

(iv) Now, draw a line from point A to O and extend it to reach the opposite end of constant S circle. This point is represented as normalized load admittance point B. Here, the normalized admittance is $y_R = 2.1 + j2.1$. Further, extend the line AOB to the outer periphery of the chart to reach point B'.

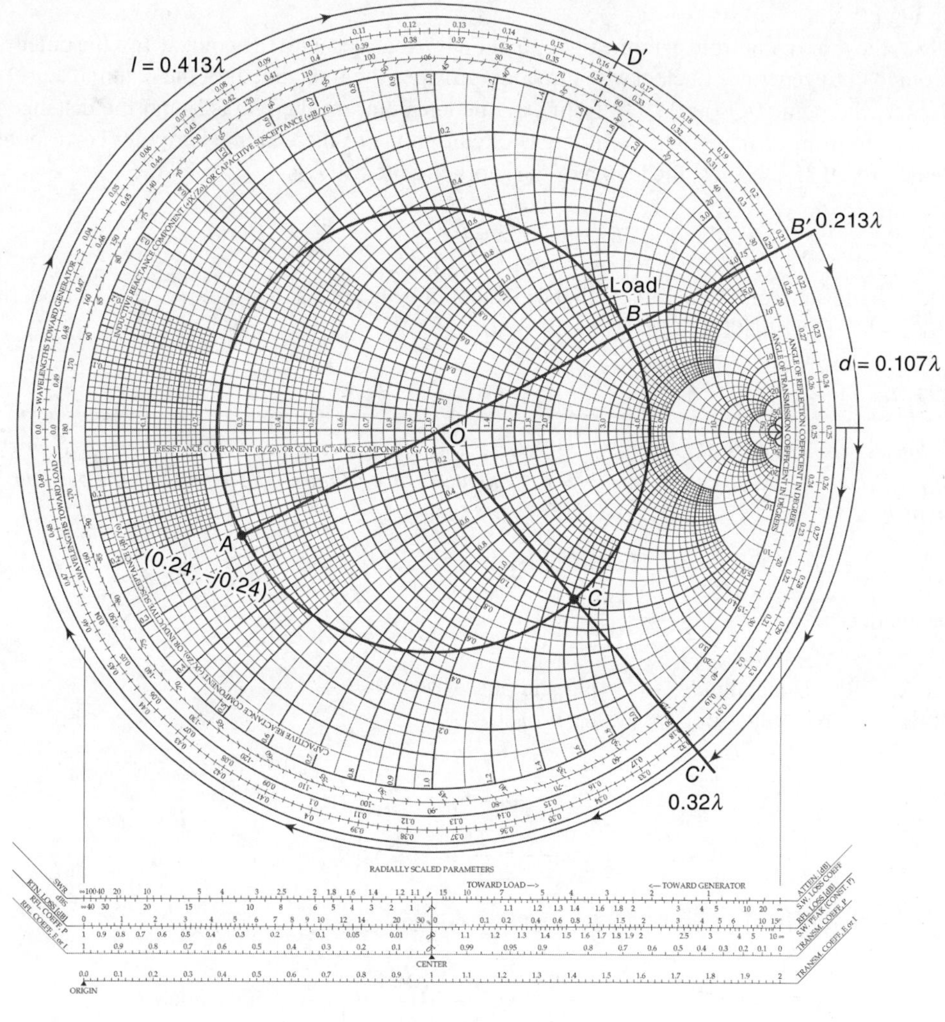

Figure E9.21

(v)   Moving along the constant S circle from load to generator in the clockwise direction to reach a point C at which constant S-circle intersects the unity circle $\left(\dfrac{Y}{G_0}=1\right)$. Draw a line from center point O to C and also, extend the line to point C' on the outer periphery.

(vi) Now, the distance of the stub from the load is obtained from $B'C'$ as
$$d = \text{arc } B'C' = 0.32\lambda - 0.213\lambda = 0.107\lambda$$

(vii) At point C, the normalized admittance value is $1 + j1.65$. This is the location where the stub is to be connected. So, the stub should provide an opposite susceptance of $-j1.65$.

(viii) The susceptance of $-j1.65$ is represented as point D' in the chart and is located above real axis as shown in Fig E9.21.

(ix) Now, the movement from extreme right point on the real axis upto the point D' (on the outer periphery) from load to generator in clockwise direction provides the total length of the required stub.

(x)   Hence, the point D' is at 0.163λ from extreme left point on the real axis and the distance along the outer rim from extreme right point (short circuit point) to the extreme left point corresponds to $\lambda/4$ length i.e., 0.25λ. Hence, the length of the short circuited stub is
$$l = \frac{\lambda}{4} + 0.163\lambda = 0.25\lambda + 0.163\lambda = 0.413\lambda$$

Here, a short circuited stub of length 0.413λ should be located at a distance of 0.107λ from the load of $100\angle{-45°}\ \Omega$ with $300\ \Omega$ line.

Example 9.22

An UHF lossless transmission line working at 1 GHz is connected to an unmatched line producing a voltage reflection coefficient of $0.5\angle 30°$. Calculate after deriving necessary relations, the length and the position of the stub to match the line.

Solution   Given $f = 1\ \text{GHz} = 10^9\ \text{Hz} = 10^3\ \text{MHz}$

The wavelength is, $\lambda = \dfrac{300}{f\,(\text{in MHz})} = \dfrac{300}{10^3} = 0.3\ \text{m}$

Since $K = 0.5\angle 30°$, its magnitude, $|K| = 0.5$ and phase, $\phi = 30° = \dfrac{\pi}{6}$.
Substituting the above values in Eqn. (9.96), we get

$$l_s = \frac{\lambda}{4\pi}(\phi + \pi - \cos^{-1}|K|) = \frac{0.3}{4\pi}\left(\frac{\pi}{6} + \pi - \cos^{-1}0.5\right)$$

$$= \frac{0.3}{4\pi}\left(\frac{7\pi}{6} - \frac{\pi}{3}\right) = \frac{0.3}{4\pi} \times \frac{5\pi}{6} = \frac{1}{16}\,\text{m} = 6.25\ \text{cm}$$

Similarly, substituting the $|K|$ value in Eqn. (9.97), we obtain

$$l_t = \frac{\lambda}{2\pi}\tan^{-1}\frac{\sqrt{1-|K|^2}}{2|K|} = \frac{0.3}{2\pi}\tan^{-1}\frac{\sqrt{1-(0.5)^2}}{2\times 0.5} = \frac{0.3}{2\pi}\tan^{-1}0.866$$

$$= \frac{0.3}{2\pi} \times 40.9 \times \frac{\pi}{180} = \frac{12.27}{390}\,\text{m} = 3.14\ \text{cm}$$

Example 9.23

A single stub is to match a 300 Ω line to a load of $(180 + j120)$ Ω. The wavelength is 2 m. Determine the shortest distance from the load to the stub location and the proper length of the short-circuited stub using the relevant formula.

Solution   Given $Z_0 = 300$ Ω, $Z_R = 180 + j120$ Ω and $\lambda = 2$ m.

Therefore, $$K = \frac{Z_R - Z_0}{Z_R + Z_0} = \frac{180 + j120 - 300}{180 + j120 + 300} = \frac{-120 + j120}{480 + j120} = 0.343\angle120.97°$$

Here, $|K| = 0.343$ and $\phi = 120.97°$

Substituting these values in Eqn. (9.96), we get the distance of the stub from the load as

$$l_s = \frac{\lambda}{4\pi}(\phi + \pi - \cos^{-1}|0.343|) = \frac{2}{4\pi}(120.97° + 180° - \cos^{-1}(0.343))$$

$$= \frac{1}{360°} \times 231.03° = 0.6417 \text{ m}$$

Similarly, substituting the $|K|$ value in Eqn. (9.97), we get the length of the stub as

$$l_t = \frac{\lambda}{2\pi}\tan^{-1}\frac{\sqrt{1 - |K|^2}}{2|K|} = \frac{2}{2\pi}\tan^{-1}\frac{\sqrt{1 - (0.343)^2}}{2 \times 0.343}$$

$$= \frac{1}{\pi}\tan^{-1}(1.369) = 0.2992 \text{ m}$$

Example 9.24

The characteristic impedance of a high frequency line is 100 Ω. It is terminated in an impedance of $(100 + j100)$ Ω. Using Smith chart, find the impedance one eight wavelength away from the load end.

Solution

(i)   First normalize the load impedance.

i.e, $$Z_r = \frac{Z_L}{Z_0} = \frac{100 + j100}{100} = (1 + j)$$

This normalized load impedance is plotted as point P in the Smith chart as shown in Fig. E9.24.

(ii)   With O as centre and OP as radius, draw a constant S-circle. Extend OP to cut outer periphery of the chart at point Q which represents the load of the line.

(iii)   To find the impedance $\lambda/8$ away from the load, we need to move to a distance of $\lambda/8 = 0.125\lambda$ in the clockwise direction (towards the generator) from a point Q to a point M.

(iv)   In the Smith chart, joining the center point O to point M cut the S-circle at point N. The coordinates of point N, i.e., $(2 - j)$, shows the desired normalized impedance and it is multiplied by characteristic impedance of 100 Ω results in the desired impedance.

i.e., At point N, $$\frac{Z_d}{Z_0} = (2 - j)$$

$$Z_d = 100(2 - j) = (200 - j100) \ \Omega$$

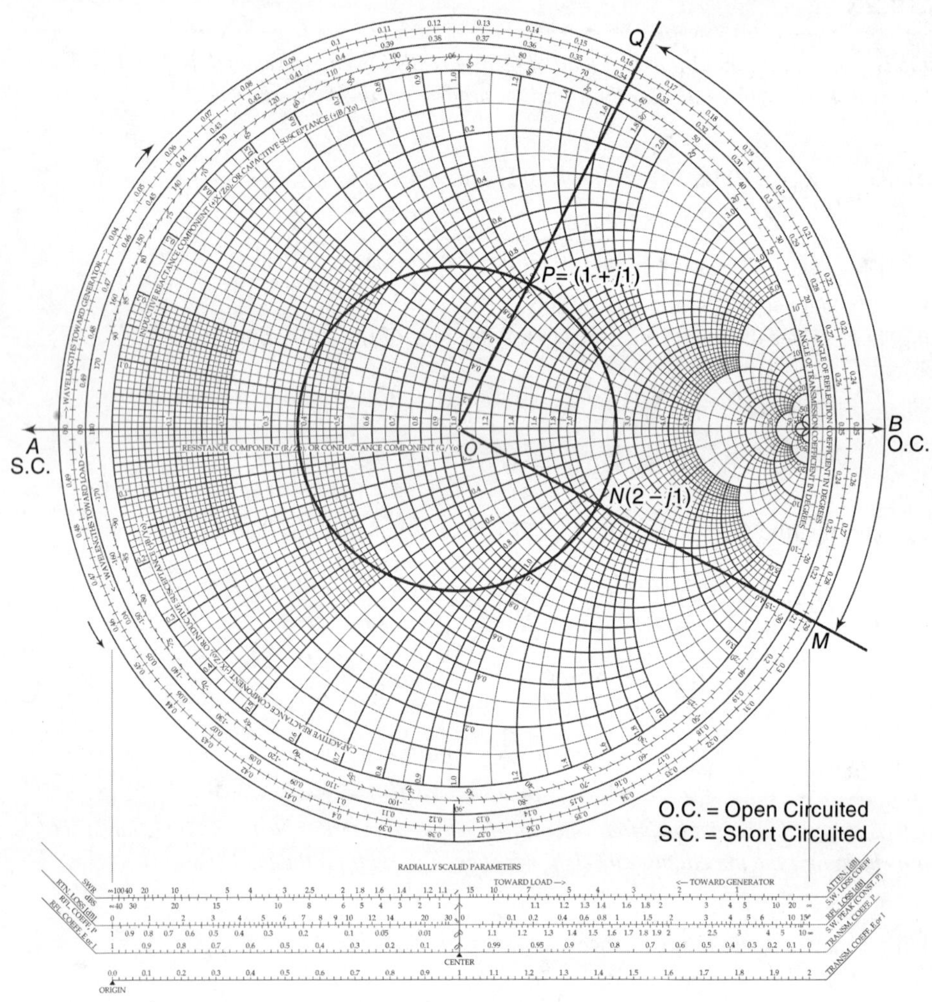

Figure E9.24

REVIEW QUESTIONS

1. Define the input impedance of a transmission line.
2. What is the input impedance of a quarter-wave length transmission line?
3. What is the input impedance of a half-wave length transmission line?
4. Discuss open and short circuited lines.
5. Discuss the impedance matching.
6. Derive the voltage reflection coefficient in a transmission line in terms of its characteristic impedance and load impedance.
7. Define the transmission coefficient in terms of the reflection coefficient.
8. What are the voltage and current magnitudes in a transmission line? How do they differ when it is short circuited and open circuited?
9. Explain the significance of reflection coefficient and insertion loss.
10. Explain the operation of quarter wave transformer and mention its important applications.
11. Derive the input impedance of a quarter wave line and discuss its applications.
12. Explain the realization of quarter wave transformer.
13. Draw and explain the operation of quarter wave line.
14. Derive the input impedance of a $\lambda/8$ line.
15. Describe the concept of a half wave length line.
16. Explain the significance of Smith chart and its application in transmission lines.
17. Explain briefly about the properties and applications of Smith chart.
18. In a transmission line, the VSWR is 2.5. The characteristic impedance 50 Ω and the line is to transmit a power of 25 W. Determine the magnitudes of the maximum and minimum voltage and current. Also, find the magnitude of the receiving end voltage when load is $(100 - j80)$ Ω.
19. The impedance (Z_R) that terminates a HF line can be determined based on the standing wave ratio, S. The characteristic impedance, Z_o and the distance from the load to the first voltage minimum is d, show that,

$$Z_R = Z_o \left\{ \frac{1 - jS \tan\left(\dfrac{2\pi d}{\lambda}\right)}{1 - j \tan\left(\dfrac{2\pi d}{\lambda}\right)} \right\}$$

20. Design a quarter waver transformer to match a load of 200 Ω to a source resistance of 500 Ω. The operating frequency is 200 MHz.
21. Determine the length and impedance of a quarter wave transformer that will match a 150 Ω load to a 75 Ω line at a frequency of 12 GHz. Derive the formula used.
22. A 75 Ω lossless transmission line is to be matched to a resistive load impedance of $Z_L = 100$ Ω via a quarter wave section. Find the characteristic impedance of the quarter wave transformer.
23. The short circuit and open circuit impedances at 800 Hz of a transmission line 40 km long are $3200\angle{-80°}$ Ω and $1300\angle{80°}$ Ω respectively. Calculate the line constants R, L, G and C.

24. Input impedance measurements of a certain transmission line 1 km long by A.C. bridge at a frequency of $\dfrac{8000}{2\pi}$ Hz yields the following results:

    Input impedance with far end short-circuited $= 49\angle 25°\ \Omega$

    Input impedance with far end open-circuited $= 2500\angle{-70°}\ \Omega$

    Calculate the values of the series impedance and shunt admittance per metre of the line. Assume the phase velocity in the transmission line to be roughly about 80,000 km/s.

25. Impedance measurement on a 500 km length of cable at $\omega = 10000$ rad/sec, under open circuited and short circuited conditions gives the following results.

    $$Z_{OC} = 2000\angle{-80°}\ \Omega \quad \text{and} \quad Z_{SC} = 20\angle 20°\ \Omega$$

    Calculate the value of Z_0, α and β.

26. An open wire transmission line having $Z_o = 650\angle{-12°}\ \Omega$ is terminated Z_o at the receiving end. If this line is supplied from a source of internal resistance 300 Ω, calculate the reflection factor and the reflection loss at the sending end terminals.

27. A transmission line of 100 m long is terminated in load of $(100 - j200)\ \Omega$. Determine the line impedance at 25 m from the load end at a frequency of 10 MHz. Assume the line impedance $Z_0 = 100\ \Omega$. Determine the input impedance and admittance using Smith chart.

28. Determine the sending end impedance of a line with negligible losses when characteristics impedance is 55 Ω and the load impedance is $115 + j75\ \Omega$ length of the line is 1.183λ by using Smith chart.

29. A 50 ohm lossless transmission line is terminated in a load impedance of $Z_L = (25 + j50)\ \Omega$. Use Smith chart to find voltage reflection coefficient, VSWR, input impedance of the line given the line of length 3.3λ and input admittance of the line.

30. A transmission line has a characteristic impedance of 300 ohms and terminated in a load impedance of $Z_L = 150 + j150\ \Omega$. Determine the following using Smith chart:

    (a) VSWR

    (b) Reflection Coefficient

    (c) Input impedance at distance 0.1λ from the load

    (d) Input admittance from 0.1λ from load.

    (e) Position of first voltage minimum and maximum from the load.

31. The transmission line has standing wave ratio $S = 2.5$ and voltage minima exists at 0.15λ from the load. Determine the load and input impedance for a line of 0.35λ length using Smith chart.

32. A low loss line with $Z_0 = 70\angle 0°\ \Omega$ is terminated in a impedance $Z_R = 115 - j80\ \Omega$. The wavelength of the transmission is 2.5 m. Using Smith chart, obtain the following:

    (i) Standing wave ratio.

    (ii) Maxima and minima line impedance

    (iii) Distance between the load and first voltage maximum.

33. A generator having an internal impedance of 50 Ω is connected to a load impedance of 250 Ω by means of a transmission line of characteristic impedance of 50 Ω. For a signal wavelength of 20 cm, find the location and length of a 75 Ω short-circuit stub for maximum transfer of energy to load using Smith chart.

34. A load has admittance $\dfrac{Y_R}{G_0} = 1.25 + j0.25$. Find the length and location for a single stub tuner, short circuited using Smith chart.

35. A line of $R_0 = 300\ \Omega$ is connected to a load of 73 Ω resistance. For a frequency of 45 MHz, calculate the length, termination and location nearest the load of a single stub to produce an impedance match.

36. An RF transmission line with a characteristic impedance of $Z_0 = 300\angle 0°\ \Omega$ terminated in an impedance of $100\angle 45°\ \Omega$. This load is to be matched to the transmission line by using a short circuited stub. With the help of Smith chart, determine the length of the stub and distance from the load.

WAVEGUIDES

10.1 INTRODUCTION

The propagation of an electromagnetic (EM) wave in any arbitrary medium should satisfy Maxwell's equations as discussed in the previous chapter. Transmission line structures such as a two-wire line and coaxial cable support only a transverse electromagnetic (TEM) wave. In such lines, the electromagnetic (EM) energy is confined and guided within the conductor boundaries satisfying Maxwell's equations.

This chapter presents the general analysis of the characteristics of the waves propagating along the uniform guiding structures. Due to skin effect, dielectric loss and conductor loss along the line, transmission lines are almost impractical to use at microwave frequencies in the GHz range. So, waveguides are employed at those frequencies to obtain low signal attenuation and large bandwidth. A waveguide is another form of transmission line structure in which the energy propagates in a rectangular or cylindrical tube without a central conductor. Rectangular waveguides have the simplest cross-section and they are easy to analyze and manufacture. In this chapter, the wave behaviour in hollow rectangular waveguides is analyzed.

In addition to TEM wave/mode that has no field components in the direction of propagation, both transverse magnetic (TM) mode with a longitudinal electric field component and transverse electric (TE) mode with a longitudinal magnetic field component can also exist. In this chapter, it is shown that a rectangular waveguide can support the TM and TE modes. Both these modes have characteristic cut-off frequencies. In a waveguide, a particular mode with frequencies below the cut-off cannot propagate, whereas the signal propagation at that mode is possible for frequencies above the cut-off. Hence, waveguides operating in TM and TE modes behave like high-pass filters. In this chapter, the TM and TE field expressions, their characteristic impedances and their field configurations inside a rectangular waveguide structure are discussed. Moreover, the characteristics of the microstrip line are also explained.

10.2 ELECTROMAGNETIC SPECTRUM AND BANDS

Electromagnetic spectrum is a family of waves, which extends from very low frequency range to ultra-high frequency range exceeding 10^{24} Hz. These include radio waves (RF), microwaves, infrared (IR), visible light, ultraviolet (UV), X-rays and gamma (γ) rays. Electromagnetic (EM) waves consist of electric and magnetic fields which oscillate at the same frequency f and travel at the velocity of light $u = c = 3 \times 10^8$ m/s.

If the sources of the fields are time harmonic, then the resultant EM wave generated is also time harmonic. The solution to wave equations represents propagation of waves. Both Maxwell's equations and Helmholtz's equations do not impose any limit on the frequency of the waves. The wavelength (λ) of an EM wave is related to its oscillation frequency (f) by $\lambda = \dfrac{c}{f}$.

Electromagnetic spectrum is divided into frequency and wavelength ranges on logarithmic scales based on their applications as shown in Figure 10.1. Different frequencies have different applications based on their excitation mechanisms. The visible part of the EM spectrum covers a very narrow wavelength from violet ($\lambda = 0.38$ µm) to red ($\lambda = 0.72$ µm).

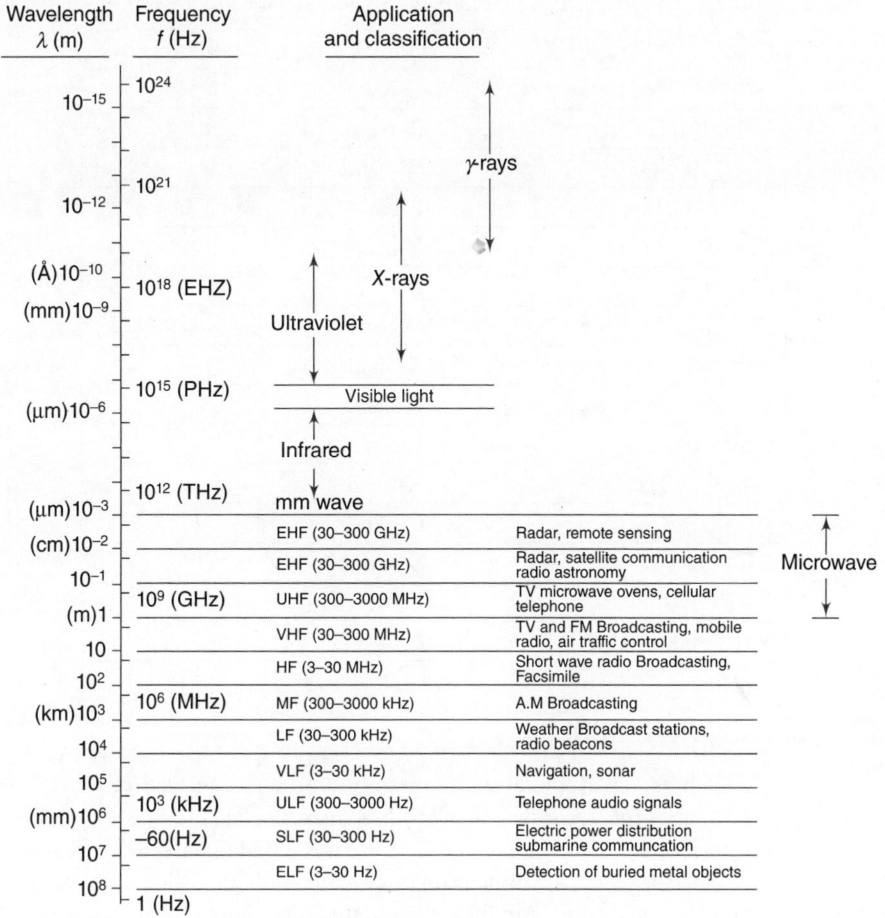

Figure 10.1 *Electromagnetic Spectrum*

The frequency range of visible light is from 4.2×10^{14} Hz to 7.9×10^{14} Hz. The ultraviolet (UV) band lies on the shorter wavelength (higher frequency) side of the visible spectrum. The infrared (IR) and the radio bands lie on the larger wavelength (lower frequency) side of the visible spectrum. Each spectral range can be specified in terms of its wavelength or frequency range.

Microwaves lie in the region between RF and IR and are used to describe EM waves with frequencies ranging from 300 MHz to 300 GHz, which correspond to wavelengths in free space from 1 m to 1 mm. EM waves with frequencies above 30 GHz and up to 300 GHz are also called millimetre waves because their wavelengths are in millimetre range (1–10 mm). Above the millimetre wave spectrum is the infrared, which consists of electromagnetic waves with wavelengths between 1 μm and 1 mm. The frequency boundary between RF and microwave is arbitrary and it depends on the particular technologies developed for the exploitation of that specific frequency range.

Microwave frequencies find the applications in radar and satellite communications and for convenience, alphabet letters are assigned to different microwave frequency bands, which are listed in Table 10.1. The properties of an electromagnetic wave propagating in a material vary from one band to another.

Table 10.1 *Band designations for microwave frequency range*

Frequency Range	Band Designation
140 – 220 GHz	G-band
110 – 170 GHz	D-band
75 – 110 GHz	W-band
60 – 90 GHz	E-band
50 – 70 GHz	V-band
40– 60 GHz	U-band
33 – 50 GHz	Q-band
26.5 – 40 GHz	Ka-band
18 – 26.5 GHz	K-band
12.4 – 18 GHz	Ku-band
8 – 12.4 GHz	X-band
4 – 8 GHz	C-band
2 – 4 GHz	S-band
1 – 2 GHz	L-band
300 – 3000 MHz	UHF-band

10.3 RECTANGULAR WAVEGUIDES

Figure 10.2 shows the rectangular waveguide with cross-section of sides a and b. Let us assume that the waveguide is filled with a source-free ($\rho_v = 0$, $\vec{J} = 0$) lossless dielectric material ($\sigma = 0$) having permittivity ε and permeability μ with perfectly conducting walls ($\sigma_c = \infty$). It is noted that the waveguide is oriented with two faces in the planes of the axes. Here, the dimension a is the height in the x direction, b is the width in the y direction. Further, the wave propagation is in the z direction and the length of the guide is assumed to be infinite in the z direction. Hence, it is reasonable to assume that all the possible fields inside the waveguide vary with time and distance z according to $e^{-\gamma z} \sin \omega t$.

10.3.1 Solution of Wave Equations in Rectangular Coordinates

The electric and magnetic fields in a charge-free dielectric medium should satisfy the following homogeneous vector Helmholtz's equations.

i.e., $\qquad \nabla^2 \tilde{E} + k^2 \tilde{E} = 0$ $\hfill (10.1)$

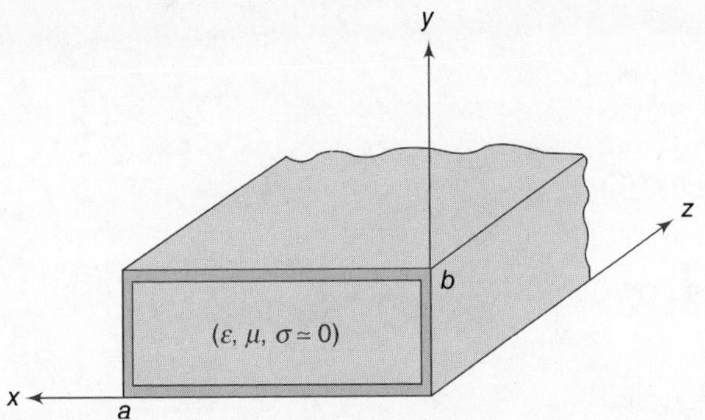

Figure 10.2 *Cross-section of a rectangular waveguide*

and
$$\nabla^2 \tilde{H} + k^2 \tilde{H} = 0 \tag{10.2}$$

where $\tilde{E}$ and $\tilde{H}$ represent the three-dimensional vector phasors and $k = \omega\sqrt{\mu\varepsilon}$ is the wavenumber. The three-dimensional Laplacian operator ∇^2 is broken into two parts, i.e., ∇^2_{xy} for the cross-sectional coordinates and ∇^2_z for longitudinal coordinate.

$$\nabla^2 \tilde{E} = (\nabla^2_{xy} + \nabla^2_z)\tilde{E} = \left(\nabla^2_{xy} + \frac{\partial^2}{\partial z^2}\right)\tilde{E}$$

$$= \nabla^2_{xy}\tilde{E} + \gamma^2\tilde{E} \tag{10.3}$$

where $\partial/\partial z = -\gamma$. Combining Eqns. (10.1) and (10.3), we get

$$\nabla^2_{xy}\tilde{E} + (\gamma^2 + k^2)\tilde{E} = 0 \tag{10.4}$$

Similarly, from Eqn. (10.2), we obtain

$$\nabla^2_{xy}\tilde{H} + (\gamma^2 + k^2)\tilde{H} = 0 \tag{10.5}$$

It is noted that the Eqns. (10.4) and (10.5) provide three second-order differential equations, one for each component of $\tilde{E}$ and $\tilde{H}$. The exact solution of these component equations depends on the cross-sectional geometry. Also, the boundary conditions for a particular field component must be satisfied at their conductor-dielectric interfaces.

Now, recalling the two Maxwell's source-free curl equations in phasor form,

$$\nabla \times \tilde{E} = -j\omega\mu\tilde{H} \tag{10.6}$$

$$\nabla \times \tilde{H} = j\omega\varepsilon\tilde{E} \tag{10.7}$$

Expanding Eqns. (10.6) and (10.7) for six components in rectangular or Cartesian coordinates, we get

$$\frac{\partial E_z^0}{\partial y} + \gamma E_y^0 = -j\omega\mu H_x^0 \tag{10.8a}$$

$$-\gamma E_x^0 - \frac{\partial E_z^0}{\partial x} = -j\omega\mu H_y^0 \tag{10.8b}$$

$$\frac{\partial E_y^0}{\partial x} - \frac{\partial E_x^0}{\partial y} = -j\omega\mu H_z^0 \tag{10.8c}$$

and
$$\frac{\partial H_z^0}{\partial y} + \gamma H_y^0 = j\omega\varepsilon E_x^0 \tag{10.9a}$$

$$-\gamma H_x^0 - \frac{\partial H_z^0}{\partial x} = j\omega\varepsilon E_y^0 \tag{10.9b}$$

$$\frac{\partial H_y^0}{\partial x} - \frac{\partial H_x^0}{\partial y} = j\omega\varepsilon E_z^0 \tag{10.9c}$$

In the above equations, the partial derivatives with respect to z are replaced by $-\gamma$. By rearranging these equations, the transverse field components H_x^0, H_y^0 and E_x^0, E_y^0 in terms of the two longitudinal components E_z and H_z can be obtained. For instance, Eqns. (10.8a) and (10.9b) can be combined to eliminate E_y^0 and express H_x^0 in terms of E_z^0 and H_z^0. Hence, the solution of wave equations in rectangular coordinates are obtained as follows:

$$H_x^0 = -\frac{1}{h^2}\left(\gamma\frac{\partial H_z^0}{\partial x} - j\omega\varepsilon\frac{\partial E_z^0}{\partial y}\right) \tag{10.10}$$

$$H_y^0 = -\frac{1}{h^2}\left(\gamma\frac{\partial H_z^0}{\partial y} + j\omega\varepsilon\frac{\partial E_z^0}{\partial x}\right) \tag{10.11}$$

$$E_x^0 = -\frac{1}{h^2}\left(\gamma\frac{\partial E_z^0}{\partial x} + j\omega\mu\frac{\partial H_z^0}{\partial y}\right) \tag{10.12}$$

$$E_y^0 = -\frac{1}{h^2}\left(\gamma\frac{\partial E_z^0}{\partial y} - j\omega\mu\frac{\partial H_z^0}{\partial x}\right) \tag{10.13}$$

where $h^2 = \gamma^2 + k^2$. For the rectangular waveguide shown in Figure 10.2, the boundary conditions are

$$E_x = E_z = 0 \text{ at } y = 0 \text{ and } y = b$$

$$E_y = E_z = 0 \text{ at } x = 0 \text{ and } x = a$$

10.3.2 TEM/TM/TE Mode

In a rectangular waveguide, the wave behaviour can be analyzed by solving Eqns. (10.4) and (10.5) for the longitudinal components E_z^0 and H_z^0 subject to boundary conditions. Further, the other transverse field components are obtained using Eqns. (10.10)–(10.13). Based on the existence of the longitudinal field components E_z or H_z, the propagation of waves in a uniform waveguide is classified into three types of field configurations. Such field configurations or patterns are called a *mode*.

1. **Transverse electromagnetic (TEM) mode**: In TEM mode, the electric and magnetic fields are transverse to the direction of wave propagation. Here, neither E_z nor H_z exists. Substituting $E_z^0 = H_z^0 = 0$ in Eqns. (10.10)–(10.13), all the transverse field components H_x^0, H_y^0 and E_x^0, E_y^0

become zero. As a result, it can be concluded that rectangular waveguide cannot support TEM wave or mode.

2. **Transverse magnetic (TM) mode**: In TM mode, the magnetic field (H_x and H_y) is transverse to the direction of wave propagation. Here, the waves contain a non-zero E_z but zero H_z as seen in Figure 10.3(a).

3. **Transverse electric (TE) mode**: In TE mode, the electric field (E_y and E_y) is transverse to the direction of wave propagation. Here, the waves contain a non-zero H_z but zero E_z as seen in Figure 10.3(b).

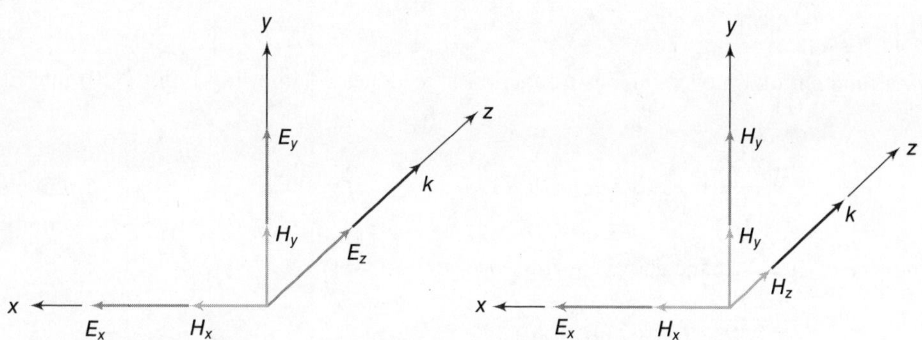

Figure 10.3 *EM field components in a rectangular waveguide (a) TM mode with $H_z = 0$ and (b) TE mode with $E_z = 0$*

In the subsequent sections, the TM and TE modes of propagation in a rectangular waveguide are examined separately.

10.4 TM MODE ANALYSIS AND FIELD EXPRESSIONS

The transverse magnetic (TM) wave does not have a component in the direction of wave propagation i.e., $H_z = 0$. The wave equation for the electric field is given by

$$\frac{\partial^2 E_z^0}{\partial x^2} + \frac{\partial^2 E_z^0}{\partial y^2} + \gamma^2 E_z^0 = -\omega^2 \mu\varepsilon E_z^0 \tag{10.14}$$

In phasor form, $\nabla_{xy}^2 E_z^0 + h^2 E_z^0 = 0$

The behaviour of TM waves is analyzed by solving the above second-order partial differential equation for E_z subject to boundary conditions of the rectangular waveguide. For TM waves, we set $H_z = 0$ in Eqns. (10.10)–(10.13) to obtain

$$H_x^0 = \frac{j\omega\varepsilon}{h^2} \frac{\partial E_z^0}{\partial y} \tag{10.15}$$

$$H_y^0 = -\frac{j\omega\varepsilon}{h^2} \frac{\partial E_z^0}{\partial x} \tag{10.16}$$

$$E_x^0 = -\frac{\gamma}{h^2}\frac{\partial E_z^0}{\partial x} \tag{10.17}$$

$$E_y^0 = -\frac{\gamma}{h^2}\frac{\partial E_z^0}{\partial y} \tag{10.18}$$

In order to solve Eqn. (10.14), apply the variable separable method and assume a product solution for E_s as

$$E_z(x, y, z) = E_z^0(x, \; y)e^{-\gamma z} \tag{10.19}$$

Let $\qquad E_z^0 = XY \tag{10.20}$

where X is a function of x alone and Y is a function of y alone. So, inserting Eqn. (10.20) into Eqn. (10.14) results in

$$Y\frac{d^2X}{dx^2} + X\frac{d^2Y}{dy^2} + \gamma^2 XY = -\omega^2 \mu\varepsilon XY$$

Substituting $\gamma^2 + \omega^2\mu\varepsilon = h^2$ in the above equation, we get

$$Y\frac{d^2X}{dx^2} + X\frac{d^2Y}{dy^2} + h^2 XY = 0$$

Dividing the above equation by XY, we obtain

$$\frac{1}{X}\frac{d^2X}{dx^2} + \frac{1}{Y}\frac{d^2Y}{dy^2} + h^2 = 0$$

Therefore, $\quad \dfrac{1}{X}\dfrac{d^2X}{dx^2} + h^2 = -\dfrac{1}{Y}\dfrac{d^2Y}{dy^2} \tag{10.21}$

Equation (10.21) equates a function of X alone to a function of Y alone. The only way in which such a relation can hold for all values of x and y is to have each of these functions equal to some constant, say A^2.

Then, $\quad \dfrac{1}{X}\dfrac{d^2X}{dx^2} + h^2 = -A^2 \tag{10.22}$

and $\quad \dfrac{1}{Y}\dfrac{d^2Y}{dy^2} = A^2 \tag{10.23}$

The solution of Eqn. (10.22) is $X = C_1 \cos Bx + C_2 \sin Bx$
where $\qquad B^2 = h^2 - A^2$
The solution of Eqn. (10.23) is $Y = C_3 \cos Ay + C_4 \sin Ay$
Therefore,

$$E_z^0 = XY = (C_1 \cos Bx + C_2 \sin Bx)(C_3 \cos Ay + C_4 \sin Ay) \tag{10.24}$$

Now the constants C_1, C_2, C_3, C_4, A and B must be selected to fit the boundary conditions, namely, $E_z^0 = 0$ when $x = 0$, $x = a$ and $y = 0$, $y = b$

To find the constants, let us apply the above boundary conditions to Eqn. (10.24).

i.e., $\left. E_z^0 \right|_{x=0} = (C_1 \cos 0 + C_2 \sin 0)(C_3 \cos Ay + C_4 \sin Ay) = 0 \Rightarrow C_1 = 0$

and $\left. E_z^0 \right|_{y=0} = C_2 \sin Bx (C_3 \cos 0 + C_4 \sin 0) = 0 \Rightarrow C_3 = 0$

Substituting $C_1 = 0$ and $C_3 = 0$ in Eqn. (10.24), we get

$$E_z^0 = C_2 C_4 \sin Bx \sin Ay = E_0 \sin Bx \sin Ay \tag{10.25}$$

where $E_0 = C_2 C_4$. From the remaining boundary conditions, we get

$$\left. E_z^0 \right|_{x=a} = E_0 \sin Bx \sin Ay = 0 \Rightarrow B = \frac{m\pi}{a}, \text{ when } m = 1, 2, 3, \ldots \tag{10.26a}$$

and $\left. E_z^0 \right|_{y=b} = E_0 \sin\left(\frac{m\pi}{a} x\right) \sin Ay = 0 \Rightarrow A = \frac{n\pi}{b}, \text{ when } n = 1, 2, 3, \ldots \tag{10.26b}$

Substituting A and B in Eqn. (10.25), the field expression for E_z^0 becomes

$$E_z^0 = E_0 \sin\left(\frac{m\pi}{a} x\right) \sin\left(\frac{n\pi}{b} y\right) \tag{10.27}$$

We know that $B^2 = h^2 - A^2$, i.e., $h^2 = B^2 + A^2$

Therefore, $h^2 = \left(\frac{m\pi}{a}\right)^2 + \left(\frac{n\pi}{b}\right)^2 \tag{10.28}$

Using Eqns. (10.15)–(10.18), the other field expressions for TM waves are obtained as

$$E_x^0 = -\frac{\gamma}{h^2}\left(\frac{m\pi}{a}\right) E_0 \cos\left(\frac{m\pi}{a} x\right) \sin\left(\frac{n\pi}{b} y\right) \tag{10.29a}$$

$$E_y^0 = -\frac{\gamma}{h^2}\left(\frac{n\pi}{b}\right) E_0 \sin\left(\frac{m\pi}{a} x\right) \cos\left(\frac{n\pi}{b} y\right) \tag{10.29b}$$

$$H_x^0 = \frac{j\omega\varepsilon}{h^2}\left(\frac{n\pi}{b}\right) E_0 \sin\left(\frac{m\pi}{a} x\right) \cos\left(\frac{n\pi}{b} y\right) \tag{10.29c}$$

$$H_y^0 = -\frac{j\omega\varepsilon}{h^2}\left(\frac{m\pi}{a}\right) E_0 \cos\left(\frac{m\pi}{a} x\right) \sin\left(\frac{n\pi}{b} y\right) \tag{10.29d}$$

The set of integers m and n provide different field pattern or mode, referred to as TM_{mn} mode in the rectangular waveguide. Here, the integer m represents the number of half-cycle variations in the x direction and integer n represents the number of half-cycle variations in the y direction. From Eqns. (10.27) and (10.29), it is noticed that if either m or n is zero and both m and n is zero, all the field components will vanish. Hence, for TM modes, neither m nor n can be zero i.e., $\text{TM}_{m,0}$ or $\text{TM}_{0,n}$ cannot exist in a waveguide. As a result, TM_{11} is the lowest order mode of all TM modes in a rectangular waveguide.

The instantaneous field expressions for TM$_{11}$ mode ($m = 1$ and $n = 1$) are obtained by multiplying the phasor expressions in Eqns. (10.27) and (10.29) with $e^{j(\omega t - \beta z)}$ and then taking the real part of the product.

i.e.,
$$E_x = \frac{\beta}{h^2}\left(\frac{\pi}{a}\right)E_0 \cos\left(\frac{\pi}{a}x\right)\sin\left(\frac{\pi}{b}y\right)\sin(\omega t - \beta z)$$

$$E_y = \frac{\beta}{h^2}\left(\frac{\pi}{b}\right)E_0 \sin\left(\frac{\pi}{a}x\right)\cos\left(\frac{\pi}{b}y\right)\sin(\omega t - \beta z)$$

$$E_z = E_0 \sin\left(\frac{\pi}{a}x\right)\sin\left(\frac{\pi}{b}y\right)\cos(\omega t - \beta z)$$

$$H_x = -\frac{\omega\varepsilon}{h^2}\left(\frac{\pi}{b}\right)E_0 \sin\left(\frac{\pi}{a}x\right)\cos\left(\frac{\pi}{b}y\right)\sin(\omega t - \beta z)$$

$$H_y = \frac{\omega\varepsilon}{h^2}\left(\frac{\pi}{a}\right)E_0 \cos\left(\frac{\pi}{a}x\right)\sin\left(\frac{\pi}{b}y\right)\sin(\omega t - \beta z)$$

$$H_z = 0$$

where
$$\beta = \sqrt{k^2 - h^2} = \sqrt{\omega^2\mu\varepsilon - \left(\frac{\pi}{a}\right)^2 - \left(\frac{\pi}{b}\right)^2}.$$

10.5 TE MODE ANALYSIS AND FIELD EXPRESSIONS

Similar to TM waves, the transverse electric (TE) wave does not have a component in the direction of wave propagation i.e., $E_z = 0$. The wave equation for the magnetic field is given by

$$\frac{\partial^2 H_z^0}{\partial x^2} + \frac{\partial^2 H_z^0}{\partial y^2} + \gamma^2 H_z^0 = -\omega^2\mu\varepsilon H_z^0$$

$$(10.30)$$

In phasor form, $\nabla_{xy}^2 H_z^0 + h^2 H_z^0 = 0$

The behaviour of TE waves is analyzed by solving the above second-order partial differential equation for H_z subject to boundary conditions of the rectangular waveguide. For TE waves, we set $E_z = 0$ in Eqns (10.10)–(10.13) to obtain

$$H_x^0 = -\frac{\gamma}{h^2}\frac{\partial H_z^0}{\partial x} \qquad (10.31)$$

$$H_y^0 = -\frac{\gamma}{h^2}\frac{\partial H_z^0}{\partial y} \qquad (10.32)$$

$$E_x^0 = -\frac{j\omega\mu}{h^2}\frac{\partial H_z^0}{\partial y} \qquad (10.33)$$

$$E_y^0 = \frac{j\omega\mu}{h^2}\frac{\partial H_z^0}{\partial x} \qquad (10.34)$$

The field expressions for TE waves ($E_z = 0$) can be derived in a manner similar to that for TM waves. As a result, H_z^0 will be found to have the same general form as Eqn. (10.24). This is differentiated with respect to x and y to find E_x^0, E_y^0, H_x^0 and H_y^0.

The solution for H_z^0 must satisfy the following boundary conditions:

$$\frac{\partial H_z^0}{\partial x} = 0 \Rightarrow E_y = 0 \text{ at } x = 0 \text{ and } x = a$$

and

$$\frac{\partial H_z^0}{\partial y} = 0 \Rightarrow E_x = 0 \text{ at } y = 0 \text{ and } y = b$$

From Eqn. (10.24), the resultant general solution for H_z^o is of the form

$$H_z^0 = XY = (C_1 \cos Bx + C_2 \sin Bx)(C_3 \cos Ay + C_4 \sin Ay) \tag{10.35}$$

To find the constants, let us apply boundary conditions to Eqn. (10.35).

i.e.,

$$\left.\frac{\partial H_z^0}{\partial x}\right|_{x=0} = (-C_1 B \sin 0 + C_2 B \cos 0)(C_3 \cos Ay + C_4 \sin Ay) = 0 \Rightarrow C_2 = 0$$

and

$$\left.\frac{\partial H_z^0}{\partial y}\right|_{y=0} = C_1 \cos Bx \,(-C_3 A \sin 0 + C_4 A \cos 0) = 0 \Rightarrow C_4 = 0$$

Substituting $C_2 = 0$ and $C_4 = 0$ in Eqn. (10.35), we get

$$H_z^0 = C_1 C_3 \cos Bx \cos Ay = H_0 \cos Bx \cos Ay \tag{10.36}$$

where $H_0 = C_1 C_3$. From the remaining boundary conditions, we get

$$\left.\frac{\partial H_z^0}{\partial x}\right|_{x=a} = -H_0 B \sin Bx \cos Ay = 0 \Rightarrow B = \frac{m\pi}{a}, \text{ when } m = 0, 1, \dots$$

and

$$\left.\frac{\partial H_z^0}{\partial y}\right|_{y=b} = -H_0 \cos\left(\frac{m\pi}{a}x\right) A \sin Ay = 0 \Rightarrow A = \frac{n\pi}{b}, \text{ when } n = 0, 1, \dots$$

Substituting A and B in Eqn. (10.36), the field expression for H_z^o becomes

$$H_z^0 = H_0 \cos\left(\frac{m\pi}{a}x\right)\cos\left(\frac{n\pi}{b}y\right) \tag{10.37}$$

Using Eqns. (10.31)–(10.34), the other field expressions for TE waves are obtained as

$$E_x^0 = \frac{j\omega\mu}{h^2}\left(\frac{n\pi}{b}\right) H_0 \cos\left(\frac{m\pi}{a}x\right)\sin\left(\frac{n\pi}{b}y\right) \tag{10.38a}$$

$$E_y^0 = -\frac{j\omega\mu}{h^2}\left(\frac{m\pi}{a}\right) H_0 \sin\left(\frac{m\pi}{a}x\right)\cos\left(\frac{n\pi}{b}y\right) \tag{10.38b}$$

$$H_x^0 = \frac{\gamma}{h^2}\left(\frac{m\pi}{a}\right) H_0 \sin\left(\frac{m\pi}{a}x\right)\cos\left(\frac{n\pi}{b}y\right) \tag{10.38c}$$

$$H_y^0 = \frac{\gamma}{h^2}\left(\frac{n\pi}{b}\right) H_0 \cos\left(\frac{m\pi}{a}x\right)\sin\left(\frac{n\pi}{b}y\right) \tag{10.38d}$$

Here, the set of integers m and n provide different field pattern or mode, referred to as TE_{mn} mode in the rectangular waveguide. From Eqns.(10.37) and (10.38), it is noticed that in TE modes, either m or n can be zero whereas when both m and n are zero, all the field components will vanish. Hence, TE_{00} mode is not possible and TE_{10} is the dominant mode in a rectangular waveguide when $a > b$. By convention, the x coordinate is assumed to coincide with the larger transverse dimension a, so the TE_{10} wave has a lower cut-off frequency than TE_{02}.

The instantaneous field expressions for TE_{10} mode ($m = 1$ and $n = 0$) are obtained by multiplying the phasor expressions in Eqns. (10.37) and (10.38) with $e^{j(\omega t - \beta z)}$ and then taking the real part of the product.

i.e., $\qquad E_x = 0$

$$E_y = \frac{\omega\mu a}{\pi} H_0 \sin\left(\frac{\pi}{a}x\right)\sin(\omega t - \beta z)$$

$$E_z = 0$$

$$H_x = -\frac{\beta a}{\pi} H_0 \sin\left(\frac{\pi}{a}x\right)\sin(\omega t - \beta z)$$

$$H_y = 0$$

$$H_z = H_0 \cos\left(\frac{\pi}{a}x\right)\cos(\omega t - \beta z)$$

where $\qquad \beta = \sqrt{k^2 - h^2} = \sqrt{\omega^2\mu\varepsilon - \left(\frac{\pi}{a}\right)^2}.$

10.6 CHARACTERISTIC EQUATION AND CUT-OFF FREQUENCIES

In a rectangular waveguide, the relationship among the propagation constant (γ), wave number (k), frequency (ω) and constitutive parameters of the medium (μ and ε) is represented by the characteristic equation. It is given by

$$\gamma^2 = h^2 - k^2 \tag{10.39}$$

where $\qquad h^2 = \left(\frac{m\pi}{a}\right)^2 + \left(\frac{n\pi}{b}\right)^2.$

Substituting h^2 term in Eqn. (10.39), the characteristic equation is written as

$$\gamma = \sqrt{\left(\frac{m\pi}{a}\right)^2 + \left(\frac{n\pi}{b}\right)^2 - k^2} \tag{10.40}$$

where $k = \omega\sqrt{\mu\varepsilon}$. We know that, in general, $\gamma = \alpha + j\beta$. From Eqn.(10.40), three cases are possible depending on k (or ω), m and n. Here, the expressions for cut-off frequency (f_c), cut-off wavelength (λ_c) and phase constant (β) are common to both TM and TE modes in a rectangular waveguide.

Case (i) Cut-off frequency:
The cut-off frequency (f_c) is the frequency at which the propagation constant becomes zero i.e., $\gamma = 0$ or α and $\beta = 0$. From Eqn. (10.39), we can obtain

$$k^2 = \omega_c^2 \mu\varepsilon = \left(\frac{m\pi}{a}\right)^2 + \left(\frac{n\pi}{b}\right)^2$$

$$\omega_c = \frac{1}{\sqrt{\mu\varepsilon}} \sqrt{\left(\frac{m\pi}{a}\right)^2 + \left(\frac{n\pi}{b}\right)^2}$$

Hence, $\quad f_c = \dfrac{1}{2\sqrt{\mu\varepsilon}} \sqrt{\left(\dfrac{m}{a}\right)^2 + \left(\dfrac{n}{b}\right)^2}$ \hfill (10.41)

Case (ii) Evanescent mode:

If there is no wave propagation in a rectangular waveguide, then such non-propagating modes are called evanescent modes. Further, these modes have only attenuation i.e., $\gamma = \alpha$ and $\beta = 0$. Therefore, for frequencies below cut-off where $f < f_c$ and γ is real, the fields are attenuated. The phase angles will remain constant and the field amplitudes will decrease rapidly with distance z according to the factor $e^{-\gamma z} = e^{-\alpha z}$ and the evanescent mode will occur when

$$k^2 = \omega^2 \mu\varepsilon < \left(\frac{m\pi}{a}\right)^2 + \left(\frac{n\pi}{b}\right)^2$$

Case (iii) Propagation mode:

In this mode, all the field components will propagate without any attenuation i.e., $\alpha = 0$ and $\gamma = j\beta$. Here, the field components have propagation according to the factor $e^{-\gamma z} = e^{-j\beta z}$. At frequencies above cut-off $f > f_c$ and γ is imaginary, the fields are propagated. Hence, propagation will occur when

$$k^2 = \omega^2 \mu\varepsilon > \left(\frac{m\pi}{a}\right)^2 + \left(\frac{n\pi}{b}\right)^2$$

Therefore, $\quad \gamma = j\beta = j\sqrt{\omega^2 \mu\varepsilon - \left(\dfrac{m\pi}{a}\right)^2 - \left(\dfrac{n\pi}{b}\right)^2} = j\sqrt{k^2 - \left(\dfrac{m\pi}{a}\right)^2 - \left(\dfrac{n\pi}{b}\right)^2}$ \hfill (10.42)

The cut-off frequency is the operating frequency below which attenuation occurs and above which propagation takes place. Hence, the waveguide acts as a high-pass filter. Also, Eqn. (10.41) can be written as

$$f_c = \frac{u'}{2} \sqrt{\left(\frac{m}{a}\right)^2 + \left(\frac{n}{b}\right)^2}$$ \hfill (10.43)

where $u' = 1/\sqrt{\mu\varepsilon}$ is the phase velocity of the plane wave propagating in the lossless dielectric medium of the rectangular waveguide. From the above equation, the cut-off frequency for TE_{10} mode ($m = 1$, $n = 0$) is obtained as

$$f_c = \frac{u'}{2a}$$

The cut-off wavelength (λ_c) is given by

$$\lambda_c = \frac{u'}{f_c} = \frac{2}{\sqrt{\left(\dfrac{m}{a}\right)^2 + \left(\dfrac{n}{b}\right)^2}}$$ \hfill (10.44)

For TE_{10} mode, the cut-off wavelength is obtained from Eqn. (10.44) as

$$\lambda_c = 2a$$

Hence, at the cut-off wavelength, the dimension a of the rectangular waveguide is just one-half wavelength i.e, $a = \lambda_c/2$.

From Eqn. (10.42), the phase shift constant (β) can be written in terms of cut-off frequency (f_c) as

$$\beta = \omega\sqrt{\mu\varepsilon}\sqrt{1 - \left(\frac{f_c}{f}\right)^2} \qquad (10.45)$$

Since the total phase shift in one wavelength is 2π radians, the guide wavelength is

$$\lambda_g = \frac{2\pi}{\beta} = \frac{2\pi}{\omega\sqrt{\mu\varepsilon}\sqrt{1 - \left(\dfrac{f_c}{f}\right)^2}} = \frac{\lambda}{\sqrt{1 - \left(\dfrac{\lambda}{\lambda_c}\right)^2}} \qquad (10.46)$$

where $\qquad \lambda = \dfrac{2\pi}{k} = \dfrac{1}{f\sqrt{\mu\varepsilon}} = \dfrac{u}{f}.$

Taking reciprocal and squaring both the sides of the above equation, we obtain

$$\frac{1}{\lambda^2} = \frac{1}{\lambda_c^2} + \frac{1}{\lambda_g^2}$$

10.7   DOMINANT AND DEGENERATE MODES

The *dominant mode* is the mode with the lowest cut-off frequency or longest cut-off wavelength. From Eqn. (10.43), the cut-off frequency for TM_{11} in a rectangular waveguide is

$$f_c = \frac{u'\sqrt{a^2 + b^2}}{2ab}$$

and it is greater than the cut-off frequency of TE_{10} mode. Therefore, TM_{11} cannot be considered as a dominant mode. It is also noted that any EM wave with frequency $f < f_{c10}$ or $\lambda > \lambda_{c10}$ is impossible to propagate in the guide.

The modes having same cut-off frequency but different field configurations are called *degenerate modes*. In a rectangular waveguide, it is seen that TE_{mn} and TM_{mn} modes (both $m \neq 0$, and $n \neq 0$,) are always degenerate. Some higher order modes may have identical cut-off frequency. In a rectangular waveguide, for the ratio of $\dfrac{a}{2} = 2$, $TE_{20}|TE_{01}$, $TE_{11}|TM_{11}$, $TE_{21}|TM_{21}$, $TE_{12}|TM_{12}$ and $TE_{22}|TM_{22}$ all have identical cut-off frequencies.

10.8   SKETCHES OF TM AND TE MODE FIELDS IN THE CROSS-SECTION

For the rectangular waveguide of cross-section shown in Figure 10.2, the field patterns of TM_{11} and TE_{10} modes are sketched in Figs 10.4 and 10.5, respectively. Figures 10.4 (a) and 10.5 (a) represent the field configurations in xy-plane, whereas Figures 10.4 (b) and 10.5 (b) represent the field configurations in yz-plane.

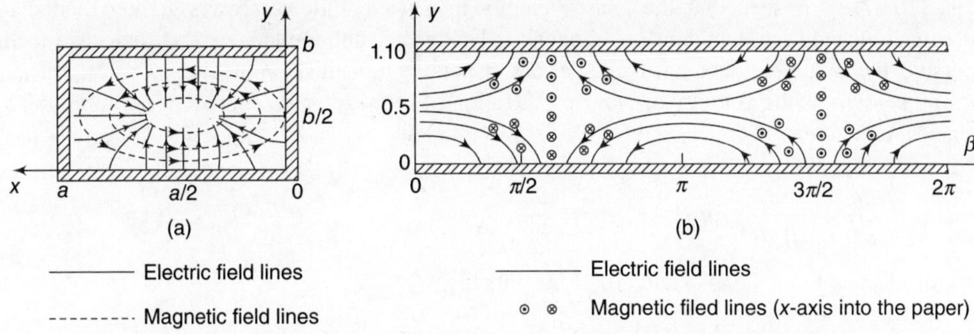

(a)

(b)

——————— Electric field lines

- - - - - - - Magnetic field lines

——————— Electric field lines

⊙ ⊗ Magnetic filed lines (*x*-axis into the paper)

Figure 10.4 *Field configuration of TM$_{11}$ mode (a) end view and (b) side view*

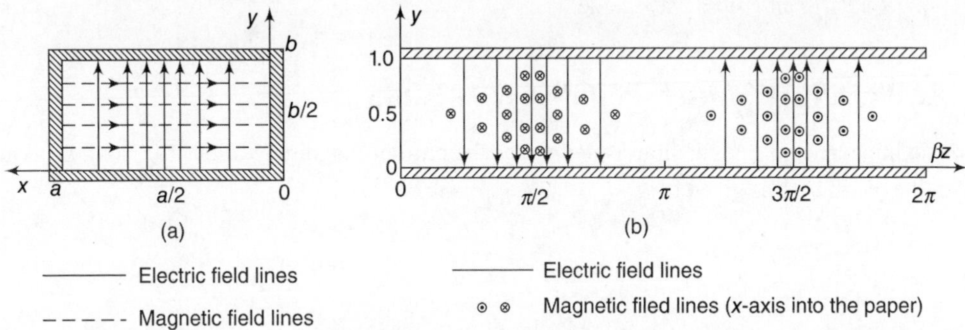

(a)

(b)

——————— Electric field lines

- - - - - Magnetic field lines

——————— Electric field lines

⊙ ⊗ Magnetic filed lines (*x*-axis into the paper)

Figure 10.5 *Field configuration of TE$_{10}$ mode (a) end view and (b) side view*

From Figure 10.4(a), it is seen that the electric and magnetic field lines are everywhere orthogonal to each other. Further, it is also noted that electric field lines are perpendicular and the magnetic field lines are parallel to the conducting guide walls. In the yz-plane, at $x = a/2$, $\sin(\pi x/a) = 1$ and $\cos(\pi x/a) = 0$, only the field H_x is present for TM$_{11}$ mode. The electric and magnetic field lines are sketched in Figure 10.4(b) for $t = 0$.

Meanwhile, from Figure 10.5(a), it is observed that both the fields E_y and H_x vary with $\sin(\pi x/a)$ and are independent of y in the xy-plane when $\sin(\omega t - \beta z) = 1$. In the yz-plane, at $x = a/2$, $\sin(\pi x/a) = 1$ and $\cos(\pi x/a) = 0$, only the fields E_y and H_x are present for TE$_{10}$ mode and both vary sinusoidally with βz. The fields of E_y and H_x are sketched in Figure 10.5(b) for $t = 0$.

10.9 PHASE AND GROUP VELOCITIES

The phase velocity u_p of a single-frequency plane wave is defined as the velocity of propagation of an equiphase wavefront. Inside the rectangular waveguide, the phase velocity of the propagating waveguide is

$$u_p = \frac{\omega}{\beta} = \frac{\omega}{\omega\sqrt{\mu\varepsilon}\sqrt{1-\left(\dfrac{f_c}{f}\right)^2}}$$

$$= \frac{u}{\sqrt{1-\left(\dfrac{f_c}{f}\right)^2}} = \frac{\lambda_g}{\lambda}u \tag{10.47}$$

From Eqn. (10.47), it is seen that the phase velocity in a waveguide is always greater than that in an unbounded medium and is dependent on frequency. Though an unbounded lossless dielectric medium is non-dispersive, the single-conductor waveguides are dispersive transmission mediums.

The group velocity is the velocity of wave propagation of the wave-packet envelope comprising a group of frequencies. It is given by

$$u_g = \frac{d\omega}{d\beta} = \frac{1}{d\beta/d\omega} = u\sqrt{1 - \left(\frac{f_c}{f}\right)^2} = \frac{\lambda}{\lambda_g}u \tag{10.48}$$

Taking the product of Eqns. (10.47) and (10.48) results in

$$u_g u_p = u^2$$

The above equation gives the relationship between the phase and group velocities. For free space or air as a dielectric medium, $u = c$, the above equation becomes $u_g u_p = c^2$. The velocity of signal propagation is equal to the group velocity in a lossless waveguide.

10.10 WAVELENGTHS AND IMPEDANCE RELATIONS

The intrinsic impedance of the medium is defined as the ratio of magnitude of electric field $\vec{E}$ to magnetic field $\vec{H}$ in the medium. It is given by

$$\eta = \frac{|\vec{E}|}{|\vec{H}|}$$

From Eqn. (10.29), the intrinsic impedance for a TM mode is

$$Z_{TM} = \eta_{TM} = \frac{E_x^0}{H_y^0} = -\frac{E_y^0}{H_x^0} = \frac{\gamma}{j\omega\varepsilon} = \frac{\beta}{\omega\varepsilon} \qquad \text{(since } \gamma = j\beta\text{)}$$

$$= \frac{\omega\sqrt{\mu\varepsilon}\sqrt{1-(f_c/f)^2}}{\omega\varepsilon} = \sqrt{\mu/\varepsilon}\sqrt{1-(f_c/f)^2}$$

Thus, $$\eta_{TM} = \eta\sqrt{1-(f_c/f)^2} = \eta\sqrt{1-(\lambda/\lambda_c)^2} \tag{10.49}$$

The above equation shows that the intrinsic impedance of propagating TM modes in a waveguide with a lossless dielectric medium is purely resistive and is always less than the intrinsic impedance of the dielectric.

From Eqn. (10.38), the intrinsic impedance for a TE mode is

$$Z_{TE} = \eta_{TE} = \frac{E_x^0}{H_y^0} = -\frac{E_y^0}{H_x^0} = \frac{j\omega\mu}{\gamma} = \frac{\omega\mu}{\beta}$$

$$= \frac{\omega\mu}{\omega\sqrt{\mu\varepsilon}\sqrt{1-(f_c/f)^2}} = \frac{\sqrt{\mu/\varepsilon}}{\sqrt{1-(f_c/f)^2}}$$

Thus, $$\eta_{TE} = \frac{\eta}{\sqrt{1-(f_c/f)^2}} = \frac{\eta}{\sqrt{1-(\lambda/\lambda_c)^2}} \tag{10.50}$$

The above equation shows that the intrinsic impedance of propagating TE modes in a waveguide with a lossless dielectric medium is purely resistive and is always greater than the intrinsic impedance of the dielectric. Hence, both the TM and TE mode impedances are purely resistive and the variation of normalized wave impedances with normalized frequency is sketched in Figure 10.6. Taking the product of Eqns. (10.49) and (10.50) results in

$$\eta_{TM}\eta_{TE} = \eta^2$$

or $$\eta = \sqrt{\eta_{TM}\eta_{TE}}$$

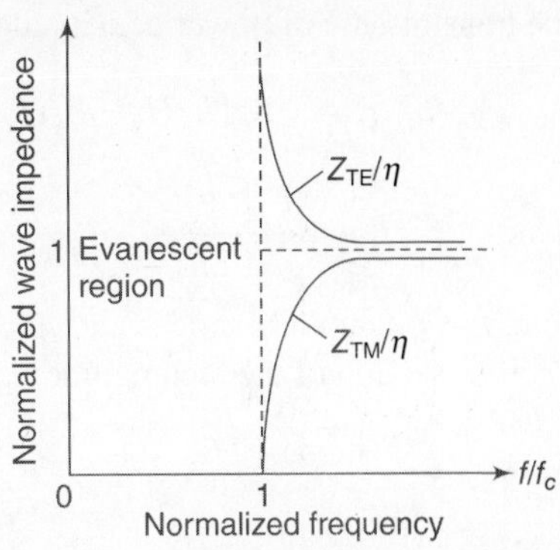

Figure 10.6 *Normalized wave impedances of TM and TE modes*

The above equation shows that the intrinsic impedance of the dielectric in the unbounded medium is the geometric mean of the wave impedances of TM and TE wave in the rectangular waveguide.

10.11 IMPOSSIBILITY OF TEM MODE

The TM and TE waves can propagate inside hollow rectangular and circular waveguides, or indeed, in cylindrical guides of any cross-section shapes. However, that the TEM wave, for which there is no axial component of either $\vec{E}$ or $\vec{H}$ cannot possibly propagate within a single conductor waveguide.

Suppose a TEM wave is assumed to exist within a hollow guide of any shape. Then, lines of $\vec{H}$ must lie entirely in the transverse plane. Also, in a non-magnetic material, $\nabla \cdot \vec{H} = 0$ which requires that the lines of $\vec{H}$ be closed loops. Therefore, if a TEM exists inside the guide, the lines of $\vec{H}$ will be closed loops in the plane perpendicular to the axis. We know that, by Maxwell's equation,

$$\nabla \times \vec{H} = \vec{J} + \frac{\partial \vec{D}}{\partial t} \quad \text{or} \quad \oint_l \vec{H} \cdot d\vec{l} = \int_s \left(\vec{J} + \frac{\partial \vec{D}}{\partial t} \right) \cdot d\vec{s}$$

The magnetomotive force around each of these closed loops must equal the axial current (conduction or displacement) through the loop. In the case of a "guide" with an inner conductor, for example, a coaxial transmission line, this axial current through the $\vec{H}$ loops is the conduction current in the inner conductor. However, for a hollow waveguide having no inner conductor, this axial current must be a displacement current. But an axial displacement current requires an axial component of $\vec{E}$, which is not present in a TEM wave. Therefore, the TEM wave cannot exist in a single conductor rectangular waveguide.

10.12 EQUATION OF POWER TRANSMISSION

The power flow in the waveguide can be determined using the time-average power density or Poynting vector.

$$\vec{S}_{(avg)} = \frac{1}{2}\text{Re}[\tilde{E} \times \tilde{H}^*]$$

The transmission of power density along the z-direction is

$$\vec{S}_{z(\text{avg})} = \frac{1}{2}\text{Re}[E_x H_y^* - E_y H_x^*]\vec{a}_z \ \text{W/m}^2$$

$$= \frac{|E_x|^2 + |E_y|^2}{2\eta}\vec{a}_z \tag{10.51}$$

Here, $\eta = \eta_{\text{TM}}$ for TM modes and $\eta = \eta_{\text{TE}}$ for TE modes. The total average power transmitted through the entire cross-section of the rectangular waveguide is given by

$$P = \int_s \vec{S}_{z(\text{avg})} \cdot d\vec{s} \ \text{W}$$

$$= \int_{x=0}^{b}\int_{y=0}^{a} \frac{|E_x|^2 + |E_y|^2}{2\eta}\, dx\, dy \tag{10.52}$$

where $d\vec{s} = dx\, dy\, \vec{a}_z$.

The power flow in a TM_{mn} mode along the z-direction can be obtained using Eqns. (10.29) and (10.51) as

$$\vec{S}_{z(\text{avg})} = \frac{\omega\varepsilon\beta E_0^2}{2h^4}\left[\left(\frac{m\pi}{a}\right)^2 \cos^2\left(\frac{m\pi}{a}x\right)\sin^2\left(\frac{n\pi}{b}y\right) + \left(\frac{n\pi}{b}\right)^2 \sin^2\left(\frac{m\pi}{a}x\right)\cos^2\left(\frac{n\pi}{b}y\right)\right]\vec{a}_z$$

Now, integrating the above equation over the waveguide cross-section, the total power flow is

$$P = \frac{\omega\varepsilon\beta E_0^2}{2h^4}\int_0^b\int_0^a\left[\left(\frac{m\pi}{a}\right)^2 \cos^2\left(\frac{m\pi}{a}x\right)\sin^2\left(\frac{n\pi}{b}y\right) + \left(\frac{n\pi}{b}\right)^2 \sin^2\left(\frac{m\pi}{a}x\right)\cos^2\left(\frac{n\pi}{b}y\right)\right]dx\, dy$$

$$= \frac{\omega\varepsilon\beta E_0^2}{h^4}\times\frac{ab}{8}\times\left[\left(\frac{m\pi}{a}\right)^2 + \left(\frac{n\pi}{b}\right)^2\right] = \frac{\omega\varepsilon\beta E_0^2 ab}{8h^2} \tag{10.53}$$

where $h^2 = (m\pi/a)^2 + (n\pi/b)^2$. Equation (10.53) shows that the total power flow for a TM_{mn} mode in a rectangular waveguide is directly proportional to its cross-sectional area (ab). Thus, the total power can be increased by increasing the physical dimensions of the waveguide or by using larger electric and magnetic fields. Here, the power is also proportional to frequency and dielectric constant of the waveguide.

Also, the time-average power flow across the cross-section of the waveguide for a TE_{10} mode can be obtained from their electric and magnetic field expressions.

For a TE_{10} mode, we know that,

$$E_y^0 = -\frac{j\omega\mu a}{\pi}H_0\sin\left(\frac{\pi}{a}x\right)$$

and $\qquad H_x^0 = \frac{\gamma a}{\pi}H_0\sin\left(\frac{\pi}{a}x\right) = \frac{j\beta a}{\pi}H_0\sin\left(\frac{\pi}{a}x\right).$

Therefore, the total power flow is

$$P = \int_0^b\int_0^a -\frac{1}{2}(E_y^0)(H_x^0)^*\, dx\, dy$$

$$= \frac{1}{2}\omega\mu\beta\left(\frac{a}{\pi}\right)^2 H_0^2\int_0^b\int_0^a \sin^2\left(\frac{\pi}{a}x\right)dx\, dy$$

$$= \omega\mu\beta ab\left(\frac{aH_0}{2\pi}\right)^2 \tag{10.54}$$

From Eqn. (10.54), it is seen that the average power flow for a TE_{10} mode in a rectangular waveguide also depends on the guide cross-sectional area.

EXAMPLE 10.1

An air-filled standard rectangular waveguide with internal dimensions of $a = 19.05$ mm and $b = 9.53$ mm propagates waves at 18 GHz.

(i) Determine the lowest possible TM mode at which the wave may be excited.

(ii) For the lowest TM mode obtained, find the guide phase constant, guide wavelength, guide phase velocity, and the wave impedance for the TM propagation at 18 GHz.

(ii) Also, determine the maximum time-averaged power transmitted through the waveguide at the lowest TM mode if the electric field intensity is not to exceed the breakdown level in air (3 MV/m).

SOLUTION

All the modes with cut-off frequencies below 18 GHz are the possible modes.

(i) For TM modes, the cut-off frequency is

$$f_c = \frac{1}{2\sqrt{\mu_0 \varepsilon_0}} \sqrt{\left(\frac{m}{a}\right)^2 + \left(\frac{n}{b}\right)^2} = \frac{3 \times 10^8}{2} \sqrt{\left(\frac{m}{0.01905}\right)^2 + \left(\frac{n}{0.00953}\right)^2}$$

where $1/\sqrt{\mu_0 \varepsilon_0} = 3 \times 10^8$ for an air-filled rectangular waveguide.
The possible cut-off frequencies below 18 GHz are as follows:

$$f_{c01} = 1.5 \times 10^8 \sqrt{\left(\frac{0}{0.01905}\right)^2 + \left(\frac{1}{0.00953}\right)^2} = 15.74 \text{ GHz}$$

$$f_{c10} = 1.5 \times 10^8 \sqrt{\left(\frac{1}{0.01905}\right)^2 + \left(\frac{0}{0.00953}\right)^2} = 7.87 \text{ GHz}$$

$$f_{c11} = 1.5 \times 10^8 \sqrt{\left(\frac{1}{0.01905}\right)^2 + \left(\frac{1}{0.00953}\right)^2} = 17.6 \text{ GHz}$$

$$f_{c20} = 1.5 \times 10^8 \sqrt{\left(\frac{2}{0.01905}\right)^2 + \left(\frac{0}{0.00953}\right)^2} = 15.75 \text{ GHz}$$

We know that, in TM_{mn} modes, either m or n cannot be zero. Therefore, out of the above four modes having cut-off frequencies below 18 GHz, only TM_{11} mode is a possible mode for wave propagation in which $m = n = 1$.

(ii) At $f = 18$ GHz, for the TM_{11} mode:

Guide phase constant

$$\beta = \omega \sqrt{\mu_0 \varepsilon_0} \sqrt{1 - \left(\frac{f_c}{f}\right)^2} = \frac{2\pi \times 18 \times 10^9}{3 \times 10^8} \sqrt{1 - \left(\frac{17.6 \times 10^9}{18 \times 10^9}\right)^2} = 79 \text{ rad/m}$$

Guide wavelength

$$\lambda_g = \frac{2\pi}{\beta} = \frac{2\pi}{79} = 0.0795 \text{ m}$$

Guide phase velocity

$$u_p = \frac{\omega}{\beta} = \frac{2\pi \times 18 \times 10^9}{79} = 1.43 \times 10^9 \text{ m/s}$$

Guide wave impedance

$$Z_{TM} = \frac{\beta}{\omega \varepsilon_0} = \frac{79}{2\pi \times 18 \times 10^9 \times 8.854 \times 10^{-12}} = 78.89 \ \Omega$$

(iii) For the TM_{mn} mode, we know that the maximum power transmitted is

$$P = \frac{\omega \varepsilon \beta E_0^2}{h^4} \times \frac{ab}{8} \times \left[\left(\frac{m\pi}{a} \right)^2 + \left(\frac{n\pi}{b} \right)^2 \right] = \frac{\omega \varepsilon \beta E_0^2 ab}{8h^2}$$

where $h^2 = \left(\dfrac{m\pi}{a} \right)^2 + \left(\dfrac{n\pi}{b} \right)^2$

Hence, for the TM_{11} mode:

$$h = \sqrt{\left(\frac{m\pi}{a} \right)^2 + \left(\frac{n\pi}{b} \right)^2} = \sqrt{\left(\frac{\pi}{0.01905} \right)^2 + \left(\frac{\pi}{0.00953} \right)^2} = 368.6 \text{ rad/m}$$

Now, the maximum total power is

$$P = \frac{\omega \varepsilon \beta E_0^2 ab}{8h^2} \qquad \text{(given } E_0 = 3 \times 10^6 \text{ V/m)}$$

$$= \frac{2\pi \times 18 \times 10^9 \times 8.854 \times 10^{-12} \times 79 \times 9 \times 10^{12} \times 0.01905 \times 0.00953}{8 \times (368.6)^2}$$

$$= 118.92 \text{ kW}$$

EXAMPLE 10.2

An air-filled rectangular waveguide has inner dimensions of $a = 2.286$ cm and $b = 1.016$ cm. Determine the cut-off frequencies of the following modes: TE_{10}, TE_{01}, TE_{20}, TE_{11}, TM_{11}, TM_{21} and TM_{12}. Also, determine the modes that will propagate along the waveguide and which of them will evanesce, when the signal frequency is 10 GHz.

SOLUTION

The cut-off frequency of a wave in a rectangular waveguide filled with air is

$$f_c = \frac{1}{2\sqrt{\mu_0 \varepsilon_0}} \sqrt{\left(\frac{m}{a} \right)^2 + \left(\frac{n}{b} \right)^2}$$

For a TE_{10} mode in which $m = 1$ and $n = 0$, the cut-off frequency is

$$f_c = \frac{c}{2} \sqrt{\left(\frac{1}{a} \right)^2} = \frac{c}{2a} = \frac{3 \times 10^8}{2 \times 2.286 \times 10^{-2}} = 6.56 \times 10^9 \text{ Hz} = 6.56 \text{ GHz}$$

For a TE_{01} mode, $f_c = \dfrac{c}{2}\sqrt{\left(\dfrac{1}{b}\right)^2} = \dfrac{c}{2b} = \dfrac{3 \times 10^8}{2 \times 1.016 \times 10^{-2}} = 14.76 \text{ GHz}$

For a TE_{20} mode, $f_c = \dfrac{c}{2}\sqrt{\left(\dfrac{2}{a}\right)^2} = \dfrac{c}{a} = \dfrac{3 \times 10^8}{2.286 \times 10^{-2}} = 13.12 \text{ GHz}$

For a TE_{11} mode, $f_c = \dfrac{c}{2}\sqrt{\left(\dfrac{1}{a}\right)^2 + \left(\dfrac{1}{b}\right)^2} = \dfrac{3 \times 10^8 \times 10^2}{2}\sqrt{\left(\dfrac{1}{2.286}\right)^2 + \left(\dfrac{1}{1.016}\right)^2} = 16.16 \text{ GHz}$

For a TM_{11} mode, the cut-off frequency will be same as TE_{11} mode frequency i.e., 16.16 GHz.

For a TM_{21} mode, $f_c = \dfrac{c}{2}\sqrt{\left(\dfrac{2}{a}\right)^2 + \left(\dfrac{1}{b}\right)^2} = \dfrac{3 \times 10^8 \times 10^2}{2}\sqrt{\left(\dfrac{2}{2.286}\right)^2 + \left(\dfrac{1}{1.016}\right)^2}$

$$= \dfrac{3 \times 10^8 \times 10^2}{2} \times \sqrt{0.765 + 0.969} = 19.75 \text{ GHz}$$

For a TM_{12} mode, $f_c = \dfrac{c}{2}\sqrt{\left(\dfrac{1}{a}\right)^2 + \left(\dfrac{2}{b}\right)^2} = \dfrac{3 \times 10^8 \times 10^2}{2}\sqrt{\left(\dfrac{1}{2.286}\right)^2 + \left(\dfrac{2}{1.016}\right)^2}$

$$= \dfrac{3 \times 10^8 \times 10^2}{2} \times \sqrt{0.191 + 3.875} = 30.25 \text{ GHz}$$

As the excitation signal frequency is 10 GHz, only modes with cut-off frequencies less than 10 GHz will propagate and the other modes will evanesce. Hence, the only possible mode that will propagate is TE_{10} mode. The other modes that will evanesce are TE_{01}, TE_{20}, TE_{11}, TM_{11}, TM_{21} and TM_{12}.

EXAMPLE 10.3

Given that $H_x = 2 \sin\left(\dfrac{2\pi}{a} x\right) \cos\left(\dfrac{3\pi}{b} y\right) \sin(\pi \times 10^{11} t - \beta z)$ A/m in a rectangular waveguide of dimensions $a = 1.5$ cm and $b = 0.8$ cm filled with a dielectric material of $\sigma = 0$, $\mu = \mu_0$ and $\varepsilon = 4\varepsilon_0$. Determine the (i) mode of operation, (ii) cut-off frequency, (iii) phase constant, (iv) propagation constant and (v) intrinsic impedance.

SOLUTION

(i) From the given expression for magnetic field, it is seen that $m = 2$ and $n = 3$ i.e., the guide is operating at TM_{23} or TE_{23} mode. So, let us select the mode as TM_{23} mode.

(ii) Cut-off frequency is

$$f_c = \dfrac{u'}{2}\sqrt{\left(\dfrac{m}{a}\right)^2 + \left(\dfrac{n}{b}\right)^2} \qquad \text{where } u' = \dfrac{1}{\sqrt{\mu\varepsilon}} = \dfrac{c}{\sqrt{\mu_r \varepsilon_r}} = \dfrac{c}{\sqrt{4}} = \dfrac{c}{2}$$

Therefore, $f_c = \dfrac{c}{4}\sqrt{\left(\dfrac{m}{a}\right)^2 + \left(\dfrac{n}{b}\right)^2} = \dfrac{3 \times 10^8 \times 10^2}{4}\sqrt{\left(\dfrac{2}{1.5}\right)^2 + \left(\dfrac{3}{0.8}\right)^2} = 29.84 \text{ GHz}$

(iii) Phase constant is

$$\beta = \omega\sqrt{\mu\varepsilon}\sqrt{1-\left(\frac{f_c}{f}\right)^2} = \frac{\omega\sqrt{\varepsilon_r}}{c}\sqrt{1-\left(\frac{f_c}{f}\right)^2}$$

where $\omega = 2\pi f = \pi \times 10^{11}$ i.e., $f = \dfrac{\pi \times 10^{11}}{2\pi} = 50$ GHz

Hence, $\beta = \dfrac{\pi \times 10^{11} \times 2}{3 \times 10^8}\sqrt{1-\left(\dfrac{29.84 \times 10^9}{50 \times 10^9}\right)^2} = 1674.67$ rad/m

(iv) Propagation constant is $\gamma = j\beta = j1674.67$/m
 (v) Intrinsic impedance for a TM mode is

$$Z_{TM} = \sqrt{\frac{\mu}{\varepsilon}}\sqrt{1-\left(\frac{f_c}{f}\right)^2} = \frac{377}{\sqrt{4}}\sqrt{1-\left(\frac{29.84 \times 10^9}{50 \times 10^9}\right)^2} = 150.8\ \Omega$$

EXAMPLE 10.4

Determine the cut-off frequencies for a TE_{10} mode in rectangular waveguides with the following inner dimensions (i) 7.214 cm $\times$ 3.404 cm (S-band) and (ii) 2.286 cm $\times$ 1.016 cm (C-band).

SOLUTION

 (i) For $a = 7.214$ cm and $b = 3.404$ cm in a rectangular waveguide, the cut-off frequency for a TE_{10} mode is

$$f_c = \frac{u}{2a} = \frac{3 \times 10^8}{2 \times 7.214 \times 10^{-2}} = 2.08 \times 10^9\ \text{Hz} = 2.08\ \text{GHz (S-band)}$$

where $u = c = 1/\sqrt{\mu_0\varepsilon_0} = 3 \times 10^8$ m/s in a waveguide filled with air.

(ii) For $a = 2.286$ cm and $b = 1.016$ cm in a rectangular waveguide, the cut-off frequency for a TE_{10} mode is

$$f_c = \frac{u}{2a} = \frac{3 \times 10^8}{2 \times 2.286 \times 10^{-2}} = 6.56 \times 10^9\ \text{Hz} = 6.56\ \text{GHz (C-band)}$$

EXAMPLE 10.5

A TE_{10} wave at 10 GHz propagates in a rectangular waveguide with inner dimensions $a = 1.5$ cm and $b = 0.6$ cm which is filled with polyethylene of $\varepsilon_r = 2.25$ and $\mu_r = 1$. Determine the (i) phase constant, (ii) guide wavelength, (iii) phase velocity, and (iv) wave impedance.

SOLUTION

At $f = 10$ GHz, the wavelength in unbounded polyethylene is

$$\lambda = \frac{u}{f} = \frac{c}{\sqrt{\varepsilon_r} \times f} = \frac{3 \times 10^8}{\sqrt{2.25} \times 10 \times 10^9} = \frac{2 \times 10^8}{10 \times 10^9} = 0.02\ \text{m}$$

The cut-off frequency for the TE_{10} mode is

$$f_c = \frac{u}{2a} = \frac{2 \times 10^8}{2 \times 1.5 \times 10^{-2}} = 6.67 \times 10^9 \text{ Hz} = 6.67 \text{ GHz}$$

(i) *Phase constant*

$$\beta = \frac{\omega}{u}\sqrt{1 - \left(\frac{f_c}{f}\right)^2} = \frac{2\pi \times 10 \times 10^9}{2 \times 10^8}\sqrt{1 - \left(\frac{6.67 \times 10^9}{10 \times 10^9}\right)^2} = 233.9 \text{ rad/m}$$

(ii) *Guide wavelength*

$$\lambda_g = \frac{2\pi}{\beta} = \frac{2\pi}{233.9} = 0.0268 \text{ m}$$

$$\text{(or)} \quad \lambda_g = \frac{\lambda}{\sqrt{1 - (f_c/f)^2}} = \frac{0.02}{\sqrt{1 - (0.667)^2}} = \frac{0.02}{0.745} = 0.0268 \text{ m}$$

(iii) *Phase velocity*

$$u_p = \frac{\omega}{\beta} = \frac{2\pi \times 10 \times 10^9}{233.9} = 2.68 \times 10^8 \text{ m/s}$$

$$\text{(or)} \quad u_p = \frac{u}{\sqrt{1 - (f_c/f)^2}} = \frac{2 \times 10^8}{0.745} = 2.68 \times 10^8 \text{ m/s}$$

(iv) **Wave impedance**

$$Z_{TE} = \frac{\omega\mu_0}{\beta} = \frac{2\pi \times 10 \times 10^9 \times 4\pi \times 10^{-7}}{233.9} = 337.22 \ \Omega$$

$$\text{(or)} \quad Z_{TE} = \frac{\sqrt{\mu/\varepsilon}}{\sqrt{1 - (f_c/f)^2}} = \frac{377/\sqrt{2.25}}{0.745} = 337.36 \ \Omega$$

EXAMPLE 10.6

A 1 cm × 3 cm rectangular air-filled waveguide operates in the TE_{12} mode at a frequency that is 20% higher than its cut-off frequency. Calculate the operating frequency, phase velocity and group velocity.

SOLUTION

Given $a = 1$ cm, $b = 3$ cm and the operating frequency $= 1.2 \times f_c$ for a TE_{12} mode.

Cut-off frequency is
$$f_c = \frac{1}{2\sqrt{\mu_0\varepsilon_0}}\sqrt{\left(\frac{m}{a}\right)^2 + \left(\frac{n}{b}\right)^2} = \frac{c}{2}\sqrt{\left(\frac{1}{a}\right)^2 + \left(\frac{2}{b}\right)^2}$$

$$= \frac{3 \times 10^8 \times 10^2}{2}\sqrt{\left(\frac{1}{1}\right)^2 + \left(\frac{2}{3}\right)^2} = 18.02 \text{ GHz}$$

Hence, the operating frequency $= 1.2 \times 18.02 \times 10^9 = 21.62$ GHz

Phase velocity is $u_p = \dfrac{c}{\sqrt{1-\left(\dfrac{f_c}{f}\right)^2}} = \dfrac{3\times10^8}{\sqrt{1-\left(\dfrac{18.02}{21.63}\right)^2}} = 5.425\times10^8 \text{ m/s}$

Group velocity is $u_g = \dfrac{c^2}{u_p} = \dfrac{9\times10^{16}}{5.425\times10^8} = 1.659\times10^8 \text{ m/s}$

EXAMPLE 10.7

A rectangular waveguide is filled with polyethylene as dielectric with $\varepsilon_r = 2.25$ and operates at 24 GHz. If the cut-off frequency of a certain TE mode is 16 GHz, find the group velocity and intrinsic impedance of the mode.

SOLUTION

For a rectangular waveguide filled with polyethylene as dielectric, the phase velocity of a TE mode is

$$u_p = \frac{c}{\sqrt{\varepsilon_r}\sqrt{1-\left(\dfrac{f_c}{f}\right)^2}} = \frac{3\times10^8}{\sqrt{2.25}\sqrt{1-\left(\dfrac{16}{24}\right)^2}} = 2.68\times10^8 \text{ m/s}$$

The relationship between the phase velocity and group velocity with polyethylene as dielectric inside the rectangular waveguide is

$$u_g u_p = \frac{c^2}{\varepsilon_r}$$

Therefore, the group velocity is

$$u_g = \frac{c^2}{\varepsilon_r u_p} = \frac{9\times10^{16}}{2.25\times2.68\times10^8} = 1.492\times10^8 \text{ m/s}$$

The intrinsic impedance of the TE mode is

$$Z_{TE} = \frac{\eta}{\sqrt{1-(f_c/f)^2}} \quad \text{where } \eta = \frac{\eta_0}{\sqrt{\varepsilon_r}} = \frac{377}{\sqrt{2.25}} = 251.33\ \Omega$$

$$= \frac{251.33}{\sqrt{1-\left(\dfrac{16}{24}\right)^2}} = 337.2\ \Omega$$

EXAMPLE 10.8

A lossless air-dielectric waveguide for an S-band radar system has the dimensions $a = 7.214$ cm and $b = 3.404$ cm. The dominant mode propagates in the +z-direction at 3 GHz. Determine the average power transmitted if the excitation level of the electric field is 10 kV/m.

SOLUTION

For the TE_{10} mode, the cut-off frequency is

$$f_c = \frac{u}{2a} = \frac{3 \times 10^8}{2 \times 7.214 \times 10^{-2}} = 2.08 \times 10^9 \text{ Hz} = 2.08 \text{ GHz}$$

Since the cut-of frequency is below 3 GHz, the possible dominant mode is TE_{10} mode and the average power transmitted for this mode is

$$P = \omega\mu\beta ab\left(\frac{aH_0}{2\pi}\right)^2 \quad (\text{Given } E_0 = 10 \times 10^3 \text{ V/m}) \tag{1}$$

Here, for air as a dielectric medium, the wave impedance is

$$\eta_0 = \frac{|E|}{|H|} \quad \Rightarrow \quad |H| = \frac{|E|}{\eta_0} = \frac{10 \times 10^3}{377} = H_0$$

and

$$\beta = \omega\sqrt{\mu_0\varepsilon_0}\sqrt{1 - \left(\frac{f_c}{f}\right)^2} = \frac{2\pi \times 3 \times 10^9}{3 \times 10^8}\sqrt{1 - \left(\frac{2.08 \times 10^9}{3 \times 10^9}\right)^2} = 45.28 \text{ rad/m}$$

Therefore, substituting the values in Eqn. (1), we get

$$P = 2\pi \times 3 \times 10^9 \times 4\pi \times 10^{-7} \times 45.28 \times 7.214 \times 3.404 \times 10^{-4} \times \left(\frac{7.214 \times 10^{-2}}{2\pi} \times \frac{10 \times 10^3}{377}\right)^2$$

$$= 236.8 \text{ W}$$

10.13 MICROSTRIP LINE

The cross-sectional view of a microstrip line is shown in Figure 10.7. It consists of a dielectric substrate with a strip conductor on one side and the ground plane on the opposite side. Unlike strip line, the microstrip is basically an open structure and requires high dielectric constant substrates to confine the electromagnetic fields near the strip conductor. Moreover, microstrip line is a non-homogeneous structure. Because of the composite nature of the dielectric interface, propagation cannot be a true TEM i.e., a pure TEM mode cannot exist. It is not possible to satisfy the boundary conditions for this mode at the surface of the dielectric. However, at low frequencies, the mode of propagation closely resembles the TEM mode, and, hence, is termed the quasi-TEM mode. The electric and magnetic field lines are concentrated predominantly in the dielectric substrate beneath the strip conductor and somewhat less in the air region above.

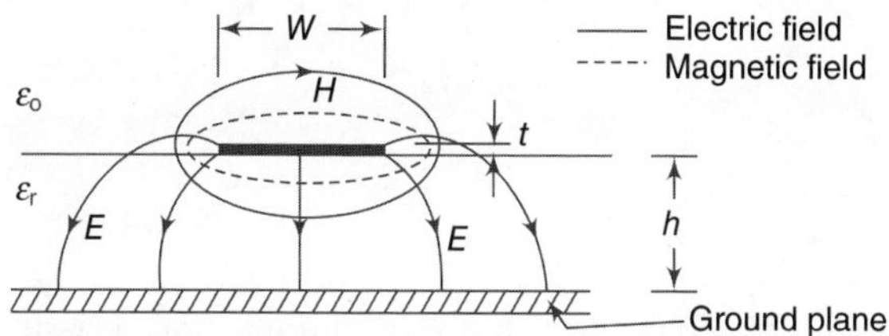

Figure 10.7 *Cross-sectional view of microstrip line*

The larger the relative dielectric constant (ε_r) of the substrate, the greater would be the concentration of energy in the substrate region.

Being an open structure, it is easily amenable for series mounting of discrete devices and to make minor adjustments after the circuit has been fabricated. However, care has to be taken to minimize the radiation loss or interference due to nearby conductors. If high dielectric constant substrates are used, it is advantageous that the phase velocity and circuit dimensions are reduced. The analysis of the microstrip line is little complicated since the structure becomes a mixed dielectric transmission line.

Microstrip is a versatile transmission line for microwave and millimetre wave integrated circuits up to 35 GHz. Its frequency range of operation can be extended up to 94 GHz by shielding the structure and using thin dielectric constant substrates.

In a microstrip line, lower dielectric constant allows higher achievable Q as well as higher operating frequency. For sufficiently small values of dielectric constant of the substrate, the maximum Q in a microstrip line can be limited due to increased radiation losses. Thinner substrates permit higher frequencies to be used, but at the expense of degradation in Q-factor, especially at lower frequencies.

A major advantage of the microstrip is that its surface is accessible for mounting passive as well as active discrete devices. It is also a versatile medium for realizing a variety of circuit forms and combining several circuit functions.

Practical microstrip circuits are housed in a shielded enclosure in order to provide electromagnetic shielding and suppress radiation. Figure 10.8 shows the cross-section of a shielded microstrip line. The dimensions of the enclosure are selected such that the waveguide modes are below cut-off, and top and sidewalls have practically no effect on the propagation characteristics.

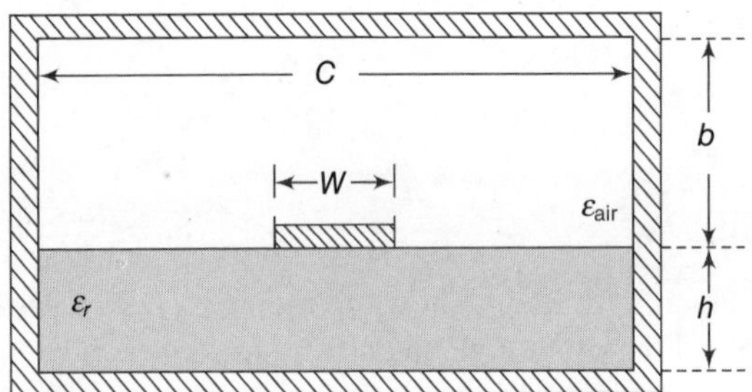

Figure 10.8   *Shielded Microstrip Line*

10.13.1   Expressions of Z_0 and λ_g

For typical microstrip lines with finite strip thickness, the characteristic impedance Z_0 is given by the following expressions according to Hammerstad:

$$Z_0 = \frac{60}{\sqrt{\varepsilon_{eff}}} \ln\left(\frac{8h}{w}\right) \Omega \qquad \left(\frac{w}{h} \leq 1\right) \tag{10.55a}$$

and

$$Z_0 = \frac{377}{\sqrt{\varepsilon_{eff}}} \left(\frac{h}{w}\right) \Omega \qquad \left(\frac{w}{h} > 1\right) \tag{10.55b}$$

where ε_{eff} is the effective dielectric constant of the substrate material. It is usually less than the value ε_r for the substrate and it takes account of the effect of the external fields. The value of ε_{eff} lies in the range $0.5\,(1 + \varepsilon_r) \leq \varepsilon_{eff} \leq \varepsilon_r$ depending on the value of w/h. For small strip widths ($w/h \ll 1$), the fields are distributed nearly equally in the substrate and air regions and hence ε_{eff} approaches the lower limit $(1 + \varepsilon_r)/2$. For large strip widths ($w/h \gg 1$), the electric field is confined mostly between the strip conductor and the ground plane. The microstrip then resembles a parallel-plate capacitor with λ_{eff} approaching ε_r.

The wavelength of propagation λ_g is given by

$$\lambda_g = \frac{\lambda_a}{\sqrt{\varepsilon_{\text{eff}}}} \tag{10.56}$$

where λ_a is the wavelength of the structure with dielectric replaced by air.

10.13.2 Losses

The propagation loss (neglecting radiation) in a practical microstrip is primarily due to two types of dissipative losses, conductor loss due to the finite resistivity of the conductor and dielectric loss due to the finite loss tangent of the dielectric substrate. If we denote α_c as the attenuation constant due to the conductor loss and α_d as the attenuation constant due to dielectric loss, both expressed in dB/unit length, then the total attenuation constant α is given by $\alpha = (\alpha_c + \alpha_d)$ dB/ unit length.

The total attenuation coefficient α is expressed by

$$\alpha \approx 8.68 \frac{R_s}{Z_0 w} \text{ dB/cm} \qquad \left(\frac{w}{h} > 1\right) \tag{10.57}$$

where R_s is the skin resistivity of the conducting surfaces and w is the strip width in cm. Figure 10.9 shows the attenuation constant α for a 50 Ω microstrip line as a function of substrate height h with ε_r as parameter.

Losses are generally greater in microstrip than in stripline but they can be reduced by using higher dielectric constant materials. Microstrip lines are usually fabricated on fibreglass or polystyrene printed circuit boards about 1.5 mm thick with copper conductors 3 mm wide. For integrated circuits, alumina, silicon or sapphire about 0.25 mm thick are used as substrates with conductors made of copper, aluminum or gold about 0.25 mm wide. Nowadays, circuits are also being manufactured with high-resistivity gallium arsenide. By using very thin substrates such as 0.1 mm quartz, the frequency limit of microstrip can be extended to about 100 GHz.

10.13.3 Dispersion

If the frequency of a signal exciting a microstrip line increases, then the effective dielectric constant, characteristic impedance and the phase constant β change. It is called dispersion. The dispersion is due to the propagation of hybrid modes along the microstrip line. Several transmission line structures exhibit this type of behaviour as shown in Figure 10.10.

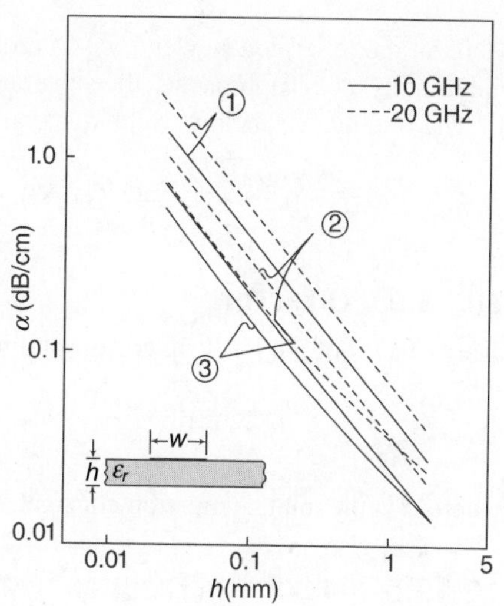

Figure 10.9 *Theoretical attenuation constant $\alpha = (\alpha_c + \alpha_d)$ for a 50 Ω microstrip line as function of substrate height h with ε_r as parameter for (1) alumina, (2) fused quartz, (3) RT/Duroid*

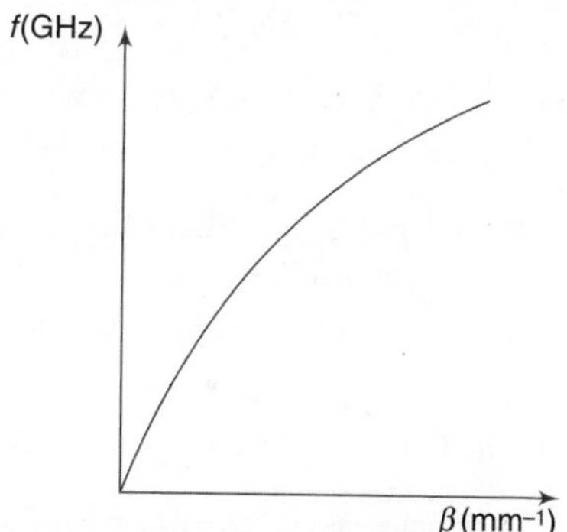

Figure 10.10 *Dispersive effect*

The dispersion effect is accounted for by defining a frequency dependant effective microstrip permittivity $\varepsilon_{\text{eff}}(f)$. Since the fields are forced into the dielectric substrate to an increasing extent as the frequency rises, $\varepsilon_{\text{eff}}(f)$ is expressed by

$$\varepsilon_{\text{eff}}(f) = \left\{ \frac{v_0}{v_{ph}(f)} \right\}^2 \tag{10.58}$$

This quantity increases the frequency and the wave is progressively slowed down.

Fundamentally, the dispersion problem consists of solving the fields in the structure for the velocity $v_{ph}(f)$. The limits of $\varepsilon_{\text{eff}}(f)$ are readily established as follows:

$$\varepsilon_{\text{eff}}(f) \to \begin{cases} \varepsilon_{\text{eff}} & as \quad f \to 0 \\ \varepsilon_r & as \quad f \to \infty \end{cases}$$

Here, at the low frequency end, $\varepsilon_{\text{eff}}(f)$ reduces to the static-TEM value of ε_{eff}. As the frequency is increased indefinitely, $\varepsilon_{\text{eff}}(f)$ approaches the substrate permittivity ε_r itself.

The frequency f_d below which dispersive effects may be neglected is given by

$$f_d = 0.3 \sqrt{\frac{Z_0}{h\sqrt{\varepsilon_r - 1}}} \; \text{GHz} \;, \text{ where } h \text{ is in cms.} \tag{10.59}$$

10.13.4 *Q*-factor

The Q-factor of a microstrip corresponding to the conductor and dielectric losses is expressed by

$$Q = \frac{\pi \sqrt{\varepsilon_{\text{eff}}(f)}}{\lambda_0 \alpha} \tag{10.60}$$

where α is the total attenuation constant specified in dB/unit length.

10.13.5 Maximum Frequency of Operation

The maximum frequency of operation in microstrip is limited primarily by the excitation of higher order modes in the form of surface waves and transverse resonances, higher losses and the requirement on stringent fabrication tolerances. The surface waves may be TM or TE modes, which propagate between the dielectric and the ground plane. The frequency at which strong coupling takes place between the quasi-TEM mode and a TM mode occurs when the two modes have the same phase velocity is given by

$$f_{TEM} = \frac{v_0 \tan^{-1}(\varepsilon_r)}{\pi h \sqrt{2(\varepsilon_r - 1)}} \tag{10.61}$$

For a wide microstrip line, a transverse-resonant mode can strongly couple to the quasi-TEM microstrip mode. The cut-off frequency for this mode is given by

$$f_c = \frac{v_0}{\sqrt{\varepsilon_r}\,(2w + 0.8h)} \tag{10.62}$$

and the mode can be suppressed by inserting slots into the metal strip.

Closed form expression for characteristic impedance and effective dielectric constant:
Using the Conformal Mapping Method, wheeler has given the design formulae as

$$\frac{w}{h} = 8 \frac{\{[\exp z_0 \sqrt{\varepsilon_r + 1}/42.4 - 1](7 + 4/\varepsilon_r)/11 + (1 + 1/\varepsilon_r)/0.81\}^{1/2}}{\exp\{(z_0\sqrt{\varepsilon_r + 1}/42.4) - 1\}}$$

This equation is suitable for design (or synthesis). For analysis, it may be reversed and put in the following form:

$$Z_0 = \frac{42.4}{\sqrt{\varepsilon_r + 1}} \ln\left\{1 + \left(\frac{4h}{w}\right)\left[\left(\frac{14 + 8/\varepsilon_r}{11}\right)\left(\frac{4h}{w}\right) + \sqrt{\left(\frac{14 + 8/\varepsilon_r}{11}\right)^2 \left(\frac{4h}{w}\right)^2 + \frac{1 + 1/\varepsilon_r}{2}\pi^2}\right]\right\}$$

The effective dielectric constant may be found by evaluating an additional value Z_a i.e., Z_0 for $\varepsilon_r = 1$. We have

$$\varepsilon_{\text{eff}} = \left(\frac{Z_a}{Z_0}\right)^2$$

Alternatively, Schneider derived an empirical expression for ε_{eff} directly in terms of ε_r, w and h. This may be written as

$$\varepsilon_{\text{eff}} = \frac{\varepsilon_r + 1}{2} + \frac{\varepsilon_r - 1}{2}\left(1 + \frac{12h}{w}\right)^{-1/2} \tag{10.63}$$

The variation of microstrip characteristic impedance Z_0 with w/h is shown in Figure 10.11(a). Here, it can be observed that there is a decrease in characteristic impedance Z_0 of the microstrip line for different values of ε_r as the ratio of w/h increases. Also, Figure 10.11(b) shows the effective dielectric constant ε_{eff} and the normalized guide wavelength λ/λ_a of the microstrip versus w/h as parameter. From Figure 10.11(b), it is noted that the effective dielectric constant ε_{eff} of the microstrip increases whereas the normalized guide wavelength

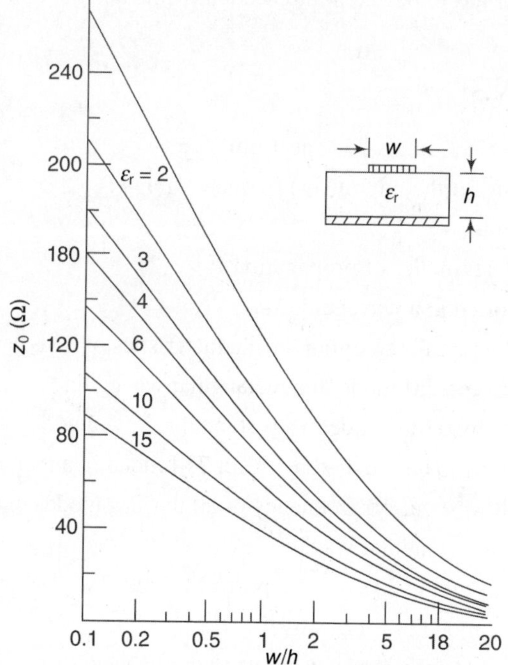

Figure 10.11(a)   *Variation of microstrip characteristic impedance with w/h*

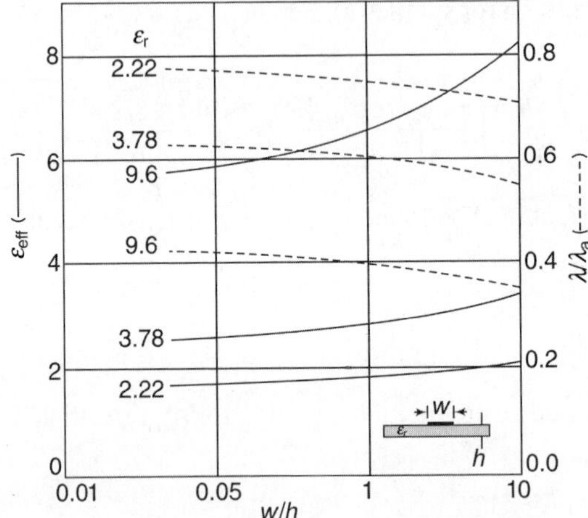

Figure 10.11(b) *Variation of ε_{eff} and normalized guide wavelength λ/λ_a of microstrip versus w/h as parameters*

λ/λ_a decreases as the ratio of *w/h* increases. It may be noted that for microstrip lines, the phase velocity u_p is given by

$$u_p = \frac{c}{\sqrt{\varepsilon_{eff}}}$$

(10.64)

Since ε_{eff} is a function of *w* and *h*, the phase velocity, and hence, the guide wavelength depends upon the line impedance also. This factor has to be taken into account while designing microstrip circuits.

REVIEW QUESTIONS

1. Discuss in detail about the electromagnetic spectrum.
2. Write the band designations for the microwave frequency range.
3. What is the use of waveguide?
4. What is meant by TM and TE modes of propagation?
5. Can a TEM wave be supported in a waveguide?
6. Discuss the analytical procedure for studying the characteristics of TM waves in a waveguide.
7. Derive the field expressions for TM mode in a rectangular waveguide.
8. Write the field components for TM_{11} mode in a rectangular waveguide.
9. State the boundary conditions to be satisfied by E_z for TM mode in a rectangular waveguide.
10. Which TM mode has the lowest cut-off frequency of all the TM modes in a rectangular waveguide?
11. Can a TM_{10} mode exist in a rectangular waveguide?
12. Show that a rectangular waveguide does not support TM_{01} and TM_{10} modes.
13. What is the lowest possible mode of a TM wave?
14. How many possible TM modes can occur in a rectangular waveguide?
15. Discuss the analytical procedure for studying the characteristics of TE waves in a waveguide.

16. Derive the field expressions for TE mode in a rectangular waveguide.

17. Write the field components for TE_{10} mode in a rectangular waveguide.

18. State the boundary conditions to be satisfied by H_z for TE mode in a rectangular waveguide.

19. Which TE mode has the lowest cut-off frequency of all the TE modes in a rectangular waveguide?

20. What is the lowest order mode of a TE mode in a waveguide?

21. Explain the differences between TM_{mn} and TE_{mn} modes.

22. Explain why single-conductor hollow or dielectric-filled waveguides cannot support TEM waves.

23. Sketch the field configurations for TM_{11} and TE_{10} in a waveguide.

24. Define cut-off frequency of a waveguide.

25. List the three basic types of propagating waves in a uniform waveguide.

26. What is meant by wave impedance?

27. Is it possible for a waveguide to have more than one cut-off frequency? On what factors does the cut-off frequency of a waveguide depend?

28. Show that in a rectangular waveguide operating in TE_{10} mode, the cut-off frequency is given by

$$f_c = \frac{c}{2a\sqrt{\varepsilon_r}}.$$

29. What is meant by an evanescent mode?

30. How does the wave impedance in a waveguide depend on frequency for a wave propagating in TEM, TE and TM mode?

31. What is the significance of a purely reactive wave impedance?

32. What are meant by the dominant and degenerate modes of a waveguide?

33. What is the cut-off wavelength of the TE_{10} mode in a rectangular waveguide?

34. Write the relationship between group velocity and phase velocity in a waveguide.

35. What are the nonzero field components for the TE_{10} mode in a rectangular waveguide?

36. Which mode is the dominant mode in a rectangular waveguide if (a) $a < b$, (b) $a > b$ and (c) $a = b$?

37. Show that in a rectangular waveguide, the guide wavelength λ_g is smaller for a dielectric-filled waveguide than an air-filled waveguide.

38. Discuss how a rectangular waveguide acts as a high-pass filter.

39. The signal propagated in a waveguide has its group velocity 1.66×10^8 m/s and the free space velocity 3×10^8 m/s. Calculate the phase velocity.

40. Draw the normalized wave impedance graph for TM and TE modes in a waveguide.

41. Write the intrinsic impedance relationship for TM and TE modes in a waveguide.

42. A rectangular waveguide has dimensions $a = 6$ cm and $b = 4$ cm. (i) Over what range of frequencies will the guide operate single-mode? (ii) Over what frequency ranges will the guide support both TE_{10} and TE_{01} modes and no others?

43. An air-filled waveguide is operating at 32.20 GHz in TM_{11} mode. Calculate the cut-off frequency, propagation constant, guide wavelength, phase velocity and the intrinsic wave impedance.

44. A 2 cm $\times$ 3 cm waveguide is filled with a dielectric material with $\varepsilon_r = 4$. If the waveguide operates at 20 GHz with TM_{11} mode, determine the (i) cut-off frequency, (ii) phase constant and (iii) phase velocity.

45. A polyethylene-filled ($\varepsilon_r = 2.5$) rectangular waveguide of $a = 1$ cm and $b = 0.5$ cm supports the TM_{11} mode when the operating frequency is 9 GHz. The amplitude of the z-component of the electric field is 1.5 kV/m at $z = 0$. Determine the (i) cut-off frequency, (ii) propagation constant, (iii) phase and group velocities, (iv) intrinsic impedance and (v) average power flow.

46. A 2 cm square waveguide operates at 12 GHz with the TM_{11} mode. Determine the (i) cut-off frequency, (ii) cut-off wavelength, (iii) guide wavelength, (iv) phase velocity, (v) group velocity, and (vi) intrinsic impedance. Also, write the general expression for the fields in time domain and phasor domain.

47. An air-filled rectangular waveguide with internal dimensions of 2.29 cm and 1.02 cm is operated in the dominant mode. Determine the cut-off frequency for the dominant mode and for the other three modes with lowest cut-off frequencies. If the operating frequency is 8.2 GHz, find the guide wavelength for the dominant mode.

48. A rectangular waveguide has internal dimensions of 7.214 cm and 3.404 cm. The operating frequency is 5 GHz. Determine the following for the first two lowest order modes: (i) phase constant, (ii) guide wavelength, and (iii) phase velocity.

49. An air-filled rectangular waveguide of $b = 1$ cm is supposed to operate at 12 GHz with $\beta_{10} = 150$ rad/m. What should a be in order to support the TE_{10} mode?

50. An X-band rectangular waveguide is filled with Teflon ($\varepsilon_r = 2.1$) and is operated at 9.5 GHz. Determine the speed of light in this material and the phase and group velocities in the waveguide.

51. The group velocity of the wave in a square waveguide operating at 3 GHz with the dominant mode is determined as 2×10^8 m/s. Determine the size of the square cross-section if the dielectric inside the guide is characterized by a permittivity of $\varepsilon = 2\varepsilon_0$.

52. The phase constant in an air-filled rectangular waveguide is 165 rad/m when it is excited with the TM_{21} mode. Calculate the wavelength of the wave if the excitation frequency is 10% higher than the cut-off frequency of the operating mode.

53. A rectangular waveguide with $a = 2$ cm and $b = 3$ cm is filled with a dielectric of $\varepsilon_r = 3$ and is operated at 50 GHz. Determine the cut-off frequency, wavelength, phase constant, group velocity and wave impedance for TE_{22} mode. Also, write the general expression for the fields in time domain and phasor domain.

54. An air-filled rectangular waveguide has cross-sectional dimensions $a = 6$ cm and $b = 3$ cm. Given that

$$E_z = 5 \sin\left(\frac{2\pi}{a} x\right) \sin\left(\frac{3\pi}{b} y\right) \cos(10^{12} t - \beta z) \text{ V/m},$$ determine the intrinsic impedance of this mode and

the average power flow in the guide.

55. An air-filled lossless rectangular waveguide with $a = 2$ cm and $b = 1$ cm operates in the TE_{10} mode at 15 GHz. Determine the magnitudes of the applied electric and magnetic fields if the average power transmitted by the waveguide is 1 kW. Write the expressions for the fields in time domain and phasor domain.

56. The magnitude of the applied electric field in an air-filled rectangular waveguide is 500 V/m when it operates with TE_{10} mode at 10 GHz. Determine the average power that is transmitted along the waveguide. The length of the waveguide is 2 m, $a = 3$ cm and $b = 2$ cm. Write expressions for the field components in time domain.

57. A 1 cm $\times$ 3 cm rectangular air-filled waveguide operates in the TE_{12} mode at a frequency that is 20% higher than the cut-off frequency. Determine the (i) operating frequency, (ii) phase velocity and (iii) group velocity.

58. In an air-filled rectangular waveguide, the cut-off frequency of a TE_{10} mode is 5 GHz, whereas that of TE_{01} mode is 12 GHz. Calculate the (i) dimensions of the guide, (ii) cut-off frequencies of the next three higher TE modes and (iii) cut-off frequency for TE_{11} mode if the guide is filled with a lossless material having $\varepsilon_r = 2.25$ and $\mu_r = 1$.

59. A rectangular waveguide is filled with polyethylene ($\varepsilon = 2.25\varepsilon_0$) and operates at 24 GHz. If the cut-off frequency of a certain TE mode is 16 GHz, find the group velocity and the intrinsic impedance of the mode.

60. A K-band rectangular waveguide with dimensions of 1.067 cm and 0.432 cm operates in the dominant mode at 18 GHz. Determine the cut-off frequency, guide wavelength, phase velocity and wave impedance, if the dielectric is air.

61. Calculate the dimensions of an air-filled rectangular waveguide for which the cut-off frequencies for TM_{11} and TE_{03} modes are both equal to 12 GHz. At 8 GHz, determine whether the dominant mode will propagate or evanesce in the waveguide.

62. A TE mode operating at 6 GHz in an air-filled rectangular waveguide has

$$E_y = 5 \sin\left(\frac{2\pi}{a}x\right) \sin\left(\frac{\pi}{b}y\right) \sin(\omega t - 12z) \text{ V/m}$$

Determine the (i) mode of operation, (ii) cut-off frequency, (iii) intrinsic impedance, and (iv) H_x.

63. The y-component of the TE mode in an air-filled rectangular waveguide with $a = 2.286$ cm and $b = 1.016$ cm is given by

$$E_y = 5 \sin\left(\frac{2\pi}{a}x\right) \cos\left(\frac{3\pi}{b}y\right) \sin(10\pi \times 10^{10}t - \beta z) \text{ V/m}$$

Determine the (i) mode of operation, (ii) propagation constant and (iii) intrinsic impedance.

64. Derive the expression for the average power transmitted down the guide for the TM_{11} mode.

65. Show how the average power flow for a TE_{10} mode in a waveguide depends on the guide dimensions.

66. Draw the cross-sectional view of the microstrip line structure.

67. Define propagation loss in a microstrip line.

68. What is meant by dispersion?

69. Write the closed form expression for characteristic impedance and effective dielectric constant of a microstrip line.

OBJECTIVE TYPE QUESTIONS

1. A rectangular waveguide acts as a

    (a) high-pass filter   (b) low-pass filter   (c) bandpass filter   (d) bandstop filter

2. A waveguide operated below the cut-off frequency can be used as

    (a) phase shifter   (b) isolator   (c) attenuator   (d) none of the above

3. If a rectangular waveguide having a cut-off frequency of 18 GHz for TE_{30} mode and dominant mode as TE_{10} mode, then the inner broad wall dimension of waveguide will be

    (a) 1.67 cm   (b) 5 cm   (c) 3.75 cm   (d) 2.5 cm

4. An evanescent mode occurs in a waveguide when the
   - (a) phase constant is real
   - (b) phase constant is zero
   - (c) phase constant is imaginary
   - (d) signal has constant frequency

5. The axial current for a hollow waveguide should necessarily be
   - (a) a combination of conduction and displacement currents
   - (b) conduction current only
   - (c) displacement current only
   - (d) time-varying conduction current and displacement current

6. An air filled rectangular waveguide has inner dimensions of 3 cm × 2 cm. Then, the wave impedance of TE_{20} mode of propagation in the waveguide at a frequency of 30 GHz is
   - (a) $300\ \Omega$
   - (b) $377\ \Omega$
   - (c) $323\ \Omega$
   - (d) $370\ \Omega$

7. If a particular mode is excited in a waveguide and there appears an extra electric field component in the direction of propagation, then the mode of wave propagation is
   - (a) traverse electric
   - (b) transverse magnetic
   - (c) transverse electromagnetic
   - (d) none of these

8. Which of the following field components exist for a TE_{11} wave propagating in z-direction?
   - (a) E_x, H_y, H_z
   - (b) E_x, E_y, H_x, H_y
   - (c) E_x, H_y, E_z
   - (d) All are present except E_z

9. If a rectangular waveguide has a as broader dimension and b as narrow dimension, then the dominant mode of wave propagation will be
   - (a) TM_{10}
   - (b) TM_{01}
   - (c) TE_{10}
   - (d) TE_{01}

10. For $a = 2b$ in a rectangular waveguide, the cut-off frequency of TE_{02} mode is 12 GHz. Then, the cut-off frequency of TM_{11} mode will be
    - (a) $3\sqrt{5}$ GHz
    - (b) 3 GHz
    - (c) 12 GHz
    - (d) $6\sqrt{5}$ GHz

11. A waveguide of dimensions $a = 1.5$ cm and $b = 1$ cm is loaded with a dielectric of $\varepsilon_r = 4$. Which one of the following statements is correct for an 8 GHz signal?
    - (a) not pass through the waveguide
    - (b) pass through the waveguide
    - (c) be absorbed in the guide
    - (d) none of the above

12. For TE or TM modes of propagation in a bounded media, the phase velocity will be
    - (a) independent of frequency
    - (b) non-linear function of frequency
    - (c) linear function of frequency
    - (d) frequency dependent or independent depending on the source

13. If the height of a waveguide is halved, then its cut-off wavelength will
    - (a) be halved
    - (b) be doubled
    - (c) be one-fourth of the previous value
    - (d) remain unchanged

14. Which of the following mode is the second dominant mode in a rectangular waveguide if $b < a/2$?
    - (a) TE_{10}
    - (b) TE_{11}
    - (c) TE_{01}
    - (d) TE_{20}

15. In a waveguide, the evanescent mode will occur if

    (a) propagation constant is imaginary   (b) propagation constant is real

    (c) only the TEM waves propagate   (d) signal has a constant frequency

16. In an air-filled waveguide of dimensions a cm $\times$ b cm, the longitudinal component of electric field of TM_{32} mode at a given frequency is of the form $E_z = 20 \sin(60\pi x)\sin(100\pi y)$. Which form would E_z have for the lowest order TM mode?

    (a) $E_z = 20 \sin(2\pi x)$ (b) $E_z = 20 \sin(20\pi y)$

    (c) $E_z = 20 \sin(20\pi x) \sin(100\pi y)$ (d) $E_z = 20 \sin(20\pi x)\sin(50\pi y)$

17. If the cut-off frequency of the dominant mode in a rectangular waveguide with aspect ratio more than 2 is 10 GHz, then the inner broad wall dimension will be

    (a) 3 cm   (b) 2 cm   (c) 2.5 cm   (d) 1.5 cm

18. The dominant TM mode for a square waveguide will be

    (a) TM_{01} (b) TM_{10}

    (c) both TM_{01} and TM_{10} (d) none of the above

19. If a rectangular waveguide of internal dimensions $a = 8$ cm, $b = 6$ cm is operated in TE_{11} mode, then the minimum operating frequency will be

    (a) 1.875 GHz   (b) 625 GHz   (c) 9.375 GHz   (d) 3.125 GHz

20. If a rectangular waveguide filled with a dielectric material of relative permittivity $\varepsilon_r = 4$ has the inside dimensions of 3 cm $\times$ 1.2 cm, then the cut-off frequency for the dominant mode is

    (a) 12.5 GHz   (b) 5 GHz   (c) 10 GHz   (d) 2.5 GHz

21. If a rectangular air-filled waveguide has a cross-section of 4 cm $\times$ 10 cm, then the minimum frequency of wave propagation in the waveguide will be

    (a) 2.5 GHz   (b) 2 GHz   (c) 1.5 GHz   (d) 3 GHz

22. A rectangular waveguide has internal dimensions of 3 cm $\times$ 4.5 cm. If a 9 GHz signal is propagated through the guide, then the cut-off wavelength for TE_{10} mode is

    (a) 9 cm   (b) 10 cm   (c) 15 cm   (d) 5 cm

23. In a rectangular waveguide, the cut-off wavelength λ_c for a TE_{20} mode is

    (a) $2/a$ (b) $2a$ (c) $2a^2$ (d) a

24. If a particular mode is excited in a waveguide and there appears an extra magnetic field component in the direction of propagation, then the mode of wave propagation is

    (a) TEM   (b) TM   (c) TE   (d) none of these

25. Which of the following is the dominant mode in rectangular waveguides?

    (a) TE_{10} (b) TE_{11} (c) TE_{01} (d) TE_{11}

26. The phase velocity u_p and the group velocity u_g in a waveguide are related as

    (a) $u_p + u_g = c$ (b) u_p/u_g (c) $u_p - u_g = c$ (d) $u_p u_g = c^2$

27. Which of the following field components exist for a TE_{30} wave propagating in z-direction?

    (a) E_x, H_y, H_z (b) E_x, H_y, H_z (c) E_y, H_x, H_z (d) E_x, E_y, H_x, H_y, H_z

28. For a wave propagating in an air-filled rectangular waveguide,

    (a) wave impendence is never less than free-space impedance

    (b) TEM mode is positive if the dimension of the guide are properly chosen

    (c) guide wavelength is never less than free-space wavelength

    (d) propagation constant is always a real quantity

29. If the operating wavelength λ is less than the cut-off wavelength λ_c in a waveguide, then the electromagnetic wave will be

    (a) attenuated   (b) guided

    (c) attenuated with some guidance   (d) guided with some attenuation

30. The cut-off wavelength λ_c for TE_{20} mode in a rectangular waveguide will be equal to

    (a) $2a$ (b) a (c) $2/a$ (d) $2a^2$

31. In a rectangular waveguide, the dominant mode is TE_{10} because it has

    (a) no attenuation   (b) no cut-off

    (c) the highest cut-off wavelength   (d) no magnetic field component

32. The phase velocity of the waves propagating in a hollow metal waveguide is

    (a) equal to the group velocity

    (b) less than the velocity of light in free space

    (c) greater than the velocity of light in free space

    (d) equal to the velocity of light in free space

33. Which of the following statements is true about degenerate modes?

    (a) The modes having the same resonant frequencies in integral multiples of other.

    (b) The modes have the cut-off frequencies in multiples of dominant mode frequency.

    (c) The modes having the same resonant frequency are called degenerate modes.

    (d) None of the above.

34. The product of wave impedance of TE_{11} and TM_{11} mode i.e., $\eta_{TE} \times \eta_{TM}$ is

    (a) 1 (b) $\sqrt{\mu/\varepsilon}$

    (c) $\omega^2\mu\varepsilon - (\pi/a)^2$ (d) μ/ε

35. A waveguide has an internal breadth of $a = 3$ cm and carries a dominant mode of unknown signal frequency. If the characteristic wave impedance is $500\ \Omega$, then the frequency will be

    (a) 762.1 GHz   (b) 76.21 GHz   (c) 0.7621 GHz   (d) 7.621 GHz

36. A rectangular waveguide of internal dimensions $a = 4$ cm and $b = 3$ cm is operated in TE_{11} mode. Then, the minimum operating frequency will be

    (a) 6.0 GHz   (b) 6.25 GHz   (c) 5.0 GHz   (d) 3.75 GHz

Answers

1. (a)	2. (c)	3. (d)	4. (b)	5. (c)	6. (b)	7. (b)	8. (d)	9. (c)	10. (a)
11. (b)	12. (b)	13. (d)	14. (d)	15. (b	16. (d)	17. (d)	18. (c)	19. (d)	20. (d)
21. (c)	22. (a)	23. (d)	24. (c)	25. (a)	26. (d)	27. (c)	28. (c)	29. (b)	30. (b)
31. (c)	32. (c)	33. (c)	34. (d)	35. (d)	36. (b)				

VALUES OF GENERAL PHYSICAL CONSTANTS

Charge of an electron (e or Q)	1.602×10^{-19} C
Mass of an electron (m)	9.11×10^{-31} kg
Velocity of light (c)	$2.998 \times 10^{8} \approx 3 \times 10^{8}$ m/s
Permittivity of free space (ε_0)	$8.854 \times 10^{-12} \approx \dfrac{1}{36\pi} \times 10^{-9}$ F/m
Permeability of free space (μ_0)	$4\pi \times 10^{-7}$ H/m
Intrinsic impedance of free space (η_0)	$120\pi \approx 377\,\Omega$
Conductivity of copper (σ)	5.8×10^{7} S/m

ELECTRIC AND MAGNETIC FIELD QUANTITIES AND THEIR UNITS

Fields	Quantities	Units
Electric field	Electric field intensity $(\vec{E})$	V/m
	Electric flux density $(\vec{D})$	C/m^2
	Scalar electric potential (V)	V
	Electric dipole moment $(\vec{p})$	$C \cdot m$
	Electric charge $(Q \text{ or } q)$	C
	Linear charge density (ρ_l)	C/m
	Surface charge density (ρ_s)	C/m^2
	Volume charge density (ρ_v)	C/m^3
Magnetic field	Magnetic field intensity $(\vec{H})$	A/m
	Magnetic flux density $(\vec{B})$	Wb/m^2 or tesla
	Vector magnetic potential $(\vec{A})$	Wb/m
	Magnetic dipole moment $(\vec{m})$	$A \cdot m^2$
	Magnetic flux (Φ)	Wb
	Current (I)	A
	Surface current density $(\vec{K} \text{ or } \vec{J}_s)$	A/m
	Volume current density $(\vec{J})$	A/m^2

CONVERSION FACTORS AND PREFIXES

Constant	Value
1 ampere (A)	1 C/s
1 angstrom unit (Å)	10^{-10} m $= 10^{-8}$ cm
1 coulomb (C)	1 A-s
1 farad (F)	1 C/V
1 henry (H)	1 V-s/A
1 hertz (Hz)	1 cycle/s
1 mil	10^{-3} inch $= 25\,\mu$m
1 micron	$1\,\mu$m $= 10^{-6}$ m
1 newton (N)	1 kg $= $ m/s^2
1 Volt (V)	1 W/A
1 watt (W)	1 J/s
1 weber (Wb)	1 V-s
1 tesla (T)	1 Wb/m^2 or 10^4 gauss
1 radian	57.296°

RECTANGULAR (CARTESIAN) COORDINATES *(x, y, z)*

Dot Product of unit vectors

$$\vec{a}_x \cdot \vec{a}_x = \vec{a}_y \cdot \vec{a}_y = \vec{a}_z \cdot \vec{a}_z = 1$$

$$\vec{a}_x \cdot \vec{a}_y = \vec{a}_y \cdot \vec{a}_z = \vec{a}_z \cdot \vec{a}_x = 0$$

Cross Product of unit vectors

$$\vec{a}_x \times \vec{a}_x = \vec{a}_y \times \vec{a}_y = \vec{a}_z \times \vec{a}_z = 0$$

$$\vec{a}_x \times \vec{a}_y = \vec{a}_z \qquad \vec{a}_y \times \vec{a}_z = \vec{a}_x \qquad \vec{a}_z \times \vec{a}_x = \vec{a}_y$$

$$\vec{a}_y \times \vec{a}_x = -\vec{a}_z \qquad \vec{a}_z \times \vec{a}_y = -\vec{a}_x \qquad \vec{a}_x \times \vec{a}_z = -\vec{a}_y$$

Cross Product of two vectors $\vec{A}$ and $\vec{B}$

$$\vec{A} \times \vec{B} = \begin{vmatrix} \vec{a}_x & \vec{a}_y & \vec{a}_z \\ A_x & A_y & A_z \\ B_x & B_y & B_z \end{vmatrix} = \left(A_y B_z - A_z B_y \right)\vec{a}_x - \left(A_x B_z - A_z B_x \right)\vec{a}_y + \left(A_x B_y - A_y B_x \right)\vec{a}_z$$

CYLINDRICAL COORDINATES (ρ, ϕ, z)

Dot Product of unit vectors

$$\vec{a}_\rho \cdot \vec{a}_\rho = \vec{a}_\phi \cdot \vec{a}_\phi = \vec{a}_z \cdot \vec{a}_z = 1$$

$$\vec{a}_\rho \cdot \vec{a}_\phi = \vec{a}_\phi \cdot \vec{a}_z = \vec{a}_z \cdot \vec{a}_\rho = 0$$

Cross Product of unit vectors

$$\vec{a}_\rho \times \vec{a}_\rho = \vec{a}_\phi \times \vec{a}_\phi = \vec{a}_z \times \vec{a}_z = 0$$

$$\vec{a}_\rho \times \vec{a}_\phi = \vec{a}_z \qquad \vec{a}_\phi \times \vec{a}_z = \vec{a}_\rho \qquad \vec{a}_z \times \vec{a}_\rho = \vec{a}_\phi$$

$$\vec{a}_\phi \times \vec{a}_\rho = -\vec{a}_z \qquad \vec{a}_z \times \vec{a}_\phi = -\vec{a}_\rho \qquad \vec{a}_\rho \times \vec{a}_z = -\vec{a}_\phi$$

Cross Product of two vectors $\vec{A}$ and $\vec{B}$

$$\vec{A} \times \vec{B} = \begin{vmatrix} \vec{a}_\rho & \vec{a}_\phi & \vec{a}_z \\ A_\rho & A_\phi & A_z \\ B_\rho & B_\phi & B_z \end{vmatrix} = \left(A_\phi B_z - A_z B_\phi\right)\vec{a}_\rho - \left(A_\rho B_z - A_z B_\rho\right)\vec{a}_\phi + \left(A_\rho B_\phi - A_\phi B_\rho\right)\vec{a}_z$$

SPHERICAL COORDINATES (r, θ, ϕ)

Dot Product of unit vectors

$$\vec{a}_r \cdot \vec{a}_r = \vec{a}_\theta \cdot \vec{a}_\theta = \vec{a}_\phi \cdot \vec{a}_\phi = 1$$

$$\vec{a}_r \cdot \vec{a}_\theta = \vec{a}_\theta \cdot \vec{a}_\phi = \vec{a}_\phi \cdot \vec{a}_r = 0$$

Cross Product of unit vectors

$$\vec{a}_r \times \vec{a}_r = \vec{a}_\theta \times \vec{a}_\theta = \vec{a}_\phi \times \vec{a}_\phi = 0$$

$$\vec{a}_r \times \vec{a}_\theta = \vec{a}_\phi \qquad \vec{a}_\theta \times \vec{a}_\phi = \vec{a}_r \qquad \vec{a}_\phi \times \vec{a}_r = \vec{a}_\theta$$

$$\vec{a}_\theta \times \vec{a}_r = -\vec{a}_\phi \qquad \vec{a}_\phi \times \vec{a}_\theta = -\vec{a}_r \qquad \vec{a}_r \times \vec{a}_\phi = -\vec{a}_\theta$$

Cross Product of two vectors $\vec{A}$ and $\vec{B}$

$$\vec{A} \times \vec{B} = \begin{vmatrix} \vec{a}_r & \vec{a}_\theta & \vec{a}_\phi \\ A_r & A_\theta & A_\phi \\ B_r & B_\theta & B_\phi \end{vmatrix} = \left(A_\theta B_\phi - A_\phi B_\theta\right)\vec{a}_r - \left(A_r B_\phi - A_\phi B_r\right)\vec{a}_\theta + \left(A_r B_\theta - A_\theta B_r\right)\vec{a}_\phi$$

VECTOR IDENTITIES

Given $\vec{A}$ and $\vec{B}$ are vector fields and V, X and Y are scalar fields, then

$$\nabla(X + Y) = \nabla X + \nabla Y$$

$$\nabla(XY) = X\nabla Y + Y\nabla X$$

$$\nabla\left(\frac{X}{Y}\right) = \frac{Y(\nabla X) - X(\nabla Y)}{Y^2}$$

$$\nabla V^n = nV^{n-1}\nabla V, \text{ where } n \text{ is an integer}$$

$$\nabla \cdot (\nabla V) = \nabla^2 V$$

$$\nabla \times (\nabla V) = 0$$

$$\nabla \cdot (V\vec{A}) = V(\nabla \cdot \vec{A}) + \vec{A} \cdot \nabla V$$

$$\nabla \times (V\vec{A}) = (\nabla V) \times \vec{A} + V(\nabla \times \vec{A})$$

$$\nabla \cdot (\nabla \times \vec{A}) = 0$$

$$\nabla(\vec{A} \cdot \vec{B}) = (\vec{A} \cdot \nabla)\vec{B} + (\vec{B} \cdot \nabla)\vec{A} + \vec{A} \times (\nabla \times \vec{B}) + \vec{B} \times (\nabla \times \vec{A})$$

$$\nabla \cdot (\vec{A} + \vec{B}) = \nabla \cdot \vec{A} + \nabla \cdot \vec{B}$$

$$\nabla \times (\vec{A} + \vec{B}) = \nabla \times \vec{A} + \nabla \times \vec{B}$$

$$\nabla \cdot (\vec{A} \times \vec{B}) = \vec{B} \cdot (\nabla \times \vec{A}) - \vec{A} \cdot (\nabla \times \vec{B})$$

$$\nabla \times (\vec{A} \times \vec{B}) = \vec{A}(\nabla \cdot \vec{B}) - \vec{B}(\nabla \cdot \vec{A}) + (\vec{B} \cdot \nabla)\vec{A} - (\vec{A} \cdot \nabla)\vec{B}$$

$$\nabla \times (\nabla \times \vec{A}) = \nabla(\nabla \cdot \vec{A}) - \nabla^2 \vec{A}$$

$$\int_v (\nabla \cdot \vec{A})\,dv = \oint_s \vec{A} \cdot d\vec{s} \qquad \text{(Divergence theorem)}$$

$$\int_v \nabla V\,dv = \oint_s V\,d\vec{s}$$

$$\int_s (\nabla \times \vec{A}) \cdot d\vec{s} = \oint_l \vec{A} \cdot d\vec{l} \qquad \text{(Stokes's theorem)}$$

$$\int_s \nabla V \times d\vec{s} = -\oint_l V\,d\vec{l}$$

$$\int_v (\nabla \times \vec{A})\,dv = -\oint_s \vec{A} \times d\vec{s}$$

RECTANGULAR (CARTESIAN) COORDINATES (x, y, z)

(i) $\nabla V = \dfrac{\partial V}{\partial x}\,\vec{a}_x + \dfrac{\partial V}{\partial y}\,\vec{a}_y + \dfrac{\partial V}{\partial z}\,\vec{a}_z$

(ii) $\nabla \cdot \vec{A} = \dfrac{\partial A_x}{\partial x} + \dfrac{\partial A_y}{\partial y} + \dfrac{\partial A_z}{\partial z}$

(iii) $\nabla \times \vec{A} = \begin{vmatrix} \vec{a}_x & \vec{a}_y & \vec{a}_z \\[4pt] \dfrac{\partial}{\partial x} & \dfrac{\partial}{\partial y} & \dfrac{\partial}{\partial z} \\[4pt] A_x & A_y & A_z \end{vmatrix}$

(iv) $\nabla^2 V = \dfrac{\partial^2 V}{\partial x^2} + \dfrac{\partial^2 V}{\partial y^2} + \dfrac{\partial^2 V}{\partial z^2}$

CYLINDRICAL COORDINATES (ρ, ϕ, z)

(i) $\nabla V = \dfrac{\partial V}{\partial \rho}\,\vec{a}_\rho + \dfrac{1}{\rho}\dfrac{\partial V}{\partial \phi}\,\vec{a}_\phi + \dfrac{\partial V}{\partial z}\,\vec{a}_z$

(ii) $\nabla \cdot \vec{A} = \dfrac{1}{\rho}\dfrac{\partial}{\partial \rho}(\rho A_\rho) + \dfrac{1}{\rho}\dfrac{\partial A_\phi}{\partial \phi} + \dfrac{\partial A_z}{\partial z}$

(iii) $\nabla \times \vec{A} = \dfrac{1}{\rho}\begin{vmatrix} \vec{a}_\rho & \rho\vec{a}_\phi & \vec{a}_z \\[4pt] \dfrac{\partial}{\partial \rho} & \dfrac{\partial}{\partial \phi} & \dfrac{\partial}{\partial z} \\[4pt] A_\rho & \rho A_\phi & A_z \end{vmatrix}$

(iv) $\nabla^2 V = \dfrac{1}{\rho}\dfrac{\partial}{\partial \rho}\left(\rho\dfrac{\partial V}{\partial \rho}\right) + \dfrac{1}{\rho^2}\dfrac{\partial^2 V}{\partial \phi^2} + \dfrac{\partial^2 V}{\partial z^2}$

SPHERICAL COORDINATES (r, θ, ϕ)

$(i)\quad \nabla V = \frac{\partial V}{\partial r}\vec{a}_r + \frac{1}{r}\frac{\partial V}{\partial \theta}\vec{a}_\theta + \frac{1}{r\sin\theta}\frac{\partial V}{\partial \phi}\vec{a}_\phi$

$(ii)\quad \nabla\cdot\vec{A} = \frac{1}{r^2}\frac{\partial}{\partial r}(r^2 A_r) + \frac{1}{r\sin\theta}\frac{\partial}{\partial \theta}(\sin\theta\, A_\theta) + \frac{1}{r\sin\theta}\frac{\partial A_\phi}{\partial \phi}$

$(iii)\quad \nabla\times\vec{A} = \frac{1}{r^2\sin\theta}\begin{vmatrix} \vec{a}_r & r\vec{a}_\theta & r\sin\theta\,\vec{a}_\phi \\ \dfrac{\partial}{\partial r} & \dfrac{\partial}{\partial \theta} & \dfrac{\partial}{\partial \phi} \\ A_r & rA_\theta & r\sin\theta A_\phi \end{vmatrix}$

$(iv)\quad \nabla^2 V = \frac{1}{r^2}\frac{\partial}{\partial r}\left(r^2\frac{\partial V}{\partial r}\right) + \frac{1}{r^2\sin\theta}\frac{\partial}{\partial \theta}\left(\sin\theta\frac{\partial V}{\partial \theta}\right) + \frac{1}{r^2\sin^2\theta}\frac{\partial^2 V}{\partial \phi^2}$

APPENDIX G

GOVERNING LAWS IN STATIC ELECTRIC FIELDS

Reference	Differential or Point form	Integral form
Gauss's law	$\nabla \cdot \vec{D} = \rho_v$	$\oint_s \vec{D} \cdot d\vec{s} = Q$
Conservative Property	$\nabla \times \vec{E} = 0$	$\oint_l \vec{E} \cdot d\vec{l} = 0$

GOVERNING LAWS IN STATIC MAGNETIC FIELDS

Reference	Differential or Point form	Integral form
Gauss's law	$\nabla \cdot \vec{B} = 0$	$\oint_s \vec{B} \cdot d\vec{s} = 0$
Ampere's law	$\nabla \times \vec{H} = \vec{J}$	$\oint_l \vec{H} \cdot d\vec{l} = I$

GOVERNING LAWS IN TIME-VARYING (DYNAMIC) FIELDS

MAXWELL'S EQUATIONS IN GENERAL FORM

Reference	Differential or Point form	Integral form
Gauss's law	$\nabla \cdot \vec{D} = \rho_v$	$\oint_s \vec{D} \cdot d\vec{s} = \int_v \rho_v \, dv$
Gauss's law for magnetism	$\nabla \cdot \vec{B} = 0$	$\oint_s \vec{B} \cdot d\vec{s} = 0$
Faraday's law	$\nabla \times \vec{E} = -\dfrac{\partial \vec{B}}{\partial t}$	$\oint_l \vec{E} \cdot d\vec{l} = -\int_s \dfrac{\partial \vec{B}}{\partial t} \cdot d\vec{s}$
Ampere's law	$\nabla \times \vec{H} = \vec{J} + \dfrac{\partial \vec{D}}{\partial t}$	$\oint_l \vec{H} \cdot d\vec{l} = \int_s \left(\vec{J} + \dfrac{\partial \vec{D}}{\partial t} \right) \cdot d\vec{s}$

MAXWELL'S EQUATIONS FOR FREE SPACE

Reference	Differential or Point form	Integral form
Gauss's law	$\nabla \cdot \vec{D} = 0$	$\oint_s \vec{D} \cdot d\vec{s} = 0$
Gauss's law for magnetism	$\nabla \cdot \vec{B} = 0$	$\oint_s \vec{B} \cdot d\vec{s} = 0$
Faraday's law	$\nabla \times \vec{E} = -\dfrac{\partial \vec{B}}{\partial t}$	$\oint_l \vec{E} \cdot d\vec{l} = -\int_s \dfrac{\partial \vec{B}}{\partial t} \cdot d\vec{s}$
Ampere's law	$\nabla \times \vec{H} = \dfrac{\partial \vec{D}}{\partial t}$	$\oint_l \vec{H} \cdot d\vec{l} = \int_s \dfrac{\partial \vec{D}}{\partial t} \cdot d\vec{s}$

IMPORTANT FORMULAE

TRIGONOMETRIC IDENTITIES

1. $e^{\pm jA} = \cos(A) \pm j\sin(A)$

2. $\left| e^{\pm jA} \right| = 1, \quad \angle e^{\pm jA} = \pm A$

3. $\cos(A) = \dfrac{\left(e^{jA} + e^{-jA} \right)}{2}$

4. $\sin(A) = \dfrac{\left(e^{jA} - e^{-jA} \right)}{2j}$

$$-1 = e^{j\pi} = e^{-j\pi} = 1\angle 180°$$

$$j = e^{j\pi/2} = 1\angle 90°$$

$$-j = -e^{j\pi/2} = e^{-j\pi/2} = 1\angle -90°$$

$$\sqrt{j} = \left(e^{j\pi/2} \right)^{1/2} = \pm e^{j\pi/4} = \pm \frac{(1+j)}{\sqrt{2}}$$

$$\sqrt{-j} = \pm e^{-j\pi/4} = \pm \frac{(1-j)}{\sqrt{2}}$$

5. $\sin(-A) = -\sin(A)$

6. $\cos(-A) = \cos(A)$

7. $\cos(A \pm B) = \cos(A)\cos(B) \mp \sin(A)\sin(B)$

8. $\sin(A \pm B) = \sin(A)\cos(B) \pm \cos(A)\sin(B)$

9. $\tan(A \pm B) = \dfrac{\tan(A) \pm \tan(B)}{1 \mp \tan(A)\tan(B)}$

10. $\cos(A)\cos(B) = \dfrac{1}{2}\left[\cos(A - B) + \cos(A + B)\right]$

11. $\sin(A)\sin(B) = \dfrac{1}{2}\left[\cos(A - B) - \cos(A + B)\right]$

12. $\sin(A)\cos(B) = \dfrac{1}{2}\left[\sin(A + B) + \sin(A - B)\right]$

13. $\cos(A)\sin(B) = \dfrac{1}{2}\left[\sin(A + B) - \sin(A - B)\right]$

14. $\sin(2A) = 2\sin(A)\cos(A) = \dfrac{2\tan(A)}{1 + \tan^2(A)}$

15. $\cos(2A) = 2\cos^2(A) - 1 = 1 - 2\sin^2(A) = \cos^2(A) - \sin^2(A) = \dfrac{1 - \tan^2(A)}{1 + \tan^2(A)}$

16. $\tan(2A) = \dfrac{2\tan(A)}{1 - \tan^2(A)}$

17. $\cos^2(A) = \dfrac{\left[1 + \cos(2A)\right]}{2}$

18. $\sin^2(A) = \dfrac{\left[1 - \cos(2A)\right]}{2}$

19. $\cos^2(A) + \sin^2(A) = 1$

20. $\sec^2(A) - \tan^2(A) = 1$

21. $\sin(A \pm 90°) = \pm\cos A$

22. $\cos(A \pm 90°) = \mp\sin A$

23. $\tan(A \pm 90°) = -\cot A$

24. $\sin(A \pm 180°) = -\sin A$

25. $\cos(A \pm 180°) = -\cos A$

26. $\tan(A \pm 180°) = \tan A$

INDEFINITE INTEGRALS

1. $\displaystyle\int x^n \, dx = \dfrac{x^{n+1}}{(n+1)} + c, \; n \neq -1$

2. $\displaystyle\int x^{-1} \, dx = \ln(x) + c$

3. $\displaystyle\int a^x \, dx = \dfrac{a^x}{\ln(a)} + c$

4. $\displaystyle\int \ln(x) \, dx = x\ln(x) - x + c$

5. $\displaystyle\int e^{ax} \, dx = \dfrac{e^{ax}}{a} + c, \; a \neq 0$

6. $\displaystyle\int x^n e^{ax} \, dx = \dfrac{x^n e^{ax}}{a} - \dfrac{n}{a}\int x^{(n-1)} e^{ax} \, dx + c$

7. $\displaystyle\int x^n e^{ax^2} \, dx = \dfrac{1}{2a} e^{ax^2} + c$

8. $\displaystyle\int \sin(ax) \, dx = -\dfrac{\cos(ax)}{a} + c$

9. $\displaystyle \int \cos(ax)\,dx = \frac{\sin(ax)}{a} + c$

10. $\displaystyle \int \tan(ax)\,dx = -\frac{1}{a}\ln\cos(ax) + c$

11. $\displaystyle \int \frac{dx}{x^2 - a^2} = \frac{1}{2}\tan^{-1}\left(\frac{x}{a}\right) + c$

12. $\displaystyle \int \frac{dx}{x^2 + a^2} = \begin{cases} \dfrac{1}{2x}\ln\left(\dfrac{x-a}{x+a}\right) + c, & x^2 > a^2 \\[2ex] \dfrac{1}{2a}\ln\left(\dfrac{a-x}{a+x}\right) + c, & x^2 < a^2 \end{cases}$

13. $\displaystyle \int \sin^2(ax)\,dx = \frac{x}{2} - \frac{\sin 2ax}{4a} + c$

14. $\displaystyle \int \cos^2(ax)\,dx = \frac{x}{2} + \frac{\sin 2ax}{4a} + c$

15. $\displaystyle \int \sin x\cos^2 x\,dx = -\frac{\cos^3 x}{3} + c$

16. $\displaystyle \int e^{ax}\sin(bx)\,dx = \frac{e^{ax}\left[a\sin\left[(bx)-b\cos(bx)\right]\right]}{\left(a^2+b^2\right)} + c$

17. $\displaystyle \int e^{ax}\cos(bx)\,dx = \frac{e^{ax}\left[a\cos\left[(bx)+b\sin(bx)\right]\right]}{\left(a^2+b^2\right)} + c$

18. $\displaystyle \int x^n \sin(ax)\,dx = \frac{-x^n\cos(ax)+n\int x^{n-1}\cos(ax)\,dx}{a}$

19. $\displaystyle \int x^n \cos(ax)\,dx = \frac{x^n\sin(ax)-n\int x^{n-1}\sin(ax)\,dx}{a}$

20. $\displaystyle \int \cos(ax)\cos(bx)\,dx = \frac{\sin\left[(a-b)x\right]}{2(a-b)} + \frac{\sin\left[(a+b)x\right]}{2(a+b)} + c,\ \ a \neq b$

21. $\displaystyle \int \sin(ax)\sin(bx)\,dx = \frac{\sin\left[(a-b)x\right]}{2(a-b)} - \frac{\sin\left[(a+b)x\right]}{2(a+b)} + c,\ \ a \neq b$

22. $\displaystyle \int \sin(ax)\cos(bx)\,dx = \frac{\cos\left[(a-b)x\right]}{2(a-b)} - \frac{\cos\left[(a+b)x\right]}{2(a+b)} + c,\ \ a \neq b$

23. $\displaystyle \int \sqrt{x^2 + a^2}\,dx = \frac{x}{2}\sqrt{x^2+a^2} + \frac{a^2}{2}\ln\left(x + \sqrt{x^2+a^2}\right) + c$

24. $\displaystyle \int \frac{dx}{\sqrt{x^2 + a^2}} = \ln\left(x + \sqrt{x^2 + a^2}\right) + c$

25. $\displaystyle \int \frac{x\,dx}{\sqrt{x^2 + a^2}} = \sqrt{x^2 + a^2} + c$

26. $\displaystyle \int \frac{dx}{\sqrt{a^2 - x^2}} = \sin^{-1}\left(\frac{x}{a}\right) + c$

27. $\displaystyle \int \frac{x\,dx}{\sqrt{a^2 - x^2}} = -\sqrt{a^2 - x^2} + c$

28. $\displaystyle \int \frac{dx}{\sqrt{x^2 - a^2}} = \ln\left(x + \sqrt{x^2 - a^2}\right) + c$

29. $\displaystyle \int \frac{x\,dx}{\sqrt{x^2 - a^2}} = \sqrt{x^2 - a^2} + c$

30. $\displaystyle \int \frac{dx}{\left(x^2 + a^2\right)^{3/2}} = \frac{x/a^2}{\sqrt{x^2 + a^2}} + c$

31. $\displaystyle \int \frac{x\,dx}{\left(x^2 + a^2\right)^{3/2}} = -\frac{1}{\sqrt{x^2 + a^2}} + c$

32. $\displaystyle \int \frac{x^2\,dx}{\left(x^2 + a^2\right)^{3/2}} = -\frac{x}{\sqrt{x^2 + a^2}} + \ln\left(x + \sqrt{x^2 + a^2}\right) + c$

DEFINITE INTEGRALS

1. $\displaystyle \int_0^{2\pi} \sin mx \sin nx \, dx = \int_\pi^\pi \sin mx \sin nx \, dx = \begin{cases} 0, & m \neq n \\ \pi, & m = n \end{cases}$

2. $\displaystyle \int_0^\pi \sin mx \sin nx \, dx = \int_0^\pi \cos mx \cos nx \, dx = \begin{cases} 0, & m \neq n \\ \dfrac{\pi}{2}, & m = n \end{cases}$

3. $\displaystyle \int_0^\pi \sin mx \cos nx \, dx = \begin{cases} 0, & (m+n)\text{ is even} \\ \dfrac{2m}{m^2 - n^2}, & (m+n)\text{ is odd} \end{cases}$

4. $\displaystyle \int_0^\infty \frac{\sin ax}{x} \, dx = \begin{cases} \dfrac{\pi}{2}, & a > 0 \\ 0, & a = 0 \\ -\dfrac{\pi}{2}, & a < 0 \end{cases}$

5. $\displaystyle\int_0^\infty \frac{\sin^2 ax}{x^2}\,dx = |a|\frac{\pi}{2}$

6. $\displaystyle\int_0^\infty e^{-ax}\cos bx\,dx = \frac{a}{a^2+b^2}$

7. $\displaystyle\int_0^\infty e^{-ax}\sin bx\,dx = \frac{b}{a^2+b^2}$

8. $\displaystyle\int_0^\infty x^n e^{-ax}\,dx = \frac{n!}{a^{n+1}}$, $a>0$, and n is a positive integer

9. $\displaystyle\int_0^\infty e^{-ax^2}\,dx = \frac{1}{2}\sqrt{\frac{\pi}{a}}$

10. $\displaystyle\int_{-\infty}^\infty e^{-ax^2}\,dx = \sqrt{\frac{\pi}{a}}$

11. $\displaystyle\int_{-\infty}^\infty e^{-(ax^2+bx+c)}\,dx = \sqrt{\frac{\pi}{a}}\,e^{(b^2-4ac)/4a}$

12. $\displaystyle\int_0^\infty \left[\frac{a}{a^2+x^2}\right]dx = \frac{\pi}{2}, a>0$

13. $\displaystyle\int_0^\infty x^2 e^{-ax^2}\,dx = \frac{1}{4a}\sqrt{\frac{\pi}{2a}}, a>0$

14. $\displaystyle\int_0^\infty \sin^2(nx)\,dx = \int_0^\pi \cos^2(nx)\,dx = \frac{\pi}{2}$, n is an integer

15. $\displaystyle\int_0^{\pi/2} \log(\sin x)\,dx = -\frac{\pi}{2}\log 2$

BINOMIAL SERIES

1. $(x+y)^n = x^n + nx^{n-1}y + \dfrac{n(n-1)}{2!}x^{n-2}y^2 + \dfrac{n(n-1)(n-2)}{3!}x^{n-3}y^3 + \cdots, y^2 < x^2$

2. $(1+x)^n = 1 + nx + \dfrac{n(n-1)}{2!}x^2 + \cdots, |x| < 1$

EXPONENTIAL SERIES

1. $e^x = 1 + x + \dfrac{x^2}{2!} + \dfrac{x^3}{3!} + \cdots$

2. $a^x = 1 + x\ln a + \dfrac{(x\ln a)^2}{2!} + \dfrac{(x\ln a)^3}{3!} + \cdots$

INDEX

A

Ampere's circuital law, 296–308, 345, 389, 465, 479
Amperian path, 309, 314, 317, 321
Angle of incidence, 599, 605–607, 609, 612, 613
Angle of reflection, 599, 605–606, 612
Angle of transmission, 606, 613, 614, 618, 620
Attenuation constant, 544, 553, 555, 557, 558, 564, 568–569
Average power density, 582–583, 584–585, 587, 589, 617
Azimuth angle, 15, 17

B

Bac-cab rule, 13, 362
Betatron, 534–536
Biot-Savart's law, 273–292, 296, 297, 344–345, 361
Boundary conditions, 191–200, 205, 241, 395–402, 451, 504–507, 599, 601, 608, 610, 626
Boundary-value problems, 175, 238, 240
Breakdown voltage, 184
Brewster angle, 609, 611–612, 613, 620

C

Campbell's equation, 654
Capacitance, 204–237, 246–247, 262, 267
Cartesian coordinates, 2–3, 5, 14–15, 23–25, 38, 46, 68, 238–239, 331
Charged ring, 150
Charged sphere, 118, 122–124, 219
Cylindrical coordinates, 15–17, 20, 23–25, 28–29, 38–39, 43, 48, 57, 58–48, 92, 100, 189, 239, 299, 309, 336
Circular polarization, 594–595
Coaxial cable, 166–167, 202, 216–219, 247, 317–321, 333, 343, 432–434, 440, 592–593
Coaxial capacitor, 216–219, 228, 474, 476, 528
Coefficient of coupling, 416–421, 532
Complex permittivity, 553
Complex number, 514
Components of a vector, 15
Composite capacitor, 223, 224
Conductance, 201, 202, 407

D

Conduction current, 177, 178–179, 467–468, 469, 474, 475, 479, 523–524
Conduction current density, 178–179, 465, 472–475, 501, 523, 524, 525
Conductivity, 175–176, 179, 180–181, 504, 505, 516
Conservative field, 136, 337–338
Constitutive parameters, 175, 452, 544, 548, 555, 595, 605
Continuity equation, 187–191, 466, 502
Continuous charge distribution, 89–107
Convection current, 177–178, 523, 524
Coulomb's law, 77–85, 90, 96, 119, 120, 134, 237, 255, 256, 351
Critical angle, 607, 612
Cross product, 9–12, 13, 15, 16, 18, 22, 351, 352
Curl, 54–63, 70–72, 292, 297, 298–299, 329, 330, 390, 508, 509, 513
Current density, 176–179, 187–188, 196–200, 275, 297, 298, 314, 315, 390, 465, 501
Cylindrical coordinates, 15–16, 20, 23–25, 27, 28–29, 38–39, 43, 57–58, 103–104, 117, 247–248, 309

D

Degenerate mode, 732
Del operator, 38, 41, 43, 48, 298
Diamagnetic materials, 382–383
Dielectric breakdown, 184
Dielectric constant, 78, 183–186
Dielectric material, 175, 184–185, 194, 222, 223, 501
Dielectric polarization, 182–183
Dielectric strength, 183–186
Differential surface, 28, 30, 34, 108, 124, 317, 379, 388, 389, 436
Differential volume, 27–28, 29–30, 36, 50, 106, 110, 388, 389, 436
Dipole moment, 155–156, 157, 183, 368–369, 371, 380, 382–383, 388–389
Directional derivative, 43, 44
Dispersion, 745

Displacement current, 465–477, 523, 524, 526
Displacement current density, 466, 468, 469–471, 473–474, 480, 501, 523, 524, 525–528
Distance vector, 5–6, 42, 78, 79, 86, 92, 97, 100, 109, 183, 257, 259, 273–274, 286
Distortionless line, 650
Divergence, 45–50
Divergence theorem, 50–54, 63, 71, 111–117, 240, 323, 477, 478, 580
Dominant mode, 732
Dot product, 6–9, 12, 16, 18, 22, 35

E

Eighth-wave line, 686
Electric boundary conditions, 191–200
Electric dipole, 107, 108, 127, 154–156, 182, 252, 322
Electric field intensity, 85–89
Electric field strength, 85, 218, 594
Electric flux, 107–108, 109, 209, 322, 477
Electric flux density, 107–108, 109, 111, 112, 119, 120, 122–124, 126, 132, 163, 192, 196, 200, 238, 322, 501, 528
Electric flux lines, 107–108, 322
Electric permittivity, 78, 175
Electric potential, 2, 77, 126, 134–158, 507, 508
Electric susceptibility, 184, 185
Electromagnetic boundary conditions, 504–507
Electromagnetic induction, 453–454
Electromagnetic spectrum, 529–530
Electromotive force, 407, 451, 453, 479, 502
Electrostatic deflection, 264–266
Electrostatic energy density, 163–167
Electrostatic field, 77, 136, 137, 180, 191, 255, 256, 329, 360, 436, 477–478
Electrostatic potential energy, 158–163
Electrostatic voltmeter, 267,
Elliptical polarization, 595
Equipotential surfaces, 126–127, 128, 239, 255, 256,
Evanescent mode, 731
External inductance, 432, 433

F

Faraday disc generator, 463
Faraday's law, 453–454, 455, 456, 477, 478–479, 480, 483, 484, 487, 490, 502, 508, 515, 522
Ferrimagnetic materials, 384
Ferromagnetic materials, 383
Field lines, 45,. 54, 108, 127–128, 194, 205, 288, 299, 381
Field pattern, 107, 288, 381, 422
Flux density, 45, 107–108, 196–200, 322–328
Flux linkage, 414, 415–416, 417, 422, 432–435, 453, 478

Free space, 78, 126, 177, 178, 184, 195, 255, 309, 322, 386, 480, 500, 530, 535, 556–557, 558
Frequency distortion, 650

G

Gaussian surface, 109, 110, 114, 118–121, 122, 124–125, 126, 245, 255, 432, 434
Gauss's divergence theorem, 111–117
Gauss's law, 109–111, 112, 114, 118–126, 134–135, 141, 180, 192, 237–238, 245, 296, 322, 396, 477–478, 479, 480, 515
Gauss's law for magnetism, 479, 480, 515
Gradient, 42–45, 54, 67, 68, 70–71, 136, 137, 144, 151, 224, 255, 329, 508
Gradient operator, 38, 43, 48
Group velocity, 573

H

Half-wave line, 688
Hall effect, 443–445
Hall effect voltage, 443–444
Helmholtz's equation, 516, 530, 543, 551
Helmholtz's theorem, 71–73
Hole drift velocity, 179
Hole mobility, 179
Homogeneous medium, 188, 238, 397, 515, 553, 554, 595
Horizontal polarization, 598
Hysteresis, 386
Hysteresis loop, 384–387

I

Ideal transformer, 531–534
Incident angle, 599, 605–607, 609, 612, 613
Incident wave, 595–597, 598–599, 603–604, 605, 606, 611
Inductance, 414–436, 531
Infinite line, 645
Infinite line charge, 93, 118, 119, 259
Infinite line current, 309–314
Infinite sheet of charge, 100, 101, 102, 120–122
Infinite sheet of current, 314
Ink-jet printer, 266
Insertion loss, 684
Instantaneous power density, 581, 582, 593
Insulators, 175, 176, 555
Internal inductance, 432–433
Intrinsic impedance of free space, 544–545, 550, 552, 554, 556, 557, 561, 581–582, 596, 599, 603, 606, 608, 627
Irrotational field, 302
Isolated sphere, 219, 220, 233
Isotropic, 184, 238, 451–452, 513, 515

J

Joule's law, 203–204

K

Kirchhoff's voltage law, 502, 503

L

Laplace's equation, 68, 238–255, 329
Laplacian operator, 67–70, 238
Lenz's law, 453, 455, 465
Line charge, 90, 91–99, 118, 119, 160
Line charge density, 90, 98, 110, 119, 213, 259
Line current, 275, 309–314, 330, 340, 344
Line integral, 31–34, 54, 55–56, 63, 70, 135
Linear polarization, 594
Loading, 652
Lorentz force, 352, 535
Loss tangent, 555, 565–566, 570, 573
Lossless dielectric, 548–552
Lossy dielectric, 552–556, 562, 573, 582, 617

M

Magnetic boundary conditions, 395–402, 504–507
Magnetic circuits, 403–414, 437
Magnetic dipole, 288, 379–382, 383, 388–389
Magnetic field intensity, 273–274, 278–279, 281–284, 286, 287, 296–298, 309, 314–315, 318–319, 321, 322, 345, 402, 406, 422, 426, 436, 452, 501, 600, 601, 603, 608, 610
Magnetic field strength, 273, 291, 379, 381
Magnetic flux, 322–328, 331, 403, 404, 407, 415, 433, 453, 478
Magnetic flux density, 322–328, 344, 345, 361, 367, 368, 380, 381, 385, 386, 403, 408, 422, 426, 432, 434, 440–441, 443, 501, 508, 534, 535, 536
Magnetic permeability, 387–395
Magnetic potential, 328–344, 379, 403, 508, 509
Magnetic susceptibility, 390
Magnetic torque, 369, 370, 371
Magnetization, 387–395
Magnetization curve, 384, 386
Magnetomotive force, 403, 407, 411
Magnetostatic deflection, 443
Magnetostatic energy, 453
Magnetostatic energy density, 437
Magnetostatic field, 451–453, 478
Mass spectrometer, 445
Maxwell's equations, 297, 323, 451–536, 541, 547
Method of images, 255–262
Microstrip line, 743

Mobility, 178, 179, 180
Motional emf, 454–465
Mutual inductance, 415–416, 417

N

Newton's law, 178
Non-uniform field, 127–134
Normal incidence, 595–598, 602
Null Identities, 70–71

O

Oblique incidence, 598–602, 605–610
Ohm's law, 179, 180, 201, 404, 407, 501, 524, 541
Orthogonal coordinate systems, 14–27

P

Parallel polarization, 601–602, 610–612, 620
Parallel-plate capacitor, 101, 166, 468
Paramagnetic materials, 383
Permeability, 322, 387–395, 404, 407, 417, 437
Permeance, 403, 407, 413
Permittivity, 78, 119, 120, 175, 184, 191, 194, 195, 205, 206, 223, 224, 553, 062, 609
Perpendicular polarization, 598–601, 607–609, 610, 612, 619–620
Phase, 544, 549, 555, 594, 595, 608
Phase constant, 544, 545, 553, 555, 556, 557, 558, 596, 603
Phase distortion, 650
Phase shift, 555
Phase velocity, 544, 556, 558, 567, 569, 574
Phasor, 514–518, 520, 522, 548–549, 552, 569, 574, 582, 594, 595, 596–604, 608, 610
Plane of incidence, 598, 607, 610
Plane wave, 545, 547–579, 581, 594, 595–626
Point charge, 77–79, 81–83, 85, 86–87, 89–90, 107–108, 109, 118–119, 144–149, 154, 159–160, 255, 256, 322
Poisson's equation, 175, 238–255, 331, 453, 509
Polarization, 182–183, 594–595, 598–602, 607–612, 620
Position vector, 5–6, 22, 32, 79, 85–86, 118
Potential difference, 135–136, 205, 213, 220–221, 239, 249, 267
Potential functions, 72, 507–509
Power density, 203–204, 581–583
Power loss, 628–630
Poynting vector, 579–593
Poynting's theorem, 579–593
Principle of superposition, 79
Propagation constant, 542, 543, 544, 553, 565, 566, 627
Propagation mode, 731
Propagation vector, 551

Q

Quarter-wave line, 687

R

Rectangular coordinates, 4, 5, 14–15, 20, 27–28, 43, 67, 297, 305

Reflected wave, 595–597, 598, 599, 063, 605

Reflection coefficient, 603, 604, 605, 609, 611

Reflection factor, 684

Reflection loss, 684

Refracted wave, 605, 607

Refractive index, 606

Relative permeability, 382, 384, 390, 404, 437

Relative permittivity, 78, 184, 199

Relaxation time, 187–191, 206

Reluctance, 403, 404–405, 406, 407–408, 411–414

Resistance, 200–204, 206, 207, 217, 220, 404, 405, 407, 628, 629

Resistivity, 179, 407, 628

Retarded potential, 511

Right hand rule, 9, 55, 71, 274, 280, 281, 296, 311, 314, 352, 369, 454

Right hand screw rule, 9, 274

S

Scalar electric potential, 134, 328, 502, 507–509, 510

Scalar field, 2, 32, 34, 36, 42–45, 67–71, 77, 136

Scalar magnetic potential, 328–344

Scalar product, 6, 204, 580

Scalar triple product, 12–13

Self-inductance, 532

Semiconductor, 176, 177, 179, 443, 444

Single stub matching, 691

Skin depth, 558–579, 628, 629–630

Skin effect, 558

Smith chart, 689

Snell's law of refraction 606–607, 608, 609, 611

Snell's law of reflection, 599–600, 605, 607, 608

Solenoid, 290, 403, 414, 422–425, 438–439

Solid angle, 109

Spherical capacitor, 220–222

Spherical coordinates, 17–27, 29–31, 39–42, 106, 124, 144, 155, 156, 239, 305, 379, 510

Standing wave, 596–598

Standing wave ratio, 604–605

Stokes's theorem, 63–67, 70, 292–296, 345, 458, 466, 478

Superconductors, 176, 382, 396

Surface charge density, 90, 91, 100, 103, 105, 110, 193, 223, 234, 251, 259, 504

Surface current, 275, 356, 367, 505, 626–628

Surface current density, 275, 314–315, 330, 391, 396, 504, 626–627, 629

Surface impedance, 628, 629–630

Surface integral, 34–36, 50, 63, 64, 70, 71, 111, 119, 120, 163, 292, 297, 466, 479

T

Time-harmonic fields, 514–529

Time varying fields, 451–536

Toroid, 321, 403, 408, 410, 426–432

Torque, 155–158, 367–379

Total reflection, 607

Transformer, 454–465, 431–434

Transformer emf, 455–458

Transmission coefficient, 604, 609, 611

Transmission lines, 213–215, 434–436

Transmission line equations, 642

Transmitted wave, 602, 605–607

Transverse electric wave, 637

Transverse magnetic wave, 637

Transverse electromagnetic wave, 551–552

Travelling wave, 544, 549, 604

U

Uniform field, 54, 127–134

Uniform plane wave, 547–548, 551, 552, 581, 594, 595, 602, 605, 607, 610

Uniqueness theorem, 239–240

Unit vector, 2–3, 7, 9–10, 15–16, 18, 19–20, 22–23, 28, 47, 78, 90, 155, 192, 276, 368, 369

V

Vacuum, 77, 177, 62, 451, 556

Vector addition, 3–5

Vector differential operator, 38–42

Vector field, 2, 13, 25, 34–35, 36, 37, 45–50, 54–63, 68, 70–72, 111, 136

Vector identity, 163, 239, 329–330, 331, 466, 509, 542, 543

Vector magnetic potential, 328–344, 345, 379, 507–508, 510, 511

Vector multiplication, 6–14

Vector product, 6, 9–10, 330, 345, 368

Vector subtraction, 3–5

Vector transformation, 19, 20, 39, 41, 57

Vector triple product, 13–14

Vertical polarization, 601

Volume charge density, 90–91, 109, 122, 160, 177, 87, 203, 238, 322, 355, 444, 452, 507–508, 509

Volume current density, 178, 187, 204, 275, 330, 367, 508, 509

Volume integral, 31–37, 50, 64, 71, 111, 323, 478, 580

W

Wave equations, 509, 510–513, 516, 530, 541–543, 548, 552–554

Wave number, 516, 544, 548, 549, 551, 555, 574

Wave parameters, 544–547

Wave velocity, 560, 571

Waveguides, 722

Wavelength, 529, 530, 544, 549, 564, 565, 574, 575, 597, 598, 600, 602

Work, 127, 135–136, 137–138, 159–160, 161, 162–163, 203, 267

Z

Zenith angle, 17